EDUCATIONAL

2nd Canadian Edition

PSYCHOLOGY

Anita E. Woolfolk   The Ohio State University

Philip H. Winne   Simon Fraser University

Nancy E. Perry   University of British Columbia

Toronto

National Library of Canada Cataloguing in Publication Data

Woolfolk, Anita
    Educational psychology / Anita E. Woolfolk, Philip H. Winne,
    Nancy E. Perry. — 2nd Canadian ed.

Includes bibliographical references and index.
ISBN 0-205-36068-8

1. Educational psychology. I. Winne, Philip H. II. Perry, Nancy Ellen, 1962- III. Title.

LB1051.W73 2002   370.15   C2002-902818-3

ISBN 0-205-36068-8

Vice-President, Editorial Director: Michael J. Young
Acquisitions Editor: Lori Will
Senior Developmental Editor: Martina van de Velde
Managing Editor: Tracy Bordian
Copy Editor: Cheryl Cohen
Proofreader: Judy Phillips
Production Manager: Wendy Moran
Page Layout: Phyllis Seto/Hermia Chung
Permissions Research: Susan Wallace-Cox
Photo Research: Lisa Brant
Art Director: Mary Opper
Interior and Cover Design: Sarah Battersby
Cover Image: Alex Telfer Photography/photonica

  2 3 4 5   07 06 05 04 03

Printed and bound in the United States of America.

Statistics Canada information is used with permission of the Minister of Industry, as Minister responsible for Statistics
Canada. Information on the availability of the wide range of data from Statistics Canada can be obtained from Statistics
Canada's Regional Offices, its World Wide Web site at www.statcan.ca, and its toll-free access number 1-800-263-1136.

Brief Contents

Contents

3 Personal, Social, and Emotional Development   60

Part Two *Individual Variations*

4 Learner Differences 104

Culture and Community 155

Part Three *Learning: Theory and Practice*

6 Behavioural Views of Learning 194

Cognitive Views of Learning   230

8 Complex Cognitive Processes
268

Overview 269

What Would You Do? 270

9 Social Cognitive and Constructivist Views of Learning   310

12 Teaching for Learning   444

Part Five *Assessing Student Learning*

13 Standardized Testing in Canada 486

14 Classroom Assessment and Grading 526

Student Preface

Many of you reading this book will be enrolled in an educational psychology course as part of your professional preparation for teaching, counselling, speech therapy, or psychology. Others of you, while not planning to become teachers, are reading this book because you are interested in what educational psychology has to say about teaching and learning in a variety of settings. The material in this text should be of interest to everyone who is concerned about education and learning, from the nursery school volunteer to the instructor in a community program for adults with learning disabilities. No background in psychology or education is necessary to understand this material. It is as free of jargon and technical language as possible, and many people have worked to make this edition clear, relevant, and interesting.

Since the original edition of *Educational Psychology* appeared, there have been many exciting developments in the field. This second Canadian edition incorporates new insights and current trends in Canada while retaining the best features of the previous work. The second Canadian edition continues to emphasize the educational implications and applications of research on child development, cognitive science, learning, and teaching. Theory and practice are not separated but are considered together; we show how information and ideas drawn from research in educational psychology can be applied to solve the everyday problems of teaching. To help you explore the connections between knowledge and practice, we have included many examples, lesson segments, case studies, guidelines, and practical tips from experienced teachers. Throughout the text you will be challenged to think about the value and use of the ideas in each chapter and you will see principles of educational psychology in action. Professors and students find these features very helpful. But what about the new developments?

In this second Canadian edition, we include up-to-date statistics about our population and the implications for education in a rapidly changing Canadian mosaic. We also highlight the latest research on uniquely Canadian issues concerning programming for students with special needs; multicultural education; and second-language learning. Our provinces are world leaders in criterion-referenced standardized testing, which we introduce in some detail. As well, we present excerpts from an actual psychoeducational assessment report, which illustrate information that teachers need to understand to provide effective instruction for exceptional students.

As you read Educational Psychology, Second Canadian Edition, you will notice that the authors are referred to by name as they share their personal experiences. Anita Woolfolk, Phil Winne, and Nancy Perry have been studying, researching, and practising the strategies, methods, and theories discussed in this text for many years. We hope you enjoy these experiences and use them to gain insights into your own.

A host of Canadian citations in this Canadian edition bring prospective teachers the most current information. Topics include:

- the brain and learning
- Vygotsky and sociocultural theories of development
- the role of adults and peers in cognitive development
- personal and collective self-esteem
- bullies and victims
- navigating the transitions in school
- person-first language as alternatives to labelling students

- emotional intelligence and tacit knowledge
- ADHD
- positive behaviour support
- collaborative teaching for inclusion classrooms
- Canadian education and cultural issues
- stereotype threat
- culturally relevant pedagogy
- learning strategies
- sociocognitive theory and self-efficacy
- problem-based learning
- cooperative learning
- interest and emotions in learning
- self-schemas and motivation
- conceptual change teaching in science
- constructivist approaches in mathematics
- creating learning communities
- dealing with conflict and violence
- revised taxonomies for learning
- criterion-referenced standardized testing
- grading rubrics
- psychoeducational assessment
- authentic assessment
- portfolios

The Plan of the Book. The introductory chapter begins with you and the questions you may be asking yourself about teaching. What is good teaching, and what does it take to become an excellent teacher? How can educational psychology help you to understand what good teaching is and, if you choose a career in teaching, to become such a teacher? Part One, "Students," focuses on the learners. How do they develop mentally, physically, emotionally, and socially, and how do all these aspects fit together? Where do individual differences come from, and what do they mean for teachers? How can teachers adapt instruction for students with special needs? What does it mean to create a culturally compatible classroom, one that makes learning accessible to all students? Part Two, "Learning," looks at learning from three major perspectives—behavioural, cognitive, and constructivist—with an emphasis on the last two. Learning theories have important but different implications for instruction at every level. Cognitive research is particularly vital right now and promises to be a wellspring of ideas for teaching in the immediate future. The new chapter, "Sociocognitive and Constructivist Views of Learning," examines the role of social and cultural influences in learning. Part Three, "Motivating and Teaching," discusses the ever-present, linked issues of motivating, managing, and teaching today's students. The material in these chapters is based on the most recent research in real classrooms and includes information on both teacher-centred and student-centred approaches to teaching. Part Four, "Assessing," looks at many ways to assess and evaluate students' learning.

Aids to Understanding. At the beginning of each chapter you will find an outline of the key topics with page numbers for quick reference. An overview begins with a question asking about a subject related to the chapter. Before you read each chapter, take a moment to reflect on the questions raised. Your answers to the questions and the overview, along with a list of learning objectives (also useful for review later), provide an "orientation" to the chapter topics.

When you turn the page you confront another question, "What Would You Do?" about a real-life classroom situation related to the information in the chapter. By the time you reach the Teachers' Casebook at the end of the chapter, you should have even more ideas about how to solve the problem raised, so be alert as you read.

Within the chapter, headings point out themes, questions, and problems as they arise, so you can look up information easily. These can also serve as a quick review of important points. When a new term or concept is introduced, it appears in boldface type along with a brief margin definition. These Key Terms are also defined in a Glossary at the end of the book. After every major section of the chapter, Checkpoints ask you to review and apply your learning. Can you answer these questions? If not, you might review the material. Throughout the book, graphs, tables, photos, and cartoons have been chosen to clarify and extend the text material—and to add to your enjoyment. Finally, Weblinks also provides a list of Web sites where you can further explore each chapter's information.

Each chapter ends with a Summary of the main ideas keyed to the Checkpoint questions in each main heading, and an alphabetical list of the Key Terms from the chapter, along with the page number where each is discussed.

Other Text Features. Every chapter includes Guidelines, the Teachers' Casebook, and Point/Counterpoints on such issues as inclusion, "paying" kids to learn, and alternatives to direct teaching.

Guidelines. An important reason for studying educational psychology is to gain skills in solving classroom problems. Often texts give pages of theory and research findings, but little assistance in translating theory into practice. This text is different. Included in each chapter are several sets of Guidelines, teaching tips, and practical suggestions based on the theory and research discussed in the chapter. Each suggestion is clarified by two or three specific examples. Although the Guidelines cannot cover every possible situation, they do provide a needed bridge between knowledge and practice and should help you transfer the text's information to new situations. In addition, every chapter after the first has one set of Guidelines that gives ideas for working with families and the community—an area of growing importance today.

Connect & Extend. Connect and Extend features appear in the margins several times throughout each chapter, linking content to teaching, students' thinking, research, and the news. They are valuable components for promoting deep-level processing and transferring theory to authentic classroom settings.

Teachers' Casebook. At the end of each chapter, master teachers from across Canada offer their own solutions to the problem you encountered at the beginning of each chapter. Teachers' Casebook: What Would They Do? gives you insights into the thinking of expert teachers; compare their solutions to the ones you devised. Their ideas truly show educational psychology at work in a range of everyday situations. The Teachers' Casebook brings to life the topics and principles discussed in each chapter.

Point/Counterpoint. There is a section in each chapter called Point/Counterpoint, a debate that examines two contrasting perspectives on an important question or controversy related to research or practice in educational psychology. Many of the topics considered in these Point/Counterpoints have been in the news recently and are central to the discussions of educational reformers.

Becoming a Professional. At the end of each chapter, beginning with Chapter 2, is a section called "Becoming a Professional" that gives you guidance for developing a professional teaching portfolio and a resource file for your future classrooms.

Companion Web Site. We've also created a Companion Web Site to accompany this Canadian edition. There, you'll find tips about how to make the best use of learning aids in the text, some of students' most frequently asked questions (and answers!), an online study guide with chapter objectives and practice test questions, and other aids to help you learn the most you can about educational psychology.

Student Responses. You are invited to respond to any aspect of this text. We welcome your feedback. You may wish to criticize the solutions in the Teachers' Casebook, for example, or suggest topics or materials you think should be added to future editions. We would also like to know what you think of the text features and student supplements (see Web site). Please send letters to:

Woolfolk/Winne/Perry
Educational Psychology, Second Canadian Edition
Pearson Education Canada
26 Prince Andrew Place
Don Mills, ON M3C 2T8

Personal Acknowledgments

Our work on this project benefited immensely from consultations with friends and colleagues. Especially, we thank Anita Woolfolk for supporting this Canadian adaptation of her excellent textbook, Nancy Hutchinson (Queen's University) for providing material for Chapters 4 and 5, and Louise Mercer (University of British Columbia) for supplying a psychoeducational report, which we abridged for Chapter 13. Also, we thank Robin Cull-Hewitt and Dianne Jamieson-Noel (Simon Fraser University), and Lynda Hutchinson and Karen VandeKamp (University of British Columbia) for their help in locating Canadian statistics and reference materials. Lynda Hutchinson deserves special mention for completing the tedious but important tasks of matching in-text references with those in the bibliography, and chapter key terms with those in the glossary.

The following Canadian reviewers contributed thoughtful comments:

Diane Galambos, Sheridan College
Patrick Walton, University College of the Cariboo
Larry Morton, University of Windsor
Vera Woloshyn, Brock University
Heather Higgins, Acadia University
Gretchen Hess, University of Alberta

Thanks to Andrew Wellner for inviting us to be a part of this project and Martina van de Velde for guiding us through production, offering just the right mix of help and direction. The entire team at Pearson Education is a model in their field.

A Great Way to Learn and Instruct Online

The Pearson Education Canada Companion Website is easy to navigate and is organized to correspond to the chapters in this textbook. Whether you are a student in the classroom or a distance learner you will discover helpful resources for in-depth study and research that empower you in your quest for greater knowledge and maximize your potential for success in the course.

Companion Website

[www.pearsoned.ca/woolfolk]
Enter

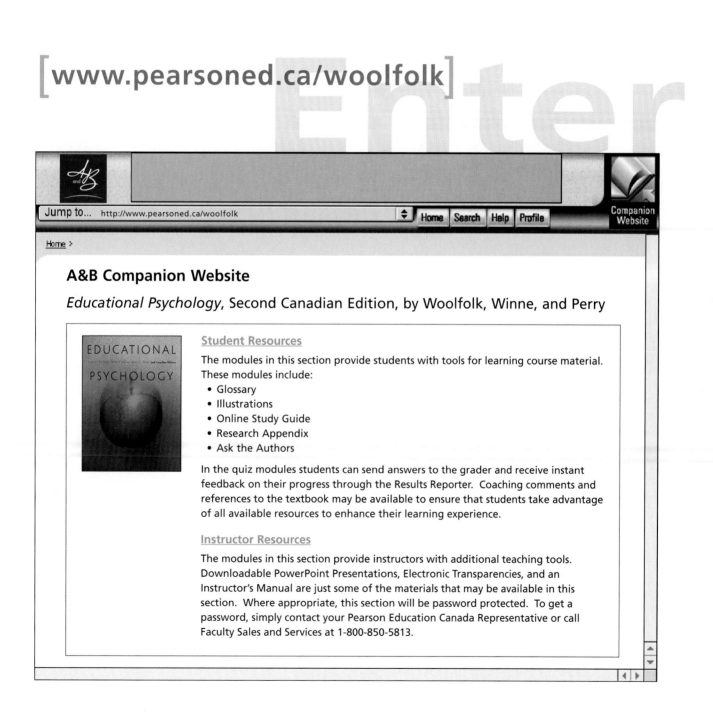

Jump to... http://www.pearsoned.ca/woolfolk | Home | Search | Help | Profile |

Companion Website

Home >

A&B Companion Website

Educational Psychology, Second Canadian Edition, by Woolfolk, Winne, and Perry

Student Resources

The modules in this section provide students with tools for learning course material. These modules include:

- Glossary
- Illustrations
- Online Study Guide
- Research Appendix
- Ask the Authors

In the quiz modules students can send answers to the grader and receive instant feedback on their progress through the Results Reporter. Coaching comments and references to the textbook may be available to ensure that students take advantage of all available resources to enhance their learning experience.

Instructor Resources

The modules in this section provide instructors with additional teaching tools. Downloadable PowerPoint Presentations, Electronic Transparencies, and an Instructor's Manual are just some of the materials that may be available in this section. Where appropriate, this section will be password protected. To get a password, simply contact your Pearson Education Canada Representative or call Faculty Sales and Services at 1-800-850-5813.

EDUCATIONAL

2nd Canadian Edition

PSYCHOLOGY

Teachers, Teaching, and Educational Psychology

ake a minute to remember the names of the best teachers you ever had, inside or outside a classroom. What was it about these teachers that made you remember them over the years? What effects did they have on you?

If you are like many students, you begin this course with a mixture of anticipation and wariness. Perhaps you are required to take educational psychology as part of a program in teacher education, speech therapy, nursing, or counselling. You may have chosen this class as an elective because you are interested in education or psychology. Whatever your reason for enrolling, you probably have questions about teaching, schools, students—or even about yourself—that you hope this course may answer. The second Canadian edition of *Educational Psychology* has been written with questions such as these in mind.

In this first chapter, we begin not with educational psychology but with education—more specifically, with the state of teaching today. Only when you are aware of the challenges teachers face can you appreciate the contributions of educational psychology. After a brief introduction to the world of the teacher, we turn to a discussion of educational psychology itself. We will consider what educational psychology is and why you should study it. How can principles identified by educational psychologists benefit teachers, therapists, parents, and others who are interested in teaching and learning? What exactly is the content of educational psychology, and where does this information come from?

By the time you have finished this chapter, you will be in a much better position to answer these questions and many others, such as:

- ▶ What is good teaching?
- ▶ Would teaching be a good career for me?
- ▶ What do expert teachers know?
- ▶ What are the greatest concerns of beginning teachers?
- ▶ Why should I study educational psychology?
- ▶ What roles do theory and research play in this field?
- ▶ What kinds of problems will the study of educational psychology help me to solve?

What Would You Do?

TEACHERS' CASEBOOK

It is your second year as a teacher at John A. Macdonald Public School (kindergarten–Grade 8). One of your colleagues has been nominated for a Prime Minister's Award for Teaching Excellence. This person has been a role model to you in your first two years as a teacher, providing advice and encouragement, and you would like to support her by writing a letter of recommendation highlighting her exemplary teaching practices, commitment, and leadership.

▶ How will you prepare?

▶ What do you need to know about teaching to complete this task?

▶ What are some indicators of excellent teaching? Do different philosophies of teaching provide different answers to this question?

▶ What are your recommendations, and how would you back them up?

Describing teachers who made a difference in his life, Harvard professor Robert Coles (1990) said:

> I mention these teachers in my life because, in fact, they continue to be a great big part of it still. Their voices are in my head and are part of my voice, I am sure. Their thoughts and values inform what I consider and call my own thoughts and values. Their example—the things they did, the style of their teaching, the strategies they employed—continue to inform the way I work. . . .
>
> In a sense, then, all good teachers rescue us from the death of boredom, apathy, self-preoccupation, and self-satisfaction: the teacher as an intellectual and moral life saver who fortunately has come our way and, of course, the teacher as one who is rescued by rescuing others. (p. 59)

What Is Good Teaching?

Connect & Extend
To your own philosophy
What are the goals of education, real and ideal? What does it mean to be an educated person? What makes a teacher effective? Describe the most effective teacher you ever had. How do you learn best? What do you hope to gain from this course? Your answers will provide the basis for developing a philosophy of teaching.

There are hundreds of answers to this question, including ideas based on your own experience. This question has been examined by educators, psychologists, philosophers, novelists, journalists, mathematicians, scientists, historians, policy makers, and parents, to name only a few groups. And good teaching is not confined to classrooms—it occurs in homes and hospitals, museums and sales meetings, therapists' offices and summer camps. In this book, we are primarily concerned with teaching in classrooms, but much of what you will learn applies to other settings as well.

Inside Four Classrooms

To begin our examination of good teaching, let's step inside the classrooms of several outstanding teachers. All the situations that follow are real.

A Multilingual First Grade. Anne Lee-Hawman teaches Grade 1 in Mississauga, Ontario. Of the 22 children in her classroom, half speak English as a second language (ESL). As is true for most linguistically diverse students in Canada, they spend 100 percent of their school day using English as opposed to their native language. This immersion, or submersion, approach to second-language learning contrasts with the bilingual approaches used in many American states.

The ESL teacher helps Anne to integrate these children by working in Anne's classroom each day. Together they support students in small groups and make modifications to the curriculum that enable students who speak ESL to participate in all the activities of the classroom. One strategy they have found useful is to make information available through visual materials (e.g., pictures, diagrams, and word or concept maps). Also, Anne makes use of peer tutors and, whenever possible, offers one-on-one instruction to students who need it.

In addition to supporting students' acquisition of English, Anne encourages students and their parents to continue talking, reading, and writing in their first language at home. Also, she fosters an appreciation for diverse languages and cultures in her classroom by celebrating multicultural holidays, and by having students compare and contrast their home/community experiences and practices during classroom discussions and sharing times.

Anne makes a point of learning as much as she can about her students' linguistic and cultural heritages. She recognizes how important it is for teachers to understand the way(s) that issues of language and culture influence children's learning, so they don't misinterpret children's motivation and behaviour. This year, five languages are represented in Anne's classroom: English, Hindi, Punjabi, Chinese, and Malaysian. She has a lot of learning to do.

A Suburban Sixth Grade. Ken teaches Grade 6 in a suburban elementary school. He emphasizes "process writing." His students complete first drafts, discuss them with others in the class, revise, edit, and "publish" their work. The students also keep daily journals and often use these to share personal concerns with Ken. They tell him of problems at home, fights, and fears; he always takes the time to respond in writing. The study of science is also placed in the context of the real world. The students use a National Geographic Society computer network to link with other schools in order to identify acid rain patterns around the world. For social studies, the class played two simulation games that focused on the first half of the 1800s. They "lived" as trappers collecting animal skins, and as pioneers heading west.

Throughout the year Ken is very interested in the social and emotional development of his students—he wants them to learn about responsibility and fairness as well as science and social studies. This concern is evident in the way he develops his class rules at the beginning of the year. Rather than specifying dos and don'ts, Ken and his students generate a list of rights and responsibilities for their class. This list covers most of the situations that might need a "rule."

Two Advanced Math Classes. Hilda Borko and Carol Livingston (1989) describe two expert secondary-school mathematics teachers. In one lesson for her advanced mathematics class, Ellen had her students identify any three problems about ellipses from their text. She asked if there were any questions or uncertainties about these problems. Ellen answered student questions, worked two of the problems, and then used the three problems to derive all the concepts and equations the students needed to understand the material. Ellen's knowledge of the subject and of her students was so thorough that she could create the explanations and derive the formulas on the spot, no matter which problems the students chose.

Another teacher, Randy, worked with his students' confusion to construct a review lesson about strategies for doing integrals. When one student said that a particular section in the book seemed "haphazard," Randy led the class through a process of organizing the material. He asked the class for general statements about useful strategies for doing integrals. He clarified their suggestions, elaborated on some, and helped students improve others. He asked the students to tie their ideas to passages in the text. Even though he accepted all reasonable suggestions, he listed only the key strategies on the board. By the end of the period, the students had transformed the disorganized material from the book into an ordered and useful outline to guide their learning. They also had a better idea about how to read and understand difficult material.

What do you see in these classrooms? The teachers are committed to their students. They must deal with a wide range of student abilities and challenges:

Connect & Extend
To real life
Nearly everyone can name a favourite teacher—someone who had a real impact on their life. The B.C. Teachers' Federation went out and asked British Columbians to describe special teachers, and the difference they had made. Here's what some people said about their favourite teachers:

"Ms. Finlayson . . . she was wonderful. She stuck by me through my high school years."
"He cared not only about my performance in class but also about how I was feeling as a person."
"She demanded a lot, but she was very fair."
"Mr.s Cooper, my first Canadian teacher, he made me feel very at home."
"Mr. Jones awoke a talent in me that I didn't even realize I had."
"He changed my life. Things he said to me made me a better person . . . just made me think more about things."
"He just wanted me to believe more in myself than I did."
 From the BCTF Web site:
www.BCTeachersforBCKids. ca/sa-main.html

Connect & Extend
To other chapters
Ken's process writing, student publishing, and journal writing are examples of a "whole language" approach, discussed in **Chapter 12**. Ken's "Bill of Rights" is an example of an innovative approach to setting class rules, discussed in **Chapter 11**.

Connect & Extend
To the research
Borko, H., & Livingston, C. (1989). Cognition and improvisation: Differences in mathematics instruction by expert and novice teachers. *American Educational Research Journal, 26*, 473–498.

different languages, different home lives, different needs. These teachers must understand their subjects and their students' thinking so well that they can spontaneously create new examples and explanations when students are confused. They must make the most abstract concepts, such as negative numbers, real and understandable for their particular students. And then there is the challenge of new technologies and techniques. The teachers must use them appropriately to accomplish important goals, not just to entertain the students. The whole time that these experts are navigating through the academic material, they also are taking care of the emotional needs of their students, propping up sagging self-esteem and encouraging responsibility. If we followed these individuals from the first day of class, we would see that they carefully plan and teach the basic procedures for living and learning in their classes. They can efficiently correct and collect homework, regroup students, give directions, distribute materials, collect lunch money, and deal with disruptions—and do all of this while also making a mental note to check why one of their students is so tired.

Anne, Ken, Ellen, and Randy are examples of **expert teachers**, the focus of much recent research in education and psychology. For another perspective on the question "What is good teaching?" let's examine the research on what expert teachers know.

Expert Knowledge

Expert teachers have elaborate systems of knowledge for understanding problems in teaching. For example, when a beginning teacher is faced with students' wrong answers on math or history tests, all the wrong answers may seem about the same—wrong. The inexperienced teacher may have trouble connecting other facts or ideas with the students' wrong answers. But for an expert teacher, wrong answers are part of a rich system of knowledge that could include how to recognize several types of wrong answers; the misunderstanding or lack of information behind each kind of mistake; the best way to reteach and correct the misunderstanding; materials and activities that have worked in the past; and several ways to test whether the reteaching was successful (Floden & Klinzing, 1990; Leinhardt, 1988). Peterson and Comeaux (1989) argue that it is the quality of teachers' professional knowledge and their ability to be aware of their own thinking that make them expert.

What do expert teachers know that allows them to be so successful? Lee Shulman (1987) has studied this question, and he has identified seven areas of professional knowledge. Expert teachers know:

1. The academic subjects they teach.
2. General teaching strategies that apply in all subjects (such as the principles of classroom management, effective teaching, and evaluation that you will discover in this book).
3. The curriculum materials and programs appropriate for their subject and grade level.
4. Subject-specific knowledge for teaching: special ways of teaching certain students and particular concepts, such as the best ways to explain negative numbers to lower-ability students.
5. The characteristics and cultural backgrounds of learners.
6. The settings in which students learn—pairs, small groups, teams, classes, schools, and the community.
7. The goals and purposes of teaching.

This is quite a list. Obviously, one course cannot give you all the information you need to teach. In fact, a whole program of courses won't make you an expert. That takes time and experience. But studying educational psychology can add to

Connect & Extend
To the research
Carter, K., Sabers, D., Cushing, K., Pinnegar, S., & Berliner, D. (1987). Processing and using information about students: A study of expert, novice, and postulant teachers. *Teaching and Teacher Education, 3,* 147–157.

Connect & Extend
To other chapters
Teachers' knowledge of their own thinking is an example of metacognitive knowledge, discussed in **Chapter 7**.

Expert Teachers: Experienced, effective teachers who have developed solutions for common classroom problems. Their knowledge of teaching processes and content is extensive and well organized.

your professional knowledge. In this book we will focus on general teaching strategies, the characteristics of students, and settings for learning. We will also touch on learning goals and subject-specific knowledge for teaching.

How do you grow from beginning teacher to expert? Can you learn to be an expert teacher, or are really great teachers just born? Is good teaching an art or a science? Answers to this last question provide another perspective on good teaching.

*T*eaching: Artistry, Technique, and a Lot of Work

Because researchers have identified a number of effective teaching techniques, some educators argue that all teachers should learn these practices and be tested on them to earn or to keep their teaching certificates. Other educators believe that the mark of an excellent teacher is not the ability to apply techniques but the artistry of being **reflective**—thoughtful and inventive—about teaching (Schon, 1983). Educators who adopt this view tend to be more concerned with how teachers solve problems, create instruction, make decisions, and plan than they are with the specific techniques teachers apply. They believe teaching is a complicated, demanding activity that requires creative thinking and a commitment to lifelong learning (Borko, 1989; Peterson & Comeaux, 1989).

Most people agree that teachers must be both technically competent and inventive. They must be able to use a range of strategies, and they must also be able to invent new strategies. They must have some simple routines that work for managing classes, but they must also be willing and able to break from the routine when the situation calls for change. New problems arise all the time, and when the old solutions do not work, something else is needed.

With the growing understanding that teaching is a complex problem-solving activity has come a call to give teachers more freedom and responsibility. A number of educational reform movements seek to involve teachers in designing curricula and assessments, and making decisions for themselves and their students, as you can see in the Point/Counterpoint section.

You may be thinking that all this talk about expert teachers and expert knowledge, artistry, and technique is a bit idealistic and abstract. Right now, you may have other, more down-to-earth, concerns about becoming a teacher. You are not alone!

▲ *Expert teachers not only know the content of the subjects they teach, they also know how to relate this content to the world outside the classroom and how to keep students involved in learning.*

Connect & Extend
To the research
Jean Piaget (1973) had this to say about teaching: "The art of education is like the art of medicine: it is an art that cannot be practised without special 'gifts,' but one that assumes exact and experimental knowledge relating to the human beings on which it is exercised" (*To understand is to invent: The future of education.* New York: Grossman, p. 94).

Concerns of Beginning Teachers

Beginning teachers everywhere share many concerns. A review of studies conducted around the world found that beginning teachers regard their most serious challenges to be maintaining classroom discipline, motivating students, accommodating differences among students, evaluating student work, and dealing with parents. Many teachers also experience what has been called "reality shock" when they take their first jobs and confront the "harsh and rude reality of everyday classroom life" (Veenman, 1984, p. 143). One source of shock may be that teachers really cannot ease into their responsibilities. On the first day in the classroom, the beginning teacher faces the same tasks as teachers with years of experience. Student teaching, while a critical element, does not really prepare prospective teachers for starting a school year with a new class. And schools usually offer little chance for helpful contact between novice and experienced teachers, making mutual support and assistance difficult. If you have had any of these concerns, you shouldn't be troubled. It comes with the job of being a beginning teacher (Calderhead & Robson, 1991; Cooke & Pang, 1991; Veenman, 1984).

Reflective: Thoughtful and inventive. Reflective teachers think back over situations to analyze what they did and why, and to consider how they might improve learning for their students.

Connect & Extend
To the research

- Read and discuss the article by Sparks—Langer, G. M., & Colton, A. S. B. (1991). Synthesis of research on teachers' reflective thinking. *Educational Leadership, 48*(6), 37–44. *Focus Questions:* What does it mean to be a reflective teacher? Why is reflection important in teaching?

- For a slightly longer discussion of the value of technique versus reflective thinking in teacher preparation, see pages 109–111 of Hoy, W. K., & Woolfolk, A. E. (1989). Supervising student teachers. In A. Woolfolk (Ed.), *Research perspectives on the graduate preparation of teachers* (pp. 108–131). Boston: Allyn & Bacon.

- See the article by Murphy, J., Evertson, C. M., & Radnofsky, M. L. (1991). Restructuring schools: Fourteen elementary and secondary teachers' perspectives on reform. *Elementary School Journal, 92*, 135–148. *Focus Question:* Are teachers becoming more involved in school decisions?

▲ *Teaching is one of the few professions in which a new teacher is expected to assume all the responsibilities of an experienced "pro" during the first week on the job. Veteran teachers can be a source of support and guidance to new teachers during these early weeks.*

CHECKPOINT

What Is Good Teaching?

Review

▷ What do expert teachers know?

▷ What are the artistic and scientific aspects of teaching?

▷ What are the concerns of beginning teachers?

Apply

▷ Analyze one of your current teachers in terms of Shulman's seven kinds of knowledge.

▷ How are your concerns about teaching similar to or different from those reported in studies of beginning teachers?

With experience, however, most teachers meet the challenges that seem difficult for beginners. They have more time to experiment with new methods or materials. Finally, as confidence grows, seasoned teachers can focus on the students' needs. Are my students learning? Are they developing positive attitudes? Is this the best way to teach the slower learners to write a persuasive essay? At this advanced stage, teachers judge their success by the successes of their students (Feiman-Nemser, 1983; Fuller, 1969).

We talk about good teachers because that is what many of you are planning to become. But all good teaching begins with an understanding of *students* and *learning*. As you will see throughout this text, today there is great interest in studying how people understand and apply knowledge. Just as educational psychologists have investigated how expertise develops in teaching, they have also explored how students come to be experts in particular subjects. Many of the chapters in this book are concerned with these issues.

ℐhe Ultimate Goal of Teaching: Lifelong Expert Learning

Today, people change jobs an average of seven times before they retire. Many of these career changes require new knowledge and skills (Weinstein, 1994). Thus,

Teachers at the Centre of Educational Reform

Many current efforts to restructure schools recommend a shift from assembly—line models of teaching to instructional activities that foster strategic and independent thought by *all* students. The informed and reflective teacher is at the centre of such reforms. As professionals, teachers can apply their "knowledge and time to commanding the essential core of educational practice: curriculum, instruction, and assessment" (Calfee & Hiebert, 1991, p. 107). How can this recommendation become a reality? What happens when teachers are given opportunities to extend and use their expertise to redesign instruction for their students?

▶ **POINT** *Teachers take charge of their professional development.*

In fall 1995, a group of intermediate teachers lobbied administrators in Coquitlam School District, BC, for funds to support their action research project. Action research involves teachers in investigating and experimenting with their own teaching practices. By March 1998, action research had become a district-wide approach to teacher development and self-directed professional growth. Approximately 10 percent of Coquitlam's teachers were involved in 14 action research groups of 12 to 14 teachers each, and the district administration and teachers' association were exploring ways to involve more teachers in action research and to support teachers' involvement from year to year.

For one afternoon each month during the school year, the district released teachers from their classrooms to meet with their action research groups. In these meetings, teachers discussed mutually agreed-upon questions about some aspect of teaching and learning. For example, members of one group focused on teaching and learning in math. They also designed action plans, which

they enacted and evaluated between meetings. Some teachers formed smaller groups within the action research groups to address more specific goals and interests. These smaller groups met between the larger group's meetings. Although each action research group identified a unique topic of inquiry (e.g., math instruction, assessment of early literacy), the common goal among groups was to enhance student learning by improving teaching practices.

What did teachers have to say about their action research experience?

It's a great form of professional development. It allows you to set a goal or area of focus that is relevant to your needs and your learners . . . . The support from others in the group is an added bonus that may not be there when you undertake it alone.

A really wonderful thing is [students'] awareness of all this—of me modelling for them my ongoing learning through this project . . . [it's] brought home to them the genuine commitment to learning everybody needs to have throughout their life.

◀ **COUNTERPOINT** *Teacher—directed professional development poses some challenges.*

In fall 1996, Nancy Perry approached Coquitlam's assistant superintendent about the possibility of collaborating with Coquitlam teachers to design, implement, and interpret assessments of young children's literacy. She was then invited to facilitate one action research group of 10 primary teachers (kindergarten through Grade 3) and three remedial/resource teachers. The group had a wide range of beliefs and experiences concerning literacy instruction and assessment.

Over the year, most teachers gained valuable insights from one another and confidence in their ability to make professional judgments. Also, most developed high—quality assessments of their students' literacy development. However, there were occasions when Nancy was concerned about what teachers were learning from one another and how she should introduce current theory and research without seeming to undermine teachers' authority. Some teachers chose not to participate in some of the group's activities. A few others never identified a focus for their professional development or realized tangible changes in their teaching practices or resources. Finally, as is true of most educational innovations, funding for action research meetings was limited to one year for individual teachers.

The district hoped that experiences like this would "hook" teachers so they would continue working with their groups on their own time. This was true for some teachers (Nancy worked with five teachers for three years), but others felt it was too much to ask given all the other demands on their time.

Do these challenges deny the overall efficacy of action research as one method for increasing teachers' professionalism and enhancing students' learning? Or are these problems worth solving so that teachers can meet their professional potential? One administrator in the Coquitlam School District believes the latter. She continues to provide her teachers with time each month to meet and work on action research. To accommodate this work, she teaches their students in the gymnasium while the teachers meet in the library (one group for an hour and a half in the morning, another group for the same length of time in the afternoon).

one goal of teaching should be to free students from the need for teachers so the students can continue to learn independently throughout their lives.

The Ultimate Goal of Teaching: Lifelong Expert Learn

Connect & Extend
To the research
Evidence for the importance of technique and reflection in teaching can be found in a study of a teacher education program in the Netherlands that strongly emphasizes the development of reflective thinking: Korthagen, F. A. J. (1985). Reflective teaching and preservice teacher education in the Netherlands. *Journal of Teacher Education, 36*(5), 11–15. More than 50 percent of the program's graduates who responded to a survey said they had been insufficiently prepared for handling problems of motivation and management. Many of these graduates found that they had to abandon their attempts at analysis and inquiry in their early teaching years to develop ways to handle the day—to—day teaching problems. Beginning teachers need to master some basic teaching techniques and procedures in order to protect the capacity for reflection. Otherwise, they may spend all their time in the first years of teaching just learning to survive.

To continue learning independently throughout life, you must be a self-regulated learner. **Self-regulated learners** have a combination of academic learning skills and self-control that makes learning easier, so they are more motivated; in other words, they have the *skill* and the *will* to learn (McCombs & Marzano, 1990; Murphy & Alexander, 2000). The concept of self-regulated learning integrates much of what is known about effective learning and motivation. Three factors influence skill and will: knowledge, motivation, and self-discipline or volition.

Knowledge

To be self-regulated learners, students need *knowledge* about themselves, the subject, the task, strategies for learning, and the contexts in which they will apply their learning. "Expert" students know about *themselves* and how they learn best. For example, they know their preferred learning styles, what is easy and what is hard for them, how to cope with the hard parts, what their interests and talents are, and how to use their strengths (see Chapter 4 of this book). These experts also know quite a bit about the *subject* being studied—and the more they know, the easier it is to learn more (Alexander, 1997). They probably understand that different *learning tasks* require different approaches on their part. A simple memory task, for example, might require a mnemonic strategy (see Chapter 7) while a complex comprehension task might be approached by means of concept maps of the key ideas (see Chapter 8). Also, these self-regulated learners know that learning often is difficult and knowledge is seldom absolute—there usually are different ways of looking at problems as well as different solutions (Pressley, 1995; Winne, 1995).

These expert students not only know what each task requires, they can also apply the *strategy* needed. They can skim or read carefully. They can use memory strategies or reorganize the material. As they become more knowledgeable in a field, they apply many of these strategies automatically. In short, they have mastered a large, flexible repertoire of learning strategies and tactics (see Chapter 8).

Finally, expert learners think about the *contexts* in which they will apply their knowledge—when and where they will use their learning—so they can set motivating goals and connect present work to future accomplishments (Wang & Palincsar, 1989; Weinstein, 1994; Winne, 1995).

Motivation

Self-regulated learners are *motivated* to learn (see Chapters 10 and 11). They find many tasks in school interesting because they value learning, not just performing well in the eyes of others. But even if they are not intrinsically motivated by a particular task, they are serious about getting the intended benefit from it. They know *why* they are studying, so their actions and choices are self-determined and not controlled by others. However, knowledge and motivation are not always enough. Self-regulated learners need volition or self-discipline. "Where motivation denotes commitment, volition denotes follow-through" (Corno, 1992, p. 72).

Volition

When Anita originally wrote this chapter, it was a Friday night. She had been writing almost all day, even though she was suffering with a head cold. She wanted to keep writing because the deadline for this chapter was very near. She had knowl-

---

CHECKPOINT

The Ultimate Goal of Teaching: Lifelong Expert Learning

Review

▶ Describe self-regulated learning.

Apply

▶ What aspects of teachers' professional knowledge can you hope to develop by studying educational psychology?

Self-regulated Learners: Learners who have a combination of academic learning skills and self—control that makes learning easier; they have the *skill* and the *will* to learn.

Volition: Willpower, self-discipline.

edge and motivation, but to keep going she needed a good dose of volition. **Volition** is an old-fashioned word for willpower. Self-regulated learners know how to protect themselves from distractions—where to study, for example, so they are not interrupted. They know how to cope when they feel anxious, drowsy, or lazy (Corno, 1992, 1995; Snow, Corno, & Jackson, 1996). And they know what to do when tempted to stop working and take a nap—the temptation Anita was facing on that Friday night—or indulge in a large bowl of (low-fat) chips and salsa. Obviously, not all of your students will be self-regulated learners. In fact, some psychologists suggest that you think of this capacity as an individual difference characteristic (Snow, Corno, & Jackson, 1996). Some students are much better at it than others. How can you help more students become self-regulated learners? That is where educational psychology and this book can help.

Connect & Extend
To the research
The spring 1992 issue of *Educational Psychologist, 27*(2), has a special section on "The Nature and Mission of Educational Psychology" with articles by Merle Wittrock, David Berliner, Robert Calfee, and Carol Goodenow.

*T*he Role of Educational Psychology

We begin our consideration of the role of educational psychology by defining the term. For as long as educational psychology has existed—about 90 years—there have been debates about what it really is. Some people believe educational psychology is simply knowledge gained from psychology and applied to the activities of the classroom. Others believe it involves applying the methods of psychology to study classroom and school life (Clifford, 1984a; Grinder, 1981).

The view generally accepted today is that **educational psychology** is a distinct discipline with its own theories, research methods, problems, and techniques. "Educational psychology is distinct from other branches of psychology because it has the understanding and improvement of education as its primary goal" (Wittrock, 1992, p. 138). Educational psychologists "study what people think and do [and perhaps feel] as they teach and learn a particular curriculum in a particular environment where education and training are intended to take place" (Berliner, 1992, p. 145). Merle Wittrock sums it up well, saying that educational psychology focuses on "the psychological study of the everyday problems of education, from which one derives principles, models, theories, teaching procedures, and practical methods of instruction and evaluation, as well as research methods, statistical analyses, and measurement and assessment procedures appropriate for studying the thinking and affective processes of learners and the socially and culturally complex processes of schools." But are the findings of educational psychologists really that helpful for teachers? After all, most teaching is just common sense, isn't it? Let's take a few minutes to examine these questions.

Is It Just Common Sense?

In many cases, the principles set forth by educational psychologists—after spending much thought, research, and money—sound pathetically obvious. People are tempted to say, and usually do say, "Everyone knows that!" Consider these examples:

Taking Turns. What method should a teacher use in selecting students to participate in a primary-grade reading class?

Common Sense Answer. Teachers should call on students randomly so that everyone will have to follow the lesson carefully. If a teacher were to use the same order every time, the students would know when their turn was coming up.

Answer Based on Research. Research by Ogden, Brophy, and Evertson (1977) indicates that the answer to this question is not so simple. In Grade 1 reading classes, for example, going round the circle in order and giving each child a chance to read led to better overall achievement than calling on students randomly. The critical factor in going round the circle may be that each child has a chance to partic-

Educational Psychology: The discipline concerned with teaching and learning processes; applies the methods and theories of psychology and has its own as well.

ipate. Without a system for calling on everyone, many students can be overlooked or skipped. Research suggests there are better alternatives for teaching reading than going around the circle, but if teachers choose this alternative, they should make sure that everyone has the chance for practice and feedback (Tierney, Readence, & Dishner, 1990).

Classroom Management. Students are engaged in an appropriate and educationally meaningful task, but still, some students are repeatedly out of their seats without permission, wandering around the room. What should the teacher do?

Common Sense Answer. Each time the wanderers get up, the teacher should remind students to remain in their seats. These repeated reminders will help overactive students remember the rule. If the teacher does not remind them and lets them get away with breaking the rules, both the out-of-seat students and the rest of the class may decide the teacher is not really serious about the rule.

Answer Based on Research. In a now-classic study, Madsen, Becker, Thomas, Koser, and Plager (1968) found that the more often a teacher told students to sit down when they were out of their seats, the more often the students got out of their seats without permission. When the teacher ignored students who were out of their seats and praised students who were sitting down, the rate of out-of-seat behaviour dropped greatly. When the teacher returned to the previous system of telling students to sit down, the rate of out-of-seat behaviour increased once again. It seems that—at least under some conditions—the more a teacher says "Sit down!" the more the students stand up!

Skipping Grades. Should a school encourage exceptionally bright students to skip grades or to enter university or college early?

Common Sense Answer. No! Very intelligent students who are a year or two younger than their classmates are likely to be social misfits. They are neither physically nor emotionally ready for dealing with older students and would be miserable in the social situations that are so important in school, especially in the later grades.

Answer Based on Research. Maybe. According to Samuel Kirk and his colleagues (1993), "From early admissions to school to early admissions to college, research studies invariably report that children who have been accelerated have adjusted as well as or better than have children of similar ability who have not been accelerated" (p. 105). Whether acceleration is the best solution for a student depends on many specific individual characteristics, including the intelligence and maturity of the student, and on the other available options. For some students, moving quickly through the material and working in advanced courses with older students is a very good idea.

Connect & Extend
To the research
Read and discuss the article by Gage, N. L. (1991). The obviousness of social and educational research results. *Educational Researcher, 20*(1), 10–16. Focus Questions: What makes findings in educational research seem "obvious"? What is the danger in this kind of thinking?

Lily Wong (1987) demonstrated that just seeing research results in writing can make them seem obvious. She selected 12 findings from research on teaching; one of them was the "taking turns" result noted above. She presented six of the findings in their correct form and six in *exactly the opposite form* to college students and to experienced teachers. Both the college students and teachers rated about half of the *wrong* findings as "obviously" correct. In a follow-up study, other participants were shown the 12 findings and their opposites and were asked to pick which ones were correct. For 8 of the 12 findings, the participants chose the wrong result more often than the right one.

You may have thought that educational psychologists spend their time discovering the obvious. The examples above point out the danger of this kind of thinking. When a principle is stated in simple terms, it can sound simplistic. A similar phenomenon takes place when we see a gifted dancer or athlete perform; the well—trained performer makes it look easy. But we see only the results of the training, not all the work that went into mastering the individual movements. And bear in mind that any research finding—or its opposite—may sound like common sense. The issue is not what *sounds* sensible, but what is demonstrated when the principle is put to the test (Gage, 1991).

Using Research to Understand and Improve Teaching

Conducting research to test possible answers is one of two major tasks of educational psychology. The other task is combining the results of various studies into theories that attempt to present a unified view of such things as teaching, learning, and development.

Descriptive Studies.   Educational psychologists design and conduct many different kinds of research studies in their attempts to understand teaching and learning. Some of these studies are "descriptive," that is, their purpose is to describe events in a particular class or several classes. Reports of **descriptive studies** often include survey results, interview responses, samples of actual classroom dialogue, or records of class activities.

One descriptive approach, classroom **ethnography**, is borrowed from anthropology. Ethnographic methods involve studying naturally occurring events in the life of a group and trying to understand the meaning of these events to the people involved. For example, the descriptions of expert high school mathematics teachers in the opening pages of this chapter were taken from an ethnographic study by Hilda Borko and Carol Livingston (1989). The researchers made detailed observations in the teachers' classes and analyzed these observations, along with audio recordings and information from interviews with the teachers, in order to describe differences between novice and expert teachers.

In some descriptive research, researchers carefully analyze videotapes of classes to identify recurring patterns of teacher and student behaviour. In other studies, the researcher uses **participant observation** and works within the class or school to understand the actions from the perspectives of the teacher and the students. Researchers also may employ case studies. A **case study** investigates in depth how a teacher plans courses, for example, or how a student tries to learn specific material.

Correlational Studies.   Often the results of descriptive studies include reports of correlations. We will take a minute to examine this concept, because you will encounter many correlations in the coming chapters. A **correlation** is a number that indicates both the strength and the direction of a relationship between two events or measurements. Correlations range from 1.00 to —1.00. The closer the correlation is to either 1.00 or —1.00, the stronger the relationship. For example, the correlation between height and weight is about .70 (a strong relationship); the correlation between height and number of languages spoken is about .00 (no relationship at all).

The sign of the correlation tells the direction of the relationship. A **positive correlation** indicates that the two factors increase or decrease together. As one gets larger, so does the other. Height and weight are positively correlated because greater height tends to be associated with greater weight. A **negative correlation** means that increases in one factor are related to decreases in the other. For example, the correlation between outside temperature and the weight of clothing worn is negative, since people tend to wear clothing of increasing weight as the temperature decreases.

It is important to note that correlations do not prove cause and effect (see Figure 1.1). Height and weight are correlated—taller people tend to weigh more than shorter people. But gaining weight obviously does not cause you to grow taller. Knowing a person's height simply allows you to make a general prediction about that person's weight. Educational psychologists identify correlations so they can make predictions about important events in the classroom.

Descriptive Studies: Studies that collect detailed information about specific situations, often using observation, surveys, interviews, recordings, or a combination of these methods.

Ethnography: A descriptive approach to research that focuses on life within a group and tries to understand the meaning of events to the people involved.

Participant Observation: A method for conducting descriptive research in which the researcher becomes a participant in the situation in order to better understand life in that group.

Case Study: Intensive study of one person or one situation.

Correlation: Statistical description of how closely two variables are related.

Positive Correlation: A relationship between two variables in which the two increase or decrease together. Example: calorie intake and weight gain.

Negative Correlation: A relationship between two variables in which a high value on one is associated with a low value on the other. Example: height and distance from top of head to the ceiling.

▲ *These students are conducting field observations and measurements as part of a science lesson. What will they learn using this approach? Can research shed light on this question?*

Connect & Extend
To real life
Perfect positive (1.0) correlation: the radius of a circle and its circumference. Perfect negative (-1.0) correlation: the number of minutes of daylight and the number of minutes of dark each day. Less than perfect positive correlation: the cost of a car and the cost of insuring it; child's IQ score and school grades: .39 (Sattler, 1992). Less than perfect negative correlation: cost of a theatre ticket and distance from the stage. Zero correlation: population of India and the winning percentage of the New York Yankees.

Experimental Studies. A second type of research—**experimentation**—allows educational psychologists to go beyond predictions and actually study cause and effect. Instead of just observing and describing an existing situation, the investigators introduce changes and note the results. First, a number of comparable groups of subjects are created. In psychological research, the term **subjects** generally refers to the people being studied—teachers or Grade 8 students, for example—not to subjects such as math or science. One common way to make sure that groups of subjects are essentially the same is to assign each subject to a group using a random procedure. **Random** means each subject has an equal chance to be in any group.

In one or more of these groups, the experimenters change some aspect of the situation to see if this change or "treatment" has an expected effect. The results in each group are then compared. Usually statistical tests are conducted to see if the differences between the groups are significant. When differences are described as **statistically significant**, it means that they probably did not happen simply by chance. A number of the studies we will examine attempt to identify cause—and—effect relationships by asking questions such as this: If teachers ignore students who are out of their seats without permission and praise students who are working hard at their desks (cause), will students spend more time working at their desks (effect)?

In many cases, both descriptive and experimental research occur together. The study by Ogden, Brophy, and Evertson (1977) described at the beginning of this section is a good example. In order to answer questions about the relationship between how students are selected to read in a primary—grade class and their achievement in reading, these investigators first observed students and teachers in a number of classrooms and then measured the reading achievement of the students. They found that having students read in a predictable order was associated, or correlated, with gains in reading scores. With a simple correlation such as this, however, the researchers could not be sure that the strategy was actually causing the effect. In the second part of the study, Ogden and her colleagues asked several teachers to call on each student in turn. They then compared reading achievement in these groups with achievement in groups where teachers used other strategies. This second part of the research was thus an experimental study.

Experimentation: Research method in which variables are manipulated and the effects recorded.

Subjects: People or animals participating in a study.

Random: Without any definite pattern; following no rule.

Statistically Significant: Not likely to be a chance occurrence.

Theories for Teaching. The major goal of educational psychology is understanding teaching and learning, and research is a primary tool. Reaching this goal is a slow process; there are very few landmark studies that answer a question once and for all. Human beings are too complicated. Instead, research in educational psychology examines limited aspects of a situation—perhaps a few variables at a time,

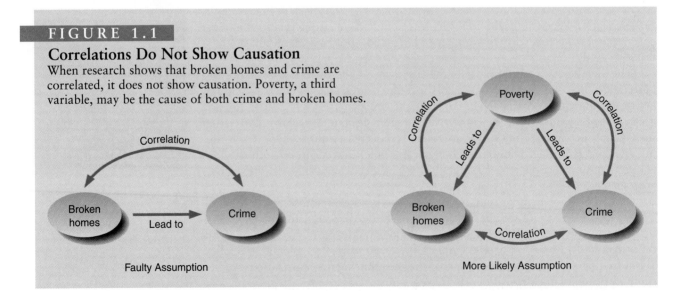

FIGURE 1.1

Correlations Do Not Show Causation
When research shows that broken homes and crime are correlated, it does not show causation. Poverty, a third variable, may be the cause of both crime and broken homes.

Correlation
Broken homes — Lead to → Crime
Faulty Assumption

Poverty
Correlation   Correlation
Leads to   Leads to
Broken homes   Crime
Correlation
More Likely Assumption

or life in one or two classrooms. If enough studies are completed in a certain area and findings repeatedly point to the same conclusions, we eventually arrive at a **principle**. This is the term for an established relationship between two or more factors—between a certain teaching strategy, for example, and student achievement.

Another tool for building a better understanding of the teaching and learning processes is **theory**. The common-sense notion of theory (as in "Oh well, it was only a theory") is "a guess or hunch." But the scientific meaning of theory is quite different. According to Keith Stanovich at the Ontario Institute for Studies in Education, "A theory in science is an interrelated set of concepts that is used to explain a body of data and to make predictions about the results of future experiments" (1992, p. 21). Given a number of established principles, educational psychologists have developed explanations for the relationships among many variables and even whole systems of relationships. There are theories to explain how language develops, how differences in intelligence occur, and, as noted earlier, how people learn.

Few theories explain and predict perfectly. In this book, you will see many examples of educational psychologists taking different theoretical positions and disagreeing on the overall explanations of such issues as learning and motivation. Since no one theory offers all the answers, it makes sense to consider what each has to offer.

So why, you may ask, is it necessary to deal with theories? Why not just stick to principles? The answer is that both are useful. Principles of classroom management, for example, will give you help with specific problems. A good theory of classroom management, on the other hand, will give you a new way of thinking about discipline problems; it will give you tools for creating solutions to many different problems and for predicting what might work in new situations. A major goal of this book is to provide you with the best and the most useful theories for teaching—those that have solid evidence behind them. Although you may prefer some theories over others, consider them all as ways of understanding the challenges teachers face.

Connect & Extend
To what you know
Are the following studies descriptive (D) or experimental (E)?
1. Researchers observe teachers of classes that have high achievement in order to determine how these teachers are alike.(D) 2. Teachers give three groups of impulsive children different types of training to determine which type of training is most effective in reducing impulsivity.(E) 3. Researchers administer IQ tests to a group of boys and girls to determine if there is a relationship between gender and verbal ability.(D) 4. Teachers use two different methods of instruction for two similar groups of math students to determine which method leads to higher scores on a math achievement test.(E)

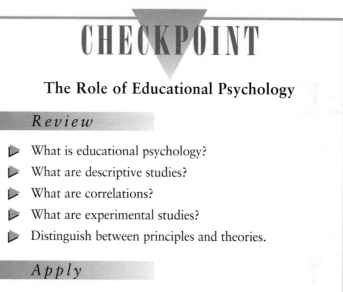

CHECKPOINT

The Role of Educational Psychology

Review

▷ What is educational psychology?

▷ What are descriptive studies?

▷ What are correlations?

▷ What are experimental studies?

▷ Distinguish between principles and theories.

Apply

▷ What would you say to someone who asserts that "teaching is just common sense"?

*T*he Contents of This Book

Part One of this text focuses on the students. In Part One, we examine the ways in which students develop. Because children may differ from adolescents and adults in their thinking, language, and images about themselves, they may require different kinds of teaching. As a teacher, you will want to take into account the mental, physical, emotional, and social abilities and limitations of your students.

Also, Part One discusses how children differ from one another in their abilities, previous learning, learning styles and preferences, and in the ways that they have been prepared for schools by their cultural experiences. Classrooms today are becoming more and more diverse. Teachers are expected to work with students with learning disabilities and visual or hearing impairments, for example, and with students who have developmental disabilities or who are gifted or developmentally advanced. And most classrooms today are multicultural, with students who speak different languages and come from a variety of cultural backgrounds.

Connect & Extend
To the research
Killion, J. P., & Todnem, G. R. (1991). A process for personal theory building. *Educational Leadership, 48*(6), 14–16. *Focus Question:* Why do teachers need a personal theory for teaching?

Principle: Established relationship between factors.

Theory: Integrated statement of principles that attempts to explain a phenomenon and make predictions.

Teachers must be able to recognize, respect, and adapt to these individual and group differences and to create classroom communities that allow students to belong and to thrive.

Having introduced the students, we will move to one of the most important topics in both educational psychology and the classroom: human learning. Part Two explores the three approaches to the study of learning: behavioural, cognitive, and sociocognitive and constructivist. We will also see how these approaches can be applied in a number of practical ways, including strategies for teaching and classroom management and instruction in various subject areas. An understanding of how students learn is the basis for teachers' professional knowledge about both general and specific teaching strategies.

Having covered the dual foundations of teaching—the students and the processes of learning—we can concentrate in Part Three on actual practice. Here we examine theories of motivation and their applications to teaching. There is no learning without attention and engagement, so teachers and students must understand and incorporate the motivational factors that support active, engaged, independent learning. Because most learning and teaching happen in groups, we will examine how to organize and manage a classroom full of active learners. And because teachers deal with individuals as well as groups, we will spend some time discussing communication and interpersonal relationships. In this part of the book, we also look at instruction from two perspectives: a teacher—focused view that emphasizes the teacher's role in planning, providing, and monitoring instruction, and a student—centred view that emphasizes the students' active construction of understanding. Teachers owe it to their students to design powerful environments for learning, so teachers must understand how different approaches can influence students' learning.

In Part Four, we consider how to evaluate what has been taught. Because to learn is to become more knowledgeable and competent, teachers must have at their disposal ways to assess knowledge and competence in order to guide students and give them useful information so they can guide themselves. We will look at standardized tests, teacher—made tests, grading systems, and various alternatives to the traditional systems of evaluation and grading.

How This Book Can Help *You* Learn

Earlier, you were encouraged to "take this book personally"—to use it to learn more about learning, motivation, goal setting, studying, test taking, and self—regulation so you can apply the knowledge to your life now. In addition, if you are a teacher or prospective teacher, this text will help you build a knowledge base for teaching. The structure as well as the content support learning. Here is how you might use the different elements of the book to help you develop a base of knowledge for use as a student now and always and as a teacher later.

Getting Ready to Learn. Each chapter begins with several features to help you get ready for learning. You are asked several questions to start you thinking about a topic related to the chapter. Your answers may bring to mind information you already know about the topics in the chapter. You will soon see that all learning begins with what students already know and believe. The chapter *outline* and the *overview* give you a snapshot of the organization of the material to come. Next you encounter a *What Would You Do?* scenario, asking you to project yourself into a classroom and decide how you would handle a problem situation. As you consider possible actions, you will be confronting issues from the upcoming chapter. So, as you read the chapter, you can check out and perhaps expand your ideas for handling the situation. Reading with a purpose in mind aids comprehension. We hope the What Would You Do? problem gives you good reasons and purposes for reading that tie knowledge in educational psychology to classroom practice.

Connect & Extend
To real life
A national survey of 750 Canadian elementary and secondary—school teachers indicates Canada's teachers are committed professionals and lifelong learners. The New Approaches to Lifelong Learning (NALL) study (2000), conducted by researchers at the University of Toronto and funded by the Social Sciences and Humanities Research Council of Canada, indicates that, on average, Canadian teachers work 47 to 55 hours each week, more than most other professional and managerial groups in Canada. How do teachers spend this time? The survey reveals that, on average, teachers spend about 28 hours each week on direct teaching activities, and 19 hours on other school work. Outside class time, teachers are preparing courses, planning lessons, marking students' work, and meeting with students and parents. In addition, the survey found that the majority of teachers spend several hours each week engaged in extracurricular activities, such as coaching sports and running school clubs. Finally, the survey found that more than 90 percent of Canada's teachers participate in coursework, professional workshops, and informal learning activities that are connected with their current teaching duties and keep them current with best practices in their field.
Discuss the validity of these results with the rest of your class. Do you think they are representative of the work teachers do? What are some potential biases? You might want to continue the discussion by noting the need to be "critical consumers" of research results, particularly those reported in the press. (National survey finds heavy teacher workloads. *Retrieved from*
http://gleneagle.vr9.com/go/ resources/staff/teacherworkload-study.html)

Aids to Understanding. Throughout the text, you will find other aids to understanding and application. Use them fully to get the most from this book. Notice the headings and subheadings as you read. These headings show the structure of the chapter, the main ideas, and the related ideas under each main idea. Key terms are highlighted in bold and defined in the margin the first time they are used. There is a list of key terms at the end of each chapter. When you finish reading, test yourself to see if you can briefly explain these terms in your own words. Also, after each main section of the chapter are *Checkpoint* boxes, asking you to check your understanding of higher—level principles. At the end of the chapter is a *Summary* that reflects the contents in the Checkpoint boxes.

Teaching Portfolio: A depiction of you as a teacher, usually including a curriculum vitae, statement of teaching philosophy, examples of your teaching plans and activities, example assignments and tests, students' work, and even videos or CD excerpts of teaching.

Applying Knowledge. If the ideas in this book are to be valuable, they need to be used to think about and act on problems of teaching and learning—both your own and those of your students. That emphasis is clear at the beginning of each chapter when you are asked to consider, What Would You Do? Throughout every chapter after this one are *Guidelines*, principles that can be applied in teaching. Each principle includes a few examples to encourage you to think about applications. One set of Guidelines focuses on families as partners in teaching—an important consideration today. Every chapter also contains a *Point/Counterpoint* debate about a critical issue in educational psychology. You will see that educators do not always agree about the meaning of research findings or how those findings should be applied. At the end of every chapter after this one is a section called *Becoming a Professional* that gives you guidance for:

- ▶ Developing a personal study guide.
- ▶ Organizing a professional **teaching portfolio.**
- ▶ Developing a resource file.

Finally, we return to the What Would You Do? situation to see what several experienced teachers around the country would do. Compare your ideas with theirs and with the information in the chapter. Do you agree? What would you add?

Becoming a Good Beginning Teacher. Becoming an expert teacher takes time and experience, but you can start now by becoming a good beginner. You can develop a repertoire of effective principles and practices for your first years of teaching so that some activities quickly become automatic. You can also develop the habit of questioning and analyzing these accepted practices and your own teaching so you can solve new problems when they arise. You can learn to look behind the effective techniques identified in research to ask: Why did this approach work with these students? What else might be as good or better? The answers to these questions and your ability to analyze the situations are much more important than the specific techniques themselves. As you ask and answer questions, you will be refining your personal theories of teaching.

The goal of this book is to help you become an excellent beginning teacher, one who can both apply and improve many techniques. Even more important, we hope this book will cause you to think about students and teaching in new ways, so you will have the foundation for becoming an expert as you gain experience.

CHECKPOINT

How This Book Can Help *You* Learn

Review

▷ What methods will you use to learn educational psychology?

*S*ummary

What Is Good Teaching?

What do expert teachers know?

It takes time and experience to become an expert teacher. These teachers have a rich store of well—organized knowledge about the many specific situations of teaching. This includes knowledge about the subjects they teach, their students, general teaching strategies, subject-specific ways of teaching, settings for learning, curriculum materials, and the goals of education.

What are the artistic and scientific aspects of teaching?

Teaching is both an art and a science. Effective teaching requires an understanding of research findings on learning and instruction and knowledge of effective techniques and routines. Teaching also calls for the creativity, talent, and judgment of an artist.

Teaching: Artistry, Technique, and a Lot of Work

What are the concerns of beginning teachers?

Learning to teach is a gradual process. The concerns and problems of teachers change as they progress. During the beginning years, attention tends to be focused on survival. Maintaining discipline, motivating students, evaluating students' work, and dealing with parents are universal concerns for beginning teachers. The more experienced teacher can move on to concerns about professional growth and effectiveness with a wide range of students.

The Ultimate Goal of Teaching: Lifelong Expert Learning

What is self-regulated learning?

One important goal of teaching is to prepare students for lifelong learning. To reach this goal, students must be self-regulated learners; that is, they must have a combination of the knowledge, motivation to learn, and volition that provides the skill and will to learn independently and effectively. Knowledge includes an understanding of self, subject, task, learning strategy, and contexts for application. Motivation to learn provides the commitment, and volition is the follow-through that combats distraction and protects persistence.

The Role of Educational Psychology

What is educational psychology?

The goals of educational psychology are to understand and to improve the teaching and learning processes. Educational psychologists develop knowledge and methods; they also use the knowledge and methods of psychology and other related disciplines to study learning and teaching in everyday situations.

Descriptive studies.

Reports of descriptive studies often include survey results, interview responses, samples of actual classroom dialogue, or records of the class activities. One descriptive approach, classroom ethnography, is borrowed from anthropology. Ethnographic methods involve studying the naturally occurring events in the life of a group and trying to understand the meaning of these events to the people involved. Researchers also may employ case studies. A case study investigates in depth how a teacher plans courses, for example, or how a student tries to learn specific material. Both descriptive studies and experimental research can provide valuable information for teachers.

What are correlations?

Correlations allow you to predict events that are likely to occur in the classroom. A correlation is a number that indicates both the strength and the direction of a relationship between two events or measurements. Correlations range from 1.00 to -1.00. The closer the correlation is to either 1.00 or -1.00, the stronger the relationship.

Experimental studies.

Experimental studies can indicate cause—and—effect relationships and should help teachers introduce useful changes. Instead of simply observing and describing an existing situation, the investigators introduce changes and note the results.

What is the difference between principles and theories?

A principle is an established relationship between two or more factors—between a certain teaching strategy, for example, and student achievement. A theory is an interrelated set of concepts that is used to explain a body of data and to make predictions about the results of future experiments. There are theories to explain how language develops, how differences in intelligence occur, and, as noted earlier, how people learn. The principles from research offer a number of possible answers to specific problems, and the theories offer perspectives for analyzing almost any situation that may arise. The process of analyzing research and theory will encourage you to think critically about teaching.

How This Book Can Help *You* Learn

Becoming a good teacher means being a good learner. Much of the information in this text will help you become a more expert learner if you take the ideas personally and apply them to your own life. Take advantage of the book's features—the overviews, outlines, What Would You Do? questions, chapter Checkpoints and Summaries, organizational headings, Guidelines, and Teachers' Casebooks—to become an expert learner.

Key Terms

case study, *p. 13*

correlation, *p. 13*

descriptive studies, *p. 13*

educational psychology, *p. 11*

ethnography, *p. 13*

experimentation, *p. 14*

expert teachers, *p. 6*

negative correlation, *p. 13*

participant observation, *p. 13*

positive correlation, *p. 13*

principle, *p. 15*

random, *p. 14*

reflective, *p. 7*

self-regulated learners, *p. 10*

statistically significant, *p. 14*

subjects, *p. 14*

teaching portfolio, *p. 17*

theory, *p. 15*

volition, *p. 10*

Weblinks

www.cmec.ca/educmin.stm

This site lists links for the education ministry in every province. Ministry sites offer a wealth of practical, legal, and political material that provides context for the application of educational psychology in the country's schools.

http://ericir.syr.edu/Eric

The ERIC database, the world's largest source of education information, contains more than 950 000 abstracts of documents and journal articles on education research and practice. By searching AskERIC's Web—based version of the ERIC database, you can access the ERIC abstracts that are also found in the printed medium, *Resources in Education and Current Index to Journals in Education*. The database is updated monthly, ensuring that the information you receive is timely and accurate.

www.mhhe.com/socscience/education/edpsych/edpsytop.html

This site is a collection of links to extensive information on the Web that relates directly or indirectly to educational psychology.

www.schoolnet.ca/home/e

Established in 1993, Canada's SchoolNet is designed to promote the effective use of information technology among Canadians by helping all Canadian public schools and libraries to connect to the Internet. SchoolNet is a collaborative initiative among provincial and territorial governments, universities and colleges, education associations, the telecommunications industry, and other private—sector representatives. The SchoolNet Web site showcases innovative, award—winning, Internet—based educational resources and services that provide teachers and learners alike with a single platform from which to access the information highway.

http://tip.psychology.org

The Theory Into Practice (TIP) database is a tool intended to make learning and instructional theory more accessible to educators. The database briefly summarizes 50 major theories of learning and instruction. These theories can also be accessed by learning domains and concepts.

What Would They Do?

Here is how some practising teachers responded to the teaching situation presented at the beginning of this chapter about writing a letter of recommendation for a colleague who has been nominated for a Prime Minister's Award for Teaching Excellence.

SALLY BENDER

George Fitton School
Brandon, Manitoba

While, individually, we have our ideas about what an exemplary teacher is and should be, it is important to look at what the profession is saying about the same issue. Taking time to read the professional journals and other literature would help in determining what a letter describing a colleague's performance should include. The granting of such a prestigious award could well depend on your words.

To prepare for writing the letter, I would list qualities describing my colleague's commitment to the profession and to the children whose lives are touched by excellent teaching practice. The list would include the following:

▶ builds close relationships with students and the school community through respect and example;

▶ creates a classroom that encourages and honours diversity in thinking and response;

▶ provides ongoing opportunities for children to take responsibility and ownership for what happens in the classroom and beyond;

▶ knows about child growth and development and uses that knowledge to drive the teaching and learning that occurs in the classroom;

▶ manages the classroom with respect for the rights of the children and encourages them to take responsibility for their own actions at all times;

▶ is flexible enough to respond to "teachable moments" by giving up the "teaching" agenda for the "learning" one;

▶ models patience, tolerance, and respect for all;

▶ shares learning and teaching practice with colleagues;

▶ works as a team member and shares responsibility;

▶ is enthusiastic, challenging, and responsive to all students and colleagues;

▶ has consistent expectations and evaluates regularly the learning that is taking place for all students;

▶ provides a positive and encouraging atmosphere where children are free to take risks while learning and to learn from and through their mistakes;

▶ sees learning as a process that results in better performance;

▶ is knowledgeable about learning styles and uses that knowledge when planning lessons and learning experiences for all children;

▶ provides opportunities for learning that begin with the child's experiences and develop from the child's perspective;

▶ plans activities where cooperation is a necessity, for it is a life skill;

▶ ensures a classroom environment that is rich in print and language—stimulating possibilities;

▶ provides a balance between teacher—directed and child—initiated experiences;

▶ encourages parent support through regular communication.

By determining the qualities that you value in your colleague, you will be better prepared to write the letter of recommendation to accompany the nomination for such a prestigious award.

BARB POPOFF

Lord Baden—Powell Elementary
Coquitlam, British Columbia

Following are the qualities that I consider important in being an effective teacher.

An effective teacher:

▶ demonstrates his or her love of teaching and working with children by providing a warm and caring environment for learning. In a positive learning environment, children take risks without feeling threatened or insecure. They feel safe making decisions about their learning. A happy environment balances hard work and fun.

▶ considers the self-esteem of children and provides opportunities for children to feel successful and to take pride in their accomplishments. Balancing encouragement, motivation, and constructive criticism allows self—esteem to grow within the structure of the curriculum.

▶ knows the children—their strengths and their needs. An effective teacher is flexible and can modify the curriculum or teaching lesson to fit the needs and/or strengths of the children. Such a learning environment accommodates children with learning problems, as well as those who need to be challenged.

▶ works cooperatively and collaboratively with colleagues. The teaching profession can be quite overwhelming, especially to a teacher just starting out. Advising, encouraging, and showing direction and support lessens the anxiety and confusion felt by beginning teachers.

▶ continues to develop professionally and seeks self—improvement by attending regular professional seminars and conferences. Growth and learning are lifelong, and new ideas and skills are an asset and an exciting part of teaching in any classroom.

Cognitive Development and Language

hink for a moment about how you would explain the concept of "symbol" to a 6-year-old and to a 14-year-old. Would you use words? Pictures? Specific examples? What kind? What do you know about how younger and older children differ in their thinking?

The material in this chapter will help you answer these questions and many others about how young people think and how their thinking changes over time. These changes in thinking and understanding are called *cognitive development*.

In this chapter, we begin with a discussion of the general principles of human development and a brief look at the human brain. Then we will examine the ideas of two of the most influential cognitive developmental theorists, Jean Piaget and Lev Vygotsky. Piaget's ideas have implications for teachers about what their students can learn and when the students are ready to learn it. We will examine important criticisms of his ideas as well.

The work of Lev Vygotsky, a Russian psychologist, is becoming more and more influential. His theory highlights the important role teachers and parents play in the cognitive development of the child. Finally, we will explore language development and discuss the role of the school in developing and enriching language skills.

By the time you have completed this chapter, you should be able to:

▶ State three general principles of human development, and give examples of each.

▶ Explain how children's thinking differs at each of Piaget's four stages of development.

▶ Summarize the implications of Piaget's theory for teaching students of different ages.

▶ Contrast Piaget's and Vygotsky's ideas about cognitive development.

▶ Give implications of Vygotsky's theory for teaching students of any age.

▶ Describe briefly the stages of language development.

▶ Suggest ways a teacher can help children expand their language use and comprehension.

What Would You Do?

TEACHERS' CASEBOOK

The provincial curriculum guide calls for a unit on poetry, including lessons on *symbolism* in poems. You are concerned that many of your Grade 5 students may not be ready to understand this abstract concept. To test the waters, you ask a few students to describe a symbol.

"It's sorta like a big metal thing that you bang together." Tracy waves her hands like a drum major.

"Yeah," Sean adds, "My sister plays one in the high school band."

You realize they are on the wrong track here, so you try again. "I was thinking of a different kind of symbol, like a ring as a symbol of marriage or a heart as a symbol of love, or . . ."

You are met with blank stares.

Trevor ventures, "You mean like the Olympic torch?"

"And what does that symbolize, Trevor?" you ask.

"I said, the torch." Trevor wonders how you could be so dense.

▶ What do these students' reactions tell you about children's thinking?

▶ How would you approach this unit?

▶ What more would you do to "listen" to your students' thinking so you could match your teaching to their level of thinking?

▶ How would you give your students concrete experience with symbolism?

▶ How will you decide if the students are not developmentally ready for this material?

A Definition of Development

The term **development** in its most general psychological sense refers to certain changes that occur in human beings (or animals) between conception and death. The term is not applied to all changes, but rather to those that appear in orderly ways and remain for a reasonably long period of time. A temporary change caused by a brief illness, for example, is not considered a part of development. Psychologists also make a value judgment in determining which changes qualify as development. The changes, at least those that occur early in life, are generally assumed to be for the better and to result in behaviour that is more adaptive, more organized, more effective, and more complex (Mussen, Conger, & Kagan, 1984).

Human development can be divided into a number of different aspects. **Physical development**, as you might guess, deals with changes in the body. **Personal development** is the term generally used to describe changes in an individual's personality. **Social development** refers to changes in the way an individual relates to others. **Cognitive development** implies changes in thinking.

Many changes during development are simply matters of growth and maturation. **Maturation** refers to changes that occur naturally and spontaneously and that are, to a large extent, genetically programmed. Such changes emerge over time and are relatively unaffected by environment, except in cases of malnutrition or severe illness. Much of a person's physical development falls into this category. Other changes are brought about through learning, as individuals interact with their environment. Such changes make up a large part of a person's social development. But what about the development of thinking and personality? Most psychologists agree that in these areas, both maturation and interaction with the environment (or nature and nurture, as they are sometimes called) are important, but they disagree about the amount of emphasis to place on each.

Development: Orderly, adaptive changes we go through from conception to death.

Physical Development: Changes in body structure that take place as one grows.

Personal Development: Changes in personality that take place as one grows.

Social Development: Changes over time in the ways we relate to others.

Cognitive Development: Gradual, orderly changes by which mental processes become more complex and sophisticated.

Maturation: Genetically programmed, naturally occurring changes over time.

General Principles of Development

Although there is disagreement about what is involved in development and about the way it takes place, there are a few general principles almost all theorists would support.

1. *People develop at different rates.* In your own classroom, you will have a whole range of examples of different developmental rates. Some students will be larger, better coordinated, or more mature in their thinking and social relationships. Others will be much slower to mature in these areas. Except in rare cases of very rapid or very slow development, such differences are normal and to be expected in any large group of students.

2. *Development is relatively orderly.* People develop certain abilities before others. In infancy they sit before they walk, babble before they talk, and see the world through their own eyes before they can begin to imagine how others see it. In school, they will master addition before algebra, Bambi before Shakespeare, and so on. Theorists may disagree on exactly what comes before what, but they all seem to find a relatively logical progression.

3. *Development takes place gradually.* Very rarely do changes appear overnight. A student who cannot manipulate a pencil or answer a hypothetical question may well develop this ability, but the change is likely to take time.

The Brain and Cognitive Development

If you have taken an introductory psychology class, you have read about the brain and nervous system. You probably remember, for example, that there are several different areas of the brain and that certain areas are involved in particular functions. For example, the feathery-looking cerebellum coordinates and orchestrates smooth, skilled movements—from the graceful gestures of the dancer to the every-day action of eating without stabbing yourself in the nose with a fork. The cerebellum may also play a role in higher cognitive functions such as learning. The thalamus is involved in our ability to learn new information, particularly if it is verbal. The reticular formation plays a role in attention and arousal, blocking some messages and sending others on to higher brain centres for processing (Wood & Wood, 1999).

The outer 0.3-cm-thick covering of the cerebrum is the wrinkled-looking cerebral cortex—the largest area of the brain. The cerebral cortex accounts for about 85 percent of the brain's weight and contains the greatest number of neurons—the tiny structures that store and transmit information; this part of the brain allows the greatest human accomplishments. This crumpled sheet of neurons serves three major functions: receiving signals from sense organs (such as visual or auditory signals), controlling voluntary movement, and forming associations. In humans, this area of the brain is much larger than in lower animals. The cortex is the last part of the brain to develop, so it is believed to be more susceptible to environmental influences than other areas of the brain. In addition, all parts of the cortex do not mature at the same rate. The part of the cortex that controls physical motor movement develops or matures first, then the areas that control complex senses such as vision and hearing, and last, the frontal lobe that controls higher-order thinking processes (Berk, 2000; Meece, 1997).

Connect & Extend
To the news
See the May 1, 2001, issue of *Maclean's* for the cover story, "How we think." Montrealer Steven Pinker is challenging other fellow neuroscientists with provocative theories about how evolution has changed the human brain. He and other researchers are probing the mysteries of learning, emotions, and how the brain functions.

Specialization and Integration

Different areas of the cortex seem to have different functions, as shown in Figure 2.1. Even though different functions are found in different areas of the

FIGURE 2.1

A View of the Cerebral Cortex

This is a simple representation of the left side of the human brain, showing the cerebral cortex. The cortex is divided into different areas or lobes, each having a variety of regions with different functions. A few of the major functions are indicated here.

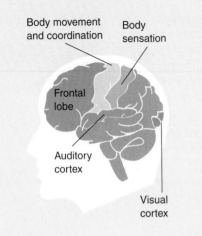

brain, these specialized functions are quite specific and elementary. To accomplish more complex functions such as speaking or reading, the various areas of the cortex must work together (Byrnes & Fox, 1998). For example, many areas of the cortex are necessary in processing language. To answer a question, you must first hear it. This involves the primary auditory cortex. Movements controlled by the motor cortex are required to speak your response. Broca's area (near the area that controls the lips, jaw, and tongue) has a role in setting up a grammatical way of expressing an idea, and Wernicke's area (near the auditory cortex) is necessary for connecting meaning with particular words. A person with a functioning Broca's area but a damaged Wernicke's area will say meaningless things in a grammatical structure. Damage limited to Broca's area, on the other hand, is associated with short, ungrammatical sentences, but the words are appropriate (Anderson, 1995a).

Another aspect of brain functioning that has implications for cognitive development is **lateralization**, or the specialization of the two hemispheres of the brain. We know that each half of the brain controls the opposite side of the body. Damage to the right side of the brain will affect movement of the left side of the body and vice versa. In addition, certain areas of the brain affect particular behaviour. For most of us, the left hemisphere of the brain is the major factor in language processing, and the right hemisphere handles most of the spatial-visual information and emotions (non-verbal information). For some left-handed people, the relationship may be reversed, but for most left-handers there is less hemispheric specialization altogether (Berk, 2000). In addition, females on average seem to show less hemispheric specialization than males (O'Boyle & Gill, 1998).

These differences in brain hemisphere performance are more relative than absolute, however; one hemisphere is just more efficient than the other in performing certain functions. Nearly any task, particularly the complex skills and abilities that concern teachers, requires participation of many different areas of the brain. For example, the right side of the brain is better at figuring out the meaning of a story, but the left side is where grammar and syntax are understood, so both sides of the brain have to work together in reading. "The primary implication of these findings is that the practice of teaching to 'different sides of the brain' is not supported by the neuroscientific research" (Byrnes & Fox, 1998, p. 310). Thus, beware of educational approaches based on simplistic views of brain functioning—what Keith Stanovich (1998), a professor at the University of Toronto, has called "the left-brain–right-brain nonsense that has inundated education through workshops, inservices, and the trade publications" (p. 420).

Storing and Transferring Information

Neurons (nerve cells that store and transfer information) send messages by releasing chemicals that jump across the synapses (the tiny spaces between the neuron fibres) from one neuron fibre to another. By the time we are born, we have all the neurons we will ever have, about 100 to 200 billion (Baron, 1998). However, the fibres that reach out from the neurons and the synapses between the fibre ends do increase during the first years of life, perhaps into adolescence.

Neurons that are stimulated and used continue to add new synapses, making new connections, but unstimulated neurons lose connections and die off. In fact, animal studies have shown that rats raised in stimulating environments (with toys, tasks for learning, and human handling) develop 25 percent more synapses than rats that are raised with little stimulation (Greenough, Black, & Wallace, 1987). Early stimulation is important for humans as well. It is clear that extreme

Lateralization: The specialization of the two hemispheres (sides) of the brain cortex.

deprivation of stimulation can have negative effects on brain development, but this does not mean that extra stimulation will improve development for young children who are getting adequate or typical amounts of stimulation (Byrnes & Fox, 1998; Kolb & Whishaw, 1998). Of course, many factors besides stimulus deprivation, such as the mother's intake of drugs (including alcohol and caffeine) during pregnancy, toxins in the infant's environment, or poor nutrition, can have negative effects on brain development.

Another factor that influences thinking and learning is **myelination**, or the coating of neuron fibres with an insulating fatty covering. This process is something like coating bare electrical wires with rubber or plastic. The myelin coating makes message transmission faster and more efficient. Myelination happens quickly in the early years but continues gradually into adolescence and is the reason the child's brain grows rapidly in the first few years of life.

Myelination: The process by which neural fibres are coated with a fatty sheath called *myelin* that makes message transfer more efficient.

In the next decade we should see increasing research on the brain, development, learning, and teaching. For example, in 1998, there was a special issue of *Educational Psychology Review* on cognitive neuroscience and education. The authors of this volume emphasized that the brain is a complex collection of systems working together to construct understanding, detect patterns, create rules, and make sense of experience. These systems change over the lifetime as the individual matures and develops. We turn next to examine this process of change.

The first theory of cognitive development we will consider was developed by a biologist turned psychologist, Jean Piaget.

CHECKPOINT

A Definition of Development

Review

▷ Summarize three principles describing how development takes place.

▷ What part of the brain is associated with higher mental functions?

▷ What is lateralization, and why is it important?

Apply

▷ What aspect of development is involved in Trevor's understanding of "symbolism" at the opening of this chapter?

Piaget's Theory of Cognitive Development

During the past half-century, Swiss psychologist Jean Piaget devised a model describing how humans go about making sense of their world by gathering and organizing information (Piaget, 1954, 1963, 1970a, 1970b). We will examine Piaget's ideas closely, because they provide an explanation of the development of thinking from infancy to adulthood.

According to Piaget (1954), certain ways of thinking that are quite simple for an adult are not so simple for a child. Sometimes all you need to do to teach a new concept is to give a student a few basic facts as background. At other times, however, all the background facts in the world are useless. The student simply is not ready to learn the concept. With some students, you can discuss the general causes of wars and then ask why they think the Second World War broke out in 1939. But suppose the students respond with "When is 1939?" Obviously their concepts of time are different from your own. They may think, for example, that they will some day catch up to a sibling in age, or they may confuse the past and the future.

Influences on Development

As you can see, cognitive development is much more than the addition of new facts and ideas to an existing store of information. According to Piaget, our thinking

▲ Jean Piaget was a Swiss psychologist whose insightful descriptions of children's thinking changed the way we understand cognitive development.

Connect & Extend
To your students' thinking
To experience some of the ways children differ from adults in their thinking, ask children of various ages the following questions:

What does it mean to be alive?
Can you name some things that are alive?
Is the moon alive?
Where do dreams come from?
Where do they go?
What is farther, to go from the bottom of the hill all the way to the top or to go from the top of the hill all the way to the bottom?
Can a person live in Toronto and Ontario at the same time?
Will you be just as old as your big brother some day?
When is yesterday?
Where does the sun go at night?

▲ *According to Piaget, the first step from action to thinking is the internalization of action, performing an action mentally rather than physically.*

Organization: Ongoing process of arranging information and experience into mental systems or categories.

Adaptation: Adjustment to the environment.

Schemes: Mental systems or categories of perception and experience.

processes change radically, though slowly, from birth to maturity because we constantly strive to make sense of the world. How do we do this? Piaget identified four factors—biological maturation, activity, social experiences, and equilibration—that interact to influence changes in thinking (Piaget, 1970a). Let's briefly examine the first three factors. We'll return to a discussion of equilibration in the next section.

One of the most important influences on the way we make sense of the world is *maturation,* the unfolding of the biological changes that are genetically programmed in each human being at conception. Parents and teachers have little impact on this aspect of cognitive development, except to be sure that children get the nourishment and care they need to be healthy.

Activity is another influence. With physical maturation comes the increasing ability to act on the environment and learn from it. When a young child's coordination is reasonably developed, for example, the child may discover principles about balance by experimenting with a see-saw. Thus, as we act on the environment—as we explore, test, observe, and eventually organize information—we are likely to alter our thinking processes at the same time.

As we develop, we are also interacting with the people around us. According to Piaget, our cognitive development is influenced by *social transmission,* or learning from others. Without social transmission, we would need to reinvent all the knowledge already offered by our culture. The amount people can learn from social transmission varies according to their stage of cognitive development.

Maturation, activity, and social transmission all work together to influence cognitive development. How do we respond to these influences?

Basic Tendencies in Thinking

As a result of his early research in biology, Piaget concluded that all species inherit two basic tendencies, or "invariant functions." The first of these tendencies is toward **organization**—the combining, arranging, recombining, and rearranging of behaviour and thoughts into coherent systems. The second tendency is toward **adaptation**, or adjusting to the environment.

Organization. People are born with a tendency to organize their thinking processes into psychological structures. These psychological structures are our systems for understanding and interacting with the world. Simple structures are continually combined and coordinated to become more sophisticated and thus more effective. Very young infants, for example, can either look at an object or grasp it when it comes in contact with their hands. They cannot coordinate looking and grasping at the same time. As they develop, however, infants organize these two separate behavioural structures into a coordinated higher-level structure of looking at, reaching for, and grasping the object. They can, of course, still use each structure separately (Ginsburg & Opper, 1988; Miller, 1993).

Piaget gave a special name to these structures: **schemes**. In his theory, schemes are the basic building blocks of thinking. They are organized systems of actions or thought that allow us to mentally represent or "think about" the objects and events in our world. Schemes may be very small and specific—for example, the sucking-through-a-straw scheme or the recognizing-a-rose scheme. Or they may be larger and more general—the drinking scheme or the categorizing-plants scheme. As a person's thinking processes become more organized and new schemes develop, behaviour also becomes more sophisticated and better suited to the environment.

Adaptation. In addition to the tendency to organize their psychological structures, people also inherit the tendency to adapt to their environment. Two basic processes are involved in adaptation: assimilation and accommodation.

Assimilation takes place when people use their existing schemes to make sense of events in their world. Assimilation involves trying to understand something new by fitting it into what we already know. At times, we may have to distort the new information to make it fit. For example, the first time many children see a skunk, they call it a "kitty." They try to match the new experience with an existing scheme for identifying animals.

Accommodation occurs when a person must change existing schemes to respond to a new situation. If data cannot be made to fit any existing schemes, more appropriate structures must be developed. We adjust our thinking to fit the new information, instead of adjusting the information to fit our thinking. Children demonstrate accommodation when they add the scheme for recognizing skunks to their other systems for identifying animals.

People adapt to their increasingly complex environments by using existing schemes whenever these schemes work (assimilation) and by modifying and adding to their schemes when something new is needed (accommodation). In fact, both processes are required most of the time. Even using an established pattern such as sucking through a straw may require some accommodation if the straw is of a different size or length than the type you are used to. If you have tried drinking juice from box packages, you know that you have to add a new skill to your sucking scheme—don't squeeze the box or you will shoot juice through the straw, straight up into the air and into your lap. Whenever new experiences are assimilated into an existing scheme, the scheme is enlarged and changed somewhat, so assimilation involves some accommodation.

There are also times when neither assimilation nor accommodation is used. If people encounter something that is too unfamiliar, they may ignore it. Experience is filtered to fit the kind of thinking a person is doing at a given time. For example, if you overhear a conversation in a foreign language, you probably will not try to make sense of the exchange unless you have some knowledge of the language.

Equilibration. According to Piaget, organizing, assimilating, and accommodating can be seen as a kind of complex balancing act. In his theory, the actual changes in thinking take place through the process of **equilibration**—the act of searching for a balance. Piaget assumed that people continually test the adequacy of their thinking processes in order to achieve that balance.

Briefly, the process of equilibration works like this: if we apply a particular scheme to an event or situation and the scheme works, equilibrium exists. If the scheme does not produce a satisfying result, **disequilibrium** exists, and we become uncomfortable. This motivates us to keep searching for a solution through assimilation and accommodation, and thus our thinking changes and moves ahead. In order to maintain a balance between our schemes for understanding the world and the data the world provides, we continually assimilate new information using existing schemes, and we accommodate our thinking whenever unsuccessful attempts to assimilate produce disequilibrium.

Assimilation: Fitting new information into existing schemes.

Accommodation: Altering existing schemes or creating new ones in response to new information.

Equilibration: Search for mental balance between cognitive schemes and information from the environment.

Disequilibrium: In Piaget's theory, the "out-of-balance" state that occurs when a person realizes that his or her current ways of thinking are not working to solve a problem or understand a situation.

Four Stages of Cognitive Development

Now we turn to the actual differences that Piaget hypothesized for children as they grow. Piaget's four stages of cognitive development are called sensorimotor, preoperational, concrete operational, and formal operational. Piaget believed that all people pass through the same four stages in exactly the same order. These stages are generally associated with specific ages, as shown in Table 2.1. When you see ages linked to stages, remember that these are only general guidelines, not labels for all children of a certain age. Piaget was interested in the kinds of thinking abilities people are able to use, not in labelling. Often, people can use one level of thinking to solve one kind of problem and a different level to solve another. Piaget noted that individuals may go through long periods of transition between stages

TABLE 2.1 Piaget's Stages of Cognitive Development

Stage	Approximate Age	Characteristics
Sensorimotor	0–2 years	Begins to make use of imitation, memory, and thought.
		Begins to recognize that objects do not cease to exist when they are hidden.
		Moves from reflex actions to goal-directed activity.
Preoperational	2–7 years	Gradually develops use of language and ability to think in symbolic form.
		Able to think operations through logically in one direction.
		Has difficulties seeing another person's point of view.
Concrete Operational	7–11 years	Able to solve concrete (hands-on) problems in logical fashion.
		Understands laws of conservation and is able to classify and seriate.
		Understands reversibility.
Formal Operational	11–adult	Able to solve abstract problems in logical fashion.
		Becomes more scientific in thinking.
		Develops concerns about social issues, identity.

Source: From *Piaget's Theory of Cognitive and Affective Development,* 4/e by Barry J. Wadsworth. Copyright © 1971, 1979, 1984, 1989. Adapted by permission of Addison-Wesley Educational Publishers Inc.

and that a person may show characteristics of one stage in one situation but characteristics of a higher or lower stage in other situations. Therefore, knowing a student's age is never a guarantee that you know how the child will think (Ginsburg & Opper, 1988; Orlando & Machado, 1996).

Infancy: The Sensorimotor Stage. The earliest period is called the **sensorimotor** stage, because the child's thinking involves seeing, hearing, moving, touching, tasting, and so on. During this period, the infant develops **object permanence**, the understanding that objects in the environment exist whether the baby perceives them or not. As most parents discover, before infants develop object permanence, it is relatively easy to take something away from them. The trick is to distract them and remove the object while they are not looking—"out of sight, out of mind." The older infant who searches for the ball that has rolled out of sight is indicating an understanding that objects still exist even when they are not in view. Recent research, however, suggests that infants as young as three to four months may know that the object still exists, but they do not have the memory skills to "hold on" to the location of the object or the motor skills to coordinate a search (Baillargeon & De Vos, 1991; Meece, 1997).

A second major accomplishment in the sensorimotor period is the beginning of logical, **goal-directed actions**. Think of the familiar container toy for babies. It is usually plastic, has a lid, and contains several colourful items that can be dumped out and replaced. A six-month-old baby is likely to become frustrated trying to get to the toys inside. An older child who has mastered the basics of the

Sensorimotor: Involving the senses and motor activity.

Object Permanence: The understanding that objects have a separate, permanent existence.

Goal-Directed Actions: Deliberate actions toward a goal.

sensorimotor stage will probably be able to deal with the toys in an orderly fashion. Through trial and error the child will slowly build a "container toy" scheme: (1) get the lid off; (2) turn the container upside down; (3) shake if the items jam; (4) watch the items fall. Separate lower-level schemes have been organized into a higher-level scheme to achieve a goal.

The child is soon able to reverse this action by refilling the container. Learning to reverse actions is a basic accomplishment of the sensorimotor stage. As we will soon see, however, learning to reverse thinking—that is, learning to imagine the reverse of a sequence of actions—takes much longer.

Early Childhood to the Early Elementary Years: The Preoperational Stage.

By the end of the sensorimotor stage, the child can use many action schemes. As long as these schemes remain tied to physical actions, however, they are of no use in recalling the past, keeping track of information, or planning. For this, children need what Piaget called **operations**, or actions that are carried out and reversed mentally rather than physically. The stage after sensorimotor is called **preoperational**, because the child has not yet mastered these mental operations but is moving toward mastery.

According to Piaget, the first step from action to thinking is the internalization of action, performing an action mentally rather than physically. The first type of thinking that is separate from action involves making action schemes symbolic. The ability to form and use symbols—words, gestures, signs, images, and so on—is thus a major accomplishment of the preoperational period and moves children closer to mastering the mental operations of the next stage. This ability to work with symbols, such as using the word "bicycle" or a picture of a bicycle to represent a real bicycle that is not actually present, is called the **semiotic function**.

The child's earliest use of symbols is in pretending or miming. Children who are not yet able to talk will often use action symbols—pretending to drink from empty cups or touching combs to their hair, showing that they know what each object is for. This behaviour also shows that their schemes are becoming more general and less tied to specific actions. The eating scheme, for example, may be used in playing house. During the preoperational stage, we also see the rapid development of that very important symbol system, language. Between the ages of two and four, most children enlarge their vocabulary from about 200 to 2000 words.

As the child moves through the preoperational stage, the developing ability to think about objects in symbolic form remains somewhat limited to thinking in one direction only, or using *one-way logic*. It is very difficult for the child to "think backward," or imagine how to reverse the steps in a task.

Reversible thinking is involved in many tasks that are difficult for the preoperational child, such as the conservation of matter. **Conservation** is the principle that the amount or number of something remains the same even if the arrangement or appearance is changed, as long as nothing is added and nothing is taken away. You know that if you tear a piece of paper into several pieces, you will still have the same amount of paper. To prove this, you know that you can reverse the process by taping the pieces back together.

A classic example of difficulty with conservation is found in the preoperational child's response to the following Piagetian task. Leah, a five-year-old, is shown two identical glasses, both short and wide in shape. Both have exactly the same amount of coloured water in them. The experimenter asks Leah if each glass has the same amount of water, and she answers, "Yes." The experimenter then pours the water from one of the glasses into a tall, narrow glass and asks Leah again if each glass has the same amount of water. Now she is likely to insist that there is more water in the tall, narrow glass, because the water level is higher. Notice, by the way, that Leah shows a basic understanding of identity (it's the same water) but not an understanding that the *amounts* are identical (Ginsburg & Opper, 1988).

Piaget's explanation for Leah's answer is that she is focusing, or centring, attention on the dimension of height. She has difficulty considering more than one

Operations: Actions a person carries out by thinking them through instead of literally performing the actions.

Preoperational: The stage before a child masters logical mental operations.

Semiotic Function: The ability to use symbols—language, pictures, signs, or gestures—to represent actions or objects mentally.

Reversible Thinking: Thinking backward, from the end to the beginning.

Conservation: Principle that some characteristics of an object remain the same despite changes in appearance.

The ability to manipulate concrete objects helps children understand abstract relationships such as the connection between symbols and quantity. ▼

Decentring: Focusing on more than one aspect at a time. **development:** Orderly, adaptive changes we go through from conception to death.

Egocentric: Assuming that others experience the world the way you do.

Collective Monologue: Form of speech in which children in a group talk but do not really interact or communicate.

Connect & Extend
To your students' thinking
As an example of young children's difficulties with reversibility and egocentric thinking, ask a child with only one sibling, "Do you have a brother (sister)?" The child should say, "Yes." Now ask, "Does your brother (sister) have a brother (sister)?" Young children have difficulty reversing the situation and putting themselves in their siblings' position, so they usually reply "No." Now face the child and ask the child to point to your right hand. Most young children assume your right hand is on the same side as theirs, even when they are facing you.

Connect & Extend
To your teaching
By the time children reach the concrete-operational stage of cognitive development, they have some operations and strategies that they are able to employ. Considering these new skills, how might you go about teaching a child in this stage (a) a history lesson about Canada's role in the Second World War, and (b) the importance of the five food groups for nutrition.

Concrete Operations: Mental tasks tied to concrete objects and situations.

Identity: Principle that a person or object remains the same over time.

Compensation: The principle that changes in one dimension can be offset by changes in another dimension.

Reversibility: A characteristic of Piagetian logical operations—the ability to think through a series of steps, then mentally reverse the steps and return to the starting point; also called reversible thinking.

aspect of the situation at a time, or **decentring**. The preoperational child cannot understand that increased diameter compensates for decreased height, since this would require taking into account two dimensions at once. Thus, children at the preoperational stage have trouble freeing themselves from their own perceptions of how the world appears.

This brings us to another important characteristic of the preoperational stage. Preoperational children, according to Piaget, are very **egocentric**; they tend to see the world and the experiences of others from their own viewpoints. Egocentric, as Piaget intended it, does not mean selfish; it simply means children often assume that everyone else shares their feelings, reactions, and perspectives. For example, if a little boy at this stage is afraid of dogs, he may assume that all children share this fear. Very young children centre on their own perceptions and on the way the situation appears to them. This is one reason it is difficult for these children to understand that your right hand is not on the same side as theirs when you are facing them.

Egocentrism is also evident in the child's language. You may have seen young children happily talking about what they are doing even though no one is listening. This can happen when the child is alone or, even more often, in a group of children—each child talks enthusiastically, without any real interaction or conversation. Piaget called this the **collective monologue**.

Research has shown that young children are not totally egocentric in every situation, however. Children as young as age four change the way they talk to two-year-olds by speaking in simpler sentences, and even before age two a child shows a toy to an adult by turning the front of the toy to face the other person. So young children do seem quite able to take the needs and different perspectives of others into account, at least in certain situations (Gelman, 1979; Gelman & Ebeling, 1989). The Guidelines on page 33 give ideas for working with preoperational thinkers.

Later Elementary to the Middle School Years: The Concrete-Operational Stage. Piaget coined the term **concrete operations** to describe this stage of "hands-on" thinking. The basic characteristics of the stage are the recognition of the logical stability of the physical world, the realization that elements can be changed or transformed and still conserve many of their original characteristics, and the understanding that these changes can be reversed.

Figure 2.2 shows examples of the different tasks given to children to assess conservation and the approximate age ranges when most children can solve these problems. According to Piaget, a student's ability to solve conservation problems depends on an understanding of three basic aspects of reasoning: identity, compensation, and reversibility. With a complete mastery of **identity**, the student knows that if nothing is added or taken away, the material remains the same. With an understanding of **compensation**, the student knows that an apparent change in one direction can be compensated for by a change in another direction. That is, if the liquid rises higher in the glass, the glass must be narrower. And with an understanding of **reversibility**, the student can mentally cancel out the change that has been made.

Another important operation mastered at this stage is **classification**. Classification depends on a student's abilities to focus on a single characteristic of objects in a set and group the objects according to that characteristic. Given 12 objects of assorted colours and shapes, the concrete-operational student can invariably pick out the ones that are round.

More advanced classification at this stage involves recognizing that one class fits into another. A city can be in a particular state or province and also in a particular country. As children apply this advanced classification to locations, they often become fascinated with "complete" addresses such as Lee Jary, 5116 Forest Hill Drive, Richmond Hill, Ontario, Canada, North America, Northern Hemisphere, Earth, Solar System, Milky Way, Universe.

Classification is also related to reversibility. The ability to reverse a process mentally now allows the concrete-operational student to see that there is more

GUIDELINES

Teaching the Preoperational Child

Use concrete props and visual aids whenever possible.

Examples

1. When you discuss concepts such as "part," "whole," or "one-half," use shapes on a felt board or cardboard "pizzas" to demonstrate.
2. Let children add and subtract with sticks, rocks, or coloured chips.

Make instructions relatively short, using actions as well as words.

Examples

1. When giving instructions about how to enter the room after recess and prepare for social studies, ask a child to demonstrate the procedure for the rest of the class by walking in quietly, going straight to his or her seat, and placing the text, paper, and a pencil on his or her desk.
2. Explain a game by acting out one of the parts.
3. Show children what their finished papers should look like. Use an overhead projector or display examples where children can see them easily.

Don't expect children to be consistent in their ability to see the world from someone else's point of view.

Examples

1. Avoid social studies lessons about worlds too far removed from the child's experience.
2. Avoid long lectures on sharing. Be clear about rules for sharing or use of materials, but avoid long explanations of the rationales for the rules.

Be sensitive to the possibility that children may have different meanings for the same word or different words for the same meaning. Children may also expect everyone to understand words they have invented.

Examples

1. If a child protests "I won't take a nap. I'll just rest!" be aware that a nap may mean something like "changing into pyjamas and being in my bed at home."
2. Ask children to explain the meanings of their invented words.

Give children a great deal of hands-on practice with the skills that serve as building blocks for more complex skills such as reading comprehension.

Examples

1. Provide cut-out letters to build words.
2. Supplement paper-and-pencil tasks in arithmetic with activities that require measuring and simple calculations—cooking, building a display area for class work, dividing a batch of popcorn equally.

Provide a wide range of experiences in order to build a foundation for concept learning and language.

Examples

1. Take field trips to zoos, gardens, theatres, and concerts; invite storytellers to the class.
2. Give children words to describe what they are doing, hearing, seeing, touching, tasting, and smelling.

than one way to classify a group of objects. The student understands, for example, that buttons can be classified by colour, then reclassified by size or by the number of holes.

Seriation is the process of making an orderly arrangement from large to small or vice versa. This understanding of sequential relationships permits a student to construct a logical series in which A < B < C (A is less than B is less than C) and so on. Unlike the preoperational child, the concrete-operational child can grasp the notion that B can be larger than A but smaller than C.

With the abilities to handle operations such as conservation, classification, and seriation, the student at the concrete-operational stage has finally developed a complete and very logical system of thinking. This system of thinking, however, is still tied to physical reality. The logic is based on concrete situations that can be organized, classified, or manipulated. Thus, children at this stage can imagine sev-

Classification: Grouping objects into categories.

Seriation: Arranging objects in sequential order according to one aspect, such as size, weight, or volume.

FIGURE 2.2

Some Piagetian Conservation Tasks

In addition to the tasks shown here, other tasks involve the conservation of number, length, weight, and volume. These tasks are all achieved over the concrete-operational period.

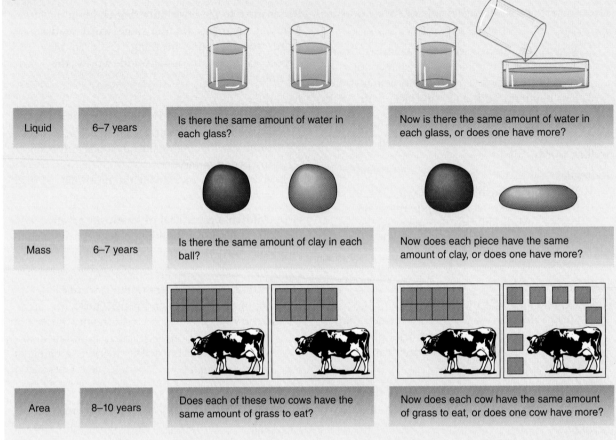

Liquid	6–7 years	Is there the same amount of water in each glass?	Now is there the same amount of water in each glass, or does one have more?
Mass	6–7 years	Is there the same amount of clay in each ball?	Now does each piece have the same amount of clay, or does one have more?
Area	8–10 years	Does each of these two cows have the same amount of grass to eat?	Now does each cow have the same amount of grass to eat, or does one cow have more?

Source: From Laura E. Berk, *Child Development*, 4/e. Copyright © 1997. All rights reserved. Adapted by permission of Allyn & Bacon.

eral different arrangements for the furniture in their rooms before they act. They do not have to solve the problem strictly through trial and error by actually making the arrangements. However, the concrete-operational child is not yet able to reason about hypothetical, abstract problems that involve the coordination of many factors at once. This kind of coordination is part of Piaget's next and final stage of cognitive development.

In any grade you teach, a knowledge of concrete-operational thinking will be helpful. In the early grades, the students are moving toward this logical system of thought. In the middle grades, it is in full flower, ready to be applied and extended by your teaching. In the high school years, it is often used by students whose thinking may not have fully developed to the next stage—the stage of formal operations. The Guidelines on page 35 should give you ideas for teaching children who can apply concrete operations.

Junior and Senior High: Formal Operations. Some students remain at the concrete-operational stage throughout their school years, even throughout life. However, new experiences, usually those that take place in school, eventually

GUIDELINES

Teaching the Concrete-Operational Child

Continue to use concrete props and visual aids, especially when dealing with sophisticated material.

Examples

1. Use timelines in history and three-dimensional models in science.
2. Use diagrams to illustrate hierarchical relationships such as branches of government and the agencies under each branch.

Continue to give students a chance to manipulate and test objects.

Examples

1. Set up simple scientific experiments like the following involving the relationship between fire and oxygen. What happens to a flame when you blow on it from a distance? (If you don't blow it out, the flame gets larger briefly, because it has more oxygen to burn.) What happens when you cover the flame with a jar?
2. Have students make candles by dipping wicks in wax, weave cloth on a simple loom, bake bread, set type by hand, or do other craft work that illustrates the daily occupations of people in the pioneer period.

Make sure presentations and readings are brief and well organized.

Examples

1. Assign stories or books with short, logical chapters, moving to longer reading assignments only when students are ready.
2. Break up a presentation with a chance to practise the first steps before introducing the next.

Use familiar examples to explain more complex ideas.

Examples

1. Compare students' lives with those of characters in a story. After reading Island of the Blue Dolphins (the true story of a girl who grew up alone on a deserted island), ask "Have you ever had to stay alone for a long time? How did you feel?"
2. Teach the concept of area by having students measure two rooms in the school that are different sizes.

Give opportunities to classify and group objects and ideas on increasingly complex levels.

Examples

1. Give students slips of paper that each have one sentence written on them and ask the students to group the sentences into paragraphs.
2. Compare the systems of the human body to other kinds of systems: the brain to a computer, the heart to a pump. Break down stories into components, from the broad to the specific: author; story; characters, plot, theme; place, time; dialogue, description, actions.

Present problems that require logical, analytical thinking.

Examples

1. Use mind twisters, brain teasers, Master Mind, and riddles.
2. Discuss open-ended questions that stimulate thinking: "Are the brain and the mind the same thing?" "How should the city deal with stray animals?" "What is the largest number?"

---

present most students with problems that they cannot solve using concrete operations. What happens when a number of variables interact, as in a laboratory experiment? In such a situation, a mental system for controlling sets of variables and working through a set of possibilities is needed. These are the abilities Piaget called **formal operations.**

At the level of formal operations, all the earlier operations and abilities continue in force; that is, formal thinking is reversible, internal, and organized in a system of interdependent elements. The focus of thinking shifts, however, from what *is* to what *might be.* Situations do not have to be experienced to be imagined. Ask a young child how life would be different if people did not sleep, and the child might say, "People have to sleep!" In contrast, the adolescent who has mastered formal operations can consider contrary-to-fact questions. In answering, the

Formal Operations: Mental tasks involving abstract thinking and coordination of a number of variables.

Hypothetico-Deductive Reasoning: A formal-operations problem-solving strategy in which an individual begins by identifying all the factors that might affect a problem and then deduces and systematically evaluates specific solutions.

Adolescent Egocentrism: Assumption that everyone else shares one's thoughts, feelings, and concerns.

adolescent demonstrates the hallmark of formal operations—**hypothetico-deductive reasoning.** The formal thinker can consider a hypothetical situation (people do not sleep) and reason deductively (from the general assumption to specific implications, such as longer workdays, more money spent on lighting, or new entertainment industries). Formal operations also include inductive reasoning, or using specific observations to identify general principles. For example, the economist observes many specific changes in the stock market and attempts to identify general principles about economic cycles. Formal-operational thinkers can form hypotheses, set up mental experiments to test them, and isolate or control variables in order to complete a valid test of the hypotheses.

The ability to consider abstract possibilities is critical for much of mathematics and science. After elementary school, most math is concerned with hypothetical situations, assumptions, and givens: "Let $x = 10$," or "Assume $x^2 + y^2 = z^2$," or "Given two sides and an adjacent angle . . ." Young children cannot reason based on symbols and abstractions, but this kind of reasoning is expected in the later grades (Bjorklund, 1989). Work in social studies and literature requires abstract thinking, too: "What did Woodrow Wilson mean when he called the First World War the 'war to end all wars'?" "What are some metaphors for hope and despair in Shakespeare's sonnets?" "What symbols of old age does T. S. Eliot use in *The Waste Land*?" "How do animals symbolize human character traits in Aesop's fables?"

The organized, scientific thinking of formal operations requires that students systematically generate different possibilities for a given situation. For example, if a child capable of formal operations is asked, "How many different meat/vegetable/salad meals can you make using three meats, three vegetables, and three salads?" the child can systematically identify the 27 possible combinations. A concrete thinker might name just a few meals, focusing on favourite foods or using each food only once. The underlying system of combinations is not yet available.

The ability to think hypothetically, consider alternatives, identify all possible combinations, and analyze one's own thinking has some interesting consequences for adolescents. Since they can think about worlds that do not exist, they often become interested in science fiction. Because they can reason from general principles to specific actions, they often are critical of people whose actions seem to contradict their principles. Adolescents can deduce the set of "best" possibilities and imagine ideal worlds (or ideal parents and teachers, for that matter). This explains why many students at this age develop interests in utopias, political causes, and social issues. They want to design better worlds, and their thinking allows them to do so. Adolescents can also imagine many possible futures for themselves and may try to decide which is best. Feelings about any of these ideals may be strong.

Another characteristic of this stage is **adolescent egocentrism.** Unlike egocentric young children, adolescents do not deny that other people may have different perceptions and beliefs; the adolescents simply become very focused on their own ideas. They analyze their own beliefs and attitudes. They reflect on others' thinking as well but often assume that everyone else is as interested as they are in their thoughts, feelings, and behaviour. This can lead to what Elkind (1981) calls the sense of an imaginary audience—the feeling that everyone is watching. Thus, adolescents believe that others are analyzing them (e.g., "Everyone noticed that I wore this shirt twice this week." "The whole class thought my answer was dumb!" "Everybody is going to love my new CD."). You can see that social blunders or imperfections in appearance can be devastating if "everybody is watching." In fact, Schonert-Reichl (1994), at the University of British Columbia, has linked adolescent egocentrism with adolescent depression. In particular, she found that girls from high socioeconomic status (SES) families tended to be overly self-conscious, and more at risk for depression. In contrast, boys from high SES families reported a heightened sense of omnipotence, uniqueness, and invulnerability. Luckily, this feeling of being "on stage" seems to peak in early adolescence, by age 14 or 15.

Connect & Extend
To your students' thinking
What are the differences (and similarities) between egocentrism in young children and egocentrism in adolescents?

Do We All Reach the Fourth Stage?

As we have just seen, most psychologists agree that there is a level of thinking more sophisticated than concrete operations. But the question of how universal formal-operational thinking actually is, even among adults, is a matter of debate.

According to Neimark (1975), the first three stages of Piaget's theory are forced on most people by physical realities. Objects really are permanent. The amount of water doesn't change when it is poured into another glass. Formal operations, however, are not so closely tied to the physical environment. They may be the product of experience and of practice in solving hypothetical problems and using formal scientific reasoning. These abilities tend to be valued and taught in literate cultures, particularly in colleges and universities.

Piaget himself (1974) suggested that most adults may be able to use formal-operational thought in only a few areas where they have the greatest experience or interest. So do not expect every student in your junior high or high school class to be able to think hypothetically about all the problems you present. Students who have not learned to go beyond

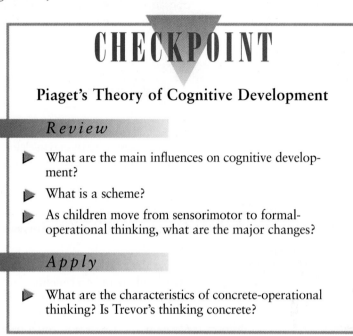

CHECKPOINT

Piaget's Theory of Cognitive Development

Review

▶ What are the main influences on cognitive development?

▶ What is a scheme?

▶ As children move from sensorimotor to formal-operational thinking, what are the major changes?

Apply

▶ What are the characteristics of concrete-operational thinking? Is Trevor's thinking concrete?

GUIDELINES

Helping Students to Use Formal Operations

Continue to use concrete-operational teaching strategies and materials.

Examples

1. Use visual aids such as charts and illustrations as well as somewhat more sophisticated graphs and diagrams.
2. Compare the experiences of characters in stories to students' experiences.

Give students the opportunity to explore many hypothetical questions.

Examples

1. Have students write position papers, then exchange these papers with the opposing side and have debates about topical social issues—the environment, the economy, national unity.
2. Ask students to write about their personal vision of a utopia; write a description of a universe that has no gender differences; write a description of Earth after humans are extinct.

Give students opportunities to solve problems and reason scientifically.

Examples

1. Set up group discussions in which students design experiments to answer questions.
2. Ask students to justify two different positions on animal rights, with logical arguments for each position.

Whenever possible, teach broad concepts, not just facts, using materials and ideas relevant to the students' lives.

Examples

1. When discussing Native land claims, consider other issues that have divided Canadians (e.g., Quebec separation).
2. Use lyrics from popular songs to teach poetic devices, to reflect on social problems, and to stimulate discussion on the place of popular music in our culture.

the information given to them are likely to fall by the wayside. Sometimes students find shortcuts for dealing with problems that are beyond their grasp; they may memorize formulas or lists of steps. These systems may be helpful for passing tests, but real understanding will take place only if students are able to go beyond this superficial use of memorization—only, in other words, if they learn to use formal-operational thinking. The Guidelines on page 37 may help you support the development of formal operations with your students.

*I*mplications of Piaget's Theory for Teachers

Piaget has taught us that we can learn a great deal about how children think by listening carefully, by paying close attention to their ways of solving problems. If we understand children's thinking, we will be better able to match teaching methods to children's abilities.

Understanding Students' Thinking

The students in any class will vary greatly both in their level of cognitive development and in their academic knowledge. As a teacher, how can you determine whether students are having trouble because they lack the necessary thinking abilities or because they simply have not learned the basic facts? To do this, Robbie Case, at the University of Toronto (1985b), suggests you observe your students carefully as they try to solve the problems you have presented. What kind of logic do they use? Do they focus on only one aspect of the situation? Are they fooled by appearances? Do they suggest solutions systematically or by guessing and forgetting what they have already tried? Ask your students how they tried to solve the problem. Listen to their strategies. What kind of thinking is behind repeated mistakes or problems? The students are the best sources of information about their own thinking abilities (Confrey, 1990a).

Matching Strategies to Abilities

An important implication of Piaget's theory for teaching is what J. M. Hunt years ago (1961) called "the problem of the match." Students must be neither bored by work that is too simple nor left behind by teaching they cannot understand. According to Hunt, disequilibrium must be kept "just right" to encourage growth. Setting up situations that lead to errors can help create an appropriate level of disequilibrium. When students experience some conflict between what they think should happen (a piece of wood should sink because it is big) and what actually happens (it floats!), they may rethink their understanding, and new knowledge may develop.

It is worth pointing out, too, that many materials and lessons can be understood at several levels and can be "just right" for a range of cognitive abilities. Classics such as *Alice in Wonderland*, myths, and fairy tales can be enjoyed at both concrete and symbolic levels. It is also possible for students to be introduced to a topic together, then work individually on follow-up activities matched to their level. Tom Good and Jere Brophy (1997) describe activity cards for three or four ability levels. These cards provide different readings and assignments, but all are directed toward the overall class objectives. One of the cards should be a good "match" for each student.

Connect & Extend
To your students' thinking
Try this test to see if your students can use formal operations by determining, in an organized way, the number of different possibilities that exist within a reasonably limited framework. Ask your students: "How many different outfits can be made with the following clothes: (1) three tops—polo shirt, dress shirt, and T-shirt; (2) three pairs of pants—jeans, shorts, slacks; and (3) three jackets—bomber, blazer, and jean jacket?" A student capable of formal operations would begin by laying out the possibilities systematically: first each jacket with the polo shirt and jeans, then each jacket with the polo shirt and slacks, then each jacket with the polo shirt and shorts, then each jacket with the polo shirt and slacks; then on to the jackets with the dress shirt and shorts, and so forth. A student at the concrete-operational stage, however, would be much less systematic; he or she might start with favourite clothes and continue in order of preference. It would not be unusual for a student operating at the concrete level to mention only three outfits, using each garment only once.

Constructing Knowledge

Piaget's fundamental insight was that individuals *construct* their own understanding; learning is a constructive process. At every level of cognitive development, you will also want to see that students are actively engaged in the learning process. They must be able to incorporate the information you present into their own schemes. To do this, they must act on the information in some way. Schooling must give the students a chance to experience the world. This active experience, even at the earliest school levels, should not be limited to the physical manipulation of objects. It should also include mental manipulation of ideas that arise out of class projects or experiments (Ginsburg & Opper, 1988). For example, after a social studies lesson on different jobs, a primary-grade teacher might show the students a picture of a woman and ask, "What could this person be?" After answers such as "teacher," "doctor," "secretary," "lawyer," "saleswoman," and so on, the teacher could suggest, "How about a daughter?" Answers such as "sister," "mother," "aunt," and "granddaughter" may follow. This should help the children switch dimensions in their classification and centre on another aspect of the situation. Next, the teacher might suggest "Canadian," "jogger," or "blonde." With older children, hierarchical classification might be involved: it is a picture of a woman, who is a human being; a human being is a primate, which is a mammal, which is an animal, which is a life form.

All students need to interact with teachers and peers in order to test their thinking, to be challenged, to receive feedback, and to watch how others work out problems. Disequilibrium is often set in motion quite naturally when the teacher or another student suggests a new way of thinking about something. As a general rule, students should act, manipulate, observe, and then talk and/or write (to the teacher and each other) about what they have experienced. Concrete experiences provide the raw materials for thinking. Communicating with others makes students use, test, and sometimes change their thinking abilities.

Discussions about the implications of Piaget's theory often centre on the question of whether cognitive development can be accelerated, as you can see in the Point/Counterpoint on page 40.

Some Limitations of Piaget's Theory

Piaget's influence on developmental psychology and education has been enormous, even though recent research has not supported all his ideas. Although most psychologists agree with Piaget's insightful descriptions of how children think, many disagree with his explanations of why thinking develops as it does.

The Trouble with Stages. Some psychologists have questioned the existence of four separate stages of thinking, even though they agree that children do go through the changes that Piaget described (Case, 1993; Gelman & Baillargeon, 1983). One problem with the stage model is the lack of consistency in children's thinking. Psychologists reason that if there are separate stages, and if the child's thinking at each stage is based on a particular set of operations, once the child has mastered the operations he or she should be somewhat consistent in solving all problems requiring those operations. In other words, once you can conserve, you ought to know that the number of blocks does not change when they are rearranged (conservation of number) and that the weight of a ball of clay does not change when you flatten it (conservation of weight). But it doesn't happen this way. Children can conserve number a year or two before they can conserve weight. Piagetian theorists have tried to deal with these inconsistencies, but not all psychologists are convinced by their explanations (Case, 1992, 1998; Orlando & Machado, 1996; Siegler, 1991).

Connect & Extend
To the research
Beilin, H. (1992). Piaget's enduring contribution to developmental psychology. *Developmental Psychology, 28,* 191–204.

Abstract
Piaget's transformation of society's conception of childhood thought and intelligence is described in four periods in the history of his research program, which spanned from the 1920s to the 1980s. The account stresses the enduring contribution to developmental psychology of Piaget's constructivism, his description of developmental mechanisms, his cognitivism, his explication of structural and functional analysis, and his addressing of epistemological issues and nontraditional methodologies.

Can Cognitive Development Be Accelerated?

Ever since Piaget described his stages of cognitive development, people have asked if progress through the stages could be accelerated. More recently, the question has focused on whether we should accelerate learning for preschoolers and young children at risk of academic failure. Can learning be accelerated, and if so, is this a good idea?

▶ **POINT** *Every child deserves a head start.*

Some of the strongest arguments in favour of "speeding up" cognitive development are based on the results of cross-cultural studies of children (studies that compare children growing up in different cultures). These results suggest that certain cognitive abilities are indeed influenced by the environment and education. Children of pottery-making families in one area of Mexico, for example, learn conservation of substance earlier than their peers in families who do not make pottery (Ashton, 1978). Furthermore, children in non-Western cultures appear to acquire conservation operations later than children in Western cultures. It seems likely that factors in the environment contribute to the rate of cognitive development.

But even if cognitive development can be accelerated, is this a good idea? Two of the most vocal (and heavily criticized) advocates of early academic training are Siegfried and Therese Engelmann (1981). In

their book, *Give Your Child a Superior Mind*, they suggest that children who learn academic skills as preschoolers will be smarter throughout their school years, are less likely to fail, and are more likely to enjoy school. They contend:

> Children respond to the environment. Their capacity to learn and what they learn depends on what the environment teaches. . . . Instead of relying on the traditional environment that is rich in learning opportunities for the child, we can take the environment a step further and mold it into a purposeful instrument that teaches and that guarantees your child will have a superior mind. (p. 10)

◀ **COUNTERPOINT** *Acceleration is ineffective and may be harmful.*

The position of Piagetian psychologists who attempt to apply his theory to education is that development should not be speeded up. This traditional view has been well summarized by Wadsworth (1978):

> The function of the teacher is not to accelerate the development of the child or speed up the rate of movement from stage to stage. The function of the teacher is to insure that development within each stage is thoroughly integrated and complete. (p. 117)

According to Piaget, cognitive development is based on the self-selected actions and thoughts of the student, not on the teacher's action. If you try to teach a student something the student is not ready to learn, he or she may learn to give the "correct" answer. But this will not really affect the way the student thinks about this problem. Therefore, why spend a long time teaching something at one stage when students will learn it by themselves much more rapidly and thoroughly at another stage?

Today the pressure is on parents and preschool teachers to create "superkids," three-year-olds who read, write, and speak a second language. David Elkind (1991) asserts that pushing children can be harmful. Elkind believes that preschool children who are given formal instruction in academic subjects often show signs of stress such as headaches. These children may become dependent on adults for guidance. Early focus on "right" and "wrong" answers can lead to competition and loss of self-esteem. Elkind asserts:

> The miseducation of young children, so prevalent in the United States today, ignores well-founded and noncontroversial differences between early education and formal education. As educators, our first task is to reassert this difference and insist on its importance. (p. 31)

Some psychologists have pointed to research on the brain to support Piaget's stage model. Epstein (1978, 1980) observed changes in rates of growth in brain weight and skull size and changes in the electrical activity of the brain between infancy and adolescence. These growth spurts occur at about the same time as transitions between the stages described by Piaget. Evidence from animal studies indicates that infant rhesus monkeys show dramatic increases in synaptic (nerve) connections throughout the brain cortex at the same time that they master the kinds of sensorimotor problems described by Piaget (Berk, 2000). This may be true in human infants as well. Transition to the higher cognitive states in humans has also been related to changes in the brain, such as production of additional synaptic connections (Byrnes & Fox, 1998). Thus, there is some neurological evidence for stages.

Underestimating Children's Abilities. It now appears that Piaget underestimated the cognitive abilities of children, particularly younger ones. The problems he gave young children may have been too difficult and the directions too confusing. His subjects may have understood more than they could show on these problems. For example, work by Gelman and her colleagues (Gelman, Meck, & Merkin, 1986; Miller & Gelman, 1983) shows that preschool children know much more about the concept of number than Piaget thought, even if they sometimes make mistakes or get confused. As long as preschoolers work with only three or four objects at a time, they can tell that the number remains the same, even if the objects are spread far apart or clumped close together. Similarly, Keenan, at the University of Toronto (Keenan, Ruffman, & Olson, 1994), found that making important task information salient helped four- and five-year-old children make inferences about what a story character knew. In other words, we may be born with a greater store of cognitive tools than Piaget suggested. Some basic understandings, such as the sense of number or understanding what other people know, may be part of our evolutionary equipment, ready for use in our cognitive development.

Piaget's theory does not explain how even young children can perform at an advanced level in certain areas where they have highly developed knowledge and expertise. For example, Porath (1997; 1996), at the University of British Columbia, found the drawings of artistically gifted children and the story plots of verbally gifted children to be far more elaborate than those of children in a same-age control group. In fact, she found that the story plots of verbally gifted six-year-olds typified those of eight-year-old children. As John Flavell (1985) noted, "the expert [child] looks very, very smart—very 'cognitively mature'—when functioning in her area of expertise" (p. 83).

Cognitive Development and Information Processing. As you will see in Chapter 7, there are alternative explanations for why children have trouble with conservation and other Piagetian tasks. These explanations focus on the child's developing information processing skills such as attention, memory capacity, and learning strategies. Siegler (1991) proposes that, as children grow older, they develop better and better rules for solving problems and for thinking logically. Teachers can help students develop their capacities for formal thinking by putting the students in situations that challenge their thinking and reveal the shortcomings of their logic. Seigler's approach is called *rule assessment* because it focuses on understanding, challenging, and changing the rules that students use for thinking. This approach assumes specific experiences, teaching, and other outside influences play a greater role than Piaget thought in children's cognitive development.

Some developmental psychologists have devised **neo-Piagetian theories** that retain Piaget's insights about children's construction of knowledge and the general trends in children's thinking, but add findings from information processing about the role of attention, memory, and strategies. For example, Robbie Case (1992, 1998) devised an explanation of cognitive development suggesting that children develop in stages within specific domains such as numerical concepts, spatial concepts, social tasks, storytelling, reasoning about physical objects, and motor development. As children practise using the schemes in a particular domain (for example, using counting schemes in the number concept area), accomplishing the schemes takes less attention. The schemes become more automatic because the child does not have to "think so hard" about it. This frees up mental resources and memory to do more. The child now can combine simple schemes into more complex ones and invent new schemes when needed (assimilation and accommodation in action).

Within each domain, children move from grasping simple schemes during the early preschool years, to merging two schemes into a unit (between about ages 4 and 6), to coordinating these scheme units into larger combinations, and finally, by about ages 9 to 11, to forming complex relationships that can be applied to

Neo-Piagetian Theories: More recent theories that integrate findings about attention, memory, and strategy use with Piaget's insights about children's thinking and the construction of knowledge.

many problems (Berk, 2000; Case, 1992, 1998). Case found that children do progress through these qualitatively different stages within each domain, but their progress is not the same across different domains. So, Case argued, progress in one domain does not automatically affect movement in another. The child must have experience and involvement with the content and the ways of thinking within each domain in order to construct increasingly complex and useful schemes and coordinated conceptual understandings about the domain.

Cognitive Development and Culture. One final criticism of Piaget's theory is that it overlooks the important effects of the child's cultural and social group. Children in Western cultures may master scientific thinking and formal operations because this is the kind of thinking required in Western schools (Artman & Cahan, 1993; Berk, 2000; Geary, 1998). Even basic concrete operations such as classification may not be so basic to people of other cultures. For example, when individuals from the Kpelle people of Africa were asked to sort 20 objects, they created groups that made sense to them—a hoe with a potato, a knife with an orange. The experimenter could not get the Kpelle to change their categories; they said this is how a wise man would do it. Finally the experimenter asked in desperation, "Well, how would a fool do it?" Then the subjects promptly created the four neat classification piles the experimenter had expected—food, tools, and so on (Rogoff & Morelli, 1989).

There is an increasingly influential view of cognitive development. Proposed years ago by Lev Vygotsky and recently rediscovered, this theory ties cognitive development to culture.

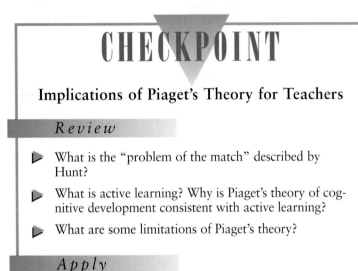

CHECKPOINT

Implications of Piaget's Theory for Teachers

Review

▶ What is the "problem of the match" described by Hunt?

▶ What is active learning? Why is Piaget's theory of cognitive development consistent with active learning?

▶ What are some limitations of Piaget's theory?

Apply

▶ How would you teach an abstract concept to students like Trevor?

V ygotsky's Sociocultural Perspective

Connect & Extend
To the research
See the spring 1995 *Educational Psychologist* for a special issue on "Lev S. Vygotsky and Contemporary Educational Psychology."

Sociocultural Theory: Emphasizes role in development of cooperative dialogues between children and more knowledgeable members of society. Children learn the culture of their community (ways of thinking and behaving) through these interactions.

Psychologists today recognize that the child's culture shapes cognitive development by determining what and how the child will learn about the world. For example, young Zinacanteco Indian girls of southern Mexico learn complicated ways of weaving cloth through informal teachings of adults in their communities. In Brazil, without going to school, children who sell candy on the streets learn sophisticated mathematics in order to buy from wholesalers, sell, barter, and make a profit. Cultures that prize cooperation and sharing teach these skills early, whereas cultures that encourage competition nurture these abilities in their children (Bakerman et al., 1990; Ceci & Roazzi, 1994; Childs & Greenfield, 1982). The stages observed by Piaget are not necessarily "natural" for all children because to some extent they reflect the expectations and activities of the children's culture (Rogoff & Chavajay, 1995).

A major spokesperson for this **sociocultural theory** (also called *sociohistoric*) was a Russian psychologist who died more than 50 years ago. Lev Semenovich Vygotsky was only 38 when he died of tuberculosis, but he had produced more than 100 books and articles. He wrote about language and thought, the psychology of art, learning and development, and educating students with special needs. His work was banned in Russia for many years because he referenced Western psychologists. But in the past 25 years, with the rediscovery of his work, Vygotsky's ideas about language, culture, and cognitive development have become major influences in psychology and education and have provided alternatives to many of Piaget's theories (John-Steiner & Mahn, 1996).

Vygotsky believed that human activities take place in cultural settings and cannot be understood apart from the settings. One of his key ideas was that our specific mental structures and processes can be traced to our interactions with others. These social interactions are more than simple influences on cognitive development—they actually create our cognitive structures and thinking processes (Palincsar, 1998). In fact, "Vygotsky conceptualized development as the transformation of socially shared activities into internalized processes" (John-Steiner & Mahn, 1996, p. 192). We will examine two themes in Vygotsky's writings that explain how social processes form learning and thinking: the social sources of individual thinking and the role of tools in learning and development, especially the tool of language (Wertsch, 1991; Wertsch & Tulviste, 1992).

▲ *Lev Vygotsky, shown here with his daughter, elaborated the sociocultural theory of development. His ideas about language, culture, and cognitive development have become major influences in the fields of psychology and education.*

The Social Sources of Individual Thinking

Vygotsky assumed that "every function in a child's cultural development appears twice: first on the social level and later on the individual level; first between people (interpsychological) and then inside the child (intrapsychological)" (1978, p. 57). In other words, higher mental processes appear first between people as they are **co-constructed** during shared activities. Then the processes are internalized by the child and become part of that child's cognitive development. For example, children first use language in activities with others, to regulate the behaviour of the others ("No nap!" or "I wanna cookie."). Later, however, the child can regulate her own behaviour using private speech ("don't spill"), as you will see in a later section. So, for Vygotsky, social interaction was more than influence, it was the origin of higher mental processes such as problem solving. Consider this example:

> A six-year-old has lost a toy and asks her father for help. The father asks her where she last saw the toy; the child says, "I can't remember." He asks a series of questions—did you have it in your room? Outside? Next door? To each question, the child answers, "no." When he says "in the car?" she says "I think so" and goes to retrieve the toy. (Tharp & Gallimore, 1988, p. 14)

Who remembered? The answer is really neither the father nor the daughter, but the two together. The remembering and problem solving was co-constructed—between people—in the interaction. But the child may have internalized strategies to use next time something is lost. At some point, the child will be able to function independently to solve this kind of problem. So, as the strategy for finding the toy indicates, higher functions appear first between a child and a "teacher" before they exist within the individual child (Kozulin, 1990).

Both Piaget and Vygotsky emphasized the importance of social interactions in cognitive development, but Piaget saw a different role for interaction. He believed that interaction encouraged development by creating disequilibrium—cognitive conflict—that motivated change. Thus, Piaget believed that the most helpful interactions were between peers because peers are on an equal basis and can challenge each other's thinking. Vygotsky (1978, 1986, 1987, 1993), on the other hand, suggested that children's cognitive development is fostered by interactions with people who are more capable or advanced in their thinking—people such as parents and teachers (Moshman, 1997; Palincsar, 1998).

Co-Constructed: Describes a social process in which people interact and negotiate (usually verbally) to create an understanding or to solve a problem. The final product is shaped by all participants.

Cultural Tools and Cognitive Development

Vygotsky believed that **cultural tools**, including real tools (such as printing presses, rulers, the abacus—today, we would add cellphones, computers, calendars, the Internet) and symbolic tools (such as numbers and mathematical systems, Braille and sign language, maps, works of art, signs and codes, and language) play very important roles in cognitive development. For example, as long as the culture provides only Roman numerals for representing quantity, certain ways of thinking mathematically—from long division to calculus—are difficult or impossible. But with a number system that has a zero, fractions, positive and negative values, and an infinite number of numbers, much more is possible. The number system is a cultural tool that supports thinking, learning, and cognitive development. This symbol system is passed from adult to child through formal and informal interactions and teachings.

Vygotsky emphasized the tools that the culture provides to support thinking. He believed that all higher-order mental processes, such as reasoning and problem solving, are *mediated* by (accomplished through and with the help of) psychological tools, such as language, signs, and symbols. Adults teach these tools to children during day-to-day activities and the children internalize them. Then the psychological tools can help students advance their own development (Karpov & Haywood, 1998). The process is something like this: as children engage in activities with adults or more capable peers, they exchange ideas and ways of thinking about or representing concepts—drawing maps, for example, as a way to represent spaces and places. These co-created ideas are internalized by children. Thus, children's knowledge, ideas, attitudes, and values develop through appropriating or "taking for themselves" the ways of acting and thinking provided by their culture and by the more capable members of their group (Kozulin & Presseisen, 1995).

In this exchange of signs and symbols and explanations, children begin to develop a "cultural tool kit" to make sense of and learn about their world (Wertsch, 1991). The kit is filled with physical tools such as pencils or paintbrushes directed toward the external world and psychological tools such as problem solving or memory strategies for acting mentally.

Vygotsky emphasized the tools that particular cultures provide to support thinking, and the idea that children use the tools they're given to construct their own understanding of the physical and social worlds. ▼

Children do not just receive the tools transmitted to them by others, however. Children transform the tools as they construct their own representations, symbols, patterns, and understandings. As we learned from Piaget, children's constructions of meaning are not the same as those of adults. In the exchange of signs and symbols such as number systems, children create their own understandings. These understandings are gradually changed as the children continue to engage in social activities and try to make sense of their world (John-Steiner & Mahn, 1996; Wertsch, 1991).

In Vygotsky's theory, language is the most important symbol system in the tool kit, and it is the one that helps to fill the kit with other tools.

The Role of Language and Private Speech

Language is critical for cognitive development. It provides a means for expressing ideas and asking questions, the categories and concepts for thinking, and the links between the past and the future (Das, 1995). When we consider a problem, we generally think in words and partial sentences. Vygotsky thought that:

the specifically human capacity for language enables children to provide for auxiliary tools in the solution of difficult tasks, to overcome impulsive action, to plan a solution to a problem prior to its execution, and to master their own behavior. (Vygotsky, 1978, p. 28)

Vygotsky placed much more emphasis than Piaget on the role of language in cognitive development. In fact, Vygotsky believed that language in the form of **private speech** (talking to yourself) guides cognitive development.

Vygotsky's and Piaget's Views Compared. If you have spent much time around young children, you know that they often talk to themselves as they play. Piaget called children's self-directed talk "egocentric speech." He assumed that this egocentric speech is another indication that young children can't see the world through the eyes of others. They talk about what matters to them, without taking into account the needs or interests of their listeners. As they mature, and especially as they have disagreements with peers, Piaget believed, children develop socialized speech. They learn to listen and exchange ideas.

Vygotsky had very different ideas about young children's private speech. He suggested that, rather than being a sign of cognitive immaturity, these mutterings play an important role in cognitive development by moving children toward self-regulation—the ability to plan, monitor, and guide your own thinking and problem solving.

Vygotsky believed that self-regulation developed in a series of stages. First the child's behaviour is regulated by others, usually parents, using language and other signs such as gestures. For example, the parent says "No!" when the child reaches toward a candle flame. Next the child learns to regulate the behaviour of others using the same language tools. The child says "No!" to another child who is trying to take away a toy, often even imitating the parent's voice tone. Along with learning to use external speech to regulate others, the child begins to use private speech to regulate her own behaviour, saying "no" quietly to herself as she is tempted to touch the flame. Finally the child learns to regulate her own behaviour by using silent inner speech (Karpov & Haywood, 1998). This series of steps is another example of how higher mental functions appear first between people as they communicate and regulate each other's behaviour, and then appear again within the individual as a cognitive process.

So children using private speech are communicating—they are communicating with themselves to guide their behaviour and thinking. In any preschool room you might hear four- or five-year-olds saying, "No, it won't fit. Try it here. Turn. Turn. Maybe this one!" while they do puzzles. As these children mature, their self-directed speech goes underground, changing from spoken to whispered speech and then to silent lip movements. Finally, the children just "think" the guiding words. The use of private speech peaks at around five to seven years of age and has generally disappeared by nine years of age. Brighter children seem to make this transition earlier (Bee, 1992).

Vygotsky identified this transition from audible private speech to silent inner speech as a fundamental process in cognitive development. Through this process the child is using language to accomplish important cognitive activities such as directing attention, solving problems, planning, forming concepts, and gaining self-control. Research supports Vygotsky's ideas (Berk & Spuhl, 1995; Bivens & Berk, 1990; Diaz & Berk, 1992; Kohlberg, Yaeger, & Hjertholm, 1969). Children tend to use more private speech when they are confused, having difficulties, or making mistakes. Inner speech not only helps us solve problems but also allows us to regulate our behaviour. Have you ever thought to yourself something like, "Let's see, the first step is . . ." or "Where did I use my glasses last?" or "If I work to the end of this page, then I can . . ."? You were using inner speech to remind, cue, encourage, or guide yourself. In a really tough situation, such as taking an important test, you might even find that you return to muttering out loud. Table 2.2 contrasts Piaget's and Vygotsky's theories of private speech. We should note that

Private Speech: Children's self-talk, which guides their thinking and action. Eventually these verbalizations are internalized as silent inner speech.

TABLE 2.2   Differences between Piaget's and Vygotsky's Theories of Egocentric or Private Speech

	Piaget	Vygotsky
Developmental Significance	Represents an inability to take the perspective of another and engage in reciprocal communication	Represents externalized thought; its function is to communicate with the self for the purpose of self-guidance and self-direction
Course of Development	Declines with age	Increases at younger ages and then gradually loses its audible quality to become internal verbal thought
Relationship to Social Speech	Negative; least socially and cognitively mature children use more egocentric speech	Positive; private speech develops out of social interaction with others
Relationship to Environmental Contexts	—	Increases with task difficulty. Private speech serves a helpful self-guiding function in situations where more cognitive effort is needed to reach a solution

Source: From L. E. Berk and R. A. Garvin. Development of private speech among low-income Appalachian children. *Developmental Psychology, 20*, p. 272. Copyright © 1984 by the American Psychological Association. Adapted by permission.

CHECKPOINT

Vygotsky's Sociocultural Perspective

Review

▷ Explain how interpsychological development becomes intrapsychological development.

▷ What are the differences between Piaget's and Vygotsky's perspectives on private speech and its role in development?

Apply

▷ Can you trace the origin of one of your problem-solving strategies to social interactions with parents or teachers? How did you learn?

Piaget accepted many of Vygotsky's arguments and came to agree that language could be used in both egocentric and problem-solving ways (Piaget, 1962).

Self-Talk and Learning. Because private speech helps students to regulate their thinking, it makes sense to allow, and even encourage, students to use private speech in school. Insisting on total silence when young students are working on difficult problems may make the work even harder for them. You may notice when muttering increases—this could be a sign that students need help. One approach, developed by Donald Meichenbaum at the University of Waterloo, is called *cognitive self-instruction.* It teaches students to use self-talk to guide learning. For example, students learn to give themselves reminders to go slowly and carefully. They "talk themselves through" tasks, saying such things as "Okay, what is it I have to do? . . . Copy the picture with the different lines. I have to go slowly and carefully. Okay, draw the line down, down, good; then to the right, that's it; now . . ." (Meichenbaum, 1977, p. 32).

The Role of Adults and Peers

Language plays another important role in development. Vygotsky believed that cognitive development occurs through the child's conversations and interactions with more capable members of the culture, adults or more able peers. These people serve as guides and teachers, providing the information and support necessary for the child to grow intellectually. The adult listens carefully to the child and pro-

Scaffolding: Support for learning and problem solving. The support could be clues, reminders, encouragement, breaking the problem down into steps, providing an example, or anything else that allows the student to grow in independence as a learner.

vides just the right help to advance the child's understanding. Thus, the child is not alone in the world "discovering" the cognitive operations of conservation or classification. This discovery is *assisted* or *mediated* by family members, teachers, and peers. Most of this guidance is communicated through language, at least in Western cultures. In some cultures, observing a skilled performance, not talking about it, guides the child's learning (Rogoff, 1990).

Jerome Bruner called this adult assistance **scaffolding** (Wood, Bruner, & Ross, 1976). The term aptly suggests that children use this help for support while they build a firm understanding that will eventually allow them to solve the problems on their own, as you will see in the next section.

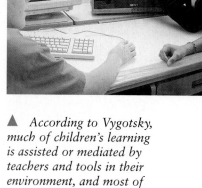

▲ *According to Vygotsky, much of children's learning is assisted or mediated by teachers and tools in their environment, and most of this guidance is communicated through language.*

Implications of Vygotsky's Theory for Teachers

There are at least three ways that cultural tools can be passed from one individual to another: imitative learning (where one person tries to imitate the other), instructed learning (where learners internalize the instructions of the teacher and use these instructions to self-regulate), and collaborative learning (where a group of peers strives to understand each other and learning occurs in the process) (Tomasello, Kruger, & Ratner, 1993). Vygotsky was most concerned with instructed learning through direct teaching or through structuring experiences that support another's learning, but his theory supports the other forms of cultural learning as well. Thus, Vygotsky's ideas are relevant for educators who teach directly and also create learning environments (Das, 1995). One major aspect of teaching in either situation is assisted learning.

Assisted Learning

Vygotsky's theory suggests that teachers need to do more than just arrange the environment so that students can discover on their own. He believed that children cannot and should not be expected to reinvent or rediscover knowledge already available in their cultures. Rather, they should be guided and assisted in their learning—so Vygotsky saw teachers, parents, and other adults as central to the child's learning and development (Karpov & Haywood, 1998).

Assisted learning, or guided participation in the classroom, requires scaffolding—giving information, prompts, reminders, and encouragement at the right time and in the right amounts, and then gradually allowing the students to do more and more on their own. Teachers can assist learning by adapting materials or problems to students' current levels; demonstrating skills or thought processes; walking students through the steps of a complicated problem; doing part of the problem (for example, in algebra, the students set up the equation and the teacher does the calculations or vice versa); giving detailed feedback and allowing revisions; or asking questions that refocus students' attention (Rosenshine & Meister, 1992). Meichenbaum's cognitive self-instruction described above is an example of assisted learning. Cognitive apprenticeships, reciprocal teaching, and instructional conversations (described in Chapter 9) are other examples. Table 2.3 gives examples of strategies that can be used in any lesson.

How can you know what kind of help to give and when to give it? One answer has to do with the student's zone of proximal development.

The Zone of Proximal Development

According to Vygotsky, at any given point in development there are certain problems that a child is on the verge of being able to solve. The child just needs some structure, clues, reminders, help with remembering details or steps, encouragement

Connect & Extend
To the research
Duncan, R. M., & Cheyne, J. A. (1999). Incidence and functions of self-reported private speech in young adults: A self-verbalization questionnaire. *Canadian Journal of Behavioural Science, 31*, 133–136.

Abstract
The present study employed a self-report approach to study the cognitive and self-regulatory functions of private speech (Vygotsky, 1934/1987, 1978) in young adults. The Self-Verbalization Questionnaire, assessing the use of self-directed speech, was administered to 1132 undergraduate university students (aged 17–47 years). In general, self-verbalization scores were high. Exploratory factors analysis produced a four-factor solution that was readily interpretable in terms of Vygotskian theory. Consistent with the view that private speech serves as a cognitive system, the highest scores were reported for questionnaire items loading highly on a factor consisting of cognitive, mnemonic, and attentional uses of self-verbalization. The scales appear to have good internal consistency, high test-retest reliability, and good content and criterion validity.

Assisted Learning: Providing strategic help in the initial stages of learning, which gradually diminishes as students gain independence.

TABLE 2.3   Assisted Learning: Strategies to Scaffold Complex Learning

- *Procedural facilitators.* These provide a "scaffold" to help students learn implicit skills. For example, a teacher might encourage students to use "signal words" such as who, what, where, when, why, and how to generate questions after reading a passage.

- *Modelling use of facilitators.* The teacher, in the above example, might model the generation of questions about the reading.

- *Thinking out loud.* This models the teacher's expert thought processes, showing students the revisions and choices the learner makes in using procedural facilitators to work on problems.

- *Anticipating difficult areas.* During the modelling and presentations phase of instruction, for example, the teacher anticipates and discusses potential student errors.

- *Proving prompt or cue cards.* Procedural facilitators are written on "prompt cards" that students keep

for reference as they work. As students practise, the cards gradually become unnecessary.

- *Regulating the difficulty.* Tasks involving implicit skills are introduced by beginning with simpler problems, providing for student practice after each step, and gradually increasing the complexity of the task.

- *Providing half-done examples.* Giving students half-done examples of problems and having them work out the conclusions can be an effective way to teach them how to ultimately solve problems on their own.

- *Reciprocal teaching.* Having the teacher and students rotate the role of teacher. The teacher provides support to students as they learn to lead discussions and ask their own questions.

- *Providing checklists.* Students can be taught self-checking procedures to help them regulate the quality of their responses.

Source: From "Effective Teaching Redux." *ASCD Update,* 32(6) p. 5. Reprinted by permission of the Association for Supervision and Curriculum Development. Copyright © 1990 by ASCD. All rights reserved.

Connect & Extend
To the research
Grigorenko, E. L., & Sternberg, R. J. (1998). *Dynamic testing. Psychological Bulletin, 124,* 75–111.

Abstract
This article evaluatively reviews the literature on dynamic testing, a collection of testing procedures designed to quantify not only the products or even the processes of learning, but also the potential to learn. The article considers a variety of approaches to dynamic testing and the strengths and weaknesses of each. Moreover, the literature on each approach is reviewed and analyzed in terms of the extent to which it fulfills the claims made for it. In all of these approaches, testing involves learning at the time of the test, rather than just static testing of what has been learned before. It is concluded that dynamic testing has the capacity to help understand people's potentials but this capacity has not yet been realized fully.

Zone of Proximal Development: Phase at which a child can master a task if given appropriate help and support.

to keep trying, and so on. Some problems, of course, are beyond the child's capabilities, even if every step is explained clearly. The **zone of proximal development** is the area where the child cannot solve a problem alone, but can be successful under adult guidance or in collaboration with a more advanced peer (Wertsch, 1991). This is the area where instruction can succeed, because real learning is possible.

We can see how Vygotsky's beliefs about the role of private speech in cognitive development fit with the notion of the zone of proximal development. Often, an adult helps a child to solve a problem or accomplish a task using verbal prompts and structuring. This scaffolding may be gradually reduced as the child takes over the guidance, perhaps first by giving the prompts as private speech and finally as inner speech. Let's move forward to a future day in the life of the girl in the earlier example who had lost her toy and *listen to* her thoughts when she realizes that a school book is missing. They might sound something like this:

"Where's my math book? Used it in class. Thought I put it in my bookbag after class. Dropped my bag on the bus. That dope Larry kicked my stuff, so maybe . . ."

The girl can now systematically search for ideas about the lost book without help from anyone else.

Assessment. One implication of Vygotsky's zone of proximal development has to do with assessment. Most standard tests measure what students can do alone. This is useful information, but may not tell teachers or parents how to help the students learn more. An alternative is dynamic assessment (Spector, 1992) or learning potential assessment (Feuerstein, 1979, 1990). The goal of these approaches is to identify the zone of proximal development by asking a child to solve a problem, and then giving prompts and hints to see how he or she learns, adapts, and uses the guidance. These prompts are systematically increased to see how much support is needed and how the child responds. The teacher watches, listens, and takes careful notes about how the child uses the help and what level of support is necessary, and then applies this information to plan instructional groupings, peer tutoring, learning tasks, assignments, and so on (Grigorenko & Sternberg, 1998).

Teaching. Students should be put in situations where they have to reach to understand, but where support from other students or from the teacher is also available. Sometimes the best teacher is another student who has just figured out the problem, because this student is probably operating in the learner's zone of proximal development. Students should be guided by explanations, demonstrations, and work with other students—opportunities for cooperative learning. Having a student work with someone who is just a bit better at the activity would also be a good idea. In addition, students should be encouraged to use language to organize their thinking and to talk about what they are trying to accomplish. Dialogue and discussion are important avenues to learning (Karpov & Bransford, 1995; Kozulin & Presseisen, 1995). The Guidelines on page 50 give more ideas for applying Vygotsky's ideas.

Clearly, language plays a major role in learning, inside and outside the classroom. Let's look at this human capability more closely.

The Development of Language

All children in every culture master the complicated system of their native language, unless severe deprivation or physical problems interfere. This knowledge is

▲ *Sometimes the best teachers are other students who have just understood a particular concept. These "teachers" may be operating in the zone of proximal development for their fellow students.*

Applying Vygotsky's Ideas in Teaching

Tailor scaffolding to the needs of students.

Examples

1. When students are beginning new tasks or topics, provide models, prompts, sentence starters, coaching, and feedback. As the students grow in competence, give less support and more opportunities for independent work.
2. Give students choices about the level of difficulty or degree of independence in projects; encourage them to challenge themselves but to seek help when they are really stuck.

Make sure students have access to powerful tools that support thinking.

Examples

1. Teach students to use learning and organizational strategies, research tools, language tools (dictionaries or computer searches), spreadsheets, and word-processing programs.
2. Model the use of tools; show students how you use an appointment book or electronic notebook to make plans and manage time, for example.

Capitalize on dialogue and group learning.

Examples

1. Experiment with peer tutoring; teach students how to ask good questions and give helpful explanations.
2. Experiment with cooperative learning strategies described in Chapters 9 and 11.

---

remarkable. At the least, sounds, meanings, words and sequences of words, volume, voice tone, inflection, and turn-taking rules must all be coordinated before a child can communicate effectively in conversations. As you might expect, there are different theories about how people master the complex process of communication.

How Do We Learn Language?

One early view of language development assumed that children learn language by repeating behaviour that leads to some kind of positive result. The child happens to say "mmm" in the presence of milk, and the parent says, "Yes, milk, milk," and gives the child a drink. The child learns to say "milk" because it leads to a happy parent and a drink of milk. Children add new words by imitating the sounds they hear and improve their use of language when they are corrected by the adults around them. The trouble with this appealing theory is that many of a child's earliest utterances are not imitations but original creations. And they are unlikely to be rewarded, because they are "incorrect," even though they make sense to the people involved. Examples are such phrases as "paper find," "car mosquito," "tooth-guy" (dentist), or "all gone kitty" (Moshman, Glover, & Bruning, 1987).

In addition, parents rarely correct pronunciation and grammar during the early stages of language development. They are much more likely to respond to the content of a child's remarks (Brown & Hanlon, 1970; Demetras & Post, 1985). Adults caring for children seem continually to adapt their language to stay just ahead of the child. As soon as a child utters identifiable words, adults simplify their language with the child. As the child progresses, adults tend to change their language to stay just a bit more advanced than the child's current level of development, thus encouraging new understanding (Bohannon & Warren-Leubecker, 1989; Fernald, 1993). In order to stretch the child's language development, adults give the kind of support, or scaffolding, that Vygotsky has recommended. By staying slightly more advanced in their language, adults may also create disequilibrium and encourage development as a result.

Even this rich learning environment cannot explain how children learn so much language so quickly and correctly. Think of all the sounds that could be combined in different orders and linked with many different meanings. Why don't children create wild languages or make crazy associations between a sound and a meaning? Why, for example, when their parents say, "Look, a rabbit," do children learn to connect the word *rabbit* with the whole animal, not with the animal's ears, or movements, or size, or fur?

Some psychologists explain this amazing accomplishment by assuming that humans are born with a special capacity for processing, understanding, and creating language (Chomsky, 1965, 1986; Eimas, 1985; Maratsos, 1989). Janet Werker (1989), at the University of British Columbia, has studied infants' sensitivity to a universal set of speech sounds. Her research indicates that humans are born with the potential to learn any language. However, this remarkable ability diminishes over time, even through the first year of life, as children acquire particular languages. It seems that humans have built-in biases and rules that constrain early sensitivity to all possible speech sounds to those required for communicating in our own language(s). These built-in constraints simplify language learning (Markman, 1990). Also, humans may share a universal grammar, a set of specifications and rules that limit the range of language created. In other words, only certain possibilities are considered as the child figures out the puzzle of language (Chomsky, 1980).

It is likely that many factors—biological and experiential—play a role in language development. The important point is that children develop language as they develop other cognitive abilities by actively trying to make sense of what they hear and by looking for patterns and making up rules to put together the jigsaw puzzle of language. In this process, built-in biases and rules may limit the search and guide the pattern recognition. Reward and correction play a role in helping children learn correct language use, but the child's thinking and creativity in putting together the parts of this complicated system are very important (Rosser, 1994).

Language Development in the School Years

By about age five or six, most children have mastered the basics of their native language. What remains for the school-age child to accomplish?

Pronunciation. The majority of first graders have mastered most of the sounds of their native language, but a few may remain unconquered. The *j*, *v*, *th*, and *zh* sounds are the last to develop. About 10 percent of eight-year-olds still have some trouble with *s*, *z*, *v*, *th*, and *zh* (Rathus, 1988). Young children may understand and be able to use many words but prefer to use the words they can pronounce easily.

Syntax. Children master the basics of word order, or **syntax**, in their native language early. But the more complicated forms, such as the passive voice ("The car was hit by the truck"), take longer to master. By early elementary school, many children can understand the meaning of passive sentences, yet they do not use such constructions in their normal conversations. Other accomplishments during elementary school include first understanding and then using complex grammatical structures such as extra clauses, qualifiers, and conjunctions.

Vocabulary and Meaning. The average 6-year-old has a vocabulary of 8000 to 14 000 words, growing to about 20 000 by age 11. It seems that the time before puberty, especially the preschool years, is a sensitive period for language growth. Research has shown that we can learn much about language after puberty, but that very positive or very negative conditions during the sensitive period before puberty can greatly help or hinder language development (Anglin, 1993; Johnson & Newport, 1989).

"WHEN I SAY 'RUNNED,' YOU KNOW I MEAN 'RAN.' LET'S NOT QUIBBLE."

© 1994 by Sidney Harris

Syntax: The order of words in phrases or sentences.

In the early elementary years, some children may have trouble with abstract words such as *justice* or *economy*. They may also take statements literally and thus misunderstand sarcasm or metaphor. Fairy tales are understood concretely simply as stories instead of as moral lessons, for example. Many children are in their preadolescent years before they are able to distinguish being kidded from being taunted or before they know that a sarcastic remark is not meant to be taken literally (Gardner, 1982b).

Metalinguistic Awareness. Around the age of five, students begin to develop **metalinguistic awareness**. This means their understanding about language and how it works becomes explicit. They have knowledge about language itself. They are ready to study and extend the rules that have been implicit—understood but not consciously expressed. This process continues throughout life, as we all become better able to manipulate and comprehend language. Teachers can develop the language abilities and knowledge of their students in a variety of ways.

Language, Literacy, and Teaching

One goal of schooling is the development of language and literacy. Literacy includes oral language as well as reading and writing. Today we know that children know a great deal about written language long before they can read or write in conventional ways:

A make-believe grocery store in a preschool has a sign announcing the daily special, "APLS BNS 5¢" (apples and bananas 5¢) (Berk, 1996).

A four-year-old recognizes the "happy birthday" sign on the wall (Crowhurst, 1994).

A four-year-old writes a story (a) and a grocery list (b) in Figure 2.3.

These students know a great deal about reading and writing. They know that letters have different forms, are associated with the sounds of spoken language,

FIGURE 2.3

A Story and a Grocery List

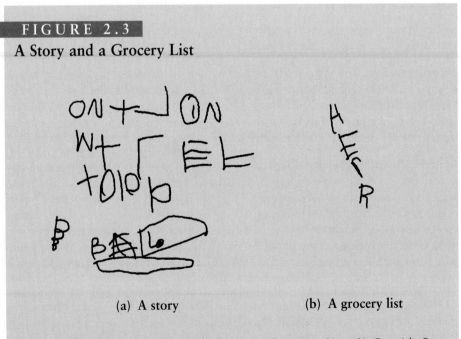

(a) A story   (b) A grocery list

Source: Lea M. McGee and Donald J. Richgels, *Literacy Beginnings,* 2/e, p. 81. Copyright © 1990 by Allyn & Bacon. Reprinted by permission.

and go together to make words. Knowledge of letter-sound correspondences and how these can be grouped to form words is phonemic awareness. This knowledge is a key predictor of early reading success (Foorman, Francis, Fletcher, Mehta, & Schaatschneider, 1998; Torgesen, Wagner, Rashotte, Rose, Lindamood, Conway, & Garvan, 1999). Also, these students know that words communicate meaning and make sentences; that writing goes from left to right and lists go down the page. Finally, they know that stories look different from shopping lists. Teachers should strive to build on this emerging literacy understanding (Paris & Cunningham, 1996).

Teachers and Literacy

The Committee on the Prevention of Reading Difficulties in Young Children (1998) and the International Reading Association (1998) assert that learning to read and write begins long before children enter school, and entering school with adequate literacy-related knowledge safeguards against reading and other academic difficulties. According to these reading specialists, effective early literacy instruction has the following characteristics:

- It presents young children with many opportunities to interact with print, and emphasizes that the primary reason for reading is to obtain meaning.

- It offers lessons about the alphabet, spelling-sound relationships, and the structure of spoken language.

- It accepts and encourages young children's reading and writing attempts, especially their use of invented spellings in their writing.

- It depends on knowledgeable and supportive teachers who understand the course of literacy development and acknowledge differences in children's rates of development and linguistic and cultural backgrounds.

Teachers can enrich students' language environment by focusing not just on correct or incorrect usage, but on the idea expressed. Probe and extend students' ideas. For example, if a student says, "I writed my name on my picture," the teacher could respond, "You wrote your name above the rocket. Where is your astronaut going?" In this way, the teacher maintains the student's interest and at the same time expands the complexity of the statement and recasts the language to a more mature form (Rice, 1989). Parents who use these strategies have children who make rapid progress in language learning (Farrar, 1990).

Cazden (1988) suggests that word meanings are most easily learned through interactions and conversations with an adult in which the adult introduces new words. For example, when a student complains, "He does that on purpose, just to make me mad!" the teacher might respond, "So you think he is intentionally tripping by your desk just to irritate you? What's your evidence for that conclusion?" Reading aloud is also a potent form of language stimulation. Reading to students often leads to conversations about the pictures or ideas in the books. The importance of one-to-one interaction with an adult in developing language abilities has been stressed by many

CHECKPOINT

Language, Literacy, and Teaching

Review

▷ How are humans predisposed to develop language? What role does learning play?

▷ Describe teacher actions and responses that encourage language development.

Apply

▷ Name two things you could do to form literacy partnerships with your students' families.

▷ How could you elaborate on and extend Trevor's understanding of "symbolism" (described at the beginning of this chapter)?

Connect & Extend
To other chapters
In **Chapter 12**, we discuss different approaches to the teaching of reading and writing.

educators and psychologists (Morrow, 1997; Rice, 1989). This is in keeping with Vygotsky's theory of cognitive development.

Partnerships with Families

Especially in the early years, the students' home experiences are central in the development of language and literacy (Roskos & Neuman, 1993; Snow, 1993; Whitehurst et al., 1994). In homes that promote literacy, parents and other adults value reading as a source of pleasure, and there are books and other printed materials everywhere. Parents read to their children, take them to bookstores and libraries, limit the amount of television everyone watches, and encourage literacy-related play such as setting up a pretend school or writing "letters" (Pressley, 1996; Roskos & Neuman, 1998; Sulzby & Teale, 1991). Of course, not all homes provide this literacy-rich environment, but teachers can help, as you will see in the Family and Community Partnerships Guidelines below.

Throughout this text you will read about other ways that teachers can encourage language development for both younger and older students. For example, we will discuss bilingual education in Chapter 5, reciprocal teaching and instructional conversations in Chapter 9, and learning to read and write in Chapter 12.

FAMILY AND COMMUNITY PARTNERSHIPS

Promoting Literacy

Communicate with families about the goals and activities of your program.

Examples

1. At the beginning of the school year, send home a description of the goals to be achieved in your class—make sure it is a clear and readable format.
2. As you start each unit, send home a newsletter describing what students will be studying—give suggestions for home activities that support the learning.

Involve families in decisions about curriculum.

Examples

1. Have planning workshops at times family members can attend—provide child care for younger siblings, but let children and families work together on projects.
2. Invite parents to come to class to read to students, take dictation of stories, tell stories, record or bind books, and demonstrate skills.

Provide home activities to be shared with family members.

Examples

1. Encourage family members to work with children to read and follow simple recipes, play language games, keep diaries or journals for the family, and visit the library. Get feedback from families or students about the activities.
2. Give families feedback sheets and ask them to help evaluate the child's school work.
3. Provide lists of good children's literature that is available locally—work with libraries, clubs, and churches to identify sources.

Source: From Lesley Mandel Morrow, *Literacy Development in the Early Years: Helping Children Read and Write*, 3/e, pp. 68–70. Copyright © 1997 by Allyn & Bacon. Adapted by permission.

Summary

A Definition of Development

What are three principles of development?

Theorists generally agree that people develop at different rates, that development is an orderly process, and that development takes place gradually.

What part of the brain is associated with higher mental functions?

The cortex is a crumpled sheet of neurons that serves three major functions: receiving signals from sense organs (such as visual or auditory signals), controlling voluntary movement, and forming associations. The part of the cortex that controls physical motor movement develops or matures first, then the areas that control complex senses such as vision and hearing, and last the frontal lobe that controls higher-order thinking processes.

What is lateralization and why is it important?

Lateralization is the specialization of the two sides, or hemispheres, of the brain. The brain begins to lateralize soon after birth. For most people, the left hemisphere is the major factor in language, and the right hemisphere is prominent in spatial and visual processing. Even though certain functions are associated with certain parts of the brain, the various parts and systems of the brain work together to learn and perform complex activities, such as reading, and to construct understanding.

Piaget's Theory of Cognitive Development

What are the main influences on cognitive development?

Piaget's theory of cognitive development is based on the assumption that people try to make sense of the world and actively create knowledge through direct experience with objects, people, and ideas. Maturation, activity, social transmission, and the need for equilibrium all influence the way thinking processes and knowledge develop. In response to these influences, thinking

processes and knowledge develop through changes in the organization of thought (the development of schemes) and through adaptation—including the complementary processes of assimilation (incorporating into existing schemes) and accommodation (changing existing schemes).

What is a scheme?

Schemes are the basic building blocks of thinking. They are organized systems of actions or thought that allow us to mentally represent or "think about" the objects and events in our world. Schemes may be very small and specific (grasping, recognizing a square), or they may be larger and more general (using a map in a new city). People adapt to their environment as they increase and organize their schemes.

As children move from sensorimotor to formal-operational thinking, what are the major changes?

Piaget believed that young people pass through four stages as they develop: sensorimotor, preoperational, concrete-operational, and formal-operational. In the sensorimotor stage, infants explore the world through their senses and motor activity, and work toward mastering object permanence and performing goal-directed activities. In the preoperational stage, symbolic thinking and logical operations begin. Children in the stage of concrete operations can think logically about tangible situations and can demonstrate conservation, reversibility, classification, and seriation. The ability to perform hypothetico-deductive reasoning, coordinate a set of variables, and imagine other worlds marks the stage of formal operations.

Implications of Piaget's Theory for Teachers

What is the "problem of the match" described by Hunt?

The "problem of the match" is that students must be neither bored by work that is too simple nor left behind by teaching they cannot

understand. According to Hunt, disequilibrium must be carefully balanced to encourage growth. Situations that lead to errors can help create an appropriate level of disequilibrium.

What is active learning? Why is Piaget's theory of cognitive development consistent with active learning?

Piaget's fundamental insight was that individuals *construct* their own understanding; learning is a constructive process. At every level of cognitive development, students must be able to incorporate information into their own schemes. To do this, they must act on the information in some way. This active experience, even at the earliest school levels, should include both physical manipulation of objects and mental manipulation of ideas. As a general rule, students should act, manipulate, observe, and then talk and/or write about what they have experienced. Concrete experiences provide the raw materials for thinking. Communicating with others makes students use, test, and sometimes change their thinking abilities.

What are some limitations of Piaget's theory?

Piaget's theory has been criticized because children and adults often think in ways that are inconsistent with the notion of invariant stages. It also appears that Piaget underestimated children's cognitive abilities. Alternative explanations place greater emphasis on students' developing information processing skills and how teachers can enhance their development. Piaget's work is also criticized for overlooking cultural factors in child development.

Vygotsky's Sociocultural Perspective

Explain how interpsychological development becomes intrapsychological development.

Higher mental processes appear first between people as they are co-constructed during shared activities. As children engage in activities with adults or more capable peers, they exchange ideas and ways of thinking about or representing concepts. These co-created ideas are internalized by children. Thus children's knowledge, ideas, attitudes, and values develop through appropriating, or "taking for themselves," the ways of acting and thinking provided by their culture and by the more capable members of their group.

What are the differences between Piaget's and Vygotsky's perspectives on private speech and its role in development?

Vygotsky's sociocultural view asserts that cognitive development hinges on social interaction and the development of language. As an example, Vygotsky describes the role of children's self-directed talk in guiding and monitoring thinking and problem solving, while Piaget suggested that private speech was an indication of the child's egocentrism. Vygotsky, more than Piaget, emphasized the significant role played by adults and more able peers in children's learning. This adult assistance provides early support while students build the understanding necessary to solve problems on their own.

Implications of Vygotsky's Theory for Teachers

What is assisted learning, and what role does scaffolding play?

Assisted learning, or guided participation in the classroom, requires scaffolding—giving information, prompts, reminders, and encouragement at the right time and in the right amounts, and then gradually allowing the students to do more and more on their own. Teachers can assist learning by adapting materials or problems to students' current levels, demonstrating skills or thought processes, walking students through the steps of a complicated problem, doing part of the problem, giving detailed feedback and allowing revisions, or asking questions that refocus students' attention.

What is a student's zone of proximal development?

At any given point in development there are certain problems that a child is on the verge of being able to solve and others that are beyond the child's capabilities. The zone of proximal development is the area where the child cannot solve a problem alone, but can be successful under adult guidance or in collaboration with a more advanced peer.

The Development of Language

How are humans predisposed to develop language? What role does learning play?

Children develop language as they develop other cognitive abilities, by actively trying to make sense of what they hear, looking for patterns, and making up rules. In this process, built-in biases and rules may limit the search and guide the pattern recognition. Reward and correction play a role in helping children learn correct language use, but the child's thought processes are very important. Metalinguistic awareness begins around age five or six and grows throughout life.

Describe teacher actions and responses that encourage language development.

Teachers have a significant role in helping children develop language ability and knowledge about language. Teachers can focus on effective communication, meaning, comprehension, and respect for language in the classroom. Reading aloud and one-on-one interactions with adults are significant in developing language abilities. Parents can play a key role in promoting literacy at home.

𝒦ey Terms

Becoming a Professional

Reflecting on the Chapter

Can you apply the ideas from this chapter on cognitive development to solve the following problems of practice?

Preschool and Kindergarten

A group of vocal parents wants you to introduce workbooks to teach basic arithmetic in your class for four- and five-year-olds. They seem to think that "play" with blocks, water, sand, clay, and so on is "wasted time." How would you respond?

Elementary and Middle School

▷ Two very concerned parents want to have a conference with you about their son's "language problems." He is in first grade and has some trouble with pronunciation. How would you prepare for the conference?

Junior High and High School

▷ The students in your class persist in memorizing definitions for many of the important abstract concepts in your class. They insist, "That's what you have to do to make a good grade in this class." Even though they can repeat the definitions precisely, they seem to have no conception of what the terms mean; they can't recognize examples of the concept in problems or give their own examples. It is almost as if they don't believe there is any real hope of understanding the ideas. Pick one important, difficult concept in your field, and design a lesson to teach it to students who believe only in memorization.

▷ It seems as if every fourth word from the mouths of your students is *like* or *you know*. Also, their understanding of the material in your class is limited, because they don't know the meaning of many words that you assumed high school students would certainly understand, such as *former* and *latter*. What would you do to encourage language development along with teaching your subject?

Check Your Understanding

▷ Be clear about the three basic principles of development.

▷ Make sure you understand the elements of Piaget's theory (assimilation, accommodation, equilibration, schemes) and his four stages of cognitive development.

▷ From Vygotsky's theory, be familiar with the ideas of zone of proximal development and assisted learning. Also, be clear about how private speech supports cognitive development.

Your Teaching Portfolio

Think about your philosophy of teaching, a question you will be asked at most job interviews. What do you believe about matching teaching to students' current level of development? Are Piaget's ideas related to "readiness to learn"? What are the roles of direct teaching and discovery in students' learning? Do Piaget and Vygotsky lead you to different philosophies?

   Add some ideas for parent involvement from this chapter to your portfolio.

Teaching Resources

Adapt Table 2.3, *Assisted Learning: Strategies to Scaffold Complex Learning*, for the grades and subjects you might teach, and add it to your teaching resources file.

Weblinks

www.piaget.org

The Jean Piaget Society, established in 1970, has an international, interdisciplinary membership of scholars, teachers, and researchers interested in exploring the nature of the developmental construction of human knowledge. The society's aim is to provide an open forum, through symposia, books, and other publications, for the presentation and discussion of scholarly work on issues related to human knowledge and its development. The society further encourages the application of advances in the understanding of development to education and other domains.

www.sasked.gov.sk.ca/docs/ela/e_literacy/index.html

This page maintained by the Saskatchewan ministry of education provides many resources concerning oral language development, learning orthography, reading, writing, and more.

http://kolar.org/vygotsky

A page of links to a wide variety of resources concerning the Russian developmental psychologist Lev Vygotsky.

TEACHERS' CASEBOOK

What Would They Do?

Here is how two practising teachers responded to the teaching situation presented at the beginning of this chapter about teaching abstract concepts such as "symbol."

JANET E. GETTINGS

Elementary Educator,
Willoughby Elementary School
Langley, British Columbia
Faculty Adviser and Sessional Instructor, University of British Columbia

The students of the class have indicated a need for scaffolded learning to enhance their understanding of the concept of symbolism.

To introduce the concept, I would build on the children's prior knowledge of homonyms by doing a quick review of commonly used word pairs, such as bear/bare, stare/stair, I/eye, pair/pear, two/to/too, followed by cymbal/symbol. With the latter example, I would explain that Tracy had defined "cymbal." I would then invite suggestions for "symbol," summarizing with a formal definition, such as "something that stands for or represents something else."

I would follow the discussion with a "Think, Pair, Share" activity. Students would be asked to think about symbols independently, then pair with a partner to share ideas. Next the partners would be invited to go on a "detective search" of the room and their desks for symbols that they could share with the class. For example, when I hang an umbrella on the door, students know they can stay in the classroom at lunch.

Another follow-up activity would be a modified game of pictionary. The class would be divided into teams of five or six and take turns being artists. Each team would send a student to the teacher to view a phrase, which the student then had to represent pictorially. Sample phrases might include "the house had not been lived in for a long time," "her face reflected pain and sadness."

At this stage, the students might be ready to move to usage of symbolism in written language. Sections of a familiar novel that included symbolic phrases to describe feelings and emotions could be shared. For example, the phrase "thunderclouds passed over her face" describes the feelings of a character in a story in language that students understand easily. I would engage the class in a discussion to share the author's message and intent.

Reading aloud humorous poetry, such as that of Jack Prelutsky, might be used to move toward the final goal of identifying the use of symbolism in poetry. Students could demonstrate their understanding by researching the use of symbolic language in the genre of poetry and by writing their own poems, incorporating symbolism into their products.

MARY LIGHTLY

Terry Fox Secondary School
Port Coquitlam, British Columbia

In planning activities for the classroom, I try to be mindful of research on effective teaching. In particular, I draw on the work of Anita Archer at the University of Oregon and Barrie Bennet at the University of Toronto. Both these researchers have written texts that summarize current research, and both relate that research to actual classroom situations.

To develop the concept of symbol, I would first design activities in which students could engage independently or in small groups. For example, I might engage students in a matching activity that required them to identify the symbolic meaning of concrete or "real life" objects. I might create a worksheet that included two lists: one list would include real world objects, such as a dove or a heart (this list might be presented as pictures); the second list would include descriptions of the symbolic meaning for each object. Students would match the picture of the dove with peace, and the picture of the heart with love. I might ask students to generate their own symbols. For example, a red rose could symbolize passion, a sword could symbolize war. Students could colour their images and display them in the classroom as a reminder of how real life objects can have symbolic meaning.

After introducing the concept in this manner, I would take the class through one or two concept attainment lessons, a strategy in which students are presented with "yes" and "no" examples of a con-cept, in this case examples and non-examples of symbols and/or symbolism. I would begin with very clear and simple examples and then increase the level of difficulty as students became more confident and skilled at recognizing symbols and symbolism.

It might take many trials and a variety of strategies but, eventually, students would be ready to look for symbolic meaning in literature.

Personal, Social, and Emotional Development

*R*eflect on a teacher who helped to shape your sense of who you are—your abilities, aspirations, or values. What did the teacher do or say that influenced you? Do you know someone whose career choice was affected by a teacher?

Schooling involves more than cognitive development. In this chapter we examine emotional, social, and moral development.

We begin with the work of Erik Erikson, whose comprehensive theory provides a framework for studying personal and social development. Next, we explore ideas about how we come to understand others and ourselves. What is the meaning of the self-concept, and how is it shaped? How do our views of others change as we grow? What factors determine our views about morality? What can teachers do to nurture honesty, cooperation, empathy, and self-esteem? We then consider three major influences on children's personal and social development: families, peers, and schools. Families today have gone through many transitions, and these changes affect the roles of teachers.

We end the chapter by examining several challenges for children—the problems and opportunities of physical development and the many risks that confront students today—such as child abuse, eating disorders, and drugs.

By the time you have completed this chapter, you should be able to:

▶ Describe Erikson's stages of psychosocial development and list several of his theory's implications for teaching.

▶ Suggest how teachers can foster self-esteem in their students.

▶ Describe the child's changing view of friendship.

▶ Describe Kohlberg's stages of moral reasoning and give an example of each.

▶ Evaluate alternatives to Kohlberg's theory.

▶ Explain the factors that encourage cheating and aggression in classrooms and discuss possible responses to each.

▶ Describe a number of challenges and risks that students face today and suggest roles for teachers in helping students respond.

What Would You Do?

One of the girls in your Grade 10 class is desperate for friends. Vanessa seems so lonely and depressed—no one ever joins her at lunch or walks with her to class. She is a reasonably good student, but just doesn't seem to fit in. On several occasions she has tried to join a group by offering help or asking questions, but these initiations never go anywhere. Even when a friendship begins, it never lasts. It seems as though Vanessa gets so excited about the possibility of a developing relationship that she pushes the new-found friend away by overwhelming her with attention, showering her with special gifts, pouring out her heart, and sharing her deepest secrets and worries. Then Vanessa always seems to be the one exploited, abandoned, or hurt. Lately her school work is careless and incomplete; she looks tired and pale.

▶ What are your concerns for this student?

▶ How do you think Vanessa feels about herself?

▶ What are some danger signs you might watch for?

▶ How would you help her form some genuine relationships?

▶ Consider the same situation, except the child is a Grade 3 student.

Erik Erikson proposed a theory of psychosocial development that describes tasks to be accomplished at different stages of life. ▼

Psychosocial: Describing the relation of the individual's emotional needs to the social environment.

Developmental Crisis: A specific conflict whose resolution prepares the way for the next stage.

The Work of Erikson

Like Piaget, Erik Erikson did not start out as a psychologist. In fact, Erikson never graduated from high school. He spent his early adult years studying art and travelling around Europe. A meeting with Sigmund Freud in Vienna led to an invitation from Freud to study psychoanalysis. Erikson then emigrated to the United States to practise his profession and to escape the threat of Hitler.

In his influential *Childhood and Society* (1963), Erikson offered a basic framework for understanding the needs of young people in relation to the society in which they grow, learn, and ultimately make their contributions. His later books, *Identity, Youth, and Crisis* (1968) and *Identity and the Life Cycle* (1980), expanded on his ideas. Although Erikson's approach is not the only explanation of personal and social development, we have chosen it to organize our discussion because Erikson emphasizes the emergence of the self, the search for identity, and the individual's relationships with others throughout life.

After studying child-rearing practices in several cultures, Erikson came to the conclusion that all humans have the same basic needs and that each society must provide in some way for those needs. Emotional changes and their relation to the social environment follow similar patterns in every society. This emphasis on the relationship of culture and the individual led Erikson to propose a **psychosocial** theory of development.

Like Piaget, Erikson saw development as a passage through a series of stages, each with its particular goals, concerns, accomplishments, and dangers. The stages are interdependent: Accomplishments at later stages depend on how conflicts are resolved in the earlier years. At each stage, Erikson suggests, the individual faces a **developmental crisis.** Each crisis involves a conflict between a positive alternative and a potentially unhealthy alternative. The way in which the individual resolves each crisis will have a lasting effect on that person's self-image and view of society. An unhealthy resolution of problems in the early stages can have potential negative repercussions throughout life, although sometimes damage can be repaired at later stages. We will look briefly at all eight stages in Erikson's theory—or, as he called them, the "eight ages of man." Table 3.1 presents the stages in summary form.

TABLE 3.1 Erikson's Eight Stages of Psychosocial Development

Stages	Approximate Age	Important Event	Description
1. Basic trust versus basic mistrust	Birth to 12–18 months	Feeding	The infant must first form a loving, trusting relationship with the caregiver or develop a sense of mistrust.
2. Autonomy versus shame/doubt	18 months to 3 years	Toilet training	The child's energies are directed toward the development of physical skills, including walking, grasping, controlling the sphincter. The child learns control but may develop shame and doubt if not handled well.
3. Initiative versus guilt	3 to 6 years	Independence	The child continues to become more assertive and to take more initiative but may be too forceful, which can lead to guilt feelings.
4. Industry versus inferiority	6 to 12 years	School	The child must deal with demands to learn new skills or risk a sense of inferiority, failure, and incompetence.
5. Identity versus role confusion	Adolescence	Peer relationships	The teenager must achieve identity in occupation, gender roles, politics, and religion.
6. Intimacy versus isolation	Young adulthood	Love relationships	The young adult must develop intimate relationships or suffer feelings of isolation.
7. Generativity versus stagnation	Middle adulthood	Parenting/Mentoring	Each adult must find some way to satisfy and support the next generation.
8. Ego integrity versus despair	Late adulthood	Reflection on and acceptance of one's life	The culmination is a sense of acceptance of oneself as one is and a sense of fulfillment.

Source: Adapted from Lester A. Lefton, *Psychology*, 5/e. Copyright © 1994 by Allyn & Bacon. Reprinted by permission.

The Preschool Years: Trust, Autonomy, and Initiative

Erikson identifies *trust versus mistrust* as the basic conflict of infancy. In the first months of life, babies begin to find out whether they can depend on the world around them. According to Erikson, the infant will develop a sense of trust if its needs for food and care are met with comforting regularity and responsiveness from caregivers. In this first year, infants are in Piaget's sensorimotor stage and are just beginning to learn that they are separate from the world around them. This realization is part of what makes trust so important: infants must trust the aspects of their world that are beyond their control (Bretherton & Waters, 1985; Isabella & Belsky, 1991).

Erikson's second stage, *autonomy versus shame and doubt*, marks the beginning of self-control and self-confidence. Young children are capable of doing more and more on their own. They must begin to assume important responsibilities for self-care such as feeding, going to the toilet, and dressing. During this period parents must tread a fine line; they must be protective—but not overprotective. If parents do not maintain a reassuring, confident attitude and do not reinforce the child's efforts to master basic motor and cognitive skills, children may begin to feel shame; they may learn to doubt their abilities to manage the world on their own terms. Erikson believes that children who experience too much doubt at this stage will lack confidence in their own powers throughout life.

For Erikson, "initiative adds to autonomy the quality of undertaking, planning, and attacking a task for the sake of being active and on the move" (Erikson, 1963, p. 255). But with **initiative** comes the realization that some activities are

Connect & Extend
To your thinking
What do you think Erikson's reply would be to the following questions?
a. Do you recommend following a rigid feeding schedule for infants?
b. Is it possible to spoil an infant by picking it up whenever it cries?
c. Should you help a child do things before the child reaches the point of frustration?
d. What advice would you give a parent who tends to be overprotective and consistently curtails a child's exploration?
e. If a child is attempting to do something, isn't it helpful to show the child the right way or a better way to do it?
f. Isn't it possible that a child will become conceited if he or she is consistently praised for accomplishments?
g. Do you think adolescents should be treated as adults before the law? Do you think it's fair to have more lenient punishments for juveniles than for adults?

Autonomy: Independence.

Initiative: Willingness to begin new activities and explore new directions.

Industry: Eagerness to engage in productive work.

▲ *Children need opportunities to learn things for themselves in order to develop a sense of initiative.*

Connect & Extend
To what you know
Relate this information to concepts you learned in Chapter 2. For example, what aspects of formal-operational thought are helpful (or perhaps necessary) in achieving identity formation? Can you think of people who seem to have established their identity but who do not seem to have achieved the formal-operational stage? Is identity formation necessarily a conscious process?

Connect & Extend
To your own philosophy
Do you agree with either of these positions? What would Erikson say about each?

a. In order to establish their identity, adolescents need to separate themselves from their parents so they can discover who they are, other than being their parents' children. If parents are very strict and controlling, children have to give so much energy to establishing the separation that they don't have the time and effort to give to defining their own identity. For this reason, parents and teachers of adolescents would be more helpful if they were lenient with teenagers.

b. Adolescents are similar to large two-year-olds in that they are egocentric and exhibit out-of-bounds behaviour. They derive a sense of security from knowing that there are limits they must observe. They are in a transition stage with no clear-cut standards of behaviour, since they are neither child nor adult. For this reason, parents and teachers of adolescents should be strict and impose rules to help a teenager make the transition more easily and safely.

forbidden. At times, children may feel torn between what they want to do and what they should (or should not) do. The challenge of this period is to maintain a zest for activity and at the same time understand that not every impulse can be acted on. Again, adults must tread a fine line, this time in providing supervision without interference. If children are not allowed to do things on their own, a sense of guilt may develop; they may come to believe that what they want to do is always "wrong." The Guidelines at the top of page 65 suggest ways of encouraging initiative.

Elementary and Middle School Years: Industry versus Inferiority

In the early school years, students are developing what Erikson calls a sense of industry. They are beginning to see the relationship between perseverance and the pleasure of a job completed. The crisis at this stage is *industry versus inferiority*. For children in modern societies, the school and the neighbourhood offer a new set of challenges that must be balanced with those at home. Interaction with peers becomes increasingly important. The child's ability to move between these worlds and to cope with academics, group activities, and friends will lead to a growing sense of competence. Difficulty with these challenges can result in feelings of inferiority. The Guidelines at the bottom of page 65 give ideas for encouraging industry.

Adolescence: The Search for Identity

The central issue for adolescents is the development of an identity that will provide a firm basis for adulthood. The individual has been developing a sense of self since infancy. But adolescence marks the first time that a conscious effort is made to answer the now-pressing question, "Who am I?" The conflict defining this stage is *identity versus role confusion.*

Identity refers to the organization of the individual's drives, abilities, beliefs, and history into a consistent image of self. It involves deliberate choices and decisions, particularly about work, values, ideology, and commitments to people and ideas (Marcia, 1987; Peneul & Wertsch, 1995). If adolescents fail to integrate all

GUIDELINES

Encouraging Initiative in Preschool Children

Encourage children to make and to act on choices.

Examples

1. Have a free-choice time when children can select an activity or game.
2. Try to avoid interrupting children who are very involved in what they are doing.
3. When children suggest an activity, try to follow their suggestions or incorporate their ideas into ongoing activities.
4. Offer positive choices: instead of saying, "You can't have the cookies now," ask, "Would you like the cookies after lunch or after naptime?"

Make sure that each child has a chance to experience success.

Examples

1. When introducing a new game or skill, teach it in small steps.
2. Avoid competitive games that highlight differences in children's abilities.

Encourage make-believe with a wide variety of roles.

Examples

1. Have costumes and props that go along with stories the children enjoy. Encourage the children to act out the stories or make up new adventures for favourite characters.
2. Monitor the children's play to be sure no one monopolizes playing "teacher," "Mommy," "Daddy," or other heroes.

Be tolerant of accidents and mistakes, especially when children are attempting to do something on their own.

Examples

1. Use cups and pitchers that make it easy to pour and hard to spill.
2. Recognize the attempt, even if the result is unsatisfactory.
3. If mistakes are made, show children how to clean up, repair, or redo.
4. Most important, help children to view errors as opportunities to learn and let them know that everyone makes mistakes (even adults, even you).

GUIDELINES

Encouraging Industry

Make sure that students have opportunities to set and work toward realistic goals.

Examples

1. Begin with short assignments, then move on to longer ones. Monitor student progress by setting up progress checkpoints.
2. Teach students to set reasonable goals. Write down goals and have students keep a journal of progress toward goals.

Give students a chance to show their independence and responsibility.

Examples

1. Tolerate honest mistakes.
2. Delegate to students tasks such as watering class plants, collecting and distributing materials, monitoring the computer lab, grading homework, keeping records of forms returned, and so on.

Provide support to students who seem discouraged.

Examples

1. Use individual charts and contracts that show student progress.
2. Keep samples of earlier work so students can see their improvements.
3. Have awards for most improved, most helpful, most hard-working.

Identity Achievement: Strong sense of commitment to life choices after free consideration of alternatives.

Identity Foreclosure: Acceptance of parental life choices without consideration of options.

Identity Diffusion: Uncentredness; confusion about who one is and what one wants.

Moratorium: Identity crisis; suspension of choices because of struggle.

these aspects and choices, or if they feel unable to choose at all, role confusion threatens.

Identity Statuses. James Marcia has suggested that there are four alternatives for adolescents as they confront their identity choices (Marcia, 1980, 1991, 1994). The first is **identity achievement**. This means that after considering the realistic options, the individual has made choices and is pursuing them. It appears that few students achieve this status by the end of high school; students who attend college or university may take a bit longer to decide. But even during college and university, about 80 percent of students change their majors at least once. And some adults may achieve a firm identity at one period in their lives, only to reject that identity and achieve a new one later. So identity, once achieved, may not be unchanging for everyone (Stephen, Fraser, & Marcia, 1992; Waterman, 1992).

Identity foreclosure describes the situation of adolescents who do not experiment with different identities or consider a range of options, but simply commit themselves to the goals, values, and lifestyles of others, usually their parents but sometimes cults or extremist groups. **Identity diffusion**, on the other hand, occurs when individuals reach no conclusions about who they are or what they want to do with their lives; they have no firm direction. Adolescents experiencing identity diffusion may have struggled unsuccessfully to make choices, or they may have avoided thinking seriously about the issues at all. They may be apathetic and withdrawn, with little hope for the future, or they may be openly rebellious. They may try to block out contact with parents or teachers by listening to music through headphones or sleeping (Berger & Thompson, 1995; Kroger, 1995).

Finally, adolescents in the midst of struggling with choices are experiencing what Erikson called a **moratorium**. He used the term to describe a delay in the adolescent's commitment to personal and occupational choices. This dzed that adolescents in complex societies undergo an *identity crisis* during moratorium. Today, the period is no longer referred to as a crisis because, for most people, the experience is a gradual exploration rather than a traumatic upheaval (Grotevant, 1998).

▲ *The search for identity is the hallmark of adolescent development. Adolescents often "try on" different roles and behaviour during this period.*

TABLE 3.2 Characteristics of the Four Identity Statuses: How Do Adolescents Differ Based on Their Progress toward Identity Achievement?

	Foreclosure	Diffusion	Moratorium	Achievement
Attitude toward parents	Loving and respectful	Withdrawn	Trying to distance self	Loving and caring
Self-esteem	Low (easily affected by others)	Low	High	High
Ethnic identity	Strong	Medium	Medium	Strong
Prejudice	High	Medium	Medium	Low
Moral stage	Preconventional or conventional	Preconventional or conventional	Postconventional	Postconventional
Dependence	Very dependent	Dependent	Self-directed	Self-directed
Cognitive processes	Simplifies complex issues; refers to others and to social norms for opinions and decisions	Complicates simple issues; refers to others in both personal and ideological choices	Thoughtful; procrastinates, especially in decisions; avoids referring to others' opinions or to social norms	Thoughtful; makes decisions by both seeking new information and considering others' opinions
College	Very satisfied	Variable	Most dissatisfied (likely to change major)	High grades
Relations with others	Stereotyped	Stereotyped or isolated	Intimate	Intimate

Source: From *The Developing Person through Childhood and Adolescence* (p. 583), by K. S. Berger and R. A. Thompson, 1995, New York: Worth. Copyright © 1995 by Worth Publishers. Reprinted with permission.

Table 3.2 summarizes characteristics of the different statuses. Both identity achievement and moratorium are considered healthy alternatives. The natural tendency of adolescents to "try on" identities, experiment with lifestyles, and commit to causes is an important part of establishing a firm identity. Adolescents who can't get past either identity diffusion or foreclosure have difficulties adjusting. For example, identity-diffused adolescents and young adults often give up, trust their lives to fate, or go along with the crowd, so they are more likely to abuse drugs (Archer & Waterman, 1990). Foreclosed adolescents tend to be rigid, intolerant, dogmatic, and defensive (Frank, Pirsch, & Wright, 1990). Schools that give adolescents experiences with community service, real-world work, internships, and mentoring foster identity formation (Cooper, 1998). The Guidelines on page 68 suggest other approaches.

Beyond the School Years

The crises of Erikson's stages of adulthood all involve the quality of human relations. The first of these stages is *intimacy versus isolation*. Intimacy in this sense refers to a

CHECKPOINT

The Work of Erikson

Review

▶ Why is Erikson's theory considered a psychosocial perspective?

▶ What are Erikson's stages of psychosocial development?

Apply

▶ How might an adolescent experiencing identity foreclosure answer the question, "Why did you choose that major?"

▶ How might Vanessa's difficulties in making friends (described at the beginning of this chapter) influence her identity achievement?

GUIDELINES

Supporting Identity Formation

Give students many models for career choices and other adult roles.

Examples

1. Point out models from literature and history. Have a calendar with the birthdays of eminent women, minority leaders, or people who made a little-known contribution to the subject you are teaching. Briefly discuss the person's accomplishments on his or her birthday.
2. Invite guest speakers to describe how and why they chose their professions. Make sure all kinds of work and workers are represented.

Help students find resources for working out personal problems.

Examples

1. Encourage them to talk to school counsellors.
2. Discuss potential outside services.

Be tolerant of teenage fads as long as they don't offend others or interfere with learning.

Examples

1. Discuss the fads of earlier eras (neon hair, powdered wigs, love beads).
2. Don't impose strict dress or hair codes.

Give students realistic feedback about themselves.

Examples

1. When students misbehave or perform poorly, make sure they understand the consequences of their behaviour—the effects on themselves and others.
2. Give students model answers or show them other students' completed projects so they can compare their work to good examples.
3. Since students are "trying on" roles, keep the roles separate from the person. You can criticize behaviour without criticizing the student.

willingness to relate to another person on a deep level, to have a relationship based on more than mutual need. Someone who has not achieved a sufficiently strong sense of identity tends to fear being overwhelmed or swallowed up by another person and may retreat into isolation.

The conflict at the next stage is *generativity versus stagnation*. **Generativity** extends the ability to care for another person and involves caring and guidance for the next generation and for future generations. While generativity frequently refers to having and nurturing children, it has a broader meaning. Productivity and creativity are essential features.

The last of Erikson's stages is *integrity versus despair,* coming to terms with death. Achieving **integrity** means consolidating your sense of self and fully accepting its unique and now unalterable history. Those unable to attain a feeling of fulfillment and completeness sink into despair.

With Erikson's theory of psychosocial development as a framework, we can now examine several aspects of personal and social development that are issues throughout childhood and adolescence.

Understanding Ourselves and Others

What is self-concept? How do we come to understand other people and ourselves? How do we develop a sense of right and wrong—and do these beliefs affect our behaviour? You will see that developments in these areas follow patterns similar to those noted in Chapter 2 for cognitive development. Children's understandings of themselves are concrete at first, and then become more abstract. Early views of self and friends are based on immediate behaviour and appearances. Children assume that others share their feelings and perceptions. Their thinking about themselves

Generativity: Sense of concern for future generations.

Integrity: Sense of self-acceptance and fulfillment.

and others is simple, segmented, and rule-bound, not flexible or integrated into organized systems. In time, children are able to think abstractly about internal processes—beliefs, intentions, values, and motivations. With these developments in abstract thinking, knowledge of self, others, and situations can incorporate more abstract qualities (Berk, 2000; Harter, 1998).

Self-Concept: Our perceptions about ourselves.

Self-Esteem: The value each of us places on our own characteristics, abilities, and behaviour.

Self-Concept and Self-Esteem

When you considered Vanessa's situation at the beginning of this chapter, was the idea of self-concept part of your analysis? The term *self-concept* is part of our everyday conversation. We talk about people who have a "low" self-concept or individuals whose self-concept is not "strong," as if self-concept were fluid levels in a car or a muscle to be developed. These actually are misuses of the term. In psychology, **self-concept** generally refers to "the composite of ideas, feelings, and attitudes people have about themselves" (Hilgard, Atkinson, & Atkinson, 1979, p. 605). We could consider self-concept to be our attempt to explain ourselves to ourselves, to build a scheme (in Piaget's terms) that organizes our impressions, feelings, and attitudes about ourselves. But this model or scheme is not permanent, unified, or unchanging. Our self-perceptions vary from situation to situation and from one phase of our lives to another.

Self-concept and self-esteem are often used interchangeably, even though they have distinct meanings. Self-concept is a cognitive structure—a belief about who you are. **Self-esteem** is an affective reaction—an evaluation of who you are. If people evaluate themselves positively—if they "like what they see"—we say that they have high *self-esteem* (Pintrich & Schunk, 1996).

The Structure of Self-Concept. The model shown in Figure 3.1 suggests that the general view of self is made up of other, more specific concepts, including the non-academic self-concept, self-concept in English, and self-concept in mathematics. Recent research indicates that self-concept for artistic abilities is another separate area (Vispoel, 1995). These self-concepts at the second level are themselves made up of more specific, separate conceptions of the self, such as conceptions about physical ability, appearance, relations with peers, and relations with family, particularly parents (Byrne & Shavelson, 1996). These conceptions are based on many experiences and events such as: sports performance; assessment of body, skin, or hair; friendships; artistic abilities; contributions to community groups; and so on.

The hierarchical structure of self-concept shown in Figure 3.1 is strongest for early adolescents. Older adolescents and adults seem to have separate, specific self-concepts, but these are not necessarily integrated into an overall self-concept. Perhaps young adolescents, faced with the challenges of different academic subjects in school and the "life task" of forming an identity, try to integrate across their many "selves" to achieve that identity. Adults are not actively involved in *all* the academic domains (math, science, social studies) and can define themselves in terms of their current interests and activities, so self-concept is more situation-specific in adults (Byrne & Worth Gavin, 1996; Pintrich & Schunk, 1996).

One important way self-concept affects learning in school is through course selection. Think back to high school. When you had a chance to choose courses, did you pick your worst subjects—those where you felt least capable? Probably not. Herbert Marsh and Alexander Yeung (1997) examined how 246 boys in early high school in Sydney, Australia, chose their courses. Academic self-concept for a particular subject (mathematics, science, etc.) was the most important predictor of course selection—more important than previous grades in the subject or overall self-concept. In fact, having a positive self-concept in a particular subject was an even bigger factor in selecting courses when self-concept in other subjects was low. The courses selected in high school put students on a path toward the future, so self-concepts about particular academic subjects can be life-changing influences.

Connect & Extend
To the research
Byrne, B. M., & Worth Gavin, D. A. (1996). The Shavelson model revisited: Testing for structure of academic self-concept across pre-, early, and late adolescents. *Journal of Educational Psychology, 88,* 215–229.

FIGURE 3.1

Structure of Self-Concept

Students have many separate but sometimes related concepts of themselves. The overall sense of self appears to be divided into at least three separate, but slightly related, self-concepts—English, mathematics, and nonacademic.

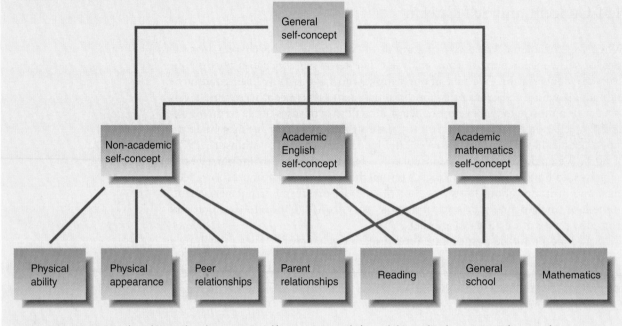

Source: From H. W. Marsh and R. J. Shavelson (1985). Self-concept: Its multifaceted, hierarchical structure. *Educational Psychologist, 20,* p. 114. Adapted by permission of the publisher and authors.

Connect & Extend
To the research
Marsh, H. W., Chessor, D., Craven, R., & Roche, L. (1995). The effects of gifted and talented programs on academic self-concept: The big fish strikes again. *American Educational Research Journal, 32,* 285–321.

Connect & Extend
To your teaching
William Glasser talks about self-concept in terms of failure and success identities. Loneliness, apathy, and withdrawal or delinquency characterize the "failure identity"; the "success identity" is characterized by the ability to give and receive love, and the feeling of doing something that is important to self or others. (Glasser, W. [1969]. *Schools without failure.* New York: Harper and Row.) Given these characteristics, what kind of experience can a teacher provide to help a student change from a failure identity to a success identity, that is, develop a more positive self-concept?

How Self-Concept Develops. The self-concept evolves through constant self-evaluation in different situations. Children and adolescents are continually asking themselves, in effect, "How am I doing?" They gauge the verbal and non-verbal reactions of significant people—parents and other family members in the early years and friends, schoolmates, and teachers later—to make judgments (Harter, 1998). Students compare their performance with their own standards and with the performances of peers. Students compare their performance in math to their performance in English and science, for example, to form self-concepts in these areas. If math is their best subject, their math self-concept may be the most positive, even if their actual performance in math is poor. But social comparisons are influential, too. Students' self-concepts in math are also shaped by how their performance compares to that of other students in their math classes (Marsh, 1994). Students who are strong in math in an average school feel better about their math skills than do students of equal ability in high-achieving schools. Marsh (1990) calls this the "Big Fish–Little Pond Effect." Participation in a gifted and talented program seems to have an opposite "Little Fish–Big Pond" effect—students who participate in gifted programs, compared to similar students who remain in regular classes, tend to show declines in academic self-concepts over time, but no changes in non-academic self-concepts (Marsh, Chessor, Craven, & Roche, 1995).

School Life and Self-Esteem

We turn now to self-esteem—the students' evaluations and feelings about themselves. For teachers, there are at least two questions to ask about self-esteem:

(1) How does self-esteem affect a student's behaviour in school? (2) How does life in school affect a student's self-esteem?

In answer to the first question, it appears that students with higher self-esteem are somewhat more likely to be successful in school (Marsh, 1990), although the strength of the relationship varies greatly, depending on the characteristics of the students and the research methods used (Ma & Kishor, 1997; Marsh & Holmes, 1990). In addition, higher self-esteem is related to more favourable attitudes toward school, more positive behaviour in the classroom, and greater popularity with other students (Cauley & Tyler, 1989; Metcalfe, 1981; Reynolds, 1980). Of course, as we discussed in Chapter 1, knowing that two variables are related (correlated) does not tell us that one is causing the other. It may be that high achievement and popularity lead to self-esteem, or vice versa. In fact, it probably works both ways (Marsh, 1987; Shavelson & Bolus, 1982).

▲ *Research indicates that awards such as "author of the week" have less impact on students' self-esteem than feedback and evaluation from the teacher or interactions with other students in class.*

What about the second question of how school affects self-esteem—is school important? A study that followed 322 Grade 6 students for two years would say yes. Hoge, Smit, and Hanson (1990) found that students' satisfaction with the school, their sense that classes were interesting and that teachers cared, and teacher feedback and evaluations influenced students' self-esteem. In physical education, teachers' opinions were especially powerful in shaping students' conceptions of their athletic abilities. Being placed in a low-ability group or being held back in school seems to have a negative impact on students' self-esteem, but learning in collaborative and cooperative settings seems to have a positive effect (Covington, 1992; Deci & Ryan, 1985). Interestingly, special programs such as "Student of the Month" or admission to advanced math classes had little effect on self-esteem. (Relate this to the "Big Fish–Little Pond Effect.")

More than 100 years ago, William James (1890) suggested that self-esteem is determined by how *successful* we are in accomplishing tasks or reaching goals we *value*. If a skill or accomplishment is not important, incompetence in that area doesn't threaten self-esteem. Susan Harter (1990) has found evidence that James was right. Children who believe an activity is important and who feel capable in that area have higher self-esteem than students who think the activity is important, but question their competence. Students must have legitimate success on tasks that matter to them. The way individuals explain their successes or failures also is important. Students must attribute their successes to their own actions, not to luck or to special assistance, in order to build self-esteem.

Teachers' feedback, grading practices, evaluations, and communication of caring for students can make a difference in how students feel about their abilities in particular subjects. But the greatest increases in self-esteem probably come when students grow more competent in areas they value—including the social areas that become so important in adolescence. Thus, a teacher's greatest challenge is to help students achieve important understandings and skills. Given this responsibility, what can teachers do? The recommendations in Table 3.3 are a beginning.

Gender, Ethnicity, and Self-Esteem

Younger children tend to have positive and optimistic views of themselves. In one study, more than 80 percent of the Grade 1 students surveyed thought they were the best students in class. As they mature, students become more realistic, but

Connect & Extend
To the research
Boileau, L., Bouffard, T., & Vezeau, C. (2000). The examination of self, goals and their impact on school achievement in sixth grade students. *The Canadian Journal of Behavioural Science, 32*, 6–17.

Abstract
The relations between perceptions of competence, self-efficacy and types of goals, and their influence on school achievement have been examined among a sample of 224 girls and 193 boys of Grade 6. Results showed that, as was expected, even though perceptions of competence and self-efficacy were related, the latter better predicts school achievement. Contrary to what was expected, no negative influence was observed for the combination of low self-efficacy and performance goals on school achievement. Finally, according to a last hypothesis, the pattern of relations between motivational variables and school achievement differs for boys and girls.

TABLE 3.3 Suggestions for Encouraging Self-Esteem

1. Value and accept all pupils, for their attempts as well as their accomplishments.

2. Create a climate that is physically and psychologically safe for students.

3. Become aware of your own personal biases (everyone has some biases) and expectations.

4. Make sure that your procedures for teaching and grouping students are really necessary, not just a convenient way of handling problem students or avoiding contact with some students.

5. Make standards of evaluation clear; help students learn to evaluate their own accomplishments.

6. Model appropriate methods of self-criticism, perseverance, and self-reward.

7. Avoid destructive comparisons and competition; encourage students to compete with their own prior levels of achievement.

8. Accept a student even when you must reject a particular behaviour or outcome. Students should feel confident, for example, that failing a test or being reprimanded in class does not make them "bad" people.

9. Remember that positive self-concept grows from success in operating in the world *and* from being valued by important people in the environment.

10. Encourage students to take responsibility for their reactions to events; show them that they have choices in how to respond.

11. Set up support groups or "study buddies" in school and teach students how to encourage each other.

12. Help students set clear goals and objectives; brainstorm about resources they have for reaching their goals.

13. Highlight the value of different ethnic groups—their cultures and accomplishments.

Sources: Information from J. Canfield (1990). Improving students' self-esteem, *Educational Leadership, 48*(1) pp. 48–50; M. M. Kash and G. Borich (1978). *Teacher behavior and student self-concept.* (Menlo Park, CA: Addison-Wesley); H. H. Marshall (1989). The development of self-concept. *Young Children, 44*(5) pp. 44–51.

many are not accurate judges of their own abilities (Paris & Cunningham, 1996). In fact, some students suffer from "illusions of incompetence"—they seriously underestimate their own competence (Phillips & Zimmerman, 1990). Gender and ethnic stereotypes can play roles here.

Gender and Self-Esteem. In the elementary grades, girls and boys have comparable perceptions of their own abilities. By Grade 9 and continuing through high school, on average, girls gradually lower their perceptions of their own abilities compared to boys (Cole, Martin, Peeke, Seroczynski, & Fier, 1999; Phillips & Zimmerman, 1990). Similar trends were noted by the Health of Canada's Youth study (King & Coles, 1992) and the Canada Youth and AIDS Study (King et al., 1988). On average, males responded more positively to questions concerning self-confidence, decisiveness, and acceptability of self, actions, and appearance. Other studies indicate that for most ethnic groups males are more confident about their abilities in school, particularly in math and science. Differences between males and females generally are small but consistent across studies (Grossman & Grossman, 1994; Kling, Hyde, Showers, & Buswell, 1999). Put these results together with the findings by Marsh and Yeung (1997) that specific academic self-concept influences course selection. Many women and ethnic minority students make decisions about courses that forever limit their options in life, and often these decisions are not based on ability but instead on "illusions of incompetence."

Personal and Collective Self-Esteem. To this point we have discussed self-esteem as a purely individual characteristic. A number of psychologists have suggested that there is another basis for self-worth and identity called the *collective self*, or the self as a member of a family, peer group, ethnic heritage, class, or team (Wright & Taylor, 1995). Perhaps our self-esteem is influenced by both individual qualities and by **collective self-esteem**—a sense of the worth of the groups to which we belong. When students are faced with daily reminders, subtle or blatant, that

Collective Self-Esteem: The sense of the value of a group, such as an ethnic group, that you belong to.

Ethnic Pride: A positive self-concept about your racial or ethnic heritage.

their ethnic or family group has less status and power, the basis for collective self-esteem can erode.

Some early research on children's perceptions seemed to indicate that children from ethnic minority groups internalized negative stereotypes. In a seminal study by Clark and Clark (1939), African American children, when confronted with a light-skinned and a dark-skinned doll, tended to choose the light-skinned doll as prettier and better on a number of dimensions. Similar findings were reported for Mexican American children (Weiland & Coughlin, 1979), Chinese American children (Aboud & Skerry, 1984), and Canadian Native children (Corenblum & Annis, 1987). However, many of these studies didn't ask the children *why* they preferred the light-skinned dolls. Some psychologists suggest that the children are simply indicating that they understand the power and status differences that surround them. The children do not think less of themselves—their self-esteem is high—but they know that majority group members tend to have more wealth and power (Spencer & Markstrom-Adams, 1990).

For all students, pride in family and community is part of the foundation for a stable identity and collective self-esteem. Because ethnic-minority students are members of both a majority culture and a subculture, it is sometimes difficult for them to establish a clear identity. Values, learning styles, and communication patterns of the students' subculture may be inconsistent with the expectations of the school and the larger society. Embracing the values of mainstream culture may seem to require rejecting ethnic values. Ethnic minority students have to "sift through two sets of cultural values and identity options" to achieve a firm identity, so they may need more time to explore possibilities (Markstrom-Adams, 1992, p. 177). In the process of establishing identity, individuals may pass through several stages (Frable, 1997):

- being unaware of, denying, or devaluing ethnic identity;
- being challenged by conflicts and discrimination to confront and examine ethnicity;
- becoming immersed in a particular ethnic or racial consciousness;
- appreciating ethnicity;
- integrating ethnicity into a full and complex bicultural identity.

Jim Cummins (1989), at the University of Toronto, encourages schools to make special efforts to encourage **ethnic pride** so these students do not get the message that differences are deficits. For example, Cummins suggests that schools display bilingual and multilingual signs, provide opportunities for students to use their first languages, and arrange for parents and community members who represent ethnic minorities to be involved in school events. Each of us has an ethnic heritage. When majority adolescents are knowledgeable and secure about their own heritage, they are also more respectful of the heritage of others. Thus, exploring the ethnic roots of all students should foster both self-esteem and acceptance of others (Rotherham-Borus, 1994).

There is a particular aspect of ethnic heritage and pride that affects schooling—language. In Chapter 5 we will examine language learning in greater depth. But while we are talking about self-esteem, consider the results of a study conducted by Stephen Wright and Donald Taylor (1995) on the impact of heritage language on personal and collective self-esteem. These researchers found that when Canadian Native (Inuit) children were educated in their heritage language for the first three years of school, they had more positive personal and collective self-esteem than the Canadian Native children in the same school who received second-language instruction (English or French) from kindergarten on. When schools value the language of all students, ethnic pride and collective self-esteem may be enhanced.

Connect & Extend
To the research
Lay, C., & Verkyten, M. (1999). Ethnic identity and its relation to personal self-esteem: A comparison of Canadian-born and foreign-born Chinese adolescents. *Journal of Social Psychology, 139*, 288–299.

Abstract
Ethnic identity and its relation to personal self-esteem were examined by comparing 31 Chinese adolescents (aged 13–18 years) who immigrated to Canada and 31 who were Canadian-born. The foreign-born adolescents were more likely to identify themselves as Chinese (rather than Chinese Canadian) and to include references to their ethnicity in response to an open-ended Who Am I Questionnaire, a variation of the 20 Statements Test (M. H. Kuhn & T. S. McPartland, 1954). For the foreign-born group only, aspects of collective self-esteem were positively related to personal self-esteem. The differences between the groups supported a contextual emphasis for associating collective self-esteem with personal self-esteem. The data were consistent with an interpretation involving collectivistic-individualistic distinctions, with the foreign-born sample being more collectivistic.

Sato, T. & Cameron, J. E. (1999). The relationship between collective self-esteem and self-construal in Japan and Canada. *Journal of Social Psychology, 139*, 426–435.

Abstract
This study examined the relationship between various facets of collective self-esteem and independent and interdependent self-construals among undergraduates in Japan (aged 18–25 years) and Canada (aged 17–48 years). Students were administered the Collective Self-Esteem Scale and the Self-Construal Scale. The results suggested that individuals with highly interdependent self-construals regarded social group memberships as self-defining, regardless of culture. Individuals with independent self-construals judged their groups positively and felt they were worthy members of their groups and that others evaluated their groups positively. Canadians who evaluated their social groups favourably may be members of groups that permitted them to be independent. In contrast, individuals in Japan who judged their groups favourably may be members of groups that promoted interdependence in addition to independence.

Perspective-Taking Ability:
Understanding that others have
different feelings and experiences.

One very important group membership for all students is their family. A study by John Fantuzzo, Gwendolyn Davis, and Marika Ginsburg (1995) capitalized on the power of families to improve students' self-esteem. The Family and Community Partnerships Guidelines list the strategies from their study that proved effective in increasing self-esteem and mathematics achievement for minority students in Grades 4 and 5.

The Self and Others

As we seek our own identity and form images of ourselves, we are also seeking and forming ways to understand the "significant others" around us. Children learn to see themselves as separate and to see others as separate people as well, with their own identities. How do we learn to interpret what others are thinking and feeling?

Intention. Around the age of two, children have a sense of intention, at least of their own intentions. They will announce, "I wanna peanut butter sandwich." They can say firmly, "I didn't break it on purpose!" By two and a half or three years of age, children extend the understanding of intention to others. Older preschoolers who get along well with their peers are able to separate intentional from unintentional actions and react accordingly. For example, they will not get angry when other children accidentally knock over their block towers. But aggressive children have more trouble assessing intention. They are likely to attack anyone who topples their towers, even accidentally (Berk, 2000; Dodge & Somberg, 1987). As children mature, they are more able to assess and consider the intentions of others.

Taking the Perspective of Others. Very young children don't understand that other people have different feelings and experiences. But this **perspective-taking ability** develops over time until it is quite sophisticated in adults. Robert Selman (1980) has developed a stage model to describe the development of perspective-

FAMILY AND COMMUNITY PARTNERSHIPS

Building Self-Esteem

1. Work with families to co-create methods for family involvement. Offer a range of possible participation methods. Make sure the plans are realistic and fit the lives of the families.
2. Maintain regular contact between home and school through telephone calls or notes. If a family has no telephone, identify a contact person (relative or friend) who can take messages. If literacy is a problem, use pictures, symbols, and codes for written communication.
3. Make all communications positive, emphasizing growth, progress, and accomplishments.
4. With the families, design family-student celebrations of the student's efforts and successes (a movie, special meal, trip to the park or library, going out for ice cream or pizza).

5. On a regular basis, send home a note in word or picture form that describes the student's progress. Ask families to indicate how they celebrated the success and to return the note.
6. Follow up with a telephone call to discuss progress, answer questions, solicit family suggestions, and express appreciation for the families' contributions.
7. Encourage families to visit the classroom.

Source: Adapted from Fantuzzo, J., Davis, G., & Ginsburg, M. (1995). Effects of parent involvement in isolation or in combination with peer tutoring on student self-concept and mathematics achievement. *Journal of Educational Psychology, 87,* 272–281.

taking. As children mature and move toward formal-operational thinking, they take more information into account. They realize that different people can react differently to the same situation. Some time between the ages of 10 and 15, most children develop the ability to analyze the perspectives of several people involved in a situation from the viewpoint of an objective bystander. Finally, older adolescents and adults can even imagine how different cultural or social values would influence the perceptions of the bystander. Even though children move through these stages, there can be great variation among children of the same age. Students who have difficulty taking the perspective of others may feel little remorse when they mistreat peers or adults. Some coaching in perspective-taking from the teacher might help (Berk, 2000).

Moral Development

If you have spent time with young children, you know that there is a period when you can say, "Eating in the living room is not allowed!" and get away with it. For young children, rules simply exist. Piaget (1965) called this the state of **moral realism**. At this stage, the child of five or six believes that rules about conduct or rules about how to play a game are absolute and can't be changed. If a rule is broken, the child believes that the punishment should be determined by how much damage is done, not by the intention of the child or by other circumstances. So accidentally breaking three cups is worse than intentionally breaking one, and in the child's eyes, the punishment for the three-cup offence should be greater.

As children interact with others, develop perspective-taking abilities, and see that different people have different rules, there is a gradual shift to a **morality of cooperation**. Children come to understand that people make rules and people can change them. When rules are broken, both the damage done and the intention of the offender are taken into account. These developmental changes and others are reflected in Kohlberg's theory of moral development, based in part on Piaget's ideas.

Kohlberg's Stages of Moral Development

Lawrence Kohlberg (1963, 1975, 1981) proposed a detailed sequence of stages of **moral reasoning**, or judgments about right and wrong. He divided moral development into three levels: (1) preconventional, where judgment is based solely on a person's own needs and perceptions; (2) conventional, where the expectations of society and law are taken into account; and (3) postconventional, where judgments are based on abstract, more personal principles that are not necessarily defined by society's laws. Each of these three levels is then subdivided into stages, as shown in Table 3.4.

Kohlberg has evaluated the moral reasoning of both children and adults by presenting them with **moral dilemmas**, or hypothetical situations in which people must make difficult decisions. Subjects are asked what the person who is caught in the dilemma should do, and why.

Connect & Extend
To the news
The June 3, 1996, issue of *U.S. News and World Report* had a cover story titled "How to Raise a Moral Child: Let's Hear It for Honesty, Self-Discipline, and Empathy" (pp. 52–59). This is an interesting mix of research and opinion and a good discussion starter.

Moral Realism: Stage of development wherein children see rules as absolute.

Morality of Cooperation: Stage of development wherein children realize that people make rules and people can change them.

Moral Reasoning: The thinking processes involved in judgments about questions of right and wrong.

Moral Dilemmas: Situations in which no single choice is clearly and indisputably right.

Connect & Extend
To your teaching
For a concise discussion of the research on moral development, see Nucci, L. (1987). Synthesis of research on moral development. *Educational Leadership, 44*(5), 86–92. Nucci's article is a nice contrast to Kohlberg's analysis of moral development. Nucci suggests that even young children can distinguish between conventions and moral issues. Conventions are rules and expectations that vary from one group to the next, such as dating practices, "politeness" norms, or rules about talking in study hall. Moral issues have to do with such actions as physically or psychologically hurting others, stealing, or lying—any activity that would be "wrong" even if there were no rule or law forbidding it. One goal of moral education should be to help children differentiate between the norms and conventions of their culture and universal moral concerns for justice, fairness, and human welfare. To help children understand these distinctions, Nucci suggests: (1) Moral education should focus on issues of justice and human welfare. (2) These concerns should be integrated into the curriculum, not taught as separate programs. (3) Moral discussion promotes moral development when students are at slightly different levels of moral development, are allowed to disagree about solutions to moral dilemmas, and really listen to each other, trying to understand, expand on, or refute each other's opinions. (4) Cooperative goal structures encourage moral development. (5) Firm, fair, flexible classroom management practices contribute to moral development.

TABLE 3.4 Kohlberg's Stage Theory of Moral Reasoning

Level 1. Preconventional Moral Reasoning

Judgment is based on personal needs and others' rules.

Stage 1 Punishment-Obedience Orientation
Rules are obeyed to avoid punishment. A good or bad action is determined by its physical consequences.

Stage 2 Personal Reward Orientation
Personal needs determine right and wrong. Favours are returned along the lines of "You scratch my back, I'll scratch yours."

Level 2. Conventional Moral Reasoning

Judgment is based on others' approval, family expectations, traditional values, the laws of society, and loyalty to country.

Stage 3 Good Boy–Nice Girl Orientation
Good means "nice." It is determined by what pleases, aids, and is approved by others.

Stage 4 Law and Order Orientation
Laws are absolute. Authority must be respected and the social order maintained.

Level 3. Postconventional Moral Reasoning

Stage 5 Social Contract Orientation
Good is determined by socially agreed-upon standards of individual rights.

Stage 6* Universal Ethical Principle Orientation
Good and right are matters of individual conscience and involve abstract concepts of justice, human dignity, and equality.

*In later work Kohlberg questioned whether stage 6 exists separately from stage 5.
Source: Adapted by permission of the *Journal of Philosophy*. From L. Kohlberg (1975). The cognitive-developmental approach to moral education. *Phi Delta Kappan, 56*, p. 671.

One of the most commonly used moral dilemmas can be summarized as follows: A man's wife is dying; there is one drug that could save her, but it is very expensive, and the druggist who invented it will not sell it at a price low enough for the man to be able to buy it. Finally, the man becomes desperate and considers stealing the drug for his wife. What should he do, and why?

At level 1 (preconventional), the child's answer might be, "It is wrong to steal because you might get caught." This answer reflects the child's basic egocentrism. The reasoning might be: "What would happen to me if I stole something? I might get caught and punished."

At level 2 (the conventional level), the subject is able to look beyond the immediate personal consequences and consider the views, and especially the approval, of others. Laws, religious or civil, are very important and are regarded as absolute and unalterable. One answer stressing adherence to rules is, "It is wrong to steal because it is against the law." Another answer, placing high value on loyalty to family and loved ones but still respecting the law, is, "It's right to steal because the man means well—he's trying to help his wife. But he will still have to pay the druggist when he can or accept the penalty for breaking the law."

At level 3 (the postconventional level), an answer might be, "It is not wrong to steal because human life must be preserved. The worth of a human life is greater than the worth of property." This response considers the underlying values that might be involved in the decision. Abstract concepts are no longer rigid, and, as the name of this level implies, principles can be separated from conventional values. A person reasoning on this level understands that what is considered right by the majority may not be considered right by an individual in a particular situation. Rational, personal choice is stressed.

Moral reasoning is related to both cognitive and emotional development. As we have seen, abstract thinking becomes increasingly important in the higher stages of moral development, as children move from decisions based on absolute rules to decisions based on abstract principles such as justice and mercy. The ability to see another's perspective, to judge intentions, and to imagine alternative bases for laws and rules also enters into judgments at the higher stages.

Alternatives to Kohlberg's Theory

Kohlberg's stage theory has been criticized, first, because the stages do not seem in reality to be separate, sequenced, and consistent. People often give reasons for moral choices that reflect several different stages simultaneously. Or a person's choices in one instance may fit one stage and his or her decisions in a different situation may reflect another stage. When asked to reason about helping someone else versus meeting their own needs, young children and adolescents reason at higher levels than when they are asked to reason about breaking the law or risking punishment (Eisenberg et al., 1987; Sobesky, 1983). Also, Kohlberg emphasized cognitive reasoning about morality, but overlooked other aspects of moral maturity, such as character and virtue, that operate to solve moral problems in everyday life (Walker & Pitts, 1998).

Social Conventions versus Moral Issues. Another criticism is that Kohlberg's theory does not differentiate between social conventions and true moral issues until the higher stages of moral reasoning. Social conventions are the social rules and expectations of a particular group or society—for example, "It is rude to eat with your hands." Such behaviour is not morally wrong, just socially inappropriate—in some cultures or situations it is acceptable to eat with your hands (in fact, try eating potato chips with a fork). True moral issues, on the other hand, involve the rights of individuals, the general welfare of the group, or the avoidance of harm. "Stealing" would be wrong, even if there were no "rule" against it; stealing is wrong, not rude. Children as young as three can distinguish between social conventions and moral issues. They know, for example, that being noisy in school would be fine if there were no rule requiring quiet, but that it would not be right to hit another child, even if there were no rule against it. So even very young children can reason based on moral principles that are not tied to social conventions and rules (Nucci, 1987; Smetana & Braeges, 1990; Turiel, 1983).

Cultural Differences in Moral Reasoning. Another criticism of Kohlberg's stage theory is that stages 5 and 6 in moral reasoning are biased in favour of Western, male values that emphasize individualism. In cultures that are more family-centred or group-oriented, the highest moral value might involve putting the opinions of the group before decisions based on individual conscience. There has been much disagreement over the "highest" moral stage. Kohlberg himself questioned the applicability of stage 6. Few people other than trained philosophers reason naturally or easily at this level. Kohlberg (1984) suggested that for all practical purposes, stages 5 and 6 might be combined.

The Morality of Caring

▲ Carol Gilligan has challenged traditional conceptions of moral development with her work on the "ethic of care."

One of the most hotly debated criticisms of Kohlberg's theory is that the stages are biased in favour of males and do not represent the way moral reasoning develops in women. Because the stage theory was based on a longitudinal study of men only, it is very possible that the moral reasoning of women and the stages of women's development are not adequately represented (Gilligan, 1982; Gilligan & Attanucci, 1988). Carol Gilligan (1982) has proposed a different sequence of moral development, an "ethic of care." Gilligan suggests that individuals move from a focus on self-interests to moral reasoning based on commitment to specific individuals and relationships, and then to the highest level of morality based on the principles of responsibility and care for all people.

The highest stage in Kohlberg's theory of moral development involves decisions based on universal principles of justice and fairness. Reasoning based on caring for others and maintaining relationships is scored at a lower level. Many of Kohlberg's early studies of moral reasoning found that most men progressed to stages 4 and 5 by adulthood, while most women "stayed" at stage 3. This makes it appear as if women are morally challenged. But recent studies find few significant differences between men and women, or boys and girls, in their level of moral reasoning as measured by Kohlberg's procedures (Eisenberg, Martin, & Fabes, 1996; Thoma, 1986).

In order to study moral reasoning as it actually happens in real life, and to get an idea about the basis for decisions, Walker and his colleagues (Walker, 1991; Walker, Pitts, Hennig, & Matsuba 1995) asked children, adolescents, and adults to describe a personal moral problem and analyze a traditional moral dilemma. For both types of problems, males and females revealed both a morality of caring and a concern with justice. Andrew Garrod and his colleagues (1990) used fables to study the moral reasoning of students in Grades 1, 3, and 5 and found that both boys and girls tended to adopt a care orientation. There were no differences between the moral reasoning of boys and girls in Grades 1 and 3. However, a few Grade 5 boys (but no girls) suggested solutions involving violence or tricks. So justice and caring seem to be important bases for moral reasoning for both genders. Even though men and women both seem to value caring and justice, there is some evidence that in everyday life, women feel more guilty about violating caring norms by being inconsiderate or untrustworthy, for example, and men feel more guilty when they show violent behaviour, such as fighting or damaging property (Williams & Bybee, 1994). Women are somewhat more likely to use a care orientation, but both men and women *can* use both orientations (Skoe, Pratt, Matthews, & Curror, 1996).

Caring for students and helping students learn to care has become a theme for many educators. For example, Nel Noddings (1995) urged that "themes of care" be used to organize the curriculum. Possible themes include "Caring for Self," "Caring for Family and Friends," and "Caring for Strangers and the World." Using the theme of "Caring for Strangers and the World," there could be units on crime, war, poverty, tolerance, ecology, or technology. Table 3.5 shows how a focus on crime and caring for strangers could be integrated into several high school classes.

Connect & Extend
To professional journals
See the May 1995 issue of *Phi Delta Kappan* for a special section on the schools and caring. Nel Noddings' article is included, as well as an article by Joyce Epstein about family-school partnerships to create caring schools.

Moral Behaviour

As people move toward higher stages of moral reasoning, they also evidence more sharing, helping, and defending of victims of injustice. This relationship between moral reasoning and moral behaviour is not very strong, however (Berk, 2000). Many other factors besides reasoning affect behaviour. Two important influences on moral behaviour are internalization and modelling.

TABLE 3.5 Using "Caring for Strangers and the World" as a Teaching Theme

Internalize: Process whereby children adopt external standards as their own.

As part of a unit on "Caring for Strangers and the World," high school students examine the issue of crime in several classes. In every class, the study of aspects of crime would be continually tied to the theme of caring and to discussions of safety, responsibility, trust in each other and in the community, and commitment to a safer future.

Subject	Elements
Mathematics	Statistics: Gather data on the location and rates of crimes, ages of offenders, and costs of crime to society. Is there a correlation between severity of punishment and incidence of crime? What is the actual cost of a criminal trial?
English and Social Studies	Read *Oliver Twist*. Relate the characters to their social and historical context. What factors contributed to crime in 19th-century England?
	Read popular mysteries. Are they literature? Are they accurate depictions of the criminal justice system?
Science	Genetics: Are criminal tendencies heritable? Are there sex differences in aggressive behaviour? Are women less competent than men in moral reasoning (and why did some social scientists think so)? How would you test this hypothesis?
Arts	Is graffiti art really art?

Source: From Nel Noddings. Teaching Themes of Care. *Phi Delta Kappan, 76,* pp. 675–679. Copyright © 1995 Phi Delta Kappan. Reprinted by permission of Phi Delta Kappan and the author.

Most theories of moral behaviour assume that young children's moral behaviour is first controlled by others through direct instruction, supervision, rewards and punishments, and correction. But in time, children **internalize** the moral rules and principles of the authority figures who have guided them; that is, children adopt the external standards as their own. If children are given reasons they can understand when they are corrected—particularly reasons that highlight the effects of actions on others—then they are more likely to internalize moral principles. They learn to behave morally even when "no one is watching" (Berk, 2000; Hoffman, 1988).

The second important influence on the development of moral behaviour is modelling. Children who have been consistently exposed to caring, generous adult models will tend to be more concerned for the rights and feelings of others (Lipscomb, MacAllister, & Bregman, 1985).

Let's consider several moral issues that arise in classrooms.

Cheating. Early research indicates that cheating seems to have more to do with the particular situation than with the general honesty or dishonesty of the individual (R. Burton, 1963). A student who cheats in math class is probably more likely to cheat in other classes, but may never consider lying to a friend or taking candy from the store. Most students will cheat if the pressure to perform well is great and the chances of being caught are slim.

There are some individual differences in cheating. Most studies of older and college-age students find that males are more likely to cheat than females; lower-

Connect & Extend
To your teaching
In a classroom discussion about stealing, the teacher finds that many students express the opinion that it is all right to steal if you don't get caught. How should a teacher respond? Would the race, culture, gender, or socioeconomic status of the student influence the teacher's response?

Connect & Extend
To your own philosophy
Moral action does not necessarily follow directly from moral judgment. But is it necessary for moral judgment to precede moral action? That is, can a person behave in a moral way even if he or she cannot make a cognitive statement about how one "should" behave?

▲ *Over time, children learn to internalize moral principles such as compassion and justice and adopt them for themselves.*

achieving students are more likely to cheat than higher achievers, students focusing on performance goals (making good grades, looking smart) as opposed to learning goals are likely to cheat; and college students in engineering, business, and science are more likely to cheat than students in the arts and humanities (Davis, Grover, Becker, & McGregor, 1992; Newstead, Franklyn-Stokes, & Armstead, 1996). Students also are particularly likely to cheat when they are behind or "cramming for tests."

The implications for teachers are straightforward. To prevent cheating, try to avoid putting students in high-pressure situations. Make sure they are well prepared for tests, projects, and assignments so they can do reasonably well without cheating. Focus on learning and not on grades. Make extra help available for those who need it. Be clear about your policies in regard to cheating, and enforce them consistently. Help students resist temptation by monitoring carefully during testing.

Aggression. **Aggression**, intentionally trying to harm others, should not be confused with assertiveness, which means affirming or maintaining a legitimate right. As Helen Bee (1981) explains, "A child who says, 'That's my toy!' is showing assertiveness. If he bashes his playmate over the head to reclaim it, he has shown aggression" (p. 350).

Two Canadian researchers, Wendy Craig and Debra Pepler, are among the leading experts on aggressive behaviour in schools, bullying. They characterize bullying as a form of social interaction in which a more dominant individual (the bully) exhibits aggressive behaviour that is intended to cause distress or harm to a less dominant individual (the victim) (Craig & Pepler, 1997, p. 42). Bullying can include relational forms of aggression (e.g., calling someone names or gossiping behind his or her back) as well as physical forms of aggression.

In a survey (Charach, Pepler, & Ziegler, 1995), 19 percent of students in Canadian schools reported being bullied twice a term, and 8 percent of students indicated that they experience aggression in school at least once each week. Craig and Pepler (1998) observed 65 elementary schoolchildren playing in the schoolyard at recess and lunch. During 48 hours of observations, they observed a total

Aggression: Bold, direct action that is intended to hurt someone else or take property; unprovoked attack.

of 314 bullying episodes, approximately 6.5 episodes every hour. They rated 84 percent of the episodes they observed as overt, indicating peers and/or adults were present. School staff were observed to intervene in only 25 percent of the episodes in which they were proximal. Clearly, aggressive behaviour in Canadian schools is a serious problem.

Modelling plays an important role in the expression of aggression (Bandura, Ross, & Ross, 1963). According to the *National Longitudinal Survey of Children and Youth* (NLSCY) in Canada (Tremblay et al., 1996), there is a strong relationship between family membership and aggressive behaviour. The survey found that children who are aggressive tend to have aggressive siblings. In general, research indicates that children who grow up in homes filled with harsh punishment and family violence are more likely to use aggression to solve their own problems (Emery, 1989; Holden & Ritchie, 1991).

One very real source of aggressive models is found in almost every home in North America—television. In the United States, 82 percent of TV programs have at least some violence. The rate for children's programs is especially high—an average of 32 violent acts per hour, with cartoons being the worst. Furthermore, in more than 70 percent of the violent scenes, the violence goes unpunished (Mediascope, 1996; Waters, 1993). Aggressive children tend to believe that violence will be rewarded, and they use aggression to get what they want. They are more likely to believe that violent retaliation is acceptable: "It's OK to shove people when you're mad" (Egan, Monson, & Perry, 1998). Seeing violent acts go unpunished on television probably affirms and encourages these beliefs.

Most children spend more time watching television than they do in any other activity except sleep (Timmer, Eccles, & O'Brien, 1988). On average, Canadian children between the ages of 2 and 11 watch 15.5 hours of television each week (Statistics Canada, 1998a). People have asked the Canadian government to impose rules that restrict youth access to violent television programs and films (Tremblay et al., 1996). In fact, a Canadian researcher, Tim Collings, is responsible for the development of the V-chip that, when inserted in television sets, allows parents to block their children's access to certain TV programs. There also are some things parents and teachers can do to reduce the negative effects of the violence seen on TV. They can emphasize to children and youth that most people do not behave in the aggressive ways shown on television; that the violent acts on TV are not real, but are created by special effects and stunts; and that there are better ways to resolve conflicts, and these are the ways most real people use to solve their problems (Huessmann, Eron, Klein, Brice, & Fischer, 1983). Also, avoid using TV viewing as a reward or punishment because that makes television even more attractive to children (Slaby et al., 1995).

Other sources of violent models include popular films and video games, which are also filled with graphic depictions of violence, often performed by the "hero." Students growing up in the inner cities see gangs and drug deals. Newspapers, magazines, and the radio are filled with stories of murders, rapes, and robberies. In some preschools the children don't play "Mommy" and "Daddy"; they pretend to sell "nickel bags" of heroin (really bags of ground-up chalk) to their playmates.

The breakdown of the family also has been suggested as a possible source of aggressive behaviour on the part of children and youth (Tremblay et al., 1996). Stress, poverty, and problems with discipline have been associated with parental separation and have been linked to aggressive tendencies. Other proposed explanations include lax discipline in schools; the availability of drugs, alcohol, and guns; and the ineffectiveness of laws concerning juvenile offenders. However, the *Canadian Criminal Code* is getting tougher on young offenders. In December 1995, Bill C-37 was passed to permit tougher sentences for violent crimes, and adolescents who commit serious violent offences, such as murder, can now be tried in adult court.

Tremblay et al. (1996) and Pepler and Sedighdeilami (1998) analyzed data from the NLSCY to examine patterns of aggressive behaviour relating to age (2–11

Connect & Extend
To your own philosophy
What about the endless hours spent in front of the television set? Are we simply robbing our children of time to play by letting them be entertained? Marie Winn has written a thought-provoking book on this subject: *The Plug-In Drug* (New York: Viking, 1985).

Connect & Extend
To the research
Galen, B. R., & Underwood, M. K. (1997). A developmental investigation of social aggression among children. *Developmental Psychology, 33,* 589–600.

Abstract
Social aggression consists of actions directed at damaging another's self-esteem, social status, or both, and includes behaviour such as facial expressions of disdain, cruel gossiping, and the manipulation of friendship patterns. In Study 1, children from Grades 4, 7, and 10 completed the Social Behaviour Questionnaire; only boys viewed physical aggression as more hurtful than social aggression, and girls rated social aggression as more hurtful than did boys. In the first phase of Study 2, girls participated in a laboratory task in which elements of social aggression were elicited and reliably coded. In the second phase of Study 2, another sample of participants (elementary, middle, and high school boys and girls) viewed samples of socially aggressive behaviour from these sessions. Girls rated the aggressor as more angry than boys, and middle school and high school participants thought the socially aggressive behaviour indicated more dislike than did elementary school children.

CHECKPOINT

Moral Development

Review

▷ What are the key differences among the preconventional, conventional, and postconventional levels of moral reasoning?

▷ Describe Gilligan's levels of moral reasoning.

▷ What influences moral behaviour?

Apply

▷ How can teachers encourage moral behaviour and caring?

▷ How might Vanessa's teacher support Vanessa's attempts to make and keep friends?

years), gender, and socioeconomic status (SES). In general, as children mature, they become less likely to respond to problem situations with physical aggression but more likely to respond with less direct forms of aggression (e.g., name-calling, bad-mouthing, or ostracizing). Also, the researchers found that, whereas boys at all ages were more physically aggressive than girls, they were less involved in indirect aggression than girls. The analyses by Tremblay and his colleagues found that boys and girls with low-SES status had the highest physical aggression scores, and that the differences between boys and girls were most pronounced among these children. Finally, the results of these researchers' analyses indicate that children who receive high ratings regarding physical aggression also tend to receive high ratings on items that reflect hyperactivity, indirect aggression, and emotional disorders. Tremblay and his colleagues suggest that efforts to reduce aggression and increase prosocial behaviour should begin early.

Victims. While some students tend to be bullies, other children are victims. Studies from Europe and the United States indicate that about 10 percent of children are chronic victims—the constant targets for physical or verbal attacks. In

GUIDELINES

Dealing with Aggression and Encouraging Cooperation

Present yourself as a non-aggressive model.

Examples

1. Do not use threats of aggression to win obedience.
2. When problems arise, model non-violent conflict-resolution strategies.

Ensure that your classroom has enough space and appropriate materials for every student.

Examples

1. Prevent overcrowding.
2. Make sure prized toys or resources are plentiful.
3. Remove or confiscate materials that encourage personal aggression, such as toy guns.

Make sure students do not profit from aggressive behaviour.

Examples

1. Comfort the victim of aggression and ignore the aggressor.

2. Use reasonable punishment, especially with older students.

Teach directly about positive social behaviour.

Examples

1. Incorporate lessons on social ethics/morality through reading selections and discussions.
2. Discuss the effects of anti-social actions such as stealing, bullying, and spreading rumours.

Provide opportunities for learning tolerance and cooperation.

Examples

1. Emphasize the similarities among people rather than the differences.
2. Set up group projects that encourage cooperation.

Canada, data from the NLSCY indicates that 5 percent of school-aged children are victims (Craig, Peters, & Konarski, 1998). Victims tend to have low self-esteem and they feel anxious, lonely, insecure, and unhappy. They often are prone to crying and withdrawal; when attacked, generally they won't defend themselves. Recent research suggests that victims may blame themselves for their situation. They believe that they are rejected because they have character flaws that they cannot change or control—no wonder they are depressed and helpless! The situation is worse for young adolescent victims whose peers seem to have little sympathy for them. Children who have been chronic victims through elementary and middle school are more depressed and more likely to attempt suicide as young adults (Graham, 1998; Hodges & Perry, 1999). In the past years we have seen tragic consequences when tormented students turned guns on their tormentors in schools in the United States and Canada.

There is a second kind of victim—highly emotional and hot-tempered students who seem to provoke aggressive reactions from their peers. This group is rejected by almost all peers and has few friends (Pellegrini, Bartini, & Brooks, 1999). The Guidelines on page 82 may give you ideas for handling aggression and encouraging cooperation.

Socialization: Family, Peers, and Teachers

Socialization is the process by which the mature members of a society, such as parents and teachers, influence the beliefs and behaviour of children, enabling them to fully participate in and contribute to the society. In this section we will consider three of the most important influences on the development and socialization of children: family, peers, and teachers.

North American Families Today

The most appropriate expectation to have about your students' families is no expectation at all. The idea of two parents, 2.2 children, Dad with the only job, and Mom in the kitchen is no longer the norm.

Increasingly, today's student may have only one or no sibling, or students may be part of **blended families**, with stepbrothers or stepsisters who move in and out of their lives. Some of your students may live with an aunt, with grandparents, with one parent, in foster or adoptive homes, or with an older brother or sister. The best advice is to drop the phrases "your parents" and "your mother and father" and to speak of "your family" when talking to students.

Many middle-class couples are waiting longer to have children and are providing more material advantages. Children in these homes may have more "things," but they may also have less time with their parents. Of course, not all students are middle-class. Twenty-one percent of Canada's children under age 18 are living in low-income families (Statistics Canada, 1996a). Many children live with one parent, usually their mother, and these families are particularly likely to have incomes below the poverty level. Your students are likely to be alone or unsupervised much of the day. The growing number of these *latchkey children* has prompted many schools to offer before- and after-school programs.

Children of Divorce. Many of your students, ready or not, have to deal with one very adult issue—divorce. According to Statistics Canada (2000), the 1998 divorce rates indicate that 36 percent of marriages will end in divorce within 30 years of the wedding.

As many of us know from experiences in our own families, separation and divorce are stressful events for all participants, even under the best circumstances. The actual separation of the parents may have been preceded by years of conflict

Connect & Extend
To the research
Graham, S. (1998). Self-blame and peer victimization in middle school: An attributional analysis. *Developmental Psychology, 34,* 587–599.

Abstract
Relations between characterological versus behavioural self-blaming attributions for victimization and maladjustment were examined in middle school students. Respondents completed a questionnaire that assessed self-perceptions of victim status, attributions for hypothetical incidents of victimization, and feelings of loneliness, social anxiety, and low self-worth. They also completed peer nomination procedures measuring perceptions of victimization in others, as well as peer acceptance and rejection. Self-perceived victimization was associated with characterological self-blame, loneliness, anxiety, and low self-worth. Peer-perceived victimization, in contrast, was related to acceptance and rejection. The data suggest that self-views are more predictive of the intrapersonal consequences of victimization (loneliness, anxiety, and low self-worth), whereas peer views are more predictive of interpersonal consequences (peer acceptance and rejection).

Socialization: The ways in which members of a society encourage positive development for the immature individuals of the group.

Blended Families: Parents, children, and stepchildren merged into families through remarriages.

in the home or may come as a shock to all, including friends and children. During the divorce itself, conflict may increase as property and custody rights are being decided.

Connect & Extend
To the research
For a concise discussion of the effects of divorce on children and suggestions for ways that teachers can help their students cope with divorce, see Rotenberg, K. J., Kim, L. S., & Herman-Stahl, M. (1998). The role of primary and secondary appraisals in the negative emotions and psychological adjustment of children of divorce. *Journal of Divorce and Remarriage, 29,* 43–66.

Effects of Divorce. After the divorce, more changes may disrupt the children's lives. Today, as in the past, the mother is most often the custodial parent, but the number of households headed by the father has been increasing, to about 17 percent by 1996 (Statistics Canada, 1996c). The parent who has custody may have to move to a less-expensive home, find new sources of income, go to work for the first time, or work longer hours. For the child, this can mean leaving behind important friendships in the old neighbourhood or school, just when support is needed the most. It may mean having just one parent, who has less time than ever to be with the children. About two-thirds of parents remarry and then half of them divorce again, so there are more adjustments ahead for the children (Furstenberg & Cherlin, 1991; Nelson, 1993). In some divorces there are few conflicts, ample resources, and the continuing support of friends and extended family. But divorce is never easy for anyone.

GUIDELINES

Helping Children of Divorce

Take note of any sudden changes in behaviour that might indicate problems at home.

Examples
1. Be alert to physical symptoms such as repeated headaches or stomach pains, rapid weight gain or loss, fatigue or excess energy.
2. Be aware of signs of emotional distress, including moodiness, temper tantrums, and difficulty in paying attention or concentrating.
3. Let parents know about the students' signs of stress.

Talk individually to students about their attitude or behaviour changes. This gives you a chance to find out about unusual stress such as divorce.

Examples
1. Be a good listener. Students may have no other adult willing to hear their concerns.
2. Let students know you are available to talk, and then let students who approach you set the agenda.

Watch your language to make sure you avoid stereotypes about "happy" (two-parent) homes.

Examples
1. Simply say "your families" instead of "your mothers and fathers" when addressing the class.
2. Avoid statements such as "We need volunteers for room mother" or "Your father can help you."

Help students maintain self-esteem.

Examples
1. Recognize a job well done.
2. Make sure the student understands the assignment and can handle the workload. This is not the time to pile on new and very difficult work.
3. The student may be angry at his or her parents, but may direct the anger at teachers. Don't take the student's anger personally.

Find out what resources are available at your school.

Examples
1. Talk to the school psychologist, guidance counsellor, social worker, or principal about students who seem to need outside help.
2. Consider establishing a discussion group, led by a trained adult, for students going through a divorce.

Be sensitive to both parents' rights to information.

Examples
1. When parents have joint custody, both are entitled to receive information and attend parent-teacher conferences.
2. The non-custodial parent may still be concerned about the child's school progress. Check with your principal about provincial laws regarding the non-custodial parent's rights.

The first two years after the divorce seem to be the most difficult period for both boys and girls. During this time, children may have problems in school, lose or gain an unusual amount of weight, develop difficulties sleeping, and so on. They may blame themselves for the breakup of their family or hold unrealistic hopes for a reconciliation (Hetherington, 1989; Pfeffer, 1981). Long-term adjustment is also affected. Boys tend to show a higher rate of behavioural and interpersonal problems at home and in school than girls in general or boys from intact families. Girls may have trouble in their dealings with males. They may become more sexually active or have difficulties trusting males. However, living with one fairly content, if harried, parent may be better than living in a conflict-filled situation with two unhappy parents. And adjustment to divorce is an individual matter; some children respond with increased responsibility, maturity, and coping skills (Amato, Loomis, & Booth, 1995; Berk, 2000). See the Guidelines on page 84 for ideas about how to help students in these situations.

Peer Relationships

Peer relationships play a significant role in healthy personal and social development. There is strong evidence that adults who had close friends as children have higher self-esteem and are more capable of maintaining intimate relationships than adults who spent lonely childhoods. The characteristics of friends and the quality of the friendships matter too. Having stable, supportive relationships with friends who are socially competent and mature enhances social development, especially during difficult times such as parents' divorce or transition to new schools (Hartup & Stevens, 1999). Adults who were rejected as children tend to have more problems, such as dropping out of school or committing crimes (Coie et al., 1995; Coie

▲ *Peer relationships in the school years appear to play a significant role in self-esteem, success in school, and success in adult life.*

Parents and Peers

A few years ago, Judith Rich Harris published a book that shocked most parents and many psychologists. *The Nurture Assumption: Why Children Turn Out the Way They Do; Parents Matter Less Than You Think and Peers Matter More* (1998) questioned the commonly held belief that parents are the major influences on their children. Her book and the subsequent controversy that rippled through talk shows and the popular press raised some important questions. Just how much influence do families have on their children compared to the possibly powerful effects of peers? How powerful are other factors such as inborn temperament?

▶ **POINT** *Parents matter less than you think.*

Contemporary behavioural genetics has established clearly that personality traits as well as abilities have a genetic component, but genes explain only about half of the variation. Harris's book challenges the deeply held belief that parents account for the other half of the influence. Writing a review of Harris's book, social psychologist and textbook author Carol Tarvis summarized five sets of findings that question the impact of parents, which is also known as the nurture assumption: (1) No child-rearing style seems to predict children's personalities outside the home. Besides, the way parents treat children often depends on the children—more permissive with cooperative children but strict with defiant ones, for example. (2) Even when parents treat their children the same way, the children often turn out much different. For instance, most children of troubled parents suffer no lasting damage, but some grow up troubled themselves. (3) There is no correlation between the personality traits of adopted children and their adoptive parents. (4) Whether children are raised by two parents or one, in day care or at home, by gay parents or

heterosexual, seems to have no impact on the children's personality. (5) Parents' behaviour seems to affect children mostly when the children are with their parents (which may be why so many parents can't believe teachers' accounts of their children's misbehaviour at school). According to Tarvis, Harris changed the discussion from nature (genes) and nurture (parents) to the older question of heredity and environment, and then documented the powerful role of one aspect of the environment—peer culture—in children's development. "Parents have long lamented the apparent cruelty of children and the obsessive conformity of teenagers, but Harris argues that they have missed the point. Children's attachment to their peer groups is not irrational, it's essential" (Tarvis, 1998, p. 14). Attachment to peers, not parents, is essential for human survival. To see the power of peers, we have to look at situations where the values and interests of parents clash with those of peers, then see whose influence dominates. In these comparisons, peers usually win. Tarvis claims, for example, that differences between black and white achievement vanish when you take peer culture into account. And the contribution of parents to the environmental influence on children's personality? About zero according to Harris, once heredity is taken into account. Harris's conclusions have been criticized, but many well-known psychologists, such as neuroscientist Robert Sapolsky of Stanford, say that her work is based on solid science (Begley, 1998).

◀ **COUNTERPOINT** *Parents are pivotal.*

Other psychologists disagree. Sharon Begley (1998) interviewed several prominent psychologists for an article in *Newsweek*. Here are a few quotes. Frank Farley of Temple University, and at the time president of the American Psychological Association, a group that had presented Harris an award

for her work, said, "She's all wrong. She is taking an extreme position based on a limited set of data. Her thesis is absurd on the face, but consider what might happen if parents believe this stuff! Will it free some to mistreat their kids, since it doesn't matter? Will it tell parents who are tired after a long day that they needn't bother even paying attention to their kid since 'it doesn't matter'?" According to Wendy Williams of Cornell, "There are many, many good studies that show parents can affect how children turn out in both cognitive abilities and behaviour. By taking such an extreme position, Harris does a tremendous disservice." Jerome Kagan of Harvard said simply, "I am embarrassed for psychology." Kagan cited one of his own studies as evidence that parents matter. He studied shy children whose parents either overprotected them or pushed them to interact with others. Children who were encouraged to play, even though they were shy, became far less fearful—so parental behaviour interacted with temperament to affect the children's personality. Also, John Gottman of the University of Washington cited evidence from his intervention studies that teach parents how to talk and listen to their children with behaviour problems. Parents who learned a new way of interacting have clear effects on their children. Finally, some psychologists questioned Harris's interpretations of the twin studies because the number of these studies is too small to warrant Harris's conclusions.

Perhaps the best lesson from this debate is that parents are not the sole source of influence—positive or negative—on their children. Harris said that she wrote the book "to lighten the burden of guilt and blame placed on the parents of 'problem children.'" Peers, other adults, and teachers all have a role to play, especially when children are away from their parents. Teachers have a chance to help shape a peer culture that can make a difference for their students.

& Dodge, 1998). Friendships are central to students' lives. When there has been a falling-out or an argument, when one child is not invited to a sleepover, when rumours are started and pacts are made to ostracize someone, the results can be devastating to the children involved. Even when students begin to mature and know intellectually that rifts will soon be healed, they may still be emotionally crushed by temporary trouble in the friendship.

A teacher should be aware of how each student gets along with the group. Are there outcasts? Do some students play the bully role? Careful adult intervention can often correct such problems, especially at the elementary and middle school levels.

A book published in 1998 caused a national debate when it claimed that peers, not parents, were the major forces shaping the personalities and behaviour of children. The Point/Counterpoint on page 86 examines this controversy.

The Point/Counterpoint on page 86 examines this controversy.

CHECKPOINT

Socialization: Family, Peers, and Teachers

Review

▷ What challenges face children whose parents are divorced?

▷ Why are peer relations important?

Apply

▷ As Vanessa's teacher, would you involve her family in dealing with her social problems?

▷ How would you decide what to do?

New Roles for Teachers

When we consider the high rate of divorce and the power of peer relationships for children, we see that teachers today are dealing with issues that once stayed outside the walls of the school. The first and most important task of the teacher is to educate, but student learning suffers when there are problems with personal and social development.

Teachers are sometimes the best source of help for students facing emotional or interpersonal problems. When students have chaotic and unpredictable home lives, they need a caring, firm structure in school. They need teachers who set clear limits, are consistent, enforce rules firmly but not punitively, respect students, and show genuine concern. As a teacher, you can be available to talk about personal problems without requiring that your students do so. One student teacher gave a boy in her class a journal titled "Very Hard Thoughts" so that he could write about his parents' divorce. Sometimes he talked to her about the journal entries, but at other times he just recorded his feelings. The student teacher was very careful to respect the boy's privacy about his writings. What can teachers do to encourage personal and social growth in school? The Guidelines on page 88 give some other ideas.

Challenges for Children

In the next few pages we examine a number of challenges children face as they mature. The first is as old as the human species—growing up, meeting the challenges of physical development. The remaining challenges are all too modern and have put students at great risk today. We will end by considering just a few of these risks.

Physical Development

For most children, at least in the early years, growing up means growing bigger, stronger, more coordinated. It also can be frightening, disappointing, exciting, and puzzling.

GUIDELINES

Supporting Personal and Social Development

Help students examine the kinds of dilemmas they are currently facing or will face in the near future.

Examples

1. In elementary school, discuss sibling rivalries, teasing, stealing, prejudice, treatment of new students in the class, behaviour toward class-mates with disabilities.
2. In high school, discuss cheating, letting friends drive when they are intoxicated, conforming to be more popular, protecting a friend who has broken a rule.

Help students see the perspectives of others.

Examples

1. Ask a student to describe his or her understanding of the views of another, and then have the other person confirm or correct the perception.
2. Have students exchange roles and try to "become" the other person in a discussion.

Help students make connections between expressed values and actions.

Examples

1. Follow a discussion of "What should be done?" with "How would you act? What would be your first step? What problems might arise?"
2. Help students see inconsistencies between their values and their own actions. Ask them to identify inconsistencies, first in others, then in themselves.

Safeguard the privacy of all participants.

Examples

1. Remind students that in a discussion they can "pass" and not answer questions.
2. Intervene if peer pressure is forcing a student to say more than he or she might like.
3. Don't reinforce a pattern of telling "secrets."

Make sure students are really listening to each other.

Examples

1. Keep groups small.
2. Be a good listener yourself.
3. Recognize students who pay careful attention to each other.

Make sure that as much as possible your class reflects concern for moral issues and values.

Examples

1. Make clear distinctions between rules based on administrative convenience (keeping the room orderly) and rules based on moral issues.
2. Enforce standards uniformly. Be careful about showing favouritism.

Source: Adapted with permission from J. W. Eiseman (1981). "What criteria should public school moral education programs meet?" *The Review of Education, 7,* pp. 226–227.

The Preschool Years. Preschool children are very active. Their **gross-motor skills,** which involve control of the large muscles, improve greatly over the years from ages two to five, as you can see in Table 3.6. Between ages two and about four or five, preschoolers' muscles grow stronger, their balance improves, and their centre of gravity moves lower, so they are able to run, jump, climb, and hop. Most of these movements develop naturally if the child has normal physical abilities and the opportunity to play. Children with physical problems, however, may need special training to develop these skills. For young children, physical activity can be an end in itself. It is fun just to improve. But preschoolers may literally run till they drop. They need periods of rest scheduled after physical exertion.

Fine-motor skills such as tying shoes or fastening buttons, which require the coordination of small movements, also improve greatly during the preschool years, as shown in Table 3.6. Children need to work with large paintbrushes, fat pencils and crayons, large pieces of drawing paper, and soft clay or playdough to accommodate their developing skills. During this time, each child will begin to show a right- or left-hand preference. Most students, about 85 percent during this time,

Gross-Motor Skills: Voluntary body movements that involve the large muscles.

Fine-Motor Skills: Voluntary body movements that involve the small muscles.

TABLE 3.6 Motor Skills Improve throughout the Preschool Years

Approximate Age	Gross-Motor Skills	Fine-Motor Skills
Birth to 3 years	sits and crawls; walks; begins to run	picks up, grasps, stacks, and releases objects
3 to 4.5 years	walks up and down stairs; jumps with both feet; throws ball	holds crayon; uses utensils; buttons; copies shapes
4.5 to 6 years	skips; rides two-wheel bicycle; catches ball; plays sports	uses pencil; makes representational drawings; cuts with scissors; prints letters

will prefer using their right hand, but those who prefer their left should not be forced to change. This means that there must be a good supply of left-handed scissors for preschool classes.

Elementary School. During the elementary school years, physical development is fairly steady for most children. They become taller, leaner, and stronger, so they are better able to master sports and games. There is tremendous variation, however. A particular child can be much larger or smaller than average and still be perfectly healthy. Because children at this age are very aware of physical differences but are not the most tactful people, you may hear comments such as "You're too little to be in Grade 5. What's wrong with you?" or "How come you're so fat?"

Throughout elementary school, many of the girls are likely to be as large as or larger than the boys in their classes. Between the ages of 11 and 14, girls are, on the average, taller and heavier than boys of the same age (Tanner, 1990). The size discrepancy can give the girls an advantage in physical activities, although some girls may feel conflict over this and, as a result, downplay their physical abilities.

Adolescence. **Puberty** marks the beginning of sexual maturity. It is not a single event, but a series of changes involving almost every part of the body. The outcome of the changes is the ability to reproduce. The sex differences in physical development we saw during the later elementary years become even more pronounced at the beginning of puberty. Generally, girls begin puberty about two years ahead of boys and reach their final height by age 16; most boys continue growing until about age 18. For the typical North American and European girl, the adolescent growth spurt begins with breast development between the ages of 10 and 11 and continues for about three years. While this is the average time frame for girls, the actual range is from 9 to 16 years. Most North American girls have their first menstrual period between the ages of 11 and 14. For the typical boy, the growth spurt begins between the ages of 12 and 13. When the growth spurt is at its peak, boys can grow 10 cm and gain 12 kg in a single year, and girls can grow 9 cm and gain 9 kg in the same time frame.

The physical changes of adolescence have significant effects on the individual's identity. Psychologists have been particularly interested in the academic, social, and emotional differences between adolescents who mature early and those who mature later. Early maturation seems to have certain special advantages for boys: the taller, broader-shouldered body type fits the cultural stereotype for the male ideal. Early-maturing boys are more likely to enjoy high social status; they tend to be popular and to be leaders. On the other hand, boys who mature late have an especially difficult time (Kaplan, 1984). However, some studies show that in

Puberty: The period in early adolescence when individuals begin to reach physical and sexual maturity.

GUIDELINES

Dealing with Differences in Growth and Development

Do not call unnecessary attention to physical differences among students.

Examples

1. Avoid seating arrangements that are obviously based on height, but try to seat smaller students so they can see and participate in class activities.
2. Avoid games that call attention to differences in height, size, or strength.
3. Don't use or allow students to use nicknames based on physical traits.

Help students obtain factual information on differences in physical development.

Examples

1. Set up science projects on sex differences in growth rates.
2. Have readings and discussions that focus on differences between early and late maturers. Make sure that you present the positives and the negatives of each.

3. Find out the school policy on sex education and on informal guidance for students. Some schools, for example, encourage teachers to talk to girls who are upset about their first menstrual period, while other schools expect teachers to send the girls to talk to the school nurse or the guidance counsellor.
4. Give the student models in literature or in their community of high-achieving individuals who do not fit the ideal physical stereotypes.

Accept that concerns about appearance and the opposite sex will occupy much time and energy for adolescents.

Examples

1. Allow students a few moments at the end of class to socialize.
2. Deal with some of these issues in curriculum-related materials.

adulthood, males who matured later tend to be more creative, tolerant, and perceptive. Perhaps the trials and anxieties of maturing late teach some boys to be better problem solvers (Brooks-Gunn, 1988; Seifert & Hoffnung, 1991).

For girls, these effects are reversed. Maturing way ahead of classmates can be a definite disadvantage. Being larger than everyone else in the class is not a valued characteristic for girls in many cultures (Simmons & Blyth, 1987). A girl who begins to mature early probably will be the first in her peer group to start the changes of puberty. This can be very upsetting to some girls, especially if they have not been prepared for the changes or if friends tease them. Later-maturing girls seem to have fewer problems, but they may worry that something is wrong with them. All students can benefit from knowing that the "normal" range in rates of maturation is great and that there are advantages for both early and late maturers. The Guidelines above give a few ideas for dealing with physical differences in the classroom.

At the same time that they are negotiating the physical transitions from childhood through adolescence, students must navigate the social and academic transitions of schooling. These changes can be uplifting, devastating, or anywhere in between for a child.

Navigating Transitions

Do you remember your first day of school? Do you remember getting your first list of required school supplies (interlined notebooks, No. 2 pencils...), buying them at a local drugstore? Did you get a free milkshake with your supplies? Today, the free milkshakes are gone—we all are watching our cholesterol. However, the transition into school is still a critical time for young children, one that, hopefully, begins a journey toward lifelong learning.

Young Children: Starting School. Between the ages of five and seven, when most children start school, cognitive development is proceeding rapidly. Children can process more information faster and their memory spans are increasing. They are moving from preoperational to concrete-operational thinking. As these internal changes progress, the children are spending hours every weekday in the new physical and social world of school. They must now re-establish Erikson's stages of psychosocial development in the unfamiliar school setting. They must learn to trust new adults, act autonomously in this more complex situation, and initiate actions in ways that fit the new rules of school. At the same time, the new psychosocial challenge of industry versus inferiority looms large. The child must master new skills and work toward new goals, while being compared to others and risking failure.

The way children cope with these challenges has implications for the rest of their school experience. Two of the best predictors of dropping out of school are low grade-point average by Grade 3 and being held back in one of the primary grades (Paris & Cunningham, 1996). Children who do well in the Grade 1 are on their way to achievement, while those who flounder are on a path toward difficulty. "How well students do in the primary grades matters more for their future success than does their school performance at any other time" (Entwisle & Alexander, 1998, p. 354).

What is this important world of school like for children? First, school requires new social roles—children must fit into the group and learn to be students. These new roles do not come easily or automatically for every child. Also, evaluation is built into school and success is not guaranteed. The basis for reward and recognition changes as children move from their families to school. In families, children generally are compared to themselves in terms of growth and development (remember, "Oh, you've gotten so much bigger since last fall!"). In school, however, children are compared to each other and someone is always bigger, faster, smarter—or so it seems (Entwisle & Alexander, 1998). In addition, different student characteristics are noticed—such as social class and ethnicity—that may not have mattered before because they were shared by family members.

As you will see in Chapter 10, teachers' judgments and expectations can have powerful effects on students. Too often ethnic and social class differences between teachers and students set the stage for miscommunication and lowered expectations. These negative cycles of lowered expectations and lowered achievement begin in Grade 1 and accumulate. By Grade 3, children's performance on achievement tests stabilizes and predicts future achievement quite well (Butler, Marsh, Sheppard, & Sheppard, 1985).

What can be done to make the transition to school positive? Research suggests a few answers. First, quality preschool and kindergarten experiences are critical for helping children, especially children from low-income homes, to do well in Grade 1. Children who achieve in Grade 1 do better in later grades, so the time to make a difference is early. Programs such as Reading Recovery and Success for All are based on early and intensive intervention. Continuity helps children become successful students, so staying in the same school for kindergarten and Grade 1, with the same peers and teachers, can be helpful. In Chapter 12, you will learn about teaching students directly how to accomplish school rules and procedures. Teachers, administrators, families, and community leaders can work together to make the transition to school positive for all children (Mangione & Speth, 1998; Paris & Cunningham, 1996).

Students in the Middle Grades: Another Transition. There are many different age configurations in schools today, but most students move from elementary to middle school or junior high between Grades 5 and 7—a time developmental psychologists call "early adolescence" (Sandrock, 1996). Again, cognitive process-es are expanding as the students develop capabilities for abstract thinking and for understanding the perspectives of others. But even greater changes are taking place in the students' physical development as they approach puberty. The students bring their new cognitive abilities and their changing bodies to the psychosocial task of identity—exploring possible selves. Who am I? Who do I want to become and who do I fear becoming? During the middle grades, students are more likely to describe themselves in terms of psychological and social traits such as "moody," "loyal," or "depressed" and political or religious orientation such as Jewish, Muslim, Christian, conservative, or libertarian. Their sense of self becomes more differen-tiated, so they know that they have many capabilities and limitations. Quite a bit is going on.

And the world is changing, too. The Carnegie Council on Adolescent Development's (1995) report, *Great Transitions: Preparing Adolescents for a New Century*, describes five changes that create a complex context for growing up today. First, as we saw earlier, the number of divorces and working parents in many countries means that young adolescents spend less time with adults and more time with peers or watching television. Second, the job future for many ado-lescents is grim as the world shifts to a knowledge-based economy, where a high school degree is not enough to earn a good salary. Why work hard in school if you will have the same dead-end job as that offered to a school dropout? Third, ado-lescents go through puberty earlier and assume adult roles later compared with previous generations. It is a strain, to say the least, to be sexually mature but socially restricted for a long time. Fourth, adolescents are surrounded by media—television, films, videos, and music—that influence their expectations, fears, and values. And finally, the world has become more diverse. About one-third of ado-lescents in North American schools today are of non-European descent, and in some regions this figure is much higher.

So, with developing minds and identities and bodies, the young adolescent must navigate the transition to the middle grades in an uncertain world. What are the results? One of the most common findings is that overall self-concept and self-esteem decline in early adolescence, as do assessments of competence in academic and non-academic areas. Just after a transition to a new school, especially the tran-sition to junior high school, students' self-concepts seem to become more negative and less stable. During the middle school or junior high years, students grow more self-conscious (remember, adolescent egocentrism and Elkind's imaginary audience discussed in Chapter 2). At this age, feelings of self-worth are more closely tied to physical appearance and social acceptance, so these years can be exceedingly diffi-cult for students such as Vanessa, described at the opening of this chapter (Wigfield, Eccles, & Pintrich, 1996). When young adolescents move from being the most mature and highest-status students in a small, familiar elementary school to being the bottom of the chain in a large, impersonal junior high school, there may be negative consequences (Graber & Brooks-Gunn, 1996; Lord, Eccles, & McCarthy, 1994; Meece, 1997; Wigfield, Eccles, MacIver, Rueman, & Midgley, 1991).

What can teachers do to make these transitions easier for middle grade stu-dents? The middle school movement is one attempt to structure schools to meet the needs of this developmental period. Some of the features of middle grade schools are interdisciplinary teams of teachers who work with a "pod" or cohort of students; integrated curricula that take into account the personal concerns of the students and build learning tasks around these concerns; advisory programs that pair every student with a teacher/advisor; and special-interest exploratory classes such as photography or computers. One more element relates to you, the teacher. Middle grade schools should have teachers who are knowledgeable about and like young adolescents (Muth & Alverman, 1999).

Children and Youth at Risk

It is a difficult time to become an adult. Many of the challenges children face threaten their safety as well as their personal and social development. We will consider only a few of the risks that students encounter. Teachers can play a role in helping students cope with these situations. In the first area—child abuse—teachers have legal responsibilities to consider.

Child Abuse. Accurate information about the number of abused children in Canada is difficult to find because many cases go unreported. In 1996, children under 18 were victims in 22 percent of the violent crimes reported to the police, and family members were responsible for 20 percent of the physical assaults and 32 percent of the sexual assaults on children (Statistics Canada, 1998b). Parents are the most likely perpetrators in familial physical and sexual abuse cases, and fathers are responsible for 73 percent of physical assaults and 98 percent of sexual assaults on children within families. About half of all abusive parents could change their destructive behaviour patterns if they received help and support. Without assistance, probably only about 5 percent of abusing parents improve (Starr, 1979). Of course, parents are not the only people who abuse children. Siblings, other relatives, and even teachers have been responsible for the physical and sexual abuse of children.

As a teacher, you must alert your principal, or school counsellor, or a school social worker if you suspect abuse. Child protection is a provincial responsibility, so be sure you understand the laws in your province concerning this important role. In British Columbia, the *Child, Family, and Community Service Act* clearly states that *anyone* who has reason to believe that a child has been or is likely to be physically or sexually abused or exploited, or neglected, has a legal responsibility to report the matter to a child-protection social worker (British Columbia Ministry for Children and Families, 1998). In British Columbia, a child is any individual under age 19. Sometimes, people don't report their suspicions because they think they need proof. That is not true. All that is required is a reasonable belief that a child is in emotional or physical danger. Each year thousands of children die because of abuse or neglect, in many cases because no one would "get involved" (Thompson & Wyatt, 1999). Table 3.7 on page 94 lists possible indicators of abuse.

Teenage Sexuality and Pregnancy. According to the *Canada Youth and AIDS Study* (King, Beazley, Warren, Hankins, Robertson, & Radford, 1998), 49 percent of Canadian men and 46 percent of Canadian women have had sexual intercourse by age 19. Twenty-one percent of 15-year-old girls report having had intercourse. The emotional impact of these early sexual experiences may have repercussions in school, both for the students involved and for fellow students who hear about the experiences. One consequence of this early sexual activity is unexpected and unwanted pregnancy. Each year, more than one million teenage girls in the United States become pregnant—30 000 of them are younger than 15 years of age (DeRidder, 1993; Scarr, Weinberg, & Levine, 1986). This adolescent pregnancy rate is twice that of England, France, and Canada, three times that of Sweden, and six times as high as the Netherlands (Berk, 1996).

A remarkable number of adolescents have little information, or indeed the wrong information, about birth control. For example, about half of the adolescent girls who become pregnant do so in their first six months of sexual activity; often, they haven't decided yet what to do about birth control, partly because they don't expect anything to happen so quickly. It can! Some adults fear that giving adolescents accurate information about sex will encourage them to experiment. Research indicates that this is not a danger. The main effect of providing the facts appears to be fewer unwanted pregnancies (Brooks-Gunn & Furstenberg, 1989; DeRidder, 1993).

Connect & Extend
To the research
Tocane, N., & Schumaker, K. (1999). Reported child sexual abuse in Canadian schools and recreational facilities: Implications for developing effective prevention strategies. *Children and Youth Service Review, 21,* 621–642.

Connect & Extend
To the research
DeRidder, L. M. (1993). Teenage pregnancy: Etiology and educational interventions. *Educational Psychology Review, 5,* 87–107. McKay, A., & Holowaty, P. (1997). Sexual health education: A study of adolescents' opinions, self-perceived needs, and current and preferred sources of information. *Canadian Journal of Human Sexuality, 6,* 29–38.

TABLE 3.7 Indicators of Child Abuse

The following are some of the signs of abuse. Not every child with these signs is abused, but these indicators should be investigated.

Physical Abuse	Physical Indicators	Behavioural Indicators	
	■ unexplained bruises (in various stages of healing), welts, human bite marks, bald spots ■ unexplained burns, especially cigarette burns or immersion burns (glove-like) ■ unexplained fractures, lacerations, or abrasions	■ self-destructive ■ withdrawn and aggressive—behavioural extremes ■ uncomfortable with physical contact ■ arrives at school early or stays late, as if afraid	■ chronic runaway (adolescents) ■ complains of soreness or moves uncomfortably ■ wears clothing inappropriate to weather, to cover body
Physical Neglect	■ abandonment ■ unattended medical needs ■ consistent lack of supervision ■ consistent hunger, inappropriate dress, poor hygiene ■ lice, distended stomach, emaciation	■ regularly displays fatigue or listlessness, falls asleep in class ■ steals food, begs from classmates ■ reports that no caretaker is at home	■ frequently absent or tardy ■ self-destructive ■ school dropout (adolescents)
Sexual Abuse	■ torn, stained, or bloodied underclothing ■ pain or itching in genital area ■ difficulty walking or sitting ■ bruises or bleeding in external genitalia ■ venereal disease ■ frequent urinary or yeast infections	■ withdrawn, chronic depression ■ excessive seductiveness ■ role reversal, overly concerned for siblings ■ poor self-esteem, self-devaluation, lack of confidence ■ peer problems, lack of involvement ■ massive weight change	■ suicide attempts (especially adolescents) ■ hysteria, lack of emotional control ■ sudden school difficulties ■ inappropriate sex play or premature understanding of sex ■ threatened by physical contact, closeness ■ promiscuity

Source: From T. Bear, S. Schenk, and L. Buckner. Supporting victims of child abuse. *Educational Leadership, 50*(4), p. 44. Reprinted with permission of the Association for Supervision and Curriculum Development. Copyright © 1993 by ASCD. All rights reserved.

Eating Disorders. Adolescents going through the changes of puberty are very concerned about their bodies. This has always been true, but today the emphasis on fitness and appearance makes adolescents even more likely to worry about how their bodies "measure up." For some, the concern becomes excessive. One consequence is eating disorders such as **bulimia** (binge eating) and **anorexia nervosa** (self-starvation), both of which are much more common in females than in males. Bulimics often binge, eating an entire litre of ice cream or a whole cake. Then, to avoid gaining weight, they force themselves to vomit, or they use strong laxatives, to purge themselves of the extra calories. Bulimics tend to maintain a normal weight, but their digestive systems can be permanently damaged.

Bulimia: Eating disorder characterized by overeating, then getting rid of the food by self-induced vomiting or laxatives.

Anorexia Nervosa : Eating disorder characterized by very limited food intake.

▲ *Naiveté about the possible consequences of early sexual activity, unwanted pregnancy, and sexually transmitted disease gives many adolescents a false sense of invincibility. "It won't happen to me."*

Anorexia is an even more dangerous disorder, for anorexics eat practically nothing or refuse to eat at all and yet often exercise obsessively. In the process they may lose 20 to 25 percent of their body weight, and some (about 5 to 10 percent) literally starve themselves to death. Anorexic students may appear pale, with brittle fingernails, and with fine, dark hairs developing all over their bodies. They are easily chilled because they have so little fat to insulate their bodies. They often are depressed, insecure, moody, and lonely. Girls may stop having their menstrual period. These eating disorders often begin in adolescence and are becoming more common—about 1 percent of adolescent girls become anorexic. These students usually require professional help—don't ignore the warning signs (Harris, 1991). Again, a teacher may be the person who begins the chain of help for students with these tragic problems.

Drug Abuse. Modern society makes growing up a very confusing process. Notice the messages from films and billboards. "Beautiful," popular people drink alcohol and smoke cigarettes with little concern for their health. We have over-the-counter drugs for almost every common ailment. Coffee wakes us up, and a pill helps us sleep. And then we tell students to "say no!" to drugs.

For many reasons, not just because of these contradictory messages, drug use has become a problem for students. Virtually all recent surveys of adolescents in North America confirm the widespread exposure of adolescents to alcohol. *The British Columbia Student Drug Use Survey* (British Columbia Ministry of Labour and Consumer Services, 1990) found 72 percent of students in Grades 8 to 12 had consumed alcohol one or more times in the past 12 months—23 percent reported drinking alcohol five or more times per month. About 13 percent of 15- to 16-year-olds and 28 percent of 17- to 19-year-olds are smokers. These proportions hold constant for youth reporting the use of marijuana.

What can be done about drug use among our students? First, we should distinguish between experimentation and abuse. Many students try something at a party but do not become regular users. The best way to help students who have trouble saying no appears to be through peer programs that teach how to say no assertively. The successful programs also teach general social skills and build self-esteem, are located in schools but run by community agencies, give intensive

Review

▶ How do students develop physically during the elementary years?

▶ Describe the worlds of the late-maturing adolescent boy and girl.

▶ What are key transitions for students?

▶ What are some danger signs of child abuse, eating disorders, and potential for suicide?

Apply

▶ How might you assess the physical and emotional risks Vanessa faces?

caring adult attention to individual students, and provide opportunities for work experiences (Lerner & Galambos, 1998). Also, the older students are when they experiment with drugs, the more likely they are to make responsible choices, so helping younger students say no is a clear benefit.

AIDS. A growing health risk for everyone, but especially for adolescents, is the spread of AIDS (acquired immune deficiency syndrome). From 1988 to 1990 in Canada, the median age of individuals infected with HIV dropped from 32 to 23. About one-fifth of all AIDS cases in the United States occur between ages 20 and 29 (Berk, 1996). In most cases, adolescents contract AIDS through intimate sexual contact or intravenous drug use. For the virus to be transmitted, people have to exchange bodily fluids without the fluids coming into contact with the air first. Obviously, this can happen a number of ways, but contact has to be more than casual. Many students do not understand that the AIDS virus is unable to survive in air or water, so AIDS cannot be transmitted by casual day-to-day touching, hugging, or sharing food—or even by being spat on (Seifert & Hoffnung, 1991). The Task Force on Pediatric AIDS of the American Psychological Association (1989) recommends education about AIDS for students, beginning in the early years and continuing through high school. In this area, education can be life-saving and does not appear to encourage experimentation.

Suicide. According to the *Adolescent Health Survey* (McCreary Centre Society, 1993), there has been a steady increase in suicide among Canada's youth over the past 25 years, and it is now among the leading causes of death for adolescents. Females are more likely to think about and attempt suicide, as are youth from minority groups (e.g., youth with disabilities and youth who are gay or lesbian). The rate of suicide among First Nations youth is 3 to 10 times the rate among non-First Nations youth.

Suicide is often a response to life problems—problems that parents and teachers sometimes dismiss. There are many warning signs that trouble is brewing. Watch for changes in eating or sleeping habits, weight, grades, disposition, activity level, or interest in friends. Students at risk sometimes suddenly give away prized possessions such as stereos, CDs, clothing, or pets. They may seem depressed or hyperactive and may say things like "Nothing matters any more," "You won't have to worry about me any more," or "I wonder what dying is like." They may start missing school or quit doing work. It is especially dangerous if the student not only talks about suicide but also has a plan for carrying out a suicide attempt.

If you suspect that there is a problem, talk to the student directly. One feeling shared by many people who attempt suicide is that no one really takes them seriously. "A question about suicide does not provoke suicide. Indeed, teens (and adults) often experience relief when someone finally cares enough to ask" (Range, 1993, p. 145). Be realistic, not poetic, about suicide. Ask about specifics, and take the student seriously. Also, be aware that teenage suicides often occur in clusters. After one student acts or when stories about a suicide are reported in the media, other teens are more likely to copy the suicide (Lewinsohn, Rohde, & Seeley, 1994). Table 3.8 lists common myths and facts about suicide.

This has been a brief, selective look at the needs of children. As we saw earlier, educators and psychologists are concerned about providing a developmentally appropriate education for preschool students. All students, whatever their age, require an education that fits their physical, cognitive, personal, and social levels of development.

TABLE 3.8 Myths and Facts about Suicide

Myth: People who talk about suicide don't kill themselves.

Fact: Eight out of 10 people who commit suicide tell someone that they're thinking about hurting themselves before they actually do it.

Myth: Only certain types of people commit suicide.

Fact: All types of people commit suicide—male and female, young and old, rich and poor, country people and city people. It happens in every racial, ethnic, and religious group.

Myth: When a person talks about suicide, you should change the subject to get his or her mind off it.

Fact: You should take them seriously. Listen carefully to what they are saying. Give them a chance to express their feelings. Let them know you are concerned. And help them get help.

Myth: Most people who kill themselves really want to die.

Fact: Most people who kill themelves are confused about whether they want to die. Suicide is often intended as a cry for help.

Sources: From R. Bell (1980). *Changing Bodies, Changing Lives: A Book for Teens on Sex and Relationships.* New York: Random House, p. 142.

Summary

The Work of Erikson

Why is Erikson's theory considered a psychosocial perspective?

Erikson was interested in the ways that individuals developed psychologically to become active and contributing members of society. He believed that all humans have the same basic needs and that each society must accommodate those needs. Erikson's emphasis on the relationship between society and the individual is a psychosocial theory of development—a theory that connects personal development (psycho) to the social environment (social).

What are Erikson's stages of psychosocial development?

Erikson believed that people go through eight life stages between infancy and old age, each of which involves a central crisis. Adequate resolution of each crisis leads to greater personal and social competence and a stronger foundation for solving future crises. In the first two stages, an infant must develop a sense of trust over mistrust and a sense of autonomy over shame and doubt. In early childhood, the focus of the third stage is on developing initiative and avoiding feelings of guilt. In the child's elementary school years, the fourth stage involves achieving a sense of industry and avoiding feelings of inferiority. In the fifth stage, identity versus role confusion, adolescents consciously attempt to solidify their identity. According to Marcia, these efforts may lead to identity achievement, foreclosure, diffusion, or moratorium. Erikson's three stages of adulthood involve struggles to achieve intimacy, generativity, and integrity.

Understanding Ourselves and Others

What is the difference between self-concept and self-esteem?

Both self-concept and self-esteem are beliefs about the self. Self-concept is our attempt to explain ourselves to ourselves, to build a scheme that organizes our impressions, feelings, and attitudes about ourselves. But this model is not fixed or permanent. Our self-perceptions vary from situation to situation and from one phase of our lives to another. Self-esteem is an affective reaction—an evaluation of who you are. If people evaluate themselves positively—if they "like what they see"—we say that they have high self-esteem. Self-concept and self-esteem are often used interchangeably, even though they have distinct meanings. Self-concept is a cognitive structure and self-esteem is an affective evaluation.

How do self-concept and self-esteem change as children develop?

Self-concept (definition of self) and self-esteem (valuing of self) become increasingly complex, differentiated, and abstract as we mature. Self-concept evolves through constant self-reflection, social interaction, and experiences in and out of school. Students develop a self-concept by comparing themselves to personal (internal) standards and social (external) standards. The self-esteem of middle and junior high school students becomes more tied to physical appearance and social acceptance. High self-esteem is related to better overall school experience, both academically and socially. Gender and ethnic stereotypes are significant factors as well. Teachers can have a profound effect on students' self-concept and self-esteem.

How do perspective-taking skills change as students mature?

An understanding of intentions develops as children mature, but aggressive students often have trouble understanding the intentions of others. Social perspective-taking also changes as we mature. Young children believe that everyone has the same thoughts and feelings they do. Later, they learn that others have separate identities and therefore separate feelings and perspectives on events.

Moral Development

What are the key differences among the preconventional, conventional, and postconventional levels of moral reasoning?

Lawrence Kohlberg's theory of moral development includes three levels: (1) a preconventional level, where judgments are based on self-interest; (2) a conventional level, where judgments are based on traditional family values and social expectations; and (3) a postconventional level, where judgments are based on more abstract and personal ethical principles. Kohlberg has evaluated the moral reasoning of both children and adults by presenting them with moral dilemmas, or hypothetical situations in which people must make difficult decisions. Critics suggest that Kohlberg's view does not account for possible sex differences in moral reasoning or differences between moral reasoning and moral behaviour.

Describe Gilligan's levels of moral reasoning.

Carol Gilligan has suggested that because Kohlberg's theory of stages was based on a longitudinal study of men only, it is very possible that the moral reasoning of women and the stages of women's development are inadequately represented. She has proposed a different sequence of moral development, an "ethic of care." Gilligan believes that individuals move from a focus on self-interests to moral reasoning based on commitment to specific individuals and relationships, and then to the highest level of morality based on the principles of responsibility and care for all people. There is some evidence that in everyday life, women feel more guilty about violating caring norms, by being inconsiderate or untrustworthy, and men feel more guilty when they show violent behaviour, such as fighting or damaging property. Women are somewhat more likely to use a care orientation, but studies also show that both men and women *can* use both orientations.

What influences moral behaviour?

Others first control young children's moral behaviour through direct instruction, supervision, rewards and punishments, and correction. In time, children internalize the moral rules and principles of the authority figures who have guided them; that is, children adopt the external standards as their own. If children are given reasons they can understand, at the time they are being instructed on correct behaviour—particularly reasons that highlight the effects of actions on others—they are more likely to internalize moral principles. A second important influence on the development of moral behaviour is modelling. Children who have been consistently exposed to caring, generous adult models will tend to be more concerned for the rights and feelings of others. The world and the media provide many negative models of behaviour. Some schools have adopted programs to increase students' capacity to care for others. Cheating and aggression are two common behaviour problems in the schools that involve moral issues.

Socialization: Family, Peers, and Teachers

What challenges face children whose parents are divorced?

During the divorce itself, conflict may increase as property and custody rights are being decided. After the divorce, the custodial parent may have to move to a less expensive home, find new sources of income, go to work for the first time, or work longer hours. For the child, this can mean leaving behind important friendships in the old neighbourhood or school just when support is needed the most, having only one parent who has less time than ever to be with the children, or adjusting to new family structures when parents remarry.

Why are peer relations important?

Peer relationships play a significant role in healthy personal and social development. There is strong evidence that adults who had close friends as children have higher self-esteem and are more capable of maintaining inti-

mate relationships than adults who spent lonely childhoods. Adults who were rejected as children tend to have more problems, such as dropping out of school or committing crimes.

Challenges for Children

How do students develop physically during the elementary years?

During the preschool years there is rapid development of children's gross- and fine-motor skills. During the elementary school years, physical development is fairly steady. Children become taller, leaner, and stronger, so they are better able to succeed at sports and games. There is tremendous variation, however. A particular child can be much larger or smaller than average and still be perfectly healthy. Throughout elementary school, many of the girls are likely to be as large as or larger than the boys in their classes. Between the ages of 11 and 14, girls are, on the average, taller and heavier than boys of the same age.

Describe the worlds of the late-maturing adolescent boy and girl.

Early maturation seems to have certain special advantages for boys. The early maturers' taller, broader-shouldered body type fits the cultural stereotype for the male ideal. Early-maturing boys are more likely to enjoy high social status; they tend to be popular and to be leaders. For girls, these effects are reversed. Being larger than everyone else in the class is not a valued characteristic for girls in many cultures. A girl who begins to mature early probably will be the first in her peer group to start the changes of puberty. This can be very upsetting to some girls. Later-maturing girls seem to have fewer problems, but they may worry that something is wrong with them. All students can benefit from knowing that the "normal" range in rates of maturation is great and that there are advantages for both early and late maturers.

What are key transitions for students?

Transition to kindergarten or Grade 1 requires new social roles—children must fit into the group and learn to

be students. Evaluation is built into school and success is not guaranteed. The basis for reward and recognition changes as children move from their families to school. In school, children are compared to each other. Different student characteristics are noticed—ones that may not have mattered before because they were shared by family members. How well students do in the primary grades matters more for their future success than does their school performance at any other time. The next transition is to middle school, just as students are undergoing great physical and cognitive changes. Just after a transition to a new school, especially the transition to junior high school, students' self-concepts seem to become more negative and less stable. When young adolescents move from being the most mature and highest-status students in a small, familiar elementary school to being the bottom of the chain in a large, impersonal junior high school, there may be negative consequences.

What are some danger signs of child abuse, eating disorders, and potential for suicide?

Signs of abuse or neglect include unexplained bruises, burns, bites, or other injuries and fatigue, depression, frequent absences, poor hygiene, inappropriate clothing, and problems with peers (see Table 3.7). Teachers must report suspected cases of child abuse and can be instrumental in helping students cope with other risks as well. Anorexic students may appear pale, have brittle fingernails, and have fine dark hairs developing all over their bodies. They are easily chilled because they have so little fat to insulate their bodies. They often are depressed, insecure, moody, and lonely. Girls may stop having their menstrual period. Students at risk of suicide may show changes in eating or sleeping habits, weight, grades, disposition, activity level, or interest in friends. They sometimes suddenly give away prized possessions such as stereos, CDs, clothing, or pets. They may seem depressed or hyperactive and may start missing school or quit doing work. It is especially dangerous if the student not only talks about suicide but also has a plan for action.

Key Terms

aggression, *p. 80*

anorexia nervosa, *p. 94*

autonomy, *p. 64*

blended families, *p. 83*

bulimia, *p. 94*

collective self-esteem, *p. 72*

developmental crisis, *p. 62*

ethnic pride, *p. 72*

fine-motor skills, *p. 88*

generativity, *p. 68*

gross-motor skills, *p. 88*

identity achievement, *p. 66*

identity diffusion, *p. 66*

identity foreclosure, *p. 66*

industry, *p. 64*

initiative, *p. 64*

integrity, *p. 68*

internalize, *p. 79*

moral dilemmas, *p. 75*

moral realism, *p. 75*

moral reasoning, *p. 75*

morality of cooperation, *p. 75*

moratorium, *p. 66*

perspective-taking ability, *p. 74*

psychosocial, *p. 62*

puberty, *p. 89*

self-concept, *p. 69*

self-esteem, *p. 69*

socialization, *p. 83*

Becoming a Professional

Reflecting on the Chapter

Can you apply the ideas from this chapter on personal/social development to solve the following problems of practice?

Preschool and Kindergarten

Elise and Donis have always been two of the most cooperative students in your four-year-old group. But both will soon have new babies in their families, and as the time draws nearer, they are becoming more and more disruptive. What would you do?

Elementary and Middle School

You notice a fairly dramatic change in one of your students. This boy seems very tired and anxious, and he is not doing his homework. The situation has gone on for a few weeks now. How would you approach this problem?

Junior High and High School

Several of your junior high school students are afraid to go to gym class because a gang of students has been extorting money and personal possessions. What steps would you take to end this situation?

You hear from one of your students that a group of seniors has a small "business" selling college application essays. What would you do?

Check Your Understanding

▷ Be clear about the difference between self-esteem and self-concept.

▷ Make sure you understand the elements of Kohlberg's theory and his three stages of moral reasoning, as well as Gilligan's alternative theory.

▷ Understand the range of family structures today.

▷ Be familiar with indicators of child abuse and neglect and your legal responsibilities.

Your Teaching Portfolio

Think about your philosophy of teaching, a question you will be asked at most job interviews. What do you believe about teaching values and moral behaviour? How can you support the development of genuine and well-founded self-esteem in your students? (Consult Table 3.3 for ideas.)

Add some ideas for parent involvement from this chapter to your portfolio.

Teaching Resources

Adapt Table 3.5, "Using 'Caring for Strangers and the World' as a Teaching Theme," for the grades and subjects you might teach and add it to your teaching resources file.

Add Table 3.7, "Indicators of Child Abuse," to your teaching resources file.

Weblinks

www.uky.edu/Subject/childev.html

This Web site provides links to a wide array of other useful sites that focus on research, policy initiatives, and other resources concerning child development.

www.nncc.org/cyfernet/cd.page.html#anchor30545785

A variety of links can be found at this Web site to topics such as ages and stages of development, emotional development, social development, thinking and learning, language and communication, creativity, play and development, and individual differences.

What Would They Do?

Here is how some practising teachers responded to the teaching situation presented at the beginning of this chapter about Vanessa, a student with few friends.

JOHN DYCK

Hugh Boyd Secondary School
Richmond, British Columbia

In dealing with a situation like this, a teacher needs to begin by understanding some of the unique social and psychological characteristics of a teenage girl in Grade 10. This is a year of transitions for girls. They are increasingly aware of the pressures of needing to do well in school, while at the same time struggling with not wanting to stand out as academic nerds. They are making important choices about the types of friendships they want and the influence these can have on their lives. Image is very important, and self-doubts and problems with self-esteem surface easily at a time like this. Vanessa's problem involves some or all of these elements.

To try to get at the root of the problem, I would first seek out a couple of trustworthy and more sensitive female students in this class and discreetly elicit their perceptions about Vanessa and her situation. I would also try to find an appropriate opportunity to discuss the changes I had been observing with Vanessa herself. Part of my job as a teacher is to be aware of changes in performance; they serve as a very good source for initiating valuable communication. These kinds of interactions depend very much on the kind of relationship a teacher has with the students.

Depending on the outcome of these conversations, I might go on to meet with Vanessa's parent(s) and/or a counsellor, possibly including Vanessa, to look for practical ways of bringing about solutions to the problem. I would also seek feedback from other teachers who work with Vanessa. I would especially consult those teachers who are particular-ly responsive to students' needs. It can be more effective to work as a team with a student on several fronts, that is, to respond in more than one classroom, and to be able to generate and implement some visible support and strategies for success for Vanessa. Ultimately, an important goal in all this would be to help Vanessa see that a group of people care about her in a very personal way and want to support her in becoming more successful in one of the most important areas of her life: relationships with people. She needs to know that she is not alone and that there is hope.

YOFI SADAKA

Herzliah High School
Montreal, Quebec

Unfortunately Vanessa's case is not unique. Not only can this problem stem from many causes, but its consequences may also be numerous.

The first thing I would need to know is whether this situation started this year, or whether Vanessa had always had trouble fitting in. A meeting with the guidance counsellor and her previous teachers might provide some answers. During such a session, we might also learn whether or not she felt more at ease in certain classes or with certain teachers. We would try to analyze her strengths and weaknesses in order to put her in a situation where she would feel more comfortable.

At the classroom level, I would encourage cooperative learning activities. I would form groups of four students and assign a project or a discussion topic in which each member had a defined role. Then, all of their efforts would be combined for a final presentation. I would try to compose this group of students who, by nature, were more helpful and positive than others. If I knew where Vanessa's strength lay, I could assign her a task that would allow her to thrive. This would not only improve her status in the group, but it would also help her self-confidence. Peers might hear of her abilities and, for the next project, offer to be partners with her.

Another solution might be to assign her a task that would affect the whole class. This could mean a responsibility in an extracurricular activity or in the classroom. For example, I could ask her to participate in class demonstrations. The assignment would first be rehearsed with the teacher, then presented to the class. I would prepare her in such a way that she might be able to answer questions from the students. This could increase her self-esteem and might change the perceptions of her classmates.

It might take time to get the desired results. One thing to avoid would be leaving Vanessa on her own. Her withdrawal might be a sign of more dangerous actions in the future. We would have to give her help and the chance to show herself at her best.

4

Learner Differences

Have you ever had the experience of being the only one in a group who had trouble doing something? How would you feel if every day in school you faced the same kind of difficulty, while everyone else seemed to find the work easier than you? What kind of support and teaching would you need to keep trying?

So far we have talked little about individuals. We have discussed principles of development that apply to everyone—stages, processes, conflicts, and tasks. Our development as human beings is similar in many ways, but not in every way. Even among members of the same family, there are marked contrasts in appearance, interests, abilities, and temperament.

We will begin our discussion of individual differences in learning with a look at names and labels that have been applied to students. Then we turn to an extended examination of intellectual abilities, which vary so greatly from individual to individual and have proved so difficult to define and measure. How can teachers work with such a wide range of abilities? Is ability grouping a good answer? What are the special needs of the gifted and how can teachers encourage creativity in all students? How do individual cognitive styles and learning preferences affect learning?

Next we explore the kinds of learning problems students may have. As we discuss each problem area, we will consider how a teacher might recognize problems, seek help from school and community resources, and plan instruction based on individuals' needs. Recent changes in provincial policies for educating exceptional learners mean that you probably will have at least one exceptional student in your class, whatever grade you teach. We will discuss these policies and how to cope with their effects.

By the time you have completed this chapter, you should be able to:

▶ Discuss the potential problems in categorizing and labelling students.

▶ Begin to develop a personal concept of intelligence.

▶ Discuss how you might recognize and teach students who are gifted.

▶ Adapt lessons for students with varying learning styles and preferences.

▶ List indicators of hearing, vision, language, and behaviour problems, as well as indicators of specific learning disabilities.

▶ Adapt learning methods to meet the needs of exceptional students.

▶ Discuss the implications of the *Canadian Charter of Rights and Freedoms* for your teaching.

What Would You Do?

One of the students in your class is the topic of conversation at this morning's school-based team (SBT) meeting. As you sip your morning coffee in the staff room, you review the results of Daryl's psychoeducational assessment, hoping they will shed some light on how you can optimize his teaching and learning environment. Nothing is jumping out at you. You wonder what sense the SBT—your administrator, the resource teacher, the school psychologist, the speech/language pathologist, and you—will make of it all. You know that Daryl's parents are hoping the results of these assessments will point to a cure for all of his learning problems. However, your experience with such assessment tools makes you doubt that this will be the case.

▶ How will you use this assessment information?

▶ What can such assessments (i.e., intelligence tests and standardized achievement tests) tell you about your students?

▶ What will you tell Daryl's parents about the assessment results and their implications for his program?

Language and Labelling

Every child is a distinctive collection of talents, abilities, and limitations. In that sense they all are "exceptional." But some students are called exceptional because they have high abilities in particular areas (e.g., music, art, math) or disabilities that interfere with learning and require special education or other services. **Exceptional students** may have developmental delays, learning disabilities, communication disorders, emotional or behavioural disorders, physical disabilities, autism, traumatic brain injury, impaired hearing, impaired vision, or advanced abilities and talents. Even though we will use these terms throughout the chapter, a caution is in order: labelling students is a controversial issue.

A label does not tell which methods to use with individual students. For example, few specific "treatments" automatically follow from a "diagnosis" of a learning disability—many different teaching strategies and materials are appropriate. Further, the labels can become self-fulfilling prophecies. Everyone—teachers, parents, classmates, and even the students themselves—may see a label as a stigma that cannot be changed. Finally, labels are mistaken for explanations, as in, "Chris gets into fights because he has a behaviour disorder." "How do you know he has a behaviour disorder?" "Because he gets into fights."

On the other hand, some educators argue that having a label protects the child. For example, if classmates know a student has a disability, they will be more willing to accept his or her behaviour. Of course, labels still open doors to some special programs, useful information, special technology and equipment, or financial assistance. Labels probably stigmatize and help students (Heward & Orlansky, 1992; Keogh & MacMillan, 1996), so until we are able to make diagnoses with greater accuracy, we should be cautious about describing a whole human being with one or two words.

Today many people object to such labels as "the developmentally delayed" or "the at-risk student," because describing a complex person in this fashion implies that the condition labelled is the most important aspect of the person. Actually the individual has many abilities, and to focus on the disability is to misrepresent the individual. An alternative is to use "person-first" language—to refer to "students with learning disabilities" or "students placed at risk." Here the emphasis is on the

Exceptional Students: Students who have abilities or problems so significant that the students require special education or other services to reach their potential.

students first, not on the special challenges they face. Figure 4.1 summarizes examples of person-first language.

One more distinction in language is important. A **disability** is just what the word implies—an inability to do something specific such as see or walk. A **handicap** is a disadvantage in certain situations. Some disabilities lead to handicaps, but not in all contexts. For example, being blind (a visual disability) is a handicap if you want to drive a car. But blindness is not a handicap when you are composing music or talking on the telephone. Stephen Hawking, the greatest living physicist, suffers from Lou Gehrig's disease and no longer can walk or talk. He once said that he is lucky that he became a theoretical physicist "because it is all in the mind. So my disability has not been a serious handicap." It is important that we do not create handicaps for people by the way we react to their disabilities. Some educators have suggested that we drop the word "handicap" altogether because the source of the word is demeaning. Handicap came from the phrase "cap-in-hand," used to describe people with disabilities who once were forced to beg just to survive (Hardman, Drew, & Egan, 1999).

In the next section we consider a concept that has provided the basis for many labels—intelligence.

Disability: The inability to do something specific such as walk or hear.

Handicap: A disadvantage in a particular situation, sometimes caused by a disability.

> # CHECKPOINT
> ## Language and Labelling
>
> ### Review
>
> ▷ What are the advantages and problems with labels?
>
> ▷ What is person-first language?
>
> ▷ Distinguish between a disability and a handicap.
>
> ### Apply
>
> ▷ Do your professors use person-first language?

FIGURE 4.1

Examples of Person-First Language

Here are some ways to be sure your language puts the student first.

Examples of Person-First Language

A student with a disability	NOT ➡	A disabled student
Children receiving special education	NOT ➡	Special education children
A man who has cerebral palsy	NOT ➡	A cerebral palsy sufferer
A child with a specific learning disability	NOT ➡	A learning disabled child
The boy with Down syndrome	NOT ➡	The Down syndrome boy
People who are physically disabled	NOT ➡	Physically disabled people
She has epilepsy	NOT ➡	She is epileptic

♦♦♦♦♦

Avoid Using Stigmatizing Terminology (Examples)

Afflicted with . . .	Hare lip	Retardate
Crippled	Hearing impaired	Trainable mentally retarded
Deviant	Mute	Victimized by . . .
Handicapped	Orthopedically impaired	

Source: Adapted from *Child and Adolescent Development for Educators,* p. 392, by J. L. Meece, 1997, New York: McGraw-Hill. Copyright © 1997 McGraw-Hill Companies. Adapted with permission.

Individual Differences in Intelligence

Because the concept of intelligence is so important in education, so controversial, and so often misunderstood, we will spend quite a few pages discussing it. Let us begin with a basic question.

What Does Intelligence Mean?

The idea that people vary in what we call **intelligence** has been with us for a long time. Plato discussed similar variations over 2000 years ago. Most early theories about the nature of intelligence involved one or more of the following three themes: (1) the capacity to learn; (2) the total knowledge a person has acquired; and (3) the ability to adapt successfully to new situations and to the environment in general.

In this century, there has been considerable controversy over the meaning of intelligence. In 1986 at a symposium on intelligence, 24 psychologists offered 24 different views about the nature of intelligence (Neisser et al., 1996; Sternberg & Detterman, 1986). More than half of the experts mentioned higher-level thinking processes—such as abstract reasoning, problem solving, and decision making—as important aspects of intelligence, and they added metacognition or knowledge of self to earlier views. However, they disagreed about the structure of intelligence—whether it is a single ability or many separate abilities (Gustafsson & Undheim, 1996; Sternberg & Kaufman, 1998).

Intelligence: One Ability or Many?

Some theorists believe intelligence is a basic ability that affects performance on all cognitively oriented tasks. An "intelligent" person will do well in computing mathematical problems, analyzing poetry, taking history essay examinations, and solving riddles. Evidence for this position comes from correlational evaluations of intelligence tests. In study after study, moderate to high positive correlations are found among all the different tests that are designed to measure separate intellectual abilities (Lohman, 1989; McNemar, 1964). What could explain these results?

Charles Spearman (1927) suggested there is one factor or mental attribute, which he called g or general intelligence, that is used to perform any mental test, but that each test also requires some specific abilities in addition to g. For example, memory for a series of numbers probably involves both g and some specific ability for immediate recall of what is heard. Spearman assumed that individuals vary in both general intelligence and specific abilities, and that together these factors determine performance on mental tasks. A current version of the general plus specific abilities theory is John Carroll's (1993) work identifying a few broad abilities (e.g., learning and memory, visual perception, verbal fluency) and at least 70 specific abilities. The most widely accepted view today is that intelligence, like self-concept, has many facets and is a hierarchy of abilities, with general ability at the top and more specific abilities at lower levels of the hierarchy (Sternberg, 1998). General ability may be related to the maturation and functioning of the frontal lobe of the brain, while specific abilities may be connected to other parts of the brain (Byrnes & Fox, 1998).

Multiple Intelligences

In spite of the correlations among the various tests of "specific abilities," some psychologists insist that there are several separate "primary mental abilities." Years ago, Edward Thurstone (1938) listed verbal comprehension, memory, reasoning,

Connect & Extend
To other views
Here are a few current ideas about the meaning of intelligence:

- goal-directed adaptive behaviour
- ability to solve novel problems
- ability to acquire and think with new conceptual systems
- problem-solving ability
- planning and other metacognitive skills
- memory access speed
- what people think intelligence is
- what IQ tests measure
- the ability to learn from bad teaching

Intelligence: Ability or abilities to acquire and use knowledge for solving problems and adapting to the world.

ability to visualize spatial relationships, numerical ability, word fluency, and perceptual speed as the major mental abilities underlying intellectual tasks. J. P. Guilford (1988) and Howard Gardner (1983) are the most prominent modern proponents of the concept of multiple cognitive abilities.

According to Gardner's (1983, 1993c) theory of **multiple intelligences**, there are at least eight separate intelligences: linguistic (verbal), musical, spatial, logical-mathematical, bodily kinesthetic (movement), interpersonal (understanding others), intrapersonal (understanding self), and naturalist (observing and understanding natural and human-made patterns and systems) (see Figure 4.2 on page 110). Gardner stresses that there may be more kinds of intelligence—eight is not a magic number. At a recent meeting of the American Psychological Association, he speculated that there may be a ninth—existential intelligence or the ability to ask big questions about the meaning of life (Gardner, 1999). He bases his notion of separate abilities in part on evidence that brain damage (e.g., from a stroke) often interferes with functioning in one area, such as language, but does not affect functioning in other areas. Also, individuals may excel in one of these eight or nine areas but have no remarkable abilities in the other seven. Still, these "separate abilities" may not be so separate after all. Recent evidence linking musical and spatial abilities has prompted Gardner to consider that there may be connections among the intelligences (Gardner, 1998). Stay tuned for more developments.

What are these intelligences? Gardner (1998, 1999) contends that an intelligence is the ability to solve problems and create products or outcomes that are valued by a culture. Varying cultures and eras of history place different values on the eight intelligences. A naturalist intelligence is critical in farming cultures, whereas verbal and mathematical intelligences are important in technological cultures. In addition, Gardner believes that intelligence has a biological basis. Intelligence "is a biological and psychological potential; that potential is capable of being realized to a greater or lesser extent as a consequence of the experiential, cultural, and motivational factors that affect a person" (1998, p. 62). Some critics suggest that Gardner's multiple intelligences are really multiple talents (Sternberg, 1985). But Gardner rejects the distinction between talent and intelligence. He believes that our common notion of intelligence "is simply a certain set of talents in the linguistic and/or logical-mathematical spheres" (1998, p. 63).

Gardner (1998) has identified a number of myths and misconceptions about multiple intelligence theory and schooling. One is that intelligences are the same as learning styles (Gardner doesn't believe that people actually have consistent

Multiple Intelligences: In Gardner's theory of intelligence, a person's eight separate abilities: logical-mathematical, linguistic, musical, spatial, bodily kinesthetic, interpersonal, intrapersonal, and naturalist.

▲ *Howard Gardner's model of multiple intelligences broadened our view of intelligent behaviour to include such factors as linguistic and music ability.*

FIGURE 4.2

Eight Intelligences

Howard Gardner's theory of multiple intelligences suggests that there are eight kinds of human abilities. An individual might have strengths or weaknesses on one or several areas.

Intelligence	End States	Core Components
Logical-mathematical	Scientist Mathematician	Sensitivity to, and capacity to discern, logical or numerical patterns; ability to handle long chains of reasoning.
Linguistic	Poet Journalist	Sensitivity to the sounds, rhythms, and meanings of words; sensitivity to the different functions of language.
Musical	Composer Violinist	Abilities to produce and appreciate rhythm, pitch, and timbre; appreciation of the forms of musical expressiveness.
Spatial	Navigator Sculptor	Capacities to perceive the visual-spatial world accurately and to perform transformations on one's initial perceptions.
Bodily-kinesthetic	Dancer Athlete	Abilities to control one's body movements and to handle objects skillfully.
Interpersonal	Therapist Salesman	Capacities to discern and respond appropriately to the moods, temperaments, motivations, and desires of other people.
Intrapersonal	Person with detailed, accurate self-knowledge	Access to one's own feelings and the ability to discriminate among them and draw on them to guide behavior; knowledge of one's own strengths, weaknesses, desires, and intelligence.
Naturalist	Botanist Farmer Hunter	Abilities to recognize plants and animals, to make distinctions in the natural world, to understand systems and define categories (perhaps even categories of intelligence).

Source: From "Multiple Intelligences Go to School," by H. Gardner and T. Hatch, 1989, *Educational Researcher, 18*(8), figure, p. 6. Copyright © 1989 by the American Educational Research Association. Reprinted with permission of the publisher. "Are There Additional Intelligences? The Case for the Naturalist, Spiritual, and Existential Intelligences," by H. Gardner (in press) in J. Kane (Ed.), *Educational Information and Transformation,* Saddle River, NJ: Prentice-Hall, Inc.

learning styles). Another misconception is that multiple intelligence theory disproves the idea of *g*. Gardner does not deny the existence of a general ability, but does question how useful *g* is as an explanation for human achievements.

Multiple Intelligences Go to School

An advantage of the multiple intelligences perspective is that it expands teachers' thinking about abilities and avenues for teaching, but the theory has been misused.

TABLE 4.1 Misuses and Applications of Multiple Intelligence Theory

Recently Howard Gardner described these negative and positive applications of his theory. The quotes are his words on the subject.

Misuses:

1. **Trying to teach all concepts or subjects using all intelligences:** "There is no point in assuming that every subject can be effectively approached in at least seven ways, and it is a waste of effort and time to attempt to do this."
2. **Assuming that it is enough just to apply a certain intelligence, no matter how you use it:** For bodily-kinesthetic intelligence, for example, "random muscle movements have nothing to do with the cultivation of the mind."
3. **Using an intelligence as a background for other activities**, such as playing music while students solve math problems. "The music's function is unlikely to be different from that of a dripping faucet or humming fan."
4. **Mixing intelligences with other desirable qualities:** For example, interpersonal intelligence "is often distorted as a license for cooperative learning," and intrapersonal intelligence "is often distorted as a rationale for self-esteem programs."
5. **Direct evaluation or even grading of intelligences without regard to context:** "I see little point in grading individuals in terms of how 'linguistic' or how 'bodily-kinesthetic' they are."

Good uses:

1. **The cultivation of desired capabilities:** "Schools should cultivate those skills and capabilities that are valued in the community and in the broader society."
2. **Approaching a concept, subject matter, discipline in a variety of ways:** Schools try to cover too much. "It makes far more sense to spend a significant amount of time on key concepts, generative ideas, and essential questions and to allow students to become familiar with these notions and their implications."
3. **The personalization of education:** "At the heart of the MI perspective—in theory and in practice—inheres in taking human difference seriously."

Source: "Reflections on Multiple Intelligences: Myths and Messages," by H. Gardner, 1998. In A. Woolfolk (Ed.), *Readings in Educational Psychology,* 2/e, pp. 64–66, Boston: Allyn & Bacon. Copyright © 1998 by Phi Delta Kappan.

Some teachers embrace a simplistic version of Gardner's theory. They include every "intelligence" in every lesson, no matter how inappropriate. Table 4.1 lists some misuses and positive applications of Gardner's work and Figure 4.3 on page 112 is an example of a lesson plan that appropriately incorporates multiple intelligences.

Many teachers and schools have embraced Gardner's ideas. However, there is not yet strong research evidence that adopting a multiple intelligences approach will enhance learning. In one of the few carefully designed evaluations, Callahan, Tomlinson, and Plucker (1997) found no significant gains in either achievement or self-concept for students who participated in START, a multiple intelligences approach to identifying and promoting talent in students who were at risk of failing. Learning is still hard work, even if there are multiple paths to knowledge.

Emotional Intelligence

We all know people who are academically or artistically talented, but unsuccessful. They have problems in school, in relationships, and on the job, but can't improve the situations. According to some psychologists, the source of the difficulties may be a lack of **emotional intelligence (EQ)**, defined as a set of capabilities to "monitor one's own and others' feelings and emotions, to discriminate among them and to use this information to guide one's thinking and actions" (Salovey & Mayer, 1990, p. 189). Daniel Goleman (1995) popularized the idea of emotional intelligence in his best-selling book on the subject. Extending the work of Peter Salovey and John Mayer (1990; Mayer & Salovey, 1993, 1997) Goleman

Emotional Intelligence (EQ): Abilities to monitor your own and others' feelings and emotions, and to use this information to guide thinking and actions.

An Example of a Lesson Plan on Solving Algebraic Equations Incorporating Multiple Intelligences in Planning

What would this lesson add to traditional approaches? What might be lost? Who might learn and who might have difficulties?

SAMPLE TWO: LESSON/UNIT PLANNING WITH THE MULTIPLE INTELLIGENCES

LESSON/UNIT TITLE: Solving Algebraic Equations

LESSON/UNIT OBJECTIVE(S): For students to learn how to solve equations through six intelligences

ANTICIPATED LEARNER OUTCOME(S): Students will be able to explain and apply the concepts and processes of solving equations

CLASSROOM RESOURCES OR MATERIALS: Textbooks, colored markers, tape and cassette player for "When Johnny Comes Marching Home"

LEARNING ACTIVITIES:

LINGUISTIC: In pairs, students read, discuss, and question textbook information.	**MATHEMATICAL-LOGICAL:** In small groups, students develop flow charts to use when solving equations.
VISUAL-SPATIAL: Teacher and students create a color-coded system for the steps in solving algebraic equations. Students solve "colored" equations.	**BODILY-KINESTHETIC:** N/A
MUSICAL: Students compose song lyrics to the tune of "When Johnny Comes Marching Home" that explain vocabulary terms such as sets, exponents, factors, variables, constants, etc.	**INTERPERSONAL:** N/A: Included in other activities but the social skills of listening well, participating, building on each other's ideas are stressed.
INTRAPERSONAL: Individually, each student might identify two variables in her life and explain how they function similarly to an equation.	**NATURALIST:** In pairs, students create algebraic equations based on variables in nature such as rabbits and foxes or caterpillars and leaves.

LESSON/UNIT SEQUENCE: 1. Visual-spatial activity 2. Linguistic activity 3. Logical-mathematical activity 4. Musical activity 5. Naturalist activity 6. Intrapersonal

ASSESSMENT PROCEDURES: 1. Assess flow charts. 2. Provide students with algebraic equations and suggest they use color coding to solve the problems. 3. Ask each student to create one equation for others to solve.

Source: From *Teaching and Learning through Multiple Intelligences* 2/e, p. 270, by L. Campbell, B. Campbell, & D. Dickinson, 1999, Boston: Allyn & Bacon. Copyright © 1999 by Allyn & Bacon. Reprinted with permission.

identified five aspects of emotional intelligence. Building upon Gardner's categories, he identified three intrapersonal abilities and two interpersonal abilities.

At the centre of emotional intelligence is the intrapersonal ability to know your own emotions. If you can't recognize what you are feeling, how can you make good choices about jobs, relationships, time management, or even entertainment (Baron, 1998)? If you don't know your own emotions, how can you communicate your feelings to others accurately? Friends keep asking "What's wrong?" and you keep saying "Nothing!" The second aspect of EQ is managing your emotions, particularly negative emotions such as anger or depression. It is useful to know you are angry, but if anger leads to rage and temper tantrums, success in school and life is more difficult. The goal is not to suppress feelings, but not to be overwhelmed by them either. The third aspect is self-motivation—the ability to focus energy, and to persist, control impulses, and delay immediate gratification in order to reach important goals. Self-motivation is critical in school. For example, four-year-old children who can delay instant gratification to work toward a goal become much better students in high school than those who act on their impulses immediately (Shoda, Mischel, & Peake, 1990).

The two interpersonal aspects of EQ are recognizing emotions in others and handling relationships. People who can recognize emotions in others (usually by reading the non-verbal cues) and can respond appropriately are more successful in working with people and often emerge as leaders (Wood & Wood, 1999).

Some researchers have criticized the notion of EQ, saying that emotional intelligence is not a cluster of capabilities but rather a set of personality traits (Nestor-Baker, 1999). Does intelligence inform emotion so we are "smart" about managing our feelings and impulses or does emotion inform intelligence so we make good decisions and understand other people? Probably both are true. The major point is that success in life requires more than cognitive skills, and teachers are important influences in helping students develop all of these capabilities.

Triarchic Theory of Intelligence: A three-part description of the mental abilities (thinking processes, coping with new experiences, and adapting to context) that lead to more or less intelligent behaviour.

Components: In an information-processing view, basic problem-solving processes underlying intelligence.

Intelligence as a Process

As you can see, the theories of Spearman, Thurstone, Gardner, and Goleman tend to describe how individuals differ in the content of intelligence—the different abilities. Recent work in cognitive psychology has emphasized instead the thinking processes that may be common to all people. How do humans gather and use information to solve problems and behave intelligently? New views of intelligence are growing out of this work.

Robert Sternberg's (1985, 1990) **triarchic theory of intelligence** is a cognitive process approach to understanding intelligence. As you might guess from the name, this theory has three parts—analytic, creative, and practical (see Figure 4.4 below).

Analytic/componential intelligence involves the mental processes of the individual that lead to more or less intelligent behaviour. These processes are defined in terms of **components**—elementary information processes that are classified by

---

Sternberg's Triarchic Theory of Intelligence

Sternberg suggests that intelligent behaviour is the product of applying thinking strategies, handling new problems creatively and quickly, and adapting to contexts by selecting and reshaping our environment.

	ANALYTIC Componential Intelligence	**CREATIVE** Experiential Intelligence	**PRACTICAL** Contextual Intelligence
Definition	Ability to think abstractly, process information; verbal abilities.	Ability to formulate new ideas and combine unrelated facts; creativity—ability to deal with novel situations and make new solutions automatic.	Ability to adapt to a changing environment and shape the environment to make the most of opportunities—problem solving in specific situations.
Examples	Solving analogies or syllogisms, learning vocabulary.	Diagnosing a problem with a car engine; finding resources for a new project.	Taking your telephone off the hook or putting a "do not disturb" sign on the door to limit distractions while studying.

Insight: The ability to deal effectively with novel situations.

Automaticity: The result of learning to perform a behaviour or thinking process so thoroughly that the performance is automatic and does not require effort.

Tacit Knowledge: Knowing how rather than knowing that—knowledge that is more likely to be learned during everyday life than through formal schooling.

the functions they serve and by how general they are. Metacomponents perform higher-order functions such as planning, strategy selection, and monitoring. Executing the strategies selected is handled by performance components. The third function—gaining new knowledge—is performed by knowledge-acquisition components, such as separating relevant from irrelevant information as you try to understand a new concept (Sternberg, 1985).

Some components are specific; that is, they are necessary for only one kind of task, such as solving analogies. Other components are very general and may be necessary in almost every cognitive task. For example, metacomponents are always operating to select strategies and keep track of progress. This may help to explain the persistent correlations among all types of mental tests. People who are effective in selecting good problem-solving strategies, monitoring progress, and moving to a new approach when the first one fails are more likely to be successful on all types of tests. Metacomponents may be a modern-day version of Spearman's *g*.

The second part of Sternberg's triarchic theory, creative/experiential intelligence, involves coping with new experiences. Intelligent behaviour is marked by two characteristics: (1) **insight**, or the ability to deal effectively with novel situations, and (2) **automaticity**—the ability to become efficient and automatic in thinking and problem solving. Thus intelligence involves solving new problems as well as quickly turning new solutions into routine processes that can be applied without much cognitive effort.

The third part of Sternberg's theory, practical/contextual intelligence, highlights the importance of choosing to live and work in a context where success is likely, adapting to that context, and reshaping it if necessary. Here, culture is a major factor in defining successful choice, adaptation, and shaping. What works in one cultural group will not work in another. For example, abilities that make a person successful in a rural farm community may be useless in the inner city or at a country club in the suburbs. People who are successful often seek situations in which their abilities will be valuable, then work hard to capitalize on those abilities and compensate for any weaknesses. Thus, intelligence in this third sense involves practical matters such as career choice or social skills.

Practical intelligence is made up mostly of action-oriented **tacit knowledge**. This tacit knowledge is more likely to be learned during everyday life than through formal schooling and "takes the form of 'knowing how' rather than 'knowing that'" (Sternberg, Wagner, Williams, & Horvath, 1995, p. 916). Recently, however, Sternberg and his colleagues have designed a program for developing practical intelligence for school success by teaching students effective strategies for reading, writing, homework, and test taking (Sternberg & Kaufman, 1998; Williams et al., 1996).

How Is Intelligence Measured?

Even though psychologists do not agree what intelligence is, they do agree that the intelligence that is recorded in standard tests is related to learning in school. Why is this so? It has to do in part with the way intelligence tests were first developed.

Binet's Dilemma. In 1904, Alfred Binet was confronted with the following problem by the minister of public instruction in Paris: how can students who will need special teaching and extra help be identified early in their school careers, before they fail in regular classes? Binet was also a political activist, very concerned with the rights of children. He believed that having an objective measure of learning ability could protect students from poor families who might be forced to leave school because they were the victims of discrimination and assumed to be slow learners.

Binet and his collaborator Theophile Simon wanted to measure not merely school achievement but the intellectual skills students needed to do well in school.

▲ *Alfred Binet developed a systematic procedure for assessing learning aptitudes. His goal was to understand intelligence and use this knowledge to help children.*

After trying many different tests and eliminating items that did not allow discrimination between successful and unsuccessful students, Binet and Simon finally identified 58 tests, several for each age group from 3 to 13. Binet's tests allowed the examiner to determine a **mental age** for a child. A child who succeeded on the items passed by most 6-year-olds, for example, was considered to have a mental age of 6, whether the child was actually 4, 6, or 8 years of age.

The concept of **intelligence quotient**, or **IQ**, was added after Binet's test was brought to North America and revised at Stanford University to give us the Stanford-Binet test. An IQ score was computed by comparing the mental-age score to the person's actual chronological age. The formula was

$$\text{Intelligence Quotient} = \text{Mental Age} \times 100 \text{ Chronological Age}$$

The early Stanford-Binet has been revised four times, most recently in 1986 (Thorndike, Hagen, & Sattler, 1986). The practice of computing a mental age has been problematic because IQ scores calculated on the basis of mental age do not have the same meaning as children get older. To cope with this problem, the concept of **deviation IQ** was introduced. The deviation IQ score is a number that tells exactly how much above or below the average a person scored on the test, compared to others in the same age group.

Group Versus Individual IQ Tests. The Stanford-Binet is an individual intelligence test. It has to be administered to one student at a time by a trained psychologist and takes about two hours. Most of the questions are asked orally and do not require reading or writing. A student usually pays closer attention and is more motivated to do well when working directly with an adult. Psychologists also have developed group tests that can be given to whole classes or schools. Compared to an individual test, a group test is much less likely to yield an accurate picture of any one person's abilities. When students take tests in a group, they may do poorly because they do not understand the instructions, because their pencils break, because they are distracted by other students, or because they do not shine on paper-and-pencil tests. As a teacher, you should be wary of IQ scores based on group tests.

What Does an IQ Score Mean?

Most intelligence tests are designed so that they have certain statistical characteristics. For example, the average score is 100; 50 percent of the people from the general population who take the tests will score 100 or above, and 50 percent will score below 100. About 68 percent of the general population will earn IQ scores between 85 and 115. Only about 16 percent of the population will receive scores below 85, and only 16 percent will score above 115. Note, however, that these figures hold true for white, native-born Americans whose first language is Standard English. Whether IQ tests should be used with ethnic minority–group students is hotly debated. Canadian teachers also need to be aware that many of these tests contain content that is not familiar to our students (e.g., math problems using imperial measures), and compare Canadian students to an American reference group. The Guidelines on page 116 will help you interpret IQ scores realistically.

Intelligence and Achievement. Intelligence test scores predict achievement in schools quite well, at least for large groups. For example, the correlation is about .65 between school achievement and scores on a popular individual intelligence test, the revised Wechsler Intelligence Scale for Children (WISC-III) (Sattler, 1992). This isn't surprising because the tests were designed to predict school achievement. Remember, Binet threw out test items that did not discriminate between good and poor students.

This boy is trying to arrange the red and white blocks so that they match the pattern in the booklet. His performance is timed. This subtest of the Wechsler Intelligence Scale for Children assesses spatial ability. ▼

GUIDELINES

Interpreting IQ Scores

Check to see if the score is based on an individual or a group test. Be wary of group test scores.

Examples

1. Individual tests include the Wechsler Scales (WPPSI, WISC-III, WAIS-R), the Stanford-Binet, the McCarthy Scales of Children's Abilities, the Woodcock-Johnson Psycho-Educational Battery, and the Kaufman Assessment Battery for Children.
2. Group tests include the Lorge-Thorndike Intelligence Tests, the Analysis of Learning Potential, the Kuhlman-Anderson Intelligence Tests, the Otis-Lennon Mental Abilities Tests, and the School and College Ability Tests (SCAT).

Remember that IQ tests are only estimates of general aptitude for learning.

Examples

1. Ignore small differences in scores among students.
2. Bear in mind that even an individual student's scores may change over time for many reasons, including measurement error.

3. Be aware that a total score is usually an average of scores on several kinds of questions. A score in the middle or average range may mean that the student performed at the average on every kind of question or that the student did quite well in some areas (for example, on verbal tasks) and rather poorly in other areas (for example, on quantitative tasks).

Remember that IQ scores reflect a student's past experiences and learning.

Examples

1. Consider these scores as predictors of school abilities, not measures of innate intellectual abilities.
2. If a student is doing well in your class, do not change your opinion or lower your expectations just because one score seems low.
3. Be wary of IQ scores for minority students and for students whose first language was not English. Even scores on "culture-free" tests are lower for disadvantaged students.
4. Check to see if Canadian norms are available for the tests used. Use caution when interpreting a student's scores on American tests normed for American students.

Do people who score high on IQ tests achieve more in life? Here the answer is less clear. There is evidence that *g*, or general intelligence, correlates with "real-world academic, social, and occupational accomplishments" (Ceci, 1991), but there is great debate about the size and meaning of these correlations (*Current Directions in Psychological Science*, 1993; McClelland, 1993). People with higher intelligence-test scores tend to complete more years of school and to have higher-status jobs. However, when the number of years of education is held constant, IQ scores and school achievement are not highly correlated with income and success in later life. Other factors such as motivation, social skills, emotional intelligence, and luck may make the difference (Goleman, 1995; Neisser et al., 1996; Sternberg & Wagner, 1993).

Intelligence: Heredity or Environment? Nowhere, perhaps, has the nature-versus-nurture debate raged so hard as in the area of intelligence. Should intelligence be seen as a potential, limited by our genetic makeup? Or does intelligence simply refer to an individual's current level of intellectual functioning, as fed and influenced by experience and education? In fact, it is almost impossible to separate intelligence "in the genes" from intelligence "due to experience." Today, most psychologists believe that differences in intelligence are due to both heredity and environment. "Genes do not fix behaviour. Rather they establish a range of possible reactions to the range of possible experiences that the environment can provide"

(Weinberg, 1989, p. 101). And environmental influences include everything from the health of a child's mother during pregnancy to the amount of lead in the child's home to the quality of teaching a child receives.

As a teacher, it is especially important for you to realize that cognitive skills, like any other skills, can always be improved. Intelligence is a current state of affairs, affected by past experiences and open to future changes. Even if intelligence is a limited potential, the potential is still quite large, and a challenge to all teachers. For example, Japanese and Chinese students know much more mathematics than North American students, but their intelligence test scores are quite similar. This superiority in math probably is related to differences in the way mathematics is taught and studied in these countries and to the self-motivation skills of many Asian students (Baron, 1998; Stevenson & Stigler, 1992).

Ability Differences and Teaching

In this section we consider how you might handle differences in academic ability in your classes. Is ability grouping a solution to the challenge of ability differences? The expressed goal of ability grouping is to make teaching more appropriate for students. As we will see, this does not always happen.

Between-Class Ability Grouping

When whole classes are formed based on ability, the process is called **between-class ability grouping** or tracking, a common practice in secondary schools and some elementary schools as well. Most high schools have "college prep" courses and "general" courses, or high-, middle-, and low-ability classes in a particular subject. Although this seems on the surface to be an efficient way to teach, research has consistently shown that segregation by ability may benefit high-ability students, but it often causes problems for low-ability students (Garmon, Nystrand, Berends, & LePore, 1995; Good & Marshall, 1984; Slavin, 1987, 1990).

Low-ability classes seem to receive lower-quality instruction in general. Teachers tend to emphasize lower-level objectives and routine procedures, with less academic focus. Often there are more management problems and, along with these problems, increased teacher stress and decreased enthusiasm. These differences in instruction and the teachers' negative attitudes may mean that low expectations are communicated to the students. Attendance may drop along with self-esteem. The lower tracks often have a disproportionate number of minority-group and economically disadvantaged students, so ability grouping, in effect, becomes segregation in school. Possibilities for friendships become limited to students in the same ability range, and assignments to classes can have long-term implications (e.g., students in modified programs may not qualify for graduation diplomas and this can limit opportunities for careers and further education).

Connect & Extend
To the research
Slavin, R. E. (1990). Achievement effects of ability grouping in secondary schools: A best-evidence synthesis. *Review of Educational Research, 60*, 471–500.

Connect & Extend
To the research
A review of the research on ability grouping is Biemiller, A. (1993, December). Lake Wobegon revisited: On diversity and education. *Educational Researcher, 22*(9), 7–12, and Biemiller, A. (1993, December). Students differ: So address differences effectively. *Educational Researcher, 22*(9), 14–15.
For a comprehensive review of research on the effects of between- and within-class ability grouping on the achievement of elementary school students, see Slavin, R. E. (1987). Ability grouping and student achievement in elementary schools: A best-evidence synthesis. *Review of Educational Research, 57*, 293–336.

Between-Class Ability Grouping: System of grouping in which students are assigned to classes based on their measured ability or their achievements.

CHECKPOINT

Ability Differences and Teaching

Review

▷ What are the problems with between-class ability grouping?

▷ What are the alternatives available for grouping in classes?

Apply

▷ If you have a wide range of academic groupings in your class, what are your options in grouping students for learning?

There are two exceptions to the general finding that between-class ability grouping leads to lower achievement. The first is found in honours or gifted classes, where high-ability students tend to perform better than comparable students in regular classes. The second exception is the **non-graded elementary school** and the related **Joplin Plan**. In these arrangements, students are grouped by ability in particular subjects, regardless of their age or grade. A reading class might therefore have students from several grades, all working at the same level in reading. Biemiller (1993) at the University of Toronto agrees that grouping students by subject ability can allow teachers to tailor instruction to students' current skill levels, and that this is sometimes necessary if we want all students to gain or demonstrate expertise in particular areas. However, he also emphasizes the need for all students to participate in a variety of ability groupings.

Within-Class Ability Grouping

A second method, **within-class ability grouping**, clustering students by ability within the same class, is another story. Many elementary school classes are grouped for reading, and some are grouped for math, even though there is no clear evidence that this approach is superior to other approaches. If you use homogeneous small groups in your class, the Guidelines on Grouping by Achievement (page 119) should make the approach more effective (Good & Brophy, 1997; Slavin, 1987).

What should teachers do when they have highly intelligent or talented students? We turn to this question next.

Creativity, Giftedness, and Talent

Creative, gifted, talented—these are terms we use every day to describe people with extraordinary abilities. As the section on multiple intelligences earlier in this chapter indicates, Gardner sees little difference between intelligence and talent. Gardner also has written extensively about **creativity**; he defines the creative individual as "a person who regularly solves problems, fashions products, or defines new questions in a domain in a way that is initially considered novel but that ultimately becomes accepted in a particular cultural setting" (Gardner, 1993a, p. 35). The notion of solving problems that are important for a particular culture is also part of his definition of intelligence. So creativity, talent, and intelligence are related; they allow us to solve important problems (Robinsin & Clinkenbeard, 1998). Let's look first at creativity.

Creativity

Most psychologists agree that there is no such thing as "all-purpose creativity"; people are creative in a particular area. But to be creative, the "invention" must be intended. An accidental spilling of paint that produces a novel design is not creative unless the artist recognizes the potential of the "accident" or uses the spilling technique intentionally to create new works (Weisberg, 1993). Although we frequently associate the arts with creativity, any subject can be approached in a creative manner.

Non-Graded Elementary School/Joplin Plan: Arrangement wherein students are grouped by ability in particular subjects, regardless of their ages or grades.

Joplin Plan: See Non-Graded Elementary School.

Within-Class Ability Grouping: System of grouping in which students in a class are divided into two or three groups based on ability in an attempt to accommodate student differences.

Creativity: Imaginative, original thinking or problem solving.

GUIDELINES

Grouping by Achievement

Form and reform groups on the basis of students' current performance in the subject being taught.

Examples

1. Use scores on the most recent reading assessments to establish reading groups, and rely on current math performance to form math groups.
2. Change group placement frequently when students' achievement changes.

Discourage comparisons between groups and encourage students to develop a whole-class spirit.

Examples

1. Don't seat groups together outside the context of their reading or math group.
2. Avoid naming ability groups—save the names for mixed-ability or whole-class teams.

Group by ability for one or, at the most, two subjects.

Examples

1. Make sure there are many lessons and projects that mix members from the groups.
2. Experiment with learning strategies in which cooperation is stressed (described in Chapters 9 and 11).

3. Keep the number of groups small (two or three at most) so that you can provide as much direct teaching as possible—leaving students alone for too long leads to less learning.

Make sure teachers, methods, and pace are adjusted to fit the needs of the group.

Examples

1. Organize and teach groups so that low-achieving students get appropriate extra instruction—not just the same material again.
2. Experiment with alternatives to grouping. There are alternatives to within-class grouping that appear more effective for some subjects. DeWayne Mason and Tom Good (1993) found that supplementing whole-class instruction in math with remediation and enrichment for students when they needed it worked better than dividing the class into two ability groups and teaching these groups separately.

Creativity and Cognition. Having a rich store of knowledge in an area is the basis for creativity, but something more is needed. For many problems, that "something more" is the ability to break away from standard thinking—**restructuring** the problem to see things in a new way, which leads to a sudden insight. Often this happens when a person has struggled with a problem or project, then sets it aside for a while. Some psychologists believe that time away from the problem allows for incubation, a kind of unconscious working through the problem. It is more likely that leaving the problem for a time interrupts rigid ways of thinking so you can restructure your view of the situation (Gleitman, Fridlund, & Reisberg, 1999). So it seems that creativity requires extensive knowledge, flexibility, and the continual reorganizing of ideas. Motivation and persistence play important roles in the creative process.

Assessing Creativity. How shall we assess creativity? One answer has been to equate creativity with divergent thinking. **Divergent thinking** is the ability to propose many different ideas or answers. **Convergent thinking** is the more common ability to identify only one answer.

E. P. Torrance has developed two types of creativity tests, verbal and graphic (Torrance, 1972; Torrance & Hall, 1980). In the verbal test, you might be instructed to think up as many uses as possible for a tin can or asked how a particular toy might be changed to make it more fun. On the graphic test, you might be given 30

Restructuring: Conceiving of a problem in a new or different way.

Divergent Thinking: Coming up with many possible solutions.

Convergent Thinking: Narrowing possibilities to a single answer.

FIGURE 4.5

A Graphic Assessment of the Creativity of an Eight-Year-Old Girl

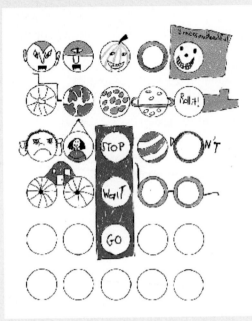

Source: Test form copyright © 1980 by Scholastic Testing Service, Inc. Reprinted by permission of Scholastic Testing Service Inc., Bensenville, IL 60106 from *The Torrance Test of Creative Thinking* by E. P. Torrence.

circles and asked to create 30 different drawings, each of which includes at least one of the circles (Sattler, 1992). Figure 4.5 shows the creativity of an eight-year-old girl in completing this task.

Responses to all these tasks are scored for originality, fluency, and flexibility, three aspects of divergent thinking. Originality is usually determined statistically. To be original, a response must be given by fewer than 5 or 10 people out of every 100 who take the test. Fluency is the number of different responses. Flexibility is generally measured by the number of different categories of responses. For instance, if you drew 30 circle pictures, but each was a face, your fluency score might be high, but your flexibility score would be quite low. Of the three measures, fluency—the number of responses—is the best predictor of divergent thinking, but there is more to real-life creativity than divergent thinking (Bjorklund, 1989).

Teachers are not always the best judges of creativity. In fact, Torrance (1972) reports that data from a 12-year follow-up study indicated no relationship between teachers' judgments of their students' creative abilities and the actual creativity these students revealed in their adult lives. A few possible indicators of creativity in your students are curiosity, concentration, adaptability, high energy, humour (sometimes bizarre), independence, playfulness, non-conformity, risk taking, attraction to the complex and mysterious, willingness to fantasize and daydream, intolerance for boredom, and inventiveness (Sattler, 1992).

Creativity in the Classroom. Today's and tomorrow's complex problems require creative solutions. How can teachers promote creative thinking? All too often, in the crush of day-to-day classroom life, teachers stifle creative ideas without realizing what they are doing. Teachers are in an excellent position to encourage or discourage creativity through their acceptance or rejection of the unusual and imaginative. "Individuals who ultimately make creative breakthroughs tend from their earliest days to be explorers, innovators, and tinkers . . . Often this adventurousness is interpreted as insubordination, though more fortunate tinkerers receive from teachers or peers some form of encouragement for their experimentation" (Gardner, 1993a, pp. 32–33).

The Brainstorming Strategy. In addition to encouraging creativity through everyday interactions with students, teachers can try **brainstorming**. The basic tenet of brainstorming is to separate the processes of creating and evaluating ideas because evaluation often inhibits creativity (Osborn, 1963). Evaluation, discussion, and criticism are postponed until all possible suggestions have been made. In this way, one idea inspires others, and people do not withhold potentially creative solutions out of fear of criticism. John Baer (1997, p. 43) gives these rules for brainstorming:

1. Defer judgment.
2. Avoid ownership of ideas. When people feel that an idea is "theirs," egos sometimes get in the way of creative thinking. They are likely to be more defensive later when ideas are critiqued, and they are less willing to allow their ideas to be modified.
3. Feel free to "hitchhike" on other ideas. This means that it's okay to borrow elements from ideas already on the table, or to make slight modifications to ideas already suggested.

Brainstorming: Generating many ideas without stopping to evaluate each one.

4. Encourage wild ideas. Impossible, totally unworkable ideas may lead someone to think of other, more possible, more workable ideas. It's easier to take a wildly imaginative bad idea and tone it down to fit the constraints of reality than to take a boring bad idea and make it interesting enough to be worth thinking about.

Individuals as well as groups may benefit from brainstorming. In writing this book, for example, we have sometimes found it helpful to list all the different topics that could be covered in a chapter, then leave the list and return to it later to evaluate the ideas.

Take Your Time—and Play! Years ago, Sigmund Freud (1959) linked creativity and play: "Might we not say that every child at play behaves like a creative writer, in that he creates a world of his own, or, rather, rearranges the things of his world in a new way which pleases him? . . . The creative writer does the same as the child at play. He creates a world of phantasy which he takes very seriously—that is, which he invests with large amounts of emotion" (pp. 143–144). There is some evidence that preschool children who spend more time in fantasy and pretend play are more creative. In fact, playing before taking a creativity test resulted in higher scores on the test for the young students in one study (Bjorklund, 1989). Teachers can encourage students of all ages to be more reflective—to take time for ideas to grow, develop, and be restructured. The Guidelines on Encouraging Creativity on page 122, adapted from Frederiksen (1984) and Sattler (1992), describe other possibilities for encouraging creativity.

▲ *Although we frequently associate the arts with creativity, it can also refer to a creative or imaginative approach to solving a problem.*

Students Who Are Gifted and Talented

There is a group of students with special educational needs that is often overlooked by the schools: students with gifts and talents. In the past, providing an enriched education for extremely bright or talented students was seen as undemocratic and elitist. Now there is a growing recognition that **gifted students** are being poorly served by most public schools. Lupart and Pyryt (1996) at the University of Calgary estimated that, in a sample of 373 students they identified as having gifts and talents, 21 percent were underachieving in school. Also, because they applied a very narrow definition of giftedness (referring to intellectual/academic talent), Lupart and Pyryt claim their estimate is fairly low. A more accurate estimate, according to these researchers, is somewhere between 40 and 50 percent.

Who Are the Gifted? There is no agreement about what constitutes a gifted student. Individuals can have many different gifts. Remember that Gardner (1983) identified eight separate kinds of "intelligences," and Guilford (1988) claims there are 180. Renzulli and Reis (1991) have defined giftedness as a combination of three basic characteristics: above-average general ability, a high level of creativity, and a high level of task commitment or motivation to achieve in certain areas. Children with gifts and talents are not the students who simply learn quickly with little effort. Their work is original, extremely advanced for their age, and potentially of lasting importance.

What do we know about these remarkable individuals? A classic study of the characteristics of individuals with gifts was started decades ago by Lewis Terman and colleagues (1925, 1947, 1959). This huge project is following the lives of 1528 gifted males and females and will continue until the year 2010. The subjects all have IQ scores in the top 1 percent of the population (140 or above on the

Gifted Student: A very bright, creative, and talented student.

GUIDELINES

Encouraging Creativity

Accept and encourage divergent thinking.

Examples
1. During class discussion, ask: "Can anyone suggest a different way of looking at this question?"
2. Reinforce attempts at unusual solutions to problems, even if the final product is not perfect.

Tolerate dissent.

Examples
1. Ask students to support dissenting opinions.
2. Make sure non-conforming students receive an equal share of classroom privileges and rewards.

Encourage students to trust their own judgment.

Examples
1. When students ask questions you think they can answer, rephrase or clarify the questions and direct them back to the students.
2. Give ungraded assignments from time to time.

Emphasize that everyone is capable of creativity in some form.

Examples
1. Avoid describing the feats of great artists or inventors as if they were superhuman accomplishments.
2. Recognize creative efforts in each student's work. Have a separate grade for originality on some assignments.

Be a stimulus for creative thinking.

Examples
1. Use a class brainstorming session whenever possible.
2. Model creative problem solving by suggesting unusual solutions for class problems.
3. Encourage students to delay judging a particular suggestion for solving a problem until all the possibilities have been considered.

▲ *Current definitions of giftedness include the characteristics of the above-average ability, creativity, and motivation to achieve. They also acknowledge that individuals, rather then being "superhumans," may be gifted in some areas and average in others.*

Stanford-Binet individual test of intelligence). They were identified on the basis of teacher recommendations and IQ tests, so they probably fall into Renzulli's academically gifted category.

Terman and colleagues found that these children were larger, stronger, and healthier than the norm. Often, they began walking sooner and were more athletic. They were more emotionally stable than their peers and became better-adjusted adults than the average. They had lower rates of delinquency, emotional difficulty, divorce, drug problems, and so on. Of course, the teachers in Terman's study who made the nominations may have selected students who were better adjusted initially.

What Problems Do the Gifted Face? In spite of Terman's findings, it would be incorrect to say that every gifted student is superior in adjustment and emotional health. Many problems confront a gifted child, including boredom and frustration in school as well as isolation (sometimes even ridicule) from peers. Schoolmates may be consumed with baseball or worried about failing math, while the gifted child is fascinated with Mozart, focused on a social issue, or totally absorbed in computers, drama, or geology. Gifted children may also find it difficult to accept their own emotions, because the mismatch between mind and emotion can be great. They may be impatient with friends, parents, and even teachers who do not share their interests or abilities. Adjustment problems seem to be greatest for the most gifted, those in the highest range of academic ability (i.e., above 180 IQ) (Keogh & MacMillan, 1996; Robinsin & Clinkenbeard, 1998). Table 4.2 lists some of the problems that can accompany the special abilities of students.

TABLE 4.2 Characteristics and Problems of Students with Special Gifts and Talents

Domains	Differentiating Characteristics	Problems
Cognitive (thinking)	Extraordinary quantity of information, unusual retentiveness	Boredom with regular curriculum; impatience with waiting for group
	High level of language development	Perceived as showoff by children of the same age
	Persistent, goal-directed behaviour	Perceived as stubborn, willful, uncooperative
	Unusual capacity for processing information	Resent being interrupted; perceived as too serious; dislike for routine and drill
Affective (feeling)	Unusual sensitivity to the expectations and feelings of others	Unusually vulnerable to criticism of others; high level of need for success and recognition
	Keen sense of humour—may be gentle or hostile	Use of humour for critical attack on others, resulting in damage to interpersonal relationships
	Unusual emotional depth and intensity	Unusual vulnerability; problem focusing on realistic goals for life's work
	Advanced levels of moral judgment	Intolerance of and lack of understanding from peer group, leading to rejection and possible isolation
Physical (sensation)	Unusual discrepancy between physical and intellectual development	Comfortable expressing themselves only in mental activity, resulting in a limited development both physically and mentally
	Low tolerance for lag between standards and athletic skills	Refusal to take part in any activities where they do not excel, limiting experience with otherwise pleasurable, constructive physical activities
Intuitive	Early involvement and concern for intuitive knowing and metaphysical ideas and phenomena	Ridiculed by peers; not taken seriously by elders; considered weird or strange
	Creativity apparent in all areas of endeavour	Seen as deviant; become bored with mundane tasks; may be viewed as troublemaker
Societal	Strongly motivated by self-actualization needs	Frustration of not feeling challenged; loss of unrealized talents
	Leadership	Lack of opportunity to use social ability constructively may result in its disappearance from child's repertoire or its being turned into a negative characteristic (e.g., gang leadership)
	Solutions to social and environmental problems	Loss to society if these traits are not allowed to develop with guidance and opportunity for meaningful involvement

Source: From *Human Exceptionality: Society, School, and Family*, 6/e, by M. L. Hardman, C. J. Drew, & M. W. Egan, 1999, Boston: Allyn & Bacon. Copyright © 1999 by Allyn & Bacon. Original source: From *Growing Up Gifted*, 5/e, by B. Clark, 1979, Upper Saddle River, NJ: Prentice-Hall, Inc. Copyright © 1979 Prentice-Hall, Inc.

A follow-up of Terman subjects 60 years later reached surprising conclusions about the relationship between popularity as a student and intellectual accomplishment as an adult. Terman's subjects who were popular and outgoing as children were less likely to maintain serious intellectual interests as adults. The authors of the study speculate that gifted students who became more accomplished as adults may have preferred adult company as children, or may have been comfortable being alone. It is possible that an active social life diverts interest away from intellectual pursuits (Tomlinson-Keasey & Little, 1990). Each path has its benefits and its liabilities for the individual.

Recognizing Students' Special Abilities. Identifying a gifted child is not always easy. Many parents provide early educational experiences for their children. A preschool or primary student coming to your class may read above grade

Connect & Extend
To the research
Feldhusen, J. F. (1989, March). Synthesis of research on gifted youth. *Educational Leadership, 46*(6), 6–12.
Highlights: Voluminous research on gifted and talented students provides several guidelines:
Identification. Schools are often ineffective in identifying gifted students, especially children from poverty and minority backgrounds, very young children, and underachievers. Multiple data sources should be used to identify giftedness.
Acceleration. Acceleration motivates gifted students by challenging them to realize their potential, and acceleration does not damage social-emotional adjustment.
Grouping. Grouping gifted and talented youth for all or part of the school day or week serves as a motivator. Mutual reinforcement of enthusiasm for academic interests prevails.
To provide for the gifted, we must upgrade instruction to fit their abilities, achievement levels, and interests. The only suitable enrichment is instruction on special topics at a high level and a fast pace.

level, play an instrument quite well, or whiz through every assignment. But even very advanced reading in the early grades does not guarantee that students will still be outstanding readers years later (Mills & Jackson, 1990). How do you separate gifted students from hard-working or parentally pressured students? In junior high and high school, some very able students deliberately earn lower grades, making their abilities even harder to recognize.

Teachers are successful only about 10 to 50 percent of the time in picking out the gifted children in their classes (Fox, 1981). These seven questions, taken from an early study of gifted students, are still good guides today (Walton, 1961):

▶ Who learns easily and rapidly?

▶ Who uses a lot of common sense and practical knowledge?

▶ Who retains easily what he or she has heard?

▶ Who knows about many things that the other children don't?

▶ Who uses a large number of words easily and accurately?

▶ Who recognizes relations and comprehends meanings?

▶ Who is alert and keenly observant and responds quickly?

Based on Renzulli and Reis's (1991) definition of giftedness, we might add:

▶ Who is persistent and highly motivated on some tasks?

▶ Who is creative, often has unusual ideas, or makes interesting connections?

Giftedness and Formal Testing. The best single predictor of academic giftedness is still the individual IQ test, but these tests are costly and time-consuming—and far from perfect. Group achievement and intelligence tests tend to underestimate the IQs of very bright children. Group tests may be appropriate for screening, but they are not appropriate for making placement decisions. Many psychologists recommend a case study approach to identifying students with gifts and talents. This means gathering many kinds of information, including test scores, grades, examples of work, projects and portfolios, letters or ratings from teachers, self-ratings, and so on (Renzulli & Reis, 1991; Sisk, 1988). Especially for recognizing artistic talent, experts in the field can be called in to judge the merits of a child's creations. Science projects, exhibitions, performances, auditions, and interviews are all possibilities. Creativity tests (discussed in the next section) may identify some children not picked up by other measures, particularly students from other minority groups who may be at a disadvantage on the other types of tests (Maker, 1987).

Teaching Gifted Students. Some educators believe that students who are gifted should be accelerated—moved quickly through the grades or through particular subjects. Other educators prefer enrichment—giving the students additional, more sophisticated, and more thought-provoking work, but keeping them with their age-mates in school. Actually, both may be appropriate (Torrance, 1986).

Many people object to acceleration, but most careful studies indicate that students who are truly gifted and who begin primary, elementary, junior high, high school, college, or even graduate school early do as well as, and usually better than, non-gifted students who are progressing at the normal pace. Social and emotional adjustment does not appear to be impaired. Students who are gifted tend to prefer the company of older playmates and may be miserably bored if kept with children of their own age. Skipping grades may not be the best solution for a particular student, but it does not deserve the bad name it has received (Jones & Southern, 1991; Kulik & Kulik, 1984; Richardson & Benbow, 1990). An alternative to skipping grades is to accelerate students in one or two particular subjects but keep them with peers for most classes (Robinsin & Clinkenbeard, 1998). However, for students who are extremely advanced intellectually (for example, those scoring 160 or higher on an individual intelligence test), the only practical solution may be to accelerate their education (Gross, 1992; Keogh & MacMillan, 1996).

Teaching methods for students who are gifted should encourage abstract thinking (formal-operational thought), creativity, and independence, not just the learning of greater quantities of facts. Teachers must be imaginative, flexible, and unthreatened by the capabilities of these students. The teacher must ask: What does this child need most? What is she ready to learn? Who can help me to challenge him? Answers might come from faculty members at nearby colleges and universities, or from books, museums, retired professionals, or older students. Strategies might be as simple as letting the child do math with the next grade. Increasingly, more flexible programs are being devised for students who are gifted: summer institutes; courses at nearby colleges; classes with local artists, musicians, or dancers; independent research projects;

CHECKPOINT

Creativity, Giftedness, and Talent

Review

▷ What is creativity, and how is it assessed?

▷ What are the characteristics of gifted students?

▷ Is acceleration a useful approach with gifted students?

Apply

▷ Think of a time that you solved a problem in a creative way. What helped you see a different approach?

▷ If you had two students in your class who were way ahead of the others in their understanding, how would you help them learn?

selected classes in high school for younger students; honours classes; and special-interest clubs. Teachers at Vancouver's University Hill Secondary School asked 33 gifted students attending their school what they would like teachers to do to provide them with the "very best learning situation for [them]" (British Columbia Ministry of Education, 1996). Students' responses are summarized in Table 4.3.

TABLE 4.3 Recommendations of Gifted Kids

Thirty-three academically gifted students at Vancouver's University Hill Secondary School were asked: "If we as teachers could provide the very best learning situation for you, what would you have us do?" Responses included:

■ Let me go ahead and work at higher levels.

■ Let us work with older kids. We can fit in.

■ It's not an age difference but an attitude difference that's important here. Older kids are more accepting.

■ Give us independent programs. Let us work ahead on our own.

■ Know that everyone has talent—and need. Provide challenge (in our talent area).

■ Have totally hands-on lessons. If we're studying elections, have a mock election.

■ Use more videos, films, and telecommunications.

■ Use humour.

■ Provide independent study opportunities—let us study something we are interested in.

Source: From British Columbia Ministry of Education, *Gifted Education: A Resource Guide for Teachers*, p. 14. Copyright © 1996 by British Columbia Ministry of Education. Reprinted by permission.

Cognitive and Learning Styles

Connect & Extend
To your teaching
When students fail a grade or a course, they are often "recycled" through the same material on the assumption that repetition will produce learning. Use the concept of cognitive style to argue against this practice.

In this section we examine individual differences that have very little to do with intelligence but can influence students' learning in school. These differences have been called cognitive styles or **learning styles**. Be aware that you may hear these terms used interchangeably. In general, educators prefer the term *learning styles*, and include many kinds of differences in this broad category. Psychologists tend to prefer the term *cognitive styles* and to limit their discussion to differences in the ways people process information (Bjorklund, 1989).

Cognitive Styles

The notion of **cognitive styles** is fairly new. It grew out of research on how people perceive and organize information from the world around them. Results from these studies suggest that individuals differ in how they approach a task, but these variations do not reflect levels of intelligence or patterns of special abilities. Instead, they have to do with "characteristic modes of perceiving, remembering, thinking, problem solving, and decision making, reflective of information-processing regularities that develop around underlying personality trends" (Messick, 1994, p. 122). For example, certain individuals respond very quickly in most situations. Others are more reflective and slower to respond, even though both types of people may be equally knowledgeable about the task at hand.

Field Dependence and Field Independence.
In the early 1940s, Herman Witkin became intrigued by the observation that certain airline pilots would fly into a bank of clouds and fly out upside down, without realizing that they had changed position. His interest led to a great deal of research on how people separate one factor from the total visual field. Based on his research, Witkin identified the cognitive styles of field dependence and field independence (Davis, 1991; Witkin, Moore, Goodenough, & Cox, 1977).

People with **field dependence** tend to perceive a pattern as a whole, not separating one element from the total visual field. They have difficulty focusing on one aspect of a situation, picking out important details, analyzing a pattern into different parts, or monitoring their use of strategies to solve problems. They tend to work well in groups, have a good memory for social information, and prefer subjects such as literature and history. In contrast, people with **field independence** are more likely to monitor their own information processing. They perceive separate parts of a total pattern and are able to analyze a pattern according to its components. They are not as attuned to social relationships as field-dependent people, but they do well in math and science, where their analytic abilities pay off.

Although you will not necessarily be able to determine all the variations in your students' cognitive styles, you should be aware that students approach problems in different ways. Some may need help learning to pick out important features and to ignore irrelevant details. They may seem lost in less structured situations and need clear, step-by-step instructions. Other students may be great at organizing but less sensitive to the feelings of others and not as effective in social situations.

Impulsive and Reflective Cognitive Styles.
Another aspect of cognitive style is impulsivity versus reflectiveness. An **impulsive** student works very quickly but makes many mistakes. The more **reflective** student, on the other hand, works slowly and makes fewer errors. As with field dependence/independence, impulsive and reflective cognitive styles are not highly related to intelligence within the normal range. However, as children grow older, they generally become more reflective, and for school-age children, being more reflective does seem to improve performance on school tasks such as reading (Kogan, 1983; Smith & Caplan, 1988).

Learning Styles: An individual's characteristic approaches to learning and studying, usually involving deep versus superficial processing of information.

Cognitive Styles: Different ways of perceiving and organizing information.

Field Dependence: Cognitive style in which patterns are perceived as wholes.

Field Independence: Cognitive style in which separate parts of a pattern are perceived and analyzed.

Impulsive: Characterized by cognitive style of responding quickly but often inaccurately.

Reflective: Characterized by cognitive style of responding slowly, carefully, and accurately.

Students can learn to be more reflective, however, if they are taught specific strategies. One that has proved successful in many situations is **self-instruction**, described in Chapter 2. This approach, developed by Meichenbaum (1986) at the University of Waterloo, capitalizes on the beneficial use of private speech described by Vygotsky. Another possibility is learning scanning strategies. For example, students taking multiple-choice tests might be encouraged to cross off each alternative as they consider it, so that no possibilities will be ignored. They might work in pairs and talk about why each possibility is right or wrong. In math classes, impulsive children need to be given specific strategies for checking their work. Just slowing down is not enough. These students must be taught effective strategies for solving the problem at hand by considering each reasonable alternative. I have also encountered several bright students who seem too reflective. They turn 30 minutes of homework into an all-night project.

▲ *People have different preferences for how and where they like to learn. Students who are distracted by noise may work better in a quiet space, even if that place is on the floor in the hall.*

Learning Styles and Preferences

Learning styles are approaches to learning and studying. Although many different learning styles have been described, one theme that unites most of the styles is differences between deep and surface approaches to processing information in learning situations (Snow, Corno, & Jackson, 1996). Individuals who have a deep-processing approach to learning see the learning materials or activities as a means for understanding some underlying concepts or meanings. These students tend to learn for the sake of learning and are less concerned about how their performance is evaluated, so motivation plays a role as well. Students who take a surface-processing approach focus on memorizing the learning materials, not understanding them. These students tend to be motivated by rewards, grades, external standards, and the desire to be evaluated positively by others. Of course, the situation can encourage deep or surface processing, but there is evidence that individuals have tendencies to approach learning situations in characteristic ways (Pintrich & Schrauben, 1992; Tait & Entwistle, in press).

Since the late 1970s a great deal has been written about differences in students' learning preferences (Dunn, 1987; Dunn & Dunn, 1978, 1987; Gregorc, 1982; Keefe, 1982). Learning preferences are usually called learning styles, but preferences is probably a more accurate label. **Learning preferences** are individual preferences for particular learning environments. They could be preferences for where, when, with whom, or with what lighting, food, or music you like to study. Think for a minute about how you learn best. Anita likes to study and write during large blocks of time, late at night. She usually makes some kind of commitment or deadline every week, so that she has to work under pressure in long stretches to finish the work. Then she takes a day off. Phil and Nancy like to write very early in the morning but, like Anita, they like to set goals. You may be similar or very different, even though we all work effectively.

There are a number of instruments for assessing students' learning preferences—for example, *The Learning Styles Inventory* (Renzulli & Smith, 1978), *Learning Style Inventory* (Dunn, Dunn, & Price, 1984), and the *Learning Style Profile* (Keefe & Monk, 1986). Tests of learning style have been criticized for lacking evidence of reliability and validity. This led Snider (1990) to conclude, "People are different, and it is good practice to recognize and accommodate individual differences. It is also good practice to present information in a variety of ways through more than one modality, but it is not wise to categorize learners and prescribe methods solely on the basis of tests with questionable technical qualities. The idea of learning styles is appealing, but a critical examination of this approach should cause educators to be skeptical" (p. 53).

It may be too much to expect the teacher to provide every student with his or her preferred setting and support for learning. But the teacher can make options available. Providing the following, for example, will allow students to work and

Connect & Extend
To other views
The Learning Styles Inventory by Renzulli and Smith (1978) asks students to indicate preferences for different types of instruction such as lecture, discussion, projects, games, and so on. *The Learning Style Inventory* by Dunn, Dunn, and Price (1984) measures preferences for 23 elements of the instructional program, including the immediate environment (temperature, noise level, etc.); emotional involvement (motivational strategies, structure, etc.); social support (working alone or with others, etc.); physical characteristics (time of day, visual versus auditory materials, etc.); and psychological inclinations (impulsive or reflective, global or analytic, etc.). The *Learning Style Profile* (Keefe & Monk, 1986) is a 126-item test based on a broad definition of learning style that includes cognitive, affective, and physiological differences.

Self-Instruction: Talking oneself through the steps of a task.

Learning Preferences: Preferred ways of studying and learning, such as using pictures instead of text, working with other people versus alone, learning in structured or in unstructured situations, and so on.

Cognitive and Learning Styles

Review

▶ Distinguish between cognitive style and learning preference.

▶ What are the advantages and disadvantages of matching teaching to individual learning styles?

Apply

▶ Are you more field dependent or field independent? How do you know?

learn in their preferred mode at least some of the time: quiet, private corners as well as large tables for working; comfortable cushions as well as straight chairs; brightly lighted desks along with darker areas; headphones for listening to music as well as earplugs; structured as well as open-ended assignments; information available from films and tapes as well as in books.

Will making these alterations lead to greater learning? Here the answer is not clear. Results of some research indicate that students learn more when they study in their preferred setting and manner (Dunn, Beaudry, & Klavas, 1989; Dunn & Dunn, 1987). There is some evidence that very bright students need less structure and prefer quiet, solitary learning (Torrance, 1986). But before you try to accommodate all your students' learning styles, remember that students, especially younger ones, may not be the best judges of how they should learn. Preference for a particular style may not always guarantee that using the style will be effective. Sometimes students, particularly low achievers, prefer what is easy and comfortable; real learning can be hard and uncomfortable. Sometimes students prefer to learn in a certain way because they have no alternatives; it is the only way they know how to approach the task. These students may benefit from developing new—and perhaps more effective—ways to learn (Weinstein & McCombs, in press).

Thus far we have focused mostly on teachers' responses to the varying abilities and styles of students. For the rest of the chapter we will consider several kinds of problems that can interfere with learning.

High-Incidence Disabilities

Teachers are more likely to encounter students with certain disabilities. As you can see in Table 4.4, these higher-incidence groups are children with learning disabilities, communication disorders, developmental disabilities, and emotional or behavioural disorders. With recent changes in the laws and new, more inclusive policies, you are likely to have children from all these categories in your classes.

More than half of all students receiving some kind of special education services in Canada are diagnosed as having learning disabilities. This is by far the largest category of students with disabilities.

Learning Disabilities

How do you explain what is wrong with a student who struggles to read, write, spell, or learn math, even though she is not developmentally delayed, emotionally disturbed, or educationally deprived, and has normal vision, hearing, and language capabilities? One explanation is that the student has a **learning disability**. This is a relatively new category of exceptional students, only 30-odd years old, according to Bernice Wong (1996) at Simon Fraser University in British Columbia. Wong is a pioneer in the field of learning disabilities. Even among experts, there is no fully agreed upon definition of learning disabilities (Wong, 1996), and there are slight differences in emphasis in the definitions used across Canada (Friend et al., 1998). However, in 1987, the Learning Disabilities Association of Canada defined learning disabilities as follows:

Connect & Extend
To other chapters
Remember that in **Chapter 2** we saw there is little evidence that people are either "right-brained" or "left-brained." For people who have normal intact brains, both hemispheres are involved in all learning tasks, even if one side may be more or less involved at any given moment. Poets write in words but paint images and patterns with their verse. Sculptors often plan analytically, think logically, and perform calculations as they sculpt (Caine & Caine, 1991). It is possible that researchers will trace certain learning problems to aspects of hemispheric specialization, but the evidence is not yet conclusive. In fact, some preliminary research indicates that the front-to-back functioning of the brain may be as important as left/right functioning in understanding learning disabilities (Jordan & Goldsmith-Phillips, 1994).

Learning Disability: Problem with acquisition and use of language; may show up as difficulty with reading, writing, reasoning, and math.

TABLE 4.4 How Many Are There? Children with Disabilities in United States Schools

During the 1992–1993 school year, there were over 4,500,000 students with disabilities in U.S. schools. As you can see with this table, about 35 percent of them were taught in regular classrooms.

Disability	Number	Percentage of Identified Students	Percentage Taught in Regular Classrooms
Specific learning disability	2,369,385	51.1	24.7
Communication disorders	1,000,154	21.6	85.5
Mental retardation	533,715	11.5	5.1
Emotional or behavioural disorders	402,668	8.7	15.8
Severe/multiple disabilities	103,215	2.2	6.2
Other health impairments	66,054	1.4	35.3
Deaf or hard of hearing	60,896	1.3	27.0
Physical disabilities	52,291	1.1	32.4
Low vision or blindness	23,811	0.5	39.6
Autism	15,527	0.3	4.7
Traumatic brain injury	3,903	0.1	7.8
Deaf-blindness	1,425	0.0	5.8
All disabilities	4,633,674	100.0	34.9

Source: U.S. Department of Education (1994).

"YOUR FEELINGS OF INSECURITY SEEM TO HAVE STARTED WHEN MARY LOU GUBLATT SAID, 'MAYBE I DON'T HAVE A LEARNING DISABILITY—MAYBE YOU HAVE A TEACHING DISABILITY.'"

(© 1975 Tony Saltzman. From Phi Delta Kappan.)

Learning disabilities refer to a number of disorders which may affect the acquisition, organization, retention, understanding or use of verbal or nonverbal information. These disorders affect learning in individuals who otherwise demonstrate at least average abilities essential for thinking and/or reasoning. As such, learning disabilities are distinct from global intellectual deficiency.

Learning disabilities result from impairments in one or more processes related to perceiving, thinking, remembering or learning. These include, but are not limited to: language processing, phonological processing, visual spatial processing, processing speed, memory and attention, and executive functions (e.g., planning and decision-making).

Learning disabilities range in severity and may interfere with the acquisition and use of one or more of the following:

• oral language (e.g., listening, speaking, understanding);
• reading (e.g., decoding, phonetic knowledge, word recognition, comprehension);
• written language (e.g., spelling and written expression); and
• mathematics (e.g., computation, problem solving).

Learning disabilities may also involve difficulties with organizational skills, social perception, social interaction and perspective taking.

Learning disabilities are lifelong. The way in which they are expressed may vary over an individual's lifetime, depending on the interaction between the demands of the environment and the individual's strengths and needs. Learning disabilities are suggested by unexpected academic under-achievement or achievement which is maintained only by unusually high levels of effort and support.

Learning disabilities are due to genetic and/or neurobiological factors or injury that alters brain functioning in a manner which affects one or more processes related to learning. These disorders are not due primarily to hearing and/or vision problems, socio-economic factors, cultural or linguistic dif-

Connect & Extend
To your teaching
Dolgins, J., Myers, M., Flynn, P. A., & Moore, J. (1984, February). How do we help the learning disabled? *Instructor,* 29–36.

Allow assignments to be typed, taped, or dictated.

Have material to be copied or directions on the child's desk rather than on the board.

Increase the time allowed or decrease the amount of writing.

Omit handwriting as a criterion for evaluating reports.

Construct tests that require minimal writing, such as multiple-choice, matching.

Tape selections that a child cannot read but can comprehend.

Provide opportunities for group projects, peer tutoring, contracts and/or learning centres.

Write summaries of reading assignments.

Decrease the number of spelling words required at one time.

To increase exposure, use spelling words that are also required in reading or science.

Avoid spelling as a criterion for evaluating assignments.

Require fewer math problems for an assignment.

Allow the use of calculators or other manipulative aids.

Provide concrete examples.

ferences, lack of motivation or ineffective teaching, although these factors may further complicate the challenges faced by individuals with learning disabilities. Learning disabilities may co-exist with various conditions including attentional, behavioural and emotional disorders, sensory impairments or other medical conditions.

For success, individuals with learning disabilities require early identification and timely specialized assessments and interventions involving home, school, community and workplace settings. The interventions need to be appropriate for each individual's learning disability subtype and, at a minimum, include the provision of:

- specific skill instruction;
- accommodations;
- compensatory strategies; and
- self-advocacy skills

This definition models one that the National Joint Committee on Learning Disabilities (NJCLD) in the United States first used in 1981. The NJCLD definition was revised in 1988 and incorporated in US Public Law 101-476, the *Individuals with Disabilities Education Act* (IDEA), in 1990.

Controversies surround the definition of learning disabilities (Hutchinson, 2001; Perry, McNamara, & Mercer, in press). In particular, many scholars believe that, in practice, too much emphasis is given to the discrepancy between students' IQ, as measured by an intelligence test, and their achievement in school. They would like to see equal, if not greater, emphasis placed on the psychological processing problems these students experience (e.g., phonological processing problems, memory problems, and problems with number sense). Linda Siegel, at the University of British Columbia, has written extensively about this topic (1989; 1999), and the Learning Disabilities Association of Ontario (2001) has proposed a new definition that emphasizes processing problems as the primary characteristic of students with learning disabilities.

TABLE 4.5 Reading Habits and Errors of Students with Learning Disabilities

Do any of your students show these signs? They could be indicators of learning disabilities.

Poor Reading Habits
- Frequently loses his or her place
- Jerks head from side to side
- Expresses insecurity by crying or refusing to read
- Prefers to read with the book held within inches from face
- Shows tension while reading; such as reading in a high-pitched voice, biting lips, and fidgeting

Word Recognition Errors
- Omitting a word (e.g., "He came to the park," is read, "He came to park")
- Inserting a word (e.g., "He came to the [beautiful] park")
- Substituting a word for another (e.g., "He came to the *pond*")
- Reversing letters or words (e.g., *was* is read *saw*)
- Mispronouncing words (e.g., *park* is read *pork*)
- Transposing letters or words (e.g., "The dog ate fast," is read, "The dog fast ate")
- Not attempting to read an unknown word by breaking it into familiar units
- Slow, laborious reading, less than 20 to 30 words per minute

Comprehension Errors
- Recalling basic facts (e.g., cannot answer questions directly from a passage)
- Recalling sequence (e.g., cannot explain the order of events in a story)
- Recalling main theme (e.g., cannot give the main idea of a story)

Source: From *Child and Adolescent Development for Educators* (p. 400), by J. L. Meece, 1997, New York: McGraw-Hill. Copyright © 1997 by McGraw-Hill Companies. Adapted with permission.

Students with Learning Disabilities

Learned Helplessness: The expectation, based on previous experiences involving lack of control, that all one's efforts will lead to failure.

Students with learning disabilities are not all alike. The most common characteristics are specific difficulties in one or more academic areas; poor coordination; problems paying attention; hyperactivity and impulsivity; problems organizing and interpreting visual and auditory information; disorders of thinking, memory, speech, and hearing; and difficulties making and keeping friends (Hallahan & Kauffman, 2000). As you can see, many students with other disabilities (such as attention-deficit/hyperactivity disorder, or ADHD) and many normal students may have some of the same characteristics. To complicate the situation even more, not all students with learning disabilities will have these problems, and few will have all of the problems.

Most students with learning disabilities have difficulties reading. Table 4.5 lists some behaviour that might signal a reading problem. Most often, these difficulties are due to phonological processing problems and insufficiently developed skills relating to phonemic awareness. Phonemic awareness refers to the sense that words are composed of separate sounds, and sounds can be combined to say (and spell) words. Math, both computation and problem solving, is the second most common problem for students with learning disabilities. The writing of some learning-disabled students is virtually unreadable, and their spoken language can be halting and disorganized. Many researchers trace some of these problems to the students' inability to use effective learning strategies such as those we will discuss in Chapter 7. Students with learning disabilities often lack effective ways to approach academic tasks. They don't know how to focus on the relevant information, get organized, apply learning strategies and study skills, change strategies when one isn't working, or evaluate their learning. They tend to be passive learners, in part because they don't know how to learn. Working independently is especially trying, so homework and seatwork are often left incomplete (Hallahan, Kauffman, & Lloyd, 1999).

Wong (1996) emphasizes the importance of early diagnosis so that students with learning disabilities get the remediation they need and do not become terribly frustrated and discouraged. The students themselves do not understand why they are having such trouble, and they may become victims of learned helplessness. Students who experience **learned helplessness** believe that they cannot control or improve their own learning. This is a powerful belief. The students never exert the effort to discover that they can make a difference in their own learning, so they remain passive and helpless.

Students with learning disabilities may also try to compensate for their problems and develop bad learning habits in the process, or they may begin avoiding certain subjects out of fear of not being able to handle the work. Research by Nancy Heath (1996; Heath & Ross, 2000) at McGill University indicates students with learning disabilities are at risk for social withdrawal and even depression. To prevent these things from happening, teachers must be sensitive to the emotional and motivational impact of students' academic difficulties.

Connect & Extend
To the research
Chapman, J. W. (1989). Learning disabled children's self-concepts. *Review of Educational Research, 58*, 347–371.
From the abstract: Studies of learning-disabled (LD) children's self-concepts show that LD students have lower self-concepts than non-disabled students. Greater decrements occur for academic self-concept than for general self-concept. Significant variations in results were found as a function of the group LD students were compared with, and the instruments used (the Piers-Harris scale of the Student's Perception of Ability Scale). For most LD children, decrements in self-concept occur by Grade 3 and remain fairly stable through high school. Mainstreamed settings did not lead to higher self-concepts than segregated settings. But unplaced LD students clearly had lower self-concepts than LD students who were receiving remedial assistance.

Teaching Students with Learning Disabilities

There is also controversy over how best to help these students. A promising approach seems to be to emphasize study skills and methods for processing information in a given subject, such as reading or math. Many of the principles of cognitive learning from Chapters 7 and 8 can be applied to help all students improve their attention, memory, and problem-solving abilities (Sawyer, Graham, & Harris, 1992). Strategic Content Learning, developed by Deborah Butler at the University of British Columbia, is one example of this approach (Butler, 1998). No set of teaching techniques will be effective for every learning-disabled child. You should work with the special education teachers in your school to design appropriate instruction for individual students. Table 4.6 summarizes problem areas and the most effective teaching approaches for learning-disabled students across their lifespan.

Connect & Extend
To other chapters
The concept of learned helplessness will be discussed again in **Chapter 5** as one explanation for the lower achievement of children of poverty and again in **Chapter 10** as a factor influencing motivation.

TABLE 4.6 Learning Disabilities across the Life Span

Learning disabilities are not limited to the school years. This table lists the problems that may occur during different phases of life and the treatments that have the strongest support from research or from expert teachers in the field.

	Preschool	Grades K–1
Problem Areas	Delay in developmental milestones (e.g., walking) Receptive language Expressive language Visual perception Auditory perception Short attention span Hyperactivity	Academic readiness skills (e.g., alphabet knowledge, quantitative concepts, directional concepts, etc.) Receptive language Expressive language Visual perception Auditory perception Gross and fine motor Attention Hyperactivity Social skills
Treatments with Most Research and/or Expert Support	Direct instruction in language skills Behavioural management Parent training	Direct instruction in academic and language areas Behavioural management Parent training

Source: From Cecil D. Mercer, *Students with Learning Disabilities*, 5/e. Copyright © 1997. Adapted by permission of Prentice-Hall Inc., Saddle River, NJ.

Hyperactivity and Attention Disorders

You have probably heard and may even have used the term **hyperactivity**. The notion is a modern one; there were no hyperactive children 50 to 60 years ago. Today, if anything, the term is applied too often and too widely. Hyperactivity is not one particular condition; it is "a set of behaviours—such as excessive restlessness and short attention span—that are quantitatively and qualitatively different from those of children of the same sex, mental age, and SES [socioeconomic status]" (O'Leary, 1980, p. 195).

Characteristics of Hyperactivity and Attention Disorders. Today most psychologists agree that the main problem for children who are labelled hyperactive is directing and maintaining attention, not simply controlling their restlessness and physical activity. The American Psychiatric Association has established the diagnostic category of **attention-deficit/hyperactivity disorder (ADHD)** to identify children with this problem. Table 4.7 lists some indicators of ADHD used by this group.

Hyperactive children are not only more physically active and inattentive than other children; they also have difficulty responding appropriately and working steadily toward goals (even their own goals), and they may not be able to control their behaviour on command, even for a brief period. The problem behaviour is generally evident in all situations and with every teacher. It is difficult to know how many children should be classified as hyperactive. The most common estimate is 3 to 5 percent of the elementary school population, but some estimates are as

Hyperactivity: Behaviour disorder marked by atypical, excessive restlessness and inattentiveness.

Attention-Deficit/Hyperactivity Disorder: Current term for disruptive behaviour disorders marked by overactivity, excessive difficulty sustaining attention, or impulsiveness.

Grades 2–6	Grades 7–12	Adult
Reading skills	Reading skills	Reading skills
Arithmetic skills	Arithmetic skills	Arithmetic skills
Written expression	Written expression	Written expression
Verbal expression	Verbal expression	Verbal expression
Receptive language	Listening skills	Listening skills
Attention span	Study skills (meta-cognition)	Study skills
Hyperactivity		Social-emotional
Social-emotional	Social-emotional-delinquency	
Direct instruction in academic areas	Direct instruction in academic areas	Direct instruction in academic areas
Behavioural management	Tutoring in subject areas	Tutoring in subject (college/university) or job area
Self-control training	Direct instruction in learning strategies (study skills)	Compensatory instruction (i.e., using aids such as tape recorder, calculator, computer, dictionary)
Parent training	Self-control training	
	Curriculum alternatives	

high as 20 percent (Friend et al., 1998). More boys than girls are identified as hyperactive. Just a few years ago, most psychologists thought that ADHD diminished as children entered adolescence, but now some researchers believe that the problems can persist into adulthood (Hallowell & Ratey, 1994). Adolescence—with the increased stresses of puberty, transition to middle or high school, more demanding academic work, and more engrossing social relationships—can be an especially difficult time for students with ADHD.

Treatment and Teaching for Students with ADHD. The most common intervention for students with ADHD is a controversial one—prescription of psychostimulant medications (e.g., Ritalin and Dexedrine). Concern has been expressed through the media that there is an increasing reliance on drug therapy for ADHD. According to a *Newsweek* headline (Leavy, 1996, March), 1.3 million American children take Ritalin—a 250 percent increase since 1990, as you can see in Figure 4.6. However, hundreds of well-designed research studies have consistently demonstrated the benefits of psychostimulant therapy in treating 70 to 80 percent of children with ADHD (Batschaw, 1997; Friend et al., 1998). In general, students with ADHD who take stimulant medication engage in less stimulant-seeking behaviour and are more able to benefit from educational and social interventions (Friend et al., 1998; Zentall, 1993). Of course, these drugs need to be carefully administered and their effects carefully monitored. Some children experience side effects such as loss of appetite or nausea, headaches, insomnia, and increased heart rate and blood pressure. For most children, these side effects are mild and can be controlled by adjusting the dosage. Finally, little is known about the long-term effects of drug therapy.

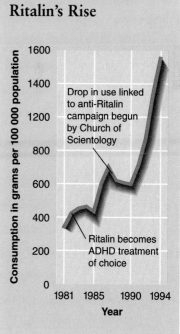

FIGURE 4.6

Ritalin's Rise

Drop in use linked to anti-Ritalin campaign begun by Church of Scientology

Ritalin becomes ADHD treatment of choice

Source: From J. Leavy, "Mother's Little Helper," Newsweek, 127, March 18, 1996, p. 52. © 1996, Newsweek Inc. All right reserved. Reprinted by permission.

TABLE 4.7 Indicators of ADHD: Attention-Deficit/Hyperactivity Disorder

Do any of your students show these signs? They could be indicators of ADHD.

Problems with *Inattention*

- Fails to give close attention to details or makes careless mistakes
- Has difficulty sustaining attention in tasks or play activities
- Does not seem to listen when spoken to directly
- Does not follow through on instructions and fails to finish schoolwork (not due to oppositional behaviour or failure to understand instructions)
- Has difficulty organizing tasks or activities
- Avoids, dislikes, or is reluctant to engage in tasks that require sustained mental effort (such as schoolwork or homework)
- Loses things necessary for tasks or activities
- Is easily distracted by extraneous stimuli
- Is forgetful in daily activities

Problems with *Impulse Control*

- Blurts out answers before questions have been completed
- Has difficulty awaiting his/her turn
- Interrupts or intrudes on others in conversations or games

Hyperactivity

- Fidgets with hands or feet or squirms in seat
- Leaves seat in classroom or in other situations in which remaining seated is expected
- Runs about or climbs excessively in situations in which it is inappropriate (in adolescents may be limited to subjective feelings of restlessness)
- Has difficulty playing or engaging in leisure activities quietly
- Talks excessively
- Acts as if "driven by a motor" and cannot remain still

Source: From *Diagnostic Statistical Manual of Mental Disorders* (DSM-IV) (pp. 83–84), 1994, Washington, DC: American Psychiatric Association. Copyright © 1994 American Psychiatric Association. Adapted with permission.

Stimulant medications in and of themselves will not improve students' learning and achievement in school. For learning to occur, they need to be paired with other effective interventions. The methods that have proven most successful for helping students with ADHD are based on behavioural principles of learning such as those described in Chapter 6. One promising approach is Positive Behaviour Support (PBS). According to Joe Lucyshyn (Lucyshyn, Horner, Dunlap, Albin, & Ben, 2002) at the University of British Columbia, PBS, which is linked to applied behaviour analysis, helps consumers (e.g., families, educators, psychologists) identify and understand the full range of variables (e.g., personal, ecological) influencing problem behaviour that interferes with learning. The goal of PBS is to foster more adaptive behaviour that supports learning. The bottom line is that even if students in your class are on medication, it is critical that they also learn the academic and social skills they will need to survive. They need to learn how and when to apply learning strategies and study skills. Also, they need to be encouraged to persist when challenged by difficult tasks and to see themselves as having control over their learning and behaviour. Medication alone will not make this happen (Kneedler, 1984).

Communication Disorders

Language is a complex learned behaviour. Language disorders may arise from many sources, because so many different aspects of the individual are involved in learning language. A child with a hearing impairment will not learn to speak normally. A child who hears inadequate language at home will learn inadequate

▲ *All students benefit from learning alternative ways of communicating, for example, sign language systems. This encourages understanding and mutual respect among students of all abilities.*

language. Children who are not listened to, or whose perception of the world is distorted by emotional problems, will reflect these problems in their language development. Because speaking involves movements, any impairment of the motor functions involved with speech can cause language disorders. And because language development and thinking are so interwoven, any problems in cognitive functioning can affect ability to use language.

Speech Impairments. The student who cannot produce sounds effectively for speaking is considered to have a speech impairment. Winzer (1999), at the University of Lethbridge, estimates that between 5 and 8 percent of school-age children have some form of **speech impairment**. Articulation problems and stuttering are the two most common problems, and about two-thirds of all children with communication disorders are boys (Winzer, 1999, p. 127).

Articulation disorders include substituting one sound for another (*thunthine* for sunshine), distorting a sound (*shoup* for soup), adding a sound (*ideer* for idea), or omitting sounds (*po-y* for pony) (Smith, 1998). Keep in mind, however, that most children are six to eight years old before they can successfully pronounce all English sounds in normal conversation. The sounds of the consonants *l, r, y, s,* and *z* and the consonant blends *sh, ch, zh,* and *th* are the last to be mastered. Also, there are dialect differences based on geography that do not represent articulation problems. A student from Newfoundland might say "ideer" for "idea" but have not speech impairment.

Stuttering generally appears between the ages of three and four. It is not yet clear what causes stuttering, but it can cause embarrassment and anxiety for the sufferer. In about 50 percent of cases, stuttering disappears during early adolescence (Wiig, 1982). If stuttering continues more than a year or so, the child should be referred to a speech therapist. Early intervention is critical (Onslow, 1992).

Voicing problems, a third type of speech impairment, include speaking with an inappropriate pitch, quality, or loudness, or in a monotone (Hallahan & Kauffman, 2000). A student with any of these problems should be referred to a speech therapist. Recognizing the problem is the first step. Be alert for students whose pronunciation, loudness, voice quality, speech fluency, expressive range, or rate is very different from that of their peers. Pay attention also to students who seldom speak. Are they simply shy, or do they have difficulties with language?

Language Disorders. Language differences are not necessarily language disorders. Students with language disorders are those who are markedly deficient in

Speech Impairment: Inability to produce sounds effectively for speaking.

Articulation Disorders: Any of a variety of pronunciation difficulties.

Stuttering: Repetitions, prolongations, and hesitations that block flow of speech.

Voicing Problems: Inappropriate pitch, quality, loudness, or intonation.

TABLE 4.8 Encouraging Language Development

- Talk about things in which the child is interested.
- Follow the child's lead. Reply to the child's initiations and comments. Share his/her excitement.
- Don't ask too many questions. If you must, use questions such as *how did/do . . . , why did/do . . . , and what happened . . .* that result in longer explanatory answers.
- Encourage the child to ask questions. Respond openly and honestly. If you don't want to answer a question, say so and explain why. *(I don't think I want to answer that question; it's very personal.)*
- Use a pleasant tone of voice. You need not be a comedian, but you can be light and humorous. Children love it when adults are a little silly.

- Don't be judgmental or make fun of a child's language. If you are overly critical of the child's language or try to catch and correct all errors, he/she will stop talking to you.
- Allow enough time for the child to respond.
- Treat the child with courtesy by not interrupting when he/she is talking.
- Include the child in family and classroom discussions. Encourage participation and listen to his/her ideas.
- Be accepting of the child and of the child's language. Hugs and acceptance can go a long way.
- Provide opportunities for the child to use language and to have that language work for him/her to accomplish his/her goals.

Source: From Robert E. Owens, Jr., *Language Disorders: A Functional Approach to Assessment and Intervention,* 2/e, p. 416. Copyright © 1995 by Allyn & Bacon. Reprinted by permission.

their ability to understand or express language, compared with other students of their own age and cultural group (Owens, 1995). Students who seldom speak, who use few words or very short sentences, or who rely only on gestures to communicate should be referred to a qualified school professional for observation or assessment. Table 4.8 gives ideas for promoting language development for all students.

Developmental Disabilities

Friend et al. (1998) characterize students with developmental delays as having significant limitations in cognitive abilities and adaptive behaviour. In general, these individuals learn at a far slower rate than other students, and may reach a point at which their learning plateaus. Often, these individuals have difficulties maintaining skills without ongoing practice, and generalizing skills learned in one context to another. Also, many of these students have difficulties carrying out tasks that involve combining or integrating multiple skills (e.g., doing the laundry).

Intelligence tests are typically used to identify developmental delays. An IQ score below 70 to 75 is one indicator of a developmental delay, but it is not enough evidence to diagnose a child as having a developmental disability. There must also be problems with adaptive behaviour, day-to-day independent living, and social functioning. This caution is especially important when interpreting the scores of students from different cultures. Defining **developmental disabilities** based on test scores alone can create what some critics call "six-hour retardates"—students who are seen as developmentally disabled only for the part of the day they attend school.

Given the limitations of formal assessments, advocates for individuals with developmental disabilities are beginning to argue that it is better to focus efforts on identifying the amount and types of services these individuals require (Friend et al., 1998). The American Association on Mental Retardation (AAMR) has developed a classification scheme to assist these efforts. It is summarized in Table 4.9. None of the ministries of education in Canada have adopted this system of levels of support. However, many ministries distinguish between supports needed for stu-

Developmental Disabilities: Significantly below-average intellectual and adaptive social behaviour, evident before age 18.

TABLE 4.9 AAMR Classification Scheme for Mental Retardation

This new scheme for classification is based on the level of support a student would need to function as completely as possible.

Intermittent	Supports on an "as needed basis." Characterized by episodic nature, person not always needing the support(s), or short-term supports needed during life-span transitions (e.g., job loss or an acute medical crisis). Intermittent supports may be high or low intensity when provided.
Limited	An intensity of supports characterized by consistency over time and time-limited but not of an intermittent nature, may require fewer staff members and less cost than more intense levels of support (e.g., time-limited employment training or transitional supports during the school-to-adult period).
Extensive	Supports characterized by regular involvement (e.g., daily) in at least some environments (such as work or home) and not time-limited (e.g., long-term home living support).
Pervasive	Supports characterized by their constancy, high intensity, provided across environments; potential life-sustaining nature. Pervasive supports typically involve more staff members and intrusiveness than do extensive or time-limited supports.

Source: From *Mental Retardation: Definition, Classification, and Systems of Support*, by AAMR Ad Hoc Committee on Terminology and Classification, 1992. Washington, DC: American Association on Mental Retardation. Copyright © 1992 by American Association on Mental Retardation. Reprinted with permission.

dents with mild and severe developmental disabilities (Hutchinson, 2001). The Ontario Ministry of Education (1995), for example, identifies students with developmental disabilities as a group with "varying degrees of general intellectual ability such that significant curriculum modification and support services for academic learning are required" (p. 11). The Ontario ministry also notes that some of these students will require support to develop social and independent living skills.

Friend et al. (1998) outline two principles on which to base instruction for students with developmental disabilities: a functional curriculum, and a community-based education. Designing a functional curriculum means setting goals and targeting skills that will help students succeed in life in and out of school. For example, it is helpful for students with developmental disabilities to learn to follow multistep directions that are essential to success in the workplace. Relating what is learned in school to community contexts is also helpful for students with developmental disabilities. For example, when students are learning to count money, arranging for them to open a bank account or do some shopping will help them to generalize those skills.

Research by Lord (1991) at the Centre for Research and Education in Human Services in Ontario found that involvement in the community was key to individuals with disabilities feeling empowered and taking charge of their own lives. These findings highlight the importance of **transition programming**—preparing individuals with disabilities for life and work in the community. As you will see later in this chapter, most provinces require that schools design an individualized education plan (IEP) for every exceptional learner. An individualized transition plan (ITP) should be part of a student's IEP at critical junctures in her or his life (e.g., transitioning from preschool to elementary school, to middle school or high school, and transitioning to life beyond school).

Transition Programming: Gradual preparation of exceptional students to move from high school into further education or training, employment, or community involvement.

GUIDELINES

Teaching Children with Below-Average General Intelligence

1. Be clear about your instructional objectives and expectations. Use instructional approaches that match those expectations and, whenever possible, make adaptations that are appropriate for the student and a natural part of your instructional environment.
2. Use heterogeneous classroom groups to support and include students with moderate and severe disabilities. Using strategies such as peer tutoring, cooperative learning, and friend support systems fosters a sense of community in the classroom, and helps students learn to value and respect one another.
3. Sometimes students with disabilities will need specialized instruction about skills that are not a part of your regular curriculum. Identify optimal times for this instruction to occur (e.g., when students are working on independent projects) and, when appropriate, involve other students in the classroom.

4. Enlist natural support systems such as older students, parents, volunteers, and teaching assistants. These individuals can reinforce your instructional objectives and support students' development of appropriate social skills.
5. Involve the students' family whenever possible. Parents can provide valuable tips about how their child learns and reinforce your goals and objectives at home.
6. Take advantage of technology. For example, students who cannot use language to communicate can be supported by various forms of augmentative communication (e.g., electronic communication boards).

Source: Adapted from M. Friend, W. Bursuck, & N. Hutchinson. (1998). *Including Exceptional Students: A Practical Guide for Classroom Teachers.* Scarborough, Ontario: Allyn & Bacon Canada.

The Guidelines above list suggestions for teaching students with below-average general intelligence.

Emotional and Behavioural Disorders

Connect & Extend
To other chapters
In **Chapter 11**, you will find ideas for dealing with mild to moderate behaviour problems.

Students with emotional and behavioural disorders can be among the most difficult to teach in a regular class. Behaviour becomes a problem when it deviates so greatly from what is appropriate for the child's age group that it significantly interferes with the child's own growth and development and/or the lives of others. Clearly, deviation implies a difference from some standard, and standards of behaviour differ from one situation, age group, culture, and historical period to another. Thus, what passes for team spirit in the football bleachers might be seen as disturbed behaviour in a bank or restaurant. In addition, the deviation must be more than a temporary response to stressful events; it must be consistent across time and in different situations.

Quay and Peterson (1987) describe six dimensions of emotional/behavioural disorders. Children who have conduct disorders are aggressive, destructive, disobedient, uncooperative, distractible, disruptive, and persistent. They have been corrected and punished for the same misbehaviour countless times. Many of these children are disliked by the adults and even the other children in their lives. The most successful strategies for helping these children include the behaviour management approaches such as those described in Chapter 6 and PBS (described above). These students need very clear rules and consequences, consistently enforced. Early intervention and school-wide initiatives are also effective (Sprague & Walker, 2000). The future is not promising for students who never learn to control their behaviour and who also fail academically. Waiting for the students to "outgrow" their problems is seldom effective (O'Leary & Wilson, 1987).

Children who are extremely anxious, withdrawn, shy, depressed, and hypersensitive, who cry easily and have little confidence, are said to have an anxiety-withdrawal disorder. These children have few social skills and consequently very few friends. The most successful approaches with them appear to involve the direct teaching of social skills (Gresham, 1981).

The third category is attentional problems immaturity. Characteristics include a short attention span, frequent daydreaming, little initiative, messiness, and poor coordination. If an immature student is not too far behind others in the class, she or he may respond to the behaviour management strategies described in Chapter 6. But if these approaches fail or if the problem is severe, you should consult the school psychologist, guidance counsellor, or another mental health professional. Related to this dimension is the category of motor excess. These students are restless and tense; they seem unable to sit still or stop talking. They share many of the same characteristics as students with ADHD.

The fifth category of behaviour disorders is socialized aggression. Students in this group are often members of gangs. They may steal or vandalize because their peer culture expects it.

Finally, some students exhibit psychotic behaviour. You are not likely to work with many of these students. Their behaviour may be bizarre, and they may express far-fetched ideas. These six categories are very general. If you are concerned about the behaviour of one of your students, it is best to consult the school psychologist or guidance counsellor.

CHECKPOINT

High-Incidence Disabilities

Review

▷ What is a learning disability?

▷ What is ADHD and how is it handled in school?

▷ What are the most common communication disorders?

Apply

▷ How would you teach the concept of "safety" to a student with a mild developmental disability?

Low-Incidence Disabilities

In this section, we discuss students with less common, perhaps more severe, disabilities. Over the course of your teaching career, it is likely that you will encounter only a few of these students. However, you can still make a difference in their lives.

Some students must have special **orthopedic devices** such as braces, special shoes, crutches, or wheelchairs to participate in a normal school program. If the school has the necessary architectural features, such as ramps, elevators, and accessible washrooms, and if teachers allow for the physical limitations of students, little needs to be done to alter the usual educational program.

Cerebral Palsy

Damage to the brain before or during birth or during infancy can cause a child to have difficulty moving and coordinating his or her body. The problem may be mild, so the child simply appears a bit clumsy, or so severe that voluntary movement is practically impossible. The most common form of **cerebral palsy** is characterized by **spasticity** (overly tight or tense muscles). But many children with cerebral palsy have secondary handicaps (Kirk, Gallagher, & Anastasiow, 1993). In the classroom, these secondary handicaps are the greatest concern—and these are generally what the regular teacher can help with most. For example, many children with cerebral palsy also have hearing impairments, speech problems, or mild

Connect & Extend
To your students
Chronic health impairments can include asthma, allergies, and even AIDS. Be aware of the students in your class who have such health problems and how they can affect students' learning. Also, be aware of the policies regarding care for these students in your school, district, and province or territory. Read the following article if you are interested in your colleagues' attitudes about teaching students with HIV/AIDS, and recommendations concerning working with these students: Lebrun, M. & Freeze, D. R. (1995). HIV-positive students in the Manitoba public school system: Are Manitoba's teachers ready? *Developmental Disabilities Bulletin 32*(2), 32–42.

Orthopedic Devices: Devices such as braces and wheelchairs that aid people with physical disabilities.

Cerebral Palsy: Condition involving a range of motor or coordination difficulties due to brain damage.

Spasticity: Overly tight or tense muscles, characteristic of some forms of cerebral palsy.

Epilepsy: Disorder marked by seizures and caused by abnormal electrical discharges in the brain.

Generalized Seizure: A seizure involving a large portion of the brain.

Absence Seizure: A seizure involving only a small part of the brain that causes a child to lose contact briefly.

Speech Reading: Using visual cues to understand language.

Sign Language: Communication system of hand movements that symbolize words and concepts.

Finger Spelling: Communication system that "spells out" each letter with a hand position.

developmental disabilities. The strategies described in this chapter should prove helpful in such situations.

A seizure is a cluster of behaviour that occurs in response to abnormal neurochemical activities in the brain (Hardman, Drew, & Egan, 1999). The effects of the seizure depend on where the discharge of energy starts in the brain and how far it spreads. People with **epilepsy** have recurrent seizures, but not all seizures are the result of epilepsy; temporary conditions such as high fevers or infections can also trigger seizures. Seizures take many forms and differ with regard to the length, frequency, and movements involved. A partial or absence seizure involves only a small part of the brain, whereas a generalized or tonic-clonic seizure includes much more of the brain.

Most **generalized seizures** (once called *grand mal*) are accompanied by uncontrolled jerking movements that ordinarily last from 2 to 5 minutes, possible loss of bowel or bladder control, and irregular breathing, followed by a deep sleep or coma. On regaining consciousness, the student may be very weary, confused, and in need of extra sleep. Most seizures can be controlled by medication. If a student has a seizure accompanied by convulsions in class, the teacher must take action so the student will not be injured. The major danger to a student having such a seizure is getting hurt by striking a hard surface during the violent jerking. Do not try to restrain the child's movements; you can't stop the seizure once it starts. Lower the child gently to the floor, away from furniture or walls. Move hard objects away. Turn the child's head gently to the side, put a soft coat or blanket under the student's head, and loosen any tight clothing. Never put anything in the student's mouth. Find out from the student's parents how the seizure is usually dealt with. If one seizure follows another and the student does not regain consciousness in between or if the seizure goes on for more than 10 minutes, get medical help right away (Hallahan & Kauffman, 2000).

Not all seizures are dramatic. Sometimes the student just loses contact briefly. The student may stare, fail to respond to questions, drop objects, and miss what has been happening for 1 to 30 seconds. These were once called *petit mal*, but they are now referred to as **absence seizures** and can easily go undetected. If a child in your class appears to daydream frequently, does not seem to know what is going on at times, or cannot remember what has just happened when you ask, you should consult the school psychologist or nurse. The major problem for students with absence seizures is that they miss the continuity of the class interaction—these seizures can occur as often as 100 times a day. If their seizures are frequent, students will find the lessons confusing. Question these students to be sure they are understanding and following the lesson. Be prepared to repeat yourself periodically.

Deaf and Hard of Hearing

You will hear the term "hearing impaired" used to describe students who have difficulties hearing, but the deaf community and researchers object to this term. Their preferred terms are *deaf* and *hard of hearing*. Signs of hearing problems are turning one ear toward the speaker, favouring one ear in conversation, or misunderstanding conversation when the speaker's face cannot be seen. Other indications include not following directions, seeming distracted or confused at times, frequently asking people to repeat what they have said, mispronouncing new words or names, and being reluctant to participate in class discussions. Take note particularly of students who have frequent earaches, sinus infections, or allergies.

In the past, educators have debated whether oral or manual approaches are better for children who are deaf or hard of hearing. Oral approaches involve **speech reading** (also called lip reading) and training students to use whatever limited hearing they may have. Manual approaches include **sign language** and **finger spelling**. Research indicates that children who learn some manual method of communicating perform better in academic subjects and are more socially mature than students who are exposed only to oral methods. Today, the trend is to combine both approaches (Hallahan & Kauffman, 2000). Technological innovations such as teletypewriters in homes and public phones and the many avenues of communication through e-mail and the Internet have expanded communication possibilities for all people with hearing problems.

Low Vision: Vision limited to close objects.

Educationally Blind: Needing Braille materials in order to learn.

Vision Impairment

Students who have difficulty seeing often hold books either very close to or very far from their eyes. They may squint, rub their eyes frequently, or complain that their eyes burn or itch. The eyes may actually be swollen, red, or encrusted. Students with vision problems may misread material on the chalkboard, describe their vision as being blurred, be very sensitive to light, or hold their heads at an odd angle (De Mott, 1982). Any of these signs should be reported to a qualified school professional.

Mild vision problems can be overcome with corrective lenses. However, students with more significant visual impairments will probably require special materials and equipment to function in general education classrooms. Most of these students will have partial or **low vision**; they have some useful vision between 20/70 and 20/200 (Friend et al., 1998). For example, a person with 20/70 vision can only see at 6 m what individuals with normal vision see at 21.3 m. An individual with 20/200 vision is considered to be legally and **educationally blind**. These students must use hearing and touch as their primary learning channels (Kirk, Gallagher, & Anastasiow, 1993).

Special materials and equipment that help visually impaired students to function in regular classrooms include large-print typewriters; variable-speed tape recorders (allowing teachers to make time-compressed tape recordings, which speed up the rate of speech without changing the voice pitch); special calculators; the abacus; three-dimensional maps, charts, and models; and special measuring devices. For students with visual problems, the quality of the print is often more important than the size, so watch out for hard-to-read handouts. Make yourself aware of local and provincial resource centres (e.g., SEFBC in British Columbia) that have resource materials and assistive technologies for students with sensory impairments.

The arrangement of the room is also an issue. Students with visual problems need to know where things are, so consistency matters—a place for everything and everything in its place. Leave plenty of space for moving around the room and make sure to monitor possible obstacles and safety hazards such as garbage cans in aisles and open cabinet doors. If you rearrange the room, give students with visual problems a chance to learn the new layout. Make sure each student has a buddy for fire drills or other emergencies (Friend et al., 1998).

If you decide that students in your class might benefit from special services, the first step is making a referral. How would you begin? Table 4.10 guides you through the referral process. In Chapter 12, when we discuss effective teaching, we will look at more ways to reach all your students.

CHECKPOINT

Low-Incidence Disabilities

Review

▶ How can schools accommodate the needs of physically disabled students?

▶ How would you handle a seizure in class?

▶ What are some signs of hearing and visual impairment?

Apply

▶ What accommodations could you make in your classroom for students with hearing or vision problems?

TABLE 4.10 Making a Referral

1. Contact the student's parents. It is very important that you discuss the student's problems with the parents *before* you refer.

2. Before making a referral, check *all* the student's school records. Has the student ever:

   - had a psychological evaluation?
   - qualified for special services?
   - been included in other special programs (e.g., for disadvantaged children; speech or language therapy)?
   - scored far below average on standardized tests?
   - been retained?

   Do the records indicate:

   - good progress in some areas, poor progress in others?
   - any physical or medical problem?
   - that the student is taking medication?

3. Talk to the student's other teachers and professional support personnel about your concern for the student. Have other teachers also had difficulty with the student? Have they found ways of dealing successfully with the student? Document the strategies that you have used in your class to meet the student's

educational needs. Your documentation will be useful as evidence that will be helpful to or required by the team of professionals who will evaluate the student. Demonstrate your concern by keeping written records. Your notes should include items such as:

- exactly what you are concerned about
- why you are concerned about it
- dates, places, and times you have observed the problem
- precisely what you have done to try to resolve the problem
- who, if anyone, helped you devise the plans or strategies you have used
- evidence that the strategies have been successful or unsuccessful

Remember that you should refer a student only if you can make a convincing case that the student may have a handicapping condition and probably cannot be served appropriately without special education. Referral for special education begins a time-consuming, costly, and stressful process that is potentially damaging to the student and has many legal ramifications.

Source: P. L. Pullen and J. M. Kaufmann (1987). *What Should I Know about Special Education? Answers for Classroom Teachers.* Austin, Texas: Pro-Ed. Reprinted by permission.

Exceptional Education and Inclusion

We have been discussing in detail the many special problems of exceptional students because, no matter what grade or subject you teach, you will encounter these students in your classroom. The trend toward including exceptional students in regular education began in the early 1970s.

Exceptional Education Laws and Policies

Education or School Act: Provincial legislation that governs education in elementary and secondary schools.

Inclusion: The practice of integrating exceptional students into regular education classrooms. The emphasis is on participation rather than placement.

Integration: Occurs when exceptional students participate in activities with their non-exceptional peers.

Canada does not have a national office of education, unlike Britain and the United States. Each province has the authority to make its own laws concerning education, including exceptional education, and each province has an **education or school act** that governs education in its elementary and secondary schools. As a teacher, you will need to become familiar with the laws and policies that govern education in your province. **Inclusion** is the current policy of the ministries of education in all of Canada's provinces and territories (Friend et al., 1998). However, provinces may vary in their definitions of inclusion. In British Columbia, for example, the principle of inclusion supports "equitable access to learning by all students and the opportunity for all students to pursue their goals in all aspects of their education" (British Columbia Special Education Branch, 1995, Section A, p. 2). However, the British Columbia Ministry of Education clarifies that **integration**— exceptional students' participation in activities with non-exceptional peers—is only one way to achieve inclusion, the preferred way. This definition of inclusion means that exceptional students need not spend 100 percent of every school day in regular education activities or classrooms. The emphasis is on meeting the educational needs of all students and this "does not preclude the appropriate use of resource rooms, self-contained classrooms, community-based training, or other specialized settings" (British Columbia Special Education Branch, 1995, Section A, p. 3).

There is one national piece of legislation that has an impact on education across Canada—the **Canadian Charter of Rights and Freedoms**, which is part of the Constitution. Section 15.1 of the Charter outlines the equality provisions that apply to education:

> Every individual is equal before and under the law and has the right to equal protection and equal benefit of the law without discrimination and, in particular, without discrimination based on race, national or ethnic origin, colour, religion, sex, age, or mental or physical disability.

According to William MacKay (1986), a law professor at Dalhousie University in Nova Scotia, there are three dimensions of "equality rights"—nondiscrimination, equal opportunity, and equal outcomes. For some students, having equal opportunities and achieving equal outcomes requires differential treatment; that is, a program that attends to and supports their exceptional learning needs.

Exceptional education in Canada has also been influenced by American legislation. In particular, Canadian practices in special education have embraced American practices of providing exceptional students with a **least restrictive placement** and an individualized education program (IEP), and of protecting the rights of exceptional students and their parents.

Least Restrictive Placement. In the United States, federal law requires that students be educated in the least restrictive environment possible. Typically, this is interpreted to mean that exceptional students should be educated in regular educational settings whenever possible, or in settings that provide as close a match as possible to regular educational settings. While there is no law requiring least restrictive placement in Canada, the principle is embodied in our practices. Some provinces (e.g., Prince Edward Island) refer to placement in the "most enabling environment," rather than the least restrictive environment (Friend et al., 1998). Consistent with Canada's goal of becoming an inclusive society, it is generally accepted that the most enabling environment for most learners most of the time is the regular education classroom. But as you can see in the Point/Counterpoint, inclusion is a hotly debated issue.

Individualized Education Program. Each exceptional student must have an educational program tailored to his or her unique needs. The **individualized education program, or IEP,** is written by a team that includes the student's teacher or teachers, a qualified school psychologist or special education supervisor, the parent(s) or guardian(s), and (when possible) the student. The program should be reviewed and updated each year and should address the following issues:

1. The student's present level of functioning.
2. Goals for the year and short-term measurable instructional objectives leading to those goals.
3. A list of specific services to be provided to the student and details of when those services will be initiated.
4. A description of how fully the student will participate in the regular school program.
5. A schedule telling how the student's progress toward the objectives will be evaluated and approximately how long the services described in the plan will be needed.

Canadian Charter of Rights and Freedoms: Legislation that protects the rights of all Canadians and, in particular, Canadians who are members of minority groups, including Canadians with disabilities.

Least Restrictive Placement: The practice of placing exceptional students in the most regular educational settings possible, while ensuring they are successful and receive support appropriate to their special needs.

Individualized Education Program (IEP): Annually revised program for an exceptional student, detailing present achievement level, goals, and strategies, drawn up by teachers, parents, specialists, and (if possible) the student.

Is Full Inclusion a Reasonable Approach to Teaching Exceptional Students?

In his booklet *Inclusion: Issues of Educating Students with Disabilities in Regular Educational Settings*, Michael Hardman (1994) summarizes the arguments for and against full inclusion.

▶ **POINT** *Full inclusion makes sense.*

Supporters of full inclusion, such as Marsha Forest, believe that:

All children need to learn with and from other children. . . . All children need to belong and feel wanted. . . . All children need to have fun and enjoy noise and laughter in their lives. . . . All children need to take risks and fall and cry and get hurt. . . . All children need to be in real families and real schools and real neighborhoods. (p. 403)

These opportunities are limited in special class placements. No matter how good the teaching, disabled students will never learn to cope with the world outside their special classroom if they are not allowed to live in that world. Furthermore, many researchers believe that special education has failed. For example, only 56 percent of students in special education earn a high school diploma and only 21 percent of these graduates go on to pursue any kind of postsecondary education. Segregation away from the mainstream, in special classes, robs disabled students of the opportunity to learn to participate fully in society, robs non-disabled students of the opportunity to develop understanding and acceptance of the disabled, and increases the likelihood that disabled individuals will be stigmatized.

◀ **COUNTERPOINT** *Full inclusion will not work.*

Just because a disabled student is physically present in a class doesn't mean that student feels a sense of belonging. Disabled students can be just as socially isolated and alone in a regular class as they would be in a "special" class across the hall or across the country. Children can be cruel, and they may not necessarily provide opportunities for their disabled peers to "have fun and enjoy noise and laughter in their lives." Furthermore, many researchers believe special education has been quite successful. Seventy-seven percent of parents of students with disabilities are satisfied with the education programs of their children (Harris, 1989). In fact, parents of children with disabilities are more satisfied with the public schools than are parents of school-age children in general (Robert Wood Johnson, 1988). And special classes cannot be held responsible for low graduation and high dropout rates among special education students. Ninety-two percent of all students with disabilities spend at least some of their time in regular classes already. Shouldn't these classes be held responsible too?

Finally, can we really expect regular teachers who are already overburdened with responsibilities for low-achieving students, students coping with family crises, and students who speak little or no English to also handle the wide range of disabilities that could confront them? Regular educators are unprepared, unsupported, and unable to handle all these challenges at once. The idea that extra support and consultation will be provided is good in theory, but will it actually come to pass in practice?

Friend et al. (1998) agree that, so far, full inclusion has been an elusive goal in education, perhaps because our social values precede our knowledge about how best to accomplish this goal, or because we haven't put adequate human and financial resources into our efforts so far, or because the nature of some students' needs requires occasional or ongoing separate programming. However, they believe that "given appropriate supports, most exceptional students can receive much or all of their education in the regular classroom . . . [and that] we must continue to commit financial and other resources to ensure that exceptional students receive quality education" (p. 18).

6. Beginning at age 16 (and as young as 14 for some students), a statement of needed transitional services to move the student toward further education or work in adult life.

Figure 4.7 is an excerpt from the IEP of a nine-year-old girl with developmental disabilities. This section of the IEP focuses on one behaviour problem and on reading.

The Rights of Students and Parents. As a teacher, you need to be aware of the expectations for parental participation in education in your province. Typically, parents are viewed as partners in the education of exceptional students. They must approve any testing and special placements concerning their child, and they have the right to see all records kept by the school board that concern their child.

An Excerpt from an Individualized Education Program (IEP)

This IEP was developed for a nine-year-old girl. This section of the plan focuses on following the teacher's directions and on reading.

Student: ___Amy North___ Age: __9__ Grade: __1__ Date: _Oct. 17, 1995_

1. Unique Characteristics or Needs: Noncompliance

Frequently noncompliant with teacher's instructions.

1. Present Levels of Performance
Complies with about 50 percent of teacher requests/commands.

2. Special Education, Related Services, and Modifications
Implemented immediately, strong reinforcement for compliance with teacher's instructions (Example: "Sure I will!" plan including precision requests and reinforcer menu for points earned for compliance, as described in The Tough Kid Book, by Rhode, Jenson, and Reavis, 1992); within three weeks, training of parents by school psychologist to use precision requests and reinforcement at home.

3. Objectives (Including Procedures, Criteria, and Schedule)
Within one month, will comply with teacher requests/commands 90 percent of the time; compliance monitored weekly by the teacher.

4. Annual Goals
Will become compliant with teacher's requests/commands.

2. Unique Characteristics or Needs: Reading

2a. Very slow reading rate
2b. Poor comprehension
2c. Limited phonics skills
2d. Limited sight-word vocabulary

1. Present Levels of Performance
2a. Reads stories of approximately 100 words of first-grade level at approximately 40 words per min.
2b. Seldom can recall factual information about stories immediately after reading them.
2c. Consistently confuses vowel sounds, often misidentifies consonants, and does not blend sounds.
2d. Has sight-word vocabulary of approximately 150 words.

2. Special Education, Related Services, and Modifications
2a–2c. Direct instruction 30 minutes daily in vowel discrimination, consonant identification, and sound blending: begin immediately, continue throughout schoolyear.
2a & 2d. Sight word drill 10 minutes daily in addition to phonics instruction and daily practice; 10 minutes practice in using phonics and sight-word skills in reading story at her level; begin immediately, continue for schoolyear.

3. Objectives (Including Procedures, Criteria, and Schedule)
2a. Within three months, will read stories on her level at 60 words per minute with two or fewer errors per story; within six months, 80 words with two or fewer errors; performance monitored daily by teacher or aide.
2b. Within three months will answer oral and written comprehension questions requiring recall of information from stories she has just read with 90 percent accuracy (e.g., Who is in the story? What happened? When? Why?) and be able to predict probable outcomes with 80 percent accuracy; performance monitored daily by teacher or aide.
2c. Within three months, will increase sight-word vocabulary to 200 words, within six months to 250 words, assessed by flashcard presentation.

4. Annual Goals
2a–2c. Will read fluently and with comprehension at beginning-second-grade level.

Source: From Daniel P. Hallahan and James M. Kauffmann, *Exceptional Learners: Introduction to Special Education,* 7/e, p. 37. Copyright © 1995 by Allyn & Bacon. Reprinted by permission.

Parents may obtain an independent evaluation, and they have the right to participate in planning their child's IEP. Schools must maintain the confidentiality of students' records and ensure that testing practices do not discriminate against students from minority cultures. Furthermore, schools should communicate with parents in their native languages (i.e., through interpreters/translators) and must have processes in place for parents to appeal any decisions made by the school about their children. Finally, students are entitled to see all records the school board keeps about them, and should, whenever possible, be involved in planning their educational programs.

Effective Teaching in Inclusive Classrooms

Connect & Extend
To the research
For a discussion of how teachers' and school administrators' attitudes toward exceptional learners and beliefs about inclusive education influence effective teaching practices, see Stanovich, P., & Jordan, A. (1998). Canadian teachers' and principals' beliefs about inclusive education as predictors of effective teaching in heterogeneous classrooms. *Elementary School Journal, 98*, 221–238.

When you think about working with disabled students, what are your concerns? Do you have enough training? Will you get the support you need from school administrators or specialists? Will working with the disabled students take time away from your other responsibilities? These are common questions, and sometimes concerns are justified. But effective teaching for exceptional students does not require a unique set of skills. It is a combination of good teaching practices and sensitivity to all your students. Disabled students need to learn the academic material, and they need to be full participants in the day-to-day life of the classroom.

To accomplish the first goal of academic learning, Larrivee (1985) concluded that effective teachers of mainstreamed students do the following:

1. Use time efficiently by having smooth management routines, avoiding discipline problems, and planning carefully.
2. Ask questions at the right level of difficulty.
3. Give supportive, positive feedback to students, helping them figure out the right answer if they are wrong but on the right track.

To accomplish the second goal of integrating disabled students into the day-to-day life of the classroom, Ferguson, Ferguson, and Bogdan (1987) give the following guidelines:

1. Mix students with disabilities into groups with non-disabled students. Avoid resegregating the disabled students into separate groups.
2. Instead of sending students out for special services such as speech therapy, remedial reading, and individualized instruction, try to integrate the special help into the class setting, perhaps during a time when the other students are working independently too.
3. Make sure your language and behaviour with disabled students is a good model for everyone.
4. Teach about differences among people as part of the curriculum. Let students become familiar with aids for the disabled, such as hearing aids, sign language, communication boards, and so on.
5. Have students work together in cooperative groups or on special projects such as role plays, biographical interviews, or lab assignments.
6. Try to keep the schedules and activity patterns of disabled and non-disabled students similar.

Connect & Extend
To the research
Lupart, J. L. (1998). Setting right the delusion of inclusion: Implications for Canadian schools. *Canadian Journal of Education, 23*, 251–264.

Abstract
Canadian schools have been subject to considerable pressure over the past few decades to adopt educational practices that support inclusive education. Accordingly, initiatives in this direction are readily apparent in schools in every province and territory. Despite this seeming progress, many students, their parents, and educators are openly concerned about quality and equity in contemporary education. Given these concerns, Lupart argues that before authentic progress toward inclusion can be realized, three key areas of education practice need to be reviewed and transformed. Lupart outlines the problems and paradoxes associated with policy, organization, and legislation on the education of students with exceptional learning needs, and discusses implications for Canadian schools and for faculties of education in particular.

Resource Rooms, Collaborative Consultation, and Cooperative Teaching. Many schools provide additional help for classroom teachers working with disabled students. A **resource room** is a classroom with special materials and equipment and a specially trained teacher. Students may come to the resource room each day for several minutes or several hours and receive instruction individually or in small groups. The rest of the day the students are in regular classes.

The resource room can also be used as a tutorial centre. Individual students may spend an hour, a day, or a week there to receive direct and intensive instruction that their classroom teacher is unable to provide. Besides working with students directly, a resource teacher may also work with them indirectly by giving the regular teacher ideas, materials, or actual demonstrations of teaching techniques.

Increasingly, special and regular educators are working together, collaborating to assume equal responsibility for the education of disabled students. The collaboration may work through consultation, planning, and problem solving about how to teach specific students, or the special education teacher might work directly alongside the regular teacher in a class made up of students with and without disabilities. The latter is called **cooperative teaching**. The teachers assume different roles, depending on the age of the students and their needs. For example, in a secondary class the regular teacher might be responsible for academic content, while the special instructor teaches study skills and learning strategies. In another classroom the regular teacher might deal with core content, while the special teacher provides remediation, enrichment, or reteaching when necessary. The two teachers might also try team teaching, where each is responsible for different parts of the lesson.

When using cooperative teaching, it is important that regular and disabled students aren't resegregated in the class, with the regular teacher always working with the "regular" students and the special teacher always working with the "mainstreamed" students. When Nancy was a resource teacher in a school district in British Columbia, she often collaborated with classroom teachers to plan and teach units of instruction. For example, she once taught research and writing strategies to a Grade 7 class that included several students with learning disabilities and a student recovering from a brain injury. While she targeted the processes involved in doing research, the classroom teacher taught content relating to Egypt. Figure 4.8 shows different ways to implement cooperative teaching.

Including Families. To create supportive learning environments for exceptional students, collaboration should extend outside the classroom to the students' families. The Family and Community Partnerships Guidelines give some ideas.

Computers and Exceptional Students

Computers have improved the education of exceptional children in countless ways. Teachers can use computers to keep records, plan programs, and manage instruction. For students who require small steps and many repetitions to learn a new concept, computers are the perfect patient tutors, repeating steps and lessons as many times as necessary. A well-designed computer instructional program is engaging and interactive—two important qualities for students with problems paying attention or with a history of failure that has eroded motivation. For example, a math or spelling program might use images, sounds, and game-like features to maintain the attention of a student with an attention-deficit disorder. Interactive videodisc programs are being developed to help hearing people use sign language. Many programs do not involve sound, so hearing-impaired students can get the full benefit from the lessons. Students who have trouble reading can use programs that will "speak" a word for them if they touch the unknown word with a light pen or the cursor. With this immediate access to help, the students are much more likely to get the reading practice they need to prevent falling further and further behind. And for the learning-disabled student whose writing can't be read, word processors produce perfect penmanship so the ideas can finally get on paper. Once the ideas are on paper, the student can reorganize and improve the writing without the agony of rewriting by hand (Hallahan & Kauffman, 1997; Hardman, Drew, & Egan, 1996; Reynolds & Birch, 1988).

For gifted students, computers can be a connection with databases and computers in universities, museums, and research labs. Computer networks allow stu-

Resource Room: Classroom with special materials and a specially trained teacher.

Cooperative Teaching: Collaboration between regular and special education teachers.

Connect & Extend
To the research
Barber, L., & Brophy, K. (1993). Parents' views on school placement procedures for their children with special needs. *Journal on Developmental Disabilities, 2,* 100–111.

Abstract
Mothers from five Ontario families with a Down Syndrome child (aged 5–10 years) were interviewed regarding their experiences in meetings with the school and as part of a partnership process concerning the identification and placement of their children, and their views of these experiences. Subjects felt that it was very important for parents to be major players in the placement process, and that schools need to take steps to ensure that parents are able to participate more fully in order that the best possible decisions are made for the child. Results also show that parents would like to see the nature of the procedure changed so that they feel more comfortable at meetings rather than intimidated. Recommendations for change are given.

FIGURE 4.8

Cooperative and Co-Teaching Approaches

There are many ways for teachers to work together in inclusion classrooms.

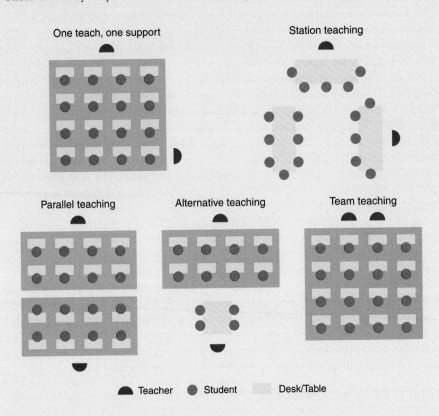

Source: From Marilyn Friend and William Bursuck, *Including Students with Special Needs: A Practical Guide for Classroom Teachers*, p. 87. Copyright © 1996 by Allyn & Bacon. Reprinted by permission.

CHECKPOINT

Exceptional Education and Inclusion

Review

▷ Describe the legislation that affects special education across Canada.

Apply

▷ What is your position on full inclusion?

▷ What should you do before referring a child for evaluation by special education professionals?

dents to work on projects and share information with others across the country. It is also possible to have gifted students write programs for students and teachers. Quite a few principals around the country rely on their students to make the technology in the school work. These are just a few examples of what technology can do. Check with the resource teachers in your district to find out what is available in your school.

▲ *Computers and other technology can support learning for disabled students so that the disabilities are less handicapping.*

FAMILY AND COMMUNITY PARTNERSHIPS

Productive Conferences

Plan and prepare for a productive conference.

Examples

1. Have a clear purpose and gather the needed information. If you want to discuss student progress, have work samples.
2. Send home a list of questions and ask families to bring the information to the conference.

Sample questions from Friend and Bursuck (1996) are:

1. What is your child's favourite class activity?
2. Does your child worry about class activities? If so, which ones?
3. What are your priorities for your child's education this year?
4. What questions do you have about your child's education in my class this year?
5. How could we at school help make this the most successful year ever for your child?
6. Are there any topics you want to discuss at the conference that I might need to prepare for? If so, please let me know.
7. Would you like other individuals to participate in the conference? If so, please give me a list of their names.
8. Is there particular school information you would like me to have available? If so, please let me know. (p. 101)

During the conference, create and maintain an atmosphere of collaboration and respect.

Examples

1. Arrange the room for private conversation. Put a sign on your door to avoid interruptions. Meet around a conference table for better collaboration. Have tissues available.
2. Address families as "Mr" and "Ms," not "Mom" and "Dad" or "Grandma." Use students' names.
3. Listen to families' concerns and build on their ideas for their children.

After the conference, keep good records and follow up on decisions.

Examples

1. Make notes to yourself and keep them organized.
2. Summarize any actions or decisions in writing and send a copy to the family and any other teachers or professionals involved.
3. Communicate with families on other occasions, especially when there is good news to share.

$\mathcal{S}$ummary

Language and Labelling

What are the advantages of and problems with labels?

Labels and diagnostic classifications of exceptional students can easily become both stigmas and self-fulfilling prophecies, but they can also open doors to special programs and help teachers develop appropriate instructional strategies.

What is person-first language?

Person-first language ("students with developmental disabilities," "students placed at risk," etc.) is an alternative to labels that describe a complex person with one or two words, implying that the condition labelled is the most important aspect of the person. With person-first language, the emphasis is on the students first, not on the special challenges they face.

Distinguish between a disability and a handicap.

A disability is an inability to do something specific such as see or walk. A handicap is a disadvantage in certain situations. Some disabilities lead to handicaps, but not in all contexts. Teachers must avoid imposing handicaps on disabled learners.

Individual Differences in Intelligence

What is g?

Spearman suggested there is one mental attribute, which he called g or general intelligence, that is used to perform any mental test, but that each test also requires some specific abilities in addition to g. Spearman assumed that individuals vary in both general intelligence and specific abilities, and that together these factors determine performance on mental tasks. A current version of the general plus specific abilities theory is Carroll's work identifying a few broad abilities (such as learning and memory, visual perception, verbal fluency), and at least 70 specific abilities.

What is Gardner's view of intelligence and his position on g?

Gardner contends that an intelligence is a biological and psychological potential to solve problems and create products or outcomes that are valued by a culture. These intelligences are realized to a greater or lesser extent as a consequence of experiential, cultural, and motivational factors. There are at least eight separate intelligences: linguistic, musical, spatial, logical-mathematical, bodily kinesthetic, interpersonal, intrapersonal (these last two are similar to the idea of emotional intelligence), naturalist, and perhaps existential. Gardner does not deny the existence of a general ability, but does question how useful g is as an explanation for human achievements.

What are the elements in Sternberg's theory of intelligence?

Sternberg's triarchic theory of intelligence is a cognitive process approach to understanding intelligence that has three parts: analytic, creative, and practical. Analytic/componential intelligence involves the mental processes that lead to more or less intelligent behaviour. These processes are defined in terms of components: metacomponents, performance components, and knowledge-acquisition components. Creative/experiential intelligence involves coping with new experiences through insight, or the ability to deal effectively with novel situations, and automaticity, or the ability to become efficient and automatic in thinking and problem solving. The third part is practical/contextual intelligence—choosing to live and work in a context where success is likely, adapting to that context, and reshaping it if necessary. Practical intelligence is made up mostly of action-oriented tacit knowledge learned during everyday life rather than formal schooling.

How is intelligence measured and what does an IQ score mean?

Intelligence is measured through individual tests (Stanford-Binet, Wechsler, Woodcock-Johnston, etc.) and group tests (Lorge-Thorndike, Analysis of Learning Potential, Otis-Lennon Mental Abilities Tests, School and College Ability Tests, etc.). Compared to an individual test, a group test is much less likely to yield an accurate picture of any one person's abilities. The average score is 100; 50 percent of the people from the general population who take the tests will score 100 or above, and 50 percent will score below 100. About 68 percent of the general population will earn IQ scores between 85 and 115. Only about 16 percent of the population will receive scores below 85, and only 16 percent will score above 115. These figures hold true for white, native-born Americans whose first language is Standard English. Intelligence predicts success in school, but is less predictive of success in life when level of education is taken into account.

Ability Differences and Teaching

What are the problems with between-class ability grouping?

Academic ability groupings can have both disadvantages and advantages for students and teachers. For low-ability students, however, between-class ability grouping generally has a negative effect on achievement, social adjustment, and self-esteem. Low-ability classes seem to receive lower-quality instruction in general. Teachers tend to emphasize lower-level objectives and routine procedures, with less academic focus. Often there are more student behaviour problems and, along with these problems, increased teacher stress and decreased enthusiasm. Low expectations may be communicated to the students. Attendance may drop along with self-esteem. The lower tracks often have a disproportionate number of minority-group and economically disadvantaged students, so ability grouping, in effect, becomes segregation in school.

What are the alternatives available for grouping in classes?

Cross-age grouping by subject can be an effective way to deal with ability differences in a school. Within-class ability grouping, if handled sensitively and flexibly, can have positive effects, but alternatives such as cooperative learning are also possible.

Creativity, Giftedness, and Talent

What is creativity and how is it assessed?

Creativity is a process that involves independently restructuring problems to see things in new, imaginative ways. Creativity is difficult to measure, but tests of divergent thinking can assess originality, fluency, and flexibility. Originality is usually determined statistically. To be original, a response must be given by fewer than 5 or 10 people out of every 100 who take the test. Fluency is the number of different responses. Flexibility is measured by the number of different categories of responses. Teachers can encourage creativity by providing opportunities for play, using brainstorming techniques, and accepting divergent ideas.

What are the characteristics of gifted students?

Terman and colleagues found that gifted children were larger, stronger, and healthier than the norm. They were more emotionally stable than their peers and became better-adjusted adults than the average. Gifted students learn easily and rapidly and retain what they have learned; use common sense and practical knowledge; know about many things that the other children don't; use a large number of words easily and accurately; recognize relations and comprehend meaning; are alert and keenly observant and respond quickly; are persistent and highly motivated on some tasks; and are creative or make interesting connections.

Is acceleration a useful approach with gifted students?

Many people object to acceleration, but most careful studies indicate that truly gifted students who are accelerated do as well as, and usually better than, non-gifted students who are progressing at the normal pace. Gifted students tend to prefer the company of older playmates and may be bored if kept with children their own age. Skipping grades may not be the best solution for a particular student, but for students who are extremely advanced intellectually (with a score of 160 or higher on an individual intelligence test), the only practical solution may be to accelerate their education.

Cognitive and Learning Styles

Distinguish between cognitive style and learning preference.

Cognitive styles are characteristic modes of perceiving, remembering, thinking, problem solving, and decision making. They reflect information-processing regularities that develop around underlying personality trends. Field dependence versus field independence and impulsive versus reflective cognitive styles are examples of these differences. Learning preferences are individual preferences for particular learning modes and environments. They could be preferences for where, when, with whom, or with what lighting, food, or music you like to study. While cognitive styles and learning preferences are not related to intelligence or effort, they may affect school performance.

What are the advantages and disadvantages of matching teaching to individual learning styles?

Results of some research indicate that students learn more when they study in their preferred setting and manner. But sometimes students, particularly low achievers, prefer what is easy and comfortable; real learning can be hard and uncomfortable. Sometimes students prefer to learn in a certain way because they have no alternatives; it is the only way they know how to approach the task. These students may benefit from developing new—and perhaps more effective—ways to learn.

High-Incidence Disabilities

What is a learning disability?

Specific learning disabilities involve significant difficulties in the acquisition and use of listening, speaking, reading, writing, reasoning, or mathematical abilities. These disorders are intrinsic to the individual, presumed to be the result of central nervous system dysfunction, and may occur across the life span. Students with learning disabilities may become victims of learned helplessness when they come to believe that they cannot control or improve their own learning and therefore cannot succeed. A focus on learning strategies often helps students with learning disabilities.

What is ADHD and how is it handled in school?

Attention-deficit/hyperactivity disorder (ADHD) is the term used to describe individuals of any age with hyperactivity and attention difficulties. Use of medication to address ADHD is effective for 70 to 80 percent of individuals who suffer from the disorder. However, it is controversial. There are negative side effects, such as headaches and nausea. Typically, these can be controlled by modifying the dosage. Also, little is known about the long-term effects of drug therapy and it is not a panacea. The drugs alone will not lead to improvements in academic learning or peer relationships, two areas where children with ADHD have great problems. Instructional methods that have proven most successful for helping students with ADHD are based on behavioural principles of learning such as those described in Chapter 6. One promising approach is Positive Behaviour Support.

What are the most common communication disorders?

Common communication disorders include speech impairments (articulation disorders, stuttering, and voicing problems) and oral language disorders.

Low-Incidence Disabilities

How can schools accommodate the needs of physically disabled students?

If the school has the necessary architectural features, such as ramps, elevators, and accessible washrooms, and if teachers allow for the physical limitations of students, little needs to be done to alter the usual educational program. Identifying a peer to help with movements and transitions can be useful.

How would you handle a seizure in class?

Do not restrain the child's movements. Lower the child gently to the floor, away from furniture or walls. Move hard objects away. Turn the child's head gently to the side, put a soft coat or blanket under the student's head, and loosen any tight clothing. Never put anything in the student's mouth. Find out from the student's parents how the seizure is usually dealt with. If one seizure follows another and the student does not regain consciousness in between or if the seizure goes on for more than 10 minutes, get medical help right away.

What are some signs of hearing and visual impairment?

Signs of hearing problems are turning one ear toward the speaker, favouring one ear in conversation, or misunderstanding conversation when the speaker's face cannot be seen. Other indications include not following directions, seeming distracted or confused at times, frequently asking people to repeat what they have said, mispronouncing new words or names, and being reluctant to participate in class discussions. Take note particularly of students who have frequent earaches, sinus infections, or allergies. Holding books very close or far away, squinting, rubbing eyes, misreading the chalkboard, and holding the head at an odd angle are possible signs of visual problems.

Exceptional Education and Inclusion

Each province or territory has an education or school act that governs education in its elementary and secondary schools. Inclusion is the current policy of all 10 provinces and 3 territories in Canada. Also, educating students in the least restrictive or most enabling environment, developing an individualized education plan (IEP) that meets the unique needs of each exceptional learner, and protecting the rights of exceptional students and their parents are principles shared by ministries of education across Canada. Only one piece of legislation has an impact on education across the country: the *Canadian Charter of Rights and Freedoms*, which is part of the Constitution.

Key Terms

absence seizure, *p. 140*

articulation disorders, *p. 135*

attention-deficit/hyperactivity disorder, *p. 132*

automaticity, *p. 114*

between-class ability grouping, *p. 117*

brainstorming, *p. 120*

Canadian Charter of Rights and Freedoms, *p. 143*

cerebral palsy, *p. 139*

cognitive styles, *p. 126*

components, *p. 113*

convergent thinking, *p. 119*

cooperative teaching, *p. 147*

creativity, *p. 118*

developmental disabilities, *p. 136*

deviation IQ, *p. 115*

disability, *p. 107*

divergent thinking, *p. 119*

educationally blind, *p. 141*

education or school act, *p. 142*

emotional intelligence (EQ), *p. 111*

epilepsy, *p. 140*

exceptional students, *p. 106*

field dependence, *p. 126*

field independence, *p. 126*

finger spelling, *p. 140*

generalized seizure, *p. 140*

gifted student, *p. 121*

handicap, *p. 107*

hyperactivity, *p. 132*

impulsive, *p. 126*

inclusion, *p. 142*

individualized education program (IEP), *p. 143*

insight, *p. 114*

integration, *p. 142*

intelligence, *p. 108*

intelligence quotient (IQ), *p. 115*

Joplin Plan, *p. 118*

learned helplessness, *p. 131*

learning disability, *p. 128*

learning preferences, *p. 127*

learning styles, *p. 126*

least restrictive placement, *p. 143*

low vision, *p. 141*

mental age, *p. 115*

multiple intelligences, *p. 109*

non-graded elementary school, *p. 118*

orthopedic devices, *p. 139*

reflective, *p. 126*

resource room, *p. 147*

restructuring, *p. 119*

self-instruction, *p. 127*

sign language, *p. 140*

spasticity, *p. 139*

speech impairment, *p. 135*

speech reading, *p. 140*

stuttering, *p. 135*

tacit knowledge, *p. 114*

transition programming, *p. 137*

triarchic theory of intelligence, *p. 113*

voicing problems, *p. 135*

within-class ability grouping, *p. 118*

Becoming a Professional

Reflecting on the Chapter

Can you apply the ideas from this chapter on individual differences to solve the following problems of practice?

Preschool and Kindergarten

▷ A little girl in your kindergarten class seldom speaks. When she does, she usually says only a word or two. She seems to understand when others talk, but almost never responds verbally. How would you approach this situation?

Elementary and Middle School

▷ The school psychologist tells you that one of your students is going to start taking medication designed to "calm him down." What would you want to know? How would you respond?

▷ The principal tells you that she is assigning two more students to your class because you are "new, and have more training in inclusion than the older teachers." One student has developmental disabilities and has problems making friends. The other is blind. How will you respond to the principal's decision? How would you prepare your class and modify your teaching for these students?

Junior High and High School

▷ A student in your fifth-period class is failing. When you look at your grade book, you see that it is the written work that is giving the student trouble. Multiple-choice test scores and class participation are fine. But his writing is hardly legible and very disorganized. Sentences are started and never finished. Ideas fly in and out like frightened birds. How would you identify the source of the problem?

▷ How would you adapt your teaching to accommodate a hearing-impaired student in your biology lab class?

Check Your Understanding

▷ Know the difference between a handicap and a disability

▷ Know the mean of standardized IQ tests and the range in which most people score.

▷ Be familiar with Gardner's theory of multiple intelligences.

▷ Know the effects of between-class ability grouping and the alternative for in-class grouping.

▷ Be aware of the alternatives for teaching gifted students, including acceleration.

▷ Be familiar with Section 15.1 of the Canadian Charter of Rights and Freedoms, as well as the human rights legislation and the school act in your province or territory.

▷ Understand the differences between cognitive styles and learning styles/preferences and how to make accommodations for differences in the classroom.

Your Teaching Portfolio

▷ Use Table 4.8 to generate ideas for developing students' language and add these to your portfolio.

▷ For your portfolio, develop a lesson plan that appropriately uses Gardner's work on multiple intelligences—see Figure 4.3 for ideas.

▷ Add Table 4.10, "Making a Referral," to your portfolio.

Teaching Resources

Add Tables 4.2, 4.3, 4.4, 4.5, 4.6, 4.7, and 4.8 to your file of teaching resources.

Weblinks

www.cec.sped.org

The site for the Council for Exceptional Children (CEC), the largest international professional organization dedicated to improving educational outcomes for individuals with exceptionalities, students with disabilities, and/or the gifted. A host of information is available, including contacts in every province.

http://educ.queensu.ca/~lda

The Learning Disabilities Association of Canada is a national non-profit voluntary organization dedicated to advancing the education, employment, social development, legal rights and general well-being of people with learning disabilities. This site provides a variety of links to research; definitions and signposts of exceptionalities; briefs prepared for government; and more.

What Would They Do?

PHELESIA HUDSON

Allion School
Lasalle, Quebec

While sitting, sipping my coffee, I compose a letter.

Dear parents,

A school-based team meeting is a wonderful opportunity for discussing your child's needs as well as the results of psychoeducational testing. However, it should be known that results of a test are but numbers on a paper. These numbers must be deciphered, taking into account Daryl's home and school experiences. They are a tool that can aid the team in making important decisions on the way Daryl will be taught (methodology), and on what he will be expected to learn (goals and objectives), based on his strengths and weaknesses.

Results, along with anecdotal records and observations from the teacher and other team members, will be used in the planning, development, and implementation of Daryl's individualized education plan (IEP). This plan will include goals that suit Daryl's abilities, as well as strategies and approaches that will help Daryl reach these objectives (decided upon by the team members, yourself included), making success attainable.

The process of meeting as a team has been set up to ensure that Daryl's individual needs be recognized and met. There are no miracle cures, and the team must meet over and over again to evaluate Daryl's progress and to continue tailoring a program to his needs.

Throughout Daryl's education, he will need you to be his strongest advocates. His teachers will change every year, as might the team members. It is therefore imperative that you become aware of the services available for your child's needs (speech therapy, psychologist, shadow, etc.) and that you insist on receiving those services.

Thank you for taking an active part in Daryl's education. I look forward to working with you, as a team.

Sincerely,

Daryl's teacher

KRISTA TULLOCH

Special Education Teacher
General Wolfe Elementary School
Vancouver, British Columbia

Before deciding how to use the assessment information, I would want answers to the following questions: What instruments were used? What data were collected? How thorough were the assessments? What qualitative statements did the assessor make about how the student participated in the process? Do those fit with how I, as the classroom teacher, typically experience the student?

Who administered them? Is this person known to the SBT, teacher, student? Was a relationship established where the child felt comfortable and able to perform to the best of their ability?

How old is the student; that is, are they able to identify their own areas of concern in the classroom or at school in general? How did they react to/describe the testing situation? How did they feel about their performance?

What areas of concern has the family identified? Are these reflected in the assessment data? What do they want 'cured'?

What was I hoping to get out of the assessment? What are my concerns about the student's level of progress in the classroom?

What was the purpose of the testing? Program placement, modifying the program in the current instructional setting, increasing support in the classroom? Why did we refer in the first place?

Has any other assessment been conducted at school or in the community? Do these new results support or refute previous findings? Has the student's vision and hearing been checked? Are there any allergies or medical conditions involved that may have educational implications? Is the child on any medication? Is there a family history of learning disability? Health problems?

What does the child's school history look like? Has he attended many schools? Moved cities multiple times? Been taught in another language or country? Had an extended absence due to illness? Have there been any family stresses that interfered with school performance?

What is the child's social experience of school? Are academic issues creating difficulties in other areas of the child's development? Is there behaviour that interferes with academic opportunities? What is that about?

What can standardized tests provide? Sometimes enhanced understanding of key areas that are specific strengths or weaknesses for a student—but only if those results show up in patterns. In the kind of assessment situations we tend to provide in schools, we don't see those patterns emerging from a single psychoeducational assessment. The patterns come out of the teacher's experience of assessing, instructing and evaluating the student; the parents' report of how the student copes at home and the student's report of managing school tasks. Tests can confirm patterns and problems you already see and help to give a name or label to them—for example, the child has low visual memory—but rarely do tests 'know' things that parents, students, and teachers don't already know about what's easy, what's hard, what's frustrating, or what's fun for the student.

In terms of what I will tell the parents about how this information will help me in planning or adapting their child's program, that depends on my knowing and understanding the child's larger context. For me, tests are just information—not good, not bad, just information. And just as I wouldn't attempt to write a paper using only one source, I wouldn't be rushing out to change an instructional program for one of my students because I got a psychoeducational report back. Assessment data provide one kind of information I can use to build a comprehensive picture of strengths, needs, goals, and plans. I'd need to look at all the information I could gather and, from it, try to see the patterns. Based on the information provided in this scenario, I'm not rushing to do anything, other than spend more time talking to the family and student to fill in the missing pieces (as described above).

Culture and Community

*W*ere there students in your junior or senior high school who spoke a different language or who were from a different racial or ethnic group than yours? How did you feel about these "different" students? Were they ever the butt of jokes in your group? Are you prepared to dedicate yourself to teaching their children and the children of other racial or ethnic groups who may seem even more unlike you?

The face of Canadian classrooms is changing. In this chapter we examine the many cultures that form the fabric of our society. We begin by tracing the schools' responses to different ethnic and cultural groups and consider the concept of multicultural education. With a broad conception of culture as a basis, we then examine three important dimensions of every student's identity: social class, ethnicity, and gender. For each dimension, we will explore the experiences of the various groups in the schools, possible differences in achievement and learning styles, and explanations for the lower achievement of some groups. Then we turn to a consideration of language and bilingual education. The last section of the chapter presents three general principles for teaching every student.

By the time you have completed this chapter you should be able to:

▶ Compare the notion of the melting pot with views about multicultural education.

▶ Define *culture* and list the various groups that make up your own cultural identity.

▶ Explain why the school achievement of low-income students often falls below that of middle- and upper-income students.

▶ Give examples of conflicts and compatibilities between home and school cultures.

▶ Describe the school's role in the development of gender differences.

▶ Describe effective teaching for culturally and linguistically diverse students.

▶ Incorporate multicultural concepts into your teaching.

▶ Give examples of culturally relevant pedagogy.

What Would You Do?

You teach in a fairly homogeneous elementary school. In fact, most of your kindergarten and Grade 1 students come from middle- or upper-middle-class families and are white. In January, a new student joins your class—she and her family have recently immigrated to Canada from Iran. After a few weeks, you notice that Fatemah is not being included in many activities. She sits by herself in the library and plays alone at recess. Then, one day, you overhear two of your higher-achieving female students talking about their "White Girls Club."

▶ Would you investigate to learn more about this "club?" How?

▶ If you found that your students had created a club that excluded non-white students, what would you do?

▶ If you teach older students, what would you do about student groups that define themselves by who *cannot* be members?

Today's Multicultural Classrooms

Who are the students in Canadian classrooms today? Here are a few statistics:

▶ 21 percent of Canadians under the age of 18 live in poverty.

▶ Many children live with one parent, usually their mother.

▶ Many children in our schools face problems that interfere with learning (e.g., they are unhealthy, neglected, physically or emotionally abused, homeless, or living with alcoholic or drug-addicted parents).

The linguistic and cultural diversity of our classrooms is increasing steadily. For example, the number of students for whom English is a second or additional language has more than tripled in British Columbia since 1990 (British Columbia Ministry of Education, 1998), and Toronto was recently named the most ethnically diverse city in the world by the United Nations (Friend et al., 1998).

Students "at risk" and students who speak English as a second language (ESL) are more likely to drop out of school than are other students.

Individuals, Groups, and Society

Mosaic: Allows individuals to maintain their culture and identity while still being a respected part of the larger society.

Melting Pot: A metaphor for the absorption and assimilation of immigrants into the mainstream of society so that ethnic differences vanish.

Multicultural Education: Education that teaches the value of cultural diversity.

Canada has always prided itself on being a multicultural society—a **mosaic** as opposed to a **melting pot**. Crealock and Bachor (1995) point out that Native people have been in North America for tens of thousands of years and have always shown collective differences in tribal beliefs, values, and rituals (p. 511). English and French Canadians settled here in the fifteenth and sixteenth centuries. In the nineteenth and early twentieth centuries, people came from Ireland, Russia, Poland, Ukraine, and Asia. Recent immigrants to Canada include individuals from Latin American countries, the Caribbean, Asia, East India, and the Middle East. Approximately 200 000 immigrants arrive in Canada each year; of these individuals, about 80 percent speak a language other than English and about 50 percent have no English proficiency (Friend et al., 1998).

As we indicated in Chapter 4, Canada aspires to be an inclusive society, and this is reflected in Canada's policy on multiculturalism. The *Canadian Multiculturalism Act* of 1989 reflects Canada's commitment to respecting and understanding our multiculturalism through the social, cultural, economic, and political institutions of our nation. Other laws that protect multiculturalism include the *Canadian Charter of Rights and Freedoms* (recall Section 15.1 from Chapter 4), the *Indian*

Act, the *Immigration Act,* the *Employment Equity Act,* and the *Canadian Human Rights Act* (Crealock & Bachor, 1995). All provinces and territories have policies and programs that support multiculturalism, bilingualism, and multilingualism in their schools (Crealock & Bachor, 1995).

Multicultural education is one response to the increasing diversity of the school population as well as to the growing demand for equality for all groups. A narrow definition of multicultural education is the expansion of educational curricula and activities to include the perspectives, histories, accomplishments, and concerns of non-European people (Hilliard, 1991/1992). A broader conception of multicultural education is that "all students, regardless of the groups to which they belong, groups such as those related to gender, ethnicity, race, culture, social class, religion, or exceptionality, should experience educational equality in the schools" (Banks, 1993X, p. 24). An examination of the alternative approaches to multicultural education is beyond the scope of an educational psychology text, but be aware that there is no general agreement about the "best" approach.

James Banks (1999) suggests that multicultural education has five dimensions, as shown in Figure 5.1 below. Many people are familiar only with the dimension of *content integration,* using examples and content from a variety of cultures when teaching a subject. Because they believe that multicultural education is simply a change in curriculum, many people assume that it is irrelevant for subjects such as science and mathematics. But if you consider the other four dimensions—helping students understand how knowledge is influenced by beliefs, reducing prejudice, creating social structures in schools that support learning and development for all students, and using teaching methods that reach

Connect & Extend
To the research
See the *Journal of Adolescent Research,* April 1994, for an article on multicultural education: LaPierriere, A., Compare, L., D'Khissy, M., Dolce, R., et al. (1994). Mutual perceptions and interethnic strategies among French, Italian, and Haitian adolescents of a multiethnic school in Montreal (pp. 193–217).
   Also see Fowler, R. (1998). Intercultural education in Canada: Glimpses from the past, hopes for the future. In K. Cushner (Ed.), *International perspectives on Intercultural Education* (pp. 302–318). Mahwah, NJ: Lawrence Erlbaum Associates.

Abstract
Describes the development of intercultural education in Canada. After describing the history of Canada, particularly as an immigrant country, the author describes the contemporary context of education and multiculturalism in Canada. The immigration policy and the persistence of nativism are described and perceptions of multiculturalism are discussed. The author argues that, as Canada has become increasingly multicultural, educators have made great strides to recognize and respond to this diversity. The author also describes issues that remain as barriers to multicultural education.

Connect & Extend
To the curriculum
Nancy Hutchinson, of Queen's University in Kingston, ON, recommends that teachers strategically apply cultural resources in their classrooms. "All students need to appreciate the role in history of the groups that make up our diverse country" (Hutchinson, 2001, p. 153), and students from minority groups need to see themselves portrayed in materials used for teaching and learning. Here are some resources she recommends:

• For social studies, see *Coming to Gum San: The History of Chinese Canadians,* written by Shehla Burney in 1995 and published by Heath Canada and the Multicultural History Society of Ontario.
• In language arts, include books such as *Lights for Gita,* written by R. Gilmore and published by Second Story Press in Toronto.
• Many ministries of education and teachers' federations have published resources to help teachers create a multicultural and antiracist learning environment. See *Multicultural Education: A Place to Start* by Keith McLeod and Eva Krugly-Smolska.

FIGURE 5.1

Banks's Dimensions of Multicultural Education

Multicultural education is more than a change in the curriculum. To make education appropriate for all students, we must consider other dimensions as well. The way the athletics and counselling programs are structured, the teaching method used, lessons about prejudice, perspectives on knowledge—these and many more elements contribute to true multicultural education.

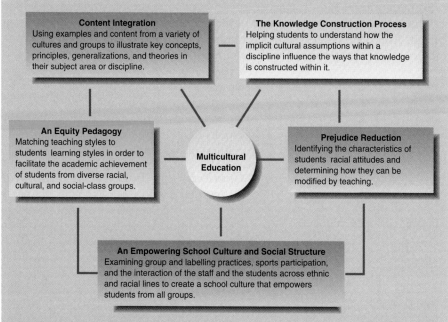

Source: From James A. Banks (1994). *Multiethnic education: Theory and practice,* 3/e, p. 5. Boston: Allyn & Bacon. Adapted with the permission of the author and the publisher.

Culture: The knowledge, values, attitudes, and traditions that guide the behaviour of a group of people and allow them to solve the problems of living in their environment.

all students—you will see that this view of multicultural education is relevant to all subjects and all students.

Multicultural education rejects the idea of the melting pot and embraces diversity. Let's take a closer look at the differences that make up the mosaic of cultural diversity.

Canadian Cultural Diversity

In this text we take a broad interpretation of culture and multicultural education, so we will examine social class, race, ethnicity, and gender as aspects of diversity. We begin with a look at the meaning of culture. Many people associate this concept with the "cultural events" section of the newspaper—art galleries, museums, Shakespeare plays, classical music, and so on. Culture has a much broader meaning: it embraces the whole way of life of a group of people.

Connect & Extend
To a specific group
For help developing a clearer understanding of culturally related learning styles of Aboriginal students and how to use these to students' advantage, see More, A. J. (1989). Native Indian students and their language styles: Research results and classroom applications. In B. Robinson (Ed.), *Culture, Style and the Educative Process* (pp. 150–166). Springfield, IL: Charles C. Thomas.

Culture and Group Membership. There are many definitions of **culture.** Most definitions include the knowledge, rules, traditions, attitudes, and values that guide behaviour in a particular group of people (Betancourt & Lopez, 1993). The group creates a culture—a program for living—and communicates the culture to members. Thus people are members of groups, they are not members of cultures. Groups can be defined along regional, ethnic, religious, racial, gender, social class, or other lines. Each of us is a member of many groups, so we all are influenced by many different cultures. Sometimes the influences are incompatible or even contradictory. For example, if you are a feminist but also a Roman Catholic, you may have trouble reconciling the two different cultures' beliefs about the ordination of women as priests. Your personal belief will be based, in part, on how strongly you identify with each group (Banks, 1994).

There are many different cultures, of course, in every modern country. In Canada, students living in the suburbs of Toronto certainly differ in a number of ways from students growing up in a Montreal high-rise apartment or on a farm in Quebec. In the United States, students growing up in a small rural town in the Deep South are part of a cultural group that is very different from that of students in a large urban centre or students in a West Coast suburb. Within those small towns in the Deep South or Quebec, the child of a gas station attendant grows up in a different culture from the child of the town doctor or dentist. Individuals of African, Asian, First Nations, or European descent have distinctive histories and traditions. The experiences of males and females are different in most ethnic and economic groups. Everyone living within a particular country shares many common experiences and values, especially because of the influence of the mass media, but other aspects of their lives are shaped by differing cultural backgrounds.

Cautions in Interpreting Cultural Differences. Before we examine the bases for cultural differences, two cautions are necessary. First, we will consider social class, ethnicity, and gender separately, because much of the available research focuses on only one of these variables. Of course, real children are not just Asian, or middle class, or female; they are complex beings and members of many groups.

The second caution comes from James Banks (1993X), who has written several books on multicultural education:

CHECKPOINT

Today's Multicultural Classrooms

Review

▶ Distinguish between the "melting pot" and multiculturalism.

▶ What is multicultural education?

▶ What is culture?

Apply

▶ What cultural groups affect your identity?

Although membership in a gender, racial, ethnic, social-class, or religious group can provide us with important clues about an individual's behaviour, it cannot enable us to predict behaviour *Membership in a particular group does not determine behaviour but makes certain types of behaviour more probable.* (pp. 13–14)

Keep this in mind as you read about characteristics of economically disadvantaged students or Asian Canadians or males. The information we will examine reflects tendencies and probabilities. It does not tell you about a specific person. Remember that you will be teaching individual students. Each child is a unique product of many influences, a member of a variety of groups. For example, if a minority-group student in your class consistently arrives late, you should not assume that the student's behaviour reflects a cultural difference in beliefs about punctuality. It may be that the student has a job before school or must walk a long distance, or that he or she is simply not a morning person.

Social Class Differences

The term used by sociologists for variations in wealth, power, and prestige is **socioeconomic status**, or **SES**. In modern societies, levels of wealth, power, and prestige are not always consistent. Some people—for instance, university professors—are members of professions that are reasonably prestigious but provide little wealth or power. Other people have political power though they are not wealthy. No single variable, not even income, is an effective measure of SES. The *National Longitudinal Survey of [Canada's] Children and Youth* (NLSCY) considered family income, parents' occupations, and parents' education to arrive at an overall indicator of SES (Lipps & Frank, 1997). Five equally sized groups (or quintiles) were created to reflect five levels of SES: lower, lower-middle, middle, upper-middle, and highest.

Social class is a significant dimension of cultural differences, often overpowering other differences such as ethnicity or gender. For example, upper-class individuals from a variety of ethnic groups typically find that they have more in common with each other than they have with lower-class individuals from their own ethnic groups. (Gollnick & Chinn, 1994).

Who Are the Poor?

In Canada in 1992, more than 50 percent of single mothers and over 20 percent of children under the age of 18 lived below the poverty line (Winzer, 1999). The United States has the highest rate of poverty for children (over 25 percent) of all developed nations, but Canada is not far behind. According to Margaret Winzer (1999) at the University of Lethbridge, poverty is a significant risk factor for children's physical, social-emotional, and intellectual development. For example, poor children are more likely to suffer the consequences of poor nutrition (e.g., they may be underweight or suffer from allergies), and their lives at home are more often filled with stress. At school, they are at risk for reading and writing difficulties, and they make up a large percentage of the students who repeat a grade, get referred for special education services, or drop out of school.

Children from minority cultures are more likely than those from majority cultures to be poor, and students from minority cultures who also have limited English proficiency have historically done poorly in school (Winzer, 1999). These students are more likely than their peers from majority cultures to experience social isolation, increasing academic failure as they move through school, disproportionate referrals for special education, lower scores on tests, high dropout rates, and lower rates of college attendance (Winzer & Mazurek, 1998).

SES and Achievement

There are many relationships between SES and school performance. For example, it is well documented that high-SES students of all ethnic groups show higher average levels of achievement and stay in school longer than low-SES students (Alwin & Thornton, 1984; Conger, Conger, & Elder, 1997; McLoyd, 1998). The relationship between high SES and higher levels of achievement is shown in Figure 5.2. However, when SES is measured solely in terms of parents' education, income, or occupation, the relationship between SES and achievement is weaker than when it is measured in terms that include family atmosphere variables such as parents' attitudes toward education, the aspirations of parents for their children, or the intellectual activities of the family (Laosa, 1984; Peng & Lee, 1992; White, 1982). This is an encouraging result. It indicates that lack of income may not be as important for school achievement as the actual attitudes and behaviour of the child's family life.

Poverty during a child's preschool years appears to have the greatest negative impact. Unfortunately, families with young children are the most likely to be poor because young parents have the lowest-paying jobs or no jobs at all (Bronfenbrenner, McClelland, Wethington, Moen, & Ceci, 1996). And the longer the child is in poverty, the stronger the impact on achievement. For example, even when we take into account parents' education, the chance that children will be retained in grades or placed in special education increases by 2 to 3 percent for every year the children live in poverty (Sherman, 1994).

What are the effects of low socioeconomic status that might explain the lower school achievement of many low-SES students? Many factors maintain a cycle of poverty. Poor health care for

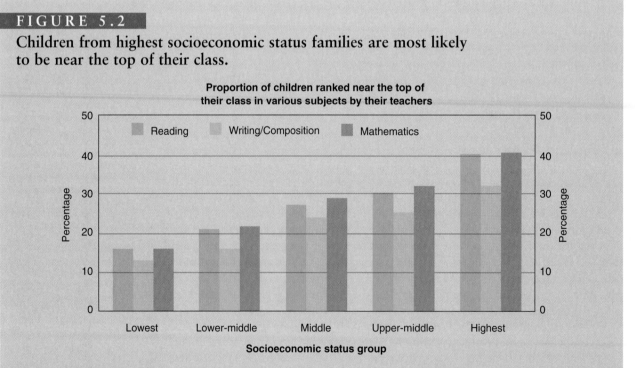

FIGURE 5.2

Children from highest socioeconomic status families are most likely to be near the top of their class.

Source: Adapted from Statistics Canada, *Education Quarterly Review, 1997,* Catalogue no. 81-003, Vol. 4, no. 2, p. 55. From the *National Longitudinal Survey of Children and Youth, 1994–95: Initial Results from the School Component.*

mother and child, limited resources, family stress, interruptions in schooling, exposure to violence, overcrowding, homelessness, discrimination, and other factors lead to school failures, low-paying jobs, and another generation born in poverty. Garcia (1991) and McLoyd (1998) describe other possible explanations. Let's take a closer look at each of them.

Poor Health Care. Families in poverty have less access to good prenatal and infant health care and nutrition. Over half of all adolescent mothers receive no prenatal care at all. Poor mothers and adolescent mothers are more likely to have premature babies, and prematurity is associated with many cognitive and learning problems. Children in poverty are more likely to be exposed to legal drugs (nicotine, alcohol) and illegal drugs (cocaine, heroin) before birth. Children whose mothers take drugs during pregnancy can have problems with organization, attention, and language skills. Children who live in older houses with lead paint and lead-soldered pipes, which exist in many inner-city areas, have greater concentrations of lead in their blood. This lead poisoning is associated with lower school achievement and long-term neurological impairment (McLoyd, 1998).

Low Expectations—Low Self-Esteem. Because low-SES students may wear old clothes, speak ungrammatically, or be less familiar with books and school activities, teachers and other students may assume that these students are not bright. The teacher may avoid calling on them to protect them from the embarrassment of giving wrong answers or because they make the teacher uncomfortable. The children come to believe that they aren't very good at schoolwork (Elrich, 1994).

Learned Helplessness. Low-SES children may be the victims of learned helplessness, described in the previous chapter. That is, low-SES students (or any students who fail continually) may come to believe that doing well in school is impossible for them. Many of their friends and relatives never finished school, so it seems normal to quit. Many of these students drop out of school before earning a high school diploma and go on to experience a life of failure (Friend et al., 1998). Without a high school diploma, these students find few rewards awaiting them in the work world. Many available jobs barely pay a living wage. Low-SES children, particularly those who also encounter racial discrimination, "become convinced that it is difficult if not impossible for them to advance in the mainstream by doing well in school" (Goleman, 1988).

Peer Influences and Resistance Cultures. Some researchers have suggested that low-SES students may become part of a **resistance culture**. To members of this culture, making it in school means selling out and trying to act "middle class." In order to maintain their identity and their status within the group, low-SES students must reject the behaviour that would make them successful in school—studying, cooperating with teachers, even coming to class (Bennett, 1995; Ogbu, 1987, 1997). John Ogbu linked identification in a resistance culture to poor Hispanic American, Native American, and African American groups, but similar reactions have been noted for poor white students both in the United States and in England (Willis, 1977). This is not to say that all low-SES students resist achievement. Adolescents whose parents value academic achievement tend to select friends who also share those values (Berndt & Keefe, 1995) and many young people are high achievers in spite of their economic situation or negative peer influences (O'Connor, 1997).

Tracking. Another explanation for the lower achievement of many low-SES students is that these students experience **tracking** and, therefore, have a different academic socialization—they are actually taught differently (Oakes, 1990). If they are tracked into "low-ability" or "general" classes, they may be taught to memorize and be passive. Their classes may be low-level and teacher-dominated. Middle-class students are more likely to be encouraged to think and create in their classes (Anyon, 1980). When low-SES students receive an inferior education, their

Resistance Culture: Group values and beliefs about refusing to adopt the behaviour and attitudes of the majority culture.

Tracking: Assignment to different classes and academic experiences based on achievement.

Connect & Extend
To other chapters
The concepts of teacher expectation effects and self-fulfilling prophecies are very important in consideration of cultural differences in the classroom. These concepts are discussed fully in **Chapter 10**.

Connect & Extend
To other chapters
The concept of learned helplessness was discussed in Chapter 4 as one explanation for the lower achievement of students with learning disabilities and will be discussed again in **Chapter 10** as a factor influencing motivation.

Connect & Extend
To professional journals
For a discussion of the possible clashes between school cultures and students' home cultures, see Crago, M. B., Eriks-Brophy, A., Pesco, D., & Mcalpine, L. (1997). Culturally based miscommunication in the classroom. *Language, Speech and Hearing Services in Schools, 28,* 245–254.

Connect & Extend
To other chapters
Related information on the effects of ability grouping and tracking appears in **Chapter 4**.

Connect & Extend
To the research
For a description and evaluation of a program for at-risk children that avoids the use of a "pull-out" orientation by using regrouping and tutoring, see Slavin, R. E., Madden, N. A., Karweit, N. L., Livermon, B. J., & Dolan, L. (1990). Success for all: First-year outcomes of a comprehensive plan for reforming urban education. *American Educational Research Journal, 27,* 255–278.

academic skills are inferior and their life chances are limited. In an interview with Marge Scherer (1993), Jonathan Kozol, a well-known author, former teacher, and advocate for American children living in poverty, described the cruel predictive side of tracking:

> [T]racking is so utterly predictive. The little girl who gets shoved into the low reading group in 2nd grade is very likely to be the child who is urged to take cosmetology instead of algebra in the 8th grade, and most likely to be in vocational courses, not college courses, in the 10th grade, if she hasn't dropped out by then (p. 8).

Child-Rearing Styles. The oldest explanation for the academic problems of low-SES children is that their home environment does not give them the head start in school provided by middle- and upper-class homes. Adjustment to school may be more difficult for these children, because schools tend to value and expect the behaviour more often taught in middle-class homes. For example, studies have shown that middle-class mothers talk more; give more verbal guidance; help their children understand the causes of events, make plans, and anticipate consequences; direct their children's attention to the relevant details of a problem; and, rather than impose solutions, encourage children to solve problems themselves (Hess & Shipman, 1965; L. Hoffman, 1984; Willerman, 1979). Contrast these two interactions as a mother works with a child on a puzzle:

> "No, that piece goes here!"

> "What shape is that piece? Can you find a spot that is straight like the piece? Yes, that's straight, but look at the colour. Does the colour match? No? Look again for a straight, red piece. Yes—try that one. Good for you! You finished the corner."

By assisting their children in these ways, mothers are actually following Lev Vygotsky's advice to provide intellectual support, or scaffolding, in the children's zone of proximal development, as we discussed in Chapter 2. You can see how the second approach is more likely to encourage learning concepts (straight, shape, colour, corner, match) and problem solving. Hess and McDevitt (1984) studied mothers and children over an eight-year period and found evidence that this "teaching as opposed to telling" style, often used by middle-class mothers, is related to higher achievement test scores for children aged 4 through 12. These differences in parental interaction styles may account for some of the differences among children from various SES groups.

You should be wary, however, of prejudging families based on their socioeconomic status. Recent research indicates that higher-control parenting is linked to better grades for Asian and African American students (Glasgow, Dornbusch, Troyer, Steinberg, & Ritter, 1997). Parenting that is strict and directive, with clear rules and consequences, combined with high levels of warmth and emotional support, is associated with higher academic achievement for inner-city children (Jarrett, 1995). Differences in cultural values and in the danger of neighbourhoods may make more parental control useful and appropriate.

Home Environment and Resources. Recent research has focused on the home and neighbourhood resources of families—books, computers, libraries, trips, museums, and so on. These home and neighbourhood resources seem to have the greatest impact on children's achievement when school is not in session—during the summer or before students enter school. For example, Entwisle, Alexander, and Olson (1997) found that low- and high-SES students made comparable gains in reading and math when schools were open, but the low-SES students lost ground during summer while the high-SES students continued to improve academically. Another study found that lack of emotional support and cognitive stimulation in the home accounted for one-third to one-half of the disadvantages in verbal, reading, and math skills of poor children in the United States (Korenman, Miller, & Sjaastad, 1995).

When families stress the value of reading and learning, their children are usually at an advantage in school. ▼

Again, not all low-income families lack resources. Many of these families provide rich learning environments for their children. When parents of any SES level support and encourage their children—by reading to them, providing books and educational toys, taking the children to the library, making time and space for learning—the children tend to become better, more enthusiastic readers (Morrow, 1983; Peng & Lee, 1992; Shields, Gordon, & Dupree, 1983). Remember, White (1982) found that the actual behaviour of the parents were more predictive of their children's school achievement than income level or parents' occupation.

CHECKPOINT

Social Class Differences

Review

▷ What is SES?

▷ What is the relationship between SES and school achievement?

Apply

▷ What changes might you need to make in your classroom to help low-SES students succeed?

Ethnic and Racial Differences

Ethnicity is used to refer to "groups that are characterized in terms of a common nationality, culture, or language" (Betancourt & Lopez, 1993, p. 631). This shared sense of identity may be based on geography, religion, race, or language. We all have some ethnic heritage, whether our background is Italian, Jewish, Ukrainian, Hmong, Chinese, Japanese, Iranian, Cree, Inuit, German, Jamaican, or Irish—to name only a few. **Race**, on the other hand, is defined as "a category composed of men and women who share biologically transmitted traits that are defined as socially significant" such as skin colour or hair texture (Macionis, 1991, p. 308). Depending on the traits you measure and the theory you follow, there are between 3 and 300 races. In effect, race is a label people apply to themselves and to others based on appearances. There are no biologically pure races (Betancourt & Lopez, 1993).

Sociologists sometimes use the term **minority group** to label a group of people that receives unequal or discriminatory treatment. Strictly speaking, however, the term refers to a numerical minority compared to the total population. Referring to particular racial or ethnic groups as "minorities" is technically incorrect in some situations, because in certain places the "minority" group is actually the majority—for example, students from Pacific Rim countries in some of the inner-city schools in Vancouver. So the practice of referring to people as "minorities" because of their racial or ethnic heritage has been criticized because it can be misleading.

The Changing Demographics: Cultural Differences

Table 5.1 shows how ethnically diverse Canada has become. In 1997–1998, 194 351 immigrants arrived in Canada. It is estimated that by the year 2016, 20 percent of Canada's population will be members of a visible minority group (Winzer, 1999).

Ricardo Garcia (1991) compares culture to an iceberg. One-third of the iceberg is visible; the rest is hidden and unknown. The visible signs of culture, such as costumes and marriage traditions, represent only a small portion of the differences among cultures. Many of the differences are below the surface—implicit, unstated, even unconscious biases and beliefs. Each cultural group teaches its members certain "lessons" about living (Casanova, 1987; Kagan, 1983).

Cultures differ in rules for conducting interpersonal relationships, for example. In some groups listeners give a slight affirmative nod of the head and perhaps an

Ethnicity: A cultural heritage shared by a group of people.

Race: A group of people who share common biological traits that are seen as self-defining by the people of the group.

Minority Group: A group of people who have been socially disadvantaged—not always a minority in actual numbers.

TABLE 5.1   Recent Immigrants by Country of Last Residence[1]

	1993–1994	1994–1995	1995–1996	1996–1997	1997–1998
	Number of Immigrants				
Total Immigrants	234 457	220 123	216 988	224 870	194 351
Africa	13 460	14 598	14 862	14 226	14 649
Asia	146 629	135 509	133 912	148 198	115 475
India	19 450	15 802	19 511	20 764	17 572
Hong Kong	41 524	39 873	28 500	29 516	12 115
Vietnam	7 799	4 696	3 151	1 899	1 748
Philippines	20 919	16 745	14 165	11 775	7 799
Other Asian Countries	56 937	58 393	68 585	84 244	76 241
Australasia	1 276	969	1 173	1 325	1 345
Europe	40 072	41 110	41 166	37 506	41 225
Great Britain	7 059	6 203	6 299	5 440	4 299
France	3 369	3 506	3 792	2 868	3 400
Germany	1 988	2 093	2 618	2 241	2 030
Netherlands	643	583	820	1 004	660
Greece	402	337	293	291	248
Italy	689	588	709	555	525
Portugal	989	746	837	708	635
Poland	4 791	2 869	2 231	1 867	1 678
Other European Countries	20 142	24 185	23 567	22 532	27 750
United States, West Indies	19 070	15 397	15 465	13 872	12 292
United States	6 705	5 851	5 466	5 462	4 696
West Indies	12 365	9 546	9 999	8 410	7 596
Other North and Central American Countries	4 545	3 212	3 070	3 459	3 166
South America	8 102	8 279	6 534	5 582	5 618
Other Countries	1 303	1 049	806	702	581

From July 1 of one year to June 30 of the next year.

Source: Statistics Canada. CANSIM database, Matrix No. 2, April 15, 1999. Available at **http://cansima.statcan.ca/cgi-win/ CNSMCGI.EXE.table051-006**, Table 051,006.

occasional "uh-huh" to indicate they are listening carefully. But members of other cultures listen without giving acknowledgment, or with eyes downcast, as a sign of respect. In some cultures high-status individuals initiate conversations and ask the questions, and low-status individuals only respond. In other cultures, the pattern is reversed.

Cultural influences are widespread and pervasive. Some psychologists even suggest that culture defines intelligence. For example, physical grace is essential in Balinese social life, so the ability to master physical movements is a mark of intelligence in that culture. Manipulating words and numbers is important in Western societies, so in these cultures such skills are indicators of intelligence (Gardner, 1983).

Cultural Conflicts. The above are just a few areas where cultures may teach different lessons about living. The differences may be obvious, such as holiday customs, or they may be subtle, such as how to get your turn in conversations. The more subtle and unconscious the difference, the more difficult it is to change or even recognize (Casanova, 1987). Cultural conflicts are usually about below-the-surface differences, because when subtle cultural differences meet, misunderstandings are common. Thus, the members of a different culture may be misperceived as rude, slow, or disrespectful.

For example, Erickson and Shultz (1982) studied school counsellors working with students from the same culture and students from different cultures. The researchers found that the culturally different students did not nod and say "uh-huh" as they listened to the counsellors. Not having received this expected feedback, the counsellors assumed that the culturally different students had not understood, and so the counsellors repeated their remarks in simpler form. Again no nod, so the counsellors simplified and repeated once more. When the students were interviewed afterward, many said that the counsellors had made them feel stupid. In fact, the counsellors had decided that these students were not very bright. Neither participant realized that a subtle cultural difference in how to listen was probably to blame for the impressions. In contrast, when students and counsellors shared the same background, discussions proceeded smoothly, without the cycles of simplifying and repeating. The students knew the counsellors' tacit rules for listening, because both counsellor and student had learned from the same teacher—their common culture.

▲ *The visible signs of cultural differences represent only a small portion of the differences among cultures. Many are "below the surface" and have more to do with beliefs and attitudes about life.*

Cultural Compatibility. Not all cultural differences lead to clashes, however. In a recent study by Jim Anderson (1995) at the University of British Columbia, Chinese Canadian, Indo-Canadian, and Euro-Canadian parents were asked to describe five things they were doing to promote the reading and writing development of their children (kindergarten through Grade 2). Parents in all three groups indicated that they read to their children, engaged in some form of direct teaching (e.g., teaching children how to spell, or how to decode difficult words), and tried to teach their children about the value and uses of literacy (e.g., implicitly through modelling, or through direct teaching). What was evident across all responses was that children in all three groups experienced a wide array of literacy activities. What differed among groups was the relative emphasis placed on directly teaching literacy skills versus involving children in naturally occurring literacy events. Anderson suggests that some differences across cultures may not really matter if teachers understand these differences and are willing to build upon them.

Connect & Extend
To the research
In the Chinese tradition, achievement is seen as dependent more on concentration, effort, and persistence, than on talent. Centuries ago, Xu Gan, a revered Chinese scholar, said, "Will is the teacher of study and talent is the follower of study. If a person has no talent, [achievement] is possible. But if a person has no will, it is not worth talking about study" (Hess, Chih-Mei, & McDevitt, 1987, p. 180).

Ethnic and Racial Differences in School Achievement

A major concern in schools is that some ethnic groups consistently achieve below the average for all students. For example, First Nations students are three times more likely to be labelled as learning disabled or as delinquent than are non-Native students, and 40 percent of First Nations students drop out of school between the ages of 14 and 18. Their attendance at university is less than half the national average (Crealock & Bachor, 1995).

Although there are consistent differences among ethnic groups on tests of cognitive abilities, most researchers agree that these differences are mainly the legacy of discrimination, the product of cultural mismatches, or a result of growing up in a low-SES environment. Because many minority-group students are also economically disadvantaged, it is important to separate the effects of these two sets of influences on school achievement. When we compare students from different ethnic and racial groups who are all at the same SES level, their achievement differences diminish (Gleitman, Fridlund, & Reisberg, 1999; Scarr & Carter-Saltzman, 1982).

Connect & Extend
To other chapters
Strategies for motivating minority-group students are discussed in **Chapter 10**.

Working with Families and Communities

How can you get to know the cultures of your students? The Family and Community Partnerships Guidelines give some ideas. Later in this chapter, we will explore other ways to make classrooms compatible with the home cultures of students. First, however, we need to see some of the effects of cultural conflicts and discrimination on student achievement.

FAMILY AND COMMUNITY PARTNERSHIPS

Building Learning Communities

Joyce Epstein (1995) describes six types of family/school/community partnerships. The following guidelines are based on her six categories:

Parenting Partnerships: Help all families establish home environments to support children as students.

Examples

1. Offer workshops, videos, courses, family literacy fairs, and other informational programs to help parents cope with parenting situations that they identify as important.
2. Establish family support programs to assist with nutrition, health, and social services.
3. Find ways to help families share information with the school about the child's cultural background, talents, and needs—learn from the families.

Communication: Design effective forms for school-to-home and home-to-school communication.

Examples

1. Make sure communications fit the needs of families. Provide translations, visual support— whatever is needed to make communication effective.
2. Visit families in their territory after gaining their permission. Don't expect family members to come to school until a trusting relationship is established.
3. Balance messages about problems with communications of accomplishments and positive information.

Volunteering: Recruit and organize parent help and support.

Examples

1. Do an annual postcard survey to identify family talents, interests, times available, and suggestions for improvements.
2. Establish a structure (telephone tree, etc.) to keep all families informed. Make sure families without telephones are included.

3. If possible, set aside a room for volunteer meetings and projects.

Learning at home: Provide information and ideas for families about how to help children with school work and learning activities.

Examples

1. Provide assignment schedules, homework policies, and tips on how to help with school work without doing the work.
2. Get family input into curriculum planning— have idea and activity exchanges.
3. Send home learning packets and enjoyable learning activities, especially over holidays and summers.

Decision-making partnerships: Include families in school decisions, developing family and community leaders and representatives.

Examples

1. Create family advisory committees for the school with parent representatives.
2. Make sure all families are in a network with their representative.

Community partnerships: Identify and integrate resources and services from the community to strengthen school programs, family practices, and student learning and development.

Examples

1. Have students and parents research existing resources—build a database.
2. Identify service projects for students—explore service learning.
3. Identify community members who are school alumni and get them involved in school programs.

Source: From Joyce L. Epstein. "School/Family/Community partnerships: Caring for the children we share." *Phi Delta Kappan, 76,* pp. 704–705. Copyright © 1995 by Phi Delta Kappan. Reprinted by permission of *Phi Delta Kappan* and the author.

The Legacy of Discrimination

When we considered explanations for why low-SES students have trouble in school, we listed the low expectations and biases of teachers and fellow students. This has been the experience of many ethnic-minority students as well. Imagine that the children described below are your own. What would you do?

> Almost forty years ago, in the city of Topeka, Kansas, a minister walked hand in hand with his seven-year-old daughter to an elementary school four blocks from their home. Linda Brown wanted to enroll in the 2nd grade, but the school refused to admit her. Instead, public school officials required her to attend another school two miles away. This meant that she had to walk six blocks to a bus stop, where she sometimes waited half an hour for the bus. In bad weather, Linda Brown would be soaking wet by the time the bus came; one day she became so cold at the bus stop that she walked back home. Why, she asked her parents, could she not attend the school only four blocks away? (Macionis, 1991, p. 307)

In Canada, we built residential schools for First Nations children, who were then educated off the reserve.

> [The schools] were funded by the federal government who inspected the curriculum, and operated by the Christian churches who provided administrators, teachers, and additional funds. . . . The residential schools were not successful academically, vocationally, or socially, but they persisted into the 1960s. . . . In 1961, scholars at the University of British Columbia reported to the government . . . that the schools represented a severe discontinuity in experience for the native youth. Nearly all dropped out before grade 12, few went to university, and many suffered social and emotional difficulties (Crealock & Bachor, 1995, p. 518).

Linda Brown's parents filed a suit against the Board of Education of Topeka and challenged the school segregation policy. The outcome of that landmark case, *Brown v. Topeka Board of Education*, is the basis for the principle of free and appropriate education for *all* students. In contrast, Native communities have increasingly moved to create and control schools for their children, and to inject more and more Native content into their curricula. Increasingly, bands are moving toward full responsibility for the education of children in their communities (Crealock & Bachor, 1995).

Years of research on the effects of desegregation have mostly shown that legally mandated integration is not a quick solution to the detrimental effects of centuries of racial inequality. Too often, minority-group students are resegregated in low-ability tracks even in integrated schools. Simply putting people in the same building does not mean that they will come to respect each other or even that they will experience the same quality of education (Pettigrew, 1998; Schofield, 1991). The University of British Columbia (UBC) and several other institutions across Canada have developed teacher education programs especially for preservice teachers of First Nations ancestry. The hope is that once students in the Native Indian Teacher Education Program (NITEP) at UBC complete their degrees, they will return to their band schools or teach in public schools, and provide high-quality, culturally sensitive instruction to First Nations students.

What is the legacy of unequal treatment and discrimination? Part of the testimony during the *Brown* v. *Topeka Board of Education* case in the 1950s was that when black children in a study were asked to pick the more attractive or smarter doll, they usually chose a white doll and rejected a black one. This test was replicated in 1987 with Native Canadian children and the results were the same (Corenblum & Annis, 1987).

Continuing Prejudice. The word *prejudice* is closely related to the word *prejudge*. **Prejudice** is a rigid and irrational generalization—a prejudgment—about an entire category of people (Macionis, 1994). Prejudice may be positive or negative;

Connect & Extend
To other chapters
The issue of discrimination was considered in Chapter 3 when ethnic pride was discussed.

Nine-year-old Linda Brown, the plaintiff in Brown v. Topeka Board of Education. ▼

Prejudice: Prejudgment, or irrational generalization about an entire category of people.

that is, you can have positive as well as negative irrational beliefs about a group, but the word usually refers to negative attitudes. Prejudice may target people—in particular racial, ethnic, religious, political, geographic, or language groups—or it may be directed toward the gender or sexual orientation of the individual.

The Development of Prejudice. There are many theories about how and why prejudice develops, but "no framework has yet been proposed that provides a complete explanation of prejudice" (Duckitt, 1992, p. 1182). Current explanations of prejudice combine personal and social factors. Extreme prejudice may develop as part of an **authoritarian personality**—a person who rigidly conforms to conventional values and believes that society is naturally competitive, with the "better" people rightly reaping the rewards (Duckitt, 1992, 1994; Macionis, 1994). A related source of prejudice is the human tendency to divide the social world into two categories—*us* and *them* or the *in-group* and the *out-group*. These divisions may be made on the basis of race, religion, gender, age, ethnicity, or even athletic team membership. We tend to see members of the out-group as inferior and different from us, but similar to each other—"they all look alike" (Lambert, 1995). The "White Girls Club" described at the beginning of this chapter is an example of the potential cruelty of in-groups.

But prejudice is more than a personality trait or a tendency to form in-groups: it is also a set of cultural values. Children learn about valued traits and characteristics from their families, friends, teachers, and the world around them. For years, most of the models presented in books, films, television, and advertising were middle- and upper-class European Americans. People of different ethnic and racial backgrounds were seldom the "heroes" (Gerbner, Gross, Signorelli, & Morgan, 1986). Fortunately, this is changing.

Prejudice is difficult to combat because it can be part of our thinking processes. You saw in Chapter 2 that children develop schemes or schemas as they are referred to in Chapter 7—organized bodies of knowledge—about objects, events, and actions. We have schemas that organize our knowledge about drinking from a straw, people we know, the meaning of words, and so on. We can also form schemas about groups of people. If we were to ask you to list the traits most characteristic of university students, politicians, Asian Canadians, athletes, Buddhists, lesbians, or members of Greenpeace, you probably could generate a list. That list would show that you have a **stereotype**—a schema—that organizes what you know about the group (Wyler, 1988).

As with any schema, we use our stereotype to make sense of the world. You will see in Chapter 7 that having a schema allows you to process information more quickly and efficiently, but it also allows you to distort information to make it fit your schema better (Macrae, Milne, & Bodenhausen, 1994). This is the danger in racial and ethnic stereotypes. We notice information that confirms or agrees with our stereotype—our schema—and miss or dismiss information that does not fit. For example, if a juror has a negative stereotype of Asian Canadians and is listening to evidence in the trial of an Asian Canadian, the juror may interpret the evidence more negatively. The juror may actually forget testimony in favour of the defendant but remember more damaging testimony. Information that fits the stereotype is even processed more quickly (Anderson, Klatzky, & Murray, 1990; Baron, 1998).

Continuing Discrimination. Prejudice consists of attitudes, feelings, and beliefs (usually negative) about an entire category of people. **Discrimination** is unequal treatment of particular categories of people. Members of minority groups face prejudice and discrimination in subtle or blatant ways every day. One discouraging finding is that only 4 percent of the scientists, engineers, and mathematicians in the United States are either African American or Hispanic American—whereas more than 20 percent of the total population is from one of these groups. Even though their attitudes toward science and math are more favourable than the

Authoritarian Personality: Rigidly conforming to the belief that society is naturally competitive, with "better" people reaping the rewards.

Stereotype: Schema that organizes knowledge or perceptions about a category.

Discrimination: Treating particular categories of people unequally.

attitudes of white students, black and Hispanic students begin to lose out in science and math as early as elementary school. They are chosen less often for gifted classes and acceleration or enrichment programs. They are more likely to be tracked into "basic skills" classes. As they progress through junior high, high school, and university or college, their paths take them farther and farther out of the pipeline that produces scientists. If they do persist and become scientists or engineers, as a group they—along with women—will still be paid proportionately less than whites for the same work (National Science Foundation, 1988; Oakes, 1990).

Comparable figures for Canadians of diverse ethnicity are not available. However, according to Canadian researchers Sandra Acker and Keith Oatley (1993), the "patterns of participation in mathematics, science, and technology are complex, and . . . the role of schooling in deepening or mitigating disadvantage needs much closer examination" (p. 257). In their article on gender issues in science and technology, Acker and Oatley cite evidence indicating that educational inequality relating to ethnicity, gender, religion, and class background also occurs in Canada.

There is another problem caused by stereotypes and prejudice that can undermine academic achievement—stereotype threat.

Stereotype Threat

When individuals are in situations where they might be expected to conform to a stereotype, they bear an extra emotional and cognitive burden. The burden is the possibility of confirming the stereotype, either in the eyes of others or in their own eyes. Thus when girls are asked to solve complicated mathematics problems, for example, they are at risk of confirming widely held stereotypes that girls are inferior to boys in mathematics. It is not necessary that the individual even believe the stereotype. All that matters is that the person is *aware* of the stereotype and *cares about performing* well enough to disprove its unflattering implications (Aronson, Lustina, Good, Keough, Steele, & Brown, 1999).

What are the results of **stereotype threat**? In the short run, the fear that you might confirm a negative stereotype can induce test anxiety and undermine performance (Aronson, Steele, Salinas, & Lustina, 1999). In the long term, students often develop self-defeating strategies to protect their self-esteem about academics. They withdraw, claim to not care, exert little effort—they *disidentify* or psychologically disengage from success in the domain and claim "math is for nerds" or "school is for losers." Once students define academics as "uncool," it is unlikely they will exert the effort needed for real learning.

Combatting Stereotype Threat. Stereotypes are pervasive and difficult to change. Rather than wait for changes, it may be better to acknowledge that these images exist, at least in the eyes of many, and give students ways of coping with the stereotypes. In Chapter 10 we will discuss test anxiety and how to overcome the negative effects of anxiety. Many of those strategies are appropriate for helping students resist stereotype threat.

Aronson and Fried (in press) demonstrated the powerful effects of changing beliefs about intelligence. In their study, African American and white undergraduates at Stanford University were asked to write letters to "at-risk" middle school students to encourage them to persist in school. Some of the undergraduates were given evidence that intelligence is *improvable* and encouraged to communicate this information to their pen pals. Others were given information about multiple intelligences, but not told that these multiple abilities can be improved. The middle school students were not real, but the process of writing persuasive letters about improving intelligence had a powerful effect. The African American college students, and the white students to a lesser extent, who were encouraged to believe that intelligence can be improved had higher grade-point averages and reported

Stereotype Threat: The extra emotional and cognitive burden that your performance in an academic situation might confirm a stereotype that others hold about you.

Connect & Extend
To the research
The May 1988 issue of *Elementary School Journal* (Vol. 88, No. 5) is entirely devoted to articles about minority students in the schools.

Connect & Extend
To the research
Burrell, L. F., & Christensen, C. P. (1987). Minority students' perceptions of high school: Implications for Canadian school personnel. *Journal of Multicultural Counselling and Development, 15,* 3–15.

CHECKPOINT

Ethnic and Racial Differences

Review

▷ Distinguish between ethnicity and race.

▷ How can ethnicity affect school performance?

▷ Distinguish between prejudice, discrimination, and stereotype threat.

Apply

▷ How could you as a teacher counteract stereotype threat for your students?

greater enjoyment of and engagement in school when contacted at the end of the next school quarter. Thus, believing that intelligence can be improved might inoculate students against stereotype threat.

In the next section we examine another difference that is the source of stereotypes—gender.

*F*emales and Males: Differences in the Classroom

Anita was travelling on a train while proofreading this very page for a previous edition. The conductor stopped beside her seat. He said, "I'm sorry, dear, for interrupting your homework, but do you have a ticket?" He surely would not have made the same comment to the man across the aisle writing on his legal pad. Like racial discrimination, messages of sexism can be subtle. In this section we will examine how men and women are socialized and the role of teachers in providing an equitable education for both sexes.

Gender-Role Identity

Men and women are different. Years of research on personality indicate that men *on average* are more assertive than women and have slightly higher self-esteem. Women are more extroverted, anxious, trusting, and tender-minded (Feingold, 1994). There also appear to be some differences in verbal and spatial abilities between the sexes. The origins and meanings of these differences are hotly debated. Gender-role identity is part of the discussion.

The word *gender* usually refers to judgments about masculinity and femininity, judgments that are influenced by culture and context. In contrast, *sex* refers to biological differences (Deaux, 1993). **Gender-role identity** is the image each individual has of himself or herself as masculine or feminine in characteristics—a part of self-concept. People with a "feminine" identity would rate themselves high on characteristics usually associated with females, such as "sensitive" or "warm," and low on characteristics traditionally associated with males, such as "forceful" and "competitive." Most people see themselves in gender-typed terms, as high on *either* masculine or feminine characteristics. Some children and adults, however, are more **androgynous**—they rate themselves high on *both* masculine and feminine traits. They can be assertive or sensitive, depending on the situation. Having either a masculine or an androgynous identity is associated with higher self-esteem than having a feminine identity, possibly because feminine characteristics are not as valued (Bem, 1974; Boldizar, 1991).

How do gender-role identities develop? It is likely that biology plays a role. Very early, hormones affect activity level and aggression, with boys tending to prefer active, rough, noisy play. Play styles lead young children to prefer same-sex play partners with similar styles, so by age four, children spend three times as much play time with same-sex playmates as with opposite sex playmates and by age six the ratio is 11 to 1 (Benenson, 1993; Maccoby, 1990). Of course, these are averages and individuals do not always fit the average. In addition, many other factors—social and cognitive—affect gender-role identity.

Gender-Role Identity: Beliefs about characteristics and behaviour associated with one gender as opposed to the other.

Androgynous: Having some typically male and some typically female characteristics apparent in one individual.

Both parents play more roughly and vigorously with sons than they do with daughters. Parents tend to touch male infants more at first; later, they keep male toddlers at a greater distance than females (Jacklin, DiPietro, & Maccoby, 1984). Parents are more likely to react positively to assertive behaviour on the part of their sons and emotional sensitivity in their daughters (Fagot & Hagan, 1991; Lytton & Romney, 1991). Through their interactions with family, peers, teachers, and the environment in general, children begin to form **gender schemas**, or organized networks of knowledge about what it means to be male or female (see Figure 5.3, below.). These schemas help the children make sense of the world and guide their behaviour. So a young girl whose schema for "girls" includes "girls play with dolls and not with trucks" or "girls can't be scientists" will pay attention to, remember, and interact more with dolls than trucks, and she may avoid science activities (Liben & Signorella, 1993; Martin & Little, 1990).

Gender-Role Stereotyping in the Preschool Years

Different treatment of the sexes and gender-role stereotyping continue in early childhood. Researchers have found that boys are given more freedom to roam the neighbourhood, and they are not protected for as long a time as girls from potentially dangerous activities such as playing with sharp scissors or crossing the street alone. Parents quickly come to the aid of their daughters, but are more likely to insist that their sons handle problems themselves (Block, 1983; Fagot, Hagan, Leinbach, & Kronsberg, 1985). Thus, independence and initiative seem to be encouraged more in boys than in girls.

Many student teachers are surprised when they hear young children talk about gender roles. Even in this era of great progress toward equal opportunity of the sexes, a preschool girl is more likely to tell you she wants to become a secretary than to say she wants to be an engineer. After she had given a lecture on the dangers of gender stereotyping in schools, a professor brought her young daughter to her college class. The students asked the little girl, "What do you want to be when you grow up?" The child immediately replied, "A doctor," and her professor/mother

▲ *Gender schemas often have become barriers to success when girls and boys avoid activities not associated with their gender. Recognizing these potential barriers has allowed children's choices to become less gender-driven.*

Connect & Extend
To the research
Lytton, H., & Romney, D. M. (1991). Parents' sex-related differential socialization of boys and girls: A meta-analysis. *Psychological Bulletin, 109,* 267–296.

FIGURE 5.3

Gender Schema Theory
According to *gender schema theory,* children and adolescents use gender as an organizing theme to classify and understand their perceptions about the world.

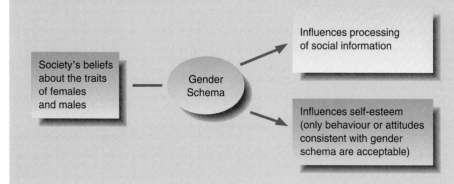

Gender Schemas: Organized networks of knowledge about what it means to be male or female.

beamed with pride. Then the girl whispered to the students in the front row, "I really want to be a nurse, but my Mommy won't let me." Actually, this is a common reaction for young children. Preschoolers tend to have more stereotyped notions of sex roles than older children, and all ages seem to have more rigid and traditional ideas about male occupations than about what females do (Martin, 1989).

Connect & Extend
To the research
Purcell, P., & Stewart, L. (1990).
Dick and Jane in 1989. *Sex Roles,
22*, 177–185. This study replicates
analyses of textbooks and children's books conducted in the
1970s. *Focus Question:* What
evidence of sexism, if any,
remains in texts today?

Gender Bias in the Curriculum. During the elementary school years, children continue to learn about what it means to be male or female. Unfortunately, schools often foster these **gender biases** in a number of ways. Most of the textbooks produced for the early grades before 1970 portrayed both males and females in sexually stereotyped roles. In a study of 2760 stories in 134 books from 16 publishers, a group called *Women on Words and Images* (1975) found that there were four times more stories about male characters than about females. Females tended to be shown in the home, behaving passively and expressing fear or incompetence. Males were usually more dominant and adventurous; they often rescued the females.

In recent years textbook publishers have recognized these problems to some extent and established guidelines to prevent them. It still makes sense to check your teaching materials for such stereotypes, however. When Purcell and Stewart (1990) used the same design as *Women on Words and Images* to analyze 62 elementary readers, they found that the numbers of male and female characters were about equal. Girls were shown in a wide range of activities, but were still portrayed as more helpless than boys. Despite new publishers' guidelines, problems have not disappeared entirely. When Scott O'Dell was looking for a publisher for his *Island of the Blue Dolphins*, he was told by several editors that he needed to make a small change—turn this story of a girl's courageous fight for survival into a story about a boy. O'Dell refused, and the book went on to win a Newbery Award for children's literature (Sadker, Sadker, & Klein, 1991).

Sex Discrimination in Classrooms. There has been quite a bit of research on teachers' treatment of male and female students. One of the best-documented findings of the past 25 years is that teachers interact more with boys than with girls. This is true from preschool to university or college. Teachers ask more questions of males, give males more feedback (praise, criticism, and correction), and give more specific and valuable comments to boys. As girls move through the grades,

Gender Biases: Different views of males and females, often favouring one gender over the other.

they have less and less to say. By the time students reach college, men are twice as likely to initiate comments as women (Bailey, 1993; Sadker & Sadker, 1994, 1986b; Serbin & O'Leary, 1975; Wingate, 1986). The effect of these differences is that from preschool through college, girls, on the average, receive 1800 fewer hours of attention and instruction than boys (Sadker, Sadker, & Klein, 1991). Of course, these differences are not evenly distributed. Some boys, generally high-achieving white students, receive more than their share. Minority-group boys, like girls, tend to receive much less attention from the teacher.

The imbalances of teacher attention given to boys and girls are particularly dramatic in science classes. In one study, boys were questioned on the subject matter 80 percent more often than girls (Baker, 1986). Boys also dominate the use of equipment in science labs, often dismantling the apparatus before the girls in the class have a chance to perform the experiments (Rennie & Parker, 1987).

Stereotypes are perpetuated in many ways, some obvious, some subtle. Guidance counsellors, parents, and teachers often do not protest at all when a bright girl says she doesn't want to take any more math or science courses, but when a boy of the same ability wants to forget about math or science, they will object. In these subtle ways, students' stereotyped expectations for themselves can be reinforced (Sadker & Sadker, 1994).

Gender Differences in Mental Abilities

Most studies find that from infancy through the preschool years there are few differences between boys and girls in overall mental and motor development or in specific abilities. During the school years and beyond, psychologists find no differences in general intelligence on the standard measures, but these tests have been designed and standardized to minimize gender differences. However, scores on some tests of specific abilities show gender differences. In the concluding article of a special issue on gender differences in cognition in the journal *Learning and Individual Differences*, Diane Halpern (1996) summarized the research:

> The data presented here and in other sources clearly show that there are some areas of cognition in which there are no male-female differences, others where the differences are small, and others where the differences are large, some favoring females and some favoring males. The "on-the-average" differences show that females excel in reading comprehension, production of written and oral language, and computation (to name a few); whereas the constellation of mathematical, mechanical, and visual information processing is often accomplished either more accurately or more quickly by males. In addition we know that there is much overlap between the sexes in these ability areas, and everyone can improve in any area with appropriate education and practice. (p. 75)

Also, the scores of males tend to be more variable in general, so there are more males than females with very high *and* very low scores on tests (Willingham & Cole, 1997).

There is a caution, however. In most studies of gender differences, race and socioeconomic status are not taken into account. When racial groups are studied separately, differences between the sexes appear to be more complicated. For example, American researchers (Grossman & Grossman, 1994; Yee, 1992) found that African American females outperformed African American males in high school mathematics, and that there is little or no difference in the performance of Asian American girls and boys in math or science.

Gender and Mathematics. Two University of Alberta researchers (Randhawa & Randhawa, 1993) have pointed to the possibility of processing differences to explain gender differences in math achievement. For example, in their examination of 253 Grade 10 students, the researchers found that reading comprehension was a significant predictor of success at solving problems for boys, but not for girls. Also,

Connect & Extend
To the research
Are females socialized to select or not select scientific careers? See Ware, N. C., & Lee, V. E. (1988). Sex differences in choice of college student majors. *American Educational Research Journal, 25*, 593–614.
Brief abstract: The process of choosing a scientific major was examined in a nationally representative sample of male and female college students of above-average ability in the United States. Women who were attending a four-year college, who reported having been influenced by high school teachers and guidance counsellors in making plans for college, and who placed a high priority upon aspects of their future family and personal lives were less likely to major in science than their female peers. High socioeconomic status, positive assessments of their high schools, and attending a four-year college predicted science majoring for men.

Connect & Extend
To the research
Linn, M. C., & Hyde, J. S. (1989). Gender, mathematics, and science. *Educational Researcher, 18*, 17–27.

Connect & Extend
To professional journals
See Latham, A. S. (1998). Gender differences on assessments. *Educational Leadership, 55*(4), 88–89.

Connect & Extend
To the research
In contrast to the Maccoby and Jacklin (1974) findings of almost three decades ago, recent findings are showing decreasing achievement differences between males and females, even in mathematics. Articles on this subject include Linn, M. C., & Hyde, J. S. (1989). Gender, mathematics, and science. *Educational Researcher, 118*, 17–28. Also Marsh, H. W. (1989). Sex differences in development of verbal and mathematics constructs: The high school and beyond study. *American Educational Research Journal, 26*, 191–225. Differences persist between academically gifted males and females in mathematics reasoning, See Mills, C. J., Ablard, K. E., & Stumpf, H. (1993). Gender differences in academically talented young students' mathematical reasoning: Patterns across age and subskills. *Journal of Educational Psychology, 85*, 340–346.

they found differences that favoured boys with regard to the processes involved in math computation, and dealing with math concepts and problem solving.

One controversial question is whether boys are better in mathematics because they take more math courses than girls. There appear to be few or no differences between boys and girls in math achievement at the beginning of high school (although differences show up earlier for academically gifted students), but during high school girls take fewer math courses (Pallas & Alexander, 1983). As soon as mathematics courses become optional, many girls avoid them. In British Columbia, females made up less than half the course enrolment in Grade 11 and Grade 12 statistics, algebra, and geometry classes in 1990 (Canadian Teachers' Federation & Ontario Women's Directorate, 1992). Similar trends have been observed in other regions of the country. The result is that Canadian women are under-represented in occupations that require knowledge of math. According to Acker and Oatley (1993), women make up only 7 percent of the workforce in fields such as architecture and engineering.

Another controversial question is whether teachers are responsible, in part, for the lower participation of girls in math and science studies. Acker and Oatley (1993) cite a Canadian survey of 7000 science teachers in the early 1980s that found teachers to be unenthusiastic about attending to the special needs of girls. Also there is some evidence that teachers treat girls and boys differently in mathematics classes. For example, some elementary school teachers spend more academic time with boys in math and with girls in reading. In one study, high school geometry teachers directed most of their questions to boys, even though the girls asked questions and volunteered answers more often. Several researchers have found that some teachers tend to accept wrong answers from girls, saying, in effect, "Well, at least you tried." But when boys give the wrong answer, the teachers are more likely to say, "Try harder! You can figure this out." These messages, repeated time and again, can convince girls that they just aren't cut out for mathematics (Girls' math achievement, 1986; Horgan, 1995).

CHECKPOINT

Females and Males: Differences in the Classroom

Review

▶ What is gender-role identity?

▶ How do gender-role identities develop?

▶ Are there gender differences in cognitive abilities?

Apply

▶ How can teachers promote gender equity in classrooms?

Connect & Extend
To the research
For a lively debate on the terminology of gender and sex, see the March 1993 issue of *Psychological Science*.

The historical disparity between male and female performance in science and technical, or so-called "hard" subjects, has diminished over the past few decades. However, teachers must monitor classroom practices to encourage all students equally in all subjects. ▶

Eliminating Gender Bias

We don't know what the situation would be like if all students, boys and girls, received appropriate instruction and encouragement in math. Acker and Oatley (1993) describe several initiatives concerned with promoting gender equity in the fields of math, science, and technology. For example, *The Better Idea Book*, compiled by the Canadian Teachers' Federation (1992), includes a comprehensive list of resource materials for teachers. Each year, Simon Fraser University in British Columbia hosts a one-day conference called "Women Do Math." Young women in Grades 9 and 10 who attend the conference are involved in workshops and discussions that stress math-related career opportunities for women. In Ontario, some school boards have organized girls-only math classes, so that teachers can tailor curricula and teaching methods to better suit girls' interests and learning preferences. According to Acker and Oatley, the keys to these successful innovations are the following: highly motivated teachers, a strong academic emphasis, the use of multiple teaching strategies, and an appreciation of the social context into which these initiatives are introduced. The Guidelines provide additional ideas about avoiding sexism in your teaching. Some are taken from Rop (1997/1998).

Connect & Extend
To professional journals
Sadker, D. (1998). Gender equity: Still knocking at the classroom door. *Educational Leadership, 56*(7), 22–27.

Connect & Extend
To real life
Do you consider commercials an influence on the development of gender roles?

GUIDELINES

Avoiding Sexism in Teaching

Check to see if textbooks and other materials you are using present an honest view of the options open to both males and females.

Examples

1. Are both males and females portrayed in traditional and non-traditional roles at work, at leisure, and at home?
2. Discuss your analyses with students, and ask them to help you find gender-role biases in other materials—magazine advertising, TV programs, news reporting, for example.

Watch for any unintended biases in your own classroom practices.

Examples

1. Do you group students by gender for certain activities? Is the grouping appropriate?
2. Do you call on one gender or the other for certain answers—boys for math and girls for poetry, for example?

Look for ways in which your school may be limiting the options open to male or female students.

Examples

1. What advice is given by guidance counsellors to students in course and career decisions?
2. Is there a good sports program for both girls and boys?
3. Are girls asked to take advanced placement courses in science and mathematics? Boys in English and foreign languages?

Use gender-free language as much as possible.

Examples

1. Do you speak of "police officer" and "letter carrier" instead of "policeman" and "mailman"?
2. Do you name a committee "head" instead of a "chairman"?

Provide role models.

Examples

1. Assign professional journal articles written by female research scientists or mathematicians.
2. Have recent female graduates who are majoring in science, math, engineering, or other technical fields come to class to talk about university.
3. Create electronic mentoring programs for both male and female students to connect them with adults working in areas of interest to the students.

Make sure all students have a chance to do complex, technical work.

Examples

1. Experiment with same-sex lab groups so girls do not always end up as the secretaries, boys as the technicians.
2. Rotate jobs in groups or randomly assign responsibilities.

Language Differences in the Classroom

In the classroom, quite a bit happens through language. Communication is at the heart of teaching, and culture affects communication. In this section, we will examine issues related to being bilingual (or multilingual).

Bilingualism

Connect & Extend
To the research
Safty, A. (1988). French immersion and the making of bilingual society: A critical review and discussion. *Canadian Journal of Education, 13,* 243–262.

Abstract
This article reviews the literature regarding French-language immersion and bilingualism. Immersion requires the exclusive use of the target language as a medium of instruction at the early grade levels. Research indicates a positive correlation between bilingualism and linguistic skills in one's first language on the one hand, and cognitive and intellectual development on the other. Bilingualism is found to provide the child with certain neurolinguistics skills that help to develop other cognitive domains. French immersion is believed to be more effective than traditional second-language teaching approaches.

Wright, S. C., Taylor, D. M., & Macarthur, J. (2000). Subtractive bilingualism and the survival of the Inuit language: Heritage versus second language education. *Journal of Educational Psychology, 92,* 63–84.

Abstract
A longitudinal study examined the impact of early heritage- and second-language education on heritage- and second-language development among Inuit, white, and mixed-heritage (Inuit/white) children. Children in an arctic community were tested in English, French, and Inuktitut at the beginning and end of each of the first three school years. Compared with Inuit in heritage-language and mixed-heritage children in a second language, Inuit in second-language classes (English or French) showed poorer heritage-language skills and poorer second-language acquisition. Conversely, Inuit children in Inuktitut classes showed heritage-language skills equal to or better than mixed-heritage children and whites educated in their heritage languages. Findings support claims that early instruction exclusively in a societally dominant language can lead to subtractive bilingualism among minority-language children, and that heritage-language education may reduce this subtractive process.

Bilingualism is a topic that sparks heated debate and touches many emotions. One reason is the changing demographics discussed earlier in this chapter. According to the 1996 census, 2 556 830 people in Canada speak a language other than English or French. In Alberta, more than 1000 children who arrive at school each year are unable to speak English (Friend et al., 1998). In some British Columbia schools, more than half the students enrolled are English learners, and many are unfamiliar with the Roman alphabet or with Western traditions, history, or lifestyles (British Columbia Ministry of Education, 1998). As a result, teachers need to focus on orienting these students to BC society, as well as teaching them English. Some students are refugees from wartorn nations and need counselling support to adapt to school and life in Canada.

Two terms that you will see associated with bilingualism are **English as a second language (ESL)**, describing classes for students whose primary language is not English, and **limited English proficiency (LEP)**, referring to students whose English skills are limited.

What Does Bilingualism Mean? There are disagreements about the meaning of bilingualism. Some definitions focus exclusively on a language-based meaning: bilingual people speak two languages. But this limited definition minimizes the significant relationship between language and culture. Consider the following descriptions of two Grade 6 students who had been in the United States for two years:

> . . . there was the eager Ting, a child of Asian ancestry, who was quite simply indomitable; she treated her halting search for English words as, at worst, an inconvenience. She had an impressive repertoire of strategies, including the dogged pursuit of clarity. She constantly monitored for sense making, striving to make connections between the concepts to which the class was being introduced and the ideas with which she was familiar.

> Then there was the reticent Manuel, a child of Latino ancestry . . . Manuel's responses in oral and written contexts, small- and large-group configurations, were sparse. Few activities or roles within the small-group problem solving contexts engaged him productively. He certainly was not a behavior problem; in fact, I would have welcomed a bit of acting out in the service of his establishing his place in this community. (Palincsar, 1996, p. 221)

Palincsar goes on to confirm what we already suspect—Ting made substantial academic gains while "Manuel's growth was modest." According to Jim Cummins (1989), at the University of Toronto, research regarding minority students' underachievement has consistently shown that those students who perform poorly in school and are over-represented in special education programs are members of minority groups who have historically been discriminated against by the "dominant" group. Furthermore, when minority students from these groups immigrate relatively late in their school experience (after the age of 10), their academic prospects are better. Cummins attributes this difference to the fact that the latecomers have not experienced the devaluation of their cultural identity in their home country. He claims that the extent to which students' language and culture are incorporated into the school program is a significant predictor of academic success, and appears to have no negative impact on their learning English.

Becoming Bilingual. Higher degrees of bilingualism are correlated with increased cognitive abilities in such areas as concept formation, creativity, knowledge of the workings of language, and cognitive flexibility. These findings seem to hold as long as there is no stigma attached to being bilingual and as long as students are not expected to abandon their first language to learn English (Galambos & Goldin-Meadow, 1990; Garcia, 1992; Hakuta & Garcia, 1989; Ricciardelli, 1992).

Learning a second language does not interfere with understanding in the first language. In fact, Cummins argues that the more proficient the speaker is in the first language, the faster she or he will master a second language (1984, 1994). If children learn two languages simultaneously as toddlers, there is a period between ages two and three when they progress more slowly because they have not yet figured out that they are learning two different languages. They may mix up the grammar of the two. But researchers believe that by age four, if they have enough exposure to both languages, they get things straight and speak as well as native **monolinguals** (Baker, 1993; Reich, 1986). The earlier we learn a second language, the more our pronunciation is near-native. After adolescence it is difficult to learn to speak a new language without an accent (Anderson & Graham, 1994).

Proficiency in a second language has two separate aspects: face-to-face communication (known as "contextualized language skills") and academic uses of language such as reading and doing grammar exercises ("decontextualized language skills") (Snow, 1987). It takes students about two to three years in a good-quality program to be able to communicate face-to-face in a second language, but mastering decontextualized, academic language skills in the new language takes five to seven years. So students who seem in conversation to "know" a second language may still have great difficulty with complex school work in that language (Cummins, 1994; Ovando, 1989).

Bilingual Education. Virtually everyone agrees that all citizens should learn the official language of their country. But when and how should instruction in that language begin? Here the debate is bitter at times. Is it better to teach non-English-speaking and limited-English-proficiency students to read first in their native language or to begin reading instruction in English? Do these children need some oral lessons in English before reading instruction can be effective? Should other subjects, such as mathematics and social studies, be taught in the primary (home) language until the children are fluent in English? On these questions there are two basic positions, which have given rise to two contrasting teaching approaches, one that focuses on making the *transition* to English as quickly as possible and one that

Connect & Extend
To professional journals
Menkart, D. J. (1999). Deepening the meaning of heritage months. *Educational Leadership, 56*(7), 19–21. This article discusses how to get past foods and festivals to increase students' understandings of heritage.

Connect & Extend
To real life
Is the increasing cultural plurality of Canada making the learning of foreign languages more important in Canadian schools than was the case in the past?

Connect & Extend
To the research
Filmore, L. W., & Valadez, C. (1986). Teaching bilingual learners. In M. Wittrock (Ed.), *Handbook of research on teaching* (pp. 648–685). New York: Macmillan.

Connect & Extend
To professional journals
Thomas, W. P., & Collier, V. P. (1998). Two languages are better than one. *Educational Leadership, 55*(4), 23–27. This article makes the case that native and non-native speakers of English benefit greatly from learning together in two languages.

◀ *Teachers in today's bilingual classrooms must help students learn skills to communicate in more than one culture.*

Bilingualism: The ability to speak two languages fluently.

English as a Second Language (ESL): Designation for programs and classes to teach English to students who are not native speakers of English.

Limited English Proficiency (LEP): Descriptive term for students who have limited mastery of English.

Monolinguals: Individuals who speak only one language.

How Should English Be Taught?

According to Jim Cummins (1994) at the University of Toronto, students who are learning English (or French) as a second language typically learn conversational skills in two years. However, being able to use English effectively in academic contexts may take between five and seven years. Supporting students' intellectual development while they make the transition to speaking English is a difficult problem for teachers. Should students receive instruction in their native languages, or should they be immersed in the new language they are learning?

▶ **POINT** *Until students are reasonably fluent in English, they should receive instruction in their native languages.*

Proponents of *native language maintenance instruction* argue that students who are forced to learn math or science in an unfamiliar language are bound to have difficulties (Gersten & Woodward, 1994; Goldenberg, 1996; Hakuta & Garcia, 1989). Imagine sitting in classrooms where the language of instruction makes the content to be learned incomprehensible. Alternatively, imagine being given a watered-down version of the content in simplified language so you can understand. Either way, your cognitive growth would be constrained. Also, you might become frustrated because you couldn't understand the teacher or communicate your thoughts, you might participate less in class, and your grades would likely decline, along with your sense of cultural validation (Gersten, 1996a).

In contrast, imagine being able to study subject matter in your first language while developing proficiency in English. According to some language learning experts, students who acquire complex academic information and skills in their native languages later apply this knowledge to subjects taught in English once their English-language skills have caught up (Gersten & Woodward, 1994; Krashen, 1981). These students don't suffer the frustration and alienation of not being able to participate fully in school. Furthermore, they maintain proficiency in their first languages, and being proficient in more than one language can be an asset in the working world.

◀ **COUNTERPOINT** *Students learning a language ought to be immersed in that language.*

Proponents of the *transmission approach* to language learning fear that valuable learning time is lost when students are taught in their native languages (Krashen, 1981). They argue that the more students are exposed to a language, the faster they will learn it. Also, they argue that bilingual education diminishes the incentive to acquire proficiency in the second language.

Bilingual classes . . . weaken [non-English-speaking students'] drive to communicate with others in English. If you have ever taught a class of immigrants, you know that only the most highly motivated will consistently respond in English if they know you speak their native language (Krashen, 1981, p. 53).

Many immigrant parents fear bilingual classes will limit their children's chances of economic and social success in the new country. "They do not believe educators who tell them their children will learn to speak English better in bilingual classes" (Krashen, 1981, p. 54).

Perhaps the most compelling argument against the native language maintenance approach to instruction is that it is just not practical in many Canadian school districts. For example, in Vancouver School District, BC, the student population speaks more than 100 languages. Organizing classes and finding teachers who speak these different languages is an insurmountable task, especially when the languages represented in and across schools change every year.

attempts to *maintain* or improve the native language and use the native language as the primary teaching language until English skills are more fully developed. The positions are described more fully in the following Point/Counterpoint.

The transition approach to learning English or French is the most common practice in Canadian schools. However, ministries and school boards are recognizing the educational, social, and economic benefits of maintaining students' first languages. They are encouraging parents and children to continue using their first languages outside the school setting, even to learn to read and write in those languages. In Ontario, the government funds native-language instruction and international-languages instruction, sometimes referred to as **Heritage Language Programs**. Through these programs, students have opportunities to receive some portion of instruction in their native languages. According to Ontario's Ministry of Education,

Heritage Language Programs: Programs that offer opportunities for students to receive instruction in their own language.

. . . it is crucial to value the first (non-English/non-French) language rather than giving the impression that it and, by extension, the student's native culture are unimportant or disposable. Support for the heritage (international) languages helps all students develop a stronger identity and appreciate the validity of all cultures and languages (Ontario Ministry of Education and Training, 1999, p. 5).

Research on Bilingual Programs. It is difficult to separate politics from practice in the debate about bilingual education. It is clear that high-quality bilingual education programs can have positive results. Students improve in the subjects that are taught in their native language, in their mastery of English, and in self-esteem as well (Crawford, 1997; Hakuta & Gould, 1987; Wright & Taylor, 1995). Similarly, English as a second language (ESL) programs seem to have positive effects on reading comprehension (Fitzgerald, 1995). However, attention today is shifting from debate about general approaches to a focus on effective teaching strategies. As you will see many times in this book, a combination of clarity of learning goals and direct instruction in needed skills—including learning strategies and tactics, teacher- or peer-guided practice leading to independent practice, authentic and engaging tasks, opportunities for interaction and conversation that are academically focused, and warm encouragement from the teacher—seems to be effective (Chamot & O'Malley, 1996; Gersten, 1996b; Goldenberg, 1996). Table 5.2 is a set of constructs for promoting learning and

---

TABLE 5.2   Ideas for Promoting Learning and Language Acquisition

Effective teaching for students in bilingual and ESL classrooms combines many strategies—direct instruction, mediation, coaching, feedback, modelling, encouragement, challenge, and authentic activities.

1. Structures, frameworks, scaffolds, and strategies
   - Provide support to students by "thinking aloud," building on and clarifying input of students
   - Use visual organizers, story maps, or other aids to help students organize and relate information
2. Relevant background knowledge and key vocabulary concepts
   - Provide adequate background knowledge to students and informally assess whether students have background knowledge
   - Focus on key vocabulary words and use consistent language
   - Incorporate students' primary language meaningfully
3. Mediation/feedback
   - Give feedback that focuses on meaning, not grammar, syntax, or pronunciation
   - Give frequent and comprehensible feedback
   - Provide students with prompts or strategies
   - Ask questions that press students to clarify or expand on initial statements
   - Provide activities and tasks that students can complete
   - Indicate to students when they are successful
   - Assign activities that are reasonable, avoiding undue frustration
   - Allow use of native language responses (when context is appropriate)
   - Be sensitive to common problems in second-language acquisition
4. Involvement
   - Ensure active involvement of all students, including low-performing students
   - Foster extended discourse
5. Challenge
   - Implicit (cognitive challenge, use of higher-order questions)
   - Explicit (high but reasonable expectations)
6. Respect for—and responsiveness to—cultural and personal diversity
   - Show respect for students as individuals, respond to things students say, show respect for culture and family, and possess knowledge of cultural diversity
   - Incorporate students' experiences into writing and language arts activities
   - Link content to students' lives and experiences to enhance understanding
   - View diversity as an asset, reject cultural deficit notions

Source: From R. Gersten (1996). Literacy instruction for language minority students: The transition years. *The Elementary School Journal, 96,* pp. 241–242. Copyright © 1996. Adapted by permission of the University of Chicago Press.

CHECKPOINT

Language Differences in the Classroom

Review

▷ What are the origins of language differences in the classroom?

▷ What is bilingual education?

Apply

▷ How can teachers accommodate different languages in their classrooms?

language acquisition that capture many of these ideas for effective instruction. We will revisit many of these ideas in later chapters.

We have dealt with a wide range of differences in this chapter. How can teachers provide an appropriate education for all their students? One response is to make the classroom compatible with the students' cultural heritage. Such a classroom is described as being culturally compatible.

Creating Culturally Compatible Classrooms

The goal of creating **culturally compatible classrooms** is to eliminate racism, sexism, and ethnic prejudice while providing equal educational opportunities for all students. According to Roland Tharp (1989), "two decades of data on cultural issues in classroom interactions and school outcomes have accumulated. When schools are changed, children's experiences and achievement also change" (p. 349). Tharp outlines several dimensions of classrooms that can be tailored to fit the needs of students. These dimensions include social organization, attention to how students approach learning, and sociolinguistics.

Social Organization

Tharp states that "a central task of educational design is to make the organization of teaching, learning, and performance compatible with the social structures in which students are most productive, engaged, and likely to learn" (p. 350). Social structure or social organization in this context means the ways people interact to accomplish a particular goal. For example, the social organization of Hawaiian society depends heavily on collaboration and cooperation. Children play together in groups of friends and siblings, with older children often caring for the younger ones. When cooperative work groups of four or five boys and girls were established in Hawaiian classrooms, student learning and participation improved. The teacher worked intensively with one group while the children in the remaining groups helped each other. Native students, especially if they have been raised with traditional values, view time as a flexible concept and don't like to be put on the spot (Crealock & Bachor, 1995). They believe that things will happen when the time is right, and that there is no need to perform until they are ready to answer. Furthermore, these students may feel awkward when they are rewarded for their performance, as many Native cultures value non-competitiveness and emotional restraint.

Approaches to Learning

Some research studies have found ethnic-group differences concerning beliefs about, and approaches to, learning. Two examples follow.

New Canadians. Jim Anderson and Lee Gunderson (1997), at the University of British Columbia, interviewed more than 60 parents and 100 students from Chinese, Iranian, and Indo-Canadian communities, and compared their beliefs and preferences concerning the teaching and learning of literate behaviour. Many

Connect & Extend
To your teaching
Barba, R. H. (1998). *Science in the multicultural classroom.* Toronto: Allyn & Bacon.
Wallace, J., & Harper, H. (1998). *Taking action: Reworking gender in school contexts.* Toronto: OADE/OWD.
Lipkin, A. (1999). *Understanding homosexuality, changing schools: A text for teachers, counselors, and administrators.* Boulder, CO: Westview Press.

Culturally Compatible Classrooms: Classrooms in which procedures, rules, grouping strategies, attitudes, and teaching methods do not cause conflicts with the students' culturally influenced ways of learning and interacting.

North American teachers support an emergent model of reading, believing that learning to read and write are imprecise processes, that approximation and invention are part of the learning process, and that adult standards for correctness and conventions will not be met in the early stages of reading and writing. This was not the view of many of the parents Anderson and Gunderson interviewed. These parents believed that accuracy and precision were important from the beginning. They criticized practices such as invented spelling and recognizing children's early attempts at reading—"It's not real reading," they said. Parents from these communities also believed that teachers should engage in more direct instruction, and that students should talk less, receive more homework, and be asked to memorize more facts.

These cultural values also were evident in students' behaviour. Consider Alice's preferences for reading and writing activities:

> Alice was an extraordinary third grader. She was an immigrant who in two years had become fluent in English; her intelligence had qualified her as an intellectually gifted student. Alice was most content at school when she was filling out pages in a workbook. She and her family believed that answering questions and filling in bubbles in multiple-choice workbook items were essential learning activities that represented the basic goal of literacy learning: to master a set of discrete skills (Anderson & Gunderson, 1997, p. 514).

Anderson and Gunderson urge teachers to recognize that there are many ways to learn reading and writing, and to encourage parents to support their children's literacy learning in ways that are familiar to them. At the same time, teachers can help parents to understand our more meaning-based view of reading and writing through regular communication and involvement in the classroom. Also, teachers can engage students in a wide range of literacy activities in the classroom, including some that build on what students experience at home.

Native Canadians.
Historically, oral communication has been the primary method of teaching among Native groups, resulting in less attention to written forms of communication (Crealock & Bachor, 1995). In fact, some Aboriginal languages are only now being coded in a manner that will standardize their written forms and make them available to Native and non-Native Canadians. Traditionally, Natives have not written books for children, and storybook reading has not been valued as a preschool activity to the extent it is in most white families. This may put First Nations students at a disadvantage, since storybook reading is considered instrumental to building understandings and skills essential for reading success in school (International Reading Association & National Association for the Education of Young Children, 1998). Furthermore, Native cultures train and reward visual-motor and spatial skills while the dominant culture trains and rewards verbal skills (Crealock & Bachor, 1995). According to Crealock and Bachor, many Native students have above-average spatial skills and high mechanical aptitude but never have these strengths reinforced in school. Ensuring these students have opportunities to engage in activities such as map-making, or making patterns or clothes, is one way to recognize these strengths.

Caveat.
We need to be careful about identifying ethnic-group differences concerning approaches to, and preferences for, learning. It is easy to move from the notion of "difference" to the idea of "deficit." Information about what's typical for an ethnic group can become just one more basis for stereotyping. We have included this information because we believe that, used sensibly, it can help you better understand your students.

It is dangerous and incorrect, however, to assume that every individual in a group shares the same learning style. The best advice for teachers is to be sensitive to individual differences in all your students and to make available alternative paths to learning. Never prejudge how a student will learn best on the basis of assumptions about the student's ethnicity or race. Get to know the individual.

Connect & Extend
To professional journals
O'Neil, J. (1990a). Link between style, culture proves divisive. *Educational Leadership, 48*(2), 8. *Focus Question:* Why do some educators argue against linking learning styles to cultural differences?

One goal of creating culturally compatible classrooms is to encourage mutual acceptance and respect among students from all backgrounds. ▶

Sociolinguistics

Connect & Extend
To the research
See Cultural differences in the classroom (1988, March). *Harvard Education Letter, 2(2),* 1–4. This article describes the KEEP program and Shirley Heath's project in the Piedmont Carolinas and offers four conclusions:

1. Interaction is the key to learning, and language is the key to interaction. "When teachers in both projects became aware of specific communication and interaction skills children were developing in their homes, they adapted classroom practice to build on these skills. In addition, teachers specifically demonstrated respect for the language of their students" (p. 3).

2. Academic standards and teacher expectations for students should not be lowered. Standard English skills were still emphasized in both projects but without devaluing the children's own dialect.

3. Schools can work with local colleges, parents, and other community members to learn more about students' home cultures.

4. By attending to students' cultures, teachers can expand and improve their teaching skills. The new ways of teaching developed in the two projects proved helpful for all the students in the classes, not just those from different cultures.

Sociolinguistics is the study of "the courtesies and conventions of conversation across cultures" (Tharp, 1989, p. 351). A knowledge of sociolinguistics will help you understand why communication sometimes breaks down in classrooms. The classroom is a special setting for communicating; it has its own set of rules for when, how, to whom, about what subject, and in what manner to use language. Sometimes the sociolinguistic skills of students do not fit the expectations of teachers.

Participation Structures. In order to be successful, students must know the communication rules; that is, they must understand the pragmatics of the classroom—when, where, and how to communicate. This is not such an easy task. As class activities change, rules change. Sometimes you have to raise your hand (during the teacher's presentation), but sometimes you don't (during storytime on the rug). Sometimes it is good to ask a question (during discussion), but at other times it isn't so good (when the teacher is scolding you). The differing activity rules are called **participation structures**. These structures define appropriate participation for each class activity. Most classrooms have many different participation structures.

To be competent communicators in the classroom, students sometimes have to read subtle, non-verbal cues telling them which participation structures are currently in effect. For example, in one classroom, when the teacher stood in a particular area of the room, put her hands on her hips, and leaned forward at the waist, the children in the class were signalled to "stop and freeze," look at the teacher, and anticipate an announcement (Shultz & Florio, 1979).

Sources of Misunderstandings. Some children are simply better than others at reading the classroom situation because the participation structures of the school match the structures they have learned at home. The communication rules for most school situations are similar to those in middle-class homes, so children from these homes often appear to be more competent communicators. They know the unwritten rules. Students from different cultural backgrounds may have learned participation structures that conflict with the behaviour expected in school. For example, one study found that the home conversation style of Hawaiian children is to chime in with contributions to a story. In school, however, this overlapping style is seen as "interrupting." When the teachers in one school learned about these differences and made their reading groups more like their students' home conversation groups, the young Hawaiian children in their classes improved in reading (Au, 1980; Tharp, 1989).

The source of misunderstanding can be a subtle sociolinguistic difference, such as how long the teacher waits to react to a student's response. White and Tharp (1988) found that when Navajo students in one class paused in giving a response, their Anglo teacher seemed to think that they had finished speaking. As a result, the teacher often unintentionally interrupted students. In another study, researchers found that Pueblo Indian students participated twice as much in classes where teachers waited longer to react. Waiting longer also helps girls to participate more freely in math and science classes (Grossman & Grossman, 1994).

It seems that even students who speak the same language as their teachers may still have trouble communicating, and thus learning school subjects, if their knowledge of pragmatics does not fit the school situation. What can teachers do? Especially in the early grades, you should make communication rules for activities clear and explicit. Do not assume students know what to do. Use cues to signal students when changes occur. Explain and demonstrate appropriate behaviour. We have seen teachers ask students to "use your inside voice" or "whisper so you won't disturb others." One teacher said and then demonstrated, "If you have to interrupt me while I'm working with other children, stand quietly beside me until I can help you." Be consistent in responding to students. If students are supposed to raise their hands, don't call on those who break the rules. In these ways you teach students how to learn in school.

Culturally Relevant Pedagogy

In the past 20 years, several researchers have focused on teachers who are especially successful with students of colour and students in poverty (Bennett, 1999; Delpit, 1995; Ladson-Billings, 1994, 1995; Moll, Amanti, Neff, & Gonzalez, 1992). The work of Gloria Ladson-Billings (1990, 1992, 1995) is a good example. For three years she studied excellent teachers in a California school district that served an African American community. In order to select the teachers, she asked parents and principals for nominations. Parents nominated teachers who respected the parents, created enthusiasm for learning in their children, and understood their children's need to operate successfully in two different worlds—the home community and the white world beyond. Principals nominated teachers who had few discipline referrals, and whose attendance rates and standardized test scores were high. Ladson-Billings was able to examine in depth eight of the nine teachers who were nominated by *both parents and principals*.

Based on her research, Ladson-Billings developed a conception of teaching excellence that encompasses but goes beyond considerations of sociolinguistics or social organizations. She uses the term **culturally relevant pedagogy** to describe teaching that rests on three propositions.

Students Must Experience Academic Success. "Despite the current social inequities and hostile classroom environments, students must develop their academic skills. The ways those skills are developed may vary, but all students need literacy, numeracy, technological, social, and political skills in order to be active participants in a democracy" (Ladson-Billings, 1995, p. 160).

Develop/Maintain Their Cultural Competence. As they become more academically skilled, students still retain their cultural competence. "Culturally relevant teachers utilize students' culture as a vehicle for learning" (Ladson-Billings, 1995, p. 161). For example, a teacher might use "non-offensive" rap music to teach about literal and figurative meaning, rhyme, alliteration, and onomatopoeia

Sociolinguistics: The study of formal and informal rules for how, when, about what, to whom, and how long to speak in conversations within cultural groups.

Participation Structures: The formal and informal rules for how to take part in a given activity.

Culturally Relevant Pedagogy: Excellent teaching for students of colour that includes academic success and developing/maintaining cultural competence and critical consciousness to challenge the status quo.

CHECKPOINT

Creating Culturally Compatible Classrooms

Review

▶ What are the elements of a culturally compatible classroom?

▶ What is culturally relevant pedagogy?

Apply

▶ How do participation structures affect students' access to learning in classrooms?

▶ How can you move "beyond the basics" in teaching all your students?

in poetry. He or she might bring in a representative from a community to work with students on a project that has cultural significance (e.g., researching and experimenting with an art form that is linked with students' ethnic origins).

Develop a Critical Consciousness to Challenge the Status Quo. In addition to developing academic skills while encouraging cultural competence, excellent teachers help students "develop a broader sociopolitical consciousness that allows them to critique the social norms, values, mores, and institutions that produce and maintain social inequities" (Ladson-Billings, 1995, p. 162). For example, in one school students were upset that their textbooks were out of date. They mobilized to investigate the funding formulas that allowed middle-class students to have newer books, wrote letters to the newspaper editor to challenge these inequities, and updated their texts with current information from other sources.

Ladson-Billings (1995) noted that many people have said her three principles "are just good teaching." She agrees that she is describing good teaching, but questions "why so little of it seems to be occurring in classrooms populated by African American students" (p. 159).

*B*ringing It All Together: Teaching Every Student

The goal of this chapter is to give you a sense of the diversity in today's and tomorrow's schools and to help you meet the challenges of teaching in a multicultural classroom. How will you understand and build on all the cultures of your students? How will you deal with many different languages? Here are a few general teaching principles to guide you in finding answers to these questions.

Know Your Students. Nothing you read in a chapter on cultural differences will teach you enough to understand the lives of all your students. If you can take other courses in college or read about other cultures, we encourage you to do it. But reading and studying are not enough. You should get to know your students' families and communities. Elba Reyes, a successful bilingual teacher for special needs children, describes her approach:

> Usually I find that if you really want to know a parent, you get to know them on their own turf. This is key to developing trust and understanding the parents' perspective. First, get to know the community. Learn where the local grocery store is and what the children do after school. Then schedule a home visit at a time that is convenient for the parents (Bos & Reyes, 1996, p. 349).

Try to spend time with students and parents on projects outside school. Ask parents to help in class or to speak to your students about their parents' jobs, hobbies, history, and heritage. In the elementary grades, don't wait until a student is in trouble to have the first meeting with a family member. Watch and listen to the ways that your students interact in large and small groups. Have students write to you, and write back to them. Eat lunch with one or two students. Spend some non-teaching time with them.

Respect Your Students. From knowledge ought to come respect for your students' learning strengths—for the struggles they face and the obstacles they overcome. For a child, genuine acceptance is a necessary condition for developing self-esteem. Pride and self-esteem are important accomplishments of the school years. Sometimes the self-image and occupational aspirations of minority children actually decline in their early years in public school, probably because of the emphasis on majority culture values, accomplishments, and history. By presenting the accomplishments of particular members of an ethnic group or by bringing that group's culture into the classroom (in the form of literature, art, music, or any cultural knowledge), teachers can help students maintain a sense of pride in their cultural group. This integration of culture must be more than the "tokenism" of sampling ethnic foods or wearing costumes. Students should learn about the socially and intellectually important contributions of the various groups. There are many excellent references that provide background information, history, and teaching strategies for different groups of students (e.g., Banks, 1997, 1999; Bennett, 1999; Ladson-Billings, 1995).

Teach Your Students. The most important thing you can do for your students is to teach them to read, write, speak, compute, think, and create. Too often, goals for low-SES or minority-group students have focused exclusively on basic skills. Students are taught words and sounds, but the meaning of the story is supposed to come later. Knapp, Turnbull, and Shields (1990) make these suggestions:

Focus on meaning and understanding from beginning to end—for example, by orienting instruction toward comprehending reading passages, communicating important ideas in written text, or understanding the concepts underlying number facts.

Balance routine skill learning with novel and complex tasks from the earliest stages of learning.

Provide context for skill learning that establishes clear reasons for needing to learn the skills.

Influence attitudes and beliefs about the academic content areas as well as skills and knowledge.

Eliminate unnecessary redundancy in the curriculum (e.g., repeating instruction in the same mathematics skills year after year). (p. 5)

And finally, teach students directly about how to be students. In the early grades this could mean directly teaching the courtesies and conventions of the classroom: how to get a turn to speak, how and when to interrupt the teacher, how to whisper, how to get help in a small group, how to give an explanation that is helpful. In the later grades it may mean teaching the study skills that fit your subject. You can ask students to learn "how we do it in school" without violating principle number two above—respect your students. Ways of asking questions around the kitchen table at home may be different from ways of asking questions in school, but students can learn both ways, without deciding that either way is superior. The Guidelines on page 188 give more ideas.

GUIDELINES

Culturally Relevant Teaching

Experiment with different grouping arrangements to encourage social harmony and cooperation.

Examples

1. Try "study buddies" and pairs.
2. Organize heterogeneous groups of four or five.
3. Establish larger teams for older students.

Provide a range of ways to learn material to accommodate a range of learning styles.

Examples

1. Give students verbal materials at different reading levels.
2. Offer visual materials—charts, diagrams, models.
3. Provide tapes for listening and viewing.
4. Set up activities and projects.

Teach classroom procedures directly, even ways of doing things that you thought everyone would know.

Examples

1. Tell students how to get the teacher's attention.
2. Explain when and how to interrupt the teacher if students need help.
3. Show which materials students can take and which require permission.
4. Demonstrate acceptable ways to disagree with or challenge another student.

Learn the meaning of different behaviour for your students.

Examples

1. Ask students how they feel when you correct or praise them. What gives them this message?
2. Talk to family and community members and other teachers to discover the meaning of expressions, gestures, or other responses that are unfamiliar to you.

Emphasize meaning in teaching.

Examples

1. Make sure students understand what they read.
2. Try storytelling and other modes that don't require written materials.
3. Use examples that relate abstract concepts to everyday experiences; for instance, relate negative numbers to being overdrawn in your chequebook.

Get to know the customs, traditions, and values of your students.

Examples

1. Use holidays as a chance to discuss the origins and meaning of traditions.
2. Analyze different traditions for common themes.
3. Attend community fairs and festivals.

Help students detect racist and sexist messages.

Examples

1. Analyze curriculum materials for biases.
2. Make students "bias detectives," reporting comments from the media.
3. Discuss the ways that students communicate biased messages about each other and what should be done when this happens.
4. Discuss expressions of prejudice such as anti-Semitism.

Summary

Today's Multicultural Classrooms

Distinguish between the "melting pot" and multiculturalism.

Statistics point to increasing cultural diversity in Canadian society. In Canada, we take pride in the emphasis on multicultural education, equal educational opportunity, and the celebration of cultural diversity.

What is multicultural education?

James Banks suggests that multicultural education has five dimensions: integrating content, helping students understand how knowledge is influenced by beliefs, reducing prejudice, creating social structures in schools that support learning and development for all students, and using teaching methods that reach all students.

What is culture?

There are many conceptions of culture, but most include the knowledge, rules, traditions, attitudes, and values that guide behaviour in a particular group of people—culture is a program for living. Everyone is a member of many cultural groups, defined in terms of geographic region, nationality, ethnicity, race, gender, social class, and religion. Membership in a particular group does not determine behaviour or values but makes certain values and kinds of behaviour more likely. Wide variations exist within each group.

Social Class Differences

What is SES?

Socioeconomic status (SES) is a term used by sociologists for variations in wealth, power, and prestige. Socioeconomic status is determined by several factors—not just income—and often overpowers other cultural differences. The majority of children in poverty are white, but disproportionate numbers of low-SES families are members of minority cultures.

What is the relationship between SES and school achievement?

Socioeconomic status and academic achievement are closely related. Low-SES students may suffer from inadequate health care, teachers' lowered expectations of them, low self-esteem, learned helplessness, participation in resistance cultures, school tracking, and understimulating child-rearing styles and home environments. A striking finding is that low-SES children lose academic ground outside school over the summer while higher-SES children continue to advance.

Ethnic and Racial Differences

Distinguish between ethnicity and race.

Ethnicity (culturally transmitted behaviour) and race (biologically transmitted physical traits) are socially significant categories people use to describe themselves and others. Minority groups (either numerically or historically unempowered) are rapidly increasing in population.

How can ethnicity affect school performance?

Conflicts between groups can arise from differences in culture-based beliefs, values, and expectations. Students in some cultures learn attitudes and behaviour that are more consistent with school expectations. Differences among ethnic groups in cognitive and academic abilities are largely the legacy of racial segregation and continuing prejudice and discrimination.

Distinguish among prejudice, discrimination, and stereotype threat.

Prejudice is a rigid and irrational generalization—a prejudgment—about an entire category of people. Prejudice may target people from particular racial, ethnic, religious, political, geographic, or language groups, or it may be directed toward the gender or sexual orientation of the individual. Discrimination is unequal treatment of particular categories of people. Stereotype threat is the extra emotional and cognitive burden that your performance in an academic situation might confirm a stereotype that others hold about you.

Females and Males: Differences in the Classroom

What is gender-role identity?

Gender-role identity is the image each individual has of himself or herself as masculine or feminine in characteristics—a part of self-concept. People with a "feminine" identity would rate themselves high on characteristics usually associated with females, such as "sensitive" or "warm," and low on characteristics traditionally associated with males, such as "forceful" and "competitive." Most people see themselves in gender-typed terms; however, some children and adults are more androgynous—they rate themselves high on *both* masculine and feminine traits.

How do gender-role identities develop?

Biology (hormones) plays a role, as does the differential behaviour of parents and teachers toward male and female children. Through their interactions with family, peers, teachers, and the environment in general, children begin to form gender schemas, or organized networks of knowledge about what it means to be male or female. Research shows that gender-role stereotyping begins in the preschool years and continues through gender bias in the school curriculum and sex discrimination in the classroom. Teachers often unintentionally perpetuate these problems.

Are there gender differences in cognitive abilities

Some measures on IQ and SAT tests have shown gender-linked differences, especially in verbal and spatial abilities and mathematics. Research on the causes of these differences has been inconclusive, except to indicate that academic socialization and teachers' treatment of male and female students in mathematics classes do play a role. Teachers can use many strategies for reducing gender bias.

Language Differences in the Classroom

What are the origins of language differences in the classroom?

Language differences among students can include dialects, bilingualism, and culture-based communication styles.

What is bilingual education?

Bilingual students speak a first language other than English, learn English as a second language, may have some degree of limitation in English proficiency, and also must often struggle with social adjustment problems relating to biculturalism. While there is much debate over the best way to help bilingual students master English, studies show it is best if they are not forced to abandon their first language. The more proficient students are in their first language, the faster they will master the second. Mastering academic language skills in any new language takes five to seven years.

Creating Culturally Compatible Classrooms

What are the elements of a culturally compatible classroom?

Culturally compatible classrooms are free of racism, sexism, and ethnic prejudice. They provide equal educational opportunities for all students. Dimensions of classroom life that can be modified to that end include social organization, teaching and learning styles and formats, and participation structures. Teachers, however, must avoid stereotypes based on cultural interpretations of learning styles or preferences. We must not assume that every individual in a group has the same preferences.

Communication may break down in classrooms because of differences in sociolinguistic styles and skills. Teachers can directly teach appropriate participation structures and be sensitive to culture-based communication rules.

What is culturally relevant pedagogy?

Gloria Ladson-Billings developed a conception of teaching excellence that encompasses considerations of sociolinguistics or social organizations, but goes beyond them. She uses the term *culturally relevant pedagogy* to describe teaching that rests on three propositions: Students must experience academic success, develop/maintain their cultural competence, and develop a critical consciousness to challenge the status quo.

Bringing It All Together: Teaching Every Student

How can teachers create classroom environments in which all students can learn?

To help create compatible multicultural classrooms, teachers must know and respect all their students, have high expectations of them, and teach them what they need to know to succeed.

Key Terms

androgynous, *p. 172*

authoritarian personality, *p. 170*

bilingualism, *p. 179*

culturally compatible classrooms, *p. 182*

culturally relevant pedagogy, *p. 185*

culture, *p. 160*

discrimination, *p. 170*

English as a second language (ESL), *p. 179*

ethnicity, *p. 165*

gender biases, *p. 174*

gender-role identity, *p. 172*

gender schemas, *p. 173*

Heritage Language Programs, *p. 180*

limited English proficiency (LEP), *p. 179*

melting pot, *p. 158*

minority group, *p. 165*

monolinguals, *p. 179*

mosaic, *p. 158*

multicultural education, *p. 158*

participation structures, *p. 185*

prejudice, *p. 169*

race, *p. 165*

resistance culture, *p. 163*

socioeconomic status (SES), *p. 161*

sociolinguistics, *p. 185*

stereotype, *p. 170*

stereotype threat, *p. 171*

tracking, *p. 163*

Becoming a Professional

Reflecting on the Chapter

Can you apply the ideas from this chapter on culture and community to solve the following problems of practice?

Elementary and Middle School

▷ Several of your students live in a low-income housing complex in the district and clearly have fewer advantages than the other students in your class. You are concerned that these students never seem to work or play with the others in the class. What would you do?

▷ Every year the number of non-English-speaking students in your class increases. This year there are four different language groups represented—and you know only about five words in each language. The school has little in the way of resources. Pick one topic and tell how you would teach it to accommodate the limited English proficiency of your students.

Junior High and High School

▷ One day you notice that the males are doing most of the talking in your classes, particularly the advanced classes. Just out of curiosity, you start to note each day how many girls and boys make contributions and ask questions. You are really surprised to see that your first impression was correct. What would you do to encourage more participation on the part of your female students?

▷ For some reason, this year there have been several racial incidents in your school. Each incident seems a bit nastier and more dangerous than the one before. What would you do in your classes to improve the situation?

Check Your Understanding

▷ Know the basic dimensions of multicultural education.

- Know the difference between prejudice and discrimination.
- Be familiar with the three propositions of culturally relevant pedagogy.
- Be familiar with research on differences in how teachers interact with male and female students.

Your Teaching Portfolio

- What is your stance on multicultural education? On tracking? Add these ideas in your philosophy of teaching statement for your portfolio.
- Include ideas for the integration of multicultural material in your portfolio.

Teaching Resources

Add Table 5.4 to your teaching resources file.

Use the Family and Community Partnerships Guidelines to brainstorm ideas for family involvement in helping your students "take their learning home."

 ## Weblinks

www.oise.utoronto.ca/~jisekebarnes/aboriginal

This Web site provides a variety of pointers to Aboriginal educational materials and programs.

www.tesl.ca

This is the home page for TESL (Teaching English as a Second Language), which is a national federation of English as a Second Language teachers, learners, and learner advocates. Click on TESL Links, then click on Teacher Tricks to view a variety of additional sources.

What Would You Do?

You were hired in January to take over the class of a teacher who moved away. This is a great school. If you do well, you might be in line for a full-time opening next fall. As you are introduced around the school, you get a number of sympathetic looks and many—too many—offers of help: "Let me know if I can do anything for you."

As you walk toward your classroom, you begin to understand why so many teachers volunteered their help. You hear the screaming when you are still halfway down the hall. "Give it back, it's MINE!" "No way—come and get it!" "I hate you." A crashing sound follows as a table full of books hits the floor. The first day is a nightmare. Evidently the previous teacher had no management system—no order. Several students walk around the room while you are talking to the class, interrupt you when you are working with a group, torment the class goldfish, and open their lunches (or other students') for a self-determined, mid-morning snack. Others listen, but ask a million questions off the topic. Simply taking roll and introducing the first activity takes an hour. You end the first day exhausted and discouraged, losing your voice and your patience.

▶ How would you approach the situation?

▶ Which problem behaviour would you tackle first?

▶ Would giving rewards or administering punishments be useful in this situation? Why or why not?

Understanding Learning

When we hear the word "learning," most of us think of studying and school. We think about subjects or skills we intend to master, such as algebra, French, chemistry, or karate. But learning is not limited to school. We learn every day of our lives. Babies learn to kick their legs to make the mobile above their cribs move, teenagers learn the lyrics to all their favourite songs, middle-aged people learn to change their diet and exercise patterns, and every few years we all learn to find a new style of dress attractive when the old styles (the styles we once loved) go out of fashion. This last example shows that learning is not always intentional. We don't try to like new styles and dislike old; it just seems to happen that way. We don't intend to become nervous when we see the dentist fill a syringe with Novocaine or when we step onto a stage, yet many of us do. So what is this powerful phenomenon called learning?

Learning: A Definition

Learning: Process through which experience causes permanent change in knowledge or behaviour.

In the broadest sense, **learning** occurs when experience causes a relatively permanent change in an individual's knowledge or behaviour. The change may be deliberate or unintentional, for better or for worse. To qualify as learning, this change must be brought about by experience—by the interaction of a person with his or her environment. Changes simply caused by maturation, such as growing taller or turning grey, do not qualify as learning. Temporary changes resulting from illness, fatigue, or hunger are also excluded from a general definition of learning. A person who has gone without food for two days does not learn to be hungry, and a person who is ill does not learn to run more slowly. Of course, learning plays a part in how we respond to hunger or illness.

Our definition specifies that the changes resulting from learning are in the individual's knowledge or behaviour. While most psychologists would agree with this statement, some tend to emphasize the change in knowledge, others the change in behaviour. Cognitive psychologists, who focus on changes in knowledge, believe learning is an internal mental activity that cannot be observed directly. As you will see in the next chapter, cognitive psychologists studying learning are interested in unobservable mental activities such as thinking, remembering, and solving problems (Schwartz & Reisberg, 1991).

The psychologists discussed in this chapter, on the other hand, favour **behavioural learning theories**. The behavioural view generally assumes that the outcome of learning is a change in behaviour and emphasizes the effects of external events on the individual. Some early behaviourists such as J. B. Watson took the radical position that because thinking, intentions, and other internal mental events could not be seen or studied rigorously and scientifically, these "mentalisms," as he called them, should not even be included in an explanation of learning. Before we look in depth at behavioural explanations of learning, let's step into an actual classroom and note the possible results of learning.

Behavioural Learning Theories: Explanations of learning that focus on external events as the cause of changes in observable behaviour.

Learning Is Not Always What It Seems

Elizabeth Chan was beginning her first day of solo teaching. After weeks of working with her cooperating teacher in a Grade 8 social studies class, she was ready to take over. As she moved from behind the desk to the front of the room, she saw another adult approach the classroom door. It was B. J. Ross, her supervisor from the university. Elizabeth's neck and facial muscles suddenly became very tense and her hands trembled.

"I've stopped by to observe your teaching," Dr. Ross said. "This will be my first of six visits. I tried to reach you last night to tell you."

Elizabeth tried to hide her reaction, but her hands trembled as she gathered the notes for the lesson.

"Let's start today with a kind of game. I will say some words, then I want you to tell me the first words you can think of. Don't bother to raise your hands. Just say the words out loud, and I will write them on the board. Don't all speak at once, though. Wait until someone else has finished to say your word. Okay, here is the first word: Métis."

"Red River." "Louis Riel." "Rebellion." The answers came very quickly, and Elizabeth was relieved to see that the students understood the game.

"All right, very good," she said. "Now try another one: Batoche."

"Duck Lake." "Fish Creek." "John A. Macdonald." "Big Mac." "Sir Ronald McDonald!" With this last answer, a ripple of laughter moved across the room.

"Ronald McDonald?" Elizabeth sighed wearily. "Get serious." Then she laughed too. Soon all the students were laughing. "Okay, settle down," Elizabeth said. "These ideas are getting a little off base!"

"Off base? Baseball," shouted the boy who had first mentioned Ronald McDonald. He stood up and started throwing balls of paper to a friend in the back of the room, simulating the style of Roger Clemens.

"Expos." "No, the Blue Jays." "The SkyDome." "Hot dogs." "Popcorn." "Hamburgers." "Ronald McDonald." The responses now came too fast for Elizabeth to stop them. For some reason, the Ronald McDonald line got an even bigger laugh the second time around, and Elizabeth suddenly realized she had lost the class.

"Okay, since you know so much about the Rebellion, close your books and take out a pen," Elizabeth said, obviously angry. She passed out the worksheet that she had planned as a cooperative, open-book project. "You have 20 minutes to finish this test!"

Are there experiences in your "learning history" that have made you anxious about speaking in public or taking tests? How might behavioural principles of learning help to explain the development of these anxieties? ▼

"You didn't tell us we were having a test!" "This isn't fair!" "We haven't even covered this stuff yet!" "I didn't do anything wrong!" There were moans and disgusted looks, even from the most mellow students. "I'm reporting you to the principal; it's a violation of students' rights!"

This last comment hit hard. The class had just finished discussing human rights as preparation for this unit on the Northwest Rebellion. As she listened to the protests, Elizabeth felt terrible. How was she going to grade these "tests"? The first section of the worksheet involved facts about events leading up to the Northwest Rebellion, and the second section asked students to create a news-style program interviewing ordinary people touched by the war.

"All right, all right, it won't be a test. But you do have to complete this worksheet for a grade. I was going to let you work together, but your behaviour this morning tells me that you are not ready for group work. If you can complete the first section of the sheet working quietly and seriously, you may work together on the second section." Elizabeth knew that her students would like to work together on writing the script for the news interview program.

It appears, on the surface at least, that very little learning of any sort was taking place in Elizabeth's classroom. In fact, Elizabeth had some good ideas; but she also made some mistakes in her application of learning principles. We will return to this episode later in the chapter to analyze various aspects of what took place. To get us started, three events can be singled out, each possibly related to a different learning process.

First, Elizabeth's hands trembled when her university supervisor entered the room. Second, the students were able to associate the phrases *Red River* and *Louis Riel* with the word *Métis*. Third, one student continued to disrupt the class with inappropriate responses. The three learning processes represented are classical conditioning, contiguity, and operant conditioning. In the following pages we will examine these three kinds of learning, starting with contiguity.

*E*arly Explanations of Learning: Contiguity and Classical Conditioning

One of the earliest explanations of learning came from Aristotle (384–322 B.C.). He said that we remember things together: (1) when they are similar, (2) when they contrast, and (3) when they are *contiguous*. This last principle is the most important, because it is included in all explanations of *learning by association*. The principle of **contiguity** states that whenever two or more sensations occur together often enough, they will become associated. Later, when only one of these sensations (a **stimulus**) occurs, the other will be remembered too (a **response**) (Rachlin, 1991; Wasserman & Miller, 1997).

Some results of contiguous learning were evident in Elizabeth's class. When she said "Métis," students associated the words "Red River" and "Louis Riel." They had heard these words together many times in a movie shown the day before. Other learning processes may also be involved when students learn these phrases, but contiguity is a factor. Contiguity also plays a major role in another learning process best known as *classical conditioning*.

Pavlov's Dilemma and Discovery: Classical Conditioning

Classical conditioning focuses on the learning of *involuntary* emotional or physiological responses such as fear, increased heartbeat, salivation, or sweating, which are sometimes called **respondents** because they are automatic responses to stimuli. Through the process of classical conditioning, humans and animals can be trained to react involuntarily to a stimulus that previously had no effect—or a very different

Contiguity: Association of two events because of repeated pairing.

Stimulus: Event that activates behaviour.

Response: Observable reaction to a stimulus.

Classical Conditioning: Association of automatic responses with new stimuli.

Respondents: Responses (generally automatic or involuntary) elicited by specific stimuli.

effect—on them. The stimulus comes to *elicit,* or bring forth, the response automatically.

Classical conditioning was discovered by Ivan Pavlov, a Russian physiologist, in the 1920s. In his laboratory, Pavlov was plagued by a series of setbacks in his experiments on the digestive system of dogs. He was trying to determine how long it took a dog to secrete digestive juices after it had been fed, but the intervals of time kept changing. At first, the dogs salivated in the expected manner while they were being fed. Then the dogs began to salivate as soon as they saw the food. Finally, they salivated as soon as they saw the scientist enter the room. The white coats of the experimenters and the sound of their footsteps all *elicited* salivation. Pavlov decided to make a detour from his original experiments and examine these unexpected interferences in his work.

In one of his first experiments, Pavlov began by sounding a tuning fork and recording a dog's response. As expected, there was no salivation. At this point, the sound of the tuning fork was a **neutral stimulus** because it brought forth no salivation. Then Pavlov fed the dog. The response was salivation. The food was an **unconditioned stimulus** (US) because no prior training or "conditioning" was needed to establish the natural connection between food and salivation. The salivation was an **unconditioned response** (UR), again because it occurred automatically—no conditioning required.

Using these three elements—the food, the salivation, and the tuning fork— Pavlov demonstrated that a dog could be conditioned to salivate after hearing the tuning fork. He did this by contiguous pairing of the sound with food. At the beginning of the experiment, he sounded the fork and then quickly fed the dog. After Pavlov repeated this several times, the dog began to salivate after hearing the sound but before receiving the food. Now the sound had become a **conditioned stimulus** (CS) that could bring forth salivation by itself. The response of salivating after the tone was now a **conditioned response** (CR).

Response Generalization, Stimulus Discrimination, and Extinction

Pavlov's work also identified three other processes in classical conditioning: *response generalization, stimulus discrimination,* and *extinction.* After the dogs learned to salivate in response to hearing one particular sound, they would also salivate after hearing similar tones that were slightly higher or lower. This process is called **response generalization** because the conditioned response of salivating generalized or occurred in the presence of similar stimuli. Pavlov could also teach the dogs **stimulus discrimination**—to respond to one tone but not to others that were similar—by making sure that food always followed only one tone, not any others. **Extinction** occurs when a conditioned stimulus (a particular tone) is presented repeatedly but is not followed by the unconditioned stimulus (food). The conditioned response (salivating) gradually fades away and finally is "extinguished"—it disappears altogether.

Pavlov's findings and those of other researchers who have studied classical conditioning have implications for teachers. It is possible that many of our emotional reactions

Neutral Stimulus: Stimulus not connected to a response.

Unconditioned Stimulus (US): Stimulus that automatically produces an emotional or physiological response.

Unconditioned Response (UR): Naturally occurring emotional or physiological response.

Conditioned Stimulus (CS): Stimulus that evokes an emotional or physiological response after conditioning.

Conditioned Response (CR): Learned response to a previously neutral stimulus.

Response Generalization: Responding in the same way to similar stimuli.

Stimulus Discrimination: Responding differently to similar, but not identical, stimuli.

Extinction: Gradual disappearance of a learned response.

CHECKPOINT

Early Explanations of Learning: Contiguity and Classical Conditioning

Review

▷ How does a neutral stimulus become a conditioned stimulus?

▷ Compare and contrast response generalization and stimulus discrimination.

Apply

▷ After several painful visits to the dentist, you feel your heart rate increase when you sit down in the dentist's chair to have your teeth cleaned. Analyze this situation in terms of classical conditioning.

GUIDELINES

Using Principles of Classical Conditioning

Associate positive, pleasant events with learning tasks.

Examples

1. Emphasize group competition and cooperation over individual competition. Many students have negative emotional responses to individual competition that may generalize to other learning.
2. Make division drills fun by having students decide how to divide refreshments equally, and then letting them eat the results.
3. Make voluntary reading appealing by creating a comfortable reading corner with pillows, colourful displays of books, and reading props such as puppets (see Morrow & Weinstein, 1986, for more ideas).

Help students to risk anxiety-producing situations voluntarily and successfully.

Examples

1. Assign a shy student the responsibility of teaching two others students how to distribute materials for map study.
2. Devise small steps toward a larger goal. For example, give ungraded practice tests daily, and then weekly, to students who tend to "freeze" in test situations.
3. If a student is afraid of speaking in front of the class, let the student read a report to a small group while seated, then read it while standing, then give the report from notes instead of reading verbatim. Next, move in stages toward having the student give a report to the whole class.

Help students recognize differences and similarities among situations so they can discriminate and generalize appropriately.

Examples

1. Explain that it is appropriate to avoid strangers who offer gifts or rides but safe to accept favours from adults when parents are present.
2. Assure students who are anxious about taking university entrance exams that this test is like all the other achievement tests they have taken.

to various situations are learned in part through classical conditioning. For example, Elizabeth's trembling hands when she saw her university supervisor might be traced to previous unpleasant experiences. Perhaps she had been embarrassed during past evaluations of her performance, and now just the thought of being observed elicits a pounding heart and sweaty palms. Remember that emotions and attitudes as well as facts and ideas are learned in classrooms. This emotional learning can sometimes interfere with academic learning. Procedures based on classical conditioning also can be used to help people learn more adaptive emotional responses, as the Guidelines above suggest.

Operant Conditioning: Trying New Responses

So far we have concentrated on the automatic conditioning of involuntary responses such as salivation and fear. Clearly, not all human learning is so automatic and unintentional. Most behaviour is not *elicited* by stimuli, but *emitted* or voluntarily enacted. People actively "operate" on their environment to produce different kinds of consequences. These deliberate actions are called **operants**. The learning process involved in operant behaviour is called **operant conditioning** because we learn to behave in certain ways as we operate on the environment.

The Work of Thorndike and Skinner

Edward Thorndike and B. F. Skinner both played major roles in developing knowledge of operant conditioning. Thorndike's (1913) early work involved cats that he

Operants: Voluntary (and generally goal-directed) behaviour emitted by a person or an animal.

Operant Conditioning: Learning in which voluntary behaviour is strengthened or weakened by consequences or antecedents.

placed in problem boxes. To escape from the box and reach food outside, the cats had to pull out a bolt or perform some other task; they had to act on their environment. During the frenzied movements that followed the closing of the box, the cats eventually made the correct movement to escape, usually by accident. After repeating the process several times, the cats learned to make the correct response almost immediately. Thorndike decided, on the basis of these experiments, that one important law of learning was the law of effect: any act that produces a satisfying effect in a given situation will tend to be repeated in that situation. Because pulling out a bolt produced satisfaction (access to food), cats repeated that movement when they found themselves in the box again.

Thorndike thus established the basis for operant conditioning, but the person generally thought to be responsible for developing the concept is B. F. Skinner (1953). Skinner began with the belief that the principles of classical conditioning account for only a small portion of learned behaviour. Much human behaviour is operant, not respondent. Classical conditioning describes only how existing behaviour might be paired with new stimuli; it does not explain how new operant behaviour is acquired.

Behaviour, like *response* or *action*, is simply a word for what a person does in a particular situation. Conceptually, we may think of behaviour as sandwiched between two sets of environmental influences: those that precede it (its **antecedents**) and those that follow it (its **consequences**) (Skinner, 1950). This relationship can be shown very simply as antecedent–behaviour–consequence, or A–B–C. As behaviour unfolds, a given consequence becomes an antecedent for the next ABC sequence. Research in operant conditioning shows that operant behaviour can be altered by changes in the antecedents, the consequences, or both. Early work focused on consequences, often using rats or pigeons as subjects.

▲ *B. F. Skinner's work on operant conditioning changed the way we think about consequences and learning.*

Types of Consequences

According to the behavioural view, consequences determine to a great extent whether a person will repeat the behaviour that led to the consequences. The type and timing of consequences can strengthen or weaken behaviour. We will look first at consequences that strengthen behaviour.

Reinforcement. While **reinforcement** is commonly understood to mean "reward," this term has a particular meaning in psychology. A **reinforcer** is any consequence that strengthens the behaviour it follows. So, by definition, reinforced behaviour increases in frequency or duration. Whenever you see a behaviour persisting or increasing over time, you can assume the consequences of that behaviour are reinforcers for the individual involved. The reinforcement process can be diagrammed as follows:

CONSEQUENCE		EFFECT
Behaviour → Reinforcer →		Strengthened or repeated behaviour

We can be fairly certain that food will be a reinforcer for a hungry animal, but what about people? It may not be clear why an event acts as a reinforcer for an individual, but there are many theories about why reinforcement works. For example, some psychologists suggest that reinforcers satisfy needs, while other psychologists believe that reinforcers reduce tension or stimulate a part of the brain (Rachlin, 1991). Whether the consequences of any action are reinforcing depends on the individual's perception of the event and the meaning it holds for her or him.

Antecedents: Events that precede an action.

Consequences: Events that are brought about by an action.

Reinforcement: Use of consequences to strengthen behaviour.

Reinforcer: Any event that follows behaviour and increases the chances that the behaviour will occur again.

Positive Reinforcement:
Strengthening behaviour by presenting a desired stimulus after the behaviour.

Negative Reinforcement:
Strengthening behaviour by removing an aversive stimulus.

Aversive: Irritating or unpleasant.

Punishment: Process that weakens or suppresses behaviour.

Presentation Punishment:
Decreasing the chances that behaviour will occur again by presenting an aversive stimulus following the behaviour; also called Type I punishment.

Connect & Extend
To real life
How can the principles of conditioning help explain the difficulty many people experience when they try to stop smoking? Outline a program for the reduction or elimination of smoking behaviour.

Connect & Extend
To real life
Positive reinforcement: Praise for good grades, bonus points on tests, a class pizza party when everyone makes above 85 on the weekly spelling test. *Negative reinforcement:* Removing a stone from your shoe; calling on a child who is madly waving his hand and shouting, "I know, I know!" (you are negatively reinforced because the noise stops); on trips, wearing a certain pair of shoes to avoid aching feet; saying "I'm really sorry" to your spouse to avoid his or her anger. *Presentation punishment:* Running extra laps; reprimands; bad grades; corporal punishment. *Removal punishment:* Fines; being grounded; missing recess; not being allowed to go on the field trip; getting fired.

Connect & Extend
To your teaching
Recall an instance of punishment that you have experienced at some time during your life. What were your feelings when you were being punished? List the feelings. (Negative feelings, such as embarrassment, resentment, hurt, anger, probably will account for 90 percent of the responses.) Does the punishment work? What are some other negative effects of punishment? If punishment is ineffective and also produces negative side effects, why do so many teachers rely on it so much?

For example, students who repeatedly get themselves sent to the principal's office for misbehaving may be indicating that something about this consequence is reinforcing for them, even if it doesn't seem rewarding to you.

Reinforcers are those consequences that strengthen the associated behaviour (Skinner, 1953, 1989). There are two types of reinforcement. The first, called **positive reinforcement**, occurs when the behaviour produces a new stimulus. Examples include a peck on the red key producing food for a pigeon, wearing a new outfit producing many compliments, or falling out of your chair producing cheers and laughter from classmates.

Notice that positive reinforcement can occur even when the behaviour being reinforced (falling out of a chair) is not "positive" from the teacher's point of view. In fact, positive reinforcement of inappropriate behaviour occurs unintentionally in many classrooms. Teachers inadvertently help maintain problem behaviour by reinforcing it. For example, Elizabeth may have unintentionally reinforced problem behaviour in her class by laughing when the boy answered, "Ronald McDonald." The problem behaviour may have persisted for other reasons, but the consequence of Elizabeth's laughter could have played a role.

When the consequence that strengthens behaviour is the *appearance* (addition) of a new stimulus, the situation is defined as positive reinforcement. In contrast, when the consequence that strengthens behaviour is the *disappearance* (subtraction) of a stimulus, the process is called **negative reinforcement**. If a particular action leads to stopping, avoiding, or escaping an **aversive** situation, the action is likely to be repeated in a similar situation. A common example is the car seat-belt buzzer. As soon as you attach your seat belt, the irritating buzzer stops. You are likely to repeat this action in the future because the behaviour made an aversive stimulus disappear. Consider students who continually "get sick" right before a test and are sent to the nurse's office. The behaviour allows the students to escape aversive situations—tests—so getting "sick" is being maintained, in part, through negative reinforcement. It is negative because the stimulus (the test) disappears; it is reinforcement because the behaviour that caused the stimulus to disappear (getting "sick") increases or repeats. It is also possible that classical conditioning plays a role. The students may have been conditioned to experience unpleasant physiological reactions to tests.

The "negative" in negative reinforcement does not imply that the behaviour being reinforced is necessarily unrewarding. The meaning is closer to that of "negative" numbers—something is subtracted. Associate positive and negative reinforcement with adding or subtracting something following a specific behaviour.

Punishment.   Negative reinforcement is often confused with punishment. The process of reinforcement (positive or negative) always involves strengthening behaviour. **Punishment**, on the other hand, always involves decreasing or suppressing behaviour. Behaviour followed by a "punisher" is less likely to be repeated in similar situations in the future. Again, it is the effect that defines a consequence as punishment, and different people have different perceptions of what is punishing. One student may find suspension from school punishing, while another student wouldn't mind at all. The process of punishment is diagrammed as follows:

CONSEQUENCE			EFFECT
Behaviour	→	Reinforcer	→	Weakened or decreased behaviour

Like reinforcement, punishment may take one of two forms. The first type has been called Type I punishment, but this name isn't very informative, so we use the term **presentation punishment**. It occurs when the appearance of a stimulus following the behaviour suppresses or decreases the behaviour. When teachers assign demerits, extra work, running laps, and so on, they are using presentation punishment. The other type of punishment (Type II punishment) we call **removal**

punishment because it involves removing a stimulus. When teachers or parents take away privileges after a young person has behaved inappropriately, they are applying removal punishment. With both types, the effect is to decrease the behaviour that led to the punishment. Figure 6.1 summarizes the processes of reinforcement and punishment.

Reinforcement Schedules

When people are first learning new behaviour, they will learn it faster if they are reinforced for every correct response. This is a **continuous reinforcement schedule**. Then, when the new behaviour has been mastered, they will maintain it best if they are reinforced intermittently rather than every time. An **intermittent reinforcement schedule** seems to help students maintain skills without expecting constant reinforcement.

There are two basic types of intermittent reinforcement schedules. One—called an **interval schedule**—is based on a time interval that passes between reinforcers. The other—a **ratio schedule**—is based on the number of responses learners make between reinforcers. Interval and ratio schedules may be either *fixed* (predictable) or *variable* (unpredictable). Table 6.1 summarizes the five possible reinforcement schedules (the continuous schedule and the four kinds of intermittent schedules).

▲ *Casino slot machines are a good example of the effectiveness of intermittent reinforcement: People "learn" to persist in losing their money on the chance that they will be rewarded with a jackpot.*

Connect & Extend
To real life
In some of his last writings, Skinner analyzed his own life in terms of his operant view of learning [Skinner, B. F. (1987). *Upon further reflection.* Englewood Cliffs, NJ: Prentice-Hall]. He noted that the older scholar doesn't need frequent reinforcement if he has been reinforced through the years on a schedule that encourages persistence.

FIGURE 6.1

Kinds of Reinforcement and Punishment

Negative reinforcement and punishment are often confused. It may help you to remember that reinforcement is always associated with increases in behaviour, and punishment always involves decreasing or suppressing behaviour.

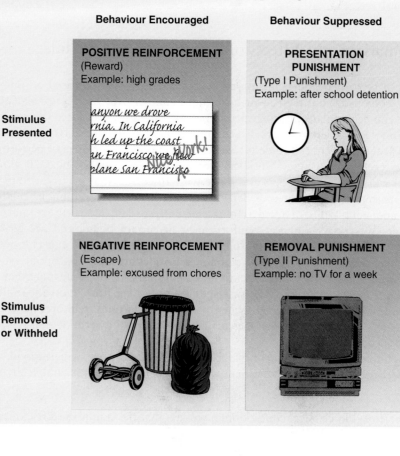

Removal Punishment: Decreasing the chances that a behaviour will occur again by removing a pleasant stimulus following the behaviour; also called Type II punishment.

Continuous Reinforcement Schedule: Presenting a reinforcer after every appropriate response.

Intermittent Reinforcement Schedule: Presenting a reinforcer after some but not all responses.

Interval Schedule: Length of time between reinforcers.

Ratio Schedule: Number of responses between reinforcers.

TABLE 6.1 Reinforcement Schedules

Schedule	Definition	Example	Response Pattern	Reaction When Reinforcement Stops
Continuous	Reinforcement after every response	Turning on the television	Rapid learning of response	Very little persistence; rapid disappearance of response
Fixed-interval	Reinforcement after a set period of time	Weekly quiz	Response rate increases as time for reinforcement approaches, then drops after reinforcement	Little persistence; rapid drop in response rate when time for reinforcement passes and no reinforcer appears
Variable-interval	Reinforcement after varying lengths of time	Pop quizzes	Slow, steady rate of responding; very little pause after reinforcement	Greater persistence; slow decline in response rate
Fixed-ratio	Reinforcement after a set number of responses	Piece work Bake sale	Rapid response rate; pause after reinforcement	Little persistence; rapid drop in response rate when expected number of responses are given and no reinforcer appears
Variable-ratio	Reinforcement after a varying number of responses	Slot machines	Very high response rate; little pause after reinforcement	Greatest persistence; response rate stays high and gradually drops off

Summarizing the Effects of Reinforcement Schedules

Connect & Extend
To your teaching
Here are a few other examples of antecedents serving as cues about what behaviour will be rewarded in a particular situation:
Antecedent: Teacher giving lecture—taking notes will be rewarded, reading a magazine will not.
Antecedent: Substitute teacher—rule breaking may not be punished in this situation.
Antecedent: Desks in a circle—discussion will be rewarded.

Speed of performance depends on control. If reinforcement is based on the number of responses you make, you have more control over the reinforcement: the faster you accumulate the correct number of responses, the faster the reinforcer will come. A teacher who says, "As soon as you complete these 10 problems correctly, you may go to the student lounge," can expect higher rates of performance than a teacher who says, "Work on these 10 problems for the next 20 minutes. Then I will check your papers and those with 10 correct may go to the lounge."

Persistence in performance depends on predictability. Continuous reinforcement and both kinds of fixed reinforcement (ratio and interval) are quite predictable. We come to expect reinforcement at certain points and are generally quick to give up when the reinforcement does not meet our expectations. To encourage persistence of response, variable schedules are most appropriate. In fact, changing the schedule gradually until it becomes very "lean"—meaning that reinforcement occurs only after many responses or a long time interval—results in people learning to work for extended periods without any reinforcement at all. Just watch gamblers playing slot machines to see how powerful a lean reinforcement schedule can be.

Reinforcement schedules influence how persistently we will respond when reinforcement is withheld. What happens when reinforcement is completely withdrawn?

Extinction. In classical conditioning, we saw that the conditioned response was extinguished (disappeared) when the conditioned stimulus appeared but the unconditioned stimulus did not follow (tone, but no food). In operant conditioning, a person or an animal will not persist in certain behaviour if the usual reinforcer is withheld. The behaviour will eventually be extinguished (stop). For example, if you go for a week without selling even one magazine door to door, you may give up. Removal of reinforcement altogether leads to extinction. The process may take a while, however, as you know if you have tried to extinguish a child's tantrums by withholding your attention. Often the child wins—you give up ignoring and instead of extinction, intermittent reinforcement occurs. This, of course, may encourage even more persistent tantrums in the future.

Antecedents and Behaviour Change

In operant conditioning, antecedents—the events preceding behaviour—provide information about which behaviour will lead to positive consequences and which to negative. Skinner's pigeons learned to peck for food when a light was on, but not to bother when the light was off, because no food followed pecking when the light was off. In other words, they learned to use the antecedent light as a cue to discriminate the likely consequence of pecking. The pigeons' pecking was under **stimulus control**, controlled by the discriminative stimulus of the light. You can see that this idea is related to discrimination in classical conditioning, but here we are talking about voluntary behaviour such as pecking, not reflexes such as salivating.

We all learn to discriminate—to read situations. When should you ask to borrow your roommate's car, after a major disagreement or after you both have had a great time at a hockey game? The antecedent cue of a school principal standing in the hall helps students discriminate the probable consequences of running or attempting to break into a locker. We often respond to such antecedent cues without fully realizing that they are influencing our behaviour. But teachers can use cues deliberately in the classroom.

Cueing. By definition, **cueing** is the act of providing an antecedent stimulus just before you want particular behaviour to take place. Cueing is particularly useful in setting the stage for behaviour that must occur at a specific time but is easily forgotten. In working with young people, teachers often find themselves correcting behaviour after the fact. For example, they may ask students, "When are you going to start remembering to?" Such reminders often lead to irritation. The mistake is already made, and the young person is left with only two choices, to promise to try harder or to say, "Why don't you leave me alone?" Neither response is very satisfying. Presenting a non-judgmental cue before this happens can help prevent these negative confrontations. When a student performs the appropriate behaviour after a cue, the teacher can reinforce the student's accomplishment instead of punishing the student's failure.

Prompting. Sometimes students need help in learning to respond to a cue in an appropriate way, so the cue becomes a discriminative stimulus. One approach is to provide an additional cue, called a **prompt**, following the first cue. There are two

Connect & Extend
To real life
Examples of stimulus control: Anita found herself (more than once) about to turn into her old office parking lot, even after her department had moved to a new building across town. The old cues kept her heading automatically to the old office. Another example is the supposedly true story of a getaway car driver in a bank robbery who sped through town, only to be caught by the police when she dutifully stopped at a red light. The stimulus of the light had come to have automatic control.

Stimulus Control: Capacity for the presence or absence of antecedents to regulate behaviour.

Cueing: Providing a stimulus that "sets up" desired behaviour.

Prompt: A reminder that follows a cue to make sure the person reacts to the cue.

FIGURE 6.2

Written Prompts: A Peer-Tutoring Checklist

By using this checklist, students are reminded how to be effective tutors. As they become more proficient, the checklist may be less necessary.

 Remember to

 _____ 1. Have the lesson ready.

 _____ 2. Talk clearly.

 _____ 3. Be friendly.

 _____ 4. Tell the student when he is right.

 _____ 5. Correct mistakes. STOP! Give the right answer.

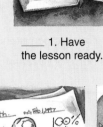 _____ 6. Praise good work!

 _____ 7. Make the lesson fun.

 _____ 8. Do not give TOO MUCH help.

_____ 9. Fill out the daily sheet.

_____ 10. Can you add a suggestion?

Source: From B. Sulzer-Azaroff and G. R. Mayer. Figure from *Achieving educational excellence: Behavior analysis for school personnel*, p. 89. Copyright © 1994 by Beth Sulzer-Azaroff and G. Roy Mayer (San Marcos, CA: Western Image, P.O. Box 427). Reprinted by permission of the authors.

Connect & Extend
To your teaching
Suggest the cues or prompts you would use to elicit the following behaviour: (1) the class looks at you to hear your directions; (2) the students open their books to the assigned page when the bell rings; (3) the students give you their full attention when you are making an important point; and (4) a student walks instead of runs to the door when the dismissal bell rings.

Applied Behaviour Analysis:
The application of behavioural learning principles to understand and change behaviour.

Behaviour Modification:
Systematic application of antecedents and consequences to change behaviour.

principles for using a cue and a prompt to teach new behaviour (Becker, Engelmann, & Thomas, 1975). First, make sure the environmental stimulus that you want to become a cue occurs immediately before the prompt you are using, so students will learn to respond to the cue and not rely only on the prompt. Second, gradually use the prompt less and less—fade it—so students do not become dependent on it.

An example of cueing and prompting is providing students with a checklist or reminder sheet. Figure 6.2 above is a checklist for the steps in peer tutoring. Working in pairs is the cue; the checklist is the prompt. As students learn the procedures, the teacher may stop using the checklist, but may remind the students of the steps. When no written or oral prompts are necessary, the students have learned to respond appropriately to the environmental cue of working in pairs— they have learned how to behave in tutoring situations. But the teacher should continue to monitor the process, recognize and reinforce good work, and correct mistakes. Before a tutoring session, the teacher might ask students to close their eyes and "see" the checklist, focusing on each step. As students work, the teacher could listen to their interactions and continue to coach students as they improve their tutoring skills.

Applied Behaviour Analysis

Applied behaviour analysis is the application of behavioural learning principles to change behaviour. The method is sometimes called **behaviour modification**, but this term has negative connotations for many people and is often misunderstood (Alberto & Troutman, 1990; Kaplan, 1991).

Ideally, applied behaviour analysis requires clear specification of the behaviour to be changed, careful recording of the behaviour, analysis of the antecedents and reinforcers that might be maintaining inappropriate or undesirable behaviour, interventions based on behavioural principles to change the behaviour, and careful measurement of changes. In research on applied behaviour analysis, a method or design called ABAB is common. That is, researchers take a baseline measurement of the behaviour (A), then apply the intervention (B), then stop the intervention to see if the behaviour goes back to the baseline level (A), and then reintroduce the intervention (B). If the behaviour during the B phases differs from the behaviour during the A phases, the consequences are effective.

In classrooms, teachers usually cannot follow all the ABAB steps, but they can do the following:

1. Clearly specify the behaviour to be changed and note the current level. For example, if a student is "careless," does this mean 2, 3, 4, or more computation errors for every 10 problems?

2. Plan a specific intervention using antecedents, consequences, or both. For example, offer the student one extra minute of computer time for every problem completed with no errors.

3. Keep track of the results, and modify the plan if necessary.

Let's consider some specific methods for accomplishing step 2—the intervention.

Methods for Encouraging Behaviour

As we discussed earlier, to increase a particular behaviour we reinforce it. There are several specific ways to encourage existing behaviour or teach new behaviour. These include praise, the Premack principle, shaping, and positive practice.

Reinforcing with Teacher Attention. Early work such as that of Madsen, Becker, and Thomas (1968) demonstrated that teachers can improve student behaviour by ignoring rule-breakers and praising students who are following the rules. On this basis, many psychologists advised teachers to "accentuate the positive"—liberally praise students for good behaviour while ignoring mistakes and misbehaviour. This praise-and-ignore approach can be helpful, but we should not expect it to solve all classroom management problems. Several studies have shown that disruptive behaviour persists when teachers use positive consequences (mostly praise) as their only classroom management strategy (Pfiffner, Rosen, & O'Leary, 1985; Rosen, O'Leary, Joyce, Conway, & Pfiffner, 1984).

There is a second consideration in using praise. The positive results found in research occur when teachers *carefully* and *systematically* praise their students. Unfortunately, praise is not always given appropriately and effectively. Merely "handing out compliments" will not improve behaviour. To be effective, praise must (1) be contingent on (immediately follow) the behaviour to be reinforced, (2) specify clearly the behaviour being reinforced, and (3) be believable (O'Leary & O'Leary, 1977). In other words, the praise should be sincere recognition of well-defined behaviour so students understand what they did to warrant the recognition. Teachers who have not received special training often violate these conditions (Brophy, 1981). Ideas for using praise effectively, based on Brophy's extensive review of the subject, are presented in the Guidelines, page 208.

Some psychologists have suggested that teachers' use of praise tends to focus students on learning to win approval rather than on learning for its own sake. Perhaps the best advice is to be aware of the potential dangers of the overuse or misuse of praise and to navigate accordingly.

Connect & Extend
To your teaching
Mr. Stevens is a Grade 2 teacher. He has been teaching for only a few weeks and is having problems. He has a class of 25 overeager children who consistently blurt and yell out their answers instead of waiting and raising their hands. He finds it difficult to respond to each student. He is pleased with their eagerness but needs a calmer setting. What would you do if you were Mr. Stevens?

Connect & Extend
To your teaching
When a teacher decides to begin ignoring behaviour that he or she wants to extinguish, the behaviour frequently increases for a short time before it decreases. How do you explain this phenomenon?

GUIDELINES

Using Praise Appropriately

Be clear and systematic in giving praise.

Examples

1. Make sure praise is tied directly to appropriate behaviour.
2. Make sure the student understands the specific action or accomplishments that is being praised. Say, "You returned this poster on time and in good condition," not, "You were very responsible."

Recognize genuine accomplishments.

Examples

1. Reward the attainment of specified goals, not just participation.
2. Do not reward uninvolved students just for being quiet and not disrupting the class.
3. Tie praise to students' improving competence or to the value of their accomplishment. Say, "I noticed that you double-checked all your problems. Your score reflects your careful work."

Set standards for praise based on individual abilities and limitations.

Examples

1. Praise progress or accomplishment in relation to the individual student's past efforts.

2. Focus the student's attention on his or her own progress, not on comparisons with others.

Attribute the student's success to effort and ability so the student will gain confidence that success is possible again.

Examples

1. Don't imply that the success may be based on luck, extra help, or easy material.
2. Ask students to describe the problems they encountered and how they solved them.

Make praise really reinforcing.

Examples

1. Don't attempt to influence the rest of the class by singling out some students for praise. This tactic frequently backfires, since students know what's really going on. In addition, you risk embarrassing the student you have chosen to praise.
2. Don't give undeserved praise to students simply to balance failures. It is seldom consoling and calls attention to the student's inability to earn genuine recognition.

Selecting Reinforcers: The Premack Principle. In most classrooms, there are many readily available reinforcers other than teacher attention, such as the chance to talk to other students or feed the class animals. But teachers tend to offer these opportunities in a haphazard way. By making privileges and rewards directly contingent on learning and positive behaviour—just as with praise—the teacher may greatly increase both learning and desired behaviour.

A helpful guide for choosing the most effective reinforcers is the Premack principle, named for David Premack (1965). According to the **Premack principle**, high-frequency behaviour (a preferred activity) can be an effective reinforcer for low-frequency behaviour (a less-preferred activity). This is sometimes referred to as "Grandma's rule": First do what I want you to do, then you may do what you want to do. Elizabeth Chan used this principle in her class when she told students they could work together on their news program after they had quietly completed the first section of the worksheet on their own.

If students didn't have to study, what would they do? The answers to this question may suggest many possible reinforcers. For most students, talking, moving around the room, sitting near a friend, being exempt from assignments or tests, reading magazines, or playing games are preferred activities. The best way to determine appropriate reinforcers for your students may be to watch what they do in their free time.

Premack Principle: Principle stating that a more-preferred activity can serve as reinforcer for a less-preferred activity.

For the Premack principle to be effective, the low-frequency (less-preferred) behaviour must happen first. In the following dialogue, notice how the teacher loses a perfect opportunity to use the Premack principle:

Students: Oh, no! Do we have to work on grammar again today? The other classes got to discuss the film we saw in the auditorium this morning.

Teacher: But the other classes finished the lesson on sentences yesterday. We're almost finished too. If we don't finish the lesson, I'm afraid you'll forget the rules we reviewed yesterday.

Students: Why don't we finish the sentences at the end of the period and talk about the film now?

Teacher: Okay, if you promise to complete the sentences later.

"HEY, WAIT A MINUTE! YOU'RE CLEANING ERASERS AS A PUNISHMENT? I'M CLEANING ERASERS AS A REWARD!"

(© 1991 Tony Saltzman)

Discussing the film could have served as a reinforcer for completing the lesson. As it is, the class may well spend the entire period discussing the film. Just as the discussion becomes fascinating, the teacher will have to end it and insist that the class return to the grammar lesson.

Some teachers use questionnaires like the one in Table 6.2 to identify effective reinforcers for their students. Remember, what works for one student may not be right for another. And students can get "too much of a good thing"—reinforcers can lose their potency if they are overused.

Shaping. What happens when students cannot gain reinforcement because they simply cannot perform a skill in the first place? Consider these examples:

▶ A Grade 4 student looks at the results of the latest mathematics test. "No credit on almost half of the problems again because I made one dumb mistake in each problem. I hate math!"

▶ A Grade 10 student tries each day to find some excuse for avoiding the softball game in gym class. The student cannot catch a ball and now refuses to try.

In both situations the students are receiving no reinforcement for their work because the end product of their efforts is not good enough. A safe prediction is that the students will soon learn to dislike the class, the subject, and perhaps the teacher and school in general. One way to prevent this problem is the strategy of **shaping**, also called **successive approximations**. Shaping involves reinforcing progress instead of waiting for perfection.

TABLE 6.2   What Do You Like? Reinforcement Ideas from Students

Name _____ Grade _____ Date_____

Please answer all the questions as completely as you can.

1. The school subjects I like best are:

2. Three things I like most to do in school are:

3. If I had 30 minutes' free time at school each day to do what I really liked, it would be:

4. My two favourite snacks are:

5. At recess I like most to (three things):

6. If I had $5 to spend on anything, I would buy:

7. Three jobs I would enjoy in the class are:

8. The two people I most like to work with in school are:

9. At home I really enjoy (three things):

Source: From G. Blackham and A. Silberman (1979). *Modification of Child and Adolescent Behavior,* 3/e, pp. 281–283. Copyright © 1979 by Wadsworth Publishing Co. Reprinted by permission of the publisher.

Shaping: Reinforcing each small step of progress toward a desired goal or behaviour.

Successive Approximations: Small components that make up complex behaviour.

Task Analysis: System for breaking down a task hierarchically into basic skills and sub-skills.

Positive Practice: Practising correct responses immediately after errors.

In order to use shaping, the teacher must break down the final complex behaviour the student is expected to master into a number of small steps. One approach identifying the small steps is **task analysis**, originally developed by R. B. Miller (1962) to help the armed services train personnel. Miller's system begins with a definition of the final performance requirement, what the trainee (or student) must be able to do at the end of the program or unit. Then the steps that will lead to the final goal are specified. The procedure simply breaks down skills and processes into sub-skills and sub-processes.

Consider an example of task analysis in which students must write a position paper based on library research. If the teacher assigned the position paper without analyzing the task in this way, what could happen? Some of the students might not know how to use the card catalogue. They might search through one or two encyclopedias, then write a summary of the issues based only on the encyclopedia articles. Another group of students might know how to use the card catalogue, tables of contents, and indexes, but have difficulty reaching conclusions. They might hand in lengthy papers listing summaries of different ideas. Another group of students might be able to draw conclusions, but their written presentations might be so confusing and grammatically incorrect that the teacher could not understand what they were trying to say. Each of the groups would have failed in fulfilling the assignment, but for different reasons.

A task analysis gives a picture of the logical sequence of steps leading toward the final goal. An awareness of this sequence can help teachers make sure that students have the necessary skills before they move to the next step. In addition, when students have difficulty, the teacher can pinpoint problem areas.

Krumboltz and Krumboltz (1972) have described the following three methods of shaping: (1) reinforce each sub-skill, (2) reinforce improvements in accuracy, and (3) reinforce longer and longer periods of performance or participation.

Much behaviour can be improved through shaping. This is especially true for skills that require persistence, endurance, increased accuracy, greater speed, or extensive practice to master. Because shaping is a time-consuming process, however, it should not be used if success can be attained through simpler methods such as cueing.

Positive Practice. A strategy for helping students replace one behaviour with another is **positive practice**. This approach is especially appropriate for dealing with academic errors. When students make a mistake, they must correct it as soon as possible and practise the correct response (Gibbs & Luyben, 1985; Kazdin, 1984). The same principle can be applied when a students breaks classroom rules. Instead of being punished, the student might be required to practise the correct alternative action.

The Guidelines on page 211 summarize approaches encouraging positive behaviour.

"OF COURSE YOU DON'T HAVE TO GO TO SCHOOL, DEAR. WOULD YOU GET SOME LIVER OUT OF THE FREEZER TO DEFROST FOR OUR LUNCH?"

(© Martha Campbell. From Phi Delta Kappan.)

Coping with Undesirable Behaviour

No matter how successful you are at accentuating the positive, there are times when you must cope with undesirable behaviour, either because other methods fail or because the behaviour itself is dangerous or calls for direct action. For this purpose, negative reinforcement, satiation, reprimands, and punishment all offer possible solutions.

Negative Reinforcement. Recall the basic principle of negative reinforcement: If an action stops or avoids something unpleasant, the action is likely to occur again in similar situations. Negative reinforcement was operating in Elizabeth

Connect & Extend
To the classroom
Examples of negative reinforcement: A Grade 10 teacher tells her class that those students who turn in sloppy, careless work will have to use their free-choice time to redo it. A Grade 1 teacher tells an angry boy that he must sit by the tree until he feels able to rejoin the kickball game without arguing.

GUIDELINES

Using Positive Reinforcement

Make sure you recognize positive behaviour in ways that students value.

Examples

1. When presenting class rules, set up positive consequences for following rules as well as negative consequences for breaking rules.
2. Recognize honest admissions of mistakes by giving a second chance: "Because you admitted that you copied your paper from a book, I'm giving you a chance to rewrite it."
3. Offer desired rewards for academic efforts, such as extra recess time, exemptions from homework or tests, extra credit on major projects.

When students are tackling new material or trying new skills, give plenty of reinforcement.

Examples

1. Find and comment on something right in every student's first drawing.
2. Reinforce students for encouraging each other. "Russian pronunciation is difficult and awkward at first. Let's help each other by eliminating all giggles when someone is brave enough to attempt a new word."

After new behaviour is established, give reinforcement on an unpredictable schedule to encourage persistence.

Examples

1. Offer surprise rewards for good participation in class.

2. Start classes with a short, written extra-credit question. Students don't have to answer, but a good answer will add points to their total for the semester.
3. Make sure the good students get compliments for their work from time to time. Don't take them for granted.

Use cueing to help establish new behaviour.

Examples

1. Put up humorous signs in the classroom to remind students of rules.
2. At the beginning of the year, as students enter class, call their attention to a list on the board of the materials they should have with them when they come to class.

Make sure all students, even those who often cause problems, receive some praise, privileges, or other rewards when they do something well.

Examples

1. Review your class list occasionally to make sure all students are receiving some reinforcement.
2. Set standards for reinforcement so that all students will have a chance to be rewarded.

Chan's classroom. When she gave in to the moans and complaints of her class and cancelled the test, her behaviour was being negatively reinforced. She escaped the unpleasant student comments by changing her assignment.

Negative reinforcement may also be used to enhance learning. To do this, you place students in mildly unpleasant situations so they can "escape" when their behaviour improves. Consider these examples:

Teacher to a Grade 3 class: "When the supplies are put back in the cabinet and each of you is sitting quietly, we will go outside. Until then, we will miss our recess."

High school teacher to a student who seldom finishes in-class assignments: "As soon as you complete the assignment, you may join the class in the auditorium. But until you finish, you must work in the study hall."

You may wonder why these examples are not considered punishment. Surely staying in during recess or not accompanying the class to a special program is punishing. But the focus in each case is on strengthening specific behaviour (putting away supplies or finishing in-class assignments). The teacher strengthens (reinforces) the behaviour by removing something aversive *as soon as the desired behaviour*

Applied Behaviour Analysis **211**

Applied Behaviour Analysis

Review

▶ What are the steps in applied behaviour analysis?

▶ How can the Premack principle help you identify reinforcers?

▶ When is shaping an appropriate approach?

▶ What are some of the possible side effects of punishment?

Apply

▶ How could you use applied behavioural analysis to change some of your behaviour such as exercising or studying?

Connect & Extend
To the classroom
Satiation: A Grade 6 teacher discovered one of his students making paper airplanes during an independent work time. He gave that student a stack of paper and told her to continue making airplanes until the stack of paper was gone. The student thought it was great fun for the first 10 minutes, but then she got weary and wanted to stop. After this experience, this student made better use of her independent work times.

Connect & Extend
To the classroom
Soft reprimands: During reading in Ms. Chandler's Grade 1 class, she noticed that Kenny wasn't concentrating on his book. She was working with a group at the time and could have called out, "Kenny, you'd better get back to work. You're not concentrating," but she decided this would embarrass him as well as disturb the concentration of others. Instead, Ms. Chandler walked over to him, asked him a couple of questions about the story, and asked him to let her know how the story ended. She achieved her goal without causing embarrassment, and she provided Kenny with an impetus and motive to concentrate on his story again.

Satiation: Requiring a person to repeat problem behaviour past the point of interest or motivation.

Reprimands: Criticisms for misbehaviour; rebukes.

occurs. Because the consequence involves removing or "subtracting" a stimulus, the reinforcement is negative.

Negative reinforcement also gives students a chance to exercise control. Missing recess and staying behind in study hall are unpleasant situations, but in each case the students retain control. As soon as students perform the appropriate behaviour, the unpleasant situation ends. In contrast, punishment occurs after the fact, and a student cannot so easily control or terminate it.

There are several rules for negative reinforcement: Describe the desired change in a positive way. Don't bluff. Make sure you can enforce your unpleasant situation. Follow through despite complaints. Insist on action, not promises. If the unpleasant situation terminates when students promise to be better next time, you have reinforced making promises, not making changes (Krumboltz & Krumboltz, 1972; O'Leary, 1995).

Satiation.   Another way to stop problem behaviour is to insist that students continue the behaviour until they are tired of doing it. This procedure, called **satiation**, should be applied with care. Forcing students to continue some behaviour may be physically or emotionally harmful or even dangerous.

An example of an appropriate use of satiation is related by Krumboltz and Krumboltz (1972). In the middle of a Grade 9 algebra class, the teacher suddenly noticed four students making all sorts of unusual motions. In response to persistent teacher questioning, the students finally admitted they were bouncing imaginary balls. The teacher pretended to greet this idea with enthusiasm and suggested the whole class do it. At first, there was a great deal of laughing and joking. After a minute this stopped, and one student even quit. The teacher, however, insisted that all the students continue. After five minutes and a number of exhausted sighs, the teacher allowed the students to stop. No one bounced an imaginary ball in that class again.

Teachers also may allow students to continue some action until they stop by themselves, if the behaviour is not interfering with the rest of the class. A teacher can do this by simply ignoring the behaviour. Remember that just responding to an ignorable behaviour may actually reinforce it.

In using satiation, a teacher must take care not to give in before the students do. It is also important that the repeated behaviour be the one you are trying to end. If the algebra teacher above had insisted that the students write, "I will never bounce imaginary balls in class again" 500 times, the students would have become satiated with writing rather than with bouncing balls.

Reprimands.   In the *Junction Journal*, Anita's daughter's elementary school newspaper, were the following lines in a story called "Why I Like School," written by a Grade 4 student. . . . "I also like my teacher. She helps me understand and learn. She is nice to everyone I like it when she gets mad at somebody, but she doesn't yell at them in front of the class, but speaks to them privately."

A study by Dan O'Leary and his associates examined the effectiveness of soft, private **reprimands** versus loud, public reprimands in decreasing disruptive behaviour (O'Leary, Kaufman, Kass, & Drabman, 1970). Reprimanding a problem student quietly so that only the student can hear seems to be much more effective. When the teacher in the study spoke to offenders loudly enough for the entire class to hear, the disruptions increased or continued at a constant level. Some students enjoy public recognition for misbehaviour. If reprimands are not used too often, and if the classroom is generally a positive, warm environment, students usually respond quickly (Kaplan, 1991; Van Houten & Doleys, 1983).

Response Cost. The concept of **response cost** is familiar to anyone who has ever paid a fine. For certain infractions of the rules, people must lose some reinforcer (money, time, privileges, pleasures). In a class, the concept of response cost may be applied in a number of ways. The first time a student breaks a class rule, the teacher gives a warning. The second time, the teacher makes a mark beside the student's name in the grade book. The student loses two minutes of recess for each mark accumulated. For older students, a certain number of marks might mean losing the privilege of working in a group or going on a class trip.

Social Isolation. One of the most controversial behavioural methods for decreasing undesirable behaviour is the strategy of **social isolation**, often called **time out** from reinforcement. The process involves removing a highly disruptive student from the classroom for 5 to 10 minutes. The student is placed in an empty, uninteresting room alone. It seems likely that the factor that actually decreases behaviour is the punishment of brief isolation from other people (O'Leary & O'Leary, 1976). A trip to the principal's office or confinement to a chair in the corner of the regular classroom does not have the same effect as sitting alone in an otherwise empty room.

Some Cautions. Punishment in and of itself does not lead to any positive behaviour. Thus, whenever you consider the use of punishment, you should make it part of a two-pronged attack. The first goal is to carry out the punishment and suppress the undesirable behaviour. The second goal is to make clear what the student should be doing instead and to provide reinforcement for those desirable actions. Thus, while the problem behaviour is being suppressed, positive alternative responses are being strengthened. The Guidelines on page 214 give ideas for using punishment for positive purposes.

▲ *This student is in "social isolation." What conditions would help make this a useful intervention?*

*B*ehavioural Approaches to Teaching and Management

The behavioural approach to learning has made several important contributions to instruction, including systems for specifying learning objectives (we will look at this topic in Chapter 13 when we discuss planning and teaching), mastery learning techniques, and class management systems such as group consequences, token economies, and contingency contracts. These approaches are useful when the goal is to learn *explicit information* or change *behaviour* and when the material is *sequential* and *factual*. As an example of a teaching approach, let's consider mastery learning.

Mastery Learning

Mastery learning is based on the assumption that, given enough time and the proper instruction, most students can master any learning objective (Bloom, 1968; Guskey & Gates, 1986). To use the mastery approach, a teacher must break a course down into small units of study. Each unit might involve mastering several

Response Cost: Punishment by loss of reinforcers.

Social Isolation: Removal of a disruptive student for 5 to 10 minutes.

Time Out: Technically, the removal of all reinforcement. In practice, isolation of a student from the rest of the class for a brief time.

Mastery Learning: An approach to teaching and grading that requires students to achieve specific objectives before moving to the next unit or topic. Based on the assumption that every student is capable of achieving most of the objectives if given enough time and proper instruction.

GUIDELINES

Using Punishment

Try to structure the situation so you can use negative reinforcement rather than punishment.

Examples

1. Allow students to escape unpleasant situations (completing additional workbook assignments, weekly test of math facts) when they reach a level of competence.
2. Insist on actions, not promises. Don't let students convince you to change terms of the agreement.

Be consistent in your application of punishment.

Examples

1. Avoid inadvertently reinforcing the behaviour you are trying to punish. Keep confrontations private, so that students don't become heroes for standing up to the teacher in a public showdown.
2. Let students know in advance the consequences of breaking the rules by posting major class rules for younger students or outlining rules and consequences in a course syllabus for older students.
3. Tell students they will receive only one warning before punishment is given. Give the warning in a calm way, then follow through.
4. Make punishment as unavoidable and immediate as is reasonably possible.

Focus on the students' actions, not on the students' personal qualities.

Examples

1. Reprimand in a calm but firm voice.
2. Avoid vindictive or sarcastic words or tones of voice. You might hear your own angry words later when students imitate your sarcasm.
3. Stress the need to end the problem behaviour instead of expressing any dislike you might feel for the student.

Adapt the punishment to the infraction.

Examples

1. Ignore minor misbehaviours that do not disrupt the class, or stop these misbehaviours with a disapproving glance or a move toward the student.
2. Don't use homework as a punishment for misbehaviours like talking in class.
3. When a student misbehaves to gain peer acceptance, removal from the group of friends can be effective, since this is really time out from a reinforcing situation.
4. If the problem behaviours continue, analyze the situation and try a new approach. Your punishment may not be very punishing, or you may be inadvertently reinforcing the misbehaviour.

specific objectives. "Mastery" usually means a score of 80 to 90 percent on a test or other assessment. The teacher informs the students of the objectives and the criteria for meeting each. Students who do not reach the minimum level of mastery or who reach this minimum but want to improve their performance (thus raising their grade) can recycle through the unit. When they are ready, they take another form of the unit test.

The challenge in mastery learning is providing the appropriate extra help for students who don't attain mastery. There are many possibilities. Students can work with peer tutors or aides inside or outside class or they can get extra help from their team members in cooperative groups. If no extra time or staff is available, mastery learning can be adapted to a regular class time frame. For example, after explaining the mastery approach, the teacher teaches the lessons, then gives an ungraded assessment to determine students' levels of understanding. Those who have reached the mastery level are given enrichment activities such as independent or group work, computer simulations, research projects, or creative problems to solve. Those who need more help work with the teacher on corrective instruction (Block & Anderson, 1975). The Keller Plan, also called the Personalized System of Instruction (PSI), is a form of mastery learning used most often in college (Sherman, Ruskin, & Semb, 1982).

Mastery learning makes the most sense when the focus is key concepts or skills that serve as a foundation for later learning. In mathematics, for example, some students will fall farther and farther behind if they have to move from addition of fractions to more advanced topics before they ever really understand addition. By the time they reach division of fractions, they are lost. Mastery learning has been successful when students get the extra time and support they need to learn—especially through corrective instruction outside class or inside class from peer tutors or members of a cooperative learning group (Guskey, 1990; Kulik, Kulik, & Bangert-Drowns, 1990; Shuell, 1996). The effects of remediation/enrichment provided only by the teacher in class, as in the Block and Anderson (1975) model, are less clear-cut and probably depend on the quality of the remediation possible using class time alone (Ellis & Fouts, 1993).

There are problems with the mastery learning approach. Teachers must have a variety of materials to allow students to recycle through objectives they failed to meet the first time. Usually, just repeating the same materials won't help. It is also important to have several assessments for each unit. In practice, mastery learning has not helped to erase achievement differences among students, as some proponents have hoped. Individual differences in achievement persist, unless the teacher holds back the faster students while the slower ones catch up—a practice that makes little sense (Arlin, 1984). Left to work at their own pace, some students will learn much more and leave a unit with much better understanding than others. Some will work much harder to take advantage of the learning opportunities (Grabe & Latta, 1981). Some will be frustrated instead of encouraged by the chance to recycle ("You mean I have to do it *again*?").

Many of the systematic applications of behavioural principles focus on classroom management. We will look at three: group consequences, token economies, and contingency contracts.

Connect & Extend
To the research
Fulk, C.L., & Smith, P. J. (1995). Students' perceptions of teachers' instructional and management adaptations for students with learning or behavior problems. *The Elementary School Journal, 95,* 409–419.
Abstract: Students from Grades 1 to 6 were interviewed individually and asked four "yes" or "no" questions about the following adaptations for some students: (1) easier work, (2) harder work, (3) rewards for good behaviour, and (4) extra chances or different rules. The majority of responses (69 percent) were positive, with students favouring both academic and behavioural adaptations when needed. However, most Grade 1, Grade 5, and Grade 6 students were opposed to some students getting more difficult work, and Grade 1 students also opposed differential handling of behaviour problems.

Group Consequences

A teacher can base reinforcement for the class on the cumulative behaviour of all members of the class, usually by adding each student's points to a class or a team total. The **good behaviour game** is an example of this approach. A class is divided into two teams. Specific rules for good behaviour are cooperatively developed. Each time a student breaks one of the rules, that student's team is given a mark. The team with the fewest marks at the end of the period receives a special reward or privilege (longer recess, first to lunch, and so on). If both teams earn fewer than a pre-established number of marks, both teams receive the reward. Most studies indicate that even though the game produces only small improvements in academic achievement, it can produce definite improvements in the behaviour listed in the good-behaviour rules.

You can also use **group consequences** without dividing the class into teams, that is, you can base reinforcement on the behaviour of the whole class. Wilson and Hopkins (1973) conducted a study using group consequences to reduce noise levels. Radio music served effectively as the reinforcer for students in a home economics class. Whenever noise in the class was below a predetermined level, students could listen to the radio; when the noise exceeded the level, the radio was turned off. Given the success of this simple method, such a procedure might be considered in any class where music does not interfere with the task at hand.

However, caution is needed in group approaches. The whole group should not suffer for the misbehaviour or mistakes of one individual if the group has no real influence over that person (Epanchin, Townsend, & Stoddard, 1994; Jenson, Sloane, & Young, 1988). Anita saw an entire class break into cheers when the teacher announced that one boy was transferring to another school. The chant "No more points! No more points!" filled the room. The "points" referred to the teacher's system of giving one point to the whole class each time anyone broke a rule. Every point meant five minutes of recess lost. The boy who was transferring had been responsible for many losses. He was not very popular to begin with, and

Good Behaviour Game:
Arrangement where a class is divided into teams and each team receives demerit points for breaking agreed-on rules of good behaviour.

Group Consequences:
Reinforcers or punishments given to a class as a whole for adhering to or violating rules of conduct.

the point system, though quite effective in maintaining order, had led to rejection and even greater unpopularity.

Peer pressure in the form of support and encouragement, however, can be a positive influence. Group consequences are recommended for situations in which students care about the approval of their peers. If the misbehaviour of several students seems to be encouraged by the attention and laughter of other students, group consequences could be helpful. Teachers might show students how to give support and constructive feedback to classmates. If a few students seem to enjoy sabotaging the system, those students may need separate arrangements.

Token Reinforcement Programs

Often it is difficult to provide positive consequences for all the students who deserve them. A **token reinforcement system** can help solve this problem by allowing all students to earn tokens for both academic work and positive classroom behaviour. The tokens may be points, checks, holes punched in a card, chips, play money, or anything else that is easily identified as the student's property. Periodically the students exchange the tokens they have earned for some desired reward (Martin & Pear, 1992).

Depending on the age of the student, the rewards could be small toys, school supplies, free time, special class jobs, or other privileges. When a "token economy," as this kind of system is called, is first established, the tokens should be given out on a fairly continuous schedule, with chances to exchange the tokens for rewards often available. Once the system is working well, however, tokens should be distributed on an intermittent schedule and saved for longer periods of time before they are exchanged for rewards.

Another variation is to allow students to earn tokens in the classroom and then exchange them for rewards at home. These plans are very successful when parents are willing to cooperate. Usually a note or report form is sent home daily or twice a week. The note indicates the number of points earned in the preceding time frame. The points may be exchanged for minutes of television viewing, access to special toys, or private time with parents. Points can also be saved up for larger rewards such as trips. Do not use this procedure, however, if you suspect the child might be severely punished for poor reports.

Token reinforcement systems are complicated and time-consuming. Generally, they should be used in only three situations: to motivate students who are completely uninterested in their work and have not responded to other approaches; to encourage students who have consistently failed to make academic progress; and to deal with a class that is out of control. Some groups of students seem to benefit more than others from token economies. Students who are developmentally challenged, slow learners, children who have failed often, students with few academic skills, and students with behaviour problems all seem to respond to the concrete, direct nature of token reinforcement.

Before you try a token system, you should be sure that your teaching methods and materials are right for the students. Sometimes class disruptions or lack of motivation indicate that teaching practices need to be changed. Maybe the class rules are unclear or are enforced inconsistently.

CHECKPOINT

Behavioural Approaches to Teaching and Management

Review

▶ What is mastery learning?

▶ Describe the managerial strategies of group consequences, token programs, and contracts.

Apply

▶ How could you use one of these management approaches to handle the situation described at the beginning of the chapter?

Maybe the text is too easy or too hard. Maybe the pace is wrong. If these problems exist, a token system may improve the situation temporarily, but the students will still have trouble learning the academic material (Jenson, Sloane, & Young, 1988).

Contingency Contract: A formal agreement, often written and signed, between the teacher and an individual student specifying what the student must do to earn a particular privilege or reward.

Contingency Contract Programs

In a **contingency contract** program, the teacher draws up an individual contract with each student, describing exactly what the student must do to earn a particular privilege or reward. In some programs, students participate in deciding on the behaviour to be reinforced and the rewards that can be gained. The negotiating process itself can be an educational experience, as students learn to set reasonable goals and abide by the terms of a contract.

An example of a contract for completing assignments that is appropriate for intermediate and upper-grade students is presented in Figure 6.3. This chart serves

FIGURE 6.3

A Contingency Contract for Completing Assignments

The teacher and student agree on the due dates for each assignment, marking them in blue on the chart. Each time an assignment is turned in, the date of completion is marked in black on the chart. As long as the actual completion line is above the planned completion line, the student earns free time or other contracted rewards.

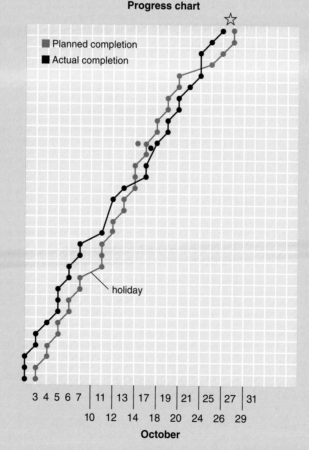

Source: From *Achieving Educational Excellence: Behavior Analysis for School Personnel* (Figure, p. 89), by B. Sulzer-Azaroff and G. R. Mayer, 1994, San Marcos, CA: Western Image, P.O. Box 427. Copyright © 1994 by Beth Sulzer-Azaroff and G. Roy Mayer. Reprinted with permission.

Connect & Extend
To the classroom
Self-management can be used to encourage social behaviour. This self-recording form is taken from Jenson, W. R., Sloane, H. N., & Young, K. R. (1988). *Applied behavior analysis in education: A structured teaching approach.* Englewood Cliffs, NJ: Prentice-Hall, p. 272.

SOCIAL SKILLS PRACTICE CARD

Name _____

Date _____

Things to remember:

Use your new skill. Take this card with you and mark it when you use the social skill.

Social skill: _____

	How many times?
WHERE?	1 2 3 4 5
1. In class	
2. On the playground	
3. At lunch	
4. At home	
5. Other	

Connect & Extend
To other chapters
Concern with self-management is not restricted to any one group or theory. Psychologists who study Vygotsky's ideas about cognitive development (**Chapter 2**) are involved, as are cognitive psychologists interested in learning strategies (**Chapters 7 and 8**) and motivational psychologists point to self-regulation as a critical factor in motivation (**Chapters 10 and 11**).

as a contract, assignment sheet, and progress record. Something like this might even help you keep track of your assignments and due dates in college.

The few pages devoted here to token reinforcement and contingency contracts can offer only an introduction to these programs. If you want to set up a large-scale reward program in your classroom, you should probably seek professional advice. Often the school psychologist, counsellor, or principal can help. In addition, remember that, applied inappropriately, external rewards can undermine the students' motivation to learn (Deci, 1975; Lepper & Greene, 1978).

Recent Approaches: Self-regulation and Cognitive Behaviour Modification

The most recent application of behavioural views of learning emphasizes **self-management**—helping students gain control of their own learning. As you will see throughout this book, the role of students in their own learning is a major concern of psychologists and educators today. This concern is not restricted to any one group or theory. Different areas of research and theory all converge on one important idea, that responsibility and the ability to learn rest within the student. No one can learn for someone else (Manning & Payne, 1996; Winne, 1995; Zimmerman, 1990; Zimmerman & Schunk, 1989).

One reason that behavioural psychologists became interested in self-management is that students taught with classic behavioural methods seldom generalized their learning to new situations. For example, some research indicates that inattentive students could learn to pay excellent attention to lessons in a small group, but when they returned to the regular classroom, they did not take their new skill back with them (Woolfolk & Woolfolk, 1974). Many behavioural psychologists decided that response generalization would be encouraged if students became partners in the behaviour change procedures. About this same time, Donald Meichenbaum (1977), of the University of Waterloo, was having success teaching impulsive students to "talk themselves through" tasks, so there was evidence that students could benefit from what Meichenbaum termed "cognitive behaviour modification" (Manning, 1991).

Self-Management

If one goal of education is to produce people who are capable of educating themselves, students must learn to manage their own lives, set their own goals, and provide their own reinforcement. In adult life, rewards are sometimes vague and goals often take a long time to reach. Think how many small steps are required to complete an education and find your first job. Life is filled with tasks that call for this sort of self-management (Kanfer & Gaelick, 1986).

Students may be involved in any or all of the steps in implementing a basic behaviour-change program. They may help set goals, observe their own work, keep records of it, and evaluate their own performance. Finally, they can select and deliver reinforcement. Such involvement can help students master all the steps so they can perform these tasks in the future (Kaplan, 1991).

Goal Setting. It appears that the goal-setting phase is very important in self-management (Pintrich & Schunk, 1996; Reeve, 1996). In fact, some research suggests that setting specific goals and making them public may be the critical elements of self-management programs. For example, S. C. Hayes and his colleagues identified college students who had serious problems with studying and then taught them how to set specific study goals. Students who set goals and announced them to the experimenters performed significantly better on tests covering the

Self-Management: Use of behavioural learning principles to change your own behaviour.

◀ *Self-management programs allow students to record and monitor their own progress and judge their performance.*

material they were studying than students who set goals privately and never revealed them to anyone (Hayes, Rosenfarb, Wulfert, Munt, Korn, & Zettle, 1985).

Higher standards tend to lead to higher performance (McLaughlin & Gnagey, 1981). Unfortunately, student-set goals have a tendency to slip lower and lower. Teachers can help students maintain high standards by monitoring the goals set and reinforcing high standards. In one study, a teacher helped Grade 1 students raise the number of math problems they set for themselves to work on each day by praising them whenever they increased their objective by 10 percent. The students maintained their new, higher work standards, and the improvements even generalized to other subjects (Price & O'Leary, 1974).

Recording and Evaluating Progress. Students may also participate in the recording and evaluation phases of a behaviour-change program. Examples of behaviour that is appropriate for self-recording include the number of assignments completed, time spent practising a skill, number of books read, and number of times out of seat without permission. Tasks that must be accomplished without teacher supervision, such as homework or private study, are also good candidates for self-monitoring. Students keep a chart, diary, or checklist recording the frequency or duration of the behaviour in question.

A progress record card can help older students break down assignments into small steps, determine the best sequence for completing the steps, and keep track of daily progress by setting goals for each day. The record card itself serves as a prompt that can be faded out (Jenson, Sloane, & Young, 1988). Because cheating on records is a potential problem, especially when students are rewarded for improvements, intermittent checking by the teacher plus bonus points for accurate recording may be helpful (Hundert & Bucher, 1978).

Self-evaluation is somewhat more difficult than simple self-recording because it involves making a judgment about quality. Very few studies have been conducted in this area, but it appears that students can learn to evaluate their behaviour with reasonable accuracy (Rhode, Morgan, & Young, 1983). One key seems to be periodically checking students' self-evaluations and giving reinforcement for accurate judgments. Older students may learn accurate self-evaluation more readily than younger students. Again, bonus points can be awarded when the teachers' and students' evaluations match (Kaplan, 1991). One teacher found that his Grade 8 science students could learn to give themselves fair and accurate grades when he used such a system.

Connect & Extend
To your teaching
One student in your class is never prepared to do his work. He doesn't have a pencil, has misplaced his book, left his homework at home, doesn't understand the assignment, forgot to buy notebook paper, and so on. The result of all this is that he seldom hands in his homework assignments. How would you approach this problem? Develop several alternative strategies, such as reward and punishment, shaping, or self-management.

Connect & Extend
To real life
A study conducted by Mark Morgan (1985. Self-monitoring of attained subgoals in private study. *Journal of Educational Psychology, 77,* 623–630) combined goal setting, self-recording, and self-evaluation. Morgan taught self-monitoring strategies to all the education students in the required educational psychology course at his college. The students who set specific short-term objectives for each study unit and monitored their progress toward the objectives outperformed the students who simply monitored study time, even though the students who monitored their time actually spent more hours studying!

Self-Reinforcement: Providing yourself with positive consequences, contingent on accomplishing particular behaviour.

Self-Reinforcement. The last step in self-management is **self-reinforcement**. There is some disagreement, however, as to whether this step is actually necessary. Some psychologists believe that setting goals and monitoring progress alone are sufficient and that self-reinforcement adds nothing to the effects (Hayes et al., 1985). Others believe that rewarding yourself for a job well done can lead to higher levels of performance than simply setting goals and keeping track of progress (Bandura, 1986). If you are willing to be tough and really deny yourself something you want until your goals are reached, the promise of the reinforcer can provide extra incentive for work. With that in mind, you may want to think now of some way you can reinforce yourself when you finish reading this chapter.

At times, families can be enlisted to help their children develop self-management abilities. Working together, teachers and parents can focus on a few goals and, at the same time, support the growing independence of the students. The Family and Community Partnerships Guidelines give some ideas.

Sometimes, teaching students self-management can solve a problem for teachers and provide fringe benefits as well. For example, the coaches of a competitive swim team with members aged 9 to 16 were having difficulty persuading swimmers to maintain high work rates. Then the coaches drew up four charts indicating the training program to be followed by each member and posted the charts near the pool. The swimmers were given the responsibility of recording their numbers of laps and completion of each training unit. Because the recording was public, swimmers could see their own progress and that of others, give and receive congratulations, and keep accurate track of the work units completed. Work output

FAMILY AND COMMUNITY PARTNERSHIPS

Student Self-Management

Introduce the system to parents and students in a positive way.

Examples

1. Invite family participation, and stress possible benefits to all family members.
2. Consider starting the program just with volunteers.
3. Describe how you use self-management programs yourself.

Help families and students establish reachable goals.

Examples

1. Provide examples of possible self-management goals for students, such as starting homework early in the evening, or keeping track of books read.
2. Show families how to post goals and keep track of progress. Encourage everyone in the family to work on a goal.

Give families ways to record and evaluate their child's progress (or their own).

Examples

1. Divide the work into easily measured steps.
2. Provide models of good work where judgments are more difficult, such as in creative writing.
3. Give families a record form or checklist to keep track of progress.

Encourage families to check the accuracy of student records from time to time, and help their children to develop forms of self-reinforcement.

Examples

1. Have many checkups when students are first learning, and fewer later.
2. Have siblings check one another's records.
3. Where appropriate, test the skills that students are supposed to be developing at home and reward students whose self-evaluations match their test performances.
4. Have students brainstorm ideas with their families on how to reward themselves for jobs well done.

increased by 27 percent. The coaches also liked the system because swimmers could begin to work immediately without waiting for instructions (McKenzie & Rushall, 1974).

Cognitive Behaviour Modification and Self-Instruction

Self-management generally means getting students involved in the basic steps of a behaviour-change program. **Cognitive behaviour modification** adds an emphasis on thinking and self-talk. For this reason, many psychologists consider cognitive behaviour modification more a cognitive than a behavioural approach. We present it here because it serves as a bridge to Chapters 7 and 8 on cognitive learning.

As noted in Chapter 2, there is a stage in cognitive development when young children seem to guide themselves through a task using private speech. They talk to themselves, often repeating the words of a parent or teacher. In cognitive behaviour modification, students are taught directly how to use self-instruction. Meichenbaum (1977) outlined the steps:

1. An adult model performs a task while talking to him- or herself out loud (cognitive modelling).
2. The child performs the same task under the direction of the model's instructions (overt, external guidance).
3. The child performs the task while instructing him- or herself aloud (overt self-guidance).
4. The child whispers the instructions to him- or herself as he/she goes through the task (faded, overt self-guidance).
5. The child performs the task while guiding his/her performance via private speech (covert self-instruction). (p. 32)

Brenda Manning and Beverly Payne (1996) list four skills that can increase student learning: listening, planning, working, and checking. How might cognitive self-instruction help students develop these skills? One possibility is to use personal booklets or class posters that prompt students to "talk to themselves" about these skills. For example, one Grade 5 class designed a set of prompts for each of the four skills and posted the prompts around the classroom. The prompts for listening included: "Does this make sense?" "Am I getting this?" "I need to ask a question now before I forget." "Pay attention!" "Can I do what he's saying to do?" Planning prompts were, "Do I have everything together?" "Do I have my friends tuned out for right now?" "Let me get organized first." "What order will I do this in?" "I know this stuff!" Posters for these and the other two skills, working and checking, are shown in Figure 6.4. Part of the power of this process is in getting students involved in thinking about and creating their own guides and prompts. Having the discussion and posting the ideas makes students more self-aware and in control of their own learning.

Actually, cognitive behaviour modification as it is described by Meichenbaum and others has many more components than just teaching students to use self-instruction. Meichenbaum's methods also include dialogue and interaction between teacher and student, modelling, guided discovery, motivational strategies, feedback, careful matching of the task with the student's developmental level, and

Review

▶ What are the steps in self-management?

Apply

▶ How could you use the elements of self-management to study in this course?

Cognitive Behaviour Modification: Procedures based on both behavioural and cognitive learning principles for changing your own behaviour by using self-talk and self-instruction.

FIGURE 6.4

Posters to Remind Students to "Talk Themselves Through" Listening, Planning, Working, and Checking in School

These four posters were designed by a Grade 5 class to help them remember to use self-instruction. Some of the reminders reflect the special world of these preadolescents.

Poster 1

While Listening:
1. Does this make sense?
2. Am I getting this?
3. I need to ask a question now before I forget.
4. Pay attention.
5. Can I do what he's saying to do?

Poster 3

While Working:
1. Am I working fast enough?
2. Stop staring at my girlfriend and get back to work.
3. How much time is left?
4. Do I need to stop and start over?
5. This is hard for me, but I can manage okay.

Poster 2

While Planning:
1. Do I have everything together?
2. Do I have my friends tuned out for right now?
3. Let me get organized first.
4. What order will I do this in?
5. I know this stuff!

Poster 4

While Checking:
1. Did I finish everything?
2. What do I need to recheck?
3. Am I proud of this work?
4. Did I write all the words? Count them.
5. I think I finished. I organized myself. Did I daydream too much?

Source: From B. H. Manning and B. D. Payne, *Self-Talk for Teachers and Students: Metacognitive Strategies for Personal and Classroom use,* p. 125. Copyright © 1996 by Allyn & Bacon. Adapted by permission.

other principles of good teaching. The student is even involved in designing the program (Harris, 1990; Harris & Pressley, 1991). Given all this, it is no surprise that students do seem to generalize skills developed through cognitive behaviour modification to new learning situations (Harris, Graham, & Pressley, in press).

Problems and Issues

The preceding sections provide an overview of several strategies for changing classroom behaviour. However, you should be aware that these strategies are tools that may be used responsibly or irresponsibly. What, then, are some issues you should keep in mind?

Ethical Issues

The ethical questions related to the use of the strategies described in this chapter are similar to those raised by any process that seeks to influence people. What are the goals? How do these goals fit with those of the school as a whole? Might students be rewarded for the "wrong" thing, though it seems "right" at first? By what criteria should strategies be chosen? What effect will a strategy have on the individuals involved? Is too much control being given to the teacher, or to a majority?

Goals. The strategies described in this chapter could be applied exclusively to teaching students to sit still, raise their hands before speaking, and remain silent at all other times (Winett & Winkler, 1972). This certainly would be an unethical use of the techniques. It is true that a teacher may need to establish some organization and order, but stopping with improvements in conduct will not ensure academic learning. On the other hand, in some situations, reinforcing academic skills may lead to improvements in conduct. Whenever possible, emphasis should be placed on academic learning. Academic improvements generalize to other situations more successfully than do changes in classroom conduct.

Strategies. Punishment can have negative side effects: it can serve as a model for aggressive responses, and it can encourage negative emotional reactions. Punishment is unnecessary and even unethical when positive approaches, which have fewer potential dangers, might work as well. When simpler, less-restrictive procedures fail, more complicated procedures should be tried.

A second consideration in the selection of a strategy is the impact of the strategy on the individual student. For example, some teachers arrange for students to be rewarded at home with a gift or activities based on good work in school. But if a student has a history of being severely punished at home for bad reports from school, a home-based reinforcement program might be very harmful to that student. Reports of unsatisfactory progress at school could lead to increased abuse at home.

Criticisms of Behavioural Methods

Properly used, the strategies in this chapter can be effective tools to help students learn academically and grow in self-sufficiency. Effective tools, however, do not automatically produce excellent work. The indiscriminate use of even the best tools can lead to difficulties. Critics of behavioural methods point to two basic problems that may arise.

Some psychologists fear that rewarding students for all learning will cause them to lose interest in learning for its own sake (Deci, 1975; Deci & Ryan, 1985; Kohn, 1993, 1996; Lepper & Greene, 1978; Lepper, Keavney, & Drake, 1996; Ryan & Deci, 1996). Studies have suggested that using reward programs with students who are already interested in the subject matter may, in fact, cause students to be less interested in the subject when the reward program ends, as you can see in the Point/Counterpoint on page 224.

Just as you must take into account the effects of a reward system on the individual, you must also consider the impact on other students. Using a reward program or giving one student increased attention may have a detrimental effect on the other students in the classroom. Is it possible that other students will learn to be "bad" in order to be included in the reward program? Most of the evidence on this question suggests that using individual adaptations such as reward programs does not have any adverse effects on students who are not participating if the teacher believes in the program and explains the reasons for using it to the non-participating students. After interviewing 98 students in Grades 1 through 6, Cindy Fulk and Paula Smith (1995) concluded that "Teachers may be more concerned about equal treatment of students than students are" (p. 416). If the conduct of some students does seem to deteriorate when their peers are involved in special programs, many of the same procedures discussed in this chapter should help them return to previous levels of appropriate behaviour (Chance, 1992, 1993).

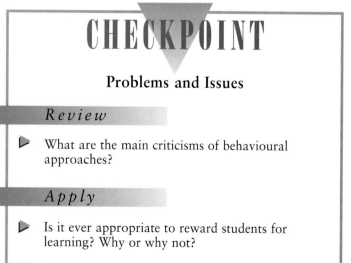

CHECKPOINT

Problems and Issues

Review

▷ What are the main criticisms of behavioural approaches?

Apply

▷ Is it ever appropriate to reward students for learning? Why or why not?

Should Students Be Rewarded for Learning?

For years educators and psychologists have debated whether students should be rewarded for school work and academic accomplishments. As an example, Judy Cameron and W. David Pierce (1996) of the University of Alberta published an article on reinforcement in the *Review of Educational Research* that precipitated extensive criticisms and rebuttals in the same journal from Mark Lepper, Mark Keavney, Michael Drake, Alfie Kohn, Richard Ryan, and Edward Deci. Earlier, Paul Chance and Alfie Kohn had exchanged opinions in several issues of *Phi Delta Kappan*: Kohn, A. (1991, March) "Caring kids: The role of the schools"; Chance, P. (1991, June) "Backtalk: A gross injustice"; Chance, P. (1992, November) "The rewards of learning"; Kohn, A. (1993, June) "Rewards versus learning: A response to Paul Chance"; Chance, P. (1993, June) "Sticking up for rewards." What are the arguments?

▶ POINT *Students are punished by rewards.*

Alfie Kohn (1993) argues that "Applied behaviorism, which amounts to saying, 'do this and you'll get that,' is essentially a technique for controlling people. In the classroom it is a way of doing things to children rather than working with them" (p. 784). Kohn goes on to contend that rewards are ineffective because when the praise and prizes stop, the behaviour stops too. "Rewards (like punishments) can get people to do what we want: buckle up, share a toy, read a book.... But they rarely produce effects that survive the rewards themselves.... They do not create an enduring commitment to a set of values or to learning; they merely, and temporarily, change what we do" (p. 784).

The problem with rewards does not stop here. According to Kohn, rewarding students for learning actually makes them less interested in the material:

All of this means that getting children to think about learning as a way to receive a sticker, a gold star, or a grade—or even worse, to get money or a toy for a grade, which amounts to an extrinsic motivator for an extrinsic motivator—is likely to turn learning from an end into a means. Learning becomes something that must be gotten through in order to receive the reward. Take the depressingly pervasive program by which children receive certificates for pizzas when they have read a certain number of books. John Nicholls of the University of Illinois comments, only half in jest, that the likely consequences of this program is "a lot of fat kids who don't like to read." (p. 785)

◀ COUNTERPOINT *Learning should be rewarding.*

According to Paul Chance (1993):

Behavioral psychologists in particular emphasize that we learn by acting on our environment. As B. F. Skinner put it: "[People] act on the world, and change it, and are changed in turn by the consequences of their actions." Skinner, unlike Kohn, understood that people learn best in a responsive environment. Teachers who praise or otherwise reward student performance provide such an environment. . . . If it is immoral to let students know they have answered questions correctly, to pat students on the back for a good effort, to show joy at a student's understanding of a concept, or to recognize the achievement of a goal by providing a gold star or a certificate—if this is immoral, then count me a sinner. (p. 788)

Do rewards undermine interest? In their review of research, Cameron and Pierce (1996) concluded, "When tangible rewards (e.g., gold star, money) are offered contingent on performance on a task [not just participation] or are delivered unexpectedly, intrinsic motivation is maintained" (p. 49). Even psychologists such as Edward Deci and Mark Lepper, who suggest that rewards might undermine intrinsic motivation, agree that rewards can also be used positively. When rewards provide students with information about their growing mastery of a subject or when the rewards show appreciation for a job well done, then the rewards bolster confidence and make the task more interesting to the students, especially students who lacked ability or interest in the task initially. Nothing succeeds like success. If students master reading or mathematics with the support of rewards, they will not forget what they have learned when the praise stops. Would they have learned without the rewards? Some would, but some might not. Would you continue working for a company that didn't pay you, even though you liked the work? Will freelance writer Alfie Kohn, for that matter, lose interest in writing because he gets paid fees and royalties?

Summary

Understanding Learning

Define learning.

Although theorists disagree about the definition of learning, most would agree that learning occurs when experience causes a change in a person's knowledge or behaviour. Behavioural theorists emphasize the role of environmental stimuli in learning and focus on behaviour—observable responses. Behavioural learning processes include contiguity learning, classical conditioning, and operant conditioning.

Early Explanations of Learning: Contiguity and Classical Conditioning

How does a neutral stimulus become a conditioned stimulus?

In classical conditioning, which was discovered by Pavlov, a previously neutral stimulus is repeatedly paired with a stimulus that evokes an emotional or physiological response. Later, the previously neutral stimulus alone evokes the response—that is, the neutral stimulus is conditioned to bring forth a conditioned response. The neutral stimulus has become a conditioned stimulus.

Discriminate between response generalization and stimulus discrimination.

Conditioned responses are subject to the processes of response generalization and stimulus discrimination. After animals or people learn to respond to one particular stimulus, they may also have similar responses to other stimuli that are similar to the original one. This process is called *response generalization* because the conditioned response has generalized or occurred in the presence of similar stimuli. Stimulus discrimination is learning to make distinctions—to respond to one stimulus but not to others that are similar.

Operant Conditioning: Trying New Responses

What defines a consequence as a reinforcer? As a punisher?

In operant conditioning, a theory of learning developed by B. F. Skinner, people learn through the effects of their deliberate responses. For an individual, the effects of consequences following an action may serve as reinforcement or punishment. A consequence is defined as a reinforcer if it strengthens or maintains the response that brought it about, while a consequence is defined as a punishment if it decreases or suppresses the response that brought it about.

How are negative reinforcement and punishment different?

Negative reinforcement is often confused with punishment. The process of reinforcement (positive or negative) always involves strengthening behaviour. The focus of negative reinforcement is strengthening specific behaviour (putting away supplies or finishing in-class assignments, etc.). The teacher strengthens (reinforces) the behaviour by removing something aversive *as soon as the desired behaviour occurs*. Because the consequence involves removing or "subtracting" a stimulus, the reinforcement is negative. Punishment, on the other hand, involves *decreasing or suppressing behaviour*. Behaviour followed by a "punisher" is *less* likely to be repeated in similar situations in the future. Negative reinforcement also gives students a chance to exercise control. As soon as they perform the appropriate behaviour, the unpleasant situation ends. In contrast, punishment occurs after the fact, and a student cannot so easily control or terminate it.

How can you encourage persistence in behaviour?

The scheduling of reinforcement influences the rate and persistence of responses. Ratio schedules (based on the number of responses) encourage higher rates of response, and variable schedules (based on varying numbers of responses or varying time intervals) encourage persistence of responses.

What is the difference between a prompt and a cue?

A cue is an antecedent stimulus just before particular behaviour is to take place. A prompt is an additional cue following the first cue. There are two principles for using a cue and a prompt to teach new behaviour. First, make sure the environmental stimulus that you want to become a cue occurs immediately before the prompt you are using, so students will learn to respond to the cue and not rely only on the prompt. Second, fade the prompt as soon as possible so students do not become dependent on it.

Applied Behaviour Analysis

What are the steps in applied behaviour analysis?

Applied behaviour analysis provides teachers with methods for encouraging positive behaviour and coping with behaviour that is undesirable. The steps are: (1) Clearly specify the behaviour to be changed and note the current level. (2) Plan a specific intervention using antecedents, consequences, or both. (3) Keep track of the results, and modify the plan if necessary.

How can the Premack principle help you identify reinforcers?

The Premack principle states that high-frequency behaviour (a preferred activity) can be an effective reinforcer for a low-frequency behaviour (a less-preferred activity). This is sometimes referred to as "Grandma's rule": First do what I want you to do, then you may do what you want to do. The best way to determine appropriate reinforcers for your students may be to watch what they do in their free time. For most students, talking, moving around the room, sitting near a friend, being exempt from assignments or tests, reading magazines, or playing games are preferred activities.

When is shaping an appropriate approach?

A lot of behaviour—especially skills that involve persistence, endurance, increased accuracy, greater speed, or extensive practice to master—can be improved through shaping. Because shaping is a time-consuming process, however, it should not be used if success can be attained through simpler methods such as cueing. Teachers can use shaping to help students develop new responses a little at a time, so shaping is useful for building complex skills or working toward difficult goals.

What are some cautions in using punishment?

Negative reinforcement, satiation, and forms of punishment—such as reprimands, response cost, and social isolation—can also help change behaviour but must be used with caution. Punishment in and of itself does not lead to any positive behaviour. Thus, whenever you consider the use of punishment, you should make it part of a two-pronged attack. The first goal is to carry out the punishment and suppress the undesirable behaviour. The second goal is to make clear what the student should be doing instead and to provide reinforcement for those desirable actions. Thus, while the problem behaviour is being suppressed, positive alternative responses are being strengthened.

Behavioural Approaches to Teaching and Management

What is mastery learning?

To use mastery learning, a teacher must break a course down into small units of study. Each unit might involve mastering several specific objectives. "Mastery" usually means a score of 80 to 90 percent on a test or other assessment. The teacher informs the students of the objectives and the criteria for meeting each. Students who do not reach the minimum level of mastery or who reach this minimum but want to improve their performance (thus raising their grade) can recycle through the unit. When they are ready, they take another form of the unit test.

Describe the managerial strategies of group consequences, token programs, and contracts.

Using group consequences involves basing reinforcement for the whole class on the behaviour of the whole class. In token programs, students earn tokens for both academic work and positive classroom behaviour. The tokens may be points, checks, holes punched in a card, chips, play money, or anything else that is easily identified as the student's property. Periodically the students exchange the tokens they have earned for some desired reward. In a contingency contract program, the teacher draws up an individual contract with each student, describing exactly what the student must do to earn a particular privilege or reward. In some programs, students participate in decid-

ing on the behaviour to be reinforced and the rewards that can be gained. A teacher must use these programs with caution, emphasizing learning and not just "good" behaviour.

Recent Approaches: Self-Regulation and Cognitive Behaviour Modification

What are the steps in self-management?

Students can apply behaviour analysis on their own to manage their own behaviour. Teachers can encourage the development of self-management skills by allowing students to participate in setting goals, keeping track of progress, evaluating accomplishments, and selecting and giving their own reinforcements. Teachers can also use cognitive behaviour modification, a behaviour-change program described by Meichenbaum in which students are directly taught how to use self-instruction.

Problems and Issues

What are the main criticisms of behavioural approaches?

The misuse or abuse of behavioural learning methods is unethical. Critics of behavioural methods also point out the danger that reinforcement could decrease interest in learning by overemphasizing rewards and could have a negative impact on other students. Guidelines do exist, however, for helping teachers use behavioural learning principles appropriately and ethically.

Key Terms

antecedents, *p. 201*

applied behaviour analysis, *p. 206*

aversive, *p. 202*

behavioural learning theories, *p. 197*

behaviour modification, *p. 206*

classical conditioning, *p. 198*

cognitive behaviour modification, *p. 221*

conditioned response (CR), *p. 199*

conditioned stimulus (CS), *p. 199*

consequences, *p. 201*

contiguity, *p. 198*

contingency contract, *p. 217*

continuous reinforcement schedule, *p. 203*

cueing, *p. 205*

extinction, *p. 199*

good behaviour game, *p. 215*

group consequences, *p. 215*

intermittent reinforcement schedule, *p. 203*

interval schedule, *p. 203*

learning, *p. 196*

mastery learning, *p. 213*

negative reinforcement, *p. 202*

neutral stimulus, *p. 199*

operant conditioning, *p. 200*

Becoming a Professional

Reflecting on the Chapter

Can you apply the ideas from this chapter on learning to solve the following problems of practice?

Preschool and Kindergarten

▶ A student in your class is terrified of the class's pet guinea pigs. The child won't get close to the cages and wants you to "give them away." How would you help the child overcome this fear?

Elementary and Middle School

▶ You want your students to improve their time management and self-management abilities so they will be prepared for the increased demands of high school next year. What would you do?

Junior High and High School

▶ You have been assigned an emotionally disturbed student. She seemed fine at first, but now you notice that when she encounters difficult work, she often interrupts or teases other students. How would you work with this student and the class to improve the situation?

▶ It takes you 10 minutes to get your class to settle down after the bell rings. Analyze this situation. What could be maintaining this problem? What could you do?

Cooperative Learning Activity

▶ Work with two or three other members of your educational psychology class to develop a plan using applied behaviour analysis to tackle one of the following problems:

1. Three students who "hang out" together in your class repeatedly say insulting and disrespectful things to you, often in front of the entire class.

2. Your class has got into the habit of ignoring due dates.

3. One of the students in your class continues to attack other students verbally and physically.

Weblinks

http://psychclassics.yorku.ca

Want to read some of the "classic" articles in the field? At this site, you'll find a search engine. Enter the name of a famous theorist, such as Pavlov or Skinner, or type in one or several theoretical terms, such as "reinforcement and reward" (using the "and" to require both terms). The engine will return a list of classic articles available online.

http://snycorva.cortland.edu/~ANDERSMD/OPER/operant.HTML

This site offers a brief tutorial about operant or Skinnerian learning theory.

www.bfskinner.org

According to this Web page, "The B. F. Skinner Foundation was established in 1987 to publish significant literary and scientific works in the analysis of behavior and to educate both professionals and the public about the science of behavior." Several resources are offered at this site.

What Would They Do?

Here is how two practising teachers responded to the teaching situation presented at the beginning of this chapter about a class out of control.

JANICE FARRELL

Colby–St. Joseph School
Sydney, Nova Scotia

Accentuate the Positive—Eliminate the Negative

What goes on in our classrooms can be productive or destructive in relation to a child's self-image. I would like children to work with me in a cooperative, positive learning environment. I would use several strategies so that children learn such skills as responsibility, cooperation, and problem solving. These skills can help students come to terms with their own behaviour, knowing what they need to do rather than being told what to do.

I would use basic "life skills" in what I do every day. These skills are valuable ways to pass the "ownership and responsibility" of actions to each individual. Through a positive, cooperative learning plan, I would be flexible in my expectations while still adhering to some basic principles. These life skills are easily integrated in all subject areas. Working within this model, children would understand they are unique, important, and special and would develop their own self-worth and self-esteem. The "strengths" of each child would be emphasized.

Teachers shouldn't be afraid to be *human*. We assume many roles in a classroom but, most importantly, the roles of teacher and friend. We learn from one another; involving the students in decisions that affect them helps them feel important and worthwhile. Look on teaching as a daily adventure in "humanity." Developing the basic life skills will help students prepare for the future.

Get to know your students and their strengths. Students and teachers should establish and achieve positive goals that will help promote a healthy learning environment. As educators, we all have the opportunity to plant a seed, but we must also be willing to nurture it so that each child will grow and develop to full potential in a safe and caring environment.

Learning is ongoing, and as teachers we need to facilitate this learning process to encourage and develop the "positive" while making efforts to eliminate the "negative." We must all try as teachers to remember that *the art of teaching lies in teaching from the heart!*

My Golden Rule *by Janice Farrell*

May I always have the strength
To stand tall and be ever so strong
So that the children I teach will realize
That I too can be wrong.
May I always have the insight
To not let the opportunity pass
To help the child that needs me
Each day within my class.
May I always have a sense of caring
Down deep within my heart
For each and every child I teach
So that I can always do my part.
May I always be ready to listen
And use love and guidance to try
To be there for my children
And to hear their gentle silent cry.
May I always value what they can offer
And know they may just need me near
To guide them along as they struggle
And help them ease away any fear.
May I always have the strength
To stand tall and be ever so strong
So that the children I teach will realize
That I too can be wrong.
May we always be ready to help one another
So that we can come to realize
When we walk along hand in hand
We all have our silent cries.

ROSEMARY DIXON

Retired
Ottawa, Ontario

This situation requires the use of both short- and long-term strategies. Positive behaviour must be rewarded immediately—by positive verbal statements and, initially, by a system of token rewards for which a larger reward, such as free time, will be given later. Whenever possible, negative behaviour must be ignored, as these children must be accepting negative attention as desirable.

Clear, explicit rules must be instituted immediately. These children should be involved in the making of these rules and in deciding on consequences for the infraction of rules. I would try to have as few rules as possible and insist that they be adhered to with absolute consistency. I would have to remind myself that learning would not take place in this class until the behaviour improved. I must not be afraid to stop the class at any time, send all the children to their seats, or call the children into a circle to discuss problems that are arising.

My first long-term strategy would be to get to know as many of the parents as possible. They could become invaluable allies. The teacher might have become a faceless name about whom horror stories were told. The parents would naturally feel more positive toward a friendly, concerned educator who had their children's best interests at heart and who was willing to involve them in the learning process.

How much help can I expect from my principal or vice-principal? It would be a good idea to find out if these colleagues would be willing to support my rewards program. A visit from the principal to the class, or by the children to the principal's office, so that praise and rewards could be given for appropriate behaviour, would probably be a pleasant and reinforcing change. For these children, previous encounters with administration have been mostly negative.

Finally, I would take up offers of help from my colleagues. Perhaps my class, or groups from the class, could be involved in cooperative or friendly competitive activities with another class.

These strategies should lead to improved self-esteem, an improved reputation within the school, increased motivation, and a return to appropriate school behaviour.

Cognitive Views of Learning

hat makes a lesson easy to learn and remember? Think about the classes you are taking this semester. What have you studied in the last two or three days that you expect to remember next week? Next year? What is different about the memorable information? Did you learn it in a different way?

In this chapter we turn from behavioural theories of learning to the cognitive perspective. This means a shift from "viewing the learners and their behaviours as products of incoming environmental stimuli" to seeing the learners as "sources of plans, intentions, goals, ideas, memories, and emotions actively used to attend to, select, and construct meaning from stimuli and knowledge from experience" (Wittrock, 1982, pp. 1–2). We will begin with a discussion of the general cognitive approach to learning and memory and the importance of knowledge in learning. To understand memory, we will consider a widely accepted cognitive model, information processing, which suggests that information moves through three different storage systems. We will briefly consider an alternative to the three-store model of memory—depth of processing. Next we will explore metacognition, a field of study that may provide insights into individual and developmental differences in learning. Then we turn to ideas about how teachers can help their students become more knowledgeable. By the time you have completed this chapter, you should be able to:

- ▶ Discuss the role of knowledge in learning.
- ▶ Describe three models of human information processing—the three-store model, levels of processing, and connectionism.
- ▶ Give examples of the roles of perception and attention in learning.
- ▶ Define declarative, procedural, and conditional knowledge.
- ▶ Explain how schemas and scripts influence learning and remembering.
- ▶ Explain the role of metacognition in learning and remembering.
- ▶ Discuss individual differences in working and long-term memory.
- ▶ Describe the stages in the development of cognitive skills.

What Would You Do?

The students in your senior history classes seem to equate understanding with memorizing. They prepare for each test by memorizing the exact words of the textbook. Even the best students seem to think that flash cards are the only learning strategy possible. In fact, when you try to get them to think about history by reading some original sources, debating issues in class, or examining art and music from the time frame you are studying, they rebel. "Will this be on the test?" "Why are we looking at these pictures—will we have to know who painted them and when?" "What's this got to do with history?" Even the students who participate in the debates seem to use words and phrases straight from the textbook without knowing what they are saying.

► What do these students "know" about history? What are their beliefs and expectations, and how do these affect their learning?

► Why do you think they insist on using the rote memory approach?

► How would you teach your students to learn in this new way?

► How will these issues affect the grade levels you teach?

TEACHERS' CASEBOOK

Connect & Extend
To life
Consider these proverbs about memory taken from Klatzky, R. L. (1984). *Memory and awareness: An information processing perspective.* New York: Freeman, p. 122.

On Learning

Learning teacheth more in one year than experience in twenty. (Roger Ascham)

What we have to learn to do, we learn by doing. (Aristotle)

On Memory

The true art of memory is the art of attention. (Samuel Johnson)

A man's memory may almost become the art of continually varying and misrepresenting his past, according to his interests in the present. (George Santayana)

On Forgetting

The mind is slow in unlearning what it has been long in learning. (Seneca)

Soon learned, soon forgotten. (Proverb)

Out of sight, out of mind. (Proverb)

An injury is much sooner forgotten than an insult. (Lord Chesterfield)

On Aging

I am too old to learn. (Shakespeare, *King Lear*)

No one is so old that he cannot still learn something. (German proverb)

An old dog will learn no new tricks. (Thomas D'Urfey)

Connect & Extend
To other chapters
Two different models of instruction based on principles of cognitive learning—Bruner's discovery learning and Ausubel's expository teaching—are described in Chapter 8.

Cognitive View of Learning:
A general approach that views learning as an active mental process of acquiring, remembering, and using knowledge.

Elements of the Cognitive Perspective

The cognitive perspective is both the oldest and the youngest member of the psychological community. It is old because discussions of the nature of knowledge, the value of reason, and the contents of the mind date back at least to the ancient Greek philosophers (Hernshaw, 1987). From the late 1800s until the late twentieth century, however, cognitive studies fell from favour and behaviourism thrived. Then, several factors—research done during the Second World War on the development of complex human skills; the computer revolution; and breakthroughs in understanding language development—all stimulated a resurgence in cognitive research. Evidence accumulated indicating that people do more than simply respond to reinforcement and punishment. For example, we plan our responses, use strategies to help us remember, and organize the material we are learning in our own unique ways (Miller, Galanter, & Pribram, 1960; Shuell, 1986). With the growing realization that learning is an active mental process, educational psychologists became interested in how people think, learn concepts, and solve problems (e.g., Ausubel, 1963; Bruner, Goodnow, & Austin, 1956).

Interest in concept learning and problem solving soon gave way, however, to interest in how knowledge is represented in the mind and particularly how it is remembered. Remembering and forgetting became major topics for investigation in cognitive psychology in the 1970s and 1980s, and the information processing model of memory dominated research.

Today, there are other models of memory besides information processing. In addition, many cognitive theorists have a renewed interest in learning, thinking, and problem solving. The **cognitive view of learning** can best be described as a generally agreed-upon philosophical orientation. This means that cognitive theorists share basic notions about learning and memory. Cognitive theorists believe, for example, that learning is the result of our attempts to make sense of the world. To do this, we use all the mental tools at our disposal. The ways we think about situations, along with our knowledge, expectations, feelings, and interactions with others and the environment, influence how and what we learn (Anderson, 1995a, 1995b; Bandura, 1986; Farnham-Diggory, 1994; Piaget, 1963).

Comparing Cognitive and Behavioural Views

The cognitive and behavioural views differ in their assumptions about what is learned. In the cognitive view, knowledge is learned, and changes in knowledge make changes in behaviour possible. In the behavioural view, the new behaviour itself is learned (Shuell, 1986). Both behavioural and cognitive theorists believe reinforcement is important in learning but for different reasons. The strict behaviourist maintains that reinforcement strengthens responses; cognitive theorists see reinforcement as a source of feedback about what is likely to happen if behaviour is repeated—as a source of information.

The cognitive view emphasizes that people are active learners who initiate experiences, seek out information to solve problems, and reorganize what they already know to achieve new insights. In fact, learning within this perspective is seen as "transforming significant understanding we already have, rather than simple acquisitions written on blank slates" (Greeno, Collins, & Resnick, 1996, p. 18). Instead of highlighting environmental events as causes of behaviour, the cognitive view stresses that people actively choose, practise, pay attention, ignore, reflect, and make many other decisions as they pursue goals. Older cognitive views emphasized the *acquisition* of knowledge, but newer approaches stress its *construction* (Anderson, Reder, & Simon, 1996; Greeno, Collins, & Resnick, 1996; Mayer, 1996).

Differences between behavioural and cognitive views are also apparent in the methods used to study learning. Most early research on learning, both behavioural and cognitive, was carried out in laboratories under rather unnatural situations. More recently, both approaches have studied learning in real-life situations. Behavioural researchers have often used rats, cats, and other species of animals as subjects in their studies, as well as people. The reverse is true in research on cognitive views of learning, where only a relatively few studies have investigated cognition in animals. In behavioural research, a single subject was usually observed in dozens and sometimes hundreds of trials—chances to observe behaviour in similar environmental conditions. In contrast, cognitive researchers most often based their studies of learning on an average description of how a group of people behaved. Because of this difference in focus on individuals versus groups, behavioural views of learning portray individual and developmental differences quite differently from cognitive views. Both approaches actually embrace a variety of distinct models— no single behavioural or cognitive model fully represents that one approach to understanding learning.

◀ *The cognitive view sees people as active learners who initiate experiences, seek out information to solve problems, and reorganize what they already know to achieve new insights.*

The Importance of Knowledge in Learning

Knowledge is the outcome of learning. If we learn a name, the history of cognitive psychology, or the rules of tennis, we know something new. But knowledge is more than the end product of previous learning; it also guides new learning. The cognitive approach suggests that one of the most important elements in the learning process is what the individual brings to the learning situation. What we already know "is a scaffold that supports the construction of all future learning" (Alexander, 1996, p. 89)—it determines to a great extent what we will pay attention to, perceive, learn, remember, and forget (Greeno, Collins, & Resnick, 1996; Shuell, 1986).

A study by Recht and Leslie (1988) shows the importance of knowledge in understanding and remembering new information. These psychologists identified junior high school students who were either very good or very poor readers, then tested the students on their knowledge of baseball. They found that knowledge of baseball was not related to reading ability. So the researchers were able to identify four groups of students: *good readers/high baseball knowledge, good readers/low baseball knowledge, poor readers/high baseball knowledge,* and *poor readers/low baseball knowledge.* Then all the students read a passage describing a baseball game and were tested in a number of ways to see if they understood and remembered what they had read.

The results demonstrated the power of knowledge. Poor readers who knew a lot about baseball remembered more than good readers with little baseball knowledge and almost as much as good readers who knew baseball. Poor readers who knew little about baseball remembered the least of what they had read. So a good basis of knowledge can be more important than good learning strategies in understanding and remembering—but extensive knowledge plus good strategies is even better.

General and Specific Knowledge. In the cognitive perspective, "knowledge emphasizes understanding of concepts and theories in different subject matter domains [such as math or history] and general cognitive abilities, such as reasoning, planning, solving problems, and comprehending language" (Greeno, Collins, & Resnick, 1996, p. 16). So, there are different kinds of knowledge. Some is general—it applies to many different situations. For example, **general knowledge** about how to read or write or use a word processor is useful in and out of school. **Domain-specific knowledge**, on the other hand, pertains to a particular task or subject. For example, knowing that the shortstop plays between second and third base is specific to the domain of baseball. Of course, there is no absolute line between general and domain-specific knowledge. When you were first learning to read, you may have studied specific facts about the sounds of letters. At that time, knowledge about letter sounds was specific to the domain of reading. But now you can use both knowledge about sounds and the ability to read in more general ways (Alexander, 1992; Schunk, 2000).

Declarative, Procedural, and Conditional Knowledge. Another way of categorizing knowledge is as declarative, procedural, or conditional (Paris & Cunningham, 1996; Paris, Lipson, & Wixson, 1983). **Declarative knowledge** is "knowledge that can be declared, usually in words, through lectures, books, writing, verbal exchange, Braille, sign language, mathematical notation, and so on" (Farnaham-Diggory, 1994, p. 468). Declarative knowledge is "knowing that" something is the case. Robert Gagné (1985) calls this category verbal information. The history students in the opening "What Would You Do?" situation were focusing exclusively on declarative knowledge about history.

The range of declarative knowledge is tremendous. You can know specific facts (the atomic weight of gold is 196.967), or generalities (leaves of some trees change colour in autumn), or personal preferences (I don't like lima beans), or

General Knowledge: Information that is useful in many different kinds of tasks; information that applies to many situations.

Domain-Specific Knowledge: Information that is useful in a particular situation or that applies only to one specific topic.

Declarative Knowledge: Verbal information; facts; "knowing that" something is the case.

TABLE 7.1   Kinds of Knowledge

	General Knowledge	Domain-Specific Knowledge
Declarative	Hours the library is open Rules of grammar	The definition of "hypotenuse" The lines of the poem "The Raven"
Procedural	How to use your word processor How to drive	How to solve an oxidation-reduction equation How to throw a pot on a potter's wheel
Conditional	When to give up and try another approach When to skim and when to read carefully	When to use the formula for calculating volume When to rush the net in tennis

personal events (what happened at my brother's wedding), or rules (to divide fractions, invert the divisor and multiply). Small units of declarative knowledge can be organized into larger units; for example, principles of reinforcement and punishment can be organized in your thinking into a theory of behavioural learning (Gagné, Yekovich, & Yekovich, 1993).

Procedural knowledge is "knowing how" to perform a task such as divide fractions or clean a carburetor—procedural knowledge must be demonstrated. Notice that repeating the rule "to divide fractions, invert the divisor and multiply" shows *declarative* knowledge—the student can state the rule. But to show *procedural* knowledge, the student must act. When faced with a fraction to divide, the student must divide correctly. Students demonstrate procedural knowledge when they translate a passage into Spanish or correctly categorize a geometric shape or craft a coherent paragraph.

Conditional knowledge is "knowing when and why" to apply your declarative and procedural knowledge. Given many kinds of math problems, it takes conditional knowledge to know when to apply one procedure and when to apply another to solve each. It takes conditional knowledge to know when to read every word in a text and when to skim. For many students, conditional knowledge is a stumbling block. They have the facts and can do the procedures, but they don't seem to apply what they know at the appropriate time.

Table 7.1 shows that we can combine our two systems for describing knowledge. Declarative, procedural, and conditional knowledge can be either general or domain-specific.

To be used, knowledge must be remembered. What do we know about memory?

CHECKPOINT

Elements of the Cognitive Experience

Review

▷ Contrast cognitive and behavioural views of learning in terms of what is learned and the role of reinforcement.

▷ How does knowledge affect learning?

Apply

▷ What do you already know that will help you in learning the material in this chapter?

Procedural Knowledge: Knowledge that is demonstrated when we perform a task; "knowing how."

Conditional Knowledge: "Knowing when and why" to use declarative and procedural knowledge.

Information Processing: The human mind's activity of taking in, storing, and using information.

The Information Processing Model of Memory

There are a number of theories of memory, but the most common are the **information processing** explanations (Hunt & Ellis, 1999; Sternberg, 1999), including neural-network or connectionist approaches (Martindale, 1991). We will use this well-researched framework for examining learning and memory.

An Overview of the Information Processing Model

Receptors: Parts of the human body that receive sensory information.

Sensory Memory: System that holds sensory information very briefly.

Information processing views of memory use the computer as a model. Like the computer, the human mind takes in information, performs operations on it to change its form and content, stores the information, retrieves it when needed, and generates responses to it. Thus, processing involves gathering and representing information, or *encoding;* holding information, or *storage;* and getting at the information when needed, or *retrieval.* The whole system is guided by *control processes* that determine how and when information will flow through each part of the system.

For some cognitive psychologists, the computer model is only a metaphor for human mental activity. But other cognitive scientists, particularly those studying artificial intelligence, try to design and program computers to "think" and solve problems like human beings (Anderson, 1995a; Schunk, 2000). Some theorists suggest that the operation of the brain resembles a large number of very slow computers, all operating in parallel (at the same time), with each computer dedicated to a different, specific task (Martindale, 1991).

Figure 7.1 is a schematic representation of a typical information processing model of memory, derived from the ideas of several theorists (Atkinson & Shiffrin, 1968; R. Gagné, 1985). Other models have been suggested, but all of the models, despite their variations, resemble flow charts. In order to understand this model, let's examine each element.

Sensory Memory

Stimuli from the environment (sights, sounds, smells, etc.) constantly bombard our receptors. **Receptors** are the body's mechanisms for seeing, hearing, tasting, smelling, and feeling. The **sensory memory**, also called the *sensory register* or *sensory information store*, holds all these sensations—very briefly.

Capacity, Duration, and Contents of Sensory Memory. The capacity of sensory memory is very large, more information than we can possibly handle at once.

FIGURE 7.1

The Information Processing System
Information is encoded in the sensory register where perception determines what will be held in working memory for further use. Thoroughly processed information becomes part of long-term memory and can be activated at any time to return to working memory.

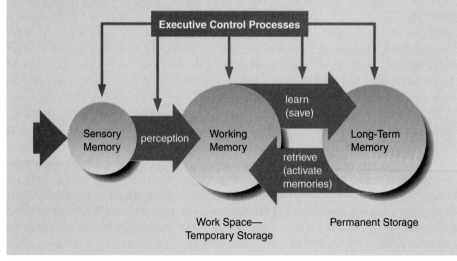

But this vast amount of sensory information is short in duration. It lasts between one and three seconds. You can experience this brief holding of sensory information in your own sensory register. Wave a pencil (or your finger) back and forth before your eyes while you stare straight ahead. See the shadowy image that trails behind the object? The sensory input remains very briefly after the stimulus has left. You can see a trace of the pencil after the actual stimulus has been removed (Lindsay & Norman, 1977). The content of sensory memory resembles the sensations from the original stimulus. Visual sensations are coded briefly by the sensory register as images, almost like photographs. Auditory sensations are coded as sound patterns, similar to echoes. It may be that the other senses also have their own codes. Thus, for a second or so, a wealth of data from sensory experience remains intact. In these instants, we have a chance to select and organize information for further processing. Perception and attention are critical at this stage.

Perception. The meaning we attach to the raw information received through our senses is called **perception**. This meaning is constructed based on both objective reality and our existing knowledge. For example, consider these marks: ᛒ. If asked what the letter is, you would say "B." If asked what the number is, you would say "13." The actual marks remain the same; the perception of them—their meaning—changes depending on whether you are asked to recognize a number or a letter. To a child without appropriate knowledge to perceive either a number or a letter, the marks would probably be meaningless (F. Smith, 1975).

Some of our present-day understanding of perception is based on studies conducted in the early twentieth century, first in Germany and then in the United States, by psychologists known as *Gestalt theorists*. **Gestalt**, which means something like pattern or configuration in German, refers to people's tendency to organize sensory information into patterns or relationships. Instead of perceiving bits and pieces of unrelated information, we perceive organized, meaningful wholes. Figure 7.2 presents a few Gestalt principles.

The Gestalt principles explain certain aspects of perception, but they are not the whole story. There are two current explanations in information processing theory for how we recognize patterns and give meaning to sensory events. The first is called *feature analysis,* or **bottom-up processing** because the stimulus must be analyzed into features or components and assembled into a meaningful pattern "from the bottom up." For example, a capital letter A consists of two relatively straight lines joined at a 45-degree angle /\ and a horizontal line (—) through the middle. Whenever we see these features, or anything close enough, including, A, A, **A**, *A*, *A*, and A, we recognize an A (Anderson, 1995a). Bottom-up processing mainly explains how we are able to read words written in other people's handwriting.

Connect & Extend
To real life
"Hidden Pictures" (a picture in which objects are concealed and the child has to find them) and "Where's Waldo?" are examples of figure-ground perception tasks. ("Hidden Pictures" can be found in *Highlights* and in other children's magazines.)

Perception: Interpretation of sensory information.

Gestalt: German for pattern or whole; Gestalt theorists hold that people organize their perceptions into coherent wholes.

Bottom-Up Processing: Perceiving based on noticing separate defining features and assembling them into a recognizable pattern.

FIGURE 7.2

Examples of Gestalt Principles
Gestalt principles of perception explain how we "see" patterns in the world around us.

a. Figure-ground
What do you see? Faces or a vase? Make one figure—the other ground.

b. Proximity
You see these lines as 3 groups because of the proximity of lines.

c. Similarity
You see these lines as an alternating pattern because of the similarity in height of lines.

d. Closure
You perceive a circle instead of dotted curved lines.

Source: From *Learning Theories: An Educational Perspective,* 2/e, by Dale H. Schunk. Copyright © 1996. Adapted by permission of Prentice-Hall, Inc., Saddle River, NJ.

Top-Down Processing:
Perceiving based on the context and the patterns you expect to occur in that situation.

Attention: Focus on a stimulus.

Connect & Extend
To the research
Flavell (1985) described four aspects of attention in developing children:

1. *Controlled:* Develop longer attention spans and ability to focus on important details, ignoring minor ones.

2. *Tailored to task:* Older children focus attention on most difficult material being learned (Berk 1994).

3. *Directive:* They develop a feel for cues (teacher's voice, gestures) telling them when/how to direct their attention.

4. *Self-monitoring:* They learn to decide if they are using the right strategy and to change if it's not working.

If all perception relied on feature analysis, learning would be very slow. Luckily, humans are capable of another type of perception, based on knowledge and expectation, called **top-down processing**. To recognize patterns rapidly, in addition to noting features, we use what we already know about the situation— what we know about words or pictures or the way the world generally operates. For example, you would not have seen the marks above as the letter A if you had no knowledge of the Roman alphabet. So, what you know also affects what you are able to perceive.

The Role of Attention. If every variation in colour, movement, sound, smell, temperature, and so on had to be perceived, life would be impossible. By paying attention to certain stimuli and ignoring others, we select from all the possibilities what we will process. But **attention** is a very limited resource. We can pay attention to only one demanding task at a time (Anderson, 1995a). For example, there was a time when Anita was learning to drive when she couldn't listen to the radio and drive at the same time. After some practice, she could listen, but had to turn the radio off when traffic was heavy. After years of practice, she can plan a class or talk on the phone as she drives. This is because many processes that initially require attention and concentration become automatic with practice. Actually, automaticity probably is a matter of degree—we are not completely automatic but rather more or less automatic in our performances depending on how much practice we have had and features of the current situation (Anderson, 1995a).

Attention and Teaching. The first step in learning is paying attention. Students cannot process something that they do not recognize or perceive. Many factors in the classroom influence student attention. Eye-catching or startling displays or actions can draw attention at the beginning of a lesson. A teacher might begin a science lesson on air pressure by blowing up a balloon until it pops. Bright colours, underlining, highlighting of written or spoken words, calling students by name, surprise events, intriguing questions, variety in tasks and teaching methods, and changes in voice level, lighting, or pacing can all be used to focus attention. And students have to maintain attention—they have to stay focused on the important features of the learning situation. The Guidelines on page 239 offer additional ideas for capturing and maintaining students' attention.

Working Memory

Once noticed and transformed into patterns of images or sounds (or perhaps other types of sensory codes), the information in sensory memory is available for further

The first step in learning is paying attention; teachers must be able to gain and maintain students' attention. ▶

GUIDELINES

Gaining and Maintaining Attention

Use signals.

Examples

1. Develop a signal that tells students to stop what they are doing and focus on you. Some teachers move to a particular spot in the room, flick the lights, or play a chord on the class piano.
2. Avoid distracting behaviour, such as tapping a pencil, that interferes with both signals and attention to learning.
3. Give short, clear directions before, not during, transitions.

Make sure the purpose of the lesson or assignment is clear to students.

Examples

1. Write the goals or objectives on the board and discuss them with students before starting. Ask students to summarize or restate the goals.
2. Explain the reasons for learning, and ask students for examples of how they will apply their understanding of the material.
3. Tie the new material to previous lessons—show an outline or map of how the new topic fits with previous and upcoming material.

Emphasize variety, curiosity, and surprise.

Examples

1. Arouse curiosity with questions such as "What would happen if. . . . ?"
2. Create shock by staging an unexpected event such as a loud argument just before a lesson on communication.
3. Alter the physical environment by changing the arrangement of the room or moving to a different setting.
4. Shift sensory channels by giving a lesson that requires students to touch, smell, or taste.
5. Use movements, gestures, and voice inflection—walk around the room, point, and speak softly and then more emphatically.

Ask questions and provide frames for answering.

Examples

1. Ask students why the material is important, how they intend to study, and what strategies they will use.
2. Give students self-checking or self-editing guides that focus on common mistakes or have them work in pairs to improve each other's work—sometimes it is difficult to pay attention to your own errors.

---

processing. **Working memory** is the "workbench" of the memory system, the component of memory where new information is held temporarily and combined with knowledge from long-term memory. Its *content* is activated information—what you are thinking about at the moment. For this reason, some psychologists consider the working memory to be synonymous with "consciousness" (Sweller, van Merrienboer, & Paas, 1998).

Capacity, Duration, and Contents of Working Memory. Working memory capacity is limited—something many of your professors seem to forget as they race through a lecture. In experimental situations based on the information processing model, it appears that the capacity of working memory is only about five to nine separate new items at once (Miller, 1956). This limitation holds true to some degree in everyday life. It is quite common to remember a new phone number after looking it up, as you walk across the room to make the call. But what if you have two phone calls to make in succession? Two new phone numbers (14 digits) are hard to store simultaneously.

Remember—put into your working memory—that we are discussing the recall of *new* information. In daily life we certainly can hold more than five to nine bits of information at once. While you are dialling that seven-digit phone number you just looked up, you are bound to have other things "on your mind"—in your working memory—such as how to use a telephone, and whom you are calling and

Working Memory: The information that you are focusing on at a given moment.

why. You don't have to pay attention to these things; they are not new knowledge. Some of the processes, such as dialling the phone, have become automatic. However, because of the working memory's limitations, if you were in a foreign country and were attempting to use an unfamiliar telephone system, you might very well have trouble remembering the phone number because you were trying to figure out the phone system at the same time. Even a few bits of new information can be too much to remember if the new information is complex or unfamiliar or if you have to integrate several elements to make sense of a situation (Sweller, van Merrienboer, & Paas, 1998).

Some psychologists argue that working memory is limited not by the number of bits of information it can store, but by the amount of information we can hold in an articulatory loop. The **articulatory loop** is a rehearsal system of about 1.5 seconds. Baddeley (1986) suggests that we can hold as much in working memory as we can rehearse (repeat to ourselves) in 1.5 seconds. The seven-digit telephone number fits this limitation.

No matter how the capacity of working memory is defined, by number of bits or by the amount you can keep in the articulatory (rehearsal) loop, it is clear that the *duration* of information is short, about 5 to 20 seconds. This is why working memory has been called *short-term* memory. It may seem to you that a memory system with a 20-second time limit is not very useful. But without this system, you would have already forgotten what you read in the first part of this sentence before you came to these last few words. This would clearly make understanding sentences difficult.

The *contents* of information in working memory may be in the form of images that resemble the perceptions in sensory memory, or the information may be structured more abstractly, based on meaning. Some recent theories suggest that there are actually two working-memory systems—one for language-based information and another for non-verbal, spatial, visual information (Baddeley, 1998; Jurden, 1995).

Retaining Information in Working Memory. Because information in working memory is fragile and easily lost, it must be kept activated to be retained. Activation is high as long as you are focusing on information, but activation decays or fades quickly when attention shifts away. Holding information in working memory is like keeping all the plates spinning on top of poles in a circus act. The performer gets one plate spinning, moves to the next, and the next, but has to return to the first before it slows down too much and falls off the pole. If we don't keep the information "spinning" in working memory—keep it activated—it will "fall off" (Anderson, 1995a, 1995b). When activation fades, forgetting follows, as

To learn the lines of a play, these students will use maintenance rehearsal. As long as they keep going over their lines, they'll probably remember them for the play. To the extent that they can connect this information with knowledge they already have in long-term memory, their recall of the lines may be stronger. ▶

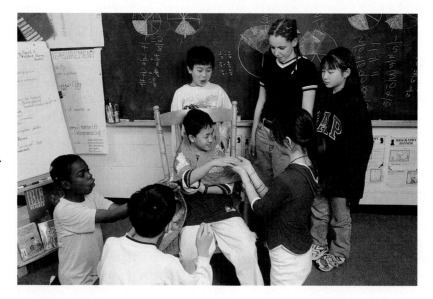

FIGURE 7.3

Working Memory

Information in working memory can be kept activated through maintenance rehearsal or transferred into long-term memory by being connected with information in long-term memory (elaborative rehearsal).

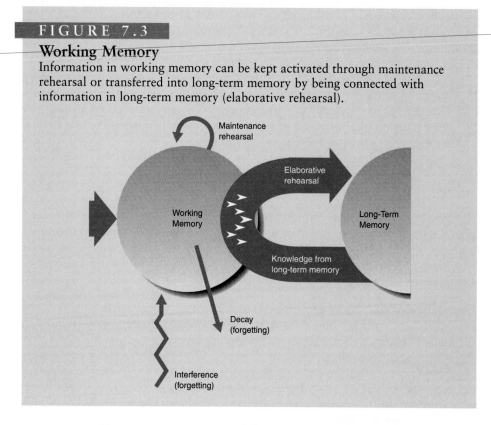

shown in Figure 7.3. To keep information activated in working memory for longer than 20 seconds, most people keep rehearsing the information mentally.

There are two types of rehearsal (Craik & Lockhart, 1972). **Maintenance rehearsal** involves repeating the information in your mind—in the articulatory loop. As long as you repeat the information, it can be maintained in working memory indefinitely. Maintenance rehearsal is useful for retaining something you plan to use and then forget, like a phone number.

Elaborative rehearsal involves connecting the information you are trying to remember with information you already know, which is stored in your long-term memory. For example, if you meet someone at a party whose name is the same as your brother's, you don't have to repeat the name to keep it in memory: you just have to make the association. This kind of rehearsal not only retains information in working memory but helps move information from short-term to long-term memory. Rehearsal is thus an "executive control process" that affects the flow of information through the information processing system.

The limited capacity of working memory can also be somewhat circumvented by the control process of **chunking**. Because the number of bits of information, not the size of each bit, is the limitation for working memory, you can retain more information if you can group individual bits of information into one or several chunks. For example, if you have to remember the six digits 3, 5, 4, 8, 7, and 0, it is easier to put them together into three chunks of two digits each (35, 48, 70) or two chunks of three digits each (354, 870). With these changes, there are only two or three chunks of information rather than six bits to hold at one time. Chunking helps you remember a telephone number or a social insurance number (Bruning, Schraw, & Ronning, 1999).

Forgetting. Information may be lost from working memory through either of two processes, interference or decay (see Figure 7.3). Interference is fairly straightforward: remembering new information interferes with or gets in the way of remembering old information. The new thought replaces the old one. As new

Maintenance Rehearsal: Keeping information in working memory by repeating it to yourself.

Elaborative Rehearsal: Keeping information in working memory by associating it with something else you already know.

Chunking: Grouping individual bits of data into meaningful larger units.

Decay: The weakening and fading of memories with the passage of time.

Long-Term Memory: Permanent store of knowledge.

thoughts accumulate, old information is lost from working memory. Information is also lost by **decay** over time. If you don't continue to pay attention to information, the activation level decays (weakens) and finally drops so low that the information cannot be reactivated—it disappears altogether.

Forgetting is very useful. Without forgetting, people would quickly overload their working memories and learning would cease. Also, it would be a problem if you remembered permanently every sentence you ever read. Finding a particular bit of information in all that sea of knowledge would be impossible. It is helpful to have a system that provides temporary storage.

Long-Term Memory

Working memory holds the information that is currently activated, such as a telephone number you have just found and are about to dial. **Long-term memory** holds the information that is well learned, such as all the other telephone numbers you know. Well-learned information is said to be high in memory strength or *durability* (Anderson, 1995b).

Capacity and Duration of Long-Term Memory. There are five main differences between working and long-term memory, as you can see in Table 7.2. Information enters working memory quickly. To move information into long-term storage requires more time and a bit of effort. Whereas the capacity of working memory is limited, the capacity of long-term memory appears to be, for all practical purposes, unlimited. In addition, once information is securely stored in long-term memory, it can remain there permanently. Theoretically, we should be able to remember as much as we want for as long as we want. Of course, the problem is to find the right information when we need it. Our access to information in working memory is immediate because we are thinking about the information at that very moment. But access to information in long-term memory requires time and effort for search and retrieval. Recently, some psychologists have suggested that there are not two separate memory stores (working and long-term). Rather, working memory is the part of long-term memory that works on (processes) currently activated information—so working memory is more about processing than storage (Baddeley, 1998).

Contents of Long-Term Memory. Allan Paivio (1971, 1986; Clark & Paivio, 1991) of the University of Western Ontario suggests that information is stored in long-term memory as either visual images or verbal units, or both. Psychologists who agree with Paivio believe that information coded both visually and verbally is easiest to learn (Mayer & Sims, 1994). This may be one reason why explaining an idea with words and representing it visually in a figure, as we do in textbooks, has

TABLE 7.2   Working and Long-Term Memory

Type of Memory	Input	Capacity	Duration	Contents	Retrieval
Working	Very fast	Limited	Very brief: 5–20 sec.	Words, images, ideas, sentences	Immediate
Long-Term	Relatively slow	Practically unlimited	Practically unlimited	Propositional networks, schemata, productions, episodes, perhaps images	Depends on representation and organization

Source: Adapted by permission of the author from F. Smith (1975), *Comprehension and Learning: A Conceptual Framework for Teachers,* published by Holt, Rinehart and Winston.

FIGURE 7.4

A Geographic Map That Supports Learning about Ancient Greece

Sources: From "Using Geographic Maps in the Classroom: The Conjoint Influence of Individual Differences and Dual coding on Learning Facts," by E. M. Diana and J. M. Webb, 1997, *Learning and Individual Differences*, 9, p. 200. Map from *The World and Its People, Europe, Africa, Asia, and Australia.* Silver Burdett Co. 1984. Reprinted with permission.

proved helpful to students. For example, Diana and Webb (1997) found that using maps such as the one in Figure 7.4 along with written text helped Grade 6 students to remember more about Ancient Greece than was possible using text alone. Paivio's ideas have some support, but critics contend that the capacity of the brain is not large enough to store all the images we have seen or can imagine. They suggest that many images are actually stored as verbal codes and then translated into visual information when an image is needed (Schunk, 2000). Most cognitive psychologists distinguish three categories of long-term memory: semantic, episodic, and procedural.

Semantic memory is memory for meaning. These memories are stored as *propositions*, *images*, and *schema*s. Because these are very important concepts for teaching, we will spend some extra time on them.

Propositions and Propositional Networks.

A **proposition** is the smallest unit of information that can be judged true or false. The statement "Ida borrowed the antique tablecloth" has two propositions:

1. Ida borrowed the tablecloth.
2. The tablecloth is an antique.

Propositions that share information, such as the two above that share information about the tablecloth (Ida borrowed the tablecloth and the tablecloth is an antique), are linked in a propositional network. A **propositional network** is

Connect & Extend
To the research
Clark, J. M., & Paivio, A. (1991). Dual coding theory and education. *Educational Psychology Review, 3,* 149–210. This is a current statement of the dual coding theory.

Connect & Extend
To real life
Why would drawing pictures of events or objects facilitate learning?

Semantic Memory: Memory for meaning.

Proposition: The smallest unit of information that can be judged true or false.

Propositional Network: Set of interconnected concepts and relationships in which long-term knowledge is held.

A Propositional Network

The sentence "Ida borrowed the antique tablecloth" has two propositions: (1) Ida borrowed the tablecloth [in the past] and (2) The tablecloth is an antique.

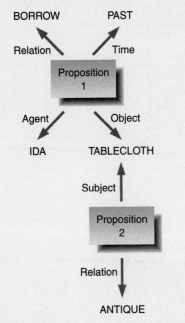

Source: Developed from material in J. Anderson (1985). *Cognitive Psychology and Its Implications*, 2/e. San Francisco: W. H. Freeman; and D. Gentner (1975). Evidence for the psychological reality of semantic components: The verbs of possession. In D. Norman and D. Rumelhart (Eds.), *Explorations in Cognition*. San Francisco: W. H. Freeman.

Images: Representations based on the physical attributes—the appearance—of information.

Schema: A basic structure for organizing information; concept.

interconnected bits of information. Different cognitive psychologists have slightly different methods for diagramming propositional networks. Figure 7.5 is a common way of representing the relationships in the sentence "Ida (the *agent*) borrowed the antique tablecloth (the *object*)." Because the verb is in the past tense, the *time* of action is in the past. The same propositional network would apply to these sentences: "The antique tablecloth was borrowed by Ida," or "Ida borrowed the tablecloth, which was an antique." The meaning is the same, and it is this *meaning* that is stored in memory as a set of relationships.

It is possible that most information is stored and represented in propositional networks. When we want to recall a bit of information, we may translate its meaning (as represented in the propositional network) into familiar phrases and sentences, or mental pictures. Also, because of the network, recall of one bit of information can trigger or *activate* recall of another. We are not aware of these networks, for they are not part of our conscious memory (Anderson, 1995a). In much the same way, we are not aware of underlying grammatical structure when we form a sentence in our own language; we don't have to diagram a sentence in order to say it.

Images.   **Images** are representations based on perceptions—on the structure or appearance of the information (Anderson, 1995a). As we form images we try to remember or recreate the physical attributes and spatial structure of information. For example, when asked how many window panes are in their living room, most people call up an image of the windows "in their mind's eye" and count the panes—the more panes, the longer it takes to respond. If the information were represented only in a proposition such as "my living room has seven window panes," then everyone would take about the same time to answer, whether the number was 1 or 24 (Mendell, 1971). However, as we saw earlier, researchers don't agree on exactly how images are stored in memory. Some psychologists believe that images are stored as pictures; others believe we store propositions in long-term memory and convert to pictures in working memory when necessary.

There probably are features of each process involved—some picture-copying memory and some memory for verbal or propositional descriptions of the image. Seeing images "in your mind's eye" is not exactly the same as seeing the actual image. It is more difficult to perform complicated transformations on mental images than on real images (Matlin & Foley, 1997). Nevertheless, images are useful in making many practical decisions such as how a molecule of water is structured or how to line up a golf shot. Images may also be helpful in abstract reasoning. Physicists, such as Faraday and Einstein, report creating images to reason about complex new problems (Gagné, Yekovich, & Yekovich, 1993).

Schemas.   Propositions and images are fine for representing single ideas and relationships. But often our knowledge about a topic combines images and propositions. "In order to deal with the fact that much of our knowledge seems integrated, psychologists have developed the idea of a schema" (Gagné, Yekovich, & Yekovich, 1993, p. 81). As mentioned in Chapter 5, schemas (sometimes called *schemata*) are abstract knowledge structures that organize large amounts of information. A **schema** (the singular form) is a pattern or guide for understanding an event, concept, or skill. Figure 7.6 is a partial representation of a schema for knowledge about an "antique."

The schema tells you what features are typical of a category, what to expect. The schema is like a pattern, specifying the "standard" relationships in an object or situation. The pattern has "slots" that are filled with specific information as we apply the schema in a particular situation. And schemas are individual. For example, your schema of an antique may be less richly developed than an antique collector's schema. You encountered the very similar concept of scheme in the discussion of Piaget's theory of cognitive development in Chapter 2.

When you hear the sentence "Ida borrowed the antique tablecloth," you know even more about the two propositions. This is because you have schemas about borrowing, tablecloths, antiques, and maybe even Ida herself. You know without being told, for example, that the lender does not have the tablecloth now, because it is in Ida's possession, and that Ida has an obligation to return the tablecloth to

FIGURE 7.6

A Schema for "Antique"
The concept of "antique" falls under the general category of "collectible object." It is related to other concepts, such as "hobby" and "travelling to flea markets," depending on the individual's experience.

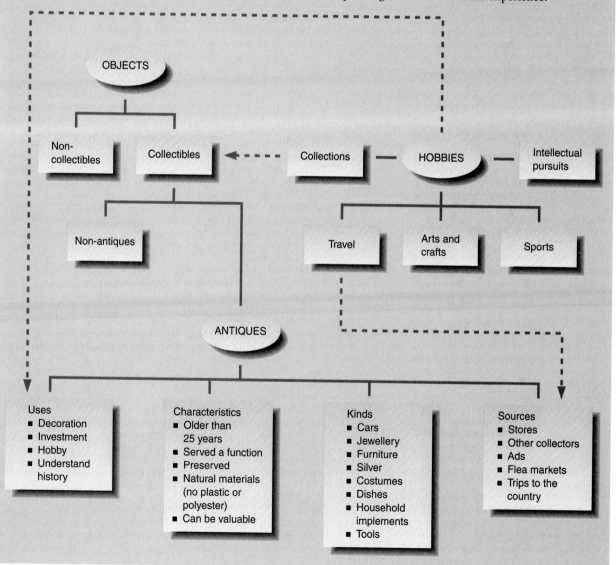

Connect & Extend
To real life
How can schemas about differences among individuals, groups, and social contexts determine how new information about people and situations is interpreted?

the lender (Gentner, 1975). None of this information is explicitly stated, but it is part of our schema for understanding the meaning of "borrow." Other schemas allow you to infer that the cloth is not plastic (if it is a real antique) and that Ida has probably invited guests for a meal. Your schema about Ida may even allow you to predict how promptly the cloth will be returned and in what condition.

Another type of schema, a **story grammar** (sometimes called a schema for text or story structure), helps students to understand and remember stories (Gagné, Yekovich, & Yekovich, 1993; Rumelhart & Ortony, 1977). A story grammar could be something like this: murder discovered, search for clues, murderer's fatal mistake identified, trap set to trick suspect into confessing, murderer takes bait—mystery solved! In other words, a story grammar is a typical general structure that could fit many specific stories. To comprehend a story, we select a schema that seems appropriate. Then we use this framework to decide which details are important, what information to seek, and what to remember. It is as though the schema is a theory about what should occur in the story. The schema guides us in "interrogating" the text, filling in the specific information we expect to find so that the story makes sense. If we activate our "murder mystery schema" we may be alert for clues or a murderer's fatal mistake (Resnick, 1981). Without the appropriate schema, trying to understand a story, textbook, or classroom lesson is a slow, difficult process, something like finding your way through a new town without a map.

A schema representing the typical sequence of events in an everyday situation is called a **script** or an *event schema*. Children as young as three have basic scripts for the familiar events in their lives (Nelson, 1986). A kindergartner's script for "lunch" might be something like the one in Figure 7.7.

Storing knowledge of the world in schemas and scripts has advantages and disadvantages. A schema can be applied in many contexts, depending on what part of the schema is relevant. You can use what you know about antiques, for example, to plan trips, decide if a particular article is worth the price asked, or enjoy a museum display. Having a well-developed schema about Ida lets you recognize her (even as her appearance changes), remember many of her characteristics, and make predictions about her behaviour. But it also allows you to be wrong. You may have incorporated incorrect or biased information into your schema of Ida. For example, if Ida is a member of an ethnic group different from yours and if you believe that group is dishonest, you may assume that Ida will keep the tablecloth. In this way, racial and ethnic stereotypes can function as schemas for misunderstanding individuals and for racial discrimination (Sherman & Bessenoff, 1999).

Episodic Memory. Memory for information tied to a particular place and time, especially information about the events of your own life, is called **episodic memory**. Episodic memory keeps track of the order of things, so it is also a good place to store jokes, gossip, or plots from films. Because it is about events we have experienced, we often can explain *when* the event happened. In contrast, we usually can't describe when we acquired a semantic memory. For example, you may have a difficult time remembering when you developed semantic memories for the meaning of the word "injustice," but you can easily remember a time that you felt unjustly treated.

FIGURE 7.7

"Lunchtime" Script

This script is typical of ones generated by children five or six years of age. Younger children give scripts that are less detailed and that contain fewer main acts.

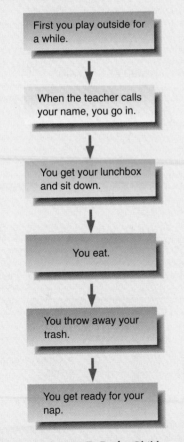

First you play outside for a while.

↓

When the teacher calls your name, you go in.

↓

You get your lunchbox and sit down.

↓

You eat.

↓

You throw away your trash.

↓

You get ready for your nap.

Source: From Laura E. Berk, *Child Development*, 2/e, p. 282. Copyright © 1991 by Allyn & Bacon. Reprinted by permission.

Procedural Memory. Memory for how to do things is called **procedural memory.** It may take a while to learn a procedure—such as how to write cursive letters, serve a tennis ball, or factor an equation—but once learned, this knowledge tends to be remembered for a long time. Procedural memories are represented as condition-action rules, sometimes called productions. **Productions** specify what to do under certain conditions: if A occurs, then do B. A production might be something like, "If you want to write smoothly, then relax your grip on the pencil," or "If your goal is to increase student attention, and a student has been paying attention a bit longer than usual, then praise the student." People can't necessarily state all their condition-action rules, but they act on them nevertheless. The more practised the procedure, the more automatic the action (Anderson, 1995a).

Storing and Retrieving Information in Long-Term Memory

Just what is done to "save" information permanently—to create semantic, episodic, or procedural memories? How can we make the most effective use of our practically unlimited capacity to learn and remember? *The way you learn information in the first place*—the way you process it at the outset—seems to affect its recall later. One important requirement is that you integrate new material with information already stored in long-term memory as you construct an understanding. Here *elaboration, organization,* and *context* play a role.

Elaboration is the addition of meaning to new information by connecting it with already existing knowledge. In other words, we apply our schemas and draw on already existing knowledge to construct an understanding and frequently change our existing knowledge in the process. We often elaborate automatically. For example, a paragraph about a historic figure in the seventeenth century tends to activate our existing knowledge about that period; we use the old knowledge to understand the new.

Material that is elaborated when first learned will be easier to recall later. First, as we saw earlier, elaboration is a form of rehearsal. It keeps the information activated in working memory long enough to have a chance for permanent storage in long-term memory. Second, elaboration builds extra links to existing knowledge. The more associations there are among bits or chunks of knowledge, the more routes there are to follow to get to the original bit. To put it another way, you have several "handles," or retrieval cues, by which you can recognize or "pick up" the information you might be seeking (Schunk, 2000). Psychologists have also found that the more precise and sensible the elaborations, the easier recall will be (Bransford, Stein, Vye, Franks, Auble, Mezynski, & Perfetto, 1982; Stein, Littlefield, Bransford, & Persampieri, 1984).

The more students elaborate new ideas, the more they "make them their own"—the deeper their understanding and the better their memory for the knowledge. We help students to elaborate when we ask them to translate information into their own words, create examples, explain to a peer, draw the relationships, or apply the information to solve new problems. Of course, if students elaborate new information by making incorrect connections or developing misguided explanations, these misconceptions will be remembered too.

Organization is a second element of processing that improves learning. Material that is well organized is easier to learn and to remember than separate bits of information, especially if the information is complex or extensive. Placing a concept in a structure will help you learn and remember either general definitions or specific examples. The structure serves as a guide back to the information when you need it. For example, Table 7.1 on page 235 organizes information about types of knowledge; Table 7.2 on page 242 gives an organized view of the capacity, duration, contents, and retrieval of information from working and long-term memory; and Figure 7.6 on page 245 organizes Anita's (limited) knowledge about antiques.

Connect & Extend
To your teaching
See the Teachers' Casebook for practising teachers' ideas about how to help students retain and retrieve information.

Episodic Memory: Long-term memory for information tied to a particular time and place, especially memory of the events in a person's life.

Procedural Memory: Long-term memory for how to do things.

Productions: The contents of procedural memory; rules about what actions to take, given certain conditions.

Elaboration: Adding and extending meaning by connecting new information to existing knowledge.

Context is a third element of processing that influences learning. Aspects of physical and emotional context—places, rooms, how we are feeling on a particular day, who is with us—are learned along with other information. Later, if you try to remember the information, it will be easier if the current context is similar to the original one. This has been demonstrated in the laboratory. Students who learned material in one type of room performed better on tests taken in a similar room than they did on tests taken in a very different-looking room (Smith, Glenberg, & Bjork, 1978). So studying for a test under "testlike" conditions may result in improved performance. Of course, you can't always go back to the same or to a similar place in order to recall something. But by picturing the setting, the time of day, and your companions, you may eventually reach the information you seek.

Levels of Processing Theories. Craik and Lockhart (1972) of the University of Toronto first proposed their **levels of processing theory** as an alternative to short- and long-term memory models, but levels of processing is particularly related to the notion of elaboration described earlier. Craik and Lockhart suggested that what determines how long information is remembered is how completely the information is analyzed and connected with other information. The more completely information is processed, the better are our chances of remembering it. For example, according to the levels of processing theory, if you are asked to sort pictures of dogs based on the colour of their coats, you might not remember many of the pictures later. But if you are asked to rate each dog on how likely it is to chase you as you jog, you probably would remember more of the pictures. To rate the dogs you must pay attention to details in the pictures, relate features of the dogs to characteristics associated with danger, and so on. This rating procedure requires "deeper" processing and more focus on the meaning of the features in the photos.

Retrieving Information from Long-Term Memory. When we need to use information from long-term memory, we search for it. Sometimes the search is conscious, as when you see a friend approaching and search for her name. At other times locating and using information from long-term memory is automatic, as when you dial a telephone number or solve a math problem without having to search for each step. Think of long-term memory as a huge library full of tools and supplies ready to be brought to the workbench of working memory to accomplish a task. The library's shelves (long-term memory) store an incredible amount, but it may be hard to find quickly what you are looking for. The workbench (working memory) is small, but anything on it is immediately available. Because it is small, however, supplies (bits of information) sometimes are lost when the workbench overflows or when one bit of information covers (interferes with) another (E. Gagné, 1985).

The size of the memory network is huge, but only one small area is activated at any one time. Only the information we are currently thinking about is in working memory. Information is retrieved in this network through the **spread of activation**. When a particular proposition or image is active—when we are thinking about it— nearby (closely associated) knowledge can be activated as well, and activation can spread through the network (Anderson, 1993; Gagné, Yekovich, & Yekovich, 1993). Thus, if you focus on the propositions "I'd like to go for a drive to see the fall leaves today," related ideas such as "I should rake leaves" and "The car needs an oil change" come to mind. As activation spreads from the car trip to the oil change, the original thought, or active memory, disappears from working memory because of the limited space. So **retrieval** from long-term memory is partly through the spreading of activation from one bit of knowledge to related ideas in the network. We often use this spreading in reverse to retrace our steps in a conversation, as in, "Before we got onto the topic of where to get the oil changed, what were we talking about? Oh yes, seeing the leaves." The learning and retrieving processes of long-term memory are diagrammed in Figure 7.8.

Context: The physical or emotional backdrop associated with an event.

Levels of Processing Theory: Theory that recall of information is based on how deeply it is processed.

Spread of Activation: Retrieval of pieces of information based on their relatedness to one another. Remembering one bit of information activates (stimulates) recall of associated information.

Retrieval: Process of searching for and finding information in long-term memory.

FIGURE 7.8

Long-Term Memory

We activate information from long-term memory to help us understand new information in working memory. With mental work and processing (elaboration, organization, context), the new information can be stored permanently in long-term memory. Forgetting is caused by interference and time decay.

Reconstruction: Recreating information by using memories, expectations, logic, and existing knowledge.

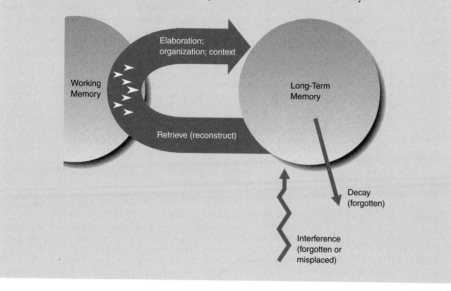

In long-term memory information is still available even when it is not activated, and even when you are not thinking about it at the moment. If spreading activation does not "find" the information we seek, we might still come up with the answer through **reconstruction**, a problem-solving process that makes use of logic, cues, and other knowledge to *construct* a reasonable answer by filling in any missing parts. Sometimes reconstructed recollections are incorrect. For example, in 1932, F. C. Bartlett conducted a series of famous studies on remembering stories. He read a complex, unfamiliar Native North American tale to students at England's Cambridge University and, after various lengths of time, asked the students to recall the story. The stories that students recalled were generally shorter than the original and were translated into the concepts and language of the Cambridge student culture. The original story told of a seal hunt, for instance, but many students remembered a "fishing trip," an activity closer to their experiences and more consistent with their schemas.

One area where reconstructed memory can play a major role is eyewitness testimony. Elizabeth Loftus and her colleagues have conducted a number of studies showing that misleading questions or other information during questioning can affect memory. For example, in a classic study, Loftus and Palmer (1974) showed subjects slides of a car wreck. Later, the experimenters asked some subjects, "How fast were the cars going when they *hit* each other?"; other subjects who saw the same slides were asked, "How fast were the cars going when they *smashed* into each other?" The difference in verbs was enough to bias the subjects' memories—the "hit" subjects estimated the cars were travelling an average of 55 km per hour, but the "smashed" subjects estimated almost 66 km per hour. And one week later, 32 percent of the "smashed" subjects remembered seeing broken glass at the scene of the wreck, while only 14 percent of the "hit" subjects remembered glass. (Broken glass was not visible in any of the slides.)

Forgetting and Long-Term Memory. If information is lost from working memory it truly disappears. No amount of effort will bring it back. But informa-

The Information Processing Model of Memory

Review

▶ Compare declarative, procedural, and conditional knowledge.

▶ Give two explanations for perception.

▶ How is information retained in working memory?

▶ How is information represented in long-term memory and what role do schemas play?

▶ What learning processes improve long-term memory?

▶ Why do we forget?

Apply

▶ A child from a large city has trouble understanding and remembering a story about endangered species in a national park. Explain this situation using information processing theory.

tion stored in long-term memory may be available, given the right cues. Some researchers believe that nothing is ever lost from long-term memory; however, recent research casts doubts on this assertion (Schwartz & Reisberg, 1991).

Information appears to be lost from long-term memory through time decay and **interference**. For example, memory for French-English vocabulary decreases for about three years after a person's last course in French, then stays level for about 25 years, then drops again for the next 25 years. One explanation for this decline is that neural connections, like muscles, grow weak without use. After 25 years, it may be that the memories are still somewhere in the brain, but they are too weak to be reactivated (Anderson, 1995a, 1995b). Finally, newer memories may interfere with or obscure older memories, and older memories may interfere with memory for new material. Even with decay and interference, long-term memory is remarkable. In a recent review of almost 100 studies of memory for knowledge taught in school, George Semb and John Ellis (1994) concluded that, "contrary to popular belief, students retain much of the knowledge taught in the classroom" (p. 279). It appears that teaching strategies that encourage student engagement and lead to higher levels of *initial* learning (such as frequent reviews and tests, elaborated feedback, high standards, mastery learning, and active involvement in learning projects) are associated with longer retention. The Guidelines on page 251 give applications of information processing for teaching.

Connectionism: An Alternative View of Memory

The most recent explanations of how memory works include **connectionist models** that assume all knowledge is stored in patterns of connections among basic processing units in a vast network of the brain. The processing of information is assumed to be distributed across this network. So connectionist models use the brain's physical network of neurons as a metaphor for memory networks. Some connectionist models, such as **parallel distributed processing (PDP)**, stay at the metaphorical level and try to describe memory in a way that is consistent with human behaviour. Brain-based theories, on the other hand, focus directly on how the nervous system might operate (Driscoll, 1994; Iran-Nejad, Marsh, & Clements, 1992).

Connectionist models have certain advantages. They can account for more than recall of information, and they can explain the slowly developing, incremental, ever-changing nature of human learning. As connections are constantly adjusted, learning occurs. When an output doesn't match a goal, the connections can be adjusted. However, connectionist models may not be developed enough to be useful for teachers except to remind us that learning involves the continued building, elaboration, and adjustment of knowledge (Driscoll, 1994; Iran-Nejad, Marsh, & Clements, 1992).

Interference: The process that occurs when remembering certain information is hampered by the presence of other information.

Connectionist Models: Views of knowledge as being stored in patterns of connections among basic processing units in the brain.

Parallel Distributed Processing (PDP): Connectionist model that uses the brain's physical network of neurons as a metaphor for memory networks.

GUIDELINES

Using Information Processing Ideas in the Classroom

Make sure you have the students' attention.

Examples

1. Develop a signal that tells students to stop what they are doing and focus on you. Make sure students respond to the signal—don't let them ignore it. Practise using the signal.
2. Move around the room, use gestures, and avoid speaking in a monotone.
3. Begin a lesson by asking a question that stimulates interest in the topic.
4. Regain the attention of individual students by walking closer to them, using their names, or asking them a question.

Help students separate essential from non-essential details and focus on the most important information.

Examples

1. Summarize instructional objectives to indicate what students should be learning. Relate the material you are presenting to the objectives as you teach: "Now I'm going to explain exactly how you can find the information you need to meet Objective One on the board—determining the tone of the story."
2. When you make an important point, pause, repeat, ask a student to paraphrase, note the information on the board in coloured chalk, or tell students to highlight the point in their notes or readings.

Help students make connections between new information and what they already know.

Examples

1. Review prerequisites to help students bring to mind the information they will need to understand new material: "Who can tell us the definition of a quadrilateral? Now, what is a rhombus? Is a square a quadrilateral? Is a square a rhombus? What did we say yesterday about how you can tell? Today we are going to look at some other quadrilaterals."

2. Use an outline or diagram to show how new information fits with the framework you have been developing. For example, "Now that you know the duties of the FBI, where would you expect to find it in this diagram of the branches of the U.S. government?"
3. Give an assignment that specifically calls for the use of new information along with information already learned.

Provide for repetition and review of information.

Examples

1. Begin the class with a quick review of the homework assignment.
2. Give frequent, short tests.
3. Build practice and repetition into games, or have students work with partners to quiz each other.

Present material in a clear, organized way.

Examples

1. Make the purpose of the lesson very clear.
2. Give students a brief outline to follow. Put the same outline on an overhead so you can keep yourself on track. When students ask questions or make comments, relate these to the appropriate section of the outline.
3. Use summaries in the middle and at the end of the lesson.

Focus on meaning, not memorization.

Examples

1. In teaching new words, help students associate the new word to a related word they already understand: "*Enmity* is from the same base as *enemy.* . . ."
2. In teaching about remainders, have students group 12 objects into sets of 2, 3, 4, 5, 6, and ask them to count the "leftovers" in each case.

Metacognition, Regulation, and Individual Differences

Connect & Extend
To the research
See the entire issue of *Learning and Individual Differences* (1996, #4) on individual differences in metacognition.

One question that intrigues many cognitive psychologists is why some people learn and remember more than others. For those who hold an information processing

Connect & Extend
To your teaching
E. Bondy (1989) describes the importance of metacognitive processes, particularly monitoring comprehension, and lists nine suggestions for educators. *Highlights:* (1) Have students keep a daily learning log. (2) Demonstrate and discuss appropriate metacognitive activity (such as estimating difficulty of task, setting goals, choosing a strategy). (3) Provide opportunities for feedback. (4) Provide instruction in self-questioning. (5) Teach students to summarize material. (6) Teach students to rate their comprehension (i.e., "I understand well," "I sort of understand," "I don't understand"). (7) Use model of learning as framework for planning instruction. (8) Teach students how to study. (9) Teach students to think aloud and systematically solve problems. [*Thinking about thinking.* In *Annual editions: Educational psychology* (pp. 83–86). Guilford, CT: Duskin.]

Executive Control Processes:
Processes such as selective attention, rehearsal, elaboration, and organization that influence encoding, storage, and retrieval of information in memory.

Metacognition: Knowledge about our own thinking processes.

view, part of the answer lies in the executive control processes shown in Figure 7.1 on page 236. **Executive control processes** guide the flow of information through the information processing system. We have already discussed a number of control processes, including attention, maintenance rehearsal, elaborative rehearsal, organization, and elaboration. These executive control processes are sometimes called *metacognitive skills,* because the processes can be intentionally used to regulate cognition.

Metacognitive Knowledge and Regulation

Donald Meichenbaum and his colleagues at the University of Waterloo describe **metacognition** as people's "awareness of their own cognitive machinery and how the machinery works" (Meichenbaum, Burland, Gruson, & Cameron, 1985, p. 5). Metacognition literally means cognition about cognition—or knowledge about knowledge. This knowledge is used to monitor and regulate cognitive processes—reasoning, comprehension, problem solving, learning, and so on (Metcalfe & Shimamura, 1994). Because people differ in their metacognitive knowledge and skills, they differ in how well and how quickly they learn (Brown, Bransord, Ferrara, & Campione, 1983; Morris, 1990).

Metacognition involves three kinds of knowledge. First, declarative knowledge describes yourself as a learner; factors that influence your learning and memory; and skills, strategies, and resources you believe are needed to perform a task. Second, knowing *what* to do—procedural knowledge—is knowing *how* to use the strategies. Third, conditional knowledge is critical to complete the task because it concerns knowing *when* and *why* to apply the strategies (Bruning, Schraw, & Ronning, 1999). Metacognition is the strategic application of this declarative, procedural, and conditional knowledge to accomplish goals and solve problems (Schunk, 2000).

Metacognitive knowledge is used to regulate thinking and learning (Brown, 1987; Nelson, 1996). Three essential skills allow us to do this: planning, monitoring, and evaluation. *Planning* involves deciding how much time to give to a task, which strategies to use, how to start, what resources to gather, what order to follow, what to skim and what to study intensely, and so on. *Monitoring* is the on-line awareness of "how I'm doing." Monitoring entails asking, "Is this making sense? Am I trying to go too fast? Have I studied enough?" *Evaluation* involves making judgments about the processes and outcomes of thinking and learning. Should I change strategies? Get help? Give up for now? Is this paper (painting, model, poem, plan, etc.) finished?

This young woman using an electronic organizer might be a good analogy for the metacognitive process. In both cases, the individual sets goals, makes plans, organizes activities, decides what procedure is needed next, selects procedures from several choices, monitors the effect of making the choice, and returns to the menu if the results are unsatisfactory. ▶

Of course, we don't have to be metacognitive all the time. Some actions become routine. Metacognition is most useful when tasks are challenging, but not too difficult. Then planning, monitoring, and evaluation can be helpful. And even when we are planning, monitoring, and evaluating, these processes are not necessarily conscious. Especially in adults, these processes can be automatic or implicit—we may use them without being aware of our efforts. Experts in a field may plan, monitor, and evaluate as second nature—they have difficulty describing their metacognitive knowledge and skills (Bargh & Chartrand, 1999; Reder, 1996).

Individual Differences in Metacognition

Some differences in metacognitive abilities are the result of development. As children grow older they are more able to exercise executive control and use strategies. For example, they are more able to determine if they have understood instructions (Markman, 1977, 1979) or if they have studied enough to remember a set of items (Flavell, Friedrichs, & Hoyt, 1970). Metacognitive abilities begin to develop around ages five to seven and improve throughout school (Flavell, 1985; Flavell, Green, & Flavell, 1995; Garner, 1990). In her work with Grades 1 and 2 students, Nancy Perry found that asking students two specific questions helped them become more metacognitive. The questions were: "What did you learn about yourself as a reader/writer today?" and "What did you learn that you can do again and again and again?" When teachers asked these questions regularly during class, even young students demonstrated fairly sophisticated levels of metacognitive understanding and action (Perry et al., 2000).

Not all differences in metacognitive abilities have to do with age or maturation. There is great variability even among students of the same developmental level, but these differences do not appear to be related to intellectual abilities. In fact, superior metacognitive skills can compensate for lower levels of ability, so these metacognitive skills can be especially important for students who often have trouble in school (Swanson, 1990).

Some individual differences in metacognitive abilities are probably caused by biological differences or by variations in learning experiences. Students can vary greatly in their ability to attend selectively to information in their environment. In fact, many students diagnosed as learning disabled actually have attention disorders (Hallahan & Kauffman, 2000), particularly with long tasks (Pelham, 1981). Attention is also influenced by the individual and cultural differences we examined in Chapters 4 and 5, such as learning abilities and preferences, cognitive styles, and cultural background. Students who are field dependent, for example, have difficulty perceiving elements in a pattern and tend to focus on the whole.

Individual Differences and Working Memory

As you might expect, there are both developmental and individual differences in working memory. Let's examine a few of each.

Developmental Differences. Research indicates that young children have very limited working memories but that their memory span improves with age. It is not clear whether these differences reflect changes in memory *capacity* or improvements in strategy use. The work of the late Robbie Case (1985a, 1985b), who was an educational psychologist at the University of Toronto, suggests that the total amount of "space" available for processing information is the same at each age, but young children must use quite a bit of this space to remember how to execute basic operations, such as reaching for a toy, finding the right word for an object, or counting. Using a new operation takes up a large portion of the child's working memory. Once an operation is mastered, however, there is more working memory available for short-term storage of new information. Biology may play a role too. As the brain and neurological system of the child mature, processing may become more efficient so that more working-memory space is available.

As children grow older, they develop more effective strategies for remembering information. Most children spontaneously discover rehearsal around age 5 or 6. Siegler (1991) describes a 9-old boy who witnessed a robbery, then mentally repeated the licence number of the getaway car until he could give the number to the police. Younger children can be taught to rehearse, and will use the strategy effectively as long as they are reminded. But they will not apply the strategy spontaneously. Children are 10 to 11 years old before they have adult-like working memories.

According to Case (1985a, 1985b), young children often use reasonable, but incorrect, strategies for solving problems because of their limited memories. They try to simplify the task by ignoring important information or skipping steps to reach a correct solution. This puts less strain on memory. For example, when comparing quantities, young children may consider only the height of the water in a glass, not the diameter of the glass, because the simpler approach demands less of their memory. According to Case, this explains young children's inability to solve the classic Piagetian conservation problem. (See Figure 2.2 on page 34).

There are several developmental differences in how students use organization, elaboration, and knowledge to process information in working memory. Around age 6, most children discover the value of using *organizational strategies* and by 9 or 10 they use these strategies spontaneously. So, given the following words to learn:

couch, orange, rat, lamp, pear, sheep, banana, rug, pineapple, horse, table, dog

an older child or an adult might organize the words into three short lists of furniture, fruit, and animals. Younger children can be taught to use organization to improve memory, but they probably won't apply the strategy unless they are reminded. Children also become more able to use elaboration as they mature, but this strategy is developed late in childhood. Creating images or stories to remember ideas is more likely for older elementary school students and adolescents (Siegler, 1991).

Individual Differences. Besides developmental differences, there are other individual variations in working memory. Some people seem to have more efficient working memories than others (Cariglia-Bull & Pressley, 1990; Di Vesta & Di Cintio, 1997; Jurden, 1995), and differences in working memory may be associated with giftedness in math and verbal areas. For example, subjects in one research study were asked to remember lists of numbers, the locations of marks on a page, letters, and words (Dark & Benbow, 1991). Subjects who excelled in mathematics remembered numbers and locations significantly better than subjects talented in verbal areas. The verbally talented subjects, on the other hand, had better memories for words. Based on these results, Dark and Benbow believe that basic differences in information processing abilities play a role in the development of mathematical and verbal talent.

Individual Differences and Long-Term Memory

The major individual difference that affects long-term memory is knowledge. Students with more *domain-specific declarative* and *procedural knowledge* are better at learning

---

CHECKPOINT

Metacognition, Regulation, and Individual Differences

Review

▷ What are the three metacognitive skills?

▷ Describe some individual differences in metacognition.

▷ How can using better metacognitive strategies improve children's memories?

Apply

▷ Give some examples of your own metacognitive abilities.

and remembering material in that domain. Think what it is like for you to read a very technical textbook in an area you know little about. Every line is difficult. You have to stop and look up words or turn back to read about concepts you don't understand. It is hard to remember what you are reading because you are trying to understand and remember at the same time. But with a good basis of knowledge, learning and remembering become easier; the more you know, the easier it is to know more. This is true in part because having knowledge improves strategy use. Another factor is related to developing domain knowledge and remembering it—interest. Alexander and her colleagues point out that to develop expert understanding and recall in a domain requires the "continuous interplay of skill (i.e., knowledge) and thrill (i.e., interest)" (Alexander, Kulikowich, & Schulze, 1994, p. 334).

Now that we have examined the information processing explanation of how knowledge is represented and remembered, let's turn to the really important question: how can teachers support the development of knowledge?

$\mathcal{B}$ecoming Knowledgeable: Some Basic Principles

Understanding a concept such as "antique" involves *declarative knowledge* about characteristics and images and *procedural knowledge* about how to apply rules to categorize specific antiques. We will discuss the development of declarative and procedural knowledge separately, but keep in mind that real learning is holistic and interrelated.

Development of Declarative Knowledge

Within the information processing perspective, to learn declarative knowledge is really to integrate new ideas with existing knowledge and construct an understanding. For example, a teacher says:

"In vitro experiments show vitamin C increases the formation of white blood cells."

Students may ignore the phrase "in vitro" because they have no existing schemas for making sense of it. But through *spreading of activation*, the concepts of "white blood cells" and "vitamin C" cue the retrieval of prior knowledge such as "vitamin C fights colds," "viruses cause colds," and "white blood cells destroy viruses." Using this prior knowledge about colds, viruses, and vitamin C, along with the new information that vitamin C increases white blood cells, the students may infer that "vitamin C fights colds *because* it increases the formation of the white blood cells." This information was neither in their long-term memories nor in the teacher's statement, but it was constructed by the students as they elaborated and organized their understanding of vitamin C. The resulting elaborated, reorganized network of knowledge includes the students' interpretations of the new information from the teacher in addition to their constructions and inferences (Gagné, Yekovich, & Yekovich, 1993). Let's examine factors that support the construction of declarative knowledge.

As you have seen, people learn best when they have a good base of knowledge in the area they are studying. With many well-elaborated schemas and scripts to guide them, new material makes more sense, and there are many possible networks for connecting new information with old. But students don't always have a good base of knowledge. In the early phases of learning, students of any age must grope around the landscape a bit, searching for landmarks and direction. Even experts in an area must use learning strategies when they encounter unfamiliar material or

Rote Memorization: Remembering information by repetition without necessarily understanding the meaning of the information.

Serial-Position Effect: The tendency to remember the beginning and the end but not the middle of a list.

Part Learning: Breaking a list of rote learning items into shorter lists.

Distributed Practice: Practice that occurs in brief periods with rest intervals.

Massed Practice: Practise for a single extended period.

Mnemonics: Techniques for remembering; also, the art of memory.

Loci Method: Technique of associating items with specific places.

What are some possible strategies? First we will discuss **rote memorization** techniques, which help students remember information that, while it has little inherent meaning, may provide the basic building blocks for other learning—the populations of the 10 largest cities in the world, for example. Next we will examine *mnemonic strategies,* which build in meaning by connecting what is to be learned with established words or images. Then we explore approaches that build on *meaning.*

Rote Memorization.   Very few things need to be learned by rote. The greatest challenge teachers face is to help students think and understand, not just memorize. Unfortunately, many students—like those in the scenario at the opening of this chapter—see memorizing and learning as the same thing (Iran-Nejad, 1990). There are times, though, when we have to memorize something word for word, such as lines in a song, poem, or play.

If you must memorize, how would you do it? If you have tried to memorize a list of items that are all similar to one another, you may have found that you tended to remember items at the beginning and at the end of the list but forgot those in the middle. This is called the **serial-position effect.** Using **part learning**—breaking the list into smaller segments—can help prevent this effect, because breaking a list into several shorter lists means there will be fewer middle items to forget.

Another strategy for memorizing a long selection or list is the use of **distributed practice.** A student who studies Hamlet's soliloquy intermittently throughout the weekend will probably do much better than a student who tries to memorize the entire speech on Sunday night. Studying for an extended period, rather than for briefer periods with rest time in between, is called **massed practice.** Distributed practice gives time for deeper processing and the chance to move information into long-term memory (Mumford, Costanza, Baughman, Threlfall, & Fleishman, 1994).

Mnemonics.   **Mnemonics** are systematic procedures for improving memory. Many mnemonic strategies use imagery (Atkinson et al., 1999; Levin, 1993).

The **loci method** derives its name from the plural of the Latin word *locus,* meaning "place." To use loci, you must first imagine a familiar place, such as your own house or apartment, and pick out particular locations. Every time you have a list to remember, the same locations serve as "pegs" on which to "hang" memories. Simply place each item from your list in one of these locations. For instance, let's say you want to remember to buy milk, bread, butter, and cereal at the store. Imagine a giant bottle of milk blocking the entry hall, a lazy loaf of bread sleeping on the living-room couch, a stick of butter melting all over the dining-room table, and dry cereal covering the kitchen floor. When you want to remember the items, all you have to do is take an imaginary walk through your house. Other **peg-type mnemonics** use a standard list of words (one is bun, two is shoe . . .) as pegs.

If you need to remember information for long periods of time, an acronym may be the answer. An **acronym** is a form of abbreviation—a word formed from the first letter of each word in a phrase, for example, NAFTA (North American Free Trade Agreement). Another method forms phrases or sentences out of the first letter of each word or item in a list, for example, Every Good Boy Does Fine to remember the lines on the G clef—E, G, B, D, F. Because the words must make sense as a sentence, this approach also has some characteristics of **chain mnemonics,** methods that connect the first item to be memorized with the second, the second item with the third, and so on. In

"HOW MANY TIMES MUST I TELL YOU—IT'S 'CAT' BEFORE 'TEMPLE' EXCEPT AFTER 'SLAVE.'"

(By permission of Bo Brown. From Phi Delta Kappan.)

one type of chain method, each item on a list is linked to the next through some visual association or story. Another chain-method approach is to incorporate all the items to be memorized into a jingle such as "*i* before *e* except after *c*," or "Thirty days hath September."

The mnemonic system that has been most extensively applied in teaching is the **keyword method**. The approach has two stages. To remember a foreign word, for example, you first choose an English word, preferably a concrete noun, that sounds like the foreign word or a part of it. Next, you associate the meaning of the foreign word with the English word through an image or sentence. For example, the French word *carte* (meaning "map") sounds like the English word "cart." Cart becomes the keyword: you make a mental picture of a shopping cart being used to move a huge collection of old maps, or you make up a sentence such as, "The cart with all the maps tipped over" (Pressley, Levin, & Delaney, 1982). Figure 7.9 offers another example of this method, as used to learn English vocabulary.

One problem, however, is that the keyword method does not work well if it is difficult to identify a keyword for a particular item. Many words and ideas that students need to remember do not lend themselves to associations with keywords (Hall, 1991; Pressley, 1991). Also, vocabulary learned with keywords may be more easily forgotten than vocabulary learned in other ways, especially if students are given keywords and images instead of being asked to supply the words and images. When the teacher provides the memory links, these associations may not fit the students' existing knowledge and may be forgotten or confused later, so remembering suffers (Wang & Thomas, 1995; Wang, Thomas, & Ouellette, 1992). Younger students have some difficulty forming their own images. For them, memory aids that rely on auditory cues—rhymes such as "*i* before *e* except after *c*" and "Thirty days hath September . . ."—seem to work better.

Many teachers use a mnemonic system to learn their students' names quickly. Until we have some knowledge to guide learning, it may help to use some rote

Peg-Type Mnemonics: Systems of associating items with cue words.

Acronym: Technique for remembering names, phrases, or steps by using the first letter of each word to form a new, memorable word.

Chain Mnemonics: Memory strategies that associate one element in a series with the next element.

Keyword Method: System of associating new words or concepts with similar-sounding cue words and images.

Connect & Extend
To your teaching
Smith, S. M. (1985). A method for teaching name mnemonics. *Teaching of Psychology, 12,* 156–158. In small groups, students create keyword mnemonics for each other's names. The name mnemonics are then presented to the whole class.

FIGURE 7.9

Using the Keyword Method to Learn English Vocabulary

Here the keyword is "purse." It is a concrete noun that sounds like "persuade" (the vocabulary word to be learned). The keyword, definition, and vocabulary word are linked in an image.

Source: From J. R. Levin, C. B. McCormick, G. E. Miller, J. K. Berry, and M. Pressley. Mnemonic versus nonmnemonic vocabulary-learning strategies for children. *American Educational Research Journal, 19,* pp. 121–136. Copyright © 1982 by the American Educational Research Association. Reprinted by permission of the publisher.

What's Wrong with Memorizing?

For years students have relied on memorization to learn vocabulary, procedures, steps, names, and facts. Is this a bad idea?

▶ **POINT** *Rote memorization creates inert knowledge.*

Years ago William James (1912) described the limitations of rote learning by telling a story about what can happen when students memorize but do not understand:

> A friend of mine, visiting a school, was asked to examine a young class in geography. Glancing at the book, she said: "Suppose you should dig a hole in the ground, hundreds of feet deep, how should you find it at the bottom—warmer or colder than on top?" None of the class replying, the teacher said: "I'm sure they know, but I think you don't ask the question quite rightly. Let me try." So, taking the book, she asked: "In what condition is the interior of the globe?" And received the immediate answer from half the class at once. "The interior of the globe is in a condition of igneous fusion." (p. 150)

The students had memorized the answer, but they had no idea what it meant. Perhaps they didn't understand the meaning of "interior," "globe," or "igneous fusion." At any rate, the knowledge was useful to them only when they were answering test questions, and only then when the questions were phrased exactly as they had been memorized.

Students often resort to memorizing the exact words of definitions when they have no hope for actually understanding the terms or when teachers take off marks for definitions that are not exact.

Most recently, Howard Gardner has been a vocal critic of rote memorization and a champion of "teaching for understanding." In an interview in *Phi Delta Kappan* (Siegel & Shaughnessy, 1994), Gardner says:

> My biggest concern about education, particularly in America, is that even our better students in our better schools are just going through the motions of education. In *The Unschooled Mind,* I review ample evidence that suggests an absence of understanding—the inability of students to take knowledge, skills, and other apparent attainments and apply them successfully in new situations. In the absence of such flexibility and adaptability, the education that the students receive is worth little. (pp. 563–564)

◀ **COUNTERPOINT** *Rote memorization can be effective.*

Memorization may not be such a bad way to learn new information that has little inherent meaning, such as foreign language vocabulary. Alvin Wang, Margaret Thomas, and Judith Ouellette (1992) compared learning Tagalog (the national language of the Philippines) using either rote memorization or the keyword approach. The keyword method is a way of creating connections and meaning for associating new words with existing words and images. In their study, even though the keyword method led to faster and better learning initially, long-term forgetting was *greater* for students who had used the keyword method than for students who had learned by rote memorization.

There are times when students must memorize and we do them a disservice if we don't teach them how. Every discipline has its own terms, names, facts, and rules. As adults, we want to work with physicians who have memorized the correct names for the bones and organs of the body or the drugs needed to combat particular infections. Of course, they can look up some information or research certain conditions, but they have to know where to start. We want to work with accountants who give us accurate information about the new tax codes, information they probably had to memorize because it changes from year to year in ways that are not necessarily rational or meaningful. We want to deal with computer sales people who have memorized their stock and know exactly which printers will work with our computer. Just because something was learned through memorization does not mean it is inert knowledge. The real question, as Gardner points out above, is whether you can *use* the information flexibly and effectively to solve new problems.

memorization and mnemonic approaches to build vocabulary and facts. Not all educators agree, as is noted in the Point/Counterpoint.

Making It Meaningful. Perhaps the best single method for helping students learn is to make each lesson as meaningful as possible. Meaningful lessons are presented in vocabulary that makes sense to the students. New terms are clarified through ties with more familiar words and ideas. Meaningful lessons are also well organized, with clear connections between the different elements of the lesson. Finally, meaningful lessons make natural use of old information to help students understand new information through examples or analogies.

The importance of meaningful lessons is emphasized in an example presented by Smith (1975). Consider the three lines below:

1. KBVODUWGPJMSQTXNOGMCTRSO
2. READ JUMP WHEAT POOR BUT SEEK
3. KNIGHTS RODE HORSES INTO WAR

Begin by covering all but the first line. Look at it for a second, close the book, and write down all the letters you remember. Then repeat this procedure with the second and third lines. Each line has the same number of letters, but the chances are great that you remembered all the letters in the third line, a good number of letters in the second line, and very few in the first line.

The first line makes no sense. There is no way to organize it in a brief glance. The second line is more meaningful. You do not have to see each letter because you bring prior knowledge of spelling rules and vocabulary to the task. The third line is the most meaningful. Just a glance and you can probably remember all of it because you bring to this task prior knowledge not only of spelling and vocabulary but also of rules about syntax and probably some historical information about knights (they didn't ride in tanks). This sentence is meaningful because you have existing schemas for assimilating it. It is relatively easy to associate the words and meaning with other information already in long-term memory (Sweller, van Merrienboer, & Paas, 1998).

The challenge for teachers is to make lessons less like learning the first line and more like learning the third line. Although this may seem obvious, think about the times when *you* have read a sentence in a text or heard an explanation from a professor that might just as well have been KBVODUWGPJMSQTXNOGMCTRSO. But remember, attempts to change the ways that students are used to learning—moving from memorizing to meaningful activities as in the opening "What Would You Do?" situation, are not always greeted with student enthusiasm. In Chapters 8, 9, and 13 we will examine a variety of ways that teachers can support meaningful learning and understanding.

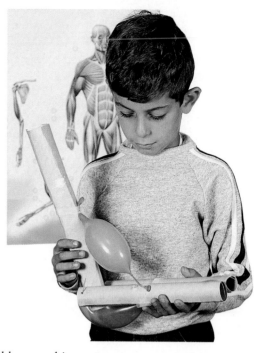

▲ *New information will be more meaningful to students, and thus will be learned more readily, if they can connect it to knowledge that they already have. This student has made a model of an elbow using materials he is familiar with such as balloons and construction paper.*

The Instructional Events Model. Robert Gagné (1977; Gagné & Driscoll, 1988) has proposed a well-developed theory of instruction based on the information processing model of learning. Table 7.3 shows Gagné's phases of learning and the "instructional events" associated with each phase.

As you can see, in the instructional events model, the first step in learning, and the first challenge for the teacher, is to gain students' attention. The next step is to set an expectancy for learning by letting the students know the goals of the lesson and perhaps arousing their curiosity or providing other motivation for learning (we will talk more about this in Chapters 10 and 11). When the students are paying attention and have appropriate expectations, they need to be reminded of what they already know that relates to the material to be learned. With this prior knowledge in their working memories, they are ready to make connections between new and old information. Now it is time to present the new material, highlighting its important aspects or key features. At this point the students should have the new material in their short-term or working memories, so they are ready to process the information and move it to long-term memory. The teacher's role now is to provide learning guidance, such as explanations and examples or a guided-discovery exercise.

But learning does not stop here. In Gagné's model, students have to demonstrate, both to the teacher and to themselves, that they really understand the material. The

Connect & Extend
To your teaching
What is the memory strategy used in each of the following examples?

a. In order to help children remember the symbol for the number eight, the teacher makes a snowman out of the figure 8 while telling a story about the snowman with eight buttons who lives for eight days.

b. To help students remember how to spell "separate," the teacher says, "There is a rat in separate."

c. Columbus sailed the ocean blue in fourteen hundred and ninety-two.

d. To remember a grocery list, Mrs. Tarent imagines cheese on her TV, limes on a soda, milk on the table, beans in the wicker basket, and tomatoes on the stove.

e. The teacher uses a timeline to show the major events before, during, and after the war of 1812.

f. Students are asked to compare their present home chores with chores they might have had if they had lived during the early 1800s.

TABLE 7.3 Gagné's Phases of Learning and the Instructional Events That Support Learning at Each Phase

Description	Learning phase	Instructional Event
Preparation for Learning	1. Attention; alertness	Gain learner's attention through unusual event, question, or change of stimulus
	2. Expectancy	Inform the learner of the objective; activate motivation
	3. Retrieval (of relevant information and/or skills) to working memory	Stimulate recall of prior knowledge
Acquisition and Performance	4. Selective perception of stimulus features	Present material; highlight distinctive features
	5. Encoding; storage in long-term memory	Provide learning guidance
	6. Retrieval and responding	Elicit performance
	7. Reinforcement	Provide informative feedback
Transfer of Learning	8. Cueing retrieval	Assess performance
	9. Generalizing	

Source: From *Learning and Instruction: Theory into Practice*, 3/e, p.125, by M. E. Gredler, 1997, Saddle River, NJ: Prentice Hall, Inc. Copyright © 1997 by Prentice-Hall, Inc. Reprinted with permission.

students must respond in some way. These responses allow the teacher and the students themselves to check understanding of the new material. Responses also provide reinforcement or corrections or both. Finally, to ensure that they can retrieve and apply their new knowledge readily, students should practise in a variety of situations. Reviews at the end of the lesson, week, and unit encourage transfer by extending practice over time.

Becoming an Expert: Development of Procedural and Conditional Knowledge

Experts in a particular field have a wealth of domain-specific knowledge, that is, knowledge that applies specifically to their area or domain. They not only have *declarative knowledge* (facts and other semantic information), but they also have at their command considerable *procedural knowledge,* an understanding of how to perform various cognitive activities. And they know when and why to apply their understandings; that is, they have *conditional knowledge,* so they can manipulate their declarative and procedural knowledge to solve problems.

Another characteristic distinguishes experts from novices in an area. Much of the expert's declarative knowledge has become "proceduralized," that is, incorporated into routines that can be applied automatically without making many demands on working memory. Skills that are applied without conscious thought are called **automated basic skills.** An example is shifting gears in a manual-transmission car. At first you had to think about every step; as you became more expert (if you did), the procedure became automatic. But not all procedures (sometimes called *cognitive skills*) can be automatic, even for experts in a particular domain. For example, no matter how expert you are in driving, you still have to consciously watch the traffic around you. This kind of conscious procedure is called a *domain-specific strategy.* Automated basic skills and domain-specific strategies are learned in different ways (Gagné, Yekovich, & Yekovich, 1993).

Automated Basic Skills. Most psychologists identify three stages in the development of an automated skill: cognitive, associative, and autonomous (Anderson, 1995; Fitts & Posner, 1967). At the **cognitive stage,** when we are first learning, we rely on declarative knowledge and general problem-solving strategies to accom-

Automated Basic Skills: Skills that are applied without conscious thought.

plish our goal. For example, to learn to assemble a bookshelf, we might try to follow steps in the instruction manual, putting a check beside each step as we complete it to keep track of progress. At this stage we have to "think about" every step and perhaps refer back to the pictures of parts to see what a "1 cm metal bolt with lock nut" looks like. The load on working memory is heavy. There can be quite a bit of trial-and-error learning at this stage, for example if the bolt we have chosen doesn't fit.

At the **associative stage**, individual steps of a procedure are combined or "chunked" into larger units. We reach for the right bolt and put it into the right hole. One step smoothly cues the next. With practice, the associative stage moves to the **autonomous stage**, where the whole procedure can be accomplished without much attention. So if you assemble enough bookshelves, you can have a lively conversation as you do, paying little attention to the assembly task. This movement from the cognitive to the associative to the autonomous stage holds for the development of basic cognitive skills in any area, but science, medicine, chess, and mathematics have been most heavily researched.

What can teachers do to help their students pass through these three stages and become more expert? In general, it appears that two factors are critical: *prerequisite knowledge* and *practice with feedback*. First, if students don't have the essential prior knowledge (schemas, skills, etc.), the load on working memory will be too great. In order to compose a poem in a foreign language, for example, you must know some of the vocabulary and grammar of that language, and you must have some understanding of poetry forms. To learn the vocabulary, grammar, *and* forms as you also try to compose the poem would be too much.

Second, practice with feedback allows you to form associations, recognize cues automatically, and combine small steps into larger condition-action rules or *productions*. Even from the earliest stage, some of this practice should include a simplified version of the whole process in a real context. Practice in real contexts helps students learn not only *how* to do a skill but also *why* and *when* (Collins, Brown, & Newman, 1989; Gagné, Yekovich, & Yekovich, 1993). Of course, as every athletic coach knows, if a particular step, component, or process is causing trouble, that element might be practised alone until it is more automatic, and then put back into the whole sequence, to lower the demands on working memory (Anderson, Reder, & Simon, 1996).

Domain-Specific Strategies.   As we saw earlier, some procedural knowledge, such as monitoring the traffic while you drive, is not automatic because conditions are constantly changing. Once you decide to change lanes, the manoeuvre may be fairly automatic, but the decision to change lanes was conscious, based on the traffic conditions around you. **Domain-specific strategies** are these consciously applied skills of organizing thoughts and actions to reach a goal. To support this kind of learning, teachers need to provide opportunities for practice in many different situations—for example, practise reading with newspapers, package labels, magazines, books, letters, operating manuals, and so on. In the next chapter's discussion of problem solving, we will examine other ways to help students develop domain-specific strategies.

CHECKPOINT

Becoming Knowledgeable: Some Basic Principles

Review

▷ Describe three ways to develop declarative knowledge.

▷ Describe some procedures for developing procedural knowledge.

Apply

▷ How would you use the keyword method to teach the exports of foreign countries?

Cognitive Stage: The initial learning of an automated skill when we rely on general problem-solving approaches to make sense of steps or procedures.

Associative Stage: Individual steps of a procedure are combined or "chunked" into larger units.

Autonomous Stage: Final stage in the learning of automated skills. The procedure is fine-tuned and becomes "automatic."

Domain-Specific Strategies: Consciously applied skills to reach goals in a particular subject or problem area.

Learning Outside School

The last several sections of this chapter have described many ideas for helping students become knowledgeable—memory strategies, mnemonics, metacognitive skills such as planning or monitoring comprehension, and cognitive skills. Some students have an advantage in school because they learn these strategies and skills at home. The Family and Community Partnerships Guidelines give ideas for working with families to give all your students more support and practice in developing these skills.

Summary

Elements of the Cognitive Perspective

Contrast cognitive and behavioural views of learning in terms of what is learned and the role of reinforcement.

Cognitive learning theorists focus on the human mind's active attempts to make sense of the world. In the cognitive view, knowledge is learned, and changes in knowledge make changes in behaviour possible. In the behavioural view, the new behaviour itself is learned. Both behavioural and cognitive theorists believe reinforcement is important in learning, but for different reasons. The strict behaviourist maintains that reinforcement strengthens responses; cognitive theorists see reinforcement as a source of feedback about what is likely to happen if behaviour is repeated—as a source of information.

How does knowledge affect learning?

The cognitive approach suggests that one of the most important elements in the learning process is what the individual brings to the learning situation. Knowledge is the outcome of learning and the power of knowledge is the driving element in learning. What we already know determines to a great extent what we will pay attention to, perceive, learn, remember, and forget.

The Information Processing Model of Memory

Compare declarative, procedural, and conditional knowledge.

Declarative knowledge is knowledge that can be declared, usually in words or other symbols. Declarative knowledge is "knowing that" something is the case. Small units of declarative knowledge can be organized into larger units. Procedural knowledge is "knowing how" to do something; procedural knowledge must be demonstrated. Conditional knowledge is "knowing when and why" to apply your declarative and procedural knowledge.

Give two explanations for perception.

The Gestalt principles are valid explanations of certain aspects of perception, but there are two other kinds of explanations in information processing theory for how we recognize patterns and give meaning to sensory events. The first is called *feature analysis*, or *bottom-up processing*, because the stimulus must be analyzed into features or components and assembled into a meaningful pattern. The second type of perception, *top-down processing*, is based on knowledge and expectation. To recognize patterns rapidly, in addition to noting features, we use what we already know about the situation.

How is information retained in working memory?

To keep information activated in working memory for longer than 20 seconds, people use maintenance rehearsal (mentally repeating the information in the articulatory loop) and elaborative rehearsal (connecting the information you are trying to remember with information from long-term memory). This kind of rehearsal not only retains information in working memory but helps move information from short-term to long-term memory. The limited capacity of working memory can also be somewhat circumvented by the control process of chunking.

How is information represented in long-term memory, and what role do schemas play?

Long-term memory seems to hold an unlimited amount of information permanently. Information may be part of our semantic, episodic, or procedural memories. In long-term memory, bits of information may be stored and interrelated in terms of propositional networks and in schemas (such as story grammars and scripts) that are data structures that allow us to represent large amounts of complex information, make inferences, and understand new information.

What learning processes improve long-term memory?

The way you learn information in the first place affects its recall later. One important requirement is to integrate new material with information already stored in long-term memory using elaboration, organization, and context. Elaboration is the addition of meaning to new information through its connection with already existing knowledge. Material that is well organized is easier to learn and to remember, especially if the information is complex or extensive. Aspects of physical and emotional context are learned along with other information. Another view of memory is the levels of processing theory, in which recall of information is determined by how completely it is processed.

Why do we forget?

Information lost from working memory truly disappears, but information stored in long-term memory may be available, given the right cues. Information appears to be lost from long-term memory through time decay (neural connections, like muscles, grow weak without use) and interference (newer memories may interfere with or obscure older memories, and older memories may interfere with memory for new material).

Metacognition, Regulation, and Individual Differences

What are the three metacognitive skills?

The three metacognitive skills used to regulate thinking and learning are planning, monitoring, and evaluation. Planning involves deciding how much time to give to a task, which strategies to use, how to start, and so on. Monitoring is the on-line awareness of "how I'm doing." Evaluation involves making judgments about the processes and outcomes of thinking and learning and acting on those judgments.

Describe some individual differences in metacognition.

As children develop cognitively, they are more able to exercise executive control and use strategies. Also, some individual differences in metacognitive abilities probably are caused by biological differences or by variations in learning experiences. Students can vary greatly in their ability to attend selectively to information in their environment, and to plan and execute strategies.

How can using better metacognitive strategies improve children's memories?

Younger children can be taught to use organization to improve memory, but they probably won't apply the strategy unless they are reminded. Children also become more able to use elaboration as they mature, but this strategy is developed late in childhood. Creating images or stories to remember ideas is more likely for older elementary school students and adolescents.

Becoming Knowledgeable: Some Basic Principles

Describe three ways to develop declarative knowledge.

Declarative knowledge develops as we integrate new information with our existing understanding. The least effective way to accomplish this is rote memorization, which can best be improved by part learning and distributed practice. Mnemonics as memorization aids include peg-type approaches such as the loci method, acronyms, chain mnemonics, and the keyword method. The best way to learn and remember is to understand and use information. Making the information to be remembered meaningful is important and often is the greatest challenge for teachers.

Describe some procedures for developing procedural knowledge.

Automated basic skills and domain-specific strategies—two types of procedural knowledge—are learned in different ways. There are three stages in the development of an automated skill: cognitive (following steps or directions guided by declarative knowledge), associative (combining individual steps into larger units), and autonomous (where the whole procedure can be accomplished without much attention). Prerequisite knowledge and practice with feedback help students move through these stages. Domain-specific strategies are consciously applied skills of organizing thoughts and actions to reach a goal. To support this kind of learning, teachers need to provide opportunities for application in many different situations.

Key Terms

Becoming a Professional

Reflecting on the Chapter

Can you apply the ideas from this chapter on cognitive views of learning to solve the following problems of practice?

Preschool and Kindergarten

▶ The Grade 1 teachers believe that the kindergarten teachers could do a better job of preparing their students to "pay attention" in class. As a kindergarten teacher, what would you do? How would you justify your plans to the Grade 1 teachers?

Elementary and Middle School

▶ Several students in your class are recent immigrants and have limited knowledge of the kinds of experiences described in your basal reader series (county fairs, zoos, trips to the beach, shopping malls, etc.). The students speak and read English, but still have difficulty understanding and remembering what they read. What would you do?

Junior High and High School

▶ You have reached a complicated chapter in your text—one that is difficult for students every year. How would you make the highly abstract concepts (such as sovereignty and jurisprudence) understandable for your students?

Check Your Understanding

▶ Understand the role of prior knowledge in learning.

▶ Know what a schema is and how schemas affect attention, learning, and remembering.

▶ Know how metacognitive skills affect learning and remembering.

- Be familiar with some common mnemonic strategies.

Your Teaching Portfolio

Use the section on the differences between behavioural and cognitive approaches to learning to refine your teaching philosophy. How will you answer the job-interview question "What is your theory of learning and why?"

Teaching Resources

Use the section on mnemonics to generate ideas for helping your students learn key vocabulary in science or social studies subjects and include these ideas in your teaching resources file.

Are there maps such as the one in Figure 7.4 that would help your students learn important relationships?

 # Weblinks

www.frii.com/~geomanda/mnemonics.html

Do you like to make up mnemonics to help you remember? Here's a site that provides hundreds of mnemonics for subjects ranging from auto mechanics to spelling. The site includes links to other mnemonics sites.

http://tip.psychology.org/theories.html

This is a database of learning concepts that are hyperlinked to one another and to theories of learning. It provides brief descriptions and several references. Use your browser's back button or history tool to return to the top-level list.

What Would They Do?

Here is how two practising teachers responded to the teaching situation presented at the beginning of this chapter about history students intent on memorizing.

JUDITH RUTLEDGE

Eastern High School of Commerce
Toronto, Ontario

I'd recognize the importance of marks, first of all. Frequently, students have to produce a piece of writing that asks them for much more than memorized facts. While memorizing has many advantages, I'd also explore the limitations of using that as a primary learning strategy. In fact, for an interim period, I'd guarantee students their old marks and hold out the possibility of higher ones if they were willing to expand their ways of thinking.

People who are very concerned with marks often have high aspirations. They are also interested in other people who have achieved remarkable goals, and in how they did it; it's not hard to demonstrate the advantages of creative and critical thinking, and to set up some exercises that let the students experiment deliberately with a variety of thinking techniques. I'd explore the kind of thinking that goes on at the highest levels of human endeavour. We'd look at the factors that go into decision making, intellectual breakthroughs and discoveries, wise government, and good citizenship. Contemporary events invariably offer excellent case studies.

It's also interesting to examine the idea of what constitutes a "fact," that is, what can be memorized with perfect assurance that it won't subsequently be challenged. Dividing the class into different groups and getting them to present the views of various people involved in a historical moment can be pretty illuminating. It provides an opportunity to think about who writes history; which views and values prevail; and whose voices are not heard at all. This kind of reflection can be very meaningful for students as they wonder about their own position and purpose in the world. They can see that it's fun and ultimately more useful and rewarding than attempting to simply memorize what one textbook has presented. They are in control of their learning, not just blind consumers.

CLAIRE FRANKEL-SALAMA

Bishops College
St. John's, Newfoundland

Most students are motivated to obtain good marks and, for many, these have been achieved through rote learning. True learning through the association of ideas has not been part of their school experience. Why is this the case? Why is the rote memory approach still the favoured method of "learning"?

In many schools, teachers have to deal with the unpleasant logistical realities of extremely large classes, multiple preparations, heavy course loads, and extracurricular activities. In the interest of expedience, there is a strong emphasis on multiple-choice and factually strict questioning techniques that afford little room for independent thinking and development of good writing skills. In fact, the increased use of standardized testing has only served to exacerbate this problem by precluding more pedagogically sound qualitative forms of evaluation and feedback. Teachers feel increasingly pressured to prepare students for the exam rather than to develop keen, critical minds.

How can we, as educators, deal with these realities and still work toward a more synthetic approach to learning?

Certainly it is valuable to consider an interdisciplinary approach to teaching, especially at the high school level, where courses tend to be taught as separate units. Meetings between departments should take place, and multidisciplinary projects should be encouraged. For example, it may be possible to accommodate a history presentation or essay in a literature or even a science assignment. This should not be considered cheating; indeed, such an effort should have the cooperation of all departments involved. In this way, the student begins to realize the impact of science on literature, of music on history, of mathematics on art, etc. A co-directed paper on socialism in literature will surely have more intellectual impact than a simple research paper in one restricted area.

Another effective way to encourage analysis and synthesis involves the use of authentic documents and oral histories. A reading of Rabelais's recommendation of a good Renaissance education helps us to question our own. The study of caricatures from different sources regarding the same historical event deepens understanding of different political viewpoints. A survivor's account of the Triangle Shirtwaist Factory fire helps us "feel" the need for labour reform. A study of socialist art and its relationship to an economic system will explain what the ideology is really about. The comprehension of contextualities will certainly deepen understanding.

Teachers should not despair nor think that these efforts will bear no fruit. After all, wisdom comes with age and experience. It is not unusual to receive visits or letters from former students thanking a teacher for introducing a particular author, some interesting paintings, a meaningful destination, or previously unheard music. Germination requires a confluence of several seemingly unrelated conditions. Eventually, some seeds will bloom, perhaps even beyond expectations.

Complex Cognitive Processes

hink of a concept you learned lately in a class. How did you learn it? If you learned from a text or a teacher, were examples provided? What kinds? Do you understand the concept well enough to define it in your own words? Can you apply it to solve a problem?

In the previous chapter we focused on the development of knowledge—how people make sense of and remember information and ideas. In this chapter we will focus on understanding, problem solving, and thinking. We will be concerned with the implications of cognitive theories for the day-to-day practice of teaching, particularly for the development of students' thinking and understanding.

Because the cognitive perspective is a philosophical orientation and not a unified theoretical model, teaching methods derived from it are varied. In this chapter, we will first examine four important areas in which cognitive theorists have made suggestions for learning and teaching: concept learning, problem solving, learning strategies and tactics, and thinking. Finally, we will explore the question of how to encourage the transfer of learning from one situation to another to make learning more useful.

By the time you have completed this chapter, you should be able to:

▶ Design a lesson for teaching a key concept in your subject area.

▶ Describe the steps for solving complex problems, and explain the role of problem representation.

▶ Give examples of algorithms and heuristics for problem solving.

▶ Apply new learning strategies and tactics to prepare for tests and assignments in your current courses.

▶ Discuss the implications of cognitive theories for teaching critical thinking.

▶ List three ways a teacher might encourage positive transfer of learning.

What Would You Do?

The directions seem perfectly clear to you: Read two poems about nature (selected from eight poems you read together last week), then write a one-page compare-and-contrast analysis of the two poems. The students enjoyed reading the poetry last week. But their first attempt to write about the poems is a disaster. They jot down a few lines, giving superficial descriptions of each poem and then tell which one they liked best. Most don't even give reasons why they chose one over the other. There is not comparison, no contrast, no critical thinking or analysis. The students must have spent all their time worrying about spelling and grammar. The form is fine, but the students don't really have anything to say. As you hand back the papers, you can see the disappointment in their faces. The grades are clearly lower than they expected.

▶ How would you explain what is missing in their papers?

▶ Where would you go from here?

▶ How would you encourage the students to think critically in analyzing the two poems? How will these issues affect the grades you will teach?

TEACHERS' CASEBOOK

Connect & Extend
To the field
"The greatest enemy of understanding is coverage. As long as you are determined to cover everything, you actually ensure that most kids are not going to understand." Howard Gardner in Brandt, R. (1993). On teaching for understanding: A Conversation with Howard Gardner. *Educational Leadership, 50*(7), 7.

The Importance of Understanding

The previous chapter examined basic learning and memory processes such as attention, knowledge representation, memory, and forgetting. In this chapter we consider complex cognitive processes that lead to understanding. Understanding is more than memorizing. It is more than retelling in your own words. Howard Gardner (1993b) defines understanding as:

> the capacity to take knowledge, skills, and concepts and apply them appropriately in new situations. If someone only parrots back what he or she has been taught, we do not know whether the individual understands. If that person applies the knowledge promiscuously, regardless of whether it is appropriate, then I would not say he or she understands either. . . . But if that person knows where to apply and where not to apply, and can do it to new situations, he or she understands. (p. 2)

David Perkins and Tina Blythe (1994) have a similar view of understanding. They believe that understanding means "being able to do a variety of thought-demanding things with a topic—like explaining, finding evidence and examples, generalizing, applying, analogizing, and representing the topic in new ways" (p. 6). So understanding involves appropriately *transforming* and *using* knowledge, skills, and ideas. You will see in the next chapter that these understandings are considered "higher-level cognitive objectives" in a commonly used taxonomy of educational objectives (Bloom, Engelhart, Frost, Hill, & Krathwohl, 1956).

In the following sections we will explore what is known about different aspects of thinking: learning concepts, problem solving, critical thinking, using learning strategies, and how teachers can support these paths to understanding. We begin with a discussion of the building blocks of thinking—concepts.

Learning and Teaching about Concepts

Concept: A general category of ideas, objects, people, or experiences whose members share certain properties.

Most of what we know about the world involves concepts and relations among concepts (Schwartz & Reisberg, 1991). But what exactly is a concept? A **concept** is a category used to group similar events, ideas, objects, or people. When we talk about the concept *student,* for example, we refer to a category of people who are similar to one another—they all study a subject. The people may be old or young, in school or not; they may be studying hockey or Bach, but they can all be categorized as students. Concepts are abstractions; they do not exist in the real world. Only individual examples of concepts exist. Concepts help us organize vast amounts of information into manageable units. For instance, there are about 7.5 million distinguishable differences in colours. By categorizing these colours into some dozen or so groups, we manage to deal with this diversity quite well (Bruner, 1973).

Connect & Extend
To your teaching
According to Piaget, a person cannot think in abstract terms until the stage of formal operations is reached. How then can a child learn abstract concepts such as "yesterday" and "happy"?

Views of Concept Learning

Traditionally, psychologists have assumed that members of a category share a set of **defining attributes**, or distinctive features: students all study; textbooks all contain pages that are bound together in some way. The defining attributes theory of concepts suggests that we recognize specific examples by noting key required features.

Since about 1970, however, these long-popular views about the nature of concepts have been challenged (Benjafield, 1992). While some concepts, such as equilateral triangle, have clear-cut defining attributes, most concepts do not. Take the concept of *party.* What are the defining attributes? You might have difficulty listing these attributes, but you probably recognize a party when you see or hear one (unless, of course, we are talking about political parties, or the other party in a lawsuit, where the sound might not help you recognize the "party"). What about the concept of *bird?* Your first thought might be that birds are animals that fly. But is an ostrich a bird? What about a penguin?

Prototypes and Exemplars

According to critics of the traditional view of concept learning, we have in our minds a prototype of a party and a bird—an image that captures the essence of each concept. A **prototype** is the best representative of its category. For instance, the best representative of the "birds" category for many Canadians might be a robin (Rosch, 1973). Other members of the category may be very similar to the prototype (sparrow) or similar in some ways but different in others (chicken, ostrich). At the boundaries of a category, it may be difficult to determine if a particular instance really belongs. For example, is a telephone a piece of "furniture"? Is an elevator a "vehicle"? Is an olive a "fruit"? Whether something fits into a category is a matter of degree. Thus, categories have fuzzy boundaries and **graded membership** (Schwartz & Reisberg, 1991). Some events, objects, or ideas are simply better examples of a concept than others.

Another explanation of concept learning suggests that we identify members of a category by referring to exemplars. **Exemplars** are our actual memories of specific birds, parties, furniture, and so on that we use to compare with an item in question to see if that item belongs in the same category as our exemplar. For example, if you see a strange steel-and-stone bench in a public park, you may compare it to the sofa in your living room to decide if the uncomfortable-looking creation is still for sitting or if it has crossed a fuzzy boundary into "sculpture."

Prototypes probably are built from experiences with many exemplars. This happens naturally because episodic memories of particular events tend to blur together over time, creating an average or typical sofa prototype from all the sofa exemplars you have experienced (Schwartz & Reisberg, 1991).

"CITY CHILDREN HAVE TROUBLE WITH THE CONCEPT OF HARVEST."

(© Martha Campbell. From Phi Delta Kappan.*)*

Defining Attributes: Distinctive features shared by members of a category.

Prototype: Best representative of a category.

Graded Membership: The extent to which something belongs to a category.

Exemplar: A specific example of a given category that is used to classify an item.

Connect and Extend
To the research
Tennyson, R. D., & Cocchiarella, M. M. (1986). An empirically based instructional design theory for teaching concepts. *Review of Educational Research, 56,* 40–71. Abstract: An instructional design theory views concept learning as a two-phase process: (a) formation of conceptual knowledge, and (b) development of procedural knowledge. Two fundamental components of the proposed theoretical model are content structure variables and instructional design variables. A rational combination of these components provides the means for the selection of one of four basic instructional design strategies. The theoretical model is described with reference to instructional methods and cognitive processes.

Concepts and Schemas

In addition to prototypes and exemplars, a third element is involved when we recognize a concept—our schematic knowledge related to the concept. How do we know that counterfeit money is not "real" money, even though it perfectly fits our "money" prototype and exemplars? We know because of its history. It was printed by the "wrong" people. So our understanding of the concept of money is connected with such concepts as crime, forgery, and the Bank of Canada.

Strategies for Teaching Concepts

Most of the current approaches to teaching concepts still rely heavily on the traditional analysis of defining attributes. Interest is growing, however, in the prototypes view of concept learning, partly because children first learn many concepts in the real world from best examples or prototypes, pointed out by adults (Tennyson, 1981). The teaching of concepts can combine both distinctive features and prototypes.

One approach to teaching about concepts is called *concept attainment*—a way of helping students construct an understanding of specific concepts and practise thinking skills such as hypothesis testing (Joyce & Weil, 1998; Klausmeier, 1992).

An Example Concept-Attainment Lesson. Here is how a Grade 5 teacher helped his students learn about a familiar concept and practise thinking skills at the same time (Eggen & Kauchak, 1996, pp. 105–107). The teacher began a lesson by saying that he had an idea in mind and wanted students to "figure out what it is." He placed two signs on a table—one said "Examples" and the other said "Non-examples." Then from a bag he removed an apple and placed it in front of the "Examples" sign. Next he put a rock in front of the "Non-examples" sign. He asked his students, "What do you think the idea might be?" "Things we eat" was the first suggestion. The teacher wrote "HYPOTHESES" on the board and, after a brief discussion of the meaning of "hypotheses," listed "things we eat" under this heading. Next he asked for other hypotheses—"living things" and "things that grow on plants" came next. After some discussion of the differences between living things and things that grow on plants, the teacher brought out two more objects, a tomato for the "Examples" side and a carrot for the "Non-examples." Animated reconsideration of all the hypotheses followed these additions and a new hypothesis—"red things"—was suggested. Throughout the discussion, the teacher asked students to explain their conclusions—"We eat carrots, but a carrot is not an example, so the idea can't be things we eat." The teacher added an avocado as an example and celery as a non-example (thus ruling out the "red" hypothesis). Through discussion of more examples (peach, squash, orange) and non-examples (lettuce, artichoke, potato), the students narrowed their hypothesis to "things with seeds in the parts you eat." The students had "constructed" the concept of "fruit"—foods we eat with seeds in the edible parts (or, a more advanced definition, any engorged ovary, such as a pea pod, nut, tomato, pineapple, or the edible part of the plant developed from a flower).

Connect & Extend
To your teaching
Can abstract concepts be taught through the use of prototypes?

Lesson Components. Whatever strategy you use for teaching concepts, you will need four components in any lesson: examples and non-examples, relevant and irrelevant attributes, the name of the concept, and a definition (Joyce & Weil, 1998). In addition, visual aids such as pictures, diagrams, or maps can improve learning of many concepts (Anderson & Smith, 1987).

Examples are essential in teaching concepts. More examples are needed in teaching complicated concepts and in working with younger or less-able students. Both examples and non-examples (sometimes called *positive* and *negative instances*) are necessary to make the boundaries of the category clear. So a discussion of why a bat (non-example) is not a bird will help students define the boundaries of the bird concept.

The identification of relevant and irrelevant attributes is another aspect of teaching concepts. The ability to fly, as we've seen, is not a relevant attribute for classifying animals as birds. Even though many birds fly, some birds do not (ostrich, penguin), and some non-birds do (bats, flying squirrels). The ability to fly would have to be included in a discussion of the bird concept, but students should understand that flying does not define an animal as a bird.

The name of the concept is important for communicating, but it is somewhat arbitrary. Simply learning a label does not mean the person understands the concept, although the label is necessary for the understanding. In the example above, students probably already used the "fruit" name but may not have understood that squash and avocados are fruits.

A definition helps make the nature of the concept clear. A good definition has two elements: a reference to any more *general category* that the new concept falls into, and a statement of the new concept's *defining attributes* (Klausmeier, 1976). For example, a fruit is food we eat (general category) with seeds in the edible parts (defining attributes). An equilateral triangle is a plane, simple, closed figure (general category), with three equal sides and three equal angles (defining attributes). This kind of definition helps place the concept in a schema of related knowledge.

In teaching some concepts, "a picture is worth a thousand words"—or at least a few hundred. Seeing and handling specific examples, or pictures of examples, helps young children learn concepts. For students of all ages, the complex concepts in history, science, and mathematics can often be illustrated in diagrams or graphs. For example, Anderson and Smith (1983) found that when the students they taught only read about the concept, just 20 percent could understand the role of reflected light in our ability to see objects. But when the students worked with diagrams such as the one in Figure 8.1 on page 274, almost 80 percent understood the concept.

Lesson Structure. The fruit lesson described earlier is an example of good concept teaching for several reasons. First, examining examples and non-examples before discussing attributes or definitions appears to be the more effective method of teaching (Joyce & Weil, 1998). Start your concept lesson with prototypes, or best examples, to help the students establish the category. The teacher began with the classic fruit example, an apple, then moved to less typical examples, such as tomatoes and squash. These examples show the wide range of possibilities the category includes and the variety of irrelevant attributes within a category. This information helps students avoid focusing on an irrelevant attribute as a defining feature. The peach example tells students that fruit can have one seed as well as many. The squash and avocado examples indicate that fruits do not have to be sweet. Including fruits of different colours that have one seed or many, a sweet taste or not, and thick or thin skin will prevent **undergeneralization**, or the exclusion of some foods from their rightful place in the category fruit.

Non-examples should be very close to the concept, but miss by one or just a few critical attributes. For instance, sweet potatoes and rhubarb are not fruits, even though sweet potatoes are sweet and rhubarb is used to make pies. Including non-examples will prevent **overgeneralization**, or the inclusion of substances that are not fruits.

After the students seem to have grasped the concept under consideration, it is useful to ask them to think about the ways that they formed and tested their hypotheses. Some students may consider one example at a time while other students may work with several simultaneously. Some older students may make systematic tests and eliminate one hypothesis at a time, keeping written records, while others are more global and scattered. Thinking back helps students develop their metacognitive skills and shows them that different people approach problems in different ways (Joyce & Weil, 1998). Table 8.1 summarizes the stages of concept teaching.

Undergeneralization: Exclusion of some true members from a category; limiting a concept.

Overgeneralization: Inclusion of nonmembers in a category; overextending a concept.

Connect & Extend
To your teaching
How can a teacher determine if a student has learned a concept?

FIGURE 8.1

Understanding Complex Concepts

Illustrations can help students grasp a difficult concept.

Q. When sunlight strikes the tree it helps the boy to see the tree. How does it do this?

Q. When sunlight strikes the tree it helps the boy to see the tree. How does it do this?

A. Some of the light bounces (is reflected) off the tree and goes to the boy's eyes.

Source: From *The Educator's Handbook: A Research Perspective*, edited by Virginia Richardson-Koehler. Copyright © 1987. Reprinted by permission of Addison-Wesley Educational Publishers, Inc.

Extending and Connecting Concepts. Once students have a good sense of a concept, they should use it. This might mean writing, reading, explaining, doing exercises, solving problems, or engaging in any other activity that requires them to

---

TABLE 8.1   Phases of the Concept Attainment Model

There are three main phases in concept attainment teaching. First the teacher presents examples/non-examples and students identify the concept, then the teacher checks for understanding, and finally students analyze their thinking strategies.

Phase One: Presentation of Data and Identification of Concept	Phase Two: Testing Attainment of the Concept	Phase Three: Analysis of Thinking Strategies
Teacher presents labelled examples.	Students identify additional unlabelled examples as yes or no.	Students describe thoughts.
Students compare attributes in positive and negative examples.	Teacher confirms hypotheses, names concept, and restates definitions according to essential attributes.	Students discuss role of hypotheses and attributes.
Students generate and test hypotheses.	Students generate examples.	Students discuss type and number of hypotheses.
Students state a definition according to the essential attributes.		

Source: From Bruce R. Joyce and Marsha Weil, *Models of Teaching*, 5/e, p. 173. Copyright © 1996 by Allyn & Bacon. Reprinted by permission.

apply their new understanding. This will connect the concept into the students' web of related schematic knowledge. One approach that you may see in texts and workbooks for students above the primary grades is **concept mapping** (Novak & Musonda, 1991). Students "diagram" their understanding of the concept, as Amy has in Figure 8.2 below. Amy's map shows a reasonable understanding of the concept of molecule, but also indicates that Amy holds one misconception. She thinks that there is no space between the molecules in solids.

Teaching Concepts through Discovery

Jerome Bruner's early research on thinking (Bruner, Goodnow, & Austin, 1956) stirred his interest in educational approaches that encourage concept learning and the development of thinking. Bruner's work emphasized the importance of understanding the structure of a subject being studied, the need for active learning as the basis for true understanding, and the value of **inductive reasoning** in learning.

Structure and Discovery. Subject structure refers to the fundamental ideas, relationships, or patterns of the field—the essential information. Because structure

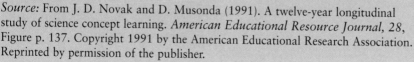

▲ *Concept mapping has students "diagram" their understanding of a concept. What are examples of the concept of music for this student?*

Connect & Extend
To your teaching
See the **Teachers' Casebook** for ideas about how to conduct discovery lessons so that everyone, not just the brightest or quickest, makes discoveries.

FIGURE 8.2

Amy's Molecule

Amy, in Grade 8, has drawn a map to represent her understanding of the concept of "molecule." Her concept includes one misconception—that there is no space between molecules in solids.

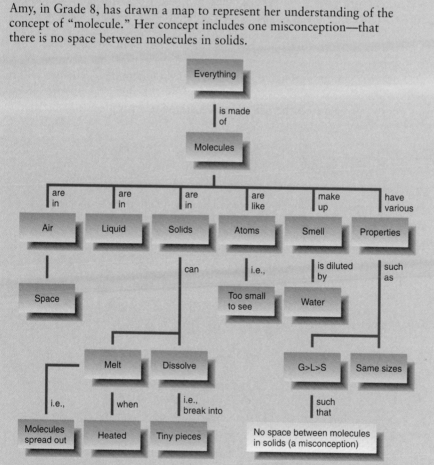

Source: From J. D. Novak and D. Musonda (1991). A twelve-year longitudinal study of science concept learning. *American Educational Resource Journal, 28,* Figure p. 137. Copyright 1991 by the American Educational Research Association. Reprinted by permission of the publisher.

Concept Mapping: Student's diagram of his or her understanding of a concept.

Inductive Reasoning: Formulating general principles based on knowledge of examples and details.

Coding System: A hierarchy of ideas or concepts.

Discovery Learning: Bruner's approach, in which students work on their own to discover basic principles.

Eg-Rule Method: Teaching or learning by moving from specific examples to general rules.

Intuitive Thinking: Making imaginative leaps to correct perceptions or workable solutions.

does not include specific facts or details about the subject, the essential structure of an idea can be represented simply as a diagram, set of principles, or formula. According to Bruner, learning will be more meaningful, useful, and memorable for students if they focus on understanding the structure of the subject being studied. For example, if you learned the concepts figure, plane, simple, closed, quadrilateral, isosceles, scalene, equilateral, and right, you would be on your way to understanding one aspect of geometry. But how do these terms relate to one another? If you can place the terms into a **coding system** such as the one in Figure 8.3, you will have a better understanding of the basic structure of this part of geometry.

A coding system is a hierarchy of related concepts. At the top of the coding system is the most general concept, in this case *plane, simple, closed figure*. More specific concepts are arranged under the general concept.

In order to grasp the structure of information, Bruner believes, students must be active—they must identify key principles for themselves rather than simply accepting teachers' explanations. He believes that teachers should provide problem situations stimulating students to question, explore, and experiment. This process has been called **discovery learning**. In discovery learning, the teacher presents examples and the students work with the examples until they discover the interrelationships—the subject's structure. Thus, Bruner believes that classroom learning should take place through inductive reasoning, that is, by using specific examples to formulate a general principle. For instance, if students are presented with enough examples of triangles and non-triangles, they will eventually discover what the basic properties of any triangle must be. Encouraging inductive thinking in this way is sometimes called the **eg-rule method**, from the Latin e.g., meaning "for example." The concept attainment lesson on fruit above used this approach.

Discovery in Action. An inductive approach requires **intuitive thinking** on the part of students. Bruner suggests that teachers can nurture this intuitive thinking by encouraging students to make guesses based on incomplete evidence and then to confirm or disprove the guesses systematically (Bruner, 1960). After learning about ocean currents and the shipping industry, for example, students might be

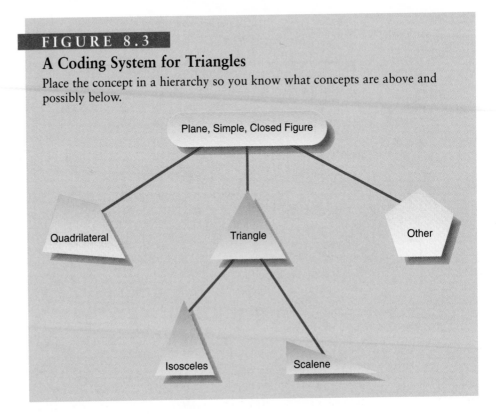

FIGURE 8.3

A Coding System for Triangles

Place the concept in a hierarchy so you know what concepts are above and possibly below.

Bruner's ideas about discovery learning emphasize the importance of active learning as a basis for true understanding.

shown old maps of three harbours and asked to guess which one became a major port. Then students could check their guesses through systematic research. Unfortunately, educational practices often discourage intuitive thinking by punishing wrong guesses and rewarding safe but uncreative answers.

Notice that in Bruner's discovery learning, a teacher organizes the class so that the students learn through their own active involvement. A distinction is usually made between discovery learning, in which the students work on their own to a great extent, and **guided discovery**, in which the teacher provides some direction. Unguided discovery is appropriate for preschool children, but in a typical elementary or secondary classroom, unguided activities usually prove unmanageable and unproductive. For these situations, guided discovery is preferable. Students are presented with intriguing questions, baffling situations, or interesting problems: Why does the flame go out when we cover it with a jar? Why does this pencil seem to bend when you put it in water? What is the rule for grouping these words together? Instead of explaining how to solve the problem, the teacher provides the appropriate materials and encourages students to make observations, form hypotheses, and test solutions. Feedback must be given at the optimal moment, when students can either use it to revise their approach or take it as encouragement to continue in the direction they've chosen. The Guidelines on page 278, ashould help you apply Bruner's suggestions.

Discovery learning appears to have many advantages, but even Bruner believes that it is not appropriate in every situation. The Point/Counterpoint section on page 279 examines the pros and cons of this approach.

Teaching Concepts through Exposition

David Ausubel's (1963, 1977) view of learning offers an interesting contrast to that of Bruner. According to Ausubel, people acquire knowledge primarily through reception rather than through discovery. Concepts, principles, and ideas are presented and understood, not discovered. As you saw in Chapter 7, the more organized and focused the presentation, the more thoroughly the person will learn.

Ausubel stresses what is known as **meaningful verbal learning**—verbal information, ideas, and relationships among ideas, taken together. Rote memorization is not considered meaningful learning, because material learned by rote is not connected with existing knowledge. Ausubel has proposed his **expository teaching** model to encourage meaningful rather than rote reception learning. (Here, exposition

Guided Discovery: An adaptation of discovery learning, in which the teacher provides some direction.

Meaningful Verbal Learning: Focused and organized relationships among ideas and verbal information.

Expository Teaching: Ausubel's method—teachers present material in complete, organized form, moving from broadest to more specific concepts.

GUIDELINES

Applying Bruner's Ideas

Present both examples and non-examples of the concepts you are teaching.

Examples

1. In teaching about mammals, include people, kangaroos, whales, cats, dolphins, and camels as examples, and chickens, fish, alligators, frogs, and penguins as non-examples.
2. Ask students for additional examples and non-examples.

Help students see connections among concepts.

Examples

1. Ask questions such as these: What else could you call this apple? (Fruit.) What do we do with fruit? (Eat.) What do we call things we eat? (Food.)
2. Use diagrams, outlines, and summaries to point out connections.

Pose a question and let students try to find the answer.

Examples

1. How could the human hand be improved?
2. What is the relation between the area of one tile and the area of the whole floor?

Encourage students to make intuitive guesses.

Examples

1. Instead of giving a word's definition, say, "Let's guess what it might mean by looking at the words around it."
2. Give students a map of Ancient Greece and ask where they think the major cities were.
3. Don't comment after the first few guesses. Wait for several ideas before giving the answer.
4. Use guiding questions to focus students when their discovery has led them too far astray.

Connect & Extend
To other chapters
What characteristics of cognitive development would support the statement that expository teaching is more appropriate for the secondary than the elementary level?

Ausubel's principles of expository teaching and reception learning emphasizes the concepts, principles, and ideas as presented by the teacher and then understood by students. ▼

means *explanation*, or the setting forth of facts and ideas.) In this approach, teachers present materials in a carefully organized, sequenced, and somewhat finished form, and students thus receive the most usable material in the most efficient way. Ausubel does agree with Bruner that people learn by organizing new information into hierarchies or coding systems. Ausubel calls the general concept at the top of the system the *subsumer,* because all other concepts are subsumed under it, as in Figure 8.3. However, Ausubel believes that learning should progress, not inductively as Bruner recommends, but deductively: from the general to the specific, or from the rule or principle to examples. The **deductive reasoning** approach is sometimes called the **rule-eg method.**

Advance Organizers. Optimal learning generally occurs when there is a potential fit between the student's schemas and the material to be learned. To make this fit more likely, a lesson following Ausubel's strategy always begins with an advance organizer. This is an introductory statement of a relationship or a high-level concept broad enough to encompass all the information that will follow. The function of advance organizers is to provide scaffolding or support for the new information. You can also see the advance organizer as a kind of conceptual bridge between new material and students' current knowledge (Faw & Waller, 1976). Textbooks often contain advance organizers—the chapter overviews in this book are examples. The organizers can serve three purposes: they direct your attention to what is important in the coming material; they highlight relationships among ideas that will be presented; and they remind you of relevant information you already have.

In general, advance organizers fall into one of two categories, *comparative* and *expository* (Joyce & Weil, 1998; Mayer, 1979, 1984). Each fulfills an important function. Comparative organizers *activate* (bring into working memory) already existing schemas. They remind you of what you already know but may not realize is relevant. A comparative advance organizer for a history lesson on revolutions might be a statement that contrasts military uprisings with the physical and social

Is Discovery Learning Effective?

Most psychologists and educators agree that students must make sense of information to learn and remember it. Simply memorizing lists and facts leads to superficial understanding and rapid forgetting. When students struggle with perplexing problems, test possible solutions, and finally discover for themselves the fundamental structure of a key concept, they are more likely to understand and remember the information. But critics of discovery learning raise important questions. Is discovery learning an effective method?

▶ POINT *Discovery learning matches cognitive development.*
Educators favouring discovery learning note that this approach is consistent with the ways that people learn and develop. For example, Jerome Bruner (1966, 1971) identified three stages of cognitive growth, similar to the stages identified by Piaget. Bruner believes that children move from an *enactive* stage to an *iconic* stage and finally to a *symbolic* stage. In the enactive stage (similar to Piaget's sensorimotor stage), the child represents and understands the world through actions—to understand something is to manipulate it, taste it, throw it, break it, and so on. At the iconic stage, the child represents the world in images—appearances dominate. This stage corresponds to Piaget's preoperational thinking, in which the higher the water level, the more

water there must be in the glass, because that's what appears to be true. At the final level, the child is able to use abstract ideas, symbols, language, and logic to understand and represent the world. Actions and images can still be used in thinking, but they do not dominate.

Discovery learning allows students to move through these three stages as they encounter new information. First the students manipulate and act on materials; then they form images as they note specific features and make observations; and finally they abstract general ideas and principles from these experiences and observations. Because they have experienced each stage of representation, Bruner believes, the students will have a better understanding of the topic. When students are motivated and really participate in the discovery project, discovery learning leads to superior learning (Strike, 1975).

◀ COUNTERPOINT *Discovery learning is impractical.*
In theory, discovery learning seems ideal, but in practice there are problems. To be successful, discovery projects often require special materials and extensive preparations. And these preparations can't guarantee success. For example, a discovery lesson on the effects of light on plants takes many hours and often falls flat because the plants grown in darkness and those grown in light don't always

behave as they should—many factors other than light affect growth (Anderson & Smith, 1987).

To benefit from a discovery situation, students must have basic knowledge about the problem and must know how to apply problem-solving strategies. Without this knowledge and skill, they will flounder and grow frustrated. Instead of learning from the materials, they may simply play with them. The brightest students may make discoveries, while the others lose interest or just wait passively for someone else to complete the project. Instead of benefiting from a teacher's organized explanation, these "non-discovering" students may get an inadequate explanation from a fellow student who can't quite communicate his or her discoveries. Everyone may grow frustrated as the teacher seems to withhold the solutions and explanations needed.

Critics believe that discovery learning is so inefficient and so difficult to organize successfully that other methods are preferable. This seems especially true for lower-ability students. Discovery methods may make too many demands on these students, because they lack the background knowledge and problem-solving skills needed to benefit. Some research has shown that discovery methods are ineffective and even detrimental for lower-ability students (Corno & Snow, 1986; Slavin, Karweit, & Madden, 1989).

changes involved in the Industrial Revolution; you could also compare the common aspects of the French, English, Mexican, Russian, Iranian, and American revolutions (Salomon & Perkins, 1989).

In contrast, *expository organizers* provide *new* knowledge that students will need to understand the upcoming information. An expository organizer is thus a statement of a subsumer, a definition of a general concept. In an English class, you might begin a large thematic unit on rites of passage in literature with a broad statement of the theme and why it has been so central in literature—something like, "A central character coming of age must learn to know himself or herself, often makes some kind of journey of self-discovery, and must decide what in the society is to be accepted and what rejected."

Deductive Reasoning: Drawing conclusions by applying rules or principles; logically moving from a general rule or principle to a specific solution.

Rule-Eg Method: Teaching or learning by moving from general principles to specific examples.

The following advance organizer is taken from Joyce, B., & Weil, M. (1988). *Models of teaching* (3/e). Englewood Cliffs, NJ: Prentice-Hall, pp. 70–71.

Connect & Extend
To life

A guide, beginning a tour of an art museum with a group of high school students, says, "I want to give you an idea that will help you understand the paintings and sculpture we are about to see. The idea is simply that art, although it is a personal expression, reflects in many ways the culture and times in which it was produced. This may seem obvious to you at first when you look at the difference between Oriental and Western art. However, it is also true that, within each culture, as the culture changes, so the art will change—and that is why we can speak of periods of art. The changes are often reflected in the artists' techniques, subject matter, colours, and style. Major changes are often reflected in the forms of art that are produced." In the tour that follows, as the students look at paintings and sculpture, the guide points out to them the differences.

The general conclusion of research on advance organizers is that they do help students learn, especially when the material to be learned is quite unfamiliar, complex, or difficult (Corkill, 1992; Mayer, 1984; Shuell, 1981). Of course, the effects of advance organizers depend on how good they are and how students actually use them. First, to be effective, the organizer must be processed and understood by the students. This was demonstrated dramatically in a study by Dinnel and Glover (1985). They found that instructing students to paraphrase an advance organizer—which, of course, requires them to understand its meaning—increased the effectiveness of the organizer. Second, the organizer must really be an organizer: it must indicate relations among the basic concepts and terms that will be used. In other words, a true organizer isn't just a statement of historical or background information. No amount of student processing can make a bad organizer more effective. Concrete models, diagrams, or analogies seem to be especially good organizers (Mayer 1983a, 1984).

Steps in an Expository Lesson. After presenting an advance organizer, the next step in a lesson using Ausubel's approach is to present content in terms of basic similarities and differences, using specific examples. To learn any new material, students must see not only the similarities between the material presented and what they already know but also the differences so that interference—the confusion of old and new material—can be avoided.

It is often helpful in an expository lesson to ask students to supply similarities and differences themselves. In a grammar lesson, you might ask, "What are the differences between the way commas and semicolons are used?" Or suppose in teaching the coming-of-age theme in literature, you choose *The Diary of Anne Frank* and *Paddle-to-the-Sea* as the basic material for the unit. As the students read the first book, you might ask them to compare the central character's growth, state of mind, and position in society with characters from other novels, plays, and films.

When the class moves on to the second book, you can start by asking students to compare Anne Frank's inner journey with Paddle's journey through the Great Lakes to the Atlantic Ocean. As comparisons are made, whether within a single class lesson or during an entire unit, it is useful to underscore the goal of the lesson and occasionally to repeat the advance organizer (with amendments and elaborations).

Along with the comparisons, specific examples must come into play. You can see that the best way to point out similarities and differences is with examples. There must be specific examples of comma and semicolon usage; the specific elements of Paddle's and Anne Frank's dilemmas must be clear. Finally, when all the material has been presented, ask students to discuss how the examples can be used to expand on the original advance organizer. The phases of expository teaching are summarized in Figure 8.4.

CHECKPOINT

Learning and Teaching about Concepts

Review

▶ Distinguish between prototypes and exemplars.

▶ What are the four elements needed in concept teaching?

▶ What are the key characteristics of Bruner's discovery learning?

▶ What are the stages of Ausubel's expository teaching?

Apply

▶ What are the defining attributes of the concept of "cup"? What attributes are irrelevant?

Making the Most of Expository Teaching. Another consideration with expository teaching is the age of the students. This approach requires students to manipulate ideas mentally, even if the ideas are simple and based on physical realities such as rocks and minerals. Expository teaching is therefore more developmentally appropriate for students at or above later elementary school, that is,

Applying Ausubel's Ideas

Use advance organizers.

Examples

1. English: Shakespeare used the social ideas of his time as a framework for his plays—*Julius Caesar*, *Hamlet*, and *Macbeth* dealt with concepts of natural order, a nation as the human body, etc.
2. Social studies: Geography dictates economy in pre-industrialized regions or nations.
3. History: Important concepts during the Renaissance were symmetry, admiration of the classical world, the centrality of the human mind.

Use a number of examples.

Examples

1. In mathematics class, ask students to point out all the examples of right angles that they can find in the room.

2. In teaching about islands and peninsulas, use maps, slides, models, postcards.

Focus on both similarities and differences.

Examples

1. In a history class, ask students to list the ways in which Canada was the same and different before and after Confederation.
2. In a biology class, ask students how they would transform spiders into insects or an amphibian into a reptile.

---

around Grades 5 or 6 (Luiten, Ames, & Ackerson, 1980). The Guidelines above should help you follow the main steps in expository teaching.

Problem Solving

"Educational programs," Robert Gagné has written, "have the important ultimate purpose of teaching students to solve problems—mathematical and physical problems, health problems, social problems, and problems of personal adjustment" (1977, p. 177). A **problem** has an initial state, the current situation; a goal, the desired outcome; and a path for reaching the goal, including operations or activities that move you toward the goal. Problem solvers often have to set and reach sub-goals as they move toward the final solution. For example, if your goal is to drive to the lake, but at the first stop sign you skid through the intersection, you may have to reach a sub-goal of fixing your brakes before you can continue toward the original goal (Schunk, 2000). Also, problems can range from well-structured to ill-structured, depending on how clear-cut the goal is and how much structure is provided for solving the problem. Most arithmetic problems are well-structured but finding the right university major is ill-structured—many different solutions and paths to solutions are possible.

Problem solving is usually defined as formulating new answers, going beyond the simple application of previously learned rules to achieve a goal. Problem solving is what happens when no solution is obvious—when, for example, you can't afford new brakes (Mayer & Wittrock, 1996). Some psychologists suggest that most human learning involves problem solving (Anderson, 1993).

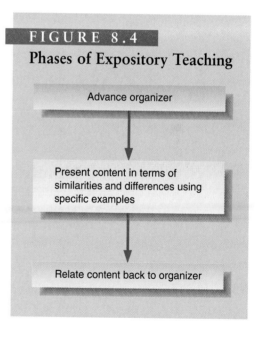

FIGURE 8.4

Phases of Expository Teaching

Advance organizer

↓

Present content in terms of similarities and differences using specific examples

↓

Relate content back to organizer

Problem: Any situation in which you are trying to reach some goal and must find a means to do so.

Problem Solving: Creating new solutions for problems.

Problem Solving: General or Domain-Specific?

Connect & Extend
To history
You might want to note that, although interest in problem solving is great today, many of the early ideas of John Dewey are consistent with the recent emphasis on teaching students to be effective problem solvers.

There is an interesting debate about problem solving. Some psychologists believe that effective problem-solving strategies are specific to the problem area. That is, the problem-solving strategies in mathematics are unique to math, the strategies in art are unique to art, and so on. Becoming an expert problem solver in an area requires that you master the strategies of the area. The other side of the debate claims that there are some general problem-solving strategies that can be useful in many areas.

There is evidence for both sides of the argument. In fact, it appears that people move between general and specific approaches, depending on the situation and their level of expertise. Early on, when we know little about a problem area or domain, we may rely on general learning and problem-solving strategies to make sense of the situation. As we gain more domain-specific knowledge (particularly procedural knowledge about how to do things in the domain), we need the general strategies less and less. But if we encounter a problem outside our current knowledge, we may return to relying on general strategies to attack the problem (Alexander, 1992, 1996; Perkins & Salomon, 1989; Shuell, 1990).

A General Problem-Solving Strategy

Think of a general problem-solving strategy as a beginning point, a broad outline. Such strategies usually have five stages (Derry, 1991; Derry & Murphy, 1986; Gallini, 1991; Gick, 1986). John Bransford and Barry Stein (1993) use the acronym IDEAL to identify the five steps:

I   Identify problems and opportunities.

D   Define goals and represent the problem.

E   Explore possible strategies.

A   Anticipate outcomes and Act.

L   Look back and Learn.

We will examine each of these steps because they are found in many approaches to problem solving.

Identifying: Problem Finding

The first step, identifying that a problem exists and treating the problem as an opportunity, begins the process. This is not always straightforward. There is a story describing tenants who were angry about the slow elevators in their building. Consultants hired to "fix the problem" reported that the elevators were no worse than average and that improvements would be expensive. Then one day, as the building supervisor watched people waiting impatiently for an elevator, he realized that the problem was not slow elevators but the fact that people were bored; they had nothing to do while they waited. When the problem was redefined as boredom and seen as an opportunity to improve the "waiting experience," the simple solution of installing a mirror on each floor eliminated complaints.

Identifying the problem is a critical first step. Research indicates that people often hurry through this important step and "leap" to naming the first problem that comes to mind ("the elevators are too slow!"). Experts in a field are more likely to spend time carefully considering the nature of the problem (Bruning, Schraw, & Ronning, 1999). Finding a solvable problem and turning it into an opportunity is the process behind thousands of successful inventions, including the ballpoint pen, appliance timer, alarm clock, self-cleaning oven, and garbage disposal. A walk through the kitchen section of Sears or the Bay will give you examples of problems turned into opportunities to sell you things you didn't know you needed—until you saw the creative solution!

Once a solvable problem is identified, what next? We will examine steps D, E, A, and L in some detail, because they make up the heart of the process.

Defining Goals and Representing the Problem

Let's take a real problem: the machines designed to pick tomatoes are damaging the tomatoes. What to do? If we represent the problem as a faulty machine design, the goal is to improve the machine. But if we represent the problem as a faulty design of the tomatoes, the goal is to develop a tougher tomato. The problem-solving process follows two entirely different paths, depending on which representation and goal are chosen (Bransford & Stein, 1993). To represent the problem and set a goal, you have to focus on relevant information, understand the elements of the problem, and activate the right *schema* to understand the whole problem.

Focusing Attention.   Representing the problem often requires finding the relevant information and ignoring the irrelevant details. For example, consider the following problem adapted from Sternberg and Davidson (1982):

> If you have black socks and white socks in your drawer, mixed in the ratio of four to five, how many socks will you have to take out to make sure of having a pair the same colour?

What information is relevant to solving this problem? Did you realize that the information about the four-to-five ratio of black socks to white socks is irrelevant? As long as you have only two different colours of socks in the drawer, you will have to remove only three socks before two of them have to match.

Understanding the Words.   The second task in representing a story problem is **linguistic comprehension**, understanding the meaning of each sentence (Mayer, 1983a, 1983b, 1992b). Take, for example, the following sentence from an algebra story problem:

> The riverboat's rate in still water is 19 km per hour more than the rate of the river current.

This is a *relational proposition*. It describes the relationship between two rates, that of the riverboat and that of the current. Here is another sentence from a story problem:

> The cost of the candy is $6.05 per kg.

This is an *assignment proposition*. It simply assigns a value to something, in this case the cost of one unit of candy.

Research shows that relational propositions are harder to understand and remember than assignment propositions. In one study, when students had to recall relational and assignment propositions such as those above, the error rate for recalling relational propositions was about three times higher than the error rate for assignment propositions (Mayer, 1982). If you misunderstand the meaning of individual statements in a problem, you will have a hard time representing the whole problem correctly and setting a goal.

The main stumbling block in representing many word problems is the students' understanding of *part-whole relations* (Cummins, 1991). Students have trouble figuring out what is part of what, as evident in this dialogue between a teacher and a Grade 1 student:

Teacher: Pete has three apples; Ann also has some apples; Pete and Ann have nine apples altogether; how many apples does Ann have?

Student: Nine.

Connect & Extend
To other chapters
Piaget (**Chapter 2**) identified children's difficulties with part-whole relations years ago when he asked questions such as, "There are six daisies and two daffodils; are there more daisies or flowers?" Young children usually answer, "Daisies!"

Linguistic Comprehension: Understanding of the meaning of sentences in word problems.

Teacher: Why?

Student: Because you just said so.

Teacher: Can you retell the story?

Student: Pete had three apples; Ann also had some apples; Ann had nine apples; Pete also has nine apples. (Adapted from De Corte & Verschaffel, 1985, p. 19)

The student interprets "altogether" (the whole) as "each" (the parts).

Understanding the Whole Problem. The third task in representing a problem is to assemble all the relevant information and sentences into an accurate understanding or translation of the total problem. Even if you understand every sentence, you may still misunderstand the problem as a whole. Consider this example:

> Two train stations are 50 miles apart. At 2 P.M. one Saturday afternoon two trains start toward each other, one from each station. Just as the trains pull out of the stations, a bird springs into the air in front of the first train and flies ahead to the front of the second train. When the bird reaches the second train it turns back and flies toward the first train. The bird continues to do this until the trains meet. If both trains travel at the rate of 25 miles per hour and the bird flies at 100 miles per hour, how many miles will the bird have flown before the trains meet? (Posner, 1973)

Your interpretation of the problem is called a *translation* because you translate the problem into a schema that you understand. If you translate this as a *distance* problem and set a goal ("I have to figure out how far the bird travels before it meets the oncoming train and turns around, then how far it travels before it has to turn again, and finally add up all the trips back and forth..."), then you have a very difficult task on your hands. But there is a better way to structure the problem. You can represent it as a question of *time* and focus on the time the bird is in the air. If you figure out how long the bird is in the air, then you can easily determine the distance it will cover, because you know exactly how fast it flies. The solution could be stated like this:

> Because the stations are 50 miles apart and the trains are moving toward each other at the same speed, the trains will meet in the middle, 25 miles from each station. Because they are traveling 25 mph, it will take the trains one hour to reach the meeting point. In the one hour it takes the trains to meet, the bird will cover 100 miles because it is flying at 100 miles per hour. Easy!

Research shows that students can be too quick to decide what a problem is asking. The subjects in one study made their decisions about how to categorize standard algebra problems after reading only the first few sentences of a problem (Hinsley, Hayes, & Simon, 1977). Once a problem is categorized—"Aha, it's a distance problem!"—a particular schema is activated. The schema directs attention to relevant information and sets up expectations for what the right answer should look like (Robinson & Hayes, 1978).

When students do not have the necessary schemas to represent problems, they often rely on surface features of the situation and represent the problem incorrectly—like the student who wrote "15 + 24 = 39" as the answer to the question, "Josée has 15 bonus points and Louise has 24. How many more does Louise have?" This student saw two numbers and the word "more," so he applied the *add to get more* procedure. When students use the wrong schema, they overlook critical information, use irrelevant information, and may even misread or misremember critical information so that it fits the schema. Errors in representing the problem and difficulties in solving it are the results. But when students use the proper schema for representing a problem, they are less likely to be confused by irrelevant information or tricky wording, such as *more* in a problem that really requires *subtraction* (Resnick, 1981). Figure 8.5 gives examples of different ways students might represent a simple mathematics problem.

Four Different Ways to Represent a Problem

A teacher asks, "How many wildlife stamps will Jane need to fill her book if there are three empty pages and each page holds 30 stamps?" The teacher gives the students supplies such as squared paper, number lines, and place-value frames and encourages them to think of as many ways as possible to solve the problem. Here are four different solutions, based on four different but correct representations:

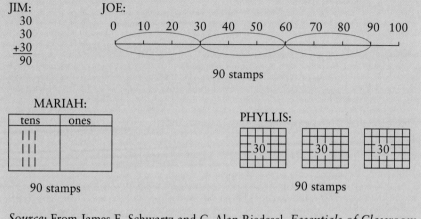

JIM:
```
  30
  30
 +30
  90
```

JOE:

90 stamps

MARIAH:

90 stamps

PHYLLIS:

90 stamps

Source: From James E. Schwartz and C. Alan Riedesel. *Essentials of Classroom Teaching: Elementary Mathematics*, pp. 123–124. Copyright © 1994 by Allyn & Bacon. Reprinted by permission.

Translation and Schema Training. How can students improve translation and schema selection? To answer this question, we often have to move from general to area-specific problem-solving strategies because schemas are specific to content areas. In mathematics, for example, it appears that students benefit from seeing many different kinds of example problems worked out correctly for them. The common practice of showing students a few examples, then having students work many problems on their own, is less effective. Especially when problems are unfamiliar or difficult, worked-out examples are helpful (Cooper & Sweller, 1987). The most effective examples seem to be those that do not require students to integrate several sources of information, such as a diagram and a set of statements about the problem. This kind of attention splitting may put too much strain on the working memory. When students are learning, worked examples should deal with one source of information at a time (Marcus, Cooper, & Sweller, 1996). Ask students to compare examples. What is the same about each solution? What is different? Why? The same procedures may be effective in areas other than mathematics. Adrienne Lee and Laura Hutchinson (1998) found that undergraduate students learned more when they had examples of chemistry-problem solutions that were annotated to show an expert problem solver's thinking at critical steps. Asking students to reflect on the examples helped too, so explanation and reflection can make worked examples more effective.

How else might students develop the schemas they will need to represent problems in a particular subject area? Mayer (1983b) has recommended giving students practice in the following: (1) Recognizing and categorizing a variety of problem types; (2) representing problems—either concretely in pictures, symbols, or graphs, or in words; and (3) selecting relevant and irrelevant information in problems.

The Results of Problem Representation. There are two main outcomes of the problem representation stage of problem solving, as shown in Figure 8.6. If your representation of the problem suggests an immediate solution, your task is done.

FIGURE 8.6

Diagram of the Problem-Solving Process

There are two paths to a solution. In the first, the correct schema is activated and the solution is apparent. But if no schema is available, searching and testing may become the path to a solution.

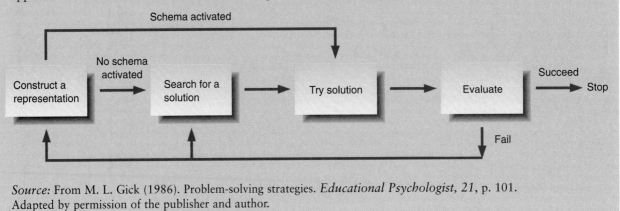

Source: From M. L. Gick (1986). Problem-solving strategies. *Educational Psychologist, 21,* p. 101. Adapted by permission of the publisher and author.

In the language of the cognitive scientist, you have activated the right schema and the solution is apparent because it is part of the schema. In one sense, you haven't really solved a new problem, you have simply recognized the new problem as a "disguised" version of an old problem that you already know how to solve. Mary Gick (1986) of Carleton University called this **schema-driven problem solving,** a kind of matching between the situation and your store of systems for dealing with different problems. In terms of Figure 8.6, you have taken the schema-activated route and proceeded directly to a solution. But what if you have no existing way of solving the problem or if your activated schema fails? Time to search for a solution!

Exploring Possible Solution Strategies

If you do not have existing schemas that suggest an immediate solution, you must take the *search-based route* indicated in Figure 8.4. Obviously, this path is not as efficient as activating the right schema, but sometimes it is the only way. In conducting your search for a solution, you have available two general kinds of procedures: algorithmic and heuristic.

Algorithms. An **algorithm** is a step-by-step prescription for achieving a goal. It usually is domain-specific, that is, tied to a particular subject area. In solving a problem, if you choose an appropriate algorithm and implement it properly, a correct answer is guaranteed. Unfortunately, students often apply algorithms haphazardly. They try first this, then that. They may even happen on the right answer, but not understand how they found it. For some students, applying algorithms haphazardly could be an indication that formal operational thinking and the ability to work through a set of possibilities systematically, as described by Piaget, is not yet developed.

In math classes you probably experienced some success applying algorithms. As long as you were careful in your computations, you were able to solve even complicated problems. Later, if you were given geometry proofs to verify or algebraic equations to factor, you soon discovered that there were no algorithms guaranteeing a solution. At that point, if you did not learn some heuristics, you probably bailed out of math classes as soon as possible.

Heuristics. A **heuristic** is a general strategy that might lead to the right answer. Because many of life's problems are fuzzy, with ill-defined problem statements and

Schema-Driven Problem Solving: Recognizing a problem as a "disguised" version of an old problem for which one already has a solution.

Algorithm: Step-by-step procedure for solving a problem; prescription for solutions.

Heuristic: General strategy used in attempting to solve problems.

no apparent algorithms, the discovery or development of effective heuristics is important. Let's examine a few.

In **means-ends analysis**, the problem is divided into a number of intermediate goals or sub-goals and then a means of solving each is figured out. For example, writing a 20-page term paper can loom as an insurmountable problem for some students. They would be better off breaking this task into several intermediate goals, such as selecting a topic, locating sources of information, reading and organizing the information, making an outline, and so on. As they attack a particular intermediate goal, they may find that other goals arise. For example, locating information may require that they find someone to refresh their memory about using the library computer search system. Keep in mind that psychologists have yet to discover an effective heuristic for students who are just starting their term paper the night before it is due.

A second aspect of means-ends analysis is *distance reduction,* or pursuing a path that moves directly toward the final goal. People tend to look for the biggest difference between the current state of affairs and the goal and then search for a strategy that reduces the difference. We resist taking detours or making moves that are indirect as we search for the quickest way to reach the goal. So when you realize that reaching the goal of completing a term paper may require a detour of relearning the library computer search system, you may resist at first because you are not moving directly and quickly toward the final goal (Anderson, 1995b).

Some problems lend themselves to a **working-backward strategy**, in which you begin at the goal and move back to the unsolved initial problem. Working backward is sometimes an effective heuristic for solving geometry proofs. It can also be a good way to set intermediate deadlines ("Let's see, if I have to submit this chapter in three weeks, it has to be in the mail by the 28th, so I should have a first draft by the 11th").

Another useful heuristic is **analogical thinking** (Copi, 1961), which limits your search for solutions to situations that have something in common with the one you currently face. When submarines were first designed, for example, engineers had to figure out how battleships could determine the presence and location of vessels hidden in the depths of the sea. Studying how bats solve an analogous problem of navigating in the dark led to the invention of sonar.

Analogical reasoning can lead to faulty problem solving too. When they were first learning to use a word processor, some people used the analogy of the typewriter and failed to take advantage of the features of a computer. A common mistake was "typing" a return at the end of every line instead of using the word processor's wrap feature. It seems that people need knowledge both in the problem

Means-Ends Analysis: Heuristic in which a goal is divided into sub-goals.

Working-Backward Strategy: Heuristic in which one starts with the goal and moves backward to solve the problem.

Analogical Thinking: Heuristic in which a person limits the search for solutions to situations that are similar to the one at hand.

◄ *One advantage of working in groups is the opportunity to explain your problem-solving strategy to someone else—putting solutions into words often improves problem solving.*

Connect & Extend
To the research
Vosniadou, S., & Schommer, M. (1988). Explanatory analogies can help children acquire information from expository text. *Journal of Educational Psychology, 80,* 524–536.
This article describes the results of an experiment in which analogies were used to help young children learn new information from science texts. For example, "an infection is like a war," "a stomach is like a blender." Results showed that children in the analogy condition communicated more information than those in the control condition. Implication: Analogies can facilitate learning.

Connect & Extend
To your teaching
A student was given the problem "Find the value of *x* and *y* that solves both equations":

$$8x + 4y = 284x + 2y = 10$$

The student quickly responded $x = 2$, $y = 3$, correctly addressing the first problem, but neglecting to check the solution on the second. How could you help the student be more reflective?

domain and the analogy domain in order to use an analogy effectively (Gagné, Yekovich, & Yekovich, 1993).

Putting your problem-solving plan into words and giving reasons for selecting it can lead to successful problem solving (Cooper & Sweller, 1987; Lee & Hutchinson, 1998). You may have discovered the effectiveness of this **verbalization** process accidentally, when a solution popped into your head as you were explaining a problem to someone else. Gagné and Smith (1962) found that when students from Grades 9 and 10 were instructed to state a reason for each step they were taking, they were much more successful in solving the problem than students who did not state reasons.

Anticipating, Acting, and Looking Back

After representing the problem and exploring possible solutions, the next step is to select a solution and *anticipate the consequences*. For example, if you decide to solve the damaged-tomato problem by developing a tougher tomato, how will consumers react? If you take time to learn a new graphics program to enhance your term paper (and your grade), will you still have enough time to finish the paper?

After you choose a solution strategy and implement it, evaluate the results by checking for evidence that confirms or contradicts your solution. Many people tend to stop working before reaching the best solution and simply accept an answer that works in some cases. In mathematical problems, evaluating the answer might mean applying a checking routine, such as adding to check the result of a subtraction problem or, in a long addition problem, adding the column from bottom to top instead of top to bottom. Another possibility is estimating the answer. For example, if the computation was 11×21, the answer should be around 200, since 10×20 is 200. A student who reaches an answer of 2311 or 23 or 562 should quickly realize such an answer cannot be correct. Estimating an answer is particularly important when students rely on calculators or computers, because they cannot go back and spot an error in the figures.

Factors That Hinder Problem Solving

Consider the following situation:

> You enter a room. There are two ropes suspended from the ceiling. You are asked by the experimenter to tie the two ends of the ropes together and are assured that the task is possible. On a nearby table are a few tools, including a hammer and pliers. You grab the end of one of the ropes and walk toward the other rope. You immediately realize that you cannot possibly reach the end of the other rope. You try to extend your reach using the pliers but still cannot grasp the other rope. What can you do? (Maier, 1933)

Functional Fixedness. This problem can be solved by using an object in an unconventional way. If you tie the hammer or the pliers to the end of one rope and start swinging it like a pendulum, you will be able to catch it while you are standing across the room holding the other rope, as shown in Figure 8.7. You can use the weight of the tool to make the rope come to you instead of trying to stretch the rope. People often fail to solve this problem because they seldom consider unconventional uses for materials that have a specific function. This difficulty is called **functional fixedness** (Duncker, 1945). Problem solving requires seeing things in new ways. In your everyday life, you may often exhibit functional fixedness. Suppose a screw on a dresser-drawer handle is loose. Will you spend 10 minutes searching for a screwdriver? Or will you think to use another object not necessarily designed for this function, such as a ruler edge or a dime?

Verbalization: Putting your problem-solving plan and its logic into words.

Functional Fixedness: Inability to use objects or tools in a new way.

FIGURE 8.7

Overcoming Functional Fixedness

In the two-string problem, the subject must set one string in motion in order to tie both strings together.

Response set. Another block to effective problem solving is **response set**. Consider the following:

> In each of the four matchstick arrangements below, move only one stick to change the equation so that it represents a true equality such as V = V.

V=VII   VI=XI   XII=VII   VI=II

You probably figured out how to solve the first example quite quickly. You simply move one matchstick from the right side over to the left to make VI = VI. Examples two and three can also be solved without too much difficulty by moving one stick to change the V to an X or vice versa. But the fourth example (taken from Raudsepp & Haugh, 1977) probably has you stumped. To solve this problem you must change your response set or switch schemas, because what has worked for the first three problems will not work this time. The answer here lies in changing from Roman numerals to Arabic numbers and using the concept of square root. By overcoming response set, you can move one matchstick from the right to the left to form the symbol for square root; the solution reads √T = I which is simply the symbolic way of saying that the square root of 1 equals 1.

The Importance of Flexibility. Functional fixedness and response set point to the importance of flexibility in understanding problems. If you get started with an inaccurate or inefficient representation of the true problem, it will be difficult—or at least very time-consuming—to reach a solution (Wessells, 1982). Sometimes it is helpful to play with the problem. Ask yourself: "What do I know? What do I need to know to answer this question? Can I look at this problem in other ways?" Try to think conditionally rather than rigidly and divergently rather than convergently. Ask, "What could this be?" instead of "What is it?" (Benjafield, 1992).

If you open your mind to multiple possibilities, you may have what the Gestalt psychologists called an insight. Insight is the sudden reorganization or reconceptualization of a problem that clarifies the problem and suggests a feasible solution. The supervisor described earlier, who suddenly realized that the problem in his building was not slow elevators but impatient, bored tenants, had an insight that allowed him to reach the solution of installing mirrors by the elevators.

Response Set: Rigidity; tendency to respond in the most familiar way.

Connect & Extend
To your teaching
The following five heuristics that might help students solve postsecondary level math problems are from Schoenfeld, A. H. (1979). Explicit heuristic training as a variable in problem solving performance. *Journal for Research in Mathematics Education, 10,* 173–187.
1. Draw a diagram, if possible.
2. If the problem has an "N" that takes on integer values, try substituting numbers such as 1, then 2, then 3, then 4 for the "N," and look for a pattern in the results.
3. If you are trying to prove a statement, for example, "If X is true, then Y is true," try proving the contrapositive, "If X is false, then Y is false," or try assuming the statement you want to prove is false and look for a contradiction.
4. Try solving a similar problem with fewer variables.
5. Try to set up sub-goals.

Effective Problem Solving: What Do the Experts Do?

Most psychologists agree that effective problem solving is based on an ample store of knowledge about the problem area. In order to solve the matchstick problem, for example, you had to understand Roman and Arabic numbers as well as the concept of square root. You also had to know that the square root of 1 is 1. Let's take a moment to examine this expert knowledge.

Expert Knowledge. The modern study of expertise began with investigations of chess masters (Simon & Chase, 1973). Results indicated that masters can quickly recognize about 50 000 different arrangements of chess pieces. They can look at one of these patterns for a few seconds and remember where every piece on the board was placed. It is as though they have a "vocabulary" of 50 000 patterns. Michelene Chi (1978) demonstrated that chess experts in Grades 3 through 8 had a similar ability to remember chess-piece arrangement. For all the masters, patterns of pieces are like words. If you were shown any word from your vocabulary store for just a few seconds, you would be able to remember every letter in the word in the right order (assuming you could spell the word).

But a series of letters arranged randomly is hard to remember, as you saw in Chapter 7. An analogous situation holds for chess masters. When chess pieces are placed on a board randomly, masters are no better than average players at remembering the positions of the pieces. The master's memory is for patterns that make sense or could occur in a game.

A similar phenomenon occurs in other fields. There may be an intuition about how to solve a problem based on recognizing patterns and knowing the "right moves" for those patterns. Experts in physics, for example, organize their knowledge around central principles, whereas beginners organize their smaller amounts of physics knowledge around the specific details stated in the problems. For instance, when asked to sort physics problems from a textbook in any way they wanted, novices sorted based on superficial features such as the kind of apparatus mentioned—a lever or a pulley—while the experts grouped problems according to the underlying physics principle needed to solve the problem, such as Boyle's or Newton's laws (Hardiman, Dufresne, & Mestre, 1989). And the experts can recognize the patterns needed to solve a particular problem very quickly, so they literally don't have to think as hard (Glaser, 1981).

In addition to representing a problem very quickly, experts know what to do next. They have a large store of productions or condition-action schemas about what action to take in various situations. Thus, the steps of understanding the problem and choosing a solution happen simultaneously and fairly automatically (Ericsson & Smith, 1991). Of course, this means that they must have many, many schemas available. A large part of becoming an expert is simply acquiring a great store of *domain knowledge* or knowledge that is knowledge about a particular to a field (Alexander, 1992). To do this, you must encounter many different kinds of problems in that field, see problems solved by others, and practise solving many yourself. Some estimates are that it takes 10 years or 10 000 hours of study to become an expert in most fields (Simon, 1995).

Experts' rich store of knowledge is *elaborated* and *well practised,* so that it is easy to retrieve from long-term memory when needed (Anderson, 1995b). Experts can use their extensive knowledge to *organize* information for easier learning and retrieval. Among Grade 4 students, those who were soccer experts learned and remembered far more new soccer terms than those with little knowledge of soccer, even though the abilities of the two groups to learn and remember non-soccer terms were the same. The soccer experts organized and clustered the soccer terms to aid in recall (Schneider & Bjorklund, 1992). Even very young children who are experts on a topic can use strategies to organize their knowledge. A good example of the use of category knowledge about dinosaurs is Anita's nephews (only three or four years old at the time) who promptly ran down the list of large and small plant- and meat-eating dinosaurs, from the well-known stegosaurus (large plant-eater) to the less familiar ceolophysis (small meat-eater).

With organization comes planning and monitoring. Experts spend more time analyzing problems, drawing diagrams, breaking large problems down into sub-problems, and making plans. While a novice might begin immediately—writing equations for a physics problem or drafting the first paragraph of a paper, experts plan out the whole solution and often make the task simpler in the process. As they work, experts monitor progress, so time is not lost pursuing dead ends or weak ideas (Gagné et al., 1993).

Chi, Glaser, and Farr (1988) summarize the superior capabilities of experts. Experts (1) perceive large, meaningful patterns in given information, (2) perform tasks quickly and with few errors, (3) deal with problems at a deeper level, (4) have superior short- and long-term memories, (5) take a great deal of time to analyze a given problem, and (6) are better at monitoring their performance. When the area of problem solving is fairly well defined, such as chess or physics or computer pro-gramming, these skills of expert problem solvers hold fairly consistently. But when the problem-solving area is less well-defined and has fewer clear underlying prin-ciples, such as problem solving in economics or psychology, the differences between experts and novices are not as clear-cut (Alexander, 1992).

Expert Teachers.   Studies of expert teachers identify many of the characteristics described above. Expert teachers have a sense of what is typical in classrooms, of what to expect during certain activities or times of the day. Many of their teaching routines have become automatic—they don't even have to think about how to dis-tribute materials, take roll, move students in and out of groups, or assign grades. This gives the teachers more mental and physical energy for being creative and focusing on their students' progress. For example, one study found that expert math teachers could go over the previous day's work with the class in 2 or 3 min-utes, compared to 15 minutes for novices (Leinhardt, 1986).

Expert teachers work from integrated sets of principles instead of dealing with each new event as a new problem. They look for patterns revealing similarities in situations that seem quite different at first glance. Experts focus more than begin-ners on analyzing a problem and mentally applying different principles to develop a solution. In one study of solutions to discipline problems, the expert teachers spent quite a bit of time framing each problem, forming questions, deciding what information was necessary, and considering alternatives (Swanson, O'Conner, & Cooney, 1990).

Expert teachers have a deep and well-organized knowledge of the subjects they teach. A study by François Tochon of the Université de Sherbrooke and Hugh Munby of Queen's University (1993) clearly showed that expert teachers, in con-trast to novices, deliberately avoid rigid plans. Expert teachers improvise lessons on the spot to accommodate the needs of their students in ways such as inventing explanations and generating additional examples (see also Borko & Livingston, 1989; Sabers, Cushing, & Berliner, 1991). And as we saw in Chapter 1, expert teachers also know a great deal about their students, the curriculum, teaching strategies, and ways to make the curriculum understandable and accessible to the students.

Novice Knowledge.   Studies of the differences between experts and novices in particular areas have revealed surprising information about how novices under-stand and misunderstand a subject. Physics again provides many examples. Most beginners approach physics with a great deal of misinformation, partly because many of their intuitive ideas about the physical world are wrong. Most elementary school children believe that light helps us see by brightening the area around objects. They do not realize that we see an object because the light is reflected by the object to our eyes. This concept does not fit with the everyday experience of

Connect & Extend
To the research
Joshua, S., & Dupin, J. J. (1987). Taking into account student con-ceptions in instructional strategy: An example in physics. *Cognition and Instruction, 4,* 117–135. *abstract:* Several studies have emphasized the predominant influence of students' conceptions in the learning process in physics. But, more often than not, these conceptions are somehow consid-ered in a negative way, as "errors." This article describes taking stu-dents' conceptions as an active basis for scientific reasoning in real class situations with groups [of students aged] approximately 12 and 14 years.
   The subject matter taught was basic electricity. The article shows how pre-instruction conceptions were actually used (or not used) by the students to explain the electricity phenomena, and how these conceptions subsequently changed, increasing in internal consistency, without moving closer to scientific conceptions. Analogical explanation helped overcome this situation.

Review

▶ What are the steps in the general problem-solving process?

▶ Why is the representation stage of problem solving so important?

▶ Describe factors that can interfere with problem solving.

▶ What are the differences between expert and novice knowledge in a given area?

▶ How do misconceptions interfere with learning?

Apply

▶ What are some common misconceptions about being an expert?

turning on a light and "brightening" the dark area. Researchers found that even after completing a unit on light in which materials explicitly stated the idea of reflected light and vision, most Grade 5 students—about 78 percent—continued to cling to their intuitive notions. But when new materials were designed that directly confronted the students' misconceptions, only about 20 percent of the students failed to understand (Eaton, Anderson, & Smith, 1984).

It seems quite important for science teachers to understand their students' intuitive models of basic concepts. If the students' intuitive model includes misconceptions and inaccuracies, the students are likely to develop inadequate or misleading representations of a problem. (You should note that some researchers don't use the term "misconception" but refer to *naive* or *intuitive conceptions* to describe students' beginning knowledge in an area.) To learn new information and solve problems, students must sometimes "unlearn" common-sense ideas

GUIDELINES

Problem Solving

Ask students if they are sure they understand the problem.

Examples
1. Can they separate relevant from irrelevant information?
2. Are they aware of the assumptions they are making?
3. Encourage them to visualize the problem by diagramming or drawing it.
4. Ask them to explain the problem to someone else. What would a good solution look like?

Encourage attempts to see the problem from different angles.

Examples
1. Suggest several different possibilities yourself and then ask students to offer some.
2. Give students practice in taking and defending different points of view on an issue.

Help students develop systematic ways of considering alternatives.

Examples
1. Think out loud as you solve problems.

2. Ask, "What would happen if?"
3. Keep a list of suggestions.

Teach heuristics.

Examples
1. Ask students to explain the steps they take as they solve problems.
2. Use analogies to solve the problem of limited parking in the downtown area. How are other "storage" problems solved?
3. Use the working-backward strategy to plan a party.

Let students do the thinking; don't just hand them solutions.

Examples
1. Offer individual problems as well as group problems, so that each student has the chance to practise.
2. Give partial credit if students have good reasons for "wrong" solutions to problems.
3. If students are stuck, resist the temptation to give too many clues. Let them think about the problem overnight.

(Joshua & Dupin, 1987). Changing your intuitive ideas about concepts involves motivation too. Pintrich, Marx, and Boyle (1993) suggest that four conditions are necessary for people to change basic concepts: (1) Students have to be dissatisfied with the current concept; that is, their existing concept must be seen as inaccurate, incomplete, or not useful. (2) Students must understand the new concept. (3) The new concept must be plausible—it must fit in with what the students already know. (4) The new concept must be fruitful—it must be seen as useful in solving problems or answering questions.

The Guidelines on page 292 give some ideas for helping students become expert problem solvers.

▼ *B*ecoming an Expert Student: Learning Strategies and Study Skills

As we saw in Chapter 7, the way something is learned in the first place greatly influences how readily we remember and how appropriately we can apply the knowledge later. First, students must be *cognitively engaged* in order to learn—they have to focus attention on the relevant or important aspects of the material. Second, they have to *invest effort,* make connections, elaborate, translate, organize, and reorganize in order to *think and process deeply*—the greater the practice and processing, the stronger the learning. Finally, students must *regulate and monitor* their own learning—keep track of what is making sense and notice when a new approach is needed. The emphasis today is on helping students develop effective learning strategies and tactics that *focus attention and effort, process information deeply, and monitor understanding.* Some students will develop good strategies for organizing and learning on their own, but most need help.

Learning Strategies and Tactics

Learning strategies are ideas for accomplishing learning goals, a kind of overall plan of attack. **Learning tactics** are the specific techniques that make up the plan (Winne & Perry, 1994). Your strategy for learning the material in this chapter might include the tactics of using mnemonics to remember key terms, skimming the chapter to identify the organization, and then writing answers to possible essay questions. Your use of strategies and tactics reflects metacognitive knowledge.

Fortunately, teaching these procedural skills has become a high priority in education, and several important principles have been identified.

Connect & Extend
To your teaching
Brainstorm about intuitive models in other fields besides science and mathematics. What are some common misconceptions about cultural differences, history, government, or educational psychology?

Connect & Extend
To other chapters
The guidelines for study skills apply to everyone who wishes to become an expert learner and involve the metacognitive abilities and executive control processes discussed in **Chapter 7**.

Learning Strategies: General plans for approaching learning tasks.

Learning Tactics: Specific techniques for learning, such as using mnemonics or outlining a passage.

Connect & Extend
To other chapters
See Chapter 7 for a discussion of declarative, procedural, and conditional knowledge.

1. Students must be exposed to a number of *different strategies,* not only general learning strategies but also specific tactics, such as the graphic strategies described later in this chapter.

2. *Teach conditional knowledge* about when, where, and why to use various strategies (Pressley, 1986). Although this may seem obvious, teachers often neglect this step, either because they do not realize its significance or because they assume students will make inferences on their own. A strategy is more likely to be maintained and employed if students know when, where, and why to use it.

3. Students may know when and how to use a strategy, but unless they also *develop the desire to employ these skills,* general learning ability will not improve. Several learning strategy programs (Borkowski, Johnston, & Reid, 1986; Dansereau, 1985) include a motivational training component. In Chapters 10 and 11 we look more closely at this important issue of motivation.

4. *Direct instruction in schematic knowledge* is often an important component of strategy training. To identify main ideas—a critical skill for a number of learning strategies—you must have an appropriate schema for making sense of the material. Table 8.2 summarizes several tactics for learning declarative (verbal) knowledge and procedural skills (Derry, 1989).

Deciding What Is Important. You can see from the first entry in Table 8.2 that learning begins with focusing attention—deciding what is important. But distinguishing the main idea from less important information is not always easy. Often students focus on the "seductive details" or the concrete examples, perhaps because these are more interesting (Dole, Duffy, Roehler, & Pearson, 1991;

TABLE 8.2   Examples of Learning Tactics

	Examples	Use When?
Tactics for Learning Verbal Information	1. Attention Focusing ■ Making outlines, underlining ■ Looking for headings and topic sentences	 With easy, structured materials; for good readers For poorer readers; with more difficult materials
	2. Schema Building ■ Story grammars ■ Theory schemas ■ Networking and mapping	 With poor text structure, goal is to encourage active comprehension
	3. Idea Elaboration ■ Self-questioning ■ Imagery	 To understand and remember specific ideas
Tactics for Learning Procedural Information	1. Pattern Learning ■ Hypothesizing ■ Identifying reasons for actions	 To learn attributes of concepts To match procedures to situations
	2. Self-instruction ■ Comparing own performance to expert model	 To tune, improve complex skills
	3. Practice ■ Part practice ■ Whole practice	 When few specific aspects of a performance need attention To maintain and improve skill

Source: Based on S. Derry (1989). Putting learning strategies to work, *Educational Leadership, 47*(5), pp. 5–6.

Gardner, Brown, Sanders, & Menke, 1992). You may have had the experience of remembering a joke or an intriguing example from a lecture but not being clear about the larger point the professor was trying to make. Finding the central idea is especially difficult if students lack prior knowledge in an area and the amount of new information provided is extensive. Teachers can give students practice using signals in texts such as headings, bold words, outlines, or other indicators to identify key concepts and main ideas. Teaching students to summarize material can be helpful too.

Summaries.   Creating summaries can help students learn, but students have to be taught how to summarize (Byrnes, 1996; Dole et al., 1991; Palincsar & Brown, 1984). Jeanne Ormrod (1999, p. 333) summarizes these suggestions for helping students create summaries:

▶ Begin doing summaries of short, easy, well-organized readings. Introduce longer, less organized, and more difficult passages gradually.

* For each summary, ask students to
* find or write a *topic sentence* for each paragraph or section,
* identify *big ideas* that cover several specific points,
* find some *supporting information* for each big idea, and
* delete any *redundant information* or unnecessary details.
* Ask students to compare their summaries and discuss what ideas they thought were important and why—what's their evidence?

Two other study strategies that are based on identifying key ideas are *underlining* texts and *taking notes*.

Underlining and Highlighting.   Do you underline or highlight key phrases in textbooks? Are these words turning yellow or pink at this very moment? What about outlining or taking notes? Underlining and note taking are probably two of the most commonly used strategies among college students. Yet few students receive any instruction in the best ways to take notes or underline, so it is not surprising that many students use ineffective strategies.

One common problem is that students underline or highlight too much. It is far better to be selective. In studies that limit how much students can underline—for example, only one sentence per paragraph—learning has improved (Snowman, 1984). In addition to being selective, you also should actively transform the information into your own words as you underline or take notes. Don't rely on the words of the book. Note connections between what you are reading and other things you already know. Draw diagrams to illustrate relationships. Finally, look for organizational patterns in the material and use them to guide your underlining or note taking (Irwin, 1991; Kiewra, 1988).

Taking Notes.   As you sit in class, filling your notebook with words or furiously trying to keep up with a lecturer, you may wonder if taking notes makes a difference. The answer appears to be yes—taking notes serves at least two important functions:

▶ Taking notes focuses attention during class and helps encode information so it has a chance of making it to long-term memory. In order to record key ideas in your own words, you have to translate, connect, elaborate, and organize. Even if students don't review notes before a test, taking notes in the first place appears to aid learning, especially for those who lack prior knowledge in an area. Of course, if taking notes distracts you from actually listening to and making sense of the lecture, then note taking may not be effective (Di Vesta & Gray, 1972; Kiewra, 1989; Van Metter, Yokoi, & Pressley, 1994).

Connect & Extend
To your teaching
Weinstein, C., Ridley, D. S., Dahl, T., & Weber, E. S. (1988/1989). Helping students develop strategies for effective learning. *Educational Leadership, 46*(4), 17–19.

The authors give many examples of elaboration strategies.

What is the main idea of this story?

If this principle were not true, what would that imply?

What does this remind me of?

How could I use this information in the project I am working on?

How could I represent this in a diagram?

How do I feel about the author's opinion?

How could I put this in my own words?

What might be an example of this?

If I were going to interview the author, what would I ask her?

How does this apply to my life?

▶ Notes provide extended external storage that allows you to return and review. Students who use their notes to study tend to perform better on tests, especially if they take many high-quality notes—more is better as long as you are capturing key ideas, concepts, and *relationships*, not just intriguing details (Kiewra, 1985, 1989).

In an extensive interview study of 252 college students, Peggy Van Metter, Linda Yokoi, and Mike Pressley (1994) concluded that understanding is served when students use note taking to focus attention on important ideas and construct a representation in the notes that reflects the organization of the lecture. As the course progresses, the expert student matches all notes to their anticipated use and makes modifications in strategies after tests or assignments; uses personal codes to flag material that is unfamiliar or difficult; fills in holes by consulting relevant sources (including other students in the class); records information verbatim only when a verbatim response will be required; and generally is strategic about taking and using notes.

To help students organize their note taking, some teachers provide matrices or maps, such as the one in Figure 8.8. When students are first learning to use these maps, you might fill in some of the spaces for them. If you use such an approach with your students, you might encourage students to exchange their filled-in maps and explain their thinking to each other.

FIGURE 8.8

A Map to Guide Note Taking

The compare/contrast map below allows students to organize their listening or reading as they consider two ideas, concepts, time periods, authors, experiments, theories, and so on.

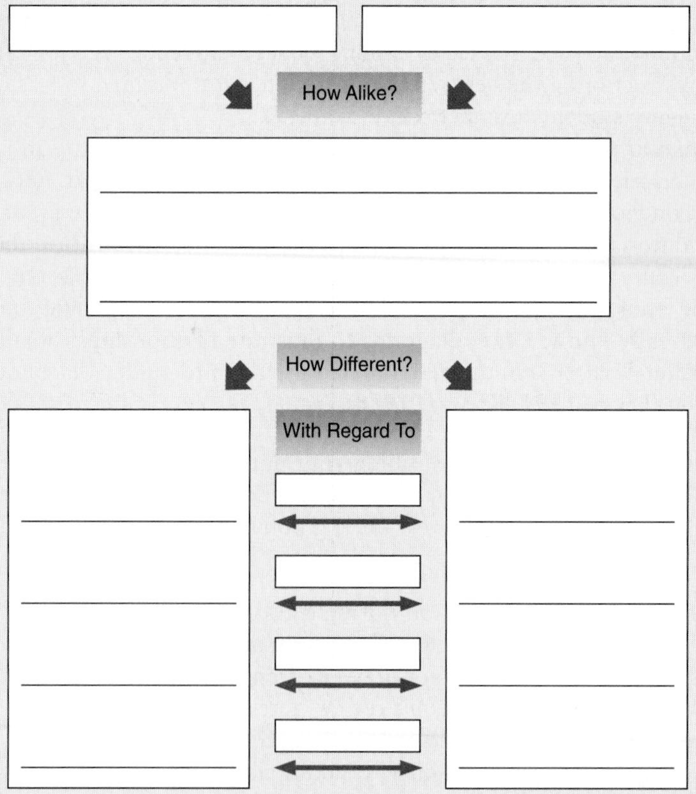

Source: From S. Parks and H. Black, *Organizing Thinking: Book 1.* 1992, published by Critical Thinking Books and Software. Reprinted by permission.

Visual Tools for Organizing

To use underlining and note taking effectively you must identify main ideas. In addition, effective use of underlining and note taking depends on understanding the organization of the text or lecture—the connections and relationships among ideas. Some visual strategies have been developed to help students with this key element. There is some evidence that creating graphic organizers such as maps or charts is more effective than outlining in learning from texts (Robinson, 1998; Robinson & Kiewra, 1995). Armbruster and Anderson (1981) taught students specific techniques for diagramming relationships among ideas presented in a text. "Mapping" these relationships by noting causal connections, comparison/contrast connections, and examples improved recall. Davidson (1982) suggested that students compare one another's "maps" and discuss the differences. The map in Figure 8.9 is a complex web about Holden Caulfield, the main character of J. D. Salinger's

FIGURE 8.9

A Map to Organize Studying and Learning

This map represents one student's (Brian Cooper's) analysis of *Catcher in the Rye*. The map was produced using software called "Inspiration."

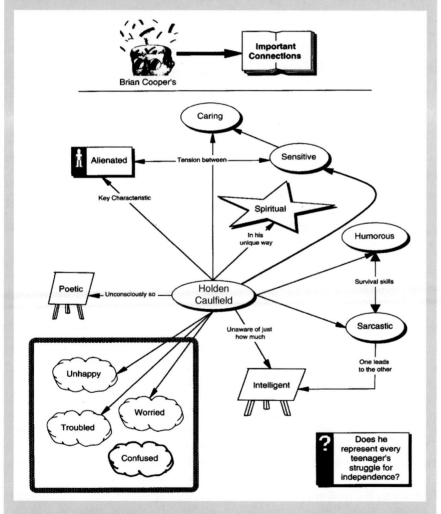

Source: From D. Helfgott, M. Westhaver, and B. Hoof, *Inspiration Software: User's Guide manual,* 1992, Inspiration Software, Inc., 1-800-877-4292 or 503-297-3004. Reprinted by permission.

Catcher in the Rye, developed using Inspiration software. Amy's molecule (Figure 8.2) is a hierarchical graphic depiction of the relationships among concepts. Other ways to visualize organization include *Venn diagrams* showing how ideas or concepts overlap, or *tree diagrams* showing how ideas branch off each other. Timelines organize information in sequence and are useful in classes such as history or geology.

Connect & Extend
To other chapters
Direct instruction in learning strategies is especially important for students with learning disabilities as described in **Chapter 4**.

Reading Strategies. As we saw earlier, effective learning strategies and tactics should help students focus attention; invest effort (elaborate, organize, summarize, connect, translate) so that they process information deeply; and monitor their understanding. There are a number of strategies that support these processes in reading. Many use mnemonics to help students remember the steps involved. For example, one strategy for any grade above later elementary is **READS**:

R   *Review* headings and subheadings

E   *Examine* boldface words

A   *Ask,* "What do I expect to learn?"

D   *Do* it—Read!

S   *Summarize* in your own words (Friend & Bursuck, 1996).

READS is similar to a well-known strategy you might have encountered in school, called **PQ4R** (Thomas & Robinson, 1972). In this system the extra *R* is for reflection, and the *P* stands for preview. So the acronym stands for: Preview, Question, Read, Reflect, Recite, and Review. To use PQ4R to study this chapter, you would:

1. *Preview.* Introduce yourself to the chapter you are about to read by surveying the major topics and sections. Read the overview, the objectives, the section headings and subheadings, the summary, and perhaps the initial sentences of the major sections. All of these procedures will help activate schemas so you can interpret and remember the text that follows. Previewing also allows you to formulate your own general purpose for reading each section, whether it is to identify the main idea or to note the general biases of the author.

2. *Question.* For each major section, write questions that are related to your reading purposes. One way is to turn the headings and subheadings into questions. For example, in this chapter you might ask: "Why are thinking and understanding important in learning?"

3. *Read.* At last! The questions you have formulated can be answered through reading. Pay attention to the main ideas, supporting details, and other data in keeping with your purposes. You may have to adjust your reading speed to suit the difficulty of the material and your purpose in reading.

4. *Reflect.* While you are reading, try to think of examples or create images of the material. Elaborate and try to make connections between what you are reading and what you already know.

5. *Recite.* After reading each section, sit back and think about your initial purposes and questions. Can you answer the questions without looking at the book? In doing this, you give your mind a second chance to connect what you have read with what you already know. If your mind is blank after reading the section, it may have been too difficult to read comfortably, or you may have been daydreaming. Reciting helps you to monitor your understanding and tells you when to reread before moving on to the next section. Reciting should take place after each headed section, but you may need to do it more often when you are reading difficult material.

6. *Review.* Effective review incorporates new material more thoroughly into your long-term memory. As study progresses, review should be cumulative, including the sections and chapters you read previously. Rereading is one

READS: A five-step reading strategy: *Review* headings; *Examine* boldface words; *Ask* "What do I expect to learn?"; *Do* it—Read; *Summarize* in your own words.

PQ4R: A method for studying text that involves six steps: Preview, Question, Read, Reflect, Recite, Review.

form of review, but trying to answer key questions without referring to the book is the best way. Wrong answers can direct you to areas that need more study, especially before an exam.

A strategy that can be used in reading literature is **CAPS**:

C   Who are the *characters*?

A   What is the *aim* of the story?

P   What *problem* happens?

S   How is the problem *solved*?

Many of the cooperating teachers we work with use a strategy called **KWL Plus** to guide reading and inquiry in general. This general framework can be used with most grade levels from middle elementary upward. The steps are:

K   What do I already *know* about this subject?

W   What do I *want* to know?

L   At the end of the reading or inquiry, what have I *learned*?

No matter what strategies you use, students have to be taught how to use them. Direct teaching, explanation, modelling, and practice with feedback are necessary. Here is how one teacher used modelling and discussion to teach the KWL strategy. After reviewing the steps, the teacher models an example and a non-example of using KWL to learn about "crayons" (Friend & Bursuck, 1996):

Teacher: What do we do now that we have a passage assigned to read? First, I brainstorm, which means I try to think of anything I already know about the topic and write it down.

The teacher writes on the board or overhead known qualities of crayons, such as "made of wax," "come in many colors," "can be sharpened," "several different brands."

Teacher: I then take this information I already know and put it into categories, like "what crayons are made of" and "crayon colors." Next, I write down any questions I would like to have answered during my reading, such as "Who invented crayons? When were they invented? How are crayons made? Where are they made?" At this point, I'm ready to read, so I read the passage on crayons. Now I must write down what I learned from this passage. I must include any information that answers the questions I wrote down before I read and any additional information. For example, I learned that colored crayons were first made in the United States in 1903 by Edwin Binney and E. Harold Smith. I also learned that the Crayola Company owns the company that made the original magic markers. Last, I must organize this information into a map so I can see the different main points and any supporting points.

At this point, the teacher draws a map on the chalkboard or overhead.

Teacher: Let's talk about the steps I used and what I did before and after I read the passage.

A class discussion follows.

Teacher: Now I'm going to read the passage again, and I want you to evaluate my textbook reading skills based on the KWL Plus strategy we've learned.

The teacher then proceeds to demonstrate the strategy *incorrectly*.

Teacher: The passage is about crayons. Well, how much can there really be to know about crayons besides there are hundreds of colors and they always seem to break in the middle? Crayons are for little kids, and I'm in junior high so I don't need to know that much about them. I'll just skim the passage and go ahead and answer the question. Okay, how well did I use the strategy steps?

The class discusses the teacher's inappropriate use of the strategy. (Friend & Bursuck, 1996, pp. 342–343)

CAPS: A strategy that can be used in reading literature: *Characters, Aim* of story, *Problem, Solution.*

KWL Plus: A strategy to guide reading and inquiry: Before— What do I already *know*? What do I *want* to know? After— What have I *learned*?

Anderson (1995a) suggests several reasons why strategies such as READS and PQ4R are effective. First, following the steps makes students more aware of the organization of a given chapter. How often have you skipped reading headings entirely and thus missed major clues to the way the information was organized? Next, these steps require students to study the chapter in sections instead of trying to learn all the information at once. This makes use of distributed practice. Creating and answering questions about the material forces students to process the information more deeply and with greater elaboration (Doctorow, Wittrock, & Marks, 1978; Hamilton, 1985).

As you may have guessed, methods PQ4R are most appropriate for older children. Very little is known about teaching study skills to students in the early elementary grades. The effective application of study skills probably requires

GUIDELINES

Becoming an Expert Student

Make sure you have the necessary declarative knowledge (facts, concepts, ideas) to understand new information.

Examples
1. Keep definitions of key vocabulary available as you study.
2. Review required facts and concepts before attempting new material.

Find out what type of test the teacher will give (essay, short answer), and study the material with that in mind.

Examples
1. For a test with detailed questions, practise writing answers to possible questions.
2. For a multiple-choice test, use mnemonics to remember definitions of key terms.

Make sure you are familiar with the organization of the materials to be learned.

Examples
1. Preview the headings, introductions, topic sentences, and summaries of the text.
2. Be alert for words and phrases that signal relationships, such as *on the other hand, because, first, second, however, since.*

Know your own cognitive skills and use them deliberately.

Examples
1. Use examples and analogies to relate new material to something you care about and understand well, such as sports, hobbies, or films.
2. If one study technique is not working, try another—the goal is to stay involved and be as

effective as you can, not to use any particular strategy.

Study the right information in the right way.
Examples
1. Be sure you know exactly what topics and readings the test will cover.
2. Spend your time on the important, difficult, and unfamiliar material that will be required for the test or assignment.
3. Keep a list of the parts of the text that give you trouble and spend more time on those pages.
4. Process the important information thoroughly by using mnemonics, forming images, creating examples, answering questions, making notes in your own words, and elaborating on the text. Do not try to memorize the author's words—use your own.

Monitor your own comprehension.

Examples
1. Use questioning to check your understanding.
2. When reading speed slows down, decide if the information in the passage is important. If it is, note the problem so you can reread or get help to understand. If it is not important, ignore it.
3. Check your understanding by working with a friend and quizzing one another.

Source: Adapted from B. B. Armbruster and T. H. Anderson. Research synthesis on study skills. *Educational Leadership, 39,* pp. 154–156. Reprinted by permission of the Association for Supervision and Curriculum Development. Copyright © 1981 by ASCD. All rights reserved.

cognitive and metacognitive tools that are difficult for very young children to use (Winne, 1997). And of course, young children are still focusing much of their attention on learning the basics of word recognition.

The Guidelines on page 300 provide a summary of ideas about studying.

Teaching for Transfer

CHECKPOINT

Becoming an Expert Student: Learning Strategies and Study Skills

Review

▷ Distinguish between learning strategies and tactics.

▷ What key functions do learning strategies play?

▷ Describe some procedures for developing learning strategies.

Apply

▷ How would you use study skills to study this chapter?

▷ How could you improve your strategies for taking notes?

Teaching for Transfer

Think back for a moment to a class in one of your high school subjects that you did not go on to study in college. Imagine the teacher, the room, the textbook. Now remember what you actually studied in class. If it was a science class, what were some of the formulas you learned? Oxidation reduction? If you are like most of us, you may remember that you learned these things, but you will not be quite sure exactly what you learned. Were those hours wasted? These questions are about the transfer of learning.

Defining Transfer

Whenever something previously learned influences current learning or when solving an earlier problem affects how you solve a new problem, **transfer** has occurred (Mayer & Wittrock, 1996). If students learn a mathematical principle in first block and use it to solve a physics problem in third block, positive transfer has taken place. Even more rewarding for teachers is when a math principle learned in October is applied to a physics problem in March. However, the effect of past learning on present learning is not always positive. *Functional fixedness* and *response set* are examples of negative transfer because they involve the attempt to apply familiar but *inappropriate* strategies to a new situation.

Specific transfer occurs when a rule, fact, or skill learned in one situation is applied in another, very similar situation—for example, applying rules of punctuation to write a job-application letter or using knowledge of the alphabet to find a word in the dictionary. General transfer involves applying to new problems the principles and attitudes learned in other, often dissimilar situations. Thus, general transfer might mean using problem-solving heuristics to solve issues in your personal life—for example, applying working backward to decide when to call for an appointment to have a dentist check a sore tooth in time to get any necessary treatment done before you leave for spring break.

A Contemporary View of Transfer

Gavriel Salomon and David Perkins (1989) describe two kinds of transfer, termed low-road and high-road transfer. **Low-road transfer** "involves the spontaneous, automatic transfer of highly practised skills, with little need for reflective thinking" (p. 118). The key to low-road transfer is practising a skill often, in a variety of situations, until your performance becomes automatic. So if you worked one summer for a temporary secretarial service and were sent to many different offices to work on all kinds of typewriters and word processors, by the end of the summer

"I DON'T GET IT! THEY MAKE US LEARN READING, WRITING AND ARITHMETIC TO PREPARE US FOR A WORLD OF VIDEOTAPES, COMPUTER TERMINALS AND CALCULATORS!"

(Harley Schwadron. From Phi Delta Kappan.)

Connect & Extend
To your teaching
What transfer in learning the sound "o" could be expected from learning to read the following words?
First group: does oh Spot good dog
Second group: hot stop clock pop Tom
Which group of words is more likely to be found in a Grade 1 basal reading program?

Connect & Extend
To your teaching
What principles do you anticipate teaching that could be expected to have general transfer?

you probably would be able to handle most machines easily. Your practice with many machines would let you transfer your skill automatically to a new situation.

High-road transfer, on the other hand, involves consciously applying abstract knowledge learned in one situation to a different situation. This can happen in one of two ways. You may learn a principle or a strategy, intending to use it in the future. For example, if you plan to apply what you learn in anatomy class this semester to work in a life-drawing course you will take next semester, you may search for principles about human proportions, muscle definition, and so on. This is called *forward-reaching transfer,* because you are looking forward to applying the knowledge gained. *Backward-reaching transfer* occurs when you are faced with a problem and look back on what you have learned in other situations to help you in this new one. Analogical thinking is an example of this kind of transfer. You search for other, related situations that might provide clues to the current problem. The key to high-road transfer is *mindful abstraction,* or the deliberate identification of a principle, main idea, strategy, or procedure that is not tied to one specific problem or situation but could apply to many. Such an abstraction becomes part of your metacognitive knowledge, available to guide future learning and problem solving.

There is one last kind of transfer that is especially important for students—the transfer of learning strategies. As we have seen several times in this book, students may learn new strategies for reading, studying, problem solving, or remembering, and then fail to use those strategies outside the situations where they were learned. But the idea of learning strategies and tactics is that they be applied across a wide range of situations. What gets in the way of strategy transfer? Sometimes students simply don't understand that a particular strategy applies in new situations or they don't know how to adapt it to fit. Perhaps they have practised with only one kind of material or problem and never had the chance to apply the strategy to new material (Schunk, 1996a). Table 8.3 summarizes the types of transfer.

Teaching for Positive Transfer

Years of research and experience show that teachers cannot expect students to automatically transfer what they learn to new problems. Students will master new knowledge, problem-solving procedures, and learning strategies but not use them unless prompted or guided. For example, studies of real-world mathematics show that people do not always apply math procedures learned in school to solve practical problems in their homes or grocery stores (Lave, 1988; Lave & Wenger, 1991). This is because learning is *situated,* that is, learning happens in specific situations. We learn solutions to particular problems, not general all-purpose solutions that can fit any problem. Because knowledge is learned as a tool to solve particular problems, we may not realize that the knowledge is relevant when we

TABLE 8.3   Kinds of Transfer

	Low-Road Transfer	High-Road Transfer
Definition	Automatic transfer of highly practised skill	Conscious application of abstract knowledge to a new situation
Key Conditions	Extensive practice Variety of settings and conditions Overlearning to automaticity	Mindful focus on abstracting a principle, main idea, procedure that can be used in many situations
Examples	Driving many different cars Finding your gate in an airport	Applying PQ4R in reading texts Applying procedures from math in designing a page layout for the school newspaper

encounter a problem that seems different, at least on the surface. We tend to use knowledge only in situations where it is obviously appropriate (Driscoll, 1994; Singley & Anderson, 1989). How can you make sure your students will use what they learn, even when situations change?

What Is Worth Learning? First you must answer the question "What is worth learning?" Learning basic skills such as reading, writing, computing, cooperating, and speaking will definitely transfer to other situations, because these skills are necessary for later work both in and out of school—writing job applications, reading novels, paying bills, working on a team, locating and evaluating health care services, among others. All later learning depends on positive transfer of these basics to new situations.

Teachers must also be aware of what the future is likely to hold for their students, both as a group and as individuals. What will society require of them as adults? What will their careers require of them? As a child, Anita studied nothing about computers. Now she spends hours at her word processor. Computer programming and word processing were not part of her high school curriculum, but learning to use a slide rule was taught. Now calculators and computers have made this skill obsolete. Undoubtedly changes as extreme and unpredictable as these await the students you will teach. For this reason, the general transfer of principles, attitudes, learning strategies, and problem solving will be just as important to your students as the specific transfer of basic skills.

How Can Teachers Help? To have something to transfer, students must first learn and understand. Students will be more likely to transfer information to new situations if they have been actively involved in the learning process. They must be encouraged to form abstractions that they will apply later. For example, Salomon and Perkins (1989) give this advice for teaching history:

> [The] history teacher can introduce direct discussion of contemporary events. To provoke forward-reaching transfer, the teacher can select an episode in history and encourage students to seek contemporary analogs. To provoke backward-reaching transfer, the teacher can choose a current phenomenon. . . and urge students to reach into their historical repertoires for analogies and disanalogies. (p. 136)

Greater transfer can also be ensured by **overlearning**, practising a skill past the point of mastery. Many of the basic facts students learn in elementary school, such as the multiplication tables, are traditionally overlearned. Overlearning helps students retrieve the information quickly and automatically when it is needed.

Stages of Transfer for Strategies. Gary Phye (1992; Phye & Sanders, 1994) suggests we think of the transfer of learning strategies as a tool to be used in a "mindful" way to solve academic problems. He describes three stages in developing strategic transfer. In the acquisition phase, students should not only receive instruction about a strategy and how to use it, but they should also rehearse the strategy and practise being aware of when and how they are using it. In the retention phase, more practice with feedback helps students hone their strategy use. In the transfer phase, the teacher should provide new problems that can be solved with the same strategy, even though the problems appear different on the surface. To enhance motivation, point out to students how using the strategy will help them solve many problems and accomplish different tasks. These steps help build both procedural and conditional knowledge—how to use the strategy as well as when and why.

Newly mastered concepts, principles, and strategies must be practised and applied in a wide variety of situations. Positive transfer is encouraged when skills are used under authentic conditions, similar to those that will exist when the skills are needed later. Students can learn about multiplication by figuring how many

▲ *A challenge for every generation of teachers and learners is to be able to transfer the knowledge they acquire in school and while growing up to situations they'll face in the future.*

Connect & Extend
To life
Why is information that is over-learned resistant to forgetting? Do we overlearn all information that is practised and rehearsed?

Connect & Extend
To the research
Garner, R. (1990). When children and adults do not use learning strategies: Toward a theory of settings. *Review of Educational Research, 60,* 517–530.

Overlearning: Practising a skill past the point of mastery.

Teaching for Transfer

Review

▶ Distinguish between specific and general transfer.

▶ Distinguish between low-road and high-road transfer.

Apply

▶ Why is it important to ask students to apply new knowledge to both well-defined and ill-defined problems?

ways they can make $1.67 using only dimes and pennies. They can learn to write by corresponding with e-mail pen pals in other countries. They can learn historical research methods by researching their own families. Some of these applications should involve complex, ill-defined, unstructured problems, because many of the problems to be faced in later life, in school and out, will not come to students complete with instructions, and applications should include situations outside school. The Family and Community Partnerships Guidelines give ideas for enlisting the support of families in encouraging transfer.

This chapter has covered quite a bit of territory, partly because the cognitive perspective has so many implications for instruction. Although they are varied, you can see that most of the cognitive ideas for teaching concepts, problem-solving skills, and learning strategies emphasize the role of the student's prior knowledge and the need for active, mindful learning.

FAMILY AND COMMUNITY PARTNERSHIPS

Promoting Transfer

Keep families informed about their child's curriculum so they can support learning.

Examples

1. At the beginning of units or major projects, send a letter summarizing the key goals, a few of the major assignments, and some common problems students have in learning the material for that unit.
2. Ask parents for suggestions about how their child's interests could be connected to the curriculum topics.

Give families ideas for how they might practise, extend, or apply learning from school.

Examples

1. To extend writing, ask parents to encourage their children to write letters or e-mail to companies or civic organizations asking for information or free products. Provide a shell letter form for structure and ideas and include addresses of companies that provide free samples or information.
2. Ask family members to include their children in some projects that require measurement, halving or doubling recipes, or estimating costs.

3. Suggest students work with grandparents to do a family memory book. Combine historical research and writing.

Show connections between learning in school and life outside.

Examples

1. Ask families to talk about and show how they use the skills their children are learning in jobs, hobbies, or community involvement projects.
2. Ask family members to come to class to demonstrate how they use reading, writing, science, math, or other knowledge in their work.

Make families partners in practising learning strategies.

Examples

1. Focus on one learning tactic at a time—ask families to simply remind their children to use a particular tactic with homework that week.
2. Develop a lending library of books and videotapes to teach families about learning strategies.
3. Give parents a copy of the Becoming an Expert Student Guidelines on page 300, rewritten for your grade level.

Summary

Learning and Teaching about Concepts

Distinguish between prototypes and exemplars.

Concepts are categories used to group similar events, ideas, people, or objects. A prototype is the best representative of its category. For instance, the best representative of the "birds" category for many Canadians might be a robin. Exemplars are our actual memories of specific birds and so on that we use to compare with an item in question to see if that item belongs in the same category as our exemplar. We probably learn concepts from prototypes or exemplars of the category, understand in terms of our schematic knowledge, and then refine concepts through our additional experience of relevant and irrelevant features.

What are the four elements needed in concept teaching?

Lessons about concepts include four basic components: concept name, definition, attributes, and examples (along with non-examples). The concept attainment model is one approach to teaching concepts that asks students to form hypotheses about why particular examples are members of a category and what that category (concept) might be.

What are the key characteristics of Bruner's discovery learning?

In discovery learning, the teacher presents examples and the students work with the examples until they discover the interrelationships—the subject's structure. Bruner believes that classroom learning should take place through inductive reasoning, that is, by using specific examples to formulate a general principle. Encouraging inductive thinking in this way is sometimes called the eg-rule method.

What are the stages of Ausubel's expository teaching?

Ausubel believes that learning should progress deductively: from the gener-al to the specific, or from the rule or principle to examples. After presenting an advance organizer, the next step in a lesson using Ausubel's approach is to present content in terms of basic similarities and differences, using specific examples. Finally, when all the material has been presented, ask students to discuss how the examples can be used to expand on the original advance organizer.

Problem Solving

What are the steps in the general problem-solving process?

Problem solving is both general and domain-specific. The five stages of problem solving are: identifying the problem (and perhaps seeing the problem as an opportunity); understanding the problem through representation and setting goals; exploring possible solutions; anticipating possible consequences of the strategies and then implementing one strategy; and evaluating the results and learning from the results. Bransford and Stein use the acronym IDEAL to identify the five steps: Identify the problem, Define goals and represent the problem, Explore possible strategies, Anticipate outcomes and Act, Look back and Learn.

Why is the representation stage of problem solving so important?

A critical element in solving problems in school is representing the problem accurately, showing understanding of both the whole problem and its discrete elements. Schema training may improve this ability. The problem-solving process follows entirely different paths, depending on what representation and goal are chosen. If your representation of the problem suggests an immediate solution, the task is done: the new problem is recognized as a "disguised" version of an old problem with a clear solution. But if there is no existing way of solving the problem or if the activated schema fails, students must search for a solu-tion. The application of algorithms and heuristics—such as means-ends analysis, analogical thinking, working backward, and verbalization—may help students solve problems.

Describe factors that can interfere with problem solving.

Factors that hinder problem solving include functional fixedness or rigidity (response set). These disallow the flexibility needed to represent problems accurately and to have insight into solutions.

What are the differences between expert and novice knowledge in a given area?

Expert problem solvers have a rich store of declarative, procedural, and conditional knowledge. They organize this knowledge around general principles or patterns that apply to large classes of problems. They work faster, remember relevant information, and monitor their progress better than novices. The same is true for expert teachers. Accomplishing many classroom tasks has become automatic, so that routines are smooth. Less class time is wasted. Experts have a rich store of well-organized knowledge about the many specific situations of teaching.

How do misconceptions interfere with learning?

If the students' intuitive models include misconceptions and inaccuracies, then the students are likely to develop inadequate or misleading representations of a problem. To learn new information and solve problems, students must sometimes "unlearn" common-sense ideas.

Becoming an Expert Student: Learning Strategies and Study Skills

Distinguish between learning strategies and tactics.

Learning strategies are ideas for accomplishing learning goals, a kind of overall plan of attack. Learning tactics are the specific techniques that make up the plan. A strategy for learning might include a pattern of several tactics, such as mnemonics to remember key terms, skimming to identify the organization, and then writing answers to possible essay questions. Using tactics and strategies reflects metacognitive knowledge.

What key functions do learning strategies play?

Learning strategies help students *become cognitively engaged*—focus attention on the relevant or important aspects of the material. Second, they encourage students to *invest effort*, make connections, elaborate, translate, organize, and reorganize to *think and process deeply*—the greater the practice and processing, the stronger the learning. Finally, strategies help students *monitor and regulate* their own learning—keep track of what is making sense and notice when a new approach is needed.

Describe some procedures for developing learning strategies.

Expose students to a number of different tactics and strategies, not only general learning strategies but also specific tactics, such as the graphic tactics. Teach conditional knowledge about when, where, and why to use various strategies. Develop motivation to use the strategies and tactics by showing students how their learning and performance can be improved. Provide direct instruction in content knowledge needed to use the strategies.

Teaching for Transfer

Distinguish between specific and general transfer.

Specific transfer occurs when a rule, fact, or skill learned in one situation is applied in another, very similar, situation; for example, applying rules of punctuation to write a job-application letter. General transfer involves applying to new problems the principles and attitudes learned in other, often dissimilar, situations.

Distinguish between low-road and high-road transfer.

Transfer involving spontaneity and automaticity in familiar situations has been called *low-road* transfer. *High-road* transfer involves reflection and conscious application of abstract knowledge to new situations. Teachers can promote thinking and learning skills by teaching for mastery and for the positive, general transfer of knowledge. In addition, teachers can help students transfer learning strategies by teaching strategies directly, providing practice with feedback, and then expanding the application of the strategies to new and unfamiliar situations.

*K*ey Terms

Becoming a Professional

Reflecting on the Chapter

Can you apply the ideas from this chapter on complex cognitive processes to solve the following problems of practice?

Preschool and Kindergarten

▶ Several students in your class still have trouble discriminating between simple shapes. What would you do to help them understand?

Elementary and Middle School

▶ Students in your class are having a really hard time with the concepts of heat and energy. What would you do?

Junior High and High School

▶ Students in your math class can solve problems for homework, but become confused on tests that cover several chapters. They don't seem to know when to apply one procedure and when to use another. How would you help them?

▶ You decide to give an essay test that requires original thinking and creativity. Your students perform very poorly and protest loudly that the test is "unfair." They want to use the definitions and facts they have so carefully memorized. What would you do?

Check Your Understanding

▶ Know the basic features of concept teaching.

▶ Know the five common steps in problem solving.

▶ Be familiar with the notion of intuitive or naive conceptions.

▶ Be familiar with a range of learning strategies and tactics.

Your Teaching Portfolio

Use Table 8.2 plus the section titled *Learning Strategies and Tactics* to generate ideas for appropriate learning strategies and tactics for the students you will teach and include these ideas in your portfolio.

Teaching Resources

Add Figures 8.5 "Four Different Ways to Represent a Problem," 8.8 "A Map To Guide Note Taking," 8.9 "A Map to Organize Studying and Learning," and Table 8.2 to your file of teaching resources.

Use the Family and Community Partnerships Guidelines to brainstorm ideas for family involvement in helping your students "take their learning home."

Weblinks

http://library.usask.ca/ustudy/critical/index.html

At this site developed at the University of Saskatchewan, you'll find information about critical thinking and problem solving. The site includes several references.

www.cloudnet.com/~edrbsass/edcreative.htm

How do classroom teachers plan lessons for problem solving? Try out your skill at finding correspondences between research findings and classrooms at this site. It provides sketches for lots(!) of lesson plans that teachers have generated to involve their students in learning problem solving.

www.muskingum.edu/~cal/database/database.html

This site presents the Learning Strategies Database, a collection of information on learning strategies compiled over a 10-year period. Sources include books, professional journals, and presentations from professional meetings.

TEACHERS' CASEBOOK

What Would They Do?

Here is how two practising teachers responded to the teaching situation presented at the beginning of this chapter about a discovery lesson that went wrong.

PATRICIA BELL

Prime Minister's Award for Teaching Excellence, Certificate of Excellence
Centennial Collegiate Vocational Institute
Guelph, Ontario

Investigating the causes for poor results on an assignment and working toward a solution can be as rewarding as a teacher evaluation survey! I am constantly learning from my students.

This particular assignment, a comparison contrast demanding a personal evaluation, requires higher-level thinking skills. This cannot be achieved in a single step. These students should have written a critical analysis on one poem; received teacher comments positively reinforcing personal insights supported by evidence from the poem; discussed, in class, tactics for comparing two poems; examined and evaluated sample pieces of writing that demonstrate assignment expectations; practised comparison writing in class; done peer marking of the comparison piece—all before finally submitting a polished comparison to the teacher.

I would re-examine the steps I used leading up to the assignment; determine if there was adequate foundation for the assignment; and divide the process up into smaller, more manageable units of writing for this class, to lead them progressively to an assignment requiring synthesis. I would also ask myself if the students were engaged in the process. Perhaps I could capture their interest by having them compare two popular songs, with emphasis on providing evidence from the songs to support their personal attitudes. I would use a variety of teaching strategies each step of the way to meet the needs of students with various learning styles.

In the end, I would encourage and reassure the students, and explain that the process is as important as the product and that they will be progressing from this initial experience toward better results on similar assignments.

JANICE ADAMS

Vaters Junior High
St. John's, Newfoundland

The problem with this assignment, as I see it, is twofold. First, there is a lack of previous experience talking and writing about poems. Second, there is an absence of what I call "scaffolding" experiences, which are necessary when introducing a new writing form, in this case, the compare/contrast essay.

Before I would expect students to compare-contrast two poems, we would have had a variety of experiences with poetry, some of them spontaneous, fuelled by student questions after the daily reading of our "poem for the week"; and other teacher-guided group discussions that resulted in more formal responses to a particular poem.

My goal is for students to see that poetry, like any literature, is the writer's attempt to capture an experience, real or fictitious. The experience might involve an event, a story, an emotion, a scene, a contemplation, an idea, or maybe a realization. Discussing who might be speaking in the poem, to whom she or he might be speaking, and why, are crucial in helping students connect with the poem. Also important is identifying language devices, forms, word choice, and uses of figurative language the poet has chosen to "capture" her or his thoughts. As well, students should consider possible reasons for, and alternatives to, these choices. Not only do such experiences foster a comfortableness with poetry, but they also build a store of knowledge about this genre.

Because I feel compare-contrast is such a valuable cross-curricular writing form, I sequence and structure the initial writing experience very carefully. First, we would experience two different treatments of a subject or a book. In my mystery and wonder unit, which I entitled "Things Are Not Always What They Appear to Be," we read Chris Van Allsburg's *Jumanji* and then watch the film. Next, I pass out a sheet that has one column for noting the similarities and one for the differences. The differences column is subdivided for notes on the book and those on the movie. As a class, we write down as many similarities and differences as we can generate. Often, I will have the students rank these prewriting notes to determine which ones are most significant.

On a second page, I have examples of a paragraph dealing with similarities and one showing contrasts. I emphasize the use of appropriate transitional language, such as *first, second, in addition, finally*, etc. I emphasize, too, the importance of using words that signal contrast, such as *while, however*, and *unlike*. Third, the students write out drafts of these two paragraphs using their selected notes. Fourth, I introduce the introductory paragraph with its lead sentence and a simple thesis statement. We then work on a closing paragraph, which might include an account of what version they preferred or reasons why they thought the book and the movie were so different.

The students must then combine all these first-draft paragraphs into a final essay. I pass out a sheet outlining the evaluation criteria that must be attached to the final piece. With this step-by-step process, it's rare to find a student who can't succeed in a first attempt at comparing and contrasting two texts.

By the spring, when I require the students to write a compare-contrast essay on two poems, the students have a structure in place and many ways of looking at poems that allow most of the students to handle this task successfully.

![9]

Social Cognitive and Constructivist Views of Learning

What have you heard about cognitive apprenticeships? Inquiry? Cooperative learning? Reciprocal teaching? What comes to mind when you hear these terms?

In the past three chapters we analyzed different aspects of learning. We considered behavioural and information processing explanations of what people learn and how they learn it. We also examined complex cognitive processes such as concept learning and problem solving. These explanations about learning focus on the individual and what is happening in his or her "head." But recent perspectives on learning have called attention to two other aspects of learning that are critical—social factors and cultural factors. In this chapter we look at the role of other people and the cultural context in learning.

Two general theoretical frames include social and cultural factors as major elements: social learning or social cognitive views, and sociocultural constructivist theories. Rather than debating the merits of each approach, we will consider the contributions of different models of instruction, grounded in different theories of learning. Don't feel that you must choose the "best" approach—there is no such thing. The goal of all the different models is to create situations in which students learn, understand, and remember. Even though theorists argue about which model is best, most excellent teachers learn from all the approaches and apply them as appropriate.

By the time you have completed this chapter, you should be able to:

▶ Summarize the elements of social cognitive theory.

▶ Describe situations in which a teacher might use modelling.

▶ Explain three constructivist perspectives on learning.

▶ Incorporate into your teaching inquiry learning, problem-based learning, and cooperative groups.

▶ Design lessons that include instructional conversations and apprenticeships in thinking.

What Would You Do?

You have finally landed a job teaching English and writing in a high school. Over the summer, you plan your World Literature course, pick books you really enjoyed in high school, and add new selections that relate to recent films. The first day of class, you discover that a number of students appear to have limited English proficiency. You make a mental note to meet with them to determine how much and what kind of reading they can handle. To get a sense of the class's interest, you ask students to write a "review" of the last book they read, as if they were on TV doing a "Book Beat" program. There is a bit of grumbling, but the students seem to be writing, so you take a few minutes to try to talk with one of the students for whom English is not a first language.

That night you look over the "book reviews." Either the students are giving you a hard time or no one has read anything lately. Two students try to write about the Bible but they refuse to review it. Several mention a text from another class but their reviews are one-sentence evaluations—usually containing the words "lame" or "useless" (often misspelled). If the paragraphs are any indication, these students can't put four sentences together and stay on the same topic. The papers of three students form a stark contrast—they are a pleasure to read, worthy of publication in the school literary magazine (if there were one), and reflect a fairly sophisticated understanding of good literature.

▶ How would you adapt your plans for this group?

▶ What will you do tomorrow?

▶ What teaching approaches do you think will work with this class?

▶ How will you work with the three students who are more advanced?

Social Processes in Learning

When you consider the English class just described, do you think about social and cultural influences on the students' learning? Reading and books seem to have very different meanings among students in the class. And the students probably have seen different models of reading in their lives outside school. In the following pages we will discuss how people learn through interactions with others and how observation, modelling, dialogue, and culture affect learning. Understanding the role of social processes in learning has become increasingly important in educational psychology. As Carol Goodenow (1993) noted almost a decade ago:

> Education is fundamentally a social and interpersonal process. Although individuals can and do learn many things through isolated observation of the world around them, personal experimentation and experience, and solitary reading, for the most part what we term education (i.e., "schooling") occurs in the company of others. (p. 177)

The first perspective we will examine that adds social considerations to an explanation of learning is the work of Albert Bandura (1977, 1986, 1997), a Canadian who teaches at Stanford University in California. In the early 1960s he demonstrated that people can learn by observing the actions and consequences of others.

Social Learning and Social Cognitive Theories

In Chapter 6 we discussed behavioural views of learning. Although Bandura's early work on learning was grounded in behavioural principles of reinforcement and

Connect & Extend
To your teaching
Here is a common example of the use of modelling. In Mrs. B's Grade 2 classroom, the use of vicarious reinforcement brings many positive results: improved concentration, neater work habits, responsible behaviour, interest, and enthusiasm for extra projects. As the children were working on a social studies project, Mrs. B. noticed that at a table with four children, two were concentrating and two were fooling around. Her comments to the two children who were working helped the other two children to focus their attention back onto their tasks. "Why, Christine and Robert, you're doing such a fine job on your map. I can tell you're concentrating and putting your best effort into it." When she noticed that the other two had gone back to work, she commented, "I'm happy to see that you're both working so well. You do such a nice job when you concentrate." All four children worked responsibly throughout the rest of the period. Similar procedures are used to help achieve neat work habits and responsible behaviour.

punishment, he challenged and expanded behavioural conceptions of learning by adding social factors. He believed that the traditional behavioural views of learning were accurate but incomplete. Behavioural views overlooked important elements, particularly social influences on learning. Bandura's early work focused on social behaviour, particularly the behaviour of others. For this reason, his earlier work was labelled **social learning theory** and was considered a *neo-behavioural* approach (Bandura, 1977).

To explain some limitations of the behavioural model, Bandura distinguishes between the *knowledge* (learning) that people have acquired and the *observable performance based on that knowledge* (behaviour). In other words, Bandura suggested that we may know more than we show. An example is found in one of Bandura's early studies (1965). Preschool children saw a film in which a model, a child of the same age, kicked and punched a metre-tall, inflatable "Bobo" doll. (Bobo was the brand name of this toy.) One group saw the model rewarded for this aggressive behaviour. Another group saw the model punished, and a third group saw no consequences. When the children who watched one of these three films were moved to a room with the doll, the children who had seen punching and kicking rewarded on the film were the most aggressive toward the doll. Those who had seen the attacks punished were the least aggressive. But when the children were promised rewards for imitating the model's aggression, all of them demonstrated that they had learned the behaviour. The incentives affected performance. Even though learning may have occurred, it may not be demonstrated until the learner perceives that the situation is "right," that is, when there are incentives to perform. This might explain why some students don't perform "bad behaviour" such as swearing or smoking that are modelled by their peers. For these students, personal consequences may discourage performing the behaviour. It's important to note that social consequences are not necessarily the whole story. Children may have learned how to write the alphabet but perform badly because their limited fine-motor coordination prevents writing neatly—their poor performance is not an indication of their learning. Students may have learned how to simplify fractions but perform badly on a test because they are anxious or ill or misread the problem.

Recently, Bandura's research has focused on cognitive factors such as beliefs, self-perceptions, and expectations, so, his theory is now called a **social cognitive theory**. Social cognitive theory distinguishes between enactive and vicarious learning. *Enactive learning* is gaining knowledge by doing and personally experiencing the consequences of your actions. This may sound like operant conditioning all over again, but it is not. The difference has to do with the role of consequences. Proponents of operant conditioning believe that consequences strengthen or weaken behaviour. In enactive learning, however, consequences are seen as providing information to the learner. Our interpretations of the consequences create expectations, influence motivation, and shape beliefs (Schunk, 2000). We will see many examples of enactive learning—learning by doing—later in the chapter when we consider inquiry learning, problem-based learning, cognitive apprenticeships, and other approaches.

Vicarious learning is gaining knowledge by observing others. People and even animals can learn merely by observing another person or animal learn. This fact challenges the behaviourist idea that cognitive factors are unnecessary in an explanation of learning. If people can learn by watching, they must be focusing their attention, constructing images, remembering, analyzing, and making decisions that affect what they do later. A lot goes on mentally before performance and reinforcement can even take place.

In both the earlier and the more recent versions of Bandura's theory, the role of observation in learning is an important factor.

▲ *Albert Bandura expanded on behavioural theories to develop the social cognitive theory of learning.*

Social Learning Theory: Theory that emphasizes learning through observation of others.

Social Cognitive Theory: Theory that adds concern with cognitive factors such as beliefs, self-perceptions, and expectations to social learning theory.

Learning by Observing Others

Through **observational learning** we learn not only how to perform a behaviour but also what is likely to happen to us in specific situations if we do perform it. Observation can be a very efficient learning process. Let's look more closely at how observational learning occurs. Bandura (1986) notes that there are four important elements to be considered in observational learning. They are *paying attention*, *retaining information or impressions*, *producing behaviour*, and *being motivated* to repeat the behaviour.

Attention. To learn through observation, we have to pay attention. In teaching, you will have to ensure students' attention to critical features of the lesson by making clear presentations and highlighting important points. In demonstrating a skill (for example, threading a sewing machine or focusing a microscope), you may need to have students look over your shoulder or along your forearm as you demonstrate. Seeing your hands from the same perspective as they see their own helps direct their attention to the essential features of the situation and makes observational learning easier.

Retention. To imitate the behaviour of a model, you have to remember it. This involves mentally representing the model's actions in some way, probably as verbal steps ("Hwa-Rang, the eighth form in tae kwan do, is a palm-heel block, then a middle riding stance punch, then . . ."), or as visual images, or both. Retention can be improved by mentally rehearsing (imagining imitating the behaviour) as well as by actual practice. In the retention phase of observational learning, practice helps us remember the elements of the desired behaviour, such as the sequence of steps.

Production. Once we "know" how a behaviour should look and feel, and remember the elements or steps, we still may not perform it smoothly. Sometimes we need a great deal of practice, feedback, and coaching about subtle points before we can reproduce the behaviour of the model. In the production phase, practice with feedback about how we are performing makes the behaviour smoother and more expert.

Social cognitive theories of learning consider the importance of learning by doing and learning by observing others. ▼

Motivation and Reinforcement. As mentioned earlier, social learning theory distinguishes between acquisition and performance. We may acquire a new skill or behaviour through observation, but we may not perform that behaviour until there is some motivation or incentive to do so. Reinforcement can play several roles in observational learning. If we anticipate being reinforced for imitating the actions of a model, we may be more motivated to pay attention, remember, and reproduce the behaviour. In addition, reinforcement is important in maintaining learning. A person who tries a new behaviour is unlikely to persist without reinforcement (Barton, 1981; Ollendick, Dailey, & Shapiro, 1983). For example, if an unpopular student adopted the dress style of the "in" group but was greeted with teasing and ridicule, it is unlikely that the imitation would continue.

Bandura identifies three forms of reinforcement that can encourage observational learning. First, of course, the observer may reproduce the behaviour of the model and receive direct reinforcement, as when a

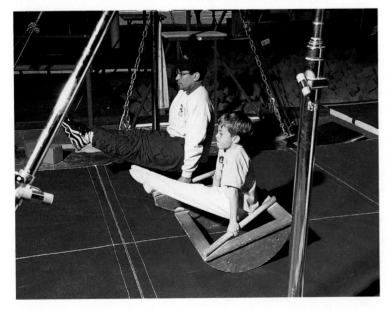

gymnast successfully executes a front flip/round-off combination and the coach/model says, "Excellent!"

But the reinforcement need not be direct—it may be **vicarious reinforcement**. The observer may simply see others reinforced for a particular behaviour and then increase his or her production of that behaviour. For example, if you compliment two students during class on the attractive illustrations in their lab reports, several other students who observe your compliments may turn in illustrated lab reports next time. Most TV ads hope for this kind of effect. People in commercials become deliriously happy when they drive a particular car or drink a specific brand of juice, and the viewer is supposed to do the same: the viewer's behaviour is reinforced vicariously by the actors' obvious pleasure. Punishment can also be vicarious: you may hesitate to ask questions in a seminar after observing classmates being put down for doing the same.

The final form of reinforcement is self-reinforcement, that is, controlling your own reinforcers. This sort of reinforcement is important for both students and teachers. We want our students to improve not only because it can lead to external rewards but also because the students value and enjoy their growing competence. For a teacher, sometimes self-reinforcement is the main thing that keeps you going.

Factors That Influence Observational Learning. What causes an individual to learn and perform modelled behaviour and skills? Several factors play a role, as shown in Table 9.1. The developmental level of the observer makes a difference. As children grow older, they are able to focus attention for longer periods of time, use memory strategies to retain information, and motivate themselves to practise. A second influence is the status of the model. Children are more likely to imitate the actions of others who seem competent, powerful, and prestigious. So, depending on the age and interests of the child, models may include parents, teachers, older siblings, Barney, athletes, action heroes, rock stars, and TV personalities. Third, by watching others, we also learn which behaviour is appropriate for people like ourselves, so we most readily imitate models whom we see as similar to us.

Vicarious Reinforcement: Increasing the chances that we will repeat a behaviour by observing another person being reinforced for that behaviour.

TABLE 9.1   Factors That Affect Observational Learning

Characteristic	Effects on Modelling
Developmental Status	Improvements with development include longer attention and increased capacity to process information, use strategies, compare performances with memorial representations, and adopt intrinsic motivators.
Model Prestige and Competence	Observers pay greater attention to competent, high-status models. Consequences of modeled behaviours convey information about functional value. Observers attempt to learn actions they believe they will need to perform.
Vicarious Consequences	Consequences to models convey information about behavioural appropriateness and likely outcomes of actions. Valued consequences motivate observers. Similarity in attributes or competence signals appropriateness and heightens motivation.
Outcome Expectations	Observers are more likely to perform modeled actions they believe are appropriate and will result in rewarding outcomes.
Goal Setting	Observers are likely to attend to models who demonstrate behaviours that help observers attain goals.
Self-efficacy	Observers attend to models when they believe they are capable of learning or performing the modelled behaviour. Observation of similar models affects self-efficacy ("If they can do it, I can too").

Source: From *Learning Theories: An Education Perspective,* 3/e, p. 121, by D. H. Schunk, 2000, Saddle River, NJ: Prentice-Hall, Inc. Copyright © 2000 by Prentice-Hall, Inc. Adapted with permission.

All students need to see successful, capable models who look and sound like them, no matter what their ethnicity, socioeconomic status, or sex.

The last three influences involve goals and expectations. If observers expect that certain of a model's actions will lead to particular outcomes (for example, particular practice regimens leading to improved athletic performance), and, if the observers value those outcomes or goals, the observers are more likely to pay attention to the models and try to reproduce their behaviour. Finally, observers are more likely to learn from models if the observers have a high level of **self-efficacy**—that is, if they believe they are capable of doing the actions needed to reach the goals, or they are capable at least of learning how to become capable (Bandura, 1997; Pintrich & Schunk, 1996). We will discuss goals, expectations, and self-efficacy in greater depth in the chapter on motivation.

Observational Learning in Teaching

There are five possible outcomes of observational learning: directing attention, encouraging existing behaviour, changing inhibitions, teaching new behaviour and attitudes, and arousing emotions. Let's look at each of these as they occur in classrooms.

Directing Attention. By observing others, we not only learn about actions, but we also notice the objects involved in the actions. For example, in a preschool class, when one child plays enthusiastically with a toy that has been ignored for days, many other children may want to have the toy, even if they play with it in different ways or simply carry it around. This happens, in part, because the children's attention has been drawn to that particular toy.

Fine-Tuning Already-Learned Behaviour. All of us have had the experience of looking for cues from other people when we find ourselves in unfamiliar situations. Observing the behaviour of others tells us which of our already-learned behaviour to use: the proper fork for eating the salad, when to raise your hand to ask a question, what kind of language is appropriate, and so on. Adopting the dress and grooming styles of TV idols is another example of this kind of effect.

Strengthening or Weakening Inhibitions. If class members witness one student breaking a class rule and getting away with it, they may learn that undesirable consequences do not always follow rule breaking. The students may be less inhibited in the future about breaking the class rule. If the rule breaker is a well-liked, high-status class leader, the effect of the modelling may be even more pronounced. One psychologist has called this phenomenon the **ripple effect** (Kounin, 1970). The ripple effect can work to the teacher's benefit. When the teacher deals effectively (not necessarily harshly) with a rule breaker, especially a class leader, the idea of breaking the rule may be inhibited for other students who view the interaction. This does not mean that teachers must reprimand each student who breaks a rule. But once a teacher has called for a particular action, following through is an important part of capitalizing on the ripple effect.

Teaching New Behaviour. Modelling has long been used, of course, to teach

Teachers must draw students' attention to the critical features of a lesson by making clear presentations and highlighting important details. Good demonstrations allow students to focus on the important features and make observational learning easier. ▼

dance, sports, and crafts, as well as skills in subjects such as home economics, chemistry, and industrial arts. Modelling can also be applied deliberately in the classroom to teach cognitive skills and to broaden horizons—to teach new ways of thinking. Teachers serve as models for a vast range of behaviour, from pronouncing vocabulary words, to reacting to the seizure of a student with epilepsy, to being enthusiastic about learning. For example, a teacher might model thinking skills by thinking "out loud" about a student's question. Or a high school teacher concerned about girls who seem to have stereotyped ideas about careers might invite women with non-traditional jobs to speak to the class.

Modelling, when applied deliberately, can be an effective and efficient means of teaching new behaviour (Bandura, 1986; Schunk, 1987). Studies indicate that modelling can be most effective when the teacher makes use of all the elements of observational learning described in the previous section, especially reinforcement and practice with feedback about how to improve the behaviour that leads to a result or product (Butler & Winne, 1995).

Models who are the same age as the students may be particularly effective. For example, Schunk and Hanson (1985) compared two methods for teaching subtraction to Grade 2 students who had difficulties learning this skill. One group of the students observed other Grade 2 students learning the procedures, then participated in an instructional program on subtraction. Another group of students watched a teacher's demonstration, then participated in the same instructional program. Of the two groups, the students who observed peer models learning not only scored higher on tests of subtraction after instruction, but also gained more confidence in their own ability to learn. For students who doubt their own abilities, a good model is a low-achieving student who keeps trying and ultimately masters the material (Schunk, 2000).

Arousing Emotion. Finally, through observational learning people may develop emotional reactions to situations they have never experienced personally, such as flying or driving. A child who watches a friend falling from a swing and breaking an arm may become fearful of swings. Students may be anxious when they are assigned to a certain teacher because they've heard frightening stories about how "mean" that teacher is. Note that hearing and reading about a situation are forms of observation. Some terrible examples of modelling occur with "copy-cat killings" in schools. When frightening things happen to people who are similar in age or circumstances to your students, they may need to talk about their emotions. The Guidelines on page 318 will give you some ideas about using observational learning in the classroom.

Reciprocal Determinism

In social cognitive theory both internal and external factors are important. Environmental events, personal factors, and behaviour are seen as interacting in the process of learning. Personal factors (beliefs, expectations, attitudes, and knowledge), the physical and social environment (resources, other people, physical settings, and consequences of actions), and behaviour (individual actions, choices, and verbal statements) all influence and are influenced by each other. Bandura calls this mutual interaction of forces reciprocal determinism.

> In the social cognitive view people are neither driven by inner forces, nor are they automatically shaped and controlled by external stimuli. Rather, human functioning is explained in terms of a model of triadic reciprocity in which behaviour, cognitive and other personal factors, and environmental events all operate as interacting determinants of each other. (Bandura, 1986, p. 18)

Think for a minute about the power of reciprocal determinism in human interactions. If personal factors, behaviour, and the environment are in constant interaction, cycles of events are progressive and self-perpetuating. For example, a

"DAD, CAN YOU READ?"

GUIDELINES

Using Observational Learning

Model behaviour and attitudes you want your students to learn.

Examples
1. Show enthusiasm for the subject you teach.
2. Be willing to demonstrate both the mental and the physical tasks you expect the students to perform. Anita once saw a teacher sit down in the sandbox while her four-year-old students watched her demonstrate the difference between "playing with sand" and "throwing sand."
3. When reading to students, model good problem solving. Stop and say, "Now let me see if I remember what happened so far," or "That was a hard sentence. I'm going to read it again."
4. Model good problem solving—think out loud as you work through a difficult problem.

Use peers, especially class leaders, as models.

Examples
1. In group work, pair students who do well with those who are having difficulties.
2. Ask students to demonstrate the difference between "whispering" and "silence—no talking."

Make sure students see that positive behaviour leads to reinforcement for others.

Examples
1. Point out the connections between positive behaviour and positive consequences in stories.
2. Be fair in giving reinforcement. The same rules for rewards should apply to the problem students as to the good students.

Enlist the help of class leaders in modelling behaviour for the entire class.

Examples
1. Ask a well-liked student to be friendly to an isolated, fearful student.
2. Let high-status students lead an activity when you need class cooperation or when students are likely to be reluctant at first. Popular students can model dialogues in foreign-language classes or be the first to tackle dissection procedures in biology.

---

new student walks into class late. The student has a tattoo and several visible pierced body parts. The student is actually anxious and hopes to do better at this new school, but the teacher's initial reaction to the late entry and dramatic appearance is a bit hostile. The student feels insulted and responds in kind. So, the teacher begins to form expectations about the student, is more vigilant and less trusting, and the student decides that this school will be just as worthless as his previous one—so why bother to try. The teacher sees the student's disengagement, invests less effort in teaching him, and on and on.

Social cognitive theories study the impact of social factors on individuals—the direction of the influence is from social processes outside the learner to the mind inside the learner. But there are other perspectives on learning that include a much wider range of social processes, such as cultural and historical factors. These other perspectives focus on constructions of knowledge that occur between people, not just within them. Many of these ideas began

CHECKPOINT

Social Learning and Social Cognitive Theories

Review

▷ Distinguish between social learning and social cognitive theories.

▷ Distinguish between enactive and vicarious learning.

▷ What are the elements of observational learning?

▷ What is reciprocal determinism?

Apply

▷ Describe how observational learning and modelling might be used to help the students described at the beginning of the chapter to write better book reviews.

in anthropology or sociology and have been brought into educational psychology to help us paint a more complete picture of learning. Because these are influential theories, we will spend the rest of the chapter learning more about them.

Constructivism: View that emphasizes the active role of the learner in building understanding and making sense of information.

Constructivism and Situated Learning

Consider this situation:

> A young child who has never been to the hospital is in her bed in the pediatric wing. The nurse at the station down the hall calls over the intercom above the bed, "Hi Chelsea, how are you doing? Do you need anything?" The girl looks puzzled and does not answer. The nurse repeats the question with the same result. Finally, the nurse says emphatically, "Chelsea, are you there? Say something!" The little girl responds tentatively, "Hello wall—I'm here."

Chelsea has encountered a new situation—a talking wall. The wall is persistent. It sounds like a grown-up wall. She shouldn't talk to strangers, but she is not sure about walls. She uses what she knows and what the situation provides to *construct* meaning and to act. Constructivist theories of learning focus on how people make meaning.

Connect & Extend
To the research
Marshall, H. H. (Ed.) (1992).
*Redefining Student Learning:
Roots of educational Change.*
Norwood, NJ: Ablex.

Constructivist Views of Learning

Constructivism, "a vast and woolly area in contemporary psychology, epistemology, and education" (von Glaserfeld, 1997, p. 204), is a broad term used by philosophers, curriculum designers, psychologists, educators, and others. Most people who use the term emphasize "the learner's contribution to meaning and learning through both individual and social activity" (Bruning, Schraw, & Ronning, 1999, p. 215). Constructivist perspectives are grounded in the research of theorists such as Jean Piaget, Lev Vygotsky, F. C. Bartlett, Jerome Bruner, and the Gestalt psychologists, as well as the educational philosophy of John Dewey, to mention just a few of the intellectual roots.

There are a variety of constructivist theories of learning. Most theories in contemporary cognitive science include some kind of constructivism because they assume that individuals construct their own cognitive structures as they interpret their experiences in particular situations (Palincsar, 1998). There are constructivist approaches in science education, literacy, in educational psychology and

◀ *Constructivist and situated views of learning challenge other perspectives that see the learner as "receiver and processor of knowledge." Constructivist views see learners as having more interactive roles.*

anthropology, and in computer-based education. But even though many psychologists and educators use the term "constructivism," they often mean quite different things (Marshall, 1996; Phillips, 1997). Some constructivist views focus on how individuals make meaning; others emphasize the *shared, social construction of knowledge* (Driscoll, 1994; Iran-Nejad, 1990; Perkins, 1991; Spiro, Feltovich, Jacobson, & Coulson, 1991; Tobin, 1990; von Glaserfeld, 1990; Wittrock, 1992). Thus, one way to organize constructivist views is to talk about two forms of constructivism: psychological constructivism and social constructivism (Palincsar, 1998; Phillips, 1997).

Psychological/Individual Constructivism. Psychological constructivists "are concerned with how *individuals* build up certain elements of their cognitive or emotional apparatus" (Phillips, 1997, p. 153). These constructivists are interested in individual knowledge, beliefs, self-concept, or identity, so they are sometimes called *individual* constructivists. They all focus on the inner psychological life of people. Using these standards, the most recent information processing theories are constructivist (Mayer, 1996). Information processing approaches to learning regard the human mind as a symbol processing system. This system converts sensory input into structures of symbols (propositions, images, or schemas), and then processes (rehearses or elaborates) those symbol structures so knowledge can be held in memory and retrieved. According to this view, the outside world is a source of input but, once the sensations are perceptually processed and enter working memory, the important work is assumed to be happening "inside the head" of the individual (Schunk, 2000; Vera & Simon, 1993; Winne, 1995).

Even though information processing theorists talk about meaning and knowledge construction, many psychologists believe that information processing is "trivial constructivism" because the individual's only constructive contribution is to build accurate representations of the outside world (Derry, 1992; Garrison, 1995; Marshall, 1996). In contrast, Piaget's psychological constructivist perspective is less concerned with "correct" representations and more interested in meaning as the individual constructs it. As we saw in Chapter 2, Piaget proposed a sequence of cognitive stages through which all humans pass. Thinking at each stage builds on and incorporates previous stages as it becomes more organized and adaptive, and less tied to concrete events. Piaget's special concern was with logic and how people construct universal knowledge that cannot be learned directly from the environment—knowledge such as conservation or reversibility (Miller, 1993). Such knowledge comes from reflecting on and coordinating our own cognitions or thoughts, not from mapping external reality. Piaget saw the social environment as an important factor in development but did not believe that social interaction was the main mechanism for changing thinking (Moshman, 1997).

Vygotsky's Social Constructivism. As you also saw in Chapter 2, Vygotsky believed that social interaction, cultural tools, and activity shape an individual's development and learning. By participating in a broad range of activities with others, learners appropriate (internalize or take for themselves) the outcomes produced by working together; "they acquire new strategies and knowledge of the world and culture" (Palincsar, 1998, pp. 351–352). Some theorists categorize Vygotsky as a psychological constructivist because he was primarily interested in development within the individual (Moshman, 1997; Phillips, 1997). But because his theory relies heavily on social interactions and the cultural context to explain learning, most psychologists classify Vygotsky as a social constructivist (Palincsar, 1998; Prawat, 1996). In a sense, he is both. One advantage of his theory of learning is that it gives us a way to consider both the psychological and the social; he bridges both camps. For example, Vygotsky's concept of the zone of proximal development—the range of problems a child can solve with the help (scaffolding) of an adult or more able peer—has been called a place where culture and cognition create each other (Cole, 1985). Culture creates cognition when the adult uses

Connect & Extend
To the research
The 2000 Yearbook of the National Society for the Study of Education (NSSE) is devoted to the examination of constructivism. Phillips, D. C. (Ed.) (2000). *Constructivism in Education: Opinions and Second Opinions on Controversial Issues.* Chicago, IL: University of Chicago Press.

tools and practices from the culture (language, maps, computers, looms, or music) to steer the child toward goals that are culturally valued (reading, writing, computers, dance). Cognition creates culture as the adult and child together generate new practices and solutions to problems that can be added to the cultural group's repertoire (Serpell, 1993).

The term *constructivism* is sometimes used to talk about how public knowledge is created. Although this is not our main concern in educational psychology, it is worth a quick look.

Sociological Constructivism. Sociological constructivists (sometimes called construc*tionists*) do not focus on individual learning. Their concern is how public knowledge in disciplines such as science, math, economics, or history is constructed. Beyond this kind of academic knowledge, sociological constructivists also are interested in how common-sense ideas, everyday beliefs, and commonly held understandings about the world are communicated to new members of a sociocultural group (Gergen, 1997; Phillips, 1997). Questions raised might include who determines what constitutes history or the proper way to behave in public, or how does a person get elected class president. According to sociological constructionists, all of knowledge is socially constructed, and, more important, some people have more power than others do in defining what will count as knowledge. Relationships between and among teachers, students, families, and the community are the central issues. Collaboration to understand diverse viewpoints is encouraged and traditional bodies of knowledge often are challenged (Gergen, 1997). Vygotsky's theory, with its attention to how cognition creates culture, has elements in common with sociological constructivism.

The various perspectives on constructivism raise some general questions and differ on the answers. These questions can never be fully resolved, but different theories tend to favour particular positions.

How Is Knowledge Constructed?

One tension among different approaches to constructivism is based on *how* knowledge is constructed. Moshman (1982) describes three explanations.

1. *The realities and truths of the external world direct knowledge construction.* Individuals *reconstruct* outside reality by building accurate mental representations such as propositional networks, concepts, cause-and-effect patterns, and condition-action production rules that reflect "the way things really are." Information processing models emphasize this view of knowledge as an entity that is constructed in one situation and applied in another (Cobb & Bowers, 1999).

2. *Internal processes such as Piaget's organization, assimilation, and accommodation direct knowledge construction.* New knowledge is abstracted from old knowledge. Knowledge is not a mirror of reality but rather an abstraction that grows and develops with cognitive activity. Knowledge is not true or false; it just grows more internally consistent and organized with development.

3. *Both external and internal factors direct knowledge construction.* Knowledge grows through the *interactions* that involve internal (cognitive) and external (environmental and social) factors. Vygotsky's description of cognitive development through the appropriation and use of cultural tools such as language is consistent with this view (Bruning, Schraw, & Ronning, 1999). Another example is Bandura's theory of reciprocal interactions between people, behaviour, and environments (Schunk, 2000). Table 9.2 summarizes the three general explanations about how knowledge is constructed.

TABLE 9.2 How Knowledge Is Constructed

Type	Assumptions about Learning and Knowledge	Example Theories
External Direction	Knowledge is acquired by constructing a representation of the outside world. Direct teaching, feedback, and explanation affect learning. Knowledge is accurate to the extent that it reflects the "way things really are" in the outside world.	Information processing
Internal Direction	Knowledge is constructed by transforming, organizing, and reorganizing previous knowledge. Knowledge is not a mirror of the external world, even though experience influences thinking and thinking influences knowledge. Exploration and discovery are more important than teaching	Piaget
Both External and Internal Direction	Knowledge is constructed based on social interactions and experience. Knowledge reflects the outside world as filtered through and influenced by culture, language, beliefs, interactions with others, direct teaching, and modelling. Guided discovery, teaching, models, and coaching as well as the individual's prior knowledge, beliefs, and thinking affect learning.	Vygotsky

Is the World Knowable?

Most constructivists believe that people cannot perceive the world directly but must filter it through their understandings, like Chelsea did when she answered the wall. But some perspectives, such as information processing, assume the world is knowable. There is an objective reality "out there" and an individual can grasp it, even though knowledge constructions are personal and may include misconceptions about how the world operates. For example, young children sometimes construct a subtraction procedure that says, "subtract the smaller number from the larger number, no matter which number in a problem is on top." Other constructivists, including Piaget and Vygotsky, don't talk about accurate conceptions but instead about logical or sound interpretations. Still, they believe that we can know about the world because knowledge construction is a rational process and, thus, some constructions are better than others—more logical, justifiable, or defensible, for example (Moshman, 1997).

Many of the more extreme constructivist perspectives, on the other hand, do not assume that the world is knowable. The theorists who take this stance, often called **radical constructivists**, suggest that all knowledge is individually constructed within cultural and social contexts. Radical constructivists are not concerned with accurate, "true" representations of the world.

> Radical constructivists hold that we live in a relativistic world that can only be understood from individually unique perspectives, which are constructed through experimental activity in the social/physical world. No individual's viewpoint thus constructed should be viewed as inherently distorted or less correct than another's, although it is certainly true that one individual perspective can be more useful than another. (Derry, 1992, p. 415)

A difficulty with this position is that, when pushed to the extreme of relativism, all knowledge and beliefs are equal because all are constructed. There are problems with this thinking for educators. First, teachers have a professional responsibility to emphasize some values, such as honesty or justice, over others such as bigotry. All beliefs are not equal. As teachers we ask students to work hard to learn. If learning cannot advance understanding because all understandings are equally good, notes David Moshman (1997), "we might just as well let students continue to believe whatever they believe" (p. 230). Also, it appears that some knowledge, such as counting and one-to-one correspondence, is not constructed

Radical Constuctivism: Theory of knowledge and learning asserting that all knowledge is individually constructed and equally valid.

but universal. Knowing one-to-one correspondence is part of being human (Geary, 1995; Schunk, 2000).

Knowledge: Situated or General?

A final question that cuts across many constructivist perspectives is whether knowledge is internal, general, and transferable; or bound to the time and place in which it is constructed. Psychologists who emphasize the social construction of knowledge and **situated learning** affirm Vygotsky's notion that learning is inherently social and embedded in a particular cultural setting (Cobb & Bowers, 1999). What is true in one time and place—such as the "fact" before Columbus's time that the Earth was flat—becomes false in another time and place. Particular ideas may be useful within a specific **community of practice**, such as fifteenth-century navigation, but useless outside that community. What counts as new knowledge is determined in part by how well the new idea fits with current accepted practice. Over time, the current practice may be questioned and even overthrown but, until such major shifts occur, current practice will shape what is considered useful.

Situated learning emphasizes that being in the real world outside school differs importantly from studying in school. The real world outside school often is more like an apprenticeship where novices, with the support of an expert guide and model, take on more and more responsibility until they are able to function independently. For those who take a situated learning view, this explains learning in factories, around the dinner table, in high school halls, in street gangs, in the business office, and on the playground.

Situated learning is often described as "enculturation" or adopting the norms, behaviour, skills, beliefs, language, and attitudes of a particular community. The community might be mathematicians or gang members or writers or students in your Grade 8 class or hockey players—any group that has particular ways of thinking and doing. Knowledge is seen *not* as an individual's cognitive structures but as a creation of the community over time. The practices of the community— the ways of interacting and getting things done, as well as the tools the community has created—constitute the knowledge of that community. Learning means becoming more able to participate in those practices and use the tools (Cognition and Technology Group at Vanderbilt, 1990, 1993; Derry, 1992; Garrison, 1995; Greeno, Collins, & Resnick, 1996).

Situated Learning: The idea that skills and knowledge are tied to the situation in which they were learned, and are difficult to apply in new settings.

Community of Practice: Social situation or context in which ideas are judged useful or true.

Connect & Extend
To the research
Background: Gardner, H. (1991). *The Unschooled Mind: How Children Think and How Schools Should Teach.* New York: Basic Books. Gardner, H. (1993b). *Educating the Unschooled Mind: A science and public policy seminar.* Washington, DC: American Educational Research Association. Brandt, R. (1993). On teaching for understanding: A conversation with Howard Gardner. *Educational Leadership, 50*(7), 4–7.

◀ *Constructivist approaches may involve, among other things, authentic or real-life tasks, social negotiation, and shared responsibility as part of learning.*

Constructivism and Situated Learning **323**

At the most basic level, "situated learning. . . emphasizes the idea that much of what is learned is specific to the situation in which it is learned" (Anderson, Reder, & Simon, 1996, p. 5). Thus, some would argue, learning to do calculations in school may help students do more school calculations, but this may not help them balance a chequebook because the skills can be applied only in the context in which they were learned, namely school (Lave, 1988; Lave & Wenger, 1991).

There is evidence that much of what we learn is tied to the situation in which it was learned. But it also is the case that knowledge and skills can be applied across contexts that were not part of the initial learning situation—for example, when you use your ability to calculate and read to do your income taxes, even though income tax forms were not part of your high school curriculum (Anderson, Reder, & Simon, 1996). So learning that is situated in school does not have to be doomed or irrelevant. As you saw in Chapter 8, a major question in educational psychology and education in general concerns *specific* and *general* knowledge and the *transfer* of knowledge from one situation to another. How can you encourage this transfer? Help is on the way in the next section.

Common Elements of Constructivist Perspectives

We have looked at some areas of disagreement among the constructivist perspectives, but what about areas of agreement? Even though there is no single constructivist theory, many constructivist approaches recommend:

▶ complex, challenging learning environments and authentic, real-world tasks;

▶ social negotiation and shared responsibility as a part of learning;

▶ multiple representations of content;

▶ understanding that knowledge is constructed; and

▶ student-centred instruction (Driscoll, 1994; Marshall, 1992).

Before we discuss particular teaching approaches, let's look more closely at these dimensions of constructivist teaching.

Connect & Extend
To professional journals
Special issue on Authentic Learning: *Educational Leadership*, April 1993. There are 25 articles in this issue—everything from an interview with Howard Gardner to descriptions of American Civil War re-enactments.

Complex Learning Environments: Problems and learning situations that mimic the ill-structured nature of real life.

Social Negotiation: Aspect of learning process that relies on collaboration with others and respect for different perspectives.

Complex Learning Environments and Authentic Tasks. Constructivists believe that students should not be given stripped-down, simplified problems and basic-skills drills, but instead should encounter **complex learning environments** that deal with "fuzzy," ill-structured problems. The world beyond school presents few simple problems or step-by-step directions, so schools should be sure that *every* student has experience solving complex problems. Complex problems are not merely difficult ones. Complex problems have many parts. There are multiple, interacting elements in the problems and multiple solutions are possible. There is no one right way to reach a conclusion, and each solution may bring a new set of problems. These complex problems should be embedded in authentic tasks and activities, the kinds of situations that students will face as they apply what they are learning to the real world (J. S. Brown, 1990; Needles & Knapp, 1994; Resnick, 1987). Students may need support as they work on these complex problems, helping them find resources, keeping track of their progress, breaking larger problems down into smaller ones, and so on. This aspect of constructivist approaches is consistent with situated learning in emphasizing learning in *situations* where the learning will be applied.

Social Negotiation. Many constructivists share Vygotsky's belief that higher mental processes develop through **social negotiation** and interaction, so collaboration in learning is valued. The Language Development and Hypermedia Group (1992) suggests that a major goal of teaching is to develop students' abilities to establish and defend their own positions while respecting the positions of others and working together to negotiate or co-construct meaning. To accomplish this exchange, students must talk and listen to each other. It is a challenge for children in cultures that are individualistic and competitive, such as much of Canada, to adopt what has been called an **intersubjective attitude** about negotiation and joint construction of meaning. An intersubjective attitude is a commitment to build shared meaning by finding common ground and exchanging interpretations.

Connect & Extend
To the research
Confrey, J. (1990b). What constructivism implies for teaching. In R. Davis, C. Maher, and N. Noddings (Eds.), *Constructivist views on the teaching and learning of mathematics* (pp. 107–122). Monograph 4 of the National Council of Teachers of Mathematics, Reston, VA.

Multiple Representations of Content. When students encounter only one model, one analogy, one way of understanding complex content, they often oversimplify as they try to apply that one approach to every situation. Anita saw this happen in her educational psychology class when six students were presenting an example of guided discovery learning. The students' presentation was a near-copy of a guided discovery demonstration she had given earlier in the semester, but with some major misconceptions. Her students knew only one way to represent discovery learning. Resources for the class should have provided **multiple representations of content** (guided discovery) using different analogies, examples, and metaphors.

Rand Spiro and his colleagues (1991) suggest that "revisiting the same material, at different times, in rearranged contexts, for different purposes, and from different conceptual perspectives is essential for attaining the goals of advanced knowledge acquisition" (p. 28). This idea is consistent with Bruner's (1966) **spiral curriculum**, a structure for teaching that introduces the fundamental structure of all subjects—the "big ideas"—early in the school years, then revisits the subjects in more and more complex forms over time.

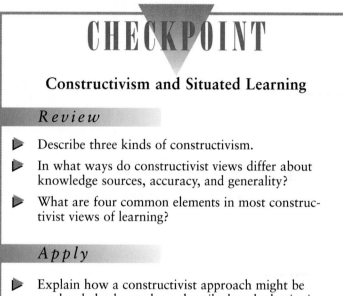

CHECKPOINT

Constructivism and Situated Learning

Review

▷ Describe three kinds of constructivism.

▷ In what ways do constructivist views differ about knowledge sources, accuracy, and generality?

▷ What are four common elements in most constructivist views of learning?

Apply

▷ Explain how a constructivist approach might be used to help the students described at the beginning of the chapter write better book reviews.

Understanding the Knowledge Construction Process. Throughout this text you have encountered the concept of metacognition—knowledge of your own mental processes and how you learn. Constructivist approaches often go beyond helping students understand their own metacognitive processes to making them aware of their own role in constructing knowledge (Cunningham, 1992). The assumptions we make, our beliefs, and our experiences shape what each of us comes to "know" about the world. Different assumptions and different experiences lead to different knowledge. Constructivists stress the importance of understanding the process of constructing knowledge so that students will be aware of influences that shape their thinking; thus they will be able to choose, develop, and defend positions in a self-critical way while respecting the positions of others.

Student-Centred Instruction. "While there are several interpretations of what [constructivist] theory means, most agree that it involves a dramatic change in the focus of teaching, putting the students' own efforts to understand at the center of the educational enterprise" (Prawat, 1992, p. 357). Student-centred instruction does not mean that the teacher abandons responsibility for instruction. Because the design of teaching is a central issue in this book, we spend the rest of this chapter discussing examples of student-centred instruction.

Intersubjective Attitude: A commitment to build shared meaning with others by finding common ground and exchanging interpretations.

Multiple Representations of Content: Considering problems using various analogies, examples, and metaphors.

Spiral Curriculum: Bruner's structure for teaching that introduces the fundamental structure of all subjects early in the school years, then revisits the subjects in more and more complex forms over time.

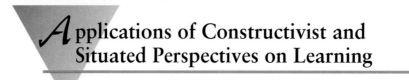

Applications of Constructivist and Situated Perspectives on Learning

In this section we will examine four specific teaching approaches that put the student at the centre: inquiry learning and problem-based learning, cooperative learning, dialogue and instructional conversations, and cognitive apprenticeships.

Inquiry Learning and Problem-Based Learning

John Dewey described the basic **inquiry learning** format in 1910. There have been many adaptations of this strategy, but the form usually includes these elements (Pasch, Sparks-Langer, Gardner, Starko, & Moody, 1991).

The teacher presents a puzzling event, question, or problem. The students:

▶ formulate hypotheses to explain the event or solve the problem;

▶ collect data to test the hypotheses;

▶ draw conclusions; and

▶ reflect on the original problem and the thinking processes needed to solve it.

Examples of Inquiry. In one kind of inquiry, teachers present a problem and students ask yes/no questions to gather data and test hypotheses. This allows the teacher to monitor students' thinking and guide the process. Here is an example:

1. *Teacher presents discrepant event* (after clarifying ground rules). The teacher blows softly across the top of a letter-sized sheet of paper, and the paper rises. She tells students to figure out why it rises.

2. *Students ask questions* to gather more information and to isolate relevant variables. Teacher answers only "yes" or "no." Students ask if temperature is important (no). They ask if the paper is of a special kind (no). They ask if air pressure has anything to do with the paper rising (yes). Questions continue.

3. *Students test causal relationships.* In this case, they ask if the nature of the air on top causes the paper to rise (yes). They ask if the fast movement of the air results in less pressure on the top (yes). Then they test out the rule with other materials—for example, thin plastic.

4. *Students form a generalization* (principle): "If the air on the top moves faster than the air on the bottom of a surface, the air pressure on top is lessened, and the object rises." Later lessons expand students' understanding of the principles and physical laws through further experiments.

5. The teacher leads students in a discussion of their thinking processes. What were the important variables? How did you put the causes and effects together? and so on. (Pasch et al., 1991, pp. 188–189)

Shirley Magnuson and Annemarie Palincsar have developed a teachers' guide for planning, implementing, and assessing the different phases of inquiry science units (Palincsar, Magusson, Marano, Ford, & Brown, 1998). The model, called *Guided Inquiry Supporting Multiple Literacies* or GIsML, is shown in Figure 9.1.

The teacher first identifies a curriculum area and some general guiding questions, puzzles, or problems. For example, an elementary teacher chooses communication as the area and asks this general question: "How and why do humans and animals communicate?" Next, several specific focus questions are posed. "How do whales communicate?" "How do gorillas communicate? The focus questions have to be carefully chosen to guide students toward important understandings. One key idea in understanding animal communication is the relationship between the

Connect & Extend
To your teaching
John Cronin lists these four common misconceptions about authentic learning:
Misconception #1: If you can't take 'em to Spain, they might as well not learn Spanish at all. The fact that living with native speakers is the best way to learn Spanish does not make using the language in classroom conversations a poor alternative. Look for the small and obvious ways to make learning more authentic—especially if your can't take 'em to Spain.
Misconception #2: If you don't have your chef's licence, you'll have to starve. You don't need special training or materials to create authentic instruction. Good teachers have been doing it for years.
Misconception #3: If it isn't real fun, it isn't real. Important learning and valuable life skills are not always fun to learn or fun to use. Self-discipline is part of growing up authentically.
Misconception #4: If you want to learn to play the piano, you must start with mastering Chopin. Not all learning has to be complicated; some important life skills are simple.
From Cronin, J. F. (1993). Four misconceptions about authentic learning. *Educational Leadership, 50*(7), 78–80.

Inquiry Learning: Approach in which the teacher presents a puzzling situation and students solve the problem by gathering data and testing their conclusions.

FIGURE 9.1

A Model to Guide Teacher Thinking about Inquiry-Based Science Instruction

The straight lines show the sequence of phases in instruction and the curved lines show cycles that might be repeated during instruction.

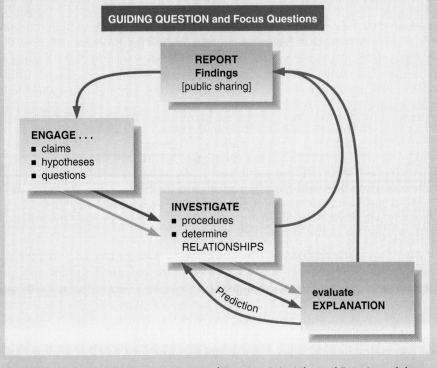

Source: From "Designing a Community of Practice: Principles and Practices of the GIsML Community," by A. S. Palincsar, S. J. Magnuson, N. Marano, D. Ford, and N. Brown, 1998, *Teaching and Teacher Education, 14*, p. 12. Adapted with permission.

animals' structures, survival functions, and habitats. Animals have specific *structures*, such as large ears or echo-locators, that *function* to find food or attract mates or identify predators, and these structures and functions are related to the animals' *habitats*. So focus questions must ask about animals with different structures for communication, different functional needs for survival, and different habitats. Questions about animals with the same kinds of structures or the same habitats would not be good focus points for inquiry (Magnusson & Palincsar, 1995).

The next phase is to engage students in the inquiry, perhaps by playing different animal sounds, having students make guesses and claims about communication, and asking the students questions about their guesses and claims. Then the students conduct both first- and second-hand investigations. *First-hand investigations* are direct experiences and experiments—for example, measuring the size of bats' eyes and ears in relation to their bodies (using pictures or videos, not real bats!). In *second-hand investigations*, students consult books, the Internet, interviews with experts, and so on to find specific information or get new ideas. As part of investigating, the students begin to identify patterns. The curved line in Figure 9.1 shows that cycles can be repeated. In fact, students might go through several cycles of investigation, pattern identification, and reporting results before moving on to constructing explanations and making final reports. Another possible cycle is to evaluate explanations before reporting by making and then checking predictions, and applying the explanation to new situations.

Problem-Based Learning:
Methods that provide students with realistic problems that don't necessarily have "right" answers.

Inquiry teaching allows students to learn content and process at the same time. In the examples above, students learned about animal communication and habitats, the effects of air pressure, and how airplanes fly. In addition, they learned the inquiry process itself—how to solve problems, evaluate solutions, and think critically. Inquiry has much in common with guided discovery learning and shares its advantages and disadvantages. Like discovery learning, inquiry methods require great preparation, organization, and monitoring to be sure everyone is engaged and challenged (Kindsvatter, Wilen, & Ishler, 1988).

Problem-Based Learning. In **problem-based learning**, students are confronted with a real problem that has meaning for them. This problem launches their inquiry as they collaborate to find solutions. In true problem-based learning, the problem is real and the students' actions matter. For example, one teacher capitalized on current affairs to encourage student reading, writing, and social studies problem solving:

> Cathie's elementary class learned about the Alaskan oil spill. She brought a newspaper article to class that sequenced in logbook fashion the events of the oil spill in Prince William Sound. To prepare her students to understand the article, she had her students participate in several background-building experiences. First, they used a world map, an encyclopedia, and library books to gather and share relevant information. Next, she simulated an oil spill by coating an object with oil. By then, the class was eager to read the article. (Espe, Worner, & Hotkevich, 1990, p. 45)

After they read and discussed the newspaper article, the teacher asked the class to imagine how the problem might have been prevented. Students had to explain and support their proposed solutions. The following week the students read another newspaper article about how people in their state were helping with the cleanup efforts in Alaska. The teacher asked if the students wanted to help, and they replied with an enthusiastic "Yes!" The students designed posters and made speeches requesting donations of clean towels to be used to clean the oil-soaked animals in Prince William Sound. The class sent four large bags of towels to Alaska to help in the cleanup. The teacher's and the students' reading, writing, research, and speaking were directed toward solving a real-life problem (Espe, Worner, & Hotkevich, 1990). Other authentic problems that might be the focus for student projects are pollution in local rivers, student conflicts in school, raising money for class projects, or building a playground for young children. The teacher's role in problem-based learning is summarized in Table 9.3.

Some problems are not authentic in the sense that they affect the students' lives, but they are engaging. For example, the Cognition and Technology Group at Vanderbilt University (CTGV, 1990, 1993) has developed a videodisc-based learning environment that focuses on mathematics instruction for Grades 5 and 6. The series, called *The Adventures of Jasper Woodbury*, presents complex situations that require students to identify problems; set sub-goals; and apply math, science, history, and literature concepts to solve problems. Even though the situations are complex and lifelike, the problems can be solved using data embedded in the stories presented. For example, in one adventure, Jasper sets out in a small motorboat, headed to Cedar Creek to inspect an old cruiser he is thinking of buying. Along the way Jasper has to consult maps, use his marine radio, deal with fuel and repair problems, buy the cruiser, and finally determine if he has enough fuel and time to sail his purchase home before sundown. Often the adventures have real-life follow-up problems that build on the knowledge developed. For example, after designing a playground for a hypothetical group of children in one Jasper adventure, students can tackle building a real playhouse for a preschool class.

There are 12 different adventures. Research indicates that students from Grade 4 through to high school can work with the adventures (CTGV, 1990). Students are highly motivated as they work in groups to solve the problems; even group members with limited math skills can contribute to the solutions because

TABLE 9.3 The Teacher's Role in Problem-Based Learning

Phase	Teacher Behaviour
Phase 1 Orient students to the problem	Teacher goes over the objectives of the lesson, describes important logistical requirements, and motivates students to engage in self-selected problem-solving activity.
Phase 2 Organize students for study	Teacher helps students define and organize study tasks related to the problem.
Phase 3 Assist independent and group investigation	Teacher encourages students to gather appropriate information, conduct experiments, and search for explanations and solutions.
Phase 4 Develop and present artifacts and exhibits	Teacher assists students in planning and preparing appropriate artifacts such as reports, videos, and models and helps them share their work with others. for study
Phase 5 Analyze and evaluate the problem-solving process	Teacher helps students to reflect on their investigations the processes they used.

Source: From *Classroom Instruction and Management* (p. 161), by R. I. Arends, New York: McGraw-Hill. Copyright © 1997 McGraw-Hill. Reprinted with permission.

they might notice key information in the video or suggest innovative ways to approach the situation.

The Vanderbilt group calls its problem-based approach **anchored instruction**. The *anchor* is the rich, interesting situation. This anchor provides a focus—a reason for setting goals, planning, and using mathematical tools to solve problems. The intended outcome is to develop knowledge that is useful and flexible, not inert. Inert knowledge is information that is memorized but seldom applied (CTVG, 1996; Whitehead, 1929).

Group Work and Cooperation in Learning

The terms *group learning* and *cooperative learning* often are used as if they meant the same thing. Actually, "group" work simply refers to several students working together—they may or may not be cooperating.

Working in Groups. Many activities can be completed in groups. For example, students can work together in conducting local surveys. How do people feel about the plan to build a new mall that will bring more shopping and more traffic? Would the community support or oppose the building of a nuclear power plant? If students must learn 10 new definitions in a biology class, why not let students divide up the terms and definitions and teach one another? Be sure, however, that everyone in the group can handle the task. Sometimes a group effort ends with one or two students doing the work of the entire group.

Group work can be useful, but true **cooperative learning** requires much more than simply putting students in groups, as you will see in the next few pages.

Beyond Groups to Cooperation. Collaboration and cooperative learning have a long history in North American education. In the early 1900s, John Dewey criticized the use of competition in education and encouraged educators to structure schools as democratic learning communities. These ideas fell from favour in the

Connect & Extend
To your teaching
Cooperative learning (1986, September). *Harvard Education Letter 2*(5), 4–6. This article describes STAD and the approach of Roger and David Johnson. One advantage of cooperative learning, as noted by Nel Noddings of Stanford University, is that "children solve problems at a more thoughtful, deliberate pace than they do when working as a class. Without any teacher to approve or reject a proposed solution, they debate strategies for some time." Noddings notes how often children in groups call out "Wait, wait!" and wonders how many would like to slow down the pace of full-class instruction so they could feel that they really understood.

Connect & Extend
To the research
Slavin, R. R. (1991). Synthesis of research on cooperative learning. *Educational Leadership, 48*(5), 71–82. Focus Question: When is cooperative learning most effective, and with which students?

Connect & Extend
To professional journals
Cooperative learning (1990, special section). *Educational Leadership, 47*(4), 4–67, and Cooperative Learning (1991, special section). *Educational Leadership, 48*, 71–95.

Anchored Instruction: A type of problem-based learning that uses a complex interesting situation as an anchor for learning.

Cooperative Learning: Arrangement in which students work in mixed-ability groups and are rewarded on the basis of the success of the group.

1940s and 1950s, replaced by a resurgence of competition. In the 1960s, there was a swing back to individualized and cooperative learning structures, stimulated in part by concern for civil rights and interracial relations (Webb & Palincsar, 1996).

Today, evolving constructivist perspectives on learning fuel interest in collaboration and cooperative learning. As you have seen, two characteristics of constructivist teaching are *complex, real-life learning environments* and *social interaction*. As educators focus on learning in real contexts, "there is a heightened interest in situations where elaboration, interpretation, explanation, and argumentation are integral to the activity of the group and where learning is supported by other individuals" (Webb & Palincsar, 1996, p. 844).

Different constructivist approaches favour cooperative learning for different reasons. Information processing theorists point to the value of group discussion in helping participants rehearse, elaborate, and expand their knowledge. As group members question and explain, they have to organize their knowledge, make connections, and review—all processes that support information processing and memory. Advocates of a Piagetian perspective suggest that the interactions in groups can create the cognitive conflict and disequilibrium that lead an individual to question his or her understanding and try out new ideas—or, as Piaget (1985) said, "to go beyond his current state and strike out in new directions" (p. 10). Constructivists who favour Vygotsky's theory suggest that social interaction is important for learning because higher mental functions such as reasoning, comprehension, and critical thinking originate in social interactions and are then internalized by individuals. Children can accomplish mental tasks with social support before they can do them alone. Thus cooperative learning provides the social support and scaffolding that students need to move learning forward. Table 9.4 summarizes the functions of cooperative learning from different constructivist perspectives, and describes some of the elements of each kind of group.

To benefit from the dimensions of cooperative learning listed in Table 9.4, groups must *be cooperative*—all members must participate. But, as any teacher or parent knows, cooperation is not automatic when students are put into groups. Angela O'Donnell and Jim O'Kelly describe a teacher who claimed to be using "cooperative learning" by asking students to work in pairs on a paper, each writing one part. Unfortunately, the teacher allowed no time to work together and pro-

Connect & Extend
To other chapters
The need for belonging is the third level of Maslow's hierarchy, discussed in **Chapter 10**. The need to maintain relationships is strong. Anita was reminded of this when her daughter was reprimanded by her Grade 4 teacher for passing notes during class. Liz's explanation was that there had been a fight during lunch, "and we had to work it out!"

TABLE 9.4 Different Forms of Cooperative Learning for Different Purposes

Different forms of cooperative learning fit different purposes, need different structures, and have their own potential problems and possible solutions.

Considerations	Elaboration	Piagetian	Vygotskian
Group size	Small (2–4)	Small	Dyads
Group composition	Heterogeneous/homogeneous	Heterogeneous	Heterogeneous
Tasks	Rehearsal/integrative	Exploratory	Skills
Teacher role	Facilitator	Facilitator	Model/guide
Potential problems	Poor help-giving	Inactive	Poor help-giving
	Unequal participation	No cognitive conflict	Providing adequate time/dialogue
Averting Problem	Direct instruction in help-giving	Structuring controversy	Direct instruction in help-giving
	Modelling help-giving		Modelling help-giving
	Scripting interaction		

Source: From A. M. O'Donnell and J. O'Kelly, Learning from peers: Beyond the rhetoric of positive results. *Educational Psychology Review,* 6, 1994, p. 327. Reprinted by permission of Plenum Publishing Corporation.

vided no guidance or preparation in cooperative social skills. Students got a grade for their individual part and a group grade for the whole project. One student received an A for his part, but a C for the group project because his partner earned an F—he never turned in any work. So one student was punished with a C for a situation he could not control while the other was rewarded with a C for doing no work at all. This was not cooperative learning—it wasn't even group work (O'Donnell & O'Kelly, 1994). Let's look at what can go wrong with cooperative learning—then we can consider how to avoid these problems.

What Can Go Wrong: Misuses of Group Learning. Without careful planning and monitoring by the teacher, group interactions can hinder learning and reduce rather than improve social relations in classes. For example, if there is pressure in a group for conformity—perhaps because rewards are being misused or one student dominates the others—interactions can be unproductive and unreflective. Misconceptions might be reinforced or the worst, not the best, ideas may be combined to construct a superficial understanding (Battistich, Solomon, & Delucci, 1993). Also, the ideas of low-status students may be ignored or even ridiculed while the contributions of high-status students are accepted and reinforced, regardless of the merit of either set of ideas (Anderson, Holland, & Palincsar, 1997; Cohen, 1986). Mary McCaslin and Tom Good (1996) list several other disadvantages of group learning:

▶ Students often value the process or procedures over the learning. Speed and finishing take precedence over thoughtfulness and learning.

▶ Rather than challenging and correcting misconceptions, students support and reinforce misunderstandings.

▶ Socializing and interpersonal relationships may take precedence over learning.

▶ Students may simply shift dependency from the teacher to the "expert" in the group—learning is still passive and what is learned can be wrong.

▶ Status differences may be increased rather than decreased. Some students learn to "loaf" because the group progresses with or without their contributions. Others are even more convinced that they are helpless to understand without the support of the group.

The next sections examine how teachers can avoid these problems and encourage true cooperation.

Making Cooperative Learning Work

David and Roger Johnson (1999a) list five elements that define true cooperative learning groups:

- ▶ Face-to-face interaction
- ▶ Positive interdependence
- ▶ Individual accountability
- ▶ Collaborative skills
- ▶ Group processing

Students *interact face-to-face* and close together, not across the room. Group members experience *positive interdependence*—they need each other for support, explanations, and guidance. Even though they work together and help each other, members of the group must ultimately demonstrate learning on their own—they are held *individually accountable* for learning, often through individual tests or other assessments. *Collaborative skills* are necessary for effective group functioning. Often these skills, such as giving constructive feedback, reaching consensus, and involving every member, must be taught and practised before the groups tackle a learning task. Finally, members monitor *group processes* and relationships to make sure the group is working effectively and to learn about the dynamics of groups. They take time to ask, "How are we doing as a group? Is everyone working together?"

Setting Up Cooperative Groups. How large should a cooperative group be? The answer depends on your learning goals. If the purpose is for the group members to review, rehearse information, or practise, four to five or six students is about the right size. But if the goal is to encourage each student to participate in discussions, problem solving, or computer learning, then groups of two to four members work best. Also, in setting up cooperative groups, it often makes sense to balance the number of boys and girls. Some research indicates that when there are just a few girls in a group, they tend to be left out of the discussions unless they are the most able or assertive members. By contrast, when there are only one or two boys in the group, they tend to dominate and be "interviewed" by the girls unless these boys are less able than the girls or are very shy. In general, for very shy and introverted students, individual learning may be a better approach (O'Donnell & O'Kelly, 1994; Webb, 1985; Webb & Palincsar, 1996). Whatever the case, teachers must monitor groups to make sure everyone is contributing and learning.

In practice, the effects of learning in a group vary, depending on what actually happens in the group and who is in it. If only a few people take responsibility for the work, these people will learn, but the non-participating members probably will not. Students who ask questions, get answers, and attempt explanations are more likely to learn than students whose questions go unasked or unanswered. In fact, there is evidence that the more a student provides elaborated, thoughtful explanations to other students in a group, the more the *explainer* learns. Giving good explanations appears to be even more important for learning than receiving explanations (Webb & Palincsar, 1996). To explain, you have to organize the information, put it into your own words, think of examples and analogies (which connect the information to things you already know), and test your understanding by answering questions. These are excellent learning strategies (King, 1990; O'Donnell & O'Kelly, 1994).

Some teachers assign roles to students to encourage cooperation and full participation. Several roles are described in Table 9.5 on page 333. If you use roles, be sure that the roles support learning. In groups that focus on practice, review, or mastery of basic skills, roles should support persistence, encouragement, and participation. In groups that focus on higher-order problem solving or complex learning, roles should encourage thoughtful discussion, sharing of explanations and

TABLE 9.5   Possible Student Roles in Cooperative Learning Groups

Depending on the purpose of the group and the age of the participants, having these assigned roles might help students cooperate and learn. Of course, students may have to be taught how to enact each role effectively, and roles should be rotated so students can participate in different aspects of group learning.

Role	Description
Encourager	Encourages reluctant or shy students to participate
Praiser/Cheerleader	Shows appreciation of other's contributions and recognizes accomplishments
Gate Keeper	Equalizes participation and makes sure no one dominates
Coach	Helps with the academic content, explains concepts
Question Commander	Makes sure all students' questions are asked and answered
Checker	Checks the group's understanding
Taskmaster	Keeps the group on task
Recorder	Writes down ideas, decisions, and plans
Reflector	Keeps group aware of progress (or lack of progress)
Quiet Captain	Monitors noise level
Materials Monitor	Picks up and returns materials

Source: Adapted from Spencer Kagan, *Cooperative learning.* San Clemente, CA: Kagan Cooperative Learning, 1994, 1 (800) WEE CO-OP.

insights, probing, brainstorming, and creativity. Make sure that you don't communicate to students that the major purpose of the groups is simply to do the procedures—the roles. Roles are supports for learning, not ends in themselves (Woolfolk Hoy & Tschannen-Moran, 1999).

Jigsaw. An early format for cooperative learning that emphasizes high interdependence is **jigsaw**. Each group member is given part of the material to be learned by the whole group and becomes an "expert" on his or her piece. Students have to teach each other, so everyone's contribution is important. A more recent version, Jigsaw II, adds expert groups where the students who have the same material from each learning group confer to make sure they understand their assigned part and then plan ways to teach the information to their learning-group members. Next, students return to their learning groups, bringing their expertise to the sessions. In the end, students take an individual test covering all the material and earn points for their learning-team score. Teams can work for rewards or simply for recognition (Slavin, 1995).

Judy Pitts (1992) describes a lesson about how to do library research that has a jigsaw format. The overall project for each group is to educate the class about a different country. Groups have to decide what information to present and how to make it interesting for their classmates. In the library, each group member is responsible for mastering a particular resource (*Readers' Guide, NewsBank*, reference sets, almanacs, etc.) and teaching other group members, if the need arises. Students learning about each resource meet first in expert groups to be sure all the "teachers" know how to use the resource.

In this class, students confront complex, real-life problems, and not simplified worksheets. They learn by doing and by teaching others. The students must take positions and argue for them—how should our group educate the class about Turkey, for example—while being open to the ideas of others. They may encounter different representations of the same information—graphs, databases, maps, interviews, or encyclopedia articles—and have to integrate information from different sources. This lesson exemplifies many of the characteristics of constructivist approaches. But the most important characteristic of the lesson is that students have a good chance of learning how to do library research by actually doing it.

Jigsaw: A cooperative structure in which each member of a group is responsible for teaching other members one section of the material.

Connect & Extend
To the research
King, A. (1990). Enhancing peer interaction and learning in the classroom through reciprocal questioning. *American Educational Research Journal, 27*, 664–687.

Connect & Extend
To professional resources
For more information on instructional conversations, including examples of class transcripts and instruments to assess instructional conversations, contact: Dissemination Center, National Center for Research on Cultural Diversity and Second Language Learning, Center for Applied Linguistics, 1118 22nd Street NW, Washington, DC 20037.

Reciprocal Questioning. Another cooperative approach can be used with a wide range of ages and subjects. **Reciprocal questioning** requires no special materials or testing procedures. After a lesson or presentation by the teacher, students work in pairs or triads to ask and answer questions about the material (King, 1990, 1994). The teacher provides question stems (see Figure 9.2), and then students are taught how to develop specific questions on the lesson material using the generic question stems. The students create questions, then take turns asking and answering. This process has proven more effective than traditional discussion groups because it seems to encourage deeper thinking about the material. Questions such as those on the "Prompt Cards" in Figure 9.2 which encourage students to make connections between the lesson and previous knowledge or experience, seem to be the most helpful.

Scripted Cooperation. Donald Dansereau and his colleagues have developed a method for learning in pairs called **scripted cooperation**. Students work together on almost any task, including reading a selection of text, solving math problems, or editing writing drafts. In reading, for example, both partners read a passage, and then one student gives an oral summary. The other partner comments on the summary, noting omissions or errors. Next, the partners work together to elaborate on the information—create associations, images, mnemonics, ties to previous work, examples, analogies, and so on. The partners switch roles of summarizer and listener for the next section of the reading, and then continue to take turns until they finish the assignment (Dansereau, 1985; O'Donnell & O'Kelly, 1994).

There are many other forms of cooperative learning. In Chapter 11 you will find methods that emphasize increasing motivation through teamwork and interteam competition. Spencer Kagan (1994) has written extensively on the subject and developed many formats.

Another constructivist approach that relies heavily on interaction is instructional conversations.

FIGURE 9.2

Reciprocal Questioning Prompt Cards to Guide Dialogue

After studying material or participating in a lesson, pairs of students use the "Prompt Cards" below to develop questions and then share answers.

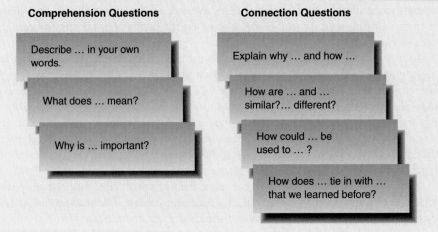

Source: Adapted from Alison King, Guiding knowledge construction in the classroom. Effects of teaching children how to question and how to explain. *American Educational Research Journal, 31*, p. 345. Copyright 1994 by the American Educational Research Association. Reprinted by permission of the publisher.

Reciprocal Questioning: Approach where groups of two or three students ask and answer each other's questions after a lesson or presentation.

Scripted Cooperation: A learning strategy in which two students take turns summarizing material and criticizing the summaries.

Dialogue and Instructional Conversations

One implication of Vygotsky's theory of cognitive development is that important learning and understanding require interaction and conversation. Students need to grapple with problems in their zone of proximal development, and they need the scaffolding provided by interaction with a teacher or other students. Instructional conversations provide these opportunities. **Instructional conversations** are *instructional* because they are designed to promote learning, but they are *conversations*, not lectures or traditional discussions. Here is a segment of conversation from a literature group in a bilingual Grade 3 classroom (Moll & Whitmore, 1993). The conversation shows how the participants mediate each other's learning through dialogue about the shared experience.

> **T:** *Sylvester and the Magic Pebble.* What did you think about this story?
>
> **Rita:** I think they cared a lot for him.
>
> **T:** What do you mean? You mean his parents?
>
> **Rita:** Yes.
>
> **T:** What made you think that when you read the story?
>
> **Rita:** Because they really worried about him.
>
> **T:** Who else wants to share something? I'd like to hear everybody's ideas. Then we can decide what we want to talk about. Sarah?
>
> **Sarah:** I think he got the idea of it when he was little, or maybe one of his friends got lost or something?
>
> **T:** What do you mean, he got the idea?
>
> **Sarah:** He got the idea for his parents to think that Sylvester got lost.
>
> **T:** You're talking about where William Steig might have gotten his ideas.
>
> **Sarah:** Yes.
>
> **T:** That maybe something like this happened to him or someone he knew. A lot of times authors get their ideas from real life things, don't they? Jon, what did you think about this story?
>
> **Jon:** It was like a moral story. It's like you can't wish for everything. But, in a sense, everything happened to him when he was panicking.
>
> **T:** When did you think he panicked?
>
> **Jon:** Well, when he saw the lion, he started to panic.
>
> **Richard:** And he turned himself into a rock.
>
> **Jon:** Yeah. He said, "I wish I were a rock."
>
> **T:** Right. And it happened, didn't it?
>
> **Richard:** It was stupid of him.
>
> **T:** So maybe he wasn't thinking far enough ahead? What would you have wished instead of a rock? (pp. 24–25)

The conversation continues as the students contribute different levels of interpretation of the story. The teacher notes these interpretations in her summary: "Look at all the different kinds of things you had to say. Rita talked about the characters in the story and what they must be feeling. Sarah took the author's point of view. And you saw it as a particular kind of story, Jon, a moral story."

In instructional conversations, the teacher's goal is to keep everyone cognitively engaged in a substantive discussion. In the above conversation, the teacher takes almost every other turn. As the students become more familiar with this learning approach, we would expect them to talk more among themselves with less teacher talk. These conversations do not have to be long. Even taking up lunch money can be an opportunity for an instructional conversation.

Instructional Conversation: Situation in which students learn through interactions with teachers and/or other students.

During the first few minutes of the day, Ms. White asked how many children wanted hot lunches that day. Eighteen children raised their hands. Six children were going to eat cold lunches. Ms. White asked, "How many children are going to eat lunch here today?"

By starting with 18 and counting on, several children got to the answer of 24. One child got out counters and counted out a set of 18 and another set of 6. He then counted all of them and said "24."

Ms. White then asked, "How many more children are eating hot lunch than are eating cold lunch?"

Several children counted back from 18 to 12. The child with the blocks matched 18 blocks with 6 blocks and counted the blocks left over.

Ms. White asked the children who volunteered to tell the rest of the class how they got the answer. Ms. White continued asking for different solutions until no one could think of a new way to solve the problem. (Peterson, Fennema, & Carpenter, 1989, p. 45)

This teacher is creating an environment in which students can make sense of mathematics and use mathematics to make sense of the world. To accomplish these goals, teaching begins with the student's current understanding. Teachers can capitalize on the natural use of counting strategies to see how many different ways students can solve a problem. The emphasis is on mathematical thinking, not on math "facts" or on learning the one best (teacher's) way to solve the problem. The teacher is a guide, helping students construct their own understandings through dialogue (Putnam & Borko, 1998). Table 9.6 on page 337 summarizes the elements of productive instructional conversations.

Cognitive Apprenticeships

Over the centuries, apprenticeships have proved to be an effective form of education. By working alongside a master and perhaps other apprentices, young people have learned many skills, trades, and crafts. Apprenticeships are powerful teaching and learning opportunities and can be beneficial to both master and apprentice. More knowledgeable guides provide models, demonstrations, and corrections, as well as a personal bond that is motivating. The performances required of the learner are real and important and grow more complex as the learner becomes more competent (Collins, Brown, & Holum, 1991; Collins, Brown, & Newman, 1989). In addition, both the newcomers to learning and the old-timers contribute to the community of practice by mastering and remastering skills—and sometimes improving these skills in the process (Lave & Wenger, 1991).

Allan Collins and his colleagues (1989) suggest that knowledge and skills learned in school have become too separated from their use in the world beyond school. To correct this imbalance, some educators recommend that schools adopt many of the features of apprenticeships. But rather than focusing on learning to sculpt or dance or build a cabinet, apprenticeships in school would focus on cognitive objectives such as reading comprehension, writing, or mathematical problem solving. There are many cognitive apprenticeship models, but most share six features:

▶ Students observe an expert (usually the teacher) *model* the performance.

▶ Students get external support through *coaching* or tutoring (including hints, feedback, models, and reminders).

▶ Students receive conceptual *scaffolding*, which is then gradually faded as the student becomes more competent and proficient.

▶ Students continually *articulate* their knowledge—putting into words their understanding of the processes and content being learned.

▶ Students *reflect* on their progress, comparing their problem solving to an expert's performance and to their own earlier performances.

TABLE 9.6 Elements of the Instructional Conversation

Good instructional conversations must have elements of both instruction and conversation.

Instructional

1. *Thematic focus.* Teacher selects a theme on which to focus the discussion and has a general plan for how the theme will unfold, including how to "chunk" the text to permit optimal exploration of the theme.

2. *Activation and use of background knowledge.* Teacher either "hooks into" or provides students with pertinent background knowledge necessary for understanding a text, weaving the information into the discussion.

3. *Direct teaching.* When necessary, teacher provides direct teaching of a skill or concept.

4. *Promotion of more complex language and expression.* Teacher elicits more extended student contributions by using a variety of elicitation techniques: invitations to expand, questions, restatements, and pauses.

5. *Promotion of bases for statements or positions.* Teacher promotes students' use of text, pictures, and reasoning to support an argument or position, by gently probing: "What makes you think that?" or "Show us where it says _____."

Conversational

6. *Fewer "known-answer" questions.* Much of the discussion centres on questions for which there might be more than one correct answer.

7. *Responsiveness to student contributions.* While having an initial plan and maintaining the focus and coherence of the discussion, teacher is also responsive to students' statements and the opportunities they provide.

8. *Connected discourse.* The discussion is characterized by multiple, interactive, connected turns; succeeding utterances build on and extend previous ones.

9. *Challenging, but non-threatening, atmosphere.* Teacher creates a challenging atmosphere that is balanced by a positive affective climate. Teacher is more collaborator than evaluator and students are challenged to negotiate and construct the meaning of the text.

10. *General participation, including self-selected turns.* Teacher does not hold exclusive right to determine who talks; students are encouraged to volunteer or otherwise influence the selection of speaking turns.

Source: From Claude Goldenberg (1991). *Instructional Conversations and Their Classroom Application*, p. 7. Santa Cruz, CA and Washington, DC: National Center for Research on Cultural Diversity and Second Language Learning. Reprinted by permission.

▶ Students are required to *explore* new ways to apply what they are learning—ways that they have not practised at the master's side.

As students learn, they are challenged to master more complex concepts and skills and to perform them in many different settings (Roth & Bowen, 1995; Shuell, 1996).

How can teaching provide **cognitive apprenticeships?** In some schools, for example, students of different ages work side by side for part of every day on a "pod" designed to have many of the qualities of an apprenticeship. The pods might focus on a craft or a discipline. Examples include gardening, architecture, and "making money." Many levels of expertise are evident in the students of different ages, so students can move at a comfortable pace, but still have the model of a master available. Community volunteers, including many parents, visit to demonstrate a skill that is related to the pod topic.

Another successful example of cognitive apprenticeships is the reciprocal teaching approach.

Cognitive Apprenticeship: A relationship in which a less experienced learner acquires knowledge and skills under the guidance of an expert.

An Example of a Cognitive Apprenticeship: Reciprocal Teaching

▲ *Annemarie Palincsar's research has focused attention on strategies that improve reading comprehension.*

Connect & Extend
To the research
Rosenshine, B., and Meister, C. (1994). Reciprocal teaching: A review of the research. *Review of Educational Research, 64,* 479–530.

The goal of **reciprocal teaching** is to help students understand and think deeply about what they read (Palincsar, 1986; Palincsar & Brown, 1984, 1989). To accomplish this goal, students in small reading groups are taught four tactics: *summarizing* the content of a passage, *asking a question* about the central point, *clarifying* the difficult parts of the material, and *predicting* what will come next. These are tactics that skilled readers apply almost automatically, but poor readers seldom do—or they don't know how. To use the tactics effectively, poorer readers need direct instruction, modelling, and practice in actual reading situations.

Palincsar (1986) characterizes reciprocal teaching as "a dialogue between teachers and students in which participants take turns assuming the role of teacher" (p. 77). The "teacher"—whether the adult teacher or a student—leads a dialogue that is structured in terms of the four strategies. Initially the classroom teacher introduces the four strategies, perhaps focusing on one strategy each day. The introduction explains each strategy and the teacher models it. Next, students have opportunities to practise and receive feedback from the teacher on using the strategy. As students become more adept with each strategy for understanding text, the teacher gradually shifts onto them the responsibility for leading the discussion. The role of the teacher transforms into the role of a coach who offers guidance and feedback only as needed. Palincsar (1986) stresses that "the rate at which this transfer occurs will vary among students," but each student should be given the level of support necessary to carry out the strategies successfully (p. 78). In this way, the teacher is providing what Bruner (Wood, Bruner, & Ross, 1976) calls scaffolded instruction. According to Palincsar, the "hallmark of scaffolded instruction is its interactive nature. . . [where dialogue] is the means by which support is provided and adjusted" (p. 75).

An Example of Reciprocal Teaching.   Let's look at examples of reciprocal teaching. First, let's see how one teacher introduced her students to reciprocal teaching (Palincsar, 1986, p. 84).

> T: . . . Does anyone remember those four activities that we were talking about when we were talking about thinking as we listen to the story?
>
> S1: We give a summary.
>
> T: One was summary, right. And what do we do when we talk about summarizing? T__?
>
> S2: Tell about the story.
>
> T: Yes, and you don't have to tell all about it, just the most important ideas. What was another thing we talked about? B__?
>
> S3: Questions.
>
> T: Yes. . . What do we ask questions about? Anything at all?
>
> S3: About the story and see if we understand.
>
> T: Right. . .
> . . .
>
> T: . . .We're going to start today with some stories and we're going to use those four different activities. . . summaries, questioning, predicting, and clarifying to help us understand the story.

Notice how this teacher refines her questions and elaborates her students' responses, scaffolding their understanding of the strategies they will be using to comprehend text. In the following examples, teachers and students are applying the strategies, first, in an early lesson and, then, after 19 lessons (Palincsar, 1986, pp. 89–93). In this early lesson, the classroom teacher leads the discussion.

> T: Today we're going to have a new story about a new animal. We will still be doing the same things. . . summariz[ing]. . . The title of today's story

Reciprocal Teaching: A method, based on modelling, to teach reading comprehension strategies.

is "Cats Do Talk." Any predictions about what you think this story is going to tell us?

S3: That cats can talk.

T: Exactly. . . How do you think they talk, R__?

S3: They move their tails.

T: Any other predictions? Let's see if R__'s predictions are right. . .

Reading

T: How do cats show their feelings?

S4: They talk. They make a sound.

T: Did the paragraph tell us about any other way they can talk to us?

S1: They come up to you.

T: So, through their movements they can show you whether they need something?

S2: They come up to your arm.

. . .

T: Very good. If I were going to summarize, I would say. . . [summarizes]. There was a word here that I'm not quite sure if I understand. [Asks students to clarify.]

In the next example, taken from the 19th lesson, S6 leads the discussion.

S6: [After reading.] What does the daddy-long-legs do when something comes around it?

S1: Use that odour and. . .

S6: Yeah. C___?

S2: When an animal comes along, he puts out his odour and they get too sick to catch him.

S6: Yeah. M__?

S4: Or too weak.

S3: They feel too weak and too sick.

S6: Everybody gave me good answers.

T: Very good.

S6: I will summarize. . .

Applying Reciprocal Teaching. Research on reciprocal teaching has shown some dramatic results. Although reciprocal teaching seems to work with almost any age student, most of the research has been done with younger adolescents who can read aloud fairly accurately but who are far below average in reading comprehension. After 20 hours of practice with this approach, many students who were in the bottom quarter of their class moved up to the average or above-average level on tests of reading comprehension. Based on the results of several studies, Palincsar has identified three guidelines for effective reciprocal teaching (Palincsar & Brown, 1984; "When the Student Becomes the Teacher," 1986):

1. *Shift gradually.* The shift from teacher control to student responsibility must be gradual.

2. *Match demands to abilities.* The difficulty of the task and the responsibility must match the abilities of each student and grow as these abilities develop.

3. *Diagnose thinking.* Teachers should carefully observe the "teaching" of each student for clues about how the student is thinking and what kind of instruction the student needs.

In reciprocal teaching, Annemarie Palincsar and Ann Brown have made four significant contributions to education. First, they remind us that procedures for fostering and monitoring comprehension must be taught—not all students develop

Stand-Alone Thinking Skills Programs: Programs that teach thinking skills directly without need for an extensive knowledge of subject matter.

these tactics on their own. Second, Palincsar and Brown focused attention on 4 rather than 40 or more tactics, as some sources have suggested. Third, they emphasized practising these 4 tactics in the context of actual reading—reading literature and reading texts. Finally, they refined and developed the idea of scaffolding and gradually moving the student toward independent and fluid reading comprehension (Rosenshine & Meister, 1994).

With a consideration of reciprocal teaching, we are moving toward instructional approaches that emphasize social interaction and students' active construction of meaning.

Cognitive Apprenticeships in Thinking

Many educational psychologists believe that good thinking can and should be developed in school. But clearly, the teaching of thinking entails much more than the standard classroom practices of answering "thought" questions at the end of the chapter or participating in teacher-led discussions. What else is needed? One approach has been to focus on the development of *thinking skills,* either through stand-alone programs that teach skills directly, or through indirect methods that embed development of thinking in the regular curriculum.

Stand-Alone Programs for Developing Thinking. There are many different programs that teach thinking skills directly. A resource book for educators (Costa, 1985) lists more than 15 different programs, including *de Bono's CoRT* system; *Odyssey: A Curriculum for Thinking*; *Winocur's Project Impact*; *Lipman's Philosophy for Children*; and *Meeker's SOI.* In these programs students learn skills such as comparing, ordering, classifying, and making inferences. The advantage of these **stand-alone thinking skills programs** is that students do not need extensive knowledge of subject matter to master the skills. Students who have had trouble with the traditional curriculum may achieve success—and perhaps an enhanced sense of self-efficacy—through these programs. As you saw in Chapter 8, encouraging students to transfer knowledge and skills to new situations is a challenge for all teachers (Mayer & Wittrock, 1996; Prawat, 1991). The disadvantage is that the general skills often are not used outside the program unless teachers make a concerted effort to show students how to apply the skills in specific subjects, as you can see in the Point/Counterpoint discussion.

"WE DID THAT LAST YEAR—HOW COME WE HAVE TO DO IT AGAIN THIS YEAR?"

(© W. A. Vanselown. From Phi Delta Kappan.)

Developing Thinking in Every Class. Another way to develop students' thinking is to provide cognitive apprenticeships in analysis, problem solving, and reasoning through the regular lessons of the curriculum. David Perkins and his colleagues (Perkins, Jay, & Tishman, 1993) propose that teachers do this by creating a *culture of thinking* in their classrooms. This means that there is a spirit of inquisitiveness and critical thinking, a respect for reasoning and creativity, and an expectation that students will learn and understand. In such a classroom, education is seen as *enculturation*, a broad and complex process of acquiring knowledge and understanding consistent with Vygotsky's theory of mediated learning. We all learned language by being a member of a particular cultural group. We also learned ways of interacting, norms of appropriate behaviour, and many other complicated rules and procedures through living in a culture that supports certain knowledge and values. Just as our home culture taught us lessons about the use of language, the culture of a classroom can teach lessons about thinking by giving us *models* of good thinking; providing *direct instruction* in thinking processes; and encouraging *practice* of those thinking processes through *interactions* with others.

Let's consider how this might happen in a classroom described by Perkins, Jay, and Tishman (1993).

Suppose a Grade 8 teacher wants her students to learn how to construct explanations that involve *multiple causes*. The class is studying the agriculture of eastern Asia, specifically the important rice crops. The teacher introduces a lesson by *modelling* good thinking about multiple causes:

> Have you noticed that the roses in the park bloomed early this year? I'm asking myself why. What factors caused these early blooms? I recall it was a warm winter. That was probably an important factor. But certainly there are other factors involved—probably some hidden ones—and I know it is important to search for them. In fact, now that I have stopped to think, I remember that we had very heavy rains in March. This may be a factor too. (Perkins, Jay, & Tishman, 1993, p. 80)

After providing this model, the teacher points out other effects that have multiple causes, such as winning a skating contest or staying healthy. Next, the teacher gives straightforward, *direct instruction* about how to analyze causes, such as considering how causal factors may work together or separately. She teaches the students to draw diagrams that depict multiple causes. Then she gives the students *practice* in analyzing multiple causes by asking them to diagram the causes involved in rice growth and how the causes work together or separately to produce rice. The teacher stimulates their thinking by suggesting that the students cast a wide net and consider many factors, such as weather, soil, insects, and farming practices. One student's diagram is presented in Figure 9.3 on page 343.

When the students finish their diagrams, the teacher asks them to each discuss their analysis with a partner. She guides the *interaction* with questions such as "How did you identify causes?" "Was it hard to figure out if causes worked together or alone?" "What questions can you invent about this multifactor causal analysis game?" "Can you envision other situations where you could use this kind of causal analysis?"

In this lesson, the four factors of modelling, direct instruction, practice, and interaction help students become expert members of the thinking community.

The Language of Thinking. How many words can you find in the above lesson that describe aspects of thinking? A quick look finds "search," "asking why," "hidden factors," "analyze," "identify," "figure out," "envision," "effects," "causes," and "invent." Phil's computer's thesaurus just found over 100 more words when he highlighted "thinking." The language of thinking consists of natural language terms that refer to mental processes and mental products—"words like *think, believe, guess, conjecture, hypothesis, evidence, reasons, estimate, calculate, suspect, doubt,* and *theorize*—to name just a few" (Tishman, Perkins, & Jay, 1993, p. 8). The classroom should be filled with a clear, precise, and rich vocabulary of thinking. Rather than saying, "What do you think about Jamie's answer?" the teacher might ask questions that expand thinking, such as "What evidence can you give to refute or support Sandeep's answer?" and "What assumptions is Sandeep making?" "What are some alternative explanations?" Students surrounded by a rich language of thinking are more likely to think deeply about thinking. Students learn more when they engage in talk that is interpretive and that analyzes

Connect & Extend
To the research
Adams, M. J. (1989). Thinking skills curricula. *Educational Psychologist, 24*, 25–27. This article addresses the explosion of interest in the teaching of thinking. What content or processes should a thinking-skills curriculum include? How should it be organized? In what ways would such a curriculum differ in force or effect from thoughtful delivery of conventional school topics? This article concludes that the direct teaching of thinking offers an important complement to the conventional school regimen for all students, and is invaluable for those with scholastic difficulties.

Connect & Extend
To the research
Perkins, D., Jay, E., and Tishman, S. (1993). New conceptions of thinking: From ontology to education. *Educational Psychologist, 28,* 67–85; see also Tishman, S., Perkins, D., and Jay, E. (1995). *The thinking classroom: Learning and teaching in a culture of thinking.* Boston: Allyn and Bacon.

Connect & Extend
To what you know
List all the different words related to thinking that you hear during one of your university or college classes. You might contrast the "thinking language" in a class that seems to challenge you to think with a class that focuses on skills and facts.

Should Schools Teach Critical Thinking and Problem Solving?

The question of whether schools should focus on process or content, problem-solving skills or core knowledge, higher-order thinking skills or academic information has been debated for years. Some educators suggest that students must be taught how to think and solve problems, while other educators assert that students cannot learn to "think" in the abstract. They must be thinking about something—some content. Should teachers focus on knowledge or thinking?

▶ **POINT** *Problem solving and higher-order thinking can and should be taught.*

An article in the April 28, 1995, issue of the *Chronicle of Higher Education* makes this claim:

> Critical thinking is at the heart of effective reading, writing, speaking, and listening. It enables us to link together mastery of content with such diverse goals as self-esteem, self-discipline, multicultural education, effective cooperative learning, and problem solving. It enables all instructors and administrators to raise the level of their own teaching and thinking. (p. A-71)

How can students learn to think critically? Some educators recommend teaching thinking skills directly with widely used techniques such as CoRT (Cognitive Research Trust) or the Productive Thinking Program. Other researchers argue that learning computer programming languages such as LOGO will improve

students' minds and teach them how to think logically. For example, Papert (1980) believes that when children learn through discovery how to give instructions to computers in LOGO, "powerful intellectual skills are developed in the process" (p. 60). Finally, because expert readers automatically apply certain metacognitive strategies, many educators and psychologists recommend directly teaching novice or poor readers how to apply these strategies. Michael Pressley's Good Strategy User model and Palincsar and Brown's (1984) reciprocal teaching approach are successful examples of direct teaching of metacognitive skills. Research on these approaches generally shows improvements in achievement and comprehension for students of all ages who participate (Pressley, Barkowski, & Schneider, 1987; Rosenshine & Meister, 1994).

◀ **COUNTERPOINT** *Thinking and problem-solving skills do not transfer.*

According to E. D. Hirsch Jr., a vocal critic of critical thinking programs:

> But whether such direct instruction of critical thinking or self-monitoring *does* in fact improve performance is a subject of debate in the research community. For instance, the research regarding critical thinking is not reassuring. Instruction in critical thinking has been going on in several countries for over a hundred years. Yet researchers found that students from nations as

varied as Israel, Germany, Australia, the Philippines, and the United States, including those who have been taught critical thinking continue to fall into logical fallacies. (1996, p. 136)

The CoRT program has been used in more than 5000 classrooms in 10 nations. But Polson and Jeffries (1985) report that "after 10 years of widespread use we have no adequate evidence concerning. . . the effectiveness of the program" (p. 445). In addition, Mayer and Wittrock (1996) note that field studies of problem solving in real situations show that people often fail to apply the mathematical problem-solving approaches they learn in school to actual problems encountered in the grocery store or home.

Even though educators have been more successful in teaching metacognitive skills, critics still caution that there are times when such teaching hinders rather than helps learning. Robert Siegler (1993) suggests that teaching self-monitoring strategies to low-achieving students can interfere with the students' development of adaptive strategies. Forcing students to use the strategies of experts may put too much burden on working memory as the students struggle to use an unfamiliar strategy and miss the meaning or content of the lesson. For example, rather than teach students strategies for figuring out words from context, it may be helpful for students to focus on learning more vocabulary words.

and gives explanations. Talk that just describes but doesn't explain, give reasons, identify parts, make a case, defend a position, or evaluate evidence is less helpful in learning (Palincsar, 1998).

Critical Thinking: Evaluating conclusions by logically and systematically examining the problem, the evidence, and the solution.

Critical Thinking. Critical thinking skills are useful in almost every life situation—even in evaluating the media ads that constantly bombard us. To evaluate the claim that 99 out of 100 dentists prefer a particular brand of toothpaste, you must consider such questions as: Which dentists were polled? How were they chosen? Was the toothpaste company involved in the polling process? If so, how

FIGURE 9.3

A Multicausal Analysis of Factors Affecting Rice Growth

Students are taught how to use the *and/or* convention to diagram causes that work together *(and)* or separately *(or)* to produce an effect; in this case, the growth of rice.

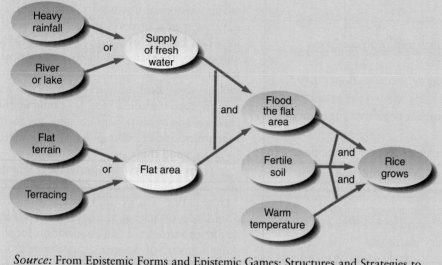

Source: From Epistemic Forms and Epistemic Games: Structures and Strategies to Guide Inquiry, by A. Collins and W. Ferguson, 1993, *Educational Psychologist,* 28, p. 35. Adapted by permission of the publisher and the authors.

▲ *This girl appears to be engrossed in her reading, but how does her teacher know that she is making sense of what she is reading, or what her understanding of the text is?*

could this bias the results of the poll? Or when you see a group of gorgeous people extolling the virtues of a particular brand of orange juice as they frolic in skimpy bathing suits, you must decide if sex appeal is a relevant factor in choosing a fruit drink. Psychologists have not been able to agree on the skills that constitute critical thinking, but Table 9.7 provides a representative list of skills.

Connect & Extend
To professional journals
Educational Leadership (1988, April), Vol. 45, No. 7, has a special section called "Teaching Thinking Throughout the Curriculum."

Connect & Extend
To the research
Greeno, J. G. (1989). A perspective on thinking. American Psychologist, 44, 134–141.
   Abbreviated abstract: Research on general thinking abilities—productive, higher-order, critical, and creative thinking—has progressed slowly compared with the rapid progress in the study of cognitive structures and procedures. Three framing assumptions for the study of thinking are proposed, involving situated cognition, personal and social epistemologies, and conceptual competence; topics in the psychology of thinking are discussed in relation to the assumptions.

TABLE 9.7   Examples of Critical Thinking Skills

Defining and Clarifying the Problem

1. Identify central issues or problems.
2. Compare similarities and differences.
3. Determine which information is relevant.
4. Formulate appropriate questions.

Judfing Information Related to the Problem

5. Distinguish among fact, opinion, and reasoned judgment.
6. Check consistency.
7. Identify unstated assumptions.
8. Recognize stereotypes and clichés.
9. Recognize bias, emotional factors, propaganda, and semantic slanting.
10. Recognize different value systems and ideologies.

Solving Problems/Drawing Conclusions

11. Recognize the adequacy of data.
12. Predict probable consequences.

Source: From "California Assesses Critical Thinking," by P. Kneedler. In A. Costa (Ed.), *Developing Minds: A Resource Book for Teaching Thinking*, p. 277. Copyright © 1985 by the Association for Supervision and Curriculum Development and the author. Reprinted with permission. All rights reserved.

FAMILY AND COMMUNITY PARTNERSHIPS

Communicating about Innovations

Be confident and honest.

Examples

1. Write out your rationale for the methods you are using—consider likely objections and craft your responses.
2. Admit mistakes or oversights—explain what you have learned from them.

Treat parents as equal partners.

Examples

1. Listen carefully to parents' objections, take notes, and follow up on requests or suggestions—remember, you both want the best for the child.
2. Give parents the telephone number of an administrator who will answer their questions about a new program or initiative.
3. Invite families to visit your room or assist in the project in some way.

Communicate effectively.

Examples

1. Use plain language and avoid jargon. If you must use a technical term, define it in accessible ways. Use your best teaching skills to educate parents about the new approach.
2. Encourage local newspapers or television stations to do stories about the "great learning" going on in your classroom or school.

3. Create a lending library of articles and references about the new strategies.

Have examples of projects and assignments available for parents when they visit your class.

Examples

1. Encourage parents to try math activities. If they have trouble, show them how your students (and their child) are successful with the activities and highlight the strategies the students have learned.
2. Keep a library of students' favourite activities to demonstrate for parents.

Develop family involvement packages.

Examples

1. Once a month, send families, via their children, descriptions and examples of the math, science, or language to be learned in the upcoming unit. Include activities children can do with their parents.
2. Make the family project count, for example, as a homework grade.

Source: From Addressing Parents' Concerns over Curriculum Reform, by M. Meyer, M. Delgardelle, and J. Middleton, 1996, *Educational Leadership*, 53(7), p. 57. Copyright © 1996 by the Association for Supervision and Curriculum Development. Adapted with permission. All rights reserved.

Summary

Social Learning and Social Cognitive Theories

Distinguish between social learning and social cognitive theories.

Social learning theory was an early neo-behavioural theory that expanded behavioural views of reinforcement and punishment. In behavioural views, reinforcement and punishment directly affect behaviour. In social learning theory, seeing another person, a model, reinforced or punished can have similar effects on the observer's behaviour. Social cognitive theory expands social learning theory to include cognitive factors such as beliefs, expectations, and perceptions of self.

Distinguish between enactive and vicarious learning.

Enactive learning is learning by doing and experiencing the consequences of your actions. *Vicarious learning* is learning by observing. It challenges the behaviourist idea that cognitive factors are unnecessary in an explanation of learning. If people can learn by watching, they must be focusing their attention, constructing images, remembering, analyzing, and making decisions that affect learning. Thus much is going on mentally before performance and reinforcement can even take place.

What are the elements of observational learning?

The elements are *paying attention, retaining information or impressions, producing behaviour,* and *being motivated* to repeat the behaviour. To learn through observation, we have to pay attention to aspects of the situation that will help us learn. To imitate the behaviour of a model, you have to retain the information. This involves mentally representing the model's actions in some way, probably as verbal steps. In the production phase, practice makes the behaviour smoother and more expert. Sometimes we need a great deal of practice, feedback, and coaching about subtle points before we can reproduce the behaviour of the model. Finally, motivation shapes observational learning through incentives and reinforcement. We may acquire a new skill or behaviour through observation, but we may not perform that behaviour until there is some motivation or incentive to do so. Reinforcement can play several roles in observational learning, including focusing attention, encouraging reproduction or practice, and supporting maintenance of the new learning.

What is reciprocal determinism?

Environmental events, personal factors, and behaviour interact in the process of learning. Personal factors (beliefs, expectations, attitudes, and knowledge), the physical and social environment (resources, consequences of actions, other people, and physical settings), and behaviour (individual actions, choices, and verbal statements) all influence and are influenced by each other.

Constructivism and Situated Learning

Describe three kinds of constructivism.

Psychological constructivists are concerned with how *individuals* make sense of their worlds. These constructivists might be interested in individual knowledge, beliefs, self-concept, or identity, so they are sometimes called *individual* constructivists; they all focus on the inner psychological life of people. Piaget is an example of an individual constructivist. *Social* constructivists believe that social interaction, cultural tools, and activity shape individual development and learning. By participating in a broad range of activities with others, learners appropriate (take for themselves) the outcomes produced by working together; they acquire new strategies and knowledge of their world. Most psychologists classify Vygotsky as a social constructivist. Finally, sociological constructivists are interested in how public knowledge in disciplines such as science, math, economics, or history is constructed as well as how everyday beliefs and commonly held understandings about the world are communicated to new members of a sociocultural group.

In what ways do constructivist views differ about knowledge sources, accuracy, and generality?

Constructivists debate whether knowledge is constructed by mapping external reality, by adapting and changing internal understandings, or by an interaction of external forces and internal understandings. Most psychologists posit a role for both internal and external factors, but differ in how much they emphasize one or the other. Some constructivists argue that the world is knowable and that humans can construct accurate, logical, or warranted models of reality. Others argue that all constructions are equally valid and correct, even though some may be more useful than others. Also, there is discussion about whether knowledge can be constructed in one situation and applied to another or whether knowledge is so specific and tied to the context in which it was learned that it cannot be used successfully in another context. Situated learning emphasizes the latter view—the importance of physical and social contexts in learning.

What are some common elements in most constructivist views of learning?

Even though there is no single constructivist theory, many constructivist approaches recommend complex, challenging learning environments and authentic tasks; social negotiation and shared responsibility as a part of learning; multiple representations of content; understanding that knowledge is constructed; and student-centred instruction.

Applications of Constructivist and Situated Perspectives on Learning

Distinguish between inquiry and problem-based learning.

There have been many adaptations of inquiry, but the strategy begins when the teacher presents a puzzling event, question, or problem. The students then formulate hypotheses to explain the event or solve the problem; collect data to test the hypotheses; draw conclusions; and reflect on the original problem and the thinking processes needed to solve it. Problem-based learning may follow a similar path, but the learning begins with an authentic problem—one that matters to the students. The goal is to learn math or science or history or some other important subject while seeking a real solution to the problem.

Describe five elements that define true cooperative learning.

Students *interact face to face* and close together, not across the room. Group members experience *positive interdependence*—they need each other for support, explanations, and guidance. Even though they work together and help each other, members of the group must ultimately demonstrate learning on their own—they are held *individually accountable* for learning, often through individual tests or other assessments. If necessary, the *collaborative skills* important for effective group functioning, such as giving constructive feedback, reaching consensus, and involving every member, are taught and practised before the groups tackle a learning task. Finally, members monitor *group processes* and relationships to make sure the group is working effectively and to learn about the dynamics of groups.

Describe six features that most cognitive apprenticeship approaches share.

There are many cognitive apprenticeship models, but most share six features: Students observe an expert (usually the teacher) *model* the performance. Students get external support through *coaching* or tutoring (including hints, feedback, models, and reminders). Students receive conceptual *scaffolding*, which is then gradually faded as the student becomes more competent and proficient. Students continually *articulate* their knowledge—putting into words their understanding of the processes and content being learned. Students *reflect* on their progress, comparing their problem solving to an expert's performance and to their own earlier performances. Students are required to *explore* new ways to apply what they are learning—ways that they have not practised at the master's side.

Describe the use of dialogue in reciprocal teaching.

The goal of reciprocal teaching is to help students understand and think deeply about what they read. To accomplish this goal, students in small reading groups learn four strategies: *summarizing* the content of a passage, *asking a question* about the central point, *clarifying* the difficult parts of the material, and

predicting what will come next. These strategies are practised in a classroom dialogue about the readings. In these dialogues, teachers first take a central role, but as the discussion progresses, the students take more and more control.

What is meant by thinking as enculturation?

Enculturation is a broad and complex process of acquiring knowledge and understanding consistent with Vygotsky's theory of mediated learning. We all learned language, norms of appropriate behaviour, and many other complicated rules by being a member of a particular cultural group. Just as our home culture taught us lessons about the use of language, the culture of a classroom can teach lessons about thinking by giving us *models* of good thinking; providing *direct instruction* in thinking processes; and encouraging *practice* of those thinking processes through *interactions* with others.

Looking Back at Learning

What do different views of learning add to our understanding?

Rather than debating the merits of each approach, consider their contributions to understanding learning and improving teaching. Different views of learning can be used together to create productive learning environments. Behavioural theory helps us understand the role of cues in setting the stage for behaviour and the role of consequences in encouraging or discouraging behaviour. But much of humans' lives and learning is more than behaviour. Language and higher-order thinking require complex information processing and memory—something the cognitive models of the thinker-as-computer helped us understand. And what about the person as a creator and constructor of knowledge, not just a processor of information? Here, constructivist perspectives have much to offer.

𝒦ey Terms

anchored instruction, *p. 329*

cognitive apprenticeship, *p. 337*

community of practice, *p. 323*

complex learning environments, *p. 324*

constructivism, *p. 319*

cooperative learning, *p. 329*

critical thinking, *p. 342*

inquiry learning, *p. 326*

instructional conversation, *p. 335*

intersubjective attitude, *p. 325*

jigsaw, *p. 333*

multiple representations of content, *p. 325*

observational learning, *p. 314*

problem-based learning, *p. 328*

radical constructivism, *p. 322*

reciprocal questioning, *p. 334*

reciprocal teaching, *p. 338*

ripple effect, *p. 316*

scripted cooperation, *p. 334*

self-efficacy, *p. 316*

situated learning, *p. 323*

social cognitive theory, *p. 313*

social learning theory, *p. 313*

social negotiation, *p. 324*

spiral curriculum, *p. 325*

stand-alone thinking skills programs, *p. 340*

vicarious reinforcement, *p. 315*

ℬecoming a Professional

Reflecting on the Chapter

Can you apply the ideas from this chapter on social cognitive and constructivist views of learning to solve the following problems of practice?

Preschool and Kindergarten

▷ One of your students is very fearful of taking risks or attempting any task that does not have a right answer. The child tries to

tell other students "the right way" to do everything. How would you help the student tolerate uncertainty and take risks in her thinking?

Elementary and Middle School

▷ How would you help Grade 3 students understand negative numbers?

▷ You want to use cooperative learning with your students, but they are used to individual work. How would you begin?

Junior High and High School

▷ Your school librarian wants to help all the history classes learn to use the print and database resources in the library. How would you take advantage of this opportunity?

▷ Brainstorm ways to "understand your students' understanding" in a particular content area. What would you do before, during, and after a class to make your students' knowledge and thinking processes visible to both you and them?.

Check Your Understanding

▷ Know elements of observational learning.

▷ Know the five common teaching recommendations shared by most constructivist views.

▷ Be able to recognize examples of inquiry, problem-based learning, cognitive apprenticeships, and instructional conversations.

Your Teaching Portfolio

Use Table 9.8 to think about your own philosophy of learning. Would you incorporate elements from different theoretical approaches into your personal conception of learning?

Teaching Resources

Use the Family and Community Partnerships Guidelines to brainstorm ideas for how you would explain your teaching innovations to families. Experiment by drafting a "Newsletter."

Add Table 9.5, "Possible Student Roles in Cooperative Learning Groups," Table 9.6, "Elements of an Instructional Conversation," and Figure 9.2, "Reciprocal Questioning Prompt Cards to Guide Dialogue," to your teaching resources file.

Weblinks

www.towson.edu/csme/mctp/Essays.html

A site that lists a wide variety of online essays about constructivism. Here, you can find everything from sold research to bandwagon parades. A good spot for material you can use to flex your analytic muscle.

www.human.waseda.ac.jp/~djscott/situated.html

A variety of theory and research papers on situated learning can be found here. Some have been published while others are solely online resources. Several leading researchers are covered.

What Would They Do?

Here is how two practising teachers responded to the teaching situation presented at the beginning of this chapter about the awful "book reviews."

ELAINE A. TAN

Lakeview Elementary School
Burnaby, British Columbia

As a new teacher myself, I understand the initial excitement this teacher was feeling. Rather than feel helpless at this point, remember that these reviews reflect only one type of assessment—the written form. Today's multi-ability-level classrooms require a variety of assessment methods to address diverse backgrounds and learning styles, and to give students more opportunities to demonstrate progress. The key here is to focus less on what needs to be covered and more on how it will be covered—process over content!

The first assignment might have caused some students to feel incapable because they lacked English grammar and writing skills, and had an underdeveloped vocabulary. The key for ESL students is to provide lower-language and higher-interest visuals; for example, to use key words that connect ideas, sentence frames, or line maps. All students will benefit from vocabulary building. Select key vocabulary in each lesson and have students discuss, use, and apply those words.

The teacher should also adapt various instructional methods. For example, supplement long novels with videos or short stories written at appropriate levels to access different learning styles and means of understanding; integrate fine art to access another learning style. Try the same activity again by grouping students in twos and threes, providing each with an interesting article she or he can relate to and write about. Prepare in advance a set of sentence frames to be completed for the students' articles.

Make use of the capable students, since all students benefit from shared learning experiences. Assign these three students as peer tutors in small groups. Cooperative learning groups assist with the inherent behavioural management challenge and help to reduce the isolation, boredom, and fear of sharing some students feel. Small groups also provide the ESL learner with a fluent English speaker, while simultaneously building the confidence and self-esteem of the peer tutor.

Where possible, assign world literature selections based on students' countries of origin to heighten interest and attention span. ESL students may want to write responses in their first languages. Have peer tutors assist in translating ideas into English. This provides major language and interpersonal benefits for both groups of students, along with challenges for the advanced students.

LESLEY PETERSON

Sister High School
Winnipeg, Manitoba

The first thing to determine is whether this writing task was a reasonably reliable diagnostic tool. Did you check that the students were familiar with the conventions of the review form, or fail to make your expectations clear? It might be worth assigning another writing task, before deciding that the students whose papers were lacking in coherence were, in fact, unable to write coherent papers. However, in my experience weak students tend to interpret every writing task as an invitation to retell the story. If these students have failed to do even that coherently, the problem is probably a real one.

How to proceed with the very weak students, then, assuming that their weaknesses are real, requires reference to the program policy and course outline. Also, if the course is required for university entrance or is a prerequisite for such a course, you cannot solely grade on effort and improvement. There must be standards. You should be prepared to differentiate your teaching in terms of the material that students read, the assignments they may choose, and the criteria by which they are evaluated. Differentiating instruction is still a good strategy for the "standards-driven" curriculum while retaining the same evaluation criteria for all students.

Central to the design of courses like this is a strong emphasis on the writing process. You should plan to teach writing, reading, and revision strategies that will be helpful to all or most students. If this is your goal, however, I strongly suggest changing this first assignment. Instead, ask the students to write reviews of the "best" book they have ever read. Knowing what they consider the "best" is invaluable to planning for a wide range of readings that engage students' interest. If you're well and widely read in world literature, you'll be able to find novels, short stories, and poems that intersect with what engages students. It's that old basic principle of teaching: find out where they are, then meet them, and take them forward from there.

If this is a university-entrance course, you should gather more data on the students who appear weak. Check their final marks in the prerequisite course, and talk to previous English teachers. If you still feel the student does not have the reading, writing, and thinking skills necessary for success in this course, consider conferencing with the student's parents. Advise them that this course will be a struggle for their child. An early recommendation to see a guidance counsellor or to change a timetable can be a real favour to the student. Better that the student enrol in an appropriate course now than sit in the wrong one, have her or his self-esteem battered for months, and then drop the course.

As for the really advanced writers, they need to be recognized, supported, and challenged. Nurture and challenge their love of literature and writing. Easy assignments can hurt self-esteem and lead to under-achievement (not to mention boredom). Encourage these students to get involved in whatever writing communities are available. If there isn't a school magazine, encourage them to start one. Many cities have organizations similar to the Manitoba Writers' Guild, which sponsors readings and open-microphone sessions, organizes workshops, etc.

Teaching a separate gifted program for three students is more work than most English teachers have time for. But there are community resources you can access. Does your town library or college have a writer in residence? If your school has a work experience coordinator, can she hook up these students with a professional journalist? Our local theatre gave one of my students a volunteer position reading and making recommendations on scripts. It changed her life.

Find out what kind of writing these students are most interested in and introduce them to other people who care about it as much as they do. You definitely shouldn't punish them for their ability by giving them extra work. It might be possible for them to earn a separate credit for their extra involvement—talk to a guidance counsellor, work experience coordinator, or administrator to find out what's available. And have the grace to admit that these students might learn more if you let them spend part of your class time in the library. They'll respect you more for it, not less.

Motivation: Issues and Explanations

hy are you reading this chapter? Did you open the book because you are curious about motivation and interested in the topic? Or is there a test in your near future? Do you need this course to earn a teaching certificate? To graduate? Maybe you believe you have a good chance to do well in this class, and that belief keeps you working. Perhaps it is some combination of these reasons. What motivates you to study motivation?

Most educators agree that motivating students is a critical task of teaching. We begin with the question "What is motivation?" and examine some answers that have been proposed. This leads to a discussion of intrinsic and extrinsic motivation and four general theories of motivation: behavioural, humanistic, cognitive, and sociocultural. The next major sections of the chapter examine in some detail factors common to contemporary views of motivation: goal orientations; interests and emotions, including curiosity and anxiety; and self-schemas including the important concept of self-efficacy. We end the chapter by examining factors the teacher controls in creating environments, situations, and relationships that can affect students' motivation to learn in school.

Once you have completed this chapter, you should be able to:

▶ Give examples of intrinsic and extrinsic motivation, and of motivation to learn.

▶ Define the concept of motivation from the behavioural, humanistic, cognitive, and sociocultural points of view.

▶ Discuss the possible motivational effects of success and failure and how these effects relate to beliefs about ability.

▶ Set motivating goals for yourself and your students.

▶ Describe the roles of interests and emotions in motivation.

▶ Explain the relationship between self-efficacy, self-determination, and motivation.

▶ Describe the characteristics of mastery-oriented, failure-avoiding, and failure-accepting students.

▶ Define motivation to learn.

▶ Explain how ambiguity and risk of the learning task affect motivation.

▶ Discuss how the value of a task affects motivation to learn.

▶ Describe the characteristics of classrooms that support students' autonomy.

▶ Explain how evaluation procedures and grouping arrangements, particularly cooperative learning, can influence motivation.

▶ Describe potential effects of teachers' expectations on students.

What Would You Do?

This year, many students in your Grade 7 class seem defeated about learning. They look at assignments and protest, "This is too long (too hard, too much)!" "We can't do this by tomorrow (Monday, next week)!" Because they don't exert much effort, of course, they prove themselves right every time—they can't do the work. Neither pep talks nor punishments for incomplete work are making a dent in the students' defeatist attitudes. Even the better students are starting to drag their feet, protest longer assignments, and invest minimal effort in class. You suspect a few students have even started to cheat on tests to save their sinking grades. A few teachers blame the students' negative attitudes on social and economic challenges they face in their community. However, your colleague, who teaches in a high-socioeconomic-status neighbourhood, observes some of the same attitudes and behaviour in her students, perhaps for different reasons.

▶ Are these students "unmotivated"?

▶ Why might they be so pessimistic about learning?

▶ What could you do to change students' attitudes in your class?

▶ How can you save your own sinking motivation?

▶ How will these issues affect the way you teach?

What Is Motivation?

Motivation is usually defined as an internal state that arouses, directs, and maintains behaviour. Psychologists studying motivation have focused on five basic questions (Graham & Weiner, 1996; Pintrich, Marx, & Boyle, 1993):

1. *What choices do people make about their behaviour?* Why do some students, for example, focus on their homework while others watch television?

2. *How long does it take to get started?* Why do some students who choose to do their homework start right away, while others procrastinate?

3. *What is the intensity or level of involvement in the chosen activity?* Once the book bag is opened, is the student absorbed and focused or just going through the motions?

4. *What causes a person to persist or to give up?* Will a student read the entire Shakespeare assignment or just a few pages?

5. *What is the individual thinking and feeling while engaged in the activity?* Is the student enjoying Shakespeare or worrying about an upcoming test?

Answering these questions about real students in classrooms is a challenge. As you will see in this chapter and the next, many factors influence motivation.

Intrinsic and Extrinsic Motivation

We all know how it feels to be motivated, to move energetically toward a goal. We also know what it is like to work hard, even if we are not fascinated by the task. What energizes and directs our behaviour? The explanation could be drives, needs, incentives, fears, goals, social pressure, self-confidence, interests, curiosity, beliefs, values, expectations, and more. Some psychologists have explained motivation in terms of personal *traits* or persistent individual characteristics. Certain people, so the theory goes, have a strong need to achieve, a fear of tests, or an enduring interest in art, so they behave accordingly. They work hard to achieve, avoid tests, or

---

Connect & Extend
To the research
For a thorough discussion of the many terms and concepts related to motivation, see Murphy, P. K., & Alexander, P. A. (2000). A motivated exploration of motivation terminology. *Contemporary Educational Psychology, 25,* 3–53.

Connect & Extend
To the research
Weiner, B. (1990). History of motivational research in education. *Journal of Educational Psychology, 82,* 616–622.
Focus Questions: How are the behavioural and cognitive views of learning reflected in the various theories of motivation? What is the current conception of motivation?

Motivation: An internal state that arouses, directs, and maintains behaviour.

spend hours in art galleries. Other psychologists see motivation more as a *state*, a temporary situation. If, for example, you are reading this paragraph because you have a test tomorrow, you are motivated (at least for now) by the situation. In fact, the motivation we experience at any given time is a combination of trait and state. You may be studying because you value learning *and* because your professor gives pop quizzes.

As you can see, some explanations of motivation rely on internal, personal factors such as needs, interests, curiosity, and enjoyment. Other explanations point to external, environmental factors—rewards, social pressure, punishment, for example. Motivation that stems from internal factors is called **intrinsic motivation**. Intrinsic motivation is the tendency to seek out and persist with challenges as we pursue personal interests and exercise our capabilities (Deci & Ryan, 1985; Reeve, 1996). When we are intrinsically motivated, we do not need external incentives or punishments—*the activity itself is rewarding.* James Raffini (1996) puts it well: intrinsic motivation is "what motivates us to do something when we *don't have* to do anything" (p. 3).

In contrast, when we do something to earn a grade or reward, avoid punishment, please the teacher, or for some other reason that has little to do with the task itself, we experience **extrinsic motivation**. We are not really interested in the activity for its own sake; we care only about what we gain by doing it.

You can't tell just by looking if a behaviour is motivated intrinsically or extrinsically. The essential difference between the two types of motivation is the student's reason for acting, that is, whether the location or **locus of causality** for the action is internal or external—inside or outside the person. Students who read or practise their backstroke may be reading or swimming because they freely chose the activity based on personal interests (*internal locus* of causality/intrinsic motivation), or because someone or something else outside is influencing them (*external locus* of causality/extrinsic motivation) (Reeve, 1996).

Is your motivation for reading this chapter intrinsic or extrinsic? Is your locus of causality internal or external? As you answer this question, you probably realize that these descriptions are not all-or-nothing. Our activities fall along a continuum from fully *self-determined* (internal locus of causality/intrinsic motivation) to fully *determined by others* (external locus of extrinsic motivation). For example, students may freely choose to work hard on activities that they don't find particularly enjoyable because they believe the activities are important for reaching a valued goal. They may spend hours studying anatomy to become a physician. Is this intrinsic or extrinsic motivation? Actually it is in between—the student is freely choosing to respond to outside causes such as medical school requirements. The person has *internalized an external cause.*

In school, both intrinsic and extrinsic motivation are important. Many activities are, or could be, interesting to students. Teaching can encourage students' intrinsic motivation by stimulating their curiosity and making them feel more competent as they learn. But this won't work all the time. Did you find long division or grammar inherently interesting? Was your curiosity piqued by the provinces and their capitals? Teachers will be disappointed if they count on intrinsic motivation to energize every student all the time. In some situations, incentives and external supports are necessary. Teachers must encourage and nurture intrinsic motivation while making sure that extrinsic motivation supports learning (Brophy, 1988; Deci, Koestner, & Ryan, 1999; Ryan & Deci, 1996). To do this, they need to know about factors that influence motivation.

◢our General Approaches to Motivation

Motivation is a vast, complicated subject encompassing many theories. Some theories were developed through work with animals in laboratories. Others are based

"WHAT DO I GET FOR JUST NEATNESS?"

(© Glenn Bernhardt)

▲ A basic question in motivation is "Where does it come from—within or outside the individual?" Why do these children raise their hands in class—because they are interested in the subject or because they want to earn a good grade? The answer is probably much more complicated than either alternative.

What Is Motivation?

▶ Define motivation.

▶ What is the difference between intrinsic and extrinsic motivation?

▶ How does locus of causality apply to motivation?

▶ It is sometimes suggested that one way of improving education would be to pay students for successful school achievement. What would be the likely effects of doing this?

Reward: An object or event that we think is attractive and provide as a consequence of a behaviour.

Incentive: An object or event that encourages or discourages behaviour.

Hierarchy of Needs: Maslow's model of seven levels of human needs, from basic physiological requirements to the need for self-actualization.

Humanistic Views: Approaches to motivation that emphasize personal freedom, choice, self-determination, and striving for personal growth.

Deficiency Needs: Maslow's four lower-level needs, which must be satisfied first.

Being Needs: Maslow's three higher-level needs, sometimes called growth needs.

Self-Actualization: Fulfilling one's potential.

---

on research with humans in situations that used games or puzzles. Some theories grow out of work done in clinical or industrial psychology. Our examination of the field is necessarily selective.

Behavioural Approaches to Motivation

Behaviourists explain motivation with concepts such as "reward" and "incentive." A **reward** is an object or event supplied as a consequence of a particular behaviour that *we* think is attractive. For example, a chemistry teacher might believe bonus points are rewards for students who make neat sketches of lab apparatus in their notebooks. An **incentive** is an object or event that actually motivates a person's behaviour. Students who value bonus points view points as an incentive. Receiving bonus points will motivate these students—they will make neat sketches in their lab reports. According to the behavioural view, then, understanding student motivation requires probing students' views about what they count as incentives and distinguishing these from what we may think are rewards.

If we are consistently reinforced for certain behaviour, we may develop habits or tendencies to act in certain ways. If a student is regularly reinforced by social recognition or privileges on earning letters in volleyball but receives little recognition for studying, that student will probably work longer and harder on perfecting her serve than understanding geometry. Providing grades for learning—or demerits for misbehaviour—is an attempt to motivate students by extrinsic means. Whether this works depends on whether grades are incentives. Of course, in any individual case, other factors can affect how a student behaves.

Humanistic Approaches to Motivation

The **humanistic view** is sometimes called "third-force" psychology because it developed in the 1940s in reaction to two other dominant forces at that time: behaviourism and Freudian psychoanalysis. Proponents of humanistic psychology such as Abraham Maslow and Carl Rogers believed that neither behavioural nor Freudian psychology adequately explained why people act as they do.

Humanistic theories of motivation share a belief that people are continually motivated by inherent needs to fulfill their potential for "self-actualization" (Maslow, 1968, 1970), the inborn "actualizing tendency" (Rogers & Freiberg, 1994), or "self-determination" (Deci, Vallerand, Pelletier, & Ryan, 1991). From the humanistic perspective, motivating students means encouraging their inner resources (Reeve, 1996).

Maslow's Hierarchy. Maslow (1970) suggested people have a **hierarchy of needs.** Lower-order needs must be met before higher-order needs can be addressed. Four lower-order needs—for survival, safety, belongingness and love, and esteem—are categorized as **deficiency needs** because meeting them decreases one's focus on them. Three higher-order needs—knowing and understanding, aesthetic appreciation, and ultimately self-actualization—are called **being needs** because, as these needs are met, people strive for more of these kinds of fulfillment. **Self-actualization** is Maslow's term for self-fulfillment, the realization of personal potential. Maslow's theory has been criticized because people do not always behave as it pre-

What Should Schools Do to Encourage Students' Self-Esteem?

James Beane (1991) begins his article "Sorting Out the Self-Esteem Controversy" with this statement: "In the '90s, the question is not whether schools should enhance students' self-esteem, but how they propose to do so" (p. 25). The attempts to improve students' self-esteem have taken three main forms: personal development activities such as sensitivity training; self-esteem programs where the curriculum focuses directly on improving self-esteem; and structural changes in schools that place greater emphasis on cooperation, student participation, community involvement, and ethnic pride.

▶ **POINT** *The self-esteem movement has problems.*

Attempts to encourage self-esteem directly through sensitivity training or self-esteem courses have not proven very successful. As Beane notes, "Saying 'I like myself and others' in front of a group is not the same as actually feeling that way, especially if I am only doing it because I am supposed to. Being nice has a place in enhancing self-esteem, but it is not enough" (p. 26). Many of the self-esteem courses are commercial packages—costly for schools but without solid evidence that they make a difference for students (Crisci, 1986; Leming, 1981).

Sensitivity training and self-esteem courses share a common conceptual problem. They assume that we encourage self-esteem by changing the individual's beliefs, making the young person work harder against the odds. But what if the student's environment is truly unsafe, debilitating, and unsupportive? Some people have overcome tremendous problems, but to expect everyone to do so "ignores the fact that having positive self-esteem is almost impossible for many young people, given the deplorable conditions under which they are forced to live by the inequities in our society" (Beane, 1991, p. 27).

Because many attempts to encourage self-esteem have been superficial, commercial, and filled with "pop psychology," the self-esteem movement has become an easy target for critics in magazine articles such as "Education: Doing Bad and Feeling Good" (*Time*, February 5, 1990) and "The Trouble with Self-Esteem" (*U.S. News and World Report*, April 2, 1990).

◀ **COUNTERPOINT** *The self-esteem movement has promise.*

Beyond the "feel-good psychology" of some aspects of the self-esteem movement is a basic truth: "Self-esteem is a central feature of human dignity and thus an inalienable human entitlement. As such, schools and other agencies have a moral obligation to help build it and avoid debilitating it" (Beane, 1991, p. 28). If we view self-esteem accurately as a product of our thinking and our actions—our values, ideas, and beliefs as well as our interactions with others—then we see a significant role for the school. Practices that allow authentic participation, cooperation, problem solving, and accomplishment should replace policies that damage self-esteem, such as tracking and competitive grading.

Beane suggests four principles to guide educators:

First, being nice is surely a part of this effort, but it is not enough. Second, there is a place for some direct instruction regarding affective matters, but this is not enough either. Self-esteem and affect are not simply another school subject to be placed in set-aside time slots. Third, the negative affect of "get tough" policies is not a promising route to self-esteem and efficacy. This simply blames young people for problems that are largely not of their own making. Fourth, since self-perceptions are powerfully informed by culture, comparing self-esteem across cultures without clarifying cultural differences is distracting and unproductive. (pp. 29–30)

Source: From "Sorting Out the Self-Esteem Controversy," by J. A. Beane, 1991, *Educational Leadership, 49*(1), pp. 25–30. Copyright © 1991 by the Association for Supervision and Curriculum Development. Reprinted with permission. All rights reserved.

dicts. For example, some people deny themselves lower-order safety needs or friendship needs to achieve knowledge or understanding. Criticisms aside, Maslow's theory does invite looking at the whole person whose physical, emotional, and intellectual needs are interrelated. It helps us understand that, if the classroom is a fearful, unpredictable place, students are likely to be more concerned with safety and less with needs to know and understand.

Cognitive Approaches to Motivation

Cognitive theories of motivation also developed in reaction to behavioural views. Cognitive theorists hold that behaviour is determined by our thinking, not simply

Attribution Theories:
Descriptions of how individuals' explanations, justifications, and excuses influence their motivation and behaviour.

▲ *The needs for safety and belonging are among Maslow's hierarchy of needs.*

by whether we have been reinforced or punished (Schunk, 1996b; Stipek, 1993). Behaviour is initiated and regulated by mental plans (Miller, Galanter, & Pribram, 1960), goals (Locke & Latham, 1990), schemas (Ortony, Clore, & Collins, 1988), expectations (Vroom, 1964), and attributions (Weiner, 1992). One central assumption in cognitive approaches to motivation is that people do not respond directly to external events or physical conditions such as hunger but, rather, to their interpretations of these events. You may have had the experience of being so involved in a project that you skipped a meal, not realizing you were hungry until you noticed the time. Food deprivation did not automatically motivate you to seek food.

In cognitive theories, people are seen as active and curious searchers for information to solve personally relevant problems. They work hard because they enjoy the work and because they want to understand. Thus, cognitive theories, such as Bernard Weiner's attribution theory, emphasize intrinsic motivation.

Attribution Theory. Attribution theory's explanation of motivation begins by assuming we all ask "Why?" as we try to understand our successes and failures. "Why did I flunk my mid-term?" "Why did I do so well this grading period?" Students *attribute* their successes and failures to various factors: ability, effort, mood, knowledge, luck, help, interest, clarity of instructions, the interference of others, unfair policies, and so on. **Attribution theories** of motivation describe how these explanations, justifications, and excuses influence motivation. Bernard Weiner is one major theorist who relates attribution theory to school learning (Weiner, 1979, 1986, 1992, 1994a, 1994b; Weiner & Graham, 1989). According to Weiner, every cause to which students attribute successes or failures can be characterized using three dimensions together:

1. *locus*, the location of the cause as internal or external to the person,
2. *stability*, whether the cause stays the same or can change with context, and
3. *responsibility*, whether the person can control the cause.

For example, luck is external (locus), unpredictable (stability), and can't be controlled (responsibility). Table 10.1 shows common attributions for success or failure on a test.

Weiner believes these three dimensions have important implications for motivation. The *internal/external locus*, for example, is closely related to emotions and self-esteem (Weiner, 1980). If a student attributes success or failure to internal

Connect & Extend
To the research
Graham, S. (1991). A review of attribution theory in achievement contexts. *Educational Psychology Review, 3,* 5–39. This article reviews several major principles of attribution theory as they relate to achievement strivings, including the antecedents to particular self-ascriptions; the emotional consequences of causal attributions for success and failure; help-seeking and help-giving, peer acceptance and rejection; achievement evaluation; and attributional process in African American populations.

TABLE 10.1 Weiner's Theory of Causal Attribution

There are many explanations students can give for why they fail a test. Below are eight reasons representing the eight combinations of locus, stability, and responsibility in Weiner's model of attributions.

Dimension Classification	Reason for Failure
Internal-stable-uncontrollable	Low aptitude
Internal-stable-controllable	Never studies
Internal-unstable-uncontrollable	Sick the day of the exam
Internal-unstable-controllable	Did not study for this particular test
External-stable-uncontrollable	School has hard requirements
External-stable-controllable	Instructor is biased
External-unstable-uncontrollable	Bad luck
External-unstable-controllable	Friends failed to help

Source: From *Human Motivation: Metaphors, Theories and Research* (p. 253), by B. Weiner, 1992, Newbury Park, CA: Sage Publications. Copyright © 1992 by Sage Publications. Adapted with permission.

factors, success leads to feelings of pride and increased motivation, but failure lowers self-esteem. The *stability* dimension is closely related to expectations about the future. If students attribute failures to stable factors, such as the difficulty of the subject matter, they will expect to fail in that subject in the future. But if they attribute outcomes to unstable factors, such as mood or luck, they can hope for better outcomes in the future.

The *responsibility* dimension is related to emotions such as anger, pity, gratitude, or shame (Weiner, 1994a). If students feel responsible for their failures, they may feel guilt. If they feel responsible for successes, they may feel proud. Failing at a task we cannot control can lead to shame or anger toward the person or institution that is in control. Succeeding at uncontrollable tasks leads to feelings of gratefulness or being lucky.

When failure is attributed to lack of ability and the student considers ability to be *uncontrollable*, the sequence of motivation is:

Failure → Lack of Ability → Uncontrollable → Not Responsible → Shame, Embarrassment → Withdraw → Performance Declines

When failure is attributed to lack of effort, the sequence is:

Failure → Lack of Effort → Controllable → Responsible → Guilt → Engagement → Performance Improves

Feeling in control of your learning may lead to choosing more complex academic tasks, applying more effort, and persisting longer in school work (Schunk, 1996b; Weiner, 1994a, b). On the negative side, if people feel they cannot control their lives, self-esteem is likely to be diminished. Continual discrimination against women, people of colour, and individuals with special needs can have this effect (Beane, 1991). Weiner's locus and responsibility dimensions are closely related to Deci's concept of *locus of causality* which is discussed later in the chapter.

Attributions in the Classroom. When regularly successful students fail, they often make attributions to internal, controllable factors: they misunderstood the directions, lacked the necessary knowledge, or simply did not study hard enough, for example. When students see themselves as capable and attribute failure to lack of effort or insufficient knowledge—controllable causes—they usually focus on

Connect & Extend
To your teaching
What are the implications of attribution theories of motivation? Consider the following, taken from "Why can't Susie and Johnny do math?" (1987, July). *Harvard Education Letter, 3*(4), 6–7.
Dale Schunk identified 40 elementary school children who were having trouble with subtraction, divided them into four groups, and set them to working. A monitor checked groups A, B, and C every eight minutes. To each child in the A group she commented, "You've been working hard." To children in the B group she said, "You need to work hard." Children in the C group got no comment at all, and children in the D group had contact with the proctor only when she read them instructions.
The results were unambiguous: youngsters who were told that they had been working hard completed 63 percent more problems than their fellows. They got three times as many subtraction problems right on the test that followed training.

strategies for succeeding next time. This adaptive, mastery-oriented response often leads to achievement, pride, and a greater feeling of control (Ames, 1992).

Difficult motivational problems arise when students attribute failures to stable, uncontrollable causes. Such students may seem resigned to failure, depressed, helpless—"unmotivated" (Weiner, 1994a, 1994b; Weiner, Russell, & Lerman, 1978). Such students respond to failure by focusing even more on their inadequacy; their attitudes toward school work may deteriorate even further (Ames, 1992). Apathy is a logical reaction to failure if students believe its causes are stable and beyond their control. As well, students who view their failures in this light are less likely to seek help—they believe nothing and no one can help (Ames & Lau, 1982).

Teacher Actions and Student Attributions.

How do students determine causes of their successes and failures? Their teachers' behaviour provides cues. When a teacher assumes a student's failure is attributable to forces beyond the student's control, the teacher often responds with sympathy and avoids punishments. If, however, failure is attributed to a controllable factor, especially lack of effort, the teacher's response is likely to be anger and punishments may follow. These tendencies seem to be consistent across time and cultures (Weiner, 1986).

What do students make of their teachers' actions? Graham (1991, 1996) gives some surprising answers. When teachers respond to students' mistakes with pity, give praise for a "good try," or offer help the student hasn't asked for, students are more likely to attribute failure to an uncontrollable cause—usually lack of ability. For example, Graham and Barker (1990) asked students of various ages to rate the effort and ability of two boys on a videotape. On the tape, a teacher was circulating around the class while students worked. The teacher stopped to look at the two boys' papers, did not comment to the first boy but said to the second, who had not asked for help and did not appear to be stumped by the problem, "Let me give you a hint. Don't forget to carry your tens." Peers and even quite young students perceived the helped boy was lower in ability than the boy who did not get help. It is as if they read the teacher's behaviour to say, "You poor child, you just don't have the ability to do this hard work, so I will help."

Does this mean teachers should withhold help or be critical? Of course not! But it does show that praise as a "consolation prize" (Brophy, 1985) or oversolicitous help can give unintended messages. Graham (1991) suggests that many minority-group students are victims of well-meaning compassion from teachers. Seeing the very real problems some students face, teachers may ease up on requirements so students can "experience success" and "feel good about themselves." But a subtle message may accompany such compassion, praise, and extra help: "You don't have the ability to do this, so I will overlook your failure." Sympathetic feedback, even if well-intended, can be a subtle form of discrimination if it is prompted by stereotypes about students with exceptionalities or from other cultures.

Expectancy x Value Theories.

Theories that blend behaviourists' focus on behaviour with cognitivists' attention to thinking are **expectancy x value theories.** In these theories, motivation is produced by two main thoughts: the individual's expectation of reaching a goal, and the value of that goal. "If I try hard, can I succeed?" "If I succeed, is the outcome valuable or rewarding to me?" Motivation is a product of both factors. If either factor is zero, there is no motivation to work toward the goal. For example, if Cindy believes she has a good chance of winning a prize in the science fair (high expectation), and if that prize is very important to her (high value), her motivation should be strong. But if either factor is near zero (she believes she hasn't much chance of winning, or she couldn't care less about science fair prizes), her motivation will be nil. Albert Bandura's social cognitive theory, discussed later in this chapter, is an example of an expectancy x value approach to motivation (Feather, 1982; Pintrich & Schunk, 1996).

Connect & Extend
To the research
Blumenfeld, P. C., Pintrich, P. R., & Hamilton, V. L. (1986). Children's concepts of ability, effort, and conduct. *American Educational Research Journal, 23*, 95-104. *Brief abstract:* Children's self-perceptions of ability may reflect assessments of their effort and good conduct as well as academic performance. In a study of 158 second and sixth graders, ability was generally linked to effort and effort to conduct, but not ability to conduct, in either ratings or judgment criteria. Children generally used absolute standards in judging ability and did so almost exclusively in judging effort and conduct. The results suggest that children's judgments of ability, effort, and conduct are interrelated but distinguishable.

Connect & Extend
To your teaching
Read Clifford, M. M. (1990). Students need challenge, not easy success. *Educational Leadership 48*(1), 22–26. Evaluate Clifford's claim that students need some experience with failure. For whom is this experience most needed?

Connect & Extend
To your teaching
Based on expectancy theory, predict the level of motivation in each of the following situations:
a. Perceived probability of success under minimum effort is high; incentive value is high.
b. Perceived probability of success under maximum effort is high; incentive value is moderate.
c. Perceived probability of success under maximum effort is low; incentive value is moderate.

Expectancy x Value Theories: Explanations of motivation that emphasize individuals' expectations for success combined with their valuing of the goal.

Sociocultural Conceptions of Motivation

According to **sociocultural views of motivation**, people engage in activities to maintain their identities and their interpersonal relations within a community, which is often referred to as a community of practice. To learn is to participate in the practices, the life of the community. Thus, students are motivated to learn if they are members of a classroom or school community that values learning. We learn to speak and dress and conduct ourselves in museums or theatres by watching and learning from more capable members of our culture. Similarly, students learn how to be students by watching and learning from classmates and peers in the school community. In other words, we learn by the company we keep (Greeno, Collins, & Resnick, 1996).

The concept of identity is central in sociocultural views of motivation. When students see themselves as budding computer scientists or violinists or newspaper editors, they have an identity within a group. Part of socialization is moving from being a member or participant on the edge or periphery of these groups to a central place in the group's activities. The concept of **legitimate peripheral participation** means that beginners are genuinely involved in the work of the group, even if their abilities are undeveloped and their contributions are small at first. Each task is a piece of the real work of the expert. The novice computer scientist learns about surfing the Web before learning how to code elegant Web pages, just as the novice teacher learns to tutor one child before working with a whole class. The identities of both the novice and the expert are bound up in their participation in the community. To strengthen their identities as community members, they are motivated to learn the values and carry out the practices of their community (Lave & Wenger, 1991).

Classrooms can be intentionally structured as learning communities. For example, Brown and Campione (1996) developed learning communities for middle school students around research projects in science. Scardamalia and Bereiter (1996), colleagues at the University of Toronto, designed a learning community where students use a computer system, called Knowledge Forum, that supports collaboration among students about questions, hypotheses, methods of inquiry, and findings. Because motivation arises from identity and identity develops through legitimate participation, the challenge in designs for learning communities is to be sure that all students can progress from positions of legitimate peripheral participation to become full participants in the community.

The behavioural, humanistic, cognitive, and sociocultural approaches to motivation are summarized in Table 10.2 on page 362. These theories differ in their answers to the question "What is motivation?" but each contributes in its own way toward a comprehensive understanding of human motivation.

To organize the many ideas about motivation, let's examine three broad areas emphasized in most contemporary explanations of motivation: goals, interests and emotions, and self-perceptions (Murphy & Alexander, 2000). We will look closely at each of these areas with an emphasis on implications for teaching and learning.

Sociocultural Views of Motivation: Perspectives that emphasize participation, identities, and interpersonal relations within communities of practice.

Legitimate Peripheral Participation: Genuine involvement in the work of the group, even if your abilities are undeveloped and contributions are small.

CHECKPOINT

Four General Approaches to Motivation

Review

▸ What are the key factors in a behavioural viewpoint? A cognitive viewpoint? A humanistic viewpoint? A sociocultural viewpoint?

▸ Distinguish between deficiency needs and being needs in Maslow's theory.

▸ What are the three dimensions of attributions in Weiner's theory?

▸ What are expectancy x value theories?

▸ What is legitimate peripheral participation?

Apply

▸ Use Maslow's theory to explain why a student who is upset about events in his or her family might not be motivated to study.

▸ How does participation and identity in a group affect your motivation?

TABLE 10.2 Four Views of Motivation

	Behavioural	Humanistic	Cognitive	Sociocultural
Source of Motivation	Extrinsic	Intrinsic	Intrinsic	Intrinsic
Important Influences	Reinforcers, rewards, incentives, and punishers	Need for self-esteem, self-fulfillment, and self-determination	Beliefs, attributions for success and failure, expectations	Engaged participation in learning communities; maintaining identity through participation in activities of group
Key Theorists	Skinner	Maslow Deci	Weiner Graham	Lave Wenger

Goal Orientation and Motivation

Connect & Extend
To the research
Ames, C. (1992). Classrooms: Goals, structures, and student motivation. *Journal of Educational Psychology, 84,* 261–271. This article integrates many concepts about goals and provides a frame for the next chapter in this text. For an elaboration of Ames's ideas, see Blumenfeld, P. C. (1992). Classroom learning and motivation: Clarifying and expending goal theory. *Journal of Educational Psychology, 84,* 272–281.

A **goal** is what an individual is striving to accomplish (Locke & Latham, 1990). When students strive to understand a math problem or make a 4.0 grade-point average, this is *goal-directed behaviour.* In pursuing goals, students are generally aware of some current condition (I haven't even opened my book), some ideal condition (I have read and understood every page), and the discrepancy between the current and ideal situations. Goals motivate people to act to reduce the discrepancy between where they are and where they want to be.

Goal setting is usually effective for most people. It is often a good idea to set goals for each day. For example, "Today I intend to review this chapter, gather library references for my history paper, and jog."

According to Locke and Latham (1990), there are four main reasons why goal setting improves performance. First, goals direct our attention to the tasks at hand. (If your mind wanders while reviewing the chapter, your goal helps direct your attention back to the task.) Second, goals mobilize effort. (The harder the goal, up to a point, the greater the effort.) Third, goals increase persistence. (When we have a clear goal we are less likely to be distracted or to give up until we reach the goal.) Finally, when old strategies fall short, goals invite developing new strategies. For example, if your goal is making an A and you don't reach that goal on your first quiz, you might drop the strategy of reviewing once a month and try a new approach to studying, such as explaining the key points every week to a friend in a study group.

Types of Goals

The types of goals we set influence our motivation. Goals that are specific, moderately difficult, and likely to be reached in the relatively near future tend to enhance motivation and persistence (Pintrich & Schunk, 1996; Stipek, 1996). Specific goals provide clearer standards for judging performance. If performance falls short, we keep going. For example, instead of working on an entire essay, you may decide to write an introduction. Because it is clear when you are finished (your introduction is done), you know when you have met the goal. Anything short of finishing the introduction means "keep working." Moderate difficulty provides a challenge but not an unreasonable one. You can finish your introduction if you stay with it. Finally, goals that can be reached fairly soon are not likely to be pushed aside by

Goal: What an individual strives to accomplish.

more immediate concerns. Self-help groups that encourage their members to make progress "one day at a time" are aware of this property of short-term goals.

Four Kinds of Goals. Educational psychologists have discovered that students categorize goals in terms of one of four main general views or orientations: learning goals, performance goals, work-avoidance goals, and social goals (Murphy & Alexander, 2000). Among these *goal orientations*, the most common distinction relating to classroom learning is between learning goals (sometimes called task goals or mastery goals) and performance goals (also termed ability goals or ego goals). The point of a **learning goal** is to improve, to learn, regardless of mistakes you make or how awkward you appear. Students who set learning goals tend to seek challenges and persist when they encounter difficulties. Nicholls and Miller (1984) call these students **task-involved learners** because they are concerned with mastering the task and are not worried about how their performance measures up compared to others. We often say that these people "get lost in their work." In addition, task-involved learners are more likely to seek appropriate help, and they report using deeper cognitive processing strategies and better study strategies (Butler & Neuman, 1995; Young, 1997).

Students who hold a **performance goal** are focused on how they are judged by others. They want to look smart and avoid seeming incompetent by getting good grades. Or they may be more concerned with winning and outdoing other students (Wolters, Yu, & Pintrich, 1996). Students holding performance goals undermine learning by doing things just to look smart, such as reading easy books to "read the most books" (Young, 1997). If success seems impossible, they may adopt defensive, failure-avoiding strategies—they pretend not to care, make a show of "not really trying," cheat, or may simply give up (Jagacinski & Nicholls, 1987; Pintrich & Schunk, 1996). Nicholls and Miller (1984) refer to these students as **ego-involved learners** because they are preoccupied with themselves. Deborah Stipek (1996) lists this behaviour as indicative of a student who is too ego-involved with classwork:

▶ Cheats/copies from classmates' papers.

▶ Seeks attention for good performance.

▶ Works hard only on graded assignments.

▶ Is upset by and hides papers with low grades.

▶ Compares grades with classmates.

▶ Chooses tasks most likely to result in positive evaluations.

▶ Is uncomfortable with assignments that have unclear evaluation criteria.

Some students don't want to learn or to look smart; they just want to avoid work. These students try to complete assignments and activities as quickly as possible without exerting much effort (Schunk & Pintrich, 1996). Nicholls called these students **work-avoidant learners**—they feel successful when they don't have to try hard, when the work is easy, or when they can "goof off."

The final category of goals, **social goals**, becomes more important as students get older. As students move into adolescence, their social networks change to include more peers. Non-academic activities such as athletics, dating, and "hanging out" compete with school work (Urdan & Maehr, 1995). Social goals include a wide variety of needs and motives with different relationships to learning—some help, but others hinder learning. For example, adolescents' goal of maintaining friendly relations in a cooperative learning group can interfere with learning if group members don't challenge friends' wrong answers or misconceptions because they are afraid to hurt their feelings (Anderson, Holland, & Palincsar, 1997). Certainly, pursuing goals such as having fun with friends or avoiding being labelled a "nerd" can get in the way of learning. But goals of bringing honour to your family or team by working hard can support learning (Urdan & Maehr, 1995).

Connect & Extend
To your teaching
Are students with learning goals more likely to: (1) be internal or external in locus of control; (2) have internal and stable or internal and unstable attributions; (3) be failure-avoiders or success-seekers?

Learning Goal: A personal intention to improve abilities and understand, no matter how performance suffers.

Task-Involved Learners: Students who focus on mastering the task or solving the problem.

Performance Goal: A personal intention to seem competent or perform well in the eyes of others.

Ego-Involved Learners: Students who focus on how well they are performing and how they are judged by others.

Work-Avoidant Learners: Students who don't want to learn or to look smart, but just want to avoid work.

Social Goals: A wide variety of needs and motives to be connected to others or part of a group.

▲ *If this girl's goal is to improve and not worry about mistakes, she may attempt more difficult pieces and welcome criticism. If her goal is to simply look good, she may avoid difficulty and criticism.*

We talk about goals in separate categories but students have to coordinate their goals as they decide what to do and how to act. Sometimes social and academic goals are incompatible. For example, academic failure may be interpreted positively by some minority-group students because noncompliance with the majority culture's norms and standards is seen as an accomplishment. Thus it would be impossible to simultaneously succeed in both school and the peer group (Ogbu, 1987; Wentzel, 1999). And succeeding in the peer group is important—the need for social relationships is basic and strong for most people.

The Need for Relatedness. The need to establish close emotional bonds and attachments with the important people in our lives is relatedness (Ryan, 1991). When teachers and parents are responsive and demonstrate they care about children's interests and well-being, children show high intrinsic motivation. But, when children are denied the interpersonal involvement they seek from adults—when adults, for example, are unresponsive to their needs—the children lose intrinsic motivation (Grolnick, Ryan, & Deci, 1991). As well, emotional and physical problems ranging from eating disorders to suicide are more common among people lacking social relationships (Baumeister & Leary, 1995).

Relatedness has two components: involvement and autonomy support. Involvement is the degree to which teachers and parents are interested in and knowledgeable about their children's activities and experiences, and devote time to them. When students feel a sense of belonging and personal support from teachers, they are more interested in class work and find it more valuable (Goodenow, 1993; Stipek, 1996). Autonomy support is the degree to which teachers and parents encourage children to make their own choices rather than apply pressure to control the children's behaviour. When teachers and parents show high involvement and autonomy support, children show greater competence, academic achievement, and responsibility, as well as less aggression (Grolnick & Ryan, 1989; Grolnick, Ryan, & Deci, 1991).

Feedback and Goal Acceptance

Goal setting in the classroom is effective because it helps focus on the task, create supportive social relationships, and identify specific, challenging, attainable learning goals—but there are two other good reasons as well. The first is *feedback*. To be motivated to resolve a discrepancy between where you are and where you want to be, you need an accurate sense of where you are and how far you have to go. When feedback tells a student that current efforts fall short of the goal, and if the feedback describes how to do better, the student can exert more effort or has an idea of what to do (Butler & Winne, 1995). When feedback describes accomplishment in relation to goals, the student can feel satisfied and competent, and may even set a slightly higher goal for the future. In one study, feedback to some adults emphasized they had accomplished 75 percent of the standards set; other adults were told they had fallen short of the standards by 25 percent. When the feedback highlighted accomplishment, the subjects' self-confidence, analytic thinking, and performance were all enhanced (Bandura, 1997).

The second factor affecting motivation to pursue a goal is *goal acceptance*. When students accept goals their teachers set or establish their own goals, the power of goal setting to motivate learning can be tapped. But if students reject goals set by others or refuse to set their own goals, motivation suffers. Generally, students are more willing to adopt goals that others set when the goals seem realistic, reasonably difficult, and meaningful (Erez & Zidon, 1984); and if good reasons are given about the value of the goals. Goal acceptance might be greater (and goals more appropriate) if you work with students' families to identify and monitor the goals. The Family and Community Partnerships Guidelines give some ideas.

Goals: Lessons for Teachers

Students are more likely to work toward goals that are clear, specific, reasonable, moderately challenging, and attainable within a relatively short time frame. If teachers overstress student performance, high grades, competition, and achievement, they may encourage students to set performance goals. This undermines students' learning and task involvement (Anderman & Maehr, 1994). Be aware that some students may not be expert at setting their own goals or keeping their goals in mind—encouragement and accurate feedback are necessary. If you use a reward system, be sure the goal you set is to *learn and improve*, not just to perform well or look smart. And be sure the goal is not too difficult.

Most people are more motivated when tasks give them a chance to form positive relationships with others. Students, like adults, are more likely to stick with tasks or respond well to teachers who make them feel secure and competent. But take care to be honest in giving feedback so that attributions are made to controllable factors.

CHECKPOINT

Goal Orientation and Motivation

Review

▶ What kinds of goals are the most motivating?

▶ Describe learning, performance, work-avoidant, and social goals.

▶ What makes goal setting effective in the classroom?

Apply

▶ A teacher says to the class, "I want all of you to study hard so you can make good scores on the provincial exams next June." Predict the effects of this goal-setting statement. Are students likely to be motivated by the goal? Why or why not?

FAMILY AND COMMUNITY PARTNERSHIPS

Setting Goals

Understand family goals for children.

Examples

1. In an informal setting, around a coffee pot or snacks, meet with families individually or in small groups to listen to what they want for their children.

2. Mail out questionnaires or send response cards home with students, asking what skills the families believe their children most need to work on. Pick one goal for each child and develop a plan for working toward the goal both inside and outside school. Share the plan with the families and ask for feedback.

Identify student and family interests that can be related to goals.

Examples

1. Ask a member of the family to share a skill or hobby with the class.

2. Identify "family favourites"—favourite foods, music, vacations, sports, colours, activities, hymns, movies, games, snacks, recipes, memories. Tie class lessons to interests. Give families a way to track progress toward goals.

Examples

1. Provide simple "progress charts" or goal cards that can be posted on the refrigerator.

2. Ask for feedback (and mean it) about parents' perceptions of your effectiveness in helping students reach goals.

Interests and Emotions

Students' interest in and excitement about what they're learning is one of the most important factors in education. ▼

How do you feel about learning? Excited, bored, curious, fearful? Today, researchers emphasize that learning involves not only the *cold cognition* of reasoning and problem solving. Learning and information processing also involve emotion, invitingly called *hot cognition* (Miller, 1993; Pintrich, Marx, & Boyle, 1993). Students are more likely to pay attention to, learn, and remember material that provokes appropriate emotional responses (Alexander & Murphy, 1998; Cowley & Underwood, 1998; Reisberg & Heuer, 1992) or that relates to their personal interests (Renninger, Hidi, & Krapp, 1992). How can we use these findings to support learning in school?

Tapping Interests

When Walter Vispoel and James Austin (1995) asked more than 200 middle school students to rate reasons for their successes and failures in different school subjects, lack of interest in the topic was rated highest as an explanation for failures. For explaining successes, interest was second only to effort. It seems logical that learning experiences should be related to the interests of students, and interests increase when students feel competent. So, even if students are not initially interested in a subject or activity, they may develop interest as they experience success (Stipek, 1996).

One source of interest is fantasy. For example, Cordova and Lepper (1996) found that students learned more math facts during a computer exercise when they were challenged, as captains of starships, to navigate through space by solving math problems. The students got to name their ships, stock the (imaginary) galley with their favourite snacks, and name all the crew members after their friends. The Guidelines on page 367 give other ideas.

However, there are cautions about responding to students' interests. Ruth Garner (1992) found that the presence of "seductive details" can hinder learning. Seductive details are interesting bits of information that are not central to the curriculum. Some examples might be details about the life of a scientist that do not help you understand her theories. Interesting puzzles or manipulatives that don't directly support learning objectives can also be seductive. The research is quite clear: students remember these seductive details at the expense of the curriculum they should know. So, if you dress up like the author of a book, as described in the Guidelines, make sure any details you share about "your" life connect directly to your objectives for students' learning.

Arousal: Excitement and Anxiety in Learning

We all know what it is like to be aroused—we feel alert, wide awake, even excited. **Arousal** involves both psychological and physical reactions—changes in brainwave patterns, blood pressure, heart rate, and breathing rate. To understand the effects of arousal on motivation, think of two extremes. The first is late at night. You are struggling for the third time to understand a chapter (hopefully not ours!) but you are so sleepy. Your attention drifts and your eyes droop. But you're not done. You decide to go to bed and get up early to study (a plan you know seldom works). At the other extreme, imagine a scholarship exam tomorrow. As you try to go to sleep, you worry about doing well. You know you need a good night's

Arousal: Physical and psychological reactions causing a person to be alert, attentive, wide awake.

GUIDELINES

Building on Students' Interests

Relate content objectives to student experiences.

Examples

1. With a teacher in another school, city, or province, establish pen pals across the classes. Through writing letters or e-mail, students exchange personal experiences, photos, drawings, written work, and ask and answer questions ("Have you learned cursive writing yet?" "What are you doing in math now?" "What are you reading?"). Letters can be mailed in one large mailer to save stamps.
2. Identify classroom experts for different assignments or tasks. Who knows how to use the computer for graphics? How to search the Net? How to cook? How to use an index?
3. Have a "Switch Day" when students each exchange roles with a member of the school staff or a support person. Students must research the role by interviewing their staff members, prepare for the job, dress the part for the day they take over, and then evaluate their success after the switch.

Identify student interests, hobbies, and extracurricular activities that can be incorporated into class lessons and discussions.

Examples

1. Have students design and conduct interviews and surveys to learn about each other's interests.
2. Keep the class library stocked with books that connect to students' interests and hobbies.

Support instruction with humour, personal experiences, and anecdotes that show the human side of the content.

Examples

1. Share your own hobbies, interests, and favourites.
2. Tell students there will be a surprise visitor; then dress up as the author of a story and tell about "yourself" and your writing.

Source: Adapted from *150 Ways to Increase Intrinsic Motivation in the Classroom*, by J. P. Raffini, 1996, Boston: Allyn & Bacon. Copyright © 1996 by Allyn & Bacon.

---

sleep, but you are wide awake. In the first case, arousal is too low; in the second, it's too high.

There appears to be an optimum level of arousal for most activities, as shown in Figure 10.1 (Yerkes & Dodson, 1908) on page 368. Generally, moderately high arousal is helpful on simple tasks where thinking is automated, but lower levels of arousal are better for novel and complex tasks. Let's look for a moment at how to increase arousal by arousing curiosity.

Curiosity: Novelty and Complexity. Psychologists suggested more than 30 years ago that individuals are naturally motivated to seek novelty, surprise, and complexity (Berlyne, 1966). Research has since found that variety in teaching approaches and diversity in tasks can support learning (Brophy & Good, 1986; Stipek, 1996). For younger students, the chance to manipulate and explore objects, provided they are relevant to objectives, is an effective way to stimulate curiosity. For older students, well-constructed questions, logical puzzles, and paradoxes can have the same effect. Example: ranchers killed the wolves on their land; the following spring, their sheep population was smaller—how could this be since wolves hunt sheep but fewer wolves means more sheep? Searching to solve this paradox, students learn about ecological systems: without wolves to eliminate weaker and sicker sheep, the sheep population exceeds the winter food supply needed to sustain the flocks. Many sheep died of starvation.

George Lowenstein (1994) suggests that gaps in knowledge can "produce the feeling of deprivation labeled *curiosity*. The curious person is motivated to obtain the missing information to reduce or eliminate the feeling of deprivation" (p. 87).

FIGURE 10.1

Arousal and Quality of Performance

On a simple or well-practised task, the best performance occurs when arousal is moderately high. But on a complex task, lower arousal leads to better performance—as long as the arousal isn't *too* low.

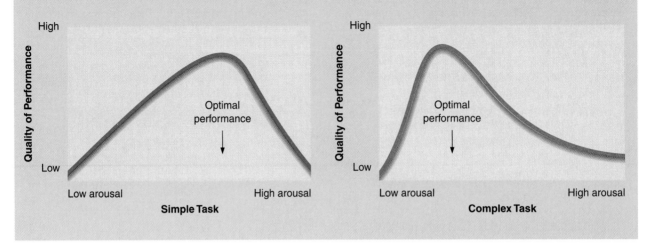

Connect & Extend
To the research
Meece, J. L., Wigfield, A., & Eccles, J. (1990). Predictors of math anxiety and its influence on young adolescents' course enrolment intentions and performance in mathematics. *Journal of Educational Psychology, 92,* 6–70. This study found that math anxiety was most directly related to students' math ability perceptions, performance expectancies, and value perceptions. Students' performance expectancies predicted subsequent math grades, whereas their value perception predicted course enrolment intentions.

This idea is similar to Piaget's concept of disequilibrium, discussed in Chapter 2, and has several implications for teaching. First, students need some base of knowledge before they can experience gaps in knowledge that spark curiosity. Second, students must be aware of those gaps for curiosity to result. Asking students to make guesses and then providing feedback can help them recall what they know and expose gaps. Also, mistakes, if appropriately handled, can stimulate curiosity by pointing to missing knowledge. Finally, the more we learn about a topic, the more curious we may become about it. As Maslow (1970) predicted, the need for more knowledge is often stimulated by learning.

As we noted earlier, sometimes arousal is too high, not too low. Because classrooms are places where students are tested and graded, anxiety can also be a factor in classroom motivation.

Anxiety in the Classroom. At one time or another, everyone has experienced **anxiety**, a "general uneasiness, a sense of foreboding, a feeling of tension" (Hansen, 1977, p. 91). Over the entire last century, "researchers have consistently reported a negative correlation between virtually every aspect of school achievement and a wide range of anxiety measures" (Covington & Omelich, 1987, p. 393). Anxiety can be both a cause and an effect of school failure—students do poorly because they are anxious, and their poor performance further increases their anxiety. Anxiety probably is both a trait and a state. Some students tend to be anxious in many situations (*trait anxiety*) but some situations are especially anxiety-provoking (*state anxiety*) (Covington, 1992).

Anxiety has both cognitive and affective components. The cognitive side includes worry and negative thoughts—for example, thinking about how bad it would be to fail and worrying (predicting) that you will. The affective side involves physiological elements such as sweaty palms, upset stomach, and racing heartbeat, as well as emotional reactions such as fear (Schunk, 2000; Zeidner, 1995).

In the classroom, the conditions surrounding a test or answering questions in class can influence the performance of highly anxious students. For example, Hill and Eaton (1977) found that, when there was no time limit for solving arithmetic problems, very anxious grade 5 and 6 students worked as quickly and accurately

Anxiety: General uneasiness, a feeling of tension.

as their less-anxious classmates. With a time limit, however, very anxious students made three times as many errors as classmates, spent about twice as much time on each problem, and cheated twice as often as their less-anxious peers. Whenever pressures to perform are coupled with severe consequences for failure, and when competitive comparisons are emphasized, anxiety may be elevated (Wigfield & Eccles, 1989).

How Does Anxiety Interfere with Achievement? Sigmund Tobias (1985) suggests a model to explain how anxiety interferes at three points in the learning and performance cycle. When students are learning new material, they must pay attention to it. Highly anxious students divide their attention between new material and nervous feelings. Instead of concentrating on a lecture or on what they are reading, they keep noticing their laboured breathing and thinking, "I'm so tense, I'll never understand this stuff!" Much of their attention is taken up with thoughts about performing poorly, being criticized, and feeling embarrassed. From the beginning, anxious students may miss much of the information they are supposed to learn because their thoughts are focused on their own worries (Hill & Wigfield, 1984; Paulman & Kennelly, 1984).

But the problems do not end here. Even if they are paying attention, many anxious students have trouble learning material that requires them to rely on their memory. Unfortunately, much material in school is this way. Anxious students also are more easily distracted by irrelevant or incidental aspects of the task at hand. They have trouble focusing on significant details (Hill & Wigfield, 1984). In addition, many highly anxious students have poor study habits. Simply learning to be more relaxed will not automatically improve these students' performance; their learning strategies and study skills must be improved as well (Naveh-Benjamin, 1991).

Finally, anxious students often know more than they can demonstrate on a test or other high-stakes setting. They may lack useful test-taking skills, or they may have learned the materials but "freeze and forget." Thus anxiety can interfere at one or all three points: attention, learning, and testing (Naveh-Benjamin, McKeachie, & Lin, 1987).

Coping with Anxiety. When students face stressful situations in school, they can use three kinds of coping strategies—problem solving, emotional management, and avoidance. Problem-focused strategies might include planning a study schedule, borrowing good notes, or finding a protected place to study. Emotion-focused strategies are attempts to reduce anxious feelings—for example, by using relaxation exercises or describing the feelings to a friend. Of course, the latter might become an avoidance strategy, along with going out for pizza or suddenly launching an all-out desk-cleaning attack—"Can't study until you get organized!" Different strategies are helpful at different points—for example, problem solving before and emotion management during an exam. Different strategies fit different people and situations (Zeidner, 1995).

Anxious students left on their own often select either extremely difficult or extremely easy tasks. In the first case, they are likely to fail, which will increase their sense of hopelessness and anxiety about school. In the second case, they will probably succeed on the easy tasks, but they will miss the sense of satisfaction that could encourage greater effort, ease their fears about school work, and nur-

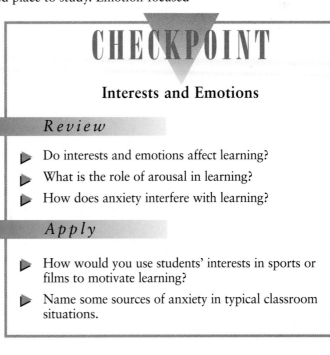

CHECKPOINT

Interests and Emotions

Review

▶ Do interests and emotions affect learning?

▶ What is the role of arousal in learning?

▶ How does anxiety interfere with learning?

Apply

▶ How would you use students' interests in sports or films to motivate learning?

▶ Name some sources of anxiety in typical classroom situations.

ture a sense of self-efficacy. Teachers should guide anxious students to set appropriate short- and long-term goals. Goal cards, progress charts, or goal-planning journals may help here.

Anxious students may also need help working at a moderate pace, especially when taking tests. Often, anxious students work too quickly and make many careless errors or work too slowly and never finish. If possible, consider eliminating time limits on important tests. Because anxiety appears to interfere with both attention and retention (Wittrock, 1978), highly anxious students (at least those of average or high ability) benefit most from instruction that is quite well structured and allows for repetition of parts of the lesson that are missed or forgotten (Seiber, O'Neil, & Tobias, 1977; Wigfield & Eccles, 1989).

Interests and Emotions: Lessons for Teachers

Try to keep the level of arousal right for the task at hand. If students are going to sleep, energize them by introducing variety, piquing their curiosity, surprising them, or giving them a brief chance to be physically active. Learn about their interests and incorporate interests into lessons and assignments. If arousal is too great, follow the Guidelines on below for dealing with anxiety.

GUIDELINES

Coping with Anxiety

Use competition carefully.

Examples

1. Monitor activities to make sure no students are being put under undue pressure.
2. During competitive games, make sure all students involved have a reasonable chance of succeeding.
3. Experiment with cooperative learning activities.

Avoid situations in which highly anxious students will have to perform in front of large groups.

Examples

1. Ask anxious students questions that can be answered with a simple yes or no, or some other brief reply.
2. Give anxious students practice in speaking before smaller groups.

Make sure all instructions are clear. Uncertainty can lead to anxiety.

Examples

1. Write test instructions on the board or on the test itself instead of giving them orally.
2. Check with students to make sure they understand. Ask several students how they would do the first question, exercise, or sample question on a test. Correct any misconceptions.

3. If you are using a new format or starting a new type of task, give students examples or models to show how it is done.

Avoid unnecessary time pressures.

Examples

1. Give occasional take-home tests.
2. Make sure all students can complete classroom tests within the period given.

Remove some of the pressures from major tests and exams.

Examples

1. Teach test-taking skills; give practice tests; provide study guides.
2. Avoid basing most of a report-card grade on one test.
3. Make extra-credit work available to add points to course grades.
4. Use different types of items in testing because some students have difficulty with particular formats.

Develop alternatives to written tests.

Examples

1. Try oral, open-book, or group tests.
2. Have students do projects, organize portfolios of their work, make oral presentations, or create a finished product.

$\mathcal{S}$elf-Schemas

Thus far, we have examined goals, interests, and emotions, but there is another factor that must be considered in explaining motivation. What do students believe about themselves? Let's start with a basic question—What do they believe about their ability?

Incremental View of Ability: Belief that ability is a set of skills that can be changed.

Entity View of Ability: Belief that ability is a fixed characteristic that cannot be changed.

Beliefs about Ability

Young children tend to hold an exclusively **incremental view of ability** (Nicholls & Miller, 1984), a view that ability is unstable and controllable—"an ever-expanding repertoire of skills and knowledge" (Dweck & Bempechat, 1983, p. 244). By hard work, study, or practice, knowledge can be increased and thus ability can be improved. Through the early elementary grades, most students believe effort is the same as intelligence. Smart people try hard and trying hard makes you smart. If you fail, you aren't smart and you didn't try hard; if you succeed, you must be a smart, hard worker (Stipek, 1998). As children reach the age of 11 or 12, they begin to differentiate among effort, ability, and performance. About this time, they come to believe that someone who succeeds without working at all must be really smart. This is when beliefs about ability begin to influence motivation (Anderman & Maehr, 1994).

Students who hold an **entity view of ability** assume that ability is a *stable, uncontrollable* trait—an individual difference that is unchangeable. According to this view, some people have more ability than others but the amount each person has is fixed. Students with this view tend to set performance goals and seek situations where they can look smart and protect their self-esteem. They keep doing what they can do well without expending too much effort or risking failure, because either one—working hard or failing—indicates (to them) low ability. To work hard but still fail would be a devastating blow to their sense of competence.

Another protective strategy is to make a point of not trying at all. If you fail after not trying, no one can accuse you of being dumb. Just before a test a student might say, "I didn't study at all!" or "All I want to do is pass." Then, any grade above passing is a success. Procrastination is another self-protective strategy. Low grades do not imply low ability if the student can claim, "I did okay considering I didn't start the term paper until last night." Some evidence suggests that blaming anxiety for poor test performance can also be a self-protective strategy (Covington & Omelich, 1987). Of course, even though these strategies may help students avoid the negative implications of failure, very little learning is going on.

Students who are incremental theorists, in contrast, tend to set learning goals and seek situations in which they can improve their skills, since improvement means getting smarter. Failure is not devastating; it simply indicates more work is needed. Ability is not threatened. Incremental theorists tend to set moderately difficult goals, the kind we have seen are the most motivating.

One of the most powerful influences on motivation to achieve is another kind of belief—self-efficacy.

Beliefs about Self-Efficacy

Bandura (1986, 1997) suggests that critical sources of motivation are predictions about possible outcomes of behaviour. "Will I succeed or fail? Will I be liked or laughed at?" We imagine future consequences based on past experiences and our observations of others. These predictions are affected by self-efficacy. Bandura (1997) defines self-efficacy as "beliefs in one's capabilities to organize and execute the courses of action required to produce given attainments" (p. 3).

Self-Efficacy, Self-Concept, and Self-Esteem. Most people assume self-efficacy is the same as self-concept or self-esteem, but it isn't. Self-efficacy involves predictions about capabilities *specific to a particular task* (Pajares, 1997). The question is whether you can do the task, not how well you do it compared to another person. Self-concept is more global. It refers to a variety of perceptions about the self, including self-efficacy. Self-concept develops along two "lines." The first is through external comparisons to other people or other aspects of the self as frames of reference. The second is through internal comparisons among your various abilities for accomplishing particular tasks—the question is whether you can do English better than math, not how well others might do either (Marsh, Walker, & Debus, 1991). Another difference is that self-efficacy beliefs are strong predictors of behaviour, but self-concept has weaker predictive power (Bandura, 1997).

Compared to self-concept, self-efficacy concerns judgments of particular personal capabilities; self-concept concerns judgments of overall self-worth. There is no direct relationship between self-concept and self-efficacy. You might feel highly efficacious in one area and still not have high self-concept, or vice versa. For example, Phil has quite low self-efficacy for singing but his self-concept is not affected, probably because his life does not require singing (thank goodness!). But if his self-efficacy for teaching his graduate course started dropping after several bad experiences, his self-esteem would suffer.

Sources of Self-Efficacy. Bandura identified four sources of expectations about self-efficacy: mastery experiences, physiological and emotional arousal, vicarious experiences, and social persuasion. **Mastery experiences** are our direct experiences. These are the most powerful source of efficacy information. Successes raise efficacy expectations; failures lower them. Level of arousal affects self-efficacy depending on how the arousal is interpreted. As you face the task, are you anxious and worried (lowers efficacy) or excited and "psyched" (raises efficacy) (Bandura, 1997; Pintrich & Schunk, 1996).

In **vicarious experiences**, we watch someone else model accomplishments. Usually, the more closely the student identifies with the model, the greater the impact on self-efficacy. When the model performs well, the student's efficacy increases but when the model performs poorly, efficacy expectations decrease. Although mastery experiences generally are acknowledged as the most influential source of efficacy beliefs in adults, Keyser and Barling (1981) found that children (Grade 6 students) may rely more on modelling as a source of self-efficacy information.

▲ *Students' beliefs about their own ability to succeed influence achievement. These beliefs are affected in one way or another by family, teachers, and others.*

Social persuasion may be a "pep talk" or specific performance feedback. Social persuasion alone can't create enduring increases in self-efficacy, but a persuasive boost in self-efficacy can lead a student to make an effort, attempt new strategies, or try hard enough to succeed (Bandura, 1982). Social persuasion can counter occasional setbacks that might bring about self-doubt and interrupt persistence. The potency of persuasion depends on the credibility, trustworthiness, and expertise of the persuader (Bandura, 1986).

Efficacy and Motivation. Greater efficacy leads to greater effort and persistence in the face of setbacks. Self-efficacy also influences motivation through goal setting. If we have a high sense of efficacy for a given task, we set higher goals, are less afraid of failure, and search for new strategies if old ones fail. If our sense of efficacy is low, however, we may avoid a task altogether or give up easily if difficulties arise (Bandura, 1993, 1997; Zimmerman, 1995).

Self-efficacy and attributions affect each other. If success is attributed to internal or controllable causes such as ability or effort, self-efficacy is enhanced. But if success is attributed to luck or the intervention of others, self-efficacy may not be strengthened. Efficacy affects attributions, too. People with a strong sense of self-efficacy for a given task ("I'm good at math") tend to attribute their failures to lack of effort ("I should have double-checked my work"). But people with a low sense of self-efficacy ("I'm terrible at math") tend to attribute their failures to lack of ability ("I'm just dumb"). So, having a strong sense of self-efficacy for a certain task encourages controllable attributions, and controllable attributions increase self-efficacy. Thus, if a student held an entity view of ability (ability is stable and uncontrollable, thus cannot be changed) and a low sense of self-efficacy, motivation would be destroyed when failures were attributed to lack of ability ("I just can't do this and I'll never be able to learn!") (Bandura, 1997; Pintrich & Schunk, 1996).

There is evidence that a high sense of self-efficacy supports motivation even when efficacy is unrealistically high. Children and adults who are optimistic about the future, believe they can be effective, and have high expectations are more mentally and physically healthy, less depressed, and more motivated to achieve (Flammer, 1995).

Research on self-efficacy and achievement suggests that performance in school is improved and self-efficacy is increased when students: (a) adopt short-term goals so it is easier to judge progress; (b) are taught to use specific learning strategies such as outlining or summarizing that help them focus attention; and (c) receive rewards based on performance, not just engagement, because performance rewards signal increasing competence (Graham & Weiner, 1996).

Teacher Efficacy. Much of Anita's research has focused on **teaching efficacy**, a teacher's belief that he or she can help all students learn (Hoy & Woolfolk, 1990, 1993; Tschannen-Moran, Woolfolk Hoy, & Hoy, 1998; Woolfolk & Hoy, 1990; Woolfolk, Rosoff, & Hoy, 1990). Teaching efficacy appears to be one of the few personal characteristics of teachers that correlates with student achievement. Self-efficacy theory predicts that teachers with a high sense of efficacy work harder and persist longer even when students are difficult to teach, in part because these teachers believe in themselves and in their students.

We have found that prospective teachers' sense of efficacy tends to increase as a consequence of completing student teaching. Teachers' sense of personal efficacy is higher in schools where other teachers and administrators have high expectations for students and where teachers receive help from their principals in solving instructional and management problems (Hoy & Woolfolk, 1993). Another important conclusion from this research is that efficacy grows from real success with students, not just from the moral support of professors or cheerleading by colleagues. Experiences or training that helps you succeed in teaching's day-to-day tasks will provide a foundation for developing a sense of efficacy in your career.

Self-Determination: The need to experience choice and control in what we do and how we do it.

Cognitive Evaluation Theory: Suggests that events affect motivation through the individual's perception of the events as controlling behaviour or providing information.

The perception of control is a significant element in having a sense of efficacy. Sense of control is also an element in a current humanistic theory of motivation—self-determination.

Self-Determination

Self-determination is the need to experience choice and control in what we do and how we do it. It is the desire to self-direct rather than have external rewards or pressures determine our actions (Deci & Ryan, 1985; Deci, Vallerand, Pelletier, & Ryan, 1991). People strive to be in charge of their own behaviour, even to the point of rejecting help from others to remain in command (deCharms, 1976, 1983).

To capture the difference between self- and other-determination, Richard deCharms created the metaphor of "origins" and "pawns." Origins are people who perceive themselves as the origin or source of their intention to act. Pawns see themselves as powerless participants in a game controlled by others. For pawns, play becomes work, leisure feels like obligation, and intrinsic motivation becomes extrinsic motivation (Lepper & Greene, 1978).

DeCharms witnessed that some students are too little governed by their own intrinsic motivation and too powerless over external controls and demands. As origins, students are active and responsible; but as pawns, they are passive and take little responsibility for school work. DeCharms developed programs to help teachers support student self-determination that emphasized setting realistic goals; personal planning about how to reach the goals; personal responsibility for actions; and feelings of self-confidence. Some studies show that when students feel more like origins and less like pawns, they have higher self-esteem, feel more competent and in charge of their learning, score higher on standardized tests, and are absent less (deCharms, 1976; Ryan & Grolnick, 1986).

Self-Determination in the Classroom. From Grade 1 through graduate school, classroom environments that support student self-determination and autonomy are associated with greater student interest, sense of competence, creativity, conceptual learning, and preference for challenge. These relationships appear to hold (Ryan & Grolnick, 1986; Williams, Wiener, Markakis, Reeve, & Deci, 1993). When students can make choices, they more often believe their work is important, even if it is not "fun." Thus, they tend to internalize educational goals. Ruth Garner (1998) sums up the value of self-determination: "It is through this self determination . . . that wise teachers allow each of their students to guide them to what the students find particularly enjoyable and worth learning" (p. 236).

Controlling environments tend to improve performance mainly on rote recall tasks. When students are pressured to perform, they often seek the quickest, easiest solution. A discomforting finding, however, is that both students and parents seem to prefer more controlling teachers, even though the students learn more when their teachers support autonomy (Flink, Boggiano, & Barrett, 1990). Are you willing to risk going against popular images to support student autonomy? If so, focus on information, not control, in your interactions with students.

Information and Control. Many things happen to students throughout the school day. They are praised and criticized, reminded of deadlines, assigned grades, given choices, lectured about rules, and so on. **Cognitive evaluation theory** (Deci & Ryan, 1985; Deci, Vallerand, Pelletier, & Ryan, 1991) explains how these events influence the students' intrinsic motivation by affecting their sense of self-determination and competence. According to this theory, all events have two aspects, controlling and informational. If an event is highly controlling, if it pressures students to act or feel a certain way, then students experience less control and their *intrinsic motivation* diminishes. If, on the other hand, the event provides information that increases the students' sense of competence and efficacy, then intrinsic motivation increases. Of course, if the information provided makes students feel less competent, it is likely that motivation decreases.

For example, a teacher might praise a student by saying, "Good for you! You got an A because you finally followed my instructions correctly." This is a highly controlling statement. The credit goes to the teacher and thus undermines the student's sense of self-determination and intrinsic motivation. The teacher could say instead, "Good for you! Your understanding of the author's use of metaphors has improved tremendously. You earned an A." This statement provides information about the student's growing competence and should increase intrinsic motivation.

How can teachers support student autonomy? Two important steps are to limit controlling messages to students and make sure information you provide highlights students' growing competence. Unfortunately, when teachers are under pressure and "controlled" by the school administration, they are likely to treat students the same way. In one study, teachers who were told to "make sure" their students performed well in solving problems were more critical and gave students more hints and less time for independent work than teachers who were told that their job was to "help" the students learn how to solve the problems themselves. Moreover, students of the pressured teachers actually performed worse (Boggiano, Flink, Shields, Seelbach, & Barrett, 1993). The Guidelines on page 376 give ideas about how to support students' self-determination and autonomy.

Learned Helplessness

Connect & Extend
To other chapters
The concept of learned helplessness was first introduced in **Chapter 4** during the discussion of learning disabilities. Learned helplessness is also an issue for at-risk students, as described in **Chapter 5**. Consider the many factors in a classroom that might lead to learned helplessness, including physical or cognitive disabilities, racial prejudice, sex-role stereotyping, poverty, and so on.

Whatever the label, most theorists agree that a sense of efficacy, control, or self-determination is essential to intrinsic motivation. Unfortunately, some people believe that events and outcomes in their lives are mostly uncontrollable; they experience learned helplessness (Seligman, 1975). To understand the power of learned helplessness, consider this experiment (Hiroto & Seligman, 1975): Some subjects were given a series of solvable puzzles while others were given unsolvable ones. Next, all subjects were given a series of solvable puzzles. Those who struggled with unsolvable problems in the first phase of the experiment solved significantly fewer puzzles in the second phase. They had learned that they could not control the outcome, so why even try?

Learned helplessness has several harmful effects. Students who feel hopeless are unmotivated. They are reluctant to attempt work because they expect to fail. Why try? Because they are pessimistic about learning, these students miss opportunities to elaborate knowledge and practise skills. So, they develop cognitive deficits. Finally, they often suffer from affective problems such as depression, anxiety, and listlessness (Alloy & Seligman, 1979). Once learned helplessness is established, it is very difficult to undo. As we saw in Chapters 4 and 5, learned helplessness is a particular hazard for students with learning disabilities and those victimized by discrimination.

Self-Worth

What are the connections between attributions for success and failure, and beliefs about ability, self-efficacy, and self-worth? Covington and his colleagues suggest these factors come together in three kinds of motivational sets, shown in Table 10.3 on page 379: *mastery-oriented*, *failure-avoiding*, and *failure-accepting* (Covington, 1992; Covington & Omelich, 1984, 1987).

Mastery-oriented students tend to value achievement and see ability as improvable (an incremental view). They focus on learning goals to increase their skills and abilities. They are not fearful of failure because failing does not threaten their sense of competence and self-worth. This allows them to set moderately difficult goals, take risks, and cope constructively with failure. They generally attribute success to their own effort and thus they assume responsibility for learn-

Mastery-Oriented Students: Students who focus on learning goals because they value achievement and see ability as improvable.

GUIDELINES

Supporting Self-Determination and Autonomy

Allow and encourage students to make choices.

Examples

1. Design several different ways to meet a learning objective (e.g., a paper, a compilation of interviews, a test, a news broadcast) and let students choose one. Encourage them to explain the reasons for their choice.
2. Appoint student committees to make suggestions about streamlining procedures such as caring for class pets or distributing equipment.
3. Provide time for independent and extended projects.

Help students plan actions to accomplish self-selected goals.

Examples

1. Experiment with goal cards. Students list their short- and long-term goals and then record three or four specific actions that will move them toward the goals. Goal cards are personal—like credit cards.
2. Encourage middle and high school students to set goals in each subject area, record them in a goal book or on a floppy disk, and check progress toward the goals on a regular basis.

Hold students accountable for the consequences of their choices.

Examples

1. If students choose to work with friends and do not finish a project because too much time was spent socializing, grade the project as it deserves and help the students see the connection between lost time and poor performance.
2. When students choose a topic that captures their imagination, discuss the connections between their investment in the work and the quality products that follow.

Provide rationales for limits, rules, and constraints.

Examples

1. Explain reasons for rules.
2. Respect rules and constraints in your own behaviour.

Acknowledge that negative emotions are valid reactions to teacher control.

Examples

1. Communicate that it is okay (and normal) to feel bored waiting for a turn, for example.
2. Communicate that sometimes important learning involves frustration, confusion, weariness.

Use non-controlling, positive feedback.

Examples

1. See poor performance or behaviour as a problem to be solved, not a target of criticism.
2. Avoid controlling language—"should," "must," "have to."

Source: Adapted from *150 Ways to Increase Intrinsic Motivation in the Classroom*, by J. P. Raffini, 1996, Boston: Allyn & Bacon, and *Motivating Others: Nurturing Inner Motivational Resources* (pp. 29–31), by J. Reeve, 1996, Boston: Allyn & Bacon. Copyright © 1996 by Allyn & Bacon.

ing and have a strong sense of self-efficacy. They perform very well in competitive situations, learn quickly, have more self-confidence and energy, are more aroused, welcome concrete feedback (it does not threaten them), and are eager to learn "the rules of the game" so they can succeed. All these factors make for persistent, successful learning (Alderman, 1985; McClelland, 1985; Morris, 1991).

Failure-avoiding students tend to hold an entity view of ability. They set performance goals. They lack a strong sense of competence and self-worth and they base these beliefs only on how well they perform. They feel only as smart as their last test grade, so they do not develop a solid sense of self-efficacy. To feel competent, they must protect themselves (and their self-images) from failure. If they have been generally successful, they may avoid failure by taking few risks and "sticking with what they know." If, on the other hand, they have experienced some successes but also many failures, they may adopt strategies such as procrastination, feeble efforts, setting very low or ridiculously high goals, or claiming not to care.

Failure-Avoiding Students: Students who avoid failure by sticking to what they know, by not taking risks, or by claiming not to care about their performance.

Unfortunately, as we have seen, failure-avoiding strategies are self-defeating, generally leading to the very failure students were trying to avoid. If failure continues and excuses wear thin, these students may finally decide they are incompetent. This is what they feared in the first place. Now, they come to accept it. Their sense of self-worth and self-efficacy deteriorate. They give up and become **failure-accepting students**. They are convinced their problems are due to low ability, and they can no longer protect themselves from this conclusion. As we saw earlier, students who attribute failure to low ability and believe ability is fixed are likely to become depressed, apathetic, and helpless. They have little hope for change.

Teachers may be able to prevent some failure-avoiding students from becoming failure-accepting by helping them to set new and more realistic goals. Also, some students may need support in aspiring to higher levels in the face of sex or ethnic stereotypes about what they "should" want or what they "should not" be able to do well. This kind of support could make all the difference. Instead of pitying or excusing these students, teach them tactics for learning and then hold them accountable.

Self-Schemas: Lessons for Teachers

If students believe they lack ability to deal with a subject, they will probably act on this belief even if their actual abilities are well above average. These students are likely to have little motivation to tackle advanced topics because they expect to do poorly in these areas. If students believe that failing means they are stupid, they are likely to adopt self-protective, but also self-defeating, strategies. Simply telling students to "try harder" is not particularly effective. Students need real evidence that effort will pay off, that setting a higher goal will not lead to failure, that they can improve, and that abilities change. They need authentic mastery experiences. The Guidelines on page 378 offer ideas for encouraging self-efficacy and self-worth.

How can we put together all this information about motivation? How can teachers create environments, situations, and relationships that encourage motivation? We address these questions next.

CHECKPOINT

Self-Schemas

Review

▷ How do beliefs about ability affect motivation?

▷ What is self-efficacy, and how is it different from other self-schemas?

▷ What are the sources of self-efficacy, and how does efficacy affect motivation?

▷ How does self-determination affect motivation?

▷ How does self-worth influence motivation?

Apply

▷ Explain how beliefs about the nature of ability might be associated with students' self-protective, self-defeating behaviour such as procrastination or not trying.

▷ Describe the development of learned helplessness. What kinds of goals would a student set if the student felt helpless?

Initiating Motivation to Learn

Jere Brophy (1988) describes **motivation to learn** as "a student tendency to find academic activities meaningful and worthwhile and to try to derive the intended academic benefits from them. Motivation to learn can be construed as both a general trait and a situation-specific state" (pp. 205–206). Elements that make up motivation to learn include: planning, concentration on the goal, metacognitive awareness of what you intend to learn and how you intend to learn it, active search for new information, clear perceptions of feedback, pride and satisfaction in achievement, and minimal anxiety or fear of failure (Johnson & Johnson, 1985). In short, motivation to learn involves wanting or intending to learn *plus* positive

GUIDELINES

Encouraging Self-Efficacy and Self-Worth

Emphasize students' progress in a particular area.

Examples

1. Return to earlier material in reviews and show how "easy" it is now.
2. Encourage students to improve projects when they have learned more.
3. Keep examples of particularly good work in portfolios.

Make specific suggestions for improvement, and revise grades when improvements are made.

Examples

1. Return work with comments noting what the students did right, what they did wrong, and why they might have made the mistakes.
2. Experiment with peer editing.
3. Show students how their revised, higher grade reflects greater competence and raises their class average.

Stress connections between past efforts and past accomplishments.

Examples

1. Have individual goal-setting and goal-review conferences with students, in which you ask students to reflect on how they solved difficult problems.

2. Confront self-defeating, failure-avoiding strategies directly.

Set learning goals for your students, and model a mastery orientation for them.

Examples

1. Recognize progress and improvement.
2. Share examples of how you have developed your abilities in a given area and provide other achievement models who are similar to your students—no supermen or superwomen whose accomplishments seem unattainable.
3. Read stories about students who overcame physical, mental, or economic challenges.
4. Don't excuse failure because a student has problems outside school. Help the student succeed inside school.

views about learning *plus* thoughtful, active study strategies such as summarizing, elaborating the basic ideas, outlining in your own words, or drawing graphs of the key relationships (Brophy, 1988).

To engender motivation to learn, teachers should pursue three major goals. First, involve students productively in class work by creating a *state* of motivation to learn. Second, over the long term, help students develop the *trait* of being motivated to learn "to educate themselves throughout their lifetime" (Bandura, 1993, p. 136). Finally, invite students to be deeply and actively cognitively engaged, to be *thoughtful* (Blumenfeld, Puro, & Mergendoller, 1992).

Earlier, we examined intrinsic and extrinsic motivation, attributions, goals, interests, emotions, and self-schemas in motivation. Table 10.3 shows how each of these relates to motivation to learn. Now, what can teachers do to encourage and support motivation to learn? We organize our discussion using the TARGETT model.

Connect & Extend
To professional journals
Ames, C. (1992). Classrooms: Goals, structures, and student motivation. *Journal of Educational Psychology, 84*, 261–271.

On TARGETT for Learning

Carol Ames (1990, 1992) identified six areas of teachers' decisions that influence student motivation to learn: the *task* set for students; the *autonomy* students are

TABLE 10.3 Building a Concept of Motivation to Learn

	Need for Achievement	Goals Set	Attributions	View of Ability	Strategies
Mastery-oriented	High need for achievement; low fear of failure	Learning goals: moderately difficult and challenging	Effort, use of right strategy, sufficient knowledge is cause of success	Incremental; improvable	Adaptive strategies: e.g., try another way, seek help, practise/study more
Failure-avoiding	High fear of failure	Performance goals; very hard or very easy	Lack of ability is cause of failure	Entity; set	Self-defeating strategies: e.g., make a feeble effort, pretend not to care
Failure-accepting	Expectation of failure; depression	Performance goals or no goals	Lack of ability is cause of failure	Entity; set	Learned helplessness; likely to give up

allowed in working; how students are *recognized* for accomplishments; *grouping* practices; *evaluation* procedures; and how *time* is scheduled in classes. Epstein (1989) coined the acronym TARGET for these six areas. We add a seventh area, *teacher expectations*, to create a TARGETT model for motivation to learn that appears in Table 10.4. Now, let's examine each area more closely.

Tasks for Learning

Features of an **academic task** can affect students' motivation. Tasks can be interesting or boring. Tasks concern subject content and involve cognitive operations such as *memorizing*, *inferring*, *classifying*, *applying*, and so on. As students work on tasks, they learn content and practise tactics for learning. Tasks also vary in

▲ *Students may differ in the degree to which they are willing to take risks—or risk being "wrong"—in classroom activities.*

Connect & Extend
To the research
Maehr, M. L., & Anderman, E. M. (1993). Reinventing schools for early adolescents: Emphasizing task goals. *Elementary School Journal, 93,* 593–610. This article describes how the TARGET model can be used to reform middle schools to support learning goals.

Connect & Extend
To the research
Graham, S., & Golan, S. (1991). Motivational influences on cognition: Task involvement, ego involvement, and depth of information processing. *Journal of Educational Psychology, 83,* 187–194.

Academic Tasks: The work the student must accomplish, including the content covered and the mental operations required.

On TARGETT for Learning   379

terms of how clear or ambiguous they are and how much risk is involved in doing them (Doyle, 1983). Finally, tasks have a certain value to students, determined in part by their meaningfulness to the students. We will investigate more closely each of these aspects of tasks.

Task Operations Imply Risk and Ambiguity. Doyle (1983) categorized academic tasks by operations they require. *Memory* tasks require students to recognize or reproduce something they have encountered before, such as matching provinces and capitals. *Routine procedures* involve following steps or rules to solve a problem—using πr^2 to calculate the area of a circle, for example. *Comprehension* tasks require students to go beyond information explicitly given by combining several ideas, originating a procedure, or writing in a particular style. *Opinion* tasks ask students to state a personal preference of belief, such as which character in a story is the bravest. The operations a task calls for determine

---

TABLE 10.4 The TARGETT Model for Supporting Student Motivation to Learn

Teachers make decisions in many areas that can influence motivation to learn. The TARGETT acronym highlights task, autonomy, recognition, grouping, evaluation, time, and teacher expectations.

TARGETT Area	Focus	Objectives	Examples of Possible Strategies
Task	How learning tasks are structured—what the student is asked to do	Enhance intrinsic attractiveness of learning tasks Make learning meaningful	Encourage instruction that relates to students' backgrounds and experience Avoid payment (monetary or other) for attendance, grades, or achievement Foster goal setting and self-regulation
Autonomy/ Responsibility	Student participation in learning/school decisions	Provide optimal freedom for students to make choices and take responsibility	Give alternatives in making assignments Ask for student comments on school life—and take them seriously Encourage students to take initiatives and evaluate their own learning Establish leadership opportunities for *all* students
Recognition	The nature and use of recognition and reward in the school setting	Provide opportunities for all students to be recognized for learning Recognize progress in goal attainment Recognize challenge seeking and innovation	Foster "personal best" awards Reduce emphasis on "honour rolls" Recognize and publicize a wide range of school-related activities of students
Grouping	The organization of school learning and experiences	Build an environment of acceptance and appreciation of all students Broaden the range of social interaction, particularly of at-risk students Enhance social skills development	Provide opportunities for cooperative learning, problem solving, and decision making Encourage multiple group membership to increase range of peer interaction Eliminate ability-grouped classes

Source: From M. L. Maehr and E. M. Anderman. Reinventing schools for early adolescents: Emphasizing task goals. *The Elementary School Journal, 93,* pp. 604–605. Copyright © 1993. Adapted by permission of The University of Chicago Press.

Calvin and Hobbes
by Bill Watterson

TARGETT Area	Focus	Objectives	Examples of Possible Strategies
Evaluation	The nature and use of evaluation and assessment procedures	Grading and reporting processes	Reduce emphasis on social comparisons of achievement
		Practices associated with use of standardized tests	Give students opportunities to improve their performance (e.g., study skills, classes)
		Definition of goals and standards	Establish grading/reporting practices that portray student progress in learning
			Encourage student participation in the evaluation process
Time	The scheduling of the school day	Allow the learning task and student needs to dictate scheduling	Allow students to progress at their own rate whenever possible
		Provide opportunities for extended and significant student involvement in learning tasks	Encourage flexibility in the scheduling of learning experiences
			Give teachers greater control over time usage through, for example, block scheduling
Teacher Expectations	Beliefs and predictions about students' abilities	Hold appropriate but high expectations for all students	Give all students the chance to revise and improve their work
		Communicate that you expect growth	Monitor who gets which opportunities
			Make sure materials show diversity in achievement

Connect & Extend
To the research
Nolen, S. B. (1988). Reasons for studying: Motivational orientations and study strategies. *Cognition and Instruction,5*, 269–288.

Brief Abstract: This study of Grade 8 students explored the relationship among (a) individual differences in three motivational or goal orientations and (b) valuing and use of study strategies. Task orientation was positively correlated with both valuing and use of strategies requiring deep processing of information. Ego orientation was positively related to valuing and use of surface-level strategies only. Work avoidance was negatively related to valuing and use of both kinds of strategies. Analysis indicated that task orientation, more than perceived ability or knowledge of the value of deep-processing strategies, predicts the spontaneous use of these strategies. The predication held over four to six weeks, suggesting the importance of individual differences in motivational orientation.

In the same issue are two commentaries on this study:
Lepper, M. R. (1988). Motivational considerations in the study of instruction. *Cognition and Instruction, 5*, 289–310.

Brown, A. L. (1988). Motivation to learn and understand: Taking charge of one's own learning. *Cognition and Instruction, 5*, 311–322.

how ambiguous and risky the task is. In turn, this affects student motivation, as you will soon see.

Some tasks involve less risk than others because failure is unlikely. Opinion tasks are low-risk—there are no right or wrong answers. Simple memory or procedural tasks also have low risk—to answer correctly, just follow the steps (if you remember them!). However, the stakes can be high for memory or procedural tasks that are longer and more complex. Reciting 100 lines from Shakespeare is a lot to memorize; thus, it's risky.

A task's *ambiguity* is how clear-cut its expected answer is. Opinion and understanding tasks are ambiguous: it's difficult to predict the right answer (if there is one) or know how to create it. Memory and procedural tasks, in contrast, are unambiguous. The solution to a quadratic inequality has one clear "right" answer, even though the task may be difficult. Figure 10.2 summarizes how tasks can be categorized by risk and ambiguity.

How do risk and ambiguity relate to motivation? Most students strive to *lower risk* and *decrease ambiguity* in school work, especially highly anxious students or those trying to avoid failure. For example, a complicated *comprehension* task can offer lots for students to learn but can be ambiguous and risky. Students will want more guidance in the form of models, rules, or formulas: "How many pages?" "Will we have to know dates and names?" "Can you give us a model we can follow?"

Often, students try to *negotiate the task*. Acceding to student negotiations transforms a *comprehension* task into a *procedural* one. Risk and ambiguity are reduced. This produces a temporary *state* of motivation, but it is motivation to perform, to get the grade. Little has been done to foster an enduring *trait* of motivation to learn. Equally important, the task is now misaligned with objectives. The procedural task does less to extend problem-solving and critical-thinking skills the teacher had intended to develop. Also, because students learn operations they practise, negotiating students have learned a procedure—how to negotiate with teachers (Doyle, 1983). Moreover, negotiations can lead to management problems and, if students remain confused, they may become discouraged or lose interest.

FIGURE 10.2

Ambiguity and Risk Associated with Academic Tasks in Classrooms

Academic tasks can be characterized by their levels of risk and ambiguity. Because students often find high-ambiguity/high-risk tasks very threatening, they need extra support and fewer pressures when completing them.

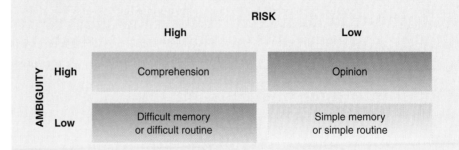

Source: From W. Doyle (1983). Academic work. *Review of Educational Research, 53*, Figure p. 183. Copyright 1983 by the American Educational Research Association. Adapted by permission of the publisher.

What to do? Teachers must make wise choices and then stick with them, even when students try to negotiate changes. Instructions should be clear, but not too restricting. Penalties for taking a risk or making a mistake should not be too great. Finally, tasks must have value to students. What affects the value of classroom tasks?

Task Value. Expectancy-value theories suggest that the strength of motivation in a particular situation is determined by our *expectation* of success and the *value* we ascribe to that success. There are three kinds of task-related values (Eccles & Wigfield, 1985). **Attainment value** is the importance of doing well. It is closely tied to an individual's needs—the need to be competent and well-liked, for example—and the meaning of success to that person. For instance, if a student has a strong need to appear smart and believes that a high test grade shows that, the test has high attainment value for that student. A second kind of task-related value is **intrinsic or interest value**. This is the enjoyment of the activity itself. Some students like learning; others enjoy the feeling of effort or the challenge of solving puzzles. Third, tasks have **utility value**; that is, they are useful in achieving a goal. **Authentic tasks** that reflect elements of real-life problems can highlight utility value. Most school tasks have elements of authenticity. Helping students perceive these elements can elevate the task's utility value for them.

Problem-based learning is one example of teaching using authentic tasks. In problem-based learning, according to Stepien and Gallagher (1993), "Students meet an ill-structured problem before they receive any instruction. In place of covering the curriculum, learners probe deeply into issues searching for connections, grappling with complexity, and using knowledge to fashion solutions" (p. 26). Teachers act as coaches and tutors, asking questions, modelling thinking, helping students organize and monitor their problem solving. An example of such a problem appropriate for Grade 7 or 8 students would be, Where should we locate a new landfill? Students would research the situation, perhaps interview experts, and develop recommendations to present to their municipal council. The novelty of the problem, its challenge, the opportunity to pursue diverse solutions, and its real-life meaning help motivate students.

Supporting Autonomy and Recognizing Accomplishment

The second area in the TARGETT model concerns how much choice and autonomy students are allowed. Choice is not the norm in schools. Students spend thousands of hours in schools where other people decide what will happen and "where raised hands are sometimes ignored, questions to teachers are fairly frequently brushed aside, and permission to go somewhere else to do something else is quite routinely refused" (Garner, 1998, p. 232). Yet, as we saw earlier, self-determination and an internal locus of causality are keys to intrinsic motivation. What can teachers do to support choice without inviting chaos?

Supporting Choices

Like totally unguided discovery learning, unstructured or unguided choice can be counterproductive for learning (Garner, 1998). For example, Dyson (1997) found children became anxious and upset if their teachers asked them to draw or write about anything they wanted in any way they wanted. Unbounded choice was perceived as a "scary void." The alternative is bounded choice—give students a range of options that set valuable tasks for them but also allow them to follow personal interests. The balance must be just right: "too much autonomy is bewildering and

Connect & Extend
To the research
The January 1988 issue of *Elementary School Journal* is devoted to the topic "schoolwork and academic tasks."

Connect & Extend
To the research
Vispoel, W. P., & Austin, J. R. (1995). Success and failure in junior high school: A critical incident approach to understanding students' attributional beliefs. *American Educational Research Journal, 32*, 377–412.

Connect & Extend
To the research
Lowenstein, G. (1994). The psychology of curiosity: A review and reinterpretation. *Psychological Bulletin, 117*, 75–98. This article connects curiosity to perceived gaps in information.

Connect & Extend
To professional journals
See the special April 1993 issue of *Educational Leadership* devoted to "authentic learning."

Connect & Extend
To the research
The June 1998 issue of *Educational Psychology Review*, edited by Karen Harris and Patricia Alexander, has a series of articles describing models of integrated teaching that include student choice. One article by Ruth Garner (pp. 227–238) describes the power of bounded choices.

Attainment Value: The importance of doing well on a task; how success on the task meets personal needs.

Intrinsic or Interest Value: The enjoyment a person gets from a task.

Utility Value: The contribution of a task to meeting one's goals.

Authentic Tasks: Tasks that have some connection to real-life problems the students will face outside the classroom.

too little is boring" (Guthrie, Cox, Anderson, Harris, Mazzoni, & Rach (1998, p. 185).

Students also can exercise autonomy about feedback from the teacher or classmates. Figure 10.3 illustrates a strategy called "Check It Out." Students specify a set of skills that they want evaluated in a particular assignment. Over a unit, all the skills have to be "checked out," but students can choose when each skill is evaluated. How else can teachers support student self-determination? According to a study by Reeve, Bolt, and Cai (1999), compared to controlling teachers, autonomy-supporting teachers listened more, resisted solving problems for students, gave fewer directives, and asked more questions about what students wanted to do.

Recognizing Accomplishment

The third TARGETT area is *recognition*. How should students' accomplishments be acknowledged and rewarded? In Chapter 6 we described authentic praise that focuses on progress, growing competence, and independence. But praise can have paradoxical effects at times. Some students may view a teacher's feedback, whether praise or criticism, as a cue about capabilities: praise means I'm not very smart—when I succeed, the teacher has to recognize it. Criticism means my teacher thinks I'm smart and I could do better (Stipek, 1996).

What sort of recognition leads to engagement? In a study by Ruth Butler (1987), Grade 5 and 6 students were given interesting divergent thinking tasks followed by either individual comments, standardized praise ("very good"),

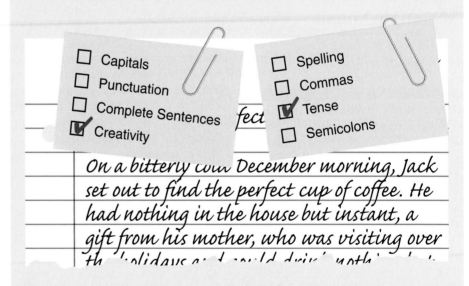

FIGURE 10.3

Student Autonomy: Check It Out

Using this technique to support student autonomy, the teacher decides on a set of skills that will be developed over a unit, but the student decides which skill(s) will be evaluated on any given assignment. Over the course of the unit, all the skills have to be "checked out." This student has indicated that she wants the teacher to "check out" her creativity and verb tense.

Source: From *150 Ways to Increase Intrinsic Motivation in the Classroom* (pp. 33–34) by J. P. Raffini, 1996, Boston: Allyn & Bacon. Copyright © Allyn & Bacon, Inc. Adapted with permission.

grades, or no feedback. Interest, performance, attributions to effort, and task involvement were higher after personal comments. Ego-involved motivation (the desire to look good or do better than others) was greater after grades and standard praise. We recommend recognizing students for self-referenced improvement, for tackling difficult tasks, for persistence, and for creativity.

Grouping, Evaluation, and Time

Relationships with other people can have considerable motivational power, according to David and Roger Johnson (1985):

> Motivation to learn is inherently interpersonal. It is through interaction with other people that students learn to value learning for its own sake, enjoy the process of learning, and take pride in their acquisition of knowledge and development of skill. Of the interpersonal relationships available in the classroom, peers may be the most influential on motivation to learn. (p. 250)

The ways students relate to peers are influenced by the goal structure of activities and tasks the teacher creates.

Grouping and Goal Structures

Students in the classroom are part of a group where motivation is influenced by the ways they relate to group mates who are also involved in accomplishing a particular goal (Johnson & Johnson, 1999). This interpersonal factor is the **goal structure** of the task. There are three such structures: cooperative, competitive, and individualistic, as shown in Figure 10.4.

In Chapter 9, we described advantages of cooperative goal structures. When the task involves complex learning and problem-solving skills, cooperation can lead to higher achievement than competition, especially for low-ability students (Johnson & Johnson, 1985; Slavin, 1995). Well-designed cooperative learning also improves the ability to see the world from another person's point of view, enhances relations among ethnic groups in classrooms, increases self-esteem, increases willingness to help and encourage fellow students, and elevates acceptance of students with disabilities and low-achieving students (Slavin, 1995; Stipek, 1996; Webb & Palincsar, 1996). Students learn to set attainable goals and negotiate. They become more altruistic. The interaction with peers that students enjoy becomes a part of the learning process. The result? The need for belonging described by Maslow is more likely to be met and motivation is increased.

There are many approaches to peer learning or group learning, as you saw in Chapter 9. **Teams-Games-Tournaments,** or TGT (Slavin, 1995), is an approach designed specifically to enhance motivation. After the teacher introduces a topic and poses problems, students move into heterogeneous teams to help each other figure out answers. Instead of taking written tests, each student meets once a week at a "tournament table" with two other students of comparable ability from the other teams. The three students at each tournament table compete, answering questions similar to the problems they practised in their study teams. The winner at each table earns six points for his or her team. Each week the participants at the tournament tables change—winners are "bumped" up to a higher-ability table to keep the competition fair. This way, students all have the chance to contribute equally to their team's total score (Slavin, 1990).

Research on Teams-Games-Tournaments raises a caution about cooperative learning that involves teams. Bette Chambers and Philip Abrami (1991) of Concordia University in Montreal found that members of successful teams learned more than members of unsuccessful teams, but also they were happier about the outcome and rated their ability higher than members of losing teams. For low-

Connect & Extend
To the research
Butler, R. (1987). Task-involving and ego-involving properties of evaluation: Effects of different feedback conditions on motivational perceptions, interest, and performance. *Journal of Educational Psychology, 79,* 474–482.
Brief Abstract: Does the impact of information about performance on subsequent intrinsic motivation depend significantly on the degree to which this information promotes task-involved or an ego-involved motivational orientation? Two hundred Grade 5 and 6 students were given interesting divergent thinking tasks in each of three sessions. Individual comments, numerical grades, standardized praise, or no feedback were received after Sessions 1 and 2. At Session 3 (post-test), interest, performance, and attributions of effort, outcome, and the impact of evaluation to task-involved causes were highest after receipt of comments. Ego-involved attributions were highest after receipt of grades and praise. These findings support the conceptualization of feedback conditions as task-involving (comments), ego-involving (grades and praise), or neither (no feedback).

Goal Structure: The way students relate to others who are also working toward a particular goal.

Teams-Games-Tournaments (TGT): Learning arrangement in which team members prepare cooperatively, then meet comparable individuals of competing teams in a tournament game to win points for their team.

FIGURE 10.4

Different Goal Structures

Each goal structure is associated with a different relationship between the individual and the group. This relationship influences motivation to reach the goal.

	Cooperative	Competitive	Individualistic
Definition	Students believe their goal is attainable only if other students will also reach the goal.	Students believe they will reach their goal if and only if other students do not reach the goal.	Students believe that their own attempt to reach a goal is not related to other students' attempts to reach the goal.
Examples	Team victories—each player wins only if all the team members win; a relay race; a quilting bee; a barn raising; a symphony; a play.	Golf tournament, singles tennis match, a 100-metre dash; valedictorian.	Lowering your handicap in golf, jogging, learning a new language, enjoying a museum, losing or gaining weight, stopping smoking.

Source: From D. Johnson and R. Johnson (1975). *Learning Together and Alone: Cooperation, Competition and Individualization.* Adapted by permission of Allyn & Bacon.

Connect & Extend
To the research
Slavin, R. R. (1991). Synthesis of research on cooperative learning. *Educational Leadership, 48*(5), 71–82. *Focus Question:* When is cooperative learning most effective, and with which students?

Connect & Extend
To the research
For a thorough review of research on different forms of cooperative learning, asee O'Donnell, A. M., & O'Kelly, J. (1994). Learning from peers: Beyond the rhetoric of positive results. *Educational Psychology Review, 6,* 321–350. a

Connect & Extend
To your teaching
Design a lesson plan using a cooperative learning format. The assignment should consist of (1) a description of how to prepare the students for this lesson; (2) a summary of the expected results; (3) the topic of the lesson and the information that would be given to members of the groups; and (4) the actual test or means of assessment that would be used to determine learning. If possible, you should actually teach the lesson in a school classroom.

achieving students who tend to be anxious, failure-accepting, or helpless, being on a losing team could make matters worse. Chambers and Abrami suggest experimenting with cooperation both within and between teams. For example, the whole class might earn recognition if each team reaches a specified level of learning.

Table 10.4 gave ideas for fostering motivation through peer relations. Besides the use of cooperative learning, ideas include allowing time and opportunity for peer interaction in school, using project-based learning, and encouraging the development of teams and "schools within schools."

The nature of the goal structure—cooperative, competitive, or individualistic—has implications for the next two TARGETT areas, *evaluation* and *time*.

Evaluation

Emphasizing competitive evaluation and grading means that more students will focus on performance goals rather than learning goals and more will be ego-involved as opposed to task-involved. In this situation, students look on classroom work as "an exchange of performance for grades" (Doyle, 1983, p. 181). Grading here refers to more than just report card marks. It includes teachers' formal as well as informal evaluations.

Of course, not all students are caught up in an exchange of performance for grades. Low-achieving students who have little hope of "making the grade" or mastering the tasks may simply want to finish. In a study of Grade 1 students, when the work was too challenging, low-achieving students made up answers, filled in the page with patterns, or copied from other students, just to get through their seatwork. As one student said when she finished a word-definition matching exercise, "I don't know what it means, but I did it" (Anderson, Brubaker, Alleman-Brooks, & Duffy, 1985, p. 132).

How can teachers avoid these negative effects? De-emphasize grades and emphasize learning. Students should understand the value of their work. Instead of saying, "You will need to know this for the test," tell students what they learn will be useful in solving problems they want to solve. Suggest that the lesson will

Connect & Extend
To the research
Chambers, B., & Abrami, P. C. (1991). The relationship between student team learning outcomes and achievement, causal attributions, and affect. *Journal of Educational Psychology, 83,* 140–146.

▲ *Students working in teams can support each other's learning and motivation. Immediate help is available for learning problems and encouragement can help overcome lagging interest.*

answer some interesting questions. Communicate that understanding is more important than finishing. And follow through on these "promises" in the ways you set tasks, interact with students, and give feedback.

Unfortunately, many teachers do not follow this advice. Brophy (1988) and several colleagues spent about 100 hours observing how six teachers introduced their lessons. Most introductions were routine, apologetic, or unenthusiastic, with teachers describing procedures, making threats, emphasizing finishing, or promising tests on the material:

> "You don't expect me to give you baby work to do every day, do you?"
> "My talkers are going to get a third page to do during lunch."
> "If you are done by 10 o'clock, you can go outside." (Brophy, 1988, p. 204)

Other teachers are dissimilar to the six Brophy studied. Hermine Marshall (1987) described a few elementary school teachers who seemed to establish a *learning orientation* in their classrooms. They stressed understanding instead of performing, being graded, or finishing work. In Chapter 12, we will examine strategies for establishing such an orientation in your class.

One way to emphasize learning rather than grades is to use self-evaluation. This strategy also supports autonomy. For exam-

CHECKPOINT

On TARGETT for Learning

Review

▶ What does TARGETT stand for?

▶ How do tasks and task value affect motivation?

▶ What does it mean for students to "negotiate a task"?

▶ Distinguish between bounded and unbounded choices.

▶ How can recognition undermine motivation and a sense of self-efficacy?

▶ What determines whether a goal structure is cooperative, competitive, or individualistic?

▶ How does evaluative climate affect goal setting?

▶ What are some effects of time on motivation?

Apply

▶ Name some ways other than problem-based learning to make learning tasks more authentic.

▶ Why would providing rationales for class rules help students feel more autonomous?

▶ Describe a cooperative learning structure that is designed to support student motivation.

▶ How can evaluation procedures help to create a learning-oriented classroom?

Connect & Extend
To your teaching
A recent addition to the list of cooperative learning techniques is Cooperative Integrated Reading and Composition (CIRC). This system supports the traditional approach of using ability-based reading groups. Students are assigned to teams made up of pairs from each reading group in the class. While the teacher works with one reading group, the teams work in their pairs using many of the methods of reciprocal teaching described in Chapter 9—reading aloud, making predictions, asking questions, summarizing, and writing about the stories they are reading. Team members help each other prepare for tests, write and edit work, and often "publish" team books. Teams are rewarded based on the average performance of all their members on all the reading and writing assignments. Thus, there is equal opportunity for success, group support for learning, and individual accountability for final performance. These three elements are characteristic of many cooperative learning strategies (Slavin, 1995).

Connect & Extend
To other chapters
Chapter 11 discusses how to make more time for learning by decreasing disruptions, smoothing transitions, and avoiding discipline problems.

Self-Fulfilling Prophecy: A groundless expectation that is confirmed because it has been expected.

Pygmalion Effect: Exceptional progress by a student as a result of high teacher expectations for that student; named for the mythological king who made a statue, then caused it to be brought to life.

Sustaining Expectation Effect: Student performance maintained at a certain level because teachers don't recognize improvements.

ple, the sheet for self-evaluating and goal planning in Figure 10.5 could be adapted for almost any grade.

Time

Most experienced teachers know there is too much work and not enough time in the school day. Students seldom can stick with an activity. Even if they become engrossed in a project, they must stop and turn to another subject when the block is over or the schedule demands. Furthermore, students must progress as a group. If some individuals can move faster or if they need more time, they still have to follow the pace of the whole group. Scheduling often interferes with motivation by making students move faster or slower than is appropriate or by interrupting their involvement. It is difficult to develop persistence and a sense of self-efficacy in the face of these conditions. One challenge to you as a teacher will be to schedule time for engaged and persistent learning. Some elementary classrooms have time for DEAR—Drop Everything And Read—to give extended periods when everyone, even the teacher, reads. Some middle and high schools have teachers work in teams to plan larger blocks of time where students pursue interdisciplinary projects.

Now let's add the last T—teacher expectations.

$\mathcal{T}$eacher Expectations

Robert Rosenthal and Lenore Jacobson (1968) captured the attention of the media more than 30 years ago with a study described in their book *Pygmalion in the Classroom*. They chose several students at random in a number of elementary school classrooms, then told the teachers that these randomly chosen students probably would make significant intellectual gains during the year. Even though randomly chosen students should not make larger gains than normal, that year they did. The researchers explained this as a **self-fulfilling prophecy**, a groundless expectation that comes true simply because one expects it. According to this explanation, the teachers' beliefs about students' abilities or behaviour brought about the very behaviour the teacher expected. Controversy over this finding, dubbed the **Pygmalion effect**, continues today (Babad, 1995; Brophy, 1982; Cooper & Good, 1983; Elashoff & Snow, 1971; Good, 1988; Rosenthal, 1987, 1995; Snow, 1995).

Two Kinds of Expectation Effects

The self-fulfilling prophecy is one kind of expectation effect. A second kind occurs when teachers are reasonably accurate in initially estimating students' abilities and respond to students appropriately. So far, so good. Problems arise, though, when students improve but teachers do not raise their expectations correspondingly. This is a **sustaining expectation effect**—the teacher's unchanged expectation sustains the student's achievement at the initial (lower) expected level because teaching is not adjusted to be appropriate to the students' new level of achievement. Sustaining effects are more common than self-fulfilling prophecy effects (Cooper & Good, 1983). This may be especially true for withdrawn children who provide little information about themselves. Teachers may sustain their expectations about these children for lack of new input (Jones & Gerig, 1994).

Sources of Expectations

Expectations and beliefs focus attention and organize memory, so teachers may selectively attend to information that fits initial expectations and remember only that (Fiske, 1993; Hewstone, 1989). When student performance does not fit expectations, the teacher may rationalize and attribute it to external causes beyond the student's control. For example, the low-ability student who did well on a test must have cheated, or the high-ability student who failed must have been upset that day. Expectations often endure even in the face of considerable information to the contrary (Brophy, 1982). Other sources of teachers' expectations (e.g., see Braun, 1976) include test scores, sex, ethnic background, knowledge of older siblings, socioeconomic class, physical attractiveness, and notes from previous teachers or psychological reports in permanent record files.

Teacher Behaviour and Student Reaction

Table 10.6 on page 391 shows six dimensions of teacher communication toward students that may be influenced by expectations. These dimensions include both instructional practices and interpersonal interactions.

FIGURE 10.5

Self-Evaluation and Goals Planning

By completing this form, students evaluate their own work in relation to their goals and set new goals for the future.

Name ____________________ Advisor ____________________

Subject ____________________ Quarter ____________________

1. Self-Evaluation:

a. How am I doing in this course? ____________________

b. What difficulties have I been having? ____________________

c. How much time and effort have I been spending in this course? ____________________

d. Do I need more help in this course? __________ If yes, how have I tried to get it?

2. Academic Goal

a. My goal to achieve before the end of the quarter is ____________________

b. I want to work on this goal because ____________________

c. I will achieve this goal by ____________________

3. Behaviour or Social Goal

a. My goal to achieve before the end of the quarter is ____________________

b. I want to work on this goal because ____________________

c. I will achieve this goal by ____________________

Variations

Advisors may choose to use this activity at the beginning of each quarter and adapt self-evaluation and goal planning sheets to specific grade levels. Follow-up conferences are also useful for helping students evaluate their plans.

Source: From *150 Ways to Increase Intrinsic Motivation in the Classroom* (p. 67), by J. P. Raffini, 1996, Boston: Allyn & Bacon. Copyright © 1996 Allyn & Bacon. Adapted with permission.

Connect & Extend
To the research
Babad, E. (1995). The "teachers' pet" phenomenon, students' perceptions of differential behavior, and students' morale. *Journal of Educational Psychology, 87,* 361–374.
Brief Abstract: The relationships among the teacher's pet phenomenon, students' perceptions of teacher's differential behaviour, and students' morale were investigated in 80 upper-elementary Israeli classrooms. The intensity of the teacher's pet phenomenon (rate of students' consensus in identifying teacher's pets in each classroom) was related to perceived teachers' differential behaviour, particularly to teachers' differential (also preferential) affect. In turn, teachers' perceived differential affect was negatively related to students' morale and satisfaction. In classrooms of teachers who had pets who were not popular, students demonstrated lower morale, whereas students in "popular-pet" classrooms did not demonstrate lower morale. Previous findings on the teacher's pet phenomenon and on students' and teachers' perceptions of teachers' differential behaviour were replicated.

Connect & Extend
To the research
Is there any reason why teachers should not have high expectations for all of their students? What about the distinction between "high expectations" and "reasonable expectations?"

Connect & Extend
To your own philosophy
Should you read your students' cumulative foalders at the beginning of the school year? If so, how can you keep from forming low expectations?

Connect & Extend
To the research
For a complete discussion of teacher expectations and student learning, see Good, T. (1987). Teacher expectations. In D. Berliner & B. Rosenshine (Eds.), *Talks to teachers* (pp. 159–200). New York: Random House.

Instructional Strategies. As we have seen, different grouping practices may have a marked effect on students. And some teachers leave little to the imagination: they make their expectations all too clear. For example, Alloway (1984) recorded comments such as these directed to low-achieving groups:

"I'll be over to help you slow ones in a minute."
"The blue group will find this hard."

By these remarks the teacher not only tells the students that they lack ability but also communicates that finishing the work, not understanding, is the goal.

Once teachers assign students to ability groups, they usually assign different learning activities to each group. To the extent that the different activities challenge students and increase achievement, these differences are probably necessary. Activities become inappropriate, however, when the sustaining expectation effect crops up—when students who are ready for more challenging work are not given the opportunity to try it because teachers believe they cannot handle it.

Teacher-Student Interactions. However the class is grouped and whatever the assignments, the quantity and quality of teacher-student interactions affect stu-

TABLE 10.5 Six Dimensions of Teaching That Can Communicate Expectations

Dimension	Students believed to be MORE capable have:	Students believed to be LESS capable have:
Task environment curriculum, procedures, task definition, pacing, qualities of environment	More opportunity to perform publicly on meaningful tasks.	Less opportunity to perform publicly, especially on meaningful tasks (supplying alternate endings to a story vs. learning to pronounce a word correctly).
	More opportunity to think.	Less opportunity to think, analyze (since much work is aimed at practice).
Grouping practices	More assignments that deal with comprehension, understanding (in higher-ability groups).	Less choice on curriculum assignments—more work on drill-like assignments.
Locus of responsibility for learning	More autonomy (more choice in assignments, fewer interruptions).	Less autonomy (frequent teacher monitoring of work, frequent interruptions).
Feedback and evaluation practices	More opportunity for self-evaluation.	Less opportunity for self-evaluation.
Motivational strategies	More honest/contingent feedback.	Less honest/more gratuitous/less contingent feedback.
Quality of teacher relationships	More respect for the learner as an individual with unique interests and needs.	Less respect for the learner as an individual with unique interests and needs.

Source: From T. Good and R. Weinstein, "Teaching expectations: A framework for exploring classrooms." In K. Zumwalt (Ed.), *Improving teaching* (The ASCD 1986 Yearbook). Reprinted by permission of the Association for Supervision and Curriculum Development. Copyright © 1986 by ASCD. All rights reserved.

dents. Research shows that students who are expected to achieve tend to be asked more and harder questions, given more chances and a longer time to respond, and interrupted less often than students who are expected to do poorly. Teachers also give high-expectation students cues and prompts, communicating their belief that the students can answer the question (Allington, 1980; Good & Brophy, 1997; Rosenthal, 1995). Teachers tend to be more encouraging in general toward those students for whom they have high expectations. They smile at these students more often and show greater warmth through such non-verbal responses as leaning toward the students and nodding their heads as the students speak (Woolfolk & Brooks, 1983, 1985). In contrast, with low-expectation students, teachers ask easier questions, allow less time for answering, and are less likely to give prompts.

CHECKPOINT

Teacher Expectations

Review

▶ What are some sources of teacher expectations?

▶ What are the two kinds of expectation effects and how do they happen?

▶ What are the different avenues for communicating teacher expectations?

Apply

▶ How can teacher expectations set up a cycle of expectation and confirmation?

Feedback and reinforcement also seem to depend somewhat on teacher expectations. Good and Brophy (1997) noted that teachers demand better performance from high-achieving students, are less likely to accept poor answers from them, and praise them more for good answers. Teachers are more likely to respond with sympathetic acceptance or even praise to inadequate answers from low-achieving students, but to criticize these same students for wrong answers. Even more disturbing, low-achieving students receive less praise than high-achieving students for similar correct answers. When an answer on a test is "almost right," the teacher is more likely to give the benefit of the doubt (and thus the better grade) to high-achieving students (Finn, 1972). This inconsistent feedback can be very confusing for low-ability students. Imagine how hard it would be to learn if your wrong answers were sometimes praised, sometimes ignored, and sometimes criticized, and your right answers received little recognition (Good 1983a, b).

You may be promising yourself that you will never communicate low expectations to your students in these not-so-subtle ways, especially now that you know about the dangers involved. Of course, not all teachers form inappropriate expectations or act on their expectations in unconstructive ways (Babad, Inbar, & Rosenthal, 1982). But avoiding the problem may be more difficult than it seems. In general, low-expectation students also tend to be the most disruptive students. (Of course, low expectations can reinforce their desire to disrupt or misbehave.) Teachers may call on these students less, wait a shorter time for their answers, and give them less praise for right answers, partly to avoid the wrong, careless, or silly answers that can cause disruptions, delays, and digressions (Cooper, 1979). The challenge is to deal with these very real threats to classroom management without communicating low expectations to some students or fostering their own low expectations of themselves. And sometimes, low expectations become part of the culture of the school—beliefs shared by teachers and administrators alike (Weinstein, Madison, & Kuklinski, 1995). The Guidelines on page 392 may help you avoid some of these problems.

GUIDELINES

Avoiding the Negative Effects of Teacher Expectations

Use information about students from tests, cumulative folders, and other teachers very carefully.

Examples
1. Some teachers avoid reading cumulative folders at the beginning of the year.
2. Be critical and objective about the reports you hear from other teachers.

Be flexible in your use of grouping strategies.

Examples
1. Review the work of students often and experiment with new groupings.
2. Use different groups for different subjects.
3. Use mixed-ability groups in cooperative exercises.

Make sure all the students are challenged.

Examples
1. Don't say, "This is easy, I know you can do it."
2. Offer a wide range of problems, and encourage all students to try a few of the harder ones for extra credit. Find something positive about these attempts.

Be especially careful about how you respond to low-achieving students during class discussions.

Examples
1. Give them prompts, cues, and time to answer.
2. Give ample praise for good answers.
3. Call on low achievers as often as high achievers.

Use materials that show a wide range of ethnic groups.

Examples
1. Check readers and library books. Is there ethnic diversity?
2. If few materials are available, ask students to research and create their own, based on community or family sources.

Make sure that your teaching does not reflect racial, ethnic, or sexual stereotypes or prejudice.

Examples
1. Use a checking system to be sure you call on and include all students.

2. Monitor the content of the tasks you assign. Do boys get the "hard" math problems to work out at the board? Do you avoid having students with limited English give oral presentations?

Be fair in evaluation and disciplinary procedures.

Examples
1. Make sure equal offences receive equal punishment. Find out from students in an anonymous questionnaire whether you seem to be favouring certain individuals.
2. Try to grade student work without knowing the identity of the student. Ask another teacher to give you a "second opinion" from time to time.

Communicate to all students that you believe they can learn—and mean it.

Examples
1. Return papers that do not meet standards with specific suggestions for improvements.
2. If students do not have the answers immediately, wait, probe, and then help them think through an answer.

Involve all students in learning tasks and in privileges.

Examples
1. Use some system to make sure you give each student practice in reading, speaking, and answering questions.
2. Keep track of who gets to do what job. Are some students always on the list while others seldom make it?

Monitor your non-verbal behaviour.

Examples
1. Do you lean away or stand farther away from some students? Do some students get smiles when they approach your desk while others get only frowns?
2. Does your tone of voice vary with different students?

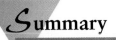

Summary

What Is Motivation?

Define motivation.

Motivation is an internal state that arouses, directs, and maintains behaviour. Studies of motivation focus on how and why people initiate actions directed toward specific goals, how intensively they are involved in the activity, how persistent they are in their attempts to reach these goals, and what they think and feel along the way. Explanations of motivation include both personal and environmental factors as well as intrinsic and extrinsic sources of motivation.

What is the difference between intrinsic and extrinsic motivation?

Intrinsic motivation is the natural tendency to seek out and conquer challenges as we pursue personal interests and exercise capabilities—it is motivation to do something when we don't have to. Extrinsic motivation is based on factors not related to the activity itself. We are not really interested in the activity for its own sake; we care only about what it will gain us.

How does locus of causality apply to motivation?

The essential difference between intrinsic and extrinsic motivation is the person's reason for acting, that is, whether the locus of causality for the action (the location of the cause) is internal or external—inside or outside the person. If the locus in internal, motivation is intrinsic; if the locus is external, motivation is extrinsic. Most motivation has elements of both.

Four General Approaches to Motivation

What are key factors in motivation according to a behavioural viewpoint? A humanistic viewpoint? A cognitive viewpoint? A sociocultural viewpoint?

Behaviourists emphasize extrinsic motivation caused by incentives, rein-forcers, and punishment. Humanistic views stress intrinsic motivation created by needs such as personal growth, fulfillment, and self-determination. Cognitive views stress a person's active search for meaning, understanding, and competence, plus the power of the individual's attributions and interpretations. Sociocultural views emphasize legitimate engaged participation and identity within a community.

Distinguish between deficiency needs and being needs in Maslow's theory.

Maslow called four lower-order needs—survival, safety, belonging, and self-esteem—deficiency needs. When these needs are satisfied, motivation for fulfilling them decreases. He labelled the three higher-order needs—intellectual achievement, aesthetic appreciation, and self-actualization—being needs. When they are met, a person's motivation does not cease; instead, it increases to seek further fulfillment.

What are the three dimensions of attributions in Weiner's theory?

According to Weiner, most of the attributed causes for successes or failures can be characterized in terms of three dimensions: *locus* (location of the cause internal or external to the person), *stability* (whether the cause stays the same or can change), and *responsibility* (whether the person can control the cause). The greatest motivational problems arise when students attribute failures to stable, uncontrollable causes. These students may seem resigned to failure, depressed, helpless—what we generally call "unmotivated."

What are expectancy x value theories?

Expectancy x value theories suggest that motivation to reach a goal is the product of our expectations for success and the value of the goal to us. If either is zero, motivation is zero also.

What is legitimate peripheral participation?

Legitimate peripheral participation means that beginners are genuinely involved in the work of the community, even if their abilities are undeveloped and their contributions are small. The identities of novices and experts are defined by their participation in the community. They are each motivated to learn the values and practices of their community to develop their identity as community members.

Goal Orientation and Motivation

What kinds of goals are the most motivating?

Goals increase motivation if they are specific, moderately difficult, and able to be reached in the near future (proximal).

Describe learning, performance, work-avoidant, and social goals.

A learning goal is an intention to gain knowledge and master skills. Students who set learning goals tend to seek challenges and persist when they encounter difficulties. A performance goal is an intention to get good grades or to appear smart or more capable than others. Students who set performance goals are preoccupied with themselves and how they appear. Work-avoidant learners simply want to find the easiest way to handle the situation. Students with social goals can be supported or hindered in their learning, depending on the specific goal (e.g., have fun with friends or bring honour to the family).

What makes goal setting effective in the classroom?

For goal setting to be effective in the classroom, students need accurate feedback about their progress toward goals and they must accept the goals set. Generally, students are more willing to adopt goals that seem realistic, reasonably difficult, and meaningful, and if good reasons are given for the value of the goals.

Interests and Emotions

Do interests and emotions affect learning?

Learning and information processing are influenced by emotion. Students are more likely to pay attention to, learn from, and remember events, images, and readings that provoke emotional responses or that are related to their personal interests. However, there are cautions in responding to students' interests. "Seductive details," interesting bits of information that are not central to the learning, can hinder learning.

What is the role of arousal in learning?

There appears to be an optimum level of arousal for most activities. Generally, higher arousal is helpful on simple tasks but less arousal is better for complex tasks. Severe anxiety is an example of arousal that is too high for optimal learning. When arousal is too low, teachers can stimulate curiosity by pointing out gaps in knowledge or using variety in activities.

How does anxiety interfere with learning?

Anxiety can be the cause and the result of poor performance; it can interfere with attention to, learning of, and retrieval of information. Many anxious students need help to develop effective skills for taking tests and studying.

Self-Schemas

How do beliefs about ability affect motivation?

When people hold an entity theory of ability they believe ability is fixed. They tend to set performance goals and strive to protect themselves from failure. People who hold an incremental theory of ability believe ability can be improved. They tend to set learning goals and handle failure constructively.

What is self-efficacy and how is it different from other self-schemas?

Self-efficacy is distinct from other self-schemas in that it involves judg-ments of capabilities *specific to a par-ticular task*. Self-concept is a more global construct that contains many perceptions about the self, including self-efficacy. Self-concept develops as a result of external and internal com-parisons, using other people or other aspects of the self as frames of refer-ence. Self-efficacy is concerned with judgments of personal capabilities; self-esteem is concerned with judg-ments of self-worth.

What are the sources of self-efficacy and how does efficacy affect motivation?

Four sources of efficacy expectations are mastery experiences (direct expe-riences), level of arousal about the task, vicarious experiences (accom-plishments modelled by someone else), and social persuasion (a "pep talk" or specific performance feed-back). Greater efficacy leads to greater effort and persistence in the face of setbacks. Efficacy also influ-ences motivation through goal setting. People with a high sense of efficacy in a given area set higher goals, are less afraid of failure, and search for new strategies when old ones fail. If sense of efficacy is low, people may avoid a task altogether or give up easily when problems arise.

How does self-determination affect motivation?

When students experience self-determination, they are intrinsically motivated—they are more interested in their work, have a greater sense of self-esteem, and learn more. Whether students experience self-determina-tion depends in part on the teacher's communications with students: is the teacher providing information or seeking to control students? In addi-tion, teachers must acknowledge the students' perspective, offer choices, provide rationales for limits, and treat poor performance as a problem to be solved rather than a target for criticism.

How does self-worth influence motivation?

Mastery-oriented students tend to value achievement and view ability as improvable, so they focus on learning goals to increase their skills and abil-ities. They are not fearful of failure, because failing does not threaten their sense of competence and self-worth. This allows them to take risks and cope with failure constructively. A low sense of self-worth seems to be linked with the failure-avoiding and failure-accepting strategies intended to protect the individual from the consequences of failure. These strate-gies may seem to help in the short term but are damaging to motivation and self-esteem in the long run.

Define motivation to learn.

Teachers are interested in a particular kind of motivation—student motiva-tion to learn. This is both a trait and a state that involves taking academic work seriously, trying to get the most from it, and applying appropriate learning strategies in the process.

On TARGETT for Learning

What does TARGETT stand for?

TARGETT is an acronym for seven areas where teachers make decisions that influence student motivation to learn: the nature of *tasks* that are set for students; the *autonomy* students are allowed in working; the way that students are *recognized* for their accomplishments; *grouping* practices; *evaluation* procedures; the way *time* is scheduled in the classroom; and the communication of *teacher expecta-tions*.

How do tasks affect motivation?

Tasks that teachers set affect motiva-tion. When students encounter tasks that relate to their interests, stimulate curiosity, or connect to real-life situa-tions, motivation to learn is more like-ly. Difficult tasks that require critical thinking are risky and ambiguous.

What does it mean for students to "negotiate a task?"

A complicated *comprehension* task is both ambiguous and risky. But the students want more guidance, so they ask for models, rules, minimums, or formulas. If students are very con-fused, they may become restless, turn to other students for help, get dis-couraged, or lose interest. Under these conditions, a teacher sometimes responds by transforming the *comprehension* task into a *procedural* one. Risk and ambiguity are reduced and motivation may seem to increase, at least temporarily, but the task itself is not as interesting. So the results of the "task negotiation" may be a temporary *state* of motivation to perform, to get the grade, rather than motivation to learn.

What are the three kinds of task value?

Tasks can have attainment, intrinsic, or utility value for students. Attainment value is the importance to the student of succeeding. Intrinsic value is the enjoyment the student gets from the task. Utility value is how much the task contributes to reaching short- or long-term goals.

Supporting Antonomy and Recognizing Accomplishment

Distinguish between bounded and unbounded choices.

Unstructured or unguided choices can be counterproductive for learning. The alternative is bounded choice— give students a range of options that set valuable tasks for them and allow them to follow personal interests. The balance must be just right so students are not bewildered by too much choice or bored by too little.

How can recognition undermine motivation and a sense of self-efficacy?

Recognition in the classroom will support motivation to learn if it is for personal progress rather than competitive victories. Praise should focus on students' growing competence. At times praise can have paradoxical effects because students use praise (and criticism) as cues about capabilities. For example, if two students succeed and the teacher praises only

one, the message, to older children at least, may be that the praised student had less ability and had to work harder to succeed, thus earning praise. The unpraised student was simply "doing what comes naturally," succeeding based on high ability.

Grouping, Evaluation, and Time

What determines whether a goal structure is cooperative, competitive, or individualistic?

How students relate to peers in the classroom is influenced by the goal structure of the activities. Goal structures can be competitive (I reach my goal only if others do not), individualistic (reaching my goals is unrelated to whether others reach theirs), or cooperative (I reach my goals only if others reach theirs). Cooperative goal structures can encourage motivation and increase learning, especially for low-achieving students.

How does evaluative climate affect goal setting?

The more competitive the grading, the more students set performance goals and focus on "looking competent;" that is, the more they are ego-involved. When the focus is on performing rather than learning, students often see the goal of classroom tasks as simply finishing, especially if the work is difficult.

What are some effects of time on motivation?

To foster motivation to learn, teachers should use time flexibly. Students forced to move faster or slower than they should or who are interrupted as they become involved in a project are not likely to develop persistence for learning.

Teacher Expectations

What are some sources of teacher expectations?

Sources include intelligence test scores; gender; notes from previous teachers and the medical or psychological reports found in cumulative folders; ethnic background; knowledge of older brothers and sisters; physical characteristics; previous achievement; socioeconomic class; and the actual behaviour of the student.

What are the two kinds of expectation effects and how do they happen?

The first is the self-fulfilling prophecy—the teacher's beliefs about students' abilities have no basis in fact but student behaviour comes to match the initially inaccurate expectation. The second is a sustaining expectation effect—the teacher is fairly accurate in an initial reading of students' abilities and respond to students appropriately. Problems arise when students show some improvement but the teacher does not alter expectations based on the improvement. Then, the teacher's unchanging expectation can sustain the student's achievement at the level of the initial expectation. Sustaining effects are more common than self-fulfilling prophecy effects.

What are the different avenues for communicating teacher expectations?

Based on views of how well students are likely to do, some teachers treat students differently. Differences in treatment toward low-expectation students may include setting less challenging tasks, focusing on lower-level learning, giving fewer choices, providing inconsistent feedback, and communicating less respect and trust. Students may behave accordingly, fulfilling teachers' predictions or staying at an expected level of achievement.

*K*ey Terms

academic tasks, *p. 379*
anxiety, *p. 368*

arousal, *p. 366*
attainment value, *p. 383*

attribution theories, *p. 358*
authentic tasks, *p. 383*

*B*ecoming a Professional

Reflecting on the Chapter

Can you apply the ideas from this chapter on motivation to solve the following problems of practice?

Preschool and Kindergarten

▷ How could you help young students build a foundation for self-efficacy in school?

▷ What would you do to help students develop persistence without discouraging spontaneity and enthusiasm?

Elementary and Middle School

▷ Several of your students seem to have given up in science. They almost expect to fail. This is especially troubling because a number of the students are girls who believe "girls are no good in science." What would you do?

▷ How would you respond to mistakes without communicating to students that their mistakes are the result of low ability? You also want to avoid being unrealistic about what they can do or implying that the material is "easy."

▷ You are talking to the parents of one of your lower-achieving students. You really like the student, but he seems not to apply himself to the work. Suddenly the boy's mother says, "We think our son is doing badly in your class because you don't like him. You just seem to expect him to fail!" What would you do?

Junior High and High School

▷ You are the faculty adviser for the student newspaper. Your students have grand ideas for stories and features, but they seem to run out of steam and never quite finish. The production of the paper is always last-minute and rush-rush. How would you help the students stay motivated and work steadily?

▷ As the time to take provincial exams nears, a few of your students are becoming so anxious that you wonder if they will make it through the tests. What can you do to help them?

▷ You want to prepare your senior classes for the kind of independent work they will face in university, so you assign a research project. As soon as you have set the assignment, the questions begin: "How many sources?" "How many pages?" "What exactly do you mean by 'support your conclusions with evidence'?" "What kind of evidence?" How do you make the assignment clear without spoon-feeding?

Check Your Understanding

▷ Be clear about the kinds of goals that are most motivating.

▷ Make sure you understand the difference between intrinsic and extrinsic motivation.

▷ Understand the elements of attribution theory.

▷ Know ways to enhance self-efficacy in students.

▷ Know about the role of choice in motivation.

▷ Understand the difference between a self-fulfilling prophecy and a sustaining expectation effect.

▷ Be familiar with several approaches to cooperative learning.

Your Teaching Portfolio

Think about your philosophy of teaching, a question you will be asked at most job interviews. What do you believe about motivating hard-to-reach students? How can you support the development of genuine and well-founded self-efficacy in your students? (Consult the Guidelines for ideas.)

Add some ideas for parent involvement from this chapter to your portfolio.

Use the section on the TARGETT model to refine your teaching philosophy. How will you answer the job-interview question "What would you do to motivate difficult-to-reach students?"

Teaching Resources
Adapt all the Guidelines from the chapter for the age group you plan to teach.

Use the TARGETT model (Table 10.4) to generate motivational strategies for the grade you will teach.

Weblinks

---

www.mcrel.org/resources/noteworthy/barbaram.asp

A paper by Barbara L. McCombs, "Understanding the Keys to Motivation to Learn." It includes references.

www.valdosta.edu/~whuitt/psy702/files/selfeff.html

This is the full text of a thorough review of research on self-efficacy: Pajares, F. (1996). *Review of Educational Research*, 66(4), 543–578.

www.mcrel.org/resources/noteworthy/loycec.asp

How do teachers' verbal interactions with students affect motivation? An article by Loyce Caruthers addresses teacher expectations, how these take shape in teachers' interactions with students, and what happens as a result.

www.clcrc.com

The Cooperative Learning Center at the University of Minnesota is directed by two of the most prolific researchers in this area. The centre's site features a wide variety of information about this form of learning.

What Would They Do?

Here is how two practising teachers responded to the teaching situation presented at the beginning of this chapter about unmotivated students.

LORI ULRIKSEN

Gordon Denny School
La Ronge, Saskatchewan

When dealing with a problem like this, you'll need to consider many variables: yourself, your students, and the assignment or activities.

Foremost, you set the classroom rules, expectations, and, inevitably, the classroom atmosphere. Involve students in this process, and clarify your expectations concerning work and behaviour. Explain that behaviour such as whining will not be tolerated, as it is contagious and detrimental to everyone.

Select a wide variety of teaching strategies, activities, materials, and assignments. This allows you to meet individual learning styles and interests. Although variety is essential, it is equally important to incorporate structure and routine into your daily schedule. Most students need routines to feel secure, successful, and confident.

Get to know your students' capabilities and interests. This gives you the confidence that your students can succeed at assigned tasks. If students are weak academically, you may have to modify assignments. Give your students choices within assignments to accommodate learning styles. Break down large assignments into smaller, more manageable tasks, and ensure that students have prerequisite skills. For example, before assigning a large research project, make sure that your students can locate and use resources, organize information, write paragraphs, etc.

If complaining continues to be a "nagging" problem, try other strategies. Involve students in making fair choices about assignments. Show them what has to be covered, and the time available. With practice, you can guide students to choose appropriately.

At times, using peer pressure can be an effective tool. Inform students that if everyone starts working immediately and diligently, you'll give them a few extra minutes to finish, if necessary. If they don't, it's homework! The students will then monitor themselves and usually finish quickly and quietly.

Instead of using materialistic rewards, you may want to consider using incentives that build pride and classroom harmony. Examples of ways to reward hard work may include fitting in baseball on a nice day, granting free time, or helping younger students. Many strategies will work if you are consistent and follow through. Experiment until you find what works for you and your current class.

Overall, teachers have to realize that not all students will like every activity or aspect of the curriculum, no matter how exciting. Don't set yourself up with the expectation that you have to "entertain" your students from 9:00 to 3:30. You may burn out and take it too personally when students don't like your idea of fun!

LYNN DRUMMOND

R. C. MacDonald Elementary School
Coquitlam, British Columbia

What would I do if my students seemed defeated about learning and protested when they looked at a new assignment?

Unless I had started with a class in the middle of the school year, I hope that I would not find myself in such a position. Negative attitudes toward school and learning have many sources, but I believe that if students feel respected as individuals and supported as learners, many of these negative attitudes can be eliminated. The first few weeks of school are crucial in developing in each student a sense of belonging so that a support system evolves that will enable students to take risks as learners.

Creating a positive, encouraging learning atmosphere in a classroom at the beginning of the school year takes time, but it is time well spent. During this initial stage, academic pursuits are secondary. The goal is for students to begin to feel included and valued as members of the group. The teacher plays a very important role in the beginning by establishing class norms, and procedures are established for students to get to know each other and to interact with a variety of classmates. Social skills and problem-solving skills are taught, modelled, and practised. Accountability is established at this time as students learn that everyone must contribute. In this initial phase, students are given the tools they will need to become successful learners.

As the group becomes more cohesive, the shift from a teacher-centred classroom to a student-centred classroom begins. With the continued emphasis on developing strong social skills, students learn to interact positively with their peers. In all areas, not just the academic, "experts" are identified to whom the students can turn when they need help. This empowers students as they begin to share leadership within the class. As pride in their abilities and accomplishments develops, they become motivated learners and the need for extrinsic motivation diminishes.

Frequent use of cooperative learning games allows students to practise leadership skills, as well as learn accountability, both as individual learners and as members of a group. Shy and passive students have opportunities to develop important skills and increase their self-esteem. Outgoing, dominant, or aggressive students learn to share leadership. During this second phase, conflict resolution strategies, which are important life skills, are taught, frequently modelled, and their practice encouraged.

With the social and emotional issues having been addressed, more weight is gradually given to academic goals. A variety of groupings are employed. Whole class instruction is used for teaching new concepts and for modelling processes, such as research. Small groups then work together on that process. Partner groupings provide excellent opportunities for students to edit their work before turning in assignments, or practise skills. Individual work time provides an opportunity to demonstrate what they have learned. At any given time in my classroom, children might be found working with a partner, working in small groups, or working independently.

As the students learn to accept more responsibility for their own learning, they are given more choices. Learning activities must be meaningful and, whenever possible, different learning styles should be recognized. Students begin to become aware of how they learn, not just what they are learning. This introduction to metacognition encourages them to set goals, to think about their mistakes and get back on track, to identify their strengths and weaknesses, and to seek feedback on their learning.

An observer coming into my class mid-year might think it very unstructured. However, the opposite is true. These carefully built structures provide the framework for the students' learning. Once the structures are in place, students have a safe, supportive, encouraging environment in which they can focus on learning. My role as teacher is no longer that of authority figure but of facilitator, whom the students views as just one of many people in the classroom they can turn to for help. The students are on their way to becoming confident, motivated learners.

Model taken from Schmuck, P. A., & Schmuck, R. A. (1992), *Group processes in the classroom.* Dubuque, IA: Wm. C. Brown Publishers.

Creating Learning Environments

hen you imagine facing 25 or 30 students on the first day of class, what are your concerns? List the management problems that you find most difficult. What are your strengths in dealing with classroom management problems?

This chapter examines the ways that teachers create social and physical environments for learning. We will look at classroom management—one of the main concerns of teachers, particularly beginning teachers.

The very nature of classes, teaching, and students makes good management a critical ingredient of success; we will look at why this is true. Next, we will turn to the goals of classroom management. Successful managers create more time for learning, involve more students, and help students to become self-managing.

A positive learning environment must be established and maintained throughout the year. One of the best ways to do this is to try to prevent problems from occurring at all. But when problems arise—as they always do—an appropriate response is important. What will you do when students challenge you openly in class, when one student asks your advice on a difficult personal problem, or when another withdraws from all participation? We will examine the ways that teachers can communicate effectively with their students in these and many other situations.

By the time you have completed this chapter, you should be able to:

▶ Describe the special managerial demands of classrooms and relate these demands to students of different ages.

▶ Create a list of rules and procedures for a class.

▶ Arrange the physical environment of your classroom to fit your learning goals and teaching methods.

▶ Develop a plan for organizing your first week of teaching.

▶ Explain Jacob Kounin's suggestions for preventing management problems.

▶ Describe how you might respond to a student who seldom completes work.

▶ Suggest two different approaches for dealing with a conflict between teacher and student, or between two students.

What Would You Do?

There are students from four different ethnic groups in the middle school "pod" you are working with this year. Last week, the principal added a student with pretty severe emotional/behavioural problems and a student with cerebral palsy to the group as part of an experiment in full inclusion. The boy with cerebral palsy is in a wheelchair and has some difficulties with language and hearing. Students from each of the four ethnic groups seem to stick together, never making friends with students from "outside." When you ask people to work together for projects, the divisions are strictly on ethnic lines. Many of the subgroups communicate in their native language—one you don't understand—and you assume that often the joke is on you because of the looks and laughs directed your way. Clarise, the emotionally disturbed student, is making matters worse by telling ethnic jokes to anyone who will listen in a voice loud enough to be overheard by half the class. There are rumours of an ambush after school to "teach Clarise a lesson." You agree that she—and the whole class for that matter—needs a lesson, but not this kind.

▶ How would you structure the class to help the students feel more comfortable together?

▶ What are your first goals in working on this problem?

▶ Is conflict negotiation called for here? How would you handle the situation?

▶ How will these issues affect the grade levels you will teach?

The Need for Organization

In the United States, *Phi Delta Kappan* publishes annual Gallup Polls of the public's attitude toward public schools. In 1999, as in almost every year since 1969, "lack of discipline" was named as the number one problem facing the schools (Rose & Gallup, 1999). Canada does not have this kind of national survey but it's not hard to find articles in our major papers (e.g., the *Vancouver Sun* or the *Globe and Mail*) about the problem of discipline in our schools. Clearly, the public sees discipline as an important challenge for teachers. In order to understand the role of management in teaching, let's take a closer look at the classroom itself.

The Ecology of Classrooms

The word *ecology* is usually associated with nature. But classrooms are ecological systems too. The environment of the classroom and the inhabitants of that environment—students and teachers—are constantly interacting. Each aspect of the system affects all others. The characteristics of classrooms, the tasks of teaching, and the needs of students all influence classroom management (Epanchin, Townsend, & Stoddard, 1994).

Characteristics of Classrooms. Classes are particular kinds of environments. They have "distinctive properties affecting participants regardless of how students are organized for learning or what educational philosophy the teacher espouses" (Doyle, 1986, p. 394). Let's look at six of the features described by Doyle.

Classrooms are *multidimensional.* Many individuals, all with differing goals, preferences, and abilities, must share resources, accomplish various tasks, use and reuse materials without losing them, move in and out of the room, keep track of

TEACHERS' CASEBOOK

Connect & Extend
To your teaching
Many computer programs exist to help teachers manage their own activities inside and outside the classroom. Typical activities include online standard forms, IEPs, student home and school databases, student reports, letters to parents, archiving and locating information, electronic mail, financial planning, and scheduling. Complete classroom management systems and computer-managed instruction (CMI) are also available. For more information see: Bitter, G. G. & Pierson, M. E. (1999). *Using technology in the classroom*, 3/e. Boston: Allyn & Bacon.

Connect & Extend
To your own philosophy
Some educators object to the metaphor of teacher as manager. These critics suggest that the image brings with it notions of manipulation and detachment. Is the metaphor of manager an appropriate choice? What other metaphors can you suggest for teachers acting to maintain order and discipline? Anita's research into this area, presented at the annual meeting of the American Educational Research Association (AERA) in 1993, suggests that images of group leaders (coaches, guides, etc.), problem solvers (physicians, chess players), and nurturers (mothers, fathers, gardeners) are common for beginning teachers.

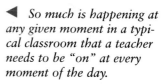

So much is happening at any given moment in a typical classroom that a teacher needs to be "on" at every moment of the day.

what is happening, and so on. In addition, actions can have multiple effects. Calling on low-ability students may encourage their participation and thinking but may slow the discussion and lead to management problems if the students cannot answer.

Classrooms also are *simultaneous*. Everything happens at once. A teacher explaining a concept must also notice if students are following the explanation, decide whether two whispering youngsters should be ignored or stopped, determine if there is enough time to start the next topic, and decide who should answer the question that Jill just asked. Action is fast-paced and *immediate*. Teachers have literally hundreds of exchanges with students during a single day. In this rapid-fire existence, events are *unpredictable*. Even when plans are carefully made, the overhead projector is in place, and the handouts are ready, the lesson can still be interrupted by a burned-out bulb in the projector, a child who suddenly becomes ill, or a loud, angry discussion right outside the classroom.

Because classrooms are *public,* the way the teacher handles these unexpected intrusions is seen and judged by all. Students are always noticing if the teacher is being "fair." Is there favouritism? What happens when a rule is broken? Finally, classrooms have *histories*. The meaning of a particular teacher's or student's actions depends in part on what has happened before. The 15th time a student arrives late requires a different response from the teacher than the first late arrival. In addition, the history of the first few weeks of school affects life in the class all year.

The Basic Task: Gain Their Cooperation. No productive activity can take place in a group without the cooperation of all members. This obviously applies to classrooms. Even if some students don't participate, they must allow others to do so. (You have probably seen one or two students bring an entire class to a halt.) So the basic management task for teachers is to achieve order and harmony by gaining and maintaining student cooperation in class activities (Doyle, 1986). Given the multidimensional, simultaneous, immediate, unpredictable, public, and historical nature of classrooms, this is quite a challenge.

Gaining student cooperation means much more than dealing effectively with misbehaviour. It means planning activities, having materials ready, having developmentally appropriate expectations for behaviour and academics, giving clear signals to students, accomplishing transitions smoothly, foreseeing problems and stopping them before they start, selecting and sequencing activities so that flow and interest are maintained, establishing a climate of trust and respect, and much more. Also, different activities require different managerial skills. For example, a new or complicated activity may be a greater threat to classroom organization and management than a familiar or simple activity.

Age-Related Needs. Obviously, gaining the cooperation of kindergartners is not the same task as gaining the cooperation of students in Grade 12. Jere Brophy and Carolyn Evertson (1978) have identified four general stages of classroom management, defined by age-related needs. Let's look briefly at each.

During kindergarten and the first few years of elementary school, children are learning how to go to school. They are being socialized into a new role. Direct teaching of classroom rules and procedures is important during this stage. Little learning will take place until the children master these basics.

Children in the middle elementary years are usually familiar with the student role, even if they are not always perfect examples of it. Many school and classroom routines have become relatively automatic. Specific new rules and procedures for a particular activity may have to be taught directly, however. And you may hear the familiar refrain, "My teacher last year didn't do it that way!" Still, at this stage you will spend more time monitoring and maintaining the management system than teaching it directly.

Toward the end of elementary school and middle school and the beginning of high school, friendships and status within peer groups take on tremendous importance. Pleasing the teacher may be replaced by pleasing peers. Some students begin to test and defy authority. The management challenges at this stage are to deal productively with these disruptions and to motivate students who are becoming less concerned with teachers' opinions and more interested in their social lives.

By the end of high school, the focus of most students returns to academics. By this time, unfortunately, many of the students with overwhelming behavioural problems have dropped out. At this stage the challenges are to manage the curriculum, fit academic material to students' interests and abilities, and help students become more self-managing in their learning. The first few classes each semester may be devoted to teaching particular procedures for using materials and equipment, or for keeping track of and submitting assignments. But most students know what is expected.

The Goals of Classroom Management

Classroom management, according to Jack Martin and Jeff Sugarman of Simon Fraser University, concerns "those activities . . . that create a positive classroom climate within which effective teaching and learning can occur" (1993, p. 9). But order for its own sake is an empty goal. As we discussed in Chapter 6, it is unethical to use class management techniques just to keep students docile and quiet. What, then, is the point of working so hard to manage classrooms? There are at least three reasons why management is important.

More Time for Learning. If you were to use a stopwatch to time the commercials during a TV quiz show, you'd likely find that almost half of the program was devoted to commercials. Then, if you timed all the "small talk," you'd find that very little quizzing takes place. If you used a similar approach in classrooms, timing all the different activities throughout the day, you might be surprised by how little actual teaching takes place. Many minutes are lost each day through interruptions, disruptions, late starts, and rough transitions (Karweit, 1989; Karweit & Slavin, 1981).

Obviously, students will learn only the material they have a chance to learn. Almost every study examining time and learning has found a significant relationship between time spent on content and student learning (Berliner, 1988). In fact, the correlations between content studied and student learning are usually larger than the correlations between specific teacher behaviour and student learning (Rosenshine, 1979). So one important goal of classroom management is to expand

Classroom Management: Techniques used to maintain a healthy learning environment, relatively free of behaviour problems.

the sheer number of minutes available for learning. This is sometimes called **allocated time.**

Simply making more time for learning will not automatically lead to achievement. To be valuable, time must be used effectively. As you saw in the chapters on cognitive learning, the way students process information is a central factor in what they learn and remember. Basically, students will learn what they practise and think about (Doyle, 1983). The time spent actively involved in specific learning tasks is often called **engaged time,** or sometimes **time on task.**

Again, however, engaged time doesn't guarantee learning. Students may be struggling with material that is too difficult or using the wrong learning strategies. When students are working with a high rate of success—really learning and understanding—we call the time spent **academic learning time.** A second goal of class management is to increase academic learning time by keeping students *actively engaged in worthwhile, appropriate learning activities.* Figure 11.1 shows how the 1000+ hours of time mandated for school can become only about 333 hours of quality academic learning time for a typical student.

Access to Learning. Each classroom activity has its own rules for participation. Sometimes these rules are clearly stated by the teacher, but often they are implicit and unstated. Teacher and students may not even be aware that they are following different rules for different activities (Berliner, 1983). The differences are

Allocated Time: Time set aside for learning.

Engaged Time: Time spent actively learning.

Time on Task: Time spent actively engaged in the learning task at hand.

Academic Learning Time: Time when students are actually succeeding at the learning task.

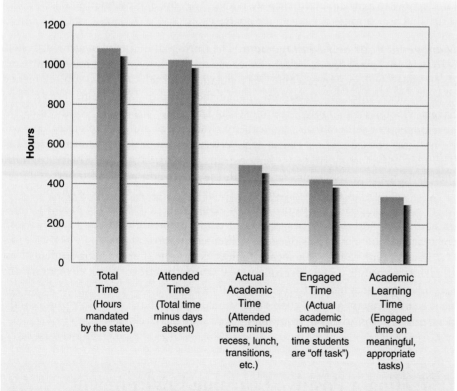

FIGURE 11.1

Who Knows Where the Time Goes

The over 1000 hours per year of instruction students receive can represent only 300 or 400 hours of quality academic learning time.

Source: From C. S. Weinstein and A. J. Mignano, Jr. *Elementary Classroom Management.* Copyright © 1993 by The McGraw-Hill Companies. Adapted with permission of The McGraw-Hill Companies.

Checkpoint

The Need for Organization

Review

▶ What are the challenges of classroom management?

▶ What are the goals of good classroom management?

Apply

▶ Explain how you would increase academic learning time in your classroom.

Connect & Extend
To your teaching
Are there cultural differences in the verbal and non-verbal ways that students show respect, pay attention, and bid for a turn in conversation? How can cultural differences in interaction styles and expectations make classroom management more challenging?

sometimes quite subtle. For example, in a reading group students may have to raise their hands to make a comment, but in a show-and-tell circle in the same class they may simply have to catch the teacher's eye.

As we saw in Chapter 5, the rules defining who can talk; what they can talk about; and when, to whom, and how long they can talk are often called participation structures. In order to participate successfully in a given activity, students must understand the participation structure. Some students, however, seem to come to school less able to participate than others. The participation structures they learn at home in interactions with siblings, parents, and other adults do not match the participation structures of school activities (Tharp, 1989). But teachers are not necessarily aware of this conflict. Instead, the teachers see that a child doesn't quite fit in, always seems to say the wrong thing at the wrong time, or is very reluctant to participate, and they are not sure why.

What can we conclude? In order to involve all your students, you must make sure that everyone knows *how* to participate in each specific activity. The key is awareness. What are your rules and expectations? Are they understandable, given your students' cultural backgrounds and home experiences? What unspoken rules or values may be operating? Are you clear and consistent in signalling your students about how to participate? To reach the second goal of good classroom management—giving all students access to learning—you must make sure everyone knows how to participate in class activities. This means teaching, signalling, and practising appropriate ways to participate.

Management for Self-Management. The third goal of any management system is to help students become better able to manage themselves. The movement from demanding obedience to teaching self-regulation and self-control is a fundamental shift in discussions of classroom management today (Weinstein, 1999). Tom Savage (1999) says simply, "the most fundamental purpose of discipline is the development of self-control. . . . Academic knowledge and technological skill will be of little consequence if those who possess them lack self-control" (p. 11). Through self-control, students demonstrate *responsibility*—the ability to fulfill their own needs without interfering with the rights and needs of others (Glasser, 1990). Students learn self-control by making choices and dealing with the consequences, setting goals and priorities, managing time, collaborating to learn, mediating disputes and making peace, and developing trusting relations with trustworthy teachers and classmates (Rogers & Freiberg, 1994).

Encouraging self-management requires extra time, but teaching students how to take responsibility is an investment well worth the effort. When elementary and secondary teachers have effective class management systems but neglect to set student self-management as a goal, their students often have trouble working independently after graduating from these "well-managed" classes.

Creating a Positive Learning Environment

In making plans for your class, much of what you have already learned in this book should prove helpful. You know, for example, that problems are prevented when individual variations, such as those discussed in Chapters 2, 3, 4, and 5, are taken into account in instructional planning. Sometimes students become disruptive because the work assigned is too difficult. And students who are bored by lessons well below their ability levels may be interested in finding more exciting activities to fill their time.

In one sense, teachers prevent discipline problems whenever they make an effort to motivate students. A student involved in learning is usually not involved in a clash with the teacher or other students at the same time. All plans for motivating students are steps toward preventing problems. We will discuss strategies for motivating students later in this chapter.

Some Research Results

What else can teachers do to be good managers? For several years, educational psychologists at the University of Texas at Austin studied classroom management quite thoroughly (Emmer, Evertson, & Anderson, 1980; Emmer, Evertson, & Worsham, 2000; Evertson, 1988; Evertson, Emmer, & Worsham, 2000). Their general approach was to study a large number of classrooms, making frequent observations during the first weeks of school and less frequent visits later in the year. After several months there were dramatic differences among the classes. Some had very few management problems, while others had many. The most and least effective teachers were identified on the basis of the quality of classroom management and student achievement later in the year.

Next, the researchers looked at their observation records of the first weeks of class to see how the effective teachers got started. Other comparisons were made between the teachers who ultimately had harmonious, high-achieving classes and those whose classes were fraught with problems. On the basis of these comparisons, management principles were developed. The researchers then taught these principles to a new group of teachers; the results were quite positive. Teachers who applied the principles had fewer problems; their students spent more time learning and less time disrupting; and achievement was higher. The findings of these studies formed the basis for two books on classroom management (Emmer et al., 2000; Evertson et al., 2000). Many of the ideas in the following pages are from these books.

Rules and Procedures Required

At the elementary school level, teachers must lead 20 to 30 students of varying abilities through many different activities each day. Without efficient rules and procedures, a great deal of time is wasted answering the same question over and over. "My pencil broke. How can I do my math?" "I'm finished with my story. What should I do now?" "Steven hit me!" "I left my homework in my locker."

At the secondary school level, teachers must deal daily with more than 100 students who use dozens of materials and often change rooms for each class. Secondary school students are also more likely to challenge teachers' authority. The effective managers studied by Emmer, Evertson, and their colleagues had planned procedures and rules for coping with these situations.

Procedures.   How will materials and assignments be distributed and collected? Under what conditions can students leave the room? How will grades be determined? What are the special routines for handling equipment and supplies in science, art, or vocational classes? **Procedures** describe how activities are accomplished in classrooms, but they are seldom written down; they are simply the ways of getting things done in class. Experts recommend that teachers establish procedures to cover the following areas (Weinstein, 1996; Weinstein & Mignano, 1997):

1. *Administrative routines,* such as taking attendance.
2. *Student movement,* such as entering and leaving or going to the bathroom.

Connect & Extend
To other chapters
In **Chapter 12** you will learn about the importance of careful planning and clear objectives. Good planning is an important aspect of classroom management.

Connect & Extend
To other chapters
Motivation and classroom management are closely related. The motivational strategies described in **Chapters 10** and **12** are good first steps in effective class management.

Connect & Extend
To the research
For a description of a study that tested the Emmer/Evertson management principles along with other approaches, such as reinforcement strategies with adolescents in several schools, see Gottfredson, D. C., Gottfredson, G. D., & Hybl, L. G. (1993). Managing adolescent behavior: A multiyear, multischool study. *American Educational Research Journal, 30,* 179–217. Generally, the application of these principles improved behaviour.

Procedures: Prescribed steps for an activity.

3. *Housekeeping,* such as watering plants or storing personal items.
4. *Routines for accomplishing lessons,* such as how to collect assignments or return homework.
5. *Interactions between teacher and student,* such as how to get the teacher's attention when help is needed.
6. *Talk among students,* such as giving help or socializing.

You might use these six areas as a framework for planning your class procedures and routines. The Guidelines below should help you as you plan.

GUIDELINES

Establishing Class Procedures

Determine procedures for student upkeep of desks, classroom equipment, and other facilities.

Examples
1. Some teachers set aside a cleanup time each day or once a week in self-contained classes.
2. You might demonstrate and have students practise how to push chairs under the desk, take and return materials stored on shelves, sharpen pencils, use the sink or water fountain, assemble lab equipment, and so on.
3. In some classes a rotating monitor is in charge of equipment or materials.

Decide how students will be expected to enter and leave the room.

Examples
1. How will students know what they should do as soon as they enter the room? Some teachers have a standard assignment ("Have your homework out and be checking it over").
2. Under what conditions can students leave the room? When do they need permission?
3. If students are late, how do they gain admission to the room?
4. Many teachers require students to be in their seats and quiet before they can leave at the end of class. The teacher, not the bell, dismisses class.

Establish a signal and teach it to your students.

Examples
1. In the classroom, some teachers flick the lights, sound a chord on a piano or recorder, move to the podium and stare silently at the class, use a phrase such as "Eyes, please," take out their grade books, or move to the front of the class.

2. In the halls, a raised hand, one clap, or some other signal may mean "Stop."
3. On the playground, a raised hand or whistle may mean "Line up."

Set procedures for student participation in class.

Examples
1. Will you have students raise their hands for permission to speak or simply require that they wait until the speaker has finished?
2. How will you signal that you want everyone to respond at once? Some teachers raise a cupped hand to an ear. Others preface the question with "Everyone."
3. Make sure you are clear about differences in procedures for different activities: reading group, learning centre, discussion, teacher presentation, seatwork, film, peer learning group, library, and so forth.
4. How many students at a time can be at the pencil sharpener, teacher's desk, learning centre, sink, bookshelves, reading corner, or bathroom?

Determine how you will communicate, collect, and return assignments.

Examples
1. Some teachers reserve a particular corner of the board for listing assignments. Others write assignments in coloured chalk. For younger students it may be better to prepare assignment sheets or folders, colour-coding them for math workbook, reading packet, and science kit.
2. Some teachers collect assignments in a box or bin; others have a student collect work while they introduce the next activity.

Rules. Rules specify expected and forbidden actions in the class. They are the dos and don'ts of classroom life. Unlike procedures, rules are often written down and posted. In establishing rules, you should consider what kind of atmosphere you want to create (Martin & Sugarman, 1993). What student behaviour will help you teach effectively? What limits do the students need to guide their behaviour? The rules you set should be consistent with school rules, and also in keeping with principles of learning. For example, we know from the research on small group learning that students benefit when they explain work to peers. They learn as they teach. A rule that forbids students to help each other may be inconsistent with good learning principles. Or a rule that says "No erasures when writing" may make students focus more on preventing mistakes than on communicating clearly in their writing (Burden, 1995; Weinstein & Mignano, 1997).

Having a few general rules that cover many specifics is better than listing all the dos and don'ts. But, if specific actions are forbidden, such as chewing gum in class or smoking in the bathrooms, a rule should make this clear.

Rules for Elementary School.

Evertson and her colleagues (2000) give five examples of general rules for elementary school classes:

1. *Be polite and helpful.* This applies to behaviour toward adults (including substitute teachers) and children. Examples of polite behaviour include waiting your turn, saying "please" and "thank you," and not fighting or calling names.

2. *Respect other people's property.* This might include picking up litter; returning library books; not marking walls, desks, or buses; and getting permission before using other people's things.

3. *Listen quietly while others are speaking.* This applies to the teacher and other students, in large-class lessons or small-group discussions.

4. *Do not hit, shove, or hurt others.* Make sure you give clear explanations of what you mean by "hurt." Does it apply to hurt feelings as well as hurt bodies?

5. *Obey all school rules.* This reminds students that all school rules apply in your classroom. Then students cannot claim, for example, that they thought it was okay to chew gum or listen to a radio in your class, even though doing so would be against school rules, "because you never made a rule against it for us."

Whatever the rule, students need to be taught the behaviour that the rule includes and excludes. Examples, practice, and discussion will be needed before learning is complete.

As you've seen, different activities often require different rules. This can be confusing for elementary students until they have thoroughly learned all the rules. To prevent confusion, you might consider making signs that list the rules for each activity. Then, before the activity, you can post the appropriate sign as a reminder. This provides clear and consistent cues about participation structures so all students, not just the "well-behaved," know what is expected. Of course, these rules must be explained and discussed before the signs can have their full effect.

Rules for Secondary School.

Emmer and colleagues (2000) suggest six examples of rules for secondary students:

1. *Bring all needed materials to class.* The teacher must specify the type of pen, pencil, paper, notebook, texts, and so on.

2. *Be in your seat and ready to work when the bell rings.* Many teachers combine this rule with a standard beginning procedure for the class, such as a warm-up exercise on the board or a requirement that students have paper with a proper heading ready when the bell rings.

Rules: Statements specifying expected and forbidden behaviour; dos and don'ts.

Connect & Extend
To your teaching
Visit elementary school classes and note the rules posted by different teachers at the same grade level. Identify rules that are common to all or most classes, as well as those that are unusual.

Connect & Extend
To your teaching
What are the differences between procedures and rules? What rewards and penalties are appropriate for the grade levels you will teach?

Connect & Extend
To your teaching
Here are some tips for using consequences, taken from Richard Curwin (1992). *Rediscovering hope: Our greatest teaching strategy.* Bloomington, IN: National Educational Service, pp. 79–80.

- Always implement a consequence when a rule is broken.
- Select the most appropriate consequence from the list of alternatives, taking into account the offense, situation, student involved, and the best means of helping that student.
- State the rule and consequence to the offending student. Nothing more need be said.
- Be private. Only the student(s) involved should hear.
- Do not embarrass the student.
- Do not think of the situation as win-lose. This is not a context. Do not get involved in a power struggle.
- Control your anger. Be calm and speak quietly, but accept no excuses from the student.
- Sometimes it is best to let the student choose the consequence.
- The professional always looks for ways to help the client.

Source: From Richard Curwin. *Rediscovering Hope: Our Greatest Teaching Strategy*, Copyright 1992, pp. 79–80. Permission to excerpt granted by the National Education Service, Bloomington, IN. To obtain a copy, contact the NES at 1-800-733-6786 or FAX 812-336-7790 or e-mail NES@Bluemarble.net. All rights reserved by NES.

3. *Respect and be polite to everyone.* This rule covers fighting, verbal abuse, and general troublemaking.

4. *Respect other people's property.* This means property belonging to the school, the teacher, or other students.

5. *Listen and stay seated while someone else is speaking.* This applies when the teacher or other students are talking.

6. *Obey all school rules.* As with the elementary class rules, this covers a variety of behaviour and situations, so you do not have to repeat every school rule for your class. It also reminds the students that you will be monitoring them inside and outside your class. Make sure you know all the school rules. Some secondary students are adept at convincing teachers that their misbehaviour "really isn't against the rules."

▲ *Consequences for breaking rules are posted in this classroom. How about consequences for following the rules?*

Consequences. As soon as you decide on your rules and procedures, you must consider what you will do when a student breaks a rule or does not follow a procedure. It is too late to make this decision after the rule has been broken. For many infractions, the logical consequence is having to go back and "do it right." Students who run in the hall may have to return to where they started and walk properly. Incomplete papers can be redone. Materials left out should be put back (Charles, 1996). Sometimes consequences are more complicated. In their case studies of four expert elementary school teachers, Weinstein and Mignano (1997) found that the teachers' consequences for problem behaviour fell into seven categories, as shown in Table 11.1. The main point here is that decisions about conse-

---

TABLE 11.1 Seven Categories of Consequences for Students

1. *Expressions of disappointment.* If students like and respect their teacher, then a serious, sorrowful expression of disappointment may cause students to stop and think about their behaviour.

2. *Loss of privileges.* Students can lose free time. If they have not completed homework, for example, they can be required to do it during a free period or recess.

3. *Exclusion from the group.* Students who distract their peers or fail to cooperate can be separated from the group until they are ready to cooperate. Some teachers give a student a pass for 10 to 15 minutes. During this time, the student goes to another class or study hall, where the other students and teachers ignore them. Some students may perceive this consequence as a reward.

4. *Written reflections on the problem.* Students can write in journals, write essays about what they did and how it affected others, or write letters of apology—if this is appropriate. Another possibility is to ask students to describe objectively what they did; then the teacher and the student can discuss and sign and date this statement. These records are

available if parents or administrators need evidence of the students' behaviour.

5. *Detentions.* Detentions can be very brief meetings after school, during a free period, or at lunch. The main purpose is to talk about what has happened. (In high school, detentions often are used as punishments; suspensions and expulsions are available as more extreme measures.)

6. *Visits to the principal's office.* Expert teachers tend to use this consequence rarely, but they do use it when the situation warrants. Some schools require students to be sent to the office for certain offences, such as fighting. If you tell a student to go to the office and the student refuses, you might call the office saying the student has been sent. Then the student has the choice of either going to the office or facing the principal's penalty for "disappearing" on the way.

7. *Contact with parents.* If problems become a repeated pattern, most teachers contact the student's family. This is done to seek support for helping the student, not to blame the parents or punish the student.

Source: From *Elementary Classroom Management,* 2/e, by C. S. Weinstein and A. J. Mignano, Jr., New York: McGraw-Hill. Copyright © 1997 by The McGraw-Hill Companies. Adapted with permission.

TABLE 11.2 A Bill of Rights for Students and Teachers

Students' Bill of Rights

Students in this class have the following rights:

To whisper when the teacher isn't talking or asking for silence.

To celebrate authorship or other work at least once a month.

To exercise outside on days there is no physical education class.

To have 2-minute breaks.

To have healthy snacks during snack time.

To participate in choosing a table.

To have privacy. Get permission to touch anyone else's possessions.

To be comfortable.

To chew gum without blowing bubbles or making a mess.

To make choices about the day's schedule.

To have free work time.

To work with partners.

To talk to the class without anyone else talking.

To work without being disturbed.

Teacher's Bill of Rights

The Teacher has the following rights:

To talk without anyone else talking, moving about, or disturbing the class.

To work without being disturbed.

To have everyone's attention while giving directions.

To punish someone who is not cooperating.

To send someone out of the group or room, or to the office.

Source: From *Elementary Classroom Management* 2/e, by C. S. Weinstein and A. J. Mignano, Jr., New York: McGraw-Hill. Copyright © 1997 by The McGraw-Hill Companies. Adapted with permission.

quences (and rewards) must be made early on, so students know before they break a rule or use the wrong procedure what this will mean for them. We encourage our student teachers to get a copy of the school rules and their cooperating teacher's rules, then plan their own.

Who Sets the Rules and Consequences? In the first chapter we described Ken, an expert teacher who worked with his students to establish a students' and teacher's "Bill of Rights" instead of defining rules. These "rights" cover most situations that might require a "rule" and help the students move toward the goal of becoming self-managing. The rights for one recent year's class are listed in Table 11.2. Developing rights and responsibilities rather than rules makes a very important point to students. "Teaching children that something is wrong *because there is a rule against it* is not the same as teaching them that there is a rule against it *because it is wrong*, and helping them to understand why this is so" (Weinstein, 1999, p. 154). Students should understand that the rules are developed so that everyone can work and learn together.

Another kind of planning that affects the learning environment is designing the physical arrangement of the class furniture, materials, and learning tools.

Connect & Extend
To other chapters
See the description of Ken's teaching approach in **Chapter 1**.

Planning Spaces for Learning

Connect & Extend
To professional journals
See the September 1998 issue of
Educational Leadership for several
articles on "Realizing a Positive
School Climate." There are descriptions of ways to improve school climate through architecture and
design, school meetings, cooperative learning, violence prevention,
parent involvement, and other
approaches.

Spaces for learning should invite and support the activities you plan in your classroom, and they should respect the inhabitants of the space. This respect begins at
the classroom door for young children by helping them identify their class—protecting them from the embarrassment and fear of getting lost. One school that has
won awards for its architecture paints each classroom door a different bright
colour, so young children can find their "home" (Herbert, 1998). Once inside,
spaces can be created that invite quiet reading, group collaboration, or independent research. If students are to use materials, they should be able to reach them.
And learning spaces should be inviting. Here's how Herb Kohl creates a positive
environment in his classes (in Scherer, 1999).

> What I do is put up the most beautiful things I know—posters, games, puz-
> zles, challenges—and let the children know these are provocations. These are
> ways of provoking them into using their minds. You have to create an envi-
> ronment that makes kids walk in and say, "I really want to see what's here. I
> would really like to look at this." (p. 9)

In terms of classroom arrangement, there are two basic ways of organizing
space: interest areas and personal territories. These are not mutually exclusive;
many teachers use a design that combines interest areas and personal territories.
Individual students' desks—their territories—are placed in the centre, with interest
areas in the back or around the periphery of the room. This allows the flexibility
needed for both large- and small-group activities. Figure 11.2 shows an elementary
classroom that combines interest area and personal territory arrangements.

Interest Areas. The design of interest areas can influence the way the areas are
used by students. For example, working with a classroom teacher, Weinstein
(1977) was able to make changes in interest areas that helped the teacher meet her
objectives of having more girls involved in the science centre and having all students experiment more with a variety of manipulative materials. In a second study,
changes in a library corner led to more involvement in literature activities throughout the class (Morrow & Weinstein, 1986).

To plan your classroom space, first decide what activities the classroom should
accommodate. For example, if you are in a self-contained elementary classroom,
you might set up interest areas for reading, arts and crafts, science, and math. If
you are teaching one particular subject at the middle or high school levels, you
might divide your room into several areas, perhaps for audiovisual activities,
small-group instruction, quiet study, and projects.

Next, you are ready to draw several possible floor plans. Use graph paper if
possible, and draw to scale. As you work, keep the Guidelines on page 414 in
mind.

Personal Territories. Can the physical setting influence teaching and learning in
classrooms organized by territories? Adams and Biddle (1970) found that verbal
interaction between teacher and students was concentrated in the centre front of
the classroom and in a line directly up the centre of the room. The data were so
dramatic that Adams and Biddle coined the term **action zone** to refer to this area
of the room. Later research modified this finding. Even though most rooms have
an action zone where participation is greatest, this area may be on one side, or near
a particular learning centre (Good, 1983a).

Front-seat location does seem to increase participation for students who are
predisposed to speak in class, whereas a seat in the back will make it more difficult to participate and easier to sit back and daydream (Woolfolk & Brooks,
1983). To "spread the action around," Weinstein and Mignano (1997) suggest that
teachers move around the room when possible, establish eye contact with students
seated far away, and direct comments to students seated at a distance.

Action Zone: Area of a classroom where the greatest
amount of interaction takes
place.

FIGURE 11.2

An Elementary Classroom Arrangement

This grade 4 teacher had designed a space that allows teacher presentations and demonstrations, small group work, computer interactions, math manipulatives activities, informal reading, art, and other projects without requiring constant rearrangement.

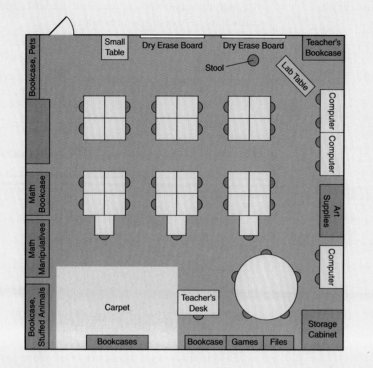

Source: From C. S. Weinstein and A. J. Mignano, Jr. *Elementary Classroom Management.* Copyright © 1993 by The McGraw-Hill Companies. Reproduced with permission of The McGraw-Hill Companies.

Many teachers vary the seating so the same students are not always consigned to the back of the room or to make the arrangement more appropriate for particular objectives and activities. Figure 11.3 is a high school mathematics class with a seating arrangement that allows focus on teacher demonstration as well as small-group work.

Horizontal rows (like the front and back rows in Figure 11.3) share many of the advantages of the traditional row and column arrangements. Both are useful for independent seatwork and teacher, student, or media presentations; they encourage students to focus on the presenter and simplify housekeeping. Horizontal rows also permit students to work more easily in pairs. However, this is a poor arrangement for large-group discussion.

Clusters of four or circle arrangements are best for student interaction. Circles are especially useful for discussions but still allow for independent seatwork. Clusters permit students to talk, help one another, share materials, and work on group tasks. Both arrangements, however, are poor for whole-group presentations and may make class management more difficult.

The fishbowl or stack special formation, where students sit close together near the focus of attention (the back row may even be standing), should be used only for short periods of time, because it is not comfortable and can lead to discipline problems. On the other hand, the fishbowl can create a feeling of group cohesion

GUIDELINES

Designing Learning Spaces

Note the fixed features and plan accordingly.

Examples

1. Remember that the audiovisual centre and computers need an electrical outlet.
2. Keep art supplies near the sink, small-group work by a blackboard.

Create easy access to materials and a well-organized place to store them.

Examples

1. Make sure materials are easy to reach and visible to students.
2. Have enough shelves so that materials need not be stacked.

Provide students with clean, convenient surfaces for studying.

Examples

1. Put bookshelves next to the reading area, games by the game table.
2. Prevent fights by avoiding crowded work spaces.

Make sure work areas are private and quiet.

Examples

1. Make sure there are no tables or work areas in the middle of traffic lanes; a person should not have to pass through one area to get to another.
2. Keep noisy activities as far as possible from quiet ones. Increase the feeling of privacy by placing partitions, such as bookcases or pegboards, between areas or within large areas.

Arrange things so you can see your students and they can see all instructional presentations.

Examples

1. Make sure you can see over partitions.
2. Design seating so that students can see instruction without moving their chairs or desks.

Avoid dead spaces and "racetracks."

Examples

1. Don't have all the interest areas around the outside of the room, leaving a large dead space in the middle.
2. Avoid placing a few items of furniture right in the middle of this large space, creating a "racetrack" around the furniture.

Provide choices and flexibility.

Examples

1. Establish private work spaces (e.g., cubicles for individual work); open tables for group work; and cushions on the floor for whole-class meetings.
2. Give students a place to keep their personal belongings. This is especially important if students don't have personal desks.

Try new arrangements, then evaluate and improve.

Examples

1. Have a "two-week arrangement," then evaluate.
2. Enlist the aid of your students. They have to live in the room, too, and designing a classroom can be a very challenging educational experience.

and is helpful when the teacher wants students to watch a demonstration, brainstorm on a class problem, or see a small visual aid.

Getting Started: The First Weeks of Class

Determining a room design, rules, and procedures are first steps toward having a well-managed class, but how do effective teachers gain students' cooperation in those first critical days and weeks? One study carefully analyzed the first weeks' activities of effective and ineffective elementary teachers, and found striking differences (Emmer, Evertson, & Anderson, 1980).

Effective Managers for Elementary Students. In the effective teachers' classrooms, the very first day was well organized. Name tags were ready. There was

FIGURE 11.3

A High School Math Classroom

This high school teacher has designed a math classroom that allows teacher presentations and demonstrations as well as small group work. Moving three tables transforms the room into four horizontal rows for independent work or testing.

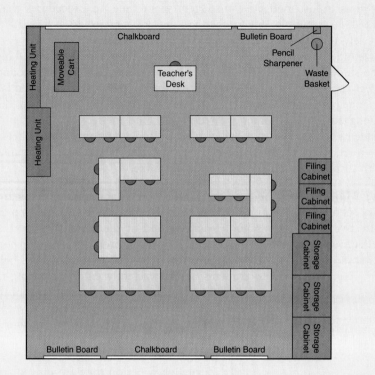

Source: From C. S. Weinstein and A. J. Mignano, Jr. *Elementary Classroom Management.* Copyright © 1993 by The McGraw-Hill Companies. Reproduced with permission of The McGraw-Hill Companies.

something interesting for each child to do right away. Materials were set up. The teachers had planned carefully to avoid any last-minute tasks that might take them away from their students. These teachers dealt with the children's pressing concerns first. "Where do I put my things?" "How do I pronounce my teacher's name?" "Can I whisper to my neighbour?" "Where is the washroom?" The effective teachers had a workable, easily understood set of rules and taught the students the most important rules right away. They taught the rules as they would any other subject, with lots of explanation, examples, and practice.

Throughout the first weeks, the effective managers continued to spend quite a bit of time teaching rules and procedures. Some used guided practice to teach procedures; others used rewards to shape behaviour. Most taught students to respond to a bell or some other signal to gain their attention. These teachers worked with the class as a whole on enjoyable academic activities. They did not rush to get students into small groups or to get them started in readers. This whole-class work gave the teachers a better opportunity to continue monitoring all students' learning of the rules and procedures. Misbehaviour was stopped quickly and firmly, but not harshly.

In the poorly managed classrooms, the first weeks were quite different. Rules were not workable; they were either too vague or very complicated. For example, one teacher made a rule that students should "be in the right place at the right

Connect & Extend
To your teaching
Five excellent and very practical discussions of classroom management are:

Evertson, C. M., Emmer, E. T., & Worsham, M. E. (2000). *Classroom management for elementary teachers,* 5/e. Boston: Allyn & Bacon.

Emmer, E. T., Evertson, C. M., Clements, B. S., & Worsham, M. E. (2000). *Classroom management for secondary teachers,* 5/e. Boston: Allyn & Bacon.

Freiberg, H. J. (Ed.). (1999). *Beyond behaviorism: Changing the classroom management paradigm.* Boston: Allyn & Bacon.

Weinstein, C. S., & Mignano, A. J., Jr. (1997). *Elementary classroom management: Lessons from research and practice,* 2/e. New York: McGraw-Hill.

Weinstein, C.S. (1996). *Secondary classroom management: Lessons from research and practice.* New York: McGraw-Hill.

Creating a Positive Learning Environment   **415**

time." Students were not told what this meant, so their behaviour could not be guided by the rule. Neither positive nor negative behaviour had clear, consistent consequences. After students broke a rule, ineffective managers might give a vague criticism, such as "Some of my children are too noisy," or issue a warning, but not follow through with the threatened consequence.

In the poorly managed classes, procedures for accomplishing routine tasks varied from day to day and were never taught or practised. Instead of dealing with these obvious needs, ineffective managers spent time on procedures that could have waited. For example, one teacher had the class practise for a fire drill the first day, but left unexplained other procedures that would be needed every day. Students wandered aimlessly and had to ask each other what they should be doing. Often the students talked to one another because they had nothing productive to do. Ineffective teachers frequently left the room. Many became absorbed in paperwork or in helping just one student. They had not made plans for how to deal with late-arriving students or other interruptions. One ineffective manager tried to teach students to respond to a bell as a signal for attention, but later let the students ignore it. All in all, the first weeks in these classrooms were disorganized and filled with surprises for teachers and students alike.

Effective Managers for Secondary Students. What about getting started in a secondary school class? It appears that many of the differences between effective and ineffective elementary school teachers hold at the secondary level as well. Again, effective managers focus on establishing rules, procedures, and expectations on the first day of class. These standards for academic work and class behaviour are clearly communicated to students and consistently enforced during the first weeks of class. Student behaviour is closely monitored, and infractions of the rules are dealt with quickly. In classes with lower-ability students, work cycles are shorter; students are not required to spend long, unbroken periods on one type of activity. Instead, during each period they are moved smoothly through several different tasks. In general, effective teachers carefully follow each student's progress, so students cannot avoid work without facing consequences (Emmer & Evertson, 1982).

With all this close monitoring and consistent enforcement of the rules, you may wonder if effective secondary teachers have to be grim and humourless. Not necessarily. The effective managers in one study also smiled and joked more with their students (Moskowitz & Hayman, 1976). As any experienced teacher can tell you, there is much more to smile about when the class is cooperative. In fact, there is another requirement for getting started, one that was evident in Ken Kowalski's class—establishing a climate of trust and respect that creates a community for learning.

CHECKPOINT

Creating a Positive Learning Environment

Review

▶ Distinguish between rules and procedures.

▶ Distinguish between personal territories and interest-area spatial arrangements.

▶ Contrast the first school week of effective and ineffective classroom managers.

Apply

▶ What basic rules would you use for your students and how would you teach them?

▶ How can the physical arrangement of the room promote learning?

Creating a Learning Community

Nel Noddings (1992, 1995) has written about the need to create caring educational environments where students take more responsibility for governing their school and classroom. As we saw in Chapter 10 when we discussed the need for relatedness, students are more intrinsically motivated when they feel that their teachers care about them (Grolnick, Ryan, & Deci, 1991). Developing supportive, caring relationships among colleagues, with parents, and among students has been a school-wide goal at Blakeburn Elementary School in Port Coquitlam, BC, since the school opened in September 2000 (Laidlaw, 2001). The school's focus is on helping students to become socially responsible. There is consistency and modelling at all levels, and the students are learning the language to solve problems, respect diversity, and contribute to the classroom and the school. In interviews, students talk about feeling safe, included, and happy to be at school. Parents say, "There is a different atmosphere at this school. . . . There is a sense of mutual trust. The expectation is that the kids will manage and get along, and they do" (p. 1).

Historically, however, North American schools have emphasized regulating students' behaviour through rules, not through relationships. One approach to developing the kind of caring and mutually trusting community that exists at Blakeburn Elementary is David and Roger Johnson's "Three Cs" of school and classroom management.

The Three Cs of Classroom Management

The three Cs for safe and productive schools are: cooperative community, constructive conflict resolution, and civic values (Johnson & Johnson, 1999b). Classroom management begins by establishing a learning community based on cooperative approaches such as those described in Chapters 9 and 10. At the heart of the community is the idea of positive interdependence—individuals working together to achieve mutual goals. Constructive conflict resolution is essential in the community because conflicts are inevitable and even necessary for learning. Jean Piaget's theory of development and the research on conceptual change teaching tell us that true learning requires cognitive conflict. And individuals trying to exist in groups will have interpersonal conflict—these can lead to learning too. Table 11.3 below shows how academic and interpersonal conflicts can be positive forces in a learning community. At the end of this chapter we will talk more about conflict resolution in schools.

TABLE 11.3 Academic and Interpersonal Conflict and Learning

Conflict, if handled well, can support learning. Academic conflicts can lead to critical thinking and conceptual change. Conflicts of interest are unavoidable, but can be handled so no one is the loser.

Academic Controversy	Conflicts of Interest
One person's ideas, information, theories, conclusions, and opinions are incompatible with those of another, and the two seek to reach an agreement.	The actions of one person attempting to maximize benefits prevents, blocks or interferes with another person maximizing her or his benefits.
Controversy Procedure	*Integrative (Problem-Solving) Negotiations*
Research and prepare positions	Describe wants
Present and advocate positions	Describe feelings
Refute opposing position and refute attacks on own position	Describe reasons for wants and feelings
Reverse perspectives	Take other's perspective
Synthesize and integrate best evidence and reasoning from all sides	Invent three optional agreements that maximize joint outcomes
	Choose one and formalize agreement

Source: From "The Three C's of School and Classroom Management," by D. Johnson and R. Johnson, 1999, in H. J. Freiberg (Ed.), *Beyond Behaviorism: Changing the Classroom Management Paradigm* (p. 133), Boston: Allyn & Bacon. Copyright © 1999 by Allyn & Bacon. Adapted by permission.

The last C is civic values—the understandings and beliefs that hold the community together. Values are learned through direct teaching, modelling, literature, group discussions, and the sharing of concerns. Some teachers have a "Concerns Box" where students can put written concerns and comments. The box is opened once a week at a class meeting and the concerns are discussed. Johnson and Johnson (1999b) give the example of a class meeting about respect. One student tells her classmates that she felt hurt during recess the day before because no one listened when she was trying to teach them the rules to a new game. The students discuss what it means to be respectful and why respect is important. Then the students share personal experiences of times when they felt respected versus not respected.

Getting Started on Community

Whether you are working as an individual or as part of a school-wide team, creating the kind of community that is now visible in the day-to-day routines at Blakeburn Elementary School does not happen automatically (Laidlaw, 2001, p. 4). It involves input from many different levels to develop a philosophy and participation structures that will foster self-control and social responsibility on the part of students. At Blakeburn, the "leadership team" met first and talked about how to create a caring and socially responsible learning community. Team members used the ministry's Performance Standards for Social Responsibility as a framework for developing a common language and set of expectations. Then they involved the children and their families. The first week of school was devoted to the articulation of what it means (for *all* members) to be part of a socially responsible community. Students participated in multi-aged, "family" groups on relevant activities. Throughout this process the staff recognized that this work must be multifaceted, and integrated in all the curricula and interactions in their classrooms and at the school. They realized that creating positive classroom and school climates requires more than the implementation of prepackaged programs at a scheduled time in the day. It involves "living the principles of inclusion and responsibility . . . all day, every day" (Laidlaw, 2001, p. 4).

CHECKPOINT

Creating a Learning Community

Review

▶ What are Johnson and Johnson's three Cs of establishing a classroom community?

Apply

▶ How would you introduce the idea of community to the students you will teach?

*M*aintaining a Good Environment for Learning

A good start is just that—a beginning. Effective teachers build on this beginning. They maintain their management system by preventing problems and keeping students motivated and engaged in productive learning activities. We have discussed several ways to keep students motivated and engaged. In Chapter 10, for example, we considered stimulating curiosity, relating lessons to student interests, encouraging cooperative learning, establishing learning goals instead of performance goals, and having positive expectations. What else can teachers do?

Encourage Engagement

The format of a lesson affects student involvement. In general, as teacher supervision increases, students' engaged time also increases (Emmer & Evertson, 1981).

For example, one study found that elementary students working directly with a teacher were on task 97 percent of the time, while students working on their own were on task only 57 percent of the time (Frick, 1990). This does not mean that teachers should eliminate independent work for students. It simply means that this type of activity usually requires careful monitoring.

When the task provides continuous cues for the student about what to do next, involvement will be greater. Activities with clear steps are likely to be more absorbing, since one step leads naturally to the next. When students have all the materials they need to complete a task, they tend to stay involved (Kounin & Doyle, 1975). If their curiosity is piqued, students will be motivated to continue seeking an answer. And, as you now know, students will be more engaged if they are involved in authentic tasks—activities that have connections to real life.

Of course, teachers can't supervise every student all the time or rely on curiosity. Something else must keep students working independently. In their study of elementary and secondary teachers, Evertson, Emmer, and their colleagues found that effective class managers at both levels had well-planned systems for encouraging students to manage their own work (Evertson et al., 2000; Emmer et al., 2000). The Guidelines below are based on their findings.

GUIDELINES

Keeping Students Engaged

Make basic work requirements clear.

Examples

1. Specify and post the routine work requirements for headings, paper size, pen or pencil use, and neatness.
2. Establish and explain rules about late or incomplete work and absences. If a pattern of incomplete work begins to develop, deal with it early; speak with parents if necessary.
3. Make due dates reasonable, and stick to them unless the student has a very good excuse for lateness.

Communicate the specifics of assignments.

Examples

1. With younger students, have a routine procedure for giving assignments, such as writing them on the board in the same place each day. With older students, assignments may be dictated, posted, or given in a syllabus.
2. Remind students of coming assignments.
3. With complicated assignments, give students a sheet describing what to do, what resources are available, due dates, and so on. Older students should also be told your grading criteria.
4. Demonstrate how to do the assignment, do the first few questions together, or provide a sample worksheet.

Monitor work in progress.

Examples

1. When you set an in-class assignment, make sure each student gets started correctly. If you check only students who raise their hands for help, you will miss those who think they know what to do but don't really understand, those who are too shy to ask for help, and those who don't plan to do the work at all.
2. Check progress periodically. In discussions, make sure everyone has a chance to respond.

Give frequent academic feedback.

Examples

1. Elementary students should get papers back the day after they are handed in.
2. Good work can be displayed in class and graded papers sent home to parents each week.
3. Students of all ages can keep records of grades, projects completed, and extra credits earned.
4. For older students, break up long-term assignments into several phases, giving feedback at each point.

Encourage Motivation and Thoughtful Learning

In classrooms that are well-managed and supportive, students gain confidence in their abilities and come to value learning. Then, the influences on students' motivation to learn in a particular situation can be summarized in three questions: Can I succeed at this task? Do I want to succeed? What do I need to do to succeed? (Eccles & Wigfield, 1985). As reflected in these questions, we want students to have confidence in their ability so they will approach learning with energy and enthusiasm. We want them to see the value of the tasks involved and work to learn, not just try to get the grade or get finished. We want students to believe that success will come when they apply good learning strategies instead of believing that their only option is to use self-defeating, failure-avoiding, face-saving strategies. When things get difficult, we want students to stay focused on the task, not get so worried about failure that they freeze. In the sections that follow, we identify some strategies for addressing these questions and encouraging students' motivation to learn.

Can I Do It? Building Confidence and Positive Expectations. One of the most important factors in building expectations for success is past success. No amount of encouragement or "cheerleading" will substitute for real accomplishment. To ensure genuine progress:

1. *Begin work at the students' level and move in small steps.* The pace should be brisk, but not so fast that students have to move to the next step before they understand the previous one. This may require assigning different tasks to different students or designing tasks that are flexible enough to allow varying processes and products. Another possibility is to have very easy and very difficult questions on every test and assignment, so all students are both successful and challenged. When grades are required, make sure all the students in class have a chance to make at least a C if they work hard.

2. *Make sure learning goals are clear, specific, and possible to reach in the near future.* When long-term projects are planned, break the work into sub-goals and help students feel a sense of progress toward the long-term goal. If possible, give students a range of goals at different levels of difficulty and let them choose.

3. *Stress self-comparison, not comparison with others.* Help students see the progress they are making by showing them how to use self-management strategies such as those described in Chapter 6. Give specific feedback and corrections. Tell students what they are doing right as well as what is wrong and *why* it is wrong. Periodically, give students a question or problem that was once hard for them but now seems easy. Point out how much they have improved.

4. *Communicate to students that academic ability is improvable* and specific to the task at hand. In other words, the fact that a student has trouble in algebra doesn't necessarily mean that geometry will be difficult or that he or she is a bad English student. Don't undermine your efforts to stress improvement by displaying only the 100-percent papers on the bulletin board.

5. *Model good problem solving*, especially when *you* have to try several approaches to get a solution. Students need to see that learning is not smooth and error-free, even for the teacher.

Do I Want to Do It? Seeing the Value of Learning. Teachers can use intrinsic and extrinsic motivation strategies to help students see the value of the learning task. In this process, the age of the student must be taken into consideration. For younger children, intrinsic or *interest value* is a greater determinant of motivation than attainment or utility value. Because younger students have a more immediate, concrete focus, they have trouble seeing the value of an activity that is linked to distant goals such as getting a good job—or even preparing for the next grade. Older students, on the other hand, have the cognitive ability to think more abstractly and connect what they are learning now with goals and future possibilities, so *utility value* becomes important to these students (Eccles & Wigfield, 1985).

Attainment and Intrinsic Value. To establish *attainment value*, we must connect the learning task with the needs of the students. First, it must be possible for students to meet their needs for safety, belonging, and achievement in our classes. The classroom should not be a frightening or lonely place. Second, we must be sure that gender or ethnic stereotypes do not interfere with motivation. For example, if students subscribe to rigid notions of masculinity and femininity, we must make it clear that both women and men can be high achievers in all subjects and that no subjects are the territory of only one sex. It is not "unfeminine" to be strong in mathematics, science, shop, or sports. It is not "unmasculine" to be good in literature, art, music, or French.

There are many strategies for encouraging *intrinsic* (interest) motivation. Several of the following are taken from Brophy (1988).

1. *Tie class activities to student interests* in sports, music, current events, pets, common problems or conflicts with family and friends, fads, television and cinema personalities, or other significant features of their lives (Schiefele, 1991). When possible, give students choices of research paper or reading topics so they can follow their own interests.

2. *Arouse curiosity.* Point out puzzling discrepancies between students' beliefs and the facts. For example, Stipek (1993) describes a teacher who asked her Grade 5 class if there were "people" on some of the other planets. When the students said yes, the teacher asked if people needed oxygen to breathe. Since the students had just learned this fact, they responded yes to this question also. Then the teacher told them that there is no oxygen in the atmosphere of the other planets. This surprising discrepancy between what the children knew about oxygen and what they believed about life on other planets led to a rousing discussion of the atmospheres of other planets, the kinds of beings that could survive in these atmospheres, and so on. A straight lecture on the atmosphere of the planets might have put the students to sleep, but this discussion led to real interest in the subject.

3. *Make the learning task fun.* Many lessons can be taught through simulations or games. For example, some Grade 8 students designed a game they called ULTRA. Students were divided into groups and formed their own "countries." Each country had to choose a name, symbol, national flower, and bird. They wrote and sang a national anthem and elected government officials. The teachers allocated different resources to the countries. To get all the materials needed for the completion of assigned projects, the countries had to establish trade with one another. There was a monetary system and a stock market. Students had to work with their fellow citizens to complete cooperative learning assignments. Some countries "cheated" in their trade with other nations, and this allowed debate about international relations, trust, and war. Students had fun, but they also learned how to work in a group without the teacher's supervision and gained a deeper understanding of world economics and international conflicts.

4. *Make use of novelty and familiarity.* Don't overuse a few teaching approaches or motivational strategies. We all need variety. Varying the goal structures of tasks (cooperative, competitive, individualistic) can help, as can using different teaching media. When the material being covered in

▲ *Learning is more interesting when students are personally involved in the task.*

Connect & Extend
To professional journals
Abi-Nader, J. (1991). Creating a vision of the future: Strategies for motivating minority students. *Phi Delta Kappan, 72,* 546–549. *Focus Questions:* Why do minority-group students sometimes find schooling unmotivating? What can be done?

class is abstract or unfamiliar to students, try to connect it to something they know and understand. For example, talk about the size of a large area, such as the Acropolis in Athens, in terms of football fields. Brophy (1988) describes one teacher who read a brief passage from *Spartacus* to personalize the unit on slavery in the ancient world.

Instrumental Value. Sometimes it is difficult to encourage intrinsic motivation, and so teachers must rely on the utility or "instrumental" value of tasks. That is, it is important to learn many skills because they will be needed in more advanced classes or because they are necessary for life outside school.

1. When these connections are not obvious, you should *explain the connections to your students*. The PLAN program makes these connections come alive for high school students (Abi-Nader, 1991). Three major strategies focus students' attention on their future: (1) working with mentors and models—often PLAN graduates—who give advice about how to choose courses, budget time, take notes, and deal with cultural differences in college; (2) storytelling about the achievements of former students—sometimes the college term papers of former students are posted on PLAN bulletin boards; and (3) filling the classroom with future-oriented talk such as "When you go to college, you will encounter these situations . . ." or, "You're at a parents' meeting—you want a good education for your children—and you are the ones who must speak up; that's why it is important to learn public speaking skills" (p. 548).

2. In some situations teachers can *provide incentives and rewards for learning* (see Chapter 6). Remember, though, that giving rewards when students are already interested in the activity may undermine intrinsic motivation. If teachers began testing and grading students on their memory of the television programs they watched the previous evening, even television viewing would lose some of its intrinsic appeal (Stipek, 1998).

3. Use *ill-structured problems and authentic tasks* in teaching. Connect problems in school to real problems outside.

What Do I Need to Do to Succeed? Staying Focused on the Task. When students encounter difficulties, as they must if they are working at a challenging level, they need to keep their attention on the task. If the focus shifts to worries about performance, fear of failure, or concern with looking smart, motivation to learn is lost. Here are some ideas for keeping the focus on learning.

1. *Give students frequent opportunities to respond* through questions and answers, short assignments, or demonstrations of skills. Make sure you check the students' answers so you can correct problems quickly. You don't want students to practise errors too long. Computer learning programs give students the immediate feedback they need to correct errors before they become habits.

2. When possible, *have students create a finished product*. They will be more persistent and focused on the task when the end is in sight. We all have experienced the power of the need for closure. We begin a project thinking, "I will work for just an hour." Then, we find ourselves still at work hours later because we want to see the finished product.

3. *Avoid heavy emphasis on grades and competition*. An emphasis on grades forces students to be ego-involved rather than task-involved. Anxious students are especially hard hit by highly competitive evaluation.

4. *Reduce task risk without oversimplifying the task*. When tasks are risky (failure is likely and the consequences of failing are grave), student motivation suffers. For difficult, complex, or ambiguous tasks, provide students

FAMILY AND COMMUNITY PARTNERSHIPS

Motivation to Learn

Work with families to build confidence and positive expectations.

Examples

1. Avoid comparing one child in a family to another during conferences and discussions with family members.
2. Ask family members to highlight strong points of homework assignments. They might attach a note to assignments describing the three best aspects of the work and one element that could be improved.

Make families partners in showing the value of learning.

Examples

1. Invite family members to the class to demonstrate how they use mathematics or writing in their work.
2. Involve parents in identifying skills and knowledge for the children to learn in school that could be applied at home and prove helpful to the family right now—for example, keeping records on service agencies, writing letters of complaint to department stores or landlords, or researching vacation destinations.

Provide resources that build skill and will for families.

Examples

1. Give family members simple strategies for helping their children improve study skills.
2. Involve older students in a "homework hotline" telephone network for helping younger students with class assignments.

Have frequent celebrations of learning.

Examples

1. Invite families to a "museum" at the end of a unit on dinosaurs. Students create the museum in the auditorium, library, or cafeteria. After visiting the museum, families go to the classroom to examine their child's portfolio for the unit.[1]
2. Place mini-exhibits of student work at local grocery stores, libraries, or community centres.

[1] R. C. Fowler and K. K. Corley (1996). Linking families, building community. *Educational Leadership, 7*(7), 24–26.

---

with plenty of time, support, resources, help, and the chance to revise or improve work.

5. *Model motivation to learn for your students.* Talk about your interest in the subject and how you deal with difficult learning problems.

6. *Teach the particular learning tactics* that students will need to master the material being studied. Show students how to learn and remember so they won't be forced to fall back on self-defeating strategies or rote memory.

The support of families and the community can be helpful as you design strategies for your students. The Family and Community Partnerships Guidelines above give ideas for working with families.

Prevention Is the Best Medicine

Jack Martin and Jeff Sugarman (1993) note that "many difficulties in classroom management can be prevented by effective teaching" (p. 51) that interests students, avoids confusion, and keeps activities moving. What else can you do to maintain your management system? The ideal way to manage problems, of course, is to prevent them in the first place. In a classic study, Jacob Kounin (1970) examined classroom management by comparing effective teachers, whose classes were relatively free of problems, with ineffective teachers, whose classes were continually plagued

Connect & Extend
To your teaching
The teacher has divided the class into small groups to work on different aspects of a class assignment. In one group there is a child who is preventing the group from completing its task because of his crazy antics and remarks. How would you set up a program that would encourage the group to take responsibility for getting the student to cooperate?

by chaos and disruption. Observing both groups in action, Kounin found that the teachers were not very different in the way they handled discipline once problems arose. The difference was that the successful managers were much better at preventing problems. Kounin concluded that effective classroom managers were especially skilled in four areas: "*withitness,*" *overlapping activities, group focusing, and movement management* (Doyle, 1977). More recent research confirms the importance of these factors (Emmer & Evertson, 1981; Evertson, 1988).

Withitness. **Withitness** means communicating to students that you are aware of everything that is happening in the classroom, that you aren't missing anything. "With-it" teachers seem to have eyes in the back of their heads. They avoid becoming absorbed or interacting with only a few students, because this encourages the rest of the class to wander. They are always scanning the room, making eye contact with individual students, so the students know they are being monitored (Brooks, 1985).

These teachers prevent minor disruptions from becoming major. They also know who instigated the problem, and they make sure the right people are dealt with. In other words, they do not make what Kounin called *timing errors* (waiting too long before intervening) or *target errors* (blaming the wrong student and letting the real perpetrators escape responsibility for their behaviour).

If two problems occur at the same time, effective managers deal with the more serious one first. For example, a teacher who tells two students to stop whispering but ignores even a brief shoving match at the pencil sharpener communicates to students a lack of awareness. Students begin to believe they can get away with almost anything if they are clever (Charles, 1996).

Overlapping and Group Focus. **Overlapping** means keeping track of and supervising several activities at the same time. For example, a teacher may have to check the work of an individual and at the same time keep a small group working by saying, "Right, go on," and stop an incident in another group with a quick "look" or reminder (Burden, 1995; Charles, 1996).

Maintaining a **group focus** means keeping as many students as possible involved in appropriate class activities and avoiding narrowing in on just one or two students. All students should have something to do during a lesson. For example, the teacher might ask everyone to write the answer to a question, then call on individuals to respond while the other students compare their answers. Choral

▲ *While this teacher is talking to a group of students, does she know what else is happening in the class? Can she "overlap" activities and still be "withit"?*

responses might be required while the teacher moves around the room to make sure everyone is participating (Charles, 1996). Some teachers have their students use small blackboards or coloured cards for responding in groups. This lets the teacher check for understanding as well. For example, during a grammar lesson the teacher might say, "Everyone who thinks the answer is *have run*, hold up the red side of your card. If you think the answer is *has run*, hold up the green side" (Hunter, 1982). This is one way teachers can ensure that all students are involved and check that they all understand the material.

Movement Management. **Movement management** means keeping lessons and the group moving at an appropriate (and flexible) pace, with smooth transitions and variety. The effective teacher avoids abrupt transitions, such as announcing a new activity before gaining the students' attention or starting a new activity in the middle of something else. In these situations, one-third of the class will be doing the new activity, many will be on the old lesson, several will be asking other students what to do, some will be taking the opportunity to have a little fun, and most will be confused.

Movement Management: Ability to keep lessons and groups moving smoothly.

Another transition problem Kounin noted is the *slowdown*, or taking too much time to start a new activity. Sometimes teachers give too many directions. Problems also arise when teachers have students work one at a time while the rest of the class waits and watches. Charles (1985, p. 26) gives this example:

> During a science lesson the teacher began, "Row 1 may get up and get their beakers. Row 2 may get theirs. Now, Row 3 . . . Now, Row 1 may line up to put some bicarbonate of soda in their beakers. Row 2 may follow them," and so forth. When each row had obtained their bicarbonate of soda the teacher had them go row by row to add water. This left the remainder of the class sitting at their desks with no direction, doing nothing or else beginning to find something with which to entertain themselves.

A teacher who successfully demonstrates withitness, overlapping activities, group focus, and movement management tends to have a class filled with actively engaged students who do not escape his or her all-seeing eye. This need not be a grim classroom. It is more likely a busy place where students are actively learning and gaining a sense of self-worth rather than misbehaving in order to get attention and achieve status.

Dealing with Discipline Problems

Being an effective manager does not mean publicly correcting every minor infraction of the rules. This kind of public attention may actually reinforce the misbehaviour, as we saw in Chapter 6. Teachers who frequently correct students do not necessarily have the best-behaved classes (Irving & Martin, 1982). The key is to know what is happening and what is important so you can prevent problems. Emmer and colleagues (2000) and Levin and Nolan (2000) suggest seven simple ways to stop misbehaviour quickly, moving from least to most intrusive:

Connect & Extend
To the research
For a description of an extensive research project examining how teachers cope with problem behaviour, see Brophy, J., & McCaslin, M. (1992). Teachers' reports of how they perceive and cope with problem students. *Elementary School Journal, 93*, 3–68.

1. *Make eye contact* with, or move closer to, the offender. Other non-verbal signals, such as pointing to the work students are supposed to be doing, might be helpful. Make sure the student actually stops the inappropriate behaviour and gets back to work. If you do not, students will learn to ignore your signals.

2. Try *verbal hints* such as "name-dropping" (simply insert the student's name into the lecture), or ask the student a question to get him or her back on task.

3. You might also ask students *if they are aware* of the negative effects of their actions or send an "I message," described later in the chapter.

"THEY'RE TESTING YOU."

(By *permission of James Warren.
From* Phi Delta Kappan.)

Connect & Extend
To your teaching
Almost every day in your Grade 6 class, Rod talks out of turn and loses the reward for his group. The other group members are giving Rod a difficult time, and the parents of two students have called you to complain that the group reward system is unfair. What would you do to resolve this problem?

Connect & Extend
To your teaching
What is a teacher's responsibility if he or she finds out that a pupil is involved in illegal acts such as selling drugs or stealing?

4. If they are not performing a class procedure correctly, *remind the students* of the procedure and have them follow it correctly. You may need to quietly collect a toy, comb, magazine, or note that is competing with the learning activities, while privately informing the students that their possessions will be returned after class.

5. In a calm, unhostile way, *ask the student to state the correct rule or procedure* and then to follow it. Glasser (1969) proposes three questions: "What are you doing? Is it against the rules? What should you be doing?"

6. Tell the student in a clear, assertive, and unhostile way to *stop the misbehaviour.* (Later in the chapter we will discuss assertive messages to students in more detail.) If students "talk back," simply repeat your statement.

7. *Offer a choice.* For example, if a student continues to call out answers during a class discussion, even after reminders to raise a hand or wait for a turn, the teacher might say, "John, I'm going to ask you to make a choice. Stop calling out answers immediately and begin raising your hand to answer, or leave the group, move to the back of the class, and you and I will have a private discussion later. You decide." (Levin & Nolan, 2000, p. 177).

If you must impose consequences, the Guidelines on page 427, taken from Weinstein and Mignano (1997), give ideas about how to do it. The examples are taken from the actual words of the expert teachers described in their book.

Special Problems with Secondary Students

Many secondary students never complete their work. Besides encouraging student responsibility, what else can teachers do to deal with this frustrating problem? Because students at this age have many assignments and teachers have many students, both teachers and students may lose track of what has and has not been completed. It often helps to teach students how to use a daily planner. In addition, the teacher must keep accurate records. The most important thing is to enforce the established consequences for incomplete work. Do not pass a student because you know he or she is "bright enough" to pass. Make it clear to these students that the choice is theirs: they can do the work and pass, or they can refuse to do the work and face the consequences.

There is also the problem of students who continually break the same rules—always forgetting materials, for example, or getting into fights. What should you do? Seat these students away from others who might be influenced by them. Try to catch them before they break the rules, but if rules are broken, be consistent in applying established consequences. Do not accept promises to do better next time (Levin & Nolan, 2000). Teach the students how to monitor their own behaviour; some of the self-management techniques described in Chapter 6 should be helpful. Finally, remain friendly with the students. Try to catch them in a good moment so you can talk to them about something other than their rule breaking.

A defiant, hostile student can pose serious problems. If there is an outbreak, try to get out of the situation as soon as possible; everyone loses in a public power struggle. One possibility is to give the student a chance to save face and cool down by saying, "It's your choice to cooperate or not. You can take a minute to think about it." If the student complies, the two of you can talk later about controlling the outbursts. If the student refuses to cooperate, you can tell him or her to wait in the hall until you get the class started on work, then step outside for a private talk. If the student refuses to leave, send another class member for the assistant principal. Again, follow through. If the student complies before help arrives, do not let him or her off the hook. If outbursts occur frequently, you might have a conference with the counsellor, parents, or other teachers. If the problem is an irreconcilable clash of personalities, the student should be transferred to another teacher.

GUIDELINES

Imposing Penalties

Delay the discussion of the situation until you and the students involved are calmer and more objective.

Examples
1. Say calmly to a student, "Sit there and think about what happened. I'll talk to you in a few minutes," or, "I don't like what I just saw. Talk to me during your free period today."
2. Say, "I'm really angry about what just happened. Everybody take out journals; we are going to write about this." After a few minutes of writing, the class can discuss the incident.

Impose consequences privately.

Examples
1. Make arrangements with students privately. Stand firm in enforcing arrangements.
2. Resist the temptation to "remind" students in public that they are not keeping their side of the bargain.
3. Move close to a student who must be disciplined and speak so that only the student can hear.

After imposing a consequence, re-establish a positive relationship with the student immediately.

Examples
1. Send the student on an errand or ask him or her for help.
2. Compliment the student's work or give a real or symbolic "pat on the back" when the student's behaviour warrants. Look hard for such an opportunity.

Set up a graded list of penalties that will fit many occasions.

Example
1. For not turning in homework: (1) receive reminder; (2) receive warning; (3) hand homework in before close of school day; (4) stay after school to finish work; (5) participate in a teacher-student-parent conference to develop an action plan.

It sometimes is useful to keep records of the incidents by logging the student's name, words and actions, date, time, place, and teacher's response. These records may help identify patterns and can prove useful in meeting with administrators, parents, or special services personnel (Burden, 1995). Some teachers have students sign each entry to verify the incidents.

Violence or destruction of property is a difficult and potentially dangerous problem. The first step is to send for help and get the names of participants and witnesses. Then get rid of any crowd that may have gathered; an audience will only make things worse. Do not try to break up a fight without help. Make sure the school office is aware of the incident; usually the school has a policy for dealing with these situations.

CHECKPOINT

Maintaining a Good Environment for Learning

Review

▷ How can teachers encourage motivation and thoughtful learning?

▷ How can teachers encourage engagement?

▷ Explain the factors identified by Kounin that prevent management problems in the classroom.

▷ Describe seven levels of intervention in misbehaviour.

Apply

▷ Will you use consequences in your class when students violate rules? What kinds?

▷ Give an example of a strategy to:
1. build student confidence
2. show the value of learning
3. help students stay focused on the task

Paraphrase Rule: Policy whereby listeners must accurately summarize what a speaker has said before being allowed to respond.

*T*he Need for Communication

Communication between teacher and students is essential when problems arise. Communication is more than "teacher talks—student listens." It is more than the words exchanged between individuals. We communicate in many ways. Our actions, movements, voice tone, facial expressions, and other non-verbal behaviour send messages to our students. Many times the messages we intend to send are not the messages our students receive.

Message Sent—Message Received

Teacher: Carl, where is your homework?

Carl: I left it in my Dad's car this morning.

Teacher: Again? You will have to bring me a note tomorrow from your father saying that you actually did the homework. No grade without the note.

Message Carl receives: I can't trust you. I need proof you did the work.

Teacher: Sit at every other desk. Put all your things under your desk. Jane and Laurel, you are sitting too close together. One of you move!

Message Jane and Laurel receive: I expect you two to cheat on this test.

A new student comes to Ms. Tung's kindergarten. The child is messy and unwashed. Ms. Tung puts her hand lightly on the girl's shoulder and says, "I'm glad you are here." Her muscles tense, and she leans away from the child. *Message student receives:* I don't like you. I think you are bad.

▲ *One of the challenges of managing elementary school children is to deal effectively with disruptive behaviour and achieve a positive outcome. In some cases, it might be appropriate to involve a student's family.*

In all interactions, a message is sent and a message is received. Sometimes teachers believe they are sending one message, but their voices, body positions, choices of words, and gestures may communicate a different message.

Students may hear the hidden message and respond to it. For example, a student may respond with hostility if she or he feels insulted by the teacher (or by another student), but may not be able to say exactly where the feeling of being insulted came from. Perhaps it was in the teacher's tone of voice, not the words actually spoken. In such cases, the teacher may feel attacked for no reason. "What did I say? All I said was . . ." The first principle of communication is that people respond to what they *think* was said or meant, not necessarily to the speaker's intended message or actual words.

There are many exercises for practising sending and receiving messages accurately. Students in Anita's classes have told her about one instructor who encourages accurate communication by using the **paraphrase rule**. Before any participant, including the teacher, is allowed to respond to any other participant in a class discussion, he or she must summarize what the previous speaker said. If the summary is wrong, indicating the speaker was misunderstood, the speaker must explain again. The respondent then tries again to paraphrase. The process continues until the speaker agrees that the listener has heard the intended message.

Paraphrasing is more than a classroom exercise. It can be the first step in communicating with students. Before teachers can deal appropriately with any student problem, they must know what the real problem is. A student who says, "This book is really dumb! Why did we have to read it?" may really be saying, "The book was too difficult for me. I couldn't read it, and I feel dumb."

Diagnosis: Whose Problem Is It?

As a teacher, you may find some student behaviour unacceptable, unpleasant, or troubling. It is often difficult to stand back from these problems, take an objective look, and decide on an appropriate response. According to Thomas Gordon (1981), the key to good teacher-student relationships is determining why you are troubled by a particular behaviour and whose problem it is. The teacher must begin by asking who "owns" the problem. The answer to this question is critical. If it is really the student's problem, the teacher must become a counsellor and supporter, helping the student find his or her own solution. But if the teacher "owns" the problem, it is the teacher's responsibility to find a solution through problem solving with the student.

Diagnosing who owns the problem is not always straightforward. Let's look at three troubling situations to get some practice in this skill:

1. A student writes obscene words and draws sexually explicit illustrations in a school encyclopedia.
2. A student tells you that his parents had a bad fight and he hates his father.
3. A student quietly reads a newspaper in the back of the room.

Why is this behaviour troubling? If you cannot accept the student's behaviour because it has a serious effect on you as a teacher—if you are blocked from reaching your goals by the student's action—then *you* own the problem. It is your responsibility to confront the student and seek a solution. A teacher-owned problem appears to be present in the first situation described above—the young pornographer—because teaching materials are damaged.

If you feel annoyed by the behaviour because it is getting in the student's own way or because you are embarrassed for the child, but the behaviour does not directly interfere with your teaching, it is probably the student's problem. The test question is: Does this student's action tangibly affect you or prevent you from fulfilling your role as a teacher? The student who hates his father would not prevent you from teaching, even though you might wish the student felt differently. The problem is really the student's, and he must find his own solution.

Situation 3 is more difficult to diagnose. There have been lengthy debates about whose problem it is when a student reads a newspaper in class. One argument is that the teacher is not interfered with in any way, so it is the student's problem. Another argument is that teachers might find reading the paper distracting during a lecture, so it is their problem, and they must find a solution. In a grey area such as this, the answer probably depends on how the teacher actually experiences the student's behaviour. Having decided who owns the problem, it is time to act.

Counselling: The Student's Problem

Let's pick up the situation in which the student found the reading assignment "dumb." How might a teacher handle this positively?

Student:	This book is really dumb! Why did we have to read it?
Teacher:	You're pretty upset. This seemed like a worthless assignment to you. [Teacher paraphrases the student's statement, trying to hear the emotions as well as the words.]
Student:	Yeah! Well, I guess it was worthless. I mean, I don't know if it was. I couldn't exactly read it.
Teacher:	It was just too hard to read, and that bothers you.
Student:	Sure, I felt really dumb. I know I can write a good report, but not with a book this tough.
Teacher:	I think I can give you some hints that will make the book easier to understand. Can you see me after school today?
Student:	Okay.

Empathetic Listening: Hearing the intent and emotions behind what another says and reflecting them back by paraphrasing.

Here the teacher used **empathetic listening** to allow the student to find a solution. (As you can see, this approach relies heavily on paraphrasing.) By trying to hear the student and by avoiding the tendency to jump in too quickly with advice, solutions, criticisms, reprimands, or interrogations, the teacher keeps the communication lines open. Here are a few *unhelpful* responses the teacher might have made:

▶ I chose the book because it is the best example of this author's style in our library. You will need to have read it before your IB English class next year. (The teacher justifies the choice; this prevents the student from admitting that this "important" assignment is too difficult.)

▶ Did you really read it? I bet you didn't do the work, and now you want out of the assignment. (The teacher accuses; the student hears, "The teacher doesn't trust me!" and must defend herself or himself or accept the teacher's view.)

▶ Your job is to read the book, not ask me why. I know what's best. (The teacher pulls rank, and the student hears, "You can't possibly decide what is good for you!" The student can rebel or passively accept the teacher's judgment.)

Empathetic, active listening can be a helpful response when students bring problems to you. You must reflect back to the student what you hear him or her saying. This reflection is more than a parroting of the student's words; it should capture the emotions, intent, and meaning behind them. Sokolove, Garrett, Sadker, and Sadker (1986, p. 241) have summarized the components of active listening: (1) blocking out external stimuli; (2) attending carefully to both the verbal and nonverbal messages; (3) differentiating between the intellectual and the emotional content of the message; and (4) making inferences regarding the speaker's feelings.

When students realize they really have been heard and not evaluated negatively for what they have said or felt, they feel freer to trust the teacher and to talk more openly. Sometimes the true problem surfaces later in the conversation.

Confrontation and Assertive Discipline

Now let's assume a student is doing something that actively interferes with teaching. The teacher decides the student must stop. The problem is the teacher's. Confrontation, not counselling, is required.

"I" Messages. Gordon (1981) recommends sending an **"I" message** in order to intervene and change a student's behaviour. Basically, this means telling a student in a straightforward, assertive, and non-judgmental way what she or he is doing, how it affects you as a teacher, and how you feel about it. The student is then free to change voluntarily, and often does so. Here are two "I" messages:

▶ If you leave your book bags in the aisles, I might trip and hurt myself.

▶ When you all call out, I can't concentrate on each answer, and I'm frustrated.

Assertive Discipline. Lee and Marlene Canter (1992; Canter, 1989) suggest other approaches for dealing with a teacher-owned problem. They call their method **assertive discipline**. Teachers are assertive when they make their expectations clear and follow through with established consequences. Students then have a straightforward choice: they can follow the rules or accept the consequences. Many teachers are ineffective with students because they are either wishy-washy and passive or hostile and aggressive.

The *passive style* can take several forms. Instead of telling the student directly what to do, the teacher tells, or often asks, the student to *try* or to *think about* the appropriate action. The passive teacher might comment on the problem behaviour without actually telling the child what to do differently: "Why are you doing that?

Connect & Extend
To professional debates
Read Canter, L. (1989). Assertive discipline—More than names on the board and marbles in a jar. *Phi Delta Kappan, 71*(1), 41–56. Evaluate Canter's claims for his "assertive discipline" approach. What are the similarities between the criticism of behavioural approaches to learning and the criticisms of assertive discipline? A special feature on discipline can be found in the 1989 issue of *Educational Leadership, 46*(6), 72–83. This feature presents a debate between supporters and critics of assertive discipline.

"I" Message: Clear, non-accusatory statement of how something is affecting you.

Assertive Discipline: Clear, firm, unhostile response style.

Don't you know the rules?" or "Sam, are you disturbing the class?" Or teachers may clearly state what should happen, but never follow through with the established consequences, giving the students "one more chance" every time. Finally, teachers may ignore behaviour that should receive a response or may wait too long before responding.

A *hostile response style* involves different mistakes. Teachers may make "you" statements that condemn the student without stating clearly what the student should be doing: "You should be ashamed of the way you're behaving!" or "You never listen!" or "You are acting like a baby!" Teachers may also threaten students angrily but follow through too seldom, perhaps because the threats are too vague—"You'll be very sorry you did that when I get through with you!"—or too severe. For example, a teacher tells a student in a physical education class that he will have to "sit on the bench for *three weeks*." A few days later the team is short one member and the teacher allows the student to play, never returning him to the bench to complete the three-week sentence. Often a teacher who has been passive becomes hostile and explodes when students persist in misbehaving.

In contrast to both the passive and hostile styles, an *assertive response* communicates to the students that you care too much about them and the process of learning to allow inappropriate behaviour to persist. Assertive teachers clearly state what they expect. To be most effective, the teachers often look into a student's eyes when speaking and address the student by name. Assertive teachers' voices are calm, firm, and confident. They are not sidetracked by accusations such as "You just don't understand!" or "You don't like me!" Assertive teachers do not get into a debate about the fairness of the rules. They expect changes, not promises or apologies.

Even though many teachers and school administrators have given enthusiastic testimonies about the assertive discipline approach, some educators and psychologists question its effectiveness. The Point/Counterpoint further explores the issue.

Confrontations and Negotiations. If "I" messages or assertive responses fail and a student persists in misbehaving, teacher and student are in a conflict. Several pitfalls now loom. The two individuals become less able to perceive each other's behaviour accurately. Research has shown that the angrier you get with another person, the more you see the other as the villain and yourself as an innocent victim. Because you feel the other person is in the wrong, and he or she feels just as strongly that the conflict is all your fault, very little mutual trust is possible. A cooperative solution to the problem is almost impossible. In fact, by the time the discussion has gone on a few minutes, the original problem is lost in a sea of charges, countercharges, and self-defence (Johnson & Johnson, 1994).

There are three methods of resolving a conflict between teacher and student. One is for the teacher to impose a solution. This may be necessary during an emergency, as when a defiant student refuses to go to the hall to discuss a public outbreak, but it is not a good solution for most conflicts. The second method is for the teacher to give in to the student's demands. You might be convinced by a particularly compelling student argument, but again, this should be used sparingly. It is generally a bad idea to be talked out of a position, unless the position was wrong in the first place. Problems arise when either the teacher or the student gives in completely.

Gordon recommends a third approach, which he calls the "no-lose method." Here the needs of both the teacher and the students are taken into account in the solution. No one person is expected to give in completely; all participants retain respect for themselves and each other. The no-lose method is a six-step, problem-solving strategy:

1. *Define the problem.* What exactly is the behaviour involved? What does each person want? (Use active listening to help students pinpoint the real problem.)

Does Assertive Discipline Work?

Lee Canter, the developer of "assertive discipline," describes his observations of effective teachers:

I found that, above all, the master teachers were assertive; that is they taught students how to behave. They established clear rules for the classroom, they communicated those rules to the students, and they taught students how to follow them. (1989, p. 58)

Is assertive discipline effective? There are strong opinions both against and in favour of the approach, as you will see. Researchers are skeptical, but some practitioners are committed to assertive discipline.

▶ POINT Research results do not support assertive discipline.

In an article entitled "What Research Really Shows about Assertive Discipline," Gary Render, Je Neil Padilla, and H. Mark Krank (1989) note that very little unbiased information is available about the effectiveness of this approach. Even though reports claim that 500 000 people have been trained in assertive discipline, Render and his colleagues were able to find only 16 systematic studies of assertive discipline. Their analysis of these studies has led them to conclude that:

The claims made by Canter (1988) . . . are simply not supported by the existing and available literature. We would agree that Assertive Discipline could be helpful in severe cases where students are behaving inappropriately more than 96 percent of the time, as in the study by Mandlebaum et al. (1983). We would also argue that teachers such as the one in that study would benefit from any intervention. However, we can find no evidence that Assertive Discipline is an effective approach deserving schoolwide or districtwide adoption. (p. 72)

A second criticism of assertive discipline is that while it may stop misbehaviour in the short run, the long-term effects on students are damaging. Richard Curwin and Allen Mendler (1988) remind teachers that classroom management systems not only manage behaviour, they also teach students lessons about their own self-worth, their ability to act responsibly and solve problems, how much control they have over their own lives, and how to use that control. What lessons are taught by systems such as assertive discipline? "If Richard shapes up after the third mark on the chalkboard because the fourth means a call home to an abusive parent, did the program improve his self-control, or did it simply transfer the inner turmoil of a child caught in a dysfunctional family?" (Curwin & Mendler, 1988, p. 68). This concern is echoed by John Covaleskie (1992): "What helps children become moral is not knowledge of the rules, or even obedience to the rules, but discussions about the reasons for acting in certain ways" (p. 56).

◀ COUNTERPOINT: Practitioners know that assertive discipline works.

In response to the assertion by Render and his colleagues that research does not support assertive discipline, Sammie McCormack (1989) says, "The decision to implement a program should be based on many factors, in addition to research; from a practitioner's standpoint, Assertive Discipline works" (p. 77). McCormack reports the reactions of more than 8700 teachers. In these schools, 78 to 99 percent of the teachers saw improvements in student behaviour as a consequence of using assertive discipline. McCormack does not explain how these particular samples were selected or if teachers in other schools had different reactions.

In response to Curwin and Mendler's (1988) concerns that classroom management models such as assertive discipline may undermine students' self-worth and sense of responsibility, Lee Canter (1988) notes that several studies have found improvements in both teachers' and students' self-concepts after the introduction of assertive discipline. Further, Canter states that the basis of assertive discipline is giving students choices and that it is through making choices and accepting the consequences that students learn about responsibility.

2. *Generate many possible solutions.* Brainstorm, but remember, don't allow any evaluations of ideas yet.

3. *Evaluate each solution.* Any participant may veto any idea. If no solutions are found to be acceptable, brainstorm again.

4. *Make a decision.* Choose one solution through consensus, not voting. In the end, everyone must be satisfied with the solution.

5. *Determine how to implement the solution.* What will be needed? Who will be responsible for each task? What is the timetable?

6. *Evaluate the success of the solution.* After trying the solution for a while, ask, "Are we satisfied with our decision? How well is it working? Should we make some changes?"

Many of the conflicts in classrooms are between students. These can be important learning experiences for all concerned.

Student Conflicts and Confrontations

Handling conflict is difficult for most of us—for young people it can be even harder. Given the public's concern about violence in schools, it is surprising how little we know about conflicts among students (Rose & Gallup, 1999; Johnson, Johnson, Dudley, Ward, & Magnuson, 1995). There is some evidence that in elementary schools, conflicts most often centre on disputes over resources (school supplies, computers, athletic equipment, or toys) and over preferences (which activity to do first or what game to play). More than 20 years ago, a large study of more than 8000 junior and senior high students and 500 faculty from three major US cities concluded that 90 percent of the conflicts among students are resolved in destructive ways or never resolved at all (DeCecco & Richards, 1974). The few studies since that time have reached similar conclusions. Avoidance, force, and threats seem to be the major strategies for dealing with conflict (Johnson et al., 1995).

Conflicts: Goals and Needs. When people are in conflict, they have two major concerns. The first is to satisfy their needs and meet their goals. This usually is the source of the conflict—the needs or goals of one person or group clash with the needs or goals of others. The second concern is to maintain an appropriate relationship with the other party in the conflict. Both of these concerns can be placed on a continuum from not very important to critically important. Different strategies are called for, depending on the importance of the goals and the relationships, as shown in Table 11.4 (Johnson & Johnson, 1994).

The message here is that different strategies make sense in different situations. Without guidance and practice, however, students may always use the same strategy—they may not be able to fit strategy to situation.

Connect & Extend
To the research
Carter, S. P., and Stewin, L. L. (1999). School violence in the Canadian context: An overview and model for intervention. *International Journal for the Advancement of Counselling, 21,* 267–277.

Abstract:
School violence and the incidence of violent crimes among Canadian youth is seen to be increasing. While more research is being conducted in the area of school violence, little has previously been done to examine psychopathology as a possible factor influencing violent student behaviour. A recent study conducted by S. P. Carter . . . using the Behavior Assessment System for Children and a structured interview showed a high incidence of psychopathology among violent junior high male students. A comprehensive model for intervention is described in which several factors are presented. Implications of current research includes the need to develop intervention strategies that are consistent with diagnostic findings and the need for early identification and intervention before behaviour patterns become fixed in adolescence.

▲ *Conflict arises in the classroom when one student's needs conflict with another's. What is the basis of this conflict? How would you help these students resolve their differences?*

TABLE 11.4 Strategies for Managing Conflict

Different situations call for different strategies. But any strategy can be used inappropriately. For example, withdrawing may be used inappropriately to avoid all conflict or appropriately to postpone confrontation until constructive discussions are possible.

Goal Important?	Relationship Important?	Strategy	Appropriate Uses	Inappropriate Uses
No	No	Withdraw	Postpone until constructive discussion is possible	Avoid conflict, hide
No	Yes	Smooth/Give in	When other's needs are more important	Give in just to be liked
Yes	No	Force	Seldom appropriate, perhaps when others' safety is your responsibility	To intimidate, win at all costs, overpower
Yes	Yes	Confront	Resolve conflict—strengthen relationship—protect both parties' goals	Generally appropriate
Moderately	Moderately	Compromise	When mutual sacrifices are required for the common good	When confrontation could satisfy both parties' goals

Violence in the Schools. Violence in Canadian schools is a serious and growing concern among students, parents, and teachers. Sillars (1995, p. 37) recently reported that "Nearly one-third of Calgary junior and senior high students have carried a weapon to school in the past year, according to a school violence survey by the Canadian Research Institute for Law and the Family (CRILF). . . . Four-fifths claim they have been struck, threatened, or had something stolen at school last year. More than half admitted to committing seriously delinquent acts." This problem has many causes; it is a challenge for every element of society. What can the schools do?

One answer is prevention. Some gang members have reported that they turned to gang activities when their teachers insulted them, called them names, humiliated them publicly, belittled their culture, ignored them in class, or blamed all negative incidents on particular students. These students reported joining gangs for security and to escape teachers who treated them badly or expected little of them because they were members of minority groups (Padilla, 1992; Parks, 1995). Other studies have found that gang members respected teachers who insisted on academic performance in a caring way (Huff, 1989). Anita once asked a gifted educator in an urban high school which teachers were most effective with the really tough students. He said there are two kinds, teachers who can't be intimidated or fooled and expect their students to learn, and teachers who really care about the students. When asked, "Which kind are you?" he answered "Both!"

Besides prevention, schools can also establish mentoring programs, conflict resolution training, social skills training, more relevant curricula, and parent and community involvement programs (Padilla, 1992; Parks, 1995). One intervention that seems to be helpful is peer mediation.

Peer Mediation. David Johnson and his colleagues (1995) provided conflict resolution training to 227 students in Grades 2 through 5. Students learned a five-step negotiating strategy:

1. *Jointly define the conflict.* Separate the person from the problem and the actions involved, avoid win-lose thinking, and get both parties' goals clear.

2. *Exchange positions and interests.* Present a tentative proposal and make a case for it; listen to the other person's proposal and feelings; and stay flexible and cooperative.

3. *Reverse perspectives.* See the situation from the other person's point of view and reverse roles and argue for that perspective.

4. *Invent at least three agreements that allow mutual gain.* Brainstorm, focus on goals, think creatively, and make sure everyone has power to invent solutions.

5. *Reach an integrative agreement.* Make sure both sets of goals are met. If all else fails, flip a coin, take turns, or call in a third party—a mediator.

CHECKPOINT

The Need for Communication

Review

▷ What is meant by "empathetic listening"?

▷ Distinguish among assertive, passive, and hostile response styles.

▷ What are some options for dealing with student-student and student-teacher conflicts?

Apply

▷ Describe how you might use Gordon's problem-solving approach to handle a classroom problem you have witnessed.

▷ How will you involve families in creating a learning community in your classroom?

In addition to learning conflict resolution, all students in Johnson and Johnson's study were trained in mediation strategies. The role of the mediator was rotated—every day the teacher chose two students to be the class mediators and to wear the mediators' T-shirts. Johnson and his colleagues found that students learned the conflict resolution and mediation strategies and used them successfully, both in school and at home, to handle conflicts in a more productive way. For details of the strategies, see Johnson and Johnson (1994), Miller, (1994), or Smith (1993).

Peer mediation has also been successful with older students and those with serious problems (Sanchez & Anderson, 1990). In one program, selected gang members were given mediation training, then all members were invited to participate voluntarily in the mediation process, supervised by school counsellors. Strict rules governed the process leading to written agreements signed by gang representatives. Sanchez and Anderson (1990) found that gang violence in the school was reduced to a bare minimum—"The magic of the mediation process was communication" (p. 56).

Respect and Protect. One system that has been developed to combat violence in the schools is Respect and Protect from the Johnson Institute, Minneapolis, Minnesota. The program is founded on five ideas: First, everyone is obliged to respect and protect the rights of others. Second, violence is not acceptable. Third, the program targets the violence-enabling behaviour of staff, students, and parents, such as denying, rationalizing, justifying, or blaming others for violence. Fourth, there is a clear definition of what constitutes violence that distinguishes two kinds of violence—bully/victim violence and violence that arises from normal conflicts. Finally, the program has both adult-centred prevention that improves the school climate and student-centred interventions that give students choices and clear consequences (Rembolt, 1998). Table 11.5 gives an overview of the levels of choices and consequences.

Connect & Extend
To the research
Johnson, D. W., Johnson, R., Dudley, B., Ward, M., & Magnuson, D. (1995). The impact of peer mediation training on the management of school and home conflicts. *American Educational Research Journal, 32,* 829–844.

Abstract
A peer mediation program in a midwestern, suburban US school was examined to determine the types of conflicts that occurred, the strategies students used to resolve their conflicts, and the types of resolutions in both school and home settings. The impact of the peer mediation program on the strategies used to manage conflicts and the resolutions of conflicts was also examined. A significant difference between the types of conflict occurring in the school and in the home was found. The training had significant impact on the strategies students used and the resulting resolutions.

TABLE 11.5 Respect and Protect

This table shows measured responses to each level of violence.

Overview of Choices, Consequences, and Contracts Intervention Process

Violence Level	Level One	Level Two	Level Three	Level Four	Level Five
Violation	Rule Violation (Minor infraction)	Misuse of Power (Repeat violation)	Abuse of Power (Serious)	Continued Abuse (Severe)	Pathology (Intractable)
Staff Action	Confront behaviour	Confront behaviour	Confront behaviour	Confront behaviour	Confront behaviour
	Stop violence	Stop violence	Stop violence	Stop violence	Stop violence
	Deal with problem	Refer to office	Refer to office	Refer to office	Refer to office
	File intervention report	File intervention report	File intervention report	File intervention report	File intervention report
	Review No Violence rule	Try to assess type of conflict	Try to assess type of conflict	Assess type of conflict	Follow psychosocial recommendations
	Suggest anger management, conflict resolution, peer mediation, or class meeting	Evaluate for talk with parent	Parent conference	Do psychosocial evaluation	Hold parent conference
			Suggest parenting program	Hold parent conference	Mandate parenting program
				Mandate parenting program	Suggest intensive therapy or treatment for student
				Suggest family counselling	
Student Consequences	Review of activity for violence	Office referral	Office referral	Office referral	Office referral
	Parent notified (optional)	Life Skills worksheet	Parent notified	Parent notified	Parent notified
	Restitution	Parent notified	Minimum time-out	Maximum time-out	Maximum time-out
	Legal action	Restricted until worksheet finished	Violence Group	Violence Group	Placement into an alternative setting
		Restitution	Anger management	Reconnections	Restitution
		Legal action	Connections	Restitution	Legal action
			Empowerment	Legal action	
			Restitution		
			Legal action		
Contracts*	Verbal Promise	Simple Contract	Turf Contract I	Turf Contract II	Bottom-Line Contract

Students are placed at Levels 1–5 depending on the frequency and severity of their violent behaviour. Students may stay at a particular level as the situation warrants. Any violent act that is racial, sexual, involves physical fighting, or is committed against staff results in the student being placed immediately at Level 3 or higher. The program manual provides lists of behaviours that correlate with each level of violence.

Source: From "Making Violence Unacceptable," by C. Rembolt, 1998, *Educational Leadership*, 56(1), p. 36. Copyright © 1998 by *Educational Leadership*. Adapted with permission.

*See source for a complete description on the different contracts.

FAMILY AND COMMUNITY PARTNERSHIPS

Classroom Management

Make sure families know the expectations and rules of your class and school.

Examples

1. At a Family Fun Night, have your students do skits showing the rules—how to follow them and what breaking them "looks like" and "sounds like."
2. Make a poster for the refrigerator at home that describes, in a light way, the most important rules and expectations.
3. For older students, give families a list of due dates for the major assignments, along with tips about how to encourage quality work by pacing the effort—avoiding last-minute panic.
4. Communicate in appropriate ways—use the family's first language when possible. Tailor messages to the reading level of the home.

Make families partners in recognizing good citizenship.

Examples

1. Send positive notes home when students, especially students who have had trouble with classroom management, work well in the classroom.
2. Give ideas for ways any family, even those with few economic resources, can celebrate accom-plishment—a favourite food; the chance to choose a video to rent; a comment to a special person such as an aunt, grandparent, or minis-ter; the chance to read to a younger sibling.

Identify talents in the community to help build a learning environment in your class.

Examples

1. Have students write letters to carpet and furni-ture stores asking for donations of remnants to carpet a reading corner.
2. Find family members who can build shelves or room dividers, paint, sew, laminate manipula-tives, write stories, repot plants, or network computers.
3. Contact businesses for donations of computers, printers, or other equipment.

Seek cooperation from families when behaviour problems arise.

Examples

1. Talk to families over the phone or in their home. Have good records about the problem behaviour.
2. Listen to family members and solve problems with them.

Communicating with Families about Classroom Management

As we have seen throughout this book, families are important partners in educa-tion. This statement applies to classroom management as well. When parents and teachers share the same expectations and support each other, they can create a more positive classroom environment and more time for learning. The Family and Community Partnerships Guidelines give ideas for working with families and the community.

$\mathcal{S}$ummary

The Need for Organization

What are the challenges of classroom management?

Classrooms are by nature multidimensional, full of simultaneous activities, fast-paced and immediate, unpredictable, public, and affected by the history of students' and teachers' actions. A manager must juggle all these elements every day. Productive classroom activity requires students' cooperation. Maintaining cooperation is different for each age group. Young students are learning how to "go to school" and need to learn the general procedures of school. Older students need to learn the specifics required for working in different subjects. Working with adolescents requires teachers to understand the power of the adolescent peer group.

What are the goals of good classroom management?

The goals of effective classroom management are to make ample time for learning; improve the quality of time use by keeping students actively engaged; make sure participation structures are clear, straightforward, and consistently signalled; and encourage student self-management, self-control, and responsibility.

Creating a Positive Learning Environment

Distinguish between rules and procedures.

The most effective teachers set rules and establish procedures for handling predictable problems. Rules are the specific dos and don'ts of classroom life. They usually are written down or posted. Procedures cover administrative tasks, student movement, housekeeping, routines for running lessons, interactions between students and teachers, and interactions among students. Rules can be written in terms of rights and students may benefit from participating in establishing these rules. Consequences should be established for following and breaking the rules and procedures so that the teacher and the students know what will happen.

Distinguish between personal territories and interest-area spatial arrangements.

There are two basic kinds of spatial organization, territorial (the traditional classroom arrangement) and functional (dividing space into interest or work areas). Flexibility is often the key. Important considerations in the teacher's choice of physical arrangements include access to materials; convenience; privacy when needed; ease of supervision; and a willingness to re-evaluate plans.

What do effective classroom managers do during the first week of school?

Effective classroom managers spent the first days of class teaching basic rules and procedures. Students were occupied with organized, enjoyable activities and learned to function cooperatively in the group. Quick, firm, clear, and consistent responses to infractions of the rules characterized effective teachers. Materials were set up. The teachers had planned carefully to avoid any last-minute tasks that might have taken them away from their students. These teachers dealt with the children's pressing concerns first. They had a workable, easily understood set of rules and taught the students the most important rules right away. They taught the rules like any other subject, with lots of explanation, examples, and practice.

Creating a Learning Community

What are Johnson and Johnson's three Cs of establishing a classroom community?

The three Cs are cooperative community, constructive conflict resolution, and civic values. Classroom management begins by establishing a community based on cooperative learning. At the heart of the community is the idea of positive interdependence—individuals working together to achieve mutual goals. Constructive conflict resolution is essential in the community because conflicts are inevitable and even necessary for learning. The last C is civic values—the understandings and beliefs that hold the community together. Values are learned through direct teaching, modelling, literature, group discussions, and the sharing of concerns.

Maintaining a Good Environment for Learning

How can teachers encourage engagement?

The format of a lesson affects student involvement. In general, as teacher supervision increases, students' engaged time also increases. When the task provides continuous cues for the student about what to do next, involvement will be greater. Activities with clear steps are likely to be more absorbing, because one step leads naturally to the next. Making work requirements clear and specific, providing needed materials, and monitoring activities all add to engagement.

How can teachers encourage motivation and thoughtful learning?

The influences on students' motivation to learn in a particular situation can be summarized in three questions: Can I succeed at this task? Do I want to succeed? What do I need to do to succeed? When students are confident they can succeed, they will approach learning with energy and enthusiasm. When they value tasks assigned, they work to learn, not to get the grade or get finished. As teachers, we should promote the belief that success will come to students who apply effective learning strategies, and discourage students' use of self-defeating, failure-avoiding, face-saving strategies. Finally, we should encourage students to persist when they are faced with challenging tasks, not to be afraid to make mistakes. In fact, we should encourage students to view errors as opportunities to learn.

Explain the factors identified by Kounin that prevent management problems in the classroom.

To create a positive environment and prevent problems, teachers must take individual differences into account, maintain student motivation, and reinforce positive behaviour. Successful problem preventers are skilled in four areas described by Kounin: "withitness," overlapping, group focusing, and movement management. When penalties have to be imposed, teachers should impose them calmly and privately.

Describe seven levels of intervention in misbehaviour.

Teachers can first make eye contact with the student or use other nonverbal signals, then try verbal hints such as simply inserting the student's name into the lecture. Next the teacher asks if the offender is aware of the negative effects of the actions, then reminds the student of the procedure and has her or him follow it correctly. If this does not work, the teacher can ask the student to state the correct rule or procedure and then to follow it, and then moves to telling the student in a clear, assertive, and unhostile way to stop the misbehaviour. If this fails too, the teacher can offer a choice—stop the behaviour or meet privately to work out the consequences.

The Need for Communication

What is meant by "empathetic listening"?

Communication between teacher and student is essential when problems arise. All interactions between people, even silence or neglect, communicate some meaning. Empathetic, active listening can be a helpful response when students bring problems to teachers. Teachers must reflect back to the students what they hear them saying. This reflection is more than a parroting of words; it should capture the emotions, intent, and meaning behind them.

Distinguish among assertive, passive, and hostile response styles.

The *passive style* can take several forms. Instead of telling the student directly what to do, the teacher simply comments on the behaviour, asks the student to *think about* the appropriate action, or threatens but never follows through. In a *hostile response style*, teachers may make "you" statements that condemn the student without stating clearly what the student should be doing. An *assertive response* communicates to the students that the teacher cares too much about them and the process of learning to allow inappropriate behaviour to persist. Assertive teachers clearly state what they expect.

What are some options for dealing with student-student and student-teacher conflict?

Students need guidance in resolving conflicts. Different strategies are useful, depending on whether the goal, the relationship, or both are important to those experiencing conflict. It can help to reverse roles and see the situation through the eyes of the other. In dealing with serious problems, prevention and peer mediation might be useful. No matter what the situation, the cooperation of families can help to create a positive learning environment in the classroom and school.

Key Terms

*B*ecoming a Professional

Reflecting on the Chapter

Can you apply the ideas from this chapter on creating learning environments to solve the following problems of practice?

Preschool and Kindergarten

▷ Your class is larger than ever this year, and it is very difficult to get everyone dressed for play outside. How would you handle the situation?

Elementary and Middle School

▷ It takes your class 15 minutes to settle down each morning and begin work. What would you do?

▷ A few students in your class always seem to be out of step with the rest of the class. They call out answers when they shouldn't, interrupt others, and get up and walk around when they should be seated and working. What would you do?

Junior High and High School

▷ You tell a student to put away a CD player, and she says, "Try and make me!" What would you do?

▷ One of your bright and able students has stopped doing homework. What would you do?

Check Your Understanding

▷ Be familiar with Kounin's terms of *withitness, overlapping activities, group focusing,* and *movement management.*

▷ Know the basic room arrangements of rows, circles, clusters, and horseshoes and the activities for which each is best suited.

▷ Understand a range of consequences for minor to major misbehaviour.

▷ Be familiar with alternatives for communicating with students, such as empathetic listening, "I" messages, and problem solving.

Your Teaching Portfolio

Think about your philosophy of teaching, a question you will be asked at most job interviews. What is your philosophy of classroom management? What rules will you set and how will you establish them? (Consult the Guidelines for ideas.)

Add some ideas for parent involvement from this chapter to your portfolio.

Teaching Resources

Adapt the rules on pages 409 and 410 for students you will teach.

Add the floor plans from Figures 11.2 and 11.3 to your teaching resources file.

Add Table 11.5 on graduated responses to school violence to your teaching resources file.

 **Weblinks**

http://ss.uno.edu/SS/homePages/CManage.html

At this site you'll find a variety of links expanding on topics of classroom management. Sites referenced here include "Solutions for Handling 117 discipline problems in the classroom" and "Tips for Using the Computer for Classroom Management."

http://education.indiana.edu/cas/tt/v1i2/table.html

This is a special issue of the online journal *Teacher Talk*, a publication for secondary teachers. It presents several approaches to classroom management.

www.ncsu.edu.cpsv/index.html

This Web site for the Center for the Prevention of School Violence provides a variety of links and information on this important topic.

What Would They Do?

Here is how two practising teachers responded to the teaching situation presented at the beginning of this chapter about bringing together a class with many conflicts and cliques.

VICKI DEN OUDEN

Learning Assistance Teacher
Surrey Christian School
Surrey, British Columbia

It is crucial to establish the right atmosphere in a classroom in order for successful learning to take place. Ideally, the students and teacher should feel mutual respect, trust, and acceptance. It is up to the teacher to develop this in her classroom. This can be done through carefully planned lessons and discussions. In this situation, since the teacher is already overwhelmed, she should team up with her colleagues and the school counsellor for some positive solutions.

One idea might be to teach a unit on multiculturalism, discrimination, or racism. Collaborative learning activities, peer teaching, and role playing should be included in the planning. This would allow the students to share their own views instead of feeling the teacher is just "preaching" at them. Of course, the teacher would need to carefully and sensitively guide the discussions. There are many excellent books and videos on these topics, some told from a teenager's point of view. The school librarian or school district resource centre can help locate such materials. The unit should culminate with a related project (e.g., posters, a play), thereby putting the words into action. Working together on a project can develop a sense of ownership, pride, and community among the students.

The student with cerebral palsy could participate fully in the activities with the help of his special education assistant, although some modifications to the assignments might be needed. The teacher should check his individualized education program (IEP) in this regard. If he is able or wishes to, the boy could eventually share his feelings about his disability or possible experiences of discrimination. (Taking his language/speech difficulties into consideration, the teacher may find the boy chooses to share his views through a poem or a computer journal.) This could occur only once an atmosphere of trust and caring had been established. The student would need to feel safe in sharing such personal feelings. Once this had been achieved, the sharing could be a tremendously unifying force for the class.

Clarise's emotional/behavioural problems require some individual attention outside of the class. The school counsellor or resource teacher would be instrumental in this. Direct instruction in social skills would be most beneficial.

Also, the potential risk to Clarise's safety would need to be addressed immediately. The principal or school counsellor could be consulted on procedures to deal with bullying and conflict resolution. In addition, the teacher should find out how Clarise gets home. If possible, the teacher could either accompany Clarise to the bus or ensure she had a ride home until this matter was resolved.

NELL CHOBOTAR

Shevchenko School
Vita, Manitoba

In order to become successful learners, students need to feel accepted, worthy, and safe in the classroom. At the beginning of the school year, it is imperative that teachers take the time to create a positive, non-threatening atmosphere. Considering the ever-increasing demands of the curriculum and society, this is a time-consuming task and can easily be overlooked as teachers respond to other demands.

Because "each of the four ethnic groups seems to stick together, never making friends with students from the 'outside,'" I would assume that they feel threatened by the unfamiliar and find security with their own kind. Perhaps their feelings of self-worth are not strong enough to risk mingling with outsiders. Obviously, the two new students with problems of their own will not feel readily accepted and may react, as Clarise did, to make the situation more tense.

Initially, I would introduce a theme relating to ethnic groups. I would allow each of the four groups to work cooperatively to prepare a mini "Folklorama" featuring music, dance, tapes, videos, oral presentations, and memorabilia to celebrate and share their cultures. They could invite their parents, grandparents, or members of their ethnic communities to help them prepare and present their projects. The celebration and sharing of their diverse backgrounds should enhance the students' feelings of self-worth and encourage respect for others. We would later discuss the injustices suffered by different groups in the past and present.

When the students had gained an understanding of discrimination and tolerance of others, I would continue to use cooperative grouping. However, the groups would now consist of students of mixed backgrounds, thus giving them an opportunity to mingle.

Before the arrival of the new students, the teacher should prepare the class to encourage acceptance and understanding. Perhaps a parent would be willing to speak to the class to discuss his or her child's particular needs and experiences. A wheelchair could be used to enable others to experience some of the difficulties faced by those who depend upon it.

Mainstreaming students with special needs is a challenge. However, with forethought and flexibility, it can be a rewarding and positive experience.

Teaching for Learning

*I*n the first chapter of this book we asked you to list the characteristics of those teachers you found truly outstanding. Consider what you now know about student learning and suggest why the teacher characteristics you listed might promote learning.

Much of this text has been about learning and learners, with most of Chapter 9 focused on student-centred teaching strategies. In this chapter we focus on teachers— their decisions, plans, knowledge, and actions. We look first at how teachers plan, including how to use taxonomies of learning objectives or themes as a basis for planning. With a sense of how to set goals and make plans, we move to a consideration of some general teacher-centred strategies: lecturing, seatwork, homework, questioning, recitation, and group discussion.

What else do we know about teachers? Are there particular characteristics that distinguish effective from ineffective teachers? Research on whole-class teaching points to the importance of several factors and we will explore them here. In addition, we encourage you to review strategies for meeting the diverse needs of learners in inclusive classrooms that we discussed in Chapter 4.

In the final section of this chapter, we will focus on successful teaching for different subjects—reading, writing, mathematics, and science. Educational psychologists have studied how people learn these subjects and identified implications for teaching.

By the time you have completed this chapter you should be able to:

- ▶ Write instructional objectives for your students using different taxonomies.
- ▶ Describe situations in which each of the following formats would be most appropriate: lecture, seatwork and homework, questioning, and group discussion.
- ▶ Describe a number of characteristics that effective teachers seem to share.
- ▶ List steps that can ensure clarity in presentation.
- ▶ Compare the teacher's role in direct and constructivist teaching strategies.
- ▶ Debate the merits of whole language, code-based, and balanced approaches to reading.

What Would You Do?

Your school district has adopted a whole language, integrated curriculum approach for Grades K through 6. Quite a bit of time and money was spent on workshops for teachers; buying big books and multiple copies of good children's literature; developing manipulatives for mathematics; building comfortable reading corners; making costumes, puppets, and other reading props; designing science projects; and generally supporting the innovations. Students and teachers are mostly pleased with the program. There seems to be more reading and more enjoyment of reading, at least for many children—but some students seem lost. The students' written work is longer and more creative. However, standardized tests indicate a drop in scores. The principal is clearly getting worried—this was her big project and she had to work hard to "sell it" to some members of the PTA and school board. Several parents of students in your class are complaining that they have had to hire tutors or buy commercial programs to teach their children to read.

▶ As a teacher, what would you do about the parents' complaints?

▶ Would you make any changes in your approach?

▶ What information would you need to make good decisions?

▶ Who should be involved in these decisions?

The First Step: Planning

When you thought about how to translate your principal's reading program into units and lessons for your students, you were planning. In the past few years, educational researchers have become very interested in teachers' planning. They have interviewed teachers about how they plan, asked teachers to "think out loud" while planning or to keep journals describing their plans, and even studied teachers intensively for months at a time. What have they found?

First, planning influences what students will learn, because planning transforms the available time and curriculum materials into activities, assignments, and tasks for students. When a teacher decides to devote 7 hours to language arts and 15 minutes to science in a given week, the students in that class will learn more language than science. In fact, differences as dramatic as this do occur. Nancy Karweit (1989) reported that in one school the time allocated to mathematics ranged from 2 hours and 50 minutes a week in one class to 5 hours and 55 minutes a week in a class down the hall (Clark & Peterson, 1986; Clark & Yinger, 1988; Doyle, 1983).

Second, teachers engage in several levels of planning—by the year, term, unit, week, and day. All the levels must be coordinated. Accomplishing the year's plan requires breaking the work into terms, the terms into units, and the units into weeks and days. Planning done at the beginning of the year is particularly important, because many routines and patterns are established early. For experienced teachers, unit planning seems to be the most important level, followed by weekly and then daily planning (Clark & Peterson, 1986; Clark & Yinger, 1988).

Third, plans reduce—but do not eliminate—uncertainty in teaching. Even the best plans cannot (and should not) control everything that happens in class—planning must allow flexibility (Calderhead, 1996). There is some evidence that when teachers "overplan"—fill every minute and stick to the plan no matter what—their students do not learn as much as students whose teachers are flexible (Shavelson, 1987). Chris Clark (1983) suggests that beginning teachers should think of their plans as "flexible frameworks for action, as devices for getting started in the right direction, as something to depart from or elaborate on, rather than as rigid scripts" (p. 13). So, don't proceed with a planned new unit if your in-class review shows that many students still don't understand the material in the current unit.

In order to plan creatively and flexibly, teachers need to have wide-ranging knowledge about students, their interests, and abilities; the subjects being taught; alternative ways to teach and assess understanding; working with groups; the expectations and limitations of the school and community; how to apply and adapt materials and texts; and how to pull all this knowledge together into meaningful activities. The plans of beginning teachers sometimes don't work because they lack knowledge about the students or the subject—they can't estimate how long it will take students to complete an activity, for example, or they stumble when asked for an explanation or a different example (Calderhead, 1996).

Finally, there is no one model for effective planning. For experienced teachers, planning is a creative problem-solving process (Shavelson, 1987). Experienced teachers know how to accomplish many lessons and segments of lessons. They know what to expect and how to proceed, so they don't necessarily continue to follow the detailed lesson-planning models they learned during their teacher-preparation programs. Planning is more informal—"in their heads." However, many experienced teachers think it was helpful to learn this detailed system as a foundation (Clark & Peterson, 1986).

No matter how you plan, you must have a learning goal in mind. In the next section we consider the range of goals that you might have for your students.

"AND THEN, OF COURSE, THERE'S THE POSSIBILITY OF BEING JUST THE SLIGHTEST BIT TOO ORGANIZED."

(By permission of Glen Dines. From Phi Delta Kappan.*)*

Objectives for Learning

We hear quite a bit today about visions, goals, outcomes, and standards. At a very general, abstract level are the grand goals society may have for graduates of public schools (e.g., that all graduates have effective communication and problem-solving skills). However, very general goals are meaningless as potential guidelines for instruction. Therefore, many provinces (e.g., British Columbia, Manitoba, Ontario) are developing standards that provide more specific descriptions of how students will demonstrate progress toward the attainment of grand goals (e.g., students will develop the concept of fractions, mixed numbers, and decimals and use

Connect & Extend
To your own philosophy
Cuban, L. (1990). Four stories about national goals for American education. *Phi Delta Kappan, 72*(4), 264–314. *Focus Question:* Often there is talk of creating a national agenda for education in Canada. Do you think we should have a national agenda that shapes our instructional objectives? What do you think the goals of that agenda should be?

◀ *Planning involves designating learning goals, making decisions about how to help students achieve them, and assessing their success. Tactics may or may not involve written tasks.*

Instructional Objectives: Clear statement of what students are intended to learn through instruction.

Behavioural Objectives: Instructional objectives stated in terms of observable behaviour.

Cognitive Objectives: Instructional objectives stated in terms of higher-level thinking operations.

Connect & Extend

To your own philosophy
What is your reaction to the following statement? "Behavioural objectives often may be appropriate for training (an end in itself) but seldom are appropriate for education (which is concerned with understanding)."

models to relate fractions to decimals and to find equivalent fractions). Sometimes the standards are turned into indicators such as "representing equivalent fractions." At this level, the indicators are close to being instructional objectives (Airasian, in press).

An **instructional objective** is a clear and unambiguous description of your educational intentions for your students. Norman Gronlund (2000) defines instructional objectives as "intended learning outcomes . . . the types of performance students are expected to demonstrate at the end of instruction to show that they have learned what was expected of them" (p. 4). Although there are many different approaches to writing objectives, each assumes that the first step in teaching is to decide what changes should take place in the learner—what is the goal of teaching. Objectives written by people with behavioural views focus on observable and measurable changes in the learner. **Behavioural objectives** use terms such as *list*, *define*, *add*, or *calculate*. **Cognitive objectives**, on the other hand, emphasize thinking and comprehension, so they are more likely to include words such as *understand*, *recognize*, *create*, or *apply*. Let's look at one well-developed method of writing specific objectives.

Mager: Start with the Specific. Robert Mager has developed a very influential system for writing instructional objectives. Mager's idea is that objectives ought to describe what students will be doing when demonstrating their achievement and how you will know they are doing it (Mager, 1975). Mager's objectives are generally regarded as *behavioural*. According to Mager, a good objective has three parts. First, it describes the intended student behaviour—what must the student do? Second, it lists the conditions under which the behaviour will occur—how will this behaviour be recognized or tested? Third, it gives the criteria for acceptable performance on the test. Figure 12.1 shows how the system works. This system, with its emphasis on final behaviour, requires a very explicit statement. Mager contends that often students can teach themselves if they are given well-stated objectives.

FIGURE 12.1

Mager's Three-Part System

Robert Mager believes that a good learning objective has three parts: the student behaviour, the conditions under which the behaviour will be performed, and the criteria for judging a performance.

Part	Central Question	Example
Student behaviour	Do what?	Mark statements with an *F* for fact or an *O* for opinion
Conditions of performance	Under what conditions?	Given an article from a newspaper
Performance criteria	How well?	75 percent of the statements are correctly marked

Source: From R. F. Mager, *Preparing Instructional Objectives*, 1975, Fearon, Belmont, CA. Reprinted by permission of David S. Lake Publishers.

TABLE 12.1 Gronlund's Combined Method for Creating Objectives

General Objective

For sixth grade mathematics: Student can efficiently solve real-life problems that require finding sizes of surface areas.

Specific Examples

1. Discriminates between the surface area of a figure and other quantitative characteristics of that figure (e.g., height and volume).
2. States the formula for the area of a rectangle.
3. Given the dimensions of a rectangle, computes its area.
4. Given the dimensions of a right triangle, computes its area.
5. Given the dimensions of a right cylinder, computes its surface area.
6. When confronted with a real-life problem, determines whether computing the area of a surface will help solve that problem.

Source: From *Designing Tests for Evaluating Student Achievement* by James S. Cangelosi, p. 6. Copyright © 1990. Adapted by permission of Addison-Wesley Educational Publishers, Inc.

Gronlund: Start with the General. Norman Gronlund (2000) offers a different approach, often used for writing cognitive objectives. He believes that an objective should be stated first in general terms (*understand*, *solve*, *appreciate*, etc.). Then the teacher should clarify by listing sample examples of behaviour that would provide evidence that the student has attained the objective. Look at the example in Table 12.1. The goal here really is presenting and defending a research project. The teacher does not want the student to stop with describing, summarizing, answering questions, and so on. Instead, the teacher looks at performance on these sample tasks to decide if the student can effectively present and defend. The teacher could just as well have chosen six different indicators.

Gronlund's emphasis on specific objectives as samples of more general student ability is important. A teacher could never list all the behaviour that might be involved in solving problems in the subject area, but stating an initial, general objective makes it clear that the ability to solve problems is the purpose. The most recent research on instructional objectives tends to favour approaches similar to Gronlund's. It seems reasonable to state a few central objectives in general terms and clarify them with samples of specific behaviour, as in Table 12.1 (Hamilton, 1985; Popham, 1993).

Are Objectives Useful? Providing objectives for students can promote learning with loosely organized and less-structured activities such as lectures, films, and research projects. If the importance of some information is not clear from the learning materials and activities themselves, instructional objectives will probably help focus students' attention and thus increase achievement (Duchastel, 1979). But when the task involves simply getting the gist of the passage or transferring the information to a new situation, it is better to use questions that focus on meaning, inserting the questions right before the passage to be read (Hamilton, 1985).

If the objectives are supplied in advance—and especially if students have a role in designing objectives—both students and teachers will know what the performance

Connect & Extend
To your own philosophy
Do you think behavioural objectives are really objectives in themselves, or are they a "means to an end"?

GUIDELINES

Using Instructional Objectives

Avoid "word magic"—phrases that sound noble and important but say very little, such as, "Students will become deep thinkers."

Examples

1. Keep the focus on specific changes that will take place in the students' knowledge of skills.
2. Ask students to explain the meaning of the objectives. If they can't give specific examples of what you mean, the objectives are not communicating your intentions to your students.

Suit the activities to the objectives.

Examples

1. If the goal is the memorization of vocabulary, give the students memory aids and practice exercises.

2. If the goal is the ability to develop well-thought-out positions, consider position papers, debates, projects, or mock trials.
3. If you want students to become better writers, give many opportunities for writing and rewriting.

Make sure your tests are related to your objectives.

Examples

1. Write objectives and rough drafts for tests at the same time—revise these drafts of tests as the units unfold and objectives change.
2. Weight the tests according to the importance of the various objectives and the time spent on each.

criteria are. In thinking about objectives, both teachers and students must consider what is important, what is worth learning. We have found that teachers who have clear, appropriate goals for each student often are successful in helping the students learn. Finally, many school districts still require teachers to complete lesson plans that include learning objectives. The Guidelines on instructional objectives should help you whether you decide to make thorough use of objectives or simply prepare them for certain assignments.

Flexible and Creative Plans—Using Taxonomies

Several decades ago, a group of educational evaluation experts led by Benjamin Bloom set out to improve college and university examinations. The impact of their work has touched education at all levels around the world (Anderson & Sosniak, 1994). Bloom and his colleagues developed a **taxonomy**, or classification system, of educational objectives. Objectives were divided into three domains: cognitive, affective, and psychomotor. A handbook describing the objectives in each area was eventually published. In real life, of course, behaviour from these three domains occurs simultaneously. While students are writing (psychomotor), they are also remembering or reasoning (cognitive), and they are likely to have some emotional response to the task as well (affective).

The Cognitive Domain. Six basic objectives are listed in Bloom's taxonomy of the thinking or **cognitive domain** (Bloom, Engelhart, Frost, Hill, & Krathwohl, 1956):

1. *Knowledge:* Remembering or recognizing something without necessarily understanding, using, or changing it.

2. *Comprehension:* Understanding the material being communicated without necessarily relating it to anything else.

3. *Application:* Using a general concept to solve a particular problem.

Taxonomy: Classification system.

Cognitive Domain: In Bloom's taxonomy, memory and reasoning objectives.

4. *Analysis:* Breaking something down into its parts.

5. *Synthesis:* Creating something new by combining different ideas.

6. *Evaluation:* Judging the value of materials or methods as they might be applied in a particular situation.

It is common in education to consider these objectives as a hierarchy, each skill building on those below, but this is not entirely accurate (Seddon, 1978). Some subjects, such as mathematics, do not fit this structure very well (Kreitzer & Madaus, 1994). Still, you will hear many references to *lower-level* and *higher-level objectives,* with knowledge, comprehension, and application considered lower level and the other categories considered higher level. As a rough way of thinking about objectives, this can be helpful (Gronlund, 2000).

The taxonomy of objectives can also be helpful in planning assessments because different procedures are appropriate for objectives at the various levels. Gronlund (2000) suggests that factual knowledge objectives can best be measured by true/false, short-answer, matching, or multiple-choice tests. Such tests will also work with the comprehension, application, and analysis levels of the taxonomy. For measuring synthesis and evaluation objectives, however, essays, reports, projects, and portfolios are more appropriate. Essay tests will also work at the middle levels of the taxonomy.

Bloom 2001. Bloom's taxonomy guided educators for more than 40 years. It is considered one of the most significant educational writings of the twentieth century (Anderson & Sosniak, 1994). In 1995, a group of educational researchers met to discuss revising the taxonomy (Anderson & Krathwohl, 2001). The taxonomy revisers retained the six basic levels, but they altered the order slightly and changed the names of three to indicate the cognitive processes involved. The six cognitive processes are remembering (knowledge), understanding (comprehension), applying, analyzing, evaluating, and creating (synthesizing). In addition, the revisers have added a new dimension to the taxonomy to recognize that cognitive processes must process something—you have to remember or understand or apply some form of knowledge. If you look at Table 12.2 on page 452 you will see the result. We now have six processes or verbs—the cognitive acts of remembering, understanding, applying, analyzing, evaluating, and creating. These processes act on four kinds of knowledge—factual, conceptual, procedural, and metacognitive.

Consider how this revised taxonomy might suggest objectives for a social studies/language arts class. An objective that targets *analysis of conceptual knowledge* is:

After reading an historical account of the framing of Canada's Constitution, students will be able to recognize the author's point of view or bias.

An objective for evaluating metacognitive knowledge might be:

Students will reflect on their strategies for identifying the biases of the author.

The Affective Domain. The objectives in the taxonomy of the **affective domain,** or domain of emotional response, range from least committed to most committed (Krathwohl, Bloom, & Masia, 1964). At the lowest level, a student would simply pay attention to a certain idea. At the highest level, the student would adopt an idea or a value and act consistently with that idea. There are five basic objectives in the affective domain.

1. *Receiving:* Being aware of or attending to something in the environment. This is the "I'll-listen-to-the-concert-but-I-won't-promise-to-like-it level."

2. *Responding:* Showing some new behaviour as a result of experience. At this level a person might applaud after the concert or hum some of the music the next day.

Affective Domain: Objectives focusing on attitudes and feelings.

student behaviour and skills as objectives, the teacher has overarching goals—"big ideas"—that guide planning. These goals are understandings or abilities that the teacher returns to again and again.

An Example of Constructivist Planning. Vito Perrone (1994) has these goals for his secondary history students. He wants his students to be able to:

▶ use primary sources, formulate hypotheses, and engage in systematic study;

▶ handle multiple points of view;

▶ be close readers and active writers; and

▶ pose and solve problems.

The next step in the planning process is to create a learning environment that allows students to move toward these goals in ways that respect their individual interests and abilities. Perrone (1994) suggests identifying "those ideas, themes, and issues that provide the depth and variety of perspective that help students develop significant understandings" (p. 12). For a secondary history course, a theme might be "democracy and revolution" or "fairness concerning land claims." A theme in math or music might be "patterns"; in literature, "personal identity." Perrone suggests mapping the topic as a way of thinking about how the theme can generate learning and understanding. An example of a topic map, using the theme of ecology, is shown in Figure 12.2 on page 455.

With this topic map as a guide, teacher and students can work together to identify activities, materials, projects, and performances that will support the development of the students' understanding and abilities—the overarching goals of the class. The teacher spends less time planning specific presentations and assignments and more time gathering a variety of resources and facilitating students' learning. The focus is not so much on students' products as on the processes of learning and the thinking behind the products.

Integrated and Thematic Plans. The planning map shows a way to use the theme of ecology to integrate issues in a science class. Today, teaching with themes and integrated content are major elements in planning and designing lessons and units, from kindergarten (Roskos & Neuman, 1995) through high school (Clarke & Agne, 1997). For example, middle school teachers Elaine Homestead and Karen McGinnis and college professor Elizabeth Pate (1995) designed a unit on "Human Interactions" that included studying racism, world hunger, pollution, and air and water quality. Students researched issues by reading textbooks and outside sources, learning to use databases, interviewing local officials, and inviting guest speakers into class. Students had to develop knowledge in science, mathematics, and social studies. They learned to write and speak persuasively, and in the process raised money for hunger relief in Africa.

Elementary-age students can benefit from integrated planning too. There is no reason to work on spelling skills, then listening skills, then writing skills, and then social studies or science. All these abilities can be developed together if students work to solve authentic problems. Some ideas for integrating themes with younger children are people, pets, gardens as habitats, communities, and patterns. Possibilities for older children are given in Table 12.4.

Assessment. Assessment plans differ within a constructivist classroom. Assessment is ongoing as teachers and students comment on each other's efforts. Authentic assessment in the form of exhibitions, portfolios of work, and performances (described in Chapter 14) substitutes for traditional testing. But perhaps most important, teachers and students share the authority to evaluate work. The students have a responsibility to assess their own and each other's thinking, explanations, and performances. The teachers give up control of "correctness" in the classroom and instead ask students, "Does that explanation make sense?" "Does it work to solve the problem?" "Can you improve it?" "Do you agree?" "Why?"

"NOW THAT YOU'RE ALL PRESENT AND ACCOUNTED FOR, I'LL BEGIN TODAY'S LECTURE."

(*By permission of Doug Redfern— From* Phi Delta Kappan.)

FIGURE 12.2

Planning with a Topic Map

With this map of the topic "ecology," a Grade 6 teacher can identify themes, issues, and ideas for study. Rather than "cover" the whole map, the teacher can examine a few areas in depth.

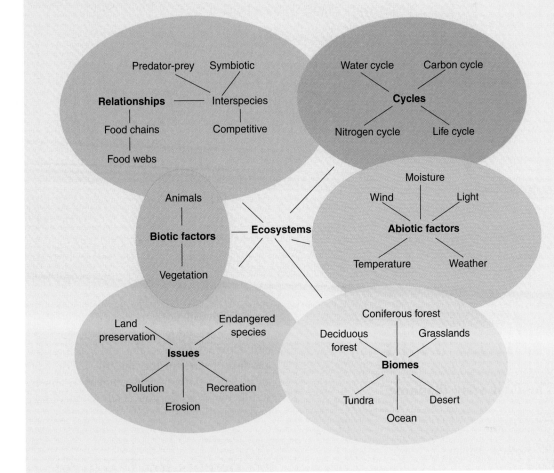

Students learn that self-assessment, judgment, and reflection are important parts of learning. Table 12.5 is a checklist that can be used to plan assessment in teaching with themes.

Let's assume you and your students have valuable and interesting plans and learning objectives as well as some appropriate ways to assess learning. What

TABLE 12.4 Some Themes for Integrated Planning for Older Children

General Systems Theory	Graphical Representations of Patterns
The Politics of Biology	Field-Based Research
Cause and Effect	Probability and Prediction
Levels of Analysis	Diversity and Variation
Conditional and Enabling Relations	Stewardship
Darwinism	Conservation of Energy and Matter

TABLE 12.5 A Checklist to Guide Assessment in Teaching with Themes

You may want to use this checklist as one of your bases of evaluation for the children's discussions, writing, and projects.

_____ Displays knowledge of content

_____ Uses theme vocabulary

_____ Understands relationships explored in theme

_____ Notes the details of the theme information

_____ Classifies and categorizes theme information

_____ Compares and contrasts books in theme

_____ Assimilates and displays knowledge of books' relationships to theme

_____ Listens to discussions and responds accordingly

_____ Recognizes different curriculum areas explored in theme

_____ Is able to work in groups and individually on activities

_____ Clarifies theme information

_____ Completes projects on a timely basis

_____ Expands theme reading independently

Source: From *Teaching with Themes* by Gare Thompson, p. 176. Copyright © 1991 by Scholastic Inc. Reprinted by permission of Scholastic Inc.

CHECKPOINT

The First Step: Planning

Review

▶ What are the levels of planning and how do they affect teaching?

▶ What is an instructional objective?

▶ Describe the three taxonomies of educational objectives.

▶ Describe teacher-centred and student-centred planning.

Apply

▶ Identify a cognitive, affective, and psychomotor objective for yourself for this week.

▶ Name a theme that could organize your planning for a grade you might teach.

next? You still need to decide what's happening on Monday. You need to design tasks and activities for teaching and learning that are appropriate for the objectives. You have an idea of *what* you want students to understand, but *how* do you teach to encourage understanding?

Formats for Teaching: Teacher Directed

This section describes a variety of general teaching strategies or formats for turning objectives into action in the classroom. These strategies are not complete models of teaching, but rather building blocks that can be used to construct lessons and units. We begin with the strategy many people associate most directly with teaching: lecturing.

Lecturing and Explaining

Some studies have found that teachers' presentations take up one-sixth to one-fourth of all classroom time. High school teachers, of course, lecture more than teachers in the lower grades. You will probably learn about how to lecture in your methods classes. Many different approaches are available, and the one you choose will depend on your objectives and the

TABLE 12.6 Three Phases in the Lecture Method

Lecturing: Organized explanation of a topic by a teacher.

Entry: Preparation for Learning

A. State objectives and rationale.

B. Provide a context for the new material to be presented.

C. Focus attention on key concept, generalization, or principle that encompasses the lecture.

Presentation

A. Sequence content from simpler to complex understandings.

B. Enhance presentation with visual aids.

C. Stimulate attention with verbal and non-verbal behaviour.

Closure: Review of Learning

A. Integrate with students' knowledge and experiences.

B. Transition to next lesson or activity.

Source: From *Dynamics of Effective Teaching, 2/e,* by Richard Kindsvatter, William Wilen, and Margaret Ishler, p. 221. Copyright © 1988 and 1992. Reprinted with permission of Addison-Wesley Educational Publishers, Inc.

subject you are teaching. You will certainly want to keep in mind the age of your students, because the younger your students, the briefer and simpler your explanations should be. You may also want to follow a basic three-part format suggested by Kindsvatter, Wilen, and Ishler (1992), shown in Table 12.6.

Lecturing is appropriate for communicating a large amount of material to many students in a short period of time. The teacher can integrate information from many sources in less time than it would take for students to integrate all the information themselves. Lecturing is a good method for introducing a new topic, giving background information, and motivating students to learn more on their own. Lecturing also helps students learn to listen accurately and critically and gives the teacher a chance to make on-the-spot changes to help students understand when they are confused (Gilstrap & Martin, 1975; Kindsvatter, Wilen, & Ishler, 1988). Lectures are therefore most appropriate for cognitive and affective objectives at the lower levels of the taxonomies described earlier: for knowledge, comprehension, application, receiving, responding, and valuing.

Scripted cooperation, described in Chapter 9, is one way of incorporating active learning into lectures. Several times during the presentation, the teacher asks students to work in pairs. One person is the summarizer and the other critiques the summary. This gives students a chance to check their understanding, organize their thinking, and translate ideas into their own words. Other possibilities are described in Table 12.7.

The lecture method also has disadvantages. You may find that some students have trouble listening for more than a few minutes at a time and that they simply tune you out. Lecturing puts the students in a passive position. It does much of the cognitive work for the students and may prevent them from asking or thinking of questions. Also, students learn and comprehend at different paces, whereas a lecture proceeds at the lecturer's own pace (Freiberg & Driscoll, 1996; Gilstrap & Martin, 1975). If your objectives include having students solve a problem; develop arguments; write essays, poems, or short stories; create paintings; or evaluate work, then you must go beyond lecturing to methods that require more active student involvement.

TABLE 12.7 Active Learning and Teacher Presentations

Here are some ideas for keeping students cognitively engaged in lessons. They can be adapted for many ages.

Question, All Write: Pose a question, ask everyone to jot an answer, then ask, "How many students would be willing to share their thoughts?"

Outcome Sentences: After a segment of presentation, ask students to finish sentences such as "I learned . . . ," "I'm beginning to wonder . . . ," "I was surprised. . . ." Share as above. Students may keep their outcome sentences in a learning log or portfolio.

Underexplain with Learning Pairs: Give a brief explanation, then ask students to work in pairs to figure out the process or idea.

Voting: Ask "How many of you . . . " questions and take a count. "How many of you agree with Raschon?" "How many of you are ready to move on?" "How many of you got 48 on this problem?"

Choral Response: Have the whole class restate in unison important facts and ideas, such as "The environment is one whole system" or "A 10-sided polygon is called a decagon."

Speak-Write: Tell students you will speak briefly, for three or four minutes. They are to listen, but not take notes. At the end of the time, ask them to write the main ideas, a summary, or questions they have about what you said.

Source: Adapted from M. Harmin (1994). *Inspiring Active Learning: A Handbook for Teachers.* Alexandria, VA: Association for Supervision and Curriculum Development.

Seatwork and Homework

In Vancouver, some parents are pressing the school board to designate one school as a "traditional" school that will, among other things, emphasize structured seatwork and increase homework (Mickleburgh, 1999). There is little research on the effects of **seatwork**, or independent classroom-desk work, but it is clear that this technique is often overused. In fact, a study found that American elementary students spend 51 percent of mathematics time in school working alone, while Japanese students spend 26 percent and Taiwanese students spend only 9 percent (Stigler, Lee, & Stevenson, 1987). Some educators point to these differences as part of the explanation for Asian students' superiority in mathematics. Seatwork should follow up a lesson and give students supervised practice. It should not be the main mode of instruction.

Making Seatwork and Homework Valuable. There is recent evidence that students who do more homework (and watch less television after school) have higher grades, even when other factors such as gender, grade level, ethnicity, SES, and amount of adult supervision are taken into consideration (Cooper, Valentine, Nye, & Lindsay, 1999). But just assigning more homework is not necessarily a good idea. The homework must be meaningful extensions of class lessons, not just busywork. The primary focus should be review and practice, not exposure to new material. Unfortunately, many workbook pages do little to support the learning of important objectives. Before you assign work, ask yourself, "Does doing this work help students learn anything that matters?" For example, consider this task, cited in the report of the Commission on Reading of the National Institute of Education (Anderson, Hiebert, Scott, & Wilkinson, 1985):

> Read each sentence. Decide which consonant letter is used the most.
> Underline it each time.

What's the point? This sort of activity communicates to students that reading isn't very important or useful. Students should see the connection between the

▲ *Individualized instruction does not necessarily mean students working alone; it refers to the idea of tailoring the pace, learning objectives, level, and assessment approach so that each individual student benefits.*

seatwork or homework and the lesson. Tell them why they are doing the work. The objectives should be clear, all the materials that might be needed should be provided, and the work should be easy enough that students can succeed on their own. Success rates should be high—near 100 percent. When seatwork is too difficult, students often resort to guessing or copying just to finish (Anderson, 1985).

Carol Weinstein and Andy Mignano (1997) describe several alternatives to workbooks, such as reading silently and reading aloud to a partner; writing for a "real" audience; writing letters or journals; transcribing conversations and punctuating them properly; making up problems; working on long-term projects and reports; solving brain teasers and puzzles; and engaging in computer activities. One of our favourites is creating a group story. Two students begin a story on the computer. Then two more add a paragraph. The story grows with each new pair's addition. The students are reading and writing, editing and improving.

Staying Engaged. To benefit from individual or group seatwork or homework, students must stay involved and do the work. The first step toward involvement is getting students started correctly by making sure they understand the assignment. It may help to do the first few questions as a class, to clear up any misconceptions. This is especially important for homework assignments, because students may have no one at home to consult if they have problems with the assignment. A second way to keep students involved is to hold them accountable for completing the work correctly, not just for filling in the page. This means the work should be checked, the students given a chance to correct the errors or revise work, and the results counted toward the class grade (Brophy & Good, 1986). Expert teachers often have ways of correcting homework quickly during the first minutes of class by having students check each other's or their own work.

Seatwork particularly requires careful monitoring. Being available to students doing seatwork is more effective than offering students help before they ask for it. To be available, you should move around the class and avoid spending too much time with one or two students. Short, frequent contacts are best (Brophy & Good, 1986; Rosenshine, 1977).

Sometimes you may be working with a small group while other students do seatwork. In these situations it is especially important for students to know what to do if they need help. One expert teacher described by Weinstein and Mignano (1997) taught students a rule, "Ask three, then me." Students have to consult three classmates before seeking help from the teacher. This teacher also spends time early in the year showing students *how* to help each other—how to ask questions and how to explain.

What about monitoring homework? If students get stuck on homework, they need help at home, someone who can scaffold their work without just "giving the answer" (Pressley, 1995). But many parents don't know how to help (Hoover-Dempsey, Bassler, & Burow, 1995). The Family and Community Partnerships Guidelines give ideas for helping parents help with homework.

Recitation and Questioning

Recitation is a common approach to teaching that has been with us for many years (Stodolsky, 1988). The teacher poses questions; students answer. The teacher's questions generally follow some sort of plan to develop a framework for the subject matter involved. The students' answers are often followed by reactions from the teacher, such as praise, correction, or requests for further information. The pattern from the teacher's point of view consists of *structure* (setting a framework), *solicitation* (asking questions), and *reaction* (praising, correcting, and expanding) (Clark, Gage, Marx, Peterson, Staybrook, Winne, 1979). These steps are repeated over and over.

Let us consider the heart of recitation, the soliciting or *questioning* phase, by looking at the different kinds of questions, when to ask them, and how to respond

Recitation: Format of teacher questioning, student response, and teacher feedback.

FAMILY AND COMMUNITY PARTNERSHIPS

Homework

Make sure families know what students are expected to learn.

Examples

1. At the beginning of a unit, send home a list of the main objectives, examples of major assignments, key due dates, homework "calendar," and a list of resources available free at libraries or on the Internet.
2. Provide a clear, concise description of your homework policy—how homework is counted toward class grades; consequences for late, forgotten, or missing homework; etc.

Help families find a comfortable and helpful role in their child's homework.

Examples

1. Remind families that "helping with homework" means encouraging, listening, monitoring, praising, discussing, brainstorming—not necessarily teaching and never doing the work for their child.
2. Encourage families to set aside a quiet time and place for everyone in the family to study. Make this time a regular part of the daily routine.
3. Have some homework assignments that are fun and involve the whole family—puzzles, family albums, watching a television program together and doing a "review."
4. At parent-teacher conferences, ask families what they need to play a more helpful role in their child's homework.

Solicit and use suggestions from families about homework.

Examples

1. Find out what responsibilities the child has at home—how much time is available for homework.
2. Periodically, have a "homework hotline" for call-in questions and suggestions.

If no one is at home to help with homework, set up other support systems.

Examples

1. Assign study buddies who can be available over the phone.
2. If students have computers, provide lists of Internet help lines.
3. Locate free help in public libraries and make these resources known.

---

to student answers. Of course, an important goal of teaching should be to encourage students to ask questions, but for now we will focus on teachers' questions, to make them as helpful as possible for students. Many beginning teachers are surprised to discover how valuable good questions can be and how difficult they are to create.

Kinds of Questions. Some educators have estimated that high school teachers ask an average of 395 questions per day (Gall, 1970). What are these questions like? Many can be categorized in terms of Bloom's taxonomy of objectives in the cognitive domain. Table 12.8 offers examples of questions at the different taxonomic levels.

Another way to categorize questioning is in terms of **convergent questions** (only one right answer) or **divergent questions** (many possible answers). Questions about concrete facts are convergent: "Who ruled England in 1540?" "Who wrote the original *Peter Pan*?" Questions dealing with opinions or hypotheses are divergent: "In this story, which character is most like you and why?" "In 100 years, which of the past five prime ministers will be most admired?"

Quite a bit of space in education textbooks has been devoted to urging teachers to ask a greater number of higher-level (analysis, synthesis, and evaluation) and divergent questions. Is this really a better way of questioning? Research has provided several surprises.

Convergent Questions: Questions that have a single correct answer.

Divergent Questions: Questions that have no single correct answer.

TABLE 12.8 Classroom Questions for Objectives in the Cognitive Domain

Questions can be posed that encourage thinking at every level of Bloom's taxonomy in the cognitive domain. Of course, the thinking required depends on what has gone before in the discussion.

Category	Type of Thinking Expected	Examples
Knowledge (recognition)	Recalling or recognizing information as learned	Define . . . What is the capital of . . . ? What did the text say about . . . ?
Comprehension	Demonstrating understanding of the materials; transforming, reorganizing, or interpreting	Explain in your own words . . . Compare . . . What is the main idea of . . . ? Describe what you saw . . .
Application	Using information to solve a problem with a single correct answer	Which principle is demonstrated in . . . ? Calculate the area of . . . Apply the rule of . . . to solve . . .
Analysis	Critical thinking; identifying reasons and motives; making inferences based on specific data; analyzing conclusions to see if supported by evidence	What influenced the writings of . . . ? Why was Ottawa chosen . . . ? Which of the following are facts and which are opinions . . . ? Based on your experiment, what is the chemical . . . ?
Synthesis	Divergent, original thinking; original plan, proposal, design, or story	What's a good name for . . . ? How could we raise money for . . . ? What would Canada be like if the New Democratic Party had been the official opposition instead of the Reform Party. . . ?
Evaluation	Judging the merits of ideas, offering opinions, applying standards	Which prime minister was the most effective? Which painting do you believe to be better? Why? Why would you favour . . . ?

Source: Adapted by permission of D. C. Heath from M. Sadker and D. Sadker (1986), "Questioning skills." In J. Cooper (Ed.), *Classroom Teaching Skills: A Handbook,* 3/e, pp. 143–160.

Fitting the Questions to the Students. Both high- and low-level questions can be effective (Gall, 1984; Redfield & Rousseau, 1981), although whether a question is actually high- or low-level depends on the student's knowledge (Winne, 1979). Different patterns seem to be better for different students, however. The best pattern for younger students and for lower-ability students of all ages is simple questions that allow a high percentage of correct answers, ample encouragement, help when the student does not have the correct answer, and praise. For high-ability students, the successful pattern includes harder questions at both higher and lower levels and more critical feedback (Berliner, 1987; Good, 1988).

Whatever their age or ability, all students should have some experience with thought-provoking questions and, if necessary, help in learning how to answer them. As we saw in Chapter 8, to master critical thinking and problem-solving skills, students must have a chance to practise the skills. They also need time to think about their answers. But research shows that teachers wait an average of only one second for students to answer (Rowe, 1974). Consider the following slice of classroom life (Sadker & Sadker, 1986a, p. 170):

Teacher: Who wrote the poem "Stopping by Woods on a Snowy Evening"? Tom?

Tom: Robert Frost.

Teacher:	Good. What action takes place in the poem? Sally?
Sally:	A man stops his sleigh to watch the woods get filled with snow.
Teacher:	Yes. Emma, what thoughts go through the man's mind?
Emma:	He thinks how beautiful the woods are . . . (She pauses for a second.)
Teacher:	What else does he think about? Joe?
Joe:	He thinks how he would like to stay and watch. (Pauses for a second.)
Teacher:	Yes—and what else? Rita? (Waits half a second.) Come on, Rita, you can get the answer to this. (Waits half a second.) Well, why does he feel he can't stay there indefinitely and watch the woods and the snow?
Sarah:	Well, I think it might be—(Pauses a second.)
Teacher:	Think, Sarah. (Teacher waits for half a second.) All right then—Mike? (Waits again for half a second.) John? (Waits half a second.) What's the matter with everyone today? Didn't you do the reading?

Very little thoughtful responding can take place in this situation. When teachers learn to pose a question, then wait at least three to five seconds before calling on a student to answer, students tend to give longer answers; more students are likely to participate, ask questions, and volunteer appropriate answers; student comments involving analysis, synthesis, inference, and speculation tend to increase; and the students generally appear more confident in their answers (Berliner, 1987; Rowe, 1974; Sadker & Sadker, 1986a; Tobin, 1987). This seems like a simple improvement in teaching, but five seconds of silence is not that easy to handle. It takes practice. You might try asking students to jot down ideas or even discuss the question with another student and formulate an answer together. This makes the wait more comfortable and gives students a chance to think. Of course, if it is clear that students are lost or don't understand the question, waiting longer will not help. When your question is met with blank stares, rephrase the question or ask if anyone can explain the confusion. Another qualification—there is some evidence that extending wait times does not affect learning in university classes (Duell, 1994), so with advanced high school students, you might conduct your own evaluation of wait time.

A word about selecting students to answer questions. If you call only on volunteers, you may get the wrong idea about how well students understand the material. Also, the same people volunteer over and over again. Many expert teachers have some systematic way of making sure that they call on everyone: They pull names from a jar or check names off a list as each student speaks (Weinstein, 1996; Weinstein & Mignano, 1997). Another possibility is to put each student's name on an index card, then shuffle the cards and go through the deck as you call on people. You can use the card to make notes about students' answers or extra help they may need.

Responding to Student Answers. What do you do after the student answers? The most common response, occurring about 50 percent of the time in most classrooms, is simple acceptance—"OK" or "Uh-huh" (Sadker & Sadker, 1986a). But there are better reactions, depending on whether the student's answer is correct, partly correct, or wrong. If the answer is quick, firm, and correct, simply accept the answer or ask another question. If the answer is correct but hesitant, give the student feedback about why the answer is correct: "That's right, Chris, the Senate is part of the legislative branch of government because the Senate. . . ." This allows you to explain the material again. If this student is unsure, others may be confused as well. If the answer is partially or completely wrong but the student has made an honest attempt, you should probe for more information, give clues, simplify the question, review the previous steps, or reteach the material. If the student's wrong answer is silly or careless, however, it is better simply to correct the answer and go on (Good, 1988; Rosenshine & Stevens, 1986).

Group Discussion

Group Discussion:
Conversation in which the teacher does not have the dominant role; students pose and answer their own questions.

Group discussion is in some ways similar to the recitation strategy described in the previous section, but should be more like the instructional conversations described in Chapter 9 (Tharp & Gallimore, 1991). A teacher may pose questions, listen to student answers, react, and probe for more information, but in a true group discussion, the teacher does not have a dominant role. Students ask questions, answer each other's questions, and respond to each other's answers (Beck, McKeown, Worthy, Sandora, & Kucan, 1996).

There are many advantages to group discussions. The students are directly involved and have the chance to participate. Group discussion helps students learn to express themselves clearly, to justify opinions, and to tolerate different views. Group discussion also gives students a chance to ask for clarification, examine their own thinking, follow personal interests, and assume responsibility by taking leadership roles in the group. Thus, group discussions help students evaluate ideas and synthesize personal viewpoints. Discussions are also useful when students are trying to understand difficult concepts that go against common sense. As we saw in Chapters 8 and 9, many scientific concepts, such as the role of light in vision or Newton's laws of motion, are difficult to grasp because they contradict common-sense notions. By thinking together, challenging each other, and suggesting and evaluating possible explanations, students are more likely to reach a genuine understanding.

Of course, there are disadvantages. Class discussions are quite unpredictable and may easily digress into exchanges of ignorance. Some members of the group may have great difficulty participating and may become anxious if forced to speak. In addition, you may have to do a good deal of preparation to ensure that participants have a background of knowledge on which to base the discussion. And large groups are often unwieldy. In many cases, a few students will dominate the discussion while the others daydream (Kindsvatter, Wilen, & Ishler, 1988). The Guidelines on productive group discussions give some ideas for facilitating a productive group discussion.

We have been looking at instructional planning and some basic teaching formats for whole classes, groups, and individuals. What about the person who is doing the planning—the teacher? What can teachers do to be effective in many different formats?

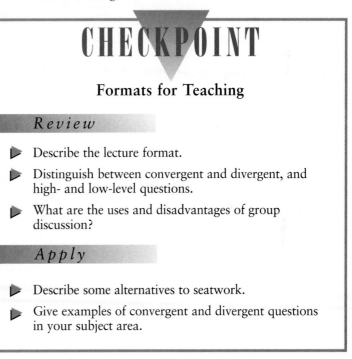

CHECKPOINT

Formats for Teaching

Review

▶ Describe the lecture format.

▶ Distinguish between convergent and divergent, and high- and low-level questions.

▶ What are the uses and disadvantages of group discussion?

Apply

▶ Describe some alternatives to seatwork.

▶ Give examples of convergent and divergent questions in your subject area.

Focus on the Teacher

How would you go about identifying the keys to effective teaching? You might ask students, principals, university or college professors of education, or experienced teachers to list the characteristics of good teachers. Or you could do intensive case studies of a few classrooms over a long period. You might observe classrooms, rate different teachers on certain characteristics, and then see which characteristics were associated with teachers whose students either achieved the most or were the most motivated to learn. (To do this, of course, you would have to decide how to assess achievement and motivation.) You could identify teachers whose students, year after year, learned more than students working with other teachers; then you could

GUIDELINES

Productive Group Discussions

Invite shy children to participate.

Examples

1. "What's your opinion, Joel? We need to hear from some other students."
2. Don't wait until there is a deadly silence to ask shy students to reply. Most people, even those who are confident, hate to break a silence.

Direct student comments and questions back to another student.

Examples

1. "That's an unusual idea, Steve. Kim, what do you think of Steve's idea?"
2. "That's an important question, John. Maura, do you have any thoughts about how you'd answer that?"
3. Encourage students to look at and talk to one another rather than wait for your opinion.

Make sure you understand what a student has said. If you are unsure, other students may be unsure as well.

Examples

1. Ask a second student to summarize what the first student said; then the first student can try again to explain if the summary is incorrect.
2. "Jasdev, I think you're saying. . . . Is that right, or have I misunderstood?"

Probe for more information.

Examples

1. "That's a strong statement. Do you have any evidence to back it up?"
2. "Tell us how you reached that conclusion. What steps did you go through?"

Bring the discussion back to the subject.

Examples

1. "Let's see, we were discussing. . . . and Sarah made one suggestion. Does anyone have a different idea?"
2. "Before we continue, let me try to summarize what has happened thus far."

Give time for thought before asking for responses.

Example

1. "How would your life be different if television had never been invented? Jot down your ideas on paper, and we will share reactions in a minute." After a minute: "Hiromi, will you tell us what you wrote?"

   When a student finishes speaking, look around the room to judge reactions.

Examples

1. If other students look puzzled, ask them to describe why they are confused.
2. If students are nodding assent, ask them to give an example of what was just said.

watch the more successful teachers, and note what they do. You might also train teachers to apply several different strategies to teach the same lesson and then determine which strategy led to the greatest student learning. You could videotape teachers, then ask them to view the tapes and report what they were thinking about as they taught and what influenced their decisions while teaching. You might study transcripts of classroom dialogue to learn what helped students understand.

All these approaches and more have been used to investigate teaching. Often researchers conduct a series of studies by making careful observations and identifying relationships between teaching and learning. The researchers then use these relationships as the basis for developing teaching approaches and testing these approaches in design experiments (Brown, 1992; Greeno, Collins, and Resnick, 1996). Let's examine some of the specific knowledge about teaching gained from these projects.

Characteristics of Effective Teachers

Some of the earliest research on effective teaching focused on the personal qualities of the teachers themselves. Researchers thought that the key to success in teaching must lie in the characteristics of teachers (Medley, 1979). Although this assumption proved incorrect—or at least incomplete—it did teach us some lessons about three teacher characteristics: knowledge, clarity, and warmth.

Teachers' Knowledge. Do teachers who know more about their subject have a more positive impact on their students? When we look at teachers' knowledge of facts and concepts, as measured by test scores and university or college grades, the relationship to student learning is unclear and may be indirect. Teachers who know more facts about their subject do not necessarily have students who learn more. But teachers who know more may make clearer presentations and recognize student difficulties more readily. They are ready for any student questions and do not have to be evasive or vague in their answers. Thus, knowledge is necessary but not sufficient for effective teaching because being more knowledgeable helps teachers be clearer and more organized.

▲ *Effective teachers must know how to transform their knowledge into examples, explanations, illustrations, and activities.*

Clarity and Organization. Students discussing a teacher are likely to make statements such as "Oh, she can really explain," or "He's so disorganized!" When Barak Rosenshine and Norma Furst (1973) reviewed about 50 studies of teaching, they concluded that clarity was the most promising teacher behaviour for future research on effective teaching. Studies confirm the importance of clarity. Teachers who provide clear presentations and explanations tend to have students who learn more and who rate their teachers more positively (Hines, Cruickshank, & Kennedy, 1985; Land, 1987). Teachers with more knowledge of the subject tend to be less vague in their explanations to the class. The less vague the teacher, the more the students learn (Land, 1987).

Planning for Clarity. Recent research offers guidelines for greater clarity in teaching (Berliner, 1987; Evertson, Emmer, & Worsham, 2000; Hines, Cruickshank, & Kennedy, 1985). When planning a lesson, try to anticipate the problems your students will have with the material. Turn to teachers' manuals and experienced teachers for help with this. You might also do the written parts of the lesson yourself to identify potential problems. Have definitions ready for new terms, and prepare several relevant examples for concepts. Think of analogies that will make ideas easier to understand. Organize the lesson in a logical sequence; include checkpoints that incorporate oral or written questions or problems to make sure the students are following the explanations.

Plan a clear introduction to the lesson. Tell students what they will be learning and how they could approach it. Often teachers are vague about both the "what" and the "how." For example, in a study by Duffy, Roehler, Meloth, and Vavrus (1986), an ineffective reading teacher began her lesson on using context in reading by saying, "Today we are going to learn about context. This skill will help you in your reading" (p. 206). This is a vague and general statement of "what" the students will learn. An effective teacher in the same study began her lesson with an explicit, precise description:

> At the end of today's lesson, you will be able to use the other words in a
> sentence to figure out the meaning of an unknown word. The skill is one
> that you use when you come to a word that you don't know and you have
> to figure out what the word means. (p. 206)

Being precise about "how" to do the work is even harder. One study found that teachers seldom, if ever, explain the cognitive processes they want their students to practise in a seatwork activity. Bright students figure out the right process, but slower students often guess or give up. For example, an *ineffective* teacher might introduce a seatwork activity on words with prefixes by saying, "Here are some words with prefixes. Write the meaning of each in the blanks." An *effective*

Explanatory Links: Words and phrases such as "because" and "in order to" that specify the relationships between ideas.

Direct Instruction/Explicit Teaching: Systematic instruction for mastery of basic skills, facts, and information.

Active Teaching: Teaching characterized by high levels of teacher explanation, demonstration, and interaction with students.

teacher, on the other hand, would demonstrate how to divide the words into a prefix and a root; how to determine the meaning of the root and the prefix; and how to put the two meanings together to make sense of the whole word (Berliner, 1987).

Clarity during the Lesson. Make clear connections between facts or concepts by using **explanatory links** such as *because, if . . . then,* or *therefore.* For example, when a teacher says, "A volume of air that is rising over a mountain becomes cooler and it expands," students are given two facts, but no connection between them. If there is a relationship between the two ideas, it should be indicated with an explanatory link as in, "A volume of air that is rising over a mountain becomes cooler because it expands." Explanatory links tie ideas together and make them easier to learn (Berliner, 1987). Explanatory links are also helpful in labelling visual material such as graphs, concept maps, or illustrations.

In general, stick with your plan and do not digress. Signal transitions from one major topic to another with phrases such as *"The next area . . . ," "Now we will turn to . . . ,"* or *"The second step is. . . ."* You might help students follow the lesson by outlining topics, listing key points, drawing concept maps on the board, or using an overhead projector. Continually monitor the group to see if everyone is following the lesson. Look for confident nods or puzzled stares. You should be able to tell if most students are keeping up.

Throughout the lesson, choose words that are familiar to the students. Define new terms and relate them to what the students already know. Be precise and check often for student understanding. Avoid vague words and ambiguous phrases: steer clear of "the somes"—*something, someone, sometime, somehow;* "the not verys"—*not very much, not very well, not very hard, not very often;* and other unspecific fillers, such as *most, not all, sort of, and so on, of course, as you know, I guess, in fact, or whatever,* and *more or less.* Use specific (and, if possible, colourful) names instead of *it, them,* and *thing.* Also, refrain from using pet phrases such as *you know, like,* and *OK?* Another idea is to record a lesson on tape to check yourself for clarity.

Warmth and Enthusiasm. As you are well aware, some teachers are much more enthusiastic than others. Some studies have found that ratings of teachers' enthusiasm for their subject are correlated with student achievement gains (Rosenshine & Furst, 1973). Warmth, friendliness, and understanding seem to be the teacher traits most strongly related to student attitudes (Murray, 1983; Ryans, 1960; Soar & Soar, 1979). In other words, teachers who are warm and friendly tend to have students who like them and the class in general. But notice, these are correlational studies. The results do not tell us that teacher enthusiasm causes student learning or that warmth causes positive attitudes, only that the two variables tend to occur together. Teachers trained to demonstrate their enthusiasm have students who are more attentive and involved but not necessarily more successful on tests of content (Gillett & Gall, 1982).

The research we have looked at has identified teacher knowledge, clarity, organization, and enthusiasm as important characteristics of effective teachers. The Guidelines on page 467 summarize the practical implications of this work for the classroom.

The Teacher in Teacher-Centred Instruction

Much of the research that focused on effective teaching in the 1970s and 1980s pointed toward a model of teaching that was related to improved student learning. Barak Rosenshine calls this approach **direct instruction** (1979) or **explicit teaching** (1986). Tom Good (1983a) uses the term **active teaching** for a similar approach. The direct instruction model fits a specific set of circumstances because it was derived from a particular approach to research. Researchers identified the elements

Connect & Extend
To your teaching
If you have observed in a primary grade, would you say that the teacher made use of direct instruction? Why or why not?

GUIDELINES

Teaching Effectively

Organize your lessons carefully.

Examples

1. Provide objectives that help students focus on the purpose of the lesson.
2. Begin lessons by writing a brief outline on the board, or work on an outline with the class as part of the lesson.
3. If possible, break the presentation into clear steps or stages.
4. Review periodically.

Strive for clear explanations.

Examples

1. Use concrete examples or analogies that relate to the students' own lives. Have several examples for particularly difficult points.

2. Give explanations at several levels so all students, not just the brightest, will understand.
3. Focus on one idea at a time and avoid digressions.

Communicate an enthusiasm for your subject and the day's lesson.

Examples

1. Tell students why the lesson is important. Have a better reason than "This will be on the test" or "You will need to know it next year." Emphasize the value of the learning itself.
2. Be sure to make eye contact with the students.
3. Vary your pace and volume in speaking. Use silence for emphasis.

of direct instruction by comparing teachers whose students learned more than expected (based on entering knowledge) with teachers whose students performed at an expected or average level. The researchers focused on existing teaching practices in American classrooms. Because the focus was on traditional forms of teaching, the research could not identify successful innovations. Effectiveness was usually defined as average improvement in standardized test scores for a whole class or school. So the results hold for large groups, but not necessarily for every student in the group. Even when the average achievement of a group improves, the achievement of some individuals may decline (Brophy & Good, 1986; Good, 1996; Shuell, 1996).

Given these conditions, you can see that direct instruction applies best to the teaching of **basic skills**—clearly structured knowledge and essential skills, such as science facts, mathematics computations, reading vocabulary, and grammar rules (Rosenshine & Stevens, 1986). These skills involve tasks that are relatively unambiguous; they can be taught step by step and tested by standardized tests. The teaching approaches described below are not necessarily appropriate for objectives such as helping students to write creatively, solve complex problems, or mature emotionally. Weinert and Helmke (1995) describe direct instruction as having the following features:

> (a) the teacher's classroom management is especially effective and the rate of student interruptive behaviors is very low; (b) the teacher maintains a strong academic focus and uses available instructional time intensively to initiate and facilitate students' learning activities; (c) the teacher insures that as many students as possible achieve good learning progress by carefully choosing appropriate tasks, clearly presenting subject-matter information and solution strategies, continuously diagnosing each student's learning progress and learning difficulties, and providing effective help through remedial instruction. (p. 138)

How would a teacher turn these themes into actions?

Basic Skills: Clearly structured knowledge that is needed for later learning and that can be taught step by step.

Connect & Extend
To your teaching
Madeline Hunter gives these examples of instructions a teacher can give to check for student understanding (Hunter, M. (1982). *Mastery Teaching.* El Segundo, CA: TIP Publications, p. 60):

"Look at the first multiple choice question. Decide which answer you would select and when I say 'show me,' place that number of fingers under your chin."
"Make a plus with your fingers if you agree with this statement, a minus if you don't and a zero if you have strong feelings."

Connect & Extend
To the research
Madeline Hunter's approaches have been remarkably popular over the years, but they are not without their critics. See the November 1986 issue of *Elementary School Journal* for five articles on a four-year Madeline Hunter follow-through project. There are findings of quantitative and qualitative analysis, commentaries by Andrew Porter and Bob Slavin, and a response from Hunter. In general, the findings show some gains in the schools that used the Hunter program, but these gains were not maintained when consultation and support for the teachers were withdrawn in the final year of the program.

Rosenshine's Six Teaching Functions. Rosenshine and his colleagues (Rosenshine, 1988; Rosenshine & Stevens, 1986) have identified six teaching functions based on the research on effective instruction. These could serve as a checklist or framework for teaching basic skills.

1. *Review and check the previous day's work.* Reteach if students misunderstood or made errors.
2. *Present new material.* Make the purpose clear, teach in small steps, provide many examples and non-examples.
3. *Provide guided practice.* Question students, give practice problems, and listen for misconceptions and misunderstandings. Reteach if necessary. Continue guided practice until students answer about 80 percent of the questions correctly.
4. *Give feedback and correctives* based on student answers. Reteach if necessary.
5. *Provide independent practice.* Let students apply the new learning on their own, in seatwork, cooperative groups, or homework. The success rate during independent practice should be about 95 percent. This means that students must be well prepared for the work by the presentation and guided practice and that assignments must not be too difficult. The point is for the students to practise until the skills become overlearned and automatic—until the students are confident. Hold students accountable for the work they do—check it.
6. *Review weekly and monthly* to consolidate learning. Include some review items as homework. Test often, and reteach material missed on the tests.

These six functions are not steps to be followed in a particular order, but all of them are elements of effective instruction. For example, feedback, review, or reteaching should occur whenever necessary and should match the abilities of the students. There are several other models of direct instruction, but most share the elements presented in Table 12.9. Madeline Hunter's Mastery Teaching (Hunter, 1982) is another example of direct instruction.

Why Does Direct Instruction Work? What aspects of direct instruction might explain its success? Linda Anderson (1989b) suggests that lessons that help students perceive links among main ideas will help them construct accurate understandings. Well-organized presentations, clear explanations, the use of explanatory links, and reviews can all help students perceive connections among ideas. If done well, therefore, a direct instruction lesson could be a resource that students use to construct understanding. For example, reviews activate prior knowledge so the student is ready to understand. Brief, clear presentations and guided practice avoid overloading the students' information processing systems and taxing their working memories. Numerous examples and explanations give many pathways and associations for building networks of concepts. Guided practice can also give the teacher a snapshot of the students' thinking and of their misconceptions, so these can be addressed directly as misconceptions rather than simply as "wrong answers."

Criticisms of Direct Instruction

Critics say that direct instruction is limited to lower-level objectives, and that it is based on traditional teaching methods, ignores innovative models, and discourages students' independent thinking. Some educational psychologists claim that the direct instruction model tells teachers to "do what works" without grounding the suggestions in a theory of student learning. Other critics disagree, saying that

TABLE 12.9 The Hunter Mastery Teaching Programs: Selected Principles

Get students set to learn.

- Make the best use of the prime time at the beginning of the lesson.
- Give students a review question or two to consider while you call the roll, pass out papers, or do other "housekeeping" chores. Follow up—listen to their answers, and correct if necessary.
- Create an *anticipatory set* to capture the students' attention. This might be an advance organizer, an intriguing question, or a brief exercise. For example, at the beginning of a lesson on categories of plants you could ask, "How is pumpkin pie similar to cherry pie but different from sweet potato pie?" Answer: Pumpkins and cherries are both fruits, unlike sweet potatoes.
- Communicate the lesson objectives (unless withholding this information for a while is part of your overall plan).

Provide information effectively.

- Determine the basic information and organize it. Use this basic structure as scaffolding for the lesson.
- Present information clearly and simply. Use familiar terms, examples, illustrations.
- Model what you mean. If appropriate, demonstrate or use analogies—"If the basketball Ann is holding were the sun, how far away do you think I would have to hold this pea to represent Pluto . . . ?"

Check for understanding, and give guided practice.

- Ask a question, and have every student signal an answer—"Thumbs up if this statement is true, down if it's false."
- Ask for a choral response: "Everyone, is this a dependent or an independent clause?"
- Sample individual responses: "Everyone, think of an example of a closed system. Jon, what's your example?"

Allow for independent practice.

- Get students started right by doing the first few questions together.
- Make independent practice brief. Monitor responses, giving feedback quickly.

To the research
For another perspective, read Berg, C. A., & Clough, M. (1991). Hunter lesson design: The wrong one for science teaching. *Educational Leadership, 48*(4), 73–78. *Focus Questions*: Why do Berg and Clough believe that the Hunter design is the wrong one for science teaching? How do students think Hunter would react? Then read Hunter, M. (1991). Hunter design helps achieve the goals of science instruction. *Educational Leadership, 48*(4), 79–81. *Focus Questions*: Evaluate Hunter's defence of her model. Do you agree that the Hunter approach can achieve the goals of science instruction?

Connect & Extend

To your teaching
Here are some ideas for ways to involve all students actively in a lesson. Ask them to:

1. Tell the answer to a neighbour.
2. Summarize the main idea in one or two sentences, writing the summary on a piece of paper and sharing this with a neighbour, or repeat the procedures to a neighbour.
3. Write the answer on a slate, then hold up the slate.
4. Raise their hands if they know the answer (thereby allowing the teacher to check the entire class).
5. Raise their hands if they agree with an answer someone else gave.
6. Raise different coloured cards when the answer is a, b, or c.

Taken from Rosenshine, B. (1987). Explicit teaching. In D. Berliner & B. Rosenshine (Eds.), *Talks to teachers* (pp. 75–62). New York: Random House.

direct instruction is based on a theory of student learning—but it is the *wrong* theory. Teachers break material into small segments, present each segment clearly, and reinforce or correct, thus *transmitting* accurate understandings from teacher to student. The student is seen as an "empty vessel" waiting to be filled with knowledge, rather than an active constructor of knowledge (Anderson, 1989a; Berg & Clough, 1991; Davis, Maher, & Noddings, 1990). These criticisms of direct instruction echo the criticisms of behavioural learning theories.

There is ample evidence, however, that direct instruction and explanation can help students learn actively, not passively. For younger and less prepared learners, student-controlled learning without teacher direction and instruction can lead to systematic deficits in the students' knowledge. Without guidance, the understandings that students construct can be incomplete and misleading (Weinert & Helmke, 1995). Deep understanding and fluid performance—whether in dance or mathematical problem solving or reading—require models of expert performance and extensive practice with feedback (Anderson, Reder, & Simon, 1995). Guided and independent practice with feedback are at the heart of the direct instruction model.

Focus on the Teacher   **469**

What direct instruction cannot do is *ensure* that students understand. If badly done, it may encourage students to memorize and mimic but never to "own" the knowledge. To help students reach this goal, Eleanor Duckworth believes that teachers must pay close attention to understanding their students' understandings (Meek, 1991). What do we know about good teaching in student-centred instruction? The next section describes this kind of effective teaching.

The Teacher in Student-Centred Instruction

Table 12.10 lists some characteristics of constructivist teaching practices described by Jacqueline Grennon Brooks and M. G. Brooks (1993). These teaching approaches are consistent with constructivist strategies such as those described in Chapter 9—inquiry, cooperative learning, instructional conversations, and cognitive apprenticeships.

Beyond Models to Outstanding Teaching

We have examined two perspectives on good teaching, one that fits direct, explicit teaching and one that is consistent with constructivist approaches. You may hear debates about the merits of these general approaches in many of your education courses. Often the debate about directive versus constructivist approaches is loudest when the students in question are at risk of failing, as you can see in the Point/Counterpoint on page 471.

TABLE 12.10 Constructivist Teaching Practices

Many constructivist practices can be incorporated into any class.

1. Constructivist teachers encourage and accept student autonomy and initiative.
2. Constructivist teachers use raw data and primary sources, along with manipulative, interactive, and physical materials.
3. When framing tasks, constructivist teachers use cognitive terminology such as "classify," "analyze," "predict," and "create."
4. Constructivist teachers allow student responses to drive lessons, shift instructional strategies, and alter content.
5. Constructivist teachers inquire about students' understandings of concepts before sharing their own understandings of those concepts.
6. Constructivist teachers encourage students to engage in dialogue, both with the teacher and with one another.
7. Constructivist teachers encourage student inquiry by asking thoughtful, open-ended questions and encouraging students to ask questions of each other.
8. Constructivist teachers seek elaboration of students' initial responses.
9. Constructivist teachers engage students in experiences that might engender contradictions to their initial hypotheses and then encourage discussion.
10. Constructivist teachers allow wait-time after posing questions.
11. Constructivist teachers provide time for students to discover relationships and create metaphors.

Source: From *"Becoming a Constructivist Teacher."* In *In Search of Understanding: The Case for Constructivist Classrooms* (pp. 101–118) by J. G. Brooks and M. G. Brooks, 1995, Association for Supervision and Curriculum Development. Copyright © 1995 by ASCD. Reprinted with permission.

What is the Best Way to Help Students at Risk of Failing?

There are many ideas and models for teaching low-achieving students—students often referred to as "at risk" for failure. Some recommendations are based on direct instruction and basic-skills teaching. Another approach bases its recommendations on cognitive theories of learning, and these recommendations question the value of direct instruction. What are the teaching strategies offered by each approach?

▶ **POINT** *Adapt direct instruction for students' needs.*

Research on effective teachers of low achievers (Ebmeier & Ziomek, 1982; Emmer, Evertson, Clements, & Worsham, 1997; Slavin, Karweit, & Madden, 1989) has identified these approaches as helpful:

Break instruction into small steps and provide short activities, chosen and sequenced by the teacher.

Cover material thoroughly and at a moderate pace. Give plenty of practice, immediate clear feedback, and specific praise.

Have students work as a whole class or in groups so the teacher can supervise. Avoid individualized, self-paced, or independent work.

Keep a level of difficulty that guarantees high rates of success.

Ask convergent questions—one correct answer.

Make sure to call on everyone and stay with a student until a question is answered.

Avoid interruptions, open-ended questions, and non-academic conversations.

Emphasize short, frequent paper-and-pencil exercises, not games, arts, crafts, discovery learning activities, and interest centres. These are less helpful for learning.

◀ **COUNTERPOINT** *Move beyond the basics.*

Educators and psychologists who hold a cognitive view of learning are critical of direct instruction. For example, Barbara Means and Michael Knapp (1991) decry the "basics" approach to teaching low achievers:

A recent summary of critiques of conventional approaches to teaching academic skills to at-risk students, offered by a group of national experts in reading, writing, and mathematics education, concluded that such approaches tend to:

underestimate what students are capable of doing; postpone more challenging and interesting work for too long—in some cases, forever; and deprive students of a meaningful or motivating context for learning or for employing the skills that are taught. (pp.

283–284)

What do critics of direct instruction offer in its place? The following are some principles recommended by Means and Knapp (1991):

Focus on complex, meaningful problems. Keep the level of tasks high enough that the purpose of the task is apparent and makes sense to students.

Embed basic skills instruction in the context of more global tasks such as class record keeping or letter writing.

Make connections with students' out-of-school experience and culture.

Model powerful thinking strategies for students; for example, think aloud as you try to figure out a difficult text passage.

Encourage multiple approaches to academic tasks. Have students describe how they reached their answers.

Provide scaffolding to enable students to accomplish complex tasks; for example, perform the calculations for students as they set up an algebra problem correctly.

Make dialogue the central medium for teaching and learning. Reciprocal teaching is one example. (See Chapter 9.)

In spite of the debates, there is no one best way to teach. Different goals require different methods. Teacher-centred instruction leads to better performance on achievement tests, while the open, informal methods such as discovery learning or inquiry approaches are associated with better performance on tests of creativity, abstract thinking, and problem solving. In addition, the open methods are better for improving attitudes toward school and for stimulating curiosity, cooperation among students, and lower absence rates (Walberg, 1990). According to these conclusions, when the goals of teaching involve problem solving, creativity, understanding, and mastering processes, many approaches besides direct instruction should be effective.

Connect & Extend
To your own philosophy
Can different formats, such as lecture or seatwork, be used in the service of different models, such as direct instruction or constructivist approaches?

CHECKPOINT

Focus on the Teacher

Review

▷ What methods have been used to study teaching?

▷ What are the general characteristics of good teaching?

▷ Contrast teaching in direct and student-centred instruction.

Apply

▷ Identify one of your teachers who exemplifies good teaching.

These guidelines are in keeping with Tom Good's conclusion that teaching should become less direct as students mature and when the goals involve affective development and problem solving or critical thinking (Good, 1983a). Of course, every subject, even college English or chemistry, can require some direct instruction. If you are teaching when to use "who" and "whom," or how to set up laboratory apparatus, direct instruction may be the best approach. Noddings (1990) reminds teachers that students may need some direct instruction in how to use various manipulative materials to get the best possible benefits from them. Students working in cooperative groups may need guidance, modelling, and practice in how to ask questions and give explanations. And to solve difficult problems, students may need some direct instruction in possible problem-solving strategies. The message for teachers is to match instructional methods to learning goals.

Focus on the Subject: Teaching Reading, Mathematics, and Science

It is clear that a teacher's knowledge of the subject is critical for teaching (Borko & Putnam, 1996). Part of that knowledge is pedagogical content knowledge, or knowing how to teach a subject to your particular students (Shulman, 1987). In the past decade, psychologists have made great progress understanding how students learn different subjects (Mayer, 1992a). Based on these findings, many approaches have been developed to teach reading, writing, science, mathematics, social studies, and all the other subjects. Many of these approaches reflect the constructivist perspectives described in Chapter 9.

Learning to Read and Write

For years, educators have debated whether students should be taught to read and write through code-based (phonics, skills) approaches that relate letters to sounds and sounds to words or through meaning-based (whole language, literature-based, emergent literacy) approaches that do not dissect words and sentences into pieces, but instead focus on the meaning of the text (Goodman, 1986; Smith, 1994; Stahl & Miller, 1989; Symons, Woloshyn, & Pressley, 1994; Vellutino, 1991).

Whole Language. Informed by theory and research in the fields of emergent literacy and developmental psychology, advocates of whole language believe that becoming literate is a natural process—much like mastering your native language—that begins long before children enter school. Also, consistent with cognitive and constructivist views of learning, whole language advocates believe that children actively create understandings of what it really means to read and to write by engaging in authentic reading and writing activities. Finally, advocates of whole language stress social aspects of learning to read and write. They emphasize how important it is for parents and teachers to model literate behaviour for developing readers and writers. From this **whole language perspective,** learning to read and write during the elementary school years is part of a continuum of learning that begins at birth and continues through adulthood (Chapman, 1997). Teachers have to be astute observers of students' literacy development to determine the supports or resources students need to learn.

In many whole language classrooms, teachers and students set goals and design curriculum together. In writing, for instance, students and teachers identify a purpose and an audience. For example, students might decide to write letters to the mayor of their city about her recycling policy. This is consistent with Lev Vygotsky's (1978) view that "writing should be incorporated into a task that is necessary and relevant for life. Only then can we be certain that it will develop not as a matter of hand and finger habits but as a really new and complex form of speech" (p. 118). Marilyn Chapman at the University of British Columbia agrees: "Children develop knowledge about writing primarily in the context of its purposeful use" (1997, p. 31). She also observes that the two main purposes for writing are to communicate with others and to facilitate students' thinking and learning (p. 33).

▲ *Contemporary learning theories have sought to understand how students learn different subjects in different ways, and in turn, how teaching methods might be adapted to these differences.*

Integrated Curricula. Another hallmark of whole language instruction is its emphasis on integrating language processes—speaking, listening, reading, writing—across curricula, and teaching language and literacy skills in the context of meaningful curricular activities. Whole language advocates design instruction according to the belief that speaking, listening, reading, and writing processes are "integrated, mutually reinforcing . . . activities" (Gunderson, 1997, p. 226) that develop concurrently (Chapman, 1997). They also hold that specific skills are better taught in a context of meaningful activities rather than in isolation. For example, Lynn (a teacher with whom Nancy worked) taught her Grade 2 and Grade 3 students how to (a) "do" research, (b) write expository text, (c) use the computer as a tool for writing, and (d) edit and proofread, all while the students were studying animals, a topic in the BC science curriculum. In addition, she used this project to reinforce social skills such as taking responsibility for self, and respecting and contributing to the work of others.

Lynn prepared students for conducting research by having a researcher from a local university visit her class at the beginning of the year. The researcher described how she studied wolves and then Lynn's class made a list of things researchers do to guide their study of different animals. Lynn also introduced a framework for writing expository text and discussed with her students how this genre differs from narrative text. Then students did what good researchers do. They gathered facts about their research topic from multiple sources and organized them under topic headings to plan their report. Students shared facts with one another and debated the pros and cons of placing a fact under one topic heading or another. After students had drafted one section of their report, Lynn taught them how to edit their writing and how to provide constructive feedback to others. Also, she demonstrated how they could use the cut-and-paste function in the computer to revise their writing. Like real writers, students revised sections of their reports multiple times until they were satisfied that their work was "publishable." Early in the year, Lynn provided explicit instruction and extensive scaffolding about how to do research and the writing process. Later in the year, Lynn shifted the responsibility for doing good research and writing to her students and encouraged them to look to one another for support. One student was an expert when it came to solving computer problems. All students became experts on the topics they studied, and all students developed as readers and writers.

Clearly, whole language approaches to instruction have much to commend them. John Shapiro (1994) at the University of British Columbia argues that

Whole Language Perspective: A philosophical approach to teaching and learning that stresses learning through authentic, real-life tasks. Emphasizes using language to learn, integrating learning across skills and subjects, and respecting the language abilities of student and teacher.

children who experience whole language approaches do become effective readers and writers.

> Their vocabulary increases, they employ varied strategies in word recognition, their comprehension abilities range from simple literal recall to more sophisticated judgments about authors' intent, they read for pleasure and information, and, perhaps more importantly, they have positive attitudes toward reading [and writing]. (p. 458–459)

However, critics argue that whole language approaches to instruction give too little emphasis to phonemic awareness and understanding the structure of language.

Do Students Need Skills and Phonics? There are now two decades of research demonstrating that skill in recognizing sounds and words supports reading. Keith Stanovich, at the Ontario Institute for Studies in Education, has conducted numerous studies that show that being able to identify many words as you read does not depend on using context to guess meaning (Stanovich, 1993/4; Stanovich, West, & Freeman, 1984). In fact, it is almost the other way around—knowing words helps you make sense of context. Identifying words as you read is a highly automatic process. The more fluent and automatic you are in identifying words, the more effective you will be in getting meaning from context (Vandervelden & Siegel, 1995). It is the poorest readers who resort to using context to help them understand meaning (Pressley, 1996).

Many studies support the code-based position. For example, three different groups reported in the *Journal of Educational Psychology* (December 1991) that alphabetic coding and awareness of letter sounds are essential skills for acquiring word identification, so some direct teaching of the alphabet and phonics is helpful in learning to read. Stanovich (1993/4) acknowledges that it is possible to "overdo the teaching of phonics," but he also contends that "some children in whole language classrooms do not pick up the alphabetic principle through simple immersion in print and writing activities, and such children need explicit instruction in alphabetic coding" (p. 285). The best approach probably makes sensible use of both phonics and whole language. After all, we want our students to be fluent *and* enthusiastic readers and writers.

Being Sensible about Reading and Writing. The results of high-quality studies suggest that:

▶ Whole language approaches to reading and writing are most effective in preschool and kindergarten. Whole language gives children a good conceptual basis for reading and writing. The social interactions around reading and writing—reading big books, writing shared stories, examining pictures, discussing meaning—are activities that support literacy and mirror the early home experiences of children who come to school prepared to learn. Whole language approaches seem to improve students' motivation, interest, and attitude toward reading and help children understand the nature and purposes of reading and writing (Graham & Harris, 1994; Shapiro, 1994).

▶ Phonemic awareness—the sense that words are composed of separate sounds and that sounds are combined to say words—in kindergarten and Grade 1 predicts literacy in later grades. If children do not have phonemic awareness in the early grades, direct teaching can dramatically improve their chances of long-term achievement in literacy (Pressley, 1996).

▶ Excellent primary school teachers balance their explicit teaching of decoding skills and their whole language instruction (Adams, Treiman, & Pressley, 1998; Vellutino, 1991; Wharton-McDonald, Pressley, & Mistretta, 1996). The Center for the Improvement of Early Reading Achievement (CIERA) has generated 10 research-based principles regarding early literacy development. These are outlined in Table 12.11.

TABLE 12.11 Improving the Reading Achievement of America's Children: CIERA's 10 Research-Based Principles

CIERA (the Center for the Improvement of Early Reading Achievement) has reviewed the research on learning to read and distilled the best findings into these 10 principles. You can read the expanded version of the principles on its Web site—www.ciera.org—under free information.

1. **Home language and literacy experiences** support the development of key print concepts and a range of knowledge prepares students for school-based learning. Programs that help families initiate and sustain these experiences show positive benefits for children's reaching achievement.

   Examples: Joint reading with a family member, parental modeling of good reading habits, monitoring homework and television viewing.

2. **Preschool programs** are particularly beneficial for children who do not experience informal learning opportunities in their homes. Such preschool experiences lead to improved reading achievement, with some effects lasting through grade 3.

   Examples: Listening to and examining books, saying nursery rhymes, writing messages, and seeing and talking about print.

3. **Skills that predict later reading success** can be promoted in kindergarten and grade 1. The two most powerful of these predictors are letter-name knowledge and phonemic awareness. Instruction in these skills has demonstrated positive effects on primary grade reading achievement, especially when it is coupled with letter-sound instruction.

   Examples: Encourage children to hear and blend sound through oral renditions of rhymes, poems, and songs, as well as writing messages and in journals.

4. **Primary-level instruction** that supports successful reading acquisition is consistent, well-designed, and focused.

   Examples: Systematic word recognition instruction on common, consistent letter-sound relationships and important but often unpredictable high-frequency words, such as *the* and *what*; teaching children to monitor the accuracy of their reading as well as their understanding of texts through strategies such as predicting, inferencing, clarifying misunderstandings, and summarizing; promoting word recognition and comprehension through repeated reading of text, guided reading and writing, strategy lessons, reading aloud with feedback, and conversations about texts children have read.

5. **Primary-level classroom environments** in successful schools provide opportunities for students to apply what they have learned in teacher-guided instruction to everyday reading and writing.

   Examples: Teachers read books aloud and hold follow-up discussions, children read independently every day, and children write stories and keep journals. These events are monitored frequently by teachers, ensuring that time is well spent and that children receive feedback on their efforts. Teachers design and revise these events based on information from ongoing assessment of children's strengths and needs.

6. **Cultural and linguistic diversity** among America's children reflects the variations within their communities and homes. This diversity is manifest in differences in the children's dispositions toward and knowledge about topics, language, and literacy.

   Examples: Effective instruction includes assessment, integration, and extension of relevant background knowledge and the use of texts that recognize diverse backgrounds. Build on the children's language when children are learning to speak, listen to, write, and read English. When teachers capitalize on the advantages of bilingualism or biliteracy, second language reading acquisition is significantly enhanced.

7. **Children who are identified as having reading disabilities** profit from the same sort of well-balanced instructional programs that benefit all children who are learning to read and write, including systematic instruction *and* meaningful reading and writing.

   Examples: Intensive one-on-one or small-group instruction, attention to both comprehension and word recognition processes, thoroughly individualized assessment and instructional planning, and extensive experiences with many types of texts.

8. **Proficient reading in third grade** and above is sustained and enhanced by programs that adhere to four fundamental features:

   Features: (1) deep and wide opportunities to read, (2) acquiring new knowledge and vocabulary, through wide reading and through explicit instruction about networks of new concepts, (3) emphasizing the influence on understanding of kinds of text (e.g., stories versus essays) and the ways writers organize particular texts, and (4) assisting students in reasoning about text.

9. **Professional opportunities** to improve reading achievement are prominent in successful schools and programs.

   Examples: Opportunities for teachers and administrators to analyze instruction, assessment, and achievement; to set goals for improvement; to learn about effective practices; and to participate in ongoing communities that deliberately try to understand both successes and persistent problems.

10. **Entire school staffs**, not just first-grade teachers, are involved in bringing children to high levels of achievement.

    Examples: In successful schools, reading achievement goals are clear, expectations are high, instructional means for attaining goals are articulated, and shared assessments monitor children's progress. Even though they might use different materials and technologies, successful schools maintain a focus on reading and writing and have programs to involve parents in their children's reading and homework. Community partnerships, including volunteer tutoring programs, are common.

If students need help cracking the code, give them what they need. Don't let ideology get in the way. You will just send more students to private tutors—if their families can afford it. But don't forget that reading and writing are for a purpose. Surround students with good literature and create a community of readers and writers.

The above discussion applies to reading and writing in the early grades, but what about the later years when comprehending difficult texts becomes important? Here reciprocal teaching (Chapter 9) and study skills (Chapter 8) can be helpful.

Learning and Teaching Mathematics

Some of the most compelling support for constructivist approaches to teaching comes from mathematics education. Critics of direct instruction believe that traditional mathematics instruction often teaches students an unintended lesson—that they "cannot understand mathematics," or worse, that mathematics doesn't have to make sense, you just have to memorize the formulas. Arthur Baroody and Herbert Ginsburg (1990, p. 62) give this example:

Sherry, a junior high student, explained that her math class was learning how to convert measurements from one unit to another. The interviewer gave Sherry the following problem:

To feed data into the computer, the measurements in your report have to be converted to one unit of measurement: metres. Your first measurement, however, is 150 cm. What are you going to feed into the computer?

Sherry recognized immediately that the conversion algorithm taught in school applied. However, because she really did not understand the rationale behind the conversion algorithm, Sherry had difficulty in remembering the steps and how to execute them. After some time she came up with an improbable answer (it was less than 1 m). Sherry knew she was in trouble and became flustered. At this point, the interviewer tried to help by asking her if there was any other way of solving the problem. Sherry responded sharply, "No!" She explained, "That's the way it has to be done." The interviewer tried to give Sherry a hint: "Look at the numbers in the problem, is there another way we can think about them that might help us figure out the problem more easily?" Sherry grew even more impatient, "This is the way I learned in school, so it has to be the way."

Sherry believed that there was only one way to solve a problem. Though Sherry knew that 100 cm was 1 m and that shifting the "invisible" decimal at the end of 150 to the left increased the unit size in metric measurements, she did not use this knowledge to solve the problem informally and quickly. Her beliefs prevented her from effectively using her existing mathematical knowledge to solve the problem. Sherry had probably been taught to memorize the steps to convert one measurement to another. How would a constructivist approach teach the same material?

The following excerpt shows how a Grade 3 teacher, Ms. Coleman, uses a constructivist approach to teach negative numbers. Notice the use of dialogue and the way the teacher asks students to justify and explain their thinking. The class has been considering one problem: $-10 + 10 = ?$ A student, Marta, has just tried to explain, using a number line, why $-10 + 10 = 0$:

Teacher: Marta says that negative ten plus ten equals zero, so you have to count ten numbers to the right. What do you think, Harold?

Harold: I think it's easy, but I don't understand how she explained it.

Teacher: OK. Does anybody else have a comment or a response to that? Tessa? (Peterson, 1992, p. 165)

Connect & Extend
To the research
Another example of how students solve mathematics problems applying rules is taken from Merseth, K. K. (1993). How old is the shepherd? An essay about mathematics education. *Phi Delta Kappan, 74*, 548–554. Merseth cites findings from research showing that three out of four students will produce some numerical answer to the problem: There are 125 sheep and 5 dogs in a flock. How old is the shepherd? Here is how one child reached an answer; notice that logic and reasoning play a role: "125 + 5 = 130 . . . this is too big, and 125 − 5 = 120 is still too big . . . while 125/5 = 25. That works! I think the shepherd is 25 years old!"

Connect & Extend
To the research
Research: Resnick, L.B. (1989). Developing mathematical knowledge. *American Psychologist, 44*, 162–169.

Brief Abstract
Research has given rise to new ideas about the nature of children's number-knowledge development. This article shows how infants' and preschoolers' implicit protoquantitative reasoning schemas combine with early counting knowledge to produce mathematical concepts of number. It also discusses elementary schoolchildren's informal and invented arithmetic, as well as implications for mathematics education.

As the discussion progresses, Ms. Coleman encourages students to talk directly to each other:

Teacher: You said you don't understand what she is trying to say?

Chang: No.

Teacher: Do you want to ask her?

Chang: What do you mean by counting to the right?

Connect & Extend
To the research
Peterson, P., Fennema, E., & Carpenter, T. (1989). Using knowledge of how students think about mathematics. *Educational Leadership, 46*(4), 42–46.

This dialogue reveals three things about learning and teaching in a constructivist classroom: the thinking processes of the students are the focus of attention; one topic is considered in depth rather than attempting to "cover" many topics; and assessment is ongoing and mutually shared by teacher and students.

Jere Confrey (1990b) analyzed an expert mathematics teacher in a class for high school girls who had difficulty with mathematics. Confrey identified five components in a model of this teacher's approach to teaching. These components are summarized in Table 12.12.

Learning Science

We have seen a number of times that by high school many students have "learned" some unfortunate lessons in school. Like Sherry, described in the preceding section, they have learned that math is impossible to understand and you just have to apply the rules to get the answers. Or they may have developed misconceptions about the world, such as the belief that the Earth is warmer in the summer because it is closer to the sun.

Many educators note that the key to understanding in science is for students to directly examine their own theories and confront the shortcomings (Hewson,

Connect & Extend
To the research
Klein, P. D. (2000). Elementary students' strategies for writing-to-learn in science. *Cognition and Instruction, 18*, 317–348.

TABLE 12.12 A Constructivist Approach to Mathematics: Five Components

1. Promote students' autonomy and commitment to their answers

   Examples:
   - Question both right and wrong student answers.
   - Insist that students at least try to solve a problem and be able to explain what they tried.

2. Develop students' reflective processes

   Examples:
   - Question students to guide them to try different ways to resolve the problem.
   - Ask students to restate the problem in their own words; to explain what they are doing and why; and to discuss what they mean by the terms they are using.

3. Construct a case history of each student

   Examples:
   - Note general tendencies in the way the student approaches problems, as well as common misconceptions and strengths.

4. If the student is unable to solve a problem, intervene to negotiate a possible solution with the student.

   Examples:
   - Based on the case study and your understanding of how the student is thinking about a problem, guide the student to think about a possible solution.
   - Ask questions such as "Is there anything you did in the last one that will help you here?" or "Can you explain your diagram?"
   - If the student is becoming frustrated, ask more direct, product-oriented questions.

5. When the problem is solved, review the solution

   Examples:
   - Encourage students to reflect on what they did and why.
   - Note what students did well and build confidence.

Source: From "What Constructivism Implies for Teaching," by J. Confrey, 1990, in *Constructivist Views on the Teaching and Learning of Mathematics* by R. Davis, C. Maher, and N. Noddings (Eds.). Monograph 4 of the National Council of Teachers of Mathematics, Reston, VA. Copyright © 1990 National Council of Teachers of Mathematics. Adapted with permission.

Connect & Extend
To the research
White, B. Y. (1993). TinkerTools: Causal models, conceptual change, and science education. *Cognition and Instruction, 10,* 1–100. Lapadat, J. C. (2000). Construction of science knowledge: Scaffolding conceptual change through discourse. *Journal of Classroom Instruction, 35,* 1–14.

Beeth, & Thorley, 1998). Only then can true learning and conceptual change happen. For change to take place, students must go through six stages: initial discomfort with their own ideas and beliefs; attempts to explain away inconsistencies between their theories and evidence presented to them; attempts to adjust measurements or observations to fit personal theories; doubt; vacillation; and finally conceptual change (Nissani & Hoefler-Nissani, 1992). You can see Piaget's notions of assimilation, disequilibrium, and accommodation operating here. Students try to make new information fit existing ideas (assimilation), but when the fit simply won't work and disequilibrium occurs, then accommodation or changes in cognitive structures follow.

The goal of **conceptual change teaching in science** is to help students pass through these six stages of learning. The two central features of conceptual change teaching are:

▶ Teachers are committed to teaching for student understanding rather than "covering the curriculum."

▶ Students are encouraged to make sense of science using their current ideas—they are challenged to describe, predict, explain, justify, debate, and defend the adequacy of their understanding. Dialogue is key. Only when intuitive ideas prove inadequate can new learning take hold (Anderson & Roth, 1989).

Conceptual change teaching has much in common with cognitive apprenticeships, inquiry learning, and reciprocal teaching described in Chapter 9—with scaffolding and dialogue playing key roles (Shuell, 1996). The Guidelines on page 479, adapted from Hewson, Beeth, and Thorley (1998), give some ideas for promoting conceptual change.

How would these guidelines look in practice? One answer comes from Michael Beeth's study of a Grade 5 classroom. Table 12.13 is a list of learning goals that the teacher presented to her students. In this classroom, the teacher typically began instruction with a question such as, "Do you have ideas? Can you talk about them? Bring them out into the open? Why do you like your ideas? Why are you attracted to them?" (Beeth, 1998, p. 1095). During her teaching she constantly asked questions that required explanation and justifications. She summarized the

Conceptual Change Teaching in Science: A method that helps students understand (rather than memorize) concepts in science by using and challenging the students' current ideas.

▲ *Conceptual change teaching in science focuses teachers' and students' attention on students' understanding rather than on "covering the curriculum." Dialogue is key.*

GUIDELINES

Teaching for Conceptual Change

Encourage students to make their ideas explicit.

Examples

1. Ask students to make predictions that might contradict their naive conceptions.
2. Ask students to state their ideas in their own words, including the attractions and limitations of the ideas for them.
3. Have students explain their ideas using physical models or illustrations.

Help students see the differences among ideas.

Examples

1. Have students summarize or paraphrase each other's ideas.
2. Encourage comparing ideas by presenting and comparing evidence.

Encourage metacognition.

Examples

1. Give a pretest before starting a unit; then have students discuss their own responses to the pretest. Group similar pretest responses together and ask students to discover what is a more general concept underlying the responses.

2. At the end of lessons, ask students: "What did you learn?" "What do you understand?" "What do you believe about the lesson?" "How have your ideas changed?"

Explore the status of ideas. Status is an indication of how much students know and accept ideas and find them useful.

Examples

1. Ask direct questions about how intelligible, plausible, and fruitful an idea is. That is, do you know what the idea means, do you believe it, and can you achieve some valuable outcome using the idea?
2. Plan activities and experiments that support and question the students' ideas, such as showing successful applications or pointing out contradictions.

Ask students for justifications of their ideas.

Examples

1. Teach students to use terms such as *logical, consistent, inconsistent*, and coherent in giving justifications.
2. Ask students to share and analyze each other's justifications.

TABLE 12.13 One Teacher's Learning Goals for Conceptual Change Teaching

The teacher in one Grade 5 class gives these questions to her students to support their thinking about science.

1. Can you state your own ideas?
2. Can you talk about why you are attracted to your ideas?
3. Are your ideas consistent?
4. Do you realize the limitations of your ideas and the possibility they might need to change?
5. Can you try to explain your ideas using physical models?
6. Can you explain the difference between understanding an idea and believing in an idea?
7. Can you apply intelligible and plausible to your own ideas?

Source: Adapted from "Teaching Science in Fifth Grade: Instructional Goals that Support Conceptual Change," by M. E. Beeth, 1998, *Journal of Research in Science Teaching, 35,* p. 1093.

students' answers, and sometimes challenged, "But do you really believe what you say?" Studies of the students in the teacher's classroom over the years showed that they had a sophisticated understanding of science concepts.

Canadian researchers Wolf-Michael Roth and Michelle McGinn add that a key to unlocking opportunities for students to construct understandings in science (and mathematics) is posing better problems (Roth & McGinn, 1997). Usually the problems students are given to solve are uncluttered with the complexities that enrich the real world. Too often, problems have pre-figured answers where "students' tasks are to disclose what the texts (or problems) hide . . . as *the* solution" (pp. 19–20) rather than learn how to do science. Roth and McGinn suggest that teachers invite students to bring problems from outside school into the classroom. Then, teachers should support students as students frame hypotheses and explore methods to investigate them. This places problems in context so that students' experiences from outside school are joined with experiences of doing science. This model, called *open inquiry*, transforms what students do to resemble what scientists do. The result? Students construct understandings about science that are genuine rather than textbookish (Roth & Bowen, 1995; Roth & Roychoudhury, 1993).

Criticisms of Constructivist Approaches to Subject Teaching

Constructivist approaches have done much to correct the excesses of tell-and-drill teaching. Some positive outcomes from constructivist teaching are better understanding of the material, greater enjoyment of literature, more positive attitudes toward school, better problem solving, and greater motivation (Harris & Graham, 1996; Palincsar, 1998). But total reliance on constructivist approaches that ignores direct teaching of skills can be detrimental for some children. For example, Harris and Graham (1996) describe the experiences of their daughter Leah in a whole language/progressive education school, where the teachers successfully developed their daughter's creativity, thinking, and understanding.

> Skills, on the other hand, have been a problem for our daughter and for other children. At the end of kindergarten, when she had not made much progress in reading, her teacher said she believed Leah had a perceptual problem or a learning disability. Leah began asking what was wrong with her, because other kids were reading and she wasn't. Finally, an assessment was done. (p. 26)

The testing indicated no learning disability, strong comprehension abilities, and poor word attack skills. Luckily, Leah's parents knew how to teach word attack skills. Direct teaching of these skills helped Leah become an avid and able reader in about six weeks.

Leah's experience is not unique. Whole language and constructivist approaches alone may not work for *all* children (Airasian & Walsh, 1997; Harris & Graham, 1996; Smith, 1994) or all kinds of learning (Weinert & Helmke, 1995). Susan Stodolsky (1988) cautions that constructivist methods may not be equally successful across all subject areas. If students fall behind because they lack specific skills, it would be unethical to withhold teaching and wait for those skills to "develop naturally," simply to be true to a particular philosophy.

Ernst von Glasersfeld (1995), a strong advocate of constructivist teaching in mathe-

CHECKPOINT

Focus on the Subject: Teaching Reading, Mathematics, and Science

Review

▷ Describe the debate about learning to read.

▷ Describe constructivist approaches to mathematics and science teaching.

Apply

▷ How would you assess students' conceptions about the science topics you will teach?

matics, believes that it is a misunderstanding of constructivism to say that memorization and rote learning always are useless. "There are, indeed, matters that can and perhaps must be learned in a purely mechanical way" (p. 5). Classrooms that integrate constructivist teaching with needed direct teaching of skills are especially good learning environments for students with special needs. Careful ongoing assessment of each student's abilities, knowledge, and motivations, followed by appropriate support should ensure that no students are lost or left behind (Graham & Harris, 1994). In the next two chapters, we look more closely at student assessment.

Summary

The First Step: Planning

What are the levels of planning and how do they affect teaching?

Teachers engage in several levels of planning—by the year, term, unit, week, and day. All the levels must be coordinated. Accomplishing the year's plan requires breaking the work into terms, the terms into units, and the units into weeks and days. The plan determines how time and materials will be turned into activities for students. There is no single model of planning, but all plans should allow for flexibility.

What is an instructional objective?

An instructional objective is a clear and unambiguous description of your educational intentions for your students. Mager's influential system for writing behavioural objectives states that objectives ought to describe what students will be doing when demonstrating their achievement and how you will know they are doing it. A good objective has three parts—the intended student behaviour, the conditions under which the behaviour will occur, and the criteria for acceptable performance. Gronlund's alternative approach suggests that an objective should be stated first in general terms, then the teacher should clarify by listing sample behaviour that would provide evidence that the student has attained the objective.

Describe the three taxonomies of educational objectives.

Bloom and others have developed taxonomies categorizing basic objectives in the cognitive, affective, and psychomotor domains. In real life, of course, behaviour from these three domains occurs simultaneously. A taxonomy encourages systematic thinking about relevant objectives and ways to evaluate them. Six basic objectives are listed in the cognitive domain: knowledge, comprehension, application, analysis, synthesis, and evaluation. A recent revision of this taxonomy keeps the same cognitive processes, but adds that these processes can act on four kinds of knowledge—factual, conceptual, procedural, and metacognitive.

Describe teacher-centred and student-centred planning.

In teacher-centred approaches, teachers select learning objectives and plan how to get students to meet those objectives. Teachers control the "what" and "how" of learning. In contrast, planning is shared and negotiated in student-centred, or constructivist, approaches. The teacher and students together make decisions about content, activities, and approaches. Rather than having specific student behaviour as objectives, the teacher has overarching goals or "big ideas" that guide planning. Integrated content and teaching with themes are often part of the planning. Assessment of learning is ongoing and mutually shared by teacher and students.

Formats for Teaching: Teacher Directed

Describe the lecture format.

The teaching format for putting objectives into action should be suited to the objectives. Lecturing is efficient for communicating a large amount of new material to a large group. There are three basic phases a lecture should follow: preparation of students; presentation of content; and review of content. However, lecturing may keep students too passive and ignore individual learning rates. The younger the student, the shorter the presentation should be. Recitation can involve various types of questions, and should fit students' abilities and motivation levels.

Distinguish between convergent and divergent and high-level versus low-level questions.

Convergent questions have only one right answer. Divergent questions have many possible answers. Higher-level questions require analysis, synthesis, and evaluation—students have to think for themselves. Teacher responses to answers should not be too hasty in most cases and should provide appropriate feedback.

What are the uses and disadvantages of group discussion?

Group discussion helps students participate directly, express themselves clearly, justify opinions, and tolerate different views. Group discussion also gives students a chance to ask for clarification, examine their own thinking, follow personal interests, and assume responsibility by taking leadership roles in the group. Thus, group discussions help students evaluate ideas and synthesize personal viewpoints. By thinking together, challenging each other, and suggesting and evaluating possible explanations, students are more likely to reach a genuine understanding. However, discussions are quite unpredictable and may easily digress into exchanges of ignorance. Some members of the group may have great difficulty participating and may become anxious if forced to speak.

Focus on the Teacher

What methods have been used to study teaching?

For years, researchers have tried to unravel the mystery of effective teaching. Researchers have used a variety of methods, including classroom observation, case studies, interviews, experimentation with different methods, and other approaches to study teaching in real classrooms. Results of research on teacher characteristics indicate that thorough and expert knowledge of a subject, organization and clarity in presentation, and enthusiasm all play important parts in effective teaching. But no one way of teaching has been found to be right for each class, lesson, or day.

What are the general characteristics of good teaching?

Teacher knowledge of the subject is necessary but not sufficient for effective teaching because being more knowledgeable helps teachers be clearer and more organized; organization and clarity are important characteristics of good teaching. Teachers who provide clear presentations and explanations tend to have students

who learn more and who rate their teachers more positively. Clarity begins with planning. Tell students what they will be learning and how they could approach it. During the lesson, avoid vague language, make clear connections between facts or concepts by using explanatory links, and check often for understanding. Finally, teacher warmth, friendliness, and understanding seem to be the traits most strongly related to positive student attitudes.

Contrast teaching in direct and student-centred instruction.

In direct instruction, the teacher gives well-organized presentations, clear explanations, carefully delivered prompts, and feedback. These actions can be resources for students as they construct understanding. In student-centred approaches, the teacher designs authentic tasks, monitors student thinking, asks questions, and prods inquiry. Both kinds of teaching may be appropriate at different times.

Focus on the Subject: Teaching Reading, Mathematics, and Science

Describe the debate about learning to read.

Today there is an ongoing debate between advocates of whole language approaches to reading and writing and

balanced approaches that include direct teaching of skills and phonics. Advocates of whole language believe children learn best when they are surrounded by good literature and read and write for authentic purposes. Advocates of a balanced approach cite extensive research indicating that skill in recognizing sounds and words—phonemic awareness—is fundamental in learning to read. Excellent primary teachers use a balanced approach combining authentic reading with skills instruction when needed.

Describe constructivist approaches to mathematics and science teaching.

Constructivist approaches to teaching mathematics and science emphasize deep understanding of concepts (as opposed to memorization), discussion and explanation, and exploration of students' implicit understandings. Many educators note that the key to understanding in science is for students to directly examine their own theories and confront the shortcomings. For change to take place, students must go through six stages: initial discomfort with their own ideas and beliefs; attempts to explain away inconsistencies between their theories and evidence presented to them; attempts to adjust measurements or observations to fit personal theories; doubt; vacillation; and finally conceptual change.

*K*ey Terms

Becoming a Professional

Reflecting on the Chapter

Can you apply the ideas from this chapter on teaching to solve the following problems of practice?

Preschool and Kindergarten

▶ You have a well-supplied science corner in your class, but your students seldom visit it. When they do, they don't seem to take advantage of the learning possibilities available with the manipulatives. How would you help students benefit from the materials?

Elementary and Middle School

▶ Your school administrator wants sample lesson plans for each of the subjects you teach. What would you include in the plans to make them useful for you?

▶ You are given a math workbook and text series and told that you must use these materials as the basis for your math teaching. What would you do to incorporate these materials into lessons that help students understand mathematical thinking and problem solving?

Junior High and High School

▶ Identify three instructional objectives for a lesson in your subject to be used in a mixed-ability Grade 10 class. How would you make these learning objectives clear to your students?

Check Your Understanding

▶ Be familiar with Bloom's taxonomy in the cognitive domain, including examples of verbs that fit each level of the domain.

▶ Know the differences between convergent and divergent questions and between higher- and lower-level questions.

▶ Be familiar with the teaching functions of direct instruction.

Your Teaching Portfolio

Think about your philosophy of teaching, a question you will be asked at most job interviews.

What is your approach to planning? How will you match teaching approaches to learning goals?

Add some ideas for parent involvement in homework from this chapter to your portfolio.

Teaching Resources

Include a summary of the cognitive, affective, and psychomotor taxonomies in your teaching resources file.

Add Table 12.2, "A Revised Taxonomy in the Cognitive Domain," to your file.

Include Table 12.7, "Active Learning and Teacher Presentations," in your file.

If you will teach elementary school, include Table 12.11, "Improving the Reading Achievement of America's Children: CIERA's 10 Research-Based Principles," in your file.

Weblinks

http://education.indiana.edu/cas/tt/v1i2/table.html

When you are setting objectives for students' learning, it's sometimes a challenge to generate your own words for what students should be able to do. This site presents a table of common terms that correspond to each of the levels in Bloom and colleagues' cognitive, affective, and psychomotor domains.

www.sasked.gov.sk.ca/docs/entre36/atibeen.html#list

Need some ideas about general formats for teaching? The Saskatchewan Ministry of Education offers a variety of ideas collected into five main categories provided as links at the bottom of the page: direct instruction, indirect instruction, experiential learning, independent study, interactive instruction.

www.nlc-bnc.ca/6/32/s32-1100-e.html

The National Library of Canada has collected a variety of teaching ideas and strategies created and approved by educators.

www.humboldt.edu/~tha1/hunter-eei.html

Madeline Hunter has developed a seven-step model for instruction. Here, you'll find an overview of her approach.

What Would They Do?

Here is how two practising teachers responded to the teaching situation presented at the beginning of this chapter about a whole language program under fire.

JANICE L. SHEETS

Assistant Principal
Mike Mountain Horse School
Lethbridge, Alberta

I would first acknowledge the concerns of the parents. I would let them know that, as a classroom teacher, I am responsible for developing a more eclectic approach to give all students every strategy available to succeed.

I would reinforce the positives of the whole language approach, especially the fact that, overall, students were enjoying literature more and spending more time reading. We usually choose to continue those things that we find enjoyable. If one goal of education is to build lifelong learners, we want to encourage this trend.

I would explain that initially it is common for spelling and penmanship to suffer because students are writing to their thinking and speaking levels, rather than limiting themselves to writing to their spelling level, which is naturally lower. This explains the discrepancy but does not help those students who are struggling.

There are several strategies I use to support students who are struggling. I continue the whole language approach, but when more independent students are doing their daily writing or reading, I build in special learning groups for students who need more directed learning.

Each morning, for 15 minutes, I teach a strategy that improves reading, spelling, or writing. Then for the remainder of the week, I have students apply the new strategy in a sentence warmup placed on the board. I make the errors and they must find and correct them. The work is taken up immediately after the time limit, and the concept is reinforced both in written form and orally each day until the majority have internalized it. I have found this extremely effective in teaching students to edit their work for errors in spelling, grammar, and the mechanics of writing.

The ideas for warmups come from curriculum expectations as well as common areas of weakness in students' reading and writing. Teaching students to peer edit, having older students buddy up with younger students to edit work, or having regular parent/community volunteers come in and help with one-on-one reading and editing are very beneficial. I always have parents listen in on my conferences with several students before I expect them to work with the students. Modelling shows parents what is expected, reinforces what you have taught, allows them to feel confident, and gives them a chance to ask clarifying questions.

Regular communication with the home is crucial, and a weekly Home and School Journal can be a good communication device. You can include quick tips for parents and recommend books that will help at home. Being proactive by establishing a daily home reading program also lets parents know that practice goes hand in hand with success. Parent workshops can promote new ideas and reinforce how parents are key to making learning enjoyable for their children.

No one strategy works all the time. One of the challenges of teaching is to find that special combination that works for each child. Parents often come up with very helpful ideas and insights that greatly help teachers in developing such programs. That kind of regular communication is the key to a winning combination for both students and parents. We are often less critical and more willing and able to help when we know that everyone is truly involved in the process.

CONNIE BUCHANAN

White City School
White City, Saskatchewan

The controversy over whole language based reading programs and phonics-based reading programs has existed for more than two decades. The situation stated here once again brings this "Great Debate" to the forefront of education circles. The pendulum continues to swing from one instructional method to the other and in this situation the decision makers have chosen to pursue the whole language curriculum more or less exclusively.

The whole language curriculum teaches the writing and reading process through the actual practice of writing and reading. This philosophy is thought to provide a more interesting and creative approach to reading and writing, and in turn, a better understanding of the text.

The phonics-based curriculum involves beginning readers learning various letter-sound relationships by using "decoding formulas." Phonics advocates feel strongly that phonics-based programs will build stronger pronunciation and word recognition.

Both philosophies have their advantages and disadvantages. Students who are self-taught readers would thrive with the whole language technique; however, any student who needs to be taught in a sequential order would simply be lost due to their need to decipher or decode the reading symbols of written text.

So what is the answer?

Unfortunately, the decision to invest in a whole language program has caused some concerns amongst the parents, administration and teachers, due to provincial test scores dropping in their school. Has this investment been a complete waste of money? Absolutely not! What the administration and teachers need to do is create balanced instruction, combining the best elements of the whole language philosophy and phonics-based instruction. In researching many long-term studies of how children need to read, you realize that not only is phonics instruction beneficial to beginning teachers, it is also crucial to involve the students in rich literature of all sorts.

The team of teachers has been successful in increasing the students' desire to read and write through the whole language initiative—what an amazing accomplishment! I truly feel that this is half the battle. The students must have an interest in literature before they will learn phonetic patterns. The love of literature adds meaning to their learning.

The principal and teacher can relate this to the parents. The love of literature is alive in their school! What they also need to express is that they will strive toward a more balanced program—one where students will be taught the relationship between sounds and letters, and exposed to interesting literature and writing at the same time.

So how can the "phonetic" component be incorporated into their present whole language curriculum?

Parents can be assured that this is not only possible but also an extremely effective way of learning. Patterns amongst stories, songs, poetry, etc., can be shared with students as you examine the letters and phonetic patterns within: graphing, charting sounds and patterns of a particular writing, or simply attending to letter/sound patterns while modelling the writing process. Teachers need to stress phoneme and phonological awareness through invented spelling, and encourage students to experiment with print while practising their learned phonetic skills. These are just a few techniques; however, it would be important for more research to be done on methods of implementing both programs successfully. Fortunately, there are many resources and studies for the administration and teachers in this situation to refer to.

The pendulum will continue to swing from whole language instruction to phonetic-based instruction. The answer is a pendulum that does not sway too far to either the left or right, but is somewhere in the middle, representing a balance in which all students learn to read and write efficiently and with enjoyment—a situation which in my mind can only happen when phonetics and whole language are used in harmony to best reach the needs of all beginning readers.

Standardized Testing in Canada

ow has standardized testing affected your life so far? What opportunities have opened or closed to you based on test scores? Was the process fair? Propose a better way to make these decisions.

Would it surprise you to learn that published tests, such as the law and medical school entrance exams and IQ tests, are creations of the twentieth century? In the nineteenth and early twentieth centuries, entrance to specialized university programs was generally based on grades, essays, and interviews. From your own experience, you know that testing has come a long way since then—too far, say some critics. They want to reshape testing as a way of reshaping the curriculum and reforming education. We will explore these new ideas.

In spite of criticisms, schools and provinces still use many standardized tests, so teachers must be knowledgeable about this kind of testing. This chapter focuses on describing and interpreting standardized tests. Understanding how standardized test scores are determined, what they really mean, and how they can be used (and misused) provides a framework for ensuring that standardized tests and testing programs contribute rather than detract from education.

First, we consider testing in general, including various methods of interpreting test scores. Then we look at different kinds of standardized tests used in Canadian schools. Finally, we examine criticisms of testing and alternatives being proposed.

By the time you have completed this chapter, you should be able to do the following:

▶ Calculate mean, median, mode, and standard deviation.

▶ Define percentile rank, standard deviation, *z* scores, grade-equivalent scores, and stanine scores.

▶ Explain how to improve reliability and validity in testing.

▶ Interpret the results of achievement, aptitude, and diagnostic tests in a realistic manner.

▶ Take a position on issues surrounding standardized testing and defend your position.

▶ Describe how to prepare students (and yourself) for taking standardized tests.

▶ Explain the strengths and weaknesses of alternative forms of assessment such as portfolios.

What Would You Do?

It is nearing the end of school and the provincial examination scores have been added into students' marks. The report cards went home last Friday, and Monday morning you get a call from the principal. The parents of one of your math students are in the office and have asked to speak with you and the principal immediately. The father is a prominent businessman and the mother is a lawyer. Their daughter received 89 percent on her Principles of Mathematics 12 examination. This student has been making Bs and Cs in your class—she seldom completes homework and has trouble with your conceptual approach to math. She just wants to know the "steps" to solve the problems so she can finish. You have tried several times over the past semester to get the parents to come in to talk about ways to support their daughter's learning, but they never had the time—until today.

You smile as you enter the principal's office, but the parents are not smiling. As soon as you sit down, the father says, "Well, you can see from our daughter's score that you have been totally wrong in the grades you have given her this year. We thought she was just weak in math, but her score on the provincial exam makes it clear you have something against her! Or maybe you just don't know how to teach math to bright young women?" The mother chimes in, "Yes, we expect you to reconsider her final grades for the year in light of her obvious ability."

▶ What would you say to the parents?

▶ What do you need to know about tests to deal with this situation?

▶ How will you approach working with this student?

▶ How will these issues affect the grade levels that you teach?

Evaluation, Measurement, and Assessment

All teaching involves **evaluation**. At the heart of evaluation is judgment, making decisions based on values. In the process of evaluation, we compare information to criteria and then make judgments. Teachers must make all kinds of judgments. "Should we use a different text this year?" "Is the film appropriate for my students?" "Will Sarah do better if she repeats the first grade?" "Should Terry get a B– or a C+ on the project?"

Measurement is evaluation put in quantitative terms—it is a numeric description of an event or characteristic. Measurement tells how much, how often, or how well by providing scores, ranks, or ratings. Instead of saying, "Sarah doesn't seem to understand addition," a teacher using measurements might say, "Sarah answered only 6 of the 15 problems correctly in her addition homework." Measurement, when done *properly*, also allows a teacher to compare one student's performance on one particular task with a standard or with the performances of the other students. The teacher might say, "She ranks 20th in her class of 24 classmates." Or, "Compared to provincial expectations, Sarah's understanding of math rates as 'needs significant improvement.'"

Not all the evaluative decisions made by teachers involve measurement. Some decisions are based on information that is difficult to express numerically: student preferences, information from parents, previous experiences, even intuition. But measurement does play a large role in many classroom decisions, and properly done, it can provide unbiased data for evaluations.

Increasingly, evaluation and measurement specialists are using the term **assessment** to describe the process of gathering information about students' learning. Assessment is a broader undertaking than testing and measurement—

Evaluation: Decision making about student performance and about appropriate teaching strategies.

Measurement: An evaluation expressed in quantitative (number) terms.

Assessment: Procedures used to obtain information about student performance.

assessment is "any of a variety of procedures used to obtain information about student performance" (Linn & Gronlund, 2000, p. 32). Assessments can be formal, such as unit tests; or they can be informal, such as observing who emerges as a leader in group work. Assessments can be designed by classroom teachers or by local, provincial, or national and international agencies. And today, assessments can go well beyond paper-and-pencil exercises to observations of performances, the development of portfolios, and the creation of artifacts (Linn & Gronlund, 2000; Popham, 1999).

In this chapter, we focus on formal assessments designed by groups and agencies outside the classroom. These assessments usually involve testing and reporting scores on those tests, so we start by examining two types of tests that are differentiated on the basis of an important principle, namely, that any score on any type of test has no meaning by itself. We must make some kind of comparison to interpret test results. There are two basic types of comparison, as we describe next.

Norm-Referenced Tests

In **norm-referenced testing**, a sample of people who have taken the test provides *norms* for determining the meaning of a given individual's score. You can think of norms as scores that describe typical levels of performance for the particular group, the norm group. By comparing the individual's raw score (the actual number of correct answers) to norms, we can determine if the score is above, below, or near average for that group.

At least three types of **norm groups** are used as reference points against which to compare an individual's score on a test. One frequently used norm group is the class or school itself. Norm groups may also be drawn from wider areas such as a school district. In this case, students' scores are compared to the scores of all other students at their grade level throughout the district. Finally, some tests have national or even international norm groups. When students take an examination of this sort, their scores are compared with the scores of students all over the country and around the world.

Norm-referenced tests cover a wide range of general objectives rather than assessing a limited number of specific objectives. These tests are especially useful in measuring overall achievement when students have studied complex material by different routes. Most norm-referenced tests used in Canada are tests of general ability or intelligence, or tests that measure specific capabilities, such as auditory discrimination. Both kinds of norm-referenced tests are almost always supplements to other information that teachers and parents gather when a student may have a learning disability or a special talent. In these instances, norm-referenced tests are used to decide whether a student should participate in instruction that complements or replaces regular classroom teaching.

Norm-referenced measurement has several limitations. The results of a norm-referenced test do not tell you where students are in a program or a curriculum. For instance, knowing that a student is in the top 3 percent of the class based on class norms on a test of algebraic concepts will not tell you if he or she is ready to move on to trigonometry. Some students clearly understand more than others, but everyone in the class may have a rather limited understanding of the algebraic concepts.

Norm-referenced tests are not typically appropriate for measuring affective and psychomotor objectives. To measure individuals' psychomotor learning, you need a clear description of standards. (Even the best gymnast in school performs certain exercises better than others and needs specific guidance about how to improve.) In affective

Norm-Referenced Testing: Testing in which scores are compared with the average performance of others.

Norm Group: A group whose average score serves as a standard for evaluating any student's score on a test.

Connect & Extend
To your teaching
Because assessment is essential to good teaching and so important to students, teachers and everyone else in the educational system must be fully aware of how assessment can be done fairly. To meet this need, nine national associations representing educators, psychologists, teachers, counsellors, school administrators, as well as representatives from all the provincial and territorial ministries developed the *Principles for Fair Student Assessment Practices for Education in Canada*, a set of standards and related guidelines about assessment practices. Based on the premise that assessments depend on professional judgment, the *Principles* identify issues to consider in exercising your professional judgment to ensure fair and equitable assessment of all students. You can get your own copy of the *Principles* on the Internet at
http://www.education.ualberta.ca /educ/psych/crame/eng_prin.pdf.

Norm-referenced testing compares an individual's score to the average score of others in a larger group. The group could be a particular classroom, school district, or international sample. ▼

Criterion-Referenced Testing:
Testing in which scores are
compared to a set standard of
performance.

areas, attitudes and values are personal; comparisons among individuals are not really appropriate. For example, how could we measure an "average" level of liberalism or support for private schools? Finally, norm-referenced tests tend to encourage competition and comparison of scores. Some students compete to be the best. Others, realizing that being the best seems impossible for them, may compete to be the worst (a dubious but nonetheless sometimes valued distinction). Either goal has its casualties.

Criterion-Referenced Tests

When test scores are compared, not to scores of others but to a given criterion or standard of performance, this is **criterion-referenced testing**. To decide who should be allowed to drive a car, it is important to determine just what standard of performance is appropriate for licensing safe drivers. It does not matter how your test results compare to others'. If your performance on the test was in the top 10 percent but you consistently ran through red lights and bumped cars while parking, you would not be a good candidate for receiving a licence, even though your score was high.

Criterion-referenced tests measure the degree of mastery of very specific objectives. The results of a criterion-referenced test should tell the teacher exactly what a student can and cannot do, at least under certain conditions. For example, a criterion-referenced test would be useful in measuring the ability to add three-digit numbers. A test could be designed with 20 different problems, and the standard for mastery could be set at 17 correct out of 20. (The standard is often somewhat arbitrary and may be based on such things as the teacher's experience.) If two students receive scores of 7 and 11, it does not matter that one student did better than the other since neither met the standard of 17. Both need more help with addition.

In teaching basic skills there are many instances where comparison to a preset standard is more important than comparison to the performance of others. It is not very comforting to know, as a parent, that your child is better in reading than most of the students in class if none of the students are able to read material suited for their grade level. Sometimes standards for meeting the criterion must be set at 100-percent correct. You would not like to have your appendix removed by a surgeon who left surgical instruments inside the body *only* 10 percent of the time.

Connect & Extend
To your teaching
A student in your Grade 4 class does poorly in the letter decoding subtest of a test standardized on a national sample of American students in Grade 4. How would your interpretation of the results differ if the test were a criterion-referenced type of score as opposed to a norm-referenced score? Explain.

Connect & Extend
To the research
Berk, R. A. (1986). A consumer's guide to setting performance standards on criterion-referenced tests. *Review of Educational Research, 56*, 137–172.

This review identifies 38 methods for setting standards or adjusting error rates. Ten criteria for technical adequacy and practicability are proposed to evaluate these methods, and specific recommendations are offered for classroom teachers.

But criterion-referenced tests are not appropriate for every situation. Some subjects cannot be analyzed into a set of specific objectives that most educators would agree on. Moreover, although standards are important in criterion-referenced testing, they sometimes can be arbitrary, as you have already seen. When deciding whether a student has mastered the addition of three-digit numbers comes down to the difference between 16 or 17 correct answers, it seems difficult to justify one particular standard over another—why 17? Why not 16 or even 18? Finally, at times it is valuable to know how students in your class compare to other students at their grade level locally, provincially, and beyond. Table 13.1 offers a comparison of norm-referenced and criterion-referenced tests. You can see that each type of test is well suited for certain situations, but each also has its limitations.

CHECKPOINT

Evaluation, Measurement, and Assessment

Review

▷ Distinguish among evaluation, measurement, and assessment.

▷ Distinguish between norm-referenced and criterion-referenced tests.

Apply

▷ The counsellor tells you that your musical aptitude is below average on a test about careers. What would you like to know about the norm group?

▷ Would you prefer a criterion-referenced or norm-referenced measure of your blood pressure? Why?

TABLE 13.1 Deciding on the Type of Test to Use

Norm-referenced tests may work best when you are

- Measuring general ability in certain areas, such as English, algebra, general science, or Canadian history.
- Assessing the range of abilities in a large group.
- Selecting top candidates when only a few openings are available.

Criterion-referenced tests may work best when you are

- Measuring mastery of basic skills.
- Determining if students have prerequisites to start a new unit.
- Assessing affective and psychomotor objectives.
- Grouping students for instruction.

Standardized Tests: Tests given, usually to large numbers of students (district-wide, provincially, or nationwide) under uniform conditions and scored according to uniform procedures.

Norming Sample: A large sample of students serving as a comparison group for scoring standardized tests.

Connect & Extend
To your teaching
Giving accurate feedback to parents is part of a teacher's job. When talking with a parent about a child's abilities, do you think the use of norm-referenced or criterion-referenced test results is more desirable?

What Do Test Scores Mean?

During their lives in school, almost all Canadian students will take **standardized tests** in the form of provincial assessments, diagnostic tests, or graduation examinations. The reason these tests are called standardized is because "the same directions are used for administering them in all classrooms and standard procedures are used for scoring and interpreting them" (Carey, 1994, p. 443). The tests are meant to be given under carefully controlled conditions so that students in any school in a province or throughout the country undergo the same experience. Standard methods of developing items, administering the test, scoring it, and reporting the scores are all implied by the term *standardized test*. When classroom teachers of the same grade or same subject share the same test items, administration procedures, scoring methods, and ways of reporting of scores, they are using standardized tests. While it is quite rarely the case in fact, the intent behind district grading policies is that grades students achieve at the same grade level or in the same subject taught at different schools will approximate the requirements of a standardized test.

Basic Concepts

In diagnostic and ability standardized testing, the test items and instructions are often tried out to make sure they work and then rewritten and retested as necessary. The final version of the test is administered to a **norming sample**, a large sample of subjects as similar as possible to the students who will be taking the test in school systems throughout the country. This norming sample serves as a comparison group for all students who take the test.

Test publishers provide one or more ways of comparing each student's raw score (number of correct answers) with the norming sample. Let's look at some of the measurements on which comparisons and interpretations are based.

While they are in school, most Canadian students will take standardized tests in the form of provincial assessments, diagnostic tests, or graduation examinations. ▼

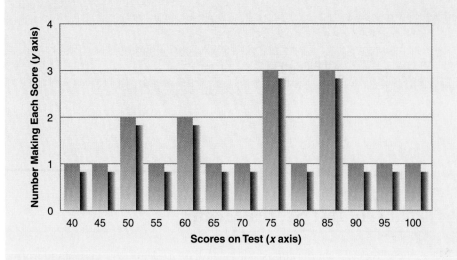

FIGURE 13.1

Histogram of a Frequency Distribution

This bar graph or histogram shows the number of people who earned each score on a test. You can quickly see, for example, that three people earned a 75 and three people earned an 85.

Frequency Distributions. A **frequency distribution** is simply a list of the number of people who obtain each score or who fall into each range of scores on a test or other measurement procedure. For example, on a spelling test 19 students made these scores: 100, 95, 90, 85, 85, 85, 80, 75, 75, 75, 70, 65, 60, 60, 55, 50, 50, 45, 40. A graph, in this case a **histogram** (bar graph), of the spelling test scores is shown in Figure 13.1, where one axis (the x, or horizontal, axis) indicates the possible scores and the other axis (the y, or vertical, axis) indicates the number of subjects who attained each score. As you can see, one student made a score of 100, three made 85, and so on.

Measurements of Central Tendency and Standard Deviation. You have probably had a great deal of experience with means. A **mean** is simply the arithmetical average of a group of scores. To calculate the mean, you add the scores and divide the total by the number of scores in the distribution. For example, the total of the 19 spelling scores is 1340, so the mean is 1340/19, or 70.53. The mean offers one way of measuring **central tendency**, the score that is typical or representative of the whole distribution of scores because it is descriptive of where to find the centre in a histogram.

Two other measures of central tendency are the median and the mode. The **median** is the middle score in the distribution, the point at which half the scores are to the left of it in an ordered (or ranked) list and half are to the right. The median of the 19 scores is the third of the three scores of 75. Nine scores in the distribution are to the left of that particular 75, and nine to the right of it. The **mode** is the score that occurs most often. The distribution in Figure 13.1 actually has two modes, 75 and 85, because each of these scores occurred three times. This makes it a **bimodal distribution**.

Each of these measures of central tendency gives a score that is representative of the group of scores, but neither tells you anything about how the scores are distributed. Two sets of scores may both have a mean of 50 but be alike in no other way. One group might contain the scores 50, 45, 55, 55, 45, 50, 50; the other group might contain the scores 100, 0, 50, 90, 10, 50, 50. In both cases the mean, median, and mode are all 50, but the distributions are very different in the shape of their histograms and in how the scores spread out.

The **standard deviation** is a measure of how widely the scores vary from the mean. The larger the standard deviation, the more spread out the scores in the distribution. The smaller the standard deviation, the more the scores are clustered near the mean. For example, in the distribution 50, 45, 55, 55, 45, 50, 50, the standard deviation is much smaller than in the distribution 100, 0, 50, 90, 10, 50, 50. Another way of saying this is that distributions with very small standard deviations have less **variability** in the scores.

The standard deviation is relatively easy to calculate. The process is similar to taking an average, but you use square roots. To calculate the standard deviation, you follow these steps:

1. Calculate the mean (written as M) of the scores.

2. Subtract the mean from each of the scores, symbolized by x. This is written as $(x - M)$.

3. Square each difference from step 2 (multiply each difference by itself). This is written $(x - M)^2$.

4. Add all the squared differences. This is written $\Sigma (x - M)^2$.

5. Divide this total by the number of scores. This is written $\dfrac{\Sigma (x - M)^2}{N}$.

6. Find the square root. This is written, $\sqrt{\dfrac{\Sigma (x - M)^2}{N}}$, otherwise known as the formula for calculating the standard deviation

Knowing the mean and the standard deviation of a set of scores gives you a better picture of the meaning of an individual score. For example, suppose you received a score of 78 on a test. You would be very pleased with the score if the mean of the test were 70 and the standard deviation were 4. In this case, your score would be 2 standard deviations above the mean, a score well above average—so high, in fact, that only about 2 in 100 students scored higher than you did.

Consider the difference if the mean of the test had remained at 70 but the standard deviation had been 20. Now, your score of 78 would be less than 1 standard deviation from the mean. You would be much closer to the middle of the group, with a score above average, but not high. Knowing the standard deviation tells you much more than simply knowing the **range** of scores from lowest to highest. No matter how the majority scored on the tests, one or two students may do very well or very poorly and thus make the range large.

The Normal Distribution. Standard deviations are very useful in understanding test results, especially if the scores on the test form a shape called a **normal distribution.** You may have met the normal distribution before. It is the bell-shaped curve, the most famous frequency distribution because it describes many naturally occurring physical and social phenomena. When scores form a normal distribution, many scores fall in the middle, giving the curve its appearance as a hill. As you move from the middle toward each end of the distribution, you find fewer and fewer scores in what are called the tails of the normal distribution.

The normal distribution has been thoroughly analyzed by statisticians. The mean of a normal distribution is the same as its midpoint, the median. Half the scores in the normal distribution are above the mean, and half are below it. In a normal distribution, the mean, median, and mode all are the same score.

A very convenient property of the normal distribution is that the percentage of scores falling within each area of the curve is known, as you can see in Figure 13.2. A person scoring within one standard deviation of the mean obviously has a lot of company. Many scores pile up here. In fact, 68 percent of all scores are located in the area between the test scores that match −1 standard deviation on the low side of the mean and +1 standard deviation on the high side. About 16 percent of the

Standard Deviation: Measure of how widely scores vary from the mean.

Variability: Degree of difference or deviation from mean.

Range: Distance between the highest and the lowest scores in a group.

Normal Distribution: The most commonly occurring distribution, in which scores are distributed evenly around the mean.

Connect & Extend
To your teaching
Which math class, A or B, is probably easier to teach, judging from the following standard score results (50 = district average)?
Class A: Mean = 57, SD = 9 Class B: Mean = 53, SD = 4
(Answer: Probably Class B because the range of students' individual differences in math achievement is not as great as in Class A.)

Connect & Extend
To your teaching
What conclusions could you draw about a test with a possible score range from 1 to 50 on which your class mean was 40 with a standard deviation of 3? You gave the same test to another class whose mean was 26 with a standard deviation of 7. How would you characterize the second class? What is the difference between the classes?

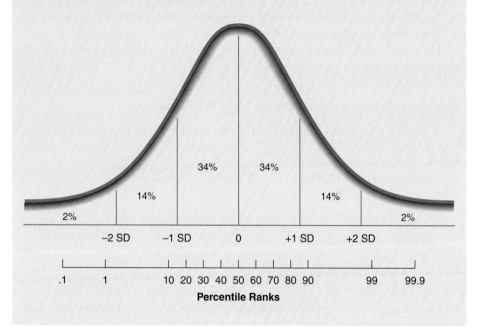

FIGURE 13.2

The Normal Distribution

The normal distribution or bell-shaped curve has certain predictable characteristics. For example, 68 percent of the scores are clustered with 1 standard deviation below to 1 standard deviation above the mean.

scores are higher than 1 standard deviation above the mean. Of this higher group, only 2 percent are better than 2 standard deviations above the mean. Similarly, only about 16 percent of the scores are less than 1 standard deviation below the mean, and of that group only about 2 percent are worse than 2 standard deviations below. At 2 standard deviations from the mean in either direction, the scorer has left the pack.

The Stanford-Binet Intelligence Test is one example of a normal distribution. The mean of this test's scores is mathematically set to be 100, and the standard deviation is 16. If you know someone who scored 132, you know they did exceptionally well on this test. Only about 2 percent of everyone who takes the test do that well, because only 2 percent of the scores are higher than 2 standard deviations above the mean in a normal distribution.

Types of Scores

Now you have enough background for a discussion of the different kinds of scores you may encounter in reports of results from standardized tests.

Percentile Rank Scores. The concept of ranking is the basis for one very common kind of score reported on standardized tests of ability or used in psychoeducational assessment, a percentile rank score. The **percentile rank** is the percentage of students in the norming sample who scored at or below a particular raw score. To find Mark's percentile rank score, compare his raw score to the list of raw scores of the students in the norming sample and determine what percent of students in the norming sample had scores the same as or lower than Mark. For example, if Mark's raw score is the same as or better than three-quarters of students in the norming sample, Mark would score at the 75th percentile or have a percentile rank of 75. Note that this does not mean Mark had a raw score of 75

Percentile Rank: Percentage of those in the norming sample whose raw scores are the same as or below an individual's raw score.

correct answers or even that Mark answered 75 percent of the questions correctly. Those are two common mistakes about interpreting percentile rank scores. Rather, the percentile rank of 75 refers to the percentage of people in the norming sample whose scores on the test were equal to or below Mark's score. A percentile rank of 50 means that a student scored as well as or better than 50 percent of the norming sample and has achieved an average score.

Figure 13.3 illustrates one important caution in interpreting percentile scores. Differences in percentile ranks do not mean the same thing in terms of raw score points in the middle of the scale as they do at the fringes. The graph shows Joan's and Alice's percentile scores on the fictitious Test of Excellence in Language and Arithmetic. Both students are about average in arithmetic skills. One equalled or surpassed 50 percent of the norming sample; the other, 60 percent. However, because their scores are near the central region of the distribution, this difference of 9 percentile ranks means a raw score difference of only a few points. Their raw scores were actually 75 and 77. In the language test, the difference of 9 percentile ranks seems to be about the same as the difference in arithmetic, since one ranked at the 90th percentile and the other at the 99th. But the difference in their raw scores on the language test is much greater. It takes a greater difference in raw score points to make a difference in percentile rank at the extreme ends of the scale. On the language test the difference in raw scores is about 10 points.

Grade-Equivalent Scores. **Grade-equivalent scores** are not used much in Canada but it's important to describe what they mean in case you should encounter them. Imagine it's September and we've developed a set 100 items to

Grade-Equivalent Score: Measure of grade level based on comparison with norming samples from each grade.

FIGURE 13.3

Percentile Ranking on a Normal Distribution Curve

Percentile scores have different meanings at different places on the scale. For example, a difference of a few raw score points near the mean might translate into a 10-point percentile difference, while it would take 6 to 7 points to make a 10-point percentile difference farther out on the scale.

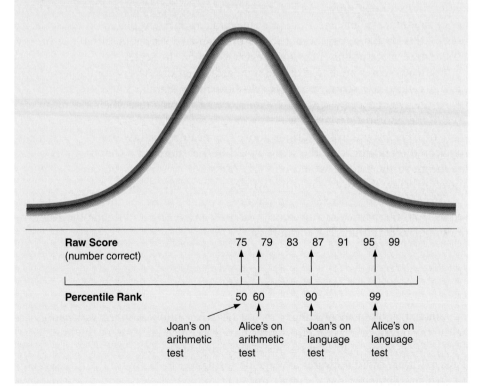

| Raw Score (number correct) | 75 79 | 83 | 87 | 91 | 95 99 |

| Percentile Rank | 50 60 | | 90 | | 99 |

Joan's on arithmetic test   Alice's on arithmetic test   Joan's on language test   Alice's on language test

Standard Score: Score based on the standard deviation.

Z Score: Standard score indicating the number of standard deviations a raw score is above or below the mean.

T Score: Standard score with a mean of 50 and a standard deviation of 10.

reflect the Grade 4 curriculum in, say, math. We administer these 100 items to nationally representative samples of students in three grades: 4, 5, and 6. Suppose all the Grade 4 students' scores on these 100 items have a mean of 52. We match this average raw score of 52 to the grade-equivalent score of 4.0. Every student who scored 52, regardless of her or his actual grade level, is assigned a grade-equivalent score of 4.0. Now, suppose the mean score of all the Grade 5 students is 77. We assign a grade-equivalent score of 5.0 to every student who scored 77, again, regardless of the student's actual grade. So, a student in Grade 4 who correctly answered 77 items on our test is assigned a grade equivalent score of 5.0. Using some mathematics, we can assign grade-equivalent scores between 4.0 and 5.0 to all the raw scores between 52 and 77. This creates grade-equivalent scores with decimals such as 4.4. The whole number refers to the grade and the decimal represents tenths of a year (roughly corresponding to the 10 months of our school year, September through June).

Suppose a student in Grade 4 received a grade equivalent score of 5.9, the same score as a Grade 5 student about to be promoted to Grade 6. Should this high-scoring Grade 4 student skip Grade 5 and be promoted to Grade 6? No. There are two powerful reasons not to recommend the Grade 4 student skip a grade. The first is that a single test should never be used to make such an important decision. No one test is "that good." The second significant reason to avoid this conclusion stems from the nature of the test. Remember that all the items on our test were drawn from the Grade 4 curriculum. The Grade 4 student who correctly answered enough test items to get a grade equivalent score of 5.9 knows a lot of the Grade 4 curriculum, even though it's only September and the school year is just beginning. But since not one test item on our test reflects the curriculum of Grade 5, we can't draw any sensible conclusions about how well the student has learned the Grade 5 material that is important preparation for Grade 6.

Grade-equivalent scores are very often misinterpreted, especially by parents. Most educators and psychologists strongly believe they should not be used at all for this single reason. Fortunately, there are several other forms of reporting available that are more appropriate.

Standard Scores. One problem with percentile ranks is the difficulty in making comparisons among ranks. As Figure 13.3 shows, a discrepancy of a certain number of raw-score points has a different meaning at different places on the scale. To remedy this problem, psychometricians use standard scores. A difference of, say, 10 standard score points is the same everywhere on the scale.

Standard scores are based on the standard deviation. A very common standard score is called the *z* score. A *z* **score** tells how many standard deviations above or below the average a raw score is. If you scored a 78 on a test where the mean was 70 and the standard deviation was 4, your *z* score would be +2 because your raw score of 78 is 2 standard deviations above the mean of the raw scores, 70. If a person scored 64 on this test, the score would be 1.5 standard deviation units *below* the mean, so the *z* score would be –1.5. A *z* score of 0 is no standard deviations above or below the mean—in other words, right at the mean.

To calculate the *z* score for a given raw score, subtract the mean of all the raw scores from the particular raw score you are considering and divide the result by the standard deviation. The formula is:

$$z = \frac{x-M}{SD}$$

Since it is often inconvenient to use negative numbers when raw scores are below the mean, other standard scores have been devised. One of the more common is the *T* **score**, which has a mean of 50 and uses a standard deviation of 10. Thus a *T* score of 50 indicates average performance. If you multiply the *z* score by 10 (which eliminates the decimal) and add 50 (which gets rid of any negative numbers), you change the z score into an equivalent *T* score. The person whose *z* score was −1.5 would have a *T* score of 35, which you calculate like this:

First multiply the *z* score by 10:   −1.5 x 10 = −15
Then add 50:   −15 + 50 = 35

The standard scores for the Stanford-Binet are based on a procedure similar to changing a *z* score into a *T* score. In the case of the Stanford-Binet, multiply *z* by 16 (the standard deviation used for Stanford-Binet scores) and add 100 (the mean set for the Stanford-Binet).

Before we leave types of standard scores, we should mention another some-times-used method. **Stanine scores** (the name comes from "standard ninths") are standard scores. There are only nine possible scores on the stanine scale, the whole numbers 1 through 9. The mean is 5, and the standard deviation is 2. Each unit from 2 to 8 is equal to half a standard deviation.

Stanine scores provide a method of considering a student's rank, since each of the nine scores includes a specific range of percentile scores in the normal distribution. For example, a stanine score of 1 is assigned to the bottom 4 percent of scores in a distribution. A stanine of 2 is assigned to the next 7 percent. Of course, some raw scores in this range of 7 percent are higher than others, but they all get a stanine score of 2.`1

Each stanine score can represent a wide range of raw scores. This has the advantage of encouraging teachers and parents to view a student's score in more general terms instead of making overly fine distinctions based on just a point or two. Figure 13.4 compares the four types of standard scores we have considered, showing how each corresponds to the others when scores form a normal distribution.

> **Stanine Scores:** Whole number scores from 1 to 9 where each stanine represents a range of raw scores that correspond to one-ninth of scale.

FIGURE 13.4

Four Types of Standard Scores on a Normal Distribution Curve
Using this figure, you can translate one type of standard into another.

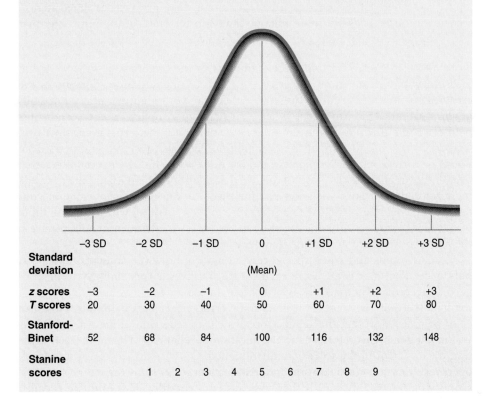

	−3 SD	−2 SD	−1 SD	0	+1 SD	+2 SD	+3 SD
Standard deviation				(Mean)			
z scores	−3	−2	−1	0	+1	+2	+3
T scores	20	30	40	50	60	70	80
Stanford-Binet	52	68	84	100	116	132	148
Stanine scores		1 2	3	4 5 6	7	8 9	

Interpreting Test Scores

Reliability: Consistency of test results.

True Score: Hypothetical average of all of an individual's scores if repeated testing under ideal conditions were possible.

It is alarming that many people in and outside schools misinterpret test scores, especially grade equivalent scores and percentile ranks. One reason this happens is because not everyone who should know about the shortcomings of tests does know about them. One all-too-common misunderstanding about test scores is that numbers are precise measurements of a student's ability or attitude or anything. No test provides a perfectly accurate description of a person's characteristics. First of all, a test is only one small sample of behaviour. Two factors are important in developing good tests and interpreting results: reliability and validity.

Reliability. If you took a test on Monday, took the same test again a week later, and received about the same score each time, you would have reason to believe the score was reliable. If 100 people took the test one day, repeated it the following week, and each individual's score on the test had about the same rank both times, you would be even more convinced the scores were reliable. (Of course, this assumes no one looks up answers or studies before the second test.) When a score has **reliability**, it represents a consistent and stable "reading" about a characteristic of a person from one occasion to the next—assuming the characteristic remains the same. A reliable thermometer works in a similar manner, giving you a reading of 100° C each time you measure the temperature of boiling water. Measuring a score's reliability in this way, by giving the test on two different occasions, indicates *stability* or, as it is often called, *test-retest reliability*. If a group of people takes two equivalent versions or forms of a test and the scores on both tests are comparable, this is called alternate-form reliability.

Reliability has several forms. It can also refer to the internal consistency of items on a test or the precision of a test's score. One of these types of reliability, known as *split-half reliability,* is calculated by comparing performance on half of the test questions with performance on the other half. If, for example, someone did quite well on all the odd-numbered items and not at all well on the even-numbered items, we could assume that the items were not very consistent or precise in measuring what they were intended to measure. The most effective way to improve reliability is to add more items to a test (assuming they are well-designed items). Generally, longer tests are more reliable than shorter ones, in the same way that larger samples are more representative of whatever they are sampled from.

Connect & Extend
To your teaching
There are many sources of error in testing: personal (e.g., illness, anxiety, misreading directions, reviewing wrong material); test-related (e.g., unclear directions, excessive length, too-high reading level); and context-related (too-competitive situation, noise, mistakes by test administrator).

True Score. All tests are imperfect estimators of the qualities or skills we try to measure with a test. There are errors in every testing situation. Sometimes the errors are in your favour, and you score higher than your ability or interest or skills might warrant. This can occur when you happen to review a key section just before a pop quiz or your guesses are lucky. Sometimes the errors go against you. You don't feel well the day of the examination, have just received bad news from home, or focused on the wrong material in your review. But if you could be tested over and over again without becoming tired and without memorizing the answers, the randomness of good luck and bad luck would even out. The average of your test scores would be very close to a true score for you. In other words, we can think of a student's **true score** as the mean of all the scores that student would receive if the test were repeated an infinite number of times.

In classrooms and when special tests are given, however, students take a test only once. That means the score each student receives is very unlikely to be 100-percent accurate. Alternatively, we can view any single score as being made up of the hypothetical true score as well as some error, either plus or minus. How can error be reduced so that the actual score is a closer reflection of the true score? As you might guess, this returns us to the question of reliability. The more reliable the test, the less error in the score actually obtained. On standardized tests, test developers take this into consideration and make estimations of how much the students' scores would probably vary if they were tested repeatedly. This estimate is called the **standard error of measurement**. It represents the *standard deviation* of the distribution of scores from our hypothetical repeated testings. When the set of scores from repeated testing spreads out a lot—that is, has a big standard error of measurement—any single score from one testing isn't likely to be representative. If there is little variability among the scores, the histogram is narrow and any particular test score won't differ much from any other. Thus a reliable test can also be defined as a test with a small standard error of measurement. As teachers and others interpret *any* test score, they must take into consideration the margin for error.

Confidence Interval. Teachers should not base an opinion of a student's ability, motivation, or achievement on just one "exact" score the student obtains. A more reasonable view of any test result is to consider it as **confidence interval** or "standard error band" that shows a range of scores around the particular score the student received. Viewing scores as a range is better because no measurement process—a test, an observation, a rating—is perfectly reliable. Scores always vary due to random influences, that is, unreliability.

Suppose, for instance, two students in your International Baccalaureate chemistry class take a standardized achievement test. One student receives a score of 77; the other, a score of 85. At first glance, these scores seem quite different. But consider the standard error bands for these scores. Suppose the standard error of measurement for this test is 3. First, calculate the length of a "leg" of the standard error band by multiplying the standard error by two: $2 \times 3 = 6$. Now, subtract this result from each score to find the lower endpoint of each score's standard error band; then, add six to each score to find the upper endpoint of each score's standard error band. The standard error band for the student who scored 77 is $77 - 6 = 71$ to $77 + 6 = 83$. This student's true score on the test is somewhere in this confidence interval. The other student's standard error band is $85 - 6 = 79$ to $85 + 6 = 91$, and the true score is somewhere between 79 and 91. As you can see, these confidence intervals overlap. It's possible that the student who obtained the "exact" score of 85 might have a true score that's actually less than that of the student whose obtained the score of 77. If these two students took the test again, they might even switch rankings.

Any significant decision about a student should take into account that every test result has some degree of unreliability. Standard error bands are a useful method for gauging that uncertainty. When selecting students for special programs, no child should be rejected simply because one obtained score missed the cutoff by a few points. The student's true score might well be on the other side of the cutoff point.

Validity. If a test is sufficiently reliable, the next question is whether it is valid, or more accurately, whether the judgments and decisions based on the test are valid. To have **validity**, the decisions and inferences based on the test must be supported by evidence. This means that validity is judged in relation to a particular use or purpose, that is, in relation to the actual decision being made and the evidence for that decision (Linn & Gronlund, 2000). A test itself never has validity. Only people's decisions and interpretations have some degree of validity.

There are different kinds of *evidence* to support a particular judgment. If the purpose of a test is to measure the skills covered in a particular course or unit, we would hope to see test questions on all the important topics and none on extraneous topics. If this condition is met, we would have *content-related evidence of validity*. Have you ever taken a test that dealt only with a few ideas from one lecture or just a few pages of the textbook? Then decisions based on that test (your grade, for instance) certainly lacked content-related evidence of validity.

Some tests are designed to predict outcomes. The LSATs (Law School Admission Test), for example, are intended to predict performance in law school. If LSAT scores correlate with academic performance as measured by, say, grade-point average in the first year, then we have *criterion-related evidence of*

Connect & Extend
To the research
Moss, P. A. (1992). Shifting conceptions of validity in educational measurement: Implications for performance assessment. *Review of Educational Research, 62,* 229–258.

Connect & Extend
To your teaching
What makes any test or measurement procedure a good predictor? Consider the relevance of the test or measurement procedure to the outcome, absence of bias, reliability, convenience, and cost.

Connect & Extend

To your teaching

Can you answer these questions adapted from Popham, W. J. (1988). *Educational evaluation,* 2/e. Englewood Cliffs, NJ: Prentice-Hall, p. 127?

Indicate which of the following types of validity is being gathered.

a. Subject-matter experts have been summoned to rate the consonance of a test's items with the objectives the test is supposed to measure.

b. A correlation is computed between a new test of student self-esteem and a previously validated and widely used test of student self-esteem.

c. Scores on a screening test (used to assign Grade 10 students to standard or enriched English classes) are correlated with English competence of first-year university students (as reflected by grades assigned at the end of first-year English).

Answers: a. content b. construct c. criterion

validity for the use of the LSAT in admissions decisions. In other words, the test scores are fairly accurate predictors of the criterion—how well the student will do in law school.

Most standardized tests are designed to measure some psychological characteristic or "construct" such as reasoning ability, reading comprehension, achievement motivation, intelligence, creativity, and so on. It is a bit more difficult to gather *construct-related evidence of validity,* yet this is a critical requirement. Construct-related evidence of validity is gathered over many years. It is indicated by a pattern of scores. For example, older children can answer more questions on intelligence tests than younger children. This fits with our construct of intelligence. If the average 5-year-old answered as many questions correctly on a test as the average 13-year-old, we would doubt that the test really measured intelligence. Construct-related evidence for validity can also be demonstrated when the results of a test correlate with the results of other well-established measures of the same construct.

Today, many educational psychologists suggest that construct-related validity is the broadest category and that gathering content- and criterion-related evidence is another way of determining if the test measures the construct it was designed to measure. And new questions are being raised about validity. What are the consequences of using a particular assessment procedure for teaching and learning? Twenty years ago Sam Messick (1975) raised two important questions to consider in making any decisions about using a test: Is the test a good measure of the characteristic it is assumed to assess? Should the test be used for the proposed purpose? The first question is about construct-related validity; the second is about ethics and values (Moss, 1992).

A number of factors may interfere with the validity of interpretations based on tests given in classroom situations. One problem has already been mentioned—a poorly planned test with weak relation to the important topics. Standardized achievement tests must be designed so that the items on the test actually measure knowledge gained in the classes. This match is absent more often than we might assume. Also, students must have the necessary skills to take the test. If students score low on a science test not because they lack knowledge about science but because they have difficulty reading the questions, do not understand the directions, or do not have enough time to finish, the test is not a valid measure of science achievement for those students.

A test must be reliable in order to be valid. For example, if, over a few months, an intelligence test yields different results each time it is given to the same child, then by definition it is not reliable. Certainly it couldn't be the basis for valid interpretations about intelligence because intelligence is assumed to be fairly stable, at least over a short timespan. However, reliability will not guarantee validity. If that intelligence test gave the same score every time for a particular child but didn't predict school achievement, speed of learning, or other characteristics associated with intelligence, then performance on the

CHECKPOINT

What Do Test Scores Mean?

Review

▶ Describe the key features of a standardized test.

▶ What are mean, median, mode, and standard deviation?

▶ Describe different kinds of scales for scores.

▶ What is test reliability?

▶ What is test validity?

Apply

▶ If all Grade 12 students in your province take a well-designed, standardized international test of science that has a mean of 70 and a standard deviation of 10, about how many should score above 80? If the standard error of measurement for this test is 4 points, would you classify a student who scored 80 as well above average?

▶ Which is better, a percentile score of 75 or a *T* score of 75? Which is easier to explain to a family member?

▶ Every time you check your weight on your bathroom scale and at the gym, you weigh 0.5 kg less at home than at the gym. Is your bathroom scale valid? Is it reliable?

Increasing Score Reliability and Validity of Interpretations

Make sure the test actually covers the content of the unit of study.

Examples

1. Compare test questions to course objectives. A behaviour-content matrix might be useful here (see Chapter 14).
2. Use local achievement tests and local norms when possible.
3. Check to see if the test is long enough to cover all important topics.
4. Are there any difficulties your students experience with the test, such as not enough time, level of reading, and so on? If so, discuss these problems with appropriate school personnel.

Make sure students know how to use all the test materials.

Examples

1. Several days before a test, do a few practice questions with a similar format.
2. Demonstrate the use of the answer sheets, especially computer-scored answer sheets.
3. Check with new students, shy students, slower students, and students who have difficulty reading to make sure they understand the questions.
4. Make sure students know if and when guessing is appropriate.

Follow instructions for administering the test exactly.

Examples

1. Practise giving the test before you actually use it.
2. Follow the time limits exactly.

Make students as comfortable as possible during testing.

Examples

1. Do not create anxiety by making the test seem like the most important event of the year.
2. Help the class relax before beginning the test, perhaps by telling a joke or having everyone take a few deep breaths. Don't be tense yourself!
3. Make sure the room is quiet.
4. Discourage cheating by monitoring the room. Don't become absorbed in your own paperwork.

Remember that no test scores are perfect.

Examples

1. Interpret scores using bands instead of a single score.
2. Ignore small differences between scores.

---

test would not be a valid indicator of intelligence. The test would be reliable—but invalid. The Guidelines should help you increase the reliability and validity of the standardized tests you give.

Standardized Tests Used in Canada's Schools

Three main kinds of standardized tests are used today in schools: tests of students' achievement, and aptitude and diagnostic psychoeducational tests that contribute toward a fuller understanding of an individual student. *Standardized tests* have two special qualities. First, they are administered to students under precisely defined—that is, standardized—conditions. Second, students' test answers are scored in a standardized way using the same method so that, as much as possible, scores can be interpreted in terms of the same benchmark. Almost every standardized **achievement test** used in Canada is criterion-referenced. This is a significant difference from standardized achievement tests that are so prominent in other countries, such as the United States, where norm-referenced interpretations

Achievement Tests: Standardized tests measuring how much students have learned in a given content area.

▲ *For a standardized test to be a valid measure of students' knowledge, the students must be familiar with procedures for taking the test—how to use the machine-scored sheets, what to do if they don't know an answer, and so on.*

dominate. In comparison, most frequently used standardized psychoeducational tests in Canada are norm-referenced. Teachers almost certainly will encounter both kinds of standardized tests, achievement and psychoeducational, though in different contexts. And the information that elementary teachers receive about their students is more likely to be based on diagnostic tests than that received by secondary teachers.

Provincial and Territorial Achievement Tests

Almost all children in Canada will take several standardized achievement tests over the course of their lives in school. Provinces and territories develop standardized achievement tests for two main purposes. One is to evaluate achievement at various levels: the whole province or territory, a region, individual school districts, and sometimes individual schools and students. Information provided by these standardized achievement tests is intended to help students, parents, and schools determine whether objectives have been reached and to identify where improvement is needed. In provinces and territories where students take standardized achievement tests in their last year of school, such as the Grade 12 examinations in British Columbia and Manitoba's examinations at the Senior 4 level, the results often form a part of students' school marks. In the case of British Columbia, the results also determine whether students receive scholarships for college or university.

The second main purpose of these large-scale standardized achievement tests is to help teachers, curriculum developers, and educational policy makers understand better how today's educational practices contribute to students' progress and achievement. Here, the intent is to shine light on areas that need work, as well as to celebrate achievements.

Quite a lot of information about testing programs is available on the Internet. At the end of the chapter, we provide a single Weblink that lists links to each province's and territory's ministry Web site. Exploring the information at these sites will be beneficial in at least two ways. First, it will introduce you to how school curricula are organized in your province or territory. This can help achieve

curriculum alignment, the qualities and degrees to which standardized achievement tests (as well as your classroom assessments) match school curricula and objectives. Curriculum alignment is a critical feature that determines how well the results of standardized achievement tests can be used in valid ways. Second, because of the expense involved in standardized achievement testing programs, as well as the important functions these programs are intended to fulfill, each province and territory strives to apply the very best and latest practices in designing the tests and developing methods for scoring them. Thus, these tests can serve as illuminating models you can use to develop and adapt assessments of your students' achievements.

We don't have space to do justice to even one province's or territory's comprehensive programs. So we will present a few snapshots of selected features that represent state-of-the-art work in standardized achievement testing.

Ontario's Educational Quality and Accountability Office Grade 3 and 6 Tests.

As of our deadline for this book, Ontario tests Grade 3 and 6 students late spring every year in reading, writing, and mathematics. These tests assess what students know and can do using real-world problems in which, as described by the *Parent Handbook 2000-2001* (Educational Quality and Accountability Office, 2001), "Students may have to argue in favour of an idea, identify the main ideas in a reading passage, or calculate the time it takes to complete a trip" (p. 5). Items for these tests are developed by teachers and school principals, examined by experts, and field-tested before being administered "for real." Parents can obtain booklets that illustrate sample test questions so they and their children know what to expect on the tests.

The September following administration of the tests, an Individual Student Report is produced for every student. Teachers in Grades 4 and 7 receive these reports for the students in their class and are encouraged to use this information as they plan for teaching. Along with the standardized achievement test results in the reports, the province provides contextual data—gathered at the same time the test was taken—from the student, teacher, and principal. These contextual data are offered as a backdrop for interpreting each student's achievement test results. Table 13.2 lists questions, copied from the *Teacher Guide* (Educational Quality and Accountability Office, October 2001), that teachers are invited to address as they analyze each student's results and consider context.

Manitoba's Grade 6 English Language Arts Test 2001–2002.

This test was developed by Grade 6 teachers working with ministry consultants. It is optional, to be administered at the discretion of each school district in Manitoba. The test is administered in early June over a three-day period, an hour each day. According to the province's *Information Bulletin* (2001), the test is designed to reflect students' achievement in five major areas of language arts: exploring thoughts, ideas, feelings, and experiences; comprehending and responding personally and critically to oral, literary, and media texts; managing ideas and information; enhancing the clarity and artistry of communication; and celebrating and building community. About 40 percent of the items are restricted-response questions in which students must demonstrate particular knowledge and skills. The remaining 60 percent of the items are open-response and involve students in selecting information, organizing their answer as they judge best, and integrating and evaluating ideas.

Teachers score the tests at their schools using a scoring **rubric**. This is a set of characteristics and rules, sometimes accompanied by examples of answers that illustrate how these are applied, to guide markers in scoring complex material such as essays. The Manitoba rubric specifies characteristics of students' answers at three ranked categories—above level, at level, and below level—with three subdivisions that they label Class 1, 2, and 3 within the "at level" rank. Each level is assessed relative to a scale that allocates a total of 10 points for content (purpose and focus, details, and language usage), 3 points for form and organization of the

TABLE 13.2 Questions Teachers are Invited to Consider Based on the Individual Student Reports Generated by Ontario's Grade 3 and 6 Assessments of Reading, Writing, and Mathematics.

Analyzing the Student's Results	Analyzing the Class's Results
▪ What strengths and weaknesses did the student demonstrate in the reading, writing, and mathematics categories and in the mathematics strands?	▪ What strengths and weaknesses did students generally demonstrate in the reading, writing, and mathematics categories and in the mathematics strands?
▪ How do these strengths and weaknesses compare with those identified at the school, board, and provincial levels? How did the student perform overall in each subject area?	▪ How do these strengths and weaknesses compare to those identified at the school, board, and provincial levels?
▪ Is it possible to identify any patterns in the student's work? What do these patterns mean?	▪ How did the class perform overall in each subject area?
▪ Are the results consistent with the student's current achievement? Do the student's booklets shed light on what may have caused any discrepancies?	▪ What patterns are evident in the class's achievement across the three subject areas? What do these patterns mean?

Interpreting the Student's Results	Interpreting the Class's Results
▪ What factors may have contributed to the strengths and weaknesses the student demonstrated on the assessment (e.g., use of a particular textbook or other resources, attendance)?	▪ What factors may have contributed to the strengths and weaknesses students demonstrated on the assessment (e.g., use of a particular textbook or other resources, class groupings, allocation of instructional time, homework)?
▪ Is the achievement reasonable in light of the student's program?	▪ What factors might account for any unexpected or inconsistent results (e.g., testing conditions, lack of familiarity with the assessment format, limits on teacher assistance, anxiety, maturity)?
▪ What factors may account for any unexpected or inconsistent results (e.g., testing conditions, lack of familiarity with the assessment format, limits on teacher assistance, anxiety, maturity)?	▪ Is it possible to identify any attitudinal factors that may be relevant?
▪ Is it possible to identify any attitudinal factors that may be relevant?	▪ What changes should be made to the classroom program to reinforce strengths and address gaps in students' learning (e.g., reprioritizing expectations, reallocating class time for various subjects, modifying teaching and assessment strategies)?
▪ What changes should be made to the student's individual program to help him or her learn better?	▪ What measures could be adopted at school?
▪ What measures could be adopted at school and at home to improve the student's achievement (e.g., reading at home, use of real-world mathematics activities)?	

answer, and 3 points for mechanics. Further details are given about how individual teachers should mark the examination. A subset of papers from each district is marked again to explore for issues in the accuracy of marking.

It is important that the every student has a full opportunity to demonstrate achievement, so the examination policies explicitly provide that the standardized methods for administering the test should be adapted to accommodate students under special circumstances. For example, if students are unable to handwrite the examination or would be disadvantaged if they were limited to writing by hand, they are allowed to use a word processor, typewriter, or Braille writing device. Students with a hearing impairment may receive instructions in American Sign Language.

What Can We Learn from Standardized Criterion-Referenced Achievement Tests? We use an example of one criterion-referenced standardized achievement test, British Columbia's Grade 12 exam in history, to highlight key features of criterion-referenced standardized tests and illustrate good practices for classroom tests.

The BC history exam consists of four parts (Student Assessment and Program Evaluation Branch, 2000). Part A is 40 multiple-choice items. Part B provides six short essay items divided into two sections. Students select one item in each section and a third item from either section. In Part C, students are presented with a few brief historical documents, quotes or other selections from historical materials, and write two brief essays based on these materials. In Part D, students write an extended essay they choose from two given topics. Having a variety of types of test items is a strength because each type contributes different information about different knowledge and skills. Multiple-choice items are quick to answer, so the curriculum can be sampled more broadly. The several types of written response items allow testing at a variety of cognitive levels and with greater authenticity. This design increases overall understanding about a student's achievement.

To help students and their teachers prepare for the history exam, the ministry publishes a booklet of specifications for the history exam (as well as similar booklets for every other exam in the Grade 12 series). The booklet describes the nature of items on the exam and how they are scored. This guide also includes a glossary of key words, which the ministry labels "command terms," that are crucial for students to understand when they analyze the tasks they are set. Some examples are:

Agree or Disagree

Support or refute a statement; give the positive or negative features; express an informed opinion one way or the other; list the advantages for or against. In today's world, dominated by science and technology, education in the humanities has little meaning. Agree or disagree with this statement.

Discuss

Present the various points of view as in a debate or argument. Points-of-view arising from the topic should be supported and/or challenged; e.g., "The first war explains the second and, in fact, caused it, insofar as one event causes another.", A. J. P. Taylor. Discuss this statement with reference to the causes of the Second World War.

Evaluate

Making a judgment which involves determining the value of a statement and/or assessing the relative significance of that idea; e.g., Most conflict in the twentieth century has been the result of the clash between totalitarianism and democratic ideologies. Evaluate this statement.

Outline

Give a description of only the main features; summarize the principal parts of a thing, idea, or event; e.g., Outline the main events of the summer of 1917 in Russia.

The booklet also provides descriptions of cognitive levels of items based on the taxonomy developed by Bloom and his colleagues (Bloom, Engelhart, Frost, Hill, & Krathwohl, 1956). Students can use the features given in these definitions and the taxonomy as standards for metacognitively monitoring their understanding of what they should do to answer items and, after drafting their answer, as checks about whether they've really answered the question.

How are items scored and what can be learned from them? Here's an item from a previous exam:

Totalitarian governments are a feature of the twentieth century. Why have some nations adopted totalitarianism?

Connect & Extend
To other chapters
Review the section on Objectives for Learning in **Chapter 9** and The Cognitive Domain of Bloom's Taxonomy in **Chapter 12**.

Each essay on the BC Grade 12 exams is scored by teachers who use a holistic scheme that assigns a score from zero to five according to the criteria in Table 13.3, which we've reproduced from page 10 of the *History 12 Examination Specifications*.

Such detailed descriptions of what "counts" in a task illuminate what it "takes" to understand a concept such as totalitarianism in rich detail. With a little bit of generalization, nearly the same standards can be applied to a wide array of other concepts in school, for example: issues in public transportation, methodologies for investigating ecological disasters, writing a current-events story for the school newspaper, or analyzing a description of supernovas. Our point is that the labour invested in developing such thorough descriptions of what students need to do to answer one item about one topic on a standardized test of history can, with a bit of extension, pay off in other areas. Students as well as teachers can use these descriptions as guides for learning and teaching.

Canada's School Achievement Indicators Program

In 1991, following a series of meetings by the ministers of education of all 10 provinces and 2 territories, an agreement was struck to carry out periodic surveys of students' achievement across the country. The School Achievement Indicators Program, or SAIP, was born. This program tests 13- and 16-year-old Canadian students in reading and writing, mathematics, and, as of 1993, science. Results are intended to satisfy the population's interest in how well our educational system is working. As well, the ministers wanted to gather information that could help them better understand what was taught in their and other provinces' curricula, to set educational priorities, and to plan improvements for educational programs.

Subjects are examined on a three-year cycle. For example, science was examined in 1996 and 1999, and, as we're finishing this book, it's scheduled again for 2002. Not all students take the tests. Instead, approximately 1000 students at each age level in each province are randomly sampled to represent the provincial population. Results are reported only at the level of whole provinces or territories. No scores are available for districts, schools, or individual students because the ministers believe that responsibilities for assessing individual students lie with the teacher, the school, and the province.

Like most of the provincial standardized achievement tests, the SAIP tests are criterion-referenced. For example, the SAIP mathematics tests are referenced to five levels of achievement in mathematics learning (National Council of Teachers of Mathematics, 1989). Items on the 1997 and the 2001 tests covered four topics: numbers and operations, algebra and functions, measurement and geometry, and managing data and statistics. Approximately 40 percent of these items assessed students' understanding of major concepts, another 30 percent examined students' knowledge of procedures, and the remaining 30 percent were problem-solving exercises that called for skills such as formulating a problem, developing a mathematical model that matched a verbal description, and verifying that a given solution was valid.

For the 2001 mathematics cycle, half the students at each age level took the test just described. As well, an entirely new test was developed and administered to the other half of students to assess mathematics problem solving. These were extended response problems that involved students in activities such as formulating problems, constructing mathematical models for verbally presented information, verifying the accuracy of solutions, and evaluating mathematical models and solutions. In addition to achievement items, the SAIP mathematics tests included a student questionnaire asking students to describe how they "lived" math instruction in their school. What was their grade level? Were their math courses full-year or semester length? Did they like math? How confident did they feel when they did

TABLE 13.3 The Holistic Scoring Scheme Used to Score Essays in British Columbia's Grade 12 History Exam (2001)

Score	Label	Qualities of Response
5	Excellent	■ Superior recall of factual content organized in a purposeful, effective and sophisticated manner. ■ Thesis is clear, relevant and valid with reference to the topic throughout the essay. ■ There is a mature, precise selection of supporting details and where evaluation is required, judgment is exemplary. ■ Expression is clear and fluent.
4	Proficient	■ Above-average recall of factual content organized in a clear and deliberate manner. ■ Good understanding of the fundamental concepts of history and where evaluation is required, judgment is sound. ■ An appropriate thesis is evident and the topic is generally addressed throughout the essay. ■ Expression is generally controlled and fluent, with a clear and appropriate selection of supporting details. There may be occasional errors, but only minor flaws in communication.
3	Acceptable	■ Satisfactory recall of factual content with some organization and planning. ■ Sufficient understanding of the fundamental concepts of history and where evaluation is required, judgment is satisfactory. ■ Thesis is identifiable but the writer may occasionally stray from the topic. ■ While the expression may be awkward, there is an adequate selection of supporting details. Errors may occasionally impede communication.
2	Limited	■ Limited and flawed recall of factual content lacking adequate organization and planning. ■ Insufficient understanding of the fundamental concepts of history and where evaluation is required, judgment is poor. ■ Thesis is irrelevant or invalid and the writer is often off the topic. ■ The expression is limited, awkward, and simplistic, with an inadequate selection of supporting details. Errors often impede communication.
1	Unsatisfactory	■ Deficient recall of factual content presented in a disorganized, error-ridden manner. ■ Inferior understanding of the fundamental concepts of history and where evaluation is required, judgment is seriously flawed. ■ Thesis is non-existent and the writer is off the topic. ■ Expression is unclear or uncontrolled and supporting details are completely lacking. Errors result in a frequent lack of communication.
0	Cannot Be Evaluated	■ While writing is evident, no discernible attempt has been made to address the topic as given or the writing is so deficient in length or legibility that it cannot be evaluated.

math questions?

The SAIP officials emphasize that even as carefully developed a test as the SAIP has limitations. First, they acknowledge that the test focuses on knowledge and skills that are measurable by paper-and-pencil tests. Second, they point out that the test doesn't completely match or align with the full curriculum in every province and territory. For example, students' ability to work with manipulatives was not assessed in the mathematics test. Also, skills in group problem solving or working on complex mathematical issues were not tested. SAIP officials suggest that dimensions of mathematics learning not represented on the SAIP test are better assessed using sound techniques for classroom assessment such as interviews, portfolios, and performance-based methods.

For those areas that are tested on the SAIP, a very careful process has been followed to develop items for the tests. In the mathematics test, for example, the items for the first version of the test were drafted by experts. Between October 1991 and November 1992, successive drafts of the test were field-tested three times. Each time, constructive criticism was sought about everything: directions, procedures for administering the test, time students had to take the test, techniques for scoring answers, and questions appearing on the questionnaire. Revisions were made and field testing was repeated. From the very first version, careful attention was paid to ensure that English and French versions of the test were comparable.

For the second round of mathematics assessment in 1997, experts representing about one-third of the provinces and territories re-examined the 1993 test. Based on analyses of the earlier version, they replaced 4 multiple-choice items and revised about another 20. The number of problem-solving items was reduced from 9 to 6, and 2 problem-solving items kept from the 1993 version were modified. This draft was field-tested once and then revised before the final version of the test was administered. To build a bridge for comparing the results of the 1993 assessment to the 1997 tests, a separate national sample of 13- and 16-year-olds was administered the 1993 version of the test in 1997. A thorough statistical analysis was done to investigate just how comparable the tests' results were.

Results of the mathematics assessment carried out in spring 2001 are not yet available as we write this text, so let's examine how Canadian students did on the mathematics assessment of 1997. A first step to answering this question was to decide what percentage of students should reach or exceed each of the five levels of performance that were identified when the tests were developed. This is a difficult question! To answer it, an 89-member panel was convened. Members represented every province and each territory, and included teachers, university professors, curriculum specialists, parents, community leaders, First Nations teacher trainers, leaders from business and industry, and representatives from national organizations such as the Canadian Society for the Study of Education. They reviewed the test, scoring criteria and procedures, and a sample of students' results. Their answer was . . . mixed.

At the lowest of the five levels of achievement in mathematics content, the panel found that the 90 percent of 13-year-old students who achieved level 1 or higher was sufficient. But too few students reached levels 2, 3, and 4. For instance, the panel expected 50 percent of students to reach at least level 3, but only 28.4 percent did. In the group of 16-year-olds, 95 percent of students scored at least at level 1 on mathematical content. However, 40 percent of this age group was expected to reach level 4, whereas only 14.5 percent did. Similar gaps were found at achievement levels 2, 3, and 5. Approximately similar judgments were made about the problem-solving section of the test (School Achievement Indicators Program, March 12, 1999, www.cmec.ca/saip/math97/Pages/App5.html). In short, we have a fairly large gap to close if students are to meet expectations for achievement in mathematics.

Psychoeducational Tests

Because of provincial policies and practices regarding inclusion and Canada's Charter of Rights and Freedoms, students in practically every Canadian classroom will display a very wide range of individual differences. It's almost certain that your classroom will include at least one exceptional student who has special needs such as those discussed in Chapter 4. Some exceptional students' needs will not be particularly perplexing. A recent immigrant to Canada who has only the most basic skills in English or French will require extra help in every arena where language and cultural understandings are keys to full participation. But other students' academic needs may be more challenging to understand because the nature of the exceptionality (or exceptionalities!) is less obvious, more complex, or both. To provide really effective instruction for these students, it may be appropriate to mobilize a school-based team. These specialists, particularly the school psychologist, have advanced training in how to administer psychoeducational tests and how to help you, parents, and others validly interpret the results of those tests.

Two categories of psychoeducational tests are often distinguished: aptitude tests and diagnostic tests. An **aptitude** is a capability for learning knowledge or skills in a relatively specific sort of situation, for example, in classrooms or on the job. **Aptitude tests** are intended to provide a score that, along with other information, helps to predict how well, how fast, or how accurately a student can learn. Some aptitude tests may seem, on the surface, to have little to do with subjects students study in school. For example, the Auditory Discrimination Test (Wepman, 1973) presents children between five and eight years old with pairs of words, some of which differ only by one phoneme, such as "cat" versus "cap." Asking students whether they hear the same word or different words isn't common as a school activity.

A **diagnosis** is a description of a student's current knowledge, skill, or ability. Straightforwardly enough, a **diagnostic test** produces a score that is a diagnosis. In the manuals that accompany diagnostic tests, relatively narrow bands of scores are sometimes matched to descriptions of problems or cognitive processing deficiencies that might cause the diagnosis. There are diagnostic tests to assess the ability to hear differences among sounds, remember spoken words or sentences, recall a sequence of symbols, separate figures from their background, express relationships, coordinate eye and hand movements, describe objects orally, blend sounds to form words, recognize details in a picture, coordinate movements, and many other abilities needed to learn, remember, and communicate learning.

To take a specific example, the Woodcock Reading Mastery Tests–Revised (Woodcock, 1987) is a commonly used diagnostic test. It includes six subtests: visual-auditory learning, letter identification, word identification, word attack,

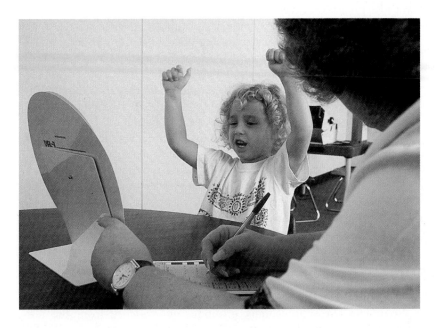

▲ *Psychoeducational assessments don't have to be a hardship for students.*

Standardized Tests Used in Canada's Schools

Review

▷ What are the main types of standardized tests used in Canada?

▷ What is a rubric and how is it used?

▷ Is there a difference between an aptitude test and a diagnostic test?

Apply

▷ How would you determine whether a year-end test you develop is aligned with the curriculum in your province?

▷ What questions would you want answered if your school's achievement in Grade 8 science was to be compared to another school's Grade 8 science achievement in another province?

word comprehension, and passage comprehension. Scores on these subtests describe the quality of performance a student would be expected to show on tasks at a known level of difficulty.

Despite their different labels, diagnostic tests and aptitude tests are really achievement tests. Even if the domain of knowledge or skill that is tested is distant from what is usually studied in school, these tests still measure what students have learned—what they know and how well they have learned to carry out tasks. The main difference among diagnostic tests, aptitude tests, and "plain" achievement tests is not so much the nature of the test itself but how people interpret students' test scores.

A Psychoeducational Assessment Report.
As a classroom teacher, you have a key role to play in meeting the needs of an exceptional student. You, along with the student's parents, are the most informed about how the student engages in learning and how well the student is achieving your objectives. Your observations, anecdotal records, and formal tests, as well as parents' concerns, will be the starting point for guiding the school-based team's work with an exceptional student. If the team should decide to refer the student for psychoeducational assessment, you can expect to receive a psychoeducational assessment report about the student.

The content of a psychoeducational assessment report will depend on the student's needs and on decisions reached by the school-based team. Since you've probably not seen anything like this before, we'll present a model report for Raymond, a fictitious Grade 2 student. It's important to note that this is a *very* condensed and edited version that we based on a real 30-page (single-spaced!) report originally prepared by Louise Mercer, a teacher and graduate student working with Nancy Perry at the University of British Columbia. We've kept something from almost every section of the real report but, for the sake of space, lots of material has been cut out that would be essential in a genuine report about a real student. Places where we made especially large deletions are marked by ellipses (. . .).

This report illustrates several good practices in using standardized tests for psychoeducational assessment. First, it is educational to its readers. Help in interpreting percentiles is provided periodically, and the reader is reminded that an average range of performance is quite broad, typically spanning a band of scores from the 25th to the 75th percentiles. The tester also approached her task a bit like she would a program of research. She used results from some early tests to hypothesize how Raymond should perform in later ones. When a hypothesis was not confirmed, she sought additional evidence to deepen her understanding of Raymond's capabilities and problems. Third, the testing plan was not rigid. When the tester noticed something potentially fruitful, such as Raymond's inconsistently gripping a pencil well, this was followed up. Also, interpretations are grounded in research literature and give background to help a novice understand why particular tests were administered. Her interpretations are carefully phrased in less than absolute terms in recognition of the error that is found in every test score, whether standardized or classroom. Finally, recommendations are presented for the classroom teacher and parents. These are solidly grounded in evidence from the tests, research, and the tester's considerable experience.

Child: Raymond Smith

Parents: Anne and Bill Smith

Address: 789 Dungeness Street, Port Pirie, BC

Dates of Assessments: 1997 December 02–12

Date of Birth: 1990 May 24

Phone: 678-1234

Age: 7 years, 7 months

Current Grade Placement: 2

Date of Report: 1998 January 06

Reason for Referral. Raymond was referred by his parents, who were concerned about his slow progress in reading, and his difficulties paying attention and remembering information, and problems he has with some manual tasks like paper cutting and colouring. They wanted to understand Raymond's "learning strengths and learning style."

Background Information. Raymond's natural parents indicate he reached developmental milestones at appropriate ages but always had difficulties with fine-motor tasks. Raymond is slow to complete written work at school. His mother reported he enjoys good health with no sleeping difficulties. His appetite is good, and vision and hearing have been checked with no difficulties recorded.

Educational History. Raymond has attended Port Pirie Elementary since kindergarten. Progress reports from kindergarten and Grade 1 indicated that in academic skills, Raymond had difficulty differentiating sounds and relating them to letters, often made letter reversals, struggled with forming letters correctly, was slow to develop basic sight vocabulary, and had difficulty memorizing songs and poems.

Present Educational Situation. Raymond is currently in Grade 2. His November progress report noted he is working within the widely held expectations for a child his age in all areas except reading and writing. Consequently, Raymond is currently receiving learning assistance four times a week for 30 minutes each session. Raymond's current teacher noted areas of concern similar to those documented in previous grades.

General Test Behaviour. Raymond is a quiet boy who remained cooperative throughout the nine days of testing sessions. He expressed enjoyment about many of the tasks . . . but was clearly frustrated by tasks that required extended verbal answers and reading.

Cognitive Functioning. Results from the Wechsler Intelligence Scale for Children–3rd Edition (WISC-III) place Raymond in the average range for students his age. His Full Scale IQ score of 98, at the 45th percentile, means that his performance was the same or better than 45 percent of students of his age. Raymond's scores were 92 on the Verbal Scale (30th percentile) and 106 on the Performance Scale (66th percentile). Both are within the average range. Although these scores seem to suggest that Raymond's ability to demonstrate knowledge nonverbally is more developed than his ability to demonstrate knowledge verbally, the difference is not statistically significant.

Overall results suggested no noteworthy general cognitive processing problems that might be contributing to Raymond's difficulties, but variable performance on subtests suggests relative strengths and weaknesses. . . . Given Raymond's overall age-appropriate intellectual aptitude, further assessments were conducted. . . .

Memory. Results on the Wide Range Assessment of Memory and Learning (WRAML) place Raymond within the average range of memory skills for students his age, consistent with his general cognitive ability measured by the WISC-III. Raymond achieved a standard score of 104, at the 61st percentile on the General Memory Index. . . . His scores on the Visual Memory Index place him at the 75th percentile, and on the Verbal Memory Index at the 55th percentile. These suggest he can retain both visual and verbal information at age-appropriate levels. . . .

Visual-Perceptual and Visual-Motor Skills. Due to referral concerns about delayed fine-motor skills and Raymond's apparent difficulties with visual-motor coordination and speed on the Coding subtest of the WISC-III, the Developmental Test of Visual Perception–2nd Edition (DTVP-2) was administered to further assess visual-perceptual and visual-motor skills. . . . Results suggest that Raymond's visual-perceptual and visual-motor skills are age-appropriate.

It was noticed that Raymond's pencil grip was inconsistent. Also, he may be slow to complete written tasks because his knowledge of letter forms is still uncertain. An informal assessment of letter knowledge revealed Raymond could name all 26 upper-case letters and 24 of the lower-case letters correctly. . . . but was able to print only 20 upper-case letters and 22 lower-case letters correctly from memory. Raymond's printing fluency may be enhanced by practice in naming and printing letters, and improving his pencil grip. Recommendations for building skills in these areas are made later in this report.

Auditory Discrimination Skills. As a result of referral concerns regarding Raymond's difficulties in paying attention, remembering information, and acquiring reading skills, the Wepman Auditory Discrimination Test–2nd Edition (ADT) was administered to assess his ability to discriminate sounds. He achieved a very high score of 29 out of 30 (91st percentile). Given Raymond's early history of high temperatures and mild ear infections, continued monitoring of his hearing is recommended.

Vocabulary and Language Skills. Raymond's general verbal abilities, measured by the WISC-III, were average for his age. . . . His language skills were further assessed because of referral concerns about paying attention and remembering information, and because Raymond had difficulty formulating oral responses on the WISC-III. It was hypothesized that his present difficulties in sustaining attention and remembering information might be related to his language development. Thus, the Clinical Evaluation of Language Fundamentals–3rd Edition (CELF-3) was administered.

Overall, results on the CELF-3 placed Raymond within the average range of language ability for students of his age. . . . His ability to understand language is somewhat stronger than his ability to use language, but both are within or above the range expected for students of his age. . . . His performance was consistent with his awkward oral responses on the WISC-III. This corroborating evidence suggests oral expression poses difficulty for Raymond. Suggestions for developing these skills will be made later in the report.

Phonological Skills. As a result of referral concerns regarding Raymond's slow progress in developing reading skills, the Phonological Awareness Profile (PAP) was administered. Phonological awareness is the ability to recognize and manipulate sounds within words. . . a powerful early predictor of later success in reading. A number of studies have demonstrated that training students in phonological awareness can benefit their reading and spelling skills.

Raymond's overall performance on the PAP is weak. . . . He experienced considerable difficulties producing the sounds of certain graphemes. . . . When asked to decode a series of non-words, Raymond again experienced difficulty with the short vowels and many of the consonant blends. Raymond eventually became so frustrated that the task was discontinued. Suggestions for strengthening Raymond's phonological awareness skills will be made later in the report.

General Knowledge. As a result of referral concerns . . . further examination was made of Raymond's ability to make connections with prior knowledge . . . a powerful predictor of success in reading comprehension. The General Information subtest of the Peabody Individual Achievement Test (PIAT) as well as the Science, Social Studies and Humanities subtests of the Woodcock-Johnson Tests of Achievement–Revised (WJ-R) were administered. . . .

Raymond's score on the General Information subtest of the PIAT indicated his general knowledge was within the average range for his age (94, 34th percentile). Domain specific knowledge scores on WJ-R Science, Social Studies and Humanities subtests suggest that his fund of general knowledge is more highly developed in science (112, 80th percentile) and social studies (115, 85th percentile) than the humanities (91, 28th percentile). . . . Raymond's fund of general knowledge, while generally age-appropriate, is somewhat limited in particular areas, such as literature and concepts of time. These areas of weakness may affect Raymond's comprehension when he reads particular topics and texts.

Academic Achievement. To assess Raymond's general academic achievement in mathematics, writing, and reading, the Woodcock-Johnson Tests of Achievement–Revised (WJ-R) were administered. . . .

Summary of Reading Achievement. Results indicate that some key reading skills are not at the level that could be expected given Raymond's overall age-appropriate intellectual, memory, and language abilities. Raymond's ability to recognize familiar words is currently below a level appropriate for his age. In particular, Raymond has not completely mastered the lower-case alphabet and he does not have an adequately developed sight vocabulary. Raymond's phonetic decoding skills need to be strengthened and he needs to make greater use of context to recognize unknown words. Typically Raymond is only using the initial consonants to decode words. In addition, word recognition difficulties are significantly affecting Raymond's fluency and impairing his comprehension. At present, Raymond has a delay of at least one grade level in his overall ability to read in English.

On the basis of these several assessments, as well as the developmental and educational information provided by Raymond's parents, Raymond . . . [has] average general cognitive abilities but delayed development in reading recognition skills (including sight vocabulary, use of context, decoding skills, and phonological awareness skills). The latter has resulted in a very slow reading rate and a concomitant impairment of his comprehension skills. Given Raymond's failure to date to develop age-appropriate reading skills, it is not surprising that he avoids reading tasks. What is surprising given Raymond's struggles with reading is that he still holds a positive attitude toward reading books. On the basis of these conclusions, and earlier observations concerning hearing and relative weaknesses in phonological awareness and spelling skills, the following recommendations are made. . . .

Discussing Test Results with Families. At times, you may be expected to explain or describe test results to your students' families. The Family and Community Partnerships Guidelines give some ideas.

FAMILY AND COMMUNITY PARTNERSHIPS

Explaining and Using Psychoeducational Test Results

Be ready to explain, in non-technical terms, what each type of score on the test report means.

Examples

1. If the test is norm-referenced, know if the comparison group was national or local, and whether it was normed using a Canadian sample. Explain that the child's score shows how he or she performed in relation to the other students in the comparison group.
2. If the test is criterion-referenced, explain that the child's scores show how well he or she performed relative to standards in specific areas.

If the test is norm-referenced, focus on the percentile scores. They are the easiest to understand.

Examples

1. Percentile scores tell what percent of students in the comparison group made the same score or lower. Higher percentiles are better, and the 99th percentile is as high as anyone can get. The 50th percentile is average.
2. Remind parents that percentile scores do not tell the "percent correct." Scores that would be bad on a classroom test (say 65 percent to 75 percent or so) are above average—even good—as percentile scores.

Be aware of errors in testing.

Examples

1. Encourage parents to think of the score not as a single point but as a range or band that includes their child's score.
2. Ignore small differences between scores. Make sure parents notice you are ignoring those differences.
3. Note that sometimes individual skills on criterion-referenced tests are measured with just a few (two or three) items. Compare test scores to actual class work in the same areas.

Use conference time to plan a learning goal for the child, one that families can support.

Examples

1. Have example questions, similar to those on the test, to show parents what their child can do easily and what kinds of questions he or she found difficult.
2. Be prepared to suggest an important skill to target.

Standardized Achievement Tests: Needed or Not?

Across the country, some teachers, parents, and professors of education are criticizing their provinces' standardized tests of achievement. Nonetheless, provinces continue to mandate these kinds of tests. In British Columbia, New Brunswick, and Nova Scotia, for example, scores on provincial standardized achievement tests must contribute to the marks students receive in their classes. Is the whole country moving toward a standardized curriculum led by the School Achievement Indicators Program (SAIP)? What should be done about standardized achievement testing?

▶ POINT *Standardized achievement testing should be scrapped.*
Critics of standardized testing state that these tests measure disjointed facts and skills that have little use or meaning in the real world. They argue that test questions are poor reflections of the full curricula students study in schools, so the tests can't measure how well students have learned the knowledge, skills, and especially the attitudes that make up a complete picture of accomplishment in school subjects.

Even when standardized achievement tests do align with the schools' curricula, they are best at measuring lower-level objectives, facts, and the most basic of skills. This leads teachers to overemphasize just what education shouldn't be emphasizing—factual knowledge and memorization—instead of teaching the critical and creative skills students will need in an unpredictable future. If this weren't bad enough, results on such tests are too often used to label students as low achievers. Self-fulfilling prophecies can be set into motion that put students into an ever-downward spiral of fading self-esteem and decreasing achievement.

Whole schools also suffer from standardized achievement testing. In some provinces, schools are ranked according to their students' test scores. Is this a valid way to measure schools' capabilities to teach the students in their communities? Or, since test scores correlate with socioeconomic status, aren't these rankings just pointing out the obvious? Communities in need are in need of more resources to serve their students better.

◀ COUNTERPOINT
Standardized achievement testing complements other assessments.
Standardized achievement testing isn't an alternative to classroom assessment. Instead, it provides an important different view of students, schools, and the province overall. Taxpayers want to know how well their tax dollars are spent on education, and provincially developed standardized tests provide a common meter stick of educational achievement. Without them, the public would have to wait until after students graduate to know whether the school systems are effective. That's too late to do anything if the school systems need support or repair.

Critics overstate their case that standardized achievement tests can't measure higher-order objectives. Well-designed multiple-choice items, written exercises, and even standardized performance items are all capable of reflecting authentic and genuinely complex accomplishments. Rather than belittle the tests of the past, critics should join with ministries in developing better standardized achievement tests.

The standardized achievement tests that provinces use are technically much stronger than the tests teachers develop for their classrooms. Teachers have been known to revise their tests by dropping items that students find "too hard," even when those items reflect central features of the subject. Changing the items on tests distorts what tests are supposed to describe. The provincial tests are very carefully aligned to the curriculum and give a clearer picture of what students really can do. As well, teachers' tests often have substantially lower reliability than the provinces'. Since valid interpretations require reliable scores, it's fairer to students when teachers can add more reliable information from standardized tests to their own information when they assign grades.

Yes, there is a correlation between a school's standardized test scores and the socioeconomic status of its community. It's wrong, however, to blame the test for it. In fact, ministries use the information from their standardized testing programs to reassess how they distribute resources to areas where they're really needed rather than allowing themselves to be swayed by the "rich and powerful." Scrapping standardized tests would open the process to too much influence from the "haves" and shut out the "have-nots."

Issues in Standardized Testing

In this section we will consider three basic issues: Can standardized achievement tests be used to compare schools, districts, and provinces? Are standardized tests biased against minority students? Can the students be taught test-taking skills?

Using Standardized Achievement Tests to Compare Schools, Districts, and Provinces

Connect & Extend
To the research
Wilson, R. J. (1999). Aspects of validity in large-scale programs of student assessment. *Alberta Journal of Educational Research, 45,* 333–343.
  Because the purposes of large-scale assessments are more extensive than the purposes of testing, validity issues that arise in the context of large-scale assessments are correspondingly more complex than those that arise in testing. This article explores what those differences are in areas such as types of items, administration of the tests and assessments, interpretations of results, and standards. It concludes with questions that need attention if large-scale assessments are to meet the goals set for them.

We believe that educators and government officials have good intentions about using standardized tests to serve students, teachers, schools, and the education ministries. But anyone's best intentions can be undermined if individuals forget or don't know about important characteristics of tests. As a result, issues can arise quickly.

In trying to serve students, teachers, schools, and the ministry, it seems logical that scores should be considered at different levels of aggregation—individual students, classes, schools, districts, regions, provinces and territories, and even the entire country. Not everyone agrees, however. In 1999 in British Columbia, for example, arguments were made that resulted in a decision not to release individual students' scores on provincial achievement tests. Anita Chapman summarized why in the British Columbia Teachers' Federation magazine, *Teacher* (1999). In essence, she argued, a single test does not sample deeply or widely enough from a curriculum, especially if it might be used to identify students' exceptionalities. A second part of her position was that a student's accomplishments could not be accurately judged because, even for these very technically sophisticated tests, the standard error band for a student's score is too wide. Finally, she believed that parents probably could not be given enough background information to interpret their children's scores meaningfully and validly.

Ministries recognize these issues. For example, in the *History 12 Examination Specifications* (2000, August) for BC's History 12 examination, it is explicitly acknowledged that

> Differences often exist between school and examination marks. School assessment measures curricular performance over time, whereas examinations evaluate those curricular areas best measured in a final testing situation. Some students perform better on examinations, others in the classroom. Thus, differences between school and examination marks should be expected.

It's also worth noting that concerns Chapman highlights apply with equal force to individual classroom tests that teachers use every day or week. We believe it particularly worthwhile to repeat ourselves on one point—whenever an individual student's score is considered, that score, like any test score, should be considered as a range described by a standard error band. No test has pinpoint accuracy.

In some jurisdictions, results of standardized achievement tests at school and district levels are made available to the public while some provinces, such as Ontario, specifically avoid this practice. Because these tests are very well constructed, field-tested, and standardized, they do allow a degree of comparability when it's of interest to compare schools or districts. These tests also have very good levels of internal consistency reliability. Along with the large number of students whose scores are averaged to describe a school or district, this results in very much narrower standard error bands for schools or districts in comparison to much wider standard error bands for an individual student.

But we remind you of one of Anita Chapman's other cautions about tests, including standardized tests—the items on any one achievement test, whether a teacher's or a province's, are only a sample of the full spectrum of a subject. Different samples of items might yield different scores. This is particularly important when comparing students or schools or provinces whose scores are not far apart. And, if one wants to compare districts in jurisdictions where teachers have latitude to choose elements of a curriculum, there is much need of evidence concerning the validity of interpretations about curriculum alignment (content) to tests.

Review

▶ What are some current issues about using standardized testing?

▶ Can students become better test-takers?

Apply

▶ What are some decisions that should *not* be based on standardized test scores?

"I HATE TAKING A TEST WITHOUT AN ERASER."

(© Martha Campbell)

Learning Propensity Assessment Device: Innovative method for testing the student's ability to benefit from teaching, consistent with Lev Vygotsky's theory of cognitive development.

Authentic Assessment: Measurement of important abilities using procedures that simulate the application of these abilities to real-life problems.

Constructed-Response Format: Assessment procedures that require the student to create an answer instead of selecting an answer from a set of choices.

A second type of training that appears to be very promising is instruction in general cognitive skills such as solving problems, carefully analyzing questions, considering all alternatives, noticing details and deciding which are relevant, avoiding impulsive answers, and checking work. These are the kinds of metacognitive and study skills we have discussed before. Training in these skills is likely to generalize to many tasks (Anastasi, 1988).

New Directions in Standardized Testing

Standardized tests continue to be controversial. In response to dissatisfaction with traditional forms of assessment, new approaches have emerged to deal with some of the most common testing problems. However, each of these approaches has its own problems. We will examine proposed procedures for measuring learning potential and for making assessment more "authentic."

Assessing Learning Potential

One criticism of traditional forms of standardized testing is that such tests are merely samples of performance at one particular point in time. These tests, critics say, fail to capture the child's potential for future learning. An alternative view of cognitive assessment is based on the assumption that the goal of assessment is to reveal potential for learning and to identify the psychological and educational interventions that will help the person realize this potential. Procedures developed by Joe Campione and Ann Brown give graduated prompts as a child works to solve a problem. The prompts are scripted, beginning with a general hint and ending with a detailed instruction for how to find the answer. The way the child uses the prompt and learns within the testing situation gives evidence of learning potential (Kozulin & Falik, 1995).

Reuven Feuerstein's *Learning Propensity Assessment Device* is another attempt to look at the process of learning rather than its product (Feuerstein, 1979; Kozulin & Falik, 1995). The assessment is a battery of 14 different instruments that include reasoning, numerical, verbal, figural, logical, and memory tasks. When necessary, the examiner teaches the child how to solve the problems and then assesses how well the child has benefited from instruction. The outcome of the assessment is not a score but descriptive information about practical teaching methods and materials for working with the child.

Both Feuerstein's and Campione and Brown's techniques reflect Vygotsky's ideas about the zone of proximal development—the range of functioning where a child cannot solve problems independently but can benefit from guidance. Results of these tests offer a thought-provoking and radically different approach to intelligence testing. Rather than focusing on where a child is, these approaches point toward where the child could go and give guidance for reaching those learning goals (Grigorenko & Sternberg, 1998).

Authentic Assessment

As the public and government demanded greater accountability in education in the 1980s and 1990s and as traditional standardized tests became the basis for important decisions, pressure to do well led many teachers and schools to "teach to the test." This tended to focus student learning on basic skills and facts. Even more troubling, say critics, the traditional standardized tests assess skills that have no equivalent in the real world. Students are asked to solve problems or answer questions they will never encounter again; they are expected to do so alone, without relying on any tools or resources and while working under extreme time limits. Real life just isn't like this. Important problems take time to solve and often require using resources, consulting other people, and integrating basic skills with creativity and high-level thinking (Kirst, 1991a; Wolf, Bixby, Glenn, & Gardner, 1991).

In response to these criticisms, the **authentic assessment** movement was born. The goal was to create standardized tests that assess complex, important, real-life outcomes. The approach is also called *direct assessment, performance assessment,* or *alternative assessment*. These terms refer to procedures that are alternatives to traditional multiple-choice standardized tests because they directly assess student performance on "real-life" tasks (Hambleton, 1996; Worthen, 1993).

Many of the suggestions for improving standardized tests will require new forms of testing, more thoughtful and time-consuming scoring, and perhaps new ways of judging the quality of the tests themselves. Standardized tests of the future may be more like writing samples and less like multiple-choice tests. Newer tests will feature more **constructed-response formats**. This means that students will create responses (essays, problem solutions, graphs, diagrams), rather than simply selecting the (one and only) correct answer. This will allow tests to measure higher-level and divergent thinking. For example, in British Columbia, the provincial examination on Principles of Mathematics 12 awards marks to written response questions. Hand-held calculators are required.

In the excitement about authentic assessment, it is important to be sensible. Just being different from traditional standardized tests will not guarantee that the alternative tests are better. Many questions have to be answered. Assume, for example, that a new assessment requires students to complete a hands-on science project. If the student does well on one science project, does this mean the student "knows" science and would do well on other projects? One study found that students' performance on three different science tasks was quite variable: a student who did well on the absorbency experiment, for example, might have trouble with the electricity task. Thus, it was hard to generalize about a student's knowledge of science based on just the three tasks. Many more tasks would be needed to get a good sense of science knowledge. But a performance assessment with many different tasks would be expensive and time-consuming (Shavelson, Gao, & Baxter, 1993).

In addition, if important decisions are based on performance assessments, will teachers begin to "teach to the assessment" by giving students practice in these particular performances? Will being a good writer bias judges in favour of a performance? Will this make performance assessments even more prone to discriminate against some groups? And how will the projects be judged? Will different judges agree on the quality? When researchers examined the results in one large portfolio-based program, they found that scorers assessing the same portfolio often gave very different ratings (Kotrez, Stecher, & Diebert, 1993). In other words, will judgments based on alternative assessments be reliable and valid? Will the assessment results generalize to tasks beyond those on the test itself? Will the new assessments have a positive effect on learning (Hambleton, 1996; Moss, 1992)?

Many jurisdictions are drafting policies that will require direct assessment of student performance to determine how well the schools, districts, and even the

▲ *In many subjects, the most reasonable test is to demonstrate the ability to produce a finished product.*

Connect & Extend
To debates on testing
Read At Odds: Performance Assessment (1991, special feature). *Phi Delta Kappan, 72*(9). This feature includes two articles: Cizek, G. J. Innovation or enervation: Performance assessment in perspective, pp. 695–699; and Wiggins, G. A response to Cizek, pp. 200–214. *Focus Questions:* Summarize the two positions on performance assessment expressed by the authors. Which position most closely represents your views? Why?

Connect & Extend
To other chapters
Chapter 14 includes a discussion of alternatives for authentic assessment, including portfolios and exhibitions.

Connect & Extend
To professional journals
Special Section on Authentic Assessment (1993, February). *Phi Delta Kappan, 74,* 444–479.

Connect & Extend
To the research
For a complete discussion of performance assessment, see Hambleton, R. K. (1996). Advances in assessment models, methods, and practices. In D. C. Berliner & R. C. Calfee (Eds.), *Handbook of Educational Psychology.* New York: Macmillan.

New Directions in Standardized Testing

Review

▶ What is learning potential assessment?

▶ What is authentic assessment?

Apply

▶ How would you judge the reliability and validity of a performance test in which a student was asked to show a knowledge of geometry by designing a tile floor using tiles of different shapes and sizes?

▶ Relate the measurement of learning potential to Vygotsky's theory of zone of proximal development.

whole province is doing. These new, authentic, or alternative assessment procedures could be used to make the same high-stakes decisions as the traditional standardized tests and thus create some of the same problems (Worthen, 1993). Because this is a new area, it will take time to develop high-quality alternative assessments for use by whole school districts or provinces. Until more is known, it may be best to focus on authentic assessment at the classroom level, as we will discuss in the next chapter.

Summary

Evaluation, Measurement, and Assessment

Distinguish among evaluation, measurement, and assessment.

In the process of evaluation, we compare information to criteria and then make judgments. Measurement is evaluation put in quantitative terms. Assessment includes measurement, but is broader because it includes all kinds of ways to sample and observe students' skills, knowledge, and abilities.

Distinguish between norm-referenced and criterion-referenced tests.

In norm-referenced tests, a student's performance is compared to the average performance of others. In criterion-referenced tests, scores are compared to a pre-established standard. Norm-referenced tests cover a wide range of general objectives and are appropriate when only the top few candidates can be admitted to a program. However, results of norm-referenced tests do not tell whether students are ready for advanced material, and they are not appropriate for affective and psychomotor objectives. Criterion-referenced tests

measure the mastery of very specific objectives—they tell the teacher exactly what the students can and cannot do, but they cannot compare students to others at their grade level either locally or nationally.

What Do Test Scores Mean?

Describe the key features of a standardized test.

Standardized tests in Canada are both norm-referenced and criterion-referenced. They have been pilot-tested and revised; norm-referenced tests are then administered in final form to a norming sample, which becomes the comparison group for scoring. Important aspects of measurement in standardized testing are the frequency distribution, the central tendency, and the standard deviation.

What are mean, median, mode, and standard deviation?

The mean (arithmetical average), median (middle score), and mode (most common score) are all measures of central tendency. The standard deviation reveals how scores spread out around the mean. A normal distribution is a frequency distribution that

is shaped like a bell-shaped curve. Many scores cluster in the middle; the farther from the midpoint, the fewer the scores. Half the scores are above the mean; half are below.

Describe different kinds of scores.

There are several basic types of standardized test scores: percentile rankings, which indicate the percentage of others who scored at or below an individual's score; grade-equivalent scores, which indicate how closely a student's performance matches average scores of students at some grade level who also achieve that score; and standard scores, which are based on the standard deviation. T and z scores are common standard scores. A stanine score is a standard score that divides the scale into ninths.

What is test score reliability?

Every test score is only an estimate of a student's hypothetical true score. Some test scores are more reliable than others; that is, they reflect more stable and consistent estimates of true score. The standard error of measurement highlights that a score is imprecise. A confidence interval based on the standard error of measurement is a helpful way to depict test reliability.

What is validity in relation to decisions based on tests?

The most important consideration about a test is the validity of interpretations and decisions based on the test's results. Some of these are more valid than others because there is strong evidence for the interpretations and decisions made. Evidence of validity can be related to content, criterion, or construct. Construct-related evidence for validity is the broadest category and encompasses the other two categories of content and criterion. Tests must be reliable to be valid, but reliability does not guarantee validity.

Standardized Tests Used in Canada's Schools

What standardized tests are used in Canada?

Three kinds of standardized tests are commonly used: achievement, and diagnostic and aptitude psychoeducational tests. Standardized criterion-referenced achievement tests are often used to gauge the overall effectiveness of education and, in some provinces, combine with classroom tests to form Grade 12 students' grades. Standardized criterion-refer-enced achievement tests often provide good models for some aspects of classroom assessment. Aptitude tests are used mainly to predict future performance, while diagnostic tests are used to describe a student's current capabilities or difficulties as a basis for designing more effective instruction. Both measure achievement, but items may sometimes seem quite different from everyday school tasks.

Issues in Standardized Testing

What are some current issues in testing?

Controversy over standardized testing has focused on the role and interpretation of achievement tests and the degree of fairness in testing. The way test results are used is a major issue for teachers. Teachers should use results to improve instruction, not to stereotype students or justify lowered expectations.

Can students become better test-takers?

Performance on standardized tests can be improved if students gain experience with this type of testing and are given training in study skills and problem solving. Many students can profit from direct instruction about how to prepare for and take tests. Involving students in designing these test preparation programs can be helpful.

New Directions in Standardized Testing

What is learning potential assessment?

An alternative goal of assessment is to reveal potential for learning and to identify educational interventions that will help the individual realize this potential. Procedures give graduated prompts as a child works to solve a problem—beginning with a general hint and ending with a detailed instruction for how to find the answer. The way the child uses the prompt and learns within the testing situation gives evidence of learning potential.

What is authentic assessment?

Authentic assessments are procedures that assess students' abilities to solve important real-life problems, think creatively, and act responsibly. Such approaches assume that assessment should reveal the potential for future learning and help identify interventions for realizing that potential. Standardized tests of the future will be more varied and will use more constructed-response formats, requiring students to generate (rather than select) answers.

Key Terms

Becoming a Professional

Reflecting on the Chapter

Can you apply the ideas from this chapter on standardized assessments to solve the following problems of practice?

Preschool and Kindergarten

▷ Jasdev has just joined your kindergarten class. A rather ill-prepared note from his preschool teacher suggests he might have problems learning to read. You plan to observe Jasdev's understanding of letter-sound correspondence and other basic literacy tasks, such as writing his name. What steps would you take to make your observations reliable and your conclusions valid?

Elementary and Middle School

▷ Your students seem very nervous about the spring provincial exams. The local paper has carried stories about the school's "low" scores last year, and there is pressure on everyone to do better this time. How would you prepare your students?

Junior High and High School

▷ The parents of one of your students are angry with you because their child was not selected for the special accelerated math group. Selection was based on both standardized test scores and class performance. How would you explain the school's decision?

Check Your Understanding

▷ This chapter describes many concepts that frequently appear on tests for teachers. Be sure you know the difference between norm-referenced and criterion-referenced tests; and the definitions of mean, median, and mode; percentile ranks, stanines, z scores, grade-equivalent scores, and T scores (not necessarily the formula but what these scores tell you); reliability and validity; high-stakes testing; test bias; and achievement, diagnostic, and aptitude tests.

Your Teaching Portfolio

Think about your philosophy of teaching, a question you will be asked at most job interviews. What do you believe about the uses of testing for children? How would you interpret the test scores of minority-group children?

Add some ideas for parent involvement from this chapter to your *portfolio*.

Using the Guidelines for preparing for a test, prepare a testing guide sheet for the grades you will teach.

Teaching Resources

Add Figure 13.4, "Four Types of Standard Scores on a Normal Distribution Curve," to your teaching resources file.

Weblinks

http://ericae.net/intass.htm

A site developed by the ERIC folks, this lists hundreds (really!) of links to issues in assessment and evaluation. A special section is provided on alternative assessment and performance-based assessment.

www.geocities.com/Athens/Parthenon/8658

A paper by a high school English teacher about performance assessments. Included are lots of links to materials about assessment in the various subject areas (physical education, social studies, etc.).

What Would They Do?

Here is how two practising teachers responded to the teaching situation presented at the beginning of this chapter about the parents who believe their daughter was graded unfairly in math.

JOYCE M. ESTABROOKS

Fredericton High School
Fredericton, New Brunswick

It is important to have a polite and non-confrontational attitude as you meet the parents. Take the approach that the school is pleased to work with the parents, since all parties have the same primary objective—the best education for the student.

The provincial examination is only one single assessment of mathematics performance. Since it is a standardized assessment for students of varying abilities, it will not include many open-ended questions or problem-solving activities requiring higher-level thinking skills. It is a summative evaluation used to ascertain the degree to which the course objectives have been met. This evaluation is thus only part of the picture and must be used with formative evaluation, which measures individual growth in skills, effort, and attitude.

One of the problems with the class assessment for this student has been her desire to just "know the steps" (and that she doesn't complete all of her homework). This is no longer an acceptable approach as the student prepares for future postsecondary courses requiring abstract and conceptual thinking skills. To raise the level of achievement on the class assessment, it is necessary to understand the concepts, make connections, and learn to apply these concepts in problem-solving situations.

This student is a bright girl, but she needs to take responsibility and apply herself to reach her potential. Assure the parents that you will be happy to work with them to help her reach that potential.

ALDONA BUSINSKUS

Burnaby South Secondary School
Burnaby, British Columbia

In general, whatever their mood, parents have their child's best interest at heart when they come to discuss an issue at school. A good teacher also has each student's best interest at heart. This is the common ground on which we meet.

Although the parents' accusatory tone makes me feel defensive, I remind myself of the above principle, and I remain determined to stay open and professional. I congratulate them on their daughter's success on the provincial exam. I expect that my principal will intervene to start off the meeting on a more business-like footing.

I do some probing to establish for myself what the parents hope for as an outcome of this meeting. (What is their goal for this meeting? Do they want to discuss the discrepancy between the marks? Are they asking for a mark change because they believe I've made a mistake? Are they accusing me of incompetence?)

On the surface, it appears that the parents' only explanation for the difference in marks is that, somehow, I am the problem. A discrepancy of 20 percent or so between the provincial exam mark and the school mark is unusual. I too would like to understand the reason for it and acknowledge that to the parents. In following this up, I want to know:

▶ What happened in their daughter's other subjects? Are the exam and school marks similar or are there significant differences?

▶ Has their daughter had other experiences where she has pulled it all together at the end but been less diligent in the day-to-day effort?

▶ Has their daughter ever told them anything to indicate that she felt her class marks were unfair? Or has she indicated that they were the marks she felt she deserved?

The parents appear to believe that the provincial exam is a better and more reliable instrument for evaluating their daughter's mathematical understanding than the classroom assessment. In fact (even though teachers are tempted to "teach to the exam"), the classroom assessment is intended to include different criteria than those measured by the exam. For example, the exam consists of short items, each of which tests a small subset of course objectives. Classroom assessment includes evaluation of a student's long-term growth in understanding, skill, and ability to apply knowledge. While there is a high correlation between the two marks, they are not meant to be "checks" of each other.

An obvious reason for the lower class mark is the lack of completed homework. I explore this area with the parents. Normally, I would offer continued support and try to work with the parents to help their daughter be more responsible for her daily work. However, since she has now completed high school, I simply stress the importance of persistence and responsibility in the future.

For myself, I will review my marks to see if this girl is the only one with such a large difference between exam and school marks, or whether there is a pattern in the comparison of my marks with the provincial exam marks in general. Any time one's practice is called into question, uncomfortable though it may be, the challenge provides an opportunity for reflection and deeper understanding.

Classroom Assessment and Grading

think back on your report cards and grades over the years. Did you ever receive a grade that was lower than you expected? How did you feel about yourself, the teacher, the subject, and school in general as a result of the lower grade? What could the teacher have done to help you understand and profit from the experience?

In this chapter, we will look at tests and grades, focusing on the effects these are likely to have on students as well as on practical means of developing more efficient methods for testing and grading.

We begin with a consideration of the many types of tests teachers prepare each year and some new approaches to assessment. Then we examine the effects grades are likely to have on students. Because there are so many grading systems, we also spend some time identifying advantages and disadvantages of one system over another. Finally, we turn to the very important topic of communication with students and parents. How will you justify the grades you give?

By the time you have completed this chapter, you should be able to:

▶ Make a plan for testing students on a unit of work.

▶ Evaluate tests that accompany textbooks and teachers' manuals.

▶ Create multiple-choice and essay test items for your subject area.

▶ Describe authentic assessment approaches, including portfolios, performances, exhibitions, and the development of scoring rubrics.

▶ Discuss the potential positive and negative effects of grades on students.

▶ Give examples of criterion-referenced and norm-referenced grading systems.

▶ Assign grades to a hypothetical group of students and defend your decisions in a class debate.

▶ Role-play a conference with parents who do not understand your grading system or their child's grades.

What Would You Do?

Your school requires that you give letter grades to students in your class. You can use any method you want, as long as an A, B, C, D, or F appears for each of the subject areas on every student's report card, every grading period. Some teachers

use worksheets, quizzes, homework, and tests. Others are assigning group work and portfolios. A few teachers are individualizing standards by grading on progress and effort more than final achievement. Some are trying contract approaches and experimenting with longer-term projects while others are relying almost completely on daily class work. Two teachers who use group work are considering giving credit toward grades for being a "good group member" or competitive bonus points for the top-scoring group. Others are planning to use improvement points for class rewards but not for grades. Your only experience with grading was using written comments and a mastery approach that rated the students as making satisfactory or unsatisfactory progress toward particular objectives. You want a system that is fair and manageable, but also encourages learning, not just performance.

▶ What would be your major graded assignments and projects?

▶ Would you include credit for such behaviour as group participation or effort?

▶ How would you put all the elements together to determine a grade for every student for every marking period?

▶ How would you justify your system to the principal and to the parents?

▶ How will these issues affect the grades that you teach?

Formative and Summative Assessment

As a teacher, you may or may not help in designing the grading system for your school or your class. Many school districts have a standard approach to grading. Still, you will have choices about how you use your district's grading system and how you assess your students' learning. Will you give tests? How many? What kinds? Will students do projects or keep portfolios of their work? How will homework influence grades? Will you grade on students' current academic performance or on their degree of improvement? How will you use the information from standardized student assessments?

There are two general uses or functions for assessment: formative and summative. **Formative assessment** occurs before or during instruction. It has two basic purposes: to guide the teacher in planning and to help students identify areas that need work. In other words, formative assessment helps form instruction. Often students are given a formative test prior to instruction, a **pretest** that helps the teacher determine what students already know. Sometimes a test is given during instruction to see what areas of weakness remain so teaching can be directed toward the problem areas. This is generally called a diagnostic test but should not be confused with the standardized diagnostic tests of more general learning abilities. A classroom diagnostic test identifies a student's areas of achievement and weakness in a particular subject. Older students are often able to apply the information from diagnostic tests to "reteach" themselves. For example, if a test on types of interpretations for test scores revealed you were fuzzy on norm-referenced interpretations, you could review the material about norm-referenced tests.

Pretests and diagnostic tests are not graded. And since formative tests do not count toward the final grade, students who tend to be very anxious on "real" tests may find this low-pressure practice in test taking especially helpful.

Formative Assessment: Ungraded testing used before or during instruction to aid in planning and diagnosis.

Pretest: Formative test for assessing students' knowledge, readiness, and abilities.

Data-Based Instruction: Assessment method using daily probes of specific-skill mastery.

Curriculum-Based Assessment (CBA): Evaluation method using frequent tests of specific skills and knowledge.

Summative Assessment: Testing that follows instruction and assesses achievement.

▲ *Testing is formative or summative depending on what is done with the results: If the results are used to plan future instruction, it is formative. If they're used to determine a final evaluation of a student, it is summative.*

Connect & Extend
To your teaching
What are some specific ways in which formative evaluations can be implemented in the classroom?

Connect & Extend
To the research
For a description of the different models of curriculum-based assessment and ideas for how it can be used with mainstreamed students, see Shapiro, E. S., & Ager, C. (1992). Assessment of special education students in regular education programs: Linking assessment to instruction. *Elementary School Journal, 92,* 283–296.

A variation of formative measurement is ongoing measurement, often called **data-based instruction** or **curriculum-based assessment (CBA)**. This approach uses frequent "probes," brief tests of specific skills and knowledge drawn from the curriculum, to give a precise picture of a student's current performance. Actually, CBA is not just one approach but a whole family of approaches for linking teaching and assessment. CBA is "any set of measurement procedures that use direct observation and recording of a student's performance in the local curriculum as a basis for gathering information to make instructional decisions" (Deno, 1987, p. 41). This method has been used primarily with students who have learning problems, because it provides systematic assessment of both student performance and the teaching methods used. The assessment probes check to see if the difficulty level and the pace of instruction are right for the student. If a student shows inadequate progress on the assessment probes, the teacher should consider modifying or switching instructional strategies or pacing (Shapiro & Ager, 1992).

Summative assessment occurs at the end of instruction. Its purpose is to let the teacher and the students know the level of accomplishment attained. Summative assessment, therefore, provides a summary of accomplishment. The final exam is a classic example.

The distinction between formative and summative assessment is based on how the results are used. The same assessment procedure can be used for either purpose. If the goal is to obtain information about student learning for planning purposes, the assessment is formative. If the purpose is to determine final achievement (and help determine a course grade), the assessment is summative.

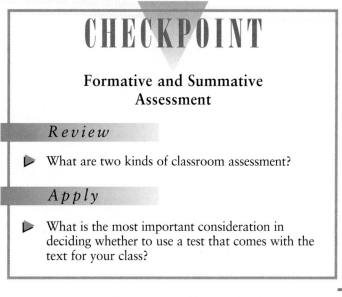

CHECKPOINT

Formative and Summative Assessment

Review

▷ What are two kinds of classroom assessment?

Apply

▷ What is the most important consideration in deciding whether to use a test that comes with the text for your class?

Getting the Most from Traditional Assessment Approaches

When most people think of assessment, they usually think of testing. As you will see shortly, teachers today have many other options, but testing is still a significant activity in most classrooms. Let's consider your options for assessing students using the traditional testing approach. In this section we will examine how to plan effective tests, how to evaluate the tests that accompany standard curriculum materials, and how to write your own test questions.

Planning for Testing

Instruction and assessment are most effective when they are well organized and planned. Creating a *behaviour-content* matrix can help. A behaviour-content matrix is a table that lists behaviour or skills as columns and key areas of the curriculum as rows. It is like a road map to the objectives you use to plan teaching and plan tests. When you use a behaviour-content matrix, you are in a better position to judge whether the content of tests aligns with the objectives you create for your curriculum.

Using a Behaviour-Content Matrix. Here is how you might use a behaviour-content matrix to design a unit test. First, decide how many items students can complete during the testing period. Divide this total into cells of a behaviour-content matrix so that more important skills and more important elements of content have more items (Berliner, 1987).

An example of a behaviour-content matrix that might be appropriate for planning a 40-question unit test in government is given in Table 14.1.

In this plan, you can see that this teacher decided the most important topic is major political issues and accordingly allotted a total of 15 questions to it. The least important topic is methods of inquiry. Also, the teacher wanted to focus on students' abilities to make generalizations (14 questions) while giving considerable attention to understanding concepts and locating information. Interpreting graphs is the least important objective, but it is not overlooked.

Once the behaviour-content matrix is filled in, write test items appropriate to each combination of skill and content. Note that this same process applies to

TABLE 14.1 Behaviour-Content Matrix for a Unit on Government

In making a test plan, begin by deciding on the total number of questions for each topic and for each kind of objective (the numbers in bold) and then allocate the number of questions to each particular combination of objective (behaviour) and topic (content).

Topics	Understanding Concepts	Making Generalizations	Locating Information	Interpreting Graphs	Total Questions
Social Trends	4	4	1	1	10
National Political Events	2	3	3	2	10
Methods of Inquiry	1	1	2	1	5
Major Political Issues	3	6	4	2	15
Total Questions	10	14	10	6	4

writing objectives for the unit. Using the same behaviour-content matrix helps to ensure your tests are validly aligned to the curriculum you teach.

When to Test? Frank Dempster (1991) examined the research on reviews and tests and reached these useful conclusions for teachers:

1. Frequent testing encourages the retention of information and appears to be more effective than a comparable amount of time spent reviewing and studying the material.
2. Tests are especially effective in promoting learning if you give students a test on the material soon after they learn it, then retest on the material later. The retests should be spaced further and further apart.
3. The use of cumulative questions on tests is a key to effective learning. Cumulative questions ask students to apply information learned in previous units to solve a new problem.

Unfortunately, the curriculum in many schools is so full that there is little time for frequent tests and reviews. Dempster argues that students will learn more if we "teach them less," that is, if the curriculum includes fewer topics, but explores those topics in greater depth and allows more time for review, practice, testing, and feedback (Dempster, 1993).

Judging Textbook Tests. Most elementary and secondary school texts today come complete with supplemental materials such as teaching manuals, handout masters, and ready-made tests. Using these tests can save time, but is this good teaching practice? The answer depends on your objectives for your students, the way you taught the material, and the quality of the tests provided (Airasian, 1996). If the textbook test matches your testing plan and the instruction you actually provided for your students, then it may be the right test to use. Table 14.2 gives key points to consider in evaluating textbook tests.

What if no tests are available for the material you want to cover, or the tests provided in your teacher's manuals are not appropriate for your students? Then it's time for you to create your own tests. We will consider the two major kinds of tests—objective and essay.

Connect & Extend
To the research
Dempster, F. N. (1991). Synthesis of research on reviews and tests. *Educational Leadership, 48*(7), 71–76.
  Focus Question: How can tests and reviews be used to encourage student learning?

Connect & Extend
To the research
Dempster, F. N. (1993). Exposing our students to less should help them learn more. *Phi Delta Kappan, 74*, 432–437.

TABLE 14.2 Key Points to Consider in Judging Textbook Tests

The decision to use a textbook test must come *after* a teacher identifies the objectives that he or she taught and now wants to assess.

Textbook tests are designed for the typical classroom, but since few classrooms are typical, most teachers deviate somewhat from the text in order to accommodate their pupils' needs.

The more classroom instruction deviates from the textbook objectives and lesson plans, the less valid the textbook tests are likely to be.

The main consideration in judging the adequacy of a textbook test is the match between its test questions and what pupils were taught in their classes:

- Are questions similar to the teacher's objectives and instructional emphases?
- Do questions require pupils to perform the behaviour they were taught?
- Do questions cover all or most of the important objectives taught?
- Is the language level and terminology appropriate for pupils?
- Does the number of items for each objective provide a sufficient sample of pupil performance?

Source: From P. Airasian. *Assessment in the Classroom*, p. 190. Copyright © 1996 by The McGraw-Hill Companies. Adapted with permission of The McGraw-Hill Companies.

Objective Testing

Objective Testing: Kinds of tests that do not require interpretation in scoring, such as multiple-choice, true/false, short-answer, and fill-in.

Stem: The question part of a multiple-choice item.

Distractors: Wrong answers offered as choices in a multiple-choice item.

Multiple-choice questions, matching exercises, true/false statements, and short-answer or fill-in items are all types of **objective testing**. The word "objective" in relation to testing means "not open to many interpretations," or "not subjective." The scoring of these types of items is relatively straightforward compared to the scoring of essay questions because the answers are more clear-cut than essay answers.

Gronlund (1993) suggests that the guiding principle for deciding which item format is best is to "use the item types that provide the most direct measures of student performance specified by the intended learning outcome" (p. 28). In other words, if you want to see how well students can write a letter, have them write a letter, don't ask multiple-choice questions about letters. But if many different item formats will work equally well, use multiple-choice questions because they are easier to score fairly and can cover many topics. Switch to other formats if writing good multiple-choice items for the material is not possible. For example, if related concepts need to be linked, such as terms and definitions, then a matching item is a better format than multiple-choice. If it is difficult to come up with several wrong answers for a multiple-choice item, try a true/false question instead. Alternatively, ask the student to supply a short answer that completes a statement (fill in the blank). Variety in objective testing can lower students' anxiety because the entire grade does not depend on one type of question that a particular student may find difficult. Here we look closely at the multiple-choice format, because it is the most versatile—and the most difficult to use well.

Connect & Extend
To other chapters
See **Chapter 11** for a discussion of Bloom's taxonomy of objectives in the cognitive domain and a recent revision of this taxonomy.

Using Multiple-Choice Tests. People often assume that multiple-choice items are appropriate only for asking factual questions. But multiple-choice items can test higher-level objectives as well, although writing higher-level items is difficult. A multiple-choice item can assess more than recall and recognition if it requires the student to deal with new material by applying or analyzing the concept or principle being tested (Gronlund, 1993). For example, the following multiple-choice item is designed to assess students' ability to recognize unstated assumptions, one of the skills involved in analyzing an idea:

A teacher's plan for improving classroom management includes making statements such as, "That's great cooperation!" and "Now that's what I call a polite way to debate." Which of the following assumptions is the teacher making?

1. Students are too often not attentive to their own behaviour. 2. Rewarding statements function as positive reinforcers. (correct answer) 3. Punishers don't have to be aversive. 4. Group work is naturally motivating.

Writing Multiple-Choice Questions. All test items require skillful construction, but good multiple-choice items are a real challenge. Some students jokingly refer to multiple-choice tests as "multiple-guess" tests—a sign that these tests are often poorly designed. Your goal in writing test items is to design them so that they measure student achievement, not test-taking and guessing skills.

The **stem** of a multiple-choice item is the part that asks the question or poses the problem. The choices that follow are called *alternatives*. The wrong answers are called **distractors** because their purpose is to distract students who have only a partial understanding of the material. If there were no good distracters, students with only a vague understanding would have no difficulty in finding the right answer.

The Guidelines adapted from Gronlund (1993) should make writing multiple-choice and other objective test questions easier.

GUIDELINES

Writing Objective Test Items

The stem should be clear and simple, and present only a single problem. Unessential details should be left out.

Poor

There are several different kinds of standard or derived scores. An IQ score is especially useful because

Better

An advantage of an IQ score is . . .

The problem in the stem should be stated in positive terms. Negative language is confusing. If you must use words such as *not*, *no*, or *except*, underline them or type them in all-capitals.

Poor

Which of the following is not a standard score?

Better

Which of the following is NOT a standard score?

Do not expect students to make extremely fine discrimination among answer choices.

Poor

The percentage of area in a normal curve falling between +1 and −1 standard deviations is about:
a. 66%. b. 67%. c. 68%. d. 69%.

Better

The percentage of area in a normal curve falling between +1 and −1 standard deviations is about:
a. 14%. b. 34%. c. 68%. d. 95%.

As much wording as possible should be included in the stem so that phrases will not have to be repeated in each alternative.

Poor

A percentile score

a. indicates the percentage of items answered correctly.
b. indicates the percentage of correct answers divided by the percentage of wrong answers.
c. indicates the percentage of people who scored at or above a given raw score.
d. indicates the percentage of people who scored at or below a given raw score.

Better

A percentile score indicates the percentage of

a. items answered correctly.
b. correct answers divided by the percentage of wrong answers.
c. people who scored at or above a given raw score.
d. people who scored at or below a given raw score.

Each alternative answer should fit the grammatical form of the stem, so that no answers are obviously right or wrong.

Poor

The Stanford-Binet test yields an

a. IQ score.
b. vocational preference.
c. reading level.
d. mechanical aptitude.

Better

The Stanford-Binet is a test of

a. intelligence.
b. reading level.
c. vocational preference.
d. mechanical aptitude.

Categorical words such as *always, all, only,* or *never* should be avoided unless they can appear consistently in all the alternatives. Most smart test-takers know that categorical answers signalled by these kinds of words are usually wrong.

Poor

A student's true score on a standardized test is

a. never equal to the obtained score.
b. always very close to the obtained score.
c. always determined by the standard error of measurement.
d. usually within a band that extends from +1 to −1 standard errors of measurement on each side of the obtained score.

Better

Which one of the statements below would most often be correct about a student's true score on a standardized test?

(continued)

a. It equals the obtained score.

b. It will be very close to the obtained score.

c. It is determined by the standard error of measurement.

d. It could be above or below the obtained score.

You should also avoid including two distractors that have the same meaning. If only one answer can be right and if two answers are the same, these two must both be wrong. This narrows down the choices considerably.

Poor

The most frequently occurring score in a distribution is called the

a. mode.

b. median.

c. arithmetical average.

d. mean.

Better

The most frequently occurring score in a distribution is called the

a. mode.

b. median.

c. standard deviation.

d. mean.

Avoid using the exact wording found in the textbook. Poor students may recognize the answers without knowing what they mean.

Avoid overuse of *all of the above* and *none of the above*. Such choices may be helpful to students who are simply guessing. In addition, using *all of the above* may trick a quick student who sees that the first alternative is correct and does not read on to discover that the others are correct, too.

Obvious patterns on a test also aid students who are guessing. The position of the correct answer should be varied, as should its length.

Evaluating Objective Test Items

How will you evaluate the quality of the objective tests you give? One way is to conduct an item analysis to identify items that are performing well and those that should be changed or eliminated. There are many techniques for item analysis but one basic approach is to calculate a *difficulty index* and a *discrimination index* for each item on the test. The difficulty index (symbolized p) of any item is simply the proportion or percentage of people who answered that item correctly. (Note, although p is called the difficulty index, it actually shows how easy an item is. A p of 1.00 describes an item that everyone answers correctly and a p of 0.00 identifies an item that no one could answer.) For tests where you want to have the best chance to identify differences among people, items with difficulty indices of around .50 are best. A simple way of calculating the difficulty index of an item when you have a large class is shown in Table 14.3 on page 535.

The discrimination index (d) tells you how well each test item differentiates between people who performed well overall on the test versus those who did poorly. The assumption here is that a test item is a better item if people who answered that item correctly also did better on the entire test; and, conversely, students who missed that item got lower scores on the test. A test item that was passed more often by the low scorers than by the high scorers would be suspect. Table 14.3 shows an uncomplicated way to estimate the discrimination index of a test item.

Essay Testing

The best way to measure some learning objectives is to require students to create answers on their own. An essay question is appropriate in these cases. The most difficult part of essay testing is judging the quality of the answers, but writing good, clear questions is not particularly easy, either. We will look at writing, administering, and grading essay tests, with most of the specific suggestions taken

TABLE 14.3 Calculating the Difficulty and Discrimination Indices for Test Items

To estimate the **Difficulty Index** (*p*) for each item:

- Rank the scores on the test from highest to lowest.
- Identify the people in the top one-third (the high-scoring group or HSG) and the people in the bottom one-third (the low-scoring group or LSG).
- For each item, count the number of people who answered correctly the HSG and the LSG combined and divide by the total in the two groups. The formula is:

$$\text{Difficulty Index of an item} = \frac{\text{number correct in HSG} + \text{number correct in LSG}}{\text{number in HSG} + \text{number in LSG}}$$

This calculation is a reasonable estimate of the proportion of students in the whole class who answered correctly. Ideally, most of the items on a norm-referenced test would have difficulty indices of .40 to .59, with only a few hard (.00 to .25) or easy (.75 to 1.00) items.

To estimate the **Discrimination Index** (*d*) for each item:

- Rank the scores on the test from highest to lowest.
- Identify the people in the top one-third of the scores (high-scoring group or HSG) and the people in the bottom one-third (low-scoring group or LSG).
- Subtract the percentage of students in the LSG who answered correctly from the percentage of students in the HSG who answered correctly. The formula is:

Discrimination
Index of = percent correct in HSG – percent correct in LSG
an item

The meaning of the discrimination index for any item is as follows:

$d = +.60$ to 1.00	*Very Strong* discriminator between high- and low-scoring students
$d = +.40$ to $.59$	*Strong* discriminator between high- and low-scoring students
$d = +.20$ to $.39$	*Moderate* discriminator between high- and low-scoring students (improve the item)
$d = -.19$ to $.19$	*Does Not* discriminate between high- and low-scoring students (improve or eliminate the item)
$d = -.20$ to -1.00	*Strong Negative* discriminator between high- and low-scoring students (check item for problems, miskeyed? two right answers? etc.)

Source: Adapted with permission from K. Linden (1992). *Cooperative Learning and Problem Solving*, pp. 207–209. Published by Waveland Press.

from Gronlund (1993). We will also consider factors that can bias the scoring of essay questions and ways you can overcome these problems.

Constructing Essay Tests. Because answering essays takes time, true essay tests necessarily cover less material than objective tests. Thus, for efficiency, essay tests should be limited to assessing the more complex learning outcomes.

An essay question should give students a clear and precise task and should indicate the elements to be covered in the answer. Gronlund suggests the following as an example of an essay question that might appear in an educational psychology course to measure an objective at the synthesis level of Bloom's taxonomy in the cognitive domain:

> For a course that you are teaching or expect to teach, prepare a complete plan for assessing student achievement. Be sure to include the procedures you would follow, the instruments you would use, and the reasons for your choices.

This question requires students to apply information and values derived from course material to produce a complex new product.

Students should be given ample time for answering. If more than one essay is being completed in the same class period, you may want to suggest time limits for each. Remember, however, that time pressure increases anxiety and may interfere with accurate assessment of some students. Whatever your approach, do not try to make up for the limited amount of material an essay test can cover by including a large number of essay questions. It would be better to plan on more frequent test-

Connect & Extend
To your teaching
One reason students prefer essay tests is that they can write down something, even if it doesn't answer the question, and receive at least partial credit for it. Do you think that granting partial credit is a common grading practice among teachers? Considering that essay questions sample only a limited amount of material, does giving partial credit seem commendable or defensible?

There are special cautions in evaluating essay tests. The challenges are to be clear with students about the criteria for grading, then apply those criteria fairly and consistently. ▶

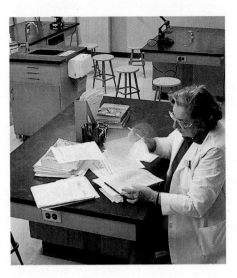

ing than to include more than two or three essay questions in a single class period. Combining an essay question with a number of objective items is one way to avoid the problem of limited sampling of course material (Gronlund, 1993).

Evaluating Essays: Dangers. In 1912, Starch and Elliot began a classic series of experiments that shocked educators into critical consideration of subjectivity in testing. These researchers wanted to find out the extent to which teachers were influenced by personal values, standards, and expectations in scoring essay tests. For their initial study, they sent copies of English examination papers written by two high school students to English teachers in 200 high schools. Each teacher was asked to score the papers according to his or her school's standards. A percentage scale was to be used, with 75 percent as a passing grade.

The results? Neatness, spelling, punctuation, and communicative effectiveness were all valued to different degrees by different teachers. The scores on one of the papers ranged from 64 to 98 percent, with a mean of 88.2. The average score for the other paper was 80.2, with a range between 50 and 97. The following year, Starch and Elliot (1913a, 1913b) published similar findings in a study involving history and geometry papers. The most important result of these studies was the discovery that the problem of subjectivity in grading was not confined to any particular subject area. The main difficulties were the individual standards of the grader and the unreliability of scoring procedures.

Certain qualities of an essay may influence grades. Teachers may reward quantity rather than quality in essays. In a series of studies described by Fiske (1981), many high school and college English teachers rated pairs of student essays that were identical in every way but linguistic style. One essay was quite verbose, with flowery language, complex sentences, and passive verbs. The other essay was written in the simple, straightforward language most teachers claim is the goal for students of writing. The teachers consistently rated the verbose essay higher.

Connect & Extend
To the research
Writing evaluation: Examining four teachers' holistic analytic scores. *Elementary School Journal, 90,* 88–95.

Evaluating Essays: Methods. Phil designs essay items to have each one target three to five key ideas. Generally, a key idea is something that requires a paragraph or two to describe. He also provides some opportunity to include a few supplementary ideas. To prepare for marking, Phil first writes out the essential parts of each key idea that every student's essay should include. Then he adds a list of other points that supplement those key ideas but aren't absolutely essential to a full and accurate answer. For each key idea, he scores a 0 if the idea is missing or wrongly described, +1 if it is mentioned but otherwise not developed, +2 if the idea is fairly well described and yet missing something small but important or is slightly off target, and +3 if the idea is fully and accurately presented. Next, he scores supplements to key ideas using a scale of 0, +1, or +2 for each one. Because these are supplements rather than key ideas, the maximum score for all the supplements is set at approximately a quarter or a third of the maximum score for key ideas, about four to five points overall. Next, Phil makes a judgment about the overall quality and organization of the student's essay, scoring this feature from 0 to +3. Then he adds up the points for key ideas, supplements, and quality. Finally, as a check that the marks make "good sense," he lays out students' papers on the floor in order of their total score. He compares close papers and, if necessary, makes scoring adjustments to be fair. This method has several advantages. It makes most essay test questions about the same "size." It reduces subjectivity by limiting the range of points assigned to any one part. It rewards students for elaborations that enrich the focus of an item. Last but not least, it recognizes that students' answers can have quality beyond just content.

Gronlund (1993) suggests several other good strategies for avoiding problems of subjectivity and inaccuracy in marking essays. When grading essay tests with several questions, it makes sense to grade all responses to one question before moving on to the next. This helps prevent the quality of a student's answer to one question from influencing your reaction to the student's other answers. After you finish reading and scoring the first question, shuffle the papers so that no students end up having all their questions graded first, last, or in the middle.

You may achieve greater objectivity if you ask students to put their names on the back of the paper, so that grading is anonymous. A final check on your fairness as a grader is to have another teacher who is equally familiar with your goals and subject matter grade your tests without knowing what grades you assigned. This can give you valuable insights into areas of bias in your grading practices.

TABLE 14.4 Comparing Objective and Essay Tests

Objective tests include any tests that ask the student to select the answer from a set of choices (multiple-choice, true/false, matching).

	Selection-Type Items	Essay Questions
Learning Outcomes Measured	Good for measuring outcomes at the knowledge, comprehension, and application levels of learning; inadequate for organizing and expressing ideas.	Inefficient for measuring knowledge outcomes; best for ability to organize, integrate, and express ideas.
Sampling of Content	The use of a large number of items results in broad coverage which makes representative sampling of content feasible.	The use of a small number of items limits coverage which makes representative sampling of content infeasible.
Preparation of Items	Preparation of good items is difficult and time consuming.	Preparation of good items is difficult but easier than selection-type items.
Scoring	Objective, simple, and highly reliable.	Subjective, difficult, and less reliable.
Factors Distorting Scores	Reading ability and guessing.	Writing ability and bluffing.
Probable Effect on Learning	Encourages students to remember, interpret, and use the ideas of others.	Encourages students to organize, integrate, and express their own ideas.

Source: From *How to Make Achievement Tests and Assessments, 5/e.* (p. 83), by N. E. Gronlund, 1993, Boston: Allyn & Bacon. Copyright © 1993 by Allyn & Bacon. Reprinted with permission.

Authentic Tests: Assessment procedures that test skills and abilities as they would be applied in real-life situations.

Now that we have examined both objective and essay testing, we can compare the two approaches. Table 14.4 presents a summary of the important characteristics of each.

*I*nnovations in Assessment

We have been considering how to make traditional testing more effective; now let's look at a few new approaches to classroom assessment. One of the main criticisms of standardized tests—that they control the curriculum, emphasizing recall of facts instead of thinking and problem solving—is a major criticism of classroom tests as well. Few teachers would dispute these criticisms. Even if you follow the guidelines we have been discussing, traditional testing can be limiting. What can be done? Should innovations in classroom assessment make traditional testing obsolete? The Point/Counterpoint section addresses this question.

One solution that has been proposed to solve the testing dilemma is to apply the concept of authentic assessment to classroom testing.

Authentic Classroom Tests

Authentic tests ask students to apply skills and abilities as they would in real life. For example, they might use fractions to enlarge or reduce recipes. The argument in favour of authentic tests goes like this:

> If tests determine what teachers actually teach and what students will study for—and they do—then the road to reform is a straight but steep one: test those capabilities and habits we think are essential, and test them in context. Make [tests] replicate, within reason, the challenges at the heart of each academic discipline. Let them be—authentic. (Wiggins, 1989, p. 41)

Wiggins goes on to say that if our instructional goals for students include the abilities to write, speak, listen, create, think critically, do research, solve problems, or apply knowledge, then our tests should ask students to write, speak, listen, create, think, solve, and apply. How can this happen?

Many educators suggest we look to the arts and sports for analogies to solve this problem. If we think of the "test" as being the recital, exhibition, game, mock court trial, or other performance, then teaching to the test is just fine. All coaches, artists, and musicians gladly "teach" to these "tests" because performing well on these tests is the whole point of instruction. Authentic assessment asks students to perform. The performances may be thinking performances, physical performances, creative performances, or other forms.

It may seem odd to talk of thinking as a performance, but there are many parallels. Serious thinking is risky, because real-life problems are not well defined. Often the outcomes of our thinking are public—our ideas are evaluated by others. Like a dancer auditioning for a theatre show, we must cope with the consequences of being evaluated. Like a sculptor looking at a lump of clay, a student facing a difficult problem must experiment, observe, redo, imagine and test solutions, apply both basic skills and inventive techniques, make interpretations, decide how to communicate results to the intended audience, and often accept criticism and improve the solution (Wolf, Bixby, Glenn, & Gardner, 1991). Table 14.5 on page 540 lists some characteristics of authentic tests.

Performance in Context: Portfolios and Exhibitions

The concern with authentic assessment has led to the development of several new approaches based on the goal of performance in context. Instead of circling

Connect & Extend
To the research
Cambourne, B., & Turbill, J. (1990). Assessment in whole-language classrooms: Theory into practice. *Elementary School Journal, 90,* 337–349.

Connect & Extend
To other chapters
See **Chapter 13** for a discussion of authentic assessment and standardized tests.

Connect & Extend
To professional journals
Wiggins, G. (1989). Teaching to the authentic test. *Educational Leadership, 46*(7), 41–47.
Focus Question: What makes tests "authentic"?

Connect & Extend
To professional journals
Aschbacher, P. R., & Winters, L. (1992). *A practical guide to alternative assessment.* Alexandria, VA: Association for Supervision and Curriculum Development.
Aschbacher, P. (1997). New directions in student assessment [Special Issue]. *Theory Into Practice, 36*(4), 194–272.

Authentic Tests: Assessment procedures that test skills and abilities as they would be applied in real-life situations.

To Test or Not to Test

We have seen the advantages and disadvantages of standardized tests, but what about classroom testing? Are traditional multiple-choice and essay tests useful in classroom assessment?

▶ **POINT** *Traditional tests are a poor basis for classroom assessment.*

In his article "Standards, Not Standardization: Evoking Quality Student Work," Grant Wiggins (1991) makes a strong case for giving students standards of excellence against which they can judge their accomplishments. But these standards should not be higher scores on multiple-choice tests. When scores on traditional tests become the standard, the message to students is that only right answers matter and the thinking behind the answers is unimportant. Wiggins notes:

> We do not judge Xerox, the Boston Symphony, the Cincinnati Reds, or Dom Perignon vineyards on the basis of indirect, easy to test, and common indicators. Nor would the workers in those places likely produce quality if some generic, secure test served as the only measure of their success in meeting a standard. Demanding and getting quality, whether from students or adult workers, means framing standards in terms of the work that we undertake and value. And it means framing expectations about that work which make quality a necessity, not an option. Consider:

- the English teacher who instructs peer-editors to mark the place in a student paper where they lost interest in it or found it slapdash and to hand it back for revision at that point;

- the professor who demands that all math homework be turned in with another student having signed off on it, where one earns the grade for one's work and the grade for the work that each person (willingly!) countersigned. (p. 22)

In a more recent article, Wiggins continues to argue for assessment that makes sense, that tests knowledge as it is applied in real-world situations. Understanding cannot be measured by tests that ask students to use skills and knowledge out of context. "In other words, we cannot be said to understand something unless we can employ our knowledge wisely, fluently, flexibly, and aptly in particular and diverse contexts" (Wiggins, 1993, p. 200).

◀ **COUNTERPOINT** *Traditional tests can play an important role.*

Most psychologists and educators would agree with Wiggins that setting clear, high, authentic standards is important, but many also believe that traditional tests are useful in this process. Learning may be more than knowing the right answers, but right answers are important. While schooling is about learning to think and solve problems, it is also about knowledge. Students must have something to think about—facts, ideas, concepts, principles, theories, explanations, arguments, images, opinions. Well-designed traditional tests can evaluate students' knowledge effectively and efficiently (Airasian, 1996; Kirst, 1991b).

Some educators believe that traditional testing should play an even greater role than it currently does. Educational policy analysts suggest that North American students, compared to students in many other developed countries, lack essential knowledge because North American schools emphasize process—critical thinking, self-esteem, problem solving—more than content. In order to teach more about content, teachers will need to determine how well their students are learning the content, and traditional testing provides useful information about content learning.

Tests are also valuable in motivating and guiding students' learning. There is research evidence that frequent testing encourages learning and retention (Nungester & Duchastel, 1982). In fact, students generally learn more in classes with more rather than fewer tests (Dempster, 1991).

Source: From "Standards, Not Standardization," by G. Wiggins, 1991, *Educational Leadership, 48*,(5), pp. 18–25. Copyright © 1991 by the Association for Supervision and Curriculum Development. Reprinted with permission.

---

answers to "factual" questions on non-existent situations, students are required to solve real problems. Facts are used in a context where they apply—for example, the student uses grammar facts to write a persuasive letter to a software company requesting donations for the class computer centre.

In Ontario's 1997 language curriculum guide (Ontario Ministry of Education and Training, 1997), one expectation for Grade 6 students in the area of media communication skills is to be able to "create a variety of media works (e.g., create a video advertisement for a book as a member of an 'advertising team')." Here's an example we created of a performance assessment and exhibition linked to this objective:

TABLE 14.5 Characteristics of Authentic Tests

A. Structure and Logistics

1. Are more appropriately public; involve an audience, a panel, and so on.

2. Do not rely on unrealistic and arbitrary time constraints.

3. Offer known, not secret, questions or tasks.

4. Are more like portfolios or a season of games (not one-shot).

5. Require some collaboration with others.

6. Recur—and are *worth* practising for, rehearsing, and retaking.

7. Make assessment and feedback to students so central that school schedules, structures, and policies are modified to support them.

B. Intellectual Design Features

1. Are "essential"—not needlessly intrusive, arbitrary, or contrived to "shake out" a grade.

2. Are "enabling"—constructed to point the student toward more sophisticated use of the skills or knowledge.

3. Are contextualized, complex intellectual challenges, not "atomized" tasks, corresponding to isolated "outcomes."

4. Involve the student's own research or use of knowledge, for which "content" is a means.

5. Assess student habits and repertoires, not mere recall or plug-in skills.

6. Are *representative* challenges—designed to emphasize depth more than breadth.

7. Are engaging and educational.

8. Involve somewhat ambiguous ("ill-structured") tasks or problems.

C. Grading and Scoring Standards

1. Involve criteria that assess essentials, not easily counted (but relatively unimportant) errors.

2. Are graded not on a "curve" but in reference to performance standards (criterion-referenced, not norm-referenced).

3. Involve demystified criteria of success that appear to **students** as inherent in successful activity.

4. Make self-assessment a part of the assessment.

5. Use a multifaceted scoring system instead of one aggregate grade.

6. Exhibit harmony with shared schoolwide aims—a *standard*.

D. Fairness and Equity

1. Ferret out and identify (perhaps hidden) strengths.

2. Strike a *constantly* examined balance between honouring achievement and native skill or fortunate prior training.

3. Minimize needless, unfair, and demoralizing comparisons.

4. Allow appropriate room for student learning styles, aptitudes, and interests.

5. Can be—should be—attempted by *all* students, with the test "scaffolded up," not "dumbed down," as necessary.

Source: From Grant Wiggins. Teaching to the authentic test. *Educational Leadership, 46*(7), p. 44. Reprinted by permission of the Association of Supervision and Curriculum Development. Copyright © 1989 by ASCD. All right reserved.

As you probably know, a lot of kids begin smoking at about your age. And you also probably know that smoking is a big threat to health, not to mention how much it costs a smoker to sustain a cigarette habit. Your assignment is to write a script for a TV "commercial" that will convince kids your age not to start smoking. Then, you and your team will produce your commercial using our classroom's video equipment—you'll create a setting for your ad and shoot actors (you!) to make your point. At the end of the month, we'll have a kind of Gemini Awards where we'll view each team's commercial and, as a class, we'll consider how to judge the effectiveness of messages like your TV commercials.

Students completing this "test" will need to use several language-related skills, such as thinking critically and writing persuasively, as they develop a script concerning this real-life issue. Group discussion skills can be examined as the team plans the script and produces the video. In their acting roles, students can demonstrate other communication skills, such as using tone of voice and gestures to persuade others. As well, students' skills in using modern communication tools, such as video cameras, and in helping one another can be observed during the shoot. When the class has its exhibition, you can evaluate students' use of high-level skills as they synthesize a method to judge the social impact of TV messages.

FIGURE 14.2

Three Ways of Rating an Oral Presentation

Numerical Rating Scale

Directions: Indicate how often the pupil performs each behaviour while giving an oral presentation. For each behaviour circle **1** if the pupil **always** performs the behaviour, **2** if the pupil **usually** performs the behaviour, **3** if the pupil **seldom** performs the behaviour, and **4** if the pupil **never** performs the behaviour.

Physical Expression

A. Stands straight and faces audience.

    1 2 3 4

B. Changes facial expression with change in the tone of the presentation.

    1 2 3 4

Graphic Rating Scale

Directions: Place an **X** on the line which shows how often the pupil did each behaviour listed while giving an oral presentation.

Physical Expression

A. Stands straight and faces the audience.

    always   usually   seldom   never

B. Changes facial expressions with change in tone of the presentation.

    always   usually   seldom   never

Descriptive Rating Scale

Directions: Place an **X** on the line at the place which best describes the pupil's performance on each behaviour.

Physical Expression

A. Stands straight and faces audience.

| stands straight, always looks at audience | weaves, fidgets, eyes roam from audience to ceiling | constant, distracting movements, no eye contact with audience |

B. Changes facial expressions with change in tone of the presentation.

| matches facial expressions to content and emphasis | facial expressions usually appropriate, occasional lack of expression | no match between tone and facial expression; expression distracts |

Source: From P. W. Airasian. *Assessment in the classroom*, p. 153. Copyright © 1996 by The McGraw-Hill Companies. Reproduced with permission of The McGraw-Hill Companies.

Scoring Rubrics. A checklist or rating scale gives specific feedback about elements of a performance. **Scoring rubrics** are more general descriptions of overall performance. For example, a rubric describing an excellent oral presentation might be:

> Pupil consistently faces audience, stands straight, and maintains eye contact; voice projects well and clearly; pacing and tone variation appropriate; well-organized; points logically and completely presented; brief summary at end. (Airasian, 1996, p. 155)

It is often helpful to have students join in developing rating scales and scoring rubrics. When students participate, they are challenged to decide what quality

Scoring Rubrics: Rules that are used to determine the quality of a student performance.

work looks or sounds like in a particular area. They know in advance what is expected. As students gain practice in designing and applying scoring rubrics, their work and their learning often improve. Figure 14.3 below is an evaluation form for self- and peer assessment of contributions to cooperative learning groups.

Performance assessment requires careful judgment on the part of teachers and clear communication to students about what is good and what needs improving. In some ways the approach is similar to the clinical method first introduced by Binet to assess intelligence: it is based on observing the student perform a variety of tasks and comparing his or her performance to a standard. Just as Binet never wanted to assign a single number to represent the child's intelligence, teachers who use authentic assessments do not try to assign one score to the student's performance. Even if rankings, ratings, and grades have to be given, these judgments are not the ultimate goals—improvement of learning is. The Guidelines for developing rubrics are taken from Goodrich (1997).

Reliability, Validity, Generalizability, and Equity. Because judgment plays such a central role in evaluating performances, issues of reliability, validity, and equity are critical considerations. Research clearly indicates that judges assessing portfolios often do not agree on ratings, so reliability may not be adequate. When raters are experienced and scoring rubrics are well developed and refined, however, reliability may improve (Herman & Winters, 1994; LeMahieu, Gitomer, & Eresh, 1993). Some of this improvement in reliability occurs because a rubric focuses the raters' attention on a few dimensions of the work and gives limited scoring levels to choose from. If scorers can give only a rating of 1, 2, 3, or 4, they

FIGURE 14.3

Self- and Peer Evaluating of Group Learning

STUDENT SELF- AND PEER EVALUATION FORM

This form will be used to assess the members of your learning group. Fill one form out on yourself. Fill one form out on each member of your group. During the group discussion, give each member the form you have filled out on them. Compare the way you rated yourself with the ways your groupmates have rated you. Ask for clarification when your rating differs from the ratings given you by your groupmates. Each member should set a goal for increasing his or her contribution to the academic learning of all group members.

Person Being Rated: _____

Write the number of points earned by the group member:
(4=Excellent, 3=Good, 2=Poor, 1=Inadequate)

____On time for class.

____Arrives prepared for class.

____Reliably completes all assigned work on time.

____Work is of high quality.

____Contributes to groupmates' learning daily.

____Asks for academic help and assistance when it is needed.

____Gives careful step-by-step explanations (doesn't just tell answers).

____Builds on others' reasoning.

____Relates what is being learned to previous knowledge.

____Helps draw a visual representation of what is being learned.

____Voluntarily extends a project.

Source: From D. W. Johnson and R. T. Johnson. "The role of cooperative learning in assessing and communicating student learning." In T. Guskey (Ed.), *ASCD 1996 Yearbook: Communicating student learning,* p. 41. Reprinted by permission of the Association for Supervision and Curriculum Development. Copyright © 1996 by ASCD. All rights reserved.

GUIDELINES

Developing a Rubric

1. *Look at models:* Show students examples of good and not-so-good work. Identify the characteristics that make the good ones good and the bad ones bad.
2. *List criteria:* Use the discussion of models to begin a list of what counts in quality work.
3. *Articulate gradations of quality:* Describe the best and worst levels of quality, then fill in the middle levels based on your knowledge of common problems and the discussion of not-so-good work.
4. *Practise on models:* Have students use the rubrics to evaluate the models you gave them in Step. 1.
5. *Use self- and peer assessment:* Give students their task. As they work, stop them occasionally for self- and peer assessment.
6. *Revise:* Always give students time to revise their work based on the feedback they get in Step 5.
7. *Use teacher assessment:* Assess students' work using the same rubrics they used in Step 4.

Step 1 may be necessary only when you are asking students to engage in a task with which they are unfamiliar. Steps 3 and 4 are useful but time-consuming; you can do these on your own, especially when you've been using rubrics for a while. A class experienced in rubric-based assessment can streamline the process so that it begins with listing criteria, after which the teacher writes out the gradations of quality, checks them with the students, makes revisions, then uses the rubric for self-, peer, and teacher assessment.

are more likely to agree than if they could score based on a 100-point scale. So the rubrics may achieve reliability not because they capture underlying agreement among raters, but because the rubrics limit options and thus limit variability in scoring (Mabry, 1999).

In terms of validity, there is some evidence that students who are classified as "master" writers on the basis of portfolio assessment are judged less capable using standard writing assessment. Which form of assessment is the best reflection of enduring qualities? There is so little research on this question, it is hard to say

▲ *To prepare for this performance, these students may have conducted historical research, written scripts, and negotiated their roles in the oral presentation. How will the teacher assess individual learning?*

Review

▶ What is authentic assessment?

▶ Describe portfolios and exhibitions.

Apply

▶ How would you assure reliability, validity, and equity in your use of authentic assessment tasks?

▶ How can checklists and rating scales be used to assess student portfolios and exhibitions?

(Herman & Winters, 1994). In addition, when rubrics are developed to assess specific tasks, the results of applying the rubrics may not predict performance on anything except very similar tasks, so what do we actually know about students' learning more generally (Haertel, 1999; Herman, 1997)?

Equity is an issue in all assessment and no less so with performances and portfolios. With a public performance there could be bias effects based on a student's appearance and speech or the student's access to expensive audio, video, or graphic resources. Performance assessments have the same potential as other tests to discriminate unfairly against students who are not wealthy or who are culturally different (McDonald, 1993). And the extensive group work, peer editing, and out-of-class time devoted to portfolios means that some students may have access to more extensive networks of support and outright help. Many students in your classes will have families with sophisticated computer-graphic and desktop-publishing capabilities. Others may have little support from home. These differences can be sources of bias and inequity.

*E*ffects of Grades and Grading on Students

Connect & Extend
To your own philosophy
Classroom evaluation is frequently referred to as the "grading game." What aspects of grading resemble a game from the student's point of view?

There is some evidence that high standards, a competitive class atmosphere, and a large percentage of lower grades are associated with increased absenteeism and dropout rates (Moos & Moos, 1978; Trickett & Moos, 1974). This seems especially likely with disadvantaged students (Wessman, 1972). Highly competitive classes may be particularly hard on anxious students or students who lack self-confidence. So, while high standards and competition do tend generally to be related to increased academic learning, it is clear that a balance must be struck between high standards and a reasonable chance to succeed.

Effects of Failure

It may sound as though low grades and failure should be avoided in school. But the situation is not that simple. After reviewing many years of research on the effects of failure from several perspectives, Margaret Clifford (1990, 1991) concluded that failure can have both positive and negative effects on subsequent performance, depending on the situation and the personality of the students involved.

For example, one study required subjects to complete three sets of problems. On the first set, the experimenters arranged for subjects to experience 0-, 50-, or 100-percent success. On the second set, it was arranged for all subjects to fail completely. On the third set of problems, the experimenters merely recorded how well the subjects performed. Those who had succeeded only 50 percent of the time before the failure experience performed the best. It appears that a history of complete failure or 100-percent success may be bad preparation for learning to cope with failure, something we must all learn. Some level of failure may be helpful for most students, especially if teachers help the students see connections between improvement and hard work that strives to repair faults in knowledge. Efforts to protect students from failure and guarantee success may be counterproductive. Clifford (1990) gives this advice to teachers:

It is time for educators to replace easy success with challenge. We must encourage students to reach beyond their intellectual grasp and allow them the privilege of learning from mistakes. There must be a tolerance for error-making in every classroom, and gradual success rather than continual success must become the yardstick by which learning is judged. (p. 23)

The more able your students, the more challenging and important it will be to help them learn to "fail successfully" (Foster, 1981).

So far, we have been talking about the effects of failing a test or perhaps a course. But what about the effect of failing an entire grade—that is, of being "held back"? Some researchers believe that being held back injures students' self-esteem and increases the chances that they will drop out of school (Grissom & Smith, 1989; Roderick, 1994). In their view, students generally do better academically when promoted. Other researchers have found some advantage for more emotionally immature children of average or above average ability who are retained in Grade 1, 2, or 3 (Kelly, 1999; Pierson & Connell, 1992), but the advantage may not last. In one study that followed many students for several years, children who could have been retained, but who were promoted, did about as well as similar children who were held back, and sometimes better (Reynolds, 1992).

No matter what, students who have trouble should get help, whether they are promoted or retained. Just covering the same material again in the same way won't solve the students' academic or social problems. As Jeannie Oakes (1999) has said, "No sensible person advocates social promotion as it is currently framed—simply passing incompetent students on to the next grade" (p. 8). The best approach may be to promote the students along with their peers, but to give them special remediation during the summer or the next year (Mantzicopoulos & Morrison, 1992; Shepard & Smith, 1989). An even better approach would be to prevent the problems before they occur by providing extra resources such as tutoring, as happens in the Reading Recovery program or Slavin's Success for All (Oakes, 1999).

Effects of Feedback

The results of several studies of feedback fit well with the notion of "successful" or constructive failure. These studies have concluded that it is more helpful to tell students why they are wrong so they can learn more appropriate strategies (Bangert-Drowns, Kulik, Kulik, & Morgan, 1991). Students often need help figuring out why their answers are incorrect and help understanding how learning skills should be applied (Butler & Winne, 1995). Without such feedback, they are likely to make the same mistakes again. Yet this type of feedback is rarely given. In one study, only about 8 percent of the teachers noticed a consistent type of error in a student's arithmetic computation and informed the student (Bloom & Bourdon, 1980).

Early research indicated that teachers' written comments on completed assignments can lead to improved performance in the future (Page, 1958). In more recent work the emphasis has been on identifying characteristics of effective written feedback. With older students (late elementary through high school), written comments are most helpful when they are personalized and when they provide constructive criticism. This means the teacher should make specific comments on errors or faulty strategies, but balance this criticism with suggestions about

Connect & Extend
To professional journals
Harvard Graduate School of Education (1999, January/February). Retention vs. social promotion: Schools search for alternatives. *Harvard Education Newsletter, 15*(1), 1–3. *Focus Question*: What are the effects of retention on students? Can you propose alternatives?

Connect & Extend
To professional journals
Two studies and a synthesis of research on grade retention: Mantzicopoulos, P., & Morrison, D. (1992). Kindergarten retention: Academic and behavioral outcomes through the end of second grade. *American Educational Research Journal, 29*, 182–198. Pierson, L. H., & Connell, J. P. (1992). Effect of grade retention on self-system processes, school engagement, and academic performance. *Journal of Educational Psychology, 84*, 300–307. Shepard, L. A., & Smith, M. L. (1990). Synthesis of research on grade retention. *Educational Leadership, 47*(8), 84–88.

Connect & Extend
To your own philosophy
What are some of your experiences in receiving feedback on papers and tests? Is it fair to give a student less than an A without indicating where improvement needs to be made?

Connect & Extend
To other chapters
See **Chapter 6** for a discussion of how to use praise effectively. These guidelines apply to written feedback as well.

◀ *Mistakes on tests can help students learn if appropriate feedback from teachers is provided so that the students can figure out why their answers were incorrect; they will be less likely to repeat the same mistake again if they know what was wrong and why.*

how to improve, and with comments on the positive aspects of the work (Butler & Nisan, 1986; Elawar & Corno, 1985). Working with Grade 6 teachers, Elawar and Corno (1985) found that feedback was dramatically improved when the teachers used these four questions as a guide: "What is the key error? What is the probable reason the student made this error? How can I guide the student to avoid the error in the future? What did the student do well that could be noted?" (p. 166). Here are some examples of teachers' written comments that proved helpful (Elawar & Corno, 1985, p. 164):

> Juan, you know how to get a percent, but the computation is wrong in this instance . . . Can you see where? (Teacher has underlined the location of errors.)

> You know how to solve the problem—the formula is correct—but you have not demonstrated that you understand how one fraction multiplied by another can give an answer that is smaller than either $(1/2 \times 1/2 = 1/4)$.

Extensive written comments may be inappropriate for younger students, but brief written comments are a different matter. Comments should help students correct errors and should recognize good work, progress, and increasing skill.

Grades and Motivation

Is there really a difference between working for a grade and working to learn? The answer depends in part on how a grade is determined. As a teacher, you can use grades to motivate the kind of learning you intend students to achieve in your course. If you test only at a simple but detailed level of knowledge, you may force students to choose between higher aspects of learning and a good grade. But when a grade reflects meaningful learning, working for a grade and working to learn become the same thing. Finally, while high grades may have some value as rewards or incentives for meaningful engagement in learning, low grades generally do not encourage greater efforts. Students receiving low grades are more likely to withdraw, blame others, decide that the work is "dumb," or feel responsible for the low grade but helpless to make improvements. Rather than give a failing grade, you might consider the work incomplete and give students support in revising or improving. Maintain high standards and give students a chance to reach them (Guskey, 1994). The Guidelines summarize the effects grades can have on students.

CHECKPOINT

Effects of Grades and Grading on Students

Review

▶ How can failure support learning?

▶ Which is better, social promotion or being "held back"?

▶ Can feedback, including grades, promote learning and motivation?

Apply

▶ How would you assess the value of the feedback you are receiving in your classes?

Grading and Reporting: Nuts and Bolts

In determining a final grade, the teacher must make a major decision. Should a student's grade reflect the amount of material learned and how well it has been learned, or should the grade reflect the student's status in comparison with the rest of the class? In other words, should grading be criterion-referenced or norm-referenced?

Connect & Extend
To your own philosophy
Given the various roles of evaluation, what is the disadvantage of a teacher giving a test and not returning the results until several weeks later? What is the disadvantage of merely posting the grade without returning the actual test? What is the disadvantage of returning the students' scored answer sheets without reviewing the correct answers?

Connect & Extend
To your own philosophy
Can grades be used as motivators for all students? What determines whether a grade is motivation? How can a teacher use grades so that they tend to be motivating instead of discouraging?

Connect & Extend
To your own philosophy
What would school be like for students if all testing were eliminated? Would most students still be motivated to learn and complete assignments?

GUIDELINES

Minimizing the Detrimental Effects of Grades

Avoid reserving high grades and high praise for answers that conform to your ideas or to those in the textbook.

Examples

1. Give extra points for correct and creative answers.
2. Withhold your opinions until all sides of an issue have been explored.
3. Reinforce students for disagreeing in a rational, productive manner.
4. Give partial credit for partly correct answers.

Make sure each student has a reasonable chance to be successful, especially at the beginning of a new task.

Examples

1. Pretest students to make sure they have prerequisite abilities.
2. When appropriate, provide opportunities for students to retest to raise their grades, but make sure the retest is as difficult as the original.
3. Consider failing efforts as "incomplete" and encourage students to revise and improve.

Balance written and oral feedback.

Examples

1. Consider giving short, lively, written comments for younger students and more extensive written comments for older students.

2. When the grade on a paper is lower than the student might have expected, be sure the reason for the lower grade is clear.
3. Tailor comments to the individual student's performance; avoid writing the same phrases over and over.
4. Note specific errors, possible reasons for errors, ideas for improvement, and work done well.

Make grades as meaningful as possible.

Examples

1. Tie grades to the mastery of important objectives.
2. Give ungraded assignments to encourage exploration.
3. Experiment with performances and portfolios.

Base grades on more than just one criterion.

Examples

1. Use essay questions as well as multiple-choice items on a test.
2. Grade oral reports and class participation.

Criterion-Referenced versus Norm-Referenced Grading

In **criterion-referenced grading**, the grade represents the quality of a list of accomplishments. If clear objectives have been set for the course, the grade may represent a certain number of objectives met satisfactorily. When a criterion-referenced system is used, criteria for each grade generally are spelled out in advance. It is then up to the student to earn the grade she or he wants to receive. Theoretically, in this system all students can achieve an A if they reach the criteria.

In **norm-referenced grading**, the major influence on a grade is the student's standing in comparison with others who also took the course. If a student studies very hard and almost everyone else does too, the student may receive a disappointing grade, perhaps a C.

Criterion-Referenced Systems. Criterion-referenced grading has the advantage of relating judgments about a student to the achievement of clearly defined instructional goals. Some school districts have developed reporting systems where report cards list objectives along with judgments about the student's attainment of each. Reporting is done at the end of each unit of instruction. The junior high report

Connect & Extend
To professional journals
Hills, J. R. (1991). Apathy concerning grading and testing. *Phi Delta Kappan, 72*(7), 540–545.

Criterion-Referenced Grading: Assessment of each student's mastery of each course objective.

Norm-Referenced Grading: Assessment of students' achievement in relation to one another or a defined group.

card shown in Figure 14.4 demonstrates the relationship between assessment and the goals of the unit.

In practice, many school systems would look suspiciously at a teacher who turned in a roster filled with As and explained that all the students had reached the class objectives. Administrators might say that if all the objectives could be so

---

FIGURE 14.4

A Criterion-Referenced Report Card

This is one example of a criterion-referenced report card. Other forms are possible, but all criterion-referenced reports indicate student progress toward specific goals.

MACKENZIE ELEMENTARY SCHOOL
GRADE 5

Student _____ Teacher _____ Principal _____Muriel Simms_____ Quarter 2 3 4

E = Excellent   S = Satisfactory   P = Making Progress   N = Needs improvement

READING PROGRAM
Materials Used: _____
_____
_____
___ Reads with understanding
___ Is able to write about what is read
___ Completes reading group work accurately and on time
___ Shows interest in reading
Reading Skills
___ Decodes new words
___ Understands new words
Independent Reading Level
Below   At Grade Level   Above

LANGUAGE ARTS
___ Uses oral language effectively
___ Listens carefully
___ Masters weekly spelling
Writing skills
___ Understands writing as process
___ Creates a rough draft
___ Makes meaningful revisions
___ Creates edited, legible final draft
Editing skills
___ Capitalizes
___ Punctuates
___ Uses complete sentences
___ Uses paragraphs
___ Demonstrates dictionary skills
Writing skill level:
Below   At Grade Level   Above

MATHEMATICS
Problem Solving
___ Solves teacher-generated problems
___ Solves Self-/Student-generated problems
___ Can create story problems
Interpreting Problems
___ Uses appropriate strategies
___ Can use more than one strategy
___ Can explain strategies in written form
___ Can explain strategies orally
Math Concepts
Understands Base Ten
Beginning Developing Sophisticated
Multiplication, Basic facts
Beginning Developing Sophisticated
2-digit Multiplication
Beginning Developing Sophisticated
Division
Beginning Developing Sophisticated
Geometry
Beginning Developing Sophisticated
Overall Math Skill Level:
Beginning Developing Sophisticated
Attitude/Work Skills
___ Welcomes a challenge
___ Persistent
___ Takes advantage of learning from others
___ Listens to others
___ Participates in discussion
It Figures
Is working on: _____
Goals: _____
Is working on achieving goal: _____

SOCIAL STUDIES
___ Understands subject matter
___ Shows curiosity and enthusiasm
___ Contributes to class discussions
___ Uses map skills
___ Demonstrates control of reading skills by interpreting text
Topics covered: individual cultures, Columbus–first English colonies

SCIENCE
___ Shows curiosity about scientific subject matter
___ Asks good scientific questions
___ Shows knowledge of scientific method
___ Uses knowledge of scientific method to help set up and run experiment(s)
___ Makes good scientific observations
___ Has researched scientific topic(s)
  Topic(s) _____
I Wonder
Is currently working on_____
_____

WORKING SKILLS
___ Listens carefully
___ Follows directions
___ Works neatly and carefully
___ Checks work
___ Completes work on time
___ Uses time wisely
___ Works well independently
___ Works well in a group
___ Takes risks in learning
___ Welcomes a challenge

HOMEWORK
___ Self-selects homework
___ Completes work accurately
___ Completes work on time

PRESENTATIONS/PROJECTS
_____
_____

HUMAN RELATIONS
___ Shows courtesy
___ Respects rights of others
___ Shows self-control
___ Interacts well with peers
___ Shows a cooperative and positive attitude in class
___ Shows a cooperative attitude when asked to work with other students
___ Is willing to help other students
___ Works well with other adults (subs, student teacher, parents, etc.)

Attendance	1st	2nd	3rd	4th
Present				
Absent				
Tardy				

Placement for next year:

Source: From K. Lake and K. Kafka. "Reporting methods in grades K–8." In T. Guskey (Ed.), *ASCD Yearbook: Communicating student learning,* p. 104. Reprinted by permission of the Association for Supervision and Curriculum Development. Copyright © 1996 by ASCD. All rights reserved.

easily attained by all the students, more or tougher objectives would be needed. Nevertheless, with effective teaching, a criterion-referenced system could well yield just such results and may be acceptable in some schools.

Norm-Referenced Systems. One common type of norm-referenced grading is called **grading on the curve**. In grading on the curve, the middle of the normal distribution or "average" performance becomes the anchor on which grading is based. In other words, teachers look at the average level of performance, assign what they consider an "average grade" for this performance, and then grade superior performances higher and inferior performances lower.

If grading were done strictly on the normal curve, there would be an equal number of As and Fs, a larger number of Bs and the same number of Ds as Bs, and an even larger number of Cs. The grades would have to form a bell-shaped curve. For example, a teacher might decide to give 10 percent As and Fs, 20 percent Bs and Ds, and 40 percent Cs. This is a very strict interpretation of grading on the curve, and will discourage students who work hard but always perform below average.

Grading on the curve can be done with varying levels of precision. The simplest approach is to rank the students' raw scores on a test from highest to lowest and use this ranked list of scores as the basis for assigning grades. Knowing that two-thirds of the scores in a normal distribution should be in the middle, you might bracket off the middle two-thirds of the scores and plan to give those students C+ and C– (or Bs, if you believed B was an average grade for the class in question). Some people prefer to use the middle one-third of the students rather than the middle two-thirds as the basis for the average grade. Based on this second approach, grades for the following scores might be:

Middle One-Third Assigned Cs

A	B	C	D	F

92 | 91 90 88 84 81 78 76 | 73 68 65 61 57 54 53 49 | 48 47 46 43 38 36 | 31 29

In the previous example the distance between one letter grade and another is sometimes one point! Given the amount of error in testing, this assignment of grades is probably not fair. You can correct some of these problems by introducing common sense into the process. For example, you may believe the following grade assignment is fairer:

Adjusted Grades

A	B	C	D	F

92 91 90 88 | 84 81 78 76 73 | 68 65 61 57 54 53 | 49 48 47 46 43 38 36 | 31 29

In this case the instructor has used the natural gaps in the range of scores to locate boundaries between grades. Between the A and B categories are seven points, between the B and C, four points, and so on. Even though this may seem fairer, many educators encourage teachers to avoid grading on the curve because this approach determines in advance that students must compete for the few good grades available (Guskey, 1994).

Table 14.6 on page 552 compares descriptions of a student's performance using criterion-referenced and norm-referenced standards and suggests a way to translate these descriptions into grades.

Preparing Report Cards

Whatever grading system you use, you will undoubtedly give several tests and you will probably assign homework or projects. Let's assume your unit assessment plan includes two short tests (mostly multiple-choice questions with one essay),

TABLE 14.6 Comparing Norm-Referenced and Criterion-Referenced Standards for Grading

Norm-referenced systems use the performance of the rest of the class as the standard for determining grades. Criterion-referenced systems use standards of subject mastery and learning to determine grades.

Grade	Criterion-referenced	Norm-referenced
A	Firm command of knowledge domain High level of skill development Exceptional preparation for later learning	Far above class average
B	Command of knowledge beyond the minimum Advanced development of most skills Has prerequisites for later learning	Above class average
C	Command of only the basic concepts of knowledge Demonstrated ability to use basic skills Lacks a few prerequisites for later learning	At the class average
D	Lacks knowledge of some fundamental ideas Some important skills not attained Deficient in many of the prerequisites for later learning	Below class average
F	Most of the basic concepts and principles not learned Most essential skills cannot be demonstrated Lacks most prerequisites needed for later learning	Far below class average

Source: From D. A. Frisbie and K. K. Waltmen. Developing a personal grading plan. *Educational Measurement: Issues and practices*, p. 37. Copyright © 1992 by the National Council on Measurement in Education. Reprinted by permission of the publisher.

Connect & Extend
To professional journals
For a summary of the considerations in developing a grading plan, see Frisbie, D. A., & Waltmen, K. K. (1992). Developing a personal grading plan. *Educational measurement: Issues and practices* (pp. 35–42). Washington, D.C.: National Council on Measurement in Education.

homework, a portfolio, and a unit test. If you use a criterion-referenced system for testing and grading, how will you convert scores on these individual performances to the overall indications of mastery on a report card such as that in Figure 14.4? What about using a norm-referenced system? How do you combine results from individual tests and assignments to yield a final distribution of scores for the unit grade?

Let us consider criterion-referenced grading first. If you adopt this system, you cannot average or combine test scores or homework grades mathematically. Since each test and assignment measures the mastery of a particular objective (or set of objectives), it would be meaningless to average, say, the students' mastery of addition of two-digit numbers with their mastery of measurement with a ruler, although both might be objectives in arithmetic. On the report card, the various objectives should be listed and the student's level of proficiency in each is indicated.

Norm-referenced grading is a different story. In order to assign grades, the teacher must merge all the scores from tests and other assignments into one final score. Final grades are based on how each student's final score compares with that of the rest of the students. But the usual procedure of simply adding up all the scores and averaging the total is often not appropriate, and it can be misleading. For example, assume two students took two tests. The tests are equally important in the overall unit. The students' scores are shown below (from Chase, 1978, p. 328).

	Test 1 Class mean = 30 Standard deviation = 8	Test 2 Class mean = 50 Standard deviation = 16	Total Raw Score
Leslie	38	50	88
Jason	30	66	96

If we compute an average or if we rank the students based on their totals, Jason will be ahead of Leslie. But if we look at the class mean and standard deviation for each test, we see a different picture. On one test, Leslie's score was one standard deviation above the mean, and on the other her score was at the mean; Jason's record is exactly the same.

If these two tests are really equally important, Jason and Leslie have identical records in relation to the rest of the class on these tests. To compare students' performances on several tests, the scores for each must be converted to a standard scale such as a T score. As you may recall from Chapter 13, a T mean is automatically 50 and the standard deviation is 10. Leslie's T score on Test 1 is 60, and her T score on test 2 is right at the mean, 50. Her total using T scores is 110. Jason's T scores are 50 on Test 1 and 60 on Test 2, for a total of 110. Most teachers do not calculate T scores for all their students, but the example illustrates the importance of using common scales in grading. Simple totals do not always reflect how well one student is doing in relation to others in the class.

The Point System

One popular system for combining grades from many assignments is a point system. Each test or assignment is given a certain number of total points, depending on its importance. A test worth 40 percent of the grade could be worth 40 points. A paper worth 20 percent could be worth 20 points. Points are then awarded on the test or paper based upon specific criteria. An A+ paper, one that meets all the criteria, could be given the full 20 points; an average paper might be given 10 points. If tests of comparable importance are worth the same number of points, are equally difficult, and cover a similar amount of material, we can expect to avoid some of the problems we encountered in assigning grades to Jason and Leslie, when the means and standard deviations of two supposedly comparable tests varied so greatly.

Let us assume a grade book indicates the scores shown in Table 14.7 on page 554. How would you assign grades to students for this unit? The most common way is to find the total number of points for each student and rank the students. Assign grades by looking for natural gaps of several points or imposing a curve (a certain percentage of As, Bs, and so on).

Percentage Grading

There is another approach to assigning grades to a group of students like those in Table 14.7. Using **percentage grading** the teacher can assign grades based on how much knowledge each student has mastered—what percentage of the total knowledge he or she understands. To do this, the teacher might score tests and other classwork with percentage scores (based on how much is correct—50 percent, 85 percent, etc.) and then average these scores to reach a course score. These scores can then be converted into letter grades according to predetermined cutoff points. Any number of students can earn any grade. This procedure is very common; you may have experienced it yourself as a student. Let us look at it more closely, because it has some frequently overlooked problems.

Percentage Grading: System of converting class performances to percentage scores and assigning grades based on predetermined cutoff points.

TABLE 14.7 Points Earned on Five Assignments

Student	Test 1 20% 20 points	Test 2 20% 20 points	Unit Test 30% 30 points	Homework 15% 15 points	Portfolio 15% 15 points	Total
Amy	10	12	16	6	7	___
Larry	12	10	14	7	6	___
Lee	20	19	30	15	13	___
Ming	18	20	25	15	15	___
Étienne	6	5	12	4	10	___
Francine	10	12	18	10	9	___
Seiko	13	11	22	11	10	___
Harv	7	9	12	5	6	___
Ivory	14	16	26	12	12	___
Nalini	20	18	28	10	15	___
Keith	19	20	25	11	12	___
Linda	14	12	20	13	9	___
Marki	15	13	24	8	10	___
Naomi	8	7	12	8	6	___
Olivia	11	12	16	9	10	___
Carlos	7	8	11	4	8	___

The grading symbols of A, B, C, D, and F are probably the most popular means of reporting. School systems often establish equivalent percentage categories for each of these letter grades. The percentages vary from school district to school district, but two typical ones are these:

90–100% = A; 80–89% = B; 70–79% = C; 60–69% = D; below 60% = F
94–100% = A; 85–93% = B; 76–83% = C; 70–75% = D; below 70% = F

As you can see, although both districts have an A to F grading system, the average achievement required for each grade is different.

Can we really say what is the total amount of knowledge available in, for example, Grade 8 science? Can we accurately measure what percentage of this body of knowledge each student has attained? Does it matter which parts of the science curriculum a student knows and doesn't know, a feature that is camouflaged by a single percentage score?

Another problem with percentage grading is the way an overall percentage is created. Most teachers simply average percentage grades from a set of assignments, even though the assignments can vary considerably in "size" and importance. In this system, every percentage score is treated as if it measures learning on an assignment that is the same "size" and importance as every other assignment. Note that the point system we just described completely avoids this particular problem.

And don't be confused—a percentage grade is not a criterion-referenced grade even though it may look like one. Moreover, as the examples just given illustrate, teachers assign grades according to cutoffs in percentage grade systems as if measurement were so accurate that a one-point difference was meaningful: "In spite of decades of research in educational and psychological measurement, which has produced more defensible methods, the concept [of percentage grading], once established, has proved remarkably resistant to change" (Zimmerman, 1981, p. 178).

Any grading system prescribed or suggested by the school can be influenced by particular concerns of the teacher. So don't be fooled by the seeming security of absolute percentages. Your own grading philosophy will continue to operate, even in this system. Because there is more concern today with specifying objectives and criterion-referenced assessment, especially at the elementary grade levels, several alternative methods for evaluating student progress against predetermined criteria have evolved. We will look at one: the contract system.

The Contract System and Grading Rubrics

When applied to the whole class, the **contract system** indicates the type, quantity, and quality of work required for each number or letter grade in the system. Rubrics describe the performance expected for each level. Students agree, or "contract," to work for particular grades by meeting the specified requirements and performing at the level specified. For example, the following standards might be established:

F: Not coming to class regularly or not turning in the required work.

D: Coming to class regularly and turning in the required work on time.

C: Coming to class regularly, turning in the required work on time, and receiving a check mark on all assignments to indicate they are satisfactory.

B: Coming to class regularly, turning in the required work on time, and receiving a check mark on all assignments except at least three that achieve a check-plus, indicating superior achievement.

A: As above, plus a successful oral or written report on one of the books listed for supplementary reading.

This example calls for more subjective judgment than would be ideal. However, contract systems reduce student anxiety about grades. The contract system can be applied to individual students, in which case it functions much like an independent study plan.

Unfortunately, the system can lead to overemphasis on the quantity of work. Teachers may be too vague about the standards that differentiate acceptable from unacceptable work. This is where scoring rubrics for each assignment can be helpful. If clear and well-developed rubrics describe the performances expected for each assignment, and if students learn to use the rubrics to evaluate their own work, then quality, not quantity, will be at the centre of grading. A teacher can modify the contract system by including a **revise option**. For example, a check mark might be worth 75 points and a check-plus 90 points; a check-plus earned after revision could be worth 85 points—more than a check, but less than a check-plus earned the first time around. This system allows students to improve their work, but also rewards getting it right the first time. Some quality control is possible, because students earn points not just for quantity but also for quality. In addition, the teacher may be less reluctant to judge a project unsatisfactory because students can improve their work (King, 1979). But beware, if a school system requires a five-point grading scale and all students contract for and achieve the highest grade (before or after revising), the teacher will wish that the principal had been consulted about the system before the grades came out.

Grading on Effort and Improvement

Grading on effort and improvement should not be a complete grading system but rather a theme that can run through most grading methods. Should teachers grade students based on how much they learn or on the final level of learning? One problem with using improvement as a standard for grading is that the best students improve the least, because they are already the most competent. Do you want to penalize these students because they knew quite a bit initially, and because teaching and testing have limited how much learning they can demonstrate? After all,

Contract System: System in which each student works for a particular grade according to agreed-upon standards.

Revise Option: In a contract system, the chance to revise and improve work.

Connect & Extend
To your own philosophy
How would you solve the following problem? You are using a contract system in one of your classes. One of the requirements for an A is "to write a book report." However, some students are reporting on books that you think they read last year, and some are handing in short, superficial reports. How can you structure the contract system so that the students will produce better-quality work?

Connect & Extend
To other chapters
See **Chapter 6** for a discussion of behaviour management contracts.

"I HOPE THIS ISN'T ANOTHER PLOY TO UP YOUR GRADE, HASKELL."

(© Art Bouthillier)

Review

▷ Describe two kinds of grading.

▷ What is the point system?

▷ Describe some alternatives to traditional grading.

▷ What are some sources of bias in grading?.

Apply

▷ What grading systems are you experiencing right now in your college classes?

▷ What are the advantages and disadvantages of contract grading? Percentage grading? Grading on the curve?

unless you assign extra work, these students will run out of opportunities to demonstrate their potential.

Many teachers try to include some judgment of effort in final grades, but effort is difficult to assess. Are you certain your perception of each student's effort is correct? Clement (1978) suggests a system called the **dual marking system** that includes a judgment about effort in the final grade. Students are assigned two grades. One, usually a letter, indicates the actual level of achievement. The other, a number, indicates the relationship of the achievement to the student's ability and effort. For example, a grade of B could be qualified as follows (Clement, 1978, p. 51):

B1: Outstanding effort, better achievement than expected, good attitude B2: Average effort, satisfactory in terms of ability B3: Lower achievement than ability would indicate, poor attitude

Of course, this system assumes that the teacher can adequately judge both true ability and effort. A grade of D1, D2, or F2 could be quite insulting. A grade of A3 or F1 should not be possible. But the system does have the advantage of recognizing hard work and giving feedback about a seeming lack of effort. An A2 or B2 might tell very bright students: "You're doing well, but I know you could do better." This could help the students to expect more of themselves and not slip by on high ability. The overall grade—A, B, C—still reflects achievement and is not changed (or biased) by teachers' subjective judgment of effort.

Cautions: Being Fair

The attributions a teacher makes about the causes of student successes or failures can affect the grades that students receive. Teachers are more likely to give higher grades for students' effort (a controllable factor) than for ability (an uncontrollable factor). Lower grades are more likely when teachers attribute a student's failure to lack of effort instead of lack of ability (Weiner, 1979). It is also possible that grades can be influenced by a **halo effect**—that is, the tendency to view particular aspects of a student based on a general impression, either positive or negative. As a teacher, you may find it difficult to avoid being affected by positive and negative halos. A very pleasant student who seems to work hard and causes little trouble may be given the benefit of the doubt (B– instead of C+), whereas a very difficult student who seems to refuse to try might be a loser at grading time (D instead of C–). The Guidelines give ideas for using any grading system in a fair and reasonable way.

Dual Marking System: System of assigning two grades, one reflecting achievement and the other effort, attitude, and actual ability.

Halo Effect: The tendency for a general impression of a person to influence our perception of any aspect of that person.

Beyond Grading: Communication

No number or letter grade conveys the totality of a student's experience in a class or course. Both students and teachers sometimes become too focused on the end point—the grade. But children and adolescents spend the majority of their waking hours for many months of the year in school, where teachers are the relevant adults. This gives teachers the opportunity and the responsibility to know their students as people.

GUIDELINES

Using Any Grading System

Explain your grading policies to students early in the course and remind them of the policies regularly.

Examples

1. Give older students a handout describing the assignments, tests, grading criteria, and schedule.
2. Explain to younger students in a low-pressure manner how their work will be evaluated.

Set reasonable standards.

Examples

1. Discuss workload and grading standards with more experienced teachers.
2. Give a few formative tests to get a sense of your students' abilities before you give a graded test.
3. Take tests yourself first to gauge the difficulty of the test and to estimate the time your students will need.

Base your grades on as much objective evidence as possible.

Examples

1. Plan in advance how and when you will test.
2. Keep a portfolio of student work. This may be useful in student or parent conferences.

Be sure students understand test directions.

Examples

1. Outline the directions on the board.
2. Ask several students to explain the directions.
3. Go over a sample question first.

Correct, return, and discuss test questions as soon as possible.

Examples

1. Have students who wrote good answers read their responses for the class; make sure they are not the same students each time.
2. Discuss why wrong answers, especially popular wrong choices, are incorrect.

3. As soon as students finish a test, give them the answers to questions and the page numbers where answers are discussed in the text.

As a rule, do not change a grade.

Examples

1. Make sure you can defend the grade in the first place.
2. DO change any clerical or calculation errors.

Guard against bias in grading.

Examples

1. Ask students to put their names on the backs of their papers.
2. Use an objective point system or model papers when grading essays.

Keep pupils informed of their standing in the class.

Examples

1. Write the distribution of scores on the board after tests.
2. Schedule periodic conferences to go over work from previous weeks.

Give students the benefit of the doubt. All measurement techniques involve error.

Examples

1. Unless there is a very good reason not to, give the higher grade in borderline cases.
2. If a large number of students miss the same question in the same way, revise the question for the future and consider throwing it out for that test.

Source: From *Problems in Middle and High School Teaching: A Handbook for Student Teachers and Beginning Teachers* (pp. 182–187), by A. M. Drayer, 1979, Boston: Allyn & Bacon. Copyright © 1979 by Allyn & Bacon. Adapted by permission of the author and publisher.

Conferences with parents are often expected of teachers in elementary school and can be equally important in junior high and high school. Schedule conferences at a time convenient for parents; confirm appointments in writing or by phone. The conference should not be a time for lecturing parents or students. As the professional, the teacher needs to take a leadership role and yet remain sensitive to the needs of the other participants. The atmosphere should be friendly and unrushed. Any observations about the student should be factual, based on first-hand

The success of a parent-teacher conference depends largely on the teacher's communication skills. Listening is an important element. ▶

observation or information from assignments. Information gained from a student or a parent should be kept confidential. Listening and problem-solving skills such as those discussed in Chapter 11 can be particularly important when you are dealing with parents or students who are angry or upset. Make sure you really hear the concerns of the participants, not just their words. The Guidelines offer some

FAMILY AND COMMUNITY PARTNERSHIPS

Conferences

Plan ahead.

Examples

What are your goals?
Problem solving?
Sharing test results?
Asking questions that you want answered?
Providing information you want to share? Emphasize the positive.
Describing your "next steps" in the classroom?
Making suggestions for use at home?

Begin with a positive statement.

Examples

"Howard has a great sense of humour."
"Giselle really enjoys materials that deal with animals."
"Sandy is sympathetic when somebody has a problem."

Listen actively.

Examples

Empathize with the parents.
Accept their feelings: "You seem to feel frustrated when Lee doesn't listen."

Establish a partnership.

Examples

Ask parents to follow through on class goals at home: "If you ask to see the homework checklist and go over it at home with Iris, I'll review it and chart her progress at school."

Plan follow-up contacts.

Examples

Write notes or make phone calls to share successes.
Keep parents informed before problems develop.

End with a positive statement.

Examples

"José has made several friends this year."
"Courtney should be a big help in the social studies play that her group is developing."

Source: From *The Successful Classroom: Management Strategies for Regular and Special Education Teachers* (p. 181), by D. P. Fromberg and M. Driscoll, 1985, New York: Teachers College Press. Copyright © 1985 by Teachers College Press. Adapted with permission.

helpful ideas for planning and conducting conferences.

You should be aware that parents have the right to view all information about their child in your files and in the school's record. In some provinces, parents can decide who else, other than their child's classroom teacher or principal, can access this material. And, in other cases, students 16 years old or older can have access to all this information. If the records contain information students or parents believe is incorrect, they can challenge such entries and have the information removed if they win the challenge. This means that the information in a student's records must be based on firm, defensible evidence. Tests must be valid and reliable. Your grades, assessments, observations, and notes must be justified by thorough testing and observation. Comments and anecdotes about students must be accurate and fair.

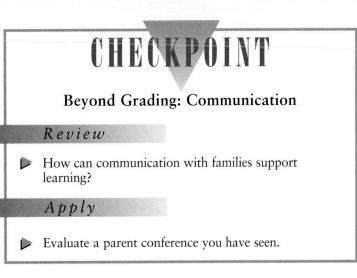

CHECKPOINT

Beyond Grading: Communication

Review

▷ How can communication with families support learning?

Apply

▷ Evaluate a parent conference you have seen.

*S*ummary

Formative and Summative Assessment

What are two kinds of classroom assessment?

Most teachers must assess students and assign grades. Many schools have policies about testing and grading practices, but individual teachers decide how these practices will be carried out. In the classroom, assessment may be formative (ungraded, diagnostic) or summative (graded). Formative assessment helps form instruction, and summative assessment summarizes students' accomplishments.

Getting the Most from Traditional Assessment Approaches

How should teachers plan for assessment?

Assessment requires planning. Learning is supported when teachers test frequently using cumulative questions that ask students to apply and integrate knowledge. With clear goals for assessment, teachers are in a better position to design their own tests or evaluate the tests provided by textbook publishers.

Describe two kinds of traditional testing.

Two traditional formats for testing are the objective test and the essay test. Objective tests, which can include multiple-choice, true/false, fill-in, and matching items, should be written with specific guidelines in mind. Writing and scoring essay questions requires careful planning and clear criteria for scoring answers that discourage bias. Essay tests are susceptible to biases such as grading essays higher when they are longer or written in elaborate prose.

Innovations in Assessment

What is authentic assessment?

Critics of traditional testing believe teachers should use authentic tests and other authentic assessment procedures. Authentic assessment requires students to perform tasks and solve problems similar to real-life performances that will be expected of them outside of school.

Describe portfolios and exhibitions.

Portfolios and exhibitions are two examples of potentially authentic assessment. A portfolio is a collection of a student's work often chosen to represent growth or improvement or to feature "best work." Exhibitions are public displays of the student's understandings. With portfolios and exhibitions there is an emphasis on carrying out real-life tasks in meaningful contexts. Evaluating alternative assessments requires careful judgment and attention to validity, reliability, generalizability, and equity, just as with other kinds of assessment.

Effects of Grades and Grading on Students

How can failure support learning?

Students need experience in coping with failure, so standards must be high enough to encourage effort. Students who don't learn how to cope with failure by persisting at learning may give up too quickly when their first efforts are unsuccessful. Occasional failure can be positive provided appropriate feedback is given.

Can feedback, including grades, promote learning and motivation?

Written or oral feedback should include specific comments on errors or faulty strategies. Learning improves when this criticism is balanced with suggestions about how to improve, along with comments on the positive aspects of the work. Grades can encourage students' motivation to learn if they are tied to meaningful learning.

Which is better, social promotion or being "held back"?

Neither retaining nor promoting a student who is having difficulty guarantees the student will learn. Unless the student is very young or emotionally immature compared to classmates, the best approach may be to promote and provide extra support such as tutoring or summer school sessions.

Grading and Reporting: Nuts and Bolts

Describe two kinds of grading.

Grading can be either criterion-referenced or norm-referenced. Criterion-referenced report cards usually indicate how well each of several objectives has been met by the student. One popular norm-referenced system is grading on the curve, based on a ranking of students in relation to the average performance level.

What are point and percentage systems?

In a point system, each assignment contribution to a grade is allocated a number of points based on each part's importance. Points are added across assignments, then students are rank ordered by total points as a guide to assigning grades. Many schools use percentage grading systems where scores of percent correct or percent mastered are averaged across assignments. This system has flaws because it treats every assignment as having the same importance.

Describe some alternatives to traditional grading.

Alternatives to traditional grading are the contract and dual marking approaches. Whatever system you use, you will have to decide whether you want to grade on effort, improvement, or some combination; and whether you want to limit the number of good grades available.

What are some sources of bias in grading?

Many factors besides quality of work can influence grades: the teacher's beliefs about the student's ability or effort or the student's general classroom behaviour, for example.

Beyond Grading: Communication

How can communication with families support learning?

Not every communication from the teacher needs to be tied to a grade. Communication with students and parents can be important in helping a teacher understand students and present effective instruction by creating a consistent learning environment. Students and parents have a legal right to see all the information in the students' records; the contents of files must be appropriate, accurate, and supported by evidence.

 ## ℯ Terms

Becoming a Professional

Reflecting on the Chapter

Can you apply the ideas from this chapter on classroom assessment and grading to solve the following problems of practice?

Preschool and Kindergarten

▷ The parents of several children in your class want a report about how their daughters and sons are "progressing" in preschool. How would you respond to their requests? What kind of assessment and reporting would be helpful for your young students?

Elementary and Middle School

▷ During a parent-teacher conference, a mother and father accuse you of playing favourites and giving their child low grades "just because he's different." How would you respond?

Junior High and High School

▷ Several students are very unhappy with the grades on their term projects. They come to you for an explanation and to try to get you to raise their grades. What would you do?

▷ Your school requires percentage grading, but you would prefer a different system. How would you make a case for your alternative?

Check Your Understanding

▷ Know the differences between formative and summative assessments.

▷ Understand the characteristics of authentic assessment.

▷ Be familiar with different ways of determining grades.

Your Teaching Portfolio

Think about your philosophy of teaching. What do you believe about testing and grading? How will you assign grades? (Consult the Guidelines for ideas.)

Develop a grading plan for the grade level you want to teach and add it to your portfolio.

Add some ideas for parent involvement from this chapter to your portfolio.

Teaching Resources

Adapt the Guidelines for developing rubrics for the age group you plan to teach.

Add Table 14.2, "Key Points to Consider in Judging Textbook Tests," and Table 14.5, "Characteristics of Authentic Tests," to your teaching resources file.

Add Figure 14.2, "Three Ways of Rating an Oral Presentation," and Figure 14.3, "Self-and Peer Evaluation of Group Learning," to your teaching resources file.

eblinks

www.bced.gov.bc.ca/exams/search/exsection.htm

British Columbia's Ministry of Education site is where you can download portable document format (.pdf) files showing you exactly what is in British Columbia's Grade 12 examinations and how they are constructed. You'll need Acrobat Reader to open these files, available at **www.adobe.com/products/acrobat/readstep2.html**

http://ericae.net/pare/Home.htm

This is the home of *Practical Assessment, Research and Evaluation*, an online journal. Here you'll find a variety of referenced articles on assessment, research, evaluation, and teaching practices. If you click the button labelled "Articles" you'll see the areas covered by articles in this publication.

http://intranet.cps.k12.il.us/Assessments/Ideas_and_Rubrics/ideas_and_rubrics.html

At this site published by the Chicago school district is helpful information about using rubrics in performance assessment. You can download examples of scoring rubrics in a variety of subjects by clicking the Rubric Bank link. Reader to open these files available at **www.adobe.com/products/acrobat/readstep2.html**

What Would They Do?

Here is how two practising teachers responded to the teaching situation presented at the beginning of this chapter about setting up a system to give letter grades.

MARCI GREEN

H. J. Alexander Community School
Toronto, Ontario

The Ontario curriculum for Grades 1 to 8 was introduced into my school in 1998. Previously, the teachers who worked in my Board of Education did not use letter grades for report cards. It has taken some time to adjust to this new system of grading and to ensure that the students are assessed fairly.

The provincial report card states that teachers must use letter grades from "A to R." The letter grade A represents the highest level of achievement that exceeds the provincial standard. The letter grade R represents "below 50," which means a student has not been able to demonstrate the required knowledge and skills.

In order to implement a grading system that is fair and manageable, I would initially review the Health and Physical Education curriculum for Grades 1 to 8. By reviewing this curriculum, I would ensure that I was teaching the required material. Then I would determine the units I would teach for each term, ensuring I had a balanced program that incorporated the requirements from the curriculum. For each unit I would develop a grid, or rubric, which would represent the expectations for each letter grade. These expectations would reflect the skills to be taught and would be clearly stated to the students, parents, and administrators before the grading period began. Posting the rubric in the gym or classroom is helpful in reminding the students of the

expectations for their report cards.

There are many ways to assess students' achievements. These consist of anecdotal records, checklists, observations, participation, and effort and tracking sheets. The students are given an appropriate amount of time to learn and practise skills before they are assessed. It is important that a variety of instructional approaches be used to ensure that students have the opportunity to learn and perform to their potential. I would make program modifications for any students with any exceptionalities. The evaluation process should be ongoing throughout the school year.

Also, reviewing the students' previous report cards may help in determining their progress or achievements throughout the school year. Once a letter grade is assigned to a student, it is important to retain any checklists, observations, etc., to help in assessing the strengths, weaknesses, and next-steps sections of the report card. It is also important to retain the information for parent-teacher interviews in case a letter grade is questioned.

PAULA BROWN

Bialik Hebrew Day School
Toronto, Ontario

Whether a teachers uses "A, B, C, D" grades, achievement levels (i.e., "beginning to develop," "developing," "developed," or "highly developed"), or anecdotal reporting, the results are the same. The teacher is judging or evaluating a child's work. Most important is to have a clear understanding of the purpose of the evaluation, to know what you are evaluating, and to provide a learning environment that will foster the student's growth academically and emotionally.

In order to understand what you are evaluating, it is important to consistently review current curriculum guidelines.

Creating a learning environment that fosters growth for all students is a challenge. I need to provide a wide variety of experiences and opportunities for learning so that each student can demonstrate an understanding of concepts.

I believe the process of learning is more important than the final product. For this reason, I like to include a self-evaluation or student's response to a peer's work. I have found that a clearly delineated rubric is a wonderful tool for encouraging and evaluating the learning process. I attach it to the assignment when it is first handed out. This way the student, the parents, and I have a clear understanding of the steps needed to successfully complete the task. When used as an evaluation tool, the rubric gives immediate, relevant feedback to the student on his or her progress, and helps provide a meaningful learning experience. This, after all, is the most important purpose of evaluation.

Absence Seizure: A seizure involving only a small part of the brain that causes a child to lose contact briefly.

Academic Learning Time: Time when students are actually succeeding at the learning task.

Academic Tasks: The work the student must accomplish, including the content covered and the mental operations required.

Accommodation: Altering existing schemes or creating new ones in response to new information.

Achievement Tests: Standardized tests measuring how much students have learned in a given content area.

Acronym: Technique for remembering names, phrases, or steps by using the first letter of each word to form a new, memorable word.

Action Zone: Area of a classroom where the greatest amount of interaction takes place

Active Teaching: Teaching characterized by high levels of teacher explanation, demonstration, and interaction with students.

Adaptation: Adjustment to the environment.

Adolescent Egocentrism: Assumption that everyone else shares one's thoughts, feelings, and concerns.

Advance Organizer: Statement of inclusive concepts to introduce and sum up material that follows.

Affective Domain: Objectives focusing on attitudes and feelings.

Aggression: Bold, direct action that is intended to hurt someone else or take property; unprovoked attack.

Algorithm: Step-by-step procedure for solving a problem; prescription for solutions.

Allocated Time: Time set aside for learning.

Analogical Thinking: Heuristic in which a person limits the search for solutions to situations that are similar to the one at hand.

Anchored Instruction: A type of problem-based learning that uses a complex interesting situation as an anchor for learning.

Androgynous: Having some typically male and some typically female characteristics apparent in one individual.

Anorexia Nervosa: Eating disorder characterized by very limited food intake.

Antecedents: Events that precede an action.

Anxiety: General uneasiness, a feeling of tension.

Applied Behaviour Analysis: The application of behavioural learning principles to understand and change behaviour.

Aptitude: Capability for learning knowledge or skills.

Aptitude Tests: Tests meant to predict future performance.

Arousal: Physical and psychological reactions causing a person to be alert, attentive, wide awake.

Articulation Disorders: Any of a variety of pronunciation difficulties.

Articulatory Loop: A memory rehearsal system of about 1.5 seconds.

Assertive Discipline: Clear, firm, unhostile response style.

Assessment: Procedures used to obtain information about student performance.

Assimilation: Fitting new information into existing schemes.

Assisted Learning: Providing strategic help in the initial stages of learning, which gradually diminishes as students gain independence.

Associative Stage: Individual steps of a procedure are combined or "chunked" into larger units.

Attainment Value: The importance of doing well on a task; how success on the task meets personal needs.

Attention: Focus on a stimulus.

Attention-Deficit/Hyperactivity Disorder: Current term for disruptive behaviour disorders marked by overactivity, excessive difficulty sustaining attention, or impulsiveness.

Attribution Theories: Descriptions of how individuals' explanations, justifications, and excuses influence their motivation and behaviour.

Authentic Assessment: Measurement of important abilities using procedures that simulate the application of these abilities to real-life problems.

Authentic Tasks: Tasks that have some connection to real-life problems the students will face outside the classroom.

Authentic Tests: Assessment procedures that test skills and abilities as they would be applied in real-life situations.

Authoritarian Personality: Rigidly conforming to belief that society is naturally competitive, with "better" people reaping the rewards.

Automated Basic Skills: Skills that are applied without conscious thought.

Automaticity: The result of learning to perform a behaviour or thinking process so thoroughly that the performance is automatic and does not require effort.

Autonomous Stage: Final stage in the learning of automated skills. The procedure is fine-tuned and becomes "automatic."

Autonomy: Independence

Aversive: Irritating or unpleasant.

Basic Skills: Clearly structured knowledge that is needed for later learning and that can be taught step by step.

Behavioural Learning Theories: Explanations of learning that focus on external events as the cause of changes in observable behaviour.

Behavioural Objectives: Instructional objectives stated in terms of observable behaviour.

Behaviour Modification: Systematic application of antecedents and consequences to change behaviour.

Being Needs: Maslow's three higher-level needs, sometimes called growth needs.

Between-Class Ability Grouping: System of grouping in which students are assigned to classes based on their measured ability or their achievements.

Bilingualism: The ability to speak two languages fluently.

Bimodal Distribution: A frequency distribution with two modes.

Blended Families: Parents, children, and stepchildren merged into families through remarriages.

Bottom-Up Processing: Perceiving based on noticing separate defining features and assembling them into a recognizable pattern.

Brainstorming: Generating many ideas without stopping to evaluate each one.

Bulimia: Eating disorder characterized by overeating, then getting rid of the food by self-induced vomiting or laxatives.

Canadian Charter of Rights and Freedoms: Legislation that protects the rights of all Canadians and, in particular, Canadians who are members of minority groups, including Canadians with disabilities.

CAPS: A strategy that can be used in reading literature: Characters, Aim of story, Problem, Solution.

Case Study: Intensive study of one person or one situation.

Central Tendency: A typical score in a distribution of scores.

Cerebral Palsy: Condition involving a range of motor or coordination difficulties due to brain damage.

Chain Mnemonics: Memory strategies that associate one element in a series with the next element.

Chunking: Grouping individual bits of data into meaningful larger units.

Classical Conditioning: Association of automatic responses with new stimuli.

Classification: Grouping objects into categories.

Classroom Management: Techniques used to maintain a healthy learning environment, relatively free of behaviour problems.

Co-Constructed: Describes a social process in which people interact and negotiate (usually verbally) to cre-

ate an understanding or to solve a problem. The final product is shaped by all participants.

Coding System: A hierarchy of ideas or concepts.

Cognitive Apprenticeship: A relationship in which a less experienced learner acquires knowledge and skills under the guidance of an expert.

Cognitive Behaviour Modification: Procedures based on both behavioural and cognitive learning principles for changing your own behaviour by using self-talk and self-instruction.

Cognitive Development: Gradual, orderly changes by which mental processes become more complex and sophisticated.

Cognitive Domain: In Bloom's taxonomy, memory and reasoning objectives.

Cognitive Evaluation Theory: Suggests that events affect motivation through the individual's perception of the events as controlling behaviour or providing information.

Cognitive Objectives: Instructional objectives stated in terms of higher-level thinking operations.

Cognitive Stage: The initial learning of an automated skill when we rely on general problem-solving approaches to make sense of steps or procedures.

Cognitive Styles: Different ways of perceiving and organizing information.

Cognitive View of Learning: A general approach that views learning as an active mental process of acquiring, remembering, and using knowledge.

Collective Monologue: Form of speech in which children in a group talk but do not really interact or communicate.

Collective Self-Esteem: The sense of the value of a group, such as an ethnic group, that you belong to.

Community of Practice: Social situation or context in which ideas are judged useful or true.

Compensation: The principle that changes in one dimension can be offset by changes in another.

Complex Learning Environments: Problems and learning situations that mimic the ill-structured nature of real life.

Components: In an information-processing view, basic problem-solving processes underlying intelligence.

Concept: A general category of ideas, objects, people, or experiences whose members share certain properties.

Concept Mapping: Student's diagram of his or her understanding of a concept.

Conceptual Change Teaching in Science: A method that helps students understand (rather than memorize) concepts in science by using and challenging the students' current ideas.

Concrete Operations: Mental tasks tied to concrete objects and situations.

Conditional Knowledge: "Knowing when and why" to use declarative and procedural knowledge.

Conditioned Response (CR): Learned response to a previously neutral stimulus.

Conditioned Stimulus (CS): Stimulus that evokes an emotional or physiological response after conditioning.

Confidence Interval: Range of scores within which an individual's particular score is likely to fall.

Connectionist Models: Views of knowledge as being stored in patterns of connections among basic processing units in the brain.

Consequences: Events that are brought about by an action.

Conservation: Principle that some characteristics of an object remain the same despite changes in appearance.

Constructed-Response Format: Assessment procedures that require the student to create an answer instead of selecting an answer from a set of choices.

Constructivism (also Constructivist Approach): View that emphasizes the active role of the learner in building understanding and making sense of information.

Context: The physical or emotional backdrop associated with an event.

Contiguity: Association of two events because of repeated pairing.

Contingency Contract: A formal agreement, often written and signed, between the teacher and an individual student specifying what the student must do to earn a particular privilege or reward.

Continuous Reinforcement Schedule: Presenting a reinforcer after every appropriate response.

Contract System: System in which each student works for a particular grade according to agreed-upon standards.

Convergent Questions: Questions that have a single correct answer.

Convergent Thinking: Narrowing possibilities to a single answer.

Cooperative Learning: Arrangement in which students work in mixed-ability groups and are rewarded on the basis of the success of the group.

Cooperative Teaching: Collaboration between regular and special education teachers.

Correlation: Statistical description of how closely two variables are related.

Creativity: Imaginative, original thinking or problem solving.

Criterion-Referenced Grading: Assessment of each student's mastery of each course objective.

Criterion-Referenced Testing: Testing in which scores are compared to a set standard of performance.

Critical Thinking: Evaluating conclusions by logically and systematically examining the problem, the evidence, and the solution.

Cueing: Providing a stimulus that "sets up" desired behaviour.

Culturally Compatible Classrooms: Classrooms in which procedures, rules, grouping strategies, attitudes, and teaching methods do not cause conflicts with the students' culturally influenced ways of learning and interacting.

Culturally Relevant Pedagogy: Excellent teaching for students of colour that includes academic success and developing/maintaining cultural competence and critical consciousness to challenge the status quo.

Cultural Tools: The real tools (computers, scales, etc.) and symbol systems (numbers, language, graphs) that allow people in a society to communicate, think, solve problems, and create knowledge.

Culture: The knowledge, values, attitudes, and traditions that guide the behaviour of a group of people and allow them to solve the problems of living in their environment.

Culture-Fair/Culture-Free Test: A test without cultural bias.

Curriculum Alignment: The quality and degree to which a standardized achievement test's items correspond to the curriculum students are taught in school.

Curriculum-Based Assessment (CBA): Evaluation method using frequent tests of specific skills and knowledge.

Data-Based Instruction: Assessment method using daily probes of specific-skill mastery.

Decay: The weakening and fading of memories with the passage of time.

Decentring: Focusing on more than one aspect at a time.

Declarative Knowledge: Verbal information; facts; "knowing that" something is the case.

Deductive Reasoning: Drawing conclusions by applying rules or principles; logically moving from a general rule or principle to a specific solution.

Deficiency Needs: Maslow's four lower-level needs, which must be satisfied first.

Defining Attributes: Distinctive features shared by members of a category.

Descriptive Studies: Studies that collect detailed information about specific situations, often using observation, surveys, interviews, recordings, or a combination of these methods.

Development: Orderly, adaptive changes we go through from conception to death.

Developmental Crisis: A specific conflict whose resolution prepares the way for the next stage.

Developmental Disabilities: Significantly below-average intellectual and adaptive social behaviour, evident before age 18.

Deviation IQ: Score based on statistical comparison of individuals' performance with the average performance of others in that age group.

Diagnosis: Description of a student's current knowledge, skills, or ability.

Diagnostic Tests: Individually administered tests to identify special learning problems.

Direct Instruction/Explicit Teaching: Systematic instruction for mastery of basic skills, facts, and information.

Disability: The inability to do something specific such as walk or hear.

Discovery Learning: Bruner's approach, in which students work on their own to discover basic principles.

Discrimination: Treating particular categories of people unequally.

Disequilibrium: In Piaget's theory, the "out-of-balance" state that occurs when a person realizes that his or her current ways of thinking are not working to solve a problem or understand a situation.

Distractors: Wrong answers offered as choices in a multiple-choice item.

Distributed Practice: Practice that occurs in brief periods with rest intervals.

Divergent Questions: Questions that have no single correct answer.

Divergent Thinking: Coming up with many possible solutions.

Domain-Specific Knowledge: Information that is useful in a particular situation or that applies only to one specific topic.

Domain-Specific Strategies: Consciously applied skills to reach goals in a particular subject or problem area.

Dual Marking System: System of assigning two grades, one reflecting achievement and the other effort, attitude, and actual ability.

Educational Psychology: The discipline concerned with teaching and learning processes; applies the methods and theories of psychology and has its own as well.

Educationally Blind: Needing Braille materials in order to learn.

Education or School Act: Provincial legislation that governs education in elementary and secondary schools.

Egocentric: Assuming that others experience the world the way you do.

Ego-Involved Learners: Students who focus on how well they are performing and how they are judged by others.

Eg-Rule Method: Teaching or learning by moving from specific examples to general rules.

Elaboration: Adding and extending meaning by connecting new information to existing knowledge.

Elaborative Rehearsal: Keeping information in working memory by associating it with something else you already know.

Emotional Intelligence (EQ): Abilities to monitor your own and others' feelings and emotions, and to use this information to guide thinking and actions.

Empathetic Listening: Hearing the intent and emotions behind what another says and reflecting them back by paraphrasing.

Engaged Time: Time spent actively learning.

English as a Second Language (ESL): Designation for programs and classes to teach English to students who are not native speakers of English.

Entity View of Ability: Belief that ability is a fixed characteristic that cannot be changed.

Epilepsy: Disorder marked by seizures and caused by abnormal electrical discharges in the brain.

Episodic Memory: Long-term memory for information tied to a particular time and place, especially memory of the events in a person's life.

Equilibration: Search for mental balance between cognitive schemes and information from the environment.

Ethnicity: A cultural heritage shared by a group of people.

Ethnic pride: A positive self-concept about one's racial or ethnic heritage

Ethnography: A descriptive approach to research that focuses on life within a group and tries to understand the meaning of events to the people involved.

Evaluation: Decision making about student performance and about appropriate teaching strategies.

Exceptional Students: Students who have abilities or problems so significant that the students require special education or other services to reach their potential.

Executive Control Processes: Processes such as selective attention, rehearsal, elaboration, and organization that influence encoding, storage, and retrieval of information in memory.

Exemplar: A specific example of a given category that is used to classify an item.

Exhibition: A performance test or demonstration of learning that is public and usually takes an extended time to prepare.

Expectancy x Value Theories: Explanations of motivation that emphasize individuals' expectations for success combined with their valuing of the goal.

Experimentation: Research method in which variables are manipulated and the effects recorded.

Expert Teachers: Experienced, effective teachers who have developed solutions for common classroom problems. Their knowledge of teaching process and content is extensive and well organized.

Explanatory Links: Words and phrases such as "because" and "in order to" that specify the relationships between ideas.

Explicit Teaching: *See* Direct Instruction.

Expository Teaching: Ausubel's method—teachers present material in complete, organized form, moving from broadest to more specific concepts.

Extinction: Gradual disappearance of a learned response.

Extrinsic Motivation: Motivation created by external factors such as rewards and punishments.

Failure-Accepting Students: Students who believe that their failures are due to low ability and that there is little they can do about it.

Failure-Avoiding Students: Students who avoid failure by sticking to what they know, by not taking risks, or by claiming not to care about their performance.

Field Dependence: Cognitive style in which patterns are perceived as wholes.

Field Independence: Cognitive style in which separate parts of a pattern are perceived and analyzed.

Fine-Motor skills: Voluntary body movements that involve the small muscles.

Finger Spelling: Communication system that "spells out" each letter with a hand position.

Formal Operations: Mental tasks involving abstract thinking and coordination of a number of variables.

Formative Assessment: Ungraded testing used before or during instruction to aid in planning and diagnosis.

Frequency Distribution: Record showing how many scores fall into set groups.

Functional Fixedness: Inability to use objects or tools in a new way.

Gender Biases: Different views of males and females, often favouring one gender over the other.

Gender-Role Identity: Beliefs about characteristics and behaviour associated with one gender as opposed to the other.

Gender Schemas: Organized networks of knowledge about what it means to be male or female.

Generalized Seizure: A seizure involving a large portion of the brain.

General Knowledge: Information that is useful in many different kinds of tasks; information that applies to many situations.

Generativity: Sense of concern for future generations.

Gestalt: German for pattern or whole; Gestalt theorists hold that people organize their perceptions into coherent wholes.

Gifted Student: A very bright, creative, and talented student.

Goal: What an individual strives to accomplish.

Goal-Directed Actions: Deliberate actions toward a goal.

Goal Structure: The way students relate to others who are also working toward a particular goal.

Good Behaviour Game: Arrangement where a class is divided into teams and each team receives demerit points for breaking agreed-on rules of good behaviour.

Graded Membership: The extent to which something belongs to a category.

Grade-Equivalent Score: Measure of grade level based on comparison with norming samples from each grade.

Grading on the Curve: Norm-referenced grading that compares students' performance to an average level.

Gross-Motor Skills: Voluntary body movements that involve the large muscles.

Group Consequences: Reinforcers or punishments given to a class as a whole for adhering to or violating rules of conduct.

Group Discussion: Conversation in which the teacher does not have the dominant role; students pose and answer their own questions.

Group Focus: The ability to keep as many students as possible involved in activities.

Guided Discovery: An adaptation of discovery learning, in which the teacher provides some direction.

Halo Effect: The tendency for a general impression of a person to influence our perception of any aspect of that person.

Handicap: A disadvantage in a particular situation, sometimes caused by a disability.

Heritage Language Programs: Programs that offer opportunities for students to receive instruction in their own language.

Heuristic: General strategy used in attempting to solve problems.

Hierarchy of Needs: Maslow's model of seven levels of human needs, from basic physiological requirements to the need for self-actualization.

High-Road Transfer: Application of abstract knowledge learned in one situation to a different situation.

Histogram: Bar graph of a frequency distribution.

Humanistic Views: Approaches to motivation that emphasize personal freedom, choice, self-determination, and striving for personal growth.

Hyperactivity: Behaviour disorder marked by atypical, excessive restlessness and inattentiveness.

Hypothetico-Deductive Reasoning: A formal-operations problem-solving strategy in which an individual begins by identifying all the factors that might affect a problem and then deduces and systematically evaluates specific solutions.

Identity: Principle that a person or object remains the same over time.

Identity Achievement: Strong sense of commitment to life choices after free consideration of alternatives.

Identity Diffusion: Uncentredness; confusion about who one is and what one wants.

Identity Foreclosure: Acceptance of parental life choices without consideration of options.

Images: Representations based on the physical attributes—the appearance—of information.

"I" Message: Clear, non-accusatory statement of how something is affecting you.

Impulsive: Characterized by cognitive style of responding quickly but often inaccurately.

Incentive: An object or event that encourages or discourages behaviour.

Inclusion: The practice of integrating exceptional students into regular education classrooms. The emphasis is on participation rather than placement.

Incremental View of Ability: Belief that ability is a set of skills that can be changed.

Individualized Education Program (IEP): Annually revised program for an exceptional student, detailing present achievement level, goals, and strategies, drawn up by teachers, parents, specialists, and (if possible) the student.

Inductive Reasoning: Formulating general principles based on knowledge of examples and details.

Industry: Eagerness to engage in productive work.

Information Processing: Human mind's activity of taking in, storing, and using information.

Initiative: Willingness to begin new activities and explore new directions.

Inquiry Learning: Approach in which the teacher presents a puzzling situation and students solve the problem by gathering data and testing their conclusions.

Insight: The ability to deal effectively with novel situations.

Instructional Conversation: Situation in which students learn through interactions with teachers and/or other students.

Instructional Objective: Clear statement of what students are intended to learn through instruction.

Integration: Occurs when exceptional students participate in activities with their non-exceptional peers.

Integrity: Sense of self-acceptance and fulfillment.

Intelligence: Ability or abilities to acquire and use knowledge for solving problems and adapting to the world.

Intelligence Quotient (IQ): Score comparing mental and chronological ages.

Interference: The process that occurs when remembering certain information is hampered by the presence of other information.

Intermittent Reinforcement Schedule: Presenting a reinforcer after some but not all responses.

Internalize: Process whereby children adopt external standards as their own.

Intersubjective Attitude: A commitment to build shared meaning with others by finding common ground and exchanging interpretations.

Interval Schedule: Length of time between reinforcers.

Intrinsic Motivation: Motivation associated with activities that are their own reward.

Intrinsic or Interest Value: The enjoyment a person gets from a task.

Intuitive Thinking: Making imaginative leaps to correct perceptions or workable solutions.

Jigsaw: A cooperative structure in which each member of a group is responsible for teaching other members one section of the material.

Joplin Plan: *See* Non-Graded Elementary School.

Keyword Method: System of associating new words or concepts with similar-sounding cue words and images.

KWL Plus: A strategy to guide reading and inquiry: Before—What do I already know? What do I want to know? After—What have I learned?

Lateralization: The specialization of the two hemispheres (sides) of the brain cortex.

Learned Helplessness: The expectation, based on previous experiences involving lack of control, that all one's efforts will lead to failure.

Learning: Process through which experience causes permanent change in knowledge or behaviour.

Learning Disability: Problem with acquisition and use of language; may show up as difficulty with reading, writing, reasoning, and math.

Learning Goal: A personal intention to improve abilities and understand, no matter how performance suffers.

Learning Preferences: Preferred ways of studying and learning, such as using pictures instead of text, working with other people versus alone, learning in structured or in unstructured situations, and so on.

Learning Propensity Assessment Device: Innovative method for testing the student's ability to benefit from teaching, consistent with Lev Vygotsky's theory of cognitive development.

Learning Strategies: General plans for approaching learning tasks.

Learning Styles: An individual's characteristic approaches to learning and studying, usually involving deep versus superficial processing of information.

Learning Tactics: Specific techniques for learning, such as using mnemonics or outlining a passage.

Least Restrictive Placement: The practice of placing exceptional students in the most regular educational settings possible, while ensuring they are successful and receive support appropriate to their special needs.

Lecturing: Organized explanation of a topic by a teacher.

Legitimate Peripheral Participation: Genuine involvement in the work of the group, even if your abilities are undeveloped and contributions are small.

Levels of Processing Theory: Theory that recall of information is based on how deeply it is processed.

Limited English Proficiency (LEP): Descriptive term for students who have limited mastery of English.

Linguistic Comprehension: Understanding of the meaning of sentences in word problems.

Loci Method: Technique of associating items with specific places.

Locus of Causality: The location—internal or external—of the cause of behaviour.

Long-Term Memory: Permanent store of knowledge.

Low-Road Transfer: Spontaneous and automatic transfer of highly practiced skills.

Low Vision: Vision limited to close objects.

Maintenance Rehearsal: Keeping information in working memory by repeating it to yourself.

Massed Practice: Practise for a single extended period.

Mastery Experiences: Our own direct experiences—the most powerful source of efficacy information.

Mastery Learning: An approach to teaching and grading that requires students to achieve specific objectives before moving to the next unit or topic. Based on the assumption that every student is capable of achieving most of the objectives if given enough time and proper instruction.

Mastery-Oriented Students: Students who focus on learning goals because they value achievement and see ability as improvable.

Maturation: Genetically programmed, naturally occurring changes over time.

Mean: Arithmetical average.

Meaningful Verbal Learning: Focused and organized relationships among ideas and verbal information.

Means-Ends Analysis: Heuristic in which a goal is divided into sub-goals.

Measurement: An evaluation expressed in quantitative (number) terms.

Median: The middle score in a group of scores.

Melting Pot: A metaphor for the absorption and assimilation of immigrants into the mainstream of society so that ethnic differences vanish.

Mental Age: In intelligence testing, a score based on average abilities for that age group.

Metacognition: Knowledge about our own thinking processes.

Metalinguistic Awareness: Understanding about one's own use of language.

Minority Group: A group of people who have been socially disadvantaged—not always a minority in actual numbers.

Mnemonics: Techniques for remembering; also, the art of memory.

Mode: The most frequently occurring score.

Modelling: Changes in behaviour, thinking, or emotions that occur through observing another person—a model.

Monolinguals: Individuals who speak only one language.

Morality of cooperation: Stage of development wherein children realize that people make rules and people can change them.

Moral dilemmas: Situations in which no single choice is clearly and indisputably right.

Moral realism: Stage of development wherein children see rules as absolute.

Moral reasoning: The thinking processes involved in judgments about questions of right and wrong.

Moratorium: Identity crisis; suspension of choices because of struggle.

Mosaic: Allows individuals to maintain their culture and identity while still being a respected part of the larger society.

Motivation: An internal state that arouses, directs, and maintains behaviour.

Motivation to Learn: The tendency to find academic activities meaningful and worthwhile and to try to benefit from them.

Movement Management: Ability to keep lessons and groups moving smoothly.

Multicultural Education: Education that teaches the value of cultural diversity.

Multiple Intelligences: In Gardner's theory of intelligence, a person's eight separate abilities: logical-mathematical, verbal, musical, spatial, bodily kinesthetic, interpersonal, intrapersonal, and naturalist.

Multiple Representations of Content: Considering problems using various analogies, examples, and metaphors.

Myelination: The process by which neural fibres are coated with a fatty sheath called myelin that makes message transfer more efficient.

Negative Correlation: A relationship between two variables in which a high value on one is associated with a low value on the other. Example: height and distance from top of head to the ceiling.

Negative Reinforcement: Strengthening behaviour by removing an aversive stimulus.

Neo-Piagetian Theories: More recent theories that integrate findings about attention, memory, and strategy use with Piaget's insights about children's thinking and the construction of knowledge.

Neutral Stimulus: Stimulus not connected to a response.

Non-Graded Elementary School/The Joplin Plan: Arrangement wherein students are grouped by ability in particular subjects, regardless of their ages or grades.

Normal Distribution: The most commonly occurring distribution, in which scores are distributed evenly around the mean.

Norm Group: A group whose average score serves as a standard for evaluating any student's score on a test.

Norming Sample: A large sample of students serving as a comparison group for scoring standardized tests.

Norm-Referenced Grading: Assessment of students' achievement in relation to one another or a defined group.

Norm-Referenced Testing: Testing in which scores are compared with the average performance of others.

Object Permanence: The understanding that objects have a separate, permanent existence.

Objective Testing: Kinds of tests that do not require interpretation in scoring, such as multiple-choice, true/false, short-answer, and fill-in.

Observational Learning: Learning by observation and imitation of others.

Operant Conditioning: Learning in which voluntary behaviour is strengthened or weakened by consequences or antecedents.

Operants: Voluntary (and generally goal-directed) behaviour emitted by a person or an animal.

Operations: Actions a person carries out by thinking them through instead of literally performing the actions.

Organization: Ongoing process of arranging information and experience into mental systems or categories.

Orthopedic Devices: Devices such as braces and wheelchairs that aid people with physical disabilities.

Overgeneralization: Inclusion of nonmembers in a category; overextending a concept.

Overlapping: Supervising several activities at once.

Overlearning: Practising a skill past the point of mastery.

Parallel Distributed Processing (PDP): Connectionist model that uses the brain's physical network of neurons as a metaphor for memory networks.

Paraphrase Rule: Policy whereby listeners must accurately summarize what a speaker has said before being allowed to respond.

Participant Observation: A method for conducting descriptive research in which the researcher becomes a participant in the situation in order to better understand life in that group.

Participation Structures: Rules for how to take part in a given activity.

Part Learning: Breaking a list of rote learning items into shorter lists.

Peg-Type Mnemonics: Systems of associating items with cue words.

Percentage Grading: System of converting class performances to percentage scores and assigning grades based on predetermined cutoff points.

Percentile Rank: Percentage of those in the norming sample whose raw scores are the same as or below an individual's raw score.

Perception: Interpretation of sensory information.

Performance Goal: A personal intention to seem competent or perform well in the eyes of others.

Personal Development: Changes in personality that take place as one grows.

Perspective-Taking Ability: Understanding that others have different feelings and experiences.

Physical Development: Changes in body structure that take place as one grows.

Portfolio: A collection of the student's work in an area, showing growth, self-reflection, and achievement.

Positive Correlation: A relationship between two variables in which the two increase or decrease together. Example: calorie intake and weight gain.

Positive Practice: Practising correct responses immediately after errors.

Positive Reinforcement: Strengthening behaviour by presenting a desired stimulus after the behaviour.

PQ4R: A method for studying text that involves six steps: Preview, Question, Read, Reflect, Recite, Review.

Prejudice: Prejudgment, or irrational generalization about an entire category of people.

Premack Principle: Principle stating that a more-preferred activity can serve as reinforcer for a less-preferred activity.

Preoperational: The stage before a child masters logical mental operations.

Presentation Punishment: Decreasing the chances that behaviour will occur again by presenting an aversive stimulus following the behaviour; also called Type I punishment.

Pretest: Formative test for assessing students' knowledge, readiness, and abilities.

Principle: Established relationship between factors.

Private Speech: Children's self-talk, which guides their thinking and action. Eventually these verbalizations are internalized as silent inner speech.

Problem: Any situation in which you are trying to reach some goal and must find a means to do so.

Problem-Based Learning: Methods that provide students with realistic problems that don't necessarily have "right" answers.

Problem Solving: Creating new solutions for problems.

Procedural Knowledge: Knowledge that is demonstrated when we perform a task; "knowing how."

Procedural Memory: Long-term memory for how to do things.

Procedures: Prescribed steps for an activity.

Productions: The contents of procedural memory; rules about what actions to take, given certain conditions.

Prompt: A reminder that follows a cue to make sure the person reacts to the cue.

Proposition: The smallest unit of information that can be judged true or false.

Propositional Network: Set of interconnected concepts and relationships in which long-term knowledge is held.

Prototype: Best representative of a category.

Psychomotor Domain: Physical ability and coordination objectives.

Psychosocial: Describing the relation of the individual's emotional needs to the social environment.

Puberty: The period in early adolescence when individuals begin to reach physical and sexual maturity.

Punishment: Process that weakens or suppresses behaviour.

Pygmalion Effect: Exceptional progress by a student as a result of high teacher expectations for that student; named for the mythological king who made a statue, then caused it to be brought to life.

Race: A group of people who share common biological traits that are seen as self-defining by the people of the group.

Radical Constuctivism: Theory of knowledge and learning asserting that all knowledge is individually constructed and equally valid.

Random: Without any definite pattern; following no rule.

Range: Distance between the highest and the lowest scores in a group.

Ratio Schedule: Number of responses between reinforcers.

READS: A five-step reading strategy: Review headings; Examine boldface words; Ask "What do I expect to learn?"; Do it—Read; Summarize in your own words.

Receptors: Parts of the human body that receive sensory information.

Reciprocal Questioning: Approach where groups of two or three students ask and answer each other's questions after a lesson or presentation.

Reciprocal Teaching: A method, based on modelling, to teach reading comprehension strategies.

Recitation: Format of teacher questioning, student response, and teacher feedback.

Reconstruction: Recreating information by using memories, expectations, logic, and existing knowledge.

Reflective: Thoughtful and inventive. Reflective teachers think back over situations to analyze what they did and why and to consider how they might improve learning for their students.

Reinforcement: Use of consequences to strengthen behaviour.

Reinforcer: Any event that follows behaviour and increases the chances that the behaviour will occur again.

Reliability: Consistency of test results.

Removal Punishment: Decreasing the chances that a behaviour will occur again by removing a pleasant stimulus following the behaviour; also called Type II punishment.

Reprimands: Criticisms for misbehaviour; rebukes.

Resistance Culture: Group values and beliefs about refusing to adopt the behaviour and attitudes of the majority culture.

Resource Room: Classroom with special materials and a specially trained teacher.

Respondents: Responses (generally automatic or involuntary) elicited by specific stimuli.

Response: Observable reaction to a stimulus.

Response Cost: Punishment by loss of reinforcers.

Response Generalization: Responding in the same way to similar stimuli.

Response Set: Rigidity; tendency to respond in the most familiar way.

Restructuring: Conceiving of a problem in a new or different way.

Retrieval: Process of searching for and finding information in long-term memory.

Reversibility: A characteristic of Piagetian logical operations—the ability to think through a series of steps, then mentally reverse the steps and return to the starting point; also called reversible thinking.

Reversible Thinking: Thinking backward, from the end to the beginning *See also* Reversibility.

Revise Option: In a contract system, the chance to revise and improve work.

Reward: An object or event that we think is attractive and provide as a consequence of a behaviour.

Ripple Effect: "Contagious" spreading of behaviour through imitation.

Rote Memorization: Remembering information by repetition without necessarily understanding the meaning of the information.

Rubric: A tool for rating a test answer by comparing it against several sets of characteristics, often with examples at each rating level.

Rule-Eg Method: Teaching or learning by moving from general principles to specific examples.

Rules: Statements specifying expected and forbidden behaviour; dos and don'ts.

Satiation: Requiring a person to repeat problem behaviour past the point of interest or motivation.

Scaffolding: Support for learning and problem solving. The support could be clues, reminders, encouragement, breaking the problem down into steps, providing an example, or anything else that allows the student to grow in independence as a learner.

Schema-Driven Problem Solving: Recognizing a problem as a "disguised" version of an old problem for which one already has a solution.

Schema(s): A basic structure for organizing information; concept.

Schemes: Mental systems or categories of perception and experience.

Scoring Rubrics: Rules that are used to determine the quality of a student performance.

Script: Schema or expected plan for the sequence of steps in a common event such as buying groceries or ordering take-out pizza.

Scripted Cooperation: A learning strategy in which two students take turns summarizing material and criticizing the summaries.

Seatwork: Independent classroom work.

Self-Actualization: Fulfilling one's potential.

Self-Concept: Our perceptions about ourselves.

Self-Determination: The need to experience choice and control in what we do and how we do it.

Self-Efficacy: A person's sense of being able to deal effectively with a particular task.

Self-Esteem: The value each of us places on our own characteristics, abilities, and behaviour.

Self-Fulfilling Prophecy: A groundless expectation that is confirmed because it has been expected.

Self-Instruction: Talking oneself through the steps of a task.

Self-Management: Use of behavioural learning principles to change your own behaviour.

Self-Regulated Learners: Learners who have a combination of academic learning skills and self-control that makes learning easier; they have the skill and the will to learn.

Self-Reinforcement: Providing yourself with positive consequences, contingent on accomplishing particular behaviour.

Semantic Memory: Memory for meaning.

Semiotic Function: The ability to use symbols—language, pictures, signs, or gestures—to represent actions or objects mentally.

Sensorimotor: Involving the senses and motor activity.

Sensory Memory: System that holds sensory information very briefly.

Serial-Position Effect: The tendency to remember the beginning and the end but not the middle of a list.

Seriation: Arranging objects in sequential order according to one aspect, such as size, weight, or volume.

Shaping: Reinforcing each small step of progress toward a desired goal or behaviour.

Sign Language: Communication system of hand movements that symbolize words and concepts.

Situated Learning: The idea that skills and knowledge are tied to the situation in which they were learned, and are difficult to apply in new settings.

Social Cognitive Theory: Theory that adds concern with cognitive factors such as beliefs, self-perceptions, and expectations to social learning theory.

Social Development: Changes over time in the ways we relate to others.

Social Goals: A wide variety of needs and motives to be connected to others or part of a group.

Social Isolation: Removal of a disruptive student for 5 to 10 minutes.

Socialization: The ways in which members of a society encourage positive development for the immature individuals of the group.

Social Learning Theory: Theory that emphasizes learning through observation of others.

Social Negotiation: Aspect of learning process that relies on collaboration with others and respect for different perspectives.

Social Persuasion: A "pep talk" or specific performance feedback—one source of self-efficacy.

Sociocultural Theory: Emphasizes role in development of cooperative dialogues between children and more knowledgeable members of society. Children learn the culture of their community (ways of thinking and behaving) through these interactions.

Sociocultural Views of Motivation: Perspectives that emphasize participation, identities, and interpersonal relations within communities of practice.

Socioeconomic Status (SES): Relative standing in the society based on income, power, background, and prestige.

Sociolinguistics: The study of formal and informal rules for how, when, about what, to whom, and how long to speak in conversations within cultural groups.

Spasticity: Overly tight or tense muscles, characteristic of some forms of cerebral palsy.

Speech Impairment: Inability to produce sounds effectively for speaking.

Speech Reading: Using visual cues to understand language.

Spiral Curriculum: Bruner's structure for teaching that introduces the fundamental structure of all subjects early in the school years, then revisits the subjects in more and more complex forms over time.

Spread of Activation: Retrieval of pieces of information based on their relatedness to one another. Remembering one bit of information activates (stimulates) recall of associated information.

Stand-Alone Thinking Skills Programs: Programs that teach thinking skills directly without need for an extensive knowledge of subject matter.

Standard Deviation: Measure of how widely scores vary from the mean.

Standard Error of Measurement: A reflection of the degree of unreliability estimated by the standard deviation of an average student's scores around that average student's true score.

Standard Score: Score based on the standard deviation.

Standardized Tests: Tests given, usually to large numbers of students (district-wide, provincially, or nation-wide) under uniform conditions and scored according to uniform procedures.

Stanine Scores: Whole number scores from 1 to 9 where each stanine represents a range of raw scores that correspond to one-ninth of scale.

Statistically Significant: Not likely to be a chance occurrence.

Stem: The question part of a multiple-choice item.

Stereotype: Schema that organizes knowledge or perceptions about a category.

Stereotype Threat: The extra emotional and cognitive burden that your performance in an academic situation might confirm a stereotype that others hold about you.

Stimulus: Event that activates behaviour.

Stimulus Control: Capacity for the presence or absence of antecedents to regulate behaviour.

Stimulus Discrimination: Responding differently to similar, but not identical, stimuli.

Story Grammar: Typical structure or organization for a category of stories.

Stuttering: Repetitions, prolongations, and hesitations that block flow of speech.

Subjects: People or animals studied.

Successive Approximations: Small components that make up complex behaviour.

Summative Assessment: Testing that follows instruction and assesses achievement.

Sustaining Expectation Effect: Student performance maintained at a certain level because teachers don't recognize improvements.

Syntax: The order of words in phrases or sentences.

T **Score:** Standard score with a mean of 50 and a standard deviation of 10.

Tacit Knowledge: Knowing how rather than knowing that—knowledge that is more likely to be learned during everyday life than through formal schooling.

Task Analysis: System for breaking down a task hierarchically into basic skills and sub-skills.

Task-Involved Learners: Students who focus on mastering the task or solving the problem.

Taxonomy: Classification system.

Teaching Efficacy: A teacher's belief that he or she can reach even the most difficult students and help them learn.

Teaching Portfolio: A depiction of you as a teacher, usually including a curriculum vitae, statement of teaching philosophy, examples of your teaching plans and activities, example assignments and tests, students' work, and even videos or CD excerpts of teaching.

Teams-Games-Tournaments (TGT): Learning arrangement in which team members prepare cooperatively, then meet comparable individuals of competing teams in a tournament game to win points for their team.

Test Bias: A potential problem with tests in which the content or procedures of administering the test discriminate against a group of students on the basis of gender, SES, race, ethnicity, etc.

Theory: Integrated statement of principles that attempts to explain a phenomenon and make predictions.

Time on Task: Time spent actively engaged in the learning task at hand.

Time Out: Technically, the removal of all reinforcement. In practice, isolation of a student from the rest of the class for a brief time.

Token Reinforcement System: System in which tokens earned for academic work and positive classroom behaviour can be exchanged for some desired reward.

Top-Down Processing: Perceiving based on the context and the patterns you expect to occur in that situation.

Tracking: Assignment to different classes and academic experiences based on achievement.

Transfer: Influence of previously learned material on new material.

Transition Programming: Gradual preparation of exceptional students to move from high school into further education or training, employment, or community involvement.

Triarchic Theory of Intelligence: A three-part description of the mental abilities (thinking processes, coping with new experiences, and adapting to context) that lead to more or less intelligent behaviour.

True Score: Hypothetical average of all of an individual's scores if repeated testing under ideal conditions were possible.

Unconditioned Response (UR): Naturally occurring emotional or physiological response.

Unconditioned Stimulus (US): Stimulus that automatically produces an emotional or physiological response.

Undergeneralization: Exclusion of some true members from a category; limiting a concept.

Utility Value: The contribution of a task to meeting one's goals.

Validity: Degree to which a test measures what it is intended to measure.

Variability: Degree of difference or deviation from mean.

Verbalization: Putting your problem-solving plan and its logic into words.

Vicarious Experiences: Accomplishments that are modelled by someone else.

Vicarious Reinforcement: Increasing the chances that we will repeat a behaviour by observing another person being reinforced for that behaviour

Voicing Problems: Inappropriate pitch, quality, loudness, or intonation.

Volition Willpower, self-discipline.

Whole Language Perspective: A philosophical approach to teaching and learning that stresses learning through authentic, real-life tasks. Emphasizes using language to learn, integrating learning across skills and subjects, and respecting the language abilities of student and teacher.

Within-Class Ability Grouping: System of grouping in which students in a class are divided into two or three groups based on ability in an attempt to accommodate student differences.

Withitness: According to Jacob Kounin, awareness of everything happening in a classroom.

Work-Avoidant Learners: Students who don't want to learn or to look smart, but just want to avoid work.

Working-Backward Strategy: Heuristic in which one starts with the goal and moves backward to solve the problem.

Working Memory: The information that you are focusing on at a given moment.

z **Score:** Standard score indicating the number of standard deviations a raw score is above or below the mean.

Zone of Proximal Development: Phase at which a child can master a task if given appropriate help and support.

AAMD Ad Hoc Committee on Terminology and Classification. (1992). *Mental retardation: Definition, classification, and systems of support* (9th ed.). Washington, DC: American Association on Mental Retardation.

Abi-Nader, J. (1991). Creating a vision of the future: Strategies for motivating minority students. *Phi Delta Kappan, 72,* 546–549.

Aboud, F., & Skerry, S. (1984). The development of ethnic identification: A critical review. *Journal of Cross-Cultural Psychology, 15,* 3–34.

Acker, S., & Oatley, K. (1993). Gender issues in education for science and technology: Current situation and prospects for change. *Canadian Journal of Education, 18,* 255–272.

Adams, M. J. (1989). Thinking skills curricula. *Educational Psychologist, 24,* 25–27.

Adams, M. J., Treiman, R., & Pressley, M. (1998). Reading, writing, and literacy. In I. Sigel & A. Renninger (Eds.) *Handbook of child psychology, Vol. 4, Child psychology in practice.* New York: Wiley.

Adams, R. S., & Biddle, B. J. (1970). *Realities of teaching: Exploration with videotape.* New York: Holt, Rinehart, & Winston.

Airasian, P. W. (1996). *Assessment in the classroom.* New York: McGraw-Hill.

Airasian, P. W. (in press). Types, uses, and critiques of objectives. In L. Anderson & D. Krathwohl (Eds.), *A taxonomy of teaching and learning: A revision of Bloom's taxonomy of educational objectives.* New York: Addison, Wesley, Longman.

Airasian, P. W., & Walsh, M. E. (1997). Constructivist cautions. *Phi Delta Kappan, 78,* 444–449.

Alberto, P., & Troutman, A. C. (1990). *Applied behavior analysis for teachers: Influencing student performance* (3rd ed.). Columbus, OH: Merrill.

Alderman, M. K. (1985). Achievement motivation and the preservice teacher. In M. Alderman & M. Cohen (Eds.), *Motivation theory and practice for preservice teachers* (pp. 37–49). Washington, DC: ERIC Clearinghouse on Teacher Education.

Alexander, P. (in press). Stages and phases of domain learning: The dynamics of subject-matter knowledge, strategy knowledge, and motivation. In C. Weinstein & B. McCombs (Eds.), *Strategic learning: Skill, will, and self-regulation.* Mahwah, NJ: Lawrence Erlbaum Associates.

Alexander, P. A. (1992). Domain knowledge: Evolving themes and emerging concerns. *Educational Psychologist, 27,* 33–51.

Alexander, P. A. (1996). The past, present, and future of knowledge research: A reexamination of the role of knowledge in learning and instruction. *Educational Psychologist, 31,* 89–92.

Alexander, P. A. (1997). Mapping the multidimensional nature of domain learning: The interplay of cognitive, motivational, and strategic forces. *Advances in Motivation and Achievement, 10,* 213–250.

Alexander, P. A., Kulikowich, J. M., & Schulze, S. K. (1994). How subject-matter knowledge affects recall and interest. *American Educational Research Journal, 31,* 313–337.

Alexander, P. A., & Murphy, P. K. (1998). The research base for APA's Learner-Centered Psychological Principles. In N. Lambert & B. McCombs (Eds.), *How students learn: Reforming schools through learner-centered education.* Washington, DC: American Psychological Association.

Allington, R. (1980). Teacher interruption behaviors during primary-grade oral reading. *Journal of Educational Psychology, 71,* 371–377.

Alloway, N. (1984). *Teacher expectations.* Paper presented at the meetings of the Australian Association for Research in Education, Perth.

Alloy, L. B., & Seligman, M. E. P. (1979). On the cognitive component of learned helplessness and depression. *The Journal of Learning and Motivation, 13,* 219–276.

Alwin, D., & Thornton, A. (1984). Family origins and schooling processes: Early versus late influence of parental characteristics. *American Sociological Review, 49,* 784–802.

Amato, L. F., Loomis, L. S., & Booth, A. (1995). Parental divorce, marital conflict, and offspring well-being during early adulthood. *Social Forces, 73,* 895–915.

American Association for the Advancement of Science (AAAS) (1993). *Benchmarks for science literacy.* Washington, DC: Author.

Ames, C. (1990). Motivation: What teachers need to know. *Teachers College Record, 91,* 409–421.

Ames, C. (1992). Classrooms: Goals, structures, and student motivation. *Journal of Educational Psychology, 84,* 261–271.

Ames, R., & Lau, S. (1982). An attributional analysis of student help-seeking in academic settings. *Journal of Educational Psychology, 74,* 414–423.

Anastasi, A. (1988). *Psychological testing* (6th ed.). New York: Macmillan.

Anderman, E. M., & Maehr, M. L. (1994). Motivation and schooling in the middle grades. *Review of Educational Research, 64,* 287–310.

Anderson, C. W., Holland, J. D., & Palincsar, A. S. (1997). Canonical and sociocultural approaches to research and reform in science education: The story of Juan and his group. *The Elementary School Journal, 97,* 359–384.

Anderson, C. W., & Roth, K. J. (1989). Teaching for meaningful and self-regulated learning of science. In J. Brophy (Ed.), *Advances in research on teaching,* (Vol. 1, pp. 265–306). Greenwich, CT: JAI Press.

Anderson, C. W., & Smith, E. L. (1983, April). *Children's conceptions of light and color: Developing the concept of unseen rays.* Paper presented at the annual meeting of the American Educational Research Association, Montreal.

Anderson, C. W., & Smith, E. L. (1987). Teaching science. In V. Richardson-Koehler (Ed.), *Educators' handbook: A research perspective* (pp. 84–111). New York: Longman.

Anderson, J. (1995). Listening to parents' voices: Cross cultural perceptions of learning to read and write. *Reading Horizons, 35,* 394–413.

Anderson, J., & Gunderson, L. (1997). Literacy learning from a multicultural perspective. *The Reading Teacher, 50,* 514–516.

Anderson, J. R. (1995a). *Cognitive psychology and its implications* (4th ed.). New York: Freeman.

Anderson, J. R. (1995b). *Learning and memory.* New York: John Wiley & Sons.

Anderson, J. R., Reder, L. M., & Simon, H. A. (1995). Applications and misapplication of cognitive psychology to mathematics education. Unpublished manuscript (accessible at www.psy.cmu.edu/~mm4b/misapplied.html).

Anderson, J. R., Reder, L. M., & Simon, H. A. (1996). Situated learning and education. *Educational Researcher, 25,* 5–11.

Anderson, L. M. (1985). What are students doing when they do all that seatwork? In C. Fisher & D. Berliner (Eds.), *Perspectives on instructional time.* New York: Longman.

Anderson, L. M., Brubaker, N. L., Alleman-Brooks, J., & Duffy, G. G. (1985). A qualitative study of seatwork in first-grade classrooms. *Elementary School Journal, 86,* 123–140.

Anderson, L. W., & Krathwohl, D. R. (Eds.) (2001). *A Taxonomy for Learning, Teaching, and Assessing: A Revision of Bloom's Taxonomy of Educational Objectives.* New York: Addison, Wesley, Longman.

Anderson, L. W., & Sosniak, L. A. (Eds.) (1994). *Bloom's Taxonomy: A forty-year retrospective.* Ninety-third yearbook for the National Society for the Study of Education: Part II. Chicago: University of Chicago Press.

Anderson, P. J., & Graham, S. M. (1994). Issues in second-language phonological acquisition among children and adults. *Topics in Language Disorders, 14,* 84–100.

Anderson, R., Hiebert, E., Scott, J., & Wilkinson, I. (1985). *Becoming a nation of readers: The report of the commission on reading.* Washington, DC: National Institute of Education.

Anderson, S. M., Klatzky, R. L., & Murray, J. (1990). Traits and social stereotypes: Efficiency differences in social information processing. *Journal of Personality and Social Psychology, 59,* 192–201.

Anglin, J. M. (1993). Vocabulary development: A morphological analysis. *Monographs of the Society for Research in Child Development, 58*(10, Serial No. 238).

Anyon, J. (1980). Social class and the hidden curriculum of work. *Journal of Education, 162,* 67–92.

Archer, S. L., & Waterman, A. S. (1990). Varieties of identity diffusions and foreclosures: An exploration of the subcategories of the identity statuses. *Journal of Adolescent Research, 5,* 96–111.

Arlin, M. (1984). Time, equality, and mastery learning. *Review of Educational Research, 54,* 65–86.

Armbruster, B. B., & Anderson, T. H. (1981). Research synthesis on study skills. *Educational Leadership, 39,* 154–156.

Aronson, J., & Fried, C. B. (in press). Reducing the effects of stereotype threat on African American college students: The role of theories of intelligence. *Journal of Experimental Social Psychology.*

Aronson, J., Lustina, M. J., Good, C., Keough, K., Steele, C. M., & Brown, J. (1999). When White men can't do math: Necessary and sufficient factors in stereotype threat. *Journal of Experimental Social Psychology, 35,* 2946.

Aronson, J., Steele, C. M., Salinas, M. F., & Lustina, M. J. (1999). The effect of stereotype threat on the standardized test performance of college students. In E. Aronson (Ed.), *Readings About the Social Animal* (8th ed.). New York: Freeman.

Artman, L., & Cahan, S. (1993). Schooling and the development of transitive inference. *Developmental Psychology, 29,* 753–759.

Aschbacher, P. (1997). New directions in student assessment [Special issue]. *Theory into Practice, 36*(4), 194–272.

Ashton, P. T. (1978). Cross-cultural Piagetian research: An experimental perspective. *Harvard Educational Review* (Reprint Series No. 13).

Atkinson, R. K., Levin, J. R., Kiewra, K. A., Meyers, T., Atkinson, L. A., Renandya, W. A., & Hwang, Y. (1999). Matrix and mnemonic text-processing adjuncts: Comparing and combining their components. *Journal of Educational Psychology, 91,* 242–257.

Atkinson, R. C., & Shiffrin, R. M. (1968). Human memory: A proposed system and its control processes. In K. Spence & J. Spence (Eds.), *The psychology of learning and motivation* (Vol. 2). New York: Academic Press.

Au, K. H. (1980). Participation structures in a reading lesson with Hawaiian children: Analysis of a culturally appropriate instructional event. *Anthropology and Education Quarterly, 11,* 91–115.

Ausubel, D. P. (1963). *The psychology of meaningful verbal learning.* New York: Grune and Stratton.

Ausubel, D. P. (1977). The facilitation of meaningful verbal learning in the classroom. *Educational Psychologist, 12,* 162–178.

Babad, E. (1995). The "teachers' pet" phenomenon, students' perceptions of differential behavior, and students' morale. *Journal of Educational Psychology, 87,* 361–374.

Babad, E. Y., Inbar, J., & Rosenthal, R. (1982). Pygmalion, Galatea, and the Golem: Investigations of biased and unbiased teachers. *Journal of Educational Psychology, 74,* 459–474.

Baddeley, A. (1998). *Human memory: Theory and practice* (Rev. ed.). Boston: Allyn & Bacon.

Baddeley, A. D. (1986). *Working memory.* Oxford, UK: Claredon Books.

Baer, J. (1997). *Creative teachers, creative students.* Boston: Allyn & Bacon.

Bailey, S. M. (1993). The current status of gender equity research in American Schools. *Educational Psychologist, 28,* 321–339.

Baillargeon, R., & De Vos, J. (1991). Object permanence in young infants: Further evidence. *Child Development, 62,* 1227–1246.

Baker, C. (1993). *Foundations of bilingual education and bilingualism.* Clevedon, England: Multilingual Matters.

Baker, D. (1986). Sex differences in classroom interaction in secondary science. *Journal of Classroom Interaction, 22,* 212–218.

Bakerman, R., Adamson, L. B., Koner, M., & Barr, R. G. (1990). !Kung infancy: The social context of object exploration. *Child Development,* 61, 794–809.

Bandura, A. (1965). Influence of models' reinforcement contingencies on the acquisition of imitative responses. *Journal of Personality and Social Psychology, 1,* 589–595.

Bandura, A. (1977). *Social learning theory.* Englewood Cliffs, NJ: Prentice-Hall.

Bandura, A. (1982). Self-efficacy mechanisms in human agency. *American Psychologist, 37,* 122–147.

Bandura, A. (1986). *Social foundations of thought and action.* Englewood Cliffs, NJ: Prentice-Hall.

Bandura, A. (1993). Perceived self-efficacy in cognitive development and functioning. *Educational Psychologist, 28,* 117–148.

Bandura, A. (1995). Exercise of personal and collective efficacy in changing societies. In A. Bandura (Ed.), *Self-efficacy in changing societies* (pp. 1–45). New York: Cambridge University Press.

Bandura, A. (1997). *Self-efficacy: The exercise of control.* New York: Freeman.

Bandura, A., Ross, D., & Ross, S. A. (1963). Vicarious reinforcement and imitative learning. *Journal of Abnormal and Social Psychology, 67,* 601–607.

Bangert-Drowns, R. L., Kulik, C. C., Kulik, J. A., & Morgan, M. (1991). The instructional effect of feedback in test-like events. *Review of Educational Research, 61,* 213–238.

Banks, J. A. (1993a). Multicultural education: Characteristics and goals. In J. Banks & C. McGee Banks (Eds.), *Multicultural education: Issues and perspectives* (2nd ed., pp. 2–26). Boston: Allyn & Bacon.

Banks, J. A. (1993b). Multicultural education: Development, dimensions, and challenges. *Phi Delta Kappan, 75,* 22–28.

Banks, J. A. (1994). *Multiethnic education: Theory and practice.* Boston: Allyn & Bacon.

Banks, J. A. (1997). *Teaching strategies for ethnic studies* (6th ed.). Boston: Allyn & Bacon.

Banks, J. A. (1999). *An introduction to multicultural education* (2nd ed.). Boston: Allyn & Bacon.

Bargh, J. A., & Chartrand, T. L. (1999). The unbearable automaticity of being. American Psychologist, 54, 462–479.

Baron, R. A. (1998). *Psychology* (4th ed.) Boston: Allyn & Bacon.

Bartlett, F. C. (1932). *Remembering: A study in experimental and social psychology.* New York: Macmillan.

Barton, E. J. (1981). Developing sharing: An analysis of modeling and other behavioral techniques. *Behavior Modification, 5,* 386–398.

Batschaw, M. L. (1997). *Children with disabilities* (4th ed.). Baltimore, ML: Brookes.

Battistich, V., Solomon, D., & Delucci, K. (1993). Interaction processes and student outcomes in cooperative groups. *Elementary School Journal, 94,* 19–32.

Baumeister, R. F., & Leary, M. R. (1995). The need to belong: Desire for interpersonal attachments as a fundamental human motivation. *Psychological Bulletin, 117,* 497–529.

Beane, J. A. (1991). Sorting out the self-esteem controversy. *Educational Leadership, 49*(1), 25–30.

Beck, I. L., McKeown, M. G., Worthy, J., Sandora, C. A., & Kucan, L. (1996). Questioning the author: A yearlong classroom implementation to engage students with text. *The Elementary School Journal, 96,* 385–414.

Becker, W. C., Engelmann, S., & Thomas, D. R. (1975). *Teaching 1: Classroom management.* Chicago: Science Research Associates.

Bee, H. (1981). *The developing child* (3rd ed.). New York: Harper & Row.

Bee, H. (1992). *The developing child* (6th ed.). New York: Harper & Row.

Beeth, M. E. (1998). Teaching science in fifth grade: Instructional goals that support conceptual change. *Journal of Research in Science Teaching, 35,* 1091–1101.

Begley, S. (1998, September 7). The parent trap. *Newsweek, 132*(10), 52–59.

Belanoff, P., & Dickson, M. (1991). *Portfolios: Process and product.* Portsmouth, NH: Heinemann, Boynton/Cook.

Bell, R. (1980). *Changing bodies, changing lives: A book for teens on sex and relationships.* New York: Random House.

Bem, S. L. (1974). The measurement of psychological androgyny. *Journal of Consulting and Clinical Psychology, 42,* 155–162.

Benenson, J. F. (1993). Greater preference among females than males for dyadic interaction in early childhood. *Child Development, 64,* 544–555.

Benjafield, J. G. (1992). *Cognition.* Englewood Cliffs, NJ: Prentice-Hall.

Bennett, C. I. (1995). *Comprehensive multicultural education: Theory and practice* (3rd ed.). Boston: Allyn & Bacon.

Bennett, C. I. (1999). *Comprehensive multicultural education: Theory and practice* (4th Ed.). Boston: Allyn & Bacon.

Berg, C. A., & Clough, M. (1991). Hunter lesson design: The wrong one for science teaching. *Educational Leadership, 48*(4), 73–78.

Berger, K. S., & Thompson, R. A. (1995). *The developing person through childhood and adolescence.* New York: Worth.

Berk, L. (1996). *Infants, children, and adolescents* (2nd ed.). Boston: Allyn & Bacon.

Berk, L. E. (1994). *Child development* (3rd ed.). Boston: Allyn & Bacon.

Berk, L. E. (1999). Infants, children, and adolescents (3rd ed). Boston: Allyn & Bacon.

Berk, L. E. (2000). *Child development* (5th ed.). Boston: Allyn & Bacon.

Berk, L. E., & Spuhl, S. T. (1995). Maternal interaction, private speech, and task performance in preschool children. *Early Childhood Research Quarterly, 10,* 145–169.

Berliner, D. (1983). Developing concepts of classroom environments: Some light on the T in studies of ATI. *Educational Psychologist, 18,* 1–13.

Berliner, D. (1987). But do they understand? In V. Richardson-Koehler (Ed.), *Educators' handbook: A research perspective* (pp. 259–293). New York: Longman.

Berliner, D. (1988). Simple views of effective teaching and a simple theory of classroom instruction. In D. Berliner & B. Rosenshine (Eds.), *Talks to teachers* (pp. 93–110). New York: Random House.

Berliner, D. (1992). Telling the stories of educational psychology. *Educational Psychologist, 27,* 143–152.

Berlyne, D. (1966). Curiosity and exploration. *Science, 153,* 25–33.

Berndt, T. J., & Keefe, K. (1995). Friends' influence on adolescents' adjustment to school. *Child Development, 66,* 1312–1329.

Betancourt, H., & Lopez, S. R. (1993). The study of culture, ethnicity, and race in American psychology. *American Psychologist, 48,* 629–637.

Biemiller, A. (1993, December). Students differ: So address differences effectively. *Educational Researcher, 22* (9), 14–15.

Bivens, J. A., & Berk, L. E. (1990). A longitudinal study of elementary school children's private speech. *Merrill-Palmer Quarterly, 36,* 443–463.

Bjorklund, D. F. (1989). *Children's thinking: Developmental function and individual differences.* Pacific Grove, CA: Brooks/Cole.

Block, J. (1983). Differential premises arising from differential socialization of the sexes: Some conjectures. *Child Development, 54,* 1335–1354.

Block, J. H., & Anderson, L. W. (1975). *Mastery learning in classroom instruction.* New York: Macmillan.

Bloom, B. S. (1968). *Learning for mastery. Evaluation Comment, 1*(2). Los Angeles: University of California, Center for the Study of Evaluation of Instructional Programs.

Bloom, B. S., Engelhart, M. D., Frost, E. J., Hill, W. H., & Krathwohl, D. R. (1956). *Taxonomy of educational objectives. Handbook I: Cognitive domain.* New York: David McKay.

Bloom, R., & Bourdon, L. (1980). Types and frequencies of teachers' written instructional feedback. *Journal of Educational Research, 74,* 13–15.

Blumenfeld, P. C. (1992). Classroom learning and motivation: Clarifying and expending goal theory. *Journal of Educational Psychology, 84,* 272–281.

Blumenfeld, P. C., Puro, P., & Mergendoller, J. R. (1992). Translating motivation into thoughtfulness. In H. Marshall (Ed.) *Redefining student learning: Roots of educational change* (pp. 207–240). Norwood, NJ: Ablex.

Boggiano, A. K., Flink, C., Shields, A., Seelback, A., & Barrett, M. (1993). Use of techniques promoting students' self-determination: Effects on students' analytic problem-solving skills. Motivation and Education, 17, 319–336.

Bohannon, J. N., III, & Warren-Leubecker, A. (1989). Theoretical approaches to language acquisition. In J. Berko Gleason (Ed.), *The development of language* (pp. 167–223). Columbus, OH: Merrill.

Boldizar, J. P. (1991). Assessing sex typing and androgyny in children: The children's sex inventory. *Developmental Psychology, 27,* 505–515.

Borko, H. (1989). Research on learning to teach: Implications for graduate teacher preparation. In A. Woolfolk (Ed.), *Research perspectives on the graduate preparation of teachers* (pp. 69–87). Boston: Allyn & Bacon.

Borko, H., & Livingston, C. (1989). Cognition and improvisation: Differences in mathematics instruction by expert and novice teachers. *American Educational Research Journal, 26,* 473–498.

Borko, H., & Putnam, R. (1996). Learning to teach. In D. Berliner & R. Calfee (Eds.), *Handbook of educational psychology* (pp. 673–708). New York: Macmillan.

Borkowski, J. G., Johnston, M. B., & Reid, M. K. (1986). Metacognition, motivation, and the transfer of control processes. In S. J. Ceci (Ed.), *Handbook of cognition: Social and neurological aspects of learning disabilities.* Hillsdale, NJ: Erlbaum.

Bos, C. S., & Reyes, E. I. (1996). Conversations with a Latina teacher about education for language-minority students with special needs. *The Elementary School Journal, 96,* 344–351.

Brandt, R. (1993). On teaching for understanding: A conversation with Howard Gardner. *Educational Leadership, 50*(7), 4–7.

Bransford, J. D., & Stein, B. S. (1993). *The IDEAL problem solver: A guide for improving thinking, learning, and creativity* (2nd ed.). New York: Freemen.

Bransford, J. D., Stein, B. S., Vye, N. J., Franks, J. J., Auble, P. M., Mezynski, K. J., & Perfetto, G. A. (1982). Differences in approaches to learning: An overview. *Journal of Experimental Psychology: General, 111,* 390–398.

Braun, C. (1976). Teacher expectation: Sociopsychological dynamics. *Review of Educational Research, 46*(2), 185–212.

Bretherton, I., & Waters, E. (1985). Growing points of attachment theory and research. *Monographs of the Society for Research in Child Development, 50* (1, 2, Serial No. 209).

British Columbia Ministry for Children and Families (1998). *The BC Handbook for Action on Child Abuse and Neglect.* Victoria, BC: Crown Publications.

British Columbia Ministry of Education (1996). *Gifted education: A resource guide for teachers.* BC: Author.

British Columbia Ministry of Education (1998). *English as a second language: Policy framework (draft document).* Victoria, BC.

British Columbia Ministry of Education (2002, March 19). Performance standards-social responsibility: A framework. Retrieved from www.bced.gov.bc.ca/classroom_assessment/perf/ stands/social_resp.htm.

British Columbia Ministry of Labour and Consumer Services (1990). *The British Columbia student drug use survey: 1990 summary report.* British Columbia: Ministry of Labour and Consumer Services. Alcohol and Drug Programs.

British Columbia Special Education Branch. (1995). *Special education services: A manual of policies, procedures, and guidelines.* Victoria: Author.

Bronfenbrenner, U., McClelland, P., Wethington, E., Moen, P., & Ceci, S. (1996). *The state of Americans: This generation and the next.* New York: Free Press.

Brooks, D. (1985). Beginning the year in junior high: The first day of school. *Educational Leadership, 42,* 76–78.

Brooks, J. G., & Brooks, M.G. (1993). Becoming a constructivist teacher. In ASCD (Ed.), *In search of understanding: The case for constructivist classrooms.* Alexandria, VA: The Association for Supervision and Curriculum Development.

Brooks-Gunn, J. (1988). The impact of puberty and sexual activity upon the health and education of adolescent boys and girls. *Peabody Journal of Education, 64,* 88–113.

Brooks-Gunn, J., & Furstenberg, F. F., Jr. (1989). Adolescent sexual behavior. *American Psychologist, 44,* 2249–2257.

Brophy, J. E. (1981). Teacher praise: A functional analysis. *Review of Educational Research, 51,* 5–21.

Brophy, J. E. (1982, March). *Research on the self-fulfilling prophecy and teacher expectations.* Paper presented at the annual meeting of the American Educational Research Association, New York.

Brophy, J. E. (1983). Conceptualizing student motivation to learn. *Educational Psychologist, 18,* 200–215.

Brophy, J. E. (1985). Teacher-student interaction. In J. Dusek (Ed.), *Teacher expectancies.* Hillsdale, NJ: Erlbaum.

Brophy, J. E. (1988). On motivating students. In D. Berliner & B. Rosenshine (Eds.), *Talks to teachers* (pp. 201–245). New York: Random House.

Brophy, J. E., & Evertson, C. (1978). Context variables in teaching. *Educational Psychologist, 12,* 310–316.

Brophy, J. E., & Good, T. (1986). Teacher behavior and student achievement. In M. Wittrock (Ed.), *Handbook of research on teaching* (3rd ed., pp. 328–375). New York: Macmillan.

Brophy, J. E., & Kher, N. (1986). Teacher socialization as a mechanism for developing student motivation to learn. In R. Feldman (Ed.), *Social psychology applied to education* (pp. 256–288). New York: Cambridge University Press.

Brown, A. (1987). Metacognition, executive control, self-regulation, and other more mysterious mechanisms. In F. Weinert & R. Kluwe (Eds.), *Metacognition, motivation, and understanding* (pp. 65–116). Hillside, NJ: Erlbaum.

Brown, A. L. (1992). Design experiments: Theoretical and methodological challenges in creating complex interventions in classroom settings. *Journal of the Learning Sciences, 2,* 141–178.

Brown, A. L., Bransford, J., Ferrara, R., & Campione, J. (1983). Learning, remembering, and understanding. In P. Mussen (Ed.), *Handbook of child psychology* (Vol. 3). New York: Wiley.

Brown, A. L., & Campione, J. C. (1996). Psychological theory and the design of innovative learning environments: On procedures, principles, and systems. In L. Schauble & R. Glasser (Eds.), *Innovations in learning: New environments for education* (pp.289–325). Mahwah, NJ: Lawrence Erlbaum Associates.

Brown, J. S. (1990). Toward a new epistemology for learning. In C. Frasson & G. Gauthier (Eds.) *Intelligent tutoring systems: At the crossroads of artificial intelligence and education.* (pp. 266–282). Norwood, NJ: Ablex.

Brown, R., & Hanlon, C. (1970). Derivational complexity and order of acquisition in child speech. In J. M. Hays (Ed.), *Cognition and the development of language.* New York: Wiley.

Bruner, J. S. (1960). *The process of education.* New York: Vintage Books.

Bruner, J. S. (1966). *Toward a theory of instruction.* New York: Norton.

Bruner, J. S. (1971). *The relevance of education.* New York: Norton.

Bruner, J. S. (1973). *Beyond the information given: Studies in the psychology of knowing.* New York: Norton.

Bruner, J. S., Goodnow, J. J., & Austin, G. A. (1956). *A study of thinking.* New York: Wiley.

Bruning, R. H., Schraw, G. J., & Ronning, R. R. (1995). *Cognitive psychology and instruction* (2nd ed.). Englewood Cliffs, NJ: Merrill/Prentice-Hall.

Bruning, R. H., Schraw, G. J., & Ronning, R. R. (1999). *Cognitive psychology and instruction* (3rd ed.). Columbus, OH: Merrill.

Burden, P. R. (1995). *Classroom management and discipline: Methods to facilitate cooperation and instruction.* White Plains, NY: Longman.

Burton, N. W., & Jones, L. V. (1982). Recent trends in achievement levels of black and white youth. *Educational Research, 11,* 10–14.

Burton, R. V. (1963). The generality of honesty reconsidered. *Psychological Review, 70,* 481–499.

Butler, D. L. (1998). A strategic content learning approach to promoting self-regulated learning by students with learning disabilities. In D. H. Schunk and B. J. Zimmerman (Eds.), *Self-regulated learning: From teaching to self-reflective practice* (pp. 160–183). NY: Guilford Press.

Butler, D. L., & Winne, P. H. (1995). Feedback and self-regulated learning: A theoretical synthesis. *Review of Educational Research, 65,* 245–281.

Butler, R. (1987). Task-involving and ego-involving properties of evaluation: Effects of different feedback conditions on motivational perceptions, interest, and performance. *Journal of Educational Psychology, 79,* 474–482.

Butler, R., & Neuman, O. (1995). Effects of task and ego achievement goals on help-seeking behaviors and attitudes. *Journal of Educational Psychology, 87,* 261–271.

Butler, R., & Nisan, M. (1986). Effects of no feedback, task-related comments, and grades on intrinsic motivation and performance. *Journal of Educational Psychology, 78,* 210–224.

Butler, S. R., Marsh, H. W., Sheppard, M. J., & Sheppard, J. L. (1985). Seven-year longitudinal study of the early prediction of reading achievement. *Journal of Educational Psychology, 77,* 349–361.

Byrne, B. M., & Shavelson, R. J. (1996). On the structure of social self-concept for pre-, early, and late adolescents: A test of the Shavelson model. *Journal of Personality and Social Psychology, 70,* 599–613.

Byrne, B. M., & Worth Gavin, D. A. (1996). The Shavelson model revisited: Testing for structure of academic self concept across pre-, early, and late adolescents. *Journal of Educational Psychology, 88,* 215–229.

Byrnes, J. P. (1996). *Cognitive development and learning in instructional contexts.* Boston: Allyn & Bacon.

Byrnes, J. P., & Fox, N. A. (1998). The educational relevance of research in cognitive neuroscience. *Educational Psychology Review, 10,* 297–342.

Caine, R. N., & Caine, G. (1991). *Making connections: Teaching and the human brain.* Alexandria, VA: Association for Supervision and Curriculum Development.

Calderhead, J. (1996) Teacher: Beliefs and knowledge. In D. Berliner & R. Calfee (Eds.), *Handbook of educational psychology* (pp. 709–725). New York: Macmillan.

Calderhead, J., & Robson, M. (1991). Images of teaching: Student teachers' early conceptions of classroom practice. *Teaching and Teacher Education, 7,* 1–8.

Calfee, R. C., & Hiebert, E. H. (1991). Teacher assessment of student achievement. In R. Stake (Ed.), *Advances in program evaluation, Vol. 1A,* 103–131. Greenwich, CT: JAI Press.

Callahan, C. M., Tomlinson, C. A., & Plucker, J. (1997). *Project STATR using a multiple intelligences model in identifying and promoting talent in high-risk students.* Storrs, CT: National Research Center for Gifted and Talented. University of Connecticut Technical Report.

Cambourne, B., & Turbill, J. (1990). Assessment in whole-language classrooms: Theory into practice. *Elementary School Journal, 90,* 337–349.

Cameron, J., & Pierce, W. D. (1996). The debate about rewards and intrinsic motivation: Protests and accusations do not alter the results. *Review of Educational Research, 66,* 39–52.

Camp, R. (1990, Spring). Thinking together about portfolios. *The Quarterly of the National Writing Project, 27,* 8–14.

Canadian Teachers' Federation & Ontario Women's Directorate. (1992). *The better idea book: A resource book on gender, culture, science and schools.* Ottawa, ON: Canadian Teachers' Federation.

Cangelosi, J. S. (1990). *Designing tests for evaluating student achievement.* New York: Longman.

Canter, L. (1988). Let the educator beware: A response to Curwin and Mendler. *Educational Leadership, 46*(2), 71–73.

Canter, L. (1989). Assertive discipline—More than names on the board and marbles in a jar. *Phi Delta Kappan, 71*(1), 41–56.

Canter, L., & Canter, M. (1992). *Lee Canter's Assertive Discipline: Positive behavior management for today's classroom.* Santa Monica: Lee Canter and Associates.

Carey, L. M. (1994). *Measuring and evaluating school learning* (2nd ed.). Boston: Allyn & Bacon.

Cariglia-Bull, T., & Pressley, M. (1990). Short-term memory differences between children predict imagery effects when sentences are read. *Journal of Experimental Child Psychology, 49,* 384–398.

Carnegie Council on Adolescent Development. (1995). *Great transitions: Preparing adolescents for a new century.* New York: Carnegie Corporation of New York.

Caroll, J. (1993). *Human cognitive abilities: A survey of factor analytic studies.* Cambridge, England: Cambridge University Press.

Casanova, U. (1987). Ethnic and cultural differences. In V. Richardson-Koehler (Ed.), *Educators' handbook: A research perspective* (pp. 370–393). New York: Longman.

Case, R. (1985a). *Intellectual development: Birth to adulthood.* New York: Academic Press.

Case, R. (1985b). A developmentally-based approach to the problem of instructional design. In R. Glaser, S. Chipman, & J. Segal (Eds.), *Teaching thinking skills* (Vol. 2, pp. 545–562). Hillsdale, NJ: Erlbaum.

Case, R. (1992). *The mind's staircase: Exploring the conceptual underpinnings of children's thought and knowledge.* Mahwah, NJ: Lawrence Erlbaum.

Case, R. (1993). Theories of learning and theories of development. *Educational Psychologist, 28,* 219–233.

Case, R. (1998). The development of conceptual structures. In D. Kuhn & R. S. Siegler (Eds.), *Handbook of child psychology: Vol. 2: Cognition, perception, and language* (pp. 745–800). New York: Wiley.

Cauley, K., & Tyler, B. (1989). The relationship of self-concept to prosocial behavior in children. *Early Childhood Research Quarterly, 4,* 51–60.

Cazden, C. B. (1988). *Classroom discourse: The language of teaching and learning.* Portsmouth, NH: Heinemann.

Ceci, S. J. (1991). How much does schooling influence intelligence and its cognitive components? A reassessment of the evidence. *Developmental Psychology, 27,* 703–720.

Ceci, S. J., & Roazzi, A. (1994). The effects of context on cognition: Postcards from Brazil. In R. J. Sternberg (Ed.), *Mind in context* (pp. 74–101). New York: Cambridge University Press.

Center for the Improvement of Early Reading Achievement (CIERA). Improving the reading achievement of America's children: 10 research-based principles. Retrieved February 12, 1999, from the CIERA Web site: www.ciera.org.

Chambers, B., & Abrami, P. C. (1991). The relationship between student team learning outcomes and achievement, causal attributions, and affect. *Journal of Educational Psychology, 83,* 140–146.

Chamot, A. U., & O'Malley, J. M. (1996). The Cognitive Academic Language Learning Approach: A model for linguistically diverse classrooms. *The Elementary School Journal, 96,* 259–274.

Chance, P. (1991). Backtalk: a gross injustice. *Phi Delta Kappan, 72,* 803.

Chance, P. (1992). The rewards of learning. *Phi Delta Kappan, 73,* 200–207.

Chance, P. (1993). Sticking up for rewards. *Phi Delta Kappan, 74,* 787–790.

Chapman, A. (1999). Assessment: Provincial learning assessment program. *Teacher, 11*(5), 10–11.

Chapman, M. L. (1997). *Weaving webs of meaning: Writing in the elementary school.* Toronto, Ontario: ITP Nelson.

Charach, A., Pepler, D. J., & Ziegler, S. (1995). Bullying at school: A Canadian perspective. *Education Canada, 35,* 12–18.

Charles, C. M. (1985). *Building classroom discipline: From models to practice* (2nd ed.). New York: Longman.

Charles, C. M. (1996). *Building classroom discipline* (5th ed.). White Plains, NY: Longman.

Chase, C. I. (1978). *Measurement for educational evaluation* (2nd ed.). Reading, MA: Addison-Wesley.

Chi, M. T. H. (1978). Knowledge structures and memory development. In R. Siegler (Ed.), *Children's thinking: What develops?* (pp. 73–96). Hillsdale, NJ: Erlbaum.

Chi, M. T. H., Glaser, R., & Farr, M. (Eds.) (1988). *The nature of expertise.* Hillsdale, NJ: Earlbaum.

Childs, C. P., & Greenfield, P. M. (1982). Informal modes of learning and teaching: The case of Zinacanteco weaving. In N. Warren (Ed.), *Advances in cross-cultural psychology* (Vol. 2, pp. 269–316). London: Academic Press.

Chomsky, N. (1965). *Aspects of a theory of syntax.* Cambridge, MA: MIT Press.

Chomsky, N. (1980). *Rules and representations.* New York: Columbia University Press.

Chomsky, N. (1986). *Knowledge of language: Its nature, origin, and use.* New York: Praeger.

Civil Rights Commission. (1973). *Teacher and students: Differences in teacher interactions with Mexican-American and Anglo students.* Washington, DC: Government Printing Office.

Cizek, G. J. (1991). Innovation or enervation: Performance assessment in perspective. *Phi Delta Kappan, 72*(9), 695–699.

Claiborn, W. L. (1969). Expectancy effects in the classroom: A failure to replicate. *Journal of Education Psychology, 60,* 377–383.

Clark, C. M. (1983). Personal communication.

Clark, C. M., Gage, N. L., Marx, R. W., Peterson, P. L., Staybrook, N. G., & Winne, P. H. (1979). A factorial experiment on teacher structuring, soliciting, and reacting. *Journal of Educational Psychology, 71,* 534–550.

Clark, C. M., & Peterson, P. L. (1986). Teachers' thought processes. In M. Wittrock (Ed.), *Handbook of research on teaching* (3rd ed., pp. 255–296). New York: Macmillan.

Clark, C. M., & Yinger, R. (1988). Teacher planning. In D. Berliner & B. Rosenshine (Eds.), *Talks to teachers* (pp. 342–365). New York: Random House.

Clark, J. M., & Paivio, A. (1991). Dual coding theory and education. *Educational Psychology Review, 3,* 149–210.

Clark, K., & Clark, M. (1939). The development of consciousness of self and the emergence of racial identification in Negro preschool children. *Journal of Social Psychology, 10,* 591–599.

Clement, S. L. (1978). Dual marking system: Simple and effective. *American Secondary Education, 8,* 49–52.

Clifford, M. M. (1984). Educational psychology. In *Encyclopedia of Education* (pp. 413–416). New York: Macmillan.

Clifford, M. M. (1990). Students need challenge, not easy success. *Educational Leadership, 48*(1), 22–26.

Clifford, M. M. (1991). Risk taking: Empirical and educational considerations. *Educational Psychologist, 26,* 263–298.

Cobb, P., & Bowers, J. (1999). Cognitive and situated learning: Perspectives in theory and practice. *Educational Researcher, 28*(2), 4–15.

Cognition and Technology Group at Vanderbilt. (1990). Anchored instruction and its relations to situated cognition. *Educational Researcher, 19*(6) 2–10.

Cognition and Technology Group at Vanderbilt. (1993). Anchored instruction and situated learning revisited. *Educational Technology, 33*(3), 52–70.

Cognition and Technology Group at Vanderbilt. (1996). Looking at technology in context: A framework for understanding technology and educational research. In D. Berliner & R. Calfee (Eds.), *Handbook of educational psychology* (pp. 807–840). New York: Macmillan.

Cohen, E. G. (1986). *Designing groupwork: Strategies for the heterogeneous classroom.* New York: Teachers College Press.

Coie, J. D., & Dodge, K. A. (1998). Aggression and antisocial behavior. In N. Eisenberg (Ed.), *Handbook of child psychology: Vol. 3. Social, emotional, and personality development* (5th ed., pp. 779–862). New York: Wiley.

Coie, J. D., Terry, R., Lenox, K., Lochman, J., & Hyman, C. (1995). Childhood peer rejection and aggression as predictors of stable patterns of adolescent disorder. *Development and Psychopathology, 7,* 697–714.

Cole, D. A., Martin, J. M., Peeke, L. A., Seroczynski, A. D., & Fier, J. (1999). Children's over- and underestimation of academic competence: A longitudinal study of gender differences, depression, and anxiety. *Child Development, 70,* 459–473.

Cole, M. (1985). The zone of proximal development: Where culture and cognition create each other. In J. V. Wertsch (Ed.), *Culture, communication, and cognition: Vygotskian perspectives* (pp. 146–161*)*. Cambridge: Cambridge University Press.

Coles, R. (1990, September). Teachers who made a difference. *Instructor,* 58–59.

Collins, A., Brown, J. S., & Holum, A. (1991). Cognitive apprenticeship: Making thinking visible. *American Educator, 15*(3), 38–39.

Collins, A., Brown, J. S., & Newman, S. E. (1989). Cognitive apprenticeship: Teaching the crafts of reading, writing, and mathematics. In L. B. Resnick (Ed.), *Knowing, learning, and instruction: Essays in honor of Robert Galser.* Hillsdale, NJ: Lawrence Earlbaum.

Committee on the Prevention of Reading Difficulties in Young Children. (1998). *Preventing reading difficulties in young children.* Washington, DC: National Academy Press.

Confrey, J. (1990a). A review of the research on students' conceptions in mathematics, science, and programming. *Review of Research in Education, 16,* 3–56.

Confrey, J. (1990b). What constructivism implies for teaching. In R. Davis, C. Maher, & N. Noddings (Eds.), *Constructivist views on the teaching and learning of mathematics* (pp. 107–122). Monograph 4 of the National Council of Teachers of Mathematics, Reston, VA.

Conger, R. D., Conger, K. J., & Elder, G. (1997). Family economic hardship and adolescent academic performance: Mediating and moderating processes. In G. Duncan & J. Brooks-Gunn (Eds.), *Consequences of growing up poor* (pp. 288–310). New York: Russell Sage Foundation.

Cooke, B. L., & Pang, K. C. (1991). Recent research on beginning teachers: Studies of trained and untrained novices. *Teaching and Teacher Education, 7,* 93–110.

Cooper, C. R. (1998). *The weaving of maturity: Cultural perspectives on adolescent development.* New York: Oxford University Press.

Cooper, G., & Sweller, J. (1987). Effects of schema acquisition and rule automation on mathematical problem-solving transfer. *Journal of Educational Psychology, 79,* 347–362.

Cooper, H. (1979). Pygmalion grows up: A model for teacher expectation communication and performance influence. *Review of Educational Research, 49,* 389–410.

Cooper, H. M., & Good, T. (1983). *Pygmalion grows up: Studies in the expectation communication process.* New York: Longman.

Cooper, H. M, Valentine, J. C., Nye, B., & Lindsay, J. J. (1999). Relationships between five after-school activities and academic achievement. *Journal of Educational Psychology, 91,* 369–683.

Cooperative learning (1986, September). *Harvard Education Letter, 2*(5), 4–6.

Cooperative learning. (1990, special edition). *Educational Leadership, 47*(4), 4–67.

Cooperative learning (1991, special edition). *Educational Leadership, 48,* 71–95.

Copi, I. M. (1961). *Introduction to logic.* New York: Macmillan.

Cordova, D. I., & Lepper, M. R. (1996). Intrinsic motivation and the process of learning: Beneficial effects of contextualization, personalization, and choice. *Journal of Educational Psychology, 88,* 715–730.

Corenblum, B., & Annis, R. C. (1987). Racial identity and preference among Canadian Indian and White children: Replication and extension. *Canadian Journal of Behavioural Science, 19,* 254–265.

Corkill, A. J. (1992). Advance organizers: Facilitators of recall. *Educational Psychology Review, 4,* 33–67.

Corno, L. (1992). Encouraging students to take responsibility for learning and performance. *The Elementary School Journal, 93,* 69–84.

Corno, L. (1995). Comments on Winne: Analytic and systemic research are both needed. *Educational Psychologist, 30,* 201–206.

Corno, L., & Snow, R. E. (1986). Adapting teaching to individual differences in learners. In M. Wittrock (Ed.), *Handbook of research on teaching* (3rd ed., pp. 605–629). New York: Macmillan.

Costa, A. L. (Ed.) (1985). *Developing minds: A resource book for teaching thinking.* Alexandria, VA: Association for Supervision and Curriculum Development.

Covaleskie, J. F. (1992). Discipline and morality: Beyond rules and consequences. *The Educational Forum, 56*(2), 56–60.

Covington, M., & Omelich, C. (1987). "I knew it cold before the exam": A test of the anxiety-blockage hypothesis. *Journal of Educational Psychology, 79,* 393–400.

Covington, M., & Omelich, C. L. (1984). An empirical examination of Weiner's critique of attribution research. *Journal of Educational Psychology, 76,* 1214–1225.

Covington, M. V. (1992). *Making the grade: A self-worth perspective on motivation and school reform.* New York: Holt, Rinehart, & Winston.

Cowley, G., & Underwood, A. (1998, June 15). Memory. *Newsweek, 131*(24), 48–54.

Craig, W. M., & Pepler, D. J. (1997). Observations of bullying and victimization in the school yard. *Canadian Journal of School Psychology, 13*, 41–60.

Craig, W. M., Peters, R. D., & Konarski, R. (1998, October). *Bullying and victimization among Canadian school children.* Working Paper Series (W-98-28E), Applied Research Branch of Strategic Policy. Hull, Quebec: Human Resources and Development Canada.

Craik, F. I. M., & Lockhart, R. S. (1972). Levels of processing: A framework for memory research. *Journal of Verbal Learning and Verbal Behavior, 11*, 671–684.

Crawford, J. (1997). *Best evidence: Research foundations of the Bilingual Education Act.* Washington, DC: National Clearinghouse for Bilingual Education.

Crealock, C., & Bachor, D. G. (1995). *Instructional strategies for students with special needs (2nd Ed.).* Scarborough, ON: Allyn & Bacon Canada.

Crisci, P. E. (1986). The Quest National Center: A focus on prevention of alienation. *Phi Delta Kappan, 67*, 440–442.

Cronin, J. F. (1993). Four misconceptions about authentic learning. *Educational Leadership, 50*(7), 78–80.

Crowhurst, M. (1994). *Language learning across the curriculum.* Scarborough, Ontario: Allyn & Bacon Canada.

Cummins, D. D. (1991). Children's interpretation of arithmetic word problems. *Cognition and Instruction, 8*, 261–289.

Cummins, J. (1984). *Bilingualism and special education.* San Diego: College Hill Press.

Cummins, J. (1989). A theoretical framework for bilingual special education. *Exceptional Children, 56*, 111–119.

Cummins, J. (1994). *The acquisition of English as a second language.* In K. Spangenberg-Urbschat & R. Prichard (Eds.), *Kids come in all languages: Reading instruction for ESL students* (pp. 36–62). Newark, DE: International Reading Association.

Cunningham, D. J. (1992) Beyond educational psychology: Steps toward an educational semiotic. *Educational Psychology Review, 4*, 165–194.

Current Directions in Psychological Science. (1993). Special Section: Controversies, 2, 1–12.

Curwin, R. L., & Mendler, A. N. (1988). Packaged discipline programs: Let the buyer beware. *Educational Leadership, 46*(2), 68–71.

Dansereau, D. F. (1985). Learning strategy research. In J. Segal, S. Chipman, & R. Glaser (Eds.), *Thinking and learning skills. Vol. I: Relating instruction to research.* Hillsdale, NJ: Erlbaum.

Dark, V. J., & Benbow, C. P. (1991). Differential enhancement of working memory with mathematical versus verbal precocity. *Journal of Educational Psychology, 83*, 48–60.

Das, J. P. (1995). Some thought on two aspects of Vygotsky's work. *Educational Psychologist, 30*, 93–97.

Davidson, J. (1982). The group mapping activity for instruction in reading and thinking. *Journal of Reading, 26*, 52–56.

Davis, J. K. (1991). Educational implications of field-dependence—independence. In S. Wapner & J. Demick (Eds.), *Field-dependence—independence: Cognitive styles across the life span.* (pp. 149–176). Hillsdale, NJ: Lawrence Erlbaum.

Davis, R. B., Maher, C. A., & Noddings, N. (Eds.) (1990). Constructivist views on the teaching and learning of mathematics. *Monograph 4 of the National Council of Teachers of Mathematics,* Reston, VA.

Davis, S. F., Grover, C. A., Becker, A. H., & McGregor, L. N. (1992). Academic dishonesty: Prevalence, determinants, techniques, and punishments. *Teaching of Psychology, 9*, 16–20.

Deaux, K. (1993). Commentary: Sorry, wrong number: A reply to Gentile's call. *Psychological Science, 4*, 125–126.

DeCecco, J., & Richards, A. (1974). *Growing pains: Uses of school conflicts.* New York: Aberdeen.

deCharms, R. (1976). *Enhancing motivation.* New York: Irvington.

deCharms, R. (1983). Intrinsic motivation, peer tutoring, and cooperative learning: Practical maxims. In J. Levine & M. Wang (Eds.), *Teacher and student perceptions: Implications for learning* (pp. 391–398). Hillsdale, NJ: Erlbaum.

Deci, E. (1975). *Intrinsic motivation.* New York: Plenum.

Deci, E., Vallerand, R. J., Pelletier, L. G., & Ryan, R. M. (1991). Motivation and education: The self-determination perspective. *Educational Psychologist, 26*, 325–346.

Deci, E. L., Koestner, R., & Ryan, R. M. (1999). A meta-analytic review of experiments examining the effects of extrinsic rewards on intrinsic motivation. *Psychological Bulletin, 125*, 627–668.

Deci, E. L., & Ryan, R. M. (1985). *Intrinsic motivation and self-determination in human behavior.* New York: Plenum.

De Corte, E., Greer, B., Verschaffel, L. (1996). Mathematics learning and teaching. In D. Berliner & R. Calfee (Eds.), *Handbook of educational psychology* (pp. 491–549). New York: Macmillan.

De Corte, E., & Verschaffel, L. (1985). Beginning first graders' initial impression of arithmetic word problems. *Journal of Mathematical Behavior, 4*, 3021.

Delpit, L. (1995). *Other people's children: Cultural conflict in the classroom.* New York: The New York Press.

Demetras, M. J. , & Post, K. N. (1985, April). *Negative feedback in mother-child dialogues.* Paper presented at the biennial meeting of the Society for Research in Child Development, Toronto.

De Mott, R. M. (1982). Visual impairments. In N. Haring (Ed.), *Exceptional children and youth.* Columbus, OH: Charles E. Merrill.

Dempster, F. N. (1981). Memory span: Sources of individual and developmental differences. *Psychological Bulletin, 89*, 63–100.

Dempster, F. N. (1991). Synthesis of research on reviews and tests. *Educational Leadership, 48*(7), 71–76.

Dempster, F. N. (1993). Exposing our students to less should help them learn more. *Phi Delta Kappan, 74*, 432–437.

Deno, S. L. (1987). Curriculum-based measurement. *Teaching Exceptional Children, 20*, 41.

DeRidder, L. M. (1993). Teenage pregnancy: Etiology and educational interventions. *Educational Psychology Review, 5*, 87–107.

Derry, S. (1991). Beyond symbolic processing: Expanding horizons for educational psychology. *Journal of Educational Psychology, 84*, 413–418.

Derry, S. J. (1989). Putting learning strategies to work. *Educational Leadership, 47*(5) 4–10.

Derry, S. J. (1992). Beyond symbolic processing: Expanding horizons for educational psychology. *Journal of Educational Psychology, 84*, 413–419.

Derry, S. J., & Murphy, D. A. (1986). Designing systems that train learning ability: From theory to practice. *Review of Educational Research, 56*, 1–39.

Dewey, J. (1910). *How we think.* Boston: D. C. Heath.

Diana, E. M., & Webb, J. M. (1997). Using geographic maps in classroom: The conjoint influence of individual differences and dual coding on learning facts. *Learning and Individual Differences, 9*, 195–214.

Diaz, R. M., & Berk, L. E. (Eds.) (1992). *Private speech: From social interaction to self-regulation.* Hillsdale, NJ: Erlbaum.

Dinnel, D., & Glover, J. A. (1985). Advance organizers: Encoding manipulations. *Journal of Educational Psychology, 77*, 514–522.

Di Vesta, F. J., & Di Cintio, M. J. (1997). Interactive effects of working memory span and text comprehension on reading comprehension and retrieval. *Learning and Individual Differences, 9*, 215–231.

Di Vesta, F. J., & Gray, G. S. (1972). Listening and notetaking. *Journal of Educational Psychology, 63*, 8–14.

Doctorow, M., Wittrock, M. C., & Marks, C. (1978). Generative processes in reading comprehension. *Journal of Educational Psychology, 70*, 109–118.

Dodge, K. A., & Somberg, D. R. (1987). Hostile attributional biases among aggressive boys are exacerbated under conditions of threats to the self. *Child Development, 58*, 213–224.

Dole, J. A., Duffy, G. G., Roehler, L. R., & Pearson, P. D. (1991). Moving from the old to the new: Research on reading comprehension instruction. *Review of Educational Research*, 61, 239–264.

Doyle, W. (1977). The uses of nonverbal behaviors: Toward an ecological model of classrooms. *Merrill-Palmer Quarterly, 23*, 179–192.

Doyle, W. (1983). Academic work. *Review of Educational Research, 53*, 159–200.

Doyle, W. (1986). Classroom organization and management. In M. C. Wittrock (Ed.), *Handbook of research on teaching* (3rd ed., pp. 392–431). New York: Macmillan.

Drayer, A. M. (1979). *Problems in middle and high school teaching: A handbook for student teachers and beginning teachers.* Boston: Allyn & Bacon.

Driscoll, M. P. (1994). *Psychology of learning for instruction.* Boston: Allyn & Bacon.

Duchastel, P. (1979). Learning objectives and the organization of prose. *Journal of Educational Psychology, 71*, 100–106.

Duckitt, J. (1992). Psychology and prejudice: A historical analysis and integrative framework. *American Psychologist, 47*, 1182–1193.

Duckitt, J. (1994). *The social psychology of prejudice.* Westport, CN: Praeger.

Duell, O. K. (1994). Extended wait time and university student achievement. *American Educational Research Journal, 31*, 397–414.

Duffy, G., Roehler, L. R., Meloth, M. S., & Vavrus, L. G. (1986). Conceptualizing instructional explanation. *Teaching and Teacher Education, 2*, 197–214.

Duncker, K. (1945). On solving problems. *Psychological Monographs, 58* (5, Whole No. 270).

Dunn, K., & Dunn, R. (1978). *Teaching students through their individual learning styles.* Reston, VA: National Council of Principals.

Dunn, K., & Dunn, R. (1987). Dispelling outmoded beliefs about student learning. *Educational Leadership, 44*(6), 55–63.

Dunn, R., Beaudry, J. S., & Klavas, A. (1989). Survey of research on learning styles. *Educational Leadership, 47*(7), 50–58.

Dunn, R., Dunn, K., & Price, G. E. (1984). *Learning Style Inventory.* Lawrence, KS: Price Systems.

Dweck, C. S., & Bempechat, J. (1983). Children's theories on intelligence: Consequences for learning. In S. Paris, G. Olson, & W. Stevenson (Eds.), *Learning and motivation in the classroom* (pp. 239–256). Hillsdale, NJ: Erlbaum.

Dyson, A. H. (1997). *Writing superheroes: Contemporary childhood, popular culture, and classroom literacy.* New York: Teachers College Press.

Eaton, J. F., Anderson, C. W., & Smith, E. L. (1984). Students' misconceptions interfere with science learning: Case studies of fifth-graders. *Elementary School Journal, 84*, 365–379.

Eccles, J., & Wigfield, A. (1985). Teacher expectations and student motivation. In J. Dusek (Ed.), *Teacher expectancies* (pp. 185–226). Hillsdale, NJ: Erlbaum.

Educational Quality and Accountability Office. (2001 October). *Grade 3 and grade 6 assessments of reading, writing and mathematics. achievement results guide, 2* (2). Toronto, ON: Author.

Educational Quality and Accountability Office. (2001). *Parent handbook 2000–2001.* Toronto, ON: Author.

Egan, S. K., Monson, T. C., & Perry, D. G. (1998). Social-cognitive influences on change in aggression over time. *Developmental Psychology, 34*, 996–1006.

Eggen, P. D., & Kauchak, D. P. (1996). *Strategies for teachers: Teaching content and thinking skills* (3rd ed.) Boston: Allyn & Bacon.

Eimas, P. D. (1985). The perception of speech in early infancy. *Scientific American, 252*, 46–52.

Eiseman, J. W. (1981). What criteria should public school moral education programs meet? *The Review of Education, 7*, 213–230.

Eisenberg, N., Martin, C. L., & Fabes, R. A. (1996). Gender development and gender effects. In D. Berliner & R. Calfee (Eds.), *Handbook of educational psychology* (pp. 358–396). New York: Macmillan.

Eisenberg, N., Shell, R., Pasernack, J., Lennon, R., Beller, R., & Mathy, R. M. (1987). Prosocial development in middle childhood: A longitudinal study. *Developmental Psychology, 23*, 712–718.

Elashoff, J. D., & Snow, R. E. (1971). *Pygmalion reconsidered.* Worthington, OH: Charles A. Jones.

Elawar, M. C., & Corno, L. (1985). A factorial experiment in teachers' written feedback on student homework: Changing teacher behavior a little rather than a lot. *Journal of Educational Psychology, 77*, 162–173.

Elkind, D. (1981). Obituary—Jean Piaget (1896–1980). *American Psychologist, 36*, 911–913.

Elkind, D. (1991). Formal education and early childhood education: An essential difference. In K. M. Cauley, F. Linder, & J. H. MacMillan (Eds.), *Annual Editions: Educational Psychology 91/92* (pp. 27–37). Guilford, CT: Duskin.

Ellis, A. K., & Fouts, J. T. (1993). *Research on educational innovations.* Princeton, NJ: Eye on Education.

Elrich, M. (1994). The stereotype within. *Educational Leadership, 51*(8), 12–15.

Emery, R. E. (1989). Family violence. *American Psychologist, 44*, 321–328.

Emmer, E. T., & Evertson, C. M. (1981). Synthesis of research on classroom management. *Educational Leadership, 38*, 342–345.

Emmer, E. T., & Evertson, C. M. (1982). Effective classroom management at the beginning of the school year in junior high school classes. *Journal of Educational Psychology, 74*, 485–498.

Emmer, E. T., Evertson, C. M., & Anderson, L. M. (1980). Effective classroom management at the beginning of the school year. *Elementary School Journal, 80*, 219–231.

Emmer, E. T., Evertson, C., Clements, B., & Worsham, M. (1997). *Classroom management for secondary teachers* (4th ed.). Boston: Allyn & Bacon.

Emmer, E. T., Evertson, C. M., & Worsham, M. E. (2000). *Classroom management for secondary teachers* (5th ed.). Boston: Allyn & Bacon.

Entwisle, D. R., & Alexander, K. L. (1998). Facilitating the transition to first grade: The nature of transition and research on factors affecting it. *The Elementary School Journal, 98*, 351–364.

Entwisle, D. R., Alexander, K., & Olson, L. (1997). *Children, schools, and inequality.* Boulder, CO: Westview Press.

Epanchin, B. C., Townsend, B., & Stoddard, K. (1994). *Constructive classroom management: Strategies for creating positive learning environments.* Pacific Grove, CA: Brooks/Cole.

Epstein, H. (1978). Growth spurts during brain development: Implications for educational policy and practice. In J. Chall & A. Mirsky (Eds.), *Education and the brain. The seventy-seventh yearbook of the National Society for the Study of Education, Part II.* Chicago: University of Chicago Press.

Epstein, H. (1980). EEG developmental stages. *Developmental Psychobiology, 13*, 629–631.

Epstein, J. L. (1989). Family structure and student motivation. In R. E. Ames & C. Ames (Eds.), *Research on motivation in education: Vol 3. Goals and cognitions* (pp. 259–295). New York: Academic Press.

Epstein, J. L. (1995). School/Family/Community partnerships: Caring for the children we share. *Phi Delta Kappan, 76*, 701–712.

Erez, M., & Zidon, I. (1984). Effects of goal acceptance on the relationship of goal difficulty to performance. *Journal of Applied Psychology, 69*, 69–78.

Erickson, F., & Shultz, J. (1982). *The counselor as gatekeeper: Social interaction in interviews.* New York: Academic Press.

Ericsson, K. A., & Smith, J. (Eds.) (1991). *Toward a general theory of expertise.* Cambridge, UK: Cambridge University Press.

Erikson, E. (1963). *Childhood and society* (2nd ed.). New York: Norton.

Erikson, E. H. (1968). *Identity, youth, and crisis.* New York: Norton.

Erikson, E. H. (1980). *Identity and the life cycle* (2nd ed.). New York: Norton.

Espe, C., Worner, C., & Hotkevich, M. (1990). Whole language— What a bargain. *Educational Leadership, 47*(6), 45.

Evertson, C. M. (1988). Managing classrooms: A framework for teachers. In D. Berliner & B. Rosenshine (Eds.), *Talks to teachers* (pp. 54–74). New York: Random House.

Evertson, C. M., Emmer, E. T., & Worsham, M. E. (2000). *Classroom management for elementary teachers* (5th ed.). Boston: Allyn & Bacon.

Fagot, B. I., & Hagan, R. (1991). Observations of parent reactions to sex-stereotyped behaviors: Age and sex effects. *Child Development, 62*, 617–628.

Fagot, B. I., Hagan, R., Leinbach, M. D., & Kronsberg, S. (1985). Differential reactions to assertive and communicative acts of toddler boys and girls. *Child Development, 56*, 1499–1505.

Fantuzzo, J., Davis, G., & Ginsburg, M. (1995). Effects of parent involvement in isolation or in combination with peer tutoring on student self-concept and mathematics achievement. *Journal of Educational Psychology, 87*, 272–281.

Farnaham-Diggory, S. (1994). Paradigms of knowledge and instruction. *Review of Educational Research, 64*, 463–477.

Farrar, M. J. (1990). Discourse and the acquisition of grammatical morphemes. *Journal of Child Language, 17*, 607–624.

Faw, H. W., & Waller, T. G. (1976). Mathemagenic behaviors and efficiency in learning from prose. *Review of Educational Research, 46*, 691–720.

Feather, N. T. (1982). *Expectations and actions: Expectancy-value models in psychology.* Hillsdale, NJ: Lawrence Erlbaum.

Feiman-Nemser, S. (1983). Learning to teach. In L. Shulman & G. Sykes (Eds.), *Handbook of teaching and policy* (pp. 150–170). New York: Longman.

Feingold, A. (1994). Gender differences in personality: A meta-analysis. *Psychological Bulletin, 116*, 429–456.

Ferguson, D. L., Ferguson, P. M., & Bogdan, R. C. (1987). If mainstreaming is the answer, what is the question? In V. Richardson-Koehler (Ed.), *Educators' handbook: A research perspective* (pp. 394–419). New York: Longman.

Fernald, A. (1993). Approval and disapproval: Infant responsiveness to vocal affect in familiar and unfamiliar languages. *Child Development, 64*, 657–674.

Feuerstein, R. (1979). *The dynamic assessment of retarded performers: The Learning Potential Assessment Device, theory, instruments, and techniques.* Baltimore: University Park Press.

Feuerstein, R. (1990). The theory of structural cognitive modifiability. In B. Presseisen (Ed.), *Learning and thinking styles: Classroom interaction* (pp. 68–134). Washington, DC: National Education Association.

Finn, J. (1972). Expectations and the educational environment. *Review of Educational Research, 42*, 387–410.

Fiske, E. B. (1981, October 27). Teachers reward muddy prose, study finds. *New York Times*, p. C1.

Fiske, E. B. (1988, April 10). America's test mania. *New York Times* (Education Life Section), pp. 16–20.

Fiske, S. T. (1993). Social cognition and social perception. *Annual Review of Psychology, 44*, 155–194.

Fitts, P. M., & Posner, M. I. (1967). *Human performance.* Belmont, CA: Brooks Cole.

Fitzgerald, J. (1995). English-as-a-second-language learners' cognitive reading process: A review of the research in the United States. *Review of Educational Research, 62*, 145–190.

Flammer, A. (1995). Developmental analysis of control beliefs. In A. Bandura (Ed.), *Self-efficacy in changing societies* (pp. 69–113). New York: Cambridge University Press.

Flavell, J. H. (1985). *Cognitive development* (2nd ed.). Englewood Cliffs, NJ: Prentice-Hall.

Flavell, J. H., Friedrichs, A. G., & Hoyt, J. D. (1970). Developmental changes in memorization processes. *Cognitive Psychology, 1*, 324–340.

Flavell, J. H., Green, F. L., & Flavell, E. R. (1995). Young children's knowledge about thinking. *Monographs of the Society for Research in Child Development, 60*(1) (Serial No. 243).

Flink, C. F., Boggiano, A. K., & Barrett, M. (1990). Controlling teaching strategies: Undermining children's self-determination and performance. *Journal of Personality and Social Psychology, 59*, 916–924.

Floden, R. E., & Klinzing, H. G. (1990). What can research on teacher thinking contribute to teacher preparation? A second opinion. *Educational Researcher, 19*(4), 15–20.

Foorman, B. F., Francis, D. J., Fletcher, J. M., Mehta, P., & Schatschneider, C. (1998). The role of instruction in learning to read: Preventing reading failure in at-risk children. *Journal of Educational Psychology, 90*, 37–55.

Foster, W. (1981, August). *Social and emotional development in gifted individuals.* Paper presented at the Fourth World Conference on Gifted and Talented, Montreal.

Fox, L. H. (1981). Identification of the academically gifted. *American Psychologist, 36*, 1103–1111.

Frable, D. E. S. (1997). Gender, Racial, ethnic, and class identities. In J. T. Spence, J. M. Darley, & D. J. Foss (Eds.) *Annual Review of Psychology* (pp. 139–162). Palo Alto, CA: Annual Reviews.

Frank, S. J., Pirsch, L. A., & Wright, V. C. (1990). Late adolescents' perceptions of their parents: Relationships among deidealization, autonomy, relatedness, and insecurity and implications for adolescent adjustment and ego identity status. *Journal of Youth and Adolescence, 19*, 571–588.

Frederiksen, N. (1984). Implications of cognitive theory for instruction in problem solving. *Review of Educational Research 54*, 363–407.

Freiberg, H. J., & Driscoll, A. (1996). *Universal teaching strategies* (2nd ed.). Boston: Allyn & Bacon.

Freud, S. (1959). Creative writers and daydreaming. In J. Strachey (Ed.), *The standard edition of the complete psychological works of Sigmund Freud* (Vol. 9). London: Hogarth Press.

Frick, T. W. (1990). Analysis of patterns in time: A method of recording and quantifying temporal relations in education. *American Educational Research Journal, 27*, 180–204.

Friend, M., & Bursuck, W. (1996). *Including students with special needs: A practical guide for classroom teachers.* Boston: Allyn & Bacon, p. 87.

Friend, M., Bursuck, W., & Hutchinson, N. (1998). *Including exceptional students: A practical guide for classroom teachers.* Scarborough, Ontario: Allyn & Bacon Canada.

Frisbie, D. A., & Waltmen, K. K. (1992). Developing a personal grading plan. *Educational Measurement: Issues and practices* (pp. 35–42). Washington, DC: National Council on Measurement in Education.

Fromberg, D. P., & Driscoll, M. (1985). *The successful classroom: Management strategies for regular and special education teachers.* New York: Teachers College Press.

Fulk, C. L., & Smith, P. J. (1995). Students' perceptions of teachers' instructional and management adaptations for students with learning or behavior problems. *The Elementary School Journal, 95*, 409–419.

Fuller, F. G. (1969). Concerns of teachers: A developmental conceptualization. *American Educational Research Journal, 6*, 207–226.

Furstenberg, F. F., & Cherlin, A. J. (1991). *Divided families.* Cambridge: Harvard University Press.

Gage, N. L. (1991). The obviousness of social and educational research results. *Educational Researcher, 20*(1), 10–16.

Gagné, E. D. (1985). *The cognitive psychology of school learning.* Boston: Little Brown.

Gagné, E. D., Yekovich, C. W., & Yekovich, F. R. (1993). *The cognitive psychology of school learning* (2nd ed.). New York: HarperCollins.

Gagné, R. M. (1977). *The conditions of learning* (3rd ed.). New York: Holt, Rinehart & Winston.

Gagné, R. M. (1985). *The conditions of learning and theory of instruction* (4th ed.). New York: Holt, Rinehart & Winston.

Gagné, R. M., & Driscoll, M. P. (1988). *Essentials of learning for instruction* (2nd ed.). Englewood Cliffs, NJ: Prentice-Hall.

Gagné, R. M., & Smith, E. (1962). A study of the effects of verbalization on problem solving. *Journal of Experimental Psychology, 63*, 12–18.

Galambos, S. J., & Goldin-Meadow, S. (1990). The effects of learning two languages on metalinguistic development. *Cognition, 34*, 1–56.

Gall, M. D. (1970). The use of questions in teaching. *Review of Educational Research, 40*, 707–721.

Gall, M. D. (1984). Synthesis of research on teachers' questioning. *Educational Leadership, 41*, 40–47.

Gallini, J. K. (1991). Schema-based strategies and implications for instructional design in strategy training. In C. McCormick, G. Miller, & M. Pressley (Eds.), *Cognitive strategies research: From basic research to educational applications*. New York: Springer-Verlag.

Garcia, E. E. (1992). "Hispanic" children: Theoretical, empirical, and related policy issues. *Educational Psychology Review, 4*, 69–94.

Garcia, R. L. (1991). *Teaching in a pluralistic society: Concepts, models, and strategies*. New York: HarperCollins.

Gardner, H. (1982a). *Art, mind, and brain: A cognitive approach to creativity*. New York: Basic Books.

Gardner, H. (1982b). *Developmental psychology* (2nd ed.). Boston: Little, Brown.

Gardner, H. (1983). *Frames of mind: The theory of multiple intelligences*. New York: Basic Books.

Gardner, H. (1991). *The unschooled mind: How children think and how schools should teach*. New York: Basic Books.

Gardner, H. (1993a). *Creating minds: An anatomy of creativity seen through the lives of Freud, Einstein, Picasso, Stravinsky, Elliot, Graham, and Gandhi*. New York: Basic Books.

Gardner, H. (1993b). *Educating the unschooled mind: A science and public policy seminar*. Washington, DC: American Educational Research Association.

Gardner, H. (1993c). *Multiple intelligences: The theory in practice*. New York: Basic Books.

Gardner, H. (1998). Reflections on multiple intelligences: Myths and messages. In A. Woolfolk (Ed.), *Readings in educational psychology* (2nd ed., pp. 61–67). Boston: Allyn & Bacon.

Gardner, H. (1999, August). *Who owns intelligence?* Invited address at the Annual Meeting of the American Psychological Association, Boston.

Gardner, R., Brown, R., Sanders, S., & Menke, D. J. (1992). "Seductive details" in learning from text. In K. A. Renninger, S. Hidi, & A. Krapp (Eds.), *The role of interest in learning and development* (pp. 239–254). Hillsdale, NJ: Erlbaum.

Garmon, A., Nystrand, M., Berends, M., & LePore. P. C. (1995). An organizational analysis of the effects of ability grouping. *American Educational Research Journal, 32*, 687–715.

Garner, R. (1990). When children and adults do not use learning strategies: Toward a theory of settings. *Review of Educational Research, 60*, 517–530.

Garner, R. (1992). Learning from school tests. *Educational Psychologist, 27*, 53–63.

Garner, R. (1998). Choosing to learn and not-learn in school. *Educational Psychology Review, 10*, 227–238.

Garrison, J. (1995). Deweyan pragmatism and the epistemology of contemporary social constructivism. *American Educational Research Journal, 32*, 716–741.

Garrod, A., Beal, C., & Shin, P. (1990). The development of moral orientation in elementary school children. *Sex Roles, 22*, 13–27.

Geary, D. C. (1995). Sexual selection and sex differences in spatial cognition. *Learning and Individual Differences, 7*, 289–303.

Geary, D. C. (1998). What is the function of mind and brain? *Educational Psychologist, 10*, 377–388.

Gelman, R. (1979). Preschool thought. *American Psychologist, 34*, 900–905.

Gelman, R., & Baillargeon, R. (1983). A review of some Piagetian concepts. In P. Mussen (Ed.), *Carmichael's manual of child psychology. Vol. 3: Cognitive development* (E. Markman & J. Flavell, Volume Eds.). New York: Wiley.

Gelman, R., Meck, E., & Merkin, S. (1986). Young children's numerical competence. *Cognitive Development, 1*, 1–29.

Gelman, S. A., & Ebeling, K. S. (1989). Children's use of nonegocentric standards in judgments of size. *Child Development, 60*, 920–932.

Gentner, D. (1975). Evidence for the psychological reality of semantic components: The verbs of possession. In D. Norman & D. Rumelhart (Eds.), *Explorations in cognition*. San Francisco: Freeman.

Gerbner, G., Gross, L. Signorelli, N., & Morgan, M. (1986). *Television's mean world: Violence Profile No. 14–15*. Philadelphia: Annenberg School of Communication, University of Pennsylvania.

Gergen, K. J. (1997). Constructing constructivism: Pedagogical potentials. *Issues in Education: Contributions from Educational Psychology, 3*, 195–202.

Gersten, R. (1996a). The language-minority students in transition: Contemporary instructional research. *The Elementary School Journal, 96*, 217–219.

Gersten, R. (1996b). Literacy instruction for language-minority students: The transition years. *The Elementary School Journal, 96*, 225–244.

Gersten, R., & Woodward, J. (1994). The language minority student and special education: Issues, trends and paradoxes. *Exceptional Children, 60*, 310–322.

Gibbs, J. W., & Luyben, P. D. (1985). Treatment of self-injurious behavior: Contingent versus noncontingent positive practice overcorrection. *Behavior Modification, 9*, 3–21.

Gick, M. L. (1986). Problem-solving strategies. *Educational Psychologist, 21*, 99–120.

Gillett, M., & Gall, M. (1982, March). *The effects of teacher enthusiasm on the at-task behavior of students in the elementary grades*. Paper presented at the annual meeting of the American Educational Research Association, New York.

Gilligan, C. (1982). *In a different voice: Psychological theory and women's development*. Cambridge, MA: Harvard University Press.

Gilligan, C., & Attanucci, J. (1988). Two moral orientations: Gender differences and similarities. *Merrill-Palmer Quarterly, 34*, 223–237.

Gilstrap, R. L., & Martin, W. R. (1975). *Current strategies for teachers: A resource for personalizing education*. Pacific Palisades, CA: Goodyear.

Ginsburg, H., & Opper, S. (1988). *Piaget's theory of intellectual development* (3rd ed.). Englewood Cliffs, NJ: Prentice-Hall.

Girls' math achievement: What we do and don't know. (1986, January). *Harvard Education Letter, 2*(1), 1–5.

Glaser, R. (1981). The future of testing: A research agenda for cognitive psychology and psychometrics. *American Psychologist, 36*, 923–936.

Glasgow, K. L., Dornbusch, S. M., Troyer, L., Steinberg, L., & Ritter, P. L. (1997). Parenting styles, adolescents' attributions, and educational outcomes in nine heterogeneous high schools. *Child Development, 68*, 507–523.

Glasser, W. (1969). *Schools without failure*. New York: Harper & Row.

Glasser, W. (1990). *The quality school: Managing students without coercion.* New York: Harper & Row.

Gleitman, H., Fridlund, A. J., & Reisberg, D. (1999). *Psychology* (5th ed.). New York: Norton.

Goldenberg, C. (1996). The education of language-minority students: Where are we, and where do we need to go? *The Elementary School Journal, 96,* 353–361.

Goleman, D. (1988, April 10). An emerging theory on blacks' I.Q. scores. *New York Times* (Education Life Section), 22–24.

Goleman, D. (1995). *Emotional intelligence.* New York: Bantam.

Gollnick, D. A., & Chinn, P. C. (1994). *Multicultural education in a pluralistic society* (4th ed.). New York: Merrill.

Good, T. (1996). Teaching effects and teacher evaluation. In J. Sikula (Ed.) *Handbook of research on teacher education* (pp. 617–665). New York: Macmillan.

Good, T. L. (1983a). Classroom research: A decade of progress. *Educational Psychologist, 18,* 127–144.

Good, T. L. (1983b). Research on classroom teaching. In L. Shulman & G. Sykes (Eds.), *Handbook of teaching and policy* (pp. 42–80). New York: Longman.

Good, T. L. (1987). Teacher expectations. In D. Berliner & B. Rosenshine (Eds.), *Talks to teachers* (pp. 159–200). New York: Random House.

Good, T. L., & Brophy, J. E. (1994). *Looking in classrooms* (6th ed.). New York: HarperCollins.

Good, T. L., & Brophy, J. E. (1997). *Looking in classrooms* (7th ed.). New York: Longman.

Good, T. L., & Marshall, S. (1984). Do students learn more in heterogeneous or homogeneous groups? In P. Peterson, L. C. Wilkinson, & M. Hallinan (Eds.), *The social context of instruction: Group organization and group processes* (pp. 15–38). Orlando, FL: Academic Press.

Goodenow, C. (1993). Classroom belonging among early adolescents: Relationships to motivation and achievement. *Journal of Early Adolescence, 13,* 21–43.

Goodman, K. S. (1986). *What's whole in whole language: A parent-teacher guide.* Portsmouth, NH: Heinemann.

Goodrich, H. (1997). Understanding rubrics. *Educational Leadership, 54(4),* 14–17.

Gordon, E. W. (1991). Human diversity and pluralism. *Educational Psychologist, 26,* 99–108.

Gordon, T. (1981). Crippling our children with discipline. *Journal of Education, 163,* 228–243.

Grabe, M., & Latta, R. M. (1981). Cumulative achievement in a mastery instructional system: The impact of differences in resultant achievement motivation and persistence. *American Educational Research Journal, 18,* 7–14.

Graber, J. A, & Brooks-Gunn, J. (1996). Transitions and turning points: Navigating the passage from childhood through adolescence. *Developmental Psychology, 32,* 768–776.

Graham, S. (1991). A review of attribution theory in achievement contexts. *Educational Psychology Review, 3,* 5–39.

Graham, S. (1996). How causal beliefs influence the academic and social motivation of African-American children. In G. G. Brannigan (Ed.), *The enlightened educator: Research adventures in the schools* (pp. 111–126). New York: McGraw-Hill.

Graham, S. (1998). Self-blame and peer victimization in middle school: An attributional analysis. *Developmental Psychology, 34,* 587–599.

Graham, S., & Barker, G. (1990). The downside of help: An attributional developmental analysis of helping behavior as a low ability cue. *Journal of Educational Psychology, 82,* 7–14.

Graham, S., & Golan, S. (1991). Motivational influences on cognition: Task involvement, ego involvement, and depth of information processing. *Journal of Educational Psychology, 83,* 187–194.

Graham, S., & Harris, K. R. (1994). The effects of whole language on children's writing: A review of the literature. *Educational Psychologist, 29,* 187–192.

Graham, S., & Weiner, B. (1996). Theories and principles of motivation. In D. Berliner & R. Calfee (Eds.), *Handbook of educational psychology* (pp. 63–84). New York: Macmillan.

Greeno, J. G., Collins, A. M., & Resnick, L. B. (1996). Cognition and learning. In D. Berliner & R. Calfee (Eds.), *Handbook of educational psychology* (pp. 15–46). New York: Macmillan.

Greenough, W. T., Black, J. E., & Wallace, C. S. (1987). Experience and brain development. *Child Development, 58,* 539–559.

Gregorc, A. F. (1982). *Gregorc Style Delineator: Development, technical, and administrative manual.* Maynard, MA: Gabriel Systems.

Gresham, F. (1981). Social skills training with handicapped children. *Review of Educational Research, 51,* 139–176.

Grigorenko, E. L., & Sternberg, R. J. (1998). Dynamic testing. *Psychological Bulletin, 124,* 75–111.

Grinder, R. E. (1981). The "new" science of education: Educational psychology in search of a mission. In F. H. Farley & N. J. Gordon (Eds.), *Psychology and education: The state of the union.* Berkeley, CA: McCutchan.

Grissom, J. B., & Smith, L. A. (1989). Repeating and dropping out of school. In L. Shepard & M. Smith (Eds.), *Flunking grades: Research and policies on retention* (pp. 34–63). Philadelphia: Falmer Press.

Grolnick, W. S., & Ryan, R. M. (1989). Parent styles associated with children's self-regulation and competence in school. *Journal of Educational Psychology, 81,* 143–154.

Grolnick, W. S., Ryan, R. M., & Deci, E. L. (1991) Inner resources for school achievement: Motivational mediators of children's perceptions of their parents. *Journal of Educational Psychology, 83,* 508–517.

Gronlund, N. E. (1993). *How to make achievement tests and assessments* (5th ed.). Boston: Allyn & Bacon.

Gronlund, N. E. (2000). *How to write and use instructional objectives* (6th ed.). Columbus: OH: Merrill.

Gross, M. U. M. (1992). The use of radical acceleration in cases of extreme intellectual precocity. *Gifted Child Quarterly, 36,* 91–99.

Grossman, H., & Grossman, S. H. (1994). *Gender issues in education.* Boston: Allyn & Bacon.

Grotevant, H. D. (1998). Adolescent development in family contexts. In N. Eisenberg (Ed.), *Handbook of child psychology: Vol 3. Social, emotional, and personality development* (5th ed., pp. 1097–1149). New York: Wiley.

Guilford, J. P. (1988). Some changes in the Structure-of-Intellect model. *Educational and Psychological Measurement, 48,* 1–4.

Gunderson, L. (1997). Whole language approaches to reading and writing. In S. A. Stahl and D. H. Hayes (Eds.), *Instructional models in reading* (pp. 221–247). Hillsdale, NJ: Erlbaum.

Guskey, T. (1990). Making the grade: What benefits students? *Educational Leadership, 52(2),* 14–21.

Guskey, T. R., & Gates, S. L. (1986). Synthesis of research on mastery learning. *Education Leadership, 43,* 73–81.

Gustafsson, J-E., & Undheim, J. O. (1996) Individual differences in cognitive functioning. In D. Berliner & R. Calfee (Eds.), *Handbook of educational psychology* (pp. 186–242). New York: Macmillan.

Guthrie, J. T., Cox, K. E., Anderson, E., Harris, K., Mazzoni, S., & Rach, L. (1998). Principles of integrated instruction for engagement in reading. *Educational Psychology Review, 10,* 227–238.

Haertel, E. H. (1999). Performance assessment and educational reform. *Phi Delta Kappan, 80,* 662–666.

Hakuta, K. (1986). *Mirror of language: The debate on bilingualism.* New York: Basic Books.

Hakuta, K., & Garcia, E. E. (1989). Bilingualism and education. *American Psychologist, 44,* 374–379.

Hakuta, K., & Gould, L. J. (1987). Synthesis of research on bilingual education. *Educational Leadership, 44(6),* 38–45.

Hall, J. W. (1991). More on the utility of the keyword method. *Journal of Educational Psychology, 83,* 171–172.

Hallahan, D. P., & Kauffman, J. M. (1997). *Exceptional learners: Introduction to special education* (7th ed.). Boston: Allyn & Bacon.

Hallahan, D. P., & Kauffman, J. M. (2000). *Exceptional learners: Introduction to special education* (8th ed.). Boston: Allyn & Bacon.

Hallahan, D. P., Kauffman, J. M., & Lloyd, J. W. (1999). *Introduction to learning disabilities* (4th ed.). Boston: Allyn & Bacon.

Hallowell, E. M., & Ratey, J. J. (1994). *Driven to distraction*. New York: Pantheon Books.

Halpern, D. F. (1996). Changing data, changing minds: What the data on cognitive sex differences tell us and what we hear. *Learning and Individual Differences, 8*, 73–82.

Hambleton, R. K. (1996). Advances in assessment models, methods, and practices. In D. C. Berliner & R. C. Calfee (Eds.), *Handbook of educational psychology* (pp. 899–925). New York: Macmillan.

Hamilton, R. J. (1985). A framework for the evaluation of the effectiveness of adjunct questions and objectives. *Review of Educational Research, 55*, 47–86.

Hansen, R. A. (1977). Anxiety. In S. Ball (Ed.), *Motivation in education*. New York: Academic Press.

Hardiman, P. T., Dufresne, R., & Mestre, J. P. (1989). The relation between problem categorization and problem solving among experts and novices. *Memory & Cognition, 17*, 627–638.

Hardman, M. L. (1994). *Inclusion: Issues of educating students with disabilities in regular educational settings*. A booklet to accompany Hardman, M. L., Drew, C. J., Egan, M. W., & Wolf, B. (1993). *Human exceptionality: Society, school, and family* (4th ed.). Boston: Allyn & Bacon.

Hardman, M. L., Drew, C. J., & Egan, M. W. (1996). *Human exceptionality: Society, school, and family* (5th ed.). Boston: Allyn & Bacon.

Hardman, M. L., Drew, C. J., & Egan, M. W. (1999). *Human exceptionality: Society, school, and family* (6th ed.). Boston: Allyn & Bacon.

Harris, J. R. (1998). The nurture assumption: Why children turn out the way they do; parents matter less than you think and peers matter more. New York: Free Press.

Harris, K. R. (1990). Developing self-regulated learners: The role of private speech and self-instruction. *Educational Psychologist, 25*, 35–50.

Harris, K. R., & Graham, S. (1996). Memo to constructivist: Skills count too. *Educational Leadership, 53*(5), 26–29.

Harris, K. R., Graham, S., & Pressley, M. (1991). Cognitive strategies in reading and written language. In N. Singh & I. Beale (Eds.), *Current perspectives in learning disabilities: Nature, theory, and treatment*. New York: Springer-Verlag.

Harris, K. R., & Pressley, M. (1991). The nature of cognitive strategy instruction: Interactive strategy construction. *Exceptional Children, 57*, 392–404.

Harris, L. (1989, June). *The ICD survey III: A report card on special education*. New York: Louis Harris & Associates.

Harris, R. T. (1991). Anorexia nervosa and bulimia nervosa in female adolescents. *Nutrition Today, 26*(2), 30–34.

Harrow, A. J. (1972). *A taxonomy of the psychomotor domain: A guide for developing behavior objectives*. New York: David McKay.

Harter, S. (1990). Issues in the assessment of self-concept of children and adolescents. In A. LaGreca (Ed.), *Through the eyes of a child* (pp. 292–325). Boston: Allyn & Bacon.

Harter, S. (1998). The development of self-representations. In N. Eisenberg (Ed.), *Handbook of child psychology: Vol 3. Social, emotional, and personality development* (5th ed., pp. 553–618). New York: Wiley.

Hartup, W. W., & Stevens, N. (1999). Friendships and adaptation across the lifespan. *Current Directions in Psychological Science, 8*, 76–79.

Harvard University (1987, January). Girls' math achievement: What we do and don't know. *Harvard Education Letter, 2*(1), 1–5.

Hayes, S. C., Rosenfarb, I., Wulfert, E., Munt, E. D., Korn, Z., & Zettle, R. D. (1985). Self-reinforcement effects: An artifact of social standard setting? *Journal of Applied Behavior Analysis, 18*, 201–214.

Heath, N. (1996). The emotional domain: Self-concept and depression in children with learning disabilities. *Advances in Learning and Behavioural Disabilities, 10*, 47–75.

Heath, N. L., & Ross, S. (2000). The prevalence and expression of depressive symptomatology in children with and without learning disabilities. *Learning Disability Quarterly, 23*, 24–36.

Herbert, E. A. (1998). Design matters: How school environment affects children. *Educational Leadership, 56*(1), 69–71.

Herman, J. (1997). Assessing new assessments: How do they measure up? *Theory Into Practice, 36*, 197–204.

Herman, J., & Winters. L. (1994). Portfolio research: A slim collection. *Educational Leadership, 52*(2), 48–55.

Hernshaw, L. S. (1987). *The shaping of modern psychology: A historical introduction from dawn to present day*. London: Routledge & Kegan Paul.

Hess, R., Chih-Mei, C., & McDevitt, T. M. (1987). Cultural variation in family beliefs about children's performance in mathematics: Comparisons among People's Republic of China, Chinese-American, and Caucasian-American families. *Journal of Educational Psychology, 79*, 179–188.

Hess, R., & McDevitt, T. (1984). Some cognitive consequences of maternal intervention techniques. A longitudinal study. *Child Development, 55*, 1902–1912.

Hess, R. D., & Shipman, V. C. (1965). Early experience and the socialization of cognitive modes in children. *Child Development, 36*, 869–886.

Hetherington, E. M. (1989). Coping with family transitions: Winners, losers, and survivors. *Child Development, 60*, 1–14.

Heward, W. L., & Orlansky, M. D. (1992). *Exceptional children* (4th ed.). Columbus, OH: Charles E. Merrill.

Hewson, P. W., Beeth, M. E., & Thorley, N. R. (1998). Teaching for conceptual change. In B. J. Fraserr & K. G. Tobin (Eds.), *International handbook of science education* (pp. 199–218). New York: Kluwer.

Hewstone, M. (1989). Changing stereotypes with disconfirming information. In D. Bar-Tal, C. Graumann, A. Kruglanski, & W. Stroebe (Eds.), *Stereotyping and prejudice: Changing conceptions* (pp. 207–223). New York: Springer-Verlag.

Hilgard, E. R., Atkinson, R. L., & Atkinson, R. C. (1979). *Introduction to psychology* (7th ed.). New York: Harcourt Brace Jovanovich.

Hill, K. T., & Eaton, W. O. (1977). The interaction of test anxiety and success-failure experiences in determining children's arithmetic performance. *Developmental Psychology, 13*, 205–211.

Hill, K. T., & Wigfield, A. (1984). Test anxiety: A major educational problem and what can be done about it. *Elementary School Journal, 85*, 105–126.

Hilliard, A. G. (1991/1992). Why we must pluralize curriculum. *Educational Leadership, 49*(4), 12–16.

Hines, C. V., Cruickshank, D. R., & Kennedy, J. J. (1985). Teacher clarity and its relation to student achievement and satisfaction. *American Educational Research Journal, 22*, 87–99.

Hinsley, D., Hayes, J. R., & Simon, H. A. (1977). From words to equations. In P. Carpenter & M. Just (Eds.), *Cognitive processes in comprehension*. Hillsdale, NJ: Erlbaum.

Hiroto, D. S., & Seligmen, M. E. P. (1975). Generality of learned helplessness in man. *Journal of Personality and Social Psychology, 31*, 311–327.

Hirsch, E. D., Jr. (1996). *The schools we need—and why we don't have them*. New York: Doubleday.

Hodges, E. V. E., & Perry, D. G. (1999). Personal and interpersonal antecedents and consequences of victimization by peers. *Journal of Personality and Social Psychology,*76, 677–685.

Hoffman, L. W. (1984). Work, family, and the socialization of the child. In R. Parke (Ed.), *Review of child development research* (Vol. 7, pp. 223–282). Chicago: University of Chicago Press.

Hoffman, M. L. (1988). Moral development. In M. Bornstein & M. Lamb (Eds.) *Developmental psychology: An advanced textbook* (2nd ed., pp. 497–548). Hillsdale, NJ: Erlbaum.

Hoge, D. R., Smit, E. K., & Hanson, S. L. (1990). School experiences predicting changes in self-esteem of sixth- and seventh-grade students. *Journal of Educational Psychology, 82,* 117–126.

Holden, G. W., & Ritchie, K. L. (1991). Linking extreme marital discord, child rearing practices, and child behavior problems: Evidence from battered women. *Child Development, 62,* 311–327.

Hoover-Dempsey, K. V., Bassler, O. C., & Burow, R. (1995). Parents' reported involvement in students' homework: Strategies and practices. *The Elementary School Journal, 95,* 435–450.

Horgan, D. D. (1995). *Achieving gender equity: Strategies for the classroom.* Boston: Allyn & Bacon.

Hoy, W. K., & Woolfolk, A. E. (1990). Organizational socialization of student teachers. *American Educational Research Journal, 27,* 279–300.

Hoy, W. K., & Woolfolk, A. E. (1993). Teachers' sense of efficacy and the organizational health of schools. *Elementary School Journal, 93,* 355–372.

Huessman, L. R., Eron, L. D., Klein, R., Brice, P., & Fischer, P. (1983). Mitigating the imitation of aggressive behaviors by changing children's attitudes about media violence. *Journal of Personality and Social Psychology, 44,* 899–910.

Huff, C. R. (1989). Youth gangs and public policy. *Crime Del, 35,* 524–537.

Hundert, J., & Bucher, B. (1978). Pupil's self-scored arithmetic performance: A practical procedure for maintaining accuracy. *Journal of Applied Behavior Analysis, 11,* 304.

Hunt, J. McV. (1961). *Intelligence and experience.* New York: Ronald.

Hunt, R. R., & Ellis, H. C. (1999). *Fundamentals of cognitive psychology* (6th ed.). New York: McGraw-Hill College.

Hunter, M. (1982). *Mastery teaching.* El Segundo, CA: TIP Publications.

Hutchinson, N. L. (2001). *Inclusion of exceptional learners in Canadian schools.* Toronto, ON: Prentice Hall.

International Reading Association & National Association for the Education of Young Children. (1998). Learning to read and write: Developmentally appropriate practices for young children. *The Reading Teacher, 52,* 193–216.

Iran-Nejad, A. (1990). Active and dynamic self-regulation of learning processes. *Review of Educational Research, 60,* 573–602.

Iran-Nejad, A., Marsh, G. E., & Clements, A. C. (1992). The figure and ground of constructive brain functioning: Beyond explicit memory processes. *Educational Psychologist, 27,* 473–492.

Irving, O., & Martin, J. (1982). Withitness: The confusing variable. *American Educational Research Journal, 19,* 313–319.

Irwin, J. W. (1991). *Teaching reading comprehension* (2nd ed.). Boston: Allyn & Bacon.

Isabella, R., & Belsky, J. (1991). Interactional synchrony and the origins of infant-mother attachment: A replication study. *Child Development, 62,* 373–384.

Jacklin, C. N., DiPietro, J. A., & Maccoby, E. E. (1984). Sex-typing behavior and sex-typing pressure in child-parent interactions. *Sex Roles, 13,* 413–425.

Jagacinski, C. M., & Nicholls, J. G. (1987). Competence and affect in task involvement and ego involvement: The impact of social comparison information. *Journal of Educational Psychology, 76,* 107–114.

James, W. (1890). *The principles of psychology.* (Vol. 2.) New York: Henry Holt.

James, W. (1912). *Talks to teachers on psychology: And to students on some of life's ideals.* New York: Holt.

Jarrett, R. (1995). Growing up poor: The family experiences of socially mobile youth in low-income African American neighborhoods. *Journal of Adolescent Research, 10,* 111–135.

Jenson, W. R., Sloane, H. N., & Young, K. R. (1988). *Applied behavior analysis in education: A structured teaching approach.* Englewood Cliffs, NJ: Prentice-Hall.

Johnson, D., & Johnson, R. (1985). Motivational processes in cooperative, competitive, and individualistic learning situations. In C. Ames & R. Ames (Eds.), *Research on motivation in education. Vol. 2: The classroom milieu* (pp. 249–286). New York: Academic Press.

Johnson, D., & Johnson, R. (1994). *Learning together and alone: Cooperation, competition, and individualization* (4th ed.). Boston: Allyn & Bacon.

Johnson. D. W., & Johnson, R. T. (1996). The role of cooperative learning in assessing and communicating student learning. In T. Guskey (Ed.), *ASCD 1996 Yearbook: Communicating student learning* (pp. 25–46). Alexandria, VA: Association for Supervision and Curriculum Development.

Johnson, D. W., & Johnson, R. (1999a). *Learning together and alone: Cooperation, competition, and individualization* (5th ed.). Boston: Allyn & Bacon.

Johnson, D. W., & Johnson, R. (1999b). The three Cs of school and classroom management. In H. J. Freiberg (Ed.), *Beyond behaviorism: Changing the classroom management paradigm* (pp. 119–144). Boston: Allyn & Bacon.

Johnson, D. W., Johnson, R., Dudley, B., Ward, M., & Magnuson, D. (1995). The impact of peer mediation training on the management of school and home conflicts. *American Educational Research Journal, 32,* 829–844.

Johnson, J. S., & Newport, E. L. (1989). Critical period effects in second language learning: The influence of maturational state on the acquisition of English as a second language. *Cognitive Psychology, 21,* 60–69.

John-Steiner, V., & Mahn, H. (1996). Sociocultural approaches to learning and development: A Vygotskian framework. *Educational Psychologist, 31,* 191–206.

Jones, E. D., & Southern, W. T. (1991). Conclusions about acceleration: Echoes of a debate. In W. Southern & E. Jones (Eds.), *The academic acceleration of gifted children* (pp. 223–228). New York: Teachers College Press.

Jones, M. G., & Gerig, T M. (1994). Silent sixth-grade students: Characteristics, achievement, and teacher expectations. *Elementary School Journal, 95,* 169–182.

Joshua, S., & Dupin, J. J. (1987). Taking into account students conceptions in instructional strategy: An example in physics. *Cognition and Instruction, 4,* 117–135.

Joyce, B., & Weil, M. (1988). *Models of teaching* (3rd ed.). Englewood, Cliffs, NJ: Prentice-Hall.

Jurden, F. H. (1995). Individual differences in working memory and complex cognition. *Journal of Educational Psychology, 87,* 93–102.

Kagan, S. (1983). Social orientation among Mexican-American children: A challenge to traditional classroom structures. In E. Garcia (Ed.), *The Mexican-American child: Language, cognition, and social development.* Tempe, AZ: Center for Bilingual Education.

Kagan, S. (1994). *Cooperative learning.* San Juan Capistrano, CA: Kagan Cooperative Learning.

Kanfer, F. H., & Gaelick, L. (1986). Self-management methods. In F. Kanfer & A. Goldstein (Eds.), *Helping people change: A textbook of methods* (3rd ed.). New York: Pergamon.

Kaplan, B. (1984). *Development and growth.* Hillsdale, NJ: Erlbaum.

Kaplan, J. S. (1991). *Beyond behavior modification* (2nd ed.). Austin, TX: Pro-Ed.

Karpov, Y. V., & Haywood, H. C. (1998). Two ways to elaborate Vygotsky's concept of mediation implications for instruction. *American Psychologist, 53,* 27–36.

Karpov, Y. V., & Bransford, J. D. (1995). L. S. Vygotsky and the doctrine of empirical and theoretical learning. *Educational Psychologist, 30,* 61–66.

Karweit, N. (1989). Time and learning: A review. In R. E. Slavin (Ed.), *School and classroom organization.* Hillsdale, NJ: Erlbaum.

Karweit, N., & Slavin, R. (1981). Measurement and modeling choices in studies of time and learning. *American Educational Research Journal, 18,* 157–171.

Kazdin, A. E. (1984). *Behavior modification in applied settings.* Homewood, IL: Dorsey Press.

Keefe, J. W. (1982). Assessing student learning styles: An overview. In *Student learning styles and brain behavior.* Reston, VA: National Association of Secondary School Principals.

Keefe, J. W., & Monk, J. S. (1986). *Learning style profile examiner's manual.* Reston, VA: National Association of Secondary School Principals.

Keenan, T., Ruffman, T., & Olson, D. R. (1994). When do children begin to understand logical inference as a source of knowledge? *Cognitive Development, 9,* 331–353.

Kelly, K. (1999). Retention vs. social promotion: Schools search for alternatives. *Harvard Education Letter, 15*(1), 1–3.

Keogh, B. K., & MacMillan, D. L. (1996). Exceptionality. In D. Berliner & R. Calfee (Eds.), *Handbook of educational psychology* (pp. 311–330). New York: Macmillan.

Keyser, V., & Barling, J. (1981). Determinants of children's self-efficacy beliefs in an academic environment. *Cognitive Therapy and Research, 5,* 29–40.

Kiewra, K. A. (1985). Investigating notetaking and review: A depth of processing alternative. *Educational Psychologist, 20,* 23–32.

Kiewra, K. A. (1988). Cognitive aspects of autonomous note taking: Control processes, learning strategies, and prior knowledge. *Educational Psychologist, 23,* 39–56.

Kiewra, K. A. (1989). A review of note-taking: The encoding storage paradigm and beyond. *Educational Psychology Review, 1,* 147–172.

Kindsvatter, R., Wilen, W., & Ishler, M. (1988). *Dynamics of effective teaching.* New York: Longman.

Kindsvatter, R., Wilen, W., & Ishler, M. (1992). *Dynamics of effective teaching* (2nd ed.). New York: Longman.

King, A. (1990). Enhancing peer interaction and learning in the classroom through reciprocal questioning. *American Educational Research Journal, 27,* 664–687.

King, A. (1994). Guiding knowledge construction in the classroom: Effects of teaching children how to question and how to explain. *American Educational Research Journal, 31,* 338–368.

King, A. J. C., Beazley, R. P., Warren, W. K., Hankins, C. A., Robertson, A. S., & Radford, J. L. (1998). *Canada Youth and AIDS study.* Kingston ON: Social Program Evaluation Group, Queen's University.

King, A. J. C., & Coles, B. (1992). *The health of Canada's youth: Views and behaviours of 11-, 13- and 15-year-olds from 11 countries.* Ottawa: Minister of Supply and Services Canada.

King, G. (1979, June). Personal communication. University of Texas at Austin.

Kirk, S., & Gallagher, J. J., & Anastasiow, N. J. (1993). *Educating exceptional children* (7th ed.). Boston: Houghton Mifflin.

Kirst, M. (1991a). Interview on assessment issues with Lorrie Shepard. *Educational Researcher, 20*(2), 21–23.

Kirst, M. (1991b). Interview on assessment issues with James Popham. *Educational Researcher, 20*(2), 24–27.

Klatzky, R. L. (1984). *Memory and awareness: An information-processing perspective.* New York: Freeman.

Klausmeier, H. J. (1976). Instructional design and the teaching of concepts. In J. Levin & V. Allen (Eds.), *Cognitive learning in children: Theories and strategies.* New York: Academic Press.

Klausmeier, H. J. (1992). Concept learning and concept teaching. *Educational Psychologist, 27,* 267–286.

Kling, K. C., Hyde, J. S., Showers, C. J., & Buswell, B. N. (1999). Gender differences in self-esteem: A meta-analysis. *Psychological Bulletin, 125,* 470–500.

Knapp, M., Turnbull, B. J., & Shields, P. M. (1990). New directions for educating children of poverty. *Educational Leadership, 48*(1), 4–9.

Kneedler, P. (1985). California assesses critical thinking. In A. Costa (Ed.), *Developing minds: A resource book for teaching thinking.* Alexandria, VA: Association for Supervision and Curriculum Development.

Kneedler, R. (1984). *Special education for today.* Englewood Cliffs, NJ: Prentice-Hall.

Kogan, N. (1983). Stylistic variation in childhood and adolescence: Creativity, metaphor, and cognitive style. In P. Mussen (Ed.), *Handbook of child psychology* (4th ed.), (Vol. 3, pp. 630–706). New York: Wiley.

Kohlberg, L. (1963). The development of children's orientations toward moral order: Sequence in the development of moral thought. *Vita Humana, 6,* 11–33.

Kohlberg, L. (1975). The cognitive-developmental approach to moral education. *Phi Delta Kappan, 56,* 670–677.

Kohlberg, L. (1981). *The philosophy of moral development.* New York: Harper & Row.

Kohlberg, L. (1984). *Essays on moral development.* San Francisco: Harper & Row.

Kohlberg, L., Yaeger, J., & Hjertholm, E. (1969). Private speech: Four studies and a review of theories. *Child Development, 39,* 691–736.

Kohn, A. (1991). Caring kids: The role of the schools. *Phi Delta Kappan, 72,* 496–506.

Kohn, A. (1993). Rewards versus learning: A response to Paul Chance. *Phi Delta Kappan, 74,* 783–787.

Kohn, A. (1996). By all available means: Cameron and Pierce's defense of extrinsic motivators. *Review of Educational Research, 66,* 1–4.

Kolb, G., & Whishaw, I. Q. (1998). Brain plasticity and behavior. In J. T. Spence, J. M. Darley, & D. J. Foss (Eds.), *Annual Review of Psychology* (pp. 43–64). Palo Alto, CA: Annual Reviews

Korenman, S., Miller, J., & Sjaastad, J. (1995). Long-term poverty and child development in the United States: Results from the NLSY. *Children and Youth Services Review, 17,* 127–155.

Kotrez, D., Stecher, B., & Diebert, E. (1993). *The reliability of scores from the 1992 Vermont Portfolio Assessment Program.* CSE Technical Report 355. Los Angeles: UCLA Center for the Study of Evaluation.

Kounin, J. (1970). *Discipline and group management in classrooms.* New York: Holt, Rinehart & Winston.

Kounin, J. S., & Doyle, P. H. (1975). Degree of continuity of a lesson's signal system and task involvement of children. *Journal of Educational Psychology, 67,* 159–164.

Kozulin, A. (1990). *Vygotsky's psychology: A biography of ideas.* Cambridge, MA: Harvard University Press.

Kozulin, A., & Falik, L. (1995). Dynamic cognitive assessment of the child. *Current Directions, 4,* 192–195.

Kozulin, A., & Presseisen, B. Z. (1995). Mediated learning experience and psychological tools: Vygotsky's and Feuerstein's perspectives in a study of student learning. *Educational Psychologist, 30,* 67–75.

Krashen, S. D. (1991). Bilingual education and second language acquisition theory. In *Schooling and language minority students: A theoretical framework.* Developed by the California State Department of Education, Office of Bilingual Bicultural Education. Los Angeles, CA: Evaluation, Dissemination, and Assessment Center, California State University.

Krathwohl, D. R., Bloom, B. S., & Masia, B. B. (1964). *Taxonomy of educational objectives. Handbook II: Affective domain.* New York: David McKay.

Kreitzer, A. E., & Madaus, G. F. (1994). Empirical investigations of the hierarchical structure of the taxonomy. In L. W. Anderson & L. A. Sosniak (Eds.), *Bloom's taxonomy: A forty-year retrospective*. Ninety-third yearbook for the National Society for the Study of Education: Part II (pp. 64–81). Chicago: University of Chicago Press.

Kroger, J. (1995). The differentiation of "firm" and "developmental" foreclosure identity statuses: A longitudinal study. *Journal of Adolescent Research, 10*, 317–337.

Krumboltz, J. D., & Krumboltz, H. B. (1972). *Changing children's behavior*. Englewood Cliffs, NJ: Prentice-Hall.

Kulik, C. L., Kulik, J. A., & Bangert-Drowns, R. L. (1990). Effectiveness of mastery learning programs: A meta-analysis. *Review of Educational Research, 60*, 265–299.

Kulik, J. A., & Kulik, C. C. (1984). Effects of accelerated instruction on students. *Review of Educational Research, 54*, 409–425.

Kulik, J. A., Kulik, C. C., & Bangert, R. L. (1984, April). Effects of practice on aptitude and achievement test scores. *American Educational Research Journal, 21*, 435–447.

Ladson-Billings, G. (1990). Like lightning in a bottle: Attempting to capture the pedagogical excellence of successful teachers of Black students. *Qualitative Studies in Education, 3*, 335–344.

Ladson-Billings, G. (1992). Culturally relevant teaching: The key to making multicultural education work. In C.A. Grant (Ed.), *Research and multicultural education* (pp. 106–121). London: Falmer Press.

Ladson-Billings, G. (1994). *The dream keepers*. San Francisco: Jossey Bass.

Ladson-Billings, G. (1995). But that is just good teaching! The case for culturally relevant pedagogy. *Theory Into Practice, 34*, 159–165.

Laidlaw, L. (2001, March). I can be happy at this school: Creating a socially responsible learning community. *Teacher, 13*(5), 1, 4.

Lambert, A. J. (1995). Stereotypes and social judgment: The consequences of group variability. *Journal of Personality and Social Psychology, 68*, 388–403.

Language Development and Hypermedia Group (1992). "Open" software design: A case study. *Educational Technology, 32*, 43–55.

Laosa, L. (1984). Ethnic, socioeconomic, and home language influences on early performance on measures of ability. *Journal of Educational Psychology, 76*, 1178–1198.

Larrivee, B. (1985). *Effective teaching behaviors for successful mainstreaming*. New York: Longman.

Lave, J. (1988). *Cognition in practice: Mind, mathematics, and culture in everyday life*. New York: Cambridge University Press.

Lave, J., & Wenger, E. (1991). *Situated learning: Legitimate peripheral participation*. Cambridge, MA: Cambridge University Press.

Learning Disabilities Association of Ontario. (2001, May 25). *Learning disabilities: A new definition*. Retrieved from www.ldao.on.ca/pei/defdraft.html.

Leavy, J. (1996, March 18). Mother's little helper. Newsweek, 127, 51–56.

Lee, A. Y., & Hutchinson, L. (1998). Improving learning from examples through reflection. *Journal of Experimental Psychology: Applied, 4*, 187–210.

Leinhardt, G. (1986). Expertise in mathematics teaching. *Educational Leadership, 43*, 28–33.

Leinhardt, G. (1988). Situated knowledge and expertise in teaching. In J. Calderhead (Ed.), *Teachers' professional learning*. London: Farmer Press.

LeMahieu, P., Gitomer, D. H., & Eresh, J. T. (1993). *Portfolios in large-scale assessment: Difficult but not impossible*. Unpublished manuscript, University of Delaware.

Leming, J. S. (1981). Curriculum effectiveness in value/moral education. *Journal of Moral Education, 10*, 147–164.

Lepper, M. R. (1988). Motivational considerations in the study of instruction. *Cognition and Instruction, 5*, 289–309.

Lepper, M. R., & Greene, D. (1978). *The hidden costs of rewards: New perspectives on the psychology of human motivation*. Hillsdale, NJ: Erlbaum.

Lepper, M. R., Keavney, M., & Drake, M. (1996). Intrinsic motivation and extrinsic reward: A commentary on Cameron and Pierce's meta-analysis. *Review of Educational Research, 66*, 5–32.

Lerner, R. M., & Galambos, N. L. (1998). Adolescent development: Challenges and opportunities for research, programs, and policies. In J. T. Spence, J. M. Darley, & D. J. Foss (Eds.), *Annual Review of Psychology* (pp. 413–446). Palo Alto, CA: Annual Reviews.

Levin, J. R. (1993). Mnemonic strategies and classroom learning: A twenty-year report card. *Elementary School Journal, 94*, 235–254.

Levin, J. R., & Nolan, J. F. (2000). *Principles of classroom management: A professional decision-making model*. Boston: Allyn & Bacon.

Lewinsohn, P. M., Rohde, P., & Seeley, J. R. (1994). Psychological risk factors for future attempts. *Journal of Consulting and Clinical Psychology, 62*, 297–305.

Liben, L. S., & Signorella, M. L. (1993). Gender-schematic processing in children: the role of initial interpretations of stimuli. *Developmental Psychology, 29*, 141–149.

Lindsay, P. H., & Norman, D. A. (1977). *Human information processing: An introduction to psychology* (2nd ed.). New York: Academic Press.

Linn, M. C., & Hyde, J. S. (1989). Gender, mathematics, and science. *Educational Researcher, 18*, 17–27.

Linn, R. L., & Gronlund, N. E. (2000). *Measurement and assessment in education* (8th ed.). Columbus, OH: Merrill.

Lipps, G., & Frank, J. (1997). The national longitudinal survey of children and youth, 1994–95: Initial results from the school component. *Statistics Canada-Catalogue No. 81-003-XPB*, Vol. 4 (2).

Lipscomb, T. J., MacAllister, H. A., & Bregman, N. J. (1985). A developmental inquiry into the effects of multiple models on children's generosity. *Merrill-Palmer Quarterly, 31*, 335–344.

Locke, E. A., & Latham, G. P. (1990). *A theory of goal setting and task performance*. Englewood Cliffs, NJ: Prentice-Hall.

Loftus, E., & Palmer, J. C. (1974). Reconstruction of automobile destruction: An example of the interaction between language and memory. *Journal of Verbal Learning and Verbal Behavior, 13*, 585–589.

Lohman, D. L. (1989). Human intelligence: An introduction to advances in theory and research. *Review of Educational Research, 59*, 333–374.

Lord, J. (1991). *Lives in transition: The process of personal empowerment*. Kitchener, ON: Centre for Research and Education in Human Services.

Lord, S., Eccles, J., & McCarthy, K. (1994). Surviving the junior high school transition: Family processes and self-perceptions as protective factors. *Journal of Early Adolescence, 14*, 162–199.

Lowenstein, G. (1994). The psychology of curiosity: A review and reinterpretation. *Psychological Bulletin, 117*, 75–98.

Lucyshyn, J. M., Horner, R. H., Dunlap, G., Albin, R. W., & Ben, K. R. (2002). Positive behavior support with families. In J. M. Lucyshyn, G. Dunlap, & R. W. Albin (Eds.), *Families and positive behavior support: Addressing problem behavior in family contexts* (pp. 3–43). Baltimore: Paul H. Brookes.

Luiten, J., Ames, W., & Ackerson, G. (1980). A meta-analysis of the effects of advance organizers on learning and retention. *American Educational Research Journal, 17*, 211–218.

Lupart, J. L., & Pyryt, M. C. (1996). "Hidden Gifted" students: Underachiever prevalence and profile. *Journal for the Education of the Gifted, 20* (1), 36–53.

Lytton, H., & Romney, D. M. (1991). Parents' sex-related differential socialization of boys and girls: A meta-analysis. *Psychological Bulletin, 109*, 267–296.

Ma, X., & Kishor, N. (1997). Attitude toward self, social factors, and achievement in mathematics: A meta-analytic review. *Educational Psychology Review, 9*, 89–120.

Mabry, L. (1999). Writing to the rubrics: Lingering effects of traditional standardized testing on direct writing assessment. *Phi Delta Kappan, 80*, 673–679.

Maccoby, E. E. (1990). Gender and relationships. *American Psychologist, 45*, 513–520.

Macionis, J. J. (1991). *Sociology* (3rd ed.). Englewood Cliffs, NJ: Prentice-Hall.

Macionis, J. J. (1994). *Sociology* (4th ed.). Englewood Cliffs, NJ: Prentice-Hall.

MacKay, A. W. (1986). The Charter's equality provisions and education: A structural analysis. *Canadian Journal of Education, 11*, 293–312.

Macrae, C. N., Milne, A. B., & Bodenhausen, C. V. (1994). Stereotypes as energy-saving devices: A peek inside the cognitive toolbox. *Journal of Personality and Social Psychology, 66*, 37–47.

Madsen, C. H., Becker, W. C., & Thomas, D. R. (1968). Rules, praise, and ignoring: Elements of elementary classroom control. *Journal of Applied Behavior Analysis, 1*, 139–150.

Madsen, C. H., Becker, W. C., Thomas, D. R., Koser, L., & Plager, E. (1968). An analysis of the reinforcing function of "sit down" commands. In R. K. Parker (Ed.), *Readings in educational psychology*. Boston: Allyn & Bacon.

Maehr, M. L., & Anderman, E. M. (1993). Reinventing schools for early adolescents: Emphasizing task goals. *The Elementary School Journal, 93*, 593–610.

Mager, R. (1975). *Preparing instructional objectives* (2nd ed.). Palo Alto, CA: Fearon.

Magusson, S. J., & Palincsar, A. S. (1995). The learning environment as a site of science reform. *Theory Into Practice, 34*, 43–50.

Maier, N. R. F. (1933). An aspect of human reasoning. *British Journal of Psychology, 24*, 144–155.

Maker, C. J. (1987). Gifted and talented. In V. Richardson-Koehler (Ed.), *Educators' handbook: A research perspective* (pp. 420–455). New York: Longman.

Mandlebaum, L. H., Russell, S. C., Krouse, J., & Gonter, M. (1983). Assertive discipline: An effective classwide behavior management program. *Behavior Disorders, 8*(4), 258–264.

Mangione, P. L., & Speth, T. (1998). The transition to elementary school: A framework for creating early childhood continuity through home, school, and community partnerships. *The Elementary School Journal, 98*, 381–397.

Manitoba Education Training and Youth. (2002, June). *2001–2002 Grade 6 English language arts, English LA—Immersion, and Anglais standards test (Optional)*. Winnipeg, MN: Author.

Manning, B. H. (1991). *Cognitive self-instruction of classroom processes*. Albany, NY: State University of New York Press.

Manning, B. H., & Payne, B. D. (1996). *Self-talk for teachers and students: Metacognitive strategies for personal and classroom use*. Boston: Allyn & Bacon.

Manning, M. L., & Baruth, L. G. (1996). *Multicultural education of children and adolescents* (2nd ed.). Boston: Allyn & Bacon.

Mantzicopolos, P., & Morrison, D. (1992). Kindergarten retention: Academic and behavioral outcomes through the end of second grade. *American Educational Research Journal, 29*, 182–198.

Maratsos, M. P. (1989). Innateness and plasticity in language acquisition. In M. L. Rice & R. L. Schiefelbusch (Eds.), *The teachability of language* (pp. 105–125). Baltimore, MD: Brooks/Cole.

Marcia, J. (1980). Ego identity development. In J. Adelson (Ed.), *The handbook of adolescent psychology*. New York: Wiley.

Marcia, J. (1987). The identity status approach to the study of ego identity development. In T. Honess & K. Yardley (Eds.), *Self and identity: Perspectives across the life span*. London: Routledge & Kagan Paul.

Marcia, J. E. (1991). Identity and self development. In R. Lerner, A. Peterson, & J. Brooks-Gunn (Eds.), *Encyclopedia of Adolescence* (Vol. 1). New York: Garland.

Marcia, J. E. (1994). The empirical study of ego identity. In H. Bosma, T. Graafsma, H. Grotebanc, & D. DeLivita (Eds.), *The identity and development*. Newbury Park, CA: Sage.

Marcus, N., Cooper, M., & Sweller, J. (1996). Understanding instructions. *Journal of Educational Psychology, 88*, 49–63.

Markman, E. M. (1977). Realizing that you don't understand: A preliminary investigation. *Child Development, 48*, 986–992.

Markman, E. M. (1979). Realizing that you don't understand: Elementary school children's awareness of inconsistencies. *Child Development, 50*, 643–655.

Markman, E. M. (1990). Constraints children place on word meanings. *Cognitive Science, 14*, 57–77.

Markstrom-Adams, C. (1992). A consideration of intervening factors in adolescent identity formation. In G. R. Adams, R. Montemayor, and T. Gullotta (Eds.), *Advances in adolescent development: Vol. 4. Adolescent identity formation* (pp. 173–192). Newbury Park, CA: Sage.

Marsh, H. W. (1987). The big-fish-little-pond effect on academic self-concept. *Journal of Educational Psychology, 79*, 280–295.

Marsh, H. W. (1990). Influences of internal and external frames of reference on the formation of math and English self-concepts. *Journal of Educational Psychology, 82*, 107–116.

Marsh, H. W. (1994). Using the National Longitudinal Study of 1988 to evaluate theoretical models of self-concept: The Self-Description Questionnaire. *Journal of Educational Psychology, 86*, 439–456.

Marsh, H. W., Chessor, D., Craven, R., & Roche, L. (1995). The effects of gifted and talented programs on academic self-concept: The big fish strikes again. *American Educational Research Journal, 32*, 285–321.

Marsh, H. W., & Holmes, I. W. M. (1990). Multidimensional self-concepts: Construct validation of responses by children. *American Educational Research Journal, 27*, 89–118.

Marsh, H. W., Walker, R., & Debus, R. (1991). Subject-specific components of academic self-concept and self-efficacy. *Contemporary Educational Psychology, 16*, 331–345.

Marsh, H. W., & Yeung, A. S. (1997). Coursework selection: Relation to academic self-concept and achievement. *American Educational Research Journal, 34*, 691–720.

Marshall, H. (1996). Implications of differentiating and understanding constructivist approaches. *Journal of Educational Psychology, 31*, 235–240.

Marshall, H. H. (1987). Motivational strategies of three fifth-grade teachers. *Elementary School Journal, 88*, 135–150.

Marshall, H. H. (Ed.) (1992). *Redefining student learning: Roots of educational change*. Norwood, NJ: Ablex.

Martin, C. L. (1989). Children's use of gender-related information in making social judgments. *Developmental Psychology, 25*, 80–88.

Martin, C. L., & Little, J. K. (1990). The relation of gender understanding to children's sex-typed preferences and gender stereotypes. *Child Development, 61*, 1427–1439.

Martin, G., & Pear, J. (1992). *Behavior modification: What it is and how to do it* (4th ed.). Englewood Cliffs, NJ: Prentice-Hall.

Martin, J., & Sugarman, J. (1993). *Models of classroom management: Principles, applications and critical perspectives* (2nd ed.). Calgary: Detselig.

Martindale, C. (1991). *Cognitive psychology: A neural-network approach*. Pacific Grove, CA: Brooks/Cole.

Maslow, A. H. (1968). *Toward a psychology of being* (2nd ed.). New York: Van Nostrand.

Maslow, A. H. (1970). *Motivation and personality* (2nd ed.). New York: Harper and Row.

Mason, D. A., & Good, T. L. (1993). Effects of two-group and whole-class teaching on regrouped elementary students' mathematics achievement. *American Educational Research Journal, 30,* 328–360.

Matlin, M. W., & Foley, H. J. (1997). *Sensation and perception* (4th ed.). Boston: Allyn & Bacon.

Mayer, J. D., & Salovey, P. (1993). The intelligence of emotional intelligence. *Intelligence, 17,* 433–442.

Mayer, J. D., & Salovey, P. (1997). What is emotional intelligence? In P. Salovey & D. Sluyter (Eds.), Emotional development, emotional literacy, and emotional intelligence. New York: Basic Books.

Mayer, R. E. (1979). Can advance organizers influence meaningful learning? *Review of Educational Research, 49,* 371–383.

Mayer, R. E. (1982). Memory for algebra story problems. *Journal of Educational Psychology, 74,* 199–216.

Mayer, R. E. (1983a). Can you repeat that? Qualitative and quantitative effects of repetition and advance organizers on learning from science prose. *Journal of Educational Psychology, 75,* 40–49.

Mayer, R. E. (1983b). *Thinking, problem solving, cognition.* San Francisco: Freeman.

Mayer, R. E. (1984). Twenty-five years of research on advance organizers. *Instructional Science, 8,* 133–169.

Mayer, R. E. (1992a). Cognition and instruction: Their historic meeting within educational psychology. *Journal of Educational Psychology, 84,* 405–412.

Mayer, R. E. (1992b). *Thinking, problem solving, and cognition* (2nd ed.). New York: Freeman.

Mayer, R. E. (1996). Learners as information processors: Legacies and limitations of educational psychology's second metaphor. *Journal of Educational Psychology, 31,* 151–161.

Mayer, R. E., & Sims, V. K. (1994). For whom is a picture worth a thousand words? Extensions of a dual-coding theory of multimedia learning. *Journal of Educational Psychology, 86,* 389–401.

Mayer, R. E., & Wittrock, M. C. (1996). Problem-solving transfer. In D. Berliner & R. Calfee (Eds.), *Handbook of educational psychology* (pp. 47–62). New York: Macmillan.

McCaslin, M., & Good, T. (1996). The informal curriculum. In D. Berliner, & R. Calfee (Eds.), *Handbook of educational psychology* (pp. 622–670). New York: Macmillan.

McClelland, D. (1985). *Human motivation.* Glenview, IL: Scott, Foresman.

McClelland, D. C. (1993). Intelligence is not the best predictor of job performance. *Current Directions in Psychological Science, 2,* 5–6.

McCombs, B. L., & Marzano, R. J. (1990). Putting the self in self-regulated learning: The self as agent in integrating skill and will. *Educational Psychologist, 25,* 51–70.

McCormack, S. (1989). Response to Render, Padilla, and Krank: But practitioners say it works! *Educational Leadership, 46*(6), 77–79.

McCreary Centre Society. (1993). *Adolescent health survey: Province of British Columbia.* Prepared by Larry Peters and Aileen Murphy. Investigators: Roger Tonkink, David Cos, and Ruth Milner. Vancouver, BC: The McCreary Centre Society.

McDonald, J. P. (1993). Three pictures of an exhibition: Warm, cool, and hard. *Phi Delta Kappan, 74,* 480–485.

McKenzie, T. L., & Rushall, B. S. (1974). Effects of self-recording on attendance and performance in a competitive swimming training environment. *Journal of Applied Behavior Analysis, 7,* 199–206.

McLaughlin, T. F., & Gnagey, W. J. (1981, April). *Self-management and pupil self-control.* Paper presented at the annual meeting of the American Educational Research Association, Los Angeles.

McLoyd, V. C. (1998). Economic disadvantage and child development. *American Psychologist, 53,* 185–204.

McMurtry, J. (1999, March). A teacher's perspective on the Surrey book ban. *Teacher: Newsmagazine of the BC Teachers' Federation, 11* (5), 15.

McNemar, Q. (1964). Lost: Our intelligence? Why? *American Psychologist, 19,* 871–882.

Means, B., & Knapp, M. S. (1991). Cognitive approaches to teaching advanced skills to educationally disadvantaged students. *Phi Delta Kappan, 73,* 282–289.

Mediascope. (1996). National television violence study: Executive summary 1994–1995. Studio City, CA: Author.

Medley, D. M. (1979). The effectiveness of teachers. In P. Peterson & H. Walberg (Eds.), *Research on teaching: Concepts, findings, and implications* (pp. 11–27). Berkeley, CA: McCutchan.

Meece, J. L. (1997). *Child and adolescent development for educators.* New York: McGraw-Hill.

Meek, A. (1991). On thinking about teaching: A conversation with Eleanor Duckworth. *Educational Leadership, 48*(b), 30–34.

Meichenbaum, D. (1977). *Cognitive behavior modification: An integrative approach.* New York: Plenum.

Meichenbaum, D. (1986). Cognitive behavior modification. In F. Kanfer & A. Goldstein (Eds.), *Helping people change: A textbook of methods* (3rd ed., pp. 346–380). New York: Pergamon.

Meichenbaum, D., Burland, S., Gruson, L., & Cameron, R. (1985). Metacognitive assessment. In S. Yussen (Ed.), *The growth of reflection in children.* Orlando, FL: Academic Press.

Mendell, P. R. (1971). Retrieval and representation in long-term memory. *Psychonomic Science, 23,* 295–296.

Messick, S. (1975). The standard problem: Meaning and values in measurement and evaluation. *American Psychologist, 35,* 1012–1027.

Messick, S. (1994). The matter of style: Manifestations of personality in cognition, learning, and teaching. *Educational Psychologist, 29,* 121–136.

Metcalfe, B. (1981). Self-concept and attitude toward school. *British Journal of Educational Psychology, 51,* 66–76.

Metcalfe, J., & Shimamura, A. P. (Eds.) (1994). *Metacognition: Knowledge about knowing.* Cambridge, MA: MIT Press.

Meyer, M., Delgardelle, M., & Middleton, J. (1996). Addressing parents' concerns over curriculum reform. *Educational Leadership, 53*(7), 54–57.

Mickleburgh, R. (1999, February 1). Parents put heat on B.C. schools: Asian immigrants behind latest drive for more structured, back-to-basics education. *Globe and Mail.* p. A3.

Miller, E. (1994). Peer mediation catches on, but some adults don't. *Harvard Education Letter, 10*(3), 8.

Miller, G. A. (1956). The magical number seven, plus or minus two: Some limits on our capacity for processing information. *Psychological Review, 63,* 81–97.

Miller, G. A., Galanter, E., & Pribram, K. H. (1960). *Plans and the structure of behavior.* New York: Holt, Rinehart & Winston.

Miller, K., & Gelman, R. (1983). The child's representation of number: A multidimensional scaling analysis. *Child Development, 54,* 1470–1479.

Miller, P. H. (1993). *Theories of developmental psychology* (3rd ed.). New York: Freeman.

Miller, R. B. (1962). Analysis and specification of behavior for training. In R. Glaser (Ed.), *Training research and education: Science edition.* New York: Wiley.

Mills, C. J., Ablard, K. E., & Stumpf, H. (1993). Gender differences in academically talented young students' mathematical reasoning: Patterns across age and subskills. *Journal of Educational Psychology, 85,* 340–346.

Mills, J. R., & Jackson, N. E. (1990). Predictive significance of early giftedness: The case of precocious reading. *Journal of Educational Psychology, 82,* 410–419.

Moll, L. C., Amanti, C., Neff, D., & Gonzalez, N. (1992). Funds of knowledge: Using a qualitative approach to connect homes and classrooms. *Theory Into Practice, 31,* 132–141.

Moll, L. C., & Whitmore, K. F. (1993). Vygotsky in classroom practice: Moving from individual transmission to social transaction. In E. Forman, N. Minick, & C. A. Stone (Eds.), *Contexts for* learning: Sociocultural dynamics in children's development (pp. 19–42). New York: Oxford University Press.

Moos, R. H., & Moos, B. S. (1978). Classroom social climate and student absences and grades. *Journal of Educational Psychology, 70*, 263–269.

Morris, C. G. (1991). *Psychology: An introduction* (7th ed.). Englewood Cliffs, NJ: Prentice-Hall.

Morris, P. F. (1990). Metacognition. In M. W. Eysenck (Ed.), *The Blackwell dictionary of cognitive psychology* (pp. 225–229). Oxford, UK: Basil Blackwell.

Morrow, L. (1983). Home and school correlates of early interest in literature. *Journal of Educational Research, 76*, 221–230.

Morrow, L., & Weinstein, C. (1986). Encouraging voluntary reading: The impact of a literature. *Reading Research Quarterly, 21*, 330–346.

Morrow, L. M. (1997). *Literacy development in the early years: Helping children to read and write* (3rd ed.). Boston: Allyn & Bacon.

Moshman, D. (1982). Exogenous, endogenous, and dialectical constructivism. *Developmental Review, 2*, 371–384.

Moshman, D. (1997). Pluralist rational constructivism. *Issues in Education: Contributions from Educational Psychology, 3*, 229–234.

Moshman, D., Glover, J. A., & Bruning, R. H. (1987). *Developmental psychology.* Boston: Little, Brown.

Moskowitz, G., & Hayman, M. L. (1976). Successful strategies of inner-city teachers: A year-long study. *Journal of Educational Research, 69*, 283–289.

Moss, P. A. (1992). Shifting conceptions of validity in educational measurement: Implications for performance assessment. *Review of Educational Research, 62*, 229–258.

Mumford, M. D., Costanza, D. P., Baughman, W. A., Threlfall, V., & Fleishman, E. A. (1994). Influence of abilities on performance during practice: Effects of massed and distributed practice. *Journal of Educational Psychology, 86*, 134–144.

Murphy, P. K., & Alexander, P. A. (2000). A motivated exploration of motivation terminology. *Contemporary Educational Psychology, 25*, 3–53.

Murray, H. G. (1983). Low inference classroom teaching behavior and student ratings of college teaching effectiveness. *Journal of Educational Psychology, 75*, 138–149.

Mussen, P., Conger, J. J., & Kagan, J. (1984). *Child development and personality* (6th ed.). New York: Harper & Row.

Muth, K. D., & Alverman, D. E. (1999). *Teaching and learning in the middle grades.* Boston: Allyn & Bacon.

National Center for Education Statistics. (1990). *Digest of Education Statistics.* Washington, DC: Center for Education Statistics.

National Council of Teachers of Mathematics (NCTM) (1989). *Curriculum and evaluation standards for school mathematics.* Reston, VA: Author.

National Joint Committee on Learning Disabilities (1989). *Letter from NJCLD to member organizations. Topic: Modifications to the NJCLD definition of learning disabilities.*

National Science Foundation (1988). *Women and minorities in science and engineering* (NSF 88–301). Washington, DC: National Science Foundation.

Naveh-Benjamin, M. (1991). A comparison of training programs intended for different types of test-anxious students: Further support for an information-processing model. *Journal of Educational Psychology, 83*, 134–139.

Naveh-Benjamin, M., McKeachie, W. J., & Lin, Y. (1987). Two types of test-anxious students: Support for an information processing model. *Journal of Educational Psychology, 79*, 131–136.

Needles, M., & Knapp, M. (1994). Teaching writing to children who are undeserved. *Journal of Educational Psychology, 86*, 339–349.

Neimark, E. (1975). Intellectual development during adolescence. In F. D. Horowitz (Ed.), *Review of child development research* (Vol. 4). Chicago: University of Chicago Press.

Neisser, U., Boodoo, G., Bouchard, A., Boykin, W., Brody, N., Ceci, S. J., Halpern, D. F., Loehlin, J. C., Perloff, R., Sternberg, R. J., & Urbina, S. (1996). Intelligence: Knowns and unknowns. *American Psychologist, 51*, 77–101.

Nelson, G. (1993). Risk, resistance, and self-esteem: A longitudinal study of elementary school-aged children from mother-custody and two-parent families. *Journal of Divorce and Remarriage, 19*, 99–119.

Nelson, K. (1986). *Event knowledge.* Hillsdale, NJ: Erlbaum.

Nelson, T. O. (1996). Consciousness and metacognition. *American Psychologist, 51*, 102–116.

Nestor-Baker, N. S. (1999). *Tacit knowledge in the superintendency: An exploratory analysis.* Unpublished doctoral dissertation, The Ohio State University, Columbus, OH.

Newby, T. J. (1991). Classroom motivation: Strategies of first-year teachers. *Journal of Educational Psychology, 83*, 195–200.

Newstead, S. E., Franklyn-Stokes, A., & Armstead, P. (1996). Individual differences in student cheating. *Journal of Educational Psychology, 88*, 229–241.

Nicholls, J. G., & Miller, A. (1984). Conceptions of ability and achievement motivation. In R. Ames & C. Ames (Eds.), *Research on motivation in education. Vol. 1: Student Motivation* (pp. 39–73). New York: Academic Press.

Nissani, M., & Hoefler-Nissani, D. M. (1992). Experimental studies of belief dependence of observations and of resistance to conceptual change. *Cognition and Instruction, 9*, 97–111.

Noddings, N. (1990). Constructivism in mathematics education. In R. Davis, C. Maher, & N. Noddings (Eds.), *Constructivist views on the teaching and learning of mathematics* (pp. 7–18). Monograph 4 of the National Council of Teachers of Mathematics, Reston, VA.

Noddings, N. (1992). *The challenge to care in schools: An alternative approach to education.* New York: Teachers College Press.

Noddings, N. (1995). Teaching themes of care. *Phi Delta Kappan, 76*, 675–679.

Nolen, S. B. (1988). Reasons for studying: Motivational orientations and study strategies. *Cognition and Instruction, 5*, 269–288.

Novak, J. D., & Musonda, D. (1991). A twelve-year longitudinal study of science concept learning. *American Educational Research Journal, 28*, 117–154.

Nucci, L. (1987). Synthesis of research on moral development. *Educational Leadership, 44*(5), 86–92.

Nungester, R. J., & Duchastel, P. C. (1982). Testing versus review: Effects on retention. *Journal of Educational Psychology, 74*, 18–22.

Oakes, J. (1990a). Opportunities, achievement, and choice: Women and minority students in science and math. *Review of Research in Education, 16*, 153–222.

Oakes, J. (1990b). *Multiplying inequities: The effects of race, social class, and tracking on opportunities to learn mathematics and science.* Santa Monica, CA: Rand.

Oakes, J. (1999). Promotion or retention: Which one is social? *Harvard Education Letter, 15*(1), 8.

O'Boyle, M. W., & Gill, H. S. (1998). On the relevance of research findings in cognitive neuroscience to educational practice. *Educational Psychology Review, 10*, 397–410.

O'Connor, C. (1997). Dispositions toward (collective) struggle and educational resilience in the inner city: A case analysis of six African American high school students. *American Educational Research Journal, 34*, 593–629.

O'Donnell, A. M., & O'Kelly, J. (1994). Learning from peers: Beyond the rhetoric of positive results. *Educational Psychology Review, 6*, 321–350.

Ogbu, J. (1987). Variability in minority school performance: A problem in search of an explanation. *Anthropology and Education Quarterly, 18*, 312–334.

Ogbu, J. U. (1997). Understanding the school performance of urban blacks: Some essential background knowledge. In H. Walberg, O.

Reyes, & R. P. Weissberg (Eds.), *Children and youth: Interdisciplinary perspectives* (pp. 140–190). Norwood, NJ: Ablex.

Ogden, J. E., Brophy, J. E., & Evertson, C. M. (1977, April). *An experimental investigation of organization and management techniques in first-grade reading groups.* Paper presented at the annual meeting of the American Educational Research Association, New York.

O'Leary, K. D. (1980). Pills or skills for hyperactive children? *Journal of Applied Behavior Analysis, 13,* 191–204.

O'Leary, S. (1995). Parental discipline mistakes. *Current Directions in Psychological Science, 4,* 11–13.

O'Leary, K. D., Kaufman, K. F., Kass, R. E., & Drabman, R. S. (1970). The effects of loud and soft reprimands on the behavior of disruptive students. *Exceptional Children, 37,* 145–155.

O'Leary, K. D., & O'Leary, S. (Eds.) (1977). *Classroom management: The successful use of behavior modification* (2nd ed.). Elmsford, NY: Pergamon.

O'Leary, K. D., & Wilson, G. T. (1987). *Behavior therapy: Application and outcome.* Englewood Cliffs, NJ: Prentice-Hall.

O'Leary, S. G., & O'Leary, K. D. (1976). Behavior modification in the schools. In H. Leitenberg (Ed.), *Handbook of behavior modification and behavior therapy.* Englewood Cliffs, NJ: Prentice-Hall.

Ollendick, T. H., Dailey, D., & Shapiro, E. S. (1983). Vicarious reinforcement: Expected and unexpected effects. *Journal of Applied Behavior Analysis, 16,* 485–491.

O'Neil, J. (1990a). Link between style, culture proves divisive. *Educational Leadership, 48*(2), 8.

Onslow, M. (1992). Choosing a treatment program for early stuttering: Issues and future directions. *Journal of Speech and Hearing Research, 35,* 983–993.

Ontario Ministry of Education (1995). *Consultation to validate: Categories of exceptionalities.* Toronto: Author.

Ontario Ministry of Education & Training. *For the love of learning,* Vol. II. Retrieved March 1999 from: http://edu. gov.on.ca/eng/general/absc/room/full/volume2/chapter 10.html.

Ontario Ministry of Education & Training. *Language: The Ontario curriculum, grades 1–8.* Retrieved March 17, 1999, from: www.edu.gov.on.ca/eng/document/curricul/curr971.html.

Orlando L., & Machado, A. (1996). In defense of Piaget's theory: A reply to 10 common criticisms. *Psychological Review, 103,* 143–164.

Ormrod, J. E. (1999). *Human learning* (3rd ed.). Upper Saddle River: NJ: Merrill/Prentice-Hall.

Ortony, A., Clore, G. L., & Collins, A. (1988). *The cognitive structure of emotions.* Cambridge: Cambridge University Press.

Osborn, A. F. (1963). *Applied imagination* (3rd ed.). New York: Scribner's.

Ovando, C. J. (1989). Language diversity and education. In J. Banks & C. McGee Banks (Eds.), *Multicultural education: Issues and perspectives* (pp. 208–228). Boston: Allyn & Bacon.

Owens, R. E. (1995). *Language disorders* (2nd ed.). Boston: Allyn & Bacon.

Padilla, F. M. (1992). *The gang as an American enterprise.* New Brunswick, NJ: Rutgers University Press.

Page, E. B. (1958). Teacher comments and student performances: A 74-classroom experiment in school motivation. *Journal of Educational Psychology, 49,* 173–181.

Paivio, A. (1971). *Imagery and verbal processes.* New York: Holt, Rinehart & Winston.

Paivio, A. (1986). *Mental representations: A dual-coding approach.* New York: Oxford University Press.

Pajares, F. (1997). Current directions in self-efficacy research. In M. L. Maehr & P. R. Pintrich (Eds.), *Advances in motivation and achievement* (Vol. 10, pp. 1–49). Greenwich, CT: JAI Press.

Palincsar, A. S. (1986). The role of dialogue in providing scaffolded instruction. In J. Levin & M. Pressley (Eds.), *Educational Psychologist, 21* (Special issue on learning strategies), 73–98.

Palincsar, A. S. (1996). Language-minority students: Instructional issues in school cultures and classroom social systems. *Elementary School Journal, 96,* 221–226.

Palincsar, A. S. (1998). Social constructivist perspectives on teaching and learning. In J. T. Spence, J. M. Darley, & D. J. Foss (Eds.), *Annual Review of Psychology* (pp. 345–375). Palo Alto, CA: Annual Reviews.

Palincsar, A. S., & Brown, A. L. (1984). Reciprocal teaching of comprehension-fostering and monitoring activities. *Cognition and Instruction, 1,* 117–175.

Palincsar, A. S., & Brown, A. L. (1989). Classroom dialogues to promote self-regulated comprehension. In J. Brophy (Ed.), *Advances in research on teaching,* (Vol. 1, pp. 35–67). Greenwich, CT: JAI Press.

Palincsar, A. S., Magnuson, S. J., Marano, N., Ford, D., & Brown, N. (1998). Designing a community of practice: Principles and practices of the GIsML community. *Teaching and Teacher Education, 14,* 5–19.

Pallas, A. M., & Alexander, K. (1983). Sex differences in quantitative SAT performance: New evidence on the differential coursework hypothesis. *American Educational Research Journal, 20,* 165–182.

Papert, S. (1980). *Mindstorms: Children, computers, and powerful ideas.* New York: Basic Books.

Paris, S. G., & Cunningham, A. E. (1996). Children becoming students. In D. Berliner & R. Calfee (Eds.), *Handbook of Educational Psychology* (pp. 117–146). New York: Macmillan.

Paris, S. G., Lipson, M. Y., & Wixson, K. K. (1983). Becoming a strategic reader. *Contemporary Educational Psychology, 8,* 293–316.

Parks, C. P. (1995). Gang behavior in the schools: Myth or reality? *Educational Psychology Review, 7,* 41–68.

Pasch, M., Sparks-Langer, G., Gardner, T. G., Starko, A. J., & Moody, C. D. (1991). *Teaching as decision making: Instructional practices for the successful teacher.* New York: Longman.

Pate, P. E., McGinnis, K., & Homestead, E. (1995). Creating coherence through curriculum integration. In M. Harmin (1994). *Inspiring active learning: A handbook for teachers* (pp. 62–70). Alexandria, VA: Association for Supervision and Curriculum Development.

Paulman, R. G., & Kennelly, K. J. (1984). Test anxiety and ineffective test taking: Different names, same construct? *Journal of Educational Psychology, 76,* 279–288.

Paulson, F. L., Paulson, P. R., & Meyer, C. A. (1991). What makes a portfolio a portfolio? *Educational Leadership, 48*(5), 60–63.

Pearson, P. D. (1989). Commentary: Reading the whole language movement. *Elementary School Journal, 90,* 231–241.

Pelham, W. E. (1981). Attention deficits in hyperactive and learning-disabled children. *Exceptional Education Quarterly, 2,* 13–23.

Pellegrini, A. D., Bartini, M., & Brooks, F. (1999). School bullies, victims, and aggressive victims: Factors relating to group affiliation and victimization in early adolescence. *Journal of Educational Psychology, 91,* 216–224.

Peneul, W. R., & Wertsch, J. V. (1995). Vygotsky and identity formation: A sociocultural approach. *Educational Psychologist, 30,* 83–92.

Peng, S., & Lee, R. (1992, April). *Home variables, parent-child activities, and academic achievement: A study of 1988 eighth graders.* Paper presented at the annual meeting of the American Educational Research Association, San Francisco.

Pepler, D. J., & Sedighdeilami, F. (1998, October). *Aggressive girls in Canada.* Working Paper Series (W-98-30E), Applied Research Branch of Strategic Policy. Hull, Quebec: Human Resources and Development Canada.

Perkins, D., & Blythe, T. (1994). Putting understanding up front. *Educational Leadership, 51*(5), 4–7.

Perkins, D., Jay, E., & Tishman, S. (1993). New conceptions of thinking: From ontology to education. *Educational Psychologist, 28,* 67–85.

Perkins, D. N. (1991, May). Technology meets constructivism: Do they make a marriage? *Educational Technology, 31,* 18–23.

Perkins, D. N., & Salomon, G. (1989). Are cognitive skills context-bound? *Educational Researcher, 18,* 16–25.

Perrone, V. (1994). How to engage students in learning. *Educational Leadership, 51*(5), 11–13.

Perry, N. E., McNamara, J. K., & Mercer, K. L. (In press). Principles, policies, and practices in special education in British Columbia. *Exceptionality Education Canada.*

Perry, N. E., VandeKamp, K., & Mercer, L. (2000, April). *Investigating teacher-student interactions that foster self-regulated learning.* In N. E. Perry (Chair), Symposium conducted at the meeting of the American Educational Research Association, New Orleans.

Peterson, P., Fennema, E., & Carpenter, T. (1989). Using knowledge of how students think about mathematics. *Educational Leadership, 46*(4), 42–46.

Peterson, P. L. (1992). Revising their thinking: Keisha Coleman and her third-grade mathematics class. In H. Marshall (Ed.), *Redefining student learning: Roots of educational change* (pp. 151–176). Norwood, NJ: Ablex.

Peterson, P. L., & Comeaux, M. A. (1989). Assessing the teacher as a reflective professional: New perspectives on teacher evaluation. In A. Woolfolk (Ed.), *Research perspectives on the graduate preparation of teachers* (pp. 132–152). Englewood Cliffs, NJ: Prentice-Hall.

Pettigrew, T. (1998). Intergroup contact theory. In J. T. Spence, J. M. Darley, & D. J. Foss (Eds.), *Annual Review of Psychology* (pp. 65–85). Palo Alto, CA: Annual Reviews.

Pfeffer, C. R. (1981). Developmental issues among children of separation and divorce. In I. Stuart & L. Abt (Eds.), *Children of separation and divorce.* New York: Van Nostrand Reinhold.

Pfiffner, L. J., Rosen, L. A., & O'Leary, S. G. (1985). The efficacy of an all-positive approach to classroom management. *Journal of Applied Behavior Analysis, 18,* 257–261.

Phillips, D. (1997). How, why, what, when, and where: Perspectives on constructivism and education. *Issues in Education: Contributions from Educational Psychology, 3,* 151–194.

Phillips, D., & Zimmerman, M. (1990). The developmental course of perceived competence and incompetence among competent children. In R. Sternberg & J. Kolligian (Eds.), *Competence considered* (pp. 41–66). New Haven, CT: Yale University Press.

Phillips, D. C. (Ed.) (2000). *Constructivism in education: Opinions and second opinions on controversial issues.* Chicago: University of Chicago Press.

Phye, G. D. (1992). Strategic transfer: A tool for academic problem solving. *Educational Psychology Review, 4,* 393–421.

Phye, G. D., & Sanders, C. E. (1994). Advice and feedback: Elements of practice for problem solving. *Contemporary Educational Psychology, 17,* 211–223.

Piaget, J. (1954). *The construction of reality in the child* (M. Cook, Trans.). New York: Basic Books.

Piaget, J. (1962). *Comments on Vygotsky's critical remarks concerning "The language and thought of the child" and "Judgment and reasoning in the child."* Cambridge, MA: MIT Press.

Piaget, J. (1963). *Origins of intelligence in children.* New York: Norton.

Piaget, J. (1965). *The moral judgment of the child.* New York: Free Press.

Piaget, J. (1970a). Piaget's theory. In P. Mussen (Ed.), *Handbook of child psychology* (3rd ed.). New York: Wiley.

Piaget, J. (1970b). *The science of education and the psychology of the child.* New York: Orion Press.

Piaget, J. (1974). *Understanding causality* (D. Miles and M. Miles, Trans.). New York: Norton.

Piaget, J. (1985). *The equilibrium of cognitive structures: The central problem of intellectual development.* (T. Brown & K. L. Thampy, Trans.). Chicago: University of Chicago Press.

Pierson, L. H., & Connell, J. P. (1992). Effect of grade retention on self-system processes, school engagement, and academic performance. *Journal of Educational Psychology, 84,* 300–307.

Pintrich (Eds.), *Advances in motivation and achievement* (Vol. 10, pp. 1–49). Greenwich, CT: JAI Press.

Pintrich, P., & Schrauben, B. (1992). Students' motivational beliefs and their cognitive engagement in academic tasks. In D. Schunk & J. Meece (Eds.), *Students' perceptions in the classroom: Causes and consequences* (pp. 149–183). Hillsdale, NJ: Erlbaum.

Pintrich, P. R., Marx, R. W., & Boyle, R. A. (1993). Beyond cold conceptual change: The role of motivational beliefs and classroom contextual factors in the process of conceptual change. *Review of Educational Research, 63,* 167–199.

Pintrich, P. R., & Schunk, D. H. (1996). *Motivation in education: Theory, research, and applications.* Columbus, OH: Merrill.

Pitts, J. M. (1992). Constructivism: Learning rethought. In J. B. Smith & J. C. Coleman, Jr. (Eds.), *School Library Media Annual* (Vol. 10, pp. 14–25). Englewood, CO: Libraries Unlimited.

Polson, P. G., & Jeffries, R. (1985). Instruction in general problem-solving skills: An analysis of four approaches. In J. Segal, S. Chipman, & R. Glaser (Eds.), *Thinking and learning skills* (Vol. 1, pp. 417–455). Mahwah, NJ: Erlbaum.

Popham, W. J. (1988). *Educational evaluation* (2nd ed.). Englewood Cliffs, NJ: Prentice-Hall.

Popham, W. J. (1999). *Classroom assessment: What teachers need to know.* Boston: Allyn & Bacon.

Porath, M. (1996). Narrative performance in verbally gifted children. *Journal for the Education of the Gifted, 19,* 276–292.

Porath, M. (1997). A developmental model of artistic giftedness in middle childhood. *Journal for the Education of the Gifted, 20,* 201–223.

Posner, M. I. (1973). *Cognition: An introduction.* Glenview, IL: Scott, Foresman.

Prawat, R. S. (1991). The value of ideas: The immersion approach to the development of thinking. *Educational Researcher, 20,* 3–10.

Prawat, R. S. (1992). Teachers beliefs about teaching and learning: A constructivist perspective. *American Journal of Education, 100,* 354–395.

Prawat, R. S. (1996). Constructivism, modern and postmodern. *Issues in Education: Contributions from Educational Psychology, 3,* 215–226.

Premack, D. (1965). Reinforcement theory. In D. Levine (Ed.), *Nebraska symposium on motivation* (Vol. 13). Lincoln, NE: University of Nebraska Press.

Pressley, M. (1986). The relevance of the good strategy user model to the teaching of mathematics. In J. Levin & M. Pressley (Eds.), *Educational Psychologist, 21* (Special issue on learning strategies), 139–161.

Pressley, M. (1991). Comparing Hall (1988) with related research on elaborative mnemonics. *Journal of Educational Psychology, 83,* 165–170.

Pressley, M. (1995). More about the development of self-regulation: complex, long-term, and thoroughly social. *Educational Psychologist, 30,* 207–212.

Pressley, M. (1996, August). *Getting beyond whole language: Elementary reading instruction that makes sense in light of recent psychological research.* Paper presented at the Annual meeting of the American Psychological Association, Toronto.

Pressley, M., Barkowski, J. G., & Schneider, W. (1987). Cognitive strategies: Good strategy users coordinate metacognition and knowledge. In R. Vasta & G. Whitehurst (Eds.), *Annals of Child Development. Vol. 4.* Greenwich, CT: JAI Press.

Pressley, M., Levin, J., & Delaney, H. D. (1982). The mnemonic keyword method. *Review of Research in Education, 52,* 61–91.

Price, G., & O'Leary, K. D. (1974). *Teaching children to develop high performance standards.* Unpublished manuscript. State University of New York at Stony Brook.

Pring, R. (1971). Bloom's taxonomy: A philosophical critique. *Cambridge Journal of Education, 1,* 83–91.

Purcell, P., & Stewart, L. (1990). Dick and Jane in 1989. *Sex Roles, 22,* 177–185.

Putnam, R. T., & Borko, H. (1998). Teacher learning: Implications of new views of cognition. In B. J. Biddle, T. L. Good, & I. F. Goodson (Eds.), *The international handbook of teachers and teaching.* Dordrecht, the Netherlands: Kluwer.

Quay, H. C., & Peterson, D. R. (1987). *Manual for the revised behavior problem checklist.* Coral Cables, FL: Author.

Rachlin, H. (1991). *Introduction to modern behaviorism* (3rd ed.), New York: W. H. Freeman.

Raffini, J. P. (1996). *150 ways to increase intrinsic motivation in the classroom.* Boston: Allyn & Bacon.

Randhawa, B. S., & Randhawa, J. S. (1993). Understanding differences in the components of mathematics achievement. *Psychological Reports, 73,* 435–444.

Range, L. M. (1993). Suicide prevention: Guidelines for schools. *Educational Psychology Review, 5,* 135–154.

Rathus, S. A. (1988). *Understanding child development.* New York: Holt, Rinehart & Winston.

Raudenbush, S. (1984). Magnitude of teacher expectancy effects on pupil IQ as a function of the credibility of expectancy induction: A synthesis of findings from 18 experiments. *Journal of Educational Psychology, 76,* 85–97.

Raudsepp, E., & Haugh, G. P. (1977). *Creative growth games.* New York: Harcourt Brace Jovanovich.

Recht, D. R., & Leslie, L. (1988). Effect of prior knowledge on good and poor readers' memory of text. *Journal of Educational Psychology, 80,* 16–20.

Reder, L. M. (1996). Different research programs on metacognition: Are the boundaries imaginary? *Learning and Individual Differences, 8,* 383–390.

Redfield, D. L., & Rousseau, E. W. (1981). A meta-analysis of experimental research on teacher questioning behavior. *Review of Educational Research, 51,* 181–193.

Reeve, J. (1996). *Motivating others: Nurturing inner motivational resources.* Boston: Allyn & Bacon.

Reeve, J., Bolt, E., & Cai, Y. (1999). Autonomy-supportive teachers: How they teach and motivate students. *Journal of Educational Psychology, 91,* 537–548.

Reich, P. A. (1986). *Language development.* Englewood Cliffs, NJ: Prentice-Hall.

Reisberg, D., & Heuer, F. (1992). Remembering the details of emotional events. In E. Winograd & U. Neisser (Eds.), *Affect and accuracy in recall: Studies of "flashbulb" memories.* Cambridge, England: Cambridge University Press.

Rembolt, C. (1998). Making violence unacceptable. *Educational Leadership, 56* (1), 32–38.

Render, G. F., Padilla, J. N. M., & Krank, H. M. (1989). What research really shows about assertive discipline. *Educational Leadership, 46*(6), 72–75.

Rennie, L. J., & Parker, L. H. (1987). Detecting and accounting for gender differences in mixed-sex and single-sex groupings in science lessons. *Educational Review, 39*(1), 65–73.

Renninger, K. A., Hidi, S., & Krapp, A. (Eds.) (1992). *The role of interest in learning and development.* Hillsdale, NJ: Lawrence Erlbaum.

Renzulli, J. S., & Reis, S. M. (1991). The schoolwide enrichment model: A comprehensive plan for the development of creative productivity. In N. Colangelo & G. Davis (Eds.), *Handbook of gifted education* (pp. 111–141). Boston: Allyn & Bacon.

Renzulli, J. S., & Smith, L. H. (1978). *The Learning Styles Inventory: A measure of student preferences for instructional techniques.* Mansfield Center, CT: Creative Learning Press.

Resnick, L. (1987). Learning in school and out. *Educational Researcher, 16*(9), 13–20.

Resnick, L. B. (1981). Instructional psychology. *Annual Review of Psychology, 32,* 659–704.

Reynolds, A. (1992). Grade retention and school adjustment: An explanatory analysis. *Educational Evaluation and Policy Analysis, 14*(2), 101–121.

Reynolds, M. C., & Birch, J. W. (1988). *Adaptive mainstreaming: A primer for teachers and principals* (3rd ed.). New York: Longman.

Reynolds, W. M. (1980). Self-esteem and classroom behavior in elementary school children. *Psychology in the Schools, 17,* 273–277.

Rhode, G., Morgan, D. P., & Young, K. R. (1983). Generalization and maintenance of treatment gains of behaviorally handicapped students from resource rooms to regular classrooms using self-evaluation procedures. *Journal of Applied Behavior Analysis, 16,* 171–188.

Ricciardelli, L. A. (1992). Bilingualism and cognitive development: Relation to threshold theory. *Journal of Psycholinguistic Research, 21,* 301–316.

Rice, M. L. (1989). Children's language acquisition. *American Psychologist, 44,* 149–156.

Richardson, T. M., & Benbow, C. P. (1990). Long-term effects of acceleration on the social-emotional adjustment of mathematically precocious youths. *Journal of Educational Psychology, 82,* 464–470.

Robert Wood Johnson (1988). *Serving handicapped children: A special report.* Princeton, NJ: Robert Wood Johnson Foundation.

Robinsin, A., & Clinkenbeard, P. R. (1998). Giftedness: An exceptionality examined. In J. T. Spence, J. M. Darley, & D. J. Foss (Eds.), *Annual Review of Psychology* (pp. 117–139). Palo Alto, CA: Annual Reviews.

Robinson, C. S., & Hayes, J. R. (1978). Making inferences about relevance in understanding problems. In R. Revlin & R. E. Mayer (Eds.), *Human reasoning.* Washington, DC: Winston.

Robinson, D. H. (1998). Graphic organizers as aids to test learning. *Reading Research and Instruction, 37,* 85–105.

Robinson, D. H., & Kiewra, K. A. (1995). Visual argument: Graphic outlines are superior to outlines in improving learning form text. *Journal of Educational Psychology, 87,* 455–467.

Roderick, M. (1994). Grade retention and school dropout: Investigating an association, *American Educational Research Journal, 31,* 729–760.

Rogers, C. R., & Freiberg, H. J. (1994). *Freedom to learn* (3rd ed.). Columbus, OH: Charles E. Merrill.

Rogoff, B. (1990). *Apprenticeship in thinking: Cognitive development in social context.* New York: Oxford University Press.

Rogoff, B., & Chavajay, P. (1995). What's become of the research on the cultural basis of cognitive development? *American Psychologist, 50,* 859–877.

Rogoff, B., & Morelli, G. (1989). Perspectives on children's development from cultural psychology. *American Psychologist, 44,* 343–348.

Rop, C. (1997/1998). Breaking the gender barrier in the physical sciences. *Educational Leadership, 55*(4), 58–60.

Rosch, E. H. (1973). On the internal structure of perceptual and semantic categories. In T. Moore (Ed.), *Cognitive development and the acquisition of language.* New York: Academic Press.

Rose, L. C., & Gallup, A. M. (1999). The 31st annual Phi Delta Kappa/Gallup Poll of the public's attitude toward the public schools. *Phi Delta Kappan, 81*(1), 41–58.

Rosen, L. A., O'Leary, S. G., Joyce, S. A., Conway, G., & Pfiffner, L. J. (1984). The importance of prudent negative consequences for maintaining the appropriate behavior of hyperactive students. *Journal of Abnormal Child Psychology, 12,* 581–604.

Rosenshine, B. (1977, April). *Primary grades instruction and student achievement.* Paper presented at the annual meeting of the American Educational Research Association, New York.

Rosenshine, B. (1979). Content, time, and direct instruction. In P. Peterson & H. Walberg (Eds.), *Research on teaching: Concepts, findings, and implications* (pp. 28–56). Berkeley, CA: McCutchan.

Rosenshine, B. (1986). Synthesis of research on explicit teaching. *Educational Leadership, 43*(7), 60–69.

Rosenshine, B. (1988). Explicit teaching. In D. Berliner & B. Rosenshine (Eds.), *Talks to teachers* (pp. 75–92). New York: Random House.

Rosenshine, B., & Furst, N. (1973). The use of direct observation to study teaching. In R. Travers (Ed.), *Second handbook of research on teaching.* Chicago: Rand McNally.

Rosenshine, B., & Meister, C. (1992, April). *The uses of scaffolds for teaching less structured academic tasks.* Paper presented at the annual meeting of the American Educational Research Association, San Francisco.

Rosenshine, B., & Meister, C. (1994). Reciprocal teaching: A review of the research. *Review of Educational Research, 64,* 479–530.

Rosenshine, B., & Stevens, R. (1986). Teaching functions. In M. Wittrock (Ed.), *Handbook of research on teaching* (3rd ed., pp. 376–391). New York: Macmillan.

Rosenthal, R. (1987). Pygmalion effects: Existence, magnitude and social importance. A reply to Wineburg. *Educational Researcher, 16,* 37–41.

Rosenthal, R. (1995). Critiquing Pygmalion: A 25-year perspective. *Current Directions in Psychological Science, 4,* 171–172.

Rosenthal, R., and Jacobson, L. (1968). *Pygmalion in the classroom.* New York: Holt, Rinehart, Winston.

Roskos, K., & Neuman, S. B. (1993). Descriptive observation of adults' facilitation of literacy in young children's play. *Early Childhood Research Quarterly, 8,* 77–98.

Roskos, K., & Neuman, S. B. (1995). Two beginning kindergarten teachers' planning for integrated literacy instruction. *Elementary School Journal, 96,* 195–215.

Roskos, K., & Neuman, S. B. (1998). Play as an opportunity for literacy. In O. N. Saracho & B. Spodek (Eds.), *Multiple perspectives on play in early childhood education* (pp. 100–115). Albany: State University of New York Press.

Rosser, R. (1994). *Cognitive development: Psychological and biological perspectives.* Boston: Allyn & Bacon.

Roth, W.-M., & Bowen, G. M. (1995). Knowing and interacting: A study of culture, practices, and resources in a grade 8 open-inquiry science guided by an apprenticeship metaphor. *Cognition and Instruction, 13,* 73–128.

Roth, W-M., & McGinn, M. K. (1997). Toward a new perspective on problem solving. *Canadian Journal of Education, 22,* 18–32.

Roth, W-M., & Roychoudhury, A. (1993). The development of science process skills in authentic contexts. *Journal of Research on Science Teaching, 30,* 127–152.

Rotherham-Borus, M. J. (1994). Bicultural reference group orientations and adjustment. In M. Bernal & G. Knight (Eds.), *Ethnic identity.* Albany, NY: State University of New York Press.

Rowe, M. B. (1974). Wait-time and rewards as instructional variables: Their influence on language, logic, and fate control. Part 1: Wait-time. *Journal of Research in Science Teaching, 11,* 81–94.

Rumelhart, D., & Ortony, A. (1977). The representation of knowledge in memory. In R. Anderson, R. Spiro, & W. Montague (Eds.), *Schooling and the acquisition of knowledge.* Hillsdale, NJ: Erlbaum.

Ryan, R. M. (1991). The nature of the self in autonomy and relatedness. In G. R. Goethals & J. Strauss (Eds.), *Multidisciplinary perspectives on the self.* New York: Springer-Verlag.

Ryan, R. M., & Deci, E. L. (1996). When paradigms clash: Comments on Cameron and Pierce's claim that rewards do not undermine intrinsic motivation. *Review of Educational Research, 66,* 33–38.

Ryan, R. M., & Grolnick, W. S. (1986). Origins and pawns in the classroom: Self-report and projective assessments of individual differences in the children's perceptions. *Journal of Personality and Social Psychology, 50,* 550–558.

Ryans, D. G. (1960). *Characteristics of effective teachers, their descriptions, comparisons and appraisal: A research study.* Washington, DC: American Council on Education.

Sabers, D. S., Cushing, K. S., & Berliner, D. C. (1991). Differences among teachers in a task characterized by simultaneity, multidi-mensionality, and immediacy. *American Educational Research Journal, 28,* 68–87.

Sadker, M., & Sadker, D. (1986a). Questioning skills. In J. Cooper (Ed.), *Classroom teaching skills* (3rd ed., pp. 143–180). Lexington, MA: D. C. Heath.

Sadker, M., & Sadker, D. (1986b). Sexism in the classroom: From grade school to graduate school. *Phi Delta Kappan, 68,* 512.

Sadker, M., & Sadker, D. (1994). *Failing at fairness: How America's schools cheat girls.* New York; Scribner.

Sadker, M., Sadker, D., & Klein, S. (1991). The issue of gender in elementary and secondary education. *Review of Research in Education, 17,* 269–334.

Salomon, G., & Perkins, D. N. (1989). Rocky roads to transfer: Rethinking mechanisms of a neglected phenomenon. *Educational Psychologist, 24,* 113–142.

Salovey, P., & Mayer, J. D. (1990). Emotional intelligence. *Imagination, Cognition, and Personality, 9,* 185–211.

Sanchez, F., & Anderson, M. L. (1990, May). Gang mediation: A process that works. *Principal,* 54–56.

Sandrock, J. W. (1996). *Adolescence.* Dubuque, IA: Brown & Benchmark.

Sattler, J. (1992). *Assessment of children* (3rd ed. revised). San Diego: Jerome M. Sattler.

Savage, T. V. (1999). *Teaching self-control through management and discipline.* Boston: Allyn & Bacon.

Sawyer, R. J., Graham, S., & Harris, K. R. (1992). Direct teaching, strategy instruction, and strategy instruction with explicit self-regulation: Effects on the composition skills and self-efficacy of learning disabled students. *Journal of Educational Psychology, 84,* 340–352.

Scardamalia, M., & Bereiter, C. (1996). Adaptation and understanding: A case for new cultures of schooling. In S. Vosniado, E. De Corte, R. Glasse, & H. Mandl (Eds.), *International perspectives on the design of technology-supported learning environments* (pp. 149–163). Hillsdale, NJ: Lawrence Erlbaum.

Scarr, S., & Carter-Saltzman, L. (1982). Genetics and intelligence. In R. Sternberg (Ed.), *Handbook of human intelligence.* New York: Cambridge University Press.

Scarr, S., Weinberg, R. A., & Levine, A. (1986). *Understanding development.* New York: Harcourt Brace Jovanovich.

Scherer, M. (1993). On savage inequalities: A conversation with Jonathan Kozol. *Educational Leadership, 50*(4), 4–9.

Scherer, M. (1999). The discipline of hope: A conversation with Herb Kohl. *Educational Leadership, 56*(1), 8–13.

Schiefele, U. (1991). Interest, learning, and motivation. *Educational Psychologist, 26,* 299–324.

Schneider, W., & Bjorklund, D. F. (1992). Expertise, aptitude, and strategic remembering. *Child Development, 63,* 416–473.

Schoenfeld, A. H. (1979). Explicit heuristic training as a variable in problem solving performance. *Journal for Research in Mathematics Education, 10,* 173–187.

Schofield, J. W. (1991). School desegregation and intergroup relations. *Review of Research in Education, 17,* 235–412.

Schon, D. (1983). *The reflective practitioner.* New York: Basic Books.

Schonert-Reichl, K. A. (1994). Gender differences in depressive symptomatology and egocentrism in adolescence. *Journal of Early Adolescence, 14,* 49–65.

School Achievement Indicators Program. *Mathematics content: Percentage of 16-year-olds by performance level and by population.* Retrieved March 12, 1999: www. cmec.ca/saip/math97/Pages/App5.html.

Schunk, D. H. (1987). Peer models and children's behavioral change. *Review of Educational Research, 57,* 149–174.

Schunk, D. H. (1996a). Goal and self-evaluative influences during children's cognitive skill learning. *American Educational Research Journal, 33,* 359–382.

Schunk, D. H. (1996b). *Learning theories: An educational perspective* (2nd ed.). Columbus, OH: Merrill.

Schunk, D. H. (2000). *Learning theories: An educational perspective* (3rd ed.). Columbus, OH: Merrill/Prentice-Hall.

Schunk, D. H., & Hanson, A. R. (1985). Peer models: Influence on children's self-efficacy and achievement. *Journal of Educational Psychology, 77,* 313–322.

Schwartz, B., & Reisberg, D. (1991). *Learning and memory.* New York: Norton.

Seddon, G. M. (1978). The properties of Bloom's taxonomy of educational objectives for the cognitive domain. *Review of Educational Research, 48,* 303–323.

Seiber, J. E., O'Neil, H. F., & Tobias, S. (1977). *Anxiety, learning, and instruction.* Hillsdale, NJ: Erlbaum.

Seifert, K. L., & Hoffnung, R. J. (1991). *Child and adolescent development.* Boston: Houghton Mifflin.

Seligman, M. E. P. (1975). *Helplessness: On depression, development, and death.* San Francisco: Freeman.

Selman, R. L. (1980). *The growth of interpersonal understanding.* New York: Academic Press.

Semb, G. B., & Ellis, J. A. (1994). Knowledge taught in school: What is remembered? *Review of Educational Research, 64,* 253–286.

Serbin, L., & O'Leary, D. (1975, January). How nursery schools teach girls to shut up. *Psychology Today,* pp. 56–58.

Serpell, R. (1993). Interface between sociocultural and psychological aspects of cognition. In E. Forman, N. Minick, & C. A. Stone (Eds.), *Contexts for learning: Sociocultural dynamics in children's development* (pp. 357–368). New York: Oxford University Press.

Shapiro, E. S., & Ager, C. (1992). Assessment of special education students in regular education programs: Linking assessment to instruction. *The Elementary School Journal, 92,* 283–296.

Shapiro, J. (1994). Research perspectives on whole language. In V. Froese (Ed.), *Whole language: Practice and theory* (pp. 433–470). Scarborough, Ontario: Allyn & Bacon Canada.

Shavelson, R. J. (1987). Planning. In M. Dunkin (Ed.), *The international encyclopedia of teaching and teacher education* (pp. 483–486). New York: Pergamon Press.

Shavelson, R. J., & Bolus, R. (1982). Self-concept: The interplay of theory and methods. *Psychology, 74,* 3–17.

Shavelson, R. J., Gao, X., & Baxter, G. (1993). *Sampling variability of performance assessments.* CSE Technical Report 361. Los Angeles: UCLA Center for the Study of Evaluation.

Shepard, L. A., & Smith, M. L. (1989). Academic and emotional effects of kindergarten retention. In L. Shepard & M. Smith (Eds.), *Flunking grades: Research and policies on retention* (pp. 79–107). Philadelphia: Falmer Press.

Sherman, A. (1994). *Wasting America's future: The Children's Defense Fund report on the costs of child poverty.* Boston: Beacon Press.

Sherman, J. G., Ruskin, R. S., & Semb, G. B. (Eds.) (1982). *The Personalized System of Instruction: 48 seminal papers.* Lawrence, KS: TRI Publications.

Sherman, J. W., & Bessenoff, G. R. (1999). Stereotypes as source-monitoring cues: On the interaction between episodic and semantic memory. *Psychological Science, 10,* 106–110.

Shields, P., Gordon, J., & Dupree, D. (1983). Influence of parent practices upon the reading achievement of good and poor readers. *Journal of Negro Education, 52,* 436–445.

Shoda, Y., Mischel, W., & Peake, P. K. (1990). Predicting adolescent cognitive and self-regulatory competencies from preschool delay of gratification. *Developmental Psychology, 26,* 978–986.

Shuell, T. (1996). Teaching and learning in a classroom context. In D. Berliner & R. Calfee (Eds.), *Handbook of educational psychology* (pp. 726–764). New York: Macmillan.

Shuell, T. J. (1981, April). *Toward a model of learning from instruction.* Paper presented at a meeting of the American Educational Research Association, Los Angeles.

Shuell, T. J. (1986). Cognitive conceptions of learning. *Review of Educational Research, 56,* 411–436.

Shuell, T. J. (1990). Phases of meaningful learning. *Review of Educational Psychology, 60,* 531–548.

Shulman, L. S. (1987). Knowledge and teaching: Foundations of the new reform. *Harvard Educational Review, 19*(2), 4–14.

Shultz, J., & Florio, S. (1979). Stop and freeze: The negotiation of social and physical space in a kindergarten/first grade classroom. *Anthropology and Education Quarterly, 10,* 166–181.

Siegel, J., & Shaughnessy, M. F. (1994). Educating for understanding: An interview with Howard Gardner. *Phi Delta Kappan, 75,* 536–566.

Siegel, L. S. (1989). I.Q. is irrelevant to the definition of learning disabilities. *Journal of Learning Disabilities, 22,* 469–479.

Siegel, L. S. (1999). Issues in the definition and diagnosis of learning disabilities. *Journal of Learning Disabilities, 32,* 304–319.

Siegler, R. S. (1991). *Children's thinking* (2nd ed.). Englewood Cliffs, NJ: Prentice-Hall.

Siegler, R. S. (1993). Adaptive and non-adaptive characteristics of low-income children's mathematical strategy use. In B. Penner (Ed.), *The challenge in mathematics and science education: Psychology's response* (pp. 341–366). Washington, DC: American Psychological Association.

Sillars, L. (1995). Studying crime in school. *Alberta Report, 22*(25), 37.

Simmons, R. G. , & Blyth, D. A. (1987). *Moving into adolescence.* New York: Aldine De Gruyter.

Simon, D. P., & Chase, W. G. (1973). Skill in chess. *American Scientist, 61,* 394–403.

Simon, H. A. (1995). The information-processing view of mind. *American Psychologist, 50,* 507–508.

Simpson, E. J. (1972). "The classification of educational objectives in the psychomotor domain." *The Psychomotor Domain. Vol 3.* Washington, Gryphon House.

Singley, K., & Anderson, J. R. (1989). *The transfer of cognitive skill.* Cambridge, MA: Harvard University Press.

Sisk, D. A. (1988). Children at risk: The identification of the gifted among the minority. *Gifted Education International, 5,* 138–141.

Sizer, T. (1984). *Horace's compromise: The dilemma of the American high school* (updated ed.). Princeton, NJ: Houghton Mifflin.

Skinner, B. F. (1950). Are theories of learning necessary? *Psychological Review, 57,* 193–216.

Skinner, B. F. (1953). *Science and human behavior.* New York: Macmillan.

Skinner, B. F. (1989). The origins of cognitive thought. *American Psychologist, 44,* 13–18.

Skoe, E. E., Pratt, M. W., Matthews, M., & Curror, S. E. (1996). The ethic of care: Stability over time, gender differences, and correlates in mid- to late adulthood. *Psychology and Aging, 11,* 280–292.

Slaby, R. G., Roedell, W. C., Arezzo, D., & Hendrix, K. (1995). *Early violence prevention.* Washington, DC: National Association for the Education of Young Children.

Slavin, R. E. (1987). Ability grouping and student achievement in elementary schools: A best-evidence synthesis. *Review of Educational Research, 57,* 293–336.

Slavin, R. E. (1990). Achievement effects of ability grouping in secondary schools: A best-evidence synthesis. *Review of Educational Research, 60,* 471–500.

Slavin, R. E. (1995). *Cooperative learning* (2nd ed.). Boston: Allyn & Bacon.

Slavin, R. E., Karweit, N. L., & Madden, N. A. (1989). *Effective programs for students at risk.* Boston: Allyn & Bacon.

Smetana, J. G., & Braeges, J. L. (1990). The development of toddlers' moral and conventional judgments. *Merrill-Palmer Quarterly, 36,* 329–346.

Smith, C. B. (Moderator) (1994). *Whole language: The debate.* Bloomington, IN: EDINFO Press.

Smith, D. D. (1998). *Introduction to special education: Teaching in an age of challenge* (3rd ed.). Boston: Allyn & Bacon.

Smith, F. (1975). *Comprehension and learning: A conceptual framework for teachers.* New York: Holt, Rinehart & Winston.

Smith, J. D., & Caplan, J. (1988). Cultural differences in cognitive style development. *Developmental Psychology, 24,* 46–52.

Smith, M. (1993). Some school-based violence prevention strategies. *NASSP Bulletin, 77*(557), 70–75.

Smith, S.M. (1985). A method for teaching name mnemonics. *Teaching of Psychology, 12,* 156–158.

Smith, S. M., Glenberg, A., & Bjork, R. A. (1978). Environmental context and human memory. *Memory and Cognition, 6,* 342–353.

Snider, V. E. (1990). What we know about learning styles from research in special education. *Educational Leadership, 48*(2), 53.

Snow, C. E. (1987). Beyond conversation: Second language learners' acquisition of description and explanation. In J. P. Lantolf & A. Labarca (Eds.), *Research in second language learning: Focus on the classroom* (pp. 3–16). Norwood, NJ: Ablex.

Snow, C. E. (1993). Families as social contexts for literacy development. In C. Daiute (Ed.), *New directions for child development* (No. 61, pp. 11–24). San Francisco: Jossey-Bass.

Snow, R. E. (1995). Pygmalion and intelligence. *Current Directions in Psychological Science, 4,* 169–171.

Snow, R. E., Corno, L., & Jackson, D. (1996) Individual differences in affective and cognitive functions. In D. Berliner & R. Calfee (Eds.), *Handbook of educational psychology* (pp. 243–310). New York: Macmillan.

Snowman, J. (1984). Learning tactics and strategies. In G. Phye & T. Andre (Eds.), *Cognitive instructional psychology.* Orlando, FL: Academic Press.

Soar, R. S., & Soar, R. M. (1979). Emotional climate and management. In P. Peterson & H. Walberg (Eds.), *Research on teaching: Concepts, findings, and implications.* Berkeley, CA: McCutchan.

Sobesky, W. E. (1983). The effects of situational factors on moral judgment. *Child Development, 54,* 575–584.

Sokolove, S., Garrett, J., Sadker, D., & Sadker, M. (1986). Interpersonal communications skills. In J. Cooper (Ed.), *Classroom teaching skills: A handbook.* Lexington, MA: D. C. Heath.

Spearman, C. (1927). *The abilities of man: Their nature and measurement.* New York: Macmillan.

Specifications for the 1999 Provincial Learning Assessment of reading comprehension. British Columbia Ministry of Education. Retrieved March 12, 1999: www.bced. gov.bc.ca/assessment/ tablespecs.htm.

Spector, J. E. (1992). Predicting progress in beginning reading: Dynamic assessment of phonemic awareness. *Journal of Educational Psychology, 84,* 353–363.

Spencer, M. B., & Markstrom-Adams, C. (1990). Identity processes among racial and ethnic-minority children in America. *Child Development, 61,* 290–310.

Spiro, R. J., Feltovich, P. J., Jacobson, M. L., & Coulson, R. L. (1991). Cognitive flexibility, constructivism, and hypertext: Random access instruction for advanced knowledge acquisition in ill-structured domains. *Educational Technology, 31*(5), 24–33.

Sprague, J., & Walker, H. (2000). Early identification and intervention for youth with antisocial and violent behavior. *Exceptional Children, 66,* 367–379.

Stahl, S. A., & Miller, P. D. (1989). Whole language and language experience approaches for beginning reading: A quantitative research synthesis. *Review of Educational Research, 59,* 87–116.

Stanovich, K. (1993/4). Romance and reality. *The Reading Teacher, 47,* 280–291.

Stanovich, K. E. (1992). *How to think straight about psychology* (3rd ed.). Glenview, IL: Scott, Foresman.

Stanovich, K. E. (1998). Cognitive neuroscience and educational psychology: What season is it? *Educational Psychology Review, 10,* 419–426.

Stanovich, K. E., West, R. F., & Freeman, D. J. (1984). A longitudinal study of sentence context effects in second-grade children: Tests of an interactive-compensatory model. *Journal of Experimental Child Psychology, 32,* 185–199.

Starch, D., & Elliot, E. C. (1912). Reliability of grading high school work in English. *Scholastic Review, 20,* 442–457.

Starch, D., & Elliot, E. C. (1913a). Reliability of grading work in history. *Scholastic Review, 21,* 676–681.

Starch, D., & Elliot, E. C. (1913b). Reliability of grading work in mathematics. *Scholastic Review, 21,* 254–259.

Starr, R. H., Jr. (1979). Child abuse. *American Psychologist, 34,* 872–878.

Statistics Canada. (1996a). "Low income families." *Canadian Census.* Retrieved March 1999 from: www.statcan.ca/english/ Pgdb/People/Families/famil60a.htm.

Statistics Canada. (1996b). "Population by language use." *Canadian Census.* Retrieved March 1999 from: www. statcan.ca/english/Pgdb/People/Population/demo29a.htm.

Statistics Canada. (1996c). "Single family households." *Canadian Census.* Retrieved March 1999: www.statcan. ca/People/Families/ famil51a.htm.

Statistics Canada. (1998a). *Average hours per week of television viewing.* Retrieved from www.statcan.ca/english/Pgdb/ People/Culture/arts23.htm.

Statistics Canada. (1998b). *Family violence in Canada: A statistical profile.* Retrieved from www.statcan.ca:80/Daily/English/ 980528/d980528.htm#ART1.

Statistics Canada. (2000, September 28). *Divorces: 1998.* Retrieved from www.statcan.ca/Daily/English/000928/d000928b.htm.

Stein, B. S., Littlefield, J., Bransford, J. D., & Persampieri, M. (1984). Elaboration and knowledge acquisition. *Memory and Cognition, 12,* 522–529.

Stephen, J., Fraser, E., & Marcia, J. E. (1992). Moratorium achievement (Mama) cycles in life span identity development: Vale orientations and reasoning system correlates. *Journal of Adolescence, 15,* 283–300.

Stepien, W., & Gallagher, S. (1993). Problem-based learning: As authentic as it gets. *Educational Leadership, 50*(7), 25–28.

Sternberg, R. (1985). *Beyond IQ: A triarchic theory of human intelligence.* New York: Cambridge University Press.

Sternberg, R. (1990). *Metaphors of mind: Conceptions of the nature of intelligence.* New York: Cambridge University Press.

Sternberg, R., & Davidson, J. (1982, June). The mind of the puzzler. *Psychology Today,* pp. 37–44.

Sternberg, R. J. (1998). Myths, countermyths, and truths about intelligence. In A. Woolfolk (Ed.), *Readings in educational psychology* (2nd ed., pp. 53–60). Boston: Allyn & Bacon.

Sternberg, R. J. (1999). *Cognitive psychology* (2nd ed.). Ft. Worth, TX: Harcourt Brace.

Sternberg, R. J., & Detterman, D. L. (Eds.) (1986). *What is intelligence? Contemporary viewpoints on its nature and definition.* Norwood, NJ: Ablex.

Sternberg, R. J., & Kaufman, J. C. (1998). Human abilities. In J. T. Spence, J. M. Darley, & D. J. Foss (Eds.), *Annual Review of Psychology* (pp. 479–502). Palo Alto, CA: Annual Reviews.

Sternberg, R. J., & Wagner, R. K. (1993). The g-ocentric view of intelligence and job performance is wrong. *Current Directions in Psychological Science, 2,* 1–5.

Sternberg, R. J., Wagner, R. K., Williams, W. M., & Horvath, J. A. (1995). Testing common sense. *American Psychologist, 50,* 912–927.

Stevenson, H. W., & Stigler, J. (1992). *The learning gap.* New York: Summit Books.

Stipek, D. J. (1993). *Motivation to learn* (2nd ed.). Boston: Allyn & Bacon.

Stipek, D. J. (1996). Motivation and Instruction. In D. Berliner & R. Calfee (Eds.), *Handbook of educational psychology* (pp. 85–109). New York: Macmillan.

Stipek, D. J. (1998). *Motivation to learn* (3rd ed.). Boston: Allyn & Bacon.

Stodolsky, S. S. (1988). *The subject matters: Classroom activity in math and social studies.* Chicago: University of Chicago Press.

Strike, K. (1975). The logic of discovery. *Review of Educational Research, 45,* 461–483.

Student Assessment and Program Evaluation Branch. (2000, August). *History 12 examination specifications September 2001.* Victoria, BC: Author.

Sulzby, E., & Teale, W. (1991). Emergent literacy. In R. Barr, M. L. Kamil, P. B. Mosenthal, & P. D. Pearson (Eds.), *Handbook of reading research,* Vol. II (pp. 727–758). New York: Longman.

Swanson, H. L. (1990). The influence of metacognitive knowledge and aptitude on problem solving. *Journal of Educational Psychology, 82,* 306–314.

Swanson, H. L., O'Conner, J. E., & Cooney, J. B. (1990). An information processing analysis of expert and novice teachers' problem solving. *American Educational Research Journal, 27,* 533–556.

Sweller, J., van Merrienboer, J. J. G., & Paas, F. G. W. C. (1998). Cognitive architecture and instructional design. *Educational Psychology Review, 10,* 251–296.

Symons, S., Woloshyn, V., & Pressley, M. (1994). The scientific evaluation of the whole language approach to literacy development [Special Issue]. *Educational Psychologist, 29*(4).

Tait, H., & Entwistle, N. J. (in press). Identifying students at risk through ineffective study strategies. *Higher Education.*

Tanner, J. M. (1990). *Foetus to man* (2nd ed.). Cambridge: Harvard University Press.

Tarvis, C. (1998, September 13). Peer pressure. [Review of the book *The nurture assumption: Why children turn out the way they do; parents matter less than you think and peers matter more.*] *New York Review of Books,* 14–15.

Task Force on Pediatric AIDS: American Psychological Association. (1989). Pediatric AIDS and human immunodeficiency virus infection: Psychological issues. *American Psychologist, 44,* 258–264.

Tennyson, R. D. (1981, April). *Concept learning effectiveness using prototype and skill development presentation forms.* Paper presented at the annual meeting of the American Educational Research Association, Los Angeles.

Tennyson, R. D., & Cocchiarella, M. J. (1986). An empirically based instructional design theory for teaching concepts. *Review of Educational Research, 56,* 40–71.

Terman, L. M., Baldwin, B. T., & Bronson, E. (1925). Mental and physical traits of a thousand gifted children. In L. M. Terman (Ed.), *Genetic studies of genius* (Vol. 1). Stanford, CA: Stanford University Press.

Terman, L. M., & Oden, M. H. (1947). The gifted child grows up. In L. M. Terman (Ed.), *Genetic studies of genius* (Vol. 4). Stanford, CA: Stanford University Press.

Terman, L. M., & Oden, M. H. (1959). The gifted group in mid-life. In L. M. Terman (Ed.), *Genetic studies of genius* (Vol. 5). Stanford, CA: Stanford University Press.

Tharp, R. G. (1989). Psychocultural variables and constants: Effects on teaching and learning in schools. *American Psychologist, 44,* 349–359.

Tharp, R. G., & Gallimore, R. (1988). *Rousing minds to life: Teaching, learning, and schooling in social context.* New York: Cambridge University Press.

The daily (May 28, 1998). *Family violence in Canada: A statistical profile.*

The scoring of essay questions: History 12 provincial examinations. British Columbia Ministry of Education. Retrieved March 12, 1999: www.bced.gov.bc.ca/exams/scoringguides/hishsp.htm.

Thoma, S. J. (1986). Estimating gender differences in the comprehension and preference of moral issues. *Developmental Review, 6,* 165–180.

Thomas, E. L., & Robinson, H. A. (1972). *Improving reading in every class: A sourcebook for teachers.* Boston: Allyn & Bacon.

Thompson, R. A., & Wyatt, J. M. (1999). Current research on child maltreatment: Implications for educators. *Educational Psychology Review, 11,* 173–202.

Thorndike, E. L. (1913). Educational psychology. In *The psychology of learning* (Vol. 2). New York: Teachers College, Columbia University.

Thorndike, R., Hagen, E., & Sattler, J. (1986). *The Stanford-Binet Intelligence Scale* (4th ed.). Chicago: Riverside.

Thurstone, E. L. (1938). Primary mental abilities. *Psychometric Monographs,* No. 1.

Tierney, R. J., Readence, J. E., & Dishner, E. K. (1990). *Reading strategies and practices: A compendium* (3rd ed.). Boston: Allyn & Bacon.

Timmer, S. G., Eccles, J., & O'Brien, K. (1988). How children use time. In F. Juster & F. Stafford (Eds.), *Time, goods, and well-being.* Ann Arbor, MI: Institute for Social Research, University of Michigan.

Tishman, S., Perkins, D., & Jay, E. (1995). *The thinking classroom: Learning and teaching in a culture of thinking.* Boston: Allyn & Bacon.

Tobias, S. (1985). Text anxiety: Interference, defective skills, and cognitive capacity. *Educational Psychologist, 20,* 135–142.

Tobin, K. (1987). The role of wait time in higher cognitive learning. *Review of Educational Research, 56,* 69–95.

Tobin, K. (1990, April). *Metaphors in the construction of teacher knowledge.* Paper presented at the Annual Meeting of the American Educational Research Association, Boston.

Tochon, F., & Munby, H. (1993). Novice and expert teachers' time epistemology: A wave function from didactics to pedagogy. *Teaching and Teacher Education, 9,* 205–218.

Tomasello, M., Kruger, A. C., & Ratner, H. H. (1993). Cultural learning. *Behavioral and Brain Sciences, 16,* 495–552.

Tomlinson-Keasey, C., & Little, T. D. (1990). Predicting educational attainment, occupational achievement intellectual skill, and personal adjustment among gifted men and women. *Journal of Educational Psychology, 82,* 442–455.

Torgesen, J. K., Wagner, R. K., Rashotte, C. A., Rose, E., Lindamood, P., Conway, T., & Garvan, C. (1999). *Journal of Educational Psychology, 91,* 579–593.

Torrance, E. P. (1972). Predictive validity of the Torrance tests of creative thinking. *Journal of Creative Behavior, 6,* 236–262.

Torrance, E. P. (1986). Teaching creative and gifted learners. In M. Wittrock (Ed.), *Handbook of research on teaching* (3rd ed., pp. 630–647). New York: Macmillan.

Torrance, E. P., & Hall, L. K. (1980). Assessing the future reaches of creative potential. *Journal of Creative Behavior, 14,* 1–19.

Tremblay, R. E., Boulerice, B., Harden, P. W., McDuff, P., Perusse, D., Pihl, R. O., & Zoccolillo, M. (1996). Do children in Canada become more aggressive as they approach adolescence? *Growing Up in Canada: National Longitudinal Survey of Children and Youth.* Human Resources Development: Statistics Canada.

Trickett, E., & Moos, R. (1974). Personal correlates of contrasting environments: Student satisfaction with high school classrooms. *American Journal of Community Psychology, 2,* 1–12.

Tschannen-Moran, M., Woolfolk Hoy, A., & Hoy, W. K. (1998). Teacher efficacy: Its meaning and measure. *Review of Educational Research, 68,* 202–248.

Turiel, E. (1983). *The development of social knowledge: Morality and convention.* New York: Cambridge University Press.

Urdan, T. C., & Maehr, M. L. (1995). Beyond a two-goal theory of motivation and achievement: A case for social goals. *Review of Educational Research, 65,* 213–243.

Vandervelden, M. C., & Siegel, L. S. (1995). Phonological recoding and phoneme awareness in early literacy: A developmental approach. *Reading Research Quarterly, 30,* 854–875.

Van Houten, R., & Doleys, D. M. (1983). Are social reprimands effective? In S. Axelrod & J. Apsche (Eds.), *The effects of punishment on human behavior.* San Diego: Academic Press.

Van Metter, P., Yokoi, L., & Pressley, M. (1994). College students' theory of note-taking derived from their perceptions of note-taking. *Journal of Educational Psychology, 86,* 323–338.

Veenman, S. (1984). Perceived problems of beginning teachers. *Review of Educational Research, 54,* 143–178.

Vellutino, F. R. (1991). Introduction to three studies on reading acquisition: Convergent findings on theoretical foundations of code-oriented versus whole-language approaches to reading instruction. *Journal of Educational Psychology, 83,* 437–443.

Vera, A. H., & Simon, H. A. (1993). Situated action: A symbolic interpretation. *Cognitive Science, 17,* 7–48.

Vispoel, W. P. (1995). Self-concept inartistic domains: An extension of the Shavelson, Hubmner, and Stanton (1976) model. *Journal of Educational Psychology, 87,* 134–153.

Vispoel, W. P., & Austin, J. R. (1995). Success and failure in junior high school: A critical incident approach to understanding students' attributional beliefs. *American Educational Research Journal, 32,* 377–412.

von Glaserfeld, E. (1990). An Exposition of constructivism: Why some like it radical. In R. Davis, C. Maher, & N. Noddings (Eds.). *Constructivist views on the teaching and learning of mathematics* (pp. 19–30). Monograph 4 of the National Council of Teachers of Mathematics, Reston, VA.

von Glaserfeld, E. (1995). A constructivist approach to teaching. In L. Steffe & J. Gale (Eds.), *Constructivism in education* (p. 5). Hillsdale, NJ: Lawrence Erlbaum.

von Glaserfeld, E. (1997). Amplification of a constructivist perspective. *Issues in Education: Contributions from Educational Psychology, 3,* 203–210.

Vroom, V. (1964). *Work and motivation.* New York: Wiley.

Vygotsky, L. S. (1978). *Mind in society: The development of higher mental process.* Cambridge, MA: Harvard University Press.

Vygotsky, L. S. (1986). *Thought and language.* Cambridge, MA: MIT Press.

Vygotsky, L. S. (1987). *Problems of general psychology.* New York: Plenum.

Vygotsky, L. S. (1993). *The collected works of L. S. Vygotsky: Vol. 2* (J. Knox & C. Stevens, Trans.). New York: Plenum.

Walberg, H. J. (1990). Productive teaching and instruction: Assessing the knowledge base. *Phi Delta Kappan, 72,* 470–478.

Walker, L. J. (1991). Sex differences in moral reasoning. In W. M. Kurtines & J. L. Gewirtz (Eds.), *Handbook of moral behavior and development* (Vol. 2, pp. 333–362). Hillsdale, NJ: Erlbaum.

Walker, L. J., & Pitts, R. C. (1998). Naturalistic conceptions of moral maturity. *Developmental Psychology, 34,* 403–419.

Walker, L. J., Pitts, R. C., Hennig, K. H., & Matsuba, M. K. (1995). Reasoning about morality and real-life moral problems. In M. Killen & D. Hart (Eds.), *Morality in everyday life: Developmental perspectives* (pp. 371–407). Cambridge, England: Cambridge University Press.

Walton, G. *Identification of the intellectually gifted children in the public school kindergarten.* Unpublished doctoral dissertation, University of California, Los Angeles, 1961.

Wang, A. Y., & Thomas, M. H. (1995). Effects of keywords on long-term retention: Help or hindrance? *Journal of Educational Psychology, 87,* 468–475.

Wang, A. Y., Thomas, M. H., & Ouellette, J. A. (1992). Keyword mnemonic and retention of second-language vocabulary words. *Journal of Educational Psychology, 84,* 520–528.

Wang, M. C., & Palincsar, A. S. (1989). Teaching students to assume an active role in their learning. In M. Reynolds (Ed.), *Knowledge base for the beginning teacher* (pp. 71–84). New York: Pergamon.

Wasserman, E. A., & Miller, R. R. (1997). What's elementary about associative learning. In J. T. Spence, J. M. Darley, & D. J. Foss (Eds.), *Annual Review of Psychology* (pp. 573–607). Palo Alto, CA: Annual Reviews.

Waterman, A. S. (1992). Identity as an affect of optimal psychological functioning. In G. Adams, T. Gullota, & R. Montemayoor (Eds.), *Adolescent identity formation.* Newbury Park, CA: Sage.

Waters, H. F. (1993, July 12). Networks under the gun. *Newsweek,* pp. 64–66.

Webb, N. (1985). Verbal interaction and learning in peer-directed groups. *Theory into Practice, 24,* 32–39.

Webb, N., & Palincsar, A. (1996). Group processes in the classroom. In D. C. Berliner & R. C. Calfee (Eds.), *Handbook of educational psychology* (pp. 841–876). New York: Macmillan.

Weiland, A., & Coughlin, R. (1979). Self-identification and preferences: A comparison of White and Mexican-American first- and third-graders. *Journal of Cross-Cultural Psychology, 10,* 356–365.

Weinberg, R. A. (1989). Intelligence and IQ. *American Psychologist, 44,* 98–104.

Weiner, B. (1979). A theory of motivation for some classroom experiences. *Journal of Educational Psychology, 71,* 3–25.

Weiner, B. (1980). The role of affect in rational (attributional) approaches to human motivation. *Educational Researcher, 9,* 4–11.

Weiner, B. (1986). *An attributional theory of motivation and emotion.* New York: Springer.

Weiner, B. (1990). History of motivational research in education. *Journal of Educational Psychology, 82,* 616–622.

Weiner, B. (1992). *Human motivation: Metaphors, theories, and research.* Newbury Park, CA: Sage.

Weiner, B. (1994a). Ability versus effort revisited: The moral determinants of achievement evaluation an achievement as a moral system. *Educational Psychologist, 29,* 163–172.

Weiner, B. (1994b). Integrating social and persons theories of achievement striving. *Review of Educational Research, 64,* 557–575.

Weiner, B., & Graham, S. (1989). Understanding the motivational role of affect: Lifespan research from an attributional perspective. *Cognition and Emotion, 4,* 401–419.

Weiner, B., Russell, D., & Lerman, D. (1978). Affective consequences of causal ascriptions. In J. H. Harvey, W. J. Ickes, & R. F. Kidd (Eds.), *New directions in attribution research* (Vol. 2). Hillsdale, NJ: Erlbaum.

Weinert, F. E., & Helmke, A. (1995). Learning from wise mother nature or big brother instructor: The wrong choice as seen from an educational perspective. *Educational Psychologist, 30,* 135–143.

Weinstein, C., Ridley, D. S., Dahl, T., & Weber, E. S. (1988/1989). Helping students develop strategies for effective learning. *Educational Leadership, 46*(4), 17–19.

Weinstein, C., Woolfolk, A., Dittmeier, L., & Shanker, U. (1994). Protector or prison guard: Using metaphors and media to explore student teachers' thinking about classroom management. *Action in Teacher Education, 16*(1), 41–54.

Weinstein, C. E. (1994). Learning strategies and learning to learn. *Encyclopedia of Education.*

Weinstein, C. E., & McCombs, B. (in press). A model of strategic learning. In C. Weinstein & B. McCombs (Eds.), *Strategic learning: Skill, will, and self-regulation.* Hillsdale, NJ: Erlbaum.

Weinstein, C. S. (1977). Modifying student behavior in an open classroom through changes in the physical design. *American Educational Research Journal, 14,* 249–262.

Weinstein, C. S. (1996). *Secondary classroom management: Lessons from research and practice.* New York: McGraw-Hill.

Weinstein, C. S. (1999). Reflections on best practices and promising programs: Beyond assertive classroom discipline. In H. J. Freiberg (Ed.), *Beyond behaviorism: Changing the classroom management paradigm* (pp. 147–163). Boston: Allyn & Bacon.

Weinstein, C. S., & Mignano, A. J., Jr. (1997). *Elementary classroom management: Lessons from research and practice* (2nd ed.). New York: McGraw-Hill.

Weinstein, R. S., Madison, S. M., & Kuklinski, M. R. (1995). Raising expectations in schools: Obstacles and opportunities for change. *American Educational Research Journal, 32,* 121–159.

Weisberg, R. W. (1993). *Creativity: Beyond the myth of genius.* New York: W. H. Freemen.

Wentzel, K. R. (1999). Social-motivational processes and interpersonal relations: Implications for understanding motivation in school. *Journal of Educational Psychology, 91,* 76–97.

Wepman, J. M. (1973). *Auditory discrimination test* (rev. ed.). Chicago: Language Research Associates.

Werker, J. F. (1989). Becoming a native listener. *American Scientist, 77,* 54–59.

Wertsch, J., & Tulviste, P. (1992). L. S. Vygotsky and contemporary developmental psychology. *Developmental Psychology, 28,* 548–557.

Wertsch, J. V. (1991). *Voices of the mind: A sociocultural approach to mediated action.* Cambridge, MA: Harvard University Press.

Wessells, M. G. (1982). *Cognitive psychology.* New York: Harper & Row.

Wessman, A. (1972). Scholastic and psychological effects of a compensatory education program for disadvantaged high school students: Project A B C. *American Educational Research Journal, 9,* 361–372.

Wharton-McDonald, R., Pressley, M., & Mistretta, J. (1996). *Outstanding literacy instruction in first grade: Teacher practices and student achievement.* Albany, NY: National Reading Research Center.

When the student becomes the teacher. (1986, March). *Harvard Education Letter, 2*(3), 5–6.

White, K. R. (1982). The relation between socioeconomic status and academic achievement. *Psychological Bulletin, 91*(3), 461–481.

White, S., & Tharp, R. G. (1988, April). *Questioning and wait-time: A cross cultural analysis.* Paper presented at the annual meeting of the American Educational Research Association, New Orleans.

Whitehead, A. N. (1929). *The aims of education.* New York: Macmillan.

Whitehurst, G. J., Epstein, J. N., Angell, A. L., Payne, A. C., Crone, D. A., & Fischel, J. E. (1994). Outcomes of an emergent literacy program in headstart. *Journal of Educational Psychology, 86,* 542–555.

Wigfield, A., & Eccles, J. (1989). Test anxiety in elementary and secondary school students. *Educational Psychologist, 24,* 159–183.

Wigfield, A., Eccles, J. S., & Pintrich, P. R. (1996). Development between the ages of 11 and 25. In D. Berliner & R. Calfee (Eds.), *Handbook of Educational Psychology* (pp. 148–185). New York: Macmillan.

Wigfield, A., Eccles, J., MacIver, D., Rueman, D., & Midgley, C. (1991). Transitions at early adolescence: Changes in children's domain-specific self-perceptions and general self-esteem across the transition to junior high school. *Developmental Psychology, 27,* 552–565.

Wiggins, G. (1989). Teaching to the authentic test. *Educational Leadership, 46*(7), 41–47.

Wiggins, G. (1991a). Assessment, authenticity, context, and validity. *Phi Delta Kappan, 75,* 200–214.

Wiggins, G. (1991b). Standards, not standardization: Evoking quality student work. *Educational Leadership, 48*(5), 18–25.

Wiggins, G. (1993). Assessment, authenticity, context, and validity. *Phi Delta Kappan, 75,* 200–214.

Wiig, E. H. (1982). Communication disorders. In H. Haring (Ed.), *Exceptional children and youth.* Columbus, OH: Charles E. Merrill.

Wilkins, W. E., & Glock, M. D. (1973). *Teacher expectations and student achievement: A replication and extension.* Ithaca, NY: Cornell University Press.

Willerman, L. (1979). *The psychology of individual and group differences.* San Francisco: Freeman.

Williams, C., & Bybee J. (1994). What do children feel guilty about? Developmental and gender differences. *Developmental Psychology, 30,* 617–623.

Williams, G. C., Wiener, M. W., Markakis, K. M., Reeve, J., & Deci, E. L. (1993). Medical student motivation for internal medicine. *Annals of Internal Medicine.*

Williams, W., Blythe, T., White, N., Li, J., Sternberg, R., & Gardner, H. (1996). *Practical Intelligence in school.* New York: HarperCollins.

Willingham, W. W., & Cole, N. S. (1997). *Gender and fair assessment.* Mahwah, NJ: Lawrence Erlbaum Associates.

Willis, P. (1977). *Learning to labor.* Lexington, MA: D. C. Heath.

Wilson, C. W., & Hopkins, B. L. (1973). The effects of contingent music on the intensity of noise in junior high home economics classes. *Journal of Applied Behavior Analysis, 6,* 269–275.

Winett, R. A., & Winkler, R. C. (1972). Current behavior modification in the classroom: Be still, be quiet, be docile. *Journal of Applied Behavior Analysis, 15,* 499–504.

Wingate, N. (1986). Sexism in the classroom. *Equity and Excellence, 22,* 105–110.

Winne, P. H. (1979). Experiments relating teachers' use of higher cognitive questions to student achievement. *Review of Educational Research, 49,* 3–50.

Winne, P. H. (1995). Inherent details in self-regulated learning. *Educational Psychologist, 30,* 173–188.

Winne, P. H. (1997). Experimenting to bootstrap self-regulated learning. *Journal of Educational Psychology, 89,* 397–410.

Winne, P. H., & Perry, N. E. (1994). Educational psychology. In V. Ramachandran (Ed.), *Encyclopedia of human behavior* (vol. 2, pp. 213–223). San Diego, CA: Academic Press.

Winzer, M. A. (1999). *Children with exceptionalities in Canadian classrooms* (5th ed.). Scarborough, ON: Prentice Hall Allyn & Bacon Canada.

Winzer, M. A., & Mazurek, K. (1998). *Special education in multicultural contexts.* Columbus, OH: Merrill.

Witkin, H. A., Moore, C. A., Goodenough, D. R., & Cox, R. W. (1977). Field-dependent and field-independent cognitive styles and their educational implications. *Review of Educational Research, 47,* 1–64.

Wittrock, M. C. (1978). The cognitive movement in instruction. *Educational Psychologist, 13,* 15–30.

Wittrock, M. C. (1982, March). *Educational implications of recent research on learning and memory.* Paper presented at the annual meeting of the American Educational Research Association, New York.

Wittrock, M. C. (1992). An empowering conception of educational psychology. *Educational Psychologist, 27,* 129–142.

Wolf, D., Bixby, J., Glenn, J., III, & Gardner, H. (1991). To use their minds well: New forms of student assessment. *Review of Research in Education, 17,* 31–74.

Wolters, C. A., Yu, S. L., & Pintrich, P. R. (1996). The relation between goal orientation and students' motivational beliefs and self-regulated learning. *Learning and Individual Differences, 8,* 211–238.

Women on Words and Images. (1975). *Dick and Jane as victims: Sex stereotyping in children's readers* (expanded ed.). Available from author, P. O. Box 2163, Princeton, NJ.

Wong, B. Y. L. (1996). *The ABCs of learning disabilities.* San Diego, CA: Academic Press.

Wong, L. (1987). Reaction to research findings: Is the feeling of obviousness warranted? *Dissertation Abstracts International,* 48/12, 3709B (University Microfilms #DA 8801059).

Wood, D., Bruner, J., & Ross, S. (1976). The role of tutoring in problem solving. *British Journal of Psychology, 66,* 181–191.

Wood, E. R. G., & Wood, S. E. (1999). The world of psychology. Boston: Allyn & Bacon.

Wood, S. E., & Wood, E. G. (1999). *The world of psychology* (3rd ed.). Boston: Allyn & Bacon.

Woodcock, R. (1987). *Woodcock Reading Mastery Tests–Revised.* Circle Pines, MN: American Guidance Service.

Woolfolk, A. E., & Brooks, D. (1983). Nonverbal communication in teaching. In E. Gordon (Ed.), *Review of research in education* (Vol. 10, pp. 103–150). Washington, DC: American Educational Research Association.

Woolfolk, A. E., & Brooks, D. (1985). The influence of teachers' nonverbal behaviors on students' perceptions and performance. *Elementary School Journal, 85,* 514–528.

Woolfolk, A. E., & Hoy, W. K. (1990). Prospective teachers' sense of efficacy and beliefs about control. *Journal of Educational Psychology, 82,* 81–91.

Woolfolk, A. E., Rosoff, B., & Hoy, W. K. (1990). Teachers' sense of efficacy and their beliefs about managing students. *Teaching and Teacher Education, 6,* 137–148.

Woolfolk, A. E., & Woolfolk, R. L. (1974). A contingency management technique for increasing student attention in a small group. *Journal of School Psychology, 12,* 204–212.

Woolfolk Hoy, A., & Tschannen-Moran, M. (1999). Implications of cognitive approaches to peer learning. In A. O'Donnell & A. King (Eds.), *Cognitive perspectives on peer learning.* Mahwah, NJ: Erlbaum.

Worthen, B. R. (1993). Critical issues that will determine the future of alternative assessment. *Phi Delta Kappan, 74,* 444–457.

Wright, S. C., & Taylor, D. M. (1995). Identity and the language of the classroom: Investigating the impact of heritage versus second language instruction on personal and collective self-esteem. *Journal of Educational Psychology, 87,* 241–252.

Wyler, R. S. (1988). Social memory and social judgment. In P. Solomon, G. Goethals, C. Kelly, & B. Stephans (Eds.), *Perspectives on memory research.* New York: Springer-Verlag.

Yee, A. H. (1992). Asians as stereotypes and students: Misperceptions that persist. *Educational Psychology Review, 4,* 95–132.

Yerkes, R. M., & Dodson, J. D. (1908). The relation of strength of stimulus to rapidity of habit formation. *Journal of Comparative Neurology, 18,* 459–482.

Young, A. J. (1997). I think, therefore I'm motivated: The relations among cognitive strategy use, motivational orientation, and classroom perceptions over time. *Learning and Individual Differences, 9,* 249–283.

Zeidner, M. (1995). Adaptive coping with test situations. *Educational Psychologist, 30,* 123–134.

Zentall, S. S. (1993). Research on the educational implications of attention deficit hyperactivity disorder. *Exceptional Children, 60,* 143–153.

Zimmerman, B. J. (1990). Self-regulated learning and academic achievement: An overview. *Educational Psychologist, 21,* 3–18.

Zimmerman. B. J. (1995). Self-efficacy and educational development. In A. Bandura (Ed.), *Self-efficacy in changing societies* (pp. 202–231). New York: Cambridge University Press.

Zimmerman, B. J., & Schunk, D. H. (Eds.) (1989). *Self-regulated learning and academic achievement: Theory, research, and practice.* New York: Springer-Verlag.

Zimmerman, D. W. (1981). On the perennial argument about grading "on the curve" in college courses. *Educational Psychologist, 16,* 175–178.

Name Index

Clifford, M., 546
Clifford, M.M., 11, 360
Clinkenbeard, P.R., 118, 122, 124
Clore, G.L., 358
Clough, M., 469
Cobb, P., 321, 323
Cocchiarella, M.M., 272
Cognition and Technology Group at Vanderbilt University (CTGV), 323, 328, 329
Cohen, E.G., 331
Coie, J.D., 85
Cole, D.A., 72
Cole, M., 320
Cole, N.S., 175
Coles, B., 72
Collier, V.P., 179
Collins, A., 261, 336, 343, 358
Collins, A.M., 233, 234, 323, 361, 464
Colton, A.S.B., 8
Comeaux, M.A., 6, 7
Committee on the Prevention of Reading Difficulties in Young Children, 53
Compare, L., 159
Confrey, J., 38, 325, 477
Conger, J.J., 24
Conger, K.J., 162
Conger, R.D., 162
Connell, J.P., 547
Connors, J., 115
Conway, G., 207
Conway, T., 53
Cooke, B.L., 7
Cooney, J.B., 291
Cooper, C.R., 67
Cooper, G., 288
Cooper, H., 391
Cooper, H.M., 388, 458
Cooper, M., 285
Copi, I.M., 287
Cordova, D.I., 366
Corenblum, B., 73, 169
Corkill, A.J., 280
Corley, K.K., 423
Corno, L., 10, 11, 127, 279, 548
Costa, A.L., 340, 343
Costanza, D.P., 256
Coughlin, R., 73
Coulson, R.L., 320
Covaleskie, J., 432
Covington, M., 368, 371, 375
Covington, M.V., 71
Cowley, G., 366
Cox, K.E., 384
Cox, R.W., 126
Crago, M.B., 163
Craig, W., 80
Craig, W.M., 83
Craik, F.I.M., 241, 248
Craven, R., 70

Crawford, J., 181
Crealock, C., 158, 159, 167, 169, 182, 183
Crisci, P.E., 357
Cronin, J.F., 326
Crowhurst, M., 51
Cruickshank, D.R., 465
CTGV. See Cognition and Technology Group at Vanderbilt University (CTGV)
Cuban, L., 447
Cummins, D.D., 283
Cummins, J., 73, 178, 179
Cunningham, A.E., 53, 72, 91, 234
Cunningham, D.J., 325
Current Directions in Psychological Science, 116
Curror, S.E., 78
Curwin, R., 409, 432
Cushing, K., 6
Cushing, K.S., 291
Cushner, K., 159

D
Dahl, T., 296
Dailey, D., 314
Dansereau, D., 334
Dansereau, D.F., 294
Dark, V.J., 254
Das, J.P., 44, 47
Davidson, J., 283, 297
Davis, G., 74
Davis, J.K., 126
Davis, R., 325, 477
Davis, R.B., 469
Davis, S.F., 80
De Corte, E., 284
De Mott, R.M., 141
De Vos, J., 30
Deaux, K., 172
Debus, R., 372
DeCecco, J., 433
deCharms, R., 374
Deci, E., 218, 224, 356
Deci, E.L., 71, 223, 355, 364, 374, 417
Delaney, H.D., 257
Delgardell, M., 346
Delpit, L., 185
Delucci, K., 331
Demetras, M.J., 50
Dempster, F., 531
Dempster, F.N., 539
Den Ouden, V., 442
Deno, S.L., 529
DeRidder, L.M., 93
Derry, S., 294
Derry, S.J., 282, 294, 320, 322, 323
Detterman, D.L., 108
Dewey, J., 326, 329
Di Cintio, M.J., 254
Di Vesta, F.J., 254, 295

Diana, E.M., 243
Diaz, R.M., 45
Dickinson, D., 112
Dickson, M., 541
Diebert, E., 519
Dinnel, D., 280
DiPietro, J.A., 173
Dishner, E.K., 12
Dixon, R., 228
D'Khissy, M., 159
Doctorow, M., 300
Dodge, K.A., 74, 85
Dodson, J.D., 367
Dolan, L., 164
Dolce, R., 159
Dole, J.A., 294, 295
Doleys, D.M., 213
Dolgins, J., 129
Dornbusch, S.M., 164
Doyle, P.H., 419
Doyle, W., 382, 386, 402, 403, 405, 424, 446
Drabman, R.S., 212
Drake, M., 223, 224
Drayer, A.M., 557
Drew, C.J., 123, 140, 147
Driscoll, A., 457
Driscoll, M., 558
Driscoll, M.P., 250, 259, 303, 320, 324
Drummond, L., 398
Duchastel, P., 449
Duchastel, P.C., 539
Duckitt, J., 170
Dudley, B., 433, 435
Duell, O.K., 462
Duffy, G., 465
Duffy, G.G., 294, 386
Dufresne, R., 290
Duncan, R.M., 47
Duncker, K., 288
Dunlap, G., 133
Dunn, K., 127, 128
Dunn, R., 127, 128
Dupin, J.J., 293
Dupree, D., 165
Dweck, C.S., 371
Dyck, J., 102
Dyson, A.H., 383

E
Eaton, J.F., 292
Eaton, W.O., 368
Ebeling, K.S., 32
Ebmeier, 471
Eccles, J., 81, 92, 367, 369, 370, 383, 420, 421
Eccles, J.S., 92
Educational Psychology Review, 27
Educational Quality and Accountability Office, 503
Egan, M.W., 123, 140, 147

Randhawa, B.S., 175
Randhawa, J.S., 175
Range, L.M., 96
Rashotte, C.A., 53
Ratey, J.J., 132
Rathus, S.A., 51
Ratner, H.H., 47
Raudsepp, E., 289
Readence, J.E., 12
Recht, D.R., 234
Reder, L.M., 233, 253, 261, 324, 469
Redfield, D.L., 461
Reeve, J., 218, 355, 356, 374, 376, 384
Reich, P.A., 179
Reid, M.K., 294
Reis, S.M., 121, 124
Reisberg, D., 119, 167, 197, 250, 270, 271, 366
Rembolt, C., 435, 436
Render, G., 432
Rennie, L.J., 175
Renninger, K.A., 366
Renzulli, J.S., 121, 122, 124, 127
Resnick, L., 324
Resnick, L.B., 233, 234, 246, 284, 323, 361, 464, 476
Reyes, E.I., 186
Reynolds, A., 547
Reynolds, M.C., 147
Reynolds, W.M., 71
Rhode, G., 219
Ricciardelli, L.A., 179
Rice, M.L., 53, 54
Richards, A., 433
Richardson, T.M., 124
Richardson-Koehler, V., 274
Richgels, D.J., 51
Ridley, D.S., 296
Riedesel, C.A., 285
Ritchie, K.L., 81
Ritter, P.L., 164
Roazzi, A., 42
Robertson, A.S., 93
Robins, B., 160
Robinsin, A., 118, 122, 124
Robinson, C.S., 284
Robinson, D.H., 297
Robinson, H.A., 298
Robson, M., 7
Roche, L., 70
Roderick, M., 547
Roehler, L.R., 294, 465
Rogers, C.R., 356, 406
Rogoff, B., 42, 47
Rohde, P., 96
Romney, D.M., 173
Ronning, R.R., 241, 252, 282, 319, 321
Rop, C., 177
Rosch, E.H., 271
Rose, E., 53

Rose, L.C., 402, 433
Rosen, L.A., 207
Rosenfarb, I., 219
Rosenshine, B., 47, 338, 340, 342, 390, 404, 459, 462, 465, 466, 467, 468, 469
Rosenthal, R., 388, 391
Roskos, K., 54, 454
Rosoff, B., 373
Ross, 81
Ross, S., 47, 131, 338
Rosser, R., 51
Rotenberg, K.J., 84
Roth, K.J., 478
Roth, W.-M., 337, 480
Rotherham-Borus, M.J., 73
Rousseau, E.W., 461
Rowe, M.B., 462
Roychoudhury, A., 480
Rueman, D., 92
Ruffman, T., 41
Rumelhart, D., 244, 246
Rushall, B.S., 220
Ruskin, R.S., 214
Russell, D., 360
Rutledge, J., 266
Ryan, R., 224
Ryan, R.M., 71, 223, 355, 356, 364, 374, 417
Ryans, D.G., 466

S
Sabers, D., 6
Sabers, D.S., 291
Sadaka, Y., 102
Sadker, D., 174, 175, 177, 430, 461, 462
Sadker, M., 174, 175, 430, 461, 462
Safty, A., 178
Salinas, M.F., 171
Salomon, G., 256, 279, 282, 301, 303
Salovey, P., 111
Sanchez, F., 435
Sanders, C.E., 303
Sanders, S., 295
Sandora, C.A., 463
Sapolsky, R., 86
Sato, T., 73
Sattler, J., 14, 115, 120, 121
Savage, T., 406
Sawyer, R.J., 131
Scardamalia, M., 361
Scarr, S., 93, 167
Schaatschneider, C., 53
Schenk, S., 94
Scherer, M., 164, 412
Schmuck, P.A., 399
Schmuck, R.A., 399
Schneider, W., 290, 342
Schoenfield, A.H., 289
Schofield, J.W., 169

Schommer, M., 288
Schon, D., 7
Schonert-Reichl, K.A., 36
School Achievement Indicators Program, 508
Schrauben, B., 127
Schraw, G.J., 241, 252, 282, 319, 321
Schulze, S.K., 255
Schumaker, K., 93
Schunk, D.H., 69, 218, 234, 236, 237, 243, 247, 252, 281, 302, 313, 315, 316, 317, 320, 321, 323, 358, 359, 360, 362, 363, 368, 372, 373
Schwartz, B., 197, 250, 270, 271
Schwartz, J.E., 285
Scott, J., 458
Seddon, G.M., 451
Sedighdeilami, F., 81
Seelback, A., 375
Seeley, J.R., 96
Seiber, J.E., 370
Seifert, K.L., 90, 96
Seligman, M.E.P., 375
Selman, R., 74
Semb, G., 250
Semb, G.B., 214
Serbin, L., 175
Seroczynski, A.D., 72
Serpell, R., 321
Shapiro, E.S., 314, 529
Shapiro, J., 473, 474
Shaughnessy, M.F., 258
Shavelson, R.J., 69, 70, 71, 446, 447, 519
Sheets, J.L., 484
Shepard, L.A., 547
Sheppard, J.L., 91
Sheppard, M.J., 91
Sherman, A., 162
Sherman, J.G., 214
Sherman, J.W., 246
Shields, A., 375
Shields, P., 165
Shields, P.M., 161, 187
Shiffrin, R.M., 236
Shimamura, A.P., 252
Shipman, V.C., 164
Shoda, Y., 113
Showers, C.J., 72
Shuell, T., 215, 232, 233, 234, 256, 280, 282, 337, 467, 478
Shulman, L., 6
Shulman, L.S., 472
Shultz, J., 167, 184
Siegel, J., 258
Siegel, L., 130
Siegel, L.S., 474
Siegler, R., 342
Siegler, R.S., 39, 41, 254
Signorella, M.L., 173
Signorelli, N., 170

Subject Index

humanistic approaches to motivation, 356–357
hyperactivity, 131–134
hypothetico-deductive reasoning, 36

I

"I" messages, 430
identity
    achievement, 66
    adolescent search for, 64–67
    crisis, 66
    diffusion, 66
    foreclosure, 66
    gender-role, 172–173
    mastery of, 32
    physical development in adolescence, 89
Identity, Youth, and Crisis (Erikson), 62
Identity and the Life Cycle (Erikson), 62
images, 244
Immigration Act, 159
impulsive cognitive style, 126
incentive, 356
inclusion
    collaborative consultation, 147
    cooperative teaching, 147
    definitions, 142–143
    effective teaching, 146–147
    families and, 147
    full inclusion, 144
    individualized education program (IEP), 143–144
    integration, 142–143
    least restrictive placement, 143
    resource room, 146–147
incremental view of ability, 371
Indian Act, 158–159
individual constructivism, 320
individual differences
    between-class ability grouping, 117–118
    cognitive styles, 126–127
    creativity, 118–121
    disabilities. *See* disabilities
    exceptional students, 106
    gifted students, 121–125
    intelligence, 108–117
    Joplin Plan, 118
    language and labelling, 106–107
    learning preferences, 127–128
    learning styles, 126, 127–128
    long-term memory, 254–255
    in metacognition, 253
    non-graded elementary school, 118
    "person-first" language, 106–107
    teaching and, 117–118
    within-class ability grouping, 118
    and working memory, 253–254
individualized education program (IEP), 143–144, 145

Individuals with Disabilities Education Act (IDEA), 129
inductive reasoning, 275
industry, 64, 65
infancy
    cognitive development, 30–31
    psychosocial development, 63–64
information, and control, 374–375
information processing
    and cognitive development, 41–42
    components, 113–114
    definition, 235
    ideas in the classroom, 251
    metacomponents, 114
    model of memory, 236
    see also memory
inhibitions, 316
initiative, 63–64, 65
inquiry learning, 326–328
insight, 114
instructional conversations, 335–336, 337
instructional events model, 259–260
instructional objective, 448
instrumental value, 422
integrated curriculum, 473–474
integrated plans, 454
integration, 142–143, 169
integrity, 68
intelligence
    and achievement, 115–116
    automaticity, 114
    below-average general intelligence, 138
    contextual, 114
    deviation IQ, 115
    emotional, 111–113
    environment and, 116–117
    general, 108
    group *vs.* individual IQ tests, 115
    heredity, 116–117
    insight, 114
    meaning of, 108
    measurement of, 114–115
    multiple intelligences, 108–111, 112
    practical, 114
    specific abilities and, 108
    tacit knowledge, 114
    triarchic theory of, 113–114
intelligence quotient (IQ), 115–117
intention, 74
interest areas, 412
interest value, 383
interests, 366
interference, 250
intermittent reinforcement schedules, 203
internal/external focus, 358–359
internalization of moral rules, 79
interval schedule, 203
intimacy, 67–68
intrinsic motivation, 355

intrinsic value, 383, 421–422
intuitive thinking, 276–277
invariant functions, 28–29

J

jigsaw, 333
Joplin Plan, 118

K

Keller Plan, 214
keyword method, 257
knowledge, 10, 17
    acquisition, 233
    conditional, 235, 260–261
    construction of, 233, 321, 322, 325
    declarative, 234–235, 254, 255–260
    domain-specific, 234, 254
    effective teachers, 465
    expert, 6–7, 290–291
    general, 234, 323–324
    importance of, 234–235
    and memory, 235
    metacognitive, 252–253
    novice, 291–293
    prerequisite, 261
    procedural, 235, 254, 260–261
    public, and constructivism, 321
    situated, 323–324
    top-down processing, 238
Kohlberg's stages of moral development, 75–77
KWL Plus, 299

L

labelling, and individual differences, 106–107
language
    see also speech
    abstract words, 52
    bilingualism, 178–182
    collective monologue, 32
    communication disorders, 134–136
    development of, 49–52
    differences, 178–182
    disorders, 135–136
    English as a second language (ESL), 178, 179
    and ethnic pride, 73
    heritage, 73
    Heritage Language Programs, 180–181
    labelling and individual differences, 106–107
    learning, 50–51
    limited English proficiency (LEP), 178, 179
    meaning, 51–52
    metalinguistic awareness, 52
    monolinguals, 179
    partnerships with families, 54

preoperational stage, 31–32, 33
prerequisite knowledge, 261
preschool years
    cognitive development, 31–32
    fine-motor skills, 88–90
    gender-role stereotyping, 173–175
    gross-motor skills, 88
    initiative, encouragement of, 65
    physical development, 88–89
    poverty, 162
    psychosocial development, 63–64
    transition into school, 91
presentation punishment, 202
pretest, 528
prevention, 423–425
principle, 15
private speech, 44–46
problem, 281
problem-based learning, 328–329, 383
problem solving
    acting, 288
    algorithms, 286
    analogical thinking, 287
    anticipation, 288
    attention, focusing, 283
    barriers to, 288–289
    definition, 281
    expert knowledge, 290–291
    expert teachers, 291
    experts' methods, 290–293
    flexibility, 289
    functional fixedness, 288
    general problem-solving strategy, 282
    general vs. domain specific, 282
    goal definition, 283–286
    guidelines, 292
    heuristics, 286–288
    identification of problem, 282–283
    linguistic comprehension, 283–284
    looking back, 288
    means-ends analysis, 287
    novice knowledge, 291–293
    possible solutions, exploration of, 286–288
    representation of problem, 283–286
    response set, 289
    schema-driven, 286
    schemas, 284, 285
    search-based route, 286
    translation of problem, 284, 285
    understanding whole problem, 284
    verbalization, 288
    working-backward strategy, 287
procedural knowledge, 235, 254, 260–261
procedural memory, 247
procedural tasks, 382
procedures, 407–408
processing theory, levels of, 248

production phase, 314
productions, 247, 261
productive conferences, 149
progress record and evaluation, 219
prompting, 205–206
pronunciation, 51
proposition, 243
propositional network, 243–244
prototype, 271
psychoeducational assessment report, 510–513
psychoeducational tests, 508–513
psychological constructivism, 320
psychomotor domain, 452–453
psychosocial development
    adolescence, 64–67
    adulthood, 67–68
    autonomy vs. shame and doubt, 63
    described, 62
    developmental crisis, 62
    elementary years, 64
    generativity vs. stagnation, 68
    identity achievement, 66
    identity diffusion, 66
    identity foreclosure, 66
    identity vs. role confusion, 64
    industry, 65
    industry vs. inferiority, 64
    initiative, 63–64, 65
    integrity vs. despair, 68
    intimacy vs. isolation, 67–68
    middle school years, 64
    moratorium, 66
    preschool years, 63–64
    stages of, 63
    trust vs. mistrust, 63
psychotic behaviour, 139
puberty, 89
punishment, 202–203, 214, 223
Pygmalion effect, 388

Q
questioning, 459–462

R
race, 165
racial differences, 165–172
radical constructivists, 322–323
random procedures, 14
range, 493
ratio schedule, 203
reading
    difficulties, 130–131
    skills, 474
    strategies, 298–301
    teaching and learning, 472–475
READS, 298–301
reality shock, 7
reasoning
    cold cognition, 366
    deductive, 278, 279

hypothetico-deductive, 36
inductive, 275
moral, 75–77
receptors, 236
reciprocal determinism, 317–319
reciprocal questioning, 334
reciprocal teaching, 338–340
recitation, 459–462
recognition of accomplishments, 384–385
reconstruction, 249
referrals, 142
reflective cognitive style, 126–127
reflective teachers, 7
reform, 9
reinforcement
    negative, 202, 210–212
    observational learning, 314–315
    operant conditioning, 201–202
    positive, 202, 211
    Premack principle, 208–209
    self-reinforcement, 220–221, 315
    shaping, 209–210
    with teacher attention, 207
    and teacher expectations, 391
    time out from, 213
    token reinforcement system, 216–217
    vicarious, 315
reinforcement schedules
    continuous, 203
    effects of, 204–205
    extinction, 204–205
    intermittent, 203
    interval schedule, 203
    ratio schedule, 203
reinforcer, 201
relatedness, 364
relational proposition, 283
reliability, 498, 500–501, 544–545
removal punishment, 202–203
report card preparation
    contract system, 555
    criterion-referenced grading, 552
    dual marking system, 556
    grading on effort and improvement, 555–556
    norm-referenced grading, 552–553
    percentage grading, 553–555
    point system, 553
    revise option, 555
reprimands, 212–213
research
    case study, 13
    correlational studies, 13
    descriptive studies, 13
    ethnography, 13
    experimental studies, 14
    participant observation, 13
    as primary tool, 14
    principle, 15
    random procedures, 14

statistical significance, 14
subjects, 14
theories. *See* theories
residential schools, 169
resistance culture, 163
resource room, 146–147
Respect and Protect system, 435–436
respondents, 198–199
response cost, 213
response generalization, 199
response set, 289, 301
responsibility dimension, 359
restructuring, 119
retention, 314
reticular formation, 25
retrieval, 236, 248–249
reversibility, 32
reversible thinking, 31
revise option, 555
reward, 356
rewards for learning, 224
ripple effect, 316
Ritalin, 133
role confusion, 64
rote memorization, 256, 258
routine procedures, 380
rubric, 503, 543–544, 545, 555
rule-eg method, 278, 279
rules, 409–410

S
SAIP tests, 506–508
satiation, 212
scaffolding, 46–47, 50
schema-driven problem solving, 286
schemas, 244–246, 272, 284, 285
schemes, 28
School Achievement Indicators
    Program (SAIP tests), 506–508
school act, 142
science, 477–480
scores. *See* test scores
scoring rubrics, 543–544, 545, 555
script, 246
scripted cooperation, 334, 457
search-based route, 286
seatwork, 458–459
second-hand investigations, 327
secondary school. *See* adolescence
seizures, 140
self-actualization, 356
self-concept
    academic, 69
    definition, 69
    development of, 70
    early views of, 68–69
    and others, 74–75
    perspective-taking ability, 74–75
    vs. self-efficacy, 372
    vs. self-esteem, 69–70
    structure of, 69, 70

self-determination, 356, 374–375, 376
self-determined activities, 355
self-efficacy, 316, 371–373, 378
self-esteem
    building, 74
    collective, 72–74
    definition, 69
    determination of, 71
    encouragement by schools, 357
    ethnic pride, 72, 73
    and family, 74
    gender and, 72
    personal, 72
    and poverty, 163
    and school life, 70–71
    vs. self-concept, 69–70
    vs. self-efficacy, 372
    victims and, 83
    in younger children, 71–72
self-evaluation, 219
self-fulfilling prophecy, 388
self-instruction, 127
self-management, 218–221, 406
self-regulated learners, 10, 45
self-reinforcement, 220–221, 315
self-schemas
    ability, beliefs about, 371
    learned helplessness, 375
    motivation to learn, 377–378
    self-efficacy, 371–373
    self-worth, 375–377
    and teaching, 377
self-talk, 46
self-worth, 375–377, 378
semantic memory, 243–246
semiotic function, 31
sensorimotor stage, 30–31
sensory information store. *See* sensory
    memory
sensory memory
    attention, 238
    bottom-up processing, 237
    capacity, 236
    content, 237
    duration, 237
    perception, 237–238
    and receptors, 236
    top-down processing, 238
sensory register. *See* sensory memory
serial-position effect, 256
seriation, 33
sexism in teaching, 177
shaping, 209–210
short-term memory. *See* working
    memory
sign language, 140
Simon, Theopile, 114–115
situated learning, 323–324
    see also constructivism
Skinner, B.F., 200–201
skipping grades, 12, 124

social class differences. *See* socioeco-
    nomic status (SES)
social cognitive theory
    definition, 313
    external factors, 317
    internal facts, 317
    observational learning, 314–317
    reciprocal determinism, 317–319
    social factors, impact of, 318–319
    vicarious reinforcement, 315
social conventions, 77
social development, 24, 88
    see also socialization
social goals, 363
social isolation, 213
social learning theory, 313
    see also social cognitive theory
social negotiation, 324–325
social persuasion, 373
social processes, 312
social sources of individual thinking,
    43
social transmission, 28
socialization
    definition, 83
    families today, 83–85
    peer relationships, 85–87
socialized aggression, 139
sociocultural theory
    adults, role of, 46–47
    applications of, 50
    assisted learning, 47, 48
    co-constructed social process, 43
    cognitive self-instruction, 46
    cultural tools, 44
    definition, 42
    implications of, for teaching,
        47–49
    language, role of, 44–46
    middle-class parents, 164
    peers, role of, 46–47
    vs. Piaget's theory of cognitive
        development, 45–47
    private speech, role of, 44–46
    scaffolding, 46–47, 50
    self-regulated learners, 45
    social sources of individual think-
        ing, 43
    zone of proximal development,
        47–49
sociocultural views of motivation,
    361
socioeconomic status (SES)
    and achievement, 162–165
    definition, 161
    and depression, 36
    home environment and resources,
        164–165
    low. *See* poverty
    poverty. *See* poverty
sociohistoric theory. *See* sociocultural
    theory